SANDERS'

ENCYCLOPAEDIA OF GARDENING

SANDERS'

ENCYCLOPAEDIA

OF GARDENING

WITH SUPPLEMENT

A DICTIONARY

*of cultivated plants, etc., giving in alpha-
betical sequence the culture and propagation of
hardy and half-hardy plants, trees and shrubs,
orchids, ferns, fruit, vegetables, hothouse and
greenhouse plants, etc., including their specific
and common names*

REVISED BY A. G. L. HELLYER

M.B.E., V.M.H., F.L.S.

COLLINGRIDGE BOOKS

LONDON · NEW YORK · SYDNEY · TORONTO

First published in 1895 by
W. H. and L. Collingridge Ltd.
Twenty-second edition, thirty-fourth
impression, 1966
Forty-first impression published in
1978 for Collingridge Books by
THE HAMLYN PUBLISHING GROUP LTD.
LONDON · NEW YORK · SYDNEY · TORONTO
Astronaut House, Feltham, Middlesex. England

Printed in Great Britain by
REDWOOD BURN LIMITED
Trowbridge & Esher

© The Hamlyn Publishing Group Ltd., 1971
ISBN 0 600 44110 5

FOREWORD

Sanders' *Encyclopaedia of Gardening* first appeared in serial form in *Amateur Gardening*. For five years from November 15th 1890 until August 10th 1895 it appeared, a column or so at a time until at last the work was completed. It was then produced as a book and had an immediate success. For the first time the gardener was provided with a comprehensive encyclopaedia which not only gave brief descriptions of all the plants he was ever likely to meet but also complete information regarding their cultivation. Moreover this encyclopaedia was so compact that it could be carried around easily and so be available as a constant source of reference indoors or out. Through the years the demand for the encyclopaedia has continued unabated. Edition after edition has been printed and there have been several revisions to keep information up to date.

A word of explanation on the methods adopted in naming plants may be of interest to the reader unversed in these matters. The present-day system was founded by Linnaeus and dates from 1753. It is based on the assumption that two names, which may be compared roughly to a surname and a Christian name, will serve to identify any species of plant without possibility of confusion with any other species. The first name denotes the genus to which the plant belongs; the second the particular species within that genus. No name applied to one genus can be used for any other genus. No name applied to one species may be used for another species within the same genus though it may be applied to a species belonging to another genus.

The analogy of Christian and surnames may be used to illustrate this point. Let us suppose that all the Smiths are related and all the Browns are likewise related. No one can be called Smith who does not belong to the family of Smiths; no one can be called Brown who does not belong to the family of Browns. It is also forbidden that there shall be two Smiths with the same Christian name; or, for that matter, two Browns. But there may be Arthur Smiths as well as Arthur Browns, George Smiths as well as George

Browns. In these instances there can be no confusion between the two Arthurs or the two Georges for their different surnames serve to distinguish them.

That is the basis of the simple scheme devised by Linnaeus. Latin or Greek names are used in place of English names because these classical languages are common to all countries. The generic name (which we may compare with the hypothetical surname) comes first and the specific name (which we have compared with a Christian name) second.

This binomial system of nomenclature (to give it its official title) was introduced to produce order and stability where formerly there had been chaos and constant change. In the main that is precisely what has been achieved and it is because of these virtues that gardeners as well as botanists have been glad to make use of the system. Popular names serve well enough for popular plants. Everyone knows what is meant by wallflower, forget-me-not and rose so long as these names are used to refer to the common wallflower or forget-me-not and the ordinary garden roses. But suppose it is not the everyday kinds to which one wishes to make reference; that the ' wallflower ' is, in fact, that curious little Moroccan species with flowers of a dull shade of purple which Farrer once described as ' sad and subtle '; or that the forget-me-not is one of the mountain species which are so spare and small and neat by comparison with our leafy woodlander; or that the rose is a wilding newly introduced from Asia? No genuine popular names exist for these. If some must be invented who is to do the inventing and how can it be assured that one name and one name only will be accepted by everyone as the true name of each plant? Of course no such thing can be guaranteed. Even in the case of old and well-established popular names they have often acquired only a local currency.

Yet another difficulty arises in the case of those immense genera, of which berberis and primula may be cited as examples, which contain hundreds of related yet totally distinct species. All may lay some claim to the popular names barberry and primrose but by what means can one distinguish between one and another? No answer can be given at once so simple and so generally satisfactory as the use of botanical names. These names are ready to hand, they have a precise application and they are relatively stable.

Nevertheless there are occasional changes even in botanical

names, and that, from the gardener's standpoint, is the one fly in the ointment.

It is not difficult to understand why some name changes may be necessary despite the simplicity and relative stability of the system devised by botanists. It may well happen that, unknown to one another, several different botanists examine and name a new plant. Perhaps they live in different countries and have been supplied with material quite independently. They may come to different conclusions as to the genus to which the newcomer belongs—that is to say as to its precise relationship to other plants already known and named. If they do, the disagreement can only be resolved by further examination of the plant and by general discussion between botanists in all parts of the world. But it is far more likely that they will come independently to the same conclusion regarding genus, but that each will then proceed to supply the new plant with what he regards as a suitable specific name. It is most unlikely that all will think of the same name. So the plant is launched on the world with several different specific names. Which is to have precedence?

Botanists have decided this problem by the very simple expedient of saying that the *first name to be published* is the valid one—always supposing, of course, that there is no good botanical reason for rejecting this name anyway. This is known as the priority rule and it works well enough on the whole. Certainly it would be difficult to think of any better way of dealing with the main problem.

But occasionally a name that is not the first to be published passes into general usage and the name with prior right is overlooked. Only years later does someone discover that Mr. Robinson coined the name *Blancus caeruleus* six months before Mr. Williams named the same plant *Blancus azureus*, the style by which it is commonly known. Under the priority rule Mr. William's name must be declared invalid and Mr. Robinson's accepted as correct.

Gardeners have urged botanists to permit exceptions to this priority rule in certain cases and it is possible that some compromise will be arranged, but it cannot be made retrospective and so many name changes made under this rule must stand.

Other name changes are made necessary by a closer examination or a better understanding of the plants themselves. It may be that a plant which at one time was believed to be closely related to certain other plants and was, therefore, placed in the genus to which they belong, is later found to have its closest affinities elsewhere. In consequence it is transferred to another genus. This means that its name must be changed.

In recent years many greenhouse plants, mainly those with ornamental foliage, have become popular as house or room plants. Their success in these circumstances depends on the conditions that can be provided. Most of them prefer a light place in a room with an equable temperature and they resent hot and dry air, draughts and fumes from gas or oil appliances. Although, in ideal conditions, the plants will flourish and grow well, they appreciate being taken into a warm greenhouse, where the atmosphere is a little more humid, for a short period. The general cultural advice given for each plant applies mainly to greenhouse conditions but these hints can also serve as a guide for plants in rooms, although many will be found to succeed in lower temperatures.

Cultural methods have not changed a great deal in the past fifty years but, in one respect at least, an entirely new conception has been introduced. It used to be supposed that, when plants were grown in pots or boxes, it was necessary to vary the soil mixture for them according to the kind of plant under consideration. In consequence recommendations for such mixtures were almost as varied as the recipes in Mrs. Beeton's cookery book. Then in the early 1930's Mr. W. J. C. Lawrence of the John Innes Horticultural Institution demonstrated that it was quite possible to grow a very wide range of totally dissimilar plants in one standard compost, and that this same compost, with slight modifications could, in fact, be made an ideal medium for *all* plants. Since then a great many greenhouse owners have discarded the old individual mixtures in favour of the standardised John Innes recommendations.

In this edition of Sanders' Encyclopaedia the individual mixtures have been retained, for it was considered that many gardeners might still wish to use them in certain instances. The John Innes mixtures may be substituted wherever desired. The basic formula for potting is as follows:

Medium loam (neither too heavy nor too light) - - - - - - 7 parts by bulk
Peat (not too dusty and averaging ⅛ inch particles) - - - - - 3 parts by bulk
Sand (coarse and grading up to ⅛ inch) 2 parts by bulk

A basic fertiliser is prepared separately to the following formula
  Hoof and horn meal ($\frac{1}{8}$ inch grist)   -   2 parts by weight
  Superphosphate of lime   -   -   -   2 parts by weight
  Sulphate of potash   -   -   -   -   1 part by weight

To prepare the standard John Innes compost used for most greenhouse plants, 4 ounces of this basic fertiliser and $\frac{3}{4}$ ounce ground chalk or limestone are added to each bushel of the loam, peat and sand-mixture. For strong-growing plants more fertiliser and chalk or limestone may be used as the plants reach the larger sizes of pot. The chalk or limestone may be omitted in the case of some lime-hating plants such as heathers and rhododendrons, though it should be observed that the basic amount ($\frac{3}{4}$ ounce per bushel) is so small that it can often be used with benefit even for these plants, especially if the loam or peat is of a rather acid nature.

A variation of this mixture is recommended for seed germination and, in some cases for the boxes or pans in which seedlings are pricked off. The basic soil mixture is as follows:

Medium loam	2 parts	
Peat	1 part	quality as for potting compost
Coarse sand	1 part	

To each bushel of this mixture add $1\frac{1}{2}$ ounces superphosphate of lime and $\frac{3}{4}$ ounce ground chalk or limestone.

ROWFANT, 1952   A. G. L. HELLYER

ENCYCLOPAEDIA

Aaron's Beard, see *Hypericum calycinum*; **-Rod,** see *Verbascum Thapsus*.

Abaca, see *Musa textilis*.

Abele Tree, see *Populus alba*.

Abelia—*Caprifoliaceae*. Slightly tender evergreen and deciduous flowering shrubs. Good maritime subjects, *A. Schumannii* and *A. grandiflora* are the most reliable. First introduced mid-nineteenth century.

CULTURE: Soil, well worked, friable; will grow in chalky loam. Position, warm sheltered wall in full sun. Plant, April or Oct. Prune slightly after flowering.

GREENHOUSE CULTURE: Compost, equal parts loam, peat, leaf-mould and silver sand. Position, well-drained pots in sunny cool house. Pot Oct. Store in cold frame till Jan. Water moderately at first, freely when in full growth, little during winter. Prune straggly growths after flowering. Stand outdoors during summer.

PROPAGATION: By layers in March; cuttings of firm shoots in cold frame in July.

SPECIES CULTIVATED: *A. chinensis* (syn. *A. rupestris*), white, fragrant, Sept., to 6 ft., deciduous, China; *floribunda*, rosy-purple, June, to 6 ft., evergreen, Mexico; *grandiflora*, pink, July-Oct., to 6 ft., semi-evergreen, hybrid; *Schumannii*, pink, Aug., to 5 ft., deciduous, China; *triflora*, cream and pink, June, to 12 ft., deciduous, Himalaya; *uniflora*, pinkish-white, summer, to 6 ft., evergreen, China.

Abeliophyllum—*Oleaceae*. Deciduous shrub of recent introduction, allied to Fontanesia and Forsythia.

CULTURE: Soil, ordinary, well drained. Position, sheltered, sunny. Prune after flowering.

SPECIES CULTIVATED: *A. distichum*, white in short racemes, February, to 3 ft., Korea.

Abies (Fir)—*Pinaceae*. Hardy coniferous evergreen trees of pyramidal habit. First introduced early seventeenth century.

CULTURE: Soil, sandy loam. Position, cool humid areas with a good depth of soil. Plant Oct. or April. *A. alba*, is a good species to plant in mixed woods as shelter for game. Timber valuable for joists, rafters and floor boards. Grows rapidly after first few years.

PROPAGATION: By seeds sown $\frac{1}{8}$ in. deep in sandy loam in temp. 55° in March, or outdoors in April.

SPECIES CULTIVATED: *A. alba* (syn. *A. pectinata*), 'Silver Fir', 100 to 120 ft., Cent. and S. Europe; *amabilis*, 100 to 250 ft., Br. Columbia; *balsamea*, 'Balsam Fir', 70 to 80 ft., N. America, var. *hudsonia*, 2 ft.; *bracteata*, 100 to 150 ft., California; *cephalonica*, 80 to 100 ft., Greece; *cilicica*, 100 ft., Asia Minor; *concolor*, 80 to 100 ft., Colorado, New Mexico, Arizona, var. *compacta*, low rounded bush, *violacea*, effective glaucous form; *firma*, 120 to 150 ft., Japan; *Forrestii*, newer species, leaves white beneath, W. China; *Fraseri*, 30 to 40 ft., Carolina; *Georgei*, newer species, W. China; *grandis*, 200 to 300 ft., California; *homolepis* (syn. *A. brachyphylla*), 120 ft., Japan; *lasiocarpa*, 'Rocky Mountain Fir', 100 ft., W. America, var. *arizonica*, slow growing, grey foliage; *Lowiana*, 200 ft., Sierra Nevada and Oregon; *magnifica*, 'Red Fir', 200 ft., Vancouver Is. to California; *Mariesii*, 40 to 50 ft., Japan; *Nordmanniana*, 100 to 200 ft., Caucasus; *Pinsapo*, 60 to 100 ft., Spain; and vars. *glauca* and *pendula*; *procera* (syn. *A. nobilis*), 200 ft., California; *sachalinensis*, 130 ft., N. Japan; *spectabilis* (syn. *A. Webbiana*), 80 to 150 ft., Himalaya; *Veitchii*, 50 to 70 ft., Japan. For Douglas Fir see Pseudotsuga.

Abobra—*Cucurbitaceae*. Half-hardy climbing, tuberous-rooted, deciduous perennial.
CULTURE: Soil, sandy. Position, south wall. Plant, June; lift tubers Oct. and store in frost-proof place.
PROPAGATION: By seeds sown in leaf-mould, loam and sand, temp. 65°, March, also by division or by cuttings in spring.
SPECIES CULTIVATED: *A. tenuifolia* (syn. *A. viridiflora*), ' Cranberry Gourd ', green, fragrant, summer, fruit egg-shaped, scarlet, 6 ft., S. America.

Abroma—*Sterculiaceae*. Stove-flowering evergreen plants. First introduced mid-eighteenth century.
CULTURE: Compost, equal parts loam, peat, sand. Pot and prune, March. Water freely in summer, moderately in winter. Temp., March to Sept. 70° to 80°; Sept. to March 60° to 65°.
PROPAGATION: By seeds sown $\frac{1}{16}$ in. deep, or cuttings of firm shoots, in fine sandy soil, March, temp. 65° to 75°.
SPECIES CULTIVATED: *A. augusta*, purple, Aug., 8 to 10 ft., Asia.

Abronia (Sand Verbena)—*Nyctaginaceae*. Half-hardy trailing plants with fragrant flowers. First introduced early nineteenth century.
CULTURE: Soil, sandy loam. Position, sunny rockery or elevated warm border. Plant, June.
PROPAGATION: By seeds sown $\frac{1}{16}$ in. deep in sandy soil, temp. 55° to 65°, March; perennials by cuttings of young shoots in similar soil and temp.
SPECIES CULTIVATED: *A. Bigelowii*, white, July, 6 to 12 in.; *A. latifolia* (syn. *A. arenaria*), lemon-yellow, July, 9 to 18 in., California; *umbellata*, rosy-pink, June and July, 6 to 18 in., California.

Abrus—*Leguminosae*. Stove deciduous climber. First introduced mid-seventeenth century.
CULTURE: Compost, two parts loam, one part peat and sand. Pot and prune March. Water freely spring and summer, moderately in autumn and winter. Temp., March to Sept. 70° to 80°; Sept. to March 60° to 65°.
PROPAGATION: By seeds sown $\frac{1}{4}$ in. deep, or cuttings of firm shoots in sandy loam, temp. 75° to 85°, Feb.
SPECIES CULTIVATED: *A. precatorius*, ' Rosary Pea ', ' Weather Plant ', pale purple, May, 9 to 12 ft. Seeds scarlet and black, used as beads for rosaries, Tropics.

Absinthium, see *Artemisia Absinthium*.

Abutilon—*Malvaceae*. Greenhouse and half-hardy herbs and shrubs.
CULTURE: Compost, two parts loam, one peat and sand. Position, sunny greenhouse. Pot and prune, March. Temp., March to Sept. 55° to 65°; Sept. to March 50° to 55°. Water freely in spring and summer, moderately in autumn and winter. May be used for summer bedding. *A. megapotamicum* is a tender climbing species for wall or greenhouse and *A. vitifolium* is hardy in the open in mild districts.
PROPAGATION: By seeds sown $\frac{1}{4}$ in. deep in cold house or frame in March, grow young plants in pots until finally planted; cuttings in sandy soil in March. Temp. 70°.
SPECIES CULTIVATED: *A. insigne*, white and carmine, Jan., 5 ft., Colombia; *hybridum*, various colours, leaves spotted, most of the garden forms belong here; *megapotamicum* (syn. *A. vexillarium*), yellow and scarlet, summer, 4 to 8 ft., Brazil; *striatum*, orange-red, all year round in greenhouse, 6 to 10 ft., Brazil; *vitifolium*, blue, mauve, shading to white, grey downy vine-like leaves, 10 to 25 ft., sometimes short-lived, Chile.

Abyssinian Banana, see *Musa Ensete*; **– Primrose,** see *Primula verticillata.*

Acacallis—*Orchidaceae.* A beautiful monotypic epiphyte. Dwarf growing, the pseudo-bulbs set at short intervals on the rhizome, flowers 1 to 2 in. across.

CULTURE: Never less than 70° F. Requires a moist atmosphere. Should be placed on a raft, the surface of which is covered with a thin layer of fibre and sphagnum moss. Enjoys frequent spraying rather than heavy watering. Shading required.

PROPAGATION: The rhizome branches and side shoots with not less than two pseudo-bulbs and a growth may be placed on separate rafts.

SPECIES CULTIVATED: *A. cyanea* (syn. *Aganisia caerulea*), light bluish, summer, 1 ft., Brazil.

Acacia (Wattle; Gum Tree)—*Leguminosae* (or *Mimosaceae*). Greenhouse evergreen flowering shrubs or small trees. First introduced mid-seventeenth century.

CULTURE: Compost, equal parts peat, loam, sand. Pot and prune, Feb. or March. Water freely in spring and summer, moderately in autumn and winter. Temp., March to Sept. 55° to 65°; Sept. to March 50° to 55°.

PROPAGATION: By seeds sown ⅛ in. deep, March, or cuttings of half-ripened shoots, in sandy peat, well-drained pots, under close frame, June to July.

SPECIES CULTIVATED: *A. alata*, yellow, winter, Australia; *armata*, ' Kangaroo Thorn ', yellow, spring, 6 to 10 ft., Australia; *Baileyana*, yellow, late winter, 15 to 20 ft., Australia; *calamifolia*, ' Broom Wattle ', Australia; *cordata*, yellow, spring, 12 to 18 in., Australia; *cultriformis*, yellow, early spring, 6 to 8 ft., Australia; *cyanophylla*, ' Blue-leaved Wattle ', golden yellow, early spring, 18 ft., Australia; *decurrens*, ' Green Wattle ', yellow, early spring, 50 ft., Australia, var. *dealbata*, ' Silver Wattle ', ' Mimosa '; *Drummondii*, yellow, April, 10 ft., Australia; *Farnesiana*, ' Popinac ', ' Cassie ', deep yellow, July, 6 to 10 ft., Tropics; *hastulata*, yellow, spring, Australia; *juniperina*, yellow, late spring and early summer, 8 to 12 ft., Australia; *leprosa*, primrose, April, 6 to 10 ft., Australia; *lineata*, yellow, spring, 6 ft., Australia; *longifolia* ' Sydney Golden Wattle ', yellow, March, 10 to 15 ft., Australia, var. *floribunda*, whitish yellow, early spring, a very distinct type; *melanoxylon*, ' Blackwood Acacia ', cream, early spring, evergreen, 20 to 30 ft., Australia; *myrtifolia*, yellow, spring, Australia; *neriifolia*, yellow, spring, 15 to 20 ft., Australia; *pendula*, ' Weeping Myall ', grey foliage, pendulous branches, 15 to 20 ft., Australia; *pubescens*, yellow, April, 6 to 12 ft., Australia; *pulchella*, yellow, March, 3 to 6 ft., Australia; *pycnantha*, ' Golden Wattle ', yellow, early spring, 15 to 20 ft., Australia; *Riceana*, yellow, May, 20 ft., Tasmania; *saligna*, yellow, spring, Australia; *verticillata*, yellow, March, 6 to 20 ft., Australia. See also the genera Albizia and Robinia.

Acaena—*Rosaceae.* Hardy trailing, low-growing, evergreen perennials. First introduced early nineteenth century.

CULTURE: Soil, sandy loam. Position, open or semi-shaded rock garden, rough banks or in paving. Plant, October to April. They are good, rapid ground coverers and excellent for planting between paving stones. Too invasive for choice neighbours. Ornamental foliage and burrs.

PROPAGATION: By seeds sown in spring; cuttings in cold frames in late summer; division of roots in spring or autumn. All in light, sandy soil.

SPECIES CULTIVATED: *A. adscendens*, purple, summer, Patagonia and N. Zealand; *argentea*, metallic bronze foliage, red burrs, Chile; *Buchananii*, silvery-green foliage, red burrs, N. Zealand; *caesiglauca* (syn. *A. glauca*, *A. Sanguisorbae caesiglauca*), blue-grey foliage, N. Zealand; *glabra*, smooth, shining foliage, N. Zealand; *laevigata*, strong, distinct, almost shrubby, glaucous, Magellan; *microphylla*, crimson burrs, N. Zealand, var. *inermis*, khaki-coloured loose mats, N. Zealand; *myriophylla*, green, feathery foliage, densely tufted, Argentine and Chile; *novae-zelandiae*, ' New Zealand Burr ', trailing, bronze foliage, red-purble purrs, N. Zealand; *Sanguisorbae*, large, silky leaves, rounded purple burrs; *sericea*, greenish, Mexico; *splendens*, hairy foliage, Chile.

3

Acalypha—(Copper-leaf)—*Euphorbiaceae.* Stove evergreen foliage plants with attractive foliage. First introduced mid-nineteenth century.
CULTURE: Compost, equal parts leaf-mould, peat, loam, sand. Pot and prune, Feb. or March. Water freely in spring and summer, moderately in autumn and winter. Temp., March to Sept. 70° to 80°; Sept. to March 60° to 65°. Suitable for summer or sub-tropical bedding.
PROPAGATION: By cuttings in sandy soil, temp. 80°, Feb. or March.
SPECIES CULTIVATED: *A. capillipes,* Australia; *fruticosa,* old world tropics; *hispida* (syn. *A. Sanderi*), ' Red-hot Cat-tail ', ' Chenille Plant ', 6 to 10 ft., New Guinea; *Godseffiana,* 1 to 3 ft., New Guinea; *Wilkesiana* (syns. *A. illustris* and *A. tricolor*), 3 to 4 ft., Fiji, and vars. *Macafeana, macrophylla, marginata, musaica, obovata* and *triumphans.*

Acampe—*Orchidaceae.* Epiphytes distributed in India, Burma, Africa, allied to Vanda, with usually hard stems and leaves. Met with in cultivation; of little value. Flowers small, fleshy, often somewhat clustered on short peduncles.
CULTURE: As for Vanda.
PROPAGATION: As for Vanda. Can seldom be effected.
SPECIES CULTIVATED: The most attractive are *A. multiflora,* 12 in., yellow, red dotted, in branched panicles, autumn, China, India; *papillosa,* 12 in. yellow, red marked, lip whitish with small excrescences, fragrant, India.

Acantholimon (Prickly Thrift)—*Plumbaginaceae.* Evergreen hardy perennials. A very large genus mostly of handsome and ornamental rock garden plants. Few of them are in cultivation. First introduced mid-nineteenth century.
CULTURE: Soil, sandy loam. Position, full sun, rock garden or a warm wall. Plant, October to April but preferably the latter.
PROPAGATION: By cuttings in a cold frame in late summer and autumn or by seeds.
SPECIES CULTIVATED: *A. acerosum,* rose, July to Aug., 6 in., Asia Minor; *Echinus* (syn. *A. androsaceum*), pink, July to Aug., 6 in., Orient; *glumaceum,* rose, July, 6 to 9 in., Armenia, the easiest and commonest; *venustum,* deep pink, summer, 9 in., Asia Minor.

Acanthopanax—*Araliaceae.* Hardy ornamental-leaved deciduous shrubs formerly included in the genus Aralia. Ivy-like fruits and usually prickly stems.
CULTURE: Soil, rich, well-drained loam. Position, warm, sheltered shrubberies, or corners of lawns. Plant in Sept. or April.
PROPAGATION: By seeds sown in heat in spring; cuttings of ripened shoots in autumn; suckers at any time.
SPECIES CULTIVATED: *A. Henryi,* 8 ft., finely toothed foliage, Central China; *Sieboldianus* (syn. *A. pentaphyllus*), 8 ft., elegant foliage, Japan, var. *variegatus,* leaves edged creamy white; *sessiliflorus,* 6 ft., leaves wrinkled, large, Japan; *Simonii,* 4 ft., attractive compound leaves, yellow spines, China. For *A. ricinifolius* see *Kalopanax pictus.*

Acanthophoenix (Prickly Date Palm)—*Palmae.* Stove evergreen palms. First introduced mid-nineteenth century.

CULTURE: Compost, two parts peat, one part loam and sand. Repot, Feb. Water freely in summer, moderately other times. Temp., March to Sept. 70° to 85°; Sept. to March 60° to 65°.
PROPAGATION: By seeds sown 1 in. deep in light soil. Temp. 80°, Feb. or March.
SPECIES CULTIVATED: *A. crinita,* 6 to 10 ft., Mauritius, Bourbon; *rubra,* 6 to 12 ft., Madagascar.

Acanthophyllum, see *Dianthus Noeanus.*

Acanthorrhiza—*Palmae.* Evergreen stove palms. First introduced mid-nineteenth century.
CULTURE: Compost, two parts loam, one part leaf-mould and sand. Repot,

Feb. Water moderately in summer, very little other times. Temp., March to Sept. 70° to 85°; Sept. to March 60° to 65°.

PROPAGATION: Like Acanthophoenix.

SPECIES CULTIVATED: *A. aculeata,* Central America; *Warscewiczii,* Panama.

Acanthus (Bear's Breech)—*Acanthaceae.* Hardy herbaceous perennial with ornamental foliage. First introduced mid-sixteenth century.

CULTURE: Soil, sandy loam. Position, warm sheltered border. Plant, Oct., March or April.

PROPAGATION: By root cuttings; seed in light soil; division of roots in Oct. or March.

SPECIES CULTIVATED: *A. Caroli-Alexandri,* white or rose, July, leaves spiny, 1 to 1½ ft., Greece; *longifolius,* purple, June, 3 to 4 ft., Dalmatia; *mollis,* white, rose, lilac, 3 to 4 ft., S. Europe, var. *latifolius,* larger and hardier form; *montanus,* tender, rosy-white, Aug., leaves spiny, 3 ft., West Africa; *Perringii,* rose, June, leaves spiny, 1 to 1½ ft., Turkey; *spinosus,* purple, July, leaves spiny, 3 to 4 ft., Levant.

Acer (Maple)—*Aceraceae.* A large genus of hardy ornamental trees, for the most part deciduous but including a few shrubby species, notably the Japanese Maple, *A. palmatum* and its varieties. All have typical winged fruits (samarae). The majority have five-lobed, palmate leaves which assume attractive autumn tints.

CULTURE: Soil, well-drained loam. Position, shrubberies or open spaces; Japanese kinds in warm borders or in pots in cool greenhouse. Plant, Oct. to March.

PROPAGATION: By seeds sown ¼ in. deep in sheltered position Oct.; grafting March; budding Aug. for choice Japanese and variegated kinds; layering Oct.

USEFUL DATA: Common Maple (*Acer campestre*) will grow to an altitude of 1,200 ft. and the Sycamore (*Acer Pseudo-Platanus*) to 1,500 ft. above sea level. Timber reaches maturity at 40 years of age. Life of trees 500 to 700 years. Timber of Sycamore used for making pattern moulds, stair-rails, turnery, etc.; that of common species and Sugar or Bird's Eye Maple (*A. saccharum*) for cabinet work. Quantity of Maple seeds required to plant an acre of ground, 14 lbs.; Sycamore, 30 lbs. Sycamore the best for hilly exposed positions.

SPECIES CULTIVATED: *A. argutum,* to 25 ft., Japan; *campestre,* 'Common Maple', to 50 ft., Britain, var. *variegatum,* leaves white and yellow, 20 ft.; *capillipes,* 35 ft., marbled bark, Japan; *carpinifolium,* 50 ft., Japan; *circinatum,* leaves scarlet in autumn, 5 ft., N.W. America; *Ginnala,* 10 to 15 ft., China, Japan, Manchuria; *griseum,* 40 ft., dark-coloured peeling bark revealing orange younger layers beneath, magnificent autumn tints, China; *Henryi,* 30 ft., spring and summer, tinted foliage, bluish-green stems, China; *Hersii,* newer species, striated bark, China; *japonicum,* 20 ft., Japan, and its vars. *aureum,* golden-leaved, and *laciniatum,* finely-cut leaves; *Maximowiczii,* handsome, newly-introduced small tree with striated bark, China; *Mono* (syn. *A. pictum*), 60 ft., Japan; *Negundo,* 'Box Elder', 40 to 70 ft., N. America, and vars. *californicum,* more vigorous, *crispum,* curled leaves, *laciniatum,* finely-cut leaves, *variegatum,* silvery leaves; *nigrum,* 'Black Maple', dark bark and orange twigs, N. America; *nikoense,* 40 ft., slow-growing, intense autumn colouring, Japan; *orientale* (syn. *A. creticum*), semi-evergreen, 10 to 15 ft., Medit. region; *palmatum,* 10 to 20 ft., Japan, and vars. *aureum, atropurpureum, septemlobum elegans, dissectum,* and *roseo-marginatum*; *pensylvanicum,* 'Snake Bark Maple', 30 ft., white-striated stems, N. America; *platanoides,* 'Norway Maple', 50 ft., Europe, and its vars. *aureo-variegatum, laciniatum, rubrum, Schwedleri; Pseudo-Platanus,* 'Sycamore', 100 ft., Central Europe, and vars. *albo-variegatum, brilliantissimum, corstorphinense, Leopoldii,* slow-growing and suitable for small gardens, *Handjeryi,* very slow-growing, *Worleei,* foliage rich yellow; *rubrum,* 'Red Maple', 80 to 100 ft., scarlet flowers, Canada; *saccharum,* 'Sugar Maple', 100 ft., maple sugar is produced from sap of this tree, N. America, var. *monumentale,* narrow erect growth; *spicatum,* 'Mountain Maple', pink fruits, brilliant autumn tints, N. America, var. *multiserratum,* attractive heart-shaped leaves; *tataricum*, 20 to 30 ft., S.E. Europe, Asia Minor; *truncatum*, 25 ft., attractive palmate leaves, China; *velutinum*, 50 ft., Caucasus N. Persia, and var. *Van-Volxemii*, vigorous tree with large palmate leaves, glaucous on the underside.

Aceranthus, see Epimedium.

Aceras (Green Man Orchis)—*Orchidaceae.* Hardy terrestrial, tuberous-rooted orchid.
CULTURE: Soil, chalky loam. Position, open and dry. Plant, Oct. to March.
PROPAGATION: By division of tubers Oct. or March.
SPECIES CULTIVATED: *A. anthropophora*, green, June, 6 to 10 in., Britain.

Achillea (Yarrow)—*Compositae.* Hardy herbaceous perennials.
CULTURE: Soil, ordinary. Position, dwarf species on rockery, tall ones in open borders. Plant Oct. to April.
PROPAGATION: By seeds sown ¼ in. deep; division of roots in autumn or spring.
SPECIES CULTIVATED: *A. ageratifolia*, close mounds, silvery leaves and stems, white, July to Aug., Greece, and var. *Aizoon* (syn. *Anthemis Aizoon*); *Ageratum*, ' Sweet Maudlin ', white, summer, 6 in., Greece; *ambigua*, silvery hummocks, white fls., June, 4 in.; *atrata*, white, Aug., 6 in., Austria; *Clavennae*, white, summer, 6 in., Austria; *clypeolata*, white-tomentose, yellow, 12 in., summer, Balkans; *filipendulina* (syn. *A. Eupatorium*), yellow, June to Sept., 4 ft., Caucasus; *Herba-rota*, neat, aromatic rock plant, white, May to June, C. Europe; *Huteri*, dwarf silvery-leaved alpine, white, May to June, Switzerland; *Jabornegii*, white, summer, 6 in., hybrid; *Kellereri*, filigreed silver leaves, white, summer, 6 in., hybrid; *Kolbiana*, white, 4 in., summer, hybrid; *Lewisii*, creamy yellow, 4 in., summer, hybrid; *Millefolium*, ' Milfoil ', white, summer, 1 to 3 ft., Britain, var. *rosea*, rose; *Ptarmica*, ' Sneezewort ', white, 2 ft., summer, Britain; *Prichardii*, white, semi-double, 4 in., summer, hybrid; *rupestris*, white, May, 3 in., Italy; *serbica*, silvery stems and foliage, May to Aug., 1 ft., Balkans; *sibirica* (syn. *A. mongolica*), narrow leaves, large white flower heads on long stems, to 3 ft., Mongolia; *tomentosa*, yellow, summer, 8 to 12 in., Europe; *umbellata*, white, June, 4 in., Greece; *Wilczekiana*, silver-serrated leaves, white, summer, 9 in., hybrid.

Achimenes—*Gesneriaceae.* Greenhouse, tuberous-rooted, deciduous perennials. First introduced mid-eighteenth century.
CULTURE: Compost, two parts peat and loam, one part leaf-mould, and sand. Pot in Feb., 1 in. apart, 2 in. deep, in pots, pans, or baskets. Water moderately at first, freely when in growth. After flowering, gradually withhold water from roots, and when foliage dies place pots on their sides in greenhouse, letting them remain till Feb.
PROPAGATION: By seeds sown ⅛ in. deep in light soil, temp. 70° to 80°, March; cuttings of young shoots and leaves April; division of scaly rhizomes, Feb.
SPECIES CULTIVATED: *A. coccinea*, scarlet, Aug., 1 ft., W. Indies; *grandiflora*, crimson, Oct., 18 in., Mexico; *heterophylla*, scarlet, July, 1 ft., Brazil; *longiflora*, violet, Aug., 1 ft., Mexico, and vars. *alba* and *major*; *patens*, violet, June, 1 ft., Mexico. A number of hybrids and varieties will be found in trade lists.

Achlys—*Berberidaceae.* Hardy herbaceous perennials.
CULTURE: Soil, cool, preferably lime-free, half shade.
PROPAGATION: Seeds or division of old plants in spring.
SPECIES CULTIVATED: *A. triphylla*, flowers inconspicuous, leaves fragrant when dried, 12 in., Western U.S.A.

Achras—*Sapotaceae.* Evergreen trees grown in tropical America for their edible fruits. Sometimes known as Calocarpum. First introduced early eighteenth century.
CULTURE: Soil, rich loamy. Position, border in warm greenhouse. Temp., March to Sept. 75° to 90°; Sept. to March 65° to 70°.
PROPAGATION: By seeds; cuttings.

Species Cultivated: *A. Ẓapota*, 'Sapote ', ' Marmalade Plum ', fruits russet-brown, to 65 ft., Cent. America.

Acidanthera—*Iridaceae.* Tender bulbous plants. First introduced late nineteenth century.

Culture: Compost, equal parts sandy loam and leaf-mould. Position, pots in cool greenhouse for *A. bicolor*, warm house for other species. Water freely during growing period, little at other times.

Propagation: By offsets treated as advised for bulbs.

Species Cultivated: *A. aequinoctialis*, white and crimson, Nov., 1½ ft., Sierra Leone; *bicolor*, white and purple, 1 to 1½ ft., Abyssinia, var. *Murieliae* (syn. *Gladiolus Murieliae*), white, blotched crimson, fragrant, 3 ft., July, Abyssinia: *candida*, white, 1 to 1½ ft., E. Trop. Africa.

Acineta—*Orchidaceae.* An epiphytic genus of considerable attraction. Pseudobulbs stout with large leaves. Flowers many in long pendent spikes, from base of pseudobulb, usually subglobose, fairly large, often fragrant.

Culture: Compost as for Cattleya with a little loam fibre added. Baskets are necessary and drainage must allow passage for the spikes. Hang near the glass, winter temp. 60° to 65°. Mature the plants in autumn by exposing to light. If ripened, water may not be required in winter. Moisture then must not be allowed to lodge on the plants or black spot may result.

Propagation: By division of plants large enough.

Species Cultivated: *A. Barkeri*, yellow or crimson marked, summer, Mexico; *chrysantha*, yellow, tip whitish, summer, Mexico; *densa* (syn. *A. erythroxantha*), yellow, crimson-spotted, spring, America; *Hrubyana*, ivory white, purple-spotted, summer, Colombia; *superba* (syn. *A. Humboldtii*), purplish crimson, lip marked yellow, spring, Colombia.

Aciphylla (Spear-grass)—*Umbelliferae.* Hardy evergreen perennials forming handsome rosettes of spiny foliage. First introduced mid-nineteenth century.

Culture: Soil, sandy loam. Position, large open rock gardens and beds. Plant, Oct., March or April.

Propagation: By seeds sown ½ in. deep in pans in cold frame, or warm position outdoors April; division of roots March.

Species Cultivated: *A. Colensoi*, white, summer, 4 to 6 ft. in Britain, 8 to 9 ft. in native haunts, N.Z.; *Lyallii*, 2 ft., sometimes more, N.Z.; *squarrosa*, ' Bayonet Plant ', white, summer, 4 to 6 ft., N.Z.

Acokanthera—*Apocynaceae.* Greenhouse evergreen flowering shrubs. Juices of both species are very poisonous. *A. spectabilis* was formerly known as *Toxicophloea spectabilis*. First introduced late eighteenth century.

Culture: Compost, two parts light loam, one part leaf-mould, and well-decayed manure, one part sand. Position, well-drained pots or border in light part of greenhouse. Water freely March to Sept., sparingly Sept. to March. Temp., March to Sept. 60° to 70°; Sept. to March 45° to 55°.

Propagation: By cuttings of young shoots in April and May, under bell-glass in gentle bottom heat.

Species Cultivated: *A. spectabilis*, ' Winter Sweet ', white, fragrant, spring, 8 to 10 ft., S. Africa; *venenata*, ' Bushman's Poison ', white, fragrant, 6 to 7 ft. S. Africa.

Aconitum (Aconite)—*Ranunculaceae.* Hardy herbaceous perennials, containing violent poisons. The flowers are hooded and foliage delphinium-like.

Culture: Soil, ordinary. Position, partly shaded borders. *A. uncinatum* is suitable for growing on pillars, arbours, etc. Plant, Oct. to March.

Propagation: By division of roots in autumn or spring; seed.

Species Cultivated: *A. anglicum*, mauve-blue, May to June, 3 ft., Britain; *Anthora*, yellow, July, 2 to 4 ft., Pyrenees; *Cammarum* (syn. *A. intromedium, A. Stoerckianum*), purple, July to Sept., 4 ft., hybrid, var. *bicolor* (syn. *A. bicolor*), purple and white, Europe; *Carmichaelii*, purple-blue, autumn, 4 ft., China, var.

Wilsonii, 6 ft.; *Fischeri*, bluish-lilac, July to Oct., variable, Asia; *japonicum*, deep violet, Sept. to Oct., 3 ft., Japan; *Lycoctonum*, ' Monkshood ', yellow, July to Sept., 3 to 4 ft., Europe, Siberia; *Napellus*, blue, July to Sept., 4 to 6 ft., very poisonous, Europe, var. *album*, white, *carneum*, flesh-colour, *pyramidale*, late flowering, and *roseum*, pink; *uncinatum* (syn. *A. volubile*), dark blue, autumn, 5 to 8 ft., partly climbing, N. America; *variegatum*, blue, and white, July to Aug., 3 to 5 ft., Europe.

Acorus—*Araceae.* Hardy aquatics. *A. Calamus* is fragrant in all its parts. Introduced by Gerard in 1596 and naturalised in Norfolk by 1660.
CULTURE: Heavy loamy soil. Position, margins of ponds; *A. gramineus* var. *pusillus* may be grown in aquariums. Plant March to July.
PROPAGATION: By division in spring.
SPECIES CULTIVATED: *A. Calamus*, ' Sweet Flag ', 3 ft., foliage resembling a flag iris, N. Temp. Regions, var. *variegatus*, leaves striped cream and green, 2 ft.; *gramineus*, 12 in., grassy, Japan, vars. *pusillus*, 3 in., *variegatus*, 12 in., leaves variegated.

Acroclinium, see Helipterum.

Acrophorus, see Davallia.

Acrophyllum—*Cunoniaceae.* Greenhouse flowering shrub. Evergreen. First introduced early nineteenth century.
CULTURE: Compost, equal parts peat and loam, little sand. Pot and prune, Feb. Water freely spring and summer, moderately other times. Temp., March to Sept. 55° to 60°; Sept. to March 45° to 50°.
PROPAGATION: By cuttings of firm shoots in sandy peat under bell-glass in a cool house in summer.
SPECIES CULTIVATED: *A. venosum*, pink, May, 6 ft., Australia.

Acrostichum—*Polypodiaceae.* Stove evergreen ferns found in tropical swamps.
CULTURE: Compost, equal parts peat, loam and leaf-mould, sand and charcoal. Pot Feb. or March. Water freely spring and summer, moderately other times. Temp., March to Sept. 70° to 85°, Sept. to March 60° to 65°.
PROPAGATION: By division of roots at potting time or by spores in spring.
SPECIES CULTIVATED: *A. aureum*, 1 to 2 ft., increasing greatly with age, Tropics; *daneaefolium* (syn. *A. excelsum*), fronds erect 5 ft. and over, Tropics.

Actaea (Baneberry)—*Ranunculaceae.* Hardy herbaceous perennials with poisonous red, white or black berries.
CULTURE: Soil, ordinary. Position, sunny border. Plant, Oct. or March.
PROPAGATION: By seeds sown outdoors in April; division of roots in March.
SPECIES CULTIVATED: *A. alba* (syn. *A. pachypoda*), white, May, berries white, 12 to 18 in., N. America; *rubra*, white, berries red, N. America; *spicata*, ' Herb Christopher ', white, May, black berries, 1 ft., Britain, var. *arguta*, taller form.

Actinea—*Compositae.* Hardy herbaceous perennials, sometimes known as Actinella.
CULTURE: Soil, light sandy. Position, rockery or open sunny border. Plant, Oct. or March.
PROPAGATION: By division of roots in March.
SPECIES CULTIVATED: *A. acaulis*, fls. rayless yellow buttons, May to June, 9 to 12 in., U.S.A.; *grandiflora*, ' Pygmy ' or ' Dwarf Sun Flower ', yellow, summer, 6 in., Rocky Mountains; *odorata*, yellow, July to Sept., 9 in. fragrant; *scaposa*, yellow, July to Sept., foliage silvery, 9 in., N. America.

Actinella, see Actinea.

Actinidia—*Actinidiaceae* (or *Dilleniaceae*). Hardy, deciduous and mostly rampant climbing, self-supporting shrubs. Flowers frequently unisexual. Fruit an insipid, gooseberry-like berry. All species from E. Asia. *A. chinensis* is the best species for gardens.

CULTURE: Soil, ordinary. Position, wall, trellis or tree stump. Plant, Oct. to March.

PROPAGATION: By seeds sown in pots in cold frame, April; layering shoots in Nov.; cuttings of half-ripened shoots in close frame.

SPECIES CULTIVATED: *A. arguta*, very vigorous, reaching the tops of tall trees, cream-coloured fragrant flowers, yellow berries; *chinensis*, vigorous, growths and fruit covered with reddish hairs; *Kolomikta*, 6 ft., foliage variegated white and pink; *polygama*, 10 ft., silver-variegated; *purpurea*, sweet-flavoured purple berries, vigorous; *rubricaulis*, red-stemmed newer species from W. China.

Actiniopteris—*Polypodiaceae*. Stove and greenhouse evergreen ferns.

CULTURE: Compost, equal parts peat, loam, charcoal, potsherds, and silver sand. Pot, Feb. or March. Good drainage and clean pots essential. Water moderately all seasons and keep atmosphere moist. Temp., March to Sept. 70° to 80°; Sept. to March 60° to 70° for *A. australis*.

PROPAGATION: By spores as for Adiantum.

SPECIES CULTIVATED: *A. australis* (syn. *A. radiata*), 3 in., India, requires stove treatment.

Actinomeris—*Compositae*. Hardy herbaceous perennial. First introduced early seventeenth century.

CULTURE: Soil, ordinary. Position, open border. Plant, Oct. or March.

PROPAGATION: By seeds sown ⅛ in. deep outdoors April; division of roots March.

SPECIES CULTIVATED: *A. alternifolia* (syn. *A. squarrosa*), 'North American Sunflower', yellow, July, 3 ft., N. America, var. *procera*, taller form.

Actinotus—*Umbelliferae*. Greenhouse or half-hardy herbaceous perennial.

INDOOR CULTURE: Compost, equal parts loam and peat, with a liberal addition of silver sand. Position, sunny part of cool greenhouse. Pot, March or April. Water freely March to Oct.; moderately afterwards. Temp., March to Sept. 55° to 65°, Sept. to March 45° to 55°.

OUTDOOR CULTURE: Soil, ordinary. Position, sunny. Sow seeds in temp. of 65° in March or April. Harden off seedlings gradually, and plant out at the end of May.

PROPAGATION: By seeds sown in a temp. of 65° in spring; or by division of the roots at potting time.

SPECIES CULTIVATED: *A. Helianthi*, 'Flannel Flower', white, June, 2 ft., Australia.

Ada—*Orchidaceae*. Epiphytic genus allied to Odontoglossum and succeeds best when grown in the Odontoglossum house. First introduced mid-nineteenth century.

CULTURE: Compost, equal parts peat or fibre and sphagnum moss. Position, pots in shade. Repot when new growth begins. Water freely during season of growth, moderately afterwards. Resting period, none. Temp., March to Sept. 55° to 60°; Sept. to March 50° night, 55° day.

PROPAGATION: By division of plant at potting time.

SPECIES CULTIVATED: *A. aurantiaca*, orange, Jan., 1 ft., Colombia; *Lehmanni*, cinnabar-orange, lip whitish, early summer, leaves grey-marked, Colombia.

× **Adaglossum**—*Orchidaceae*. A bigeneric hybrid between Ada and Odontoglossum.

Adam's Needle, see *Yucca filamentosa*.

Adder's Fern, see *Polypodium vulgare*; **-Tongue Fern,** see *Ophioglossum vulgatum*; **-Violet,** see *Goodyera pubescens*.

Adenandra—*Rutaceae*. Greenhouse, evergreen flowering shrubs. First introduced early eighteenth century.

CULTURE: Compost, equal parts loam, peat and sand. Pot, March. Water moderately Sept. to April, freely afterwards. Temp., Sept. to March 50° to 55°; March to Sept. 55° to 65°.

PROPAGATION: By cuttings of young shoots in sandy peat under bell-glass, March; also by seeds sown in similar soil at any time.

SPECIES CULTIVATED: *A. amoena*, red, June, 2 ft.; *fragrans*, 'Breath of Heaven' (syn. *Diosma fragrans*), pink, June, 2 ft., S. Africa; *coriacea*, pink, June, 18 in., S. Africa; *marginata*, flesh, June, 18 in., S. Africa; *umbellata*, pink, June, 2 ft., S. Africa; *uniflora* (syn. *Diosma uniflora*), white and pink, June, 18 in., S. Africa.

Adenanthera—*Leguminosae* (or *Mimosaceae*). Stove, evergreen flowering shrubs allied to Mimosa. First introduced mid-eighteenth century.

CULTURE: Compost, equal parts peat and loam, with a little silver sand. Position, well-drained pots in light part of stove. Pot, March. Water freely in spring and summer, and moderately in autumn and winter. Temp., March to Oct. 65° to 75°, Oct. to March 55° to 65°.

PROPAGATION: By cuttings of side shoots removed with a base of old wood and inserted in sand under bell-glass in spring.

SPECIES CULTIVATED: *A bicolor*, yellow, July, Ceylon; *pavonina*, 'Red Sandalwood Tree', 'Peacock Flower-Fence', yellow and white, July, 5 ft., China.

Adenocarpus—*Leguminosae*. Deciduous or semi-evergreen shrubs or small trees.

CULTURE: Soil, loam, peat and sand. Position, front of sheltered shrubberies. Short-lived, so young plants should be raised for replacement.

PROPAGATION: By seeds; cuttings of green wood; layers.

SPECIES CULTIVATED: *A. complicatus*, yellow, May, dense shrub, to 3 ft., S. Europe; *decorticans*, golden yellow in short dense upright racemes, May to June, 20 ft., Spain; *foliosus*, yellow, May, 4 to 6 ft., Canary Islands.

Adenophora (Gland Bell-flower)—*Campanulaceae*. Hardy perennials. First introduced late eighteenth century.

CULTURE: Soil, ordinary. Position, sunny, well-drained border, rock garden for shorter species. Plant, Oct. or March.

PROPAGATION: By seeds sown in March, in pots or pans in cold frame; division in spring.

SPECIES CULTIVATED: *A. coelestis*, pale blue, July, 1 to 2 ft., W. China; *confusa*, pale blue, summer, 18 in., W. China; *coronopifolia*, summer, pale blue, 2 to 3 ft., Manchuria; *Lamarckii*, blue, June, 1 to 2 ft., Transylvania; *latifolia*, blue, July, 18 in., Siberia; *lilifolia*, whitish blue, fragrant, Aug., 18 in., Europe; *hakusanensis*, blue, July, 18 in., Japan; *polymorpha*, pale blue, Aug., 1½ to 3 ft., E. Asia; *Potaninii*, pale blue, Aug., 2 ft., Turkistan; *stylosa*, blue, May, 1 ft., Asia; *tricuspidata* (syn. *A. denticulata*), blue, July, 18 in., China; *verticillata*, blue, June, 2 to 3 ft., Japan.

Adiantum (Maidenhair Fern)—*Polypodiaceae*. Stove, greenhouse and hardy ferns.

CULTURE: Compost, two parts peat, one part loam, silver sand, charcoal. Pot, March. Water moderately Sept. to March, freely afterwards. Position, shady at all times. Plant hardy species in April in equal parts peat and loam, in shady position. Temp. stove species, Sept. to March 60° to 70°, March to Sept. 70° to 80°; greenhouse species, Sept. to March 50° to 55°, March to Sept. 55° to 65°.

PROPAGATION: By spores sown on fine sandy peat, kept moist and shaded under bell-glass.

STOVE SPECIES CULTIVATED: *A. caudatum*, 6 to 12 in., Tropics; *cuneatum* (syn. *A. aemulum*), 8 to 12 in., Brazil; *concinnum*, 12 to 18 in., Mexico to Brazil; *cristatum*, 1½ to 3 ft., W. Indies; *curvatum*, fronds forked, Brazil; *decorum*, 8 to 12 in., Peru; *lunulatum*, fronds 1 ft. long rooting at apex, Tropics; *macrophyllum*, 12 in., Trop. America; *Moorei*, 12 in., Peru; *palmatum*, 10 in., Peru; *peruvianum*, 1 ft., Peru; *tenerum*, to 3 ft., West Indies, and var. *farleyense*, 3 ft., Barbados; *trapeziforme*, 2 to 3 ft., Trop. America, and var. *Sanctae-Catharinae*, deeper lobes.

GREENHOUSE SPECIES: *A. aethiopicum*, 6 to 8 in., Australia, Chile, California, etc.; *affine*, 12 in., New Zealand; *Capillus-Veneris*, 6 in., Temperate Zone, and numerous varieties; *diaphanum*, to 6 in., Asia to New Zealand; *excisum*, to 1 ft., Chile; *formosum*, to 2 ft., Australia; *hispidulum*, fronds forked at base, Tropics; *venustum*, 2 ft., Himalaya; *Williamsii*, 12 in., Peru.

HARDY SPECIES: *A. pedatum*, 1 to 3 ft., N. America; *venustum*, ' Don's Canadian Form', evenly-built large fronds, 1 ft.

Adlumia—*Fumariaceae.* Hardy climbing biennial. First introduced late eighteenth century.

CULTURE: Soil, light, rich. Position, warm border against south wall, or trellis in open garden. Plant, May.

PROPAGATION: By seeds sown ½ in. deep in border in April, or in pots in temp. 55° to 65°, March.

SPECIES CULTIVATED: *A. fungosa* (syn. *A. cirrhosa*), ' Climbing Fumitory ', ' Alleghany Vine ', white or purple, Aug., 10 to 15 ft., N. America.

Adonis (Pheasant's Eye)—*Ranunculaceae.* Hardy annuals and herbaceous perennials. First introduced early seventeenth century.

CULTURE: Soil, ordinary, fairly rich. Position, open border for annuals, rock garden for perennials. Plant, autumn or spring.

PROPAGATION: Annuals by seeds sown shallowly in borders in March; perennials by seeds and by division of roots in spring or autumn.

SPECIES CULTIVATED: *A. aestivalis*, crimson, June, 1 ft., annual, S. Europe; *amurensis*, yellow, Jan., 1 ft., China; *annua* (syn. *A. autumnalis*), ' Red Chamomile ', scarlet, May to Sept., 1 ft., annual, Britain; *brevistyla* (syn. *A. Davidii*, hort.), white, backs of petals blue, 9 to 12 in., summer, Tibet, W. China; *chrysocyathus*, golden-yellow, summer, 9 to 12 in., Kashmir; *pyrenaica*, yellow, July, 1 ft., Pyrenees; *vernalis*, yellow, March to May, 18 in., S. Europe.

Adromischus—*Crassulaceae.* Succulent herbs sometimes included in Cotyledon but with botanical differences.

CULTURE: Porous compost, well-lit greenhouse, temperature not below 55° F.

PROPAGATION: By leaf-cuttings.

SPECIES CULTIVATED: *A. Cooperi* (syn. *Cotyledon Cooperi*), red and greenish, to 1 ft., S. Africa; *cristatus*, to 10 in., S. Africa; *hemisphaericus*, to 14 in., S. Africa; *maculatus*, grey-green leaves blotched with red-purple, S. Africa; *rhombifolius*, grey-green scaly leaves, S. Africa.

Aechmea—*Bromeliaceae.* Stove, evergreen flowering plants. First introduced early nineteenth century.

CULTURE: Compost, equal parts of fibrous loam, rough peat, leaf-mould. Pot, March. Water freely always. Good drainage essential. Temp., Sept. to March 60° to 70°, March to Sept. 70° to 80°.

PROPAGATION: By offshoots inserted in small pots at any time.

SPECIES CULTIVATED: *A. Barleei*, yellow, July, 2 ft., W. Indies; *bromeliifolia*, Trop. America; *calyculata*, yellow, Brazil; *coelestis*, blue, July, 18 in., Brazil; *Drakeana*, rose and blue, 1½ ft., Ecuador; *fasciata*, pink and blue, Aug., 18 in., Brazil; *fulgens*, scarlet, Aug. and Sept., 18 in., French Guiana, var. *discolor*, scarlet and purple, June, 2 ft., Brazil; *hystrix*, scarlet, Feb., Brazil; *Lindenii*, scarlet and purple, Aug., 2 ft., Brazil; *Mariae-Reginae*, violet and crimson, Aug. to Dec., 2 ft., Costa Rica; *Ortgiesii* (syn. *Ortgiesia Tillandsoides*), red, 6 to 8 in., Brazil; *Pineliana*, Brazil; *polystachya*, Brazil, Argentine; *spectabilis*, rose, 2 ft., Venezuela, Colombia; *Veitchii*, red, July to Sept., 18 in., Colombia; *Weilbachii*, Brazil. See also Canistrum.

Aegle—*Rutaceae.* One species, small tree with hard greenish-yellow fruits, pulp of which is used for drinks and medicine. *A. sepiaria* has been transferred to Poncirus.

CULTURE: Soil, good. Grown in warmer citrus regions.

PROPAGATION: By seed.
SPECIES CULTIVATED: *A. Marmelos*, ' Bael Fruit ', white, April, India.

Aeonium—*Crassulaceae.* Succulent plants of Madeira and the Canary Islands, often included in the genus Sempervivum but now kept distinct.
CULTURE: Compost, equal parts loam, leaf-mould and brick rubble. Position, well-drained pots or pans in sunny part of greenhouse or window. Pot, March. Water moderately April to Oct., keep nearly dry rest of year. No stimulants, shading or syringing required. Temp., March to Oct. 55°·to 75°, Oct. to March 40° to 50°.
PROPAGATION: By seeds sown in spring in compost of equal parts sandy loam, leaf-mould and old mortar in well-drained, shallow pans, lightly covered with fine soil in temp. 55° to 65°; cuttings of shoots or leaves dried for a day or so after removal from plant and inserted in above compost in summer; division of offsets in March.
SPECIES CULTIVATED: *A. arboreum* (syn. *Sempervivum arboreum*), yellow, to 4 ft., rosettes 6 in. diameter, Mediterranean Region, var. *variegatum*, leaves variegated, *foliis purpureis*, leaves dark purple; *tabuliforme*, pale yellow, evergreen sub-shrub to 1 ft. or more, Atlantic Isles.

Aerangis, see Angraecum.

Aeranthes—*Orchidaceae.* Evergreen epiphytes native to Madagascar. The plants are practically stemless, the foliage thin, strap-shaped. Scapes thin, flowers few, solitary in some, characterised by the segments having their basal halves broad with their apices contracted into a ribbon-like tail. Green is the prevailing colour.
CULTURE: Compost half sphagnum moss, half fibre with charcoal nodules. Position, small pans, shaded from sunlight. Water throughout the year. Temp. 70° in winter, higher in summer by sun-heat.
PROPAGATION: By division, but plants seldom attain a requisite size.
SPECIES CULTIVATED: *A. arachnites*, greenish or whitish, summer; *grandiflora*, greenish or yellowish, summer; *dentiens*, green, summer; *ramosum*, olive green, racemes branched, autumn.

Aerides—*Orchidaceae.* An epiphytic genus. Most species have beautiful flowers. Stems erect, sometimes branching. Leaves distichous, persistent. Flowers, often fragrant, in axillary spikes, sometimes branched, often drooping from the upper portions of the stems. Two rather large groups are included, of which *A. odoratum* is one type, with horn-like labellums, owing to the spur-shape, and the other, *A. multiflorum*, with a flat lip. The species are given here under their familiar names. Many digressions occur, some may be localised forms, some natural hybrids; some species have terete foliage, but in the greater number, the leaves are strap-shaped, glossy green, so that the plants are not without attraction at all seasons.
CULTURE: Compost, two parts of osmunda fibre, two parts of sphagnum moss, liberally mixed with broken potsherds or broken red brick, pots very well drained, or teak cylinders may be used; the former are the better, as the fleshy roots, in many, adhere to any surface and in repotting the pots may have to be broken, creating less disturbance to the roots than if they have to be torn from wood. Position not too sunny, never gloomy. For the majority, a winter night temp. of 65° or slightly higher is required and a moist atmosphere maintained throughout the year. Summer temp. from 70° to 85°, with shading and by sun heat. The syringe may be freely used in summer and water frequently given. In winter, watering is required and the syringe occasionally used, especially if pipe heat has been excessive.
PROPAGATION: The stems emit roots, with age the lower leaves fall. The stem may then be severed, always below healthy roots and the severed leafy portion potted, guiding some of the lower roots into the compost. Perform the operation in spring. The base can remain in the original receptacle and may develop basal

growths, which can be allowed to form a specimen plant, or, when rooted, taken off and potted.

SPECIES CULTIVATED: *A. crassifolium*, amethyst-purple, summer, leaves coriaceous, Burma; *crispum*, white, rose flushed, lip rose-purple, summer, 2 to 5 ft., variable, Bombay district; *falcatum*, racemes 12 to 18 in. long, sepals and petals creamy-white, crimson-tipped, mid-lobe of lip deep purple, summer, autumn, 2 to 5 ft., handsome, variable, India, Burma; *Fieldingii*, racemes 2 ft. long, often branched, white suffused and mottled rose-purple, lip rose-purple, summer, 2 to 3 ft., Assam; *japonicum*, white or greenish-white, marked red, lip with purple spots and ridge, dwarf, fragrant, summer, Japan; *Lawrenceae*, waxlike, fragrant, white, crimson-purple, large, autumn, 1 to 4 ft., Philippines; *Leeanum*, rose-purple, amethyst, winter, East Indies; *Lobbii*, white, rose-flushed, lip violet tinted, summer, Burma; *maculosum*, fragrant, rose, purple spotted, lip rose-purple, raceme branched, summer, Bombay; *multiflorum*, variable, widely distributed, light amethyst to purple, often spotted, summer, India; *odoratum* (syn. *A. suavissimum*), variable, fragrant, white and lilac-magenta, summer, India, China; *quinquevulnerum*, variable, white, tipped and spotted amethyst-purple, lip white, mid-lobe amethyst, late summer, 2 to 5 ft., Philippines, var. *Farmeri*, white, summer; *vandarum*, leaves terete with slender tips, which thicken in succeeding years, 1 to 3 ft., flowers, very fragrant, pure white, twisted, autumn and winter, India.

Aeschynanthus—*Gesneriaceae*. Stove trailing evergreen flowering plants. First introduced early nineteenth century.

CULTURE: Compost, equal parts fibrous peat, sphagnum moss, charcoal. Position, hanging baskets, pots, or on blocks of wood or tree fern stumps. Plant, March. Water freely in summer, moderately in winter. Temp., Sept. to March 60° to 70°, March to Sept. 70° to 80°.

PROPAGATION: By cuttings, 3 in. long, of firm shoots inserted in pots of above compost mixed with sand in temp. 85°, Feb. or March.

SPECIES CULTIVATED: *A. atrosanguineus*, red, July, 1 ft., Guatemala; *Boschianus*, scarlet, July, Sumatra; *bracteatus*, scarlet and yellow, Aug., 18 in., India; *fulgens*, scarlet and yellow, June, 1 ft., E. Indies; *grandiflorus*, scarlet, Aug., 5 ft., India; *Hildebrandii*, scarlet, July, 10 in., Burma; *javanicus*, red, June, scandent, Java; *Lobbianum*, scarlet, June, 1 ft., Java; *pulcher*, scarlet, June, Java; *purpurescens*, purple and yellow, March, 1 ft., Java; *speciosus*, orange, summer, Java; *tricolor*, red and yellow, July, 1 ft., Borneo; *zebrina*, (syn. *trichosporum marmoratum*) green, spotted brown, habitat unknown.

Aesculus—*Hippocastanaceae*. Hardy, deciduous flowering trees and shrubs. Timber not of much value, used chiefly for making packing cases, carving, etc. Deer are fond of the nuts. First introduced early seventeenth century.

CULTURE: Soil, ordinary, deep. Position, shrubberies, woods, lawns, parks. Plant, Oct. to March. Prune away dead wood in winter.

PROPAGATION: By seeds sown 3 in. deep in open border soon as ripe; layering Feb.; grafting choice varieties in March or budding in July.

SPECIES CULTIVATED: *A. californica*, white, July, 20 ft., California; *carnea*, ‘Red Horse Chestnut’, red, June, 30 to 50 ft., hybrid, vars. *Briotii*, best red form, *plantierensis*, seedless form, pink flowers; *chinensis*, white, May or June, 80 to 90 ft., N. China; *glabra*, yellow, May, 30 ft., U.S.A.; *Hippocastanum*, ‘Horse Chestnut ’, white, May, 30 to 100 ft., S.E. Europe, and its vars. *Baumanii*, *Memmingeri*, *luteo-variegata*, *laciniata*, *pumila*, etc.; *indica*, white, blotched yellow and rose, June, July, up to 100 ft., Himalaya; *mutabilis*, yellow and red, June, hybrid, and vars. *Harbisonii*, long spikes of red flowers, *induta*, shrubby type with coppery pink flowers; *neglecta*, pale yellow, veined red, to 60 ft., N. Carolina, var. *georgiana*, shrubby, yellow and red flowers; *octandra*, ‘Yellow Buckeye ’, ‘Sweet Buckeye ’, yellow, May, 30 to 90 ft., S.E. United States; *parviflora* (syn. *A. macrostachya*, *Pavia alba*), ‘Dwarf Buckeye ’, 10 ft., spreading, white, U.S.A.; *Pavia*, (syn. *Pavia rubra*), ‘Red Buckeye ’ red, June, 10 to 20 ft., U.S.A.;

splendens, handsome 12 ft. shrub, scarlet, U.S.A.; *turbinata*, 'Japanese Horse Chestnut', creamy, June, to 100 ft., Japan.

Aethionema (Stone Cress)—*Cruciferae*. Hardy evergreen perennials. First introduced late eighteenth century.

CULTURE: Soil, ordinary, light. Position, sunny rockery, well drained. Plant, Oct. or March.

PROPAGATION: By cuttings of shoots inserted in pots of sandy soil in cold frame, July or Aug.

SPECIES CULTIVATED: *A. armenum*, pink, June, 6 in., Armenia and Palestine; *coridifolium*, 'Lebanon Candytuft', rose, June, 6 to 9 in., Orient; *diastrophis*, pink, summer, 9 in., Russian Armenia; *grandiflorum*, rose, May, 1 ft., Persia; *iberideum*, white, sometimes flushed lilac, June, 6 in., Levantine Alps; *oppositifolium* (*Eunomia oppositifolia*), lilac, 2 in., spring, Syria; *pulchellum*, rosy purple, June, 6 in., Armenia; *saxatile*, 'Candy Mustard', to 1 ft., small pink fls. in raceme, May to June, S. Europe; *schistosum*, pink, early summer, 6 in., Cilician Taurus; *warleyense*, 'Warley Rose', rose-pink, summer, 3 to 6 in., compact, hybrid.

African Blue Lily, see *Agapanthus africanus*; **-Corn Lily,** see Ixia; **-Cypress,** see Widdringtonia; **-Harebell,** see *Roellia ciliata*; **-Harlequin Flower,** see Sparaxis; **-Hemp,** see *Sparmannia africana*; **-Lily,** see *Agapanthus africanus*; **-Marigold,** see *Tagetes erecta*; **-Ragwort,** see Othonna; **-Tea Tree,** see *Lycium afrum*; **-Violet,** see *Saintpaulia ionantha*.

Agalmyla (Scarlet Root-blossom)—*Gesneriaceae*. Stove, trailing evergreen plants. First introduced early nineteenth century.

CULTURE: Compost, equal parts peat, sphagnum moss, and charcoal. Position, hanging baskets. Plant, March. Water freely March to Sept., moderately Sept. to March. Temp., Sept. to March 60° to 70°, March to Sept. 70° to 80°.

PROPAGATION: By cuttings of firm shoots under bell-glass, in temp. 80°, July or Aug.

SPECIES CULTIVATED: *A. longistyla*, crimson, July, 1 ft., Java; *staminea*, scarlet, June, 6 in., Java.

Aganisia—*Orchidaceae*. Stove epiphytal orchids. True Aganisias seem to have a scandent habit with pseudo-bulbs at short intervals. First introduced mid-nineteenth century.

CULTURE: Compost, fibrous peat or osmunda and sphagnum moss, equal. Position, a raft covered with a thin layer of compost is suitable. Water freely when growing, moderately when at rest. Resting period, winter. Scapes appear at base of new pseudobulb. Temp., Sept. to March 65° to 70°, March to Sept. 75° to 85° with shading.

PROPAGATION: By division of plants when new growth begins and the plants are large enough.

SPECIES CULTIVATED: *A. pulchella*, scapes erect, flowers 3 to 6, white with a purplish-red lip, British Guiana.

Agapanthus—*Liliaceae* (or *Amaryllidaceae*). Cool greenhouse, evergreen herbaceous plant. Hardy S. England, Ireland. First introduced late seventeenth century.

CULTURE: Compost, two parts loam, one part leaf-mould, dried cow manure, river sand. Position, well-drained border or rockery outdoors. Pot or plant, March. Water freely March to Sept., moderately afterwards. Temp., Sept. to March 32° to 40°, March to Sept. 45° to 55°.

PROPAGATION: By division of plant in March.

SPECIES CULTIVATED: *A africanus* (syn. *A. umbellatus*, *A. umbellatus minor*), 20 in; *campanulatus* (*A. umbellatus Mooreanus*) 20 in.; *orientalis* (*A umbellatus maximus*), var. *albus*, 2 to 3 ft., Cape, commonly cultivated as *A. umbellatus*.

Agaricus (Mushroom)—*Fungi*. Hardy esculent vegetable.

CULTURE INDOORS: On prepared beds in cellars, sheds, or other completely darkened buildings where an even temperature may be maintained.

CULTURE OUTDOORS: On steeply-ridged beds in the open or against sun-warmed wall. Mushrooms may also be cultivated with variable success in pasture grass.

PREPARING BEDS: Compost, fresh manure in a loose heap, turning it repeatedly for nine or ten days until friable and cheesy. Or use short straw or chaff thoroughly wetted and dressed with a proprietary rotting agent. Make indoor beds about a yard wide, depth 9 in., trodden or beaten thoroughly firm. Outdoor beds should have 3 ft. base, 2¼ ft. height with ridge not wider than 6 in. Cover the beds with up to 1 ft. of clean wheat straw to prevent evaporation. Test daily with thermometer thrust into middle of bed, and spawn when heat is between 75° and 80° F.

SPAWNING: Break brick of spawn into eight pieces. Bury pieces 2 in. deep at intervals of 9 in. all over bed. A fortnight later, as soon as the mycelium is seen to be running, cover with 1 in. of fine second-spit soil. Keep the casing soil moist but do not allow the water to penetrate the bed. Outdoor beds must be well thatched with straw to 6 in. thickness in summer, 1 ft. in winter. Spawn outdoor beds in July, Oct. or Jan.; indoor beds any time between midsummer and March. Bearing should commence about six to eight weeks after spawning and continue for three months or longer. Gather mushrooms by pulling the stalk from the bed; never by cutting.

CULTURE IN GRASS: Cut out pieces of turf 6 to 12 in. square, 1 in. thick, and 3 ft. apart. Stir soil below and press into it three or four lumps of spawn, about the middle of June. Replace turf and water occasionally if dry. Best results obtained where herbage is short, soil loamy and dry, and position sunny.

SPECIES CULTIVATED: *A. hortensis* (syn. *A. campestris* var. *hortensis, Psalliota hortensis, P. bispora*), now considered a species distinct from the Field Mushroom, *A. campestris* (syn. *P. campestris*).

Agastache, see Brittonastrum.

Agathaea, see Felicia.

Agave—*Amaryllidaceae* (or *Agaveaceae*). Greenhouse, evergreen flowering plants. Leaves usually stiff and spiny and yellowish green or red flowers, borne on spikes 1 to 40 ft. high when plants attain 10 to 60 years of age. In some cases the plant dies after flowering. First introduced early seventeenth century.

CULTURE: Compost, two parts loam, one part old mortar and river sand. Position, pots or tubs in greenhouses; may be stood outside June to Sept. Water moderately April to Aug., little afterwards. Pot, every five or six years; good drainage essential. Temp., winter 50° to 55°, summer 55° to 65°.

PROPAGATION: By offsets inserted in small pots at any time.

SPECIES CULTIVATED: *A. albicans,* 3 to 4 ft., Mexico; *americana,* ' American Aloe ', ' Century Plant ', 30 to 40 ft., Trop. America, and its vars. *medio-picta,* leaves yellow, edged green, and *variegata,* leaves dark green and yellow; *angustifolia* (syn. *A. vivipara*), to 8 ft., Cent. America, and var. *variegata; atrovirens,* 20 to 30 ft., S. Mexico; *attenuata* (syn. *A. glaucescens*), 6 to 10 ft., Mexico; *Botteri,* Mexico; *Celsii,* 4 ft., Mexico; *dasylirioides,* 10 ft., Guatemala; *densiflora,* 2 to 3 ft., Mexico; *ferox,* 20 to 30 ft., Mexico; *filifera* (syn. *A. filamentosa*), 10 to 15 ft., Mexico; *fourcroydes* (syns. *A. Ixtli, A. ixtlioides,* and *A. rigida*); *Ghiesbreghtii,* dwarf, Mexico, and var. *macrantha; ingens,* 20 to 30 ft., Mexico; *Kerchovei,* 12 to 18 ft., Mexico, and vars. *canaliculata, inermis, Veitchii; lophantha,* 12 to 15 ft., Mexico, and vars. *caerulescens,* glaucous leaved, and *Poselgeri,* leaves striped; *marmorata,* Mexico; *Morrisii,* Jamaica, and var. *variegata; noli-tangere* (syn. *A. horrida*), 8 ft., Mexico; *polyacantha,* 10 to 15 ft., Mexico; *potatorum* (syn. *A. Scolymus*), 12 ft., Mexico; *Roezliana,* Mexico; *Salmiana,* 30 ft., Mexico; *Shawii,* 8 to 10 ft., California; *sisalana,* ' Sisal Hemp ', 15 to 20 ft., Yucatan; *striata,* 12 ft., Mexico; *stricta* (syns. *A. hystrix* and *Bonapartea hystrix*), 10 to 12 ft., Mexico, and var. *glauca,* glaucous leaved; *utahensis,* 5 ft., Utah, Arizona; *Victoriae-*

Reginae, 10 to 12 ft., Mexico; *yuccifolia,* 20 ft., Mexico. There are many other species.

Ageratum (Floss-flower)—*Compositae.* Half-hardy annuals. First introduced early nineteenth century.

CULTURE: Soil, ordinary. Position, sunny beds or borders Plant 6 to 8 in. apart in June.

PROPAGATION: By seeds sown in light soil in temp. 60° in March, or by cuttings of young shoots from plants preserved for stock by growing in pots, pinching periodically to prevent flowering, and wintering in greenhouse temp. 50°.

SPECIES CULTIVATED: *A. Houstonianum* (syn. *A. mexicanum*), blue, summer, 18 in. to 2 ft., Tropics. Numerous dwarf forms and white varieties will be found in seed lists.

Aglaonema—*Araceae.* Stove perennials with arum-like flowers and variegated green leaves blotched with grey. First introduced mid-nineteenth century.

CULTURE: Compost, two-thirds loam, one-third leaf-mould, river sand. Position, well-drained pots, shady. Water freely when growing, little afterwards. Syringe foliage daily. Pot, March. Temp., Sept. to March 60° to 70°, March to Sept. 70° to 80°.

PROPAGATION: By division of roots in March.

SPECIES CULTIVATED: *A. angustifolium,* greenish white, July, 18 in., Straits Settlements; *commutatum,* white, July, 1 ft., Malaya; *costatum,* white, July, 6 in., Perak, and var. *virens; marantifolium,* white, 1½ ft., Malaya; *Mannii,* greenish white, July, 18 in., Trop. Africa; *modestum,* ' Chinese Evergreen ', 12 to 20 ft., Philippines. *oblongifolium,* crimson, July, 4 ft., Malaya; *pictum,* white, Aug., 18 in., Malaya; *simplex,* white, July, 18 in., Java.

Agrostemma, see Lychnis.

Agrostis—*Gramineae.* Hardy annual flowering grasses. Inflorescence light and graceful and valuable for cutting for mixing with flowers in summer, or drying for winter decoration. Also as pot plants.

CULTURE: Soil, ordinary. Position, sunny border.

PROPAGATION: By seed sown $\frac{1}{16}$ in. deep in April in open borders where plants are to grow.

SPECIES CULTIVATED: *A. alba,* ' Fiorin ', July, 2 ft., Europe; *nebulosa,* ' Cloud Grass ', July, 18 in., Spain; *stolonifera,* July, 1¾ ft., Europe. For *A. pulchella,* see *Aira elegans.*

Aichryson—*Crassulaceae.* Succulent plants of the Canary Islands intermediate between Sedum and Sempervivum and formerly included in the latter genus.

CULTURE: As Aeonium.

PROPAGATION: As Aeonium.

SPECIES CULTIVATED: *A. dichotomum,* yellow, stems hairy, annual or biennial; *domesticum* (syn. *Sempervivum tortuosum*), yellow, free flowering, erect, slightly shrubby, hybrid; *tortuosum,* golden-yellow, dense downy shrub; *villosum,* golden-yellow, to 4 in., sticky-hairy, Madeira, Azores.

Ailanthus—*Simarubaceae.* Handsome, hardy deciduous trees with ornamental foliage. First introduced mid-eighteenth century.

CULTURE: Soil, light, rich. Position, sheltered, moist. Plant Nov. *A. altissima* and its variety *pendulifolia* may be pruned to the ground annually in March to provide handsome foliage shrubs.

PROPAGATION: By portions of roots in pots of light soil in March. They should be kept close in a frame or cloche until growth starts, transplant the following spring.

SPECIES CULTIVATED: *A. altissima* (syn. *A. glandulosa*), ' Tree of Heaven ', leaves pinnate, 30 to 60 ft., China, and vars. *erythrocarpa,* fruits bright red, *pendulifolia,* leaves large and drooping, *sutchuenensis,* fruits larger.

Aipyanthus, see Arnebia.

Aira (Hair Grass)—*Gramineae*. Hardy annual ornamental grass.
CULTURE: Soil, ordinary. Sow seed in April, where plants are required. Position open. May be grown in pots in the cold greenhouse.
SPECIES CULTIVATED: *A. elegans* (syn. *A. capillaris*), 12 to 18 in., S. Europe, var. *pulchella*, awned florets.

Ajuga (Bugle)—*Labiatae*. Hardy perennials.
CULTURE: Soil, ordinary. Position, margins of half-shady beds, borders and rockeries.
PROPAGATION: By seeds sown outdoors in April, division of roots Oct. or March.
SPECIES CULTIVATED: *A. chia*, bright yellow, summer, 9 in., Cyprus; *genevensis*, blue, June, 6 in., non-trailing, Europe; *hybrida*, blue, June, 6 in., hybrid; *metallica crispa*, curiously curled, crinkled foliage of bright metallic tints; *orientalis*, blue, June, 12 to 18 in., E. Europe; *reptans*, blue, white or rose, June, 6 in., Britain, and vars. *atropurpurea*, purple leaves, *variegata*, leaves variegated, pale pink and cream, *Brockbankii*, blue.

Akebia—*Berberidaceae* (or *Lardizabalaceae*). Hardy climbing shrubs. First introduced mid-nineteenth century.
CULTURE: Soil, loam, peat and sand in equal parts. Position, south wall in S. England and Ireland; cool greenhouse other parts. Plant, Oct., Nov. in border. Prune straggling shoots after flowering. Whilst these shrubs are quite hardy, fruit is only likely to be formed in sheltered positions.
PROPAGATION: By cuttings inserted in sandy soil in gentle heat or by layers in autumn.
SPECIES CULTIVATED: *A. trifoliata* (syn. *A. lobata*), deciduous, vigorous climber, flowers purple followed by pale violet-tinted fruits, China and Japan; *quinata*, evergreen, violet or purple, fragrant, May and June, 30 to 40 ft., China and Japan.

Akee, see *Blighia sapida*.

Alabama Snow Wreath, see *Neviusia alabamensis*.

Alangium—*Alangiaceae*. Hardy shrub.
CULTURE: Ordinary light soil, moderately sheltered sunny position.
PROPAGATION: Rooted offsets in November or March.
SPECIES CULTIVATED: *A. platanifolium* (syn. *Marlea platanifolia*), deciduous, 6 ft., large maple-like leaves, small tubular white flowers, Japan.

Albizia (Pink Siris or Nemu Tree)—*Leguminosae* (or *Mimosaceae*). Slightly tender, deciduous acacia-like tree. Used as foliage plant for sub-tropical bedding as young plants. Introduced eighteenth century.
CULTURE: Ordinary light soil. Needs a high wall for successful cultivation.
PROPAGATION: Seeds sown ⅛ in. deep in March in heat.
SPECIES CULTIVATED: *A. Julibrissin*, pink, to 30 ft., not hardy in the open through average winters, W. Asia, var. *rosea*, dwarfer and hardier than the type.

Albuca—*Liliaceae*. Half-hardy bulbous plant. First introduced mid-nineteenth century.
INDOOR CULTURE: Compost, two parts loam, one part equal proportions of peat, leaf-mould, and silver sand. Position, cool greenhouse. Pot in Nov., placing five bulbs 3 in. deep in a 4½ in. pot. Cover pot with sphagnum moss or leaf-mould until growth begins, then expose to light. Water freely from time bulbs begin to grow until flowers fade, after which keep dry until Nov.
OUTDOOR CULTURE: Soil, light ordinary. Position, well-drained border at base of south greenhouse or hothouse wall. Plant 6 in. deep in Oct.
PROPAGATION: By seeds or offsets in spring.
SPECIES CULTIVATED: *A. angolensis*, yellow, 2 ft., Angola; *aurea*, yellow, June, 2 ft., S. Africa; *fastigiata*, white, May, 1½ ft., S. Africa; *Nelsonii*, white and red, fragrant, June, 2 to 3 ft., Natal.

Alchemilla (Lady's Mantle)—*Rosaceae*. Hardy herbaceous perennials with palmately-lobed or divided leaves and small greenish or yellowish flowers in corymbs.

CULTURE: Soil, ordinary, moist, well drained. Position, rock garden or front of border. Plant, autumn or spring.

PROPAGATION: By division; seeds.

SPECIES CULTIVATED: *A. alpina*, flowers green, foliage silvery, 6 in., Europe, inc. Britain; *conjuncta*, green, foliage silvery, 6 in., Alps; *mollis*, greenish-yellow, leaves green, very hairy, July, 1 to 1½ ft., S.E. Europe; *speciosa*, greenish-yellow, leaves green, July, Caucasus. Other species, e.g. *A. asterophylla, A. rigida, A. sericata, A. subsericea*, in botanic gardens.

Alder, see Alnus.

Alexandrian Laurel, see *Danae racemosa*.

Algerian Iris, see *Iris unguicularis*; **–Wax Bean,** see *Phaseolus vulgaris*.

Alisma (Water-Plantain)—*Alismaceae*. Hardy aquatic perennials with plantain-like foliage and whorled panicles of rosy flowers, apt to be weedy.

CULTURE: Soil, loam. Position, shallow water. Plant, spring.

PROPAGATION: By division; seed sown in shallow pans of loam and charcoal barely covered with water.

SPECIES CULTIVATED: *A. gramineum*, foliage ribbon-like when grown submerged, cosmopolitan; *lanceolatum*, 12 to 18 in., Europe, India, N. Africa; *Plantago-aquatica*, rose, summer, 2 to 3 ft., Britain; *rariflorum*, white, 12 in., Japan. For *A. natans*, see Luronium.

Alkanet, see Anchusa.

Allamanda—*Apocynaceae*. Stove, evergreen climbing plants. First introduced late eighteenth century.

CULTURE: Compost, two parts fibrous loam, one part leaf-mould, charcoal and coarse sand. Position, pot, tub or prepared border; shoots to be trained close to roof. Pot, Feb. Water freely April to Aug, then moderately. Temp., Sept. to March 60° to 70°, March to Sept. 70° to 80°. Prune shoots in Jan. to within one joint of main branch.

PROPAGATION: By cuttings of shoots of previous year's growth 3 in. long in pots of sandy soil in temp. 80° in spring. *A. violacea* succeeds best when grafted on to the more vigorous *A. cathartica* or one of its varieties.

SPECIES CULTIVATED: *A. cathartica*, yellow, July, 5 to 10 ft., Brazil, and vars. *grandiflora*, flowers to 4½ in. across, *Hendersonii* (syn. *A. Hendersonii*), leathery leaves, *magnifica*, 8 to 10 ft., *nobilis*, magnolia-like fragrance, *Schottii*, yellow with dark-striped throat, *Williamsii*, yellow with reddish-brown throat; *neriifolia*, yellow, June, to 3 ft., half-climbing or erect, Brazil; *violacea*, lavender, summer, 6 to 8 ft., Brazil.

Alleghany Vine, see *Adlumia fungosa*.

Alligator Apple, see *Annona palustris*; **–Pear,** see *Persea americana*.

Allium—*Liliaceae* (or *Amaryllidaceae*). Hardy and greenhouse bulbous perennials, vegetable and ornamental, with a strong onion or garlic odour.

CULTURE OF FLOWERING SPECIES AND CHIVES: Soil, ordinary, well drained. Position, sunny (for most species) borders, shrubberies and rockeries. Plant, Oct. to Nov., covering bulbs to twice diameter with soil.

PROPAGATION: By offsets or seeds in rich gritty soil in spring.

CULTURE OF GREENHOUSE SPECIES: The smaller and more delicate species of Allium, e.g. *A. acuminatum, amabile, cyaneum, Farreri, oreophilum* and *subhirsutum* are suitable for pans in the cool greenhouse and alpine house. *A. neapolitanum* is used for forcing. Compost, open. Plant dormant bulbs almost touching and plunge in ashes till growth begins. Remove to cold frame till growth is well advanced. Flower in cold greenhouse or force *A. neapolitanum* in temp. 60°. Water freely when growing, dry off after flowering. Increase by offsets removed at potting time or seeds sown in spring.

CULTURE OF ONION: Soil, rich, manured, well drained, retentive and deeply dug. Position, sunny. Prepare bed in autumn by digging deeply and working in well-rotted manure. Give balanced liquid manure during growth. Sow in boxes in greenhouse in January for early and exhibition crops, planting out in April after hardening off. Sow outdoors in August and transplant in early March with 6 to 8 in. between plants; or sow in March and thin to this distance, using large thinnings for salads. Bend over tops in mid-August to hasten ripening and dry before storing in frost-free shed.

CULTURE OF LEEKS: Soil, thoroughly dug and well manured. Sow early March to mid-April in prepared seed bed. When about 6 in. high transplant deeply into dibber holes 9 in. apart, and firm by watering. Leeks are quite hardy and can be harvested as required.

CULTURE OF SHALLOTS: Soil, deeply dug and manured. Plant bulbs 6 in. apart, pressing them into the soil until only the tip protrudes, end of Feb. Lift and dry end of July; save some small bulbs as stock for next year. May be grown from seed sown in March but these bulbs should not be planted as they will run to seed.

CULTURE OF GARLIC: Soil, rich. Plant bulbs 2 in. deep and 6 in. apart in Feb. Lift and store early August. Increase by division of bulbs.

PROPAGATION: By seed; offsets.

HARDY FLOWERING SPECIES CULTIVATED: *A. acuminatum*, lilac, June, 6 to 9 in., W.N. America; *albopilosum*, lilac, June, 1½ ft., Cent. Asia; *atropurpureum*, dark red, June, 3 ft., E. Europe; *Babingtonii*, pale red, July, 4 to 6 ft., Britain; *Beesianum*, blue, July, 1 ft., W. China; *Breweri*, violet-purple, June, 3 in., California; *bulgaricum* (syn. *Nectaroscordum bulgaricum*), whitish, May, 3 ft., S.E. Europe; *caeruleum* (syn. *A. azureum*), light blue, June to July, 1 to 3 ft., W. Siberia, Cent. Asia; *caesium*, dark blue, June to July, 1 to 3 ft., W. Siberia, Cent. Asia; *campanulatum* (syn. *A. Bidwilliae*), pale pink, June, 8 in., California; *caspium*, dull red and green, June, 1 ft., Cent. Asia; *cernuum*, rose, June to July, 1 to 1¾ ft., N. America; *Cyrilli*, lilac, June, 2 to 3 ft., S. Europe; *cyaneum*, dull blue, August, 6 in. N.W. China; *denudatum* (syn. *A. albidum*), creamy-white, July, 6 to 12 in., Caucasus, E. Europe; *Farreri*, reddish purple, June, 6 to 12 in., N.W. China; *flavum*, sulphur yellow, July, 1 ft., S. Europe; *giganteum*, lilac, June, 4 to 5 ft., Cent. Asia; *karataviense*, lilac, May to June, 9 in. Cent. Asia; *macranthum* (syn. *A. oviflorum*), purple, June to July, E. Himalaya, China; *Mairei* (syn. *A. yunnanense*), pale rose, Aug. to Sept., 4 to 8 in., W. China; *Moly*, bright yellow, June, 1 to 1½ ft., S.W. Europe; *Murrayanum*, rose, June, 1 to 1¼ ft., W.N. America; *narcissiflorum* (syn. *A. pedemontanum*), red-purple, July, 9 in., Alps; *neapolitanum*, white, June, 1 ft., S. Europe; *nigrum* (syn. *A. multibulbosum*), white, June, 2 to 3 ft., S. Europe; *nutans*, pink, July, 1½ to 2 ft., Siberia; *obliquum*, greenish-yellow, May to June, 2 to 3 ft., E. Europe, Siberia; *ochroleucum*, yellowish-white, July to Aug., 12 in., Cent. Europe; *oreophilum*, deep rose, May, 6 in., Caucasus, Cent. Asia, and var. *Ostrowskianum*, light rose; *oxyphilum*, white or pale pink, July to Aug., 10 to 20 in., Virginia; *paradoxum*, white, April, 1 ft., Caucasus; *pendulinum*, white, April to May, 6 to 9 in., S. Europe; *pulchellum*, lilac-purple, July to Aug., 1¾ ft., S. Europe; *ramosum* (syn. *A. odorum*), white and rose, June to July, 2 ft., Cent. Asia; *roseum*, light rose, June, 1 to 1¼ ft., S. Europe, var. *bulbiferum*, common in gardens; *Schubertii*, rose, June, 1 ft., W. and Cent. Asia; *scorzonerifolium*, bright yellow, June, 6 to 9 in., unknown; *siculum* (syn. *Nectaroscordum siculum*), green and dull pink, May, 3 ft., S. Europe; *sphaerocephalon*, dark red, July to Aug., 1½ to 2½ ft., Europe, inc. Britain; *stipitatum* (syn. *A. Rosenbachianum* hort.), lilac, June, 3 to 4 ft., Cent. Asia; *subhirsutum*, white, May, 6 in., S. Europe; *triquetrum*, white with green line, May, 9 in. to 1 ft., S. Europe, N. Africa; *tuberosum*, 'Chinese Chives', white, Aug. to Oct., 2 ft., China, Japan; *unifolium*, rose, June, 1 to 1½ ft., California; *ursinum*, 'Ramsons', white, May, 1 ft., Europe, inc. Britain; *Victorialis*, white, May, 1 to 2 ft., Alps; *zebdanense*, white, April to May, 1½ ft., Syria.

KITCHEN GARDEN SPECIES CULTIVATED: Most of these have been in cultivation for many hundreds of years and their exact origin is uncertain. *A. Cepa*, 'Common Onion', and vars. *aggregatum*, 'Potato Onion', *ascalonicum*, 'Shallot', *perutile,* ' Everlasting Onion ' (sometimes incorrectly called Welsh Onion), *viviparum,* ' Tree Onion ', ' Top Onion ', derived from a Cent. Asian species; *fistulosum,* ' Welsh Onion ', derived from an East Asiatic species; *Porrum,* ' Leek ', derived from a Mediterranean species; *sativum,* ' Garlic ', derived from a Cent. Asian species; *Schoenoprasum,* ' Chives ', Europe, inc. Britain, N. Asia; *Scorodoprasum,* ' Rocambole ', Europe; *tuberosum,* ' Cuchay ', ' Chinese Chives ', E. Asia.

Allspice, see *Pimenta officinalis;* **Carolina-,** see *Calycanthus floridus.*

Almond, see *Prunus Amygdalus;* **-Scented Orchid,** see *Odontoglossum madrense.*

Alnus (Alder)—*Betulaceae.* Hardy deciduous trees and shrubs. Timber of little value, except for making charcoal for gunpowder and also for its extreme durability under water.

CULTURE: Soil, ordinary. Position, damp places for *A. glutinosa;* drier spots for the others. Plant, Nov.

PROPAGATION: By seeds sown 1 in. deep in damp soil in March, transplanting the seedlings when a year old; or by suckers springing from the roots in Nov., or cuttings of firm wood after fall of leaf, inserted in open ground.

SPECIES CULTIVATED: *A. glutinosa,* ' Common Alder ', 50 to 90 ft., Britain, Europe, N. Africa and Asia, and vars. *aurea,* golden-leaved, *laciniata,* cut-leaved, and *quercifolia,* oak-leaved; *incana,* ' Grey Alder ', 50 to 70 ft., N. Temp. Zone, and vars. *aurea, pendula* and *pinnatifida.* There are others, but they are of no special interest.

Alocasia—*Araceae.* Stove plants with ornamental foliage. First introduced mid-nineteenth century.

CULTURE: Compost, equal parts peat, sphagnum moss, fibrous loam, with a little silver sand and charcoal. Pot, March, keeping base of plant above rim of pot; good drainage essential. Position, pots, shady. Water freely March to Sept., moderately afterwards. Temp., Sept. to March 60° to 70°, March to Sept. 70° to 80°.

PROPAGATION: By division of rhizomes in March.

SPECIES CULTIVATED: *A. argyrea,* 1½ ft., Trop. Asia; *Chantrieriana,* hybrid; *conspicua,* hybrid; *cucullata,* India; *cuprea,* 18 in., Borneo; *eminens,* Malaya; *esculenta,* habitat unknown; *gigas,* 5 ft., hybrid; *indica,* 4 to 6 ft., Malaya, and vars. *metallica* and *variegata;* *Korthalsii* (syn. *A. Thibautiana*), Borneo; *Lindenii,* New Guinea; *longiloba,* 1 ft., Malaya; *Lowii,* 2 ft., Borneo; *Marshallii,* India; *macrorhiza,* to 15 ft., Trop. Asia, and var. *variegata;* *Putzeysii,* Sumatra; *Sanderiana,* 18 in., Philippines; *zebrina,* 4 ft., Philippines.

Aloe—*Liliaceae.* Greenhouse, evergreen succulent plants with fleshy and more or less prickly or spiny leaves and red or yellow flowers borne on slender spikes. First introduced late sixteenth century.

CULTURE: Compost, two parts loam, one part peat, old mortar, river sand. Position, pots or tubs, sunny greenhouse. Water moderately April to Aug., little afterwards. Pot, March; good drainage indispensable. Temp., winter 50° to 55°, summer 55° to 65°.

PROPAGATION: By seeds sown in well-drained pans of sandy soil, temp. 70°.

SPECIES CULTIVATED: *A. abyssinica,* Abyssinia; *africana,* S. Africa; *arborescens,* and vars. *frutescens, natalensis, Ucriae* and *viridiflora,* S. Africa; *ciliaris,* S. Africa; *humilis,* and vars. *echinata, incurva* and *subtuberculata,* S. Africa; *Johnstonii* (syn. *A. Cooperi*), S. Africa; *Kirkii,* Zanzibar; *mitriformis,* and vars. *albispina, flavispina* and *spinulosa,* S. Africa; *striata,* S. Africa; *succotrina,* S. Africa; *variegata,* S. Africa; *vera,* Medit. Region. There are very many more species.

Alonsoa (Mask-flower)—*Scrophulariaceae.* Half-hardy shrubby perennials. First introduced late eighteenth century.

CULTURE: Compost, two parts loam, one part leaf-mould and sand. Position, pots, greenhouse, windows, or sunny beds outdoors, May to Sept. Water moderately always. Pot, March. Plant, May. Temp., Sept. to May 50° to 55°.

PROPAGATION: By seeds sown $\frac{1}{16}$ in. deep, March, temp. 60°, in sandy soil; cuttings, in pots of sandy soil, Aug.

SPECIES CULTIVATED: *A. acutifolia* (syn. *A. myrtifolia*), scarlet, and var. *alba*, white, 2 to 3 ft., Mexico; *incisifolia*, scarlet, summer, 18 in., Peru; *linearis* (syn. *A. liniflora*), scarlet, summer, 1 to 2 ft., Peru; *meridionalis* (syn. *A. Mutisii*), salmon pink, summer, 1 to 2 ft., Peru; *Warscewiczii*, scarlet summer, 18 in. to 2 ft., Chile.

Alopecurus (Lamb's-tail Grass)—*Gramineae*. Hardy perennial grasses.

CULTURE: Soil, any good light, well drained. Position, full sun.

PROPAGATION: By seeds sown when ripe in sandy soil and by division in spring.

SPECIES CULTIVATED: *A. lanatus*, woolly white, 4 to 6 in., summer, Spain; *pratense*, ' Meadow Foxtail ', 3 ft., Europe.

Aloysia, see Lippia.

Alpine Azalea, see Loiseleuria;   **-Bladder Fern,** see *Cystopteris alpina*; **-Catchfly,** see *Silene alpestris*; **-Currant,** see *Ribes alpinum*; **-Forget-me-not,** see *Myosotis alpestris*;   **-Pink,** see *Dianthus alpinus*;   **-Poppy,** see *Papaver alpinum*; **-Strawberry,** see *Fragaria vesca*;   **-Wallflower,** see Erysimum.

Alpinia—*Zingiberaceae.* Stove herbaceous perennials. First introduced late eighteenth century.

CULTURE: Compost, equal parts peat, leaf-mould and loam. Position, large pots, tubs or beds. Plant, March. Temp., March to Sept. 55° to 65°, Sept. to March 70° to 80°. Water freely March to Aug., moderately other times.

PROPAGATION: By division of roots in March.

SPECIES CULTIVATED: *A. allughas*, red, Feb., 3 to 6 ft., India; *mutica*, white, red and yellow, July and Aug., 5 ft., Malaya; *pumila*, Hong Kong; *Rafflesiana* (syn. *A. vittata*), 2 to 3 ft., Malay Peninsula; *speciosa* (syn. *A. nutans*), ' Indian Shell Flower ', white, purple and yellow, fragrant, to 12 ft., China and Japan.

Alsophila (Grove Fern)—*Cyatheaceae.* Stove and greenhouse tree ferns. A list of over ninety names has been compiled as being a complete list of Alsophila species but the majority of these have never been grown and are unlikely to be grown in this country. First introduced early nineteenth century.

CULTURE: Compost, two parts peat, one part loam, silver sand and charcoal. Pot, March. Water freely March to Sept., moderately afterwards. Position, pots or tubs, in shade. Temp. stove species, Sept. to March 60° to 70°, March to Sept. 70° to 80°; greenhouse, Sept. to March 50° to 55°, March to Sept. 55° to 60°.

PROPAGATION: By spores as Adiantum.

STOVE SPECIES CULTIVATED: *A. aspera*, 20 to 30 ft., W. Indies; *atrovirens*, 60 ft. or over, Brazil; *infesta*, 3 to 4 ft., Trop. America.

GREENHOUSE SPECIES: *A. australis*, 15 to 20 ft., Tasmania; *Colensoi*, 4 to 5 ft., New Zealand; *Cooperi*, 20 to 30 ft., Queensland; *excelsa*, ' Norfolk Island Tree Fern ', 60 to 80 ft., Norfolk Island; *quadripinnata*, 3 to 6 ft., W. Indies; *Rebeccae*, 8 ft., Queensland.

Alstroemeria (Peruvian Lily)—*Amaryllidaceae* (or *Alstroemeriaceae*). Hardy and half-hardy tuberous-rooted perennials. First introduced mid-eighteenth century.

CULTURE: Soil, rich, moist. Position, sunny, well-drained border, or pots in cool greenhouse. Plant, Oct. Water freely in summer, moderately in winter.

PROPAGATION: By seeds sown $\frac{1}{4}$ in. deep, in sandy soil, in pans in cold frame, March; division of roots, April or Oct.

SPECIES CULTIVATED: *A. aurantiaca*, orange, red and carmine, summer, 2 to 3 ft., Chile; *brasiliensis*, red, yellow and brown, summer, 3 to 4 ft., Brazil; *campaniflora* (syn. *Bomarea campaniflora*), green, summer, 4 to 5 ft., Brazil; *chilensis*, orange red, summer, 2 to 3 ft., Chile; *haemantha*, red, green and purple, summer, 2 to 3 ft., Chile; *Ligtu*, pale lilac or red and purple, $1\frac{1}{2}$ to 2 ft., Chile; *Pelegrina*, ' Lily of the Incas ', lilac, red and purple, summer, 1 ft., Chile, and var. *alba*, pure white; *psittacina* (syn. *A. pulchella* hort.), red, green and brown, summer, 2 to 3 ft., Brazil; *versicolor*, purple, maroon and green, summer, 2 to 3 ft., Peru; *violacea*, violet-mauve, summer, 3 to 5 ft., Chile.

Alternanthera (Joy-weed)—*Amaranthaceae.* Half-hardy shrubby perennials, used for carpet bedding, foliage crimson red. Sometimes known as Telanthera. First introduced mid-nineteenth century.
CULTURE: Soil, ordinary. Position, sunny beds outdoors, May to Sept. Plant, May, 2 in. apart. Lift in Sept.; store in pots or boxes in temp. 55° to 65° during winter.
PROPAGATION: By cuttings inserted in sandy soil, temp. 75°, March.
SPECIES CULTIVATED: *A. amoena*, leaves green, red and orange, 3 in., Brazil, and vars. *amabilis*, leaves orange-scarlet, *spectabilis*, and *rosea*; *Bettzickiana*, pale yellow and red leaves, 2 to 3 in., Brazil, and vars. *aurea, aurea nana compacta, magnifica*, and *spathulata*; *versicolor*, leaves coppery red, 3 in., Brazil.

Althaea (Hollyhock)—*Malvaceae.* Hardy perennial plants. Hollyhock first introduced mid-sixteenth century.
CULTURE OF HOLLYHOCK: Soil, ordinary loamy, not too light. Trench three spits deep in Oct. and work in plenty of decayed manure. Mulch surface of soil. Support with stakes standing 6 ft. out of ground. Water copiously in dry weather. Young plants yield finest flowers for exhibition. Cut down to within 6 in. of soil after flowering.
CULTURE OF OTHER SPECIES: Soil, ordinary. Position, sunny borders. Plant, Oct. or March.
PROPAGATION: Hollyhocks by seeds sown on a south border in June, thin seedlings to 6 in. apart in July. On warm soils seedlings may be transplanted direct into flowering positions in Sept., in cold districts or on wet soils pot in autumn and winter in frames, planting in April. Sow seeds in good soil in temp. 55° to 65° in Jan. or Feb., grow in pots, harden off in April, and plant out in May. Cuttings of young shoots growing out of base of flower stems inserted singly in small pots plunged in a gentle hotbed in spring; cuttings of young shoots consisting of two joints with lower leaves removed, inserted in small pots placed in a close frame in Aug. Other species by seeds sown outdoors in April.
SPECIES CULTIVATED: *A. cannabina*, rose, June, 6 ft., Europe, and var. *narbonensis*, red; *ficifolia*, 'Fig-leaved Hollyhock', yellow, June, 6 ft., Siberia; *officinalis*, 'Marsh Mallow', rose, July to Aug., 3 to 4 ft., Britain; *rosea*, 'Hollyhock', rose, 5 to 6 ft., summer, China. Many single and double flowered varieties of garden origin, for which see trade catalogues. See Hibiscus for *A. frutex*.

Alum-root, see Heuchera.

Alyssum (Madwort)—*Cruciferae.* Hardy annual and perennial herbs and sub-shrubs mostly with grey foliage. The summer bedding plant known as 'Sweet Alyssum' is now classified in the genus Lobularia. First introduced early eighteenth century.
CULTURE: Soil, ordinary. Position, open border or rockery. Plant, Oct. or April. Sow seeds of annuals where they are to grow.
PROPAGATION: By seeds for annuals; seeds and cuttings for perennials and sub-shrubs.
SPECIES CULTIVATED: *A. alpestre*, yellow, June, 3 in. Europe; *argenteum*, yellow, May to July, 1 ft., woody at base, Europe; *idaeum*, soft yellow, trailing, May to June, Crete; *Moellendorfianum*, yellow, June to July, 6 in., Bosnia; *montanum*, yellow, fragrant, summer, 2 to 4 in., Europe; *petraeum* (syn. *A. gemonense*), yellow, spring, 1 ft., woody at base, S. Europe; *pyrenaicum*, white, summer, 8 to 10 in., dwarf shrublet, Pyrenees; *saxatile*, 'Gold Dust', yellow, May, 1 ft., shrubby, Cent. and S. Europe; *spinosum*, white, June, 4 to 6 in., woody and spiny, S. Europe and N. Africa, and var. *roseum*; *Wulfenianum*, golden yellow, summer, 3 in. S. Europe.

Amaranth Feathers, see *Humea elegans.*

Amaranthus—*Amaranthaceae.* Half-hardy annuals. Foliage orange-red, crimson, green. First introduced late sixteenth century.

CULTURE: Soil, ordinary. Position, sunny bed. Plant, June.

PROPAGATION: By seeds sown $\frac{1}{16}$ in. deep, in temp. 55° to 60°, March; seedlings must be hardened off by easy stages, first on greenhouse shelf, then in frame, increasing ventilation until plants are well hardened before planting out.

SPECIES CULTIVATED: *A. caudatus,* (syns. *A. paniculatus* and *A. sanguineus*) 'Love-lies-Bleeding', 'Velvet Flower,' crimson-purple, summer, 2 to 3 ft., Tropics; *hybridus* var. *hypochondriacus,* 'Prince's Feather', crimson, summer, 4 to 5 ft., Tropics; *tricolor,* leaves carmine and yellow, India, less hardy than others, and vars. *splendens,* fine crimson foliage, best suited for pot culture in greenhouse and *salicifolius,* leaves willow-like.

Amaracus, see Origanum.

Amaryllis—*Amaryllidaceae.* Hardy bulbous plant. First introduced early eighteenth century. American authors consider the name Amaryllis should properly be applied to the American genus here called Hippeastrum; the Cape plant here called *Amaryllis Belladonna* is now known in America as *Callicrore rosea* or *Brunsvigia rosea.*

CULTURE: Compost, sandy loam, enriched with leaf-mould and cow manure. Position, well-drained border, foot of south wall. Plant bulbs 9 in. deep and 12 in. apart in September. Water freely in dry weather whilst growing. Mulch with decayed manure in spring.

PROPAGATION: By offsets.

SPECIES CULTIVATED: *A. Belladonna,* 'Belladonna Lily', rose-red, fragrant, Aug. and Sept., 18 in., Cape Colony, and various colour forms. The flowers appear before the new leaves. For greenhouse amaryllis see Hippeastrum.

Amasonia—*Verbenaceae.* Stove evergreen flowering perennial.

CULTURE: Compost, equal parts loam and leaf-mould, little silver sand. Pot, March. Position, in small pots near glass, well exposed to light; shade in summer. Water freely in spring and summer, moderately other times. Temp., March to Sept. 70° to 85°, Sept. to March 58° to 65°.

PROPAGATION: By division of the plants in March.

SPECIES CULTIVATED: *A. calycina* (syn. *A. punicea*), yellow and red, Sept., 12 to 18 in., British Guiana; *erecta,* white and pink, July, 18 in., S. America.

Amelanchier—*Rosaceae.* Hardy spring-flowering trees and shrubs. Deciduous. First introduced late sixteenth century.

CULTURE: Soil, ordinary. Position, open shrubbery. Plant, Nov. The leaves are prettily tinted in autumn. Easily grown small trees for the garden.

PROPAGATION: By seeds or layers in spring, or rooted offsets.

SPECIES CULTIVATED: *A. alnifolia,* white, April, 10 to 20 ft., N.W. America; *canadensis* (syn. *A. oblongifolia*), 'Snowy Mespilus', 'June Berry', 'Shadbush', white, April, 20 to 30 ft., N. America; *florida,* white, April, to 30 ft., N. America; *grandiflora,* a large-flowered hybrid making a small tree; *laevis,* white, May, 30 to 40 ft., N. America; *oblongifolia,* white, April, 6 to 20 ft., Eastern N. America; *ovalis* (syn. *A. vulgaris*), white, April, 15 to 20 ft., Europe; *stolonifera,* white, April, 4 to 5 ft., N. America.

American Aloe, see *Agave americana;* **-Cowslip,** see *Dodecatheon Meadia;* **-Cress** see Barbarea; **-Fox-grape,** see *Vitis Labrusca;* **-Ground Laurel,** see *Epigaea repens;* **-Ivy,** see *Parthenocissus quinquefolia;* **-Laurel,** see *Kalmia latifolia;* **-Swamp Laurel,** see *Kalmia glauca;* **-Wych-Hazel,** see *Fothergilla Gardenii;* **-Wood Lily,** see *Trillium grandiflorum.*

Ammobium—*Compositae.* Half-hardy annual, flowers valuable for cutting and drying for winter decoration. Gather when fully grown and hang head-downwards in a cool place. First introduced early nineteenth century.

CULTURE: Soil, light, rich. Position, warm border. Plant, May, 6 in. apart.

PROPAGATION: By seeds sown ⅛ in. deep in light soil, temp. 50° to 55°, March; or outdoors early in May.

SPECIES CULTIVATED: *A. alatum,* 'Everlasting Sand Flower', white, summer, 2 ft., Australia, *grandiflorum,* and var., with larger flowers.

Ammocharis—*Amaryllidaceae.* Tender bulbous plants.
CULTURE: As Brunsvigia.
PROPAGATION: As Brunsvigia.
SPECIES CULTIVATED: *A. coranica,* pink to carmine, 1 ft., S. Africa; *heterostyla,* white or pink, 6 to 12 in., Uganda, Kenya; *Tinneana* (syn. *Crinum Tinneanum*), pink to carmine or purplish red, W. Africa.

Amorpha—*Leguminosae.* Hardy deciduous flowering shrubs. First introduced early eighteenth century.
CULTURE: Soil, ordinary. Position, in the mixed shrubbery. Plant, Oct. to Feb. Prune after flowering, thinning shoots that have borne blossoms.
PROPAGATION: By cuttings in autumn; layering in summer; suckers in winter; seeds sown in cold frame.
SPECIES CULTIVATED: *A. canescens,* 'Lead Plant', blue, July, 3 ft., Missouri; *fruticosa,* 'Bastard Indigo', bluish purple, July, 6 ft., Carolina.

Amorphophallus—*Araceae.* Stove tuberous-rooted perennials. Unpleasantly scented flowers with purple or white spathes and brown spadices appearing before leaves.
CULTURE: Compost, equal parts turfy loam, peat, leaf-mould, decayed manure and silver sand. Position, well-drained pots in shade. Pot moderately firmly in pots just large enough to take tubers in Feb. to March, transfer to larger pots or tubs in April or May. Water moderately Feb. to April and Sept. to Nov.; freely April to Sept.; keep quite dry Nov. to Feb. Temp., Feb. to Sept. 70° to 80°, Sept. to Nov. 65° to 75°, Nov. to Feb. 55° to 65°.
PROPAGATION: By dividing the tubers in Feb. or March; by seeds sown in sandy soil, temp. 75°.
SPECIES CULTIVATED: *A. campanulatus* (syn. *A. virosus*), purple spathe, India; *Titanum,* purple spathe, very large, Sumatra.

Ampelopsis—*Vitaceae.* Fast-growing and ornamental, climbing, hardy deciduous shrubs, foliage brilliantly coloured in the autumn. Virginia Creeper, formerly included here, has been transferred to the genus Parthenocissus.
CULTURE: Soil, ordinary. Grown against walls and trellises. Plant Oct. to March.
PROPAGATION: By hardwood cuttings made in September and stored for planting outdoors in spring; softwood cuttings struck in frames in summer.
SPECIES CULTIVATED: *A. aconitifolia,* slender graceful vine, China; *arborea,* 'Pepper Vine', leaves dark green, colouring pale rose, U.S.A.; *brevipedunculata,* vigorous climber, N.E. Asia; *Delavayana,* vigorous, young growth reddish and hairy, China.

Amphicome—*Bignoniaceae.* Half-hardy perennial herbs, sometimes woody at base. Allied to Incarvillea and sometimes included in that genus.
CULTURE: Compost, two parts loam, one part of equal proportions of leaf-mould, decayed manure, and silver sand. Position, pots in cool greenhouse. Pot in Oct. or March. Water freely in summer, keep nearly dry in autumn and winter.
PROPAGATION: By seeds sown in a temp. of 55° in spring; cuttings of half-ripened shoots in summer.
SPECIES CULTIVATED: *A. arguta,* red, Aug., 1 ft.; *emodi* (syn. *Incarvillea emodi*), rose and orange, Aug. to Oct., 1½ ft., Himalaya.

Amsonia—*Apocynaceae.* Hardy herbaceous perennial.
CULTURE: Soil, ordinary. Position, sunny.
PROPAGATION: Seed or division.
SPECIES CULTIVATED: *A. Tabernaemonta,* blue, summer, 1 to 2 ft., Eastern U.S.A.

Amygdalus, see Prunus.

Anacampseros—*Portulacaceae.* Greenhouse succulent-leaved plant.
CULTURE: Compost, two parts sandy loam, one part of equal proportions of old mortar, small brick rubble and sand. Position, in not too large pots on shelves near the glass; no shade. Water moderately in spring and summer, keep nearly dry in autumn and winter. Dry atmosphere needed. Repot in March. Temp., 45° to 50° in winter, 50° to 60° in summer.
PROPAGATION: By seeds sown in a mixture of fine rubble and sandy loam, in heat, in spring; by cuttings, exposed to the air for a few days after removal from the plant, then inserted in fine sand in a gentle heat.
SPECIES CULTIVATED: *A. albissima*, white, S. Africa; *arachnoides*, pink, July, 12 to 18 in., S. Africa; *filamentosa*, pink, Sept., 1 ft., S. Africa; *lanceolata*, reddish, S. Africa; *papyracea*, yellow, S. Africa; *Telephiastrum*, pink, summer, 1 ft., S. Africa; *tomentosa*, bright red, S. Africa.

Anacamptis—*Orchidacea.* *A. pyramidalis* is the correct name for the English orchid known as *Orchis pyramidalis*, q. v.

Anacardium—*Anacardiaceae.* Stove evergreen tree widely cultivated in Tropics for its edible nuts. First introduced late seventeenth century.
CULTURE: Soil, light, loamy. Position, borders in warm house. Temp., March to Sept. 75° to 85°, Sept. to March 65° to 75°. Water freely during summer.
PROPAGATION: By cuttings of ripened wood, in sandy soil, under hand-glass, in warm house.
SPECIES CULTIVATED: *A. occidentale*, ' Cashew Nut ', yellow and red fruit with edible kernel, 30 to 40 ft., Trop. America.

Anacharis (Water Thyme)—*Hydrocharitaceae.* Useful oxygenating plants for pond or aquarium with narrow thyme-like leaves. It was a great pest when first introduced from N. America in 1847 but is now less vigorous.
CULTURE: Soil, aquarium compost or loam. Plant any time during spring or summer, weight clumps with lead or stone and sink in position.
PROPAGATION: Slips taken any time during growing season.
SPECIES CULTIVATED: *A. canadensis* (syn. *Elodea canadensis*), 'Canadian Water Weed', small white flowers, N. America.

Anacyclus (Mount Atlas Daisy)—*Compositae.* Perennial rock garden plants.
CULTURE: Soil, light sandy, gritty loam or scree mixture. Position, full sun, deep pocket or scree.
PROPAGATION: Seeds sown in cold frame in light, gritty soil in early spring; as the seeds are difficult to identify, the whole seed head should be rubbed up and sown chaff and all.
SPECIES CULTIVATED: *A. atlanticus*, white, spring to summer, prostrate, Morocco; *depressus*, white, backs of petals crimson, spring and summer, prostrate, N. Africa.

Anagallis (Pimpernel)—*Primulaceae.* Hardy trailing annuals and perennials.
CULTURE: Soil, light, rich. Position, sunny, well-drained borders for annuals; moist and boggy places for perennials.
PROPAGATION: Annuals by seeds sown ⅛ in. deep in temp. 65° March, transplanting seedlings outdoors in June; perennials by division of roots in March; seeds sown outdoors in April.
ANNUAL SPECIES: *A. fruticosa*, vermilion, May to Aug., 2 ft., Morocco; *indica*, blue, July, 1 ft., India.
PERENNIAL SPECIES: *A. linifolia* (syn. *A. grandiflora*), blue, July, 1 ft., Europe, and vars. *collina* and *Monellii*; *tenella*, rosy, July and Aug., Britain.

Ananas—*Bromeliaceae.* Stove evergreen plants, bearing the well-known pineapple fruits. First introduced mid-seventeenth century.
CULTURE: Compost, two parts decomposed fibrous loam, one part well-decayed manure, one part ¼ in. bones and pounded oyster shells. Position, pots plunged in a tan hotbed in stove facing south. Temp., Sept. to March 65° to 75°,

March to Sept. 75° to 90°. Full exposure to sun essential. Water moderately in winter, freely in summer. Moist atmosphere most essential in spring and summer, and a slightly dry one in winter. When fruit begins to ripen withhold water. Supply plants in fruiting pots freely with liquid manure. Plants come into bearing when two years old.

PROPAGATION: By suckers, or crowns of fruit inserted in small pots in temp. 80°, spring.

SPECIES CULTIVATED: *A. comosus* (syn. *A. sativus*), ' Pineapple ', 3 ft., Trop. America, and its vars. *variegatus*, leaves striped, and *Porteanus*, leaves with central yellow band.

Anaphalis—*Compositae*. Hardy perennials, with ' everlasting ' flowers.
CULTURE: Soil, ordinary. Position, sunny borders. Plant in Oct. or March.
PROPAGATION: By division in autumn or spring; seeds sown outdoors in April.
SPECIES CULTIVATED: *A. cinnamomea*, white flowers and foliage, cinnamon-scented, July to Sept., 1 to 2 ft., shrubby, China and Japan; *margaritacea*, ' Pearly Everlasting ', white, July and Aug., 1 ft., N. America; *triplinervis*, 12 to 18 in., white, downy leaves, Himalaya.

Anastatica—*Cruciferae*. Half-hardy annual. In its native country possesses the peculiar property of withering up in dry weather, and when rain comes of spreading itself out again, as though alive.
CULTURE: Soil, ordinary. Sow seeds in a cold frame in spring and plant in sunny border in May. Usually purchased as plants in a dry ball.
SPECIES CULTIVATED: *A. hierochuntica*, ' Rose of Jericho ', ' Resurrection Plant ', white, summer, 1 ft., Orient.

Anchusa (Alkanet, Bugloss)—*Boraginaceae*. Hardy biennials and perennials. The plant formerly known as *A. myosotidiflora* is now classified as *Brunnera macrophylla*, and *A. sempervirens* as *Pentaglottis sempervirens*.
CULTURE: Soil, ordinary. Position, sunny borders. Plant, Oct. or March. The well-known Dropmore, Opal, etc., are forms of *A. azurea*.
PROPAGATION: By seed; root cuttings in Feb.; division in Oct. for perennials; biennials, by seed in sandy soil in temp. 55° to 65° in March or outdoors in April.
SPECIES CULTIVATED: *A. azurea* (syn. *A. italica*), perennial, blue, July, 3 to 4 ft., S. France; *Barrelieri*, perennial, blue and white, June, 2 ft., Europe; *caespitosa*, gentian blue, May to August, 15 in., Crete; *capensis*, biennial, blue, July, 12 to 18 in., S. Africa; *officinalis*, biennial or perennial, rich blue, 1 to 2 ft., Europe.

Anchor Plant, see *Colletia cruciata*.

Andromeda—*Ericaceae*. Hardy evergreen flowering shrub.
CULTURE: Soil, boggy peat. Position, moist, shady borders or beds. Plant, Oct. No pruning required except to cut away dead wood.
PROPAGATION: By layering shoots in Sept.; seeds sown in peaty soil in a cold frame.
SPECIES CULTIVATED: *A. polifolia*, ' Marsh Rosemary ', pink, June, 1 ft., N. Temp. Regions, including Britain, and vars. *angustifolia*, *rosmarinifolia*, *major*, also *compacta*, a delightful form for the rockery. See Pieris, Leucothoe and Zenobia for other species formerly included in this genus.

Andropogon (Beard Grass)—*Gramineae*. Hardy ornamental flowering grass.
CULTURE. Soil, ordinary, light, and dry. Position, sunny border. Plant, Oct., March and April. Apply liquid manure occasionally in summer.
PROPAGATION: By division.
SPECIES CULTIVATED: *A. furcatus*, to 6 ft., N. America.

Androsace (Rock Jasmine)—*Primulaceae*. Hardy perennial alpine plants. First introduced mid-eighteenth century.
CULTURE: For general purposes in the rock garden, sandy loam and leaf-mould with sharp grit added generously. Plant, March or April. For those

species best suited for alpine house or cold frame cultivation, loam, leaf-mould, sand and sharp grit in equal proportions.

PROPAGATION: By seeds sown in sandy gritty soil in pans; cuttings in sandy soil in frames in spring; division of roots in spring.

SPECIES CULTIVATED: *A. alpina*, pink, summer, 1 in., Europe; *carnea*, pink, June to July, 3 in., Europe, var. *Laggeri*, pink, March to April, more densely tufted; *Chamaejasme*, white, May to June, 3 in., Europe and N. America; *ciliata*, rose-pink, June, 2 in., Pyrenees; *cylindrica*, milk-white, May to June, 2 in., Pyrenees; *helvetica*, pink, fading to white, June to July, 1 in., Europe; *hirtella*, white, May to June, 1 in., Pyrenees; *imbricata*, white, June, 1 in., Alps; *lactea*, white, yellow-eyed, June to Aug., 6 in., Switzerland, Transylvania; *lactiflora* (syn. *A. coronopifolia*), bluish-white, biennial, June to Aug., 6 in., Siberia; *lanuginosa*, rose, July, 6 in., Himalaya, var. *Leichtlinii*, white, crimson-eyed; *mucronifolia*, pink, June to July, 3 in., Kashmir; *pubescens*, white, May to June 2 in., Alps; *pyrenaica*, white, May to June, 1 in., Pyrenees; *sarmentosa*, rose, May, 3 to 4 in., Himalaya, vars. *Chumbyi*, more brightly coloured, *Watkinsii*, bright rose-red, 6 in.; *sempervivoides*, rose-red, May, 3 in., Himalaya; *villosa*, white, golden-eyed, 3 in., Europe, var. *arachnoidea*, white, June to July, 1 in., E. Europe; *Wulfeniana*, bright rose-red, April to May, 1 in., E. Alps..

Andryala—*Compositae*. Evergreen silver-leaved sub-shrubs.

CULTURE: Soil, light sandy loam, well drained. Position, sunny, sheltered.

PROPAGATION: Seeds in cold frame; cuttings in late summer in cold frame.

SPECIES CULTIVATED: *A. Agardhii*, yellow, all summer, 9 to 12 in., Spain.

Aneimia (Flower-fern; Ash-leaf Fern)—*Schizaeaceae*. Stove and greenhouse ferns. First introduced late eighteenth century. Some authorites use the name Anemidictyon in place of Aneimia.

CULTURE: Compost, equal parts loam, peat, leaf-mould, sand and charcoal. Position, shady, moist; useful for wardian cases. Pot, Feb., March. Water freely spring and summer, moderately other times. Temp., stove, March to Sept. 70° to 85°, Sept. to March 60° to 65°; greenhouse, March to Sept. 55° to 60°, Sept. to March 45° to 50°.

PROPAGATION: By spores similar to Adiantum.

STOVE SPECIES CULTIVATED: *A. adiantifolia*, 12 to 18 in., Trop. America; *collina*, 8 to 12 in., Brazil; *Dregeana*, 9 in., Natal; *rotundifolia*, 6 to 9 in., Brazil.

GREENHOUSE SPECIES CULTIVATED: *A. phyllitidis*, 1 ft., Cuba, Peru; *tomentosa* (syn. *A. chelianthoides*, *A. deltoides* and *A. flexuosa*), 1 to 2 ft., Mexico, etc.

Anemone (Windflower)—*Ranunculaceae*. Hardy herbaceous and tuberous-rooted perennials. Certain species have been placed in the genus Hepatica, and some authors separate the Pulsatilla section as an independent genus. The Japanese Anemones of gardens are hybrids of *A. hupehensis* var. *japonica* and *A. vitifolia*, now known as *A. hybrida*.

CULTURE: Soil, good ordinary, well enriched with decayed manure. Position, sunny or partly shady borders. Plant, autumn or spring.

Culture of *A. coronaria*, *fulgens*, and *hortensis*: Soil, moderately light, liberally mixed with leaf-mould and decayed manure. Position, partly shaded beds or borders. Plant tubers 3 in. deep and 6 in. apart in Oct., Nov., or Feb. to March. Lift tubers when foliage dies and store away in cool place till planting time; or in well-drained soils leave undisturbed until crowding indicates the need for lifting, separating and replanting.

PROPAGATION: Herbaceous species, by seeds in sandy soil in cold frame in spring; division of roots Oct. or March; root cuttings in spring. Tuberous-rooted species by seeds sown in prepared beds of above soil in Jan. or Feb. or in July.

SPECIES CULTIVATED: *A. albana*, white to pale blue, May, 12 in., N. Asia; *alpina* (syns. *A. acutipetala*, *Pulsatilla alpina*), white, May, 12 to 18 in., Europe, var. *sulphurea*, soft yellow; *apennina*, blue, rose and white, March, 6 in., Europe (Br.), and numerous wild and garden varieties; *baldensis*, white, tinged pink,

May to June, 6 in., Europe; *blanda*, blue, Jan. to March, 6 in., Asia Minor; *canadensis* (syn. *A. dichotoma*), white, June, 2¼ ft., E.N. America; *coronaria*, ' Poppy Anemone ', various, spring, 9 to 12 in., S. Europe; *demissa*, white, summer, 9 in., E. Asia; *Fanninii*, white, June, 3 to 4 ft., Natal; *fulgens*, ' Scarlet Windflower ', scarlet, May, 1 ft., S. Europe; *glauciifolia*, bluish-lilac, summer, 1 to 3 ft., W. China; *Halleri* (syn. *Pulsatilla Halleri*), lilac, June, to 6 in., Switzerland; *hortensis* (syn. *A. stellata*), various, spring, 1 ft., S. Europe; *hybrida* (syn. *A. elegans*), ' Japanese Windflower ', rose, 2 to 5 ft., hybrid, many named varieties from white to red; *hupehensis* (syn. *A. japonica* var. *hupehensis*), rose, summer, 1¼ to 2 ft., Cent. and W. China, var. *japonica*, semi-double, naturalised in Japan; *multifida*, yellow to purple, 6 to 18 in., S. America; *narcissiflora*, white to pink, occasionally yellow, May to June, 1 ft., Mts. of Europe; *nemorosa*, ' Wood Anemone ', white, March, 6 in., Britain, and vars. *alba, Allenii, major, Robinsoniana*, etc.; *palmata*, white and yellow, May, 6 in., Mediterranean; *patens* (syn. *Pulsatilla patens*), purple to white, May to June, 12 in., Europe, N. Asia, etc.; *pavonina*, various, to 1 ft., Balkan Peninsula, Asia Minor, and vars. *typica*, plain scarlet, *ocellata*, scarlet with yellow eye, *purpureo-violacea*, violet or rose; *Pulsatilla* (syn. *Pulsatilla vulgaris*), ' Pasque Flower ', purple, April, 1 ft., Europe (Br.), and numerous named varieties; *ranunculoides*, golden yellow, March, 9 to 12 in., Europe (Br.), Siberia; *rivularis*, white, May, 2 ft., Himalaya; *rupicola*, white, May to June, 12 in., Himalaya; *sylvestris*, ' Snowdrop Windflower ', white, April, 1 ft., Europe; *tetrasepala*, white, May to June, 2 to 4¼ ft., N. India; *tomentosa* (syns. *A. japonica* var. *tomentosa*, *A. hupehensis* var. *tomentosa*), rose, July to Sept., 3 to 5 ft., W. China; *trifolia*, white, spring, 6 in., S. Europe, var. *caerulescens*, bluish; *vernalis* (syn. *Pulsatilla vernalis*), purple, white outside, May, 6 to 9 in., Europe; *vindobonensis*, pale yellow, 6 in., March, hybrid; *vitifolia*, white, summer, 3 to 4 ft., tender, N. India, N.W. China.

Anemonella—*Ranunculaceae.* One perennial herb with tuberous roots, sometimes included in the genus Anemone.
CULTURE: Soil, light moist. Position, partly shady.
PROPAGATION: By division of roots in spring or autumn.
SPECIES CULTIVATED: *A. thalictroides* (syn. *Anemone thalictroides, Syndesmon thalictroides*), ' Rue Anemone ', white to pink, spring, 4 to 12 in., E.N. America.

Anemonopsis—*Ranunculaceae.* Hardy herbaceous perennial. First introduced mid-nineteenth century.
CULTURE: Soil, deep rich loam. Position, well-drained and partially shaded border. Plant, Oct., March.
PROPAGATION: By division of roots in Oct. or March; seeds sown in heat in March, planting seedlings out in May.
SPECIES CULTIVATED: *A. macrophylla*, lilac and purple, June and July, 2 to 3 ft., Japan.

Anemopsis (Apache Beads)—*Saururaceae.* One perennial aquatic herb. Aromatic rootstocks used medicinally and strung into necklaces as beads.
CULTURE: Soil, loamy. Position, shallow water or wet soil. Plant, spring.
PROPAGATION: By division in spring.
SPECIES CULTIVATED: *A. californica*, ' Yerba Mansa ', 18 in., rounded leaves, white, anemone-like flowers, California.

Anethum—*Umbelliferae.* Annual or biennial herbs. One species grown for seeds which are used for flavouring.
CULTURE OF DILL: Sow in April in a warm open situation in a good garden soil. Cut down when seeds begin to ripen and thresh when ripe.
SPECIES CULTIVATED: *A. graveolens* (syn. *Peucedanum graveolens*), ' Dill ', yellow, summer, to 3 ft., Europe.

Angelica—*Umbelliferae.* Perennial herbaceous herb used for flavouring confectionery and liquors, and root candied for cake decoration.
CULTURE: Soil, deep, moist loam. Position, shady.

PROPAGATION: By seeds sown ½ in. deep in March where plants are to remain. When seedlings are 3 in. high, thin them to 6 in. apart.

SPECIES CULTIVATED: *A. Archangelica*, ' Holy Ghost ', green, July, 4 to 5 ft., Europe; *sylvestris*, white, to 4 ft., Cent. Europe.

Angelonia—*Scrophulariaceae.* Stove and greenhouse herbaceous perennials. First introduced early nineteenth century.

CULTURE: Compost, equal parts of loam, peat, leaf-mould and a little sand. Position, pots in sunny parts of stove or greenhouse. Pot, March. Water freely March to Oct., moderately afterwards. Temp., March to Oct. 65° to 75°, afterwards 55° to 60° for stove species; March to Oct. 55° to 65°, Oct. to March 45° to 55° for greenhouse kinds.

PROPAGATION: By division of roots in March; cuttings of young shoots inserted in sand under bell-glass, in temp. 75° in April; seeds sown in sandy soil in spring in temp. 65° to 70°.

STOVE SPECIES CULTIVATED: *A. salicarifolia*, blue, Aug., 2 ft., S. America.

GREENHOUSE SPECIES CULTIVATED: *A. grandiflora*, lilac, 1½ to 2 ft., S. America.

Angel's Tears, see *Narcissus triandrus* var. *albus*; **-Trumpet,** see *Datura suaveolens*.

Angiopteris—*Marattiaceae.* Greenhouse, evergreen tree ferns.

CULTURE: Compost, equal parts peat, loam, leaf-mould, sand and charcoal. Pot, Feb., March. Position, pots or tubs, standing in 3 in. of water in shade. Water freely in spring and summer, moderately other times. Temp., March to Sept. 55° to 60°, Sept. to March 45° to 50°.

PROPAGATION: By offsets only.

SPECIES CULTIVATED: *A. evecta*, 10 to 15 ft., Ceylon and Pacific Isles; *Teysmanniana*, grows fronds of great length, 6 ft. being small, evergreen, Java.

Angola Hemp, see Sansevieria.

Angraecum—*Orchidaceae.* Stove epiphytal orchids, flowers fragrant in some species. Under later revision the genus has been divided into several sections which have been given generic titles. In cultivation all are known as Angraecums.

CULTURE: Compost, equal parts osmunda fibre and sphagnum moss with nodules of charcoal or finely crushed potsherds, larger for the stronger growing species. Position, shady, in suspended baskets or well-drained pans, expose to light in autumn. Pot March. Water freely March to Oct., moderately afterwards. Temp., Sept to March 65° to 70°, March to Sept. 70° to 85°. Resting period, though many differences are present in habit, must not be drastic, the compost should approach dryness in winter between waterings. Flower spikes appear in axils in the leaved species, from the ' crown ' in the leafless species, from the leaf axils or opposite them in the scandent-habited species. In a few the flowers are solitary on slender peduncles from near the base.

PROPAGATION: The stems being short in many species, and basal growths very seldom emitted, propagation can seldom be effected with the majority. The scandent-growing species, which should be placed on rafts, are readily propagated by severing the stems with three or four nodes below roots and allowing the division to remain on the raft till growth is seen.

SPECIES CULTIVATED: Dwarf or moderate size—*A. arcuatum*, white, spring, S. Africa; *articulatum*, white, May and June, 8 to 12 in., Madagascar; *bilobum*, white or rose tinged, spur orange, autumn, W. Africa; *caudatum*, white, Aug., 12 to 15 in., Trop. Africa; *citratum*, lemon-yellow, spring, 6 to 8 in., Madagascar; *Ellisii*, white, winter, 1 ft., Madagascar; *falcatum*, white, summer, 4 to 6 in., Japan; *gracilipes*, white, borne singly, various, Madagascar; *Humboltii*, white, spring, 8 to 10 in., Madagascar; *Kotschyi*, white, spurs 10 in., autumn, Trop. E. Africa; *rhodostictum*, white, column vivid scarlet, summer, ht. various, W. Africa; *Rothschildianum*, white and green, black or sepia round spur mouth, autumn, Uganda; *Scottianum*, white, spring, 1 ft., Comoro Islands; Scandent species—*A. Eichlerianum*, white and green, solitary or in twos, summer, autumn, W. Africa

Germinyanum, white, lip protracted into a tail, summer, Madagascar; *infundibulare* very large, one or two, white, green tinged, summer, autumn, W. Africa. Extra large growing species—*A. eburneum*, white, tinged green, large, on stout spikes, spurs green, Bourbon Isles; *sesquipedale*, white, 5 to 8 in. across, spur 11 in. long, 3 ft., late autumn, Madagascar.

Anguloa (Cradle Orchid)—*Orchidaceae*. Terrestrial orchids with large, fragrant, tulip-shaped flowers borne singly on bracteate scapes, with the new growths. First introduced early nineteenth century.

CULTURE: Compost, three parts good loam fibre, one part peat or osmunda fibre and a little sphagnum moss, with crushed potsherds, well mixed. Ample drainage. Position, pots in shady part of house. Pot when new growth begins. Water freely May to Sept., very seldom afterwards. Temp., April to Sept. 60° to 75°, by sun heat, Sept. to March 55°. Resting period, winter. With care in winter will withstand lower temperatures. The plicate leaves should never be syringed.

PROPAGATION: By division of large plants when repotting. When 5 bulbs or more are present, the rhizome may be severed behind the fourth bulb and the fifth then often produces a growth.

SPECIES CULTIVATED: *A. brevilabris*, much like *Ruckeri*, but smaller, greenish and dull red, summer, Peru; *Cliftonii*, large, lemon and golden, splashed with crimson-purple, lateral sepal tips attenuated and much curved, spring, Peru; *Clowesii*, yellow, May, 18 in., Colombia; *Rolfei*, a natural hybrid between *brevilabris* and *Cliftonii*, spring and early summer, Peru; *Ruckeri*, yellow and crimson, May, 18 in., Colombia, var. *sanguinea*, crimson colour deeper and on a larger area; *uniflora*, cream, white, often pink-spotted, May, 2 to 3 ft., Colombia.

× **Angulocaste**—*Orchidaceae*. Bigeneric hybrid between Anguloa and Lycaste.

Anhalonium, see Ariocarpus.

Animated Oat, see *Avena sterilis*.

Anigozanthos—*Amaryllidaceae*. Greenhouse herbaceous perennials. First introduced early nineteenth century.

CULTURE: Compost, one part loam, two parts peat, and one part silver sand. Pot in March. Position, pots in cool greenhouse fully exposed to light. Water freely in spring and summer, moderately in autumn and winter. Temp., 40° to 50° in winter, no heat at other times.

PROPAGATION: By division of the roots in spring.

SPECIES CULTIVATED: *A. flavidus*, scarlet, June, Australia; *Manglesii*, green and red, July, 3 ft., Australia; *pulcherrimus*, yellow and white, May, 2 ft., Australia; *rufus*, purple, June, 2 ft., Australia.

Ania—*Orchidaceae*. Intermediate greenhouse orchids, also known as Tainia and Ascotainia.

SPECIES CULTIVATED: *A. Hookeriana*, pale yellow streaked reddish brown, Feb. to March, to 3 ft., E. Himalaya, N. Siam; *penangiana*, very similar, Malaya.

Anise, see *Pimpinella Anisum*; **Star-,** see *Illicium verum*.

Anisostichus—*Bignoniaceae*. Slightly tender, vigorous, evergreen climber, not fully hardy but makes a wall plant in mild areas. Related to Campsis and Tecoma, and sometimes listed as Bignonia.

CULTURE: Soil, loamy. Position, south wall.

PROPAGATION: By cuttings of young shoots in well-drained soil in temp. 65° to 70°, in April.

SPECIES CULTIVATED: *A. capreolatus*, (syn. *Bignonia capreolata*) 'Cross Vine', orange-red funnel-shaped flowers, summer, to 40 ft., N. America.

Annatto, see *Bixa Orellana*.

Annona—*Annonaceae*. Stove, fragrant-leaved, evergreen shrubs cultivated for their edible fruits. First introduced late seventeenth century.

CULTURE: Compost, two parts loam, one part peat, and a little silver sand. Pot, March or April. Position, light and sunny. Water freely March to Oct., moderately afterwards. Syringe daily April to Sept. Shade from bright sunshine. Temp., March to Oct. 70° to 80°, Oct. to March 55° to 65°.

PROPAGATION: By seeds in spring, or by cuttings of firm shoots in moist sand under bell-glass in temp. 75° in summer.

SPECIES CULTIVATED: *A. Cherimola*, ' Cherimoyer ', brown, Aug., 12 to 18 ft., Trop. America; *muricata*, ' Sour Sop ', yellow, summer, 10 ft., fruits edible, Trop. America; *palustris*, ' Alligator Apple ', yellow, summer, 10 ft., Trop. America; *reticulata*, ' Custard Apple ', yellow and brown, summer, 15 to 18 ft., fruits edible, Trop. America; *squamosa*, ' Sweet Sop ', white, summer, 15 to 20 ft., fruits edible, W. Indies.

Anoectochilus (Jewel Orchid)—*Orchidaceae.* Terrestrial orchids. Anoectochilus is commonly applied to species of different genera and is so kept in this work. Cystorchis, Dossinia, Erythrodes, Eurycentrum, Haemaria, Hetaetia, Macodes and other titles are not likely to come into general use. The leaves are the attraction, the flowers being of minor interest. Variation exists, the stems may be fleshy and noded, in others swollen. Though terrestrial in general, the roots do not penetrate the soil, the plants forming colonies in suitable debris and conditions.

CULTURE: A warm, moist, sweet atmosphere, not falling below 65° or 70° in winter is essential and but little higher in summer. Shading is necessary, draughts must be avoided. Compost of osmunda or good peat fibre, the same bulk of sphagnum and a little sand and charcoal nodules. Well-drained small pans are preferable and the compost should be slightly mounded centrally. A south-western or western aspect is desirable. If a small case or large bell-glass can be given in a greenhouse, a more equable temperature can be maintained, but air must be admitted whenever conditions allow.

PROPAGATION: All the species which emit stem roots should be propagated in spring and summer, cut the stems below roots, near the plant base. If available, a case with bottom heat should be used. Stronger plants are obtained if the flower spikes are pinched out when seen. *A. discolor* and similar swollen-stemmed forms may be increased by division of the rhizomes in early spring. Usually two or three swollen stems may be obtained on the same piece of rhizome; single pieces with a piece of the rhizome and a growth will succeed.

SPECIES CULTIVATED: *A. argyroneurus*, olive, veins silvery, Java; *concinnus*, olive, veins golden, Assam; *Dawsonianus*, velvety olive, veins copper, Malay Archipelago; *Heriotii*, reddish, veins golden, India; *hieroglyphicus*, green, veins silvery, Assam; *regalis*, velvety green, veins golden, Ceylon; *setaceus*, velvety green, veins gold, Java; *Bohnhofianus*, large, olive green with golden reticulation, New Guinea; *Rollissonii*, large, rich green-shaded bronze, margined, striped and blotched pale yellow; *Sanderianus*, large, velvet-green with copper-red veins, New Guinea; *Petola*, easily grown, veined and reticulated with gold, Java. Numerous other species or forms may be found in specialists' catalogues.

Anomalesia—*Iridaceae.* Cormous plants formerly included in Antholyza.

CULTURE: Soil, light sandy. Position, sunny well-drained borders or pots in cool greenhouse. Plant in Oct. Lift in August, dry and store in a cool place till planting time.

PROPAGATION: By offsets; seeds in slight heat in spring.

SPECIES CULTIVATED: *A. Cunonia* (syn. *Antholyza Cunonia*), scarlet, July, 1 to 1½ ft., Cape.

Anomatheca, see Lapeirousea.

Anopterus—*Saxifragaceae.* Greenhouse, evergreen flowering shrub. First introduced early nineteenth century.

CULTURE: Compost, two parts loam, one part peat and sand. Pot and prune, March. Position, sunny greenhouse. Temp., Sept. to March 45° to 50°, March to Sept. 55° to 65°. Water moderately in winter, abundantly at other times.

PROPAGATION: By cuttings of firm shoots 3 in. long, in sandy peat under bell-glass in temp. 65° in summer.

SPECIES CULTIVATED: *A. glandulosus*, 'Tasmanian Laurel', white or pink, April, 2 to 3 ft., Tasmania.

Ansellia—*Orchidaceae.* Epiphytic and semi-epiphytic evergreen orchids distributed through Africa, south-east and west. Several species have been described but they are now considered variants of two types, perhaps only one. All with more or less tall, cylindrical, stem-like pseudo-bulbs, leafy on their upper halves. Prevailing floral colours yellow and brown. Spikes terminal, often branched and many-flowered.

CULTURE: Compost three parts of osmunda or peat fibre, one part sphagnum moss, a little loam fibre and finely broken potsherds. Summer temperatures may reach the tropical, particularly for the West African forms. Winter, 60° to 65°, with occasional waterings. Exposure to light should be given in autumn. Water must not be allowed to lodge in new growths.

PROPAGATION: By division of plants with eight or more bulbs.

SPECIES CULTIVATED: *A. africana*, light yellow and red-brown, winter, Sierra Leone; *confusa*, pale yellow or creamy-white, spotted brown-purple, winter, W. Africa; *congoensis*, yellow with nearly confluent red-brown blotches, various, Congo, W. Africa; *nilotica*, larger and brighter in colour, winter, E. Africa; *gigantea*, pale yellow and red-brown, autumn and winter, Natal.

Antennaria—*Compositae.* Hardy herbaceous perennials with silvery-white leaves; useful for carpet bedding, edgings to borders or clothing dry spots.

CULTURE: Soil, ordinary. Position, sunny borders or rockeries. Plant, March or Oct.

PROPAGATION: By division of roots in March.

SPECIES CULTIVATED: *A. aprica*, white or soft pink, June, 4 in., America; *dioica*, pink, June, 3 in., Europe incl. Britain; *rosea*, pink, 8 to 16 in., W.N. America.

Anthemis—*Compositae.* Hardy perennials with fully-cut, strongly-scented foliage. Flowers of the common chamomile, *A. nobilis*, are used for making chamomile tea.

CULTURE: Soil, ordinary. Position, sunny borders for tall species, rock garden for dwarf ones. Plant, October or March, common chamomile to be planted 2 ft. apart in rows 30 in. asunder in April. Gather flowers when fully expanded.

PROPAGATION: By division in March, seeds sown outdoors in April, cuttings of young growth in spring.

SPECIES CULTIVATED: *A. Biebersteiniana*, rich yellow, leaves filigree silver, June to July, 6 in., Orient; *Cupaniana*, white, all summer, 1 ft., Italy; *macedonica*, white, June, 6 to 9 in., Macedonia; *nobilis*, 'Common Chamomile', white, Aug., 1 ft., Europe; *Sancti-Johannis*, rich orange, summer, 12 to 18 in., Bulgaria; *tinctoria*, 'Dyer's' or 'Ox-eye Chamomile', yellow, Aug., 2 ft., Europe.

Anthericum—*Liliaceae.* Hardy herbaceous perennials.

CULTURE: Soil, light, rich. Position, partially shaded borders. Plant, Oct., Nov.

PROPAGATION: By seeds sown ⅛ in. deep in light soil in cold frame in Sept. or March; division of roots in Oct.

SPECIES CULTIVATED: *A. Liliago*, 'St. Bernard Lily', white, July and Aug., 12 to 18 in., S. Europe, var. *major*, a superior form; *ramosum*, white, June to Aug., 2 ft., S. Europe. See the genera Paradisea and Chlorophytum for other species formerly included in this genus.

Anthogonium—*Orchidaceae.* Usually terrestrial. Only one species seems to have appeared in cultivation. Pseudo-bulbs small, carrying two or three grass-like leaves. Flowers somewhat tubular, scapes erect.

CULTURE: Compost, three parts of fibre, two parts loam and sphagnum moss.

Temp., summer 60° and upwards, expose to light in autumn; winter 55°. Very occasional waterings if any.

PROPAGATION: By separating pseudo-bulbs.

SPECIES CULTIVATED: *A. gracilis*, rosy, as are the pedicels and ovaries, late summer, Burma, N. India.

Antholyza (Aunt Eliza)—*Iridaceae*. Cormous plants. Species formerly included here have been transferred to other genera, Anomalesia, Chasmanthe, Curtonus and Petamenes.

CULTURE: Soil, light sandy. Position, sunny well-drained borders or pots in cool greenhouse. Plant in Oct. Lift in Aug., dry and store in cool place till planting time.

PROPAGATION: By offsets; seeds in slight heat in spring.

SPECIES CULTIVATED: *A. ringens* (syn. *Babiana ringens*), crimson and greenish-yellow, summer, 1 to 1½ ft., a very remarkable plant, the upper part of the flower-stalk being flowerless and serving in its native habitat as a perch for sunbirds as they suck the nectar and pollinate the curiously-shaped blooms.

Anthony Nut, see *Staphylea pinnata*.

Anthoxanthum—*Gramineae*. Hardy perennial flowering grass. Inflorescence has the odour of newly mown hay, and is useful for winter bouquets.

CULTURE: Soil, ordinary. Plant, Oct. or March. Position, open border.

PROPAGATION: By seeds sown ⅛ in. deep where plants are to grow in April; division of roots, Oct. or March.

SPECIES CULTIVATED: *A. odoratum*, ' Sweet Vernal Grass ', 1 ft., Europe.

Anthriscus—*Umbelliferae*. Annual or perennial herbs grown for leaves which are used like parsley. First introduced mid-seventeenth century.

CULTURE: Seed germinates readily but will not transplant. Thin to 12 in. Crops in 6 to 8 weeks. Sow indoors in boxes for winter supply. May be dried.

SPECIES CULTIVATED: *A. Cerefolium*, ' Chervil ', white, annual, S.E. Europe, W. Asia; *sylvestris*, white, perennial or biennial, Europe, W. Asia. See also the genus Chaerophyllum.

Anthurium (Flamingo-plant; Tail-flower)—*Araceae*. Stove, evergreen flowering plants. First introduced early nineteenth century.

CULTURE: Compost, equal parts rough peat, sphagnum moss. Position, pots, well drained, shady. Pot, March. Water freely March to Nov., moderately afterwards. Temp., Sept. to March 60° to 65°, March to Sept. 70° to 80°.

PROPAGATION: By division of roots in March; seeds sown in a mixture of chopped sphagnum moss, charcoal and sand in temp. of 80° in spring.

SPECIES CULTIVATED, Flowering: *A. Andreanum*, scarlet and white, Colombia; *ornatum*, white and purple, Venezuela; *Scherzerianum*, scarlet, Guatemala, and vars. *album*, white, *Rothschildianum*, creamy-white spotted crimson, *Wardii*, scarlet, with extra large bracts. Ornamental-leaved—*A. crystallinum*, green, Peru; *magnificum*, green and white, Colombia; *Veitchii*, green, Colombia; *Warocqueanum*, green and white, Colombia. For varieties, which are numerous, see trade lists.

Anthyllis—*Leguminosae*. Hardy and slightly tender shrubs and perennials.

CULTURE: Soil, ordinary. Position, open or partly shaded border. Plant, Oct.

PROPAGATION: Shrubby kinds by cuttings of young shoots under bell-glass in cold frame in August; herbaceous species by seeds sown ⅛ in. deep in warm border in April; division of roots in Oct.

SPECIES CULTIVATED: *A. Barba-Jovis*, ' Jupiter's Beard ' or ' Silver Bush ', yellow shrub, to 10 ft., requires wall protection, S. Europe; *Hermanniae*, yellow, June, to 2 ft., dwarf shrub, Medit.; *montana*, pink, June, 3 to 6 in., Alps, and var. *rubra*, fine crimson; *Vulneraria*, ' Woundwort ', ' Kidney Vetch ', yellow, June to Aug., 6 to 12 in., Britain.

Antigonon (Coral Vine)—*Polygonaceae.* Tendril climbing vines for greenhouse or stove. First introduced mid-nineteenth century.

CULTURE: Compost, equal parts loam, leaf-mould and sand. Position, borders with shoots trained close to the glass in full sun. Plant, Nov. Water freely while growth is active, little during winter months. Temp., Sept. to March 60° to 65°, March to Sept. 70° to 80°.

PROPAGATION: By seeds, cuttings.

SPECIES CULTIVATED: *A. leptopus,* ' Corallita ', ' Confederate Vine ', bright pink, summer, to 30 ft., Mexico, and var. *album,* white.

Antirrhinum (Snapdragon)—*Scrophulariaceae.* Hardy perennial plants, some species grown as annuals for summer bedding. Some authors place *A. Asarina* in a separate genus as *Asarina procumbens,* and *A. Orontium* as *Misopates Orontium.*

CULTURE: Soil, ordinary. Position, warm dry borders, rockeries or walls for dwarf species. Plant, April. For massed effects plant Tom Thumb 6 in., Intermediates 1 ft., and tall varieties 1½ ft. apart.

PROPAGATION: By seed in temp. 70° in March or outdoors in April, transplanting seedlings in May; cuttings of young shoots in cold frame in Aug. Most species are best treated as annuals or biennials, fresh crops being raised every year.

SPECIES CULTIVATED: *A. Asarina,* yellow, summer, trailing, S.W. Europe; *glutinosum,* cream and yellow, June, prostrate, Spain; *majus,* ' Common Snapdragon ', pink, July, to 3 ft., Medit. Region, naturalised in Britain, many garden forms have been developed; *Orontium,* purple, summer, to 1 ft., annual, Europe, Asia.

Aotus—*Leguminosae.* Greenhouse, evergreen flowering shrub.

CULTURE: Compost, equal parts loam, peat, sand, charcoal. Pot in March. Position, pots, well drained, in light and sunny greenhouse. Water moderately in winter, freely summer. Prune shoots back after flowering. Temp., Sept. to March 45° to 50°, March to Sept. 55° to 60°.

PROPAGATION: By cuttings of firm shoots in pots of sandy soil under bell-glass, temp. 55°.

SPECIES CULTIVATED: *A. gracillima,* yellow and crimson, May, 3 ft., W. Australia.

Apache Beads, see Anemopsis.

Aphelandra—*Acanthaceae.* Stove, evergreen flowering shrubs. Flowers are surrounded by lovely coloured bracts. First introduced early eighteenth century.

CULTURE: Compost, equal parts peat, loam, leaf-mould and sand. Position, pots, moist atmosphere. Water freely in summer, moderately in winter. Prune shoots to within 1 in. of base in Feb. and repot in March. Temp., Sept. to March 60° to 65°, March to Sept. 70° to 80°.

PROPAGATION: By cuttings of firm shoots inserted in sandy soil in bottom-heat (80°), March or April.

SPECIES CULTIVATED: *A. aurantiaca,* orange, winter, 3 ft., Mexico; *pectinata,* scarlet, winter, 3 ft., S. America; *squarrosa* (syn. *A. Leopoldii*), yellow, Brazil, and var. *Louisae; tetragona,* scarlet, Aug. to Nov., 3 ft., W. Indies.

Aphelexis, see Helichrysum.

Aphyllanthes—*Liliaceae.* Hardy fibrous-rooted perennial.

CULTURE: Soil, light sandy. Position, full sun, dry.

PROPAGATION: By division of old plants; seed when obtainable.

SPECIES CULTIVATED: *A. monspeliensis,* blue, June, 9 in., S. Europe.

Apicra, see Astroloba and Poellnitzia.

Apios—*Leguminosae.* Hardy, tuberous-rooted climbing perennial. First introduced early seventeenth century.

CULTURE: Soil, ordinary. Position, warm border against south wall or trellis. Plant tubers in March.

PROPAGATION: By division of tubers in March; seeds.

Species Cultivated: *A. americana* (syn. *A. tuberosa*), brown and pink, Aug., 6 to 10 ft., N. America.

Apium—*Umbelliferae*. Hardy plants, one species grown for blanched leaf stalks as a vegetable and a variety for its edible roots. Some aquatic species chiefly used in aquariums.

Culture of Celery: Soil, ordinary, richly manured. Prepare trenches in moist site where possible, running north and south, 4 ft. apart, 15 in. wide, and 1 ft. deep for single rows, or 18 in. wide for double rows. Sow seeds in light soil, covering very thinly, in temp. 65° to 75° in Feb. for early crop; in March in similar temp. for main crop, or in cold frame in April. Seedlings in first two cases to be transplanted 2 in. apart in light soil in boxes, kept in temp. 55° to 65° for few weeks, then planted 6 in. apart in shady bed outdoors till required for planting in trenches. Plant beginning of June for early crop; end of June or July for main crop. Distance apart for plants, 8 in. for single row, and 6 in. between rows for double rows. Water and feed liberally until earthed up to ensure crisp, solid hearts. Earth up gradually from Sept. to Nov. in fine weather only, keeping soil out of heart and earthing finally right up to leaves. Lift as required. Protect with bracken during late winter.

Culture of Turnip-rooted Celery or Celeriac: Soil, rich, light. Position, sunny level border. Plant in June, 1 ft. apart in rows, 18 in. asunder. Keep all side shoots removed. Draw little soil around base of each in Aug. Water freely in dry weather. Lift roots in Oct. and store in sand till required for use. Sow and treat seedlings as advised for ordinary celery.

Culture of Aquatic Species: Soil, aquarium compost or loam. Position, submerged or shallow water at edge of pond or aquarium. Plant, spring or summer.

Propagate: By division or cuttings.

Species Cultivated: *A. graveolens* var. *dulce*, ' Celery', var. *rapaceum*, ' Celeriac ', edible root-crown; *inundatum*, dissected foliage, white flowers, aquatic; *nodiflorum*, watercress-like leaves, white flowers, aquatic.

Aponogeton—*Aponogetonaceae*. Hardy and tender aquatics, annuals and perennials. Submerged or with floating leaves, and forked or single spiked flowers floating or standing above water. Introduced late eighteenth century.

Culture: Soil, heavy loam enriched with bonemeal. Position, pond or lakes from 6 in. to 2 ft. of water, or tubs in greenhouses for tender species. Some, including *A. ulvaceum*, are used for tropical aquariums. Plant, base of pond or in pans, sinking latter into the water, March to June. *A. leptostachyus abyssinicus*. should be grown in very shallow water in pan indoors.

Propagation: Offsets, division or seed sown, directly after gathering, in sifted loam and charcoal in shallow pans.

Species Cultivated: *A. crispus*, aquarium plant with white flowers, Ceylon; *distachyus*, ' Cape Pondweed ', ' Water Hawthorn ', white, forked, fragrant flowers all summer, floating strap-like leaves, hardy, Africa, Australia; *fenestralis*, ' Madagascar Lace Plant ', leaves skeletonized to a lattice pattern, submerged, very beautiful, twin spikes, white flowers, tender and difficult to grow, Madagascar; *Krauseanus*, sulphur twin-spikes above water, hardy in south, S. Africa; *leptostachyus* var. *abyssinicus*, forked spikes, mauve, annual, Abyssinia; *spathaceus* var. *junceum*, narrow rush-like foliage, 2 to 4 in., flowers white, blue anthers, shallow water, Africa; *ulvaceus*, submerged, foliage like hart's-tongue fern, flowers sulphur, Madagascar.

Aporocactus—*Cactaceae*. Greenhouse plants with fleshy creeping stems bearing bristles. Formerly included in the genus Cereus. First introduced late seventeenth century.

Culture: Compost, two parts turfy loam, one part coarse sand and broken brick. Position, well-drained pots or pans in sunny greenhouse or window. Pot as required, water sparingly. Temp., Sept. to March 50° to 55°, March to Sept. 55° to 60°.

PROPAGATION: By seeds sown in well-drained pots or pans; cuttings of stems in sand.

SPECIES CULTIVATED: *A. flagelliformis*, red or pink, Peru; *Mallisonii*, red, summer, hybrid; *Martianus*, rosy red, Cent. America.

Apple, see Malus;   **-of Peru,** see *Nicandra Physalodes*;   **Crab-,** see *Malus floribunda.*

Aptenia—*Aizoaceae.* Greenhouse succulent plants. Formerly included in Mesembryanthemum.

CULTURE: As Mesembryanthemum.

PROPAGATION: As Mesembryanthemum.

SPECIES CULTIVATED: *A. cordifolia* (syn. *Mesembryanthemum cordifolium*), purple, summer, 1 to 2 ft., S. Africa, and var. *variegata*, variegated leaves.

Aquilegia (Columbine)—*Ranunculaceae.* Hardy perennial plants with spurred (rarely spurless) flowers and ternately-compound leaves. Graceful plants for border or rock garden.

CULTURE: Soil, sandy loam enriched with leaf-mould. Position, well-drained, partly shaded borders and rock gardens. *A. Jonesii* and *A. scopulorum* are suitable for alpine house. Plant, Oct. or March.

PROPAGATION: By seeds in sandy soil in cold frame in Aug., or in open border in April; division of roots in Oct. or April.

SPECIES CULTIVATED: *A. akitensis*, purple and cream, summer, 9 in., Japan; *alpina*, powder-blue, May to June, 12 in., Europe; *atrata*, dark blackish violet, summer, 1¼ to 2½ ft., Europe; *Bertolonii*, deep blue, early summer, 6 in., Europe; *caerulea*, ' State Flower of Colorado ', blue, summer, 12 in., America; *canadensis*, red and yellow, April to June, 1 to 2 ft., N. America, var. *nana* 6 to 9 in.; *chrysantha*, soft yellow, 2 ft., summer, America; *discolor*, blue and white, 3 in., Spain; *ecalcarata* (syn. *Semiaquilegia ecalcarata*), purplish maroon, summer, 9 to 18 in., W. China; *flabellata*, pale purple or white, summer, 1 to 1¼ ft., Japan, var. *nana-alba*, 6 to 9 in.;. *formosa* (syn. *A. arctica*), red and yellow, summer, 3 ft., N. America; *glandulosa*, blue and white, April to June, 8 to 12 in., Siberia, and var. *jucunda*, somewhat double; *grata*, mauve-violet, 6 to 18 in., summer, Yugo-slavia; *Jonesii*, blue and white, spring, 3 in., America; *longissima*, long-spurred yellow, May to June, 2 ft., America; *oxysepala*, reddish-violet and yellow, summer, 1½ to 3 ft., E. Asia; *pyrenaica*, blue, May to June, 9 in., Europe; *scopulorum*, blue, early summer, 4 to 6 in., America; *Skinneri*, yellowish green, summer, 2 to 3 ft., Mexico; *sibirica*, lilac and white, June to July, 9 in., Siberia; *Stuartii*, blue and white, June, 9 in., hybrid; *viridiflora*, chocolate and green, early summer, 9 to 12 in., Siberia; *vulgaris*, ' Common Columbine ', various, single and double, summer, 1½ to 2½ ft., Europe, incl. Britain. The popular garden aquilegias are hybrids of various species.

Arabian Jasmine, see *Jasminum Sambac.*

Arabis (Wall Cress, Rock Cress)—*Cruciferae.* Hardy annual and perennial alpine trailing plants.

CULTURE: Soil, ordinary. Position, edgings to well-drained borders or massed on sunny rock garden, carpeting beds of spring-flowering bulbs, etc. Alpine house for *A. androsacea*, *A. bryoides olympicas*. Plant, Oct. and Nov.

PROPAGATION: Seeds sown in April; cuttings inserted in shady borders in Aug.; division of roots in Oct.

SPECIES CULTIVATED: *A. androsacea*, rare, white, May to June, 1 in., Taurus; *Arendsii* (syns. *A. albida rosea*, *A.* ' Rosabella '), rose, 6 in., spring, hybrid; *aubrietioides*, rose, summer, 6 in., Asia Minor; *blepharophylla*, bright red, early spring, 4 in., America; *bryoides olympica*, rare, silver tufts and white flowers, spring, 1 in., Greece; *Ferdinandi-Coburgii*, white, early summer, 2 to 3 in., Macedonia; *procurrens*, white, spring, 4 in., Europe.

Arachis—*Leguminosae.* Stove flowering annual. After flowering, the seed pod is gradually forced into the soil to ripen its seeds, which are edible.

CULTURE: Compost, loam, leaf-mould and sand. Sow seeds in temp. of 75° to 85° in spring; plant seedlings in small pots and grow in a light position. Water moderately. Temp. 75° to 85°.

SPECIES CULTIVATED: *A. hypogaea*, ' Peanut ', ' Monkey-nut ', ' Earth-nut ', ' Ground-nut ', yellow, May, 1 ft., Tropics.

Arachnanthe, see Arachnis.

Arachnis—*Orchidaceae.* An epiphytal genus with Vanda-like habit. Flowers distinguished by the curved sickle-like shape of the petals, the lip small, fleshy, on lateral spikes. Sometimes this genus is known as Arachnanthe.

CULTURE: Compost, temperature, etc., should be as for Aerides. The often leathery leaves denote that fewer waterings are necessary in winter, but the compost should never be dried out, and rather more exposure to light in autumn benefits.

PROPAGATION: As for Aerides but can seldom be effected.

SPECIES CULTIVATED: *A. annamensis*, remarkable, rare, up to 18 in., high, flowers 3 to 8 large, 5 or 6 in. vertically, yellow, heavily blotched with deep red-brown, summer, Annam; *Cathcartii*, yellowish with thin bands of red, lip white, yellow and red, summer and autumn, 2 to 4 ft., Himalaya; *Clarkei* (syn. *Esmeralda Clarkei*), yellow-striped brown, lip yellow-spotted brown, autumn, Himalaya; *Lowii* (syns. *Vanda Lowii, Dimorphorchis Lowii*), orange-yellow spotted red, late summer, to 6 ft., Borneo; ' Scorpion Orchid ', *moschifera* (syns. *Arachnanthe moschifera, Renanthera moschifera*), yellowish, blotched with red or red-brown, musk scented, stem 12 ft. long, summer, autumn, Malaya, Java, Borneo. See Acanthopanax.

Aralia—*Araliaceae.* Hardy herbs, shrubs or trees. First introduced mid-seventeenth century.

CULTURE: Soil, rich well-drained loam. Position, shady borders for herbaceous species, margins of lakes or ponds or moist sheltered shrubberies for shrubby species. Plant, Sept. to Oct. or March to April.

PROPAGATION: By division in Oct. or March for herbaceous species; seed, suckers or root cuttings for shrubby kinds.

SPECIES CULTIVATED: *A. cachemirica*, white, summer, 6 ft., herbaceous, Himalaya; *chinensis*, ' Chinese Angelica Tree ', to 20 ft., somewhat spiny, China; *cordata* (syn. *A. edulis*), white, summer, 4 to 6 ft., young blanched shoots edible, herbaceous, Japan; *elata*, ' Japanese Angelica Tree ', to 35 ft., Manchuria; *nudicaulis*, ' Wild Sarsaparilla ', greenish, June, 3 to 4 ft., herbaceous, N. America; *racemosa*, ' American Spikenard ', greenish white, June, herbaceous, N. America; *spinosa*, ' Devil's Walking stick ', ' Hercules' Club ', to 30 ft., very spiny, N. America.

Araucaria—*Araucariaceae.* Hardy and slightly tender evergreen coniferous trees. First introduced late eighteenth century.

OUTDOOR CULTURE: Soil, deep rich loam. Position, high, dry and sheltered, away from smoky districts. Should be grown as a well-isolated specimen. Plant, Sept. to Nov.

CULTURE OF GREENHOUSE SPECIES: Compost, two parts loam, one part leaf-mould, and one part silver sand. Position, pots or tubs well drained in sunny house. Repot in March. Water freely during spring and summer, moderately at other seasons. Avoid overcrowding; give plenty of room. Temp., March to Oct. 55° to 65°, Oct. to March 45° to 55°. Requires plenty of air in summer.

PROPAGATION: Greenhouse species by means of cuttings of ends of young shoots inserted in sandy loam in a warm greenhouse in autumn; tall, overgrown plants by stem-rooting in spring. Hardy species by seeds sown 1 in. deep in light soil. Temp., Feb., March, April 65°.

GREENHOUSE SPECIES CULTIVATED: *A. Bidwillii*, ' Bunya-Bunya Tree ', 100 to 150 ft., Queensland; *columnaris* (syn. *A. Cookii*), 150 to 200 ft., New Caledonia; *Cunninghamii*, ' Moreton Bay Pine ', 70 to 100 ft., Queensland; *excelsa*, ' Norfolk Island Pine ', 100 to 120 ft., Norfolk Island, and vars. *glauca* and *robusta*; *Rulei* 50 ft., New Caledonia.

HARDY SPECIES CULTIVATED: *A. araucana*, ' Monkey Puzzle ' (syn. *A. imbricata*), 50 to 100 ft., Chile, var. *aurea*, golden-tinted foliage.

Araujia—*Asclepiadaceae*. Greenhouse, evergreen flowering climber. First introduced early nineteenth century.

CULTURE: Compost, equal parts loam, peat and leaf-mould, with sand added. Position, pots or beds in greenhouse or conservatory, shoots trained up roof or to wire trellis. Pot, Feb. to April. Water freely March to Sept., moderately afterwards. Syringe twice daily March to Aug. Prune into shape during Jan. or Feb. Temp., March to Oct. 65° to 75°, Oct. to March 55° to 65°.

PROPAGATION: By cuttings of young shoots in sandy soil in propagating case, temp. 75° to 80°, in spring.

SPECIES CULTIVATED: *A. sericofera* (syn. *Physianthus albens*), white, August, S Brazil.

Arbor-Vitae, see Thuja.

Arbutus—*Ericaceae*. Hardy ornamental foliage and fruit-bearing evergreen trees. Fruit, globular, scarlet, strawberry-like; ripe in Oct., year after flowering.

CULTURE: Soil, sandy peat. Position, sunny, sheltered. Plant, Sept. to Nov. or April.

PROPAGATION: By seeds sown 1 in. deep in well-drained pans of sandy peat in cold frame in March; or grafting on seedling stocks of *A. Unedo* in heat during spring.

SPECIES CULTIVATED: *A. Andrachne*, greenish white, April, 12 to 14 ft., Levant; *Menziesii*, ' Madrona ', white, Sept., 25 ft., with peeling bark revealing cinnamon stems, N. America; *Unedo*, ' Strawberry Tree ', useful and highly ornamental screening, evergreen, bearing white flowers and fruit like small strawberries, autumn and early winter, grows well in chalk, Europe, including Ireland, var. *rubra*, a good deep pink flowered form.

Archangelica, see *Angelica Archangelica*.

Archontophoenix—*Palmae*. Stove palms. First introduced mid-nineteenth century.

CULTURE: Compost, three parts good fibrous loam, one part decayed manure or leaf-mould and a little coarse sand. Position, well-drained pots or tubs in sunny part of heated greenhouse. Pot, Feb. or March. Water moderately Oct. to March, freely March to Oct. Temp., March to Sept. 65° to 75°, Sept. to March 55° to 65°.

PROPAGATION: By seeds sown 1 in. deep in light sandy soil under bell-glass or propagator in temp. 75°, March or April.

SPECIES CULTIVATED: *A. Alexandrae*, 20 to 80 ft., N. Australia; *Cunninghamiana* (syn. *Seaforthia elegans*), 20 to 60 ft., Queensland and New South Wales.

Arctostaphylos (Bearberry)—*Ericaceae*. Hardy, deciduous and evergreen shrubs.

CULTURE: Soil, peat, leaf-mould and loam. Position, moist, partially-shaded borders or rockeries. Plant in autumn.

PROPAGATION: By cuttings inserted in gritty soil in autumn.

SPECIES CULTIVATED: *A. manzanita*, red stems, grey foliage and pink flowers in April, 8 ft., California; *Uva-ursi*, pink, spring, succeeded by red berries, evergreen, trailing. Both natives of Scotland.

Arctotis—*Compositae*. Half-hardy annuals.

OUTDOOR CULTURE: Soil, loamy, enriched with leaf-mould. Position, preferably sunny, but will do in shade. Plant in April or May. Protect by handlights or frames in winter. Best raised from seed or cuttings annually, and grown outside in summer only.

INDOOR CULTURE: Compost, equal parts of loam and leaff-mould with a little sand. Position, well-drained pots in sunny part of greenhouse. Water liberally from March to Oct., moderately at other seasons.

PROPAGATION: By seeds sown in a temp. of 55° to 65° in March; avoid a too damp atmosphere. Also by cuttings of side shoots inserted in pots of sandy soil in a cold frame in early summer.

SPECIES CULTIVATED: *A. acaulis* (syn. *A. scapigera*), orange-carmine, etc., summer, 6 in., S. Africa; *breviscapa*, orange, summer, 6 in., S. Africa; *laevis*, brownish orange suffused red, 8 in., S. Africa; *stoechadifolia*, white, marguerite-flowers, lavender-blue reverse, summer, 2 ft., Africa and var. *grandis*.

Ardisia (Spear-flower)—*Myrsinaceae*. Stove-flowering and berry-bearing evergreen plants. First introduced early nineteenth century.

CULTURE: Compost, equal parts loam, peat, leaf-mould and sand. Pot, Feb. to April. Position, pots, in light, sunny part of stove. Water freely in summer, little in winter. Prune straggly shoots back closely in March. Temp., March to Sept. 70° to 80°, Sept. to March 55° to 65°.

PROPAGATION: By seeds sown ¼ in. deep in above compost in temp. 75° in spring; cuttings of side shoots in similar soil and temp., March.

SPECIES CULTIVATED: *A. crenata* (syn. *A. crispa*), flowers white, borne in June, followed by pretty red berries, 3 to 4 ft., Asia; *esculenta*, purplish-white, 2 to 3 ft., winter, Trop. America; *macrocarpa*, flowers flesh-coloured, followed by large vermilion berries, 5 to 6 ft., Himalaya.

Areca—*Palmae*. Stove palms. Cultivated in India and elsewhere for the nut which is chewed along with the leaf of betel pepper. First introduced late seventeenth century.

CULTURE: Compost, equal parts loam, peat, leaf-mould and sand. Position, shady, moist. Water freely at all times. Pot, Feb., March. Temp., March to Sept. 70° to 85°, Sept. to March 60° to 65°.

PROPAGATION: By seeds.

SPECIES CULTIVATED: *A. Cathecu*, ' Betel-nut Palm ', 20 to 30 ft., Trop. Asia. See also Rhopalostylis.

Arecastrum—*Palmae*. Stove palms, formerly included in Cocos.

CULTURE: As Cocos.

PROPAGATION: As Cocos.

SPECIES CULTIVATED: *A. Romanzoffianum* (syn. *Cocos Romanzoffiana, C. plumosa*), ' Queen Palm ', 30 ft., Brazil, var. *australe* (syn. *Cocos australis* of botanists).

Aregelia—*Bromeliaceae*. Stove, evergreen flowering and ornamental plants. Leaves in stiff rosettes, inner ones usually being brightly coloured.

CULTURE: Compost, equal parts fibrous loam, rough peat, leaf-mould and silver sand. Position, well-drained pots in light, moist part of stove. Pot, Feb. or March. Water moderately in winter, freely at other times. Temp., March to Sept. 70° to 80°, Sept. to March 65° to 70°.

PROPAGATION: By large-sized offshoots inserted singly in small pots of sandy peat in temp. 85°, Feb. to April.

SPECIES CULTIVATED: *A. princeps* (syn. *Karatas Meyendorfii*), violet, 1 to 1½ ft., S. Brazil; *spectabilis*, blood-red, white and pale blue, 1 ft., Brazil; *tristis*, purple, April, 1 ft., Brazil. Some of these are occasionally wrongly listed as Nidularium.

Arenaria (Sandwort)—*Caryophyllaceae*. Hardy herbaceous perennials and rock garden plants. Introduced early eighteenth century.

CULTURE: Soil, ordinary, well drained. Position, rock garden or wall. Plant, Oct. to March.

PROPAGATION: By seeds sown in sandy soil in cold frame in spring. Cuttings in spring or summer, division of roots in Oct. or March.

SPECIES CULTIVATED: *A. balearica*, white, ½ in., June, Balearic Isles; *laricifolia* (syn. *Alsine laricifolia*), white, June, 3 in., Europe; *Ledebouriana*, white, ash-grey leaves, summer, Levantine Alps; *montana grandiflora*, white, April to May, 6 in., Spain; *parnassica*, white, prostrate, spring, Greece; *purpurascens*, soft purple, summer, 2 in., Pyrenees; *Saxifraga*, glossy leaves, white, spring, 2 in., Medit.;

tetraquetra, white, Aug., 3 to 4 in., Spain;   *verna* (syn. *Alsine verna*), white, June, 2 in., Britain.

Arethusa—*Orchidaceae*. Low terrestrial orchids, native in E. North American bogs.
CULTURE: Compost, fibrous peat and loam in equal parts with a third of chopped sphagnum, sand and leaf-mould. Nearly hardy in favoured positions but a protection of leaves is required in winter. Position, rather damp.
SPECIES CULTIVATED: *A. bulbosa*, 6 to 9 in. stems bearing a single narrow leaf, terminated by a comparatively large rose-purple flower, blade of lip dilated, recurved, with a yellow beard-like crest, Carolina.

Argemone—*Papaveraceae*. Hardy annuals and perennials; usually grown as annuals. First introduced late sixteenth century.
CULTURE: Soil, sandy. Position, sunny borders, well drained. Plant in March.
PROPAGATION: By seeds sown ¼ in. deep in sandy soil outdoors in April, or in heat in March, planting outdoors in May.
SPECIES CULTIVATED: *A. grandiflora*, white, summer, 2 to 3 ft., Mexico; *mexicana*, 'Mexican Poppy', 'Prickly Poppy', yellow, June, 2 ft., annual, Mexico; *platyceras*, white or purple, summer, 1 to 4 ft., N. and S. America.

Ariocarpus (Anhalonium)—*Cactaceae*. Greenhouse succulent-stemmed perennials. Grown for the beauty of globose stems. Allied to Mammillaria.
CULTURE: Compost, equal parts sandy loam, rough old mortar and pounded bricks. Position, sunny, airy greenhouse or window. Pot, March or April, in well-drained pots just large enough to accommodate roots. Repot every third or fourth year only. Water moderately March to Sept., once a fortnight Sept. to Dec., none afterwards. Syringe on evenings of warm days, June to Sept. Apply soot water to healthy plants, June to Sept. Ventilate freely in summer. Temp., March to Sept. 60° to 70°, Sept. to March 50° to 55°.
PROPAGATION: By seeds sown ⅛ in. deep in well-drained pans or pots of sandy soil in temp. 75° in March, keeping soil moderately moist; by cuttings of the tops of the plants inserted in small pots of sandy, gritty compost in spring.
SPECIES CULTIVATED: *A. retusus* (syn. *A. prismaticus*), 6 in., Mexico; *scapharostrus*, stem to nearly 4 in. thick, Mexico.

Arisaema—*Araceae*. Stove, greenhouse and hardy tuberous-rooted perennials. Flowers, arum-like in shape. First introduced mid-eighteenth century.
CULTURE OF STOVE AND GREENHOUSE SPECIES: Compost, equal parts peat, leaf-mould, loam and sand. Position, pots in stove or greenhouse. Pot, March. Water freely March to Oct., keep dry afterwards. Temp., March to Oct. 70° to 80°, Oct. to March 60° to 65°, for stove species; Oct. to March 40° to 50°, March to Oct. 55° to 60°, for greenhouse species.
CULTURE OF HARDY SPECIES: Soil, ordinary. Position, sunny borders. Plant, Oct. or March. Top-dress with decayed manure after new growth begins. Apply liquid manure occasionally in summer.
PROPAGATION: By seeds or division of the tuberous roots—usually the latter is employed.
STOVE SPECIES CULTIVATED: *A. concinnum*, white, June, 1 to 2 ft., Himalaya; *galeata*, white, July, 1 ft., Himalaya;   *tortuosum*, white, April, 4 ft., Himalaya.
GREENHOUSE SPECIES CULTIVATED: *A. speciosum*, white, March, 1 to 2 ft., Himalaya; *triphyllum* (syn. *A. atrorubens*), green and purple, June, 1 to 2 ft., N. America.
HARDY SPECIES CULTIVATED: *A. candidissimum*, white, sometimes pale pink. July, 1½ ft., W. China;   *Griffithii*, brown, violet and green, May, 12 to 18 in., Himalaya;   *ringens*, white and green, April, 2 ft., Japan.

Arisarum—*Aracae*. Hardy tuberous-rooted perennials.
CULTURE: Soil, cool, light, enriched with leaf-mould. Position, semi-shade or north aspect.
PROPAGATION: By division of roots in spring.

Species Cultivated: A. *proboscideum*, 'Mouse-tail Plant', flowers resemble long-tailed brown mice half-hidden in round green leaves, early summer, 6 in., Italy. *vulgare*, purplish-brown, May, 6 in., Mediterranean Region.

Aristea—*Iridaceae.* Greenhouse herbaceous perennials. First introduced early nineteenth century.

Culture: Compost, two parts good peat, one part sandy loam and little sand. Position, well-drained pots in light, airy greenhouse. Pot, Feb. or March. Water copiously, April to Oct., moderately afterwards. Temp., Oct. to March 40° to 50°, March to Oct. 50° to 60°. An abundance of air required in summer, moderate amount other times.

Propagation: By seeds sown in sandy loam and peat in temp. 55° to 65° in spring; by offsets removed from parent plant March or April.

Species Cultivated: A. *corymbosa* (syn. *Witsenia corymbosa*), purple, summer, 3 ft., S. Africa.

Aristolochia (Birthwort)—*Aristolochiaceae.* Stove and hardy climbing or herbaceous plants. First introduced early eighteenth century.

Culture of Stove Species: Compost, two-thirds fibrous loam, one-third leaf-mould and sharp sand. Position, pots or borders; shoots trained close to roof of stove. Pot in March. Water freely in summer, little in winter. Temp., March to Sept. 70° to 80°, Sept. to March 60° to 65°. Prune straggly shoots only.

Culture of Hardy Species: Soil, good ordinary, well drained. Position, sunny borders for herbaceous species; south, west or east walls, or pergolas, trellises, etc., for climbing kinds. Plant in autumn or spring.

Propagation: Hardy species by cuttings of ripe shoots inserted in sandy soil in slight heat in summer, or division in spring. Stove and greenhouse species by seeds sown in light, rich soil in temp. 75° in March; cuttings in similar soil and temp., Feb. or March.

Stove Species Cultivated: A. *brasiliensis*, purple, July, 15 to 20 ft., Brazil; *elegans*, green, white and red, 8 to 10 ft., Brazil; *Goldeiana*, green and yellow, July, 10 ft., Old Calabar; *grandiflora* (syn. A. *gigas*), 'Pelican Flower', purple-spotted, June to July, 8 to 10 ft., W. Indies, Cent. and S. America, and var. *Sturtevantii* which is better than the type species; *Ruiziana* (syn. A. *Duchartrei*), yellow and brown, July, 2 to 5 ft., Upper Amazons.

Hardy Herbaceous Species: A. *Clematitis*, yellow, June to Sept., 2 to 3 ft., Europe.

Hardy Climbing Species: A. *durior* (syn. A. *Sipho*), 'Dutchman's Pipe', yellowish brown, May and June, 15 to 30 ft., N. America; *manshuriensis*, tinged brown, hardy, Korea; *tomentosa*, purple, July and Aug., downy foliage, 10 to 15 ft., N. America.

Armeria (Thrift; Sea-pink)—*Plumbaginaceae.* Dwarf perennials with narrow leaves in tufts or basal rosettes.

Culture: Soil, sandy loam. Position, edging to sunny borders or massed on rock garden. Plant, Oct. to March.

Propagation: Seeds sown in sandy soil in spring, or division of roots in early autumn or spring.

Species Cultivated: A. *juniperifolia* (syn. A. *caespitosa*), intense tufts of many rosettes, white to pink, June, Spain and Portugal, and var. *splendens*; *maritima*, 'Lady's Pincushion', 'Cushion Pink', pink, May to June, 6 in., Britain, vars. *alba*, *Laucheana* and *alpina*; *mauritanica*, glowing carmine, 2 to 3 ft., June to July, Spain and Portugal; *pseudo-armeria* (syn. A. *cephalotes*), white to dark rose-pink, June, 2 ft., Portugal; *splendens*, pink, 4 to 6 in., May, Spain; *Welwitschii*, pink, 3 in., May to June, Spain.

Armoracia—*Cruciferae.* Perennial herbs with dock-like leaves and edible roots.

Culture: Soil, ordinary deep. Plant 18 in. apart in late winter. Harvest following autumn, store in sand or ashes and replant each year for best roots.

PROPAGATION: By cuttings of pencil-thick side roots 5 in. long inserted 4 in. below surface in winter.

SPECIES CULTIVATED: *A. rusticana* (syns. *A. lapathifolia, Cochlearia Armoracia*), ' Horse Radish ', Britain, Europe.

Arnebia—*Boraginaceae.* Hardy annuals and perennials.

CULTURE: Soil, ordinary. Position, sunny rockery, well drained. Sow seeds of annuals in light soil in frames or cool houses in March, and plant out seedlings in May. Plant perennial species in Oct. or March.

PROPAGATION: Perennial species by seeds or division in spring.

SPECIES CULTIVATED: *A. cornuta,* yellow, spotted with purple, summer, 1½ to 2 ft., Turkistan, annual; *echioides* (syn. *Aipyanthus ιchioides*), ' Prophet Flower ', yellow and purple, summer, to 1 ft., Armenia, perennial.

Arnica—*Compositae.* Hardy herbaceous perennials. Tincture of *A. montana* has medicinal uses.

CULTURE: Soil, ordinary. Position, sunny border. Plant autumn or spring.

PROPAGATION: By division of roots in spring.

SPECIES CULTIVATED: *A. alpina,* bright orange-yellow, 12 in., June, N. America; *Chamissonis,* yellow, July to Sept., 2 ft., N. America; *montana,* ' Mountain Tobacco ', yellow, May to July, 1 ft., Europe; *sachalinensis,* yellow, July to Sept., 1½ ft., Sakhalin Is.

Aronia (Chokeberry)—*Rosaceae.* Deciduous shrubs with coloured autumn foliage and fruits. Formerly included in Pyrus.

CULTURE: Soil, ordinary, well drained. Position, sunny borders, thrive in chalky soil. Plant Nov. to Feb.

PROPAGATION: By seeds sown when ripe or stratified; suckers; layers; cuttings of green wood under glass.

SPECIES CULTIVATED: *A. arbutifolia,* ' RED CHOKEBERRY ', white or pale pink, May to June, pear-shaped red fruits, 5 to 10 ft., Eastern N. America; *melanocarpa,* ' Black Chokeberry ', white, May, black fruits, 1½ to 5 ft., spreading by suckers, Eastern N. America; *prunifolia* (syn. *A. floribunda*), ' Purple Chokeberry ', white, May, purplish black fruits to 12 ft., Eastern N. America.

Arpophyllum—*Orchidaceae.* Warm, greenhouse, evergreen epiphytic orchids. First introduced early nineteenth century.

CULTURE: Compost as for Cattleyas, with which they succeed, but are the better for lighter shading. More exposure to light in autumn and a more decided rest. Pot, Feb. or March. Positioι, well-drained pots in sunny part of house. Temp., Oct. to Feb. 50°, other times 60° to 80°. Water very seldom in winter, freely in summer; resting period, winter. Flowers appear at apex of new pseudo-bulb, small but numerous in cylindrical spikes. All species have the pseudo-bulbs compressed and bear a single hard fleshy leaf.

PROPAGATION: By division of fairly large plants when repotting.

SPECIES CULTIVATED: *A. cardinale,* rose, summer, 2 ft., Colombia; *giganteum,* purplish-rose, April, 2 ft. or more, Mexico; *spicatum,* purple, April, 12 to 18 in., Mexico and Guatemala.

Arrow Arum, see *Peltandra virginica;* **-head,** see Sagittaria; **-root,** see *Maranta arundinacea;* **-Wood,** see *Viburnum dentatum.*

Artemisia—*Compositae.* Hardy shrubs and herbaceous perennials, with hoary and fragrant foliage. Evergreen and deciduous.

CULTURE OF SHRUBBY AND HERBACEOUS SPECIES: Soil, ordinary. Position, sunny borders or rockeries. Plant, Oct. or March.

CULTURE OF TARRAGON: Soil, light, dryish, ordinary. Position, sunny border. Plant roots 2 to 3 in. deep, 8 in. apart in rows 18 in. asunder, March or April. Replant annually. Cut foliage off in Sept., and dry it for use in winter. Place a few roots in ordinary soil in box or large pot, and put this in warm greenhouse in Oct. to supply young shoots during winter.

Propagation: Tarragon, by cuttings of shoots inserted in ordinary soil in temp. 55° in March or April, or under hand-light outdoors in July; division of the roots in March or April. Shrubby and herbaceous species by cuttings inserted in open ground in summer; division in Oct. or March for herbaceous species; seeds sown outdoors in April for annual and other species.

Shrubby Species: *A. Abrotanum*, ' Southernwood ', ' Lad's Love ', or ' Old Man ', yellow, Aug., leaves fragrant, 2 to 4 ft., Europe; *arborescens*, 3 ft., S. Europe; *tridentata*, strongly fragrant, 6 to 8 ft., America.

Hardy Perennial Species Cultivated: *A. Absinthium*, ' Wormwood ', yellow, Aug., 18 in., Europe; *argentea*, yellow, July, 18 in., Madeira; *cana*, yellow, Aug., 2 to 3 ft., N. America; *Dracunculus*, ' Tarragon ', 2 ft., S. Europe; *gnaphalodes*, white, summer, 1 to 2 ft., N. America; *lactiflora*, cream, Aug. to Oct., 5 ft., China; *Ludoviciana*, yellow, summer, 3 ft., N. America; *pedemontana*, silver grey foliage, 4 to 6 in., Europe; *pontica*, grey foliage, 2 ft., Austria; *Stelleriana*, yellow, summer, 1 to 2 ft., N.E. Asia and N. America.

Arthropodium—*Liliaceae.* Greenhouse herbaceous perennials. First introduced early nineteenth century.

Culture: Compost, two parts sandy loam, one part peat, and a liberal quantity of silver sand. Position, well-drained pots in sunny part of greenhouse. Pot, March or April. Water freely spring and summer, moderately autumn and winter. Temp., Oct. to March 40° to 45°, March to Oct. 55° to 65°.

Propagation: By seeds sown in a mixture of equal parts sandy loam, peat, leaf-mould and sand, in a temp. of 55° to 65° in spring; also by offsets or suckers removed in spring.

Species Cultivated: *A. candidum*, white, May, 9 in., New Zealand; *cirrhatum*, white, May, 3 ft., New Zealand; *neocaledonicum*, white, May, 18 in., New Caledonia; *paniculatum*, white, May, 3 ft., New South Wales.

Artichoke, Globe, see *Cynara Scolymus*; **Jerusalem-,** see *Helianthus tuberosus*; **Chinese-,** see *Stachys affinis*.

Artillery Plant, see *Pilea microphylla.*

Artocarpus—*Moraceae.* Stove evergreen trees with large crimson or green leaves. The fruit of *A. communis* is edible. First introduced late eighteenth century.

Culture: Compost, two parts loam, one part leaf-mould and sand. Pot, Feb., March. Position, shady and moist. Prune into shape, Feb. Water freely in summer, moderately in winter. Temp., March to Sept. 65° to 75°, Sept. to March 55° to 60°.

Propagation: By stem-rooting firm shoots in Feb., March; suckers at any time.

Species Cultivated: *A. communis*, ' Bread Fruit Tree ', 50 ft., Malaya; *integra*, ' Jack Fruit ', 50 ft., India and Malaya.

Arum—*Araceae.* Hardy or half-hardy tuberous-rooted perennials. Grown more for their curiously formed flowers and showy red, poisonous berries than for their beauty. Many species formerly included here have been transferred to other genera.

Culture of Hardy Species: Soil, ordinary. Position, partially shady shrubbery borders or grassy spots. Plant, autumn or spring. Protect with a covering of leaves in winter.

Culture of Half-Hardy Species: Compost, two parts loam, one part decayed manure, and one part sand. Position, well-drained border at base of south wall, or pots in a cool greenhouse. Plant or pot in autumn. Water freely whilst growing in pots; keep dry when foliage dies.

Propagation: By offsets in autumn.

Hardy Species Cultivated: *A. italicum*, ' Italian Arum ', creamy white, spring, 1 to 1½ ft., S. Europe; *maculatum*, ' Cuckoo-pint ', ' Lords and Ladies ', yellowish green, spotted purple, 6 in., Britain.

HALF-HARDY SPECIES CULTIVATED: *A. creticum*, spathe yellowish, May, 1 ft., Crete; *palaestinum* (syn. *A. sanctum*), yellow and deep purple, May, 2 ft., Syria.

Arum Lily, see *Zantedeschia aethiopica.*

Aruncus (Goat's Beard)—*Rosaceae*. Hardy perennial, at one time included in Spiraea.
CULTURE: Soil, moist, rich. Position, part shade.
PROPAGATION: By seeds.
SPECIES CULTIVATED: *A. sylvester* (syn. *Spiraea Aruncus, S. Humboldtii*), white, summer, 4 to 6 ft., N. Temp. Regions, var. *Kneiffii*, finely dissected foliage.

Arundina—*Orchidaceae*. A terrestrial genus with reed-like leafy stems, much as in Sobralia. Inflorescence terminal, simple or paniculate.
CULTURE: Compost, three parts fibrous loam, one part peat and sphagnum moss. Water is needed throughout the year. The pots well-drained. Winter temp. 60°, summer to tropical.
PROPAGATION: By division of the plants.
SPECIES CULTIVATED: *A. chinensis*, bluish and crimson, variable, summer, China; *densa*, fragrant, rose violet to crimson, summer, Malaya, Philippines.

Arundinaria—*Gramineae*. Hardy shrubby grasses.
CULTURE: Soil, good, not too heavy and of reasonable depth. Position, sheltered from cold winds, dry root conditions are disliked.
PROPAGATION: By division.
SPECIES CULTIVATED: *A. anceps*, to 10 ft., Himalaya; *falcata*, to 20 ft., stems yellow-green, Himalaya; *gigantea*, ' Southern Cane ', ' Cane Reed ', to 25 ft., leaves to 12 in. long, finely toothed, glabrous or pubescent, N. America; *vagans* (syn. *Bambusa pygmaea* hort.), 1 to 1½ ft., runs underground, Japan. See also Chimonobambusa, Pleioblastus, Pseudosasa, Sasa, Semiarundinaria, and Sinarundinaria.

Arundo—*Gramineae*. Very tall, hardy perennial grasses.
CULTURE: Soil, well-drained sandy loam. Position, moist and sheltered in isolated groups on lawns. Plant, April. Protect crowns with covering of leaves in winter.
PROPAGATION: By division of roots in spring.
SPECIES CULTIVATED: *A. Donax*, ' Giant Reed ', reddish white, Aug., 12 ft., S. Europe, var. *versicolor*, leaves striped with white, 3 ft.

Asarina, see Antirrhinum.

Asclepias (Milkweed)—*Asclepiadaceae*. Hardy herbaceous and stove perennials. First introduced late seventeenth century.
CULTURE: Soil, rich, light peat. Position, sunny and moist borders. Plant, Oct. or April. *A. curassavica* in pots in stove with winter temp. 60° to 65°.
PROPAGATION: By division of roots in Oct. or April; also by seeds sown in temp. 50° to 75° in spring. All the hardy species require protection in severe weather.
SPECIES CULTIVATED: *A. curassavica*, red-purple, July to Sept., 2 to 3 ft., tender, Trop. America; *incarnata*, red, 2 ft., N. America; *purpurascens*, purple, July, 2 to 3 ft., Virginia; *speciosa*, purple-lilac, fragrant, July, 2 to 3 ft., N.W. America; *syriaca* (syn. *A. Cornutii*), purple, fragrant, July, 3 to 5 ft., N. America; *tuberosa*, ' Swallow-wort ', orange, July to Sept., 1 to 2 ft., N. America.

Ash, see Fraxinus; **-leaf Fern,** see *Marattia fraxinea* and Aneimia.

Asimina—*Annonaceae*. A strong, hardy, deciduous shrub of the Custard Apple family with large foliage, seldom fruits in this country.
CULTURE: Soil, ordinary, moist. Position, full sun.
PROPAGATION: By seeds (imported).
SPECIES CULTIVATED: *A. triloba*, ' Papaw ', purple, fruits fleshy, edible, to 30 ft., N. America.

Asparagus—*Liliaceae.* Climbing greenhouse foliage plants, shrubs and hardy perennials, including the edible asparagus.

CULTURE OF GREENHOUSE SPECIES: Compost, two parts loam, one part of equal proportions of leaf-mould, peat and silver sand. Position, pots, tubs, or beds, for climbers, shoots trained up roof or back walls of greenhouse; dwarf kinds in pots or baskets suspended from roof. Pot or plant in March. Water and syringe freely during the summer, moderately at other seasons. Apply weak liquid manure occasionally to established plants. Temp., Sept. to March 50° to 55°, March to Sept. 55° to 60°.

CULTURE OF EDIBLE ASPARAGUS: Soil, deep, rich sandy loam. Position, open and sunny, or in partial shade. Size of beds, 4 ft. wide; alleys, 2 ft. wide. Preparation of soil: In Oct. or Nov., trench two spits deep and break up third spit with fork. Put a thick layer of manure over third spit and work in a liberal quantity of old mortar, decayed vegetable matter, and rotted manure among upper spits. In case of heavy wet soils, put a thick layer of brick rubble under second spit. Raise beds 1 ft. above the general level unless ground very well drained. Plant in April. Spread out roots, plants to be 15 in. apart, and crowns 3 in. below surface. Three-year-old plants best for planting. Cutting: No shoots to be removed first year, moderate quantity second year, freely afterwards. Shoots should not be less than 6 in. long when cut. Cease cutting end of June. General treatment: Apply manure periodically. Keep beds free of weeds. Cut down stems early in Nov. Top-dress with decayed manure in Nov., previously lightly forking up surface. In March, rake off rough particles into alley, and leave smooth and neat. Manures: Decayed horse manure for heavy soils; cow or pig manures for light soils; seaweed mixed with above manures and applied as a top-dressing in Nov. if available; common salt, 1 oz. to a square yard occasionally.

FORCING IN FRAMES: Prepare hotbed of manure in usual way. Cover with 3 in. of light soil. Place roots on this and cover to depth of 5 in. Keep soil moist and frame closed until shoots appear, then admit a little air. Temp. 60° to 75°. Roots of no use after forcing.

PROPAGATION: Greenhouse species by seeds sown in temp. 70° in spring; division of roots, March. Edible asparagus, by seeds sown in groups of three or four in holes 1 in. deep and 15 in. apart on prepared bed, or in drills 1 in. deep and 12 in. apart in ordinary soil—March or April. Thin seedlings raised by the first method to one in each group in May; those by the second method to a foot apart when 3 in. high. Transplant latter into permanent beds when two or three years old. Seedlings ready to cut fourth year after sowing. Seeds take 20 days to germinate. A quarter-pint of seed will sow a row 50 ft. long.

GREENHOUSE SPECIES CULTIVATED: *A. acutifolius*, flowers yellow, berries red, 5 to 6 ft., almost hardy, S. Europe; *asparagoides* (syn. *Myrsiphyllum asparagoides*), 'Smilax' of florists, 6 to 10 ft., branching vine, S. Africa; *plumosus*, 'Asparagus Fern', 4 to 10 ft., S. Africa, and vars. *nanus*, dwarf, and *tenuissimus*, wiry-stemmed, all used in floristry; *scandens*, to 6 ft., S. Africa; *Sprengeri*, climbing to 6 ft., Natal; *verticillatus*, 10 ft., S. Africa.

HARDY SPECIES CULTIVATED: *A. officinalis* var. *altilis*, 'Asparagus', Europe and Asia.

Aspasia—*Orchidaceae.* A small genus of epiphytic orchids. Flowers few or solitary, produced as in Odontoglossums, with a resemblance in shape.

CULTURE: Compost and treatment as for *Odontoglossum crispum*, but the minimum winter temperature should be 55°.

PROPAGATION: As for Odontoglossum. By division of plants or from healthy back bulbs which may emit a growth if removed from the main plant and potted.

SPECIES CULTIVATED: *A. epidendroides*, with the oval pseudo-bulbs about 10 in., creamy white, brown marked, lip white, lilac or violet centrally, spring, Costa Rica, etc.; *lunata*, greenish-white barred chocolate, lip white with a violet crescent, spring, Brazil; *odorata* (syn. *A. lunata papilionacea*), similar to *lunata* but base of lip with numerous keels, spring, Costa Rica; *principissa*, lip whitish marked light mauve, spring, Cent. America. Other species are known.

Aspen, see *Populus tremula.*

Asperula—*Rubiaceae.* Hardy herbaceous perennials and annuals.

CULTURE: Soil, light, rich. Position, rockeries or in open borders. Plant, Oct., Nov.

PROPAGATION: Perennial species by division of roots in March; perennials and annuals by seeds sown ⅛ in. deep in open border in April.

PERENNIAL SPECIES CULTIVATED: *A. cynanchica*, ' Squinancy-wort ', white, June, 9 in., Europe (Britain); *Gussonei*, white, June to Sept., 6 in., Italy; *hexaphylla*, white, June to Sept., 1 ft.; *hirta*, white, changing to pink, July to Aug., 3 in., Pyrenees; *lilaciflora caespitosa*, pink, prostrate, May to June, E. Medit. For *A. odorata*, see *Galium odoratum.*

ANNUAL SPECIES CULTIVATED: *A. orientalis*, blue, summer, fragrant, 6 to 10 in., Syria.

Asphodel, see *Asphodelus ramosus.*

Asphodeline—*Liliaceae.* Hardy herbaceous perennials. First introduced late sixteenth century.

CULTURE: Soil, ordinary, rich. Position, open or shady borders. Plant, Oct. or March.

PROPAGATION: By division of roots, Oct. or March.

SPECIES CULTIVATED: *A. imperialis*, pink, July and Aug., 6 to 8 in., Cilicia; *lutea* (syn. *Asphodelus luteus*), ' King's Spear ', yellow, July and Aug., 3 to 4 ft., Medit. Region, var. *flore-pleno*, flowers double; *taurica* (syn. *Asphodelus tauricus*), white, July, 1 to 2 ft., Orient.

Asphodelus (Asphodel)—*Liliaceae.* Hardy herbaceous perennials. First introduced late sixteenth century.

CULTURE: Soil, ordinary. Position, shady or open borders. Plant in autumn or spring.

PROPAGATION: By division of roots, Oct. or April; seeds sown in a cold frame in March.

SPECIES CULTIVATED: *A. acaulis*, pink, May, 2 in., N. Africa; *albus*, white, May, 2 ft., Europe; *ramosus*, ' Silver Rod ', white, May, 4 to 5 ft., S. Europe. See Asphodeline.

Aspidistra—*Liliaceae.* Greenhouse or dwelling-room evergreen plants. Leaves large, green or variegated with cream. First introduced early nineteenth century.

CULTURE: Compost, two parts loam, one part leaf-mould and sand. Repot in March. Water freely in summer, moderately in winter. Room plants best watered by immersing pot for quarter of an hour in tepid water. Temp., min. 50°.

PROPAGATION: By division of roots in March.

SPECIES CULTIVATED: *A. elatior* (syn. *A. lurida*), ' Parlour Palm ', leaves green, 1 to 2 ft., China, var. *variegata*, leaves striped cream.

Aspidium, see Cyrtomium, Dryopteris, Polystichum.

Asplenium (Spleenwort)—*Polypodiaceae.* Stove, greenhouse and hardy ferns. Height varies from 6 in. to 4 ft.

CULTURE OF STOVE AND GREENHOUSE SPECIES: Compost, equal parts peat, loam, leaf-mould and sand. Pot March. Water freely in summer, moderately in winter. Temp. stove species, Sept. to March 60° to 70°, March to Sept. 70° to 80°; greenhouse, Sept. to March 50° to 55°, March to Sept. 55° to 65°.

CULTURE OF HARDY SPECIES: Compost, equal parts peat, loam, leaf-mould, sand and old mortar rubble. Position, old walls, rockeries; moist shady borders for Lady Ferns.

PROPAGATION: Stove and greenhouse species by spores sown in sandy peat at any time. Hardy species by spores when ripe, and division in April.

STOVE SPECIES CULTIVATED: *A. attenuatum*, New South Wales, etc.; *Belangeri*,

Java; Borneo; *caudatum*, India, Brazil; *formosum*, Trop. America; *longissimum*, Java, etc.; *Nidus*, ' Bird's-nest Fern ', Asia, Polynesia, and varieties; *viviparum*, Mauritius.

GREENHOUSE SPECIES CULTIVATED: *A. bulbiferum*, Australia and New Zealand; *Colensoi*, New Zealand; *dimorphum*, Norfolk Is.; *Hemionitis*, Spain, Canary Is.; *incisum*, Japan; *platyneuron*, N. America, S. Africa.

HARDY SPECIES CULTIVATED: *A. Adiantum nigrum*, ' French Fern ', Temp. Zones, inc. Britain; *Ceterach* (syn. *Ceterach cordatum*), ' Scale Fern ', Europe (Br.); *germanicum*, Europe (Br.); *marinum*, Europe; *Ruta-muraria*, ' Wall-Rue ', Europe; *Trichomanes*, N. America, Europe, Asia; *viride*, N. America, Europe, Asia.

Aster (Starwort, Michaelmas Daisy)—*Compositae.* Hardy herbaceous perennials. See Callistephus for China Aster; Solidaster for *A. hybridus luteus*.

CULTURE: Soil, good ordinary. Position, sunny borders, wild garden for tall species, rockeries for dwarf ones. Plant in Oct. or spring. Lift, divide and replant when overcrowded.

PROPAGATION: By seeds in heat or cold frame in spring; cuttings of young shoots in heat or cold frame in spring or summer; division in autumn or spring.

SPECIES CULTIVATED: *A. acris*, lilac-purple, Aug., 3 ft., S. Europe; *alpinus*, ' Rock Aster ', purple, July, 6 in., Europe; *Amellus*, ' Italian Starwort ', purple, Aug., 2 ft., Europe, and many varieties in shades of lavender, violet and pink; *andinus*, violet, gold disk, May to June, 3 to 6 in., N. America; *Bellidiastrum* (syn. *Bellidiastrum Michelii*), white, early summer, 6 to 9 in., Europe; *Canbyi*, lilac-blue, July to Aug., 1 ft., N. America; *cordifolius*, mauve, July, 2 ft., N. America, var. *versicolor*, light pink flowers; *diplostephioides*, rich purple, June, 1 ft., Himalaya, var. *Eichtlinii*, pale blue; *dumosus*, mauve, Oct., 18 in., N. America; *ericoides*, ' Heath Aster ', white, Oct., 2 to 3 ft., N. America; *Farreri*, violet-blue, June to July, 1 ft., China; *Frikartii*, lavender-blue, Aug. to Oct., 2 to 3 ft., hybrid; *grandiflorus*, violet, Nov., 2 to 3 ft., Virginia; *laevis*, blue, Sept., 2 ft., N. America; *lateriflorus* (syn. *A. diffusus*), white, Oct., 2 ft., N. America, var. *horizontalis*, long wide-spreading branches; *likiangensis*, royal purple, May to June, 3 in., China; *multiflorus*, white, Sept. to Nov., 3 ft., N. America; *novae-angliae*, purple, Sept., 5 to 6 ft., N. America, and numerous varieties; *novi-belgii*, blue, Sept., 4 ft., N. America, and numerous forms; *paniculatus*, pale lilac, Sept. to Oct., 3 ft., N. America; *ptarmicoides*, white, Aug., 18 in., N. America; *puniceus*, blue, Sept., 6 ft., N. America; *Shortii*, bluish, Sept., 3 ft., U.S.A.; *subcaeruleus*, violet-blue, June, 9 in., Himalaya; *Thomsonii*, pale blue, July to Nov., 1 to 2 ft., Himalaya; *Tradescantii*, white, Oct., 4 ft., N. America; *turbinellus*, mauve, Aug., 3 ft., N. America; *versicolor*, pink and white, Sept., 3 ft., N. America; *vimineus*, white, Sept., 3 ft., N. America; *yunnanensis*, lilac-blue, June to July, 9 to 12 in., Yunnan.

Asteranthera—*Gesneriaceae.* Small trailing shrub.

CULTURE: Soil, moisture-laden. Position, forest shade, creeping over mossy tree trunks.

PROPAGATION: By seed.

SPECIES CULTIVATED: *A. ovata*, red, small trailing shrub, S. Chile and Argentina.

Astilbe (False Goatsbeard)—*Saxifragaceae.* Hardy herbaceous perennials. Some species are forced for flowering early in greenhouses and often incorrectly named Spiraea.

CULTURE: Soil, loamy. Position, moist shady borders or margins of lakes or ponds. Plant in Oct. or spring. Plenty of water is required in dry weather.

INDOOR CULTURE: Compost, two parts loam, one part well-rotted manure or leaf-mould and one of silver sand. Pot roots in Sept. or Oct. Place pots in cold frame and cover with peat till Dec., when introduce to a temp. of 45° for a week or so, then transfer to temp. 55° to 60°. Water freely when growth begins. Apply weak liquid manure when flower spikes show. After flowering, harden off in cold frame till May and then plant out in garden. Lift, divide and replant following April and lift and pot in autumn. Retarded roots will flower in a cold house in about six weeks from potting.

PROPAGATION: By division; seeds.

SPECIES CULTIVATED: *A. Arendsii*, white to red, July to Aug., 2½ to 5 ft., hybrid group; *astilboides*, white, June, 2 to 3 ft., Japan; *chinensis*, white, July, 2 ft., China, and var. *pumila*, purple, dwarf; *crispa*, rich colours, dwarf, compact, hybrid; *Davidii*, rose-pink, Aug. to Sept., 4 to 5 ft., China; *japonica*, white, May, 2 ft., Japan; *Lemoinei*, white or rose, July to Aug., 2 to 3 ft., hybrid; *rivularis*, white, July, Himalaya; *simplicifolia*, white, June, 1 ft., Japan; *Thunbergii*, white, May, 1 to 2 ft., Japan.

Astragalus (Milk Vetch)—*Leguminosae*. Hardy perennial or shrubby plants. *A. Tragacantha* is a hardy, dwarf, slow-growing shrub. First introduced mid-sixteenth century.

CULTURE: Soil, ordinary. Position, open border for tall, and rockery for dwarf species. Full sun for *A. Tragacantha*. Plant, Oct., March.

PROPAGATION: By seeds sown ¼ in. deep in light soil in cold frame in March; shrubby kinds by cuttings in a cold frame in summer.

SPECIES CULTIVATED: *A. alopecuroides*, yellow, June, 3 to 5 ft., Siberia; *Durhamii*, yellow, summer, 2 to 3 ft., Balkan Peninsula; *hypoglottis* (syn. *A. danicus*), blue, June, trailing, Europe; *monspessulanus*, rosy lilac and white, June, trailing, S. Europe; *Onobrychis*, purple, July, 9 to 12 in., Persia; *Tragacantha*, 'Goat's Thorn', pale purple, May, grey leaves, 1 ft., S. Europe.

Astrantia (Masterwort)—*Umbelliferae*. Hardy herbaceous perennials. First introduced late sixteenth century.

CULTURE: Soil, ordinary. Position, shady borders or margins of woodland walks. Plant, Oct. or March.

PROPAGATION: By seeds sown in sandy loam in cold frame in April; division of roots in Oct. or March.

SPECIES CULTIVATED: *A. Biebersteinii*, white, May, 2 ft., Caucasus; *carniolica*, white, May, 1 ft., E. Europe; *major*, pink and white, 2 ft., Europe; *maxima* (syn. *A. helleborifolia*), pink, July, 2 ft., Caucasus; *minor*, white, tinted green, June, 6 in., Europe.

Astroloba—*Liliaceae*. Greenhouse, succulent-leaved dwarf plants with small whitish flowers, leafy rosettes, stem-like, elongated leaves with thorny teeth. Formerly known under the name of Apicra and closely allied to Haworthia. Natives of S. Africa.

CULTURE: As Haworthia.

PROPAGATION: As Haworthia.

SPECIES CULTIVATED: *A. aspera* (syns. *Apicra aspera, Haworthia aspera*), stem rosette erect, leaves in three compressed spiral rows; *deltoidea*, stem-like rosettes 8 to 12 in. long, prostrate; *egregia*, 4 to 6 in. high, branching from base; *foliolosa*, leaves in five twisted rows; *pentagona*, 10 in. high erect; *spiralis*, similar to *A. pentagona*, leaves in closely compressed spiral rows.

Asystasia—*Acanthaceae*. Greenhouse flowering shrub. First introduced mid-nineteenth century.

CULTURE: Compost, two parts fibrous loam, one part fibrous peat or leaf-mould, half-part dried cow manure and silver sand. Position, pots or border in light airy greenhouse. Pot, March or April. Prune after flowering, shortening lateral growth to 2 or 3 in. Disbud side shoots when inflorescences show, otherwise they fail to develop satisfactorily. Water freely March to Sept., moderately Sept. to Nov. Keep nearly dry Nov. to March. Temp., March to Oct. 55° to 65°, Oct. to March 45° to 55°.

PROPAGATION: By cuttings inserted singly in 2-in. pots filled with sandy soil, June to Aug. Repot as required until plants occupy 8 or 10 in. receptacles, or plant out in well-drained border in light position in conservatory or greenhouse.

SPECIES CULTIVATED: *A. coromandeliana* (syn. *A. gangetica*), yellow, 18 in., winter, Malaya, Ceylon, India, Arabia, Africa.

Atamasco Lily, see *Zephyranthes Atamasco*.

Atherosperma—*Monimiaceae*. Slightly tender, aromatic evergreen tree, or sometimes a bush. In Australia a kind of herb tea is brewed from parts of the plant.
CULTURE: Soil, loam and peat. Position, sheltered, with plentiful water supply.
PROPAGATION: By cuttings.
SPECIES CULTIVATED: *A. moschatum*, white, Tasmania, Victoria, New South Wales.

Athrotaxis—*Pinaceae* (or *Taxodiaceae*). Tender evergreen shrubs and trees. First introduced mid-nineteenth century.
CULTURE: Soil, good loam. Position, sheltered, only grown outside in Cornwall or Ireland. Plant, Sept. or Oct.
PROPAGATION: By seeds sown in pots in cold frame.
SPECIES CULTIVATED: *A. cupressoides*, 20 to 45 ft., Tasmania; *laxifolia*, 25 to 35 ft., Tasmania; *selaginoides*, ' Tasmanian Cedar ', 40 ft., possibly more hardy, Tasmania.

Athyrium—*Polypodiaceae*. Foliage similar to Asplenium with which genus this is sometimes united.
CULTURE: As Asplenium.
PROPAGATION: As Asplenium.
SPECIES CULTIVATED: *A. alpestre*, to 3 ft., Europe, Asia, etc.; *Filix-femina*, ' Lady Fern ', to 3 ft., Europe, Asia, N. America, etc.; *Filix-mas*, listed name; *Goeringianum*, Japan; *pycnocarpon* (syn. *Asplenium angustifolium*), 1½ ft., N. America; *thelypteroides* (syn. *Asplenium acrostichoides*), to 3 ft., N. America.

Atriplex (Salt Bush)—*Chenopodiaceae*. Hardy annuals, perennials and shrubs. *A. hortensis* occasionally grown as a substitute for spinach, the varieties used for border decoration. *A. Halimus* is a grey-leaved maritime shrub, sometimes used for hedging with tamarisk.
CULTURE OF ORACH: Soil, ordinary. Sow seeds at intervals of a few weeks from March onwards in drills 1 in. deep and 2 ft. apart. When seedlings are 3 in. high, thin them to 18 in. apart. Gather youngest and most succulent leaves for cooking.
CULTURE OF PERENNIAL AND SHRUBBY SPECIES: Soil, ordinary. Position, near the sea. *A. Halimus* suitable for hedge culture. Plant in autumn. Trim into shape April.
PROPAGATION: By cuttings in Aug.
SPECIES CULTIVATED: *A. hortensis*, ' Orach ', green, summer, 3 to 5 ft., Cent. Asia. and vars. *atrosanguinea*, *cupreata*, *rosea*, with red foliage.
EVERGREEN SPECIES CULTIVATED: *A. canescens*, ' Grey Sage Bush ', leaves light grey, 5 to 6 ft., N.W. America; *Halimus*, ' Shrubby Goosefoot ', silvery-grey leaves, 4 to 5 ft., S. Europe.

Aubergine or **Eggplant,** see *Solanum Melongena* var. *esculentum*.

Aubrieta (Purple Rock-cress)—*Cruciferae*. Hardy trailing evergreen perennials. Former spelling Aubretia. Innumerable garden varieties. First introduced early eighteenth century.
CULTURE: Soil, ordinary, loves lime. Position, sunny border, rock garden or walls. Plant, Oct. and spring. Plants will benefit from a severe trimming after flowering.
PROPAGATION. By cuttings (small) dibbled into pots of sandy soil or beneath cloche in shady borders in June; seeds sown in sandy soil in spring; division of the roots in spring. (Seeds of named garden varieties will not come true to type.)
SPECIES CULTIVATED: *A. deltoidea*, purple, spring, 2 in., S. Europe, Asia Minor; *erubescens*, purple, 3 in., spring, Macedonia; *gracilis*, pale lavender, 2 in., spring, Greece; *Kotschyi*, purple, 3 in., spring, Persia; *libanotica*, pale lavender, 3 in., spring, Syria; *Pinardii*, purple, 2 in., spring, Asia Minor.

Aucuba—*Cornaceae*. Hardy evergreen shrub. First introduced late eighteenth century.
CULTURE: Soil, ordinary. Position, open or in shade; used as a town shrub, and as a good screen beneath dense trees. Plant, Oct., Nov., April. Female aucubas bear red berries freely in winter if a male plant be placed close to them, or if a branch of male blossom be placed on female plant when in bloom. May be used for pot culture in cool greenhouses or windows in winter.
PROPAGATION: By seeds sown ¼ in. deep in cold frame in Oct.; cuttings inserted in sandy soil in sheltered border or cold frame in Sept., Oct., Nov.
SPECIES CULTIVATED: *A. japonica*, ‘ Spotted Laurel ’, ‘ Variegated Laurel ’, 6 to 10 ft., Japan, and vars. *albo-variegata, aurea, fructu-luteo, limbata, vera nana, viridis*, etc.

Aunt Eliza, see Antholyza.

Auricula, see *Primula Auricula*.

Australian Bluebell Creeper, see *Sollya heterophylla*; **-Currant,** see *Leucopogon Reichei*; **-Daisy,** see *Erigeron Karvinskianus*; **-Everlasting,** see Helipterum; **-Feather-palm,** see *Ptychosperma elegans*; **-Fleabane,** see *Erigeron Karvinskianus*; **-Fuchsia,** see Correa; **-Giant Lily,** see *Doryanthes excelsa*; **-Heath,** see Epacris; **-Honeysuckle,** see Banksia; **-Hop,** see *Daviesia alata*; **-Ivy,** see *Muhlenbeckia adpressa*; **-Lilac,** see *Hardenbergia monophylla*; **-Native Rose,** see *Boronia serrulata*; **-Pitcher Plant,** see *Cephalotus follicularis*; **-Rosemary,** see Westringia; **-Sarsaparilla Tree,** see Hardenbergia; **-Tree Fern,** see *Dicksonia antarctica*.

Austrian Briar, see *Rosa foetida*; **-Dragonshead,** see *Dracocephalum austriacum*; **-Leopard’s Bane,** see *Doronicum austriacum*; **-Pine,** see *Pinus nigra*.

Autumn Crocus, see Colchicum; **-Flowering Squill,** see *Scilla autumnalis*; **-Sneezewort,** see *Helenium autumnalis*.

Avena (Oat)—*Gramineae*. Hardy, mostly annual, grasses, native in temperate regions of the world and grown for grain, forage and hay. One species (*A. sterilis*) is grown for ornament; the awns are susceptible to change of weather and animated.
CULTURE: Sow seeds outdoors in April in ordinary soil in borders. Can be gathered when fully developed and dried for winter decoration.
SPECIES CULTIVATED: *A. sterilis*, ‘ Animated Oat ’, 2 ft., Medit. Region.

Avens, see Geum.

Avocado Pear, see *Persea americana*

Azalea, see Rhododendron; **Alpine-,** see Loiseleuria.

Azara—*Flacourtiaceae*. Half-hardy evergreen shrubs with ornamental leaves. Flowers unattractive but very fragrant. First introduced mid-nineteenth century.
CULTURE: Soil, ordinary. Position, against south wall, or in warm shrubberies in mild districts. Plant, Oct. or April.
PROPAGATION: By cuttings inserted in sandy soil in temp. 65° in March; or in close frame in Aug.
SPECIES CULTIVATED: *A. dentata*, yellow, June, 10 to 12 ft., Chile; *Gilliesii*, yellow, May, 12 to 15 ft., Chile; *microphylla*, greenish white, March, strongly vanilla-scented, the hardiest species, to 15 ft., Chile.

Azolla (Fairy Moss)—*Salviniaceae*. Hardy, floating aquatic perennials with delicate fern-like foliage.
CULTURE: Grow in shallow ponds or in indoor aquariums. Require no soil, merely to float on surface of water.
PROPAGATION: By division.
SPECIES CULTIVATED: *A. caroliniana*, pale green, turning red in autumn, lacy, Carolina; *filiculoides*, larger fronds, pale green tinted rose, S. America.

Azorella—*Umbelliferae.* Hardy, evergreen, prostrate, perennial rock plants. Flowers small, yellow and not attractive, except those of *A. trifurcata* which are handsome in a mass.
CULTURE: Soil, gritty. Position, sunny. Plant, spring.
PROPAGATION: By cuttings inserted in sandy soil in spring or summer; division of old plants.
SPECIES CULTIVATED: *A. peduncularis,* yellowish, June, 2 to 3 in., Ecuador; *trifurcata,* yellow, bronze-green rosettes, June, 2 in., Ecuador.

Babiana (Baboon-root)—*Iridaceae.* Half-hardy bulbous plants with fragrant flowers, from S. Africa. First introduced mid-eighteenth century.
OUTDOOR CULTURE: Soil, light sandy. Position, sunny, well-drained border. Plant, Sept. to Jan., placing bulbs 4 in. deep and 2 in. apart. Lift and replant bulbs annually.
INDOOR CULTURE: Compost, two parts sandy soil and one part leaf-mould or decayed cow manure. Pots, 4½ in. in diameter, well drained. Place five bulbs 3 in. deep in each pot in Nov., and cover pots with peat until growth begins. Water moderately from time bulbs begin to grow until flowers fade, then gradually withhold it, keeping bulbs dry from Sept. to Jan. Temp., Sept. to Feb. 40° to 50°, other times 50° to 60°.
PROPAGATION: By offsets.
SPECIES CULTIVATED: *B. disticha,* blue, June, 6 in.; *plicata,* blue, June, 6 in.; *ringens,* scarlet, June, 6 to 8 in.; *stricta,* white and blue, May, 6 to 8 in.

Baby Blue-eyes, see *Nemophila Menziesii.*

Baby's Tears, see Helxine.

Baccharis—*Compositae.* Hardy deciduous and evergreen shrubs of little ornamental value. Flowers unisexual. First introduced late seventeenth century.
CULTURE: Soil, ordinary. Position, sea-coast gardens. Plant, autumn.
PROPAGATION: By cuttings of young shoots in summer.
SPECIES CULTIVATED: *B. halimifolia,* 6 to 12 ft., Eastern N. America; *patagonica,* 8 to 10 ft., Magellan Straits.

Bachelor's Buttons, see *Ranunculus aconitifolius,* var. *pleniflorus* and *Achillea Ptarmica,* double forms.

Bactris—*Palmae.* Stove palms. First introduced early nineteenth century.
CULTURE: Compost, equal parts loam, leaf-mould and sand. Pot, Feb., March. Water moderately Sept. to March, freely afterwards. Position, shady and moist in summer. Temp., Sept. to March 60° to 70°, March to Sept. 70° to 80°.
PROPAGATION: By removing young plants from the bases of old ones in March, and placing these in small pots; also by seeds.
SPECIES CULTIVATED: *B. caryotaefolia,* 30 ft., Brazil; *Maraja,* ' Maraja Palm ', 30 to 50 ft., Brazil; *pallidispina,* Guiana.

Bael Fruit, see *Aegle Marmelos.*

Baeria—*Compositae.* Mostly hardy annuals. *B. macrantha* is semi-shrubby from perennial rootstock.
CULTURE: Soil, light sandy, preferably without lime. Position, full sun. Plant, spring.
PROPAGATION: By seeds; cuttings inserted in sand during summer.
SPECIES CULTIVATED: *B. aristata* (syn. *B. coronaria*), yellow, summer, trailing, California; *chrysostoma* (syn. *B. gracilis*), yellow, May, 8 to 12 in., California; *macrantha,* yellow, all summer, 6 to 9 in., perennial, N. America.

Bahia, see Eriophyllum.

Bald Cypress, see *Taxodium distichum.*

Baldmoney see *Meum athamaticum.*

Balloon Flower, see Platycodon.

Balm, see *Melissa officinalis;*   **-of-Gilead,** see *Cedronella canariensis;*   **-of-Gilead Fir,** see *Abies balsamea;*   **Bee-,** see *Monarda didyma.*

Balsam, see *Impatiens Balsamina;*   **-Apple,** see *Momordica Balsamina;*   **-Fir,** see *Abies balsamea;*   **-Pear,** see *Momordica Charantia;*   **-scented Geranium,** see *Pelargonium Radula.*

Bamboo, see Arundinaria, Bambusa, Chimonobambusa, Phyllostchysa, Pleioblastus, Pseudosasa, Sasa, Semiarundinaria, Shitataea and Sinarundinaria.

Bambusa (Bamboo)—*Gramineae.*   Tall woody grasses.
OUTDOOR CULTURE: Soil, deep rich loam.   Position, warm sheltered nook or dell.   Plant, May or June.   Protect in winter with covering of leaves.   Mulch in spring.   Water freely in dry weather.
INDOOR CULTURE: Compost, equal parts loam, leaf-mould and sand.   Position, large pots or tubs in cool greenhouse, winter temp. 40° to 50°.   Water freely spring and summer, moderately other times.
PROPAGATION: By seeds in sandy soil in heat in spring;   cuttings of rhizomes in heat in spring;   division in April or May.
SPECIES CULTIVATED: *B. angulata* (syns. *B. quadrangularis, Arundinaria quadrangularis*), 3 ft., China;   *arundinacea,* 10 to 50 ft., tender, India;   *vulgaris* (syn. *B. Thouarsii*), 'Feathery Bamboo', to 50 ft., glaucous, tender, Java.

Banana, see Musa.

Baneberry, see Actaea.

Banksia (Australian Honeysuckle)—*Proteaceae.*   Greenhouse evergreen shrubs or trees.   First introduced late eighteenth century.
CULTURE: Compost, equal parts peat, loam and sand.   Pot in spring in well-drained pots.   Water carefully in winter, moderately in summer.   Temp., Sept. to March 60° to 65°, March to Sept. 55° to 65°.
PROPAGATION: By cuttings of firm shoots in well-drained pots of sandy soil in July under bell-glass in temp. 55° to 65°;   also by seeds sown in sandy soil in temp. 60° to 65°.
SPECIES CULTIVATED: *B. collina,* 6 ft., Australia;   *dryandroides,* 6 ft., Australia;   *grandis,* 30 to 40 ft., Australia;   *integrifolia,* 10 to 12 ft., Australia;   *occidentalis,* 5 ft., Australia;   *quercifolia,* 5 ft., hardy in favoured situations, otherwise requiring cold greenhouse, Australia;   *speciosa,* 6 ft., Australia;   *serrata,* to 20 ft., Australia;   *verticillata,* 15 to 20 ft., Australia.

Banyan, see *Ficus benghalensis.*

Baptisia (False-indigo)—*Leguminosae.*   Hardy herbaceous perennials and shrubs.   First introduced early eighteenth century.
CULTURE: Soil, ordinary.   Position, sunny, well-drained border.   Plant, Oct., March or April.
PROPAGATION: By seeds sown ⅛ in. deep in sandy soil in shallow boxes in cold frame in April, or in sunny borders outdoors in May;   division in March.
SPECIES CULTIVATED: *B. alba,* white, June, 2 ft., N. America;   *australis,* blue, June, 3 to 4 ft., spreading bush, N. America;   *leucantha,* cream, July, 2 ft., N. America;   *tinctoria,* yellow, July, 2 ft., N. America.

Barbados Cherry, see *Malpighia glabra;*   **-Gooseberry,** see Pereskia;   **-Lily,** see *Hippeastram equestre;*   **-Pride,** see *Poinciana pulcherrima.*

Barbarea (American Cress)—*Cruciferae.*   Hardy perennial plants and salad vegetables.
CULTURE OF FLOWERING SPECIES: Soil, ordinary.   Position, open garden;   edgings to beds or sunny rockeries for variegated kind.
CULTURE OF WINTER CRESS: Soil, ordinary.   Position, moist, partially shaded border.   Sow seeds in shallow drills 9 in. apart in Sept. for winter use;   in March and June for summer use.   Gather tops of young leaves for salading.

PROPAGATION: By division of roots in March.

SPECIES CULTIVATED: *B. verna*, ' Winter ' or ' Land Cress ' (syn. *B. praecox*), Britain; *longirostris*, ' Thracian Cress ', pale yellow, May to June, 1 ft., Balkan Peninsula; *vulgaris*, yellow, summer, 1 to 2 ft., var. *variegata*, leaves yellow and green.

Barbary Fig, see *Opuntia vulgaris.*

Barberry, see Berberis.

Barberton Daisy, see *Gerbera Jamesonii.*

Barkeria, see Epidendrum.

Barleria—*Acanthaceae.* Stove flowering evergreen shrubs. First introduced mid-eighteenth century.

CULTURE: Compost, two parts peat and loam, one part decayed manure and sand. Plant in March in well-drained pots. Temp., Sept. to March 55° to 65°, March to Sept. 70° to 85°. Water moderately in winter, freely in summer. Prune shoots back after flowering. Syringe daily during spring and summer.

PROPAGATION: By cuttings of young shoots inserted in sandy peat under bell-glass in temp. 85°, March to July.

SPECIES CULTIVATED: *B. cristata*, purple, white, July, 2 ft., India, Burma; *flava*, yellow, winter, 18 in., Trop. Africa; *involucrata*, blue, winter, 1 to 2 ft., Ceylon; *lupulina*, yellow, Aug., 2 ft., Mauritius; *strigosa*, blue, July, 2 to 3 ft., India.

Barren Strawberry, see *Waldsteinia fragarioides*; **-wort,** see *Epimedium.*

Bartonia, see Mentzelia.

Basil, see *Ocimum Basilicum.*

Basket Grass, see *Oplismenus compositus.*

Basswood, see Tilia.

Bastard Balm, see *Melittis Melissophyllum*; **-Cedar, see** *Cedrela sinensis*; **-Indigo,** see *Amorpha fruticosa.*

Bat Willow (*Salix caerulea*).

Batemannia—*Orchidaceae.* Stove, evergreen epiphytic orchids. Pseudo-bulbs 2 to 3 in. high, dimly 4-angled, racemes arched or pendulous, flowers 1 to 5, moderately large. The flowers have the anterior portions of the lateral sepals divergent. First introduced mid-nineteenth century.

CULTURE: Compost, equal parts fibrous peat or osmunda fibre and sphagnum moss. Position, shallow basket or in pans. Repot March. Water freely in summer, in winter prevent the compost becoming dry. Winter temp. 65° to 70°, summer 70° and higher. Keep atmosphere moist, shade.

PROPAGATION: By division of old plants at potting time.

SPECIES CULTIVATED: *B. armillata*, greenish white and brown, early summer, Brazil; *Beaumontii*, greenish, yellowish, striped brown, lip white, dotted purple, summer, Brazil; *Colleyi*, 6 to 8 in., purplish-brown, lip marked red at base, August, British Guiana; *peruviana*, greenish white, and purple, spring, Peru.

Bauhinia—*Leguminosae* (or *Caesalpiniaceae*). Stove evergreen shrubs. First introduced late seventeenth century.

CULTURE: Compost, equal parts peat and loam, one-sixth sand. Pot firmly in March. Position, light, sunny, moist in summer. Water freely March to Sept., moderately other times. Temp., Sept. to March 60° to 70°, March to Sept. 70° to 80°.

PROPAGATION: By cuttings inserted in well-drained pots of sandy peat under bell-glass in temp. 75° in July.

SPECIES CULTIVATED: *B. Galpinii*, white, July, 6 ft., S. Africa; *natalensis*, white, Sept., Natal; *purpurea*, red and white, 10 to 15 ft., India, Burma, China; *tomen-*

tosa, yellow and red, 10 to 15 ft., Ceylon; *Vahlii*, white, large climber, India; *variegata*, rose, red and yellow, June, 6 to 20 ft., India, China.

Bayonet Plant, see *Aciphylla squarrosa*.

Bay Tree, see *Laurus nobilis*.

Bead Tree, see Melia.

Bean, Broad, see *Vicia Faba*;   **Butter-,** see *Phaseolus vulgaris*;   **Dutch-,** see *P. coccineus* var. *albus*;   **French-,** see *P. vulgaris*;   **Haricot-,** see *P. vulgaris*; **Kidney-,** see *P. vulgaris*;   **-Lily,** see Nymphoides;   **Scarlet Runner-,** see *P. coccineus*;   **-Tree,** see *Ceratonia Siliqua*.

Beard Tongue, see Penstemon.

Bearberry, see Arctostaphylos.

Bear's Breech, see *Acanthus mollis*;   **-Ear,** see *Primula auricula*;   **-Ear Sanicle,** see *Cortusa Matthiolii*;   **-foot Fern,** see *Humata Tyermannii*;   **-paw Fern,** see *Polypodium Meyenianum*.

Beaucarnea—*Liliaceae*. Greenhouse tree-like plants with tall trunks somewhat swollen at base, long linear leaves and small whitish flowers in panicles. Sometimes retained in the genus Nolina.

CULTURE: Compost, two parts fibrous loam, one part silver sand. Pot, March, in well-drained pots. Water freely March to Sept., moderately other times. Temp., Sept. to March 45° to 50°, March to Sept. 55° to 65°.

PROPAGATION: By seeds sown in sandy loam in temp. 65° in Feb. or March.

SPECIES CULTIVATED: *B. recurvata* (syn. *Nolina tuberculata*), leaves recurved, to 30 ft., Mexico.

Beaufortia—*Myrtaceae*. Greenhouse, evergreen flowering shrubs. First introduced early nineteenth century.

CULTURE: Compost, equal parts leaf-mould, loam and peat, one-sixth sand. Pot and prune, March; make soil quite firm and drain pots well. Water freely May to Aug., moderately at other times. Temp., Sept. to March 45° to 50°, March to Sept. 55° to 65°.

PROPAGATION: By cuttings of firm shoots inserted in sandy soil in temp. 55° to 65° in summer.

SPECIES CULTIVATED: *B. decussata*, scarlet, May, 3 ft., Australia; *purpurea*, purple, July, 2 to 3 ft., Australia; *sparsa*, red, June, 2 to 3 ft., Australia.

Beaumontia—*Apocynaceae*. Stove climber. First introduced early nineteenth century.

CULTURE: Compost, equal parts peat and loam, one-sixth sand. Position, large tub or border, well drained. Shoots to climb roof. Pot or plant, March. Water abundantly May to Aug., moderately afterwards. Temp., Sept. to March 60° to 70°; March to Sept. 70° to 80°.

PROPAGATION: By cuttings inserted in sandy soil in temp. 75° in March.

SPECIES CULTIVATED: *B. fragrans*, Cochin-China; *grandiflora*, 'Nepal Trumpet Flower', white, July to Aug., 15 to 20 ft., India; *Jerdoniana*, 15 to 20 ft., India.

Beauty Bush, see *Kolkwitzia amabilis*.

Bedstraw, see Galium.

Beech, see Fagus;   **-Fern,** see *Dryopteris Phegopteris*.

Beet, see Beta;   **Leaf** or **Spinach-,** see *B. vulgaris* var. *Cicla*;   **-root** or **Sugar-,** see *B. vulgaris*.

Beewort, see Acorus.

Begonia—*Begoniaceae*. Warm, greenhouse fibrous and tuberous-rooted perennials. Some are grown for flowers and others for ornamental foliage. First introduced mid-eighteenth century.

CULTURE OF TUBEROUS-ROOTED TYPE: Compost, equal parts loam and leaf-mould and one part of equal proportions of dried cow manure and silver sand. Start tubers to grow in Feb. or March by placing them in leaf-mould in shallow boxes in temp. 65° to 70°. When rooted, plant in small pots and afterwards transfer to large ones. Water moderately at first, fully afterwards. Feed with diluted liquid manure when growth is active. Shade from sun. After flowering, gradually withhold water and keep dry till Feb. Store in pots on their sides in temp. 50° to 55° in winter. For outdoor culture start tubers in March, and when rooting begins transplant into boxes, grow in heat till May, then plant out early in June in rich soil in partial shade. Lift tubers in Sept., place in boxes to ripen off, then store as advised for pot tubers.

CULTURE OF FIBROUS-ROOTED TYPE: Compost, same as advised for tuberous-rooted species. Sow seeds in Jan. or Feb. in temp. of 65° to 75°, or insert cuttings in pots in a similar temp. in Feb. or March. Grow the seedlings or rooted cuttings on, first in small and then larger pots in temp. 55° to 65°. Water moderately. Syringe daily. Shade from sun. Keep moist during earlier stages of growth. In autumn keep air drier and maintain temp. of 55°. Feed occasionally with liquid manure. After flowering gradually withhold water, and keep rather dry till March, when begin to give water and repot to grow and make larger plants.

CULTURE OF ORNAMENTAL-LEAVED TYPE: Compost, as advised in previous case. Pot in spring. Grow in shady position. Water freely in spring and summer, moderately in winter. Winter temp. 45° to 55°, summer temp. 55° to 65°. Feed with weak liquid manure in summer.

PROPAGATION: Ornamental-leaved type by leaf cuttings in spring or summer. Winter-flowering, by cuttings as described above or by seeds. Fibrous-rooted, by seeds or cuttings. Tuberous-rooted type by seeds sown on surface of fine sandy compost in temp. 65° to 75° in Feb., and grow seedlings on as advised for tubers; also by cuttings of young shoots in the spring.

TUBEROUS-ROOTED SPECIES CULTIVATED: *B. Bertinii*, scarlet, 1 to 2 ft., hybrid; *boliviensis*, scarlet, summer, 2 ft., Bolivia; *Clarkei*, rose, summer, Peru; *Davisii*, red, summer, Peru; *Pearcei*, yellow, summer, 1 ft., Bolivia; *rosaeflora*, rose, summer, Peru; *Veitchii*, red, summer, Peru. The foregoing were the original parents of the present race of single and double-flowered tuberous-rooted begonias grown in gardens. For names of varieties see trade lists.

FIBROUS-ROOTED SPECIES CULTIVATED: *B. albo-coccinea*, scarlet and white, winter, 18 in., India; *acutifolia*, white, spring, 3 to 4 ft., Jamaica; *angularis*, white, white-veined foliage, 8 ft., Brazil; *carminata*, scarlet, 2 ft., hybrid; *coccinea*, scarlet, April, 3 to 4 ft., Brazil; *Dregei*, white, July, 1 to 3 ft., S. Africa; *Evansiana*, pink, Sept., China; *Froebelii*, scarlet, 1 ft., Ecuador; *fuchsioides*, scarlet, winter, 4 to 6 ft., Mexico; *foliosa*, white and rose, summer, semi-pendulous, Colombia; *glaucophylla*, rose-pink, winter, pendulous or climbing, Brazil; *hydrocotylifolia*, rose-pink, summer, 1 ft., Mexico; *incarnata*, rose, winter, 2 to 3 ft., Mexico; *incana*, white, winter, 1 to 2 ft., Brazil; *Ingramii*, deep pink, 2 ft., hybrid; *kewensis*, white, 3 ft., hybrid; *manicata*, pink, winter, 9 to 12 in., Mexico; *nitida*, pale pink or rose, Sept., 3 to 5 ft., Jamaica; *Scharffiana*, white, winter, 1 to 3 ft., Brazil; *semperflorens*, rose, red or white, winter, 6 to 18 in., Brazil, and vars., of which *gigantea rosea* is very distinct, bearing large, sterile flowers; *socotrana*, rose-pink, Nov., 1 to 1½ ft., Isle of Socotra; *weltoniensis*, Dec., 18 in., hybrid; and numerous other hybrids and varieties such as Gloire de Lorraine.

ORNAMENTAL-LEAVED SPECIES CULTIVATED: *B. albo-picta*, greenish-white, foliage glossy green spotted silver, 1 to 1½ ft., Brazil; *Alleryi*, red and white, 3 to 4 ft., hybrid; *argenteo-guttata*, white and pink, foliage speckled with white, 2 to 4 ft., hybrid; *heracleifolia*, white or rose, foliage deeply lobed, 2 to 4 ft., hybrid; *imperialis*, white, foliage deep velvety green and bright green, 6 to 12 in., Mexico; *laciniata* (syn. *B. Bowringiana*), white, foliage purplish-black and green, 1½ to 2 ft., India, China; *maculata*, rose or white, foliage green dotted white, 2 to 4 ft., Brazil, and var. *Wightii*, Brazil; *metallica*, blush-white, foliage green with metallic lustre, 3 to 4 ft., Brazil; *olbia*, white, foliage bronze-green dotted white, 1 ft., Brazil; *Rex-cultosum* (*B. Rex* of horticulture), pale rose, foliage metallic green marked silver and purple, 2 ft., Assam; *ricinifolia*, rose-pink, foliage lobed, bronze-green, 2 to 4 ft., hybrid; *sanguinea*, white, foliage rich green above, blood-red beneath, 4 ft., Brazil.

Belamcanda—*Iridaceae*. Perennial with stout rootstocks cultivated for the flowers and also for the ornamental black seeds that remain when capsule splits.
    CULTURE: Soil, rich sandy. Position, sunny.
    PROPAGATION: By seeds; division.
    SPECIES CULTIVATED: *B. chinensis*, orange, spotted red, summer, to 4 ft., China, Japan; *flabellata*, light yellow, spotted orange at base, autumn, Japan.

Belladonna Lily, see *Amaryllis Belladonna*.

Bell Flower, see Campanula and Wahlenbergia;   **-Heather,** see *Erica cinerea*; **-wort,** see Uvularia.

Bellis (Daisy)—*Compositae*. Hardy herbaceous perennials.
    CULTURE: Soil, ordinary. Position, sunny or shady. Plant, Oct. or March.
    PROPAGATION: By division of old plant in June, inserting divisions 3 in. apart in shady border; seeds sown ⅛ in. deep in boxes of light soil in cold frame in March, transplanting seedlings in open border in July.
    SPECIES CULTIVATED: *B. perennis flore-pleno*, and its numerous varieties, native of Britain, etc.; *rotundifolia caerulescens*, white, tinged blue, June, 3 in., Algeria; *sylvestris*, bright red, yellow disk, June, 4 to 6 in., Medit.

Bellium (False Daisy)—*Compositae*. Hardy annuals and perennials. First introduced mid-eighteenth century.
    CULTURE: Soil, sandy loam. Position, rockery or border sheltered from north-east winds. Plant, April.
    PROPAGATION: By division of plants in March; annuals by seeds sown as for Bellis.
    SPECIES CULTIVATED: *B. bellidioides*, white, July, 3 in., Medit. Region, perennial; *minutum*, white, Aug., 3 in., Greece, annual.

Beloperone—*Acanthaceae*. Stove evergreen flowering shrubs. First introduced early nineteenth century.
    CULTURE: Compost, equal parts leaf-mould, loam and sand Pot, March, moderately firmly. Position, sunny greenhouse. Temp., Sept. to March 60° to 70°, March to Sept. 70° to 80°. Water freely May to Sept., moderately afterwards. Remove points of shoots occasionally in summer to induce dwarf growth.
    PROPAGATION: By cuttings inserted singly in small pots of light sandy soil in temp. 75° in Feb., March or April.
    SPECIES CULTIVATED: *B. guttata*, ' Shrimp Plant ', , white spotted, purple, 1½ ft., Mexico; *oblongata*, rosy purple, 3 ft., Aug., Brazil; *violacea*, violet, Aug., 3 ft., Brazil.

Benjamin Bush, see *Lindera Benzoin*.

Benthamia, see Cornus.

Benzoin, see Lindera.

Berberidopsis—*Flacourtiaceae*. Climbing shrub, hardy in warmest localities only, half-hardy in Midlands and North; evergreen. First introduced mid-nineteenth century.
    CULTURE: Soil, sandy loam. Position, against wall of any aspect including those facing north; protect in severe winter with straw or mats. Good wall shrub for cool greenhouse. Plant, Oct. or April. Prune straggly shoots only in April. Requires training.
    PROPAGATION: By seeds sown ⅛ in. deep in well-drained pots of sandy soil, in temp. 55° in March; cuttings of young shoots in similar soil and temp.; layering of shoots in the open in Sept., Oct. or Nov.
    SPECIES CULTIVATED: *B. corallina*, ' Coral Berry ', crimson, summer, 5 to 10 ft., Chile.

Berberis (Barberry)—*Berberidaceae*. An extensive family of beautiful and easily grown shrubs, evergreen and deciduous, the former grown mainly for beauty of flower and the latter for autumn colouring and fruits. Berries of the Common Barberry (*B. vulgaris*) make excellent preserve. Many species make good hedges. Some species formerly included in this genus have been transferred to Mahonia.

CULTURE: Any well-cultivated soil. Position, anywhere except in dense shade, but prefer sunny warm conditions and thrive on dry sandy or chalky formations. Plant deciduous species Oct. or March; evergreens require care, Oct. or April being best. Deciduous species are better for an occasional thinning out of older, darker coloured wood in winter; evergreen species require no pruning.

PROPAGATION: By seed sown 1 in. deep in sheltered border in Nov., resultant plants show considerable variation; cuttings of firm young shoots in sandy soil in cold frame in Sept.; layering shoots in spring.

Specific names are confused especially where stocks are raised from seed for distribution. Over 170 species known to cultivation, mostly highly ornamental, and some of the best are given here.

DECIDUOUS SPECIES CULTIVATED: *B. aggregata*, coral berries, 6 ft., China, and var. *Prattii*; *brevipaniculata*, flowers yellow, berries red, 6 ft., China; *chillanensis*, a newer species with yellow and orange flowers and black fruits, 6 ft., Andes; *Chitria*, young growths tinted copper, brilliant plum-coloured fruits, 12 ft., spreading, Himalaya; *concinna*, very large amber-red berries, 3 ft., Himalaya; *dictyophylla*, young shoots covered white bloom, red fruits, 6 ft., Yunnan; *Jamesiana*, pretty foliage spring to autumn, coral fruits, 8 ft., W. China; *Lycium*, light green foliage, showy purple fruits, 8 ft., spreading, often half-evergreen, Himalaya; *mitifolia*, crimson oblong fruits, 5 ft., China; *montana*, newer species similar to *B. chillanensis* but with larger flowers; *polyantha*, large clusters salmon-red fruits, 6 ft., W. China; *rubrostilla*, probably the finest of all fruiting Barberries, large, translucent amber-red berries, hybrid; *Sieboldii*, rounded bush, 3 ft., yellowish-red berries, Japan; *Thunbergii*, brilliant autumn foliage and red fruits, 6 ft., Japan and China, and numerous varieties; *vulgaris*, ' Common Barberry ', 10 ft., Europe inc. Britain, several named varieties; *Wilsonae*, coral red berries, 4 ft., spreading, W. China, and vars. *Stapfiana, subcaulialata* and *globosa; yunnanensis*, large bright red berries, 4 ft., spreading, W. China.

EVERGREEN SPECIES CULTIVATED: *B. actinacantha*, yellow flowers, blue fruits, 4 ft., partly evergreen, Chile; *Aquifolium*, see Mahonia; *asiatica*, rather tender, 6 ft., Himalaya; *Bergmanniae*, 6 ft., W. China; *buxifolia*, purple fruits, erect, 10 ft., Chile, var. *nana*, dwarf to 15 in., compact, seldom flowering; *candidula*, low rounded to 2 ft., bright yellow flowers, purple fruits, China; *Chenaultii*, hybrid, 5 ft.; *Coxii*, newer species similar to *B. Hookeri*, leaves white beneath, 5 ft., Burma; *Darwinii*, dense growing and suitable for hedging, flowers orange, April and May, plum-coloured fruits, 10 ft., Chile; *Gagnepainii*, handsome, compact, 5 ft., black fruits, W. China; *heterophylla*, half-evergreen, to 5 ft., Chile; *hakeoides*, to 12 ft., Chile; *Hookeri*, dense growing, to 4 ft., makes good hedge, fruits dark purple, Himalaya; *hypokerina*, similar to last, foliage white beneath, fruits violet, Burma; *japonica*, see Mahonia; *Julianae*, dense growth making good screen to 8 ft., very hardy, dark blue fruits, Cent. China; *linearifolia*, newer species, bright orange-red flowers, fruit blue-black, 8 ft., Chile; *lologensis*, natural hybrid, flowers gold suffused apricot, magnificent shrub, 8 ft., Chile; *pruinosa*, lustrous dark green leaves, purple fruits, vigorous to 8 ft., S.W. China; *Sargentiana*, similar to *B. Hookeri*, erect to 6 ft., hardy, Cent. China; *Soulieana*, similar to last, very stiff habit, Cent. China; *stenophylla*, strong-growing graceful hybrid to 10 ft., golden flowers, and numerous varieties including *coccinea* and *corallina*; *verruculosa*, arching shoots, shiny foliage, pruinose flowers, slow-growing to 3 ft.

Berchemia—*Rhamnaceae*. Hardy climbing deciduous shrubs. Scarcely meriting cultivation. First introduced early eighteenth century.

CULTURE OF HARDY SPECIES: Soil, sandy loam. Position, against south wall, well-drained border. Plant, Oct. to Feb. Prune, Feb., cutting off soft points of strong shoots and removing weak shoots altogether.

PROPAGATION: Hardy species by cuttings of shoots 6 in. long inserted half their depth and 3 in. apart in sheltered border in Oct.; greenhouse species by cuttings at any time.

SPECIES CULTIVATED: *B. racemosa*, greenish, Sept., 6 to 8 ft., Japan; *scandens* (syn. *B. volubilis*), ' Supple Jack ', white, July, 10 to 12 ft., U.S.A.

Bergamot, see *Monarda didyma*; **-Mint,** see *Mentha aquatica*.

Bergenia—*Saxifragaceae*. Hardy perennial plants with large, more or less ever-green foliage, some richly coloured in winter. Formerly known as Saxifraga and Megasea.

CULTURE: Any good, deep, fairly heavy soil. Position, light shade beneath tall trees.

PROPAGATION: By division of old plants in spring; seeds.

SPECIES CULTIVATED: *B. Beesiana*, rich rose, early summer, 12 in., Himalaya, *cordifolia* (syns. *B. Megasea* and *Saxifraga cordifolia*), pink, spring, 12 in., Siberia; and var. *purpurea*, deep reddish-purple, taller panicles; *crassifolia* (syn. *Saxifraga crassifolia*), pink, early summer, 15 in., Siberia, Mongolia; *ligulata*, white or pink, spring, 12 to 15 in., Himalaya; *Stracheyi*, white, early summer, 9 to 12 in., Himalaya.

Berkheya (South African Thistle)—*Compositae*. Ornamental thistle-like herbs.

CULTURE: Soil, porous, gritty with lime rubble. Position, hot and sunny.

PROPAGATION: By seeds in spring, pot seedlings in young state and plant in permanent quarters when well rooted.

SPECIES CULTIVATED: *B. macrocephala*, orange, July, 3 ft., Natal; *purpurea*, bluish-purple, Aug. to Sept., 3 ft., S. Africa; *radula* (syn. *B. Adlumii*), yellow, July, 3 to 6 ft., Transvaal.

Bermuda Buttercup, see *Oxalis cernua*; **-Lily,** see *Lilium longiflorum* var. *eximium*; **-Satinflower,** see *Sisyrinchium bermudiana*.

Bertolonia—*Melastomaceae*. Stove trailing foliage plants, purplish underneath and various metallic colours above. First introduced mid-nineteenth century.

CULTURE: Compost, equal parts peat, leaf-mould and sand. Position, well-drained pans in shady, close stove or warm greenhouse. Pot, Feb. or March. Temp., Sept. to March 60° to 70°, March to Sept. 75° to 85°. Water daily April to Sept., once or twice a week at other times.

PROPAGATION: By cuttings inserted in light soil in pots or pans under bell-glass in temp. 75° in spring.

SPECIES CULTIVATED: *B. Houtteana*, leaves green and carmine, 6 in., Brazil; *maculata*, leaves pink and purple, 6 in. Brazil; *marmorata*, leaves silvery white and purple, 6 in., Brazil; *pubescens*, leaves light green, with chocolate band, Ecuador.

Bessera—*Liliaceae* (or *Amaryllidaceae*). Half-hardy bulbous plant. First intro-duced mid-nineteenth century.

CULTURE: Compost, equal parts loam, leaf-mould, peat, and coarse silver sand. Position, well-drained pots in cold greenhouse. Pot, Oct. or Nov. Water freely during active growth. Keep more or less dry after foliage dies down until new growth begins. Requires plenty of sun. May be grown in well-drained border outdoors at foot of a south wall.

PROPAGATION: By offsets removed and treated as old bulbs at potting time.

SPECIES CULTIVATED: *B. elegans*, ' Coral Drops ', scarlet, summer, 18 in. to 2 ft., Mexico.

Beta (Beet)—*Chenopodiaceae*. Esculent vegetables, sometimes grown as orna-mental foliage plants. Leaves crimson, green or white. First introduced mid-sixteenth century.

CULTURE OF BEETROOT: Sandy soil manured for previous crop best. Sow globe type in April to provide early roots and make main sowing of long type for storage in mid-May in drills 1 in. deep, 15 in. apart. Thin seedlings in June to 8 in. Lift roots in Nov. and store in cool shed. Crop takes 18 weeks from time of sowing till ready for use. Seeds retain their vitality up to 10 years old. Two ounces of seed will sow a row 50 ft. long.

CULTURE OF SPINACH BEET: Sow seeds 1¼ in. deep in rows 18 in. apart in April. Thin seedlings in May to 9 in. apart in row. Use leaves only, like spinach. Soil and manure as for beetroot.

CULTURE OF ORNAMENTAL BEET: Sow seeds ¼ in. deep in boxes of light soil in temp. 60° to 70° in March; transfer seedlings to cold frame in April and plant in beds in flower garden in May.

SPECIES CULTIVATED: *B. vulgaris*, ' Beet ', ' Beetroot ', Sugar Beet ', ' Mangel ', thick roots of various forms, colours and sizes, var. *Cicla*, ' Spinach Beet ', ' Chard ', and some forms with variegated, scarlet, white and green ornamental foliage.

Betel Nut, see *Areca Cathecu.*

Bethlehem Sage, see *Pulmonaria saccharata.*

Betonica, see Stachys.

Betony, see Stachys.

Betula (Birch)—*Betulaceae.* Hardy ornamental deciduous trees and shrubs. Timber used for veneering purposes and making fish casks and bobbins. Bark used for tanning fish nets. Some 40 species are known to cultivation. The native Silver Birch, known variously as *B. alba, B. verrucosa* and *B. pendula,* should be referred to under the last of these names.

CULTURE: Soil, ordinary. Position, sheltered or exposed, in valleys, hills or mountain slopes; good seaside and town trees. Plant, Oct. to March.

PROPAGATION: By seeds sown on the surface of sandy soil in sheltered borders in March, seeds to be simply pressed in, not covered. Transplant seedlings when one year old. Dwarf birches by layering shoots in Oct., named varieties of Silver Birch by grafting on young stock of the type plant.

SPECIES CULTIVATED: *B. caerulea-grandis,* silver trunk, large foliage, 30 ft., N. Hemisphere; *Koehnei,* hybrid between *B. pendula* and *B. papyrifera; lenta,* ' Black ' or ' Cherry Bark Birch ', 70 ft., N.E. America; *lutea,* ' Yellow Birch ', yellow stems, 90 ft., N.E. America; *mandshurica,* wide spreading to 50 ft., N.E. Asia, W. China, vars. *japonica* and *szechuanica; nigra,* ' River Birch ', 60 ft., fine species with shaggy cream-coloured trunk, grows equally well near or away from water, N.E. America; *papyrifera,* ' Paper Birch ', white stem to 60 ft., bark used for making canoes, N. America, var. *kenaica,* red stems and lesser stature; *pendula,* ' Silver Birch ', 50 ft., Europe, including Britain, vars. *dalecarlica,* ' Swedish Birch ', finely cut leaves, slender weeping habit, *fastigiata,* slender upright habit, *purpurea,* leaves purple, *tristis,* tall, slender, weeping, *Youngii,* the best weeping form for small gardens.

Biarum—*Araceae.* Hardy herbaceous perennials.

CULTURE: Soil, gritty, not too rich. Position, cool, preferably slightly shaded, between rocks.

PROPAGATION: By seeds.

SPECIES CULTIVATED: *B. Davisii,* spathe yellowish-green and pinkish-brown, Nov., 3 in., Crete; *tenuifolium,* spathe dull purple and green with long worm-like purple spadix, June to July, 9 in., S. Europe.

Bidens (Bur Marigold)—*Compositae* Annual and perennial herbs.

CULTURE: Soil, ordinary. Position, sunny border. Plant perennials, Oct. or April.

PROPAGATION: Perennials by division of old plants in April; annuals by seed sown ⅛ in. deep in sandy soil in temp. 70° in March, transplanting seedlings outdoors in May.

SPECIES CULTIVATED: *B. ferulifolia,* yellow, summer, 1 to 3 ft., annual or biennial, Central America; *humilis,* yellow, July, dwarf, perennial, Mexico;

serrulata (syn. *B. grandiflora*), yellow, July, 3 ft., Mexico. For *B. atrosanguinea* and *B. dahlioides*, see Cosmos.

Bifrenaria—*Orchidaceae*. A genus of epiphytic orchids. In a few species the scapes are racemose, others have short erect spikes, with 1 to 5 large flowers, their pseudo-bulbs pyramidal, leaves usually one, hard, leathery persistent.

CULTURE: Compost, largely loam fibre with one part in three of peat and sphagnum moss. A decided rest is needed in winter in a temp. of 50°, many will withstand less if dry; summer 60° to 80°. Water may then be freely given. Drainage should be ample.

PROPAGATION: By division of plants or by healthy back bulbs taken off when repotting in the spring, and laid in a damp place till growth is seen.

SPECIES CULTIVATED: *B. atropurpurea*, purplish red, spring, summer, Brazil; *aurantiaca*, yellow, Jan. to March, S. America; *Harrisoniae*, 1 to 1½ ft., ivory white, lip purple, densely haired, winter, spring, Brazil; *inodora*, greenish yellow with purple flushes, winter, spring, Brazil; *pubigera*, white, rose-flushed, lip deeper rose, whitish haired, summer, Brazil; *tyrianthina*, purple-violet, summer, Brazil.

Bigelowia, see Chrysothamnus.

Bignonia, see Anisostichus.

Bilberry see *Vaccinium Myrtillus*.

Billardiera (Apple Berry)—*Pittosporaceae*. Half-hardy evergreen climber. First introduced early nineteenth century.

CULTURE: Soil, good ordinary, well drained. Position, south or south-west wall in mild districts only. Plant, April. Prune away all weak or dead shoots in April.

PROPAGATION: By cuttings inserted in sandy soil in a temperature of 55°; also by seeds sown in above temperature.

SPECIES CULTIVATED: *B. longiflora*, creamy-white to purple, succeeded by blue edible berries, summer, 5 ft., Tasmania.

Billbergia—*Bromeliaceae*. Stove, flowering, epiphytic, evergreen plants. First introduced early nineteenth century.

CULTURE: Compost, equal parts fibrous loam, rough peat, leaf-mould and silver sand. Pot, March. Water freely always. Good drainage essential. Temp., Sept. to March 65° to 75°, March to Sept. 70° to 80°.

PROPAGATION: By large-sized offshoots inserted singly in small pots of sandy peat in temp. 85° in April.

SPECIES CULTIVATED: *B. iridifolia*, scarlet, yellow and crimson, 18 in., Brazil; *Liboniana*, red, green and blue, 1 to 2 ft., Brazil; *Lietzei*, rosy-pink, 1 ft., Brazil; *Morelii*, blue, pink and rose, 1 ft., Brazil; *nutans*, yellowish-green with blue margins, 1½ ft., Brazil; *pallescens* (syn. *B. Bakeri*), green and violet, 18 in., Brazil; *vittata*, red and violet, 18 in. to 2 ft., Brazil; *zebrina*, 1 ft., Brazil.

Bindweed, see Convolvulus and Calystegia.

Binotia—*Orchidaceae*. A monotypic epiphyte near to Cochlioda.

CULTURE: Compost, etc., as for Odonotglossum; winter temp. should be 55°.

PROPAGATION: By division of large plants or by back bulbs as with Bifrenaria.

SPECIES CULTIVATED: *B. braziliensis*, flowers 6 to 15, green with an olive-brown suffusion, lip white, tinged green, yellow haired, autumn, Brazil.

Birch, see Betula.

Bird Cherry, see *Prunus Padus*;   **-of Paradise Flower,** see *Strelitzia Reginae*.

Birdseye Maple, see *Acer saccharinum*;   **-Primrose,** see *Primula farinosa*.

Bird's-foot Stonecrop, see *Sedum pulchellum*;   **-Trefoil,** see *Lotus corniculatus*; **-Violet,** see *Viola pedata*.

Bird's Nest Fern, see *Asplenium Nidus*.

Birthwort, see Aristolochia.

Biscutella—*Cruciferae.* Biennial or perennial plants.
CULTURE: Any reasonably good soil. Position, sunny pocket in the rock garden.
PROPAGATION: By seeds sown in light sandy soil.
SPECIES CULTIVATED: *B. laevigata,* yellow, 9 in., summer, Europe.

Bishop's Cap, see Mitella; **-Hat,** see *Epimedium alpinum.*

Bitter Almond, see *Prunus Amygdalus* var. *amara;* **-Cress,** see Cardamine; **-Nut,** see *Carya amara;* **-Root,** see *Lewisia rediviva;* **-Vetch,** see *Lathyrus vernus;* **-wort,** see Gentiana and Lewisia.

Bixa—*Bixaceae.* Stove evergreen flowering tree, source of annatto dye. First introduced late seventeenth century.
CULTURE: Compost, two parts loam, one part peat and silver sand. Pot, March. Water freely March to Sept., moderately other times. Temp., Sept. to March 60° to 70°, March to Sept. 75° to 85°.
PROPAGATION: By cuttings of shoots six to twelve months old, inserted in small pots of sandy soil in temp. 85°, June to Aug, and by seeds sown in heat.
SPECIES CULTIVATED: *B. Orellana,* ' Annatto ', pink, summer, W. Indies.

Black Hellebore, see *Helleborus niger;* **-Maple,** see *Acer saccharinum* var. *nigrum;* **-Poplar,** see *Populus nigra;* **-thorn,** see *Prunus spinosa;* **-wood Acacia,** see *Acacia melanoxylon.*

Blackberry, see Rubus; **American-** or **Cutleaved-,** see *Rubus laciniatus;* **Evergreen Thornless**-, see *R. ulmifolius* var. *inermis.*

Black-eyed Susan, see *Thunbergia alata* and *Rudbeckia hirta.*

Blacking Plant, see *Hibiscus Rosa-sinensis.*

Blackstonia (Yellow Centaury, Yellow-wort)—*Gentianaceae.* Hardy biennials. Suitable for large gardens only.
CULTURE: Soil, heavy loam. Position, moist borders.
PROPAGATION: By seeds sown ⅛ in. deep in shady beds outdoors in July, transplanting seedlings into flowering positions in Oct.
SPECIES CULTIVATED: *B. perfoliata* (syn. *Chlora perfoliata*), yellow, June, 1 ft. Britain.

Bladder Fern, see Cystopteris; **-Herb,** see *Physalis Alkekengii;* **-Nut,** see *Staphylea pinnata;* **-Senna,** see *Colutea arborescens;* **-wort,** see Utricularia.

Blaeberry, see *Vaccinium Myrtillus.*

Blandfordia—*Liliaceae.* Greenhouse, fleshy-rooted, evergreen flowering plants. First introduced early nineteenth century.
CULTURE: Compost, equal parts peat, loam and silver or river sand. Pot, Oct. Good drainage, firm potting and moderate-sized pots essential. Water freely May to Aug., moderately Aug. to Oct and Feb. to May, none at other times. Temp., Oct to Feb. 40° to 50°, Feb. to April 50° to 55°, April to Oct. 55° to 65°.
PROPAGATION: By seeds and offsets or divisions of old plants at potting time.
SPECIES CULTIVATED: *B. grandiflora* (syn. *B. Cunninghamii*), crimson, July, 2 ft., Australia; *flammea,* yellow, June, 18 in., Australia; *marginata,* crimson, summer, 2 ft., Australia; *nobilis,* orange, July, 2 ft., Australia.

Blanket Flower, see *Gaillardia aristata.*

Blazing Star, see Liatris.

Blechnum—*Polypodiaceae.* Stove, greenhouse and hardy evergreen ferns. Genus formerly known as Lomaria is included here. First introduced late seventeenth century.
CULTURE OF STOVE SPECIES: Compost, equal parts loam, leaf-mould, peat and sand. Pot, Feb. or March. Position, shady. Water abundantly April to Sept., moderately afterwards. Temp., March to Sept. 70° to 80°, Sept. to March 60°

to 70°. Syringe tree species daily Feb. to Sept. Like many other plants classed as stove plants, blechnums often thrive as well in greenhouse temperatures.

CULTURE OF GREENHOUSE SPECIES: Compost, as above. Pot, March or April. Position, shady. Water freely March to Oct., moderately afterwards. Syringe as advised for stove species. Temp., March to Sept. 55° to 65°, Sept. to March 50° to 55°.

CULTURE OF HARDY SPECIES: Soil, two parts sandy peat, one part loam and pounded limestone. Position, shady rockeries. Plant, Oct. to April. Water freely in dry weather. Protect *B. penna marina* in very severe weather.

PROPAGATION: By spores sown on fine sandy peat in well-drained pans in temp. 80° at any time; dwarf species by division of plants, Oct. or April.

STOVE SPECIES CULTIVATED: *B. attenuatum* (syn. *Lomaria attenuata*), Tropics; *blechnoides* (syn. *B. unilaterale*), 6 to 12 in., Trop. America; *fraxineum* (syn. *B. longifolium*), 1 to 2 ft., W. Indies; *gibbum* (syn. *Lomaria gibba*), to 5 ft., New Caledonia, (var. *platyptera* of the trade belongs to this species) ; *gracile*, 1 ft., Brazil; *occidentale*, 1 to 2 ft., W. Indies.

GREENHOUSE SPECIES CULTIVATED: *B. auriculatum* (syn. *B. hastatum*), 1 to 2 ft., S. America; *australe* (syn. *Lomaria pumila*), fronds to 2 ft., Cape of Good Hope; *brasiliense*, ' Brazilian Tree Fern ', 2 to 3 ft., Brazil, Peru; *capense*, (syn. *Lomaria procera*), New Zealand; *cartilagineum*, 1 to 2 ft., Australia; *discolor* (syn. *Lomaria discolor*), Australia; *glandulosum*, 2 ft., Mexico; *lanceolata* (syn. *Lomaria lanceolata*), New Zealand; *Patersonii* (syn. *Lomaria Patersonii*), dwarf, Australia; *polypodioides*, 1½ ft., Brazil; *serrulatum*, 1½ ft., Brazil; *tabulare* (syn. *Lomaria Boryana*), W. Indies.

HARDY SPECIES CULTIVATED: *B. penna marina* (syn. *Lomaria alpina*), New Zealand, Tasmania, etc.; *spicant* (syn. *Lomaria spicant*), ' Hard Fern ', ' Deer Fern ', Europe (Britain), N. America, Asia.

Bleeding Heart, see *Dicentra spectabilis*.

Blessed Thistle, see *Cnicus benedictus*.

Bletia—*Orchidaceae*. Terrestrial orchids. First introduced early eighteenth century.

CULTURE: Compost, equal parts loam and leaf-mould with crushed potsherds. Pot, March. Position, pots with 2 in. of drainage in each. Water freely March to Aug., moderately Aug. to Oct., very little, or none, afterwards. Temp., March to Sept. 65° to 75°, Sept. to March 60° to 65°. Resting period winter. Repot in early spring. Press the bulbs into the compost but do not cover. Flowers appear at base of new pseudo-bulb, several on tall slender scapes, usually brightly coloured though not large.

PROPAGATION: By division of plants after flowering.

SPECIES CULTIVATED: *B. alta* (syn. *B. verecunda*), purple, W. Indies; *catenulata*, lilac or purple-lilac, summer, Brazil, Peru; *campanulata*, deep purple, summer, Mexico; *Shepherdii*, red-purple and yellow, summer, 3 ft., Jamaica; *Sherratiana*, rose-purple and deep purple, spring, summer, New Granada; *patula*, deep violet-rose, early summer, Haiti.

Bletilla—*Orchidaceae*. A small terrestrial genus. Habit much the same as Bletia, but scapes are terminal and side lobes of the lip are convolute over the column.

CULTURE: Compost, three parts fibrous loam, one part peat with an addition of leaf-mould and sand. *B. striata*, better known as *Bletia hyacinthina*, is hardy in sheltered places in the south of England. It cannot withstand hard frost, and in other localities should be placed in a frost-proof house; should not be dried out in winter.

PROPAGATION: By division.

SPECIES CULTIVATED: *B. striata* (syn. *Bletia hyacinthina*), whitish or lilac, very variable, in some purple, in others white, summer, China, Japan.

Blighia—*Sapindaceae*. Tender tree cultivated in tropics for its edible fruits. First introduced late eighteenth century.

CULTURE: Soil, sandy loam and peat. Position, borders in warm greenhoues. Temp., March to Sept. 75° to 90°, Sept. to March 65° to 75°.

PROPAGATION: By cuttings of half-ripened shoots rooted in sandy soil under hand-glass in temp. 75° to 85°.

SPECIES CULTIVATED: *B. sapida*, 'Akee', straw- or magenta-coloured fruit 3 in. long, 30 to 40 ft., W. Africa.

Blood Berry, see *Rivina humilis*; **-Lily,** see Haemanthus; **-root,** see *Sanguinaria canadensis*.

Bloomeria—*Liliaceae* (or *Amaryllidaceae*). Half-hardy bulbous plant. First introduced mid-nineteenth century.

CULTURE: Soil, light, sandy. Position, warm border or rockery. Plant bulbs 2 to 3 in. deep, and 3 in. apart, Sept. to Nov.

PROPAGATION: By offsets planted, as directed for bulbs.

SPECIES CULTIVATED: *B. crocea* (syn. *B. aurea*), yellow, July, 1 ft., California; *Clevelandii*, yellow, July, 1 ft., California.

Blue Alpine Daisy, see *Aster alpinus*; **-Beard,** see *Caryopteris incana*; **-bell,** see *Endymion nonscriptus*; **-berry,** see *Vaccinium corymbosum*; **-Cedar,** see *Cedrus atlantica glauca*; **-Cowslip,** see *Pulmonaria angustifolia*; **-Cohosh,** see *Caulophyllum thalictroides*; **-Cupidone,** see *Catananche caerulea*; **-Dawnflower,** see *Ipomoea Leari*; **-Dicks,** see *Dicholostemma pulchellum*; **-Grass,** see Carex; **-Gum Tree,** see *Eucalyptus globulus*; **-Lace Flower,** see *Trachymene caerulea*; **-leaf Wattle,** see *Acacia cyanophylla*; **-Lotus of the Nile,** see *Nymphaea caerulea*; **-Marguerite,** see *Felicia amelloides*; **-Pincushion,** see *Brunonia australis*; **-Poppy,** see *Meconopsis betonicifolia*; **-Spiraea,** see Caryopteris; **-Willow,** see *Salix caerulea*.

Bluets, see *Houstonia caerulea*.

Blumenbachia—*Loasaceae*. Slightly tender plants with leaves armed with stinging hairs like those of nettles. First introduced early nineteenth century.

CULTURE: Soil, warm, sandy. Position, warm and sheltered.

PROPAGATION: By seeds under glass.

SPECIES CULTIVATED: *B. Hieronymii*, red, 9 to 12 in., summer, biennial, S. America; *insignis*, white, July, trailing, annual, Montevideo; *multifida*, red, July, annual, Buenos Aires.

Bocconia, see Maclaya.

Boenninghausenia—*Rutaceae*. Herbaceous perennial plants allied to Ruta.

CULTURE: Soil, deep loam, well drained. Position, warm, sheltered spot protected from the east.

PROPAGATION: By seeds sown in spring.

SPECIES CULTIVATED: *B. albiflora* (syn. *Ruta albiflora*), white, 12 to 18 in., autumn, Japan, Himalaya.

Bog Arum, see *Calla palustris*; **-Asphodel,** see Narthecium; **-Bean,** see *Menyanthes trifoliata*; **-Berry,** see *Vaccinium Oxycoccus*; **-Myrtle,** see *Myrica Gale*; **-Violet,** see *Pinguicula vulgaris*.

Bollea—*Orchidaceae*. A genus of pseudo-bulbless epiphytic orchids, at one time included in Zygopetalum. Tufted habit, scapes shorter than leaves, bearing a large single flower with a ribbed or furrowed crest on the lip.

CULTURE: Compost, two parts osmunda or similar fibre, equal quantity of sphagnum moss and an addition of crushed potsherds. Baskets or pans are preferable to pots. South-west or westerly aspect and shading in bright weather. A moist atmosphere and water throughout the year are required, avoid draughts. If necessary, repot in spring. Winter temp. at night 65° or more, summer 70°, exceeded on warm days.

PROPAGATION: By division of plants, which, however, resent disturbance.

SPECIES CULTIVATED: *B. coelestis*, bluish-violet, 3 to 4 in. across, late summer,

Colombia; *Lalindei*, rose, yellow and white, late summer, Colombia; *Lawrenceana*, white marked violet, lip passing to violet-purple, summer, Colombia; *violaceae* (syn. *Huntleya violacea*), violet, shading to white, summer, Guiana.

Boltonia—*Compositae*. Hardy herbaceous perennials. First introduced mid-eighteenth century.

CULTURE: Soil, ordinary moist loam. Position, sunny or shady borders. Plant, Oct. or April.

PROPAGATION: By division of roots in April.

SPECIES CULTIVATED: *B. asteroides*, ' False Chamomile ', white, July, 4 to 5 ft., N. America; *latisquama*, blue-violet, 2 to 8 ft., N. America.

Bomarea—*Amaryllidaceae* (or *Alstroemeriaceae*). Greenhouse, climbing, flowering perennials. First introduced early nineteenth century.

CULTURE: Compost, equal parts peat, leaf-mould, loam and sand. Pot or plant, March. Position, large pots, tubs or beds, well drained. Water freely April to Sept., moderately other times. Temp., Sept. to March 45° to 50°, March to Sept. 55° to 65°.

PROPAGATION: By seeds sown ⅛ in. deep in pots of light sandy soil in temp. 65° in March; division of roots in March.

SPECIES CULTIVATED: *B. acutifolia*, red, yellow and green, autumn, 5 to 6 ft., Mexico; *Banksii*, pink and greenish-white, spotted, hybrid; *cantabrigiensis*, reddish-orange, autumn, 8 ft., hybrid; *Carderi*, rose, autumn, 6 to 8 ft., Colombia; *edulis*, crimson, July, 5 to 6 ft., Trop. America; *multiflora*, red and orange, autumn, 6 to 8 ft., Colombia and Venezuela; *patacocensis* (syn. *B. conferta*), carmine-rose, Aug., 6 to 8 ft., Colombia.

Bona-Nox, see *Calonyction aculeatum*.

Bonavist, see *Dolichos Lablab*.

Bonstedtia, see Epimedium.

Boophone, *Amaryllidaceae*. Half-hardy or greenhouse bulbous-rooted plants. First introduced late eighteenth century. Also known as Buphane.

CULTURE: Compost, equal parts peat, loam and sand. Pot, Sept. Water only when new growth begins, then give moderate quantity; cease to give any after leaves turn yellow. Temp., Sept. to Nov. 50° to 55°, Nov. to March 55° to 65°, March to Sept. 65° to 75°. Plants must have full exposure to sun.

PROPAGATION: By offsets inserted in small pots and grown like large bulbs.

SPECIES CULTIVATED: *B. ciliaris*, purple, summer, 1 ft.; *disticha*, purple, summer, 1 ft., S. Africa.

Borago (Borage)--*Boraginaceae*. Hardy annual and perennial plants. Common species (*B. officinalis*) used for flavouring claret-cup and as a bee food.

CULTURE: Soil, ordinary. Position, sunny rockeries, dry banks. Sow seeds of common borage annually in March where required to grow, afterwards thinning seedlings to 8 in. apart.

PROPAGATION: Annuals by seeds sown as above; perennials by division of roots in April.

SPECIES CULTIVATED: *B. laxiflora*, blue, Aug., 1 ft., Corsica, perennial; *officinalis*, ' Common Borage ', annual, blue, summer, 1 to 2 ft., Britain.

Borecole or **Kale,** see *Brassica fimbriata*.

Boronia—*Rutaceae*. Greenhouse, flowering, evergreen shrubs. Flowers fragrant. First introduced late eighteenth century.

CULTURE: Compost, two parts fibrous peat, one part silver sand and pounded charcoal. Pot directly after flowering. Drain the pots well and make compost quite firm. Cut off points of young shoots when 3 in. long to promote bushy growth. Water freely April to Sept., moderately afterwards. Place plants in semi-shady position outdoors June to Aug. Temp., Sept. to March 45° to 50°, March to Sept. 50° to 60°.

PROPAGATION: By cuttings of firm young shoots inserted in sandy soil, in temp. 55° June to Aug., under bell-glass.

SPECIES CULTIVATED: *B. elatior*, rosy carmine, May, 3 to 4 ft., Australia; *heterophylla*, rose, May, 2 to 3 ft., Australia; *megastigma*, maroon and yellow, April, 18 in., Australia; *polygalifolia*, pink, 2 ft., June, Australia; *serrulata*, ' Australian Native Rose ', rose, June, 2 to 3 ft., Australia.

Boston Ivy, see *Parthenocissus tricuspidata.*

Botrychium—*Ophioglossaceae.* Hardy and half-hardy deciduous ferns.

CULTURE: Compost, equal parts sandy loam and peat. Position, moist, shady rockery, or in grass. Half-hardy species in cool greenhouse. Plant, April. Water freely in dry weather during summer.

PROPAGATION: By division of roots in April.

SPECIES CULTIVATED: *B. dissectum*, 1 ft., America; *lunaria*, ' Moonwort ', Moon Fern ', 4 to 5 in., Britain; *matricariaefolium*, 4 to 6 in., Europe; *ternatum*, 6 to 12 in., New Zealand, not hardy in Britain; *virginianum*, 16 to 18 in., N. Temp. Zone.

Bottle-brush Tree, see Callistemon.

Bougainvillea—*Nyctaginaceae.* Stove climbing deciduous plants. Coloured bracts chief floral attraction. First introduced early nineteenth century.

CULTURE: Compost, two-thirds turfy loam, one-third leaf-mould and sand. Pot or plant, Feb. Position, *B. glabra* in pots with shoots trained round wire trellis; *B. speciosa* in bed 3 ft. wide and 18 in. deep, branches and shoots being trained up roof. Prune shoots of previous year's growth tc within 1 in. of base annually in Feb. Water abundantly March to Sept., moderately Sept. to Nov., none afterwards. Temp., Feb. to May 55° to 60°, May to Sept. 65° to 75°, Sept. to Feb. 50° to 55°.

PROPAGATION: By cuttings of young shoots 3 in. long, removed with small portion of branch attached, inserted in 2 in. pots of sandy soil, under bell-glass in temp. 70° to 80°, March, April or May.

SPECIES CULTIVATED: *B.* ' Mrs. Butt ', *B.* ' Crimson Lake '), crimson, 5 to 15 ft., prob. Brazil, var. ' Mrs. McLean ' (var. ' Orange King '); *glabra*, rose, summer, 5 to 8 ft., Brazil, var. *Sanderiana*, rich rose; *spectabilis*, lilac-rose, summer, 15 ft., Brazil, var. *superba*, deep rose. There are several named varieties listed by nurserymen.

Bouncing Bet, see *Saponaria officinalis flore pleno.*

Boussingaultia—*Basellaceae.* Half-hardy tuberous-rooted climber with fragrant flowers. First introduced early nineteenth century.

CULTURE: Soil, light, sandy. Position, back wall of greenhouse or south wall or fence outdoors during summer. Plant tubers in small pots in temp. 55° in March, for transplanting outdoors in June, or in bed in Feb. for greenhouse culture. Lift outdoor tubers in Oct. and store in sand during winter; those in greenhouse bed leave undisturbed. Water freely in summer, none in winter.

PROPAGATION: By inserting tubercles removed from the stems in sandy soil in temp. 55° in spring or autumn.

SPECIES CULTIVATED: *B. baselloides*, ' Madeira Vine ', white, autumn, 6 to 8 ft., Ecuador.

Bouvardia—*Rubiaceae.* Greenhouse, flowering, evergreen shrubs with fragrant flowers. First introduced late eighteenth century.

CULTURE: Compost, equal parts fibrous loam, leaf-mould, peat and silver sand. Pot, March. Prune, Feb., shortening shoots of previous year's growth to within 1 in. of their base. Water moderately Feb. to May, and Aug. to Nov., freely May to Aug., little Nov. to Feb., Temp., Feb. to Sept. 55° to 75°, Sept. to Feb. 55° to 60°. Place plants in cold frame from June to Sept.

PROPAGATION: By cuttings of young shoots 2 in. long, inserted in pots of sandy compost in March in temp. 65°; cuttings of roots inserted in similar soil in spring; division at potting time.

SPECIES CULTIVATED: *B. angustifolia*, red, Sept., 2 ft., Mexico; *Humboldtii*, white, winter, 2 to 3 ft.; *jasminiflora*, white, winter, 2 ft., S. America; *ternifolia* (syn. *B. triphylla*), scarlet, winter, 2 ft., Mexico; and numerous hybrids as, 'The Bride', white.

Bower Plant see *Pandorea jasminioides.*

Bowkeria—*Scrophulariaceae.* Tender evergreen shrub.
CULTURE: An attractive shrub of 10 ft. for a sunny wall, in warm districts only.
PROPAGATION: By cuttings from young shoots placed in a propagator with bottom heat, or under a bell-glass in an intermediate house. Seeds, if available, are also used.
SPECIES CULTIVATED: *B. Gerardiana*, large white calceolaria-like flowers, 10 ft.

Bowstring Hemp, see Sansevieria.

Box, see Buxus;   **Brisbane-,** see *Tristania conferta*;   **-Elder,** see *Acer Negundo*; **-Holly,** see *Ruscus aculeatus*;   **-Thorn,** see Lycium.

Boykinia—*Saxifragaceae.* Hardy perennial plants with creeping rootstocks.
CULTURE: Soil, moist, deep. Position, water-side or cool border, *B. Jamesii*, in rock-garden.
PROPAGATION: By seed or division of old plants.
SPECIES CULTIVATED: *B. aconitifolia*, cream, 3 to 4 ft., summer, E. United States; *major*, creamy-white, 2 to 3 ft., summer, California; *Jamesii*, crimson, 4 to 6 in., June, Colorado.

Brachycome—*Compositae.* Half-hardy annual. First introduced early nineteenth century.
CULTURE: Soil, ordinary. Position, sunny bed or border.
PROPAGATION: By seeds sown ⅛ in. deep in shallow boxes of light soil in temp. 50° to 55° in March, transplanting seedlings outdoors in May; or outdoors in April where plants are to flower.
SPECIES CULTIVATED: *B. iberidifolia*, 'Swan River Daisy', blue or white, summer, 1 ft., Australia. Many forms of this species are now offered by seedsmen.

Brachypodium—*Gramineae.* Hardy annual flowering grass. Inflorescence suitable for drying for winter decorations.
CULTURE: Soil, ordinary. Position, sunny borders. Sow seeds outdoors in April. Cut inflorescence when in full flower.
SPECIES CULTIVATED: *B. distachyon*, 'False Brome Grass', summer, 9 in., Europe.

Brachysema—*Leguminosae.* Greenhouse, climbing, evergreen flowering plants. First introduced early nineteenth century.
CULTURE: Compost, equal parts loam, peat, leaf-mould and silver sand. Pot, Feb. Position, well-drained pots or tubs, or beds 3 ft. wide and 18 in. deep; shoots to be trained round wire trellis or up the roof and fully exposed to sun. Water freely April to Aug., moderately other times. Temp., Sept. to March 45° to 50°, March to Sept. 55° to 65°.
PROPAGATION: By seeds sown 1/16 in. deep in sandy soil in temp. 55° in March; cuttings of shoots inserted in similar soil and temp. under bell-glass in June, July or Aug.; layering shoots in Sept.
SPECIES CULTIVATED: *B. latifolium*, crimson and scarlet, April, 8 to 10 ft., Australia; *lanceolatum*, scarlet, yellow and white, spring, 3 ft., Australia; *undulatum*, violet, March, 3 to 6 ft., Australia.

Bracken, see Pteridium.

Brahea—*Palmae.* Greenhouse fan-leaved palm. First introduced mid-nineteenth century.
CULTURE: Compost, equal parts peat, loam and sand. Pot, Feb. Water freely in summer, moderately other times. Temp., Sept. to March 55° to 60°, March to Sept. 65° to 75°.

PROPAGATION: By seeds sown ½ in. deep in light soil in temp. 85° in March.
SPECIES CULTIVATED: *B. dulcis*, 3 ft., Mexico.

Brake Fern, see Pteridium.

Bramble, see Rubus.

Brasenia—*Nymphaceae* (or *Cabombacaceae*). Hardy aquatic for pond or aquarium; difficult to establish. First introduced late eighteenth century.

CULTURE: Soil, loam and charcoal. Position, shallow ponds or lakes, 1 to 1½ ft. deep, or aquarium. Plant in pots or baskets, sinking these in the water during April or May.

PROPAGATION: By offsets in May, and seed.

SPECIES CULTIVATED: *B. Schreberi*, (syn. *B. peltata*), ' Water Shield ' purple, summer, N. America, Asia, Africa, Australia.

Brassavola—*Orchidaceae*. An epiphytic genus, the majority with slender short pseudo-bulbs, bearing a longer terete leaf. Flowers, from apex of bulb, usually few, with narrow sepals and petals and a heart-shaped lip, white or green shaded, fragrant in some.

CULTURE: Cattleya compost, pans which can be suspended are preferable as several are of pendent habit. Water should be freely given while the plants are growing. In winter a long rest is beneficial, and the plants may be hung near the glass in the Cattleya house in autumn. Some confusion exists in the genus owing to the similarity of several forms given specific names.

PROPAGATION: By division when plants are large enough, in spring.

SPECIES CULTIVATED: a selection: *B. cucullata*, flowers solitary, white, with narrow sepals and petals, 4 in. long, the lip 2 in. long, its side lobes with their inner edges encircling the column, their outer edges fringed, various seasons, Venezuela, Guatemala; *fragrans*, whitish or yellow tinged, purple-spotted at base, early autumn, Brazil; *nodosa*, flowers in twos or fours, fairly large, white or green tinged, autumn, Cent. America; *Perrinii*, white, shaded green, lip veined green, early summer, Brazil. There are several other species.

Brassia—*Orchidaceae*. An epiphytic genus with showy flowers, large, but with attenuated segments. The spikes produced as in Miltonias, from the base of the pseudo-bulb, which is often compressed and carries one or two leaves.

CULTURE: Compost, as for Odontoglossum with the exception of *B. verrucosa*, *B. brachiata*, and a very small-flowered species *B. elegantula*, which succeed in the cool house; all the species mentioned require a winter temp. of 60°, higher in summer, a moist atmosphere, but avoid water lodging on the leaves. A decided rest cannot be given as growths are often present in the winter. Shading must be given in summer.

PROPAGATION: By division of plants large enough, in spring.

SPECIES CULTIVATED: *B. antherotes*, rich brown and yellow, handsome, summer, Trop. America; *brachiata*, large, greenish-white with brown-purple spots, early summer, Guatemala; *caudata*, greenish-yellow, spotted dark brown, summer, W. Indies, Brazil; *elegantula*, small, light green, white, brown flushed, summer, Mexico; *Gireoudiana*, brown, red-brown and yellow, variable, summer, Costa Rica; *Lanceana*, variable, yellow, brown-spotted, lip creamy-white, late summer, Brazil, Venezuela; *Lawrenceana*, fragrant, yellow with dark-purple spots, spring, summer, Brazil, etc., var. *longissima*, larger, sepals 7 in. long, spring, summer, Costa Rica; *maculata*, greenish-yellow, spotted brown, early summer, Jamaica; *verrucosa*, greenish with dark green warts, spring, summer, Mexico, Guatemala. Several other species and varieties are known.

Brassica—*Cruciferae*. Hardy annual and biennial plants with esculent roots or foliage. Species have been much improved by breeding and selection. The exact origin of most of the cultivated species is unknown but many have been grown in Europe, including Britain, for hundreds of years. Flowers are yellow in practically all species.

CULTURE OF BORECOLE OR KALE: Sow seeds ½ in. deep in drills 6 in. apart, in

April or May. Transplant seedlings when third leaf forms to 4 in. apart in nursery bed. Plant out permanently 18 in. apart in rows 2 ft. asunder in June or July. Season of use, Nov. to April; Hungry Gap variety is in season April to May.

CULTURE OF BROCCOLI: For autumn use sow seeds ⅛ in. deep in shallow boxes of light soil in temp. 65° in Feb.; transplant seedlings 3 in. apart in light soil in cold frame in April or May, plant out 2 ft. apart in rows 2 ft. apart in June. For winter use sow seeds of Purple Sprouting variety ¼ in. deep in drills 6 in. apart in open garden in April; transplant seedlings 6 in. apart each way in June. Plant permanently 2 ft. apart each way in July. For spring use sow seeds of late Purple Sprouting or Leamington type as for winter kinds; plant out in July.

CULTURE OF BRUSSELS SPROUTS: Sow mid-March to mid-April, and plant May to June 2 ft. apart in rows 3 ft. apart. Season of use, Nov. to April. Cut, not break, sprouts when gathering; do not remove tops till sprouts are finished.

CULTURE OF CABBAGE: Choice of varieties enables cabbage to be grown all the year round. For summer and autumn use: sow mid- to end of April, transplant 2 ft. apart each way June to July, watering in. For winter use: sow during May or early June and transplant 2 ft. apart each way July or early Aug. For spring use: sow early Aug. and transplant mid-Sept. to mid-Oct. 18 in. by 9 in. Keep ground cultivated in all cases and dress with sulphate of ammonia when in full growth. Sow Colewort in July and plant out 12 in. apart each way in Sept.

CULTURE OF CAULIFLOWER: Sow seeds ¾ in. deep during April and transplant 6 in. apart in May, plant out 18 in. apart in rows 2 ft. asunder in June. When hearts begin to form, turn leaves over them to protect from sun and frost.

CULTURE OF KOHL-RABI: Sow seeds thinly outdoors in March. Thin seedlings to 3 in. apart in May and plant out 2 ft. apart in rows 3 ft. asunder in June. Gather swollen stems for use when the size of a tennis ball.

CULTURE OF SAVOY: Sow seeds outdoors in March for early crop and at end of April for main crop. Plant dwarf varieties 12 in. apart in rows 15 in. asunder; tall kinds 2 ft. apart each way. Gather for use after autumn frost.

CULTURE OF TURNIP: Sow seeds in Feb., March, April, May, June and July for a continuous supply. Make drills ½ in. deep and 1 ft. apart, dust seedlings occasionally with lime or soot to keep off turnip flea-beetle, thin to 6 in. apart when rough leaf forms. May be forced on hotbed in Feb. or March, sow seeds broadcast and cover lightly with fine soil, keep moist. Turnips ready for use eight weeks after sowing. Swede turnips should be sown in May, thinned early, and brought to maturity for winter use.

CULTURE OF MUSTARD: Soil, ordinary. Position, open borders. Sow seeds on surface of soil, water, and cover with mats or boards till they germinate; or in drills ½ in. deep and 6 in. apart. Make first sowing end of March and follow on with successional sowings every five days until Sept. Gather for salads when 1 in. high. Two crops sufficient off one piece of ground. Indoor Culture: Sow seed on surface of light soil in shallow boxes, moisten with tepid water, cover with paper, slate or board and place in warm position in greenhouse or room. Sow every three days for succession, two crops may be grown in same soil. Seeds may be sown on flannel kept moist in a warm room at any time of year.

CULTURE OF TRONCHUDA: Soil, ordinary rich. Position, sunny. Sow seeds thinly outdoors in April. Transplant seedlings when 3 in. high, 6 in. apart in nursery bed and plant out finally 3 ft. apart each way in June. Gather outer leaves first for their midribs, and hearts last of all.

PROPAGATION: By seed.

SPECIES CULTIVATED: *B. caulorapa*, ' Kohl-rabi '; *chinensis*, ' Chinese Mustard ', ' Pak-Choi '; *fimbriata*, ' Scotch Kale ', ' Borecole '; *hirta* (syn. *B. alba*), ' White Mustard '; *juncea*, ' Leaf Mustard ', ' Indian Mustard '; *Napobrassica*, ' Swede ', ' Rutabaga '; *Napus*, ' Rape '; *nigra*, ' Black Mustard ', source of table mustard; *oleracea*, vars. *acephala*, ' Field Kale ', *botrytis*, ' Cauliflower ,' ' Broccoli ', *capitata*, ' Cabbage ', *gemmifera*, ' Brussels Sprouts ', *italica*, ' Sprouting Broccoli ', ' Calabresse '; *pekinensis*, ' Chinese Cabbage ', ' Pe-Tsai ', ' Celery

Cabbage ', leaves used as greens, white heart for salad, annual or biennial; *per-viridis*, ' Spinach Mustard '. *purpuraria*, ' Purple Mustard ', stems and ribs of leaves purple; *Tronchuda*, ' Portugal Cabbage '.

× **Brassocattleya**—*Orchidaceae*. A bigeneric hybrid between the genera Brassavola and Cattleya, requiring similar treatment to the Cattleyas.
    CULTURE: As Cattleya.
    PROPAGATION: As Cattleya.
    SPECIES CULTIVATED: *B. Lindleyana*, bluish-white, lip white marked rose, autumn, Brazil.

× **Brassocattlaelia**—*Orchidaceae*. Trigeneric hybrids between the genera Brassavola, Laelia and Cattleya, most of which have been given English vernacular names.

× **Brassolaelia**—*Orchidaceae*. Bigeneric hybrids between Brassavola and Laelia.

Bravoa—*Amaryllidaceae*. Half-hardy bulbous plant. First introduced early nineteenth century.
    OUTDOOR CULTURE: Soil, light, sandy. Position, well-drained sunny border. Plant bulbs 4 in. deep in Sept. Protect in winter with a covering of cinder ashes.
    GREENHOUSE CULTURE: Put four bulbs in a 5 in. pot, well drained, in Oct. Cover with ashes in cold frame until Jan., then remove to greenhouse. Water moderately until foliage turns yellow, then keep soil dry.
    PROPAGATION: By offsets treated as advised for bulbs.
    SPECIES CULTIVATED: *B. geminiflora*, ' Scarlet Twin Flower ', bright red, 1½ ft., Mexico; *sessiliflora*, white, May, 1¼ ft., Mexico; *singuliflora*, white, May, 2 ft., Mexico.

Brazil Nut, see *Bertholletia excelsa*.

Breadfruit, see *Artocarpus communis*.

Bredia—*Melastomaceae*. Greenhouse herbaceous perennial or shrub.
    CULTURE: As Miconia.
    PROPAGATION: As Miconia
    SPECIES CULTIVATED: *B. hirsuta*, pink, 2 to 3 ft., Japan; *tuberculata*, pink with crimson stems and leaf-stalks, Sept., 1 ft., China.

Brevoortia, see Brodiaea.

Bridal Wreath, see Francoa.

Brittonastrum—*Labiatae*. Hardy herbaceous perennial. Sometimes included in Agastache or Cedronella.
    CULTURE: Soil, ordinary. Position, sunny, open. Plant in spring or early autumn.
    PROPAGATION: By careful division in spring.
    SPECIES CULTIVATED: *B. canum*, pink, July, 3 ft., Mexico; *mexicanum* (syn. *Agastache mexicana*), purple, 2 to 3 ft., June to Aug., Mexico.

Briza—*Gramineae*. Hardy ornamental flowering grasses, the inflorescence of which is valuable for mixing with cut flowers, or drying for winter decoration.
    CULTURE: Soil, ordinary. Position, sunny beds, borders or banks.
    PROPAGATION: By seeds sown ⅛ in. deep in April where plants are required to flower. Flowers should be cut and dried for winter decoration when fully developed.
    SPECIES CULTIVATED: *B. maxima*, ' Pearl Grass ', June to July, 1 ft., Medit. Region; *media*, ' Quaking Grass ', June to July, 1 ft., Britain; *minor*, 6 in., Europe; *rotundata*, June to July, 1 ft., Mexico.

Broccoli, see *Brassica oleracea* var. *botrytis*;   **Sprouting-** or **Calabresse, see** *B. oleracea* var. *italica*.

Brodiaea—*Liliaceae* (or *Amaryllidaceae*). Hardy bulbous plants. First introduced early nineteenth century.

CULTURE: Soil, rich sandy loam. Position, warm, well-drained border. Plant in Sept and Oct., 4 in. deep and apart.

PROPAGATION: By seeds sown ⅛ in. deep in sandy soil in cold frame in March; offsets of the corms.

SPECIES CULTIVATED: These are now placed in four genera as follows:

BRODIAEA: *B. californica*, lilac or violet, June, 9 to 12 in., California; *coronaria* (syns. *B. grandiflora*, *Hookera coronaria*), lilac or violet, June, 3 to 9 in., N.W. America; *elegans*, violet, June, 6 to 12 in., Oregon, California.

DICHELOSTEMMA: *D. Ida-Maia* (syns. *Brodiaea coccinea*, *Brevoortia Ida-Maia*), ' Fire-cracker Flower ', bright red, green and white, June, 1 to 3 ft., California, Oregon; *pulchellum* (syn. *Brodiaea capitata*), violet, June, 1 to 2 ft., W.N. America; *volubile* (syns. *Brodiaea volubilis*, *Stropholirion volubile*), pink, June, 1½ to 5 ft., California.

IPHEION: *I. uniflorum* (syns. *Beauverdia uniflora*, *Brodiaea uniflora*, *Milla uniflora*, *Triteleia uniflora*), ' Spring Starflower ', pale blue or white, March to April, 6 in., has a true bulb (not corm), smells of garlic when bruised, Argentine.

TRITELEIA: *T. crocea* (syn. *Brodiaea crocea*), yellow, June, 4 to 12 in., Oregon, California; *grandiflora* (syn. *Brodiaea Douglasii*), blue, June, 9 in. to 2 ft., W.N. America; *hyacinthina* (syns. *Brodiaea hyacinthina*, *Hesperoscordum hyacinthinum*), white, sometimes lilac, July, 6 in. to 2 ft., W.N. America; *ixioides* (syn. *Brodiaea ixioides*), yellow, June, 6 in. to 2 ft., California; *laxa* (syn. *Brodiaea laxa*), blue, June, 6 in. to 2 ft., Oregon, California.

Brome Grass, see Bromus.

Bromelia—*Bromeliaceae*. Stove terrestrial herbs with stiff, spiny-margined leaves in basal rosettes and flowers in heads or panicles.

CULTURE: Compost, equal parts fibrous loam, rough peat, leaf-mould and silver sand. Pot, March. Water freely always. Good drainage essential. Temp., Sept. to March 65° to 75°, March to Sept. 70° to 80°.

PROPAGATION: By large-sized offshoots inserted singly in small pots of sandy peat in temp. 85° in April.

SPECIES CULTIVATED: *B. fastuosa*, purple, Aug., 4 ft., Brazil; *Pinguin*, red, March, 3 ft., Trop. America.

Bromheadia—*Orchidaceae*. A genus both terrestrial and epiphytic. Inflorescence terminal on dwarf or tall stems with distichous, rather rigid leaves, the size varying in different species. Only one species calls for mention.

CULTURE: Fibrous peat and sand in well-drained pots as water is required throughout the year, freely in summer. Winter temp. 70° at night, summer reaching the tropical on sunny days.

PROPAGATION: By division of the plants in spring when repotting.

SPECIES CULTIVATED: *B. palustris* (syn. *B. Finlaysonianum*), flowers fragrant, produced in succession, medium size, white or pink tinged, summer, Borneo, Malaya, etc.

Brompton Stock, see *Mathiola incana*.

Bromus (Brome Grass)—*Gramineae*. Hardy ornamental annual grass. Useful for drying for winter decoration.

CULTURE: Soil, ordinary. Position, open borders. Cut flowers when fully developed.

PROPAGATION: By seeds in Sept. or April where plants are to grow.

SPECIES CULTIVATED: *B. briziformis*, 2 ft., Caucasus.

Broom, see Cytisus and Genista; **Butcher's-,** see *Ruscus aculeatus*.

Broughtonia—*Orchidaceae*. Epiphytic orchids allied to Epidendrum. Pseudobulbs close set, often overlapping with the leaves, light glaucous green. The slender scapes, 18 in., are terminal.

CULTURE: Cattleya compost, small pans suspended near the glass. Expose early in autumn to light. Winter temp. 60°, summer 65° to 80°. Very little, if any, water in winter. A rest is necessary.

PROPAGATION: By division of plants when repotting in spring.

SPECIES CULTIVATED: *B. domingensis* (syns. *B. lilacina*, *Laeliopsis domingensis*), light rose with deeper veins, lip with white-haired crimson lines, margin fringed, summer, autumn, San Domingo; *sanguinea* (syns. *B. coccinea*, *Epidendrum sanguineum*), crimson, flowers rounded, summer, autumn, Jamaica.

Broussonetia (Paper Mulberry)—*Moraceae.* Hardy deciduous tree with ornamental foliage; leaves large, lobed, mulberry-shaped. Plants unisexual; bark used for paper-making in the Far East. First introduced mid-eighteenth century.

CULTURE: Any ordinary garden soil. Plant, Oct. to March.

PROPAGATION: By cuttings inserted in sandy soil in cold frame in Oct., or suckers in Oct. or Nov.

SPECIES CULTIVATED: *B. papyrifera*, 20 ft., China.

Browallia—*Solanaceae.* Greenhouse flowering annuals. First introduced mid-eighteenth century.

CULTURE: Compost, equal parts loam and leaf-mould, with little sand. Sow seeds $\frac{1}{16}$ in. deep in fine light soil in March in temp. 55° to 65°. When seedlings appear, transplant three or four into each 5-in. pot, keep on a shelf in greenhouse, and water moderately. Apply weak manure water in May and June. Will flower in cool greenhouse. Temp., March to June 55° to 60°. Seedlings may be planted outdoors in June to flower during summer.

SPECIES CULTIVATED: *B. americana* (syns. *B. demissa*, *B. elata*), blue, July, 9 in., Peru; *grandiflora*, blue with yellow tube, July, 2 ft., Peru; *speciosa*, purple, varying to blue, July, 2 ft., Peru; *viscosa*, violet blue, 1 to 2 ft., Colombia.

Brownea—*Leguminosae.* Stove, evergreen flowering shrubs. First introduced early nineteenth century.

CULTURE: Compost, equal parts peat and loam, little sand. Pot, Feb. or March. Water moderately in summer, occasionally at other times. Temp., Sept. to March 55° to 60°, March to Sept. 70° to 80°.

PROPAGATION: By cuttings of firm shoots inserted in sandy peat, in temp. 80° under bell-glass, in spring.

SPECIES CULTIVATED: *B. Ariza*, red, June, 10 to 20 ft., Colombia; *Birschellii*, rose, Aug., 10 ft., Venezuela; *Crawfordii*, scarlet, summer, 10 to 12 ft., hybrid; *grandiceps*, red, June, 10 ft., Venezuela.

Brown-eyed Susan, see Rudbeckia.

Brownleea—*Orchidaceae.* A small terrestrial genus closely allied to Disa.

CULTURE: Compost and position, as given for Disa, but water less frequently in winter. Winter temp. around 55°, in summer 60° and higher; shading is required.

PROPAGATION: By offsets, if they appear, in spring.

SPECIES CULTIVATED: *B. caerulea*, pale blue with violet dots, height varying between 6 and 8 in., Trop. Africa.

Bruckenthalia—*Ericaceae.* Dwarf evergreen, heath-like flowering shrub, suitable for carpeting ledges of rockery in which choice bulbs are grown.

CULTURE: Soil, peat and leaf-mould. Will grow in soil containing a moderate amount of lime. Position, sunny rockeries. Plant in spring.

PROPAGATION: By division of plants, seeds or cuttings, in spring.

SPECIES CULTIVATED: *B. spiculifolia*, ' Spike Heath ', pink, summer, **6 in.**, Cent. Europe.

Brugmansia, see Datura.

Brunfelsia—*Solanaceae.* Stove evergreen flowering shrubs. First introduced early nineteenth century.

CULTURE: Compost, four parts each fibrous peat and leaf-mould, **one part** loam and sand. Position, pots in plant stove. Pot immediately after flowering;

good drainage and firm potting essential. Prune moderately after flowering. Pinch off points of young shoots when latter are 6 in. long. Water moderately Oct. to March, freely afterwards. Syringe freely March to Aug. Apply liquid manure to healthy plants in summer. Temp., Oct. to March 50° to 55°, March to Oct. 60° to 70°.

PROPAGATION: By cuttings 2 to 3 in. long, inserted in sand under bell-glass in temp. 60° to 70°, Feb. to Aug.

SPECIES CULTIVATED: *B. americana*, pale yellow or white, June, 4 to 8 ft., W. Indies; *calycina* (SYL. *Franciscea calycina*), purple, fragrant, summer, 2 ft., Brazil, and vars. *floribunda* and *macrantha*; *latifolia*, white, lavender or purple, winter or early spring, 2 to 3 ft., Trop. America; *undulata*, white, 3 ft., Jamaica.

Brunnera—*Boraginaceae*. Small herbaceous genus formerly included in Anchusa.
CULTURE: Soil, ordinary. Position, sunny borders.
PROPAGATION: By division.
SPECIES CULTIVATED: *B. macrophylla* (syn. *Anchusa myosotidiflora*), blue, spring, 1½ ft., Siberia, Caucasus.

Brunonia—*Goodeniaceae*. Slightly tender perennial rock plant.
CULTURE: Soil, warm, sandy. Position, sheltered pocket in the rock garden.
PROPAGATION: By seeds sown in spring.
SPECIES CULTIVATED: *B. australis*, ' Blue Pincushion ', blue, 9 in., summer, Tasmania.

Brunsvigia—*Amaryllidaceae*. Greenhouse bulbous plants. First introduced mid-eighteenth century.
CULTURE: Compost, equal parts peat, loam and sand. Pot, Sept. Water only when new growth begins, then give moderate quantity; cease to give any after leaves turn yellow. Temp., Sept. to Nov. 50° to 55°, Nov. to March 55° to 65°, March to Sept. 65° to 75°. Plants must have full exposure to sun.
PROPAGATION: By offsets inserted in small pots and grown similar to large bulbs.
SPECIES CULTIVATED: *B. gigantea*, red, July, 1 ft.; *Josephinae*, scarlet, July, 18 in.; *Kirkii*, 18 in., Trop. E. Africa. Some American botanists include *Amaryllis Belladonna* (syn. *Callicrore rosea*) in this genus as *B. rosea*.

Brussels Sprouts, see *Brassica oleracea*, var. *gemmifera*.

Bryophyllum, see Kalanchoe.

Buckeye, see *Aesculus Pavia*.

Buckthorn, see Rhamnus.

Buddleia (Butterfly Bush)—*Loganiaceae*. Hardy and half-hardy evergreen and deciduous shrubs; many are fragrant and are singularly attractive to butterflies. First introduced mid-eighteenth century.
CULTURE: Any light garden soil, including chalky loam. Full sun is preferred. Tender species on west walls or in pots in cool greenhouse. Plant, Oct. or April. Prune *B. Davidii* group and *B. Fallowiana*, by cutting hard back annually before growth starts, and *B. alternifolia*, by occasionally cutting out some of the older wood immediately after flowering.
PROPAGATION: Aug. cuttings in cold frames in sandy soil. Seed may also be sown indoors in March, but *B. Davidii* and varieties will produce many worthless forms.
SPECIES CULTIVATED: *B. alternifolia*, deciduous and hardy, habit of weeping willow, to 12 ft., flowering in May on one-year-old wood, blossoms lavender, fragrant, China; *Colvilei*, half-hardy, deciduous, requiring wall protection in cold areas, large rose-coloured flowers, 20 ft., Himalaya; *Davidii*, better known as *B. variabilis*, deciduous, to 15 ft., Cent. China, var. *Veitchiana*, dark lavender, *nanhoensis*, a 3-ft. shrub for confined spaces; *Fallowiana*, powder blue, grey foliage, 8 ft., W. China; *Farreri*, deciduous, pale lavender, April, 10 ft., N.W. China; *Forrestii*, large foliage, reddish-maroon flowers, 8 ft., W. China; *globosa*, ' Orange Ball Tree ', half-evergreen, to 15 ft., Chile.

Buffalo-berry, see *Shepherdia argentea;* **-Currant,** see *Ribes aureum.*

Buffelhorn Wood, see *Burchellia capensis.*

Bugbane, see *Cimicifuga americana.*

Bugle see Ajuga:, **-Lily,** see Watsonia.

Bugloss, see Anchusa.

Bulbinella—*Liliaceae.* Hardy herbaceous tuberous-rooted perennial. First introduced mid-nineteenth century.

CULTURE: Soil, rich, well drained, containing plenty of leaf-mould. Position, partially shaded warm border. Plant in spring.

PROPAGATION: By division in spring.

SPECIES CULTIVATED: *B. Hookeri* (syn. *Chrysobactron Hookeri*), white, summer, 2 to 3 ft., New Zealand.

Bulbocodium—*Liliaceae.* Hardy bulbous plant flowering in March before the leaves. Sometimes classified under Colchicum. First introduced mid-seventeenth century.

CULTURE: Soil, ordinary. Position, sunny or shady beds or borders. Plant 3 in. deep and 3 in. apart in Sept. Lift and replant bulbs every second year.

PROPAGATION: By offsets obtained when lifting the bulbs.

SPECIES CULTIVATED: *B. vernum,* ' Spring Meadow Saffron ', purple, March, 6 in., Alps, var. *versicolor,* prettily tinted.

Bulbophyllum—*Orchidaceae.* 1,000 species or more, epiphytic, distributed widely in the East and also found in central America. The genus varies greatly, including deciduous, evergreen, minute and large-growing forms. Equal variation is seen in the flowers, the prevailing character of which is that the lip is delicately articulated at its base, so that it readily moves up and down, freedom being given to the downward motion by the lower sepals being partly twisted so leaving a space between their bases. In a number the lips are haired. A selection only of the most interesting species is given here.

CULTURE: Compost, osmunda fibre and sphagnum moss in equal quantities, mixed with finely crushed potsherds. Small pans, which can be suspended, for the smaller-growing kinds, baskets for the larger. Deciduous species and those with hard-textured pseudo-bulbs, however small, and hard leaves, require a decided rest in winter. Softer-growing kinds require water throughout the year. Discrimination must be used. A moist atmosphere with shading not too heavy, a tropical or semi-tropical temperature in summer, and a winter temperature of 65° to 70°, suits the species enumerated.

PROPAGATION: By division of the plants.

SPECIES CULTIVATED: *B. barbigerum,* purple, dusky mahogany, with dark-haired labellums, many flowers, summer, West Cent. Africa; *Binnendijkii,* spring, Borneo; *Dearei,* like *Lobbii,* but the white lip marked with purple, summer, Borneo, Philippines; *Ericssonii,* summer, New Guinea; *Fletcherianum,* red to purplish, spring, summer, leaf fleshy, up to 20 in. long, glaucous, New Guinea; *Gentilii,* peduncle 18 in., flowers in succession, yellow, purple marked, autumn, W. Africa; *grandiflorum,* large, olive-green with whitish maculations, summer, autumn, New Guinea; *lemniscatoides,* small, purplish, sepals with a white, rose-spotted, ribbon-like appendage, various seasons, Java; *lemniscatum,* deciduous, small green and maroon, each sepal-tip developed into a flattened greenish-red filament, summer, Burma; *Lobbii,* large, buff yellow, various seasons, Burma to Java, var. *colossus,* 4 in. across; *longisepalum,* large, whitish, suffused, spotted and veined with claret-red, summer, New Guinea; *mirum,* sabot-shaped in twos, yellowish, spotted and marked red purple, lip hidden, petals edged with purplish and white filaments, active in sunshine, various seasons, Sumatra; *penicilium,* greenish-brown, haired, in a swollen purplish rachis, winter, Burma; *saltatorium,* small-growing, greenish-brown, haired lip, summer, Sierra Leone; *Sillemianum,* orange yellow, lip bright mauve, Burma; *virescens,* large greenish-yellowish flowers, lips marked with red, flowers up to 12 in a circle, often 12 in. across, lower sepals pointing outward, dorsal sepals forming central cone, curious and attractive, but with unpleasant odour, various seasons, Amboina.

Other species with curious or beautiful flowers are: *B. comosum*, Burma; *Dayanum*, various seasons, Burma; *Frostii*, summer, Annam; *leopardinum*, summer, Khasia; *hirtum*, winter, Burma; *macranthum*, summer, Burma; *orthoglossum*, summer, Philippines; *vitiense*, summer, Fiji Isles, and many other species.

Bullace, see *Prunus domestica* var. *insititia*.

Bulrush, see Scirpus.

Bunya-Bunya Pine, see *Araucaria Bidwillii*.

Buphthalmum (Yellow Oxeye)—*Compositae.* Hardy herbaceous perennials. First introduced early eighteenth century.

CULTURE: Soil, ordinary. Position, open sunny border. Plant, Oct. or March. PROPAGATION: By division of old plants in Oct. or March; seeds sown outdoors in April.

SPECIES CULTIVATED: *B. salicifolium*, yellow, June, 18 in., S. Europe; *speciosissimum* (syn. *Telekia speciosissima*), yellow, June, 2 ft., Europe; *speciosum* (syn. *Telekia speciosa*), yellow, June, 5 ft., Europe.

Bupleurum—*Umbelliferae.* Slightly tender evergreen shrub and hardy perennials. *B. fruticosum* is a loose-spreading shrub to 5 ft. and is useful for windswept seaside localities, especially in chalky districts. Requires wall protection inland. First introduced late sixteenth century.

CULTURE OF SHRUBBY SPECIES: Soil, ordinary. Position, warm border. Plant, Oct. or April.

CULTURE OF PERENNIAL SPECIES: Soil, ordinary. Position, sunny borders or rockeries. Plant, Oct. or March.

PROPAGATION: Perennial species by seeds sown outdoors in April; division in March. Shrubby species by cuttings inserted in sandy peat in cold frame in Sept.; also by seeds.

SHRUBBY SPECIES CULTIVATED: *B. fruticosum*, yellow, July, 5 ft., Medit.

PERENNIAL SPECIES CULTIVATED: *B. aureum*, yellow, 9 in., June to Aug. Europe; *Candollei*, yellow, leaves glaucous, 1 ft., June to Aug., Europe, *petraeum*, yellow, June, 6 in., Europe; *stellatum*, yellow, June, 9 in., S. Europe.

Bur Marigold, see Bidens.

Burbidgea—*Zingiberaceae.* Stove herbaceous flowering perennial. First introduced mid-nineteenth century.

CULTURE: Compost, equal parts peat, leaf-mould and loam. Position, large pots, tubs or beds. Plant, March. Water freely March to Aug., moderately other times.

PROPAGATION: By division of roots in April.

SPECIES CULTIVATED: *B. nitida*, orange red, summer, 3 ft., Borneo; *schizochila*, orange-yellow, summer, Malaya.

Burchellia—*Rubiaceae.* Stove flowering evergreen shrub.

CULTURE: Compost, equal parts peat, loam, leaf-mould and sand. Pot, March. Water freely April to Sept., moderately other times. Temp., Sept to March 55° to 60°, March to Sept. 65° to 75°.

PROPAGATION: By cuttings of young shoots inserted in sandy peat under bell-glass in temp. 75° in March, April or May.

SPECIES CULTIVATED: *B. capensis*, ' Buffelhorn Wood ', scarlet, March to May, 3 ft., Cape of Good Hope.

Burnet, see Sanguisorba; **-Rose,** see *Rosa spinosissima.*

Burning Bush, see Dictamnus.

Burr Oak see *Quercus macrocarpa.*

Bush Clover, see Lespedeza; **-Honeysuckle,** see Diervilla; **-Mallow,** see *Lavatera Olbia.*

Bushman's Poison, see *Acokanthera venenata.*

Butcher's Broom, see *Ruscus aculeatus.*

Butomus (Flowering Rush)—*Butomaceae.* Pretty hardy perennial for shallow water.
CULTURE: Soil, ordinary. Position, in shallow water on margins of ponds, lakes, etc. Plant, March to May.
PROPAGATION: By division of roots in March or April.
SPECIES CULTIVATED: *B. umbellatus,* ' Flowering Rush ', rose, summer, 2 to 3 ft., Europe incl. Britain.

Butter and Eggs, see *Linaria vulgaris*; **-nut,** see *Juglans cinerea*; **-wort,** see Pinguicula.

Buttercup, see Ranunculus.

Butterfly Bush, see Buddleia; **-Flower,** see Schizanthus; **-Iris,** see Moraea; **-Orchid,** see *Oncidium Papilio*; **-Pea,** see Clitoria; **-Tulip,** see Calochortus; **-weed,** see Asclepias.

Button Bush, see *Cephalanthus occidentalis*; **-Snakeroot,** see *Liatris pycnostachya.*

Buxus (Box)—*Buxaceae.* Hardy evergreen shrubs with small stiff leaves.
CULTURE: Soil, ordinary. Position, open or shady banks or shrubberies; choice kinds on lawns. Plant, March, April, Sept. or Oct. Dwarf box (*B. sempervirens suffruticosa*) used for edgings. Plant divisions with roots attached in shallow trench 6 in. deep in Oct., Nov. or March. Allow plants to nearly touch each other and tips about 2 in. above soil. Press soil firmly. Trim plants April or Aug. Nursery yard of box will make 3 yd. of edging. Box hedges, trench soil 3 ft. deep and 3 ft. wide, add decayed manure and plant ordinary green box 12 in. high about 12 in. apart in Sept. or Oct. Trim annually in May and July.
PROPAGATION: By cuttings of young shoots 3 in. long in shady border in Aug. or Sept.; division of old plants in Oct. or March; layering in Sept. or Oct.
SPECIES CULTIVATED: *B. balearica,* 8 ft., Balearic Is.; *microphylla,* 3 ft., often prostrate, Japan, var. *japonica* has various forms; *sempervirens,* to 20 ft., Europe, N. Africa, W. Asia, and numerous varieties including *argentea, aurea, Handsworthiensis, microphylla, myrtifolia, pyramidata, rosmarinifolia, suffruticosa.*

Cabbage, see *Brassica oleracea* var. *capitata*; **-Lettuce,** see *Lactuca sativa* var. *capitata*; **-Palm,** see *Sabal Palmetto*; **Portugal-,** see *Brassica Tronchuda*; **-Rose,** see *Rosa centifolia.*

Cabomba (Fanwort)—*Nymphaeaceae.* Useful oxygenators for the cold-water aquarium, with fan-like submerged leaves and rounded floating foliage, not hardy. First introduced early nineteenth century.
CULTURE: Small slips planted in aquarium compost, or inserted as cuttings in tiny pots of loam submerged in tank, any time during growing period.
PROPAGATION: By cuttings as described.
SPECIES CULTIVATED: *C. caroliniana* (syn. *C. aquatica*), white with yellow spots, Trop. America.

Cactus, see Aporocactus, Ariocarpus, Cereus, Coryphantha, Echinocactus, Echinocereus, Echinopsis, Epiphyllum, Ferocactus, Gymnocalycium, Mammillaria, Melocactus, Nopalxochia, Notocactus, Opuntia, Pediocactus, Pelecyphora, Pereskia, Rhipsalis, Schlumbergera, Selenicereus, Stenocactus, Zygocactus.

Caesalpinia—*Leguminosae* (or *Caesalpiniaceae*). Slightly tender deciduous and stove evergreen shrubs. First introduced early eighteenth century.
CULTURE OF STOVE SPECIES: Compost, two parts peat or loam, one part leafmould, half-part silver sand. Position, pots in light part of stove or outdoors during July and Aug. Pot, Feb. or March. Water freely March to Oct..

moderately afterwards. Temp., March to Oct. 70° to 80°, Oct. to March 55° to 65°.

OTHER SPECIES: Soil, ordinary. Position, warm sheltered shrubberies or sunny walls. Plant, Oct. to Feb. Prune merely to keep in good shape.

PROPAGATION: Stove species by seeds sown in light sandy soil in temp. 75° to 85° in spring; cuttings of short young shoots inserted singly in small pots filled with pure sand under bell-glass in temp. 75° to 85° in summer. Hardier species by seeds sown in sandy soil in cold frame at any time.

SPECIES CULTIVATED: *C. Coriaria*, 'Divi-divi', 20 to 30 ft., reddish-brown pods used for dyeing and tanning, stove, S. America; *japonica*, fern-like foliage, yellow flowers with red anthers, 8 ft., Japan, the most reliable of the hardier species.

Caffer Bread, see Encephalartos.

Cakile—*Cruciferae.* Hardy annual.
CULTURE: Soil, sandy. Position, open borders.
PROPAGATION: By seeds sown $\frac{1}{16}$ in. deep where plants are to flower in March or April.
SPECIES CULTIVATED: *C. maritima*, 'Sea Rocket', lilac, June, 1 ft., Britain.

Calabresse or **Sprouting Broccoli,** see *Brassica oleracea* var. *italica.*

Caladium—*Araceae.* Stove, tuberous-rooted, deciduous perennials with arrow-shaped leaves, marked in many colours and patterns. First introduced mid-eighteenth century.
CULTURE: Compost, equal parts turfy loam, peat, leaf-mould, decayed manure, and silver sand. Position, well-drained pots in shade. Pot moderately firmly in pots just large enough to take tubers in Feb. or March; transfer to larger pots in April or May. Water moderately Feb. to April, and Sept. to Nov., freely April to Sept.; keep quite dry Nov. to Feb. Temp., Feb. to Sept. 70° to 80°, Sept. to Nov. 65° to 75°, Nov. to Feb. 55° to 65°. *C. Humboldtii* used as an edging to subtropical beds in summer.
PROPAGATION: By division of tubers in Feb. or March.
SPECIES CULTIVATED: *C. bicolor*, 18 in., S. America, and vars. *Chantinii* and *pictum*; *Humboldtii* (syn. *C. argyrites*), 9 in., Brazil; *marmoratum*, 1 ft., Trop. America; *Schomburgkii*, 18 in., Brazil; *rutescens*, Brazil; *venosum*, Brazil. Many beautiful varieties more generally grown than the species will be found in trade lists.

Calamintha, see Satureja.

Calamus (Rattan Palm)—*Palmae.* Stove, evergreen climbing or semi-climbing palms. First introduced early nineteenth century.
CULTURE: Compost, two parts turfy loam, one part leaf-mould and coarse sand. Position, well-drained pots in shade. Pot firmly in March. Water moderately Sept. to March, freely afterwards. Temp., Sept. to March 60° to 65°, March to Sept. 70° to 85°. Train shoots up trellis or rafters.
PROPAGATION: By seeds sown 1 in. deep in light soil, in temp. 80°, in March; by suckers growing from roots, inserted in small pots of light soil under bell-glass in temp. 80°.
SPECIES CULTIVATED: *C. ciliaris*, very slender, climber, Malaya; *leptospadix*, a very graceful species from the Himalaya; *Rotang*, slender, climber, India.

Calandrinia (Rock Purslane)—*Portulaceae.* Hardy, rather fleshy plants. First introduced early nineteenth century.
CULTURE: Soil, light, moderately rich. Position, sunny rockery for dwarf species; borders for tall species. Plant perennials in April.
PROPAGATION: Annuals by seeds sown $\frac{1}{16}$ in. deep in shallow boxes of light soil in temp. 55° to 60°, in March, transplant seedlings into small pots in April, and plant out in June, or sow seeds outdoors in April, where plants are to flower; perennials by seeds or division of roots in April.

SPECIES CULTIVATED: *C. Burridgei*, rose, small, to 1 ft., annual, S. America; *ciliata*, to 1 ft., purple or white, summer, annual, Peru, Equador, var. *Menziesii*, 1½ ft., crimson; *grandiflora*, light purple, summer, 1 ft., Chile; *umbellata*, magenta, all summer, 6 in., Peru.

Calanthe—*Orchidaceae*. A terrestrial and epiphytic, deciduous and evergreen, orchid. The deciduous section is the more important as hybrids have been produced between the species, their varieties, and the hybrids themselves. A race of winter and spring-flowering forms has been produced superior to the species, extending the flowering season. Their tall spikes and numerous brightly-coloured flowers are of great decorative value. The evergreen section is of less utility and includes many of negligible merit. Pseudo-bulbs in the evergreen section are much smaller, spikes usually produced in the axils of the basal leaves. The inflorescence is racemose in some, approaching corymbose in others. Habit similar to that of Phaius.

CULTURE: Deciduous forms—Compost, four parts rough fibrous loam and a fifth part of chopped sphagnum moss, sand and leaf-mould. Species and hybrids have stout, somewhat pyramidal pseudo-bulbs, often constricted centrally, the spikes being produced from the base of the new pseudo-bulb. Repotting should be effected every year, usually in March. The bulbs must not be buried but placed firmly in the top of the compost. Shade for a few days. Drainage about 2 in. Do not water until compost approaches dryness. As roots permeate the compost, water freely, in summer it may be required twice a day. Weak manure water may then be given twice a week or more frequently, varied and strength increased as growth strengthens. Towards winter the leaves will yellow and fall, water must then be decreased or withheld and spikes will be in evidence. After flowering keep quite dry in a temp. of 60°. The growing temp. after repotting should be 65° to 80° with little or no shading. The syringe should never be used. 6 or 7-in. pots will accommodate the large bulbs, which should be potted singly. Manure water must be discontinued as the foliage ripens. Evergreen section—Compost the same as for deciduous kinds but loam should be used in rougher lumps. Free drainage. Repotting every year unnecessary. The section is widely distributed, only the finer species are mentioned. A few hybrids have been raised between the evergreen species, also with deciduous group, and, from both, hybrids have been raised with Phaius. Winter temp. 60° to 65°. The species cannot be rested and compost must never be allowed to become sodden. In summer give greater heat and water more freely. Shading from bright sunshine is required.

PROPAGATION: Deciduous—A single bulb potted in spring will develop a new flowering bulb, the old bulb remaining behind it. It usually remains sound and may be separated and potted singly or several placed in a shallow box in the fore-going compost the following spring. Some will flower but, in any case, emit a basal growth. Evergreen—By division of plants at spring potting season.

DECIDUOUS SPECIES CULTIVATED (all winter-flowering): *C. labrosa*, rose purple, Burma; *rosea*, rose to dark rose, Burma; *rubens*, bright to dark red, Malaya; *vestita*, very variable, large white with yellow or red eye, India to Cochin-China, var. *Turneri* (syn. *C. Turneri Regnieri*), more numerous, smaller, variable, later, white to rose red, Cochin-China. Many hybrids, all variable, usually with red to crimson labellums and lighter sepals and petals.

EVERGREEN SPECIES CULTIVATED: *C. biloba*, purplish, lip striped white, Himalaya; *curculigoides*, orange-yellow, summer, autumn, Malacca, Java; *furcata*, white or cream-white, summer, Philippines, Java; *Fostermannii*, yellow to whitish, summer, Burma; *Masuca*, comparatively large, purple-mauve, fine variable species, summer, Ceylon, India; *veratrifolia*, very variable, white in corymbose racemes, widely distributed Ceylon to Java, Australia.

Calathea—*Marantaceae*. Stove plants with coloured basal tufted leaves. Several species were formerly known as Maranta.

CULTURE: Compost, equal parts coarse lumps of loam, peat, leaf-mould and sand. Position, well-drained pots in shade. Pot, March, moderately firmly. Water freely April to Sept., moderately afterwards. Temp., March to Sept. 70° to 80°' Sept. to March 65° to 70°.

PROPAGATION: By division of roots in March.

SPECIES CULTIVATED: *C. angustifolia*, 2 to 3 ft., Trop. America; *Bachemiana*, 9 in., Brazil; *Chantrieri* (syn. *Maranta Chantrieri*), leaves grey and dark green, 1 ft., Brazil; *Closonii*, habitat unknown; *eximia*, 2½ ft., Trop. America; *grandiflora* (syn. *C. flavescens*), 18 in. Brazil; *illustris*, 1 ft., Brazil; *insignis*, 4 to 6 ft., Brazil; *Lietzei*, 2 ft., Brazil; *leopardina*, 2 ft., Brazil; *Lindeniana*, 1 ft., Peru; *Luciana*, 3 ft., Trop. America; *Makoyana*, 3 to 4 ft., Brazil; *ornata*, 1 ft., Brazil; *picta*, 3 to 4 ft., Brazil; *pulchella* (syn. *C. tigrina*), 1 ft., Brazil; *splendida*, 1 to 1½ ft., Brazil; *Vandenheckei*, 2 to 2½ ft., Brazil; *Veitchiana*, 3 ft., Bolivia; *zebrina*, ' Zebra Plant ', 2 to 3 ft., Brazil.

Calceolaria (Slipper-flower, Slipper-wort)—*Scrophulariaceae*. Half-hardy or greenhouse, shrubby and herbaceous plants. First introduced early eighteenth century.

CULTURE OF HERBACEOUS KINDS: Sow seeds on surface of fine soil in well-drained pans or shallow boxes in July. Cover box or pan with sheet of glass, and place them under bell-glass or in cold frame. Shade from sun, and keep moderately moist. Transplant seedlings 1 in. apart in fine soil in Aug., transfer them singly into 2 in. pots in Sept., into 5 in. in Oct., and 6 or 7 in. in March. Compost, two parts sandy loam, one part leaf-mould, decayed manure and sand. Water moderately until April, then freely. Apply liquid manure from April till plants are in flower. Temp., Aug. to March 45° to 50°, March to May 50° to 55°. Discard plants after flowering.

CULTURE OF SHRUBBY KINDS: Compost, same as for herbaceous kinds. Position, pots in windows or greenhouses, or in sunny or shady beds outdoors in summer. Pot in March; plant in May. Nip off points of shoots in March to make bushy plants.

CULTURE OF HARDY KINDS: Soil, ordinary, well enriched with leaf-mould. Position, rather moist and partially shaded places in the rock garden. Plant, March or Sept. Water freely during hot, dry weather. Annual species should be sown in the open during March or April.

PROPAGATION: Shrubby kinds by cuttings 3 in. long inserted in sandy soil in cool shady frame in Sept. or Oct., or in pots or boxes in cool greenhouse or window in Sept. Cuttings to remain in frames, etc., till potting or planting time. Hardy kinds by division of roots in March or by seeds sown $\frac{1}{16}$ in. deep in pans or boxes in cold greenhouse or frame during Feb. or March.

HERBACEOUS SPECIES CULTIVATED: *C. Allardii*, yellow, spring, 1 to 2 ft., hybrid; *amplexicaulis*, yellow, summer, 1 to 2 ft., Peru; *arachnoidea*, purple, June to Sept., 1 ft., Chile; *bicolor*, pale and deep yellow, 2 ft., Peru; *Burbidgei*, yellow and white, autumn and winter, 2 to 3 ft., hybrid; *cana*, white, heavily spotted, 9 to 12 in., Chile; *corymbosa*, yellow and purple, May to Oct., 1 to 1½ ft., Chile; *crenatiflora*, yellow and orange-brown, summer, 1 to 2½ ft., Chile; *Fothergillii*, yellow and red, May to Aug., 6 in., Falkland Islands; *herbacea*, yellow, variously marked, 1 to 2 ft., April to June, garden hybrid; *Pavonii*, yellow and brown, summer, 2 to 4 ft., Peru; *purpurea*, reddish-violet, July to Sept., 1 ft., Chile.

SHRUBBY SPECIES CULTIVATED: *C. alba*, white summer, 1 ft., Chile; *fuchsiaefolia*, yellow, spring, 1 to 2 ft., Peru; *integrifolia* (syn. *C. rugosa*), yellow to red-brown, summer, 1 to 3 ft., Chile, parent of the bedding calceolaria; *thyrsiflora*, yellow, June, 1 to 2 ft., Chile.

HARDY SPECIES CULTIVATED: *C. acutifolia* (syn. *C. polyrrhiga* hort.), yellow, June to July, 6 in., Argentine; *biflora* (syn. *C. plantaginea*), yellow, June to July, 1 ft., Patagonia; *Darwinii*, bronze, yellow and white, summer, 4 in., Magellan; *scabiosaefolia*, pale yellow, summer, 1 to 2 ft., Ecuador to Chile, annual; *tenella*, yellow, June, 2 in., Chile.

Caldesia—*Alismaceae*. Waterside plants akin to Alisma. Only hardy in south of England.

CULTURE: Soil, ordinary, set crowns just below water level. Plant, spring.
PROPAGATION: By seed; division in spring.
SPECIES CULTIVATED: *C. parnassifolia*, 12 in. rounded foliage, whorls of small white flowers in July, Europe, N. Africa.

Calendula—*Compositae*. Hardy annual.
CULTURE: Soil, ordinary. Position, sunny or shady beds or borders.
PROPAGATION: By seeds sown ⅛ in. deep outdoors in March or April where plants are to flower. Reproduces itself freely from seed. Useful as a pot plant.
SPECIES CULTIVATED: *C. officinalis*, ' Pot Marigold ', ' Scotch Marigold ', orange-yellow, summer, 12 in., S. Europe. There are many varieties—see trade lists.

Calico Bush, see *Kalmia latifolia.*

Californian Bluebell, see *Phacelia Whitlavia*; **-Fuchsia,** see *Zauschneria californica*; **-Lace Fern,** see *Cheilanthes gracillima*; **-Laurel,** see *Umbellularia californica*; **-Lilac,** see *Ceanothus integerrimus*; **-Mock Orange,** see *Carpenteria californica*; **-Nutmeg,** see *Torreya californica*; **-Poppy,** see *Eschscholtzia californica*; **-Redwood,** see *Sequoia sempervirens.*

Caliphruria—*Amaryllidaceae*. Greenhouse bulbous-rooted perennial. First introduced early nineteenth century.
CULTURE: Compost, two parts sandy loam, one part leaf-mould, peat and sand. Position, well-drained pots, sunny. Pot, March, placing one bulb 3 in. deep in a 5 in. pot. Water moderately March to Oct., very little afterwards. Temp., Sept. to March 50° to 55°, March to Sept. 55° to 65°.
PROPAGATION: By offsets placed in small pots in March.
SPECIES CULTIVATED: *C. Hartwegiana*, greenish-white, June, 1 ft., Colombia.

Calla—*Araceae*. Hardy aquatic for pond margin. First introduced mid-eighteenth century.
CULTURE: Soil, rich, boggy or muddy. Position, moist bog or shallow pond. Plant, spring.
PROPAGATION: By inserting portions of creeping rootstock in boggy or muddy soil where plants are required to grow.
SPECIES CULTIVATED: *C. palustris*, ' Bog Arum ', ' Marsh Calla ', white, summer, scarlet berries, 6 in., N. Hemisphere. See also Richardia, Peltandra and Zantedeschia.

Calla Lily, see Zantedeschia.

Callianthemum—*Ranunculaceae*. Hardy, herbaceous, perennial rock plants.
CULTURE: Soil, very gritty, well drained. Position, in the rock garden. Good scree or moraine plants.
PROPAGATION: By seeds sown in compost, as above.
SPECIES CULTIVATED: *C. anemonoides*, white, 2 to 3 in., spring, Cent. Alps; *coriandrifolium*, white, 3 in., spring, Alps; *Kernerianum*, white, 2 in., spring, Europe; *rutifolium*, white—sometimes flushed pink, 2 in., spring, Alps.

Callicarpa—*Verbenaceae*. Stove, greenhouse or hardy shrubs with ornamental fruit. Berries borne abundantly in axils of leaves Nov. to May. First introduced early nineteenth century.
CULTURE OF STOVE SPECIES: Compost, equal parts peat and loam with little sand. Position, pots in sunny place. Pot, March. Prune straggly shoots into shape before potting. Water moderately Sept. to March, freely afterwards. Temp., Sept. to March 55° to 65°, March to Sept. 70° to 80°.
CULTURE OF HARDY SPECIES: Soil, ordinary loam. Position, sheltered walls with south aspect in all but mildest part of country. Plant, Nov. Prune previous year's growth fairly severely in Feb
PROPAGATION OF STOVE SPECIES: By cuttings of young shoots in 2 in. pots of sandy soil in March in temp. 80°. To ensure plenty of berries keep the points of shoots frequently pinched off and all flowers removed until the end of July.

PROPAGATION OF HARDY SPECIES: By cuttings of half-ripened wood in sandy soil under hand-glass during July or Aug.

STOVE SPECIES CULTIVATED: *C. americana*, 'French Mulberry', grey-blue, summer, berries violet-blue, 3 to 6 ft., Southern U.S.A.; *longifolia*, pink or purple, fruits white, Himalaya, China.

HARDY SPECIES CULTIVATED: *C. Bodinieri*, to 10 ft., flowers pink, fruits violet, China, var. *Giraldii*, a newer form for the open border, conspicuous berries and purple-tinted foliage in autumn, 6 ft.; *dichotoma* (syn. *C. purpurea*), to 4 ft., China, Japan; *japonica*, pale pink, Aug., berries violet, 3 to 5 ft., Japan.

Calliopsis, see Coreopsis.

Callirrhoë (Poppy Mallow)—*Malvaceae*. Hardy annuals and perennials. First introduced early nineteenth century.

CULTURE: Soil, ordinary. Position, open borders. Plant perennials Oct. or March.

PROPAGATION: Annual species by seeds sown $\frac{1}{16}$ in. deep in pans of light soil in temp. 55° to 65° in March, transplanting seedlings outdoors in May, or where plants are to flower in April; perennials by seeds sown $\frac{1}{16}$ in. deep outdoors in April, or cuttings of young shoots inserted in sandy soil in cold frame in spring.

ANNUAL SPECIES: *C. pedata*, cherry-red, summer, 2 ft., Texas, var. *compacta*, crimson, white eye.

PERENNIAL SPECIES: *C. involucrata*, crimson, summer, 6 in., N. America.

Callistemon (Bottle Brush Tree)—*Myrtaceae*. Greenhouse evergreen flowering shrubs. First introduced late eighteenth century.

CULTURE: Compost, equal parts peat, loam, and silver sand. Position, in pots, or in well-drained beds or borders with ample growing space. Pot or plant March or April. Prune shoots slightly after flowering. Water freely April to Sept., moderately afterwards. Temp., March to Sept. 55° to 65°, Sept. to March 40° to 50°.

PROPAGATION: By cuttings of firm shoots, 3 in. long, inserted in sandy peat under bell-glass, in temp. 55° to 65° during summer, or by seeds, which is a slow method of obtaining large flowering plants.

SPECIES CULTIVATED: *C. citrinus* (syn. *C. lanceolatus*), crimson, June, 8 to 10 ft., Australia; *salignus*, yellow, June, 6 ft., Australia, and vars. *albus*, white, *floribundus* and *viridiflorus*; *speciosus* (syn. *Metrosideros speciosus*), crimson, spring, 8 to 10 ft., Australia.

Callistephus (China Aster)—*Compositae*. Half-hardy annuals. First introduced early eighteenth century.

CULTURE: Soil, rich, liberally manured. Position, open, sunny, well drained. Sow seeds $\frac{1}{8}$ in. deep in light soil in temp. 50° to 60° in March, transplant seedlings in April 2 in. apart in shallow boxes or in bed of light soil in cold frame, plant out 6 to 12 in. apart in outdoor beds in May; or sow seeds same depth and soil in cold frame, or in pots in window in April and plant outdoors in May. Apply weak liquid manure twice a week during July and Aug.

POT CULTURE: Sow seeds as advised above. Transplant three seedlings into a 3 in. pot in April, into 5 in. in May, and 6 in. in June. Compost, four parts loam, one part leaf-mould or peat, with a small addition of dried cow manure and sand. Water freely, and apply liquid manure once a week when flower buds are formed. Thin out latter to three on each plant. Plants may be lifted from open ground in Aug. and placed in pots to flower if desired.

SPECIES CULTIVATED: *C. chinensis*, various colours, summer, 6 in. to 2 ft., China. Numerous types and refined strains are in commerce, and dwarf, late-flowering varieties are also available.

Callitriche (Water Starwort)—*Callitrichaceae*. Good oxygenating aquatics for ponds and aquariums.

CULTURE: Soil at base of pond, or aquarium compost. Plant, any time spring or summer.

PROPAGATION: By cuttings inserted in aquariums or in pans dropped in pond, or by weighting bunches with lead or stone and lowering these gently into water.

SPECIES CULTIVATED: *C. autumnalis*, entirely submerged, active during winter months, Europe incl. Britain; *verna*, upper leaves floating, pale green, cosmopolitan.

Callopsis—*Araceae*. Stove herbaceous perennial.
CULTURE: Compost, loam, leaf-mould and sand.
PROPAGATION: By division.
SPECIES CULTIVATED: *C. Volkensii*, spathe white, spadix yellow, July to Nov., 2 to 4 in., E. Trop. Africa.

Calluna—*Ericaceae*. Hardy evergreen flowering shrubs.
CULTURE: Soil, dry to moderately moist lime-free, preferably with peat. Position, in clumps on rockery or margins of shrubberies.
PROPAGATION: By division in Oct. or April; cuttings in August in sand and peat under bell-glass.
SPECIES CULTIVATED: *C. vulgaris*, ' Scotch Heather ', ' Ling ', purple, late summer, to 2 ft., Britain, Europe, and many horticultural varieties.

Calocarpum, see Achras.

Calocephalus—*Compositae*. Greenhouse sub-shrub with white cottony stems. Used mainly for carpet bedding.
CULTURE: Soil, ordinary. Position, sunny beds in summer only. Plant, May; lift and winter in cool greenhouse in Sept.
PROPAGATION: By cuttings inserted in cold frame in August.
SPECIES CULTIVATED: *C. Brownii* (syn. *Leucophyta Brownii*), trailing, Australia.

Calochortus (Butterfly Tulip; Star Tulip; Mariposa Lily)—*Liliaceae*. Half-hardy bulbous plants. First introduced early nineteenth century.
FRAME CULTURE: Prepare bed 12 in. deep with compost of equal parts loam, peat, leaf-mould, and sand. Plant bulbs 3 in. deep and 4 in. apart in Nov. Keep lights on in frosty weather; off night and day in fair weather. Water in dry weather. Lift and replant every three years.
POT CULTURE: Use same compost as advised for frame culture. Place a dozen bulbs 2 in. deep in a 5 in. pot in Nov. Cover pots with ashes in cold frame, and give no water. Remove pots from ashes in Jan. and place in cool greenhouse near glass. Water moderately till after flowering, then gradually withhold it. Repot annually in Nov.
OUTDOOR CULTURE: Plant bulbs in similar soil and manner to that advised for frames. Bed must be dry in winter, sunny, at foot of south wall.
PROPAGATION: By seeds sown ⅛ in. deep in pans of sandy soil in temp. 45° to 55° in March, transplanting seedlings following year into small pots and treating similarly to old bulbs; offsets planted like bulbs in Nov.
SPECIES CULTIVATED: *C. albus*, white, July, 1 ft., California; *amabilis*, yellow, July, 1 ft., California; *caeruleus*, lilac-blue, July, 6 in., California; *clavatus*, yellow, July, 2¼ ft., California; *Gunnisonii*, white, July, 2 ft., W. America; *Howellii*, white, July, 18 in., Oregon; *Kennedyi*, orange-red, July, 2½ ft., California; *luteus*, yellow, July, 1 ft., California; *macrocarpus*, pale lavender and green, July, 1½ ft., California; *Maweanus*, purple and white, June to July, 6 to 10 in., San Francisco; *monophyllus* (syn. *C. Benthamii*), yellow, July, 8 in., California; *Nuttallii*, white, June, 6 in., California; *Plummerae*, soft lavender, July, 2 ft., California; *Purdyi*, white, July, 1 ft., Washington; *splendens*, lilac, July, 1 ft., California; *uniflorus* (syn. *C. lilacinus*), lilac, July, 9 in., California; *venustus*, white, July, 18 in., California. A number of varieties will be found in specialists' lists.

Calodendrum—*Rutaceae*. Greenhouse flowering evergreen shrub. First introduced late eighteenth century.
CULTURE: Compost, two parts loam, one part peat and sand. Position, pots or tubs, sunny. Pot and prune, March. Water moderately Sept. to March, freely afterwards. Temp., Sept. to March 50° to 55°, March to Sept. 55° to 65°.

PROPAGATION: By cuttings of shoots 3 in. long inserted in sandy soil under bell-glass in temp. 60° in June or July.

SPECIES CULTIVATED: *C. capense*, 'Cape Chestnut', pink, summer, 10 ft., S. Africa.

Calonyction (Moonflower)—*Convolvulaceae*. Stove or greenhouse annual climber. First introduced mid-eighteenth century. Formerly included in Ipomoea.

CULTURE: Compost, equal parts fibrous loam, leaf-mould, decayed manure and silver sand. Position, pots in warm greenhouse, shoots supported on twiggy stakes or trellis. Plant or pot, March or April. Temp., March to Sept. 65° to 70°. Water freely when established in final pots.

PROPAGATION: By seeds ⅛ in. deep in pots in temp. 65° to 70° in March. Repot seedlings as required until they occupy 6 in. or 7 in. pots.

SPECIES CULTIVATED: *C. aculeatum* (syn. *Ipomoea Bona-Nox*), 'Good-night', night flowering, white, summer, 5 to 10 ft., Trop. America.

Calophaca—*Leguminosae*. Hardy, prostrate, deciduous flowering shrub. First introduced mid-eighteenth century.

CULTURE: Soil, ordinary. Position, open shrubbery, full sun. Plant, Oct. to Feb.

PROPAGATION: By seeds sown ½ in. deep in Nov. or March; by grafting on common laburnum in March.

SPECIES CULTIVATED: *C. wolgarica*, yellow, June, 3 ft., S. Russia.

Calopogon—*Orchidaceae*. A deciduous terrestrial genus of hardy, or nearly hardy, tuberous orchids. Flowers to 1 in. across, labellums bear a tuft of yellow hair; leaves grass-like. First introduced late eighteenth century.

CULTURE: Soil, peaty, mixed with fibrous loam, leaf-mould and sand. Position, moist sheltered rockery, not exposed to full sunshine. Plant, March or April. May also be grown in equal parts peat and loam in pots in cold frame or greenhouse.

PROPAGATION: By offsets treated as old plants.

SPECIES CULTIVATED: *C. pulchellus*, purple, July, 18 in., N. America.

Calostemma—*Amaryllidaceae*. Greenhouse flowering bulbous perennials. First introduced early nineteenth century.

CULTURE: Compost, two parts loam, one part peat and sand. Pot, Aug. Position, sunny greenhouse. Water freely March to July, moderately July to Sept., very little afterwards. Temp., Sept. to March 45° to 50°, March to Sept. 55° to 65°.

PROPAGATION: By offsets at potting time.

SPECIES CULTIVATED: *C. album*, white, May, 1 ft., N. Australia; *luteum*, yellow, Nov., 1 ft., Australia; *purpureum*, purple, Nov., 1 ft., Australia, var. *carneum*, pale purple.

Caltha (Kingcup, Water Cowslip)—*Ranunculaceae*. Hardy perennials.

CULTURE: Soil, rich. Position, damp borders, or banks of ponds, streams or lakes. Plant, Oct. or March.

PROPAGATION: By division of roots in March onwards if soil is wet.

SPECIES CULTIVATED: *C. leptosepala*, white, May, 1 ft., N.W. America; *palustris*, 'Marsh Marigold', 'Water Cowslip', 'Kingcup', yellow, April, 1 ft., Britain, and vars. *alba, monstroso-plena*; *polypetala*, yellow, 2 to 3 ft., Asia Minor.

Calvary Clover, see *Medicago Echinus*.

Calycanthus—*Calycanthaceae*. Hardy deciduous flowering shrubs.

CULTURE: Ordinary soil, not heavy, with some peat added, full sun. Plant, Oct. to March.

PROPAGATION: By seeds sown ½ in. deep in light soil in cold frame, March; by layers of shoots in July and Aug.

SPECIES CULTIVATED: *C. floridus*, 'Carolina Allspice', brownish purple, fragrant, June, 6 ft., S. United States; *fertilis* (syn. *C. glaucus*), brownish purple,

May, 6 ft., United States; occidentalis (syn. *C. macrophyllus*), red, fragrant, Aug., 9 ft., California.

Calypso—*Orchidaceae*. A monotypic, hardy, bulbous terrestrial orchid with solitary flowers terminating a stem up to 8 in. high, leaf solitary. The bulbs are entirely underground. First introduced early nineteenth century.

CULTURE: Compost, two parts leaf-mould, one part fibrous peat and coarse sand. Position, shady margins of rockwork or bog. Plant, Oct. or March. A mulch of leaves is advisable in winter, as severe frost may affect the roots.

PROPAGATION: By offsets treated as old plants at planting time.

SPECIES CULTIVATED: *C. bulbosa* (syns. *C. borealis*, *C. occidentalis*), rose-purple, lip curious, somewhat pouch-like with a tuft of golden hair in the throat, Jan., 1 ft., N. Temp. Zone.

Calystegia (Bindweed)—*Convolvulaceae*. Hardy, herbaceous trailing and climbing perennials sometimes included in the genus Convolvulus. Some species, such as *C. sepium* and *C. sylvestris* are bad weeds and should be used with care in the garden.

CULTURE: Soil, ordinary. Position, sunny border where fleshy roots can be confined and prevented from spreading over the garden. Plant, Oct. or March.

PROPAGATION: By seed in moderate heat in March or outdoors in April; division of roots in Oct. or March.

SPECIES CULTIVATED: *C. pubescens* (syn. *Convolvulus japonicus*), rose, summer, 6 ft., China, Japan; *sepium*, rose or white, July, 6 ft., Europe, Asia, N. America; *sylvestris*, white, July, 6 ft., Europe; *Soldanella*, pink, June, stems prostrate, Temp. Zone, incl. Britain; *tugorium*, white, summer, 6 ft., New Zealand, Juan Fernandez, Chile.

Camarotis—*Orchidaceae*. An epiphytic genus near Sarcochilus. Flowers small. The plants require supports.

CULTURE: Compost as for Vandas. Winter temp. 65° with moisture, no decided rest.

PROPAGATION: As for Aerides, in spring or early summer.

SPECIES CULTIVATED: *C. obtusa*, whitish, flushed rose, lip thickened, contracted apically, summer, Burma; *purpurea*, rose-purple lip dilated apically, funnel-like, summer, Burma.

Camassia (Quamash)—*Liliaceae*. Hardy bulbous plants. First introduced early nineteenth century.

CULTURE: Soil, ordinary loam. Position, beds or borders. Plant bulbs 4 in. deep and 4 in. apart in Oct. or Feb. Top-dress annually with leaf-mould or decayed manure. Lift and replant every four years.

PROPAGATION: By seeds sown ¼ in. deep in sunny position outdoors in March or ⅛ in. deep in boxes of light soil in temp. 55° in Nov.; by offset bulbs in Oct. or Feb.

SPECIES CULTIVATED: *C. Cusickii*, pale blue, June, 3 ft., Oregon; *Leichtlinii*, white, June, 3 ft., E.N. America, var. *Suksdorfii*, blue-violet; *Quamash* (syn. *C. esculenta* Lindley), blue-violet to white, June, 3 ft., E.N. America; *scilioides* (syn, *C. esculenta* Robinson, *C. Fraseri*, *C. hyacinthina*), blue-violet to white, June, 2 ft., E.N. America.

Camellia—*Theaceae* (or *Ternstroemiaceae*). Half-hardy and hardy evergreen shrubs much better suited to outdoor cultivation than has previously been supposed, particularly *C. japonica* and its vars. First introduced early eighteenth century.

CULTURE: Easily grown in lime-free soil with some shelter from wind. Excellent for shady places and for walls with north aspect.

PROPAGATION: By seed in early spring; late summer cuttings in sandy peat in close frame.

SPECIES CULTIVATED: *C. japonica*, ' Common Camellia ', for generations known as a greenhouse plant but now generally cultivated outdoors, eventually makes a small tree to 30 ft., China, Japan, numerous named varieties in white, pink to scarlet, single and double; *maliflora*, small-flowered, double pink, spring, 6 ft., China; *reticulata*, half-hardy for walls in south, 4 in., delicate red flowers, China; *saluensis*, hardy in south, for walls inland, soft pink, May onwards, China; *Sasanqua*, white, Feb., 6 ft., China; *Williamsii*, pale pink, large, hybrid.

Campanula (Bellflower)—*Campanulaceae.* **Hardy annuals, biennials, and perennials.**

CULTURE OF PERENNIAL SPECIES: Soil, ordinary rich. Position, trailing species on sunny rockeries; tall species beds and borders, sunny or shady. Plant, Oct. to April.

POT CULTURE: Compost, equal parts leaf-mould, loam and sand. Trailing kinds grow in small pots in hanging baskets. Repot them in March. Water moderately in winter, freely other times. Tall kinds grow singly in 7 in. pots or three in a 10 in. pot. Sow seeds of these in cold frame in Aug.; transplant seedlings singly in 3 in. pots in Oct., into 5 in. in April, 7 in. in May. Water moderately in winter, freely in summer.

CULTURE OF ANNUAL SPECIES: Sow seeds in gentle heat in March, transplant seedlings into boxes, harden off in cold frame in May and plant out in sunny borders early in June.

CULTURE OF CANTERBURY BELL: Sow seeds outdoors in April, May or June. Transplant seedlings when 1 in. high, 6 in. apart in nursery bed, and plant out in borders in Oct. to flower following year.

CULTURE OF BIENNIAL SPECIES: Sow seeds in pans or boxes in cool greenhouse or frame in Feb. or March. Prick out into frame when large enough to handle and plant in flowering positions in May or June.

CULTURE OF RAMPION: Sow seeds in shallow drills 6 in. apart in shady border of rich soil in May. Thin seedlings to 4 in. apart. Lift and store roots in frost-proof place in Nov. Uses: Young roots and leaves for winter salads; large roots cook and eat like parsnips.

PROPAGATION: Annuals, by seed. Perennials by seeds sown $\frac{1}{16}$ in. deep in sandy soil in temp. 55° in March or Aug.; division of roots in Oct. or April.

ANNUAL SPECIES: *C. drabifolia*, blue, July, 3 in., Greece; *macrostyla* (syn. *Sicyocodon macrostylus*), purple or mauve, July, 18 to 24 in., Asia Minor; *ramosissima* (syn. *C. Loreyi*), purple-blue, June to July, 1 ft. to 1½ ft., Italy.

BIENNIAL SPECIES: *C. longistyla*, blue-purple, summer, 1½ to 2¼ ft., Caucasus; *Medium*, 'Canterbury Bell', blue, July, 3 ft., S. Europe, and several white, rose and purple single and double vars.; *patula*, pale violet, June, 2 to 3 ft., Europe (Britain); *Rapunculus*, 'Rampion', blue or white, July, 2 to 3 ft., Europe (Britain); *speciosa*, violet, summer, 1 to 1½ ft., S. Europe; *spicata*, purple, summer, 1 ft., Alps; *thyrsoides*, straw-yellow, July, 1 to 1½ ft., Alps.

PERENNIAL SPECIES: *C. abietina*, blue, July, 1 ft., Europe; *alliariifolia*, cream, June, 24 in., Caucasus; *Allionii* (syn. *C. alpestris*), blue, June, 3 in., Europe; *alpina*, blue, June, 4 in., Europe; *ardonensis*, purple, 4 in., July, Caucasus; *arvatica*, deep blue, 2 in., June, Spain, and var. *alba*; *Aucheri*, Tyrian purple, 4 in., June, Asia Minor; *barbata*, blue, June, 9 in., Europe; *bellidifolia*, violet-purple, summer, 4 in., Caucasus; *bononiensis*, blue, June to July, 2½ ft., Europe; *caespitosa*, blue, summer, 3 in., Europe, and var. *alba*; *carpatica*, blue, summer, 12 in., E. Europe, and innumerable garden vars. and hybrids; *cashmiriana*, pale blue, 3 in., summer, Himalaya; *cenisia*, blue, prostrate, May, Alps; *cochleariifolia* (syn. *C. pusilla*), blue, July, 4 in., Alps, and numerous vars.; *collina*, blue, July, 1 ft., Caucasus; *Elatines*, purple, summer, 4 in., Piedmont, and many vars. including *fenestrellata*, violet blue, and *garganica*, light violet blue, spreading; *excisa*, blue, May, 6 in., Alps, dislikes lime; *Formanekiana*, blue or white, 12 in., July, Greece; *fragilis*, lilac, Aug., 6 in., Italy; *glomerata*, blue, summer, 12 to 18 in., Europe incl. Britain, and several vars., including *acaulis*, 4 in.; *Herminii*, pale blue, 6 in., summer, Spain; *imeretina*, purple, 9 in., July, Caucasus; *incurva*, pale blue or white, 18 in., summer, Greece; *isophylla*, lilac-blue, 4 to 6 in., July, Italy, and vars. *alba*, white, *Mayi*, mauve;   *kewensis*, blue, 4 in., July, hybrid; *Kolenatiana*, purple-blue, 9 to 12 in., late summer, Caucasus;   *laciniata*, pale blue, 18 in., July, Crete;   *lactiflora*, blue or white, 3 ft., July, Caucasus;   *lanata* (syn *C. velutina*), yellow and peach pink, 3 ft., summer, S. Europe;   *lasiocarpa*, blue, 2 in., July, Japan and U.S.A.;   *latifolia*, blue, July, 4 to 5 ft., Britain, and numerous garden vars.;   *macrorrhiza*, blue, 6 to 9 in., summer, Europe;   *malacitana*, blue, 2 in., June to July, Spain;   *michauxioides*, blue, 4 to 5 in., summer, Asia Minor;   *mirabilis*, pale blue, 9 in., summer, Caucasus;   *Morettiana*, blue, 2 to 3 in., July, Italy; *Orphanidea*, grey-blue, 4 to 6 in., July, Macedonia;   *persicifolia*, blue, June, 3 ft., Europe, and many garden vars.;   *phyctidocalyx* (syn. *C. amabilis*), purple, summer, 1 ft., Armenia;   *pilosa*, blue, 6 in., summer, Asia;   *Piperi*, dark blue, 2 in., N.W. America;   *Portenschlagiana* (syn. *C. muralis*), deep blue, June to Aug., 6 in., Macedonia;   *Poscharskyana*, grey-blue, 12 in., June, Serbia;   *pulla*, deep blue, June, 4 in., hybrid;   *pulloides*, deep blue, 4 in., June, hybrid;   *punctata* (syn. *C. nobilis*), cream, spotted red, June to July, 1 ft., Asia;   *pyramidalis*, ' Chimney Bell-flower ', blue, July, 4 to 5 ft., Dalmatia, and var. *alba*, white;   *Raddeana*, violet, July, 12 in., Caucasus;   *Raineri*, blue, June, 3 in., Alps, and var. *alba*;   *rapunculoides*, deep blue, June, 3 ft., Europe, Asia;   *rhomboidalis*, blue or white, June, 1 to 2 ft., Europe;   *rotundifolia*, ' Harebell ', blue, summer, 6 to 9 in., Britain, and many vars.;   *sarmatica*, pale blue, July, 1 ft., Caucasus;   *saxatilis*, blue, 9 to 12 in., June to July, E. Europe;   *Saxifraga*, deep blue, 6 to 9 in., June, Caucasus; *Scouleri*, blue, 12 in., June, N. America;   *Spruneriana*, blue. prostrate, June to July, Greece;   *Stansfieldii*, soft blue, 6 in., June, hybrid;   *Stevenii*, purple, May to June, 6 in., Europe, Asia;   *Tommasiniana*, blue, July, 6 in., Italy;   *Trachelium*, blue, July, 3 ft., Europe and vars. *alba*, white, *alba plena*, double white, and *flore pleno*, double blue;   *tridentata*, violet, 4 in., summer, Armenia;   *valdensis*, violet, grey leaves, 9 in., Europe;   *Vidalii* (syn. *Azorina Vidalii*), white, 2 to 6 ft., summer, Azores, shrubby greenhouse perennial;   *Wockii*, pale blue, summer, 3 in., hybrid; *Zoysii* (syn. *Favratia Zoysii*), pale blue, summer, 2 to 3 in., E. Europe.

Campernelle, see *Narcissus odorus*.

Camphor Tree, see *Cinnamomea Camphora*.

Campion, see Lychnis.

Campsis (Trumpet Creeper)—*Bignoniaceae*. Greenhouse and hardy deciduous climbing plants with orange or scarlet trumpet-shaped flowers. For many years known in gardens as either Bignonia or Tecoma, now botanically classified as Campsis. First introduced early eighteenth century.

CULTURE OF GREENHOUSE SPECIES: Compost, two parts loam, one part leaf-mould or peat, and silver sand. Position, large well-drained pots or beds in light sunny greenhouse with shoots trained up roof. Pot or plant, Feb. or March, good drainage absolutely essential. Water copiously April to Oct., slightly at other times. Temp., Oct. to March 45° to 55°, March to Oct. 55° to 65°. Prune severely by cutting all young shoots to within two buds of their base in February; permanent main stems must be trained up like a vine rod.

CULTURE OF HARDY SPECIES: Soil, good rich loam with compost or well-decayed manure added. Position, well-drained border against south wall. Plant, Sept. to March. Prune as for greenhouse species in March, support necessary for main stem.

PROPAGATION: By cuttings of firm young shoots 3 in. long in well-drained pots of sandy soil in temp. 65° to 70° in April.

GREENHOUSE SPECIES CULTIVATED: *C. grandiflora* (syn. *Bignonia* or *Tecoma chinensis*), red and yellow, summer, China, var. *Thunbergii*, orange.

HARDY SPECIES CULTIVATED: *C. radicans*, orange-red, summer, N. America, and vars. *flava*, orange-yellow, *praecox*, scarlet, June, *speciosa*, bushy growth; *Tagliabuana*, scarlet, similar to *C. grandiflora* but hardier, hybrid.

Canada Tea, see *Gaultheria procumbens*.

Canadian Wild Rice, see Zizania.

Canarina—*Campanulaceae.* Greenhouse herbaceous perennials. First introduced late seventeenth century.

CULTURE: Compost, equal parts loam, leaf-mould, decayed manure and silver sand. Position, pots or hanging basket. Pot, Feb.; good drainage very essential. Water liberally March to Aug., moderately Aug. to Nov., very little afterwards. Temp., Sept. to Feb. 45°to 55°, March to Sept. 55° to 65°.

PROPAGATION: By cuttings of young shoots inserted in sandy soil in temp. 65° in March or April; division of roots in Feb.

SPECIES CULTIVATED: *C. canariensis,* ' Canary Island Bellflower ', orange, Jan. to March, 4 ft., Canary Islands; *Eminii,* orange striped red, 4 to 5 ft. long pendent shoots, E. Africa.

Canary Creeper, see *Tropaeolum peregrinum*;   **-Grass,** see *Phalaris canariensis* **-Island Bellflower,** see *Canarina canariensis.*

Candle Plant, see *Kleinia articulata.*

Candy Mustard, see *Aethionema saxatile*;   **-tuft,** see Iberis.

Canistrum—*Bromeliaceae.* Stove evergreen flowering and ornamental plants. Flower spikes surrounded by red bracts. First introduced mid-nineteenth century.

CULTURE: Compost, equal parts of fibrous loam, rough peat, leaf-mould and silver sand. Position, well-drained pots in light, moist part of stove. Pot, Feb. or March. Water moderately in winter, freely at other times. Temp., March to Sept. 70° to 80°, Sept. to March 65° to 70°.

PROPAGATION: By large-sized offshoots inserted singly in small pots of sandy peat, in temp. of 85°, Feb. or April.

SPECIES CULTIVATED: *C. amazonicum,* greenish white, June, 1 to 1½ ft., Brazil; *aurantiacum,* orange-yellow, June to Sept., 2 ft., Brazil; *roseum,* rose, July, 18 in., Brazil; *viride,* green, 1 to 1½ ft., Brazil. See also Aechmea. Some of the above are occasionally listed as Nidularium.

Canna—*Cannaceae.* Stove herbaceous plants. First introduced mid-sixteenth century. The tubers of *C. edulis* are edible.

INDOOR CULTURE: Compost, equal parts loam, decayed manure, leaf-mould and sand. Position, pots in sunny greenhouse. Pot, March. Water freely March to Oct., very little afterwards. Temp., Sept. to March 40° to 50°, March to Sept. 65° to 85°. Apply weak liquid manure twice a week to plants in healthy growth.

OUTDOOR CULTURE: Place roots in pots in March in temp. 55° to 60°. Remove pots into temp. 55° end of April and plant outdoors early in June. Lift roots in Sept., place them in boxes filled with ordinary soil, keep latter nearly dry, and store in frost-proof position till potting time.

PROPAGATION: By seeds steeped for 24 hours in tepid water, then sown ½ in. deep in light soil in temp. 85° in Feb.; division of roots at potting time. It will facilitate germination if a slight notch be filed in the seed before sowing.

SPECIES CULTIVATED: *C. edulis,* bright red, summer, 8 to 10 ft., W. Indies and S. America; *flaccida,* yellow, summer, 4 to 5 ft., S. Carolina; *glauca,* yellow, summer, 5 to 6 ft., Mexico, W. Indies and S. America; *indica,* ' Indian Shot ', yellow and red, summer, 4 ft., W. Indies; *iridiflora,* rose, summer, 8 to 10 ft., Peru; *Warscewiczii,* scarlet, tinged blue, summer, 3 to 5 ft., Costa Rica and S. America. See trade lists for names of varieties belonging to the hybrid groups *C. generatis* and *C. orchiodes.*

Cannabis—*Moraceae.* Hardy annuals.

CULTURE: Soil, ordinary. Position, sunny borders.

PROPAGATION: By seeds sown ½ in. deep outdoors, where plants are to grow, in April, or in temp. 55° in March, transplanting seedlings in June.

SPECIES CULTIVATED: *C. sativa* (syn. *C. gigantea*), green, June, 4 to 10 ft., India.

Canterbury Bell, see *Campanula Medium.*

Cantua—*Polemoniaceae.* Greenhouse evergreen flowering shrubs. First introduced early nineteenth century.

CULTURE: Compost, two parts turfy loam, one part leaf-mould and sand. Position, pots, sunny greenhouse. Pot, March. Water moderately Sept. to March, freely March to Sept. Temp., Sept. to March 40° to 50°, March to Sept. 50° to 60°.

PROPAGATION: By cuttings of shoots inserted in silver sand under bell-glasses in temp. 50° to 55°, May to Aug.

SPECIES CULTIVATED: *C. bicolor,* yellow and red, May, 4 ft., Bolivia; *buxifolia,* ' Peruvian Magic Tree ', rose, May, 5 ft., Peru; *pyrifolia,* creamy-white, March, 3 ft., S. America.

Cape Blue Waterlily, see *Nymphaea capensis*;   **-Chestnut,** see *Calodendron capensis;* **-Cowslip,** see Lachenalia; **-Crocus,** see *Gethyllis spiralis*; **-Forget-me-not,** see *Anchusa capensis*; **-Gooseberry,** see *Physalis peruviana*; **-Honey-flower,** see *Melianthus major*; **-Honeysuckle,** see *Tecomaria capensis*; **-Jasmine,** see *Gardenia jasminoides*; **-Leadwort,** see *Plumbago capensis*; **-Lily,** see *Crinum longifolium*; **-Pondweed,** see *Aponogeton distachyus*; **-Primrose,** see Streptocarpus; **-Silver Tree,** see *Leucadendron argenteum*; **-Treasure Flower,** see *Gazania pavonia.*

Caper Bush, see *Capparis spinosa*; **-Spurge,** see *Euphorbia Lathyrus.*

Capparis—*Capparidaceae.* Slightly tender evergreen shrub. The flower buds of *C. spinosa* are pickled and sold as capers. First introduced late sixteenth century.

CULTURE: Compost, two parts turfy loam, one part leaf-mould and sand. Position, pots in sunny greenhouse. Pot, March; good drainage essential. Plant outdoors Sept. to Nov. Water moderately in pots Sept. to March, freely afterwards. Temp., Sept. to March 45° to 55°, March to Sept. 55° to 65°. May be grown outdoors in sheltered position in S. of England.

PROPAGATION: By cuttings of firm shoots in sand under bell-glasses in temp. 65° to 75°, July or Aug.

SPECIES CULTIVATED: *C. cynophallophora,* white, fragrant, 8 ft., Trop. America; *spinosa,* ' Caper Bush ', white, June, 3 ft., S. Europe, and its var. *rupestris.*

Capsicum (Red Peppers)—*Solanaceae.* Greenhouse shrubby plants usually grown as annuals. Variable many-seeded fleshy fruits differing in size, shape, colour and pungency under cultivation. Paprika is made from long, thick, bright red fruits and Cayenne from long slender form. First introduced mid-sixteenth century.

CULTURE: Soil, light rich. Position, pots in sunny greenhouse, against south wall outdoors in summer.

PROPAGATION: By seeds in temp. 80° in Feb. Transplant seedlings singly into 3 in. pots in March and into 6 in. pots in May. Water freely. Gather fruit when full colour is attained.

SPECIES CULTIVATED: *C. frutescens* (syn. *C. annuum*), ' Bird Pepper ', red fruits, Tropics, and vars. *cerasiforme,* ' Cherry Pepper ', *conoides,* ' Cone Pepper ', *fasciculatum,* ' Red Cluster Pepper ', *grossum,* ' Bell or Sweet Pepper ', *longum,* ' Long Pepper ', many types including Chilli, Cayenne, Paprika, etc.

Caragana—*Leguminosae.* Hardy flowering, deciduous, easily grown trees and shrubs. First introduced mid-eighteenth century.

CULTURE: Soil, ordinary, succeeding in poor dry areas. Position, full sun. Plant, Oct. to March.

PROPAGATION: By seeds sown 2 in. deep in ordinary soil outdoors in Nov. or March; cuttings of roots 3 in. deep outdoors in Oct.; layers of strong shoots in Sept.; grafting choice species on *C. arborescens* in March.

SPECIES CULTIVATED: *C. aborescens,* yellow, May, 15 ft., Siberia, and vars. *Lorbergii, nana, pendula*; *frutex,* yellow, April, 3 ft., Russia and Japan; *Franchetiana,* large flowers shaded maroon, 9 ft., S.W. China; *Gerardiana,* pale yellow or white, 2 to 4 ft., N.W. Himalaya; *Maximowicziana,* weeping habit, to 4 ft., W.

China; *microphylla*, yellow, May to June, 6 to 10 ft., N. Cent. Asia; *pygmaea*, yellow, May to June, 3 to 4 ft., Caucasus to Tibet; *sinica* (syn. *C. Chamlagu*, reddish yellow, May to June, 3 to 4 ft., N. China; *spinosa*, yellow, May, 4 to 6 ft., Siberia.

Caraway, see *Carum Carvi*.

Cardamine (Bitter Cress)—*Cruciferae*. Hardy herbaceous and tender aquatic plants. *C. lyrata* is a very pretty submerged aquatic not unlike Creeping Jenny.
CULTURE: Soil, ordinary. Position, moist, shady border or in the bog garden. Plant, Oct. March or April.
PROPAGATION: By seeds sown outdoors in April; division of roots in Oct.
SPECIES CULTIVATED: *C. asarifolia*, white, May, 1 ft., Italy; *cordifolia* (syn. *C. macrophylla*), pale purple, June, 1 ft., E. Asia; *lyrata*, aquatic, China, Japan; *pratense*, ' Lady-Smock ', ' Cuckoo Flower ', white to rose, May, 1 to 2 ft., Europe (Br.), Asia, etc.; *trifolia*, white, March to April, 3 to 4 in., S. Europe.

Cardinal, Flower, see *Lobelia cardinalis*; **-Monkey Flower,** see *Mimulus cardinalis*.

Cardiocrinum (Giant Lily)—*Liliaceae*. Hardy bulbous-rooted perennials formerly included in the genus Lilium. First introduced mid-nineteenth century.
CULTURE: Moist, well-drained loam with leaf-mould, peat and sand. Position, woodlands or other partially shaded places. Plant, Oct. with bulbs barely covered. Bulbs die after flowering but may leave offsets behind to flower again.
PROPAGATION: By seeds sown in sandy peat and loam in autumn. Seedlings take about seven years to flower. By removal of offsets in Oct.
SPECIES CULTIVATED: *C. cathayanum*, greenish-white, July, Aug., 1 to 4 ft., China; *cordatum*, creamy-white, July to Aug., 4 to 6 ft., Japan; *giganteum* (syn. *Lilium giganteum*), white, July to Aug., 6 to 12 ft., Himalaya.

Cardoon see *Cynara Cardunculus*.

Carex (Blue Grass; Sedge)—*Cyperaceae*. Hardy herbaceous perennial grasses.
CULTURE: Soil, ordinary. Position, margins of ponds. Plant, March. The variegated kinds may be grown in pots in ordinary good soil in cool greenhouses or in rooms.
PROPAGATION: By seeds sown where plants are to grow in March; division of roots in March.
SPECIES CULTIVATED: *C. acuta*, 2 to 3 ft., Europe; *baccans*, purple fruits, 4 ft., Trop. Asia; *depauperata*, 1 ft., Europe; *Pseudo-cyperus*, ' Bastard Cyperus ', 3 ft., Temp. Zone; *pendula*, brown inflorescence, summer, 5 to 6 ft., Britain; *riparia*, yellow foliage, 18 in., Britain; *tristachya*, leaves striped with white, 1 ft., Japan; *Vilmorinii* (syn. *C. comans*), 2 to 3 ft., New Zealand.

Carica—*Caricaceae*. Stove evergreen tree. Grown in Tropics for its edible fruits. First introduced late seventeenth century.
CULTURE: Rich loam. Position, large pots or borders in warm greenhouse. Pot or plant, March. Water freely during growing season; sparingly at other times. Temp., March to Oct. 65° to 85°, Oct. to March 55° to 65°.
PROPAGATION: By cuttings of ripened growths in sandy soil under bell-glass in temp. 80°; cuttings; grafts.
SPECIES CULTIVATED: *C. Papaya*, ' Papaya ', ' Pawpaw ', yellow, July, fruits yellow or orange, 3 to 30 in. long, 20 to 25 ft., Trop. America.

Carlina (Carline Thistle)—*Compositae*. Hardy perennials. First introduced early seventeenth century.
CULTURE: Soil, ordinary. Position, open dryish border. Plant, March or April.
PROPAGATION: By seeds sown ⅛ in. deep in April where plants are required to grow.
SPECIES CULTIVATED: *C. acanthifolia*, white, June, 18 in., S. Europe; *acaulis* (syn. *Cirsius acaule* or *Cirsium acaulis*), white, June, 9 in., Europe.

Carline Thistle, see *Carlina acanthifolia.*

Carludovica—*Cyclanthaceae.* Stove ornamental-leaved perennials with green, divided, palm-like leaves. First introduced early nineteenth century.

CULTURE: Compost, two parts peat, one part sandy loam. Position, moist, shady. Pot, March. Water moderately Nov. to March, freely afterwards. Temp., Sept. to March 55° to 65°, March to Sept. 65° to 75°.

PROPAGATION: By division of plant at potting time.

SPECIES CULTIVATED: *C. atrovirens*, 2 to 4 ft., Northern S. America; *gracilis* (syn. *C. Plumieri*), 2 ft., W. Indies; *insignis*, 3 to 6 ft., Peru; *palmata*, stemless, the leaves furnish fibre from which Panama hats are made, Peru; *rotundifolia*, 2 to 4 ft., Costa Rica.

Carmichaelia—*Leguminosae.* Greenhouse or hardy deciduous shrubs. First introduced early nineteenth century.

CULTURE: Soil, ordinary with a little sand, leaf-mould and peat. Position, sheltered borders or walls, or in borders in the cold greenhouse.

PROPAGATION: By cuttings of half-ripened side-growths inserted in sandy soil under a bell-glass in the cold greenhouse.

SPECIES CULTIVATED: *C. australis*, lilac, May to Aug., 2 to 4 ft., New Zealand; *Enysii*, violet, 1 ft., summer, New Zealand; *flagelliformis*, purplish lilac, June, 4 to 5 ft., New Zealand, and var. *corymbosa*; *grandiflora*, purple, 3 to 6 ft., June, New Zealand; *odorata*, 6 ft., rosy-lilac, June, New Zealand; *Williamsii*, greenish-yellow, 3 to 6 ft., New Zealand.

Carnation, see *Dianthus Caryophyllus.*

Carob see *Ceratonia siliqua.*

Carpenteria—*Saxifragaceae* (or *Hydrangeaceae*). Hardy to half-hardy evergreen flowering shrub. First introduced mid-nineteenth century.

CULTURE: Soil, light loamy. Position, in sheltered shrubberies in the south, but requiring wall protection in colder districts.

PROPAGATION: By cuttings of young shoots inserted in cold frame in August, or from seed sown in March.

SPECIES CULTIVATED: *C. californica*, ' Californian Mock Orange ', white, 2 in. fragrant anemone-like flowers, 6 ft., California.

Carpenter's Leaf, see *Galax aphylla.*

Carpinus—*Betulaceae.* Hardy deciduous trees frequently confused with beech, but having in our native species a rugged fluted trunk; that in the beech is smooth. Good for hedging, retaining old leaves until spring as in beech used for this purpose. Wood hard and used in manufacture of pianoforte keys and hammers.

CULTURE: Any ordinary soil including chalk. Plant Oct. to March. Use native *C. Betulus* for hedging, and plant 18 in. apart.

PROPAGATION: By seeds sown ½ in. deep in autumn in fine soil out of doors. Transplant seedlings when 1 year old. 1 lb. contains 14,000 seeds.

SPECIES CULTIVATED: *C. Betulus*, ' Hornbeam ', 50 to 80 ft., Europe, including Britain, with vars. *asplenifolia*, cut-leaved, *columnaris* and *pyramidalis*, excellent fastigiate trees, and *pendula*; *caroliniana*, ' American Hornbeam ', young growths attractive, 40 ft., America; *japonica*, sturdy pyramidal habit, 40 ft., Japan; *laxiflora*, 45 ft., Japan; *orientalis*, 20 ft., S.E. Europe; *polyneura*, graceful habit, 30 ft., W. China; *Turczaninovii* var. *ovalifolia*, similar, with tinted young growths, 25 ft., W. China.

Carpet Plant, see *Ionopsidium acaule.*

Carpobrotus—*Aizoaceae.* Half-hardy succulent plants. Formerly included in Mesembryanthemum.

CULTURE: Soil, ordinary. Position, sunny well-drained borders in sheltered districts.

PROPAGATION: By seed; cuttings in temp. 55° to 65° in March to Sept.

SPECIES CULTIVATED: *C. acinaciformis* (syn. *Mesembryanthemum acinaciforme*), reddish, August, trailing, S. Africa; *edulis* (syn. *M. edule*), 'Hottentot Fig', yellow, July, S. Africa.

Carrierea—*Flacourtiaceae.* Deciduous tree with attractive foliage and flowers in terminal racemes or panicles.
CULTURE: Soil, well drained. Position, sheltered.
PROPAGATION: By seeds; cuttings of green wood; layers; root cuttings.
SPECIES CULTIVATED: *C. calycina*, creamy-white, to 30 ft., Cent. China.

Carrion Flower, see Stapelia.

Carrot, see *Daucus Carota* var. *sativa.*

Carthamus (Distaff Thistle)—*Compositae.* Hardy annuals. First introduced mid-sixteenth century.
CULTURE: Soil, ordinary. Position, sunny border.
PROPAGATION: By seeds sown ⅛ in. deep in light soil in temp. 55° in March, transplanting seedlings where they are to flower in May.
SPECIES CULTIVATED: *C. lanatus*, yellow, July, 2 ft.; *Oxyacantha*, yellow, July, 2 ft.; *tinctorius*, 'Safflower', orange, June, 3 ft. All natives of Europe.

Cartwheel Flower, see *Heracleum villosum.*

Carum—*Umbelliferae.* Hardy thick-rooted herbs. *C. Carvi* is grown for the seeds which are used as flavouring. Oil used in kümmel.
CULTURE: Sow as soon as seed is ripe in autumn or in the following spring. Autumn-sown plants flower in the summer, spring-sown flower the following summer. Cut when seeds begin to ripen and spread in warm place to dry, then thrash and dry further. Roots also are edible.
SPECIES CULTIVATED: *C. Carvi*, 'Caraway', white, July, 2 ft., Europe.

Carya (Hickory)—*Juglandaceae.* Hardy deciduous trees. Full-grown trees bear edible nuts similar to walnuts. First introduced early seventeenth century.
CULTURE: Soil, ordinary. Position, shrubberies, woods or as single specimens on lawns and in parks. Plant, Oct. to March. Prune, Nov., thin out unsightly branches only.
PROPAGATION: By seeds, place nuts in box of soil outdoors for winter and keep soil well moistened. In March pot singly in 6 in. pots and place on gentle bottom heat; when seedlings appear harden off gradually and plant in permanent quarters before roots become potbound.
SPECIES CULTIVATED: *C. glabra* (syn. *C. porcina*), 'Pignut', 80 to 90 ft., E. America; *Pecan*, 'Pecan', 100 to 170 ft., South U.S.A.; *tomentosa*, 'Mockernut', 50 to 60 ft., E. America.

Caryolopha, see Pentaglottis.

Caryopteris—*Verbenaceae.* Hardy and half-hardy shrubs sometimes called Blue Spiraea.
CULTURE: Any garden soil, full sun. Prune previous season's shoots annually in March to two buds.
PROPAGATION: September cuttings in frame.
SPECIES CULTIVATED: *C. clandonensis*, hardy, garden hybrid, rounded bush to 2 ft., bright violet blue flowers, August, Sept.; *incana* (syn. *C. Mastacanthus*), 'Bluebeard', 4 ft., China; *mongholica*, 3 ft., China.

Caryota—*Palmae.* Stove monocarpic palms. First introduced late eighteenth century.
CULTURE: Compost, equal parts loam, leaf-mould and coarse sand. Position, pots, moist, shady. Pot, March. Water freely March to Nov., moderately afterwards. Temp., Sept. to March 55° to 65°, March to Sept. 65° to 85°.
PROPAGATION: By seeds sown 1 in. deep in light soil in temp. 85° in March; suckers removed from roots, inserted in small pots, any time.

SPECIES CULTIVATED: *C. mitis*, 20 to 25 ft., Malaya; *Rumphiana*, 20 to 30 ft., Malaya, Australia; *urens*, ' Toddy Palm ', ' Wine Palm ', 30 to 40 ft., Trop. Asia.

Cashew Nut, see *Anacardium occidentale.*

Cassava, see *Manihot esculenta.*

Cassia (Senna)—*Leguminosae* (or *Caesalpiniaceae*). Greenhouse evergreen shrubs and hardy perennials. The leaves of some species provide the medicinal senna. First introduced early eighteenth century.

CULTURE OF GREENHOUSE SPECIES: Compost, two parts loam, one part peat and sand. Position, pots in greenhouse, or well-drained border against south wall. Pot, March. Plant outdoors April. Water moderately Nov. to Feb., freely afterwards. Prune straggling shoots to within 2 in. of base in Dec. or Jan. Temp., Sept. to March 50° to 55°, March to Sept. 55° to 65°.

CULTURE OF HARDY SPECIES: Soil, ordinary well drained. Position, sunny borders. Plant, March or April. Protect in winter with covering of leaves or ashes.

PROPAGATION: By seeds sown ⅛ in. deep in light soil in temp. 75° in March; cuttings of previous year's shoots inserted in sandy soil under bell-glass in temp. 80° in March; herbaceous species by division in March.

GREENHOUSE SPECIES: *C. acutifolia*, ' Alexandrian Senna ', shrubby, 3 to 4 ft., Upper Nile; *angustifolia*, ' Indian Senna ', yellow, summer, 10 to 15 ft, Arabia; *corymbosa*, yellow, summer, 6 to 10 ft., Buenos Ayres; *Fistula*, ' Pudding Pipe Tree ', pale yellow, 20 to 30 ft., India, of economic interest, being the source of the senna pods of commerce.

HARDY SPECIES: *C. marilandica*, yellow, Sept., 3 ft., N. America.

Cassia Bark Tree, see *Cinnamomum Cassia.*

Cassie, see *Acacia Farnesiana.*

Cassinia—*Compositae.* Hardy, evergreen, flowering and ornamental-leaved shrubs of heath-like appearance.

CULTURE: Soil, ordinary. Position, sunny, dryish borders. Useful maritime shrubs which grow well in chalk. Plant in autumn.

PROPAGATION: By cuttings of young shoots inserted in sandy soil in cold frame in summer.

SPECIES CULTIVATED: *C. fulvida*, ' Golden Bush ', white, summer, 4 to 6 ft., leaves golden tinted, New Zealand; *leptophylla*, white, Aug. to Sept., 4 to 5 ft., New Zealand; *Vauvilliersii*, white, 2 to 6 ft., New Zealand.

Cassiope—*Ericaceae.* Hardy, evergreen flowering shrubs. Formerly known as Andromeda. First introduced late eighteenth century.

CULTURE: Soil, sandy peat. Position, moist, cool, north aspects.

PROPAGATION: Seeds, layers and cuttings.

SPECIES CULTIVATED: *C. fastigiata*, white, May, 9 to 12 in., Himalaya; *glandulifera*, cream-white, 12 in., May, U.S.A.; *hypnoides*, white, June, 2 in., Arctic; *lycopodioides*, white, prostrate, May, Asia; *Mertensiana*, white, 9 to 12 in., May to June, U.S.A.; *selaginoides*, white, 4 to 6 in., May to June, Asia; *Stelleriana* (syn. *Harrimanella Stelleriana*), white, prostrate, April to May, U.S.A.; *tetragona*, white, 9 in., May, Arctic Europe, America; *Wardii*, white, 9 to 12 in., May, Asia.

Castanea (Chestnut)—*Fagaceae.* Hardy deciduous trees. Bears edible nuts, which should be separated from the husks when latter fall in autumn, then be thoroughly dried in the sun or warm oven, and stored in air-tight jars or boxes in a cool, dry place. Young trees much grown as coppice wood for game shelter. Probably introduced to Britain by Romans.

CULTURE: Soil, deep, rich, dry and sandy. Position, open, sunny. Plant, Oct. to Feb. Transplant seedlings when a year old. Distance apart to plant, 25 ft. for avenues and 5 ft. apart for underwood. Useful Data: Timber most valuable in a young state; brittle when old. One bushel of seed will yield 3,000 plants. Number of seeds in a pound, 115. Weight of bushel of seed, 58 lb. Quantity of seeds to sow an acre, 600 lb. Timber reaches maturity at 50 years. Average life,

500 years. Uses: Rafters in churches, cabinet work, post and rail fencing, rustic work.

PROPAGATION: By seeds sown as soon as ripe in the open ground; choice varieties by grafting in spring on *C. sativa*.

SPECES CULTIVATED: *C. crenata*, 20 to 30 ft., Japan; *dentata* (syn. *C. americana*), 50 to 100 ft., Eastern N. America; *mollissima*, 50 ft., China and Korea; *pumila*, 10 to 20 ft., Eastern N. America; *sativa*, 'Spanish Chestnut', 50 to 60 ft., S. Europe, N. Africa, etc.; *Seguinii*, small tree, to 20 ft., sweet nuts, China.

Castanopsis—*Fagaceae*. Hardy, evergreen, ornamental-leaved tree.

CULTURE: Soil, sandy or well-drained loam, peat and leaf-mould. Position, lawns or mixed shrubberies. Plant, Oct. to March.

PROPAGATION: As advised for Sweet Chestnut.

SPECIES CULTIVATED: *C. chrysophylla* (syn. *Castanea chrysophylla*), 'Golden-leaved Chestnut', 30 to 100 ft., Oregon and California.

Castilleja—*Scrophulariaceae*. Half-hardy perennial plants with showy bracts; very difficult to grow owing to their semi-parasitic nature.

CULTURE: Compost, two parts peat, one part of equal proportions of loam, leaf-mould and sand. Position, sunny sheltered borders. Plant in April. Protect in winter.

PROPAGATION: By seeds sown in temp. 55° to 65° in March, hardening off seedlings in cold frame.

SPECIES CULTIVATED: *C. acuminata*, 'Indian Paint-brush', scarlet, N. America; *coccinea*, yellow and scarlet, July, 1 ft.; *pallida*, light purple, 1 ft., N. America.

Castor Oil Plant, see *Ricinus communis*.

Catalpa—*Bignoniaceae*. Hardy, deciduous, flowering and ornamental-leaved trees. First introduced early eighteenth century.

CULTURE: Soil, ordinary, good. Position, sunny, sheltered lawns. Plant, Oct. to April.

PROPAGATION: By cuttings of firm shoots inserted in sandy soil under bell-glass in temp. 55° to 65° in summer.

SPECIES CULTIVATED: *C. bignonioides*, 'Indian Bean', white, spotted purple and yellow, July, 25 to 50 ft., United States, and var. *aurea*, golden-leaved; *Bungei*, flowers like foxgloves, white, spotted purple, 30 ft., China; *Fargesii*, rosy pink, spotted purple, 30 to 50 ft., W. China, with its fine var. *Duclouxii* with large mauve-pink flowers; *ovata* (syn. *C. Kaempferi*), yellow, spotted red, July, 20 to 40 ft., Japan; *speciosa* (syn. *C. cordifolia*), white, June, 30 to 100 ft., Southern Central United States.

Catananche (Cupid's Dart)—*Compositae*. Hardy perennials and annuals. Flowers may be cut and dried for winter decoration; gather when fully developed. First introduced late sixteenth century.

CULTURE: Soil, ordinary. Position, warm borders. Plant, April.

PROPAGATION: By seeds sown ⅛ in. deep in light soil in temp. 55° in March, transplanting seedlings outdoors in June; by root cuttings at any time.

SPECIES CULTIVATED: *C. caerulea*, 'Blue Cupidone', blue, 2 ft., July and Aug., S. Europe, and var. *bicolor*, white and blue; *lutea*, annual, yellow, June, 1 ft., S. Europe, and var. *major*, improved double form, July to Sept., 2 ft.

Catasetum—*Orchidaceae*. Over 100 species are known in this chiefly epiphytic genus. The flowers are among the most remarkable in the order as they are dioecious. The male flowers in many have a curious adaptation of the rostellum, which is developed into two slender horns ; on touching one of these the pollen is ejected. Habit is very similar in all; stout ovoid pseudo-bulbs carrying and sheathed with plicate leaves. The spikes, generally simple, produced from the base or lower parts of the pseudo-bulbs. The male flowers, 6 to 30 are of curious shape, approaching contortion in some; the labellums generally saccate or helmet shape. The female flowers are more simple and consistent in shape, the lip more cup-shaped. In both the lip is fleshy and usually the largest of the segments. Some forms are deciduous, others are nearly so.

CULTURE: Compost as advised for Cattleyas. Baskets or pans are preferable to pots and should be suspended near the glass, especially in winter and late autumn, when exposure to full light is beneficial. Winter temp. should be 60° to 70°, when watering, if any, should be very occasional. Summer temp. 70° and upwards. Water should never be allowed to lodge on the leaves. The many garden hybrids require similar temperatures to the species, but until developed into large plants seldom have a definite resting period. Winter growths are often present and if this is the case a higher temp. and a ' growing ' atmosphere are required. When dormant, if only for a short period, give a corresponding rest.

PROPAGATION: By division of plants, each division with not less than four bulbs and a growing point in spring, when repotting should be effected if necessary.

SPECIES CULTIVATED: A selection—*C. barbatum*, variable, green, lip often whitish with fleshy filaments on the margin, various, Brazil, Demerara; *callosum*, brown-red, lip large flattish, shaded yellow, autumn, Venezuela; *Cliftonii*, usually yellow, lip shell-shaped, summer, Cent. America; *Darwinianum*, purplish-brown, autumn, Brazil; *fimbriatum*, greenish, spotted brown, lip fringed, variable, summer, Brazil, Paraguay; *Gnomus*, very variable, grotesque, greenish-red, purple spotted, various seasons, Brazil, Venezuela; *macrocarpum* (syns. *C. Claveringii*, *C. tridentatum*), greenish, spotted purple-red, lip has 3 apical teeth, summer, Brazil; *pileatum* (syn. *C. Bungerothii*), large, often white, lip broadly shell-shaped, usually autumn, Brazil, Trop. America; *Rodigasianum*, flowers many, greenish, spotted purple-brown, summer, Brazil; *Russellianum*, white, striped green, beautiful, horns absent, summer, Guatemala; *splendens*, a beautiful variable natural hybrid between *macrocarpum* and *pileatum*, autumn, various, S. America, many vars. are known; *tabulare*, greenish, spotted red-brown, lip with a large table-like callus, various seasons, Colombia, Guatemala; *Warscewiczii* (syn. *C. scurra*), much like a miniature *C. Russellianum*, spring, Demerara, Brazil, Guiana. A number of natural hybrids are known.

Catchfly, see Silene.

Catesbaea—*Rubiaceae*. Stove evergreen flowering shrub.

CULTURE: Compost, equal parts loam and peat, and a little sand. Position, well-drained pots and plenty of light. Pot in March. Water freely March to Sept., moderately afterwards. Temp., 55° to 65° Oct. to March, 75° to 85° afterwards.

PROPAGATION: By cuttings inserted in sand under bell-glass in a temp. of 75° in spring.

SPECIES CULTIVATED: *C. spinosa*, ' Lily Thorn ', yellow, May, 10 ft., W. Indies.

Cathcartia, see Meconopsis.

Catmint, see *Nepeta Cataria.*

Cat-tail, see Typha.

Cattleya—*Orchidaceae*. An important evergreen, epiphytic genus. Not only are the species appreciated but orchid collections are enriched by great numbers of hybrids derived from the species themselves, crosses between the hybrids and crosses with Laelia, Brassavola, Digbyana and Sophronitis. Hybrids have also been obtained with Epidendrum, Schomburgkia, Leptotes, etc. Cattleyas may be broadly divided into two sections, one with clavate pseudo-bulbs carrying a single large leaf, e.g. *C. labiata*. Many have flowers 6 to 8 in. across. The labellums have no definite divisions between the side lobes and frontal lobe, which is usually more richly coloured. The other group, with often tall, cylindrical stem-like pseudo-bulbs carrying two or more smaller, fleshy leaves, e.g. *C. Harrisoniana*. The inflorescence is terminal to the pseudo-bulbs. With one or two exceptions the peduncle is protected by a sheath through which it forces its way before flowering.

CULTURE: Compost, three parts osmunda fibre, cut and cleaned, one part of chopped sphagnum moss and a liberal addition of finely broken potsherds; about a quarter of the pot should be filled with clean sherds. The larger the plant the firmer should the compost be made. Often a house is given up entirely to Cattleyas and their hybrids. With the species a rest is required in winter. Water should be given occasionally, the leaves should nɯt approach flaccidity or the pseudo-bulbs shrivel. Resting temp., 55° to 60° at night; summer temp. 65° to 80°, a moist sweet atmosphere is essential, particularly in summer. Expose to light in autumn. Shading can usually be dispensed with in Sept. Avoid draughts. Repot if required when growth is expected.

PROPAGATION: By division of plants when potting. The rhizome may be cut through leaving four bulbs at least in front of the severance and an incipient ' eye ' may then grow.

SPECIES CULTIVATED: *C. Aclandiae*, olive-green, purple spotted, lip rich purple, dwarf, pans, summer, Brazil; *amethystoglossa*, rose, purple spotted, up to 20, spring, Brazil, var. *Sanderae*, pure white; *aurantiaca* (syn. *Epidendrum aurantiacum*), small, many, orange-red, summer, Mexico, Guatemala; *bicolor*, bronze-green, lip rose-purple, variable, autumn, Brazil; *Bowringiana*, variable, rose-purple, late autumn, Honduras; *citrina*, yellow, pendent, cool house, spring, Mexico; *Dormaniana* (syns. *Laelia Dormaniana*, *Laelio-cattleya Dormaniana*), olive-brown, purple dotted, lip rose-purple, summer, autumn, Brazil; *elongata* (syn. *C. Alexandrae*), dark rose, peduncle 12 in. high, spring, Brazil; *Forbesii*, yellowish-green or whitish, lip lined red, summer, Brazil; *granulosa*, olive-green, spotted purple, lip crimson, asperated, late summer, Brazil, var. *Schofieldiana*, larger; *guttata*, yellowish, spotted purple-red, lip white, rose-purple, summer, autumn, Brazil; *Harrisoniana*, light rosy-mauve, variable, summer, autumn, var. *alba*, white; *intermedia*, pale rose, lip rose-purple, summer, Brazil; *Loddigesii*, distinguished from *C. Harrisoniana* by paler colour and smooth disk of lip, various, Brazil, var. *alba*, pure white; *Schilleriana*, olive green, shaded red, lip red-purple, variable, summer, Brazil; *Skinneri*, rose-purple, early summer, Guatemala, var. *alba*, white; *velutina*, very fragrant, orange yellow, spotted and striated purple, summer, Brazil; *violacea*, purple or violet purple, lip deep violet-purple, summer, British Guiana, Brazil; *Walkeriana*, soft rose, lip purple, winter, Brazil. Clavate-bulbed section— *Dowiana*, fragrant, yellow, crimson, marked crimson-purple and old gold, summer, autumn, Costa Rica, Brazil, many vars. are known; *Eldorado*, fragrant, pale rose, rich purple, autumn, Brazil, var. *virginalis*, pure white, many other vars.; *Gaskelliana*, variable, fragrant, rose to purple-rose, June, July, Venezuela, Brazil, many vars.; *iricolor*, white with some purple streaks and 2 blotches, very rare; *labiata*, very variable, light to dark rose, the lip not distinctly lobed, crimson, October, Brazil, many vars. in varying colours; *Lueddemanniana*, rose, light or dark, lip amethyst, trumpet-shaped, summer, autumn, Venezuela; *luteola*, dwarf-growing, small, yellowish, summer, autumn, Brazil; *maxima*, pale rose, autumn, winter, Ecuador, Peru; *Mendelii*, light blush, lip often crimson-purple, May to June, Brazil, many richly coloured vars. known; *Mossiae*, light rose, lip crimson, rose and yellow, frilled, May, June, Venezuela; *Percivalliana*, rather small in comparison, rose to deep rose, lip frilled, magenta-crimson, pink, tawny-yellow and sepia markings, early winter, Venezuela; *quadricolor*, near *Trianae*, smaller, fragrant, blush-white, lip with purplish suffusions, autumn, winter, Brazil; *Rex*, creamy-white to yellow, lip crimson-red, summer, Peru, Andes; *Schroderae*, variable, fragrant, light rose, throat of lip orange, lip often purple, March to May, Brazil; *Trianae*, light rose, lip rose-purple, often deep, very variable, Dec. to Feb., Brazil; *Warneri*, rose to purple-rose, lip purple-red, May to July, Brazil; *Warscewiczii*, very large, rose, crimson and purple lip, summer, autumn, Brazil, many vars.

Cauliflower, see *Brassica oleracea* var. *botrytis*.

Caulophyllum—*Berberidaceae*. Hardy tuberous-rooted perennial. First introduced mid-eighteenth century.

CULTURE: Soil, ordinary. Position, shady. Plant, Nov.
PROPAGATION: By division of roots March to Nov.
SPECIES CULTIVATED: *C. thalictroides*, ' Blue Cohosh ', yellow, April, succeeded by blue berries in autumn, 1 ft., N. America.

Cautleya—*Zingiberaceae*. Herbaceous, semi-tuberous-rooted plants.
CULTURE: Soil, sandy, peaty, cool. Position, half-shade or north aspect.
PROPAGATION: By seed or, when possible, division of the roots in spring when growth commences.
SPECIES CULTIVATED: *C. lutea*, yellow, 12 in., summer, Himalaya.

Cayenne Pepper, see *Capsicum frutescens* var. *longum*.

Ceanothus—*Rhamnaceae*. Hardy and half-hardy evergreen and deciduous flowering shrubs. The majority of deciduous species are hardy in the open in the south, they make excellent wall shrubs and should be given this protection in colder districts. For the most part evergreen species are not really hardy. In warm localities they make fine specimens in the open but in most districts are better for wall protection. Very adaptable for training. First introduced early eighteenth century.
CULTURE: Soil, light ordinary. Position, against south or west walls or fences outdoors, in pots in cool greenhouse. Plant, Oct. to March. Pot, Oct. Prune deciduous kinds fairly severely in March, the evergreen kinds should have flowering shoots shortened as blossoms fade.
PROPAGATION: By cuttings 3 in. long in pots of sandy soil in cold frame in cool greenhouse in Sept.
SPECIES CULTIVATED: Deciduous—*C. americanus*, ' New Jersey Tea ', ' Mountain Sweet ', white, July, 5 ft., E. America; *caeruleus* (syn. *C. azureus*), blue, July to autumn frosts, 8 to 10 ft., Mexico; *Delilianus* (syn. *C. Arnouldii*), blue, July to Sept., 3 to 4 ft., hybrid, the well-known var. Gloire de Versailles belongs here; *Fendleri*, bluish white, 4 to 6 ft., Rocky Mountains; *integerrimus*, white to pale blue, June, 9 to 12 ft., California; *ovatus*, white, June to Aug., 2 to 3 ft., U.S.A. Evergreen—*C. Burkwoodii*, deep blue, hybrid; *dentatus*, blue, May, 10 ft., California; *papillosus*, blue, June, 10 to 12 ft., California; *rigidus*, rather tender, violet, April, 6 to 12 ft., California; *thyrsiflorus*, ' Californian Lilac ', blue, occasionally white, May to June, 15 to 30 ft., one of the hardiest, California; *Veitchianus*, bright blue, 10 ft., hybrid.

Cedar, see Cedrus; **-of Lebanon,** see *Cedrus libanensis*.

Cedrela—*Meliaceae*. Hardy deciduous ornamental-leaved tree with coloured wood, furnishing valuable timber. The wood of *C. odorata* is extensively used for cigar boxes. First introduced mid-nineteenth century.
CULTURE: Soil, good ordinary, well drained. Position, sheltered on lawns or in shrubberies. Plant in autumn.
PROPAGATION: By root cuttings.
SPECIES CULTIVATED: *C. odorata*, to 100 ft., flowers yellowish, W. Indies, S. America; *sinensis*, ' Bastard Cedar ', white and pink, June, 30 to 70 ft., China.

Cedronella—*Labiatae*. Rather tender shrubby herb. Leaves fragrant. First introduced late seventeenth century. See also Brittonastrum.
CULTURE: Compost, two parts sandy loam, one part leaf-mould and sand. Pot, March. Position, pots in sunny greenhouse, may be grown at base of a south wall in dryish soil in South of England. Temp., Sept. to March 50° to 55°, March to Sept. 55° to 65°. Water moderately in autumn and winter, freely other times.
PROPAGATION: By cuttings of young shoots inserted in pots of sandy soil in temp. 75° in March, April or May.
SHRUBBY SPECIES CULTIVATED: *C. canariensis*, ' Balm of Gilead ', purple, July, 3 ft., Canaries.

Cedrus—*Pinaceae*. Hardy, evergreen coniferous trees. Wood of Cedar of

Lebanon used in ancient times as incense. Oldest cedar in England at Brethby Park, Derbyshire; planted in 1676. Cones not produced by *Cedrus libani* until tree is 40 to 100 years old.

CULTURE: Soil, rich, deep, sandy. Position, well drained, elevated. *C. atlantica* does well in seaside gardens; and all are suitable for chalky soils. Plant, Sept. to Nov., or March to May.

PROPAGATION: By seeds sown ¼ in. deep in well-drained pans of light soil in cold frame in April, transplanting seedlings outdoors following spring; garden forms by grafting on seedlings of the type plant in warm house in early spring.

SPECIES CULTIVATED: *C. atlantica*, 'Mount Atlas Cedar', 80 to 100 ft., N. Africa, vars. *argentea*, foliage intense grey-blue, *aurea*, golden, *glauca*, bluish; *Deodara*, 'Deodar Cedar', 200 to 250 ft., Himalaya, and vars. *crassifolia, robusta* and *viridis*; *libanensis* (syns. *C. libani, C. libanotica*), 'Cedar of Lebanon', 80 ft., Mt. Lebanon and Asia Minor, var. *glauca*, glaucous-leaved.

Ceiba—*Bombacaceae*. Stove deciduous tree. Yields the kapok of commerce. First introduced mid-eighteenth century.

CULTURE: Compost, three parts loam, one part each leaf-mould, decayed manure and sand. Position, large pots or borders in warm greenhouse. Pot or plant, Nov. or March.

PROPAGATION: By seeds sown in Feb. in sandy soil in temp. 80° to 85°.

SPECIES CULTIVATED: *C. pentandra* (syn. *Eriodendron anfractuosum*), 'Silk-cotton Tree', white or rose, seeds with cotton-like fibre, up to 120 ft., Tropics.

Celandine, Greater, see *Chelidonium majus*;   **Lesser-,** see *Ranunculus Ficaria*; **-Poppy,** see *Stylophorum diphyllum*.

Celastrus—*Celastraceae*. Vigorous, hardy, deciduous shrubs and climbers. Grown for their attractive fruits. First introduced early eighteenth century.

CULTURE OF HARDY SPECIES: Soil, ordinary. Position, walls, arbours or clambering over trees. Plant, Oct. to March. Prune away weak shoots and tips of main shoots in Feb.

PROPAGATION: By layers of young shoots in autumn or spring.

HARDY SPECIES CULTIVATED: *C. angulatus*, green, seed capsules orange and bright red when open, 10 ft., shrubby, China; *orbiculata* (syn. *C. articulatus*), the most reliable fruiting kind, 30 ft., N.E. Asia; *scandens*, 'Staff-tree', yellow, summer, capsules orange with scarlet seeds, climbing, N. America.

Celeriac, see *Apium graveolens* var. *rapaceum.*

Celery, see *Apium graveolens*;   **-Cabbage,** see *Brassica pekinensis.*

Celmisia (New Zealand Daisy)—*Compositae*. Evergreen perennials.

CULTURE: Soil, well-drained sandy loam, deep and friable. Position, full sun, warm sheltered places.

PROPAGATION: By seeds or cuttings of side rosettes in summer.

SPECIES CULTIVATED: *C. coriacea*, white, 9 to 12 in., New Zealand; *gracilenta*, white, 6 in., May to June, New Zealand; *holosericea*, white, 12 in., summer, New Zealand; *Lyallii*, white, 12 in., June, New Zealand; *spectabilis*, white, 12 to 15 in., summer, New Zealand.

Celosia—*Amaranthaceae*. Greenhouse annuals. First introduced mid-sixteenth century.

CULTURE: Compost, two parts fibrous loam, one part leaf-mould and well-decayed cow manure and sand. Position, warm greenhouse, exposed to light. Sow seeds 1/16 in. deep in well-drained pans of light soil in temp. 75° in March. Transplant seedlings 1 in. apart when 1 in. high in light soil in well-drained pots and keep in temp. 60° to 75°. When seedlings have formed four leaves place them singly in 4 in. pots, transferring them as required to 6 in. pots. Keep plants near the glass. Water roots moderately. Syringe foliage twice daily. Apply liquid manure when flowers appear. Summer temp., 55° to 65°. May be used for summer bedding between May and Sept.

CULTURE OF COCKSCOMBS: Sow seeds as above. When seedlings appear place them close to glass and keep moderately moist. Transplant, when seedlings have formed three leaves, into 2 in. pots in above compost. Place pots on shelf near glass until ' combs ' show themselves. Select plants with finest ' combs ' and place them in 4 in. pots; plunge these to rim on gentle hotbed (temp. 65° to 75°) and keep moderately moist at root. Syringe freely. Transfer plants when pots are full of roots into 6 in. pots and treat as before. Give liquid manure when ' combs ' are well advanced. Good specimen of ' comb ' should measure 9 to 12 in. long, 3 to 6 in. wide, and plant 6 to 9 in. high.

SPECIES CULTIVATED: *C. argentea*, white, summer, 2 ft., China, var. *cristata*, ' Cockscomb ', red or crimson, summer, 2 ft., Tropics, and numerous vars. including *Childsii*, *plumosa*, *pyramidalis* and *Thompsonii*.

Celsia—*Scrophulariaceae.* Greenhouse and half-hardy annuals and perennials. First introduced mid-eighteenth century.

CULTURE: Compost, two parts fibrous loam, one part peat-moss or leaf-mould and sand. Pot, March to May or in autumn. Position, pots in sunny greenhouse or outdoors in borders. Temp., Sept. to March 45° to 55°, March to Sept. 55° to 65°. Water carefully October to March, freely at other times.

PROPAGATION: By seeds sown in pans of sandy soil in temp. 60° in March or Aug. Cuttings of perennial species in spring or autumn under bell-glass in cool house or frame.

SPECIES CULTIVATED: *C. Arcturus*, yellow with purple anthers, 1 to 2 ft., Crete; *betonicifolia*, yellow, 2 ft., Algeria; *bugulifolia*, yellow, purple-veined, 16 in., Balkan Peninsula, Asia Minor; *cretica*, ' Cretan Mullein ', yellow, 3 to 5 ft., Medit. Region; *sinuata*, yellow, 18 in., annual species of recent introduction, Medit. Region.

Celtis (Hackberry)—*Ulmaceae.* Hardy deciduous ornamental-leaved trees. First introduced mid-seventeenth century.

CULTURE: Soil, ordinary. Position, sunny shrubberies. Plant, Oct. to Feb. Prune, Nov. to Feb.

PROPAGATION: By seeds sown outdoors in spring; layering shoots in autumn or spring.

SPECIES CULTIVATED: *C. australis*, ' Nettle Tree ', May, 50 to 70 ft., S. Europe; *Bungeana* (syn. *C. Davidiana*), 15 to 25 ft., N. China; *laevigata* (syn. *C. mississippiensis*), long narrow leaves, 60 ft., S. United States; *occidentalis*, spring, 40 to 130 ft., N. America.

Centaurea—*Compositae.* Hardy and tender perennials and annuals.

CULTURE OF ANNUAL SPECIES: Sow seeds outdoors in April where plants are required to flower. Thin seedlings when an inch or so high to 4 or 6 in. apart. Ordinary rich soil and a sunny position.

CULTURE OF PERENNIAL SPECIES: Soil, ordinary good. Position, sunny borders. Plant, autumn or spring. Lift, divide, and replant every third or fourth year.

CULTURE OF TENDER SPECIES: Rear plants from seeds sown in heat in spring or summer, and grow on in pots in greenhouse; or from cuttings inserted in cold frame in July or Aug., lifting them when rooted and placing in pots in greenhouse. Plant out in beds end of May. Silvery foliage of these very striking for bedding.

PROPAGATION: By seeds sown outdoors in April, or in heat in spring, also by division of roots in autumn or spring.

ANNUAL SPECIES CULTIVATED: *C. americana*, rose or purple, Aug., 2 to 5 ft., N. America; *Cyanus*, ' Cornflower ', blue, rose, white, etc., summer, 3 ft., Britain; *moschata*, ' Sweet Sultan ', purple, summer, 2 ft., Orient, and vars. *alba*, white, *flava*, yellow, *rosea*, pink.

PERENNIAL SPECIES CULTIVATED: *C. babylonica*, yellow, July, 5 to 7 ft., Levant; *dealbata*, rose, summer, 18 in., Caucasus, var. *Steenbergii*, rose magenta, summer, 2 ft.; *glastifolia*, yellow, summer, 4 to 6 ft., Caucasus; *macrocephala*, yellow, July, 3 to 5 ft., Caucasus; *montana*, blue, July, 2 to 3 ft., Caucasus, Pyrenees, and vars. *alba*, white, *rosea*, rose; *nudicaulis*, pink, summer, 6 in., Asia Minor; *orientalis*, yellow, summer, 3 ft., Europe; *ruthenica*, pale yellow, July to Aug., 3 to 4 ft., Caucasus and Siberia.

TENDER SPECIES CULTIVATED: *C. Cineraria*, 12 to 18 in., Italy; *Clementei*, 2 to 3 ft., Spain; *gymnocarpa* (syn. *C. argentea*), 2 ft., S. Europe; *ragusina*, 2 ft., S. Europe

Centaurium (Centaury)—*Gentianaceae*. Hardy annual herbs and perennial alpine plants. Formerly known as Erythraea.

CULTURE: Soil, sandy loam. Position, sunny rockeries or borders. Plant, spring.

PROPAGATION: By cuttings or division for perennials; seeds for annuals.

SPECIES CULTIVATED: *C. portense* (syn. *Erythraea portense*), bright rose, summer, 4 in., W. Europe, incl. Britain; *Scilloides* (syn. *Erythraea Massonii*), white, summer, Azores; *vulgare* (syn. *Erythraea Centaurium*), pink, June to Sept., 6 to 12 in., Britain.

Centaury, see Centaurium.

Centipede Plant, see *Homalocladium platycladum*.

Centradenia—*Melastomaceae*. Stove flowering evergreen shrubs. First introduced early nineteenth century.

CULTURE: Compost, two parts peat, one part loam and sand. Position, sunny. Pot, Feb. Temp., Sept. to March 55° to 65°, March to Sept. 65° to 75°. Water moderately Sept. to March, freely afterwards.

PROPAGATION: By cuttings of side-shoots 2 or 3 in. long inserted in pots of sandy peat under bell-glass in temp. 85° in Feb. and March.

SPECIES CULTIVATED: *C. floribunda*, red, July, 18 in., Mexico; *grandifolia*, pink, Sept., 18 in., Mexico; *inaequilateralis* (syn. *C. rosea*), rose, April, 1 ft., Mexico.

Centranthus (Valerian)—*Valerianaceae*. Hardy herbaceous perennials and annuals. Sometimes spelled Kentranthus.

CULTURE: Soil, ordinary. Position, old walls, sunny rockeries, borders. Plant, March or April.

PROPAGATION: By seeds sown ⅛ in. deep in light soil in temp. 55° in March, transplanting seedlings outdoors in May; or in sunny positions outdoors in April or June, transplanting seedlings in May or Aug.; perennials also by division in autumn or spring.

ANNUAL SPECIES CULTIVATED: *C. macrosiphon*, red, July, 2 ft., Spain, var. *albus*, white.

PERENNIAL SPECIES CULTIVATED: *C. ruber* ' Red Valerian ', ' Spur Valerian ', red, June to Sept., 18 in., Europe incl. Britain, var. *albus*, white.

Centropogon—*Lobeliaceae*. Stove herbaceous perennial from Trop. America.

CULTURE: Compost, equal parts loam, peat, leaf-mould and a little sand. Pot, March. Position, stove Sept. to June; June to Sept. sunny frame outdoors. Temp., Oct. to Feb. 50° to 55°, Feb. to June 60° to 75°. Water moderately Sept. to Feb., freely afterwards. Prune shoots close to soil in Feb. when repotting.

PROPAGATION: By cuttings of young shoots 3 in. long, removed with a portion of stem attached, and inserted in light sandy soil in well-drained pots under bell-glass in temp. 60° to 70°.

SPECIES CULTIVATED: *C. Lucyanus*, rose, autumn, 2 ft., a hybrid.

Centrosema—*Leguminosae*. Stove evergreen climber.

CULTURE: Compost, equal parts peat, loam, leaf-mould and silver sand. Position, pots on staging, shoots trained up rafters or round a trellis or sticks. Pot in March. Water freely in spring and summer, moderately in winter. Temp., March to Sept. 75° to 85°, Sept. to March 55° to 65°.

PROPAGATION: By seeds in a temp. of 75° in March; also by cuttings in sand in a temp. of 85° in summer.

SPECIES CULTIVATED: *C. Plumieri* (syn. *Clitoria Plumieri*), red and white, autumn, 6 ft., S. America.

Century, see *Blackstonia perfoliata*; **-Plant,** see *Agave americana*.

Cephalanthera—*Orchidaceae.* Hardy terrestrial deciduous orchids with leafy stems and flowers in spikes.

CULTURE: Soil, chalky loam. Position, rather shady, open well-drained border. Plant, Sept. and Oct.

PROPAGATION: By division of plants in Sept.

SPECIES CULTIVATED: *C. Damasonium* (syns. *C. grandiflora, C. pallens*), white and yellow, June, 18 in., Britain, Europe; *falcata*, flowers yellow, sessile, in terminal spikes to 5 in. long, China, Japan; *longifolia* (syn. *C. ensifolia*), white, June, 2 ft., Britain; *rubra*, purple and white, May, 18 in., Britain.

Cephalanthus (Button-bush)—*Rubiaceae.* Hardy deciduous shrub of no great garden value. First introduced mid-eighteenth century.

CULTURE: Soil, sandy peat. Position, shrubberies, dislikes dry positions. Plant, Oct. or Nov.

PROPAGATION: By layers of shoots in Sept. or April.

SPECIES CULTIVATED: *C. occidentalis*, white, Aug., 7 ft., N. America.

Cephalaria (Giant Scabious)—*Dipsacaceae.* Hardy herbaceous scabious-like perennials. First introduced mid-eighteenth century.

CULTURE: Soil, ordinary. Position, borders or woods. Plant, March or April.

PROPAGATION: By seeds sown ⅛ in. deep in sunny position outdoors in April, transplanting seedlings in May.

SPECIES CULTIVATED: *C. alpina* (syn. *Scabiosa alpina*), yellow, July, 5 ft., Europe; *tatarica*, yellow, July, 5 ft., Siberia.

Cephalotaxus (Plum Yew)—*Taxaceae* (or *Cephalotaxaceae*). Hardy evergreen coniferous trees. Leaves similar to those of Yew. First introduced early nineteenth century.

CULTURE: Soil, ordinary. Position, sheltered shrubberies or lawns preferably in shade. Plant, Sept. to Nov. or March to May.

PROPAGATION: By seeds sown ¼ in. deep in light soil in cold frame in Sept. or March, transplanting seedlings outdoors a year after; cuttings of shoots 3 in. long inserted in sandy soil in shady cold frame, or under bell-glass or hand-light outdoors in Aug. or Sept.

SPECIES CULTIVATED: *C. drupacea*, 10 to 30 ft., Japan, and var. *prostrata*, a useful covering plant for dense shade; *Fortunei*, 10 to 20 ft., N. China.

Cephalotus—*Saxifragaceae.* Greenhouse herbaceous perennial. Pitchers, 1 to 3 in. long, dark green, purple and pink. First introduced early nineteenth century.

CULTURE: Compost, equal parts sphagnum moss, fibrous peat and silver sand. Position, pots or pans, well drained and covered with bell-glass; shady cool greenhouse or window. Temp., Oct. to March 45° to 55°, March to Oct. 50° to 55°. Water moderately Sept to April, freely afterwards.

PROPAGATION: By division of roots in March.

SPECIES CULTIVATED: *C. follicularis*, ' Australian Pitcher Plant ', 2 to 4 in., white, Australia.

Cerastium—*Caryophyllaceae.* Hardy perennials.

CULTURE: Soil, ordinary. Position, dryish borders, rockeries and edgings to flower beds. Plant, March or April.

PROPAGATION: By division of plants in March or April; cuttings of shoots 3 in. long inserted in ordinary soil in shady position outdoors in June or July; seeds sown 1/16 in. deep in shady position outdoors in April, transplanting seedlings in June or July.

SPECIES CULTIVATED: *C. alpinum*, white, June, 3 to 4 in., Britain, var. *lanatum*, prostrate, silvery woolly foliage, white, spring; *Bie*-*bersteinii*, white, June, 6 in., leaves silvery, Asia Minor; *Boissieri*, white, June, 8 to 9 in., leaves silvery; *grandiflorum*, white, July, 6 in.; *tomentosum*, ' Snow in Summer ', white, May, 6 in., leaves silvery, Europe.

Cerasus, see Prunus.

Ceratonia—*Leguminosae.* Tender evergreen tree, but only a small shrub in this country. The fleshy pods are edible. First introduced mid-sixteenth century.

CULTURE: Position, against south walls; suitable for S. and W. of England only, or in conservatories or unheated greenhouses. Plant, Sept. to Nov. or March to May.

PROPAGATION: By seeds sown 1 in. deep in pots of sandy soil in temp. 85° in March, transplanting seedlings outdoors in June; cuttings of firm shoots 4 in. long inserted in sandy soil under bell-glass in cold frame or greenhouse in Aug. or Sept.

SPECIES CULTIVATED: *C. Siliqua*, ' Carob ', ' St. John's Bread ', yellow and red, Sept., 40 to 50 ft., S. Europe.

Ceratophyllum (Hornwort)—*Ceratophyllaceae.* Submerged aquatics, with bristly foliage, for pond or cold water aquarium.

CULTURE: Soil, loam or aquarium compost. Position, base of pond or aquarium. Plant, spring and summer.

PROPAGATION: Slips inserted as cuttings or bunches of growth weighted and dropped into pond.

SPECIES CULTIVATED: *C. demersum*, dark green, forked growth, 1 to 3 ft., Europe (Britain); *submersum*, paler, Europe (Britain), Trop. Asia, Florida.

Ceratopteris (Floating Fern; Indian Fern; Water Fern)—*Ceratopteridaceae.* Only true water ferns, much used by aquarists, floating or submerged.

CULTURE: Soil, sifted loam and charcoal with a little leaf-mould. Position, in pots or pans submerged to rim in tank of water for floating kinds, submerged kinds in aquarium compost. Plant, spring or summer. All need subdued light, moist, warm atmosphere. Temp., Sept. to March 55° or 60°, March to Sept. about 75°.

PROPAGATION: By spores sown in Feb. on surface of compost in pan of water as above; viviparous forms increased by pegging down leaves into soft mud, detaching later.

SPECIES CULTIVATED: *C. pteridoides*, pale green, floating, viviparous, fleshy, S. America; *thalictroides*, ' Pod Fern ', annual, finely-cut foliage, Trop. America.

Ceratostigma—*Plumbaginaceae.* Half-hardy trailing shrub or herbaceous perennials with flowers like Plumbago.

CULTIVATION: Soil, light loam, sunny position at foot of wall or on rockery. Cut older or dying shoots hard back in April.

PROPAGATION: By removal of rooted offsets in April.

SPECIES CULTIVATED: *C. Griffithii*, blue, low, much-branched shrub, India; *plumbaginoides* (syn. *Plumbago Larpentae*), deep blue, to 1 ft., Aug., Sept., China; *Willmottianum*, makes a spreading 3 ft. bush, or may be trained to wall, sky blue flowers from June to early winter, W. China.

Cercidiphyllum—*Cercidiphyllaceae.* Hardy deciduous tree, but only a shrub to 20 ft. in this country. Good autumn tints. First introduced late nineteenth century.

CULTURE: Soil, well-drained, peaty loam. Position sheltered from early frosts and cold winds.

PROPAGATION: By seeds sown in pans or boxes in cool greenhouse or frame in March, or by layering in spring.

SPECIES CULTIVATED: *C. japonicum*, 50 to 100 ft., Japan, China.

Cercis—*Leguminosae.* Hardy, deciduous flowering trees. First introduced late sixteenth century.

CULTURE: Soil, rich, deep, sandy. Position, warm sheltered shrubberies, or on lawns. N. of England against south wall. Plant, Oct. to March.

PROPAGATION: By seeds sown ¼ in. deep in light sandy soil in temp. 55° to 65° in March, transplanting seedlings outdoors in June, or by layers of strong shoots in autumn or spring.

SPECIES CULTIVATED: *C. canadensis*, ' Red-bud ', pale rose, May to June, 15 to 40 ft., N. America; *chinensis*, pink, May, 20 to 50 ft., tender, China and Japan;

Siliquastrum, ' Judas-tree ', purple or rose, the best species for gardens, eventually a spreading tree 15 to 40 ft., flowering April before the leaves appear, S. Europe.

Cereus—*Cactaceae*. Greenhouse succulent plants. Many species formerly included in this genus have now been transferred to Aporocactus, Echinocereus, Selenicereus, etc. First introduced late seventeenth century.

CULTURE: Compost, two parts fibrous loam, one part coarse sand and broken brick. Position, well-drained pots in sunny greenhouse or window. Pot every two or three years as required. Water sparingly. Temp. Sept. to March 50° to 55°, March to Sept. 55° to 65°.

PROPAGATION: By seeds sown in well-drained pots or boxes; cuttings of stems in pots of sand kept just moist.

SPECIES CULTIVATED: *C. aethiops* (syn. *C. caerulescens*), white, July, Mexico; *kewensis*, pink and white, hybrid; *peruvianus*, red, Aug., Peru; *tetragonus*, red, to 6 ft., Brazil; *variabilis*, green and red, July, S. America.

Cerinthe (Honeywort)—*Boraginaceae*. Hardy annuals and a few perennials. First introduced mid-sixteenth century.

CULTURE: Soil, ordinary. Position, sunny well-drained beds or borders. Plant perennial species Oct. or April.

PROPAGATION: Annuals by seeds sown $\frac{1}{16}$ in. deep in April where plants are to flower, or in boxes of light sandy soil in temp. 55° to 65° in March, transplanting seedlings outdoors in May; thin outdoor-sown seedlings to 2 in. apart; perennials by seeds similar to annuals and by division of roots in April.

ANNUAL SPECIES CULTIVATED: *C. major*, ' Wax-plant ', yellow and purple, July, 1 ft., Alps; *retorta*, yellow and violet, July, 18 in., Greece.

Ceropegia—*Asclepiadaceae*. Greenhouse trailing plants.

CULTURE: Compost, equal parts peat, loam, leaf-mould and silver sand. Position, baskets or pots suspended from roof of greenhouse, or in rockeries; sunny. Pot, March. Water moderately between March and Sept., occasionally afterwards. Temp., March to Sept. 55° to 65°, afterwards 45° to 50°.

PROPAGATION: By cuttings of slender shoots inserted in silver sand, in well-drained pots, in a temp. of 65° in spring.

SPECIES CULTIVATED: *C. bulbosa*, purple and green, India; *elegans*, white, brown and purple, summer, 3 to 4 ft., India; *Gardneri*, white and purple, Ceylon; *Sandersonii*, green, autumn, 3 ft., Natal; *Thorncroftii*, green, white and red, S. Africa; *Thwaitesii*, yellow, spotted red, Ceylon; *Woodii*, white and purple, summer, 2 to 3 ft., S. Africa.

Ceropteris, see Pityrogramma.

Cestrum (Bastard Jasmine)—*Solanaceae*. Greenhouse, flowering, evergreen or semi-evergreen shrubs. Some species formerly known as Habrothamnus. First introduced late eighteenth century.

CULTURE: Compost, two parts loam, one part leaf-mould and sand. Position, pots or beds with shoots trained on wall, pillars, or roof of greenhouse. Pot, March. Prune into shape, Feb. Temp., Sept. to March 40° to 50°, March to Sept. 55° to 60°. Water moderately in winter, freely other times.

PROPAGATION: By cuttings of side-shoots 3 or 4 in. long, removed with portion of old stem attached, inserted in well-drained pots of sandy soil in temp. 65° to 75° in July, Aug. or Sept.

SPECIES CULTIVATED: *C. aurantiacum*, orange-yellow, June, 5 ft., Guatemala-*fasciculatum*, purplish-red, 5 ft., Mexico, var. *Newellii*, crimson; *Parquii*, greenish; white or yellow, June to July, 7 ft., Western S. America; *psittacinum*, orange and yellowish-green, autumn, 20 ft., C. America; *purpureum* (syn. *C. elegans*), carmine, spring, 10 ft., Mexico, and var. *Smithii*.

Ceterach, see *Asplenium Ceterach*.

Chaenomeles (Flowering Quince)—*Rosaceae*. Hardy and easily-grown shrubs of great beauty, flowering in early spring before the leaves. The quince-like fruits are useful for preserves. Formerly included in the genera Cydonia and Pyrus. *C. speciosa* is the ' Japonica ' of gardens.

CULTURE: Any garden soil. Position, sheltered if in open border, or walls of any aspect, makes attractive hedge. May be pruned in Sept. to restrict size, spur pruning as for apples.

PROPAGATION: By layering; grafting on common quince; or seed to produce new varieties.

SPECIES CULTIVATED: *C. cathayensis*, thorny bush to 10 ft., large, pink-flushed flowers, April, China; *japonica* (syn. *Cydonia Maulei*), dwarf-spreading shrub to 3 ft., blood-red, Japan, and var. *atrosanguinea*, dark red; *speciosa* (syn. *Cydonia japonica* hort., *Chaenomeles lagenaria*), spreading bush to 10 ft., or trained considerably higher, scarlet flowers, March to June, China, many named vars.

Chaenorrhinum—*Scrophulariaceae*. Annual or perennial herbs, once included in Linaria.

CULTURE: Soil, ordinary. Position, moist rockeries or margins of borders.

PROPAGATION: By division; seed.

SPECIES CULTIVATED: *C. minus*, lilac, summer, to 1 ft., annual, Europe; *origanifolium* (syn. *Linaria origanifolia*), pale purple with orange palate, summer, 6 to 9 in., France, Spain, Portugal.

Chaenostoma—*Scrophulariaceae*. Greenhouse and half-hardy evergreen plants. First introduced early nineteenth century.

CULTURE: Compost, two parts fibrous loam, one part leaf-mould with admixture of silver sand and crushed mortar rubble. Position, pots or hanging baskets in sunny greenhouse. Beds or borders out of doors, June to Sept. Water moderately Sept. to March, freely at other times. Temp., Sept. to March 50° to 55°, March to Sept. 55° to 65°.

PROPAGATION: By seeds sown in sandy soil in gentle heat during spring; cuttings of side-shoots inserted in sandy soil under bell-glass or in propagator in temp. 60° during autumn or spring.

SPECIES CULTIVATED: *C. grandiflorum* (syn. *Sutera grandiflora*), lavender-blue, scandent, summer, S. Africa.

Chaerophyllum—*Umbelliferae*. Hardy biennial. Roots carrot-like, grey or blackish with yellowish-white flesh, sweet; cooked and served as carrots.

CULTURE: Soil, ordinary. Position, sunny beds outdoors. Lift roots in Aug. and store them in dry, dark place until required for use.

PROPAGATION: By seeds sown 1 in. deep in drills 1 ft. apart in Aug. or Sept., which do not germinate until spring. Thin out seedlings to 8 in. apart in May.

SPECIES CULTIVATED: *C. bulbosum*, ' Turnip-rooted Chervil ', white, June, 2 to 3 ft., Europe. See also Anthriscus.

Chain Fern, see Woodwardia;   **-Orchid,** see Dendrochilum.

Chalk Plant, see *Gypsophila paniculata*.

Chamaecyparis (False Cypress)—*Pinaceae* (or *Cupressaceae*). Hardy evergreen coniferous trees with small scale-like leaves.

CULTURE: As Cupressus.

HEDGE CULTURE: Trench soil, 3 ft. wide and deep, adding a little well-rotted manure. Plant 2 ft. high shrubs 2 ft. apart in Sept. or Oct. Trim annually in May and July. *C. Lawsoniana* is the best species for hedging. The various coloured forms with varying degrees of vigour are useful for formal planting and stand trimming well if this is done regularly and at the correct season.

PROPAGATION: As Cupressus.

SPECIES CULTIVATED: *C. Lawsoniana*, ' Lawson's Cypress ', pyramidal habit, 100 to 150 ft., California, and vars. *Allumii*, glaucous foliage, columnar form, *argentea*, silvery foliage, *aurea*, foliage golden when young, *darleyensis*, low form, *Ellwoodii*, compact, slow-growing dwarf with grey-green foliage, *erecta*, columnar form, *Forsteckiana*, branchlets twisted, *glauca*, leaves steel-blue, *nana*, dwarf form, *nidi-*

formis, horizontal branches from dense centre, and many others; *nootkatensis*, pyramidal habit, 100 to 120 ft., Western N. America; *obtusa* (syn. *Retinospora obtusa*), spreading habit, 50 to 70 ft., Japan, and vars. *albo-spica*, *aurea*, *compacta*, *filicoides*, *gracilis*, *lycopodioides*, *magnifica*, *nana*, *pendula*, *pygmaea*, etc.; *pisifera* (syn. *Retinospora pisifera*), slender, graceful habit, 70 to 100 ft., Japan, and vars. *filifera*, *plumosa*, *squarrosa*, all dwarfer than the type; *thyoides*, ' White Cedar ', 80 to 90 ft., U.S.

Chamaedaphne—*Ericaceae*. Hardy, evergreen flowering shrubs. First introduced early eighteenth century.

OUTDOOR CULTURE: Soil, equal parts peat, leaf-mould and silver sand. Position, open sheltered borders, rockeries, or bogs. Plant, Sept. to Nov., or March. Prune straggling shoots only moderately after flowering. Water freely in dry positions during summer.

POT CULTURE: Soil, equal parts peat, leaf-mould and fine silver sand. Position, well-drained pots in cold greenhouse, Nov. to June; in shady position outdoors, June to Nov. Pot, Oct. to Nov. Water moderately, Nov. to March, freely afterwards.

PROPAGATION: By seeds sown $\frac{1}{16}$ in. deep in sandy peat in cold frame, Nov. or March; layering shoots in Sept.; division of plants, Oct. or Nov.

SPECIES CULTIVATED: *C. calyculata* (syns. *Cassandra calyculata*, *Andromeda calyculata*), white, spring, 3 ft., N. America, and var. *nana*, a more compact form to 18 in.

Chamaedorea—*Palmae*. Stove palms. Ornamental foliage. First introduced early nineteenth century.

CULTURE: Compost, two parts peat, one part loam and sand. Position, shady part of stove in pots or tubs. Pot, March. Water moderately Sept. to March, abundantly afterwards. Temp., Sept. to March 55° to 65°, March to Sept. 65° to 75°.

PROPAGATION: By seeds sown 1 in. deep in above compost in pots, in temp. 85° in March.

SPECIES CULTIVATED: *C. elatior*, 20 to 30 ft., Mexico.

Chamaelirium—*Liliaceae*. Hardy, herbaceous, tuberous-rooted perennial. Introduced mid-eighteenth century.

CULTURE: Soil, loam and leaf-mould. Position, cool, moist and shady. Best grown in colonies. Plant in March.

PROPAGATION: By seeds sown soon as ripe in loam, peat and leaf-mould in a cold frame. Division of the root-stock in March.

SPECIES CULTIVATED: *C. luteum* (syn. *C. carolinianum*), ' Fairy Wand ', yellow, June and July, 18 in., N. America.

Chamaenerion, see Epilobium.

Chamaepeuce, see Cirsium.

Chamaerops—*Palmae*. Greenhouse and half-hardy palm. Leaves, fan-shaped, green. First introduced early eighteenth century.

CULTURE: Compost, two parts rich loam, one part decayed leaf-mould and sand. Position, well-drained pots in greenhouse or sheltered well-drained beds outdoors in S. of England. Pot, March. Plant, April. Temp., Sept. to March 40° to 50°, March to Sept. 50° to 60°. Water moderately in winter, freely in summer.

PROPAGATION: By seeds sown 1 in. deep in light soil in temp. of 80° in Feb. or March; suckers removed from parent plant in April or Aug.

SPECIES CULTIVATED: *C. humilis*, ' Fan Palm ', ' European Palm ', 10 to 30 ft., S. Europe, N. Africa, and vars. *arborescens*, *bilaminata*, *dactylocarpa*, *elegans*, *macrocarpa* and *tomentosa*. See also the genus Trachycarpus.

Chamomile, see Anthemis.

Chandelier Flower, see *Brunsvigia Josephinae*.

Chaplet Flower see *Stephanotis floribunda*.

Chara (Stonewort)—*Characeae*. Submerged aquatics found in still waters in most parts of the world, sometimes used in ponds and aquariums.

CULTURE: Soil, ordinary. Position, entirely submerged. Plant, spring or summer by sinking weighted clumps.

PROPAGATION: Slips inserted as cuttings.

SPECIES CULTIVATED: *C. aspera*; *fragilis*, *hispida*, all very similar, rough to touch, Britain.

Chard, see *Beta vulgaris* var. *Cicla*.

Charieis—*Compositae*. Hardy annual. First introduced early nineteenth century.

CULTURE: Soil, ordinary. Position, sunny borders or rock gardens.

PROPAGATION: By seed.

SPECIES CULTIVATED: *C. heterophylla*, rays blue, disk yellow or blue, summer, 6 to 12 in. S. Africa.

Chasmanthe—*Iridaceae*. Cormous plants formerly included in the genus Antholyza. First introduced mid-eighteenth century.

CULTURE: Soil, light sandy. Position, sunny well-drained borders or pots in cool greenhouse. Plant, 6 in. deep and 6 in. apart in border or 6 in a 6-in. pot in Oct. Lift in Aug., dry and store in a cool place till October.

PROPAGATION: By offsets at planting time; seeds in slight heat in spring.

SPECIES CULTIVATED: *C. aethiopica* (syn. *Antholyza aethiopica*), red and yellow, June to July, 3 to 4 ft., S. Africa; *caffra* (syn. *C. intermedia*, hort.), bright red, May, 1 ft., doubtfully hardy, S. Africa; *floribunda* (syn. *A. praealta*), orange and red, May to June, 3 to 4 ft., Cape; *vittigera*, yellow and red, summer, 3 ft., Cape.

Chaste Tree, see *Vitex Agnus-castus*.

Chatham Island Forget-me-not, see *Myosotidium Hortensia*.

Cheddar Pink see *Dianthus caesius*.

Cheilanthes (Lip Fern)—*Polypodiaceae*. Stove and greenhouse ferns. First introduced late eighteenth century.

CULTURE: Compost, two parts peat, one part loam and silver sand. Position, pots in shade. Pot, Feb. or March. Water moderately Oct. to Feb., freely afterwards. Temp. stove species, Sept. to March 55° to 65°, March to Sept. 65° to 75°; greenhouse, Sept. to March 45° to 50°, March to Sept. 55° to 65°. These ferns require less moisture than most.

PROPAGATION: By spores similar to Adiantum.

STOVE SPECIES CULTIVATED: *C. farinosa*, 12 to 18 in., Abyssinia, Java, etc.; *gracillima*, 'Lace Fern', 1 ft., N. America, also thrives in greenhouse temps.; *tenuifolia*, 1 ft., New Zealand, Australia, etc.

GREENHOUSE SPECIES CULTIVATED: *C. alabamensis*, to 10 in., N. America; *gracillima*, 6 to 8 in., N. Asia, etc.; *californica*, 1 ft., California; *myriophylla*, 9 in., Cent. America; *pteridioides*, 2 to 4 in., S. Europe.

Cheiranthus (Wallflower)—*Cruciferae*. Hardy perennials. Of biennial duration only on heavy soils. Botanically not distinct from Erysimum.

CULTURE OF WALLFLOWERS: Soil, ordinary well-drained, not too heavy, add lime or old mortar. Position, sunny borders, beds or old walls. Sow either broadcast or in drills 6 in. apart and ½ in. deep in May. Transplant seedlings when third leaf has formed, 6 in. apart each way, in a bed of firm soil limed as before, and plant out finally a foot or so apart in Sept. or Oct. Make soil firm around plants to ensure sturdy firm growth. To grow on old walls, sow a pinch of seed in crevices, adding a little soil and cow manure to supply food to young plants; or plant young seedlings in similar compost in spring.

CULTURE OF DWARF SPECIES: *C. alpinus*, *kewensis* and *semperflorens* should be grown on sunny rockeries in good loamy soil and old mortar. Plant in spring. Top-dress annually in March with well-rotted cow manure.

POT CULTURE: Plant seedlings in good ordinary soil in 6 in. pots in Sept.; keep in sunny cold frame till flower buds form, then transfer to greenhouse. Water moderately. Feed with liquid manure when in flower. Throw away after blooming.

PROPAGATION: By seed; cuttings.

SPECIES CULTIVATED: *C. alpinus*, yellow, May, 6 in., Scandinavia; *Cheiri*, (syn. *Erysimum Cheiri*) ' Wallflower ', ' Gilliflower ', various colours, spring, 1 to 2 ft., Europe (Br.); *kewensis*, sulphur, orange, purple, Nov. to May, 1 ft., hybrid; *semperflorens* (syn. *C. mutabilis*), purple, spring, 1 ft., Morocco. See also Erysimum. The plant known in gardens as *Cheiranthus Allionii*, ' Siberian Wallflower ', is *Erysimum asperum*.

Cheiridopsis—*Aizoaceae. Greenhouse succulent plants*, formerly included in Mesembryanthemum.

CULTURE: As for Mesembryanthemum *except* water moderately from June to Dec., keep dry rest of year.

PROPAGATION: As for Mesembryanthemum.

SPECIES CULTIVATED: *C. candidissima* (*Mesembryanthemum candidissimum*), white or pale pink, 4 in., S.W. Africa; *C. cigarettifera* (*M. cigarettiferum*), yellow, 1½ in. S.W. Africa.

Chelidonium (Greater Celandine)—*Papaveraceae.* Hardy perennial or biennial.

CULTURE: Soil, ordinary. Position, damp shady borders. Plant, March or April.

PROPAGATION: By seeds sown ⅛ in. deep in shade outdoors in April; division of roots in April.

SPECIES CULTIVATED: *C. majus*, yellow, May, 2 ft., Britain, and vars. *flore pleno*, double, *laciniatum*, more finely divided leaves.

Chelone (Turtle-head)—*Scrophulariaceae.* Hardy herbaceous perennials. First introduced mid-eighteenth century.

CULTURE: Soil, rich, deep. Position, open borders. Plant, Oct. or March.

PROPAGATION: By seeds sown ¹⁄₁₆ in. deep in light soil in temp. 55° to 65° in March, or similar depth in soil in cold frame in April, transplanting seedlings outdoors in May and June; cuttings inserted in sandy soil in cold frame in June and July; division of plants in Aug. and Sept.

SPECIES CULTIVATED: *C. glabra*, white, Aug., 2 to 3 ft., N. America; *Lyonii*, purple, Aug., 2 to 3 ft., N. America; *obliqua*, ' Shell-flower ', purple, Aug., 2 to 3 ft., N. America. See also Penstemon.

Chenopodium—*Chenopodiaceae.* Hardy perennials and annuals grown for edible leaves and young shoots.

CULTURE OF GOOD KING HENRY: Soil, good, well trenched, and liberally manured. Position, dryish, sunny. Sow seeds 1 in. deep in drills 12 in. apart in autumn as soon as ripe, or under glass in April. Thin seedlings out to 9 in. Cover bed in October with thin layer of manure. Gather young shoots before flower develops as substitute for asparagus; leaves in May and June in lieu of spinach. Renew beds every 3 or 4 years.

CULTURE OF WHITE QUINOA: Soil, ordinary. Position, open garden. Sow seeds in drills 1 in. deep and 2 ft. apart from March onwards at intervals of a few weeks. Gather leaves, cook, and eat like spinach.

PERENNIAL SPECIES CULTIVATED: *C. Bonus-Henricus*, ' Good King Henry ', ' Lincolnshire Asparagus ', 3 ft., Britain.

ANNUAL SPECIES CULTIVATED: *C. giganteum* (syn. *C. amaranticolor*), 6 ft., India, young leaves blood-red; *Quinoa*, 4 to 5 ft., Andes.

Chequer Berry, see *Mitchella repens.*

Chequered Daffodil or **Chequered Lily,** see *Fritillaria meleagris.*

Cherimoyer, see *Annona Cherimola.*

Cherokee Rose, see *Rosa laevigata.*

Cherry, see Prunus; **-Laurel,** see *Prunus Laurocerasus;* **-Pie, see** *Heliotropium peruvianum;* **-Plum,** see *Prunus cerasifera.*

Chervil, see *Anthriscus Cerefolium*; **Turnip-rooted-,** see *Chaerophyllum bulbosum*.

Chestnut, see Castanea; **Horse-,** see *Aesculus Hippocastanum*.

Chiastophyllum—*Crassulaceae*. Succulent plant, often included in Cotyledon or Umbilicus.
CULTURE: Light soil, in sun or half shade, rock garden.
PROPAGATION: Cuttings in July to Sept. in frame, division in Sept. or March.
SPECIES CULTIVATED: *C. oppositifolium* (syn. *Cotyledon oppositifolia, C. simplicifolia, Umbilicus oppositifolius*), yellow, summer, 6 in., Caucasus.

Chickweed Wintergreen, see *Trientalis europaea*.

Chicory, see *Cichorium Intybus*.

Chile Arbor-vitae, see *Libocedrus chilensis*;   **-Bellflower,** see *Lapageria rosea;*
-Crocus, see *Tecophilaea cyanocrocus*;   **-Glory Flower,** see *Eccremocarpus scaber;*
-Jasmine, see *Mandevilla suaveolens*;   **-Pitcher Flower,** see *Sarmienta repens;*
-Rhubarb, see *Gunnera manicata*; **-Strawberry,** see *Fragaria chiloensis*.

Chilli, see *Capsicum frutescens* var. *grossum*.

Chimaphila—*Pyrolaceae*. Hardy dwarf herbaceous perennials. First introduced, mid-eighteenth century.
CULTURE: Compost, two parts leaf-mould, one part sand. Position, shady rockery outdoors. Plant, April.
PROPAGATION: By division of plants in April.
SPECIES CULTIVATED: *C. maculata*, ' Spotted Winter Green ', pink and white, June, 6 in., N. America; *umbellata*, white and pink, June, 6 in., N. America.

Chimney Bellflower, see *Campanula pyramidalis*.

Chimonanthus—*Calycanthaceae*. Hardy deciduous flowering shrub. First introduced mid-eighteenth century.
CULTURE: Soil, deep, rich, sandy. Position, against south or west walls. Plant, Feb. Prune in Feb., cutting away all shoots that have flowered to within 1 in. of base, except those required to furnish plants with branches.
PROPAGATION: By layering shoots in Sept. or Oct, or from seed in spring.
SPECIES CULTIVATED: *C. praecox* (syns. *C. fragrans* or *Calycanthus praecox*), yellow and red, fragrant, Dec., 6 to 9 ft., China and Japan, var. *grandiflorus*, larger flowered, but not so intensely fragrant.

Chimonobambusa—*Gramineae*. Shrub with creeping root-stocks formerly included in Arundinaria.
CULTURE: Soil, good, not too heavy and of reasonable depth. Position, must be sheltered from cold winds and dry root conditions are disliked.
PROPAGATION: By division in April and May.
SPECIES CULTIVATED: *C. marmorea*, 3 ft., marbled stems, Japan.

China Aster, see Callistephus; **-Rose,** see *Rosa chinensis*.

Chinaman's Breeches, see *Dicentra spectabilis*.

Chincherinchee, see *Ornithogalum lacteum*.

Chin Chin, see *Ornithogalum lacteum*.

Chinese Hawthorn, see *Photinia serrulata*;   **-Primrose,** see *Primula chinensis*;
-Rose Mallow, see *Hibiscus Rosa-sinensis*;   **-Sacred Lily,** see *Narcissus Tazetta* var. *orientalis*;   **-Yam,** see *Dioscorea Batatas*.

Chionanthus (Fringe Tree)—*Oleaceae*. Hardy deciduous flowering trees and shrubs. First introduced late eighteenth century.
CULTURE: Soil, sandy loam. Position, moist sheltered shrubbery. Plant, Oct. to Feb. *C. virginicus* suitable for pot culture for spring flowering in heated or cold greenhouses. Pot, Nov. Water moderately Nov. to April, freely afterwards. Plunge pot to rim outdoors from June to Feb.
PROPAGATION: By seeds sown in sandy soil in cold frame in April; grafting on Ash in March; budding on Ash in July.

Species Cultivated: *C. retusus*, white, June to July, 8 to 30 ft., China; *virginicus*, ' Virginia Snowflower ', white, June, 10 to 20 ft., Florida.

Chionodoxa (Glory of the Snow)—*Liliaceae*. Hardy, spring-blooming, bulbous plants. First introduced late nineteenth century.

Outdoor Culture: Soil, sandy loam. Position, sunny rockeries, well drained. Plant bulbs 1 in. apart and 3 in. deep in Sept. Lift and replant every three years.

Pot Culture: Compost, equal parts peat, loam, leaf-mould and sand. Pot, Sept., planting 12 bulbs 1 in. deep in a 3 in. pot, well drained. Cover pot with ashes outdoors or in frame until Jan., then remove to window or greenhouse. Water moderately Jan. to April, freely April to June, none afterwards.

Propagation: By seeds sown ¼ in. deep in boxes of light soil in cold frame in Aug.; offsets treated as mature bulbs.

Species Cultivated: *C. cretica*, blue and white, March, 6 in., Crete; *Luciliae*, blue and white, March, 6 in., Asia Minor, and numerous vars.; *sardensis*, intense blue, with white stamens, March, 6 in., Asia Minor.

Chionographis—*Liliaceae*. Half-hardy herbaceous perennial. First introduced late nineteenth century.

Culture: Compost, equal parts loam, leaf-mould, peat and sand. Position, warm, well-drained south border outdoors, or pot in cold frame. Plant, Oct. or Feb. Pot, Feb.

Propagation: By seeds sown ⅛ in. deep in above compost in a pot, pan, or box in March, in cold frame; division of roots in Sept.

Species Cultivated: *C. japonica*, white, May, 1 ft., Japan.

× **Chionoscilla**—*Liliaceae*. Bigeneric hybrid between Chionodoxa and Scilla.
Culture: As for Chionodoxa.
Species Cultivated: *C. Backhousei*, blue and white, early spring, 4 in.

Chirita—*Gesneriaceae*. Stove herbaceous perennial and evergreen plants. First introduced early nineteenth century.

Culture: Compost, equal parts peat and leaf-mould, half a part fibrous loam, and half a part of silver sand and charcoal. Pot, Feb. Shake away old soil from roots and put in small pots first, shifting into larger size when plants begin to grow. Water moderately at first, increasing supply when plants grow freely; keep nearly dry Oct. to Feb. Position, on shelf near glass. Liquid or artificial manure may be applied when flower buds appear. Temp., Nov. to Feb. 55° to 65°, Feb. to Nov. 70° to 85°.

Propagation: By seeds sown in well-drained pots of above compost in March. Cover seeds with sprinkle of sand, place a square of glass over each pot and put latter in temp. 75° to 85°. Keep soil moderately moist. Transplant seedlings when three leaves are formed into small pots and treat as advised for old plants. Can be propagated also by large leaves, cutting their main ribs through and laying undersides on pans of sandy soil in temp. 65° to 75° in summer.

Species Cultivated: *C. depressa*, violet, July, 6 to 8 in., China; *Horsefieldii*, white and purple, Sept., 18 in., Java; *lavandulacea*, lilac, 3 ft., Malaya and E. Indies; *lilacina*, white, blue and yellow, summer, 18 in., Chiriqui; *Marcanii*, orange, 2 to 3 ft., Siam; *Moonii*, blue and purple, June, 2 ft., Ceylon; *sinensis*, lilac, July, 6 in., China; *Walkeri*, yellow, June, 18 in., Ceylon; *zeylanica*, purple, June, 18 in., Ceylon.

Chironia—*Gentianaceae*. Greenhouse perennial plants. First introduced early nineteenth century.

Culture: Equal parts fibrous peat, loam and leaf-mould, with silver sand and crock chippings added to ensure porosity. Position, sunny part of greenhouse or frame. Temp., March to Sept. 55° to 65°, Sept. to March 45° to 55°. Water carefully at all times, particularly during winter months.

Propagation: By cuttings of side-shoots inserted in sandy soil, and placed in propagating case or under bell-glass in gentle heat in spring.

SPECIES CULTIVATED: *C. baccifera*, reddish-pink, June, 2 ft., S. Africa; *floribunda*, pink, June, 2 ft., S. Africa; *linoides*, reddish-pink, July, 1 to 2 ft., S. Africa.

Chives, see *Allium Schoenoprasum*; **Chinese-,** see *A. tuberosum.*

Chlidanthus—*Amaryllidaceae.* Half-hardy bulbous plant. First introduced early nineteenth century.

OUTDOOR CULTURE: Compost, equal parts peat, leaf-mould, loam and silver sand. Position, warm, well-drained bed or border outdoors in sandy loam and leaf-mould. Plant bulbs 3 in. deep in April. Lift bulbs in Oct. and store them in sand in frost-proof place during winter.

POT CULTURE: Plant bulbs 1 in. apart and 2 in. deep in above compost in 5 in. pots in April. Water moderately at first, freely when in active growth. Grow in cold frame or cool greenhouse. Withhold water from roots after Sept., until repotting time.

PROPAGATION: By offsets in April.

SPECIES CULTIVATED: *C. fragrans*, yellow, fragrant, June, 10 in., Peru.

Chlora, see Blackstonia.

Chloris—*Gramineae.* Hardy annual and perennial ornamental flowering grasses. Inflorescence suitable for winter decorations. Cut and dry when fully developed.

CULTURE: Soil, ordinary. Position, sunny borders. Sow seeds outdoors in April.

SPECIES CULTIVATED: *C. barbata*, 1 ft., annual E. Indies; *Gayana*, 3 ft., perennial, Africa; *truncata*, 1 ft perennial, Australia; *virgata*, 1 ft., annual S. America.

Chlorogalum—*Liliaceae.* Hardy bulbous plant. First introduced early nineteenth century.

CULTURE: Soil, light. Position, south border, well drained. Plant bulbs 4 in. deep and 3 in. apart in Oct. or March. Replant every three years.

PROPAGATION: By offsets planted similarly to old bulbs; by seeds sown ⅛ in. deep in well-drained pots of sandy soil in March.

SPECIES CULTIVATED: *C. pomeridianum*, ' Soap Plant ', white and purple, June, 2 ft., California.

Chlorophytum—*Liliaceae.* Greenhouse plants. First introduced mid-eighteenth century.

CULTURE: Compost, equal parts loam, leaf-mould, peat and sand. Position, variegated and tall kinds in pots; drooping-stemmed species in pots or baskets suspended in window or greenhouse. Pot, March. Temp., Oct. to March 45° to 50°, March to Oct. 55° to 65°. Water moderately in winter, freely other times. May be used in summer bedding displays June to Sept.

PROPAGATION: By seeds sown ⅛ in. deep in well-drained pots of light soil in temp. 65° in March; by offshoots inserted singly in small pots under bell-glass in window or greenhouse in April; by division of roots when repotting.

SPECIES CULTIVATED: *C. capense* (syns. *C. Anthericum* and *Phalangium elatum*), white, summer, 12 to 18 in., S. Africa, var. *variegatum*, leaves variegated with creamy white; *comosum* (syn. *C. Sternbergianum*), white, summer, 1 to 2 ft., S. Africa.

Chocolate Tree, see *Theobroma Cacao.·*

Choisya—*Rutaceae.* Hardy evergreen flowering shrub. First introduced early nineteenth century.

OUTDOOR CULTURE: Soil, ordinary loam with peat or leaf-mould. Position, sheltered shrubberies S. and W. of England and Ireland, against south walls N. of England. Good maritime shrub, grows well in chalky soils. Plant, Oct. or March. Prune after flowering, shortening straggling shoots only.

POT CULTURE: Compost, equal parts peat, loam, leaf-mould and sand. Pot, Sept. or Oct. Water moderately Sept. to March, freely afterwards. Keep plants in cool greenhouse Nov. to May, remainder of time outdoors.

PROPAGATION: By cuttings of shoots 3 in. long inserted in well-drained pots of sandy soil under bell-glass in temp. 55° to 65°, March to June, or in cold frame Aug. to Sept.

SPECIES CULTIVATED: *C. ternata*, ' Mexican Orange ', white, May, and usually again in autumn, 6 ft., Mexico.

Choke-berry, see Aronia;   **-Cherry,** see *Prunus virginiana.*

Chordospartium—*Leguminosae.* Small, hardy, leafless weeping tree. A rare plant from the south island of New Zealand where it grows near running water.
CULTURE: Soil, well drained, fairly dry. Position, waterside in full sun.
PROPAGATION: By seed.
SPECIES CULTIVATED: *C. Stevensonii*, whitish, tinted pale lilac, 20 ft., May to July, New Zealand.

Chorizema—*Leguminosae.* Greenhouse, flowering evergreen shrubs. First introduced early nineteenth century.
CULTURE: Compost, equal parts fibrous peat and loam, one-fourth sand. Position, pots, or in well-drained beds in greenhouses. Pot, March or June; firm potting essential. Prune straggling shoots slightly after flowering. Water freely March to Sept., moderately afterwards. Temp., March to Sept. 55° to 65°, Sept. to March 45° to 50°. Stand plants outdoors from July to Sept. to mature flowering shoots for following year.
PROPAGATION: By seeds sown $\frac{1}{16}$ in. deep in light sandy compost in temp. 65° to 70° in March; by cuttings in sandy peat under bell-glass in temp. 65° in summer.
SPECIES CULTIVATED: *C. cordatum*, red and yellow, April, 10 ft., Australia, and vars. *elatior*, red, *flavum*, orange-yellow; *diversifolium*, orange-red, May, 2 ft., Australia; *Henchmannii*, scarlet, May, 2 ft., Australia; *ilicifolium*, yellow, May, 3 ft., Australia; *varium* (syn. *C. Chandleri*), yellow and red, May, 4 ft., Australia.

Christmas Berry Tree, see *Schinus terebinthifolius*;   **-Cactus,** see Zygocactus; **-Rose,** see *Helleborus niger.*

Christ's Thorn, see *Paliurus Spina-Christi.*

Chrysalidocarpus—*Palmae.* Stove palm.
CULTURE AND PROPAGATION: As Areca.
SPECIES CULTIVATED: *C. lutescens* (syn. *Areca lutescens*), 10 to 25 ft., Madagascar.

Chrysanthemum—*Compositae.* A large genus of greenhouse and hardy perennials and hardy annuals, some woody. First introduced mid-eighteenth century.
CULTURE OF ANNUALS: Soil, ordinary rich. Position, open sunny. Plant seedlings out in May, or sow seed outdoors where plants are to flower. Gather seed in Aug.
POT CULTURE: Transplant seedlings when 2 in. high, 4 in a 5-in. or 7 in a 6-in. pot. Compost, two parts good soil, one part leaf-mould or decayed manure and sand. Grow in cold frame or greenhouse. Water moderately. Thin flower buds for fine blooms. Give liquid manure when buds appear.
CULTURE OF MARGUERITES: Compost, equal parts loam and leaf-mould and fourth part silver sand. Insert cuttings singly, or three in a 4-in. pot in April, cover with bell-glass or place in propagating box. Pot rooted cuttings in 3-in. pots, moving into 5-in. in Aug. Stand plants in full sun from July to Sept., then in cold frame till Nov., and afterwards in greenhouse in temp. 50° to 55°. Water moderately. Give liquid manure when pots are full of roots. Alternatively, young plants may be hardened off in a frame for planting outdoors at end of May in sunny beds or borders. These plants can either be discarded at the end of summer or lifted, potted and placed in a greenhouse.
CULTURE OF INDOOR CLASSES: Incurved—petals curving inwards; Anemone-flowered—dense centres and petals fringing their base; Pompons—small flowers, petals reflexed, fringed or toothed; Singles—centres open, yellow, one or more rows of guard petals; Decoratives—easily grown free-flowering doubles of moderate size; Large Flowered Exhibition (Japanese)—petals loosely arranged,

variously shaped. Compost, three parts fibrous loam, one part horse manure, one part decayed tree leaves, one part coarse silver sand, quarter-part finely ground bones, same of dissolved bones, one part charcoal, wood ashes and soot. Pot first time in 3-in. pots in March, second in 5 or 6-in. mid-April, third in 8- or 10-in. from middle to end of May. Stop main stems 4 in. from base in March to obtain bushy plants; those grown for exhibition blooms must be stopped according to variety (instructions are usually given in trade catalogues). Cut down plants intended for dwarfs to within 6 in. of pot in May. Thin flower buds to one on each shoot when size of radish seed. Stand plants in full sun May to Sept., then remove to greenhouse. Temp., while in bloom, 45° to 50°. Water freely while outdoors, moderately in greenhouse. Apply liquid manure from midsummer till flower buds show colour. Suitable liquid manures: two parts sulphate of ammonia, six parts superphosphate and one part sulphate of potash dissolved in water at the strength of $\frac{1}{2}$ oz. per gallon; one part nitrate of potash and two parts superphosphate, $\frac{1}{2}$ oz. per gallon; sheep and cow dung soaked in a sack in water till it is colour of weak tea; droppings from fowls or pigeons in weak solution. These mixtures should be alternated and applied every four or five days,

CULTURE OF OUTDOOR CHRYSANTHEMUMS: Soil, good ordinary. Position, sunny beds or borders. Plant out 3 ft. apart in May. Stop shoots when 6 in. high, disbud as for indoor varieties if large blooms are required. Water freely in summer. Give liquid manure July to Sept.

CULTURE OF HARDY PERENNIAL SPECIES: Soil, ordinary rich. Position, sunny borders. Plant, autumn or spring, *C. azaleanum, coreanum* and *rubellum* in spring. Lift, divide and replant every third year.

PROPAGATION: By cuttings in temp. 50° to 55° in Dec., Jan., Feb. or March for indoor and outdoor species; seeds in light soil in temp. 65° in March. After flowering, cut stems down and place plants in cold frame to produce cuttings, after which plant in garden or discard. Hardy perennial species: by division in March or seeds sown in warm greenhouse in Feb. or March. Marguerites by cuttings. Annuals by seed.

ANNUAL SPECIES CULTIVATED: *C. carinatum*, 'Tricolor Chrysanthemum', white, red, purple, yellow, disk purple, summer, 2 ft., N. Africa; *coronarium*, yellow and white, summer, 3 ft., S. Europe; *segetum*, 'Corn Marigold', yellow, summer, 18 in., Europe (Br.); *viscidi-hirtum*, yellow, summer, 1$\frac{1}{2}$ ft., N. Africa.

HARDY SPECIES CULTIVATED: *C. alpinum* (syn. *Leucanthemum alpinum*), white, summer, 3 to 6 in., Alps; *arcticum*, white tinged lilac, June to July, 1 ft., Arctic regions; *azaleanum*, cushion form, varied colours, double, July to Sept., 1 ft., hybrid; *cinerariifolium*, white, July to Aug., 1 to 2 ft., Dalmatia; *coccineum* (syn. *Pyrethrum roseum*), 'Pyrethrum', scarlet, summer, 2 to 3 ft., Caucasus; *hispanicum*, white, summer, 4 to 6 in., Spain, and var. *sulphureum*, yellow; *lacustre*, 'Marsh Oxeye', white, summer, 3 to 6 ft., S.W. Europe; *Leucanthemum*, 'Oxeye Daisy', white, summer, 2 ft., Europe; *maximum*, 'Shasta Daisy', white, summer, 1$\frac{1}{2}$ to 2 ft., Pyrenees, var. *laciniatum*, fringed ray-flowers; *nipponicum*, white, summer, 12 to 15 in., Japan; *Parthenium*, 'Feverfew', white, summer, 2 ft., Europe, var. *aureum*, 'Golden Feather'; *rubellum* (syn. *C. erubescens*), shades of lilac, pink, single, Sept. to Oct., 2 to 3 ft., China; *sibiricum* (syn. *C. coreanum, Leucanthemum sibiricum*), 'Korean Chrysanthemum', various, single and double, Sept. to Oct., 2 to 3 ft., Korea; *uliginosum*, 'Giant Daisy', white, autumn, 5 ft., E. Europe.

TENDER SPECIES CULTIVATED: *C. indicum*, 'Japanese Chrysanthemum', yellow, numerous in short-stemmed clusters, 2 to 3 ft., China; *frutescens*, 'Marguerite' or 'Paris Daisy', white or yellow, summer, 3 ft., Canary Is.; *morifolium* (syn. *C. sinense*), 'Florist's Chrysanthemum', various, 2 to 4 ft., China and Japan.

Chrysocoma—*Compositae*. Greenhouse, evergreen flowering sub-shrub. First introduced early eighteenth century.

CULTURE: Compost, equal parts peat, loam and silver sand. Position, well-drained pots in sunny part of greenhouse. Pot, March. Water freely in spring and summer, moderately other seasons. Temp., March to Oct. 55° to 65°, Oct. to March 45° to 50°.

PROPAGATION: By cuttings of firm shoots in silver sand under bell-glass in spring.

SPECIES CULTIVATED: *C. coma-aurea*, yellow, July, 2 ft., S. Africa. See also Aster.

Chrysogonum—*Compositae*. Hardy herbaceous perennial.

CULTURE: Compost, equal parts loam, peat and leaf-mould. Position, sunny. Plant, Oct. or March.

PROPAGATION: By division of roots in March.

SPECIES CULTIVATED: *C. virginianum*, ' Golden Star ', yellow, summer, 9 in., N. America.

Chrysophyllum—*Sapotaceae*. Stove evergreen tree. First introduced early eighteenth century.

CULTURE: Equal parts fibrous loam, leaf-mould and sand. Position, borders in warm greenhouse. Temp., March to Oct. 75° to 90°, Oct. to March 65° to 75°. Water freely during the summer months, sparingly in winter.

PROPAGATION: By cuttings of well-ripened wood in close frame and temp. 80°. Seeds sown in heat in Feb. or March.

SPECIES CULTIVATED: *C. Cainito*, ' Star Apple ', 30 to 50 ft., light green or purple fruits, 2 to 4 in. in diameter, with white pulp, Trop. America; *macrophyllum*, large leaves clothed on the under-side when young with rich golden silky hairs, which gradually turn chestnut-brown, 40 to 50 ft., Sierra Leone.

Chrysopsis (Golden Aster)—*Compositae*. Hardy herbaceous perennial.

CULTURE: Soil, ordinary. Position, sunny borders.

PROPAGATION: By division of roots in March.

SPECIES CULTIVATED: *C. villosa*, golden yellow, July to Sept., 18 in., N. America.

Chrysosplenium (Golden Saxifrage; Water Carpet)—*Saxifragaceae*. Hardy perennial semi-aquatic herbs.

CULTURE: Soil, boggy peat or wet loam. Position, damp and shady watercourses or ditches. Plant, Oct. or March.

PROPAGATION: By division of plants in March.

SPECIES CULTIVATED: *C. alternifolium*, yellow, summer, 3 in., N. Hemisphere (Br.); *americanum*, purplish-yellow, summer, 3 in., N. America; *oppositifolium*, yellow, 3 in., Europe (Br.).

Chrysothamnus—*Compositae*. Evergreen sub-shrub. Formerly known as Bigelowia.

CULTURE: Soil, well drained. Position, warmest place available, not hardy in exposed situations. Transplant from pots in spring, fasten growths to wall, spreading well.

PROPAGATION: By cuttings of young growth in gentle bottom heat, pot singly and harden off, plunge in open for first summer, return to cool house for following winter and plant out the next spring.

SPECIES CULTIVATED: *C. graveolens* (syn. *Bigelowia graveolens*), yellow, Aug. to Sept., 6 to 8 ft., Western N. America.

Chufa, see *Cyperus esculentus*.

Chysis—*Orchidaceae*. Epiphytal, deciduous or semi-deciduous orchids. Pseudobulbs swollen, slender basally, 12 in. or more high. Leaves plicate. Flowers produced with the young growths.

CULTURE: Compost, as for Cattleya, pans suspended near glass, especially in autumn when full light is necessary. Winter temp. 60.° Rest decided. In summer water freely, temp. 70° to 80°. Repot as growth appears or just before.

PROPAGATION: By division of plants in Feb. or March.

SPECIES CULTIVATED: *C. aurea*, yellow and red, spring and summer, Venezuela; *bractescens*, white and yellow, very fragrant, spring, Mexico, Guatemala, Peru;

Chelsonii, yellow and purple, spring, 1 ft., hybrid; *laevis*, yellow-orange, lip yellow and crimson, spikes arched, summer, Mexico, Guatemala.

Cibotium—*Dicksoniaceae*. A small genus of stout tree ferns akin to Dicksonias. Very few are grown in Britain, they require great space and greenhouse temp. *C. Barometz* is sometimes grown for its historical interest and is useful in its juvenile stage.

CULTURE: Usual fern compost, will eventually occupy large pots or tubs. Temp., winter 45° to 50°, increasing in spring and summer, but with free ventilation. Syringe trunks (not fronds) daily during growing season. Reduce water in winter. Repot in spring as required.

PROPAGATION: By spores.

SPECIES CULTIVATED: *C. Barometz* (syn. *C. glaucescens*), ‘ Scythian Lamb ’, stout creeping rhizome, trunkless, fronds fragrant, China, Malay, etc.; *regale*, trunk 20 ft., fronds spreading 10 to 12 ft., Mexico; *Schiedei*, trunk 10 to 15 ft., fronds finely cut, 6 to 8 ft. long, Guatemala, Mexico.

Cichorium—*Compositae*. Salad vegetables, and chicory roots used for mixing with coffee.

CULTURE OF CHICORY: Soil, rich light. Position, open, away from trees. Sow seeds ¼ in. deep in drills 15 in. asunder first week in May. Thin seedlings when an inch high to 8 in. apart in row. No liquid or artificial manures required. Force crowns for salad by placing roots close together in large pots or deep box, using ordinary soil and covering with 8 in. sand. Temp. 60°. Cut whitloof or ‘ head ’ in about a fortnight.

CULTURE OF ENDIVE: Soil, light rich. Position, open garden or on south or west borders. Sow seeds ¼ in. deep in drills 18 in. apart in June for early crop, July for main crop, Aug. for late crop. Thin to 15 in. apart or sow more thickly and transplant. Water freely in dry weather. Blanch early crop in Aug., main crop in Sept., late crop in Oct. by covering each plant with inverted pot with drainage hole plugged, or taking inside to a dark shed or cellar. Lift remaining plants in Nov. and store close together in cold frame, covering them with dry leaves to ensure blanching.

SPECIES CULTIVATED: *C. Endivia*, ‘ Endive ’, blue, July, 2 ft., Orient; *Intybus*, ‘ French Endive, ‘ Chicory ’, blue, July, 2 ft., Britain.

Cigar Flower, see *Cuphea platycentra*.

Cimicifuga (Bugbane)—*Ranunculaceae*. Hardy herbaceous perennials. Introduced early eighteenth century.

CULTURE: Soil, ordinary. Position, moist shady borders. Plant, Oct., Nov. or March.

PROPAGATION: By seeds sown 1⁄16 in. deep in light soil in cold frame in Sept.; division of roots in March.

SPECIES CULTIVATED: *C. americana*, white, Aug., 3 ft., N. America; *cordifolia*, white, July, 3 ft., N. America; *davurica*, white, July, 4 ft., China; *elata*, white, July, 3 ft., N. America; *racemosa*, ‘ Snake-root ’, white, Aug., 3 ft., N. America; *simplex*, white, Aug. to Oct., 3 ft., Kamchatka.

Cinchona (Quinine)—*Rubiaceae*. Greenhouse evergreen tree.

CULTURE: Compost, equal parts turfy loam and fibrous peat with a little sand and charcoal. Position, large pots or borders in heated greenhouse. Pot or plant, Oct. Water freely during growing season. Temp., March to Oct. 60° to 75°, Oct. to March 55° to 65°.

PROPAGATION: By cuttings of ripened wood under hand-light in temp. 75°.

SPECIES CULTIVATED: *C. officinalis*, rose, 20 to 40 ft., S. America, and its variety *condaminea*.

Cineraria, see *Senecio cruentus*.

Cinnamomum—*Lauraceae*. Stove evergreen trees and shrubs of interest on account of their economic value.

CULTURE: Compost, equal parts turfy loam and peat with a little sand. Position, large pots or borders in warm greenhouse. Water freely during growing season, and maintain a moist atmosphere. Temp., March to Oct. 70° to 80°, Oct. to March 60° to 70°.

PROPAGATION: By cuttings of young shoots in April placed in close frame and temp. 80°.

SPECIES CULTIVATED: *C. Camphora*, ' Camphor Tree ', yellow, 30 to 40 ft., China and Japan; *Cassia*, ' Cassia Bark Tree ', flowers small in silky panicles, 20 to 30 ft., China; *zeylanicum*, ' Cinnamon Tree ', yellowish white, 20 to 30 ft., India, Malaya.

Cinnamon, see *Cinnamomum zeylanicum*; **-Fern,** see *Osmunda cinnamomea*; **-Rose,** see *Rosa cinnamomea*; **-Vine,** see *Dioscorea Batatas.*

Cinquefoil, see Potentilla.

Cirrhaea—*Orchidaceae.* Dwarf-growing epiphytes. Pseudo-bulbs small with a single leaf. Spikes pendent from base of pseudo-bulbs. Flowers inverted, segments narrow.

CULTURE: Compost, three parts of osmunda fibre cut fine, one and a half parts sphagnum moss. Winter temp. 60°, only occasional waterings. Summer, water freely, 70° and upwards. Expose to full light in autumn.

PROPAGATION: By division of plants if large enough in early spring.

SPECIES CULTIVATED: *C. dependens* (syns. *C. triste, C. Warreana, C. livida, C. purpurascens*), greenish, suffused and marked purple-red, very variable, summer, autumn, Brazil; *Loddigesii*, yellowish-green or greenish, purple spotted and barred, usually summer, Brazil; *obtusata*, yellowish-white, purple spotted, lip white, tipped violet, spring; *saccata* (syn. *C. fuscolutea*), yellow or yellowish-green, lip saccate, spring, Brazil.

Cirrhopetalum—*Orchidaceae.* A large epiphytic genus, chiefly Eastern, but extending to Africa, Madagascar and Brazil. Closely allied to Bulbophyllum. In many species the flowers form a circle or part of a circle, the lower sepals elongated, turned completely over and, except at their bases and tips, joined together. Tips of upper sepal and petals frequently ornamented with filaments or hair-like tufts. Lip small, fleshy, mobile.

CULTURE: As for Bulbophyllum.

PROPAGATION: By division of plants in spring.

SPECIES CULTIVATED: A selection only—*C. appendiculatum*, flowers solitary, white and purple, tassels purple, lower sepals 6 in. long, late autumn, Bengal; *Amesianum*, old gold, single haired, lower sepals strawberry-red, various, Malaya, Philippines; *campanulatum*, yellow, lined brown-purple, fringed, lateral sepals rosy pink, deflexed, inflorescence small, pretty, Sumatra; *Collettii*, flowers 5, reddish with darker lines, tassels broad, lateral sepals 4 in. long, inflorescence fan-like, spring, summer, Burma; *Cumingii*, flowers 9 to 12, dark red, lateral sepals purplish, 1 in. long, various seasons, Philippines; *Makoyanum*, flowers, 10 or 12, circled, yellowish, lateral sepals 1¼ in. long, clear yellow, so volute as to form a tube, winter, spring, Malaya; *Mastersianum*, flowers, 6 to 10, yellow, suffused with red-brown, lateral sepals drooped; *Medusae* (syn. *Bulbophyllum Medusae*), flowers many, inflorescence globular, creamy white, lateral sepals with 4 to 5 in. long threads, summer, autumn, Malaya; *miniatum*, small, cinnabar-red, lateral sepals 2¼ in. long, summer, autumn, Annam; *ornatissimum*, flowers about five, spreading fan-like, yellowish, suffused red-purplish-brown with darker stripes, lateral sepals 3 to 5 in. long, autumn, Himalaya, Assam; *picturatum*, flowers about 10, greenish-yellow, red spotted, upper sepal with a single purple-knobbed hair, lower 2 in. long, various seasons, Burma; *psittacoides* (syn. *C. gracillimum*), flowers several, circled, crimson-red, lateral sepals curved, thread-like, autumn, Siam, Malacca; *robustum*, flowers about 10, greenish-yellow, lower sepals shaded tawny-red, 2 to 2½ in. long, summer, autumn, New Guinea; *Rothschildianum*, flowers 5, spreading fan-like, greenish-yellow, lined and suffused with red, hairs purple, lower sepals shading to purplish-red, 4 to 6 in. long, summer, various seasons, India; *refractum*, ' Windmill orchid ', greenish, purplish, bristled, lower sepals yellowish, reddish lined, narrowly oblong, often deciduous, winter, Burma; *Wendlandianum*, resembles *C. Collettii*, smaller, early summer, Burma.

Cirsium (Plumed Thistle)—*Compositae*.   Coarse prickly perennials, usually grown as biennials.

CULTURE: Soil, ordinary well drained.   Position, sunny borders.

PROPAGATION: By seed in light soil in temp. 60° to 70° in Feb. or Sept.

SPECIES CULTIVATED: *C. Casabonae*, purple, summer, 2 to 3 ft., S. Europe; *Diacantha* (syn. *Chamaepeuce Diacantha*), ' Fishbone Thistle ', purple, summer, leaves glabrous above, to 3 ft., Asia Minor; *muticum*, ' Swamp Thistle ', pink, 2 ft., summer, Medit.; *spinosissimum*, yellow, summer, 3 ft., Europe.

Cissus—*Vitaceae*.   Stove and greenhouse evergreen climbers.

CULTURE: Compost, turfy peat, loam, leaf-mould and sharp sand.   Position, pots or borders in greenhouse.   Temp. for *C. discolor*, March to Oct. 75° to 85°, Oct. to March 65° to 75°.   Others in a cool greenhouse.

PROPAGATION: By cuttings of young growth 2 in. long with heel of old wood, inserted in sandy soil under hand-glass in temp. 80°.

SPECIES CULTIVATED: *C. antarctica* (syn. *Vitis antarctica*), climbing shrub, Australia; *discolor*, strong climber, leaves velvety green mottled with white, stems coral, Java; *gongylodes* (syn. *C. pterophora*), green and red rope-like leafy branches with a terminal tuber, Brazil; *incisa* (syn. *Vitis incisa*), ' Marine Ivy ', long fleshy climber, U.S.A.   See also Rhoiocissus, Vitis.

Cistus (Rock Rose)—*Cistaceae*.   Hardy and half-hardy evergreen shrubs, mostly natives of S. Europe, but many are of garden origin.   First introduced mid-sixteenth century.

CULTURE: Hardy kinds in any soil but for preference all should have light well-drained soil and reasonably sheltered positions.   They are good rock-garden shrubs.   No pruning except removal of dead portions following severe winter.

PROPAGATION: By seeds in sandy soil in frame or unheated greenhouse in March, transplanting seedlings into small pots and planting outdoors in June; by cuttings 4 in. long in pots of sandy soil in Sept. in cold frame or greenhouse.

SPECIES CULTIVATED: *C. Aguilare*, white, brown blotches, 6 ft., strong, hybrid; *albidus*, rosy lilac, 5 ft., hardy; *corbariensis*, 3 ft., white, hardy; *crispus*, rosy red, 2 ft., comparatively hardy; *cyprius*, ' Gum Cistus ', chocolate blotches, 6 ft., hardy; *florentinus*, white, 3 ft., hybrid; *ladaniferus*, white, crimson blotches, 4 ft., *laurifolius*, hardiest white, 6 ft.; *lusitanicus*, white, carmine blotches, 3 ft., spreading; *Palinhaii*, white, June, 18 in., Portugal; *populifolius*, white, to 6 ft., var. *lasiocalyx*, pure white, 3 ft., hardy; *purpureus*, reddish purple, chocolate blotches, rather tender, 3 ft., var. Silver Pink, hardy, bright pink; *salvifolius*, white, 2 ft.; *Skanbergii*, almond pink, 4 ft., hybrid.

Citron, see *Citrus medica*; **-scented Geranium,** see *Pelargonium citriodorum*; **-scented Orchid,** see *Odontoglossum citrosum*.

Citrullus—*Cucurbitaceae*.   Tender climbing plant cultivated for its edible fruits. Requires a long warm season.   Rarely grown in England.

CULTURE: As for ordinary melon (*Cucumis melo*) except that shoots should not be pinched.

SPECIES CULTIVATED: *C. vulgaris*, ' Water Melon ', Trop. and S. Africa, var. *citroides*, citron or preserving melon.

Citrus—*Rutaceae*.   Sub-tropical, evergreen shrubs with fragrant flowers and thick-skinned, juicy, edible fruits.   Introduced here in the sixteenth century. See also Fortunella, Aegle, Poncirus.

CULTURE OF GREENHOUSE FRUITING PLANTS: Choose a lofty, well-lighted and well-ventilated greenhouse where the winter temp. can be maintained between

40° and 50°. Compost of equal parts turfy loam and well-rotted leaf-mould with a little burnt earth and charcoal added. Growth made early in the year; repot after the growth has been made. Position, in borders or in well-drained tubs or large pots. Syringe daily during the summer. Water each week Aug. to Dec. with soot water and never allow trees to become dry at the roots. Cut out any weak shoots and bare wood during the winter before growth begins. Fruits set in the spring do not ripen until the following season.

CULTURE OF DECORATIVE POT PLANTS: Seedling Citrus species make useful room plants with decorative, tough, leathery leaves that can survive a room atmosphere. *C. Limonia* and *C. taitensis* are suitable compact species. Use a standard potting compost. Put outside in summer so that the wood ripens thoroughly.

PROPAGATION: By seeds sown ½ in. deep in light soil in temp. 55° in March for producing stocks on which to graft choice kinds; cuttings inserted in small pots of sandy soil in July; layering in Oct.; budding in Aug.; grafting in March.

SPECIES CULTIVATED: *C. aurantifolia*, ' Lime ', to 10 ft., fruit thin-skinned, green, very acid, India; *Aurantium*, ' Sour or Seville Orange ', 20 ft., fruit loose skinned, orange, sour, with hollow core when ripe, Cochin-China, var. *myrtifolia*, short-jointed, narrow-leaved form useful as a pot plant; *Limonia*, ' Lemon ', to 15 ft. fruit thin skinned, pale yellow, oblong with terminal nipple, very sour, Asia; *maxima*, ' Shaddock ', ' Pummelo ', 15 to 30 ft., rind bitter, greenish-yellow, large, round, Malaya; *medica*, ' Citron ', 10 ft., fruit oval, 6 to 10 in. long, warty with scant acid pulp, used for candied peel, Asia; *nobilis*, var. *deliciosa*, ' Mandarin ' and ' Tangerine ', to 15 ft., fruit yellow or orange with loose peel and easily divided flesh, Cochin-China; *paradisi*, ' Grapefruit ', to 30 ft., fruit large, yellow, borne in clusters; *sinensis*, ' Common or Sweet Orange ', 15 ft., fruit orange, oval, with solid core and sweet pulp, China; *taitensis*, ' Otaheite Orange ', flowers pink outside, fragrant, fruit small, yellow, lemon shaped, sometimes grown as a pot plant, origin unknown.

Cladrastis (Yellow-wood)—*Leguminosae*. Hardy deciduous flowering shrubs. First introduced early nineteenth century.

CULTURE: Soil, ordinary. Position, open shrubberies, or singly on lawns. Plant, Oct. to Feb.

PROPAGATION: By seeds sown 1 in. deep in ordinary soil outdoors in March; cuttings of root inserted outdoors in spring.

SPECIES CULTIVATED: *lutea* (syn. *C. tinctoria*), white, July, 15 ft., United States; *C. sinensis;* blush-white, July, 40 to 60 ft., China. See also Maackia.

Clarkia—*Onagraceae*. Hardy annuals. First introduced early nineteenth century.

CULTURE: Soil, light, rich. Position, sunny borders or beds. Sow seeds ⅛ in. deep in April, May or June in rows or masses where plants are required to flower. Thin seedlings to 8 in. apart when 3 in. high. May be grown as a pot plant if sown in Sept., placed in small pots and grown in cool, airy conditions till spring. Pot on into loamy soil as required.

SPECIES CULTIVATED: *C. Breweri* (syn. *Eucharidum Breweri*), white, lilac and purple, summer, 8 in., California; *concinna*, purple, summer, 1 ft., California; *elegans*, rosy purple, July, 1 to 4 ft.; *pulchella*, various colours, single and double, 1 to 1½ ft. Numerous superior vars. described in trade lists, ranging in colour from purest white, through various tones of rose, pink, coral, to brilliant scarlet and crimson.

Clary, see *Salvia Sclarèa*.

Claytonia (Spring Beauty)—*Portulacaceae*. Little spring-blooming perennials. Some annual plants formerly included in this genus have been transferred to Montia. First introduced mid-eighteenth century.

CULTURE: Soil, damp, peat or bog. Position, rockery or moist, shady borders. Plant, Oct. or March.

PROPAGATION: By seed; offsets.

SPECIES CULTIVATED: *C. australasica*, white, creeping, summer, Australia, New Zealand; *caroliniana*, pink, May, 6 in., N. America; *virginica*, white, April, 6 in., N. America.

Clematis (Virgin's Bower)—*Ranunculaceae.* Greenhouse and hardy climbers and herbaceous perennials, deciduous or evergreen. The most valuable kinds for garden cultivation will be found amongst the named vars. and hybrids; it is important to remember to which class each belongs so that it may be correctly pruned.

CULTURE OF HARDY CLIMBING SPECIES: Soil, rich, deep, well-drained loam containing plenty of old mortar and decayed manure. Position, sunny trellises, arches, old tree stumps, arbours, etc., also in beds with shoots trained over surface. Plant in autumn or spring. Plant so that roots are shaded but train shoots out into the sun. Mulch liberally every spring with rich compost or old manure. Pruning: *C. montana, alpina, Flammula, Armandii, paniculata* and *tangutica* should have sufficient old growth removed to keep them within bounds; this should be done as soon as the flowers fade. *C. florida* and *C. patens* groups should be lightly thinned in Feb. *C. lanuginosa, Jackmanii* and *Viticella* groups should be pruned severely in Feb., either cutting the whole plant back to within a foot or so of the ground or else pruning each young growth to within one pair of buds of its base. *C. crispa, integrifolia, Pitcheri* and *Viorna* should have all growth that has been damaged by frost removed in Feb.

CULTURE IN POTS: Compost, two parts loam, one part of equal proportions of leaf-mould, decayed manure and sand. Plant in pots or tubs in spring. Train shoots up roof of cold or cool greenhouse or around wire trellis fixed in pots. Water freely March to Sept. Apply weak liquid manure occasionally in summer. Keep soil nearly dry in winter. Prune shoots to 3 or 4 in. from base early in the year.

CULTURE OF GREENHOUSE SPECIES: Compost, as above. Grow in pots or well-drained bed, planting in spring. Water freely during the summer, moderately in winter. Prune away weak growths and shorten rampant ones a little in Feb. Train shoots near roof. Temp., Sept. to March 45° to 55°, March to Sept. 55° to 65°. Syringe freely daily in summer.

CULTURE OF HERBACEOUS SPECIES: Soil, ordinary, rich. Position, sunny borders. Plant in autumn or spring. Top-dress in autumn with decayed manure. Prune shoots close to soil in autumn. Dwarf species best grown on sunny rockeries.

PROPAGATION: By seeds in cold frame in spring for hardy kinds, in heat in spring for greenhouse species, also by cuttings in temp. 75° in spring. Hardy climbers by grafting on roots of *C. Viticella* or *C. Vitalba* in heat in spring; layering shoots in summer; herbaceous kinds by division in autumn or cuttings of young shoots in frame in summer.

GREENHOUSE SPECIES CULTIVATED: *C. indivisa*, white, April, 15 to 20 ft., New Zealand, and var. *lobata*.

HARDY CLIMBING SPECIES CULTIVATED: *C. alpina*, 6 ft., blue, Europe; *Armandii*, vigorous evergreen, to 25 ft., white, China; *campaniflora*, vigorous, to 20 ft., lilac, small flowers in great profusion, Portugal; *Fargesii*, to 20 ft., white, China, and var. *Souliei*; *Flammula*, summer flowering, white, fragrant, Medit. area; *Jouiniana*, vigorous summer flowering with clusters of small bell-shaped flowers; *macropetala*, violet blue, 8 ft., May, China; *montana*, climber to 20 ft., white, May, Himalaya, and vars. *rubens*, clear pink, *Wilsonii*, later flowering; *orientalis*, 10 ft., yellow, slightly fragrant, Persia; *Rehderiana*, pale yellow, fragrant, China; *tangutica*, to 10 ft., yellow, N. China, var. *obtusiuscula*, yellow; *vedrariensis*, pale rose, hybrid; *Vitalba*, 'Traveller's Joy', 'Old Man's Beard', to 30 ft., greenish-white, Europe, etc.; *Viticella*, to 12 ft., blue, purple or rose-purple, S. Europe, Asia, vars. *alba*, white, *caerulea*, blue, *kermesina*, wine red.

HERBACEOUS SPECIES CULTIVATED: *C. Fremontii*, purple, summer, 1 ft., N. America; *heracleifolia* (syn. *C. tubulosa*), purple, summer, 2 ft., China, var. *Davidiana*, lavender-blue, fragrant; *integrifolia*, blue, Aug., 2 ft., S. Europe;

ochroleuca, yellow, summer, 2 ft., N. America; *recta*, white, fragrant, Aug., 2 ft., S. Europe; *stans*, white, Aug. to Sept., sometimes woody at base, Japan.

Clematoclethra—*Actinidiaceae.* Deciduous climbing shrubs.
SPECIES CULTIVATED: *C. actinidioides*, white to 20 ft., summer, W. China.

Clematopsis—*Ranunculaceae.* Half-hardy herbaceous perennials.
CULTURE: Good deep loam and full sun in large rock-garden or border.
PROPAGATION: By seeds sown as soon as ripe.
SPECIES CULTIVATED: *C. Stanleyi*, pink, 2 ft., summer, S. Africa.

Cleome—*Capparidaceae.* Stove annual. First introduced early nineteenth century.
CULTURE: Compost, equal parts loam, leaf-mould and sand. Position, pots in sunny stove. Water moderately at all times. Temp., 65° to 75°. Sow seeds $\frac{1}{16}$ in. deep in light soil in temp. 70° in March, transplanting seedlings into pots when 1 in. high.
SPECIES CULTIVATED: *C. spinosa* (syns. *C. pungens* and *C. gigantea*), 'Spider Flower', rose-purple or white, summer, 3 to 4 ft., Trop. America.

Clerodendron—*Verbenaceae.* Stove climbing and hardy flowering shrubs. First introduced late eighteenth century.
CULTURE: Compost, equal parts loam, peat, leaf-mould, decayed manure and silver sand. Pot, Feb. Prune shoots after flowering to within 2 or 3 in. of their base. Water freely March to Sept., moderately Sept. to Nov., after which keep dry. Temp., Oct. to Feb. 55° to 60°, Feb. to Oct. 65° to 85°. Plant hardy species in ordinary soil in sheltered, warm corners outdoors in Oct. or Nov.
PROPAGATION: By seeds sown $\frac{1}{8}$ in. deep in sandy soil in temp. 75° in March; cuttings of stems or shoots 3 in. long, inserted in sandy compost in temp. 70° to 75° in Jan., Feb. or March.
STOVE SPECIES CULTIVATED: *C. fragrans*, 'Glory Tree', white or blush, autumn, 6 ft., China; *myrmecophilum*, orange, 4 ft., Singapore; *speciosissimum* (syn. *C. fallax*), scarlet, Aug., 2 to 4 ft., Java; *speciosum*, dull red, summer, 10 ft., hybrid; *splendens*, scarlet, summer, 10 ft., Trop. Africa; *Thomsoniae* (syn. *C. Balfouri*), crimson, summer, 6 ft., Trop. Africa, and vars. *variegatum* and *magnificum*.
HARDY SPECIES CULTIVATED: *C. Bungei* (syn. *C. foetidum*), rose, Aug., 5 ft., China; *trichotomum*, white and red, summer, 10 to 12 ft., Japan, and var. *Fargesii*, white.

Clethra 'White Alder',—*Ericaceae.* Hardy and tender evergreen and deciduous flowering shrubs. First introduced early eighteenth century.
CULTURE: Compost, two parts loam, one part peat and sand. Position, front of shrubberies. Plant, Nov. to Feb.
PROPAGATION: By seeds sown $\frac{1}{4}$ in. deep outdoors in March, or in boxes of light soil in temp. 55° in Feb.; cuttings inserted in sandy soil in gentle heat in Aug.; layering in Oct. *C. alnifolia* suitable for forcing to flower in winter.
SPECIES CULTIVATED: *C. alnifolia*, 'Sweet Pepper Bush', white, Aug., 8 to 9 ft., Florida, var. *paniculata*, 4 ft., the hardiest; *acuminata*, white, Sept., 10 to 20 ft. Cent. U.S.A.; *barbinervis* (syn. *C. canescens*), white, Aug. 30 ft., China; *tomentosa*, white, Sept., 6 to 8 ft., South-eastern U.S.A.

Cleyera—*Theaceae* (or *Ternstroemiaceae*). Tender evergreen shrubs or small trees.
CULTURE: As for Eurya.
PROPAGATION: As for Eurya.
SPECIES CULTIVATED: *C. japonica* (syn. *Eurya ochracea*), creamy white, Japan, China.

Clianthus—*Leguminosae.* Greenhouse and half-hardy evergreen climbing shrubs or herbaceous perennials. First introduced early nineteenth century.
CULTURE: Compost, two parts fibrous loam, one part peat or leaf-mould with sharp sand, broken brick and charcoal added. Position, sunny greenhouse, in a

well-drained border, pots or hanging baskets. Pot, spring. Water carefully Oct. to March, moderately March to Oct.

PROPAGATION: By seeds sown in sandy soil in temp. 65° to 70°. Cuttings of side-shoots in sand with bottom heat. *C. Dampieri* does not thrive readily on its own roots, and is best grafted in the seedling state on to seedling stocks of *Colutea arborescens*, the latter being raised about ten days in advance of the seedling Clianthus, and established singly in small pots before grafting. Grafted plants are placed under a bell-glass in temp. 65° to 70° until union is complete and growth commences, after which they should gradually be inured to cooler conditions.

SPECIES CULTIVATED: *C. Dampieri*, ' Glory Pea ', red with black blotch, 2 to 3 ft., summer, Australia; *puniceus*, ' Parrot's Bill ', ' Red Kowhai ', scarlet, lobster-claw flowers and fern-like foliage, handsome, 3 to 6 ft., summer, New Zealand, and vars. *albus*, creamy-white, *roseus*, rosy-pink, and *magnificus*, a large form of the type species.

Cliff Brake, Fern see Pellaea.

Climbing Dahlia (*Hidalgoa Wercklei*); **-Fern** (*Lygodium scandens*); **-Fumitory** (*Adlumia fungosa*); **-Groundsel** (*Senecio scandens*); **-Hempweed** (*Mikania scandens*); **-Hydrangea** (*Schizophragma hydrangeoides*).

Clinopodium—*Labiatae*. Shrubs or herbs of the N. Temp. Zone. Some authors include this genus in Satureja.

CULTURE: Soil, ordinary. Position, sunny borders. Plant, Oct. or April.

PROPAGATION: By cuttings; division.

SPECIES CULTIVATED: *C. coccineum* (syn. *Satureja coccinea*), scarlet, to 3 ft., N. America; *dentatum*, white or purplish, to 2½ ft., N. America; *georgianum* (syn. *C. carolinianum*), white to pinkish-purple, to 2 ft., N. America.

Clintonia—*Liliaceae*. Hardy perennial herbs spreading by underground rhizomes.

CULTURE: Soil, sandy peat. Position, moist shady border. Plant, Oct. or March.

PROPAGATION: By division of roots in spring.

SPECIES CULTIVATED: *C. Andrewsiana*, rose-purple, April, berries blue, 1½ ft., California; *borealis*, yellow, May, berries blue, 1 ft., E.N. America; *umbellata*, white, spotted purple, May, berries black, 1 ft., N. America. Two plants sometimes known as Clintonia are properly *Downingia elegans* and *D. pulchella*.

Clitoria (Butterfly Pea)—*Leguminosae*. Stove evergreen flowe-ing climber. First introduced early eighteenth century.

CULTURE: Compost, equal parts peat, leaf-mould, loam and silver sand. Position, pots, tubs, or beds in light plant stove. Pot or plant, March. Water freely April to Sept., moderately afterwards. Temp., Oct. to March 55° to 65°, March to Oct. 70° to 80°.

PROPAGATION: By seeds sown ¼ in. deep in light soil in temp. 75° in March; cuttings of side shoots inserted in sandy peat in temp. 80° at any time.

SPECIES CULTIVATED: *C. heterophylla*, blue, July, 2 ft., Tropics; *ternatea*, blue, July, 10 to 12 ft., E. Indies. See also Centrosema.

Clivia (Kafir Lily)—*Amaryllidaceae*. Greenhouse evergreen flowering plants. Fleshy rooted. Formerly known by the generic name of Imantophyllum. First introduced early nineteenth century.

CULTURE: Compost, two-thirds good loam, one-third decayed manure and sand. Position, sunny, close to glass in greenhouse. Pot, Feb. Water freely March to Sept., moderately other times. Temp., March to Sept. 60° to 65°, Sept. to March 45° to 55°.

PROPAGATION: By seeds sown in light soil in temp. 75° in March; division of roots at potting time.

SPECIES CULTIVATED: *C. cyrtanthiflora*, orange, winter and early spring, hybrid; *Gardenii*, orange-yellow, Dec. to Feb., 18 in., S. Africa; *kewensis*, canary-yellow, spring, 2 ft., hybrid; *miniata*, scarlet and yellow, spring and early summer, 1 to 1½ ft., Natal; *nobilis*, red and yellow, May to July, 1 to 1½ ft., S. Africa. There are numerous vars. of *C. miniata* which are superior to the parent species.

Clove Pink or **Gilliflower,** see *Dianthus Caryophyllus*; **-Tree,** see *Eugenia aromatica*.

Clover, see Trifolium.

Club Lily, see Kniphofia; **-Moss,** see *Lycopodium clavatum*; **-Rush,** see Scirpus.

Cluster Pine, see *Pinus Pinaster*.

Clytostoma (Trumpet-flower)—*Bignoniaceae*. Greenhouse climbing plants, formerly included in the genus Bignonia. First introduced early nineteenth century.

CULTURE: Compost, two parts fibrous loam, one part peat, or leaf-soil and silver sand. Pot, Feb. to April. Position, sunny greenhouse, in bed or border with good drainage, but root production must be restricted to 3 ft. square for one plant. Prune away one-third of strong shoots and two-thirds of weak shoots in February. Water freely April to Sept., very little at other times. Shade is not necessary. Temp., Oct. to March 50° to 55°, March to Oct. 55° to 65°.

PROPAGATION: By cuttings of young shoots 3 in. long inserted in well-drained pots of sandy soil in temp. 65° to 70° in April.

SPECIES CULTIVATED: *C. binatum* (syn. *Bignonia purpurea*), mauve, May to June, 10 ft., Uruguay; *callistegioides* (syn. *Bignonia speciosa*), lavender, May, 10 to 15 ft., Brazil, Argentine.

Cnicus—*Compositae*. Thistle-like annual.

CULTURE: Soil, ordinary. Position, rock or wild garden, preferably sunny.

PROPAGATION: By seed.

SPECIES CULTIVATED: *C. benedictus*, ‘ Blessed Thistle ’, yellow, 1¼ to 2 ft., Britain, Medit. Region and Caucasus.

Cobaea—*Polemoniaceae*. Greenhouse and half-hardy climbing perennial, usually grown as an annual. First introduced late eighteenth century.

CULTURE: Compost, mainly loam, with small additions of leaf-mould and silver sand. Position, pots or beds in greenhouse, or against south or south-west walls, arches or trellises outdoors in summer. Pot, March. Plant outdoors in June. Temp., Sept. to March 50° to 55°, March to Sept. 60° to 70°. Water freely in summer, moderately other times.

PROPAGATION: Ordinary species by seeds sown ½ in. deep in light soil in temp. 60° to 65° in March; variegated species by cuttings of young side shoots inserted in sandy peat in temp. 65° in March or April.

SPECIES CULTIVATED: *C. scandens*, ‘ Cups and Saucers ’, purple, summer, 10 to 30 ft., Mexico, var. *aureo-marginata*, leaves variegated with yellow.

Cobnut, see *Corylus Avellana*.

Cobweb Houseleek, see *Sempervivum arachnoideum*.

Cochlioda—*Orchidaceae*. A small epiphytic genus. Differing from Odontoglossum chiefly by two stigmatic surfaces. Species cross with Odontoglossum, Oncidium, Miltonia, etc. *C. Noezliana* has been of great value to the hybridist and is responsible for the brilliant colours in Odontiodas. Habit that of an Odontoglossum, usually darker.

CULTURE: Compost, temps., etc., as for Odontoglossums.

PROPAGATION: By division of the plants in spring.

SPECIES CULTIVATED: *O. Noezliana*, brilliant orange-scarlet, winter, spring, Peru; *rosea* (syn. *Odontoglossum roseum*), rose-carmine, winter and spring, Peru; *sanguinea* (syn. *Mesospinidium sanguineum*), rose-pink, scape often branched, autumn, Ecuador; *vulcanica* (syn. *Mesospinidium vulcanicum*), dark rose-red to purplish, autumn, spring, Peru.

Cockscomb, see *Celosia cristata*.

Cocksfoot Grass, see Dactylis.

Cocoa Tree, see *Theobroma Cacao.*

Coconut Palm, see *Cocos nucifera.*

Cocos—*Palmae.* Stove palm producing the coconut of commerce. First introduced late seventeenth century. Some species formerly included in the genus have been transferred to Arecastrum.

CULTURE: Compost, two parts loam, equal parts peat and sand. Position, pots in shady stove. Pot, March. Water freely March to Oct, moderately at other times. Temp., March to Sept. 70° to 85°, Sept. to March 60° to 70°.

PROPAGATION: By seeds sown 1 in. deep in light soil in temp. 85° at any time.

SPECIES CULTIVATED: *C. nucifera,* ' Coconut Palm ', 40 to 100 ft., Tropics.

Codiaeum (Croton)—*Euphorbiaceae.* Stove evergreen shrubs grown extensively in hothouses for their coloured ornamental foliage. First introduced early nineteenth century.

CULTURE: Compost, two parts rich loam, one part peat and sand. Position, pots in stove close to the glass. Pot, March. Water freely March to Sept., moderately afterwards. Temp., Oct. to March 55° to 65°, March to Oct. 70° to 85°.

PROPAGATION: By cuttings of the ends of shoots inserted singly in 2 in. pots filled with sandy soil in temp. 75° at any time; stem-rooting in March or April.

SPECIES CULTIVATED: *C. variegatum,* leaves yellow and green, 3 to 10 ft., Malaya, and many vars. including *Andreanum,* broad yellow leaves, *Bergmanii,* broad creamy-yellow leaves blotched with green, *Chelsonii,* orange, red and crimson, *Evansianum,* green, yellow, crimson and scarlet, *Hawkeri,* creamy white and green, *illustre,* green and yellow, *interruptum,* yellow with red midrib, *Johannis,* green and yellow, *Laingii,* green, red and salmon, *picturatum,* green, yellow and red, *tricolor,* green, golden yellow and cream, *Warrenii,* green and orange-carmine, *Williamsii,* green, crimson and magenta, *Weismannii,* green, crimson and magenta.

Codlins and Cream, see *Epilobium hirsutum* and *Narcissus incomparabilis.*

Codonopsis—*Campanulaceae.* Hardy perennial herbs.

CULTURE: Soil, ordinary good. Position, sunny borders. Plant, autumn or spring.

PROPAGATION: By seeds sown in cold frame in spring, planting out seedlings in June; cuttings in autumn.

SPECIES CULTIVATED: *C. Bulleyana,* pale blue, June, 6 in., Tibet, Yunnan; *clematidea* (syn. *Glossocomia clematidea*), white and blue, summer, 3 ft., Cent. W. Asia; *convolvulaceae,* light lavender, climber, China to Upper Burma, var. *Forrestii* (syn. *C. tibetica*), larger flowers; *meleagris,* greenish-white outside, dull purple inside, May to June, semi-climbing, Yunnan; *mollis,* bluish-lavender, 3 ft., S. Tibet; *ovata,* blue, summer, 1 ft., Himalaya; *rotundifolia,* blue and yellow, July to Aug., 1½ ft., W. Himalaya; *Tangshen,* blue, June, semi-climbing, China; *vinciflora,* lilac, climber, Szechwan, Tibet, Himalaya; *viridiflora,* greenish-blue, summer, semi-climbing, E. Asia.

Coelia—*Orchidaceae.* A small epiphytic genus. Pseudo-bulbs globose, clustered. Flowers from their base in short, erect, bracteate spikes, small, usually densely set.

CULTURE: Temps. and compost as for Lycastes, but the winter rest less severe.

PROPAGATION: By division of plants in spring.

SPECIES CULTIVATED: *C. bella,* flowers few, large, creamy-white, magenta tipped, autumn, winter, Mexico; *macrostachya,* rose-red, height 12 to 18 in., C. America; *triptera* (syn. *C. Baueriana*), greenish-white, fragrant, summer, Mexico.

Coelogyne—*Orchidaceae.* A large epiphytic genus. Species vary greatly, small to large. Flowers solitary in some, many in others. The petals filiform in some, the lip usually crested. Spikes usually produced from the centres of the new growths, in some as the pseudo-bulbs mature.

CULTURE: Compost, three parts of cut osmunda fibre and one part, or more, sphagnum moss. Pans for the smaller growing, pots for the stronger. Baskets for those with long hanging spikes.

PROPAGATION: By division of the plants when repotting in spring. All temp. should rise higher in the summer.

SPECIES CULTIVATED: A selection only. Species requiring a decided rest and winter temp. about 50° or lower on occasion. *C. corymbosa*, white, lip white, yellow, red-marked, summer, N. India; *Mossiae*, white, lip yellow-marked, spring, Nilgiri Hills, S. India; *nervosa*, white, orange-brown keels on lip, summer, N. India; *nitida* (syn. *C. ocellata*), white, with yellow, red-margined spots in lip, spring, N. India; *ochracea*, very similar, pseudo-bulbs nearly oblong, spring, Khasia; *odoratissima*, white, lip with lemon-yellow stains, small, fragrant, early summer, Nilgiri.

Species requiring a winter temperature of 55° to 60° and more frequent watering: *C. barbata*, white, lip with brown-black hairs, winter, Assam; *cristata*, flowers pendent, white with 5 yellow keels on lip, fragrant, Feb. to April, Himalaya; *fuliginosa*, flowers 1 to 3, whitish, suffused reddish-brown, lip with blackish hairs, requires a raft, early winter, Himalaya, etc.; *Gardneriana* (syn. *Neogyne Gardneriana*), flowers pendent, white, winter, Nepal; *Lawrenceana*, flowers 1 to 2. large, tawny yellow, lip orange, sienna-brown, white, spike erect, early spring, Indo-China; *Mooreana*, large, white, with yellow hairs on lip, spring or autumn, Annam; *pulchella*, small, several, white, lip white, chocolate brown and black-brown, spring.

The following should have a winter temp. of 60° to 65°: *C. lentiginosa*, small, yellow, red-brown, orange-brown, summer, Burma; *Massangeana*, yellowish brown and chocolate brown, various, Malaya, Java; *Micholitzii*, curious, white, lip with a large, raised, corrugated, chocolate-brown process, summer, New Guinea; *Sanderiana*, white, and yellow, large, spring, Sunda Isles; *speciosa*, tawny-brown, lip yellow, white, blackish-brown with crested keels, various seasons, Malaya, Java.

For the following, winter temp. should be 70° and a moist atmosphere is needed: *C. asperata*, whitish, lip yellowish, red-brown and orange, spring, summer, Borneo, E. Indies; *Dayana*, ochre-yellow, lip white and brown, spikes pendent, long, spring, summer, Borneo; *Mayeriana*, flowers 3 to 5, green, lip with blackish markings, suitable for a tree-fern stem, late summer, Singapore; *pandurata*, large, green, lip with blackish asperities and toothed keels, place on raft, various seasons, Borneo; *tomentosa*, orange-red or brown-orange, lip shaded with white, spikes pendent, redly tomentose, summer, Borneo, Malaya; *Veitchii*, white, summer, New Guinea.

Coffea (Coffee Tree)—*Rubiaceae*. Stove evergreen shrubs. Fruit, a small reddish, fleshy berry, containing two seeds enclosed in parchment-like shell which are the ' coffee beans ' of commerce. First introduced late seventeenth century.

CULTURE: Compost, two parts turfy loam, one part leaf-mould and sand. Position, pots in moist plant stove. Pot, March. Temp., March to Sept. 75° to 85°, Sept. to March 60° to 70°. Water freely in summer, moderately other times.

PROPAGATION: By seeds sown ½ in. deep in light soil in temp. 85° in March; cuttings of firm shoots inserted in sandy soil under bell-glass in temp. 85° in summer.

SPECIES CULTIVATED: *C. arabica*, ' Arabian Coffee ', white, fragrant, Sept., 10 to 15 ft., Arabia; *hybrida*, ' Tampis Coffee ', hybrid; *liberica*, ' Liberian Coffee ', white, fragrant, 15 to 20 ft., Trop. Africa.

Coffee Tree, see Coffea.

Coix—*Gramineae*. Half-hardy ornamental flowering annual grass. First introduced late sixteenth century.

CULTURE: Soil, light, rich. Position, sunny border outdoors.

PROPAGATION: By seeds sown ½ in. deep in light soil in temp. 55° to 60° in March, transplanting seedlings outdoors in May; or similar depth outdoors in April where plants are to flower.

SPECIES CULTIVATED: *C. Lacryma-Jobi*, 'Job's Tears', 2 to 3 ft., grey pearly seeds chief attraction, Trop. Asia, var. *aurea zebrina*, variegated form.

Colchicum (Autumn Crocus)—*Liliaceae.* Hardy bulbous flowering plants.

CULTURE: Soil, light sandy loam, enriched with decayed manure or leaf-mould. Position, moist beds or rockeries, shrubbery borders, or lawns near shade of trees. Plant bulbs 3 in. deep and 3 in. apart in July or Aug. Foliage dies down in June and July, and does not reappear until after plant has flowered.

PROPAGATION: By seeds sown ⅛ in. deep in bed of fine soil outdoors in Aug. or Sept., or in pans or boxes of similar soil in cold frame at same time, transplanting seedlings 3 in. apart when two years old; division of bulbs in Aug. Seedling bulbs do not flower until four or five years old.

SPECIES CULTIVATED: *C. agrippinum*, rose-purple and white, autumn, 3 to 4 in., S. Europe; *atropurpureum*, purplish-red, autumn, 3 to 4 in., Europe; *autumnale*, ' Meadow Saffron ', purple, Sept., 8 in., Europe (Britain), and numerous vars.; *Bornmuelleri* (syn. *C. speciosum* var. *giganteum*), rosy lilac, 8 to 12 in., Asia Minor; *byzantinum*, rose and purple, Sept., 6 in., Greece; *Decaisnei*, pale rose, Oct. to Nov., Mt. Lebanon; *giganteum*, soft rose and white, autumn, hybrid; *speciosum*, lilac-purple, Sept., Caucasus, and var. *album*, white; *variegatum*, rose and purple, Sept., 6 in., E. Europe and Asia Minor.

Coleus—*Labiatae.* Stove perennials with ornamental foliage. First introduced mid-eighteenth century.

CULTURE: Compost, two parts turfy loam, one part well-decayed manure, leaf-mould and little sand. Position, pots in stove in winter, greenhouse in summer. Pot, Feb. or March, pressing soil firmly in pots. Temp., Sept. to March 60° to 70°, March to June 75° to 85°, June to Sept. 65° to 75°. Water very moderately Sept. to March, freely afterwards. Ornamental-leaved kinds require to have points of their shoots pinched off in early stage of their growth to ensure dwarf or well-shaped plants.

PROPAGATION: By seeds sown 1/16 in. deep in light soil in temp. 75° in Feb., March or April; cuttings of young shoots inserted in light soil or coconut-fibre refuse at any time; grafting in spring.

SPECIES CULTIVATED: *C. Autranii*, lavender, winter-flowering, 3 ft., Abyssinia; *barbatus*, blue, 1 to 2 ft., India, Africa; *Blumei*, white and purple, leaves bronzered, 1 to 3 ft., Java, and var. *Verschaffeltii*, *Frederici*, purplish-blue, winter-flowering, 1¼ to 2 ft., Angola; *thyrsoideus*, ' Winter-flowering Coleus ', blue, Jan. to April, 3 ft., Trop. Africa.

Colletia—*Rhamnaceae.* Half-hardy evergreen shrubs. Branches armed with formidable spines. First introduced early nineteenth century.

CULTURE: Soil, loamy. Position, sheltered, well-drained borders in S. of England. Plant in Oct.

PROPAGATION: By cuttings of firm shoots 6 in. long, inserted in well-drained pots of sandy soil in cold frame in Aug. or Sept.

SPECIES CULTIVATED: *C. armata*, white, Sept., bodkin-like spines, 10 ft., Chile; *cruciata*, ' Anchor Plant ', white, autumn, flattish, triangular spines, occasionally bodkin-like, 4 to 10 ft., Uruguay; *infausta* (syn. *C. horrida*), white, March, bodkin-like spines, 10 ft., Peru.

Collinsia—*Scrophulariaceae.* Hardy annuals. First introduced early nineteenth century.

CULTURE: Soil, ordinary. Position, open beds or borders. One of the easiest of all annuals to grow.

PROPAGATION: By seeds sown ⅛ in. deep outdoors in Sept., March or April where plants are required to flower. Thin seedlings to 6 in. apart when 2 in. high.

SPECIES CULTIVATED: *C. bartsiifolia*, white, marked lilac, 9 in., California; *bicolor*, purple and white, summer, 1 ft., California, var. *alba*, white; *grandiflora*, purple and blue, June, 18 in., N.W. America; *verna*, white and blue, May, 1 ft., N. America.

Collomia—*Polemoniaceae.* Hardy annuals. First introduced early nineteenth century.

CULTURE: Soil, ordinary. Position, open beds or borders.

PROPAGATION: By seeds sown ⅛ in. deep outdoors in Sept., March or April where plants are required to flower. Thin seedlings to 3 in. apart when 2 in. high.

SPECIES CULTIVATED: *biflora* (syn. *C. coccinea*), red, June, 18 in., Chile; *grandiflora*, buff or salmon, summer, 18 in., California.

Colocasia (West Indian Kale)—*Araceae.* Stove herbaceous plants with perennial tuberous roots, some of which are edible. Leaves, shield-like, heart or egg-shaped, deep green. First introduced mid-sixteenth century.

CULTURE: Compost, equal parts turfy loam, peat, leaf-mould and silver sand. Position, well-drained pots in shady plant stove. Plant moderately firmly in pots just large enough to take tubers in Feb. or March; transfer to larger pots in April or May. Water moderately Feb. to April and Sept. to Nov., freely April to Sept.; keep quite dry Nov. to Feb. Temp., Feb. to Sept. 70° to 80°, Sept. to Nov. 65° to 75°, Nov. to Feb. 55° to 65°.

PROPAGATION: By dividing the tubers in Feb. or March.

SPECIES CULTIVATED: *C. antiquorum*, ' Egyptian Taro ' or ' Culcas ', 2 to 4 ft., E. Indies, and vars. *illustris*, *Fontanesii* and *euchlora*; *esculenta*, 'Dasheen', 'Taro Root', 2 to 3 ft., Pacific Isles.

Columbine, see Aquilegia.

Columnea—*Gesneriaceae.* Stove evergreen trailing shrubs. First introduced mid-eighteenth century.

CULTURE: Compost, equal parts fibrous peat, sphagnum moss and charcoal. Position, hanging baskets. Plant, March. Water freely in summer, moderately in winter. Temp., Sept. to March 60° to 70°, March to Sept. 70° to 80°.

PROPAGATION: By cuttings of firm shoots 3 in. long, in pots of above compost mixed with sand, in temp. 85° Feb.

SPECIES CULTIVATED: *C. Banksii*, scarlet, May, hybrid; *gloriosa*, scarlet and yellow, June, Costa Rica, var. *purpurascens*, scarlet and yellow, purple foliage, June; *magnifica*, scarlet, May, Costa Rica; *microphylla*, scarlet and yellow, June, Costa Rica; *Schiedeana*, scarlet, summer, Mexico.

Colutea (Bladder Senna)—*Leguminosae.* Hardy deciduous flowering shrubs. First introduced mid-sixteenth century.

CULTURE: Soil, ordinary. Position, open or shady shrubberies, banks, etc. Plant, Oct. to Feb. Prune, Nov., simply cutting away weak shoots and shortening straggling ones, or may be restricted in size by annual hard pruning in spring. *C. arborescens* is the most popular species and will grow in almost any soil and situation, yellow flowers and inflated bladder-like pods.

PROPAGATION: By seeds sown 1 in. deep outdoors in Oct. or March; cuttings of firm shoots inserted in sandy soil outdoors in Oct.

SPECIES CULTIVATED: *C. arborescens*, yellow, Aug., 10 ft., S. Europe; *istria*, coppery yellow, May to Aug., 3 to 4 ft., Asia Minor; *media*, brownish red, summer, 8 to 10 ft., hybrid; *orientalis* (syn. *C. cruenta*), coppery red, June to Sept., 4 to 6 ft., Orient.

Combretum (Caffer Butter-shrub)—*Combretaceae.* Stove evergreen climbers. First introduced early nineteenth century.

CULTURE: Compost, two parts loam, one part peat and sand. Position, pots, tubs or borders in plant stove, shoots trained to pillars or roof. Pot, March. Prune side shoots to within 2 in. of base after flowering and cut away all weak ones. Water freely March to Sept., moderately afterwards. Syringe daily March to Aug. Temp., March to Sept. 70° to 85°, Sept. to March 55° to 65°.

PROPAGATION: By cuttings of side shoots 3 in. long, removed with slight portion of stem attached, and inserted in well-drained pot of sandy soil in temp. 85° in summer.

SPECIES CULTIVATED: *C. coccineum*, scarlet, autumn, 20 ft., Madagascar; *grandiflorum*, scarlet, 5 ft., Trop. Africa; *racemosum*, white, spring, Trop. Africa.

Commelina—*Commelinaceae*. Greenhouse and hardy herbaceous perennials. First introduced mid-eighteenth century.

CULTURE OF GREENHOUSE SPECIES: Compost, equal parts peat, loam, leaf-mould and sand. Position, pots in sunny greenhouse. Pot, March. Water freely March to Sept., very little afterwards. Temp., March to Sept. 55° to 65°, Sept. to March 45° to 50°.

CULTURE OF HARDY SPECIES: Soil, light, rich. Position, warm, sheltered, well-drained bed or border. Plant fleshy roots in April. Protect roots during winter on light soils with thick layer of ashes or manure. Lift roots in cold districts in Sept. and store away similarly to dahlias in frost-proof place, replanting in April.

PROPAGATION: By seeds sown ¼ in. deep in light soil in temp. 75° in March, transplanting seedlings outdoors in May to flower in Aug.; division in April.

GREENHOUSE SPECIES CULTIVATED: *C. africana*, yellow, May to Oct., 1 to 3 ft., S. Africa; *elliptica*, white, July, 2 ft., Mexico.

HARDY SPECIES CULTIVATED: *C. coelestis*, ' Day Flower ', ' Blue Spiderwort ', blue, July, 18 in., Mexico, var. *alba*, white; *tuberosa*, blue, June to July, 1 to 1½ ft., Mexico.

Comparettia—*Orchidaceae*. An epiphytic genus, small growing. Flowers brightly coloured on spikes, produced from the base of the small pseudo-bulbs. The bases of the connate lower sepals are prolonged into a spur, concealing a two-horned spur formed by the base of the lip.

CULTURE: Compost, three parts of osmunda fibre, cut fine, and one and a half parts of sphagnum. Small pans which can be suspended in a tilted position as they require water in winter, but not too frequently, and at all times it should pass away quickly. The species are so distributed that temps. require consideration. 60° is sufficient in winter and but little more in summer for those from cooler habitats. A moist atmosphere should be maintained.

PROPAGATION: By division of plants in March.

SPECIES CULTIVATED: *C. coccinea*, scarlet and orange, Aug., Brazil; *falcata*, rose-purple, autumn, Brazil to Peru, Costa Rica; *macroplectron*, rose and purple, spur 2 in. long or more, autumn, New Grenada; *speciosa*, orange and cinnabar-red, lip yellow outside, summer, Ecuador.

Comptonia—*Myricaceae*. Hardy deciduous shrub. First introduced early eighteenth century.

CULTURE: Soil, peaty loam. Position, shady borders or shrubberies. Plant, Nov.

PROPAGATION: By layers in early spring.

SPECIES CULTIVATED: *C. peregrina* (syn. *C. asplenifolia*, *Myrica asplenifolia*), ' Sweet Fern ', elegant fern-like foliage, 2 to 4 ft., Eastern N. America.

Conandron—*Gesneriaceae*. Hardy herbaceous perennial. First introduced late nineteenth century.

CULTURE: Soil, peat and loam. Position, fissures of moist, sheltered rockery. Plant, March or April. Protect in severe winters with covering of dry litter.

PROPAGATION: By seeds sown in well-drained pots of sandy peat and just covered with fine mould, in cold frame or greenhouse March or April; division of plant in March.

SPECIES CULTIVATED: *C. ramondioides*, lilac and yellow, summer, 8 to 12 in., Japan, var. *leucanthum*, white.

Cone Plant, see Conophytum.

Confederate Vine see *Antigonon leptopus*.

Coniogramme—*Polypodiaceae*. Greenhouse evergreen ferns.

CULTURE: Compost, one part fibrous peat, one part leaf-mould and loam, one part silver sand, charcoal and coarsely ground bones. Position, well-drained pots.

Pot, Feb. or March. Temp., Sept. to March 45° to 50°, March to Sept. 55° to 65°.
PROPAGATION: By spores; division.
SPECIES CULTIVATED: *C. japonica* (syn. *Gymnogramma japonica*), ' Bamboo Fern ',
fronds to 2 ft. long and 1 ft. wide, finely toothed, Japan, Formosa.

Conophytum (Cone Plant)—*Aizoaceae.* Greenhouse succulent plants.
CULTURE: Compost, six parts sharp sand, four parts rich loam, one part each
mortar rubble and brick dust. Position, well-drained pots in sunny greenhouse
or window, or bed on greenhouse staging. Plant or pot, August. Keep fairly
moist during growing period, usually Aug. to Sept., very little water Oct. to
April, quite dry May to July. Temp., Oct. to Mar. 55° to 60°, Mar. to Oct. 60°
and over.
PROPAGATION: By seeds or cuttings; as Lithops.
SPECIES CULTIVATED: *C. altile* (syn. *Mesembryanthemum altile*), purple, Aug. to
Oct., S.W. Africa; *bilobum* (syn. *M. bilobum*), yellow, Aug. to Oct., S.W. Africa;
gratum (syn. *M. gratum*), magenta, Aug. to Oct., S.W. Africa; *minutum* (syn. *M.
minutum, M. thecatum*), mauve, Aug. to Oct., S.W. Africa; *pallidum* (syn. *M.
pallidum*), purple, Sept., S.W. Africa; *tabulare*, yellow, Aug. to Oct., S.W.
Africa; *truncatellum*, yellow, Aug. to Oct., S.W. Africa.

Convallaria (Lily of the Valley; May Lily)—*Liliaceae.* Hardy herbaceous
perennial.
OUTDOOR CULTURE: Compost, equal parts loam, leaf-mould, decayed manure
and sharp sand. Position, beds or borders under shade of trees, high walls or
fences for general culture; south border for early flowering. Plant single crowns
2 or 3 in. apart, with points just below surface, in Sept. and Oct. Lift and replant
every four years, always planting largest crowns by themselves. Mulch bed
annually in Feb. with decayed manure. Apply liquid manure once a week, May
to Sept., to beds more than a year old.
POT CULTURE: Compost, equal parts good soil and leaf-mould. Plant one
clump or a dozen single crowns in a 6 in. pot, well drained, in Oct. or Nov. Place
inverted pot over crowns and stand in cold frame or under greenhouse stage until
Jan., then remove into heat, or allow to bloom naturally in greenhouse or window.
Water only when soil needs moisture in winter, freely when growth begins.
FORCING: Place single crowns close together in shallow boxes, with coconut-
fibre refuse between roots, and put boxes in temp. 80° to 85°. Cover points of
crowns with inverted box or thick layer of moss until flowers appear, then remove.
After forcing, crowns of no value for flowering again, therefore discard them.
Retarded roots flower quickly without much forcing.
PROPAGATION: By seeds sown ¼ in. deep in light soil outdoors in March;
division of crowns Sept. or Oct.
SPECIES CULTIVATED: *C. majalis*, white, spring, 6 in., Europe (Britain), etc.,
var. *Fortunei*, larger flowers, *rosea*, pink flowered.

Convolvulus (Bindweed)—*Convolvulaceae.* Hardy annual and perennial plants
mostly climbing or trailing.
CULTURE: Soil, ordinary, rich. Position, dwarf kinds in open beds and borders;
tall kinds at base of arbours, walls or trunks of trees, etc. *C. Cneorum* and *C.
mauritanicus* in sunny rock gardens. Plant perennials in March. Sow annuals in
April where required and thin seedlings to 5 in. apart when 2 in. high.
PROPAGATION: By seed outdoors in March; division of roots in March or April.
SPECIES CULTIVATED: *C. althaeoides*, rose-pink, June to Aug., 1 to 2 ft., Medit.
Region; *aureus superbus*, usually treated as annual, golden-yellow, summer, 4 to
5 ft., origin uncertain; *Cantabrica*, pale rose, June to Aug., 1 ft., Europe; *Cne-
orum*, white, tinged pink, summer, 2 to 3 ft., S. Europe; *mauritanicus*, blue, July,
trailing, S. Europe; *tricolor*, annual, various, summer, 1 ft., S. Europe. See also
Calystegia and Ipomoea.

Cooperia—*Amaryllidaceae.* Half-hardy, night-flowering, bulbous plants.
CULTURE: Compost, equal parts peat, loam and leaf-mould. Position, pots in

cool greenhouse or cold frame. Pot, Jan. or Feb. Water moderately until growth begins, then give freely; discontinue watering after Sept. and keep soil dry during winter. Temp., Sept. to Feb. 40° to 45°, Feb. to May 50° to 55°, May to Sept. 55° to 65°.

PROPAGATION: By offsets in Feb.

SPECIES CULTIVATED: *C. Drummondii*, ' Evening Star ', white, Aug., 9 in., Texas; *pedunculata*, white, Aug., 8 in., Mexico.

Coprosma—*Rubiaceae*. Rather tender evergreen shrubs.

CULTURE: Compost, two parts sandy loam, one part leaf-mould and sand. Position, pots in cool greenhouse. Repot, March. Prune straggling shoots into shape in March. Water moderately in winter, freely in summer. Temp., Sept. to March 40° to 45°, March to Sept. 55° to 65°. Hardy in sheltered positions outdoors S. of England.

PROPAGATION: By cuttings removed in March, with small portion of old wood attached, and inserted in well-drained pots of sandy soil in temp. 85° under bell-glass.

SPECIES CULTIVATED: *C. acerosa*, almost prostrate, blue translucent berries; *Baueri*, ' Tasmanian Currant ', leaves green, 10 to 25 ft., New Zealand, Norfolk Islands, var. *variegata*, leaves edged with yellow, 3 ft.; *Petriei*, prostrate, purple berries, New Zealand; *rigida*, yellow, 15 ft., New Zealand.

Coptis (Goldthread; Mouth Root)—*Ranunculaceae*. Hardy evergreen bog plants. First introduced late eighteenth century.

CULTURE: Soil, moist peat. Position, shady. Plant, Oct. or March.

PROPAGATION: By seeds sown $\frac{1}{16}$ in. deep in pans of fine sandy peat in shady, cold frame in March; division of roots in Oct. or March.

SPECIES CULTIVATED: *C. asplenifolia*, white, spring, 3 to 4 in., Japan; *quinquefolia*, white, spring, 2 to 3 in.; *trifolia*, white, April, 1 ft., N. Hemisphere.

Coral Vine, see Antigonon.

Corallita, see *Antigonon leptopus.*

Corallodiscus—*Gesneriaceae*. Evergreen, perennial, rock-garden plants at one time included in Didissandra.

CULTURE: Best grown in alpine house or cold frame in soil and under conditions similar to those required by Ramonda.

PROPAGATION: By seeds sown in gentle heat; leaf cuttings.

SPECIES CULTIVATED: *C. Forrestii*, white or deep blue, 2 to 3 in., early summer, Yunnan; *Kingianus*, violet blue, 6 in., summer, Himalaya; *lanuginosus*, lilac, 6 in., early summer, Himalaya.

Corchorus, see *Kerria japonica.*

Cordyline—*Liliaceae*. Greenhouse plants. Allied to and often called Dracaena. First introduced early nineteenth century.

CULTURE: Compost, two parts peat, one part loam and sand. Position, pots in greenhouse. Repot, March. Water moderately Oct. to March, freely afterwards. Temp., March to Sept. 55° to 65°, Sept. to March 45° to 50°.

PROPAGATION: By seeds sown 1 in. deep in pots of light soil in temp. 85° in March; cuttings of main stems cut into lengths of 1 in. and partially inserted horizontally in pots of sandy soil in March; cuttings of fleshy roots inserted 1 in. deep in pots of sandy soil, in March or April in temp. 75° to 80°; stem rooting in March or April; offsets inserted in 2 in. pots of sandy soil at any time.

SPECIES CULTIVATED: *C. australis* (syn. *Dracaena australis*), leaves broad and green, 15 to 40 ft., New Zealand; *Banksii*, ribbon-like leaves, 8 to 15 ft., New Zealand; *indivisa*, green, narrow, New Zealand; *stricta* (syn. *C. congesta*), leaves green and narrow, 6 to 10 ft., Australia; *terminalis* (syn. *Dracaena Baptistii*), leaves broad and green, 3 to 10 ft., E. Himalaya, China and E. Indies. There are many vars. with coloured or variegated leaves. See also Dracaena.

Coreopsis (Calliopsis; Tickseed)—*Compositae*. Hardy annual and perennial herbaceous plants. First introduced late seventeenth century.

CULTURE: Soil, ordinary. Position, sunny, well-drained beds or borders. Plant perennials in Oct. or March, annuals in May or June.

PROPAGATION: Annuals by seed sown ⅛ in. deep in boxes of light soil in temp. 65° to 70° in March, or outdoors in April where plants are to flower; perennials by seed sown outdoors in April, transplanting seedlings to permanent position when large enough to handle; division of roots in Oct. or March.

ANNUAL SPECIES CULTIVATED: *C. Atkinsoniana*, yellow and purple, summer, 2 to 4 ft., Western U.S.A.; *basalis* (syn. *C. cardaminifolia*), yellow and brown-purple, summer, 6 to 24 in., Southern U.S.A.; *coronata*, orange and purple, summer, 2 ft., Texas; *Drummondii*, yellow and crimson, summer, 2 ft., Texas; *tinctoria* (syn. *C. bicolor*), yellow and purple, summer, 2 ft., N. America. 4 ft., Western U.S.A.; *cardaminefolia*, yellow and brown-purple, summer, 6 to 24 in., Southern U.S.A.; *coronata*, orange and purple, summer, 2 ft., Texas; *Drummondii*, yellow and crimson, summer, 2 ft., Texas; *tinctoria* (syn. *C. bicolor*), yellow and purple, summer, 2 ft., N. America.

PERENNIAL SPECIES CULTIVATED: *C. grandiflora*, yellow, Aug., 2 to 3 ft., Southern U.S.A., var. *auriculata superba*, golden yellow with crimson centre, and *flore pleno*, double form; *lanceolata*, yellow, Aug., 2 to 3 ft., Eastern U.S.A.; *major*, deep yellow, July to Sept., 2 to 3 ft., South-eastern U.S.A.; *palmata*, orange-yellow, July to Sept., 1½ to 3 ft., Central U.S.A.; *pubescens*, yellow and purple, summer, 2 to 4 ft., Southern U.S.A., and var. *superba*, large-flowered; *rosea*, rose-pink, summer, 9 to 24 in., U.S.A.; *verticillata*, yellow, Aug., 2 ft. The plant listed in catalogues as *C. auriculata* is really *C. pubescens*.

Coriander, see *Coriandrum sativum*.

Coriandrum—*Umbelliferae*. Hardy annual herbs. One species grown for the seeds which are used in curry powder, as seasoning, in confectionery and for flavouring alcoholic drinks and junkets.

CULTURE: Soil, ordinary. Position, south border, or open ground where it can be cut with a sickle if grown on a large scale. Seed ripens in August and is threshed and dried when ripe.

PROPAGATION: By seeds sown ¼ in. deep in drills 12 in. apart in April.

SPECIES CULTIVATED: *C. sativum*, ' Coriander ', pale mauve, June, 2 to 3 ft., S. Europe.

Coriaria—*Coriariaceae*. Half-hardy deciduous flowering shrubs. Leaves and fruits poisonous.

CULTURE: Soil, ordinary. Position, sunny, sheltered borders. Plant in autumn.

PROPAGATION: By suckers or layers in autumn, or cuttings of half-ripened wood in sandy soil in frame or under hand-glass.

SPECIES CULTIVATED: *C. myrtifolia*, greenish, summer, 4 ft., S. France; *terminalis*, greenish, succeeded in autumn by waxy, currant-like berries, 4 ft., Sikkim, var. *xanthocarpa*, fruits yellow, the best one to grow. The leaves of the first yield redoul which is used in curing leather and for ink-making.

Coris—*Primulaceae*. Hardy biennial. First introduced early seventeenth century.

CULTURE: Soil, sandy peat. Position, well-drained beds on sunny rockery. Plant, March or April.

PROPAGATION: By seeds sown 1/16 in. deep in Aug. or April where plants are to grow.

SPECIES CULTIVATED: *C. monspeliensis*, lilac, May, 1 ft., S. Europe.

Cork Oak, see *Quercus Suber*.

Corkscrew Rush, see Juncus.

Corn Flag, see *Gladiolus segetum*; **-flower,** see *Centaurea Cyanus*; **-Marigold,** see *Chrysanthemum segetum*; **-Salad,** see *Valerianella Locusta*; **Indian-,** see *Zea Mays*; **Pop-,** see *Z. Mays* var. *everta*; **Sweet-,** see *Z. Mays* var. *rugosa*.

Cornel, see *Cornus sanguinea.*

Cornelian Cherry, see *Cornus mas.*

Cornus (Dogwood)—*Cornaceae.* Hardy deciduous flowering trees, shrubs and herbaceous perennials. Leaves, green or variegated with white and crimson. Some botanists divide this into a number of genera, i.e., Chamaepericlymenum (incl. *Ch. canadense* and *Ch. sirecicuan*), Cynoxylon (incl. *C. floridum* and *C. Nuttallii*), Dendrobenthamia (incl. *D. capitata*), Macrocarpium (incl. *M. mas*) and Cornus proper (incl. *C. sanguinea*).

CULTURE OF SHRUBBY SPECIES: Soil, sandy peat for dwarf, ordinary soil for others. Position, rockery for dwarf kinds, open or shady shrubberies for tall species. Plant, Oct. to Feb. The flowering species require no pruning but those grown for beauty of stem, such as *C. alba* and vars., *C. sanguinea* and *C. stolonifera*, may, if desired, be cut hard back annually in spring.

CULTURE OF HERBACEOUS SPECIES: Soil, bog or peat. Position, moist bed or rockery. Plant, March.

PROPAGATION: Shrubby kinds by cuttings of firm shoots in sandy soil outdoors in Nov.; layering shoots in spring; suckers removed from plant in Nov. and replanted at once; grafting variegated kinds in March; seeds sown outdoors in March. Herbaceous species by division in March.

SHRUBBY SPECIES CULTIVATED: *C. alba*, white, July, 8 to 10 ft., N. Asia, var. *sibirica*, coral branches, *Spaethii*, leaves edged yellow; *capitata* (syn. *Benthamia fragifera*), white, Aug., 10 ft., N. India, hardy S. of England only; *controversa*, white, June to July, 30 to 50 ft., Japan; *florida*, ' Flowering Dogwood ', May, 10 to 15 ft., a beautiful shrub with showy white bracts, N. America, and var. *rubra*, rosy red; *Kousa*, creamy white, May to June, 15 to 20 ft., Japan and China; *macrophylla*, yellowish-white, July to Aug., 30 to 50 ft., Himalaya; *mas*, ' Cornelian Cherry ', yellow, Feb., 15 ft., Europe, and vars. *aurea*, *elegantissima* and *variegata*; *Nuttallii*, creamy white, May, spice scented, pale rose bracts, Western N. America; *sanguinea*, green, June, 8 ft., branches red, Europe, Orient; *stolonifera*, ' Red Osier Dogwood ', red-stemmed, to 8 ft., N. America, var. *flaviramea*, yellow branches.

HERBACEOUS SPECIES CULTIVATED: *C. canadensis* (syns. *Chamaepericlymenum canadense, Cornella canadensis*), purplish-white, May, 6 in., N. America.

Corokia—*Cornaceae.* Half-hardy evergreen shrubs. First introduced early nineteenth century.

CULTURE: Soil, preferably poor and light, well-drained. Position, sheltered, south or west wall. Plant, Oct. to April.

PROPAGATION: By cuttings inserted in sand in well drained pan under bellglass; layering shoots in Oct.

SPECIES CULTIVATED: *C. Cotoneaster*, 6 to 8 ft., a curious shrub with twisted and contorted growth, and minute starry, yellow flowers in profusion, followed by orange berries, New Zealand.

Coronilla—*Leguminosae.* Greenhouse and hardy shrubs and hardy perennials. First introduced late sixteenth century.

CULTURE OF GREENHOUSE SPECIES: Compost, two parts loam, one part peat and sand. Position, pots in light greenhouse. Repot, March. Prune off points of shoots in spring to induce bushy growth. Water moderately Oct. to March, freely afterwards. Temp., Sept. to March 40° to 45°, March to Sept. 55° to 65°. Place plants outdoors in sunny position June to Sept.

CULTURE OF PERENNIALS: Soil, ordinary. Position, sunny rockeries or borders. Plant, Oct. or April.

CULTURE OF HARDY SHRUBS: Soil, ordinary. Position, sheltered, warm shrubberies, or south or west walls inland, or planted as maritime shrubs in exposed places and on chalk soils. Plant, Oct. Prune straggling shoots after flowering.

PROPAGATION: Greenhouse species by seeds sown ½ in. deep in light soil in temp. 75° in March, or by cuttings inserted in well-drained pots of sandy soil under bell-glass in temp. 55° from March to May; perennial species by seeds sown ⅛ in. deep outdoors in April, or division of roots in Oct.; hardy shrubs by cuttings in cold frame in autumn.

GREENHOUSE SPECIES CULTIVATED: *C. glauca*, yellow, May, 10 to 12 ft., evergreen, France.

PERENNIAL SPECIES CULTIVATED: *C. cappadocica* (syn. *C. iberica*, yellow, July, 6 in., Asia Minor; *minima*, yellow, June, 6 in., S. Europe; *varia*, ' Crown Vetch ', pink and white, summer and autumn, 1 to 2 ft., trailer, Europe.

HARDY SHRUBS CULTIVATED: *C. emeroides*, yellow, May to Aug., 4 to 5 ft., deciduous, S.E. Europe; *Emerus*, ' Scorpion Senna ', red and yellow, May to October, 7 to 9 ft., deciduous, Europe.

Correa (Australian Fuchsia)—*Rutaceae*. Greenhouse evergreen shrubs. First introduced late eighteenth century.

CULTURE: Compost, two parts peat, one part fibrous loam and sand. Position, pots, well drained, in light, airy greenhouse. Repot in July when new growth begins. Prune directly after flowering. Water moderately April to July and Oct. to April, freely July to Oct. Temp., Sept. to March 40° to 45°, March to Sept. 55° to 65°.

PROPAGATION: By cuttings inserted in well-drained pots of sandy peat under bell-glass in temp. 65° to 75° in April; grafting on *Correa alba* or *Eriostemon buxifolius* in March.

SPECIES CULTIVATED: *C. alba*, white, June, 5 to 6 ft.; *Harrisii*, scarlet, 3 ft., hybrid; *speciosa*, scarlet, June, 3 ft., Australia, vars. *Backhousiana*, *bicolor* and *pulchella*; *ventricosa*, bright salmon, 3 ft., Australia.

Cortaderia (Pampas Grass)—*Gramineae*. Large hardy perennial grasses with decorative plumes.

CULTURE: Soil, rich, light, sandy. Position, sheltered shrubberies or lawns. Plant, Oct. to April. Water freely in dry weather. Gather plumes for winter decoration directly fully developed, female plumes most durable.

PROPAGATION: By seed in sandy soil in well-drained pots in temp. 55° to 65°, Feb. to April. Transplant seedlings outdoors in Aug. or Sept.

SPECIES CULTIVATED: *C. rudiuscula* (syns. *C. Quila*, *C. jubata*, *Gynerium argenteum*), 4 to 6 ft., Ecuador to Chile and Argentina; *Selloana* (syn. *C. argentea*, *Gynerium argenteum*), 10 to 15 ft., Argentina.

Cortusa—*Primulaceae*. Hardy perennial alpine plants. First introduced late sixteenth century.

CULTURE: Soil, sandy peat. Position, shady border or rockery. Plant, March or April.

PROPAGATION: By seeds sown 1/16 in. deep in sandy peat in cold frame in March or Aug.; division of plant in March.

SPECIES CULTIVATED: *C. Matthiolii*, ' Bear's-ear Sanicle ', red, April, 1 ft., Europe, and vars. *alba*, white, *grandiflora*, purple, *pubens*, magenta-purple.

Coryanthes (Helmet or Bucket Orchids)—*Orchidaceae*. An epiphytal genus. Leaves ribbed, flowers on pendent or erect spikes from the base of the cone-shaped pseudo-bulbs. Sepals and petals flimsy, lip fleshy. First from a horizontal stalk at right angles descends a process often ribbed, this expands into a large receptacle which holds a liquid secreted by two glands at the column-base. An insect, usually a bee species, drops into this liquid and in forcing its way through a narrow passage, pollinates the next flower visited. The species are not often met with in cultivation.

CULTURE: Compost, two and a half parts of osmunda fibre, one and a half parts of sphagnum moss, and crushed potsherds. Baskets are preferable. Exposure to light in autumn benefits and though water is not required frequently in winter, a moist atmosphere should be maintained. Winter temp. 65°; summer, tropical.

PROPAGATION: By division of plants as they commence growth in spring.

SPECIES CULTIVATED: A selection only—*C. Bungerothii*, large, greenish-white, purple spotted, lip orange-yellow, yellow shaded and with red-brown spots, early summer, Venezuela; *leucocorys*, lip white, marbled and suffused with rose-purple, summer, Peru; *macrantha*, large, fragrant, yellowish, purple spotted, lip purplish, blood-red, spotted red-purple, summer, Brazil, Guiana, Venezuela; *maculata*, very variable, yellowish, spotted dull crimson, summer, Demerara, Brazil, Guiana; *speciosa* (syn. *Gongora speciosa*), variable, fragrant, yellowish, lip orange-yellow, red-brown and tawny-red, summer, Brazil, Cent. America.

Corydalis—*Fumariaceae.* Hardy annual and perennial herbs.

CULTURE: Soil, ordinary, good. Position, well-drained sunny borders, ledges of rockeries, fissures in old walls. Plant perennial and biennial species in March.

PROPAGATION: Annual species by seeds sown in April where plants are to flower; perennials by seed as for annuals, transplanting seedlings to permanent positions when large enough to handle; also by division of the plants after flowering; bulbous species by offsets in March.

PERENNIAL SPECIES CULTIVATED: *C. Allenii*, pink and white, spring, 3 to 4 in., N. America; *cashmeriana*, blue, April, 6 in., Kashmir; *cheilanthifolia*, yellow, summer, 10 in., China; *Halleri* (syn. *C. solida*), purple, April, 6 in., Europe; *lutea*, yellow, spring and summer, 1 ft., Europe; *nobilis*, yellow, May, 1 ft., Siberia; *thalictrifolia*, yellow, summer, 1 ft., China; *Wilsonii*, yellow, May, 9 in., W. China.

ANNUAL SPECIES CULTIVATED: *C. sempervirens* (syn. *C. glauca*), pale pink to purple, summer, 1½ ft., Canada.

Corylopsis—*Hamamelidaceae.* Hardy deciduous flowering shrubs. First introduced mid-nineteenth century.

CULTURE: Soil, sandy loam. Position, open, moist shrubbery in S. England; south walls in other parts of country. Plant, Oct. to Feb.

PROPAGATION: By layering shoots in Oct.

SPECIES CULTIVATED: *C. Griffithii*, yellow, March, 10 ft., rather tender, Himalaya; *pauciflora*, yellow, Feb., 3 ft., cowslip scented, not hardy in cold places, Japan; *spicata*, yellow, 3 ft., sweetly scented, Feb. to March, hardy, Japan.

Corylus (Cob-nut; Filbert)—*Betulaceae.* Hardy deciduous nut-bearing shrubs. Flowers, male—grey, female—crimson, March, April. Nuts ripe in Oct.

CULTURE: Soil, rich loam, well manured and deeply trenched. Position, open, sunny. Plant cob and hazel nuts 10 ft. apart each way, and filberts 15 ft. apart, in Oct. Prune end of March, cutting away shoots not less than two years old and shortening those of previous year's growth about one-third. Train each tree to have six main branches only. Gather nuts when husk becomes brown. Hang branches of hazel catkins (male flowers) in filbert bushes in Feb., if filbert catkins are scarce, to ensure fertilisation.

PROPAGATION: By seeds (nuts) 2 in. deep in Oct. in open garden, transplanting seedlings two years afterwards; suckers, removed from base of old plants replanted in Oct.; layering strong young shoots in Nov.; grafting on seedlings of Constantinople Nut in March to form standards, half standards, and dwarf standards.

SPECIES CULTIVATED: *C. Avellana*, ' Common Hazel ', Europe (Britain), var. *aurea*, golden-leaved, *grandis.* ' Cob-nut ' ; *Colurna*, ' Constantinople Nut ', tree, S.E. Europe; *maxima* (syn. *C. tubulosa*), ' Filbert ', S. Europe, var. *atropurpurea*, purple-leaved.

Coryphantha—*Cactaceae.* Greenhouse succulent perennials. First introduced late seventeenth century.

CULTURE: Compost, equal parts sandy loam, broken brick and mortar-rubble. Position, sunny stage or shelf in cool, airy greenhouse or window. Pot, March or April, in well-drained pots sufficiently large to accommodate the roots. Repot only when necessary, usually every third year. Water moderately March to Sept., sparingly at other times. Spray overhead in summer. Ventilate freely in summer. Temp., March to Sept. 60° to 70°, Sept. to March, 50° to 55°.

PROPAGATION: By seeds sown ⅛ in. deep in well-drained pots or pans filled with sandy soil in temp. 70° in March, keeping soil moderately moist: by cuttings of the tops of the plants inserted in small pots of sandy compost in spring; by grafting on to *Cereus speciossimus* at almost any time.

SPECIES CULTIVATED: *C. clava*, green, red and yellow, June, 1 ft., Mexico; *elephantidens*, violet-rose, autumn, 6 to 9 in., Mexico; *pectinata*, yellow, summer, 9 in., Texas, Mexico.

Cosmos—*Compositae*. Half-hardy annuals. First introduced late eighteenth century.

CULTURE: Soil, ordinary. Position, warm, dryish border.

PROPAGATION: By seeds sown in light soil in temp. of 50° to 55° in March, transplanting seedlings outdoors 2 to 3 ft. apart in May.

SPECIES CULTIVATED: *C. atrosanguineus*, dark brownish-red, Sept., 1 to 3 ft., Mexico; *bipinnatus*, ' Purple Mexican Aster ', various colours, Aug., 3 ft., Mexico; *diversifolius* (syn. *Bidens dahlioides*), lilac, Sept., 3 ft., Mexico; *sulphureus*, pale yellow, July to Aug., 3 to 4 ft., Mexico. There are many hybrids in a variety of colours.

Cossonia, see Raffenaldia.

Cotinus—*Anacardiaceae*. Deciduous shrubs or trees with yellow wood and a strong-smelling juice. Formerly included in the genus Rhus.

CULTURE: Soil, ordinary, well drained. Position, sunny borders or shrubberies. Plant, Oct. to Feb.

PROPAGATION: By seeds; root cuttings; layers.

SPECIES CULTIVATED: *C. americanus* (syn. *Rhus cotinoides*), to 20 ft., brilliant autumn colouring, Southern U.S.A.; *Coggygria* (syn. *Rhus Cotinus*), ' American Smoke Tree ', ' Wig Tree ', to 15 ft., fruiting panicle with long greenish or purplish hairs, brilliant autumn colouring, S. Europe, var. *purpureus*, panicles with intensely purple hairs and young leaves purplish.

Cotoneaster—*Rosaceae*. Hardy evergreen and deciduous shrubs and a few small trees, bearing scarlet fruits in winter. All are hardy and the wide variety of types makes them most useful for many purposes in the garden.

CULTURE: Soil, ordinary. Position, shrubberies open or in shade, trailing species against walls or growing over tree roots and rocks or bare ground under trees. Plant, Oct. to Feb.

PROPAGATION: By seeds sown 1 in. deep outdoors in March; cuttings inserted in sandy soil in frames in Sept.; layering shoots in spring.

EVERGREEN SPECIES CULTIVATED: *C. conspicua*, 4 ft., spreading habit, free berrying, W. China, var. *decora*, prostrate form; *congesta*, 18 in., miniature for rockery, Himalaya; *Dammeri*, creeping, China; *Franchetii*, 8 ft., graceful arching growth, W. China, var. *cinerescens*, more vigorous; *glabrata*, China; *glaucophylla*, half-evergreen, to 7 ft., W. China; *Harroviana*, 6 ft., China; *Henryana*, 10 ft., pendulous branches, Cent. China; *lactea*, to 10 ft., China; *microphylla*, 2 ft., trailing, for walls or rockeries, Himalaya, var. *thymifolia*, ' Rose Box ', more condensed form; *pannosa*, 10 ft., elegant growth, S.W. China; *rotundifolia*, 3 ft., spreading, scarlet fruits lasting till spring, N. India; *salicifolia* 10 ft., fast growing, elegant habit, W. China, var. *floccosa*, larger foliage, *rugosa*, similar; *serotina*, small tree, China; *turbinata*, to 6 ft., China.

DECIDUOUS SPECIES CULTIVATED: *C. acutifolia*, 10 ft., vigorous, fruit black, Cent. China, var. *villosula*, leaves pubescent beneath; *adpressa*, prostrate, W. China; *bullata*, 10 ft., spare habit, W. China; *divaricata*, 6 ft., autumn colour, spreading habit, Cent. China; *frigida*, 15 to 20 ft., vigorous, spreading, small tree, Himalaya, var. *Vicarii*, *fructu luteo*, large yellow fruits; *hebephylla*, 8 ft., spreading, purple-red fruits, S.W. China; *horizontalis*, flat, fishbone growth, on walls up to 8 ft., or as a flat bush to 3 ft., China; *lucida*, 8 ft., upright habit, black fruits, N. Asia; *melanocarpa*, to 6 ft., Europe, Asia, var. *laxiflora*, 6 ft., large clusters dark purple fruits; *moupinensis*, 12 ft., autumn foliage, black fruit, W. China; *multiflora*, early red fruits, 6 ft., China; *racemiflora*, 6 ft., slender arching habit, grey foliage, bright red oval berries, S.E. Europe, Asia; *Simonsii*, to 10 ft., upright habit, sometimes used for hedging, Himalaya; *Watereri*, 15 ft., vigorous free-fruiting hybrid; *Zabelii*, 6 ft., purple pear-shaped berries, China.

Cotton, see Gossypium; **-Grass,** see Eriophorum; **-Lavender,** see *Santolina Chamaecyparissus*; **-wood,** see *Populus deltoides*.

Cotula—*Compositae.* Hardy, evergreen, creeping, rock plants.
CULTURE: Any soil, even the poorest. Position, full sun.
PROPAGATION: By division and seeds.
SPECIES CULTIVATED: *C. acaenifolia*, flowers inconspicuous, ferny leaves in prostrate mats, New Zealand; *coronopifolia*, bronze-green carpets, S. Temp. Zone; *potentillina*, green mats of fern-like leaves, Chatham Islands; *squalida*, bronze carpets, New Zealand.

Cotyledon—*Crassulaceae.* Evergreen succulent plants. Some species formerly included here have been reclassified and will be found in the genera Chiastophyllum, Echeveria, Rosularia and Umbilicus.
CULTURE: Soil, ordinary. Position, sunny beds, rock gardens or windows. Plant, Oct. or March.
PROPAGATION: By division in March.
SPECIES CULTIVATED: *C. macrantha*, red, Dec. to spring, 1 to 2¼ ft., Cape; *orbiculata*, red, drooping, summer, to 4 ft., S. Africa; *paniculata*, red, summer, to 5 ft., S. Africa; *simplicifolia*, yellow, drooping, summer, 6 in., S. Europe; *undulata*, yellowish-red, spring to summer, S. Africa.

Cowberry, see *Vaccinium Vitis-idaea*.

Cow Parsnip, see Heracleum.

Crab Apple, see Malus; **-Cactus,** see *Zygocactus truncatus*.

Crambe (Seakale)—*Cruciferae.* Hardy herbaceous perennials and one esculent vegetable.
CULTURE OF PERENNIAL SPECIES: Soil, ordinary, rich. Position, open borders. Plant roots 3 in. deep in groups of three or six in March.
CULTURE OF SEAKALE: Soil, deep, rich, sandy. Position, open, sunny. Trench soil 2 ft. deep in autumn, incorporating an abundance of manure. Plant roots 4 to 6 in. long, 2 in. deep, upright, 18 in. apart in rows 30 in. asunder in Feb. or March. Pare off crown buds before planting. Mulch beds with stable manure in April. Apply common salt at the rate of 1 lb. to a square rod, or 1 lb. of nitrate of soda to same area in June. Lift and replant every five years. Manure and dig between rows in Nov. Blanching: Cover roots in open ground with inverted pots, dry tree leaves, or cinder ashes in Nov.
FORCING OUTDOORS: Cover roots with inverted pots in Nov. and put thick layers of fresh manure and leaves on these in Jan.
FORCING INDOORS: Lift roots in Nov., Dec. or Jan. and place them close together in large pots or boxes, with ordinary soil between, in temp. 50° to 60°. Keep roots moist and dark. Roots of no value after forcing.
PROPAGATION: By seed sown 1 in. deep in rows 12 in. apart in March, thinning seedlings to 6 in. apart in June and transplanting them to permanent beds when a year old, or by cuttings of roots as advised for planting; perennials by seeds sown ½ in. deep outdoors in March, transplanting seedlings in July; cuttings of shoots or division of roots in March. Seeds germinate in 18 to 20 days. Crop arrives at maturity two years after sowing.
SPECIES CULTIVATED: *C. cordifolia*, ' Flowering Seakale ', white, May, 5 ft., Caucasus; *maritima*, ' Seakale ', white, May and June, Europe (Britain); *orientalis*, white, fragrant, June, 4 ft., Orient.

Cranberry, see *Vaccinium Oxycoccus*; **American-,** see *V. macrocarpum*; **-Gourd,** see *Abobra viridiflora*.

Cranesbill (Geranium).

Crape Myrtle, see *Lagerstroemia indica.*

Craspedia—*Compositae.* Evergreen, perennial, rock-garden plants.
CULTURE: Soil, sandy loam. Position, full sun.
PROPAGATION: By seeds sown when ripe.
SPECIES CULTIVATED: *C. uniflora,* yellow, 9 in., summer, New Zealand.

Crassula—*Crassulaceae.* Greenhouse evergreen plants. First introduced early eighteenth century.
CULTURE: Compost, equal parts sandy loam, brick rubble, dried cow manure and river sand. Position, well-drained pots in light greenhouse, close to glass. Pot, March. Water freely April to Aug., moderately Aug. to Nov., very little afterwards. Temp., March to Sept. 55° to 65°, Sept. to March 45° to 50°.
PROPAGATION: By seeds sown in well-drained pots or pans of sandy soil, just covering seeds with fine soil, in temp. 60° to 70° in March or April, seedlings to be kept close to glass and have little water; cuttings of shoots 2 to 3 in. long, exposed to sun for few days, then inserted in June, July or Aug. in well-drained pots of sandy soil, placed on greenhouse shelf and given very little water.
SPECIES CULTIVATED: *C. arborescens,* pink, May, 2 to 10 ft., S. Africa; *argentea,* white or pink, to 10 ft., S. Africa; *columnaris,* white, summer, 6 in., S. Africa; *falcata* (syn. *Rochea falcata*), yellow and red, summer, 6 in., S. Africa; *lactea,* white, autumn, 9 in., S. Africa; *lycopodioides,* greenish, 2 ft., S. Africa; *multicava,* white, 6 in., S. Africa; *perforata,* yellowish, 4 ft., S. Africa; *pyramidalis,* white, 1 to 2 ft., S. Africa. See also Rochea.

Crataegus (Hawthorn)—*Rosaceae.* Hardy, spiny, deciduous shrubs and small trees.
CULTURE: Soil, ordinary, rich. Position, woods, shrubberies, lawns and pleasure grounds, common quick in hedges. Plant, Oct. to Feb. Prune in Nov., simply cutting into shape where necessary. Hedges: Soil, ordinary, trenched 2 ft. deep and 2 ft. wide. Plant, Nov. to March. Distance apart, 4 in., single row, 6 in. double row, 6 in. asunder. Quantity of plants required for single row 9, double row 12 per yard. Trim to shape in July and Aug.
PROPAGATION: By seed; budding choice varieties on common hawthorn; grafting in March. Berries require to be stored in sand for a year before sowing.
SPECIES CULTIVATED: *C. Azarolus,* white, fragrant, May, 15 ft., S. Europe; *Calpodendron,* white, June, 20 ft., U.S.A.; *Crus-galli,* ' Cockspur Thorn ', white, June, 20 ft., N. America; *Douglasii,* white, May, 15 ft., N.W. America; *heterophylla,* white, May to June, 20 ft., W. Asia; *intricata* (syn. *C. coccinea*), white, May, 20 ft., N. America; *Lavallei* (syn. *C. Carrierei*), white, May, 12 to 15 ft., hybrid; *macracantha,* white, May to June, 15 ft., Eastern N. America; *mollis,* white and red, May, 20 ft., U.S.A.; *monogyna,* ' Quick ', white, May, 25 to 35 ft., Britain, and var. *biflora,* ' Glastonbury Thorn '; *orientalis,* white, May, 15 ft., S.E. Europe, W. Asia; *Oxyacantha,* ' Common Hawthorn ', ' May ', white, May, 15 ft., Europe, and vars. *alba,* white, *coccinea,* crimson, *Paulii,* bright scarlet double, *plena,* double white, *punicea,* dark red, *rosea,* rose; *pinnatifida,* white, May, 15 ft., Asia; *punctata,* white, June, 25 ft., Eastern N. America; *tanacetifolia,* white, May, 15 ft., Levant.

Cream Cups, see *Platystemon californicus.*

Creeping Forget-me-not, see *Omphalodes verna;* **-Harebell,** see *Wahlenbergia hederacea;* **-Jenny,** see *Lysimachia Nummularia;* **-Sailor,** see *Saxifraga sarmentosa;* **-Speedwell,** see *Veronica repens;* **-Willow,** see *Salix repens;* **-Winter Green,** see *Gaultheria procumbens.*

Cremanthodium—*Compositae.* Hardy herbaceous plants including many dwarf, high-alpine species, but they are difficult to grow and seldom seen in cultivation.
CULTURE: Soil, deep, well-drained loam. Position, full exposure, not too arid.

PROPAGATION: By seeds sown when ripe.

SPECIES CULTIVATED: *C. nobile*, yellow, 2 ft., May to June, W. China; *reniforme*, yellow, 1 to 2 ft., summer, Himalaya.

Crepis (Hawk's Beard)—*Compositae*. Hardy herbaceous perennials and annuals.

CULTURE: Soil, ordinary, sandy. Position, sunny borders, banks or rockeries. Plant perennial species in March or April.

PROPAGATION: Annual species by seeds sown ¼ in. deep in April where plants are required to flower; perennial species by seeds sown ¼ in. deep outdoors in April, transplanting seedlings in July, or by division of roots in March or April.

SPECIES CULTIVATED: *C. aurea*, orange, autumn, 12 in., annual, Europe; *incana*, pink, 9 to 12 in., July, Greece; *rubra*, red, autumn, 1 ft., S. Europe. See also Tolpis.

Cretan Dittany, see *Origanum Dictamnus*; **-Mullein,** see *Celsia cretica*; **-Spikenard,** see *Valeriana Phu*.

Crimson Flag, see Schizostylis.

Crinodendron—*Elaeocarpaceae*. Rather tender evergreen flowering shrubs sometimes known as Tricuspidaria. First introduced mid-nineteenth century.

CULTURE: Soil, moist, lime-free loam with peat and leaf-mould. Position, in the open in mildest districts, with some shade. In other southern counties good for a partially shaded wall, even with N. aspect. Can also be grown in tubs or large well-drained pots in unheated greenhouse. Plant, or pot, Sept. to Oct. or April to May. *C. Patagua* is the more attractive species but less hardy.

PROPAGATION: By cuttings of half-ripened shoots in sandy soil under bell-glass in gentle bottom heat during July or Aug.

SPECIES CULTIVATED: *C. dependens*, white, late summer, 15 to 30 ft., Chile; *Patagua* (syn. *Tricuspidaria lanceolata*), crimson hanging lanterns, May to June, 10 to 20 ft., Chile.

Crinum—*Amaryllidaceae*. Stove, greenhouse and hardy deciduous bulbous plants. First introduced early eighteenth century.

CULTURE OF STOVE AND GREENHOUSE SPECIES: Compost, two parts turfy loam, one part peat and silver sand. Position, pots in light plant stove or greenhouse. Pot, March, in large pots or tubs, well drained. Water freely March to Oct., very little afterwards. Store pots containing bulbs on their sides in stove or greenhouse during winter. Repot every 3 or 4 years. Apply liquid manure to established bulbs in summer. Temp., March to Sept. 75° to 85° for stove, 55° to 65° for greenhouse; Sept. to March, 55° to 65° for stove, 45° to 50° for greenhouse.

CULTURE OF HARDY SPECIES: Soil, rich, deep. Position, south, well-drained border. Plant bulbs 6 in. deep in March.

PROPAGATION: By seeds sown in sandy soil in a temp. of 65° to 75° in spring; also by offsets at potting or planting time. Seedling plants take several years to flower.

STOVE SPECIES CULTIVATED: *C. amabile*, red, fragrant, summer, 3 ft., Sumatra; *erubescens*, white, purplish red and pink, July, 2 to 3 ft., Trop. America; *Kirkii*, white and red, Oct., 2 ft., Zanzibar; *Sanderianum*, white and red, 2 ft., Trop. Africa; *scabrum*, white and crimson, May, 2 to 3 ft., Trop. Africa; *zeylanicum*, white and red, July, 2 to 3 ft., Trop. Asia and Africa.

GREENHOUSE SPECIES CULTIVATED: *C. americanum*, white, July, 1 to 2½ ft., Southern U.S.A.; *asiaticum*, white, July, 2½ to 3½ ft., Trop. Asia; *Macowanii*, white and purple, autumn, 3 ft., Natal; *Moorei*, white and red, April to Oct., 2 ft., S. Africa, vars. *album*, white, *variegatum*, leaves variegated.

HARDY SPECIES CULTIVATED: *C. longifolium* (syn. *C. capense*), ' Cape Lily ', pink, summer, 3 ft., S. Africa, var. *album*, white; *Powellii*, rose, summer, 3 ft., hybrid, and vars. *album* and *rubrum*.

Crithmum—*Umbelliferae*. Hardy perennial herb. Leaves used for pickling.

Culture: Soil, sandy. Position, shady border. Sow seeds thinly in bed or ordinary sandy soil in March. Not an easy plant to grow away from the seashore.
Species Cultivated: *C. maritimum*, ' Samphire ', white, summer, 1 ft., seashores of Britain.

Crocosmia—*Iridaceae*. Hardy or half-hardy cormous plants. The common Montbretia of gardens is *C. crocosmaeflora*, a hybrid between *C. aurea* and *C. Pottsii*.
Culture: Soil, sandy loam. Position, sunny, well-drained borders. Can be treated like Gladioli or if left in the ground permanently should be lifted, divided and replanted every three years. Plants left in the ground should have a covering of leaves or ashes during winter.
Pot Culture: Compost, equal parts turfy loam, peat, leaf-mould and silver sand. Position, cold frame or greenhouse. Pot, Oct., placing six bulbs in 5-in. pot. Water when growth commences, keep moderately moist until foliage dies down, then keep dry.
Propagation: By seed; offsets.
Species Cultivated: *C. aurea*, ' Coppertip ', bright orange-yellow, to 4 ft., S, Africa; *crocosmaeflora* (syn. *Tritonia crocosmaeflora*), ' Montbretia ', orange-crimson, 2 to 3 ft., late summer, hybrid; *Pottsii* (syn. *Tritonia Pottsii*), orange-yellow, Aug., 3 ft., S. Africa.

Crocus—*Iridaceae*. Hardy bulbous flowering plants.
Outdoor Culture: Soil, light, rich. Position, margins of beds or borders or in grass plots and lawns, open or in shade, for common kinds; sunny, well-drained beds, or on rockeries, for rare and choice kinds. Plant spring-flowering species and varieties in Oct., Nov. or Dec.; autumn-flowering species in Aug. and Sept. Depth and distance: Common kinds, 3 in.; choice and rare kinds, 2 in. Leave corms undisturbed for four or five years, unless their place is wanted for other plants. Lift when necessary in June or July, drying corms in sun and storing in cool room till planting time. Foliage should not be removed until it turns yellow.
Culture in Grass: Bore holes 3 in. deep and 2 in. apart, insert a corm in bottom of each, then fill up with ordinary soil; or lift turf, fork up soil below, add a little bonemeal, place bulbs thereon and replace turf. Grass should not be cut till foliage turns yellow.
Pot Culture: Compost, light, rich, sandy soil. Position, ten in 5-in. pot, or four in a 3-in. size, in Oct. or Nov. After potting, place in cold frame or under a wall and cover with cinder ashes till growth begins, then remove to greenhouse, etc. Water freely when growth begins; give less as foliage fades. Corms of no use for flowering second time in pots, but may be planted out in garden. To force, place in temp. 55° to 65° in Dec. or Jan.
Propagation: By seeds sown ⅛ in. deep and 1 in. apart in light sandy soil in cold frame in Sept., Oct. or Nov., transplanting seedlings in Aug. of second year; offsets removed from old corms in July or Aug. and replanted 2 in. deep and 2 in. apart at same time. Seedling corms flower when three and four years old.
Species Cultivated: *asturicus*, violet, autumn, Spain; *Balansae*, orange-yellow, March, Asia Minor; *banaticus*, white and purple, March, Hungary; *biflorus*, ' Scotch Crocus ', lavender, Feb., Tuscany; *byzantinus* (syn. *C. iridiflorus*), purple and lilac, autumn, E. Europe; *cancellatus*, yellow, white and purple, autumn, Asia Minor; *chrysanthus*, orange-yellow, Jan. to March, S.E. Europe; *Clusii*, white and purple, autumn, Spain; *dalmaticus*, yellow and purple, Feb. to March, Dalmatia; *etruscus*, lilac and yellow, March, Italy; *Fleischeri*, yellow and purple, March, Asia Minor; *Imperati*, lilac, Jan. to March, Italy; *Korolkowii*, yellow, Feb. to March, Cent. Asia; *longiflorus*, lilac, yellow and purple, autumn, Italy; *Malyi*, yellow, orange and purple, March, Dalmatia; *medius*, white and purple, autumn, Italy; *minimus*, purple, March and April, Corsica; *C. moesiacus*, yellow, Feb., S.E. Europe; *nudiflorus*, purple, autumn, Pyrenees; *ochroleucus*, white and orange, autumn, Asia Minor; *pulchellus*, lavender, blue or yellow, autumn, Turkey; *reticulatus*, white, lilac and purple, March, E. Europe; *sativus*, ' Saffron Crocus ', white, lilac and purple, autumn, Western Asia; *Sieberi*,

lilac and yellow, Feb. to March, Greece; *speciosus*, lilac and purple, autumn, Cent. Europe; *suaveolens*, orange, lilac and purple, March, Italy; *susianus*, orange and brown, Feb., Crimea; *Tomasinianus*, pale sapphire-lavender, spring, Dalmatia and Serbia; *vernus*, lilac, violet and white, Feb. to April, Europe; *versicolor*, white to purple, March, France and Italy; *zonatus*, rosy lilac and yellow, autumn, S. Europe and Asia Minor. The numerous Dutch forms in cultivation were originally derived from *C. vernus*.

Crossandra—*Acanthaceae.* Stove evergreen flowering shrub. First introduced early nineteenth century.

CULTURE: Compost, equal parts loam, peat and sand. Position, pots in moist plant stove. Pot, March. Water moderately during winter, freely other times. Temp., Oct. to March 55° to 65°, March to Oct. 75° to 85°.

PROPAGATION: By cuttings of shoots 2 or 3 in. long, inserted in sand under bell-glass, in temp. of 85° at any time of year.

SPECIES CULTIVATED: *C. guineensis*, lilac, October, 6 in.; *infundibuliformis* (syn. *C. undulaefolia*), orange-red, spring, 12 to 18 in., India, Malaya; *mucronata*, scarlet, summer, 2 ft., E. Trop. Africa; *subacaulis*, orange, 6 in., spring, E. Trop. Africa.

Cross Vine, see *Bignonia capreolata*; **-wort,** see Crucianella.

Croton, see Codiaeum.

Crowberry, see Empetrum.

Crowea—*Rutaceae.* Greenhouse evergreen shrubs. First introduced early eighteenth century.

CULTURE: Compost, two parts peat, one fibrous loam, and little sand. Position, pots in light airy greenhouse. Pot, March or April. Prune straggling shoots into shape in March. Water very little Oct. to March, moderately March to Oct. Temp., Sept. to March 40° to 45°, March to Sept. 55° to 65°.

PROPAGATION: By cuttings inserted in sand under bell-glass in temp. of 65° to 75° in March or April; grafting on *Correa alba* or *Eriostemon buxifolia* in March.

SPECIES CULTIVATED: *C. angustifolia*, red, summer, 1 to 3 ft., Australia; *saligna*, pink, summer, 1 to 2 ft., Australia.

Crowfoot, see Ranunculus.

Crown Imperial, see *Fritillaria imperialis*; `-Vetch,** see *Coronilla varia.*

Crucianella (Cross-wort)—*Rubiaceae.* Hardy herbaceous perennial. First introduced early seventeenth century.

CULTURE: Soil, sandy or chalky. Position, dry banks, rockeries or borders. Plant, Oct. or March.

PROPAGATION: By seeds sown outdoors in March, transplanting seedlings to permanent positions in July or Aug.; division of roots in March, April, Oct. or Nov.

SPECIES CULTIVATED: *C. stylosa* (syn. *Phuopsis stylosa*), rose, summer, 9 to 12 in., Caucasus, and vars.

Cryophytum—*Aizoaceae.* Annual succulent plant, formerly included in Mesembryanthemum.

CULTURE: Soil, ordinary. Position, sunny bed, border or rockery. Sow seeds ⅛ in. deep in sandy soil in temp. 55° to 65° in March, transplanting seedlings outdoors in June.

PROPAGATION: By seed.

SPECIES CULTIVATED: *C. crystallinum* (syn. *Mesembryanthemum crystallinum*), ' Ice Plant ', white, July, S. Africa.

Cryptanthus—*Bromeliaceae.* Stove, epiphytic, stoloniferous herbs with flattened rosettes of stiff, prickly-margined leaves. First introduced early nineteenth century.

CULTURE: Compost, equal parts fibrous loam, rough peat, leaf-mould and silver sand. Pot, March. Water freely always; good drainage essential. Temp., Sept. to March 65° to 75°, March to Sept. 75° to 85°.

PROPAGATION: By large offsets inserted singly in small pots in temp. of 85° in April.

SPECIES CULTIVATED: *C. acaulis*, white, Aug., 6 to 8 in., Brazil, and vars. *discolor* and *ruber*; *Beuckeri*, red and white, summer, 6 in., Brazil; *bivittatus*, white, Aug., 8 to 10 in., Trop. America; *zonatus*, white, 6 in., Brazil. See also Tillandsia.

Cryptocoryne (Water Trumpet)—*Araceae*. Asiatic bog plants much used in the tropical aquarium.

CULTURE: Stove treatment and boggy soil or planted submerged in aquariums round 65°, subdued light. Soil, aquarium compost or loamy soil with slightly acid reaction.

PROPAGATION: By division.

SPECIES CULTIVATED: *C. Beckettii*, small, India; *ciliata*, 12 in., thick narrow leaves, India; *cordata*, greenish-purple, Malay; *Griffithii*, crinkled foliage, purple flowers, Malay; *Nevellii*, dwarf, India; *Wightii*, tapering leaves, curled at edges, India, Malay.

Cryptogramma—*Polypodiaceae*. Hardy deciduous fern with parsley-like fronds.

CULTURE: Soil, equal parts loam and peat with a liberal supply of broken bricks or stone, quite free from lime. Position, cool, moist rockery. Does well in moist fissures of rocks. Plant in spring.

PROPAGATION: By division in spring.

SPECIES CULTIVATED: *C. crispa* (syn. *Allosorus crispus*), ' Parsley Fern ', 3 to 6 in., mountains of Wales, Scotland, etc.; *acrostichoides*, 6 to 8 in., N. America.

Cryptomeria—*Pinaceae* (or *Taxodiaceae*). Hardy evergreen coniferous tree. Foliage bright green in spring and summer; bronzy crimson during winter. First introduced early nineteenth century.

CULTURE: Soil, deep, rich, moist loam. Position, sheltered on lawns. Plant, Oct. to April.

PROPAGATION: By seeds sown $\frac{1}{8}$ in. deep in sandy loam in temp. of 55° in March or outdoors in April; cuttings of side shoots 2 or 3 in. long, inserted in sandy soil under hand-light, or in cold frame, in Sept. or Oct.

SPECIES CULTIVATED: *C. japonica*, ' Japanese Cedar ', 70 to 100 ft., Japan, and vars. *araucarioides*, branchlets long and thin, *elegans*, delicate, glaucous green foliage changing to bronzy red in autumn, *nana*, 3 to 4 ft., *Lobbii*, branchlets stiffer and tufted, *spiralis*, dwarf, dense habit.

Cryptophoranthus—*Orchidaceae*. Small tufted epiphytes, the short stems carrying a single leaf. The small flowers, one or few, are carried at junction of stem with leaf. The sepals are connate basally and apically, leaving an aperture on each side to admit insects.

CULTURE: Compost, etc., as for Masdevallias with fewer winter waterings.

PROPAGATION: By division of the plants; occasionally small plants are produced at the bases of the old leaf blades.

SPECIES CULTIVATED: *C. atropurpureus* (syn. *Masdevallia fenestrata*), dark purple, autumn, Jamaica; *Dayanus*, yellow and red-purple, comparatively large, height 3 to 8 in., various, Colombia; *Lehmannii*, greenish-yellow and dull purple, various seasons, Brazil; *maculatus*, yellow, spotted crimson, fasciculate, summer, Brazil.

Cuchay, see *Allium tuberosum*.

Cuckoo Flower, see *Cardamine pratensis*; **-pint,** see *Arum maculatum*.

Cucumber, see *Cucumis sativus* var. *anglicus*; **Ridge-,** see *C. sativus*; **-Tree,** see *Magnolia acuminata*.

Cucumis—*Cucurbitaceae*. Half-hardy trailing, fruiting plants. Introduced late sixteenth century.

CULTURE OF CUCUMBERS IN COLD HOUSE: Build beds on the staging or grow in boxes using a compost of two parts chopped, stacked loam to one part of farmyard manure containing plenty of long straw with 1 lb. bone meal and 1 lb. lime per barrowload. Beds should be 18 in. at base and 12 in. wide at top, 10 in. high and flat-topped. Purchase plants for setting out in mid-May or sow seed direct in the bed in mid-May. Maintain a moist atmosphere by syringing. Mulch as young roots appear on surface using same compost as for beds. Training: Tie inside wires close to glass, taking main stem to required height then stopping it. Tie laterals to nearest wire and stop 2 leaves beyond first fruit. Remove male flowers and tendrils, stop secondary laterals 2 leaves beyond first fruit. Cut older leaves as they yellow to allow room for young leaves which should be pushed behind the wires to provide shade. Keep beds moist—boxes will need careful watering. Top-dress with fertiliser fortnightly, 6 weeks after planting.

CULTURE OF CUCUMBER IN FRAMES: Make compact hotbeds 3 ft. high and width greater than that of available lights. When constant night temp. of 65° is reached, place a mound of cucumber compost in each frame on hotbed and sow or plant in this. Stop when 7 leaves form and take three resulting laterals the length of the frame then stop. Allow fruit on sub-laterals and stop 2 leaves beyond each fruit. Keep moist by syringing overhead. Shade in very sunny weather.

CULTURE IN HEATED GREENHOUSE: Sow during autumn and winter in night temp. never less than 60°. Except in short days of Nov. and Dec. fruit will be out 3 months after sowing. Use open potting compost and sow single seeds in small-60 pots. Prepare beds, train plants as detailed for cold houses. Winter and spring temps., 65° night, 70° to 75° day. During May, temp. will rise to 80° by sun heat, and ventilation must be allowed. Day fire heat will be unnecessary in summer but fires should be kept very low and a little heat given at night.

CULTURE OF RIDGE CUCUMBERS AND GHERKINS: Prepare holes 18 in. square by 1 ft. deep, filling with compost of two parts soil, one manure. Set out hardened-off plants end May or sow direct in a pocket of soil. Top-dress when in flower with complete fertiliser in showery weather. Pick when small and green. Train Japanese climbing cucumber up pea sticks.

CULTURE OF MELONS: Seed sowing, preparation of beds and planting as for cucumbers. Fruits on side shoots. Allow four per plant, fertilising flowers at same time. Stop side growths as they grow into next plant. When ripening keep atmosphere buoyant. Support fruits in nets.

SPECIES CULTIVATED: *C. Anguria*, ' Bur Gherkin ', pickling; *Melo*, ' Melon ', var. *cantalupensis*, ' Cantaloup Melon ', var. *inodorus*, ' Cassaba Melon '; *sativus*, ' Ridge Cucumber ,' ' Gherkin ', var. *anglicus*, ' English Forcing Cucumber '.

Cucurbita—*Cucurbitaceae*. Half-hardy annual edible or ornamental-fruited trail-ing plants. First introduced late sixteenth century.

CULTURE OF MARROWS AND PUMPKINS: Soil, ordinary, rich. Position, beds in frames, on heaps of decayed manure or refuse, or on banks, the shoots running down the slope, or in beds in open garden formed by digging out soil 15 in. deep, filling holes with heated manure and covering this with soil. Sow seeds in a temp. of 55° in April, or where the plants are intended to grow in May. Plant, May, under hand-light, or in June without protection. Pinch out points of main shoots when 18 in. long; no pinching required afterwards. Fertilise female blooms. Water freely in dry weather. Apply liquid manure frequently after fruit is set. Fruit for preserving should be cut when yellow and then hung up in a dry room till wanted for use.

CULTURE OF GOURDS: Soil, rich, ordinary. Position, beds at base of low, sunny fences or walls, or on the summits of banks, shoots growing at will up and over the former or down the latter. Plant, June. Water freely in dry weather. Apply liquid manure occasionally when plants are laden with fruit. Gather fruit when yellow, and hang it up in dry room till wanted for use. No pinching of shoots required.

PROPAGATION: By seeds sown ½ in. deep in light soil in temp. 55° to 65° in April, or where plants are to grow in May and June.

SPECIES CULTIVATED: *C. ficifolia*, ' Malabar Gourd ', fruits green with white stripes, grown for ornament, E. Asia; *maxima*, ' Autumn and Winter Squash ', edible, origin unknown; *moschata*, ' Pumpkin ', edible, origin unknown; *Pepo*, ' Summer and Autumn Pumpkin ', ' Vegetable Marrow ', edible, origin unknown. Numerous horticultural vars. and some bush (not trailing) forms.

Cuminum—*Umbelliferae.* Half-hardy annual herb with aromatic fruits used as flavouring.
CULTURE: Soil, ordinary. Position, sunny beds or borders. Sow seeds during May where plants are required. Gather seeds in July and Aug.
SPECIES CULTIVATED: *C. Cyminum*, white or rose, 6 in., Medit. Region.

Cunila—*Labiatae.* Aromatic perennial herbs.
CULTURE: Good friable loamy soil. Position, sunny, but not too arid and sun-baked.
PROPAGATION: Seed and cuttings.
SPECIES CULTIVATED: *C. origanoides* (syn. *C. Mariana*), ' Maryland Dittany ', pink, 9 in., autumn, N. America.

Cunninghamia—*Pinaceae* (or *Taxodiaceae*). Hardy evergreen ornamental tree. One of the most ancient types of vegetation. First introduced early nineteenth century.
CULTURE: Soil, deep, well-drained loam. Position, sheltered from cold winds. Plant, Nov.
PROPAGATION: By seeds sown in sandy soil in warm greenhouse during Feb. or March.
SPECIES CULTIVATED: *C. lanceolata* (syn. *C. sinensis*), 70 to 150 ft., China.

Cunonia—*Cunoniaceae.* Greenhouse evergreen flowering tree. First introduced early nineteenth century.
CULTURE: Compost, equal parts sandy loam and peat. Position, pots in light airy greenhouse. Pot, March. Prune into shape in March. Water moderately Oct. to March, freely afterwards. Temp., March to Sept. 55° to 65°, Sept. to March 45° to 50°.
PROPAGATION: By cuttings of firm shoots inserted in sandy soil under bell-glass in temp. of 65° to 75° in summer.
SPECIES CULTIVATED: *C. capensis*, ' Red Alder ', white, Aug., to 50 ft., S. Africa.

Cup Flower, see Nierembergia; **-and Saucer Flower,** see *Cobaea scandens*; **-Plant,** see *Silphium perfoliatum.*

Cupania—*Sapindaceae.* Stove, ornamental foliage, evergreen trees. First introduced early nineteenth century.
CULTURE: Compost, equal parts loam and peat. Position, pots in moist plant stove. Pot, March. Water moderately in winter, freely other times. Prune occasionally to maintain a dwarf habit. Temp., Oct. to March 55° to 65°, March to Sept. 75° to 85°.
PROPAGATION: By cuttings of firm shoots inserted in sand under bell-glass in temp. of 85° in summer.
SPECIES CULTIVATED: *C. anacardioides*, 20 to 30 ft., Australia; *elegantissima*, 15 to 20 ft., Tropics; *grandidens*, 20 to 30 ft., Zanzibar.

Cuphea—*Lythraceae.* Greenhouse evergreen flowering plants. First introduced mid-nineteenth century.
CULTURE: Compost, equal parts loam, leaf-mould, peat and sand. Position, 5 to 6 in. pots in greenhouse, or in beds outdoors in summer. Pot, March or April. Plant outdoors in June. Water moderately Oct. to March, freely afterwards. Temp., March to Sept. 60° to 70°, Sept. to March 50° to 55°.
PROPAGATION: By seeds sown in light soil in temp. 65° to 75° in March; cuttings of young shoots inserted in sandy soil in temp. 65° to 75° in March, April or Aug.
SPECIES CULTIVATED: *C. aequipetala*, purple, June, 2 ft., Mexico; *cyanea*, yellow and red, July, 2 ft., Mexico; *Hookeriana*, vermilion and orange, July, 2 to 3 ft.,

Mexico; *lanceolata*, blue, July, 18 in., annual, Mexico; *Llavea*, bright red, summer, 2 ft., Mexico; *micropetala*, scarlet, white and red, July, 1 ft., Mexico; *platycentra*, ' Cigar Flower ' scarlet, black and white, July, 1 ft., Mexico.

Cupidone, see *Catananche caerulea.*

Cupid's Dart, see Catananche.

Cupressus (Cypress)—*Pinaceae* (or *Cupressaceae*). Hardy evergreen coniferous trees with small scale-like leaves, dark green or variegated with white or yellow. Some species formerly included in this genus have been transferred to Chamaecyparis.

CULTURE: Soil, deep, rich loam. Position, single specimens on lawns, in mixed shrubberies, etc. Plant, Sept. to Nov.

PROPAGATION: By seeds sown in pans of light soil in April, transplanting singly into small pots the following spring and planting out of doors a year afterwards; by cuttings in sandy soil in cold frame or under hand-light in Sept.

SPECIES CULTIVATED: *C. arizonica*, 30 to 40 ft., Arizona; *funebris*, ' Mourning Cypress ', weeping habit, 40 to 50 ft, China; *Goveniana*, compact habit, 20 to 30 ft., California; *lusitanica*, 100 ft., Mexico; *macrocarpa*, ' Monterey Cypress ', spreading habit, 60 to 90 ft., California; *sempervirens*, pyramidal habit, 50 to 60 ft., S. Europe, and vars. *horizontalis, indica, stricta*, etc.

Curculigo—*Amaryllidaceae*. Stove, stemless, evergreen plant. First introduced early nineteenth century.

CULTURE: Compost, equal parts lumpy peat and loam and little silver sand. Position, pots in moist plant stove. Pot, Feb. or March. Water moderately in winter, freely other times. Temp., Sept. to March 55° to 65°, March to Sept. 75° to 85°.

PROPAGATION: By suckers inserted in small pots of sandy soil in temp. 85° in March.

SPECIES CULTIVATED: *C. capitulata* (syn. *C. recurvata*), ' Weevil Plant ', 3 to 4 ft. Trop. Asia, var. *variegata*, variegated foliage.

Curcuma—*Zingiberaceae*. Stove, fleshy-rooted perennials. Turmeric, used as a condiment and dye, is obtained from *C. longa*.

CULTURE: Compost, two parts peat, one part loam and a little sand. Position, pots in warm greenhouse, well drained. Temp., March to Oct. 65° to 75°, Oct. to March 60°. Pot in Feb. Water freely during growing season. Dry off tubers after foliage dies down.

PROPAGATION: By offsets in spring treated as tubers.

SPECIES CULTIVATED: *C. albiflora*, white, 2 ft., July, Ceylon; *longa*, ' Turmeric ', yellow, 2 ft., E. Indies; *petiolata*, yellow, 1½ ft., Sept., Burma; *Roscoeana*, scarlet, 1 ft., Aug., Burma.

Currant, see Ribes; **Alpine-,** see *Ribes alpinum*; **American Black-,** see *R. americanum*; **Black-,** see *R. nigrum*; **Buffalo-,** see *R. aureum*; **Flowering-,** see *R. sanguineum*; **Red-,** see *R. rubrum*; **White-,** see *R. sativum*.

Curtonus—*Iridaceae*. Hardy cormous plants formerly included in Antholyza. Noteworthy for its arched, many-branched inflorescence.

CULTURE: Soil, light sandy. Position, sunny, well-drained borders, or pots in cool greenhouse. Plant 6 in. deep and 6 in. apart in border, or 6 in a 6-in. pot in Oct.

PROPAGATION: By offsets; seeds in slight heat in spring.

SPECIES CULTIVATED: *C. paniculatus* (syn. *Antholyza paniculata*), orange-red, July to Aug., 4 ft., Transvaal, Natal.

Cushion Pink, see *Armeria maritima* and *Silene acaulis.*

Custard Apple, see *Annona reticulata.*

Cyananthus—*Campanulaceae*. Hardy alpine herbaceous perennials. First introduced early nineteenth century.

CULTURE: Compost, equal parts sandy peat and leaf-mould. Position, sunny banks or crevices of rockeries. Plant, March or April. Protect in severe weather with ashes or leaves.

PROPAGATION: By cuttings of shoots 2 in. long inserted in sandy peat, in April, May or June, and kept under bell-glass; division of fleshy roots in March or April.

SPECIES CULTIVATED: *C. incanus*, blue, prostrate, June, Himalaya; *integer*, blue, mat-forming, June to July, Himalaya; *lobatus*, blue, June, prostrate, Himalaya, and vars. *alba*, white, *insignis*, larger flowers; *microphyllus*, blue, prostrate, June, Himalaya; *pedunculatus*, blue-violet, mat-forming, June and July, Nepal, and var. *crenatus*; *Sherriffiae*, blue, trailing, June, Himalaya.

Cyanastrum—*Cyanastraceae*. Warm-house herbaceous perennials with tuberous rootstock.

CULTURE: Compost, loam, leaf-mould and sand.

PROPAGATION: By division.

SPECIES CULTIVATED: *C. cordifolium*, blue or violet, 6 in., W. Trop. Africa.

Cyanella—*Amaryllidaceae*. Half-hardy bulbous plants with fragrant flowers. First introduced mid-eighteenth century.

CULTURE: Compost, two parts sandy soil, one part leaf-mould or decayed cow manure. Position, pots 4½ in. in diameter, well drained, in cold frame or greenhouse. Pot, Oct., placing five bulbs 2 in. deep in each pot, and covering pots with peat until growth begins. Water moderately when bulbs begin to grow; keep bulbs dry Sept. to Jan.

PROPAGATION: By offsets in Nov.

SPECIES CULTIVATED: *C. capensis*, blue, July, 1 ft., Cape of Good Hope; *lutea*, yellow, July, 1 ft., Cape of Good Hope.

Cyathea (Tree Fern)—*Cyatheaceae*. Stove and greenhouse evergreen tree ferns. First introduced late eighteenth century.

CULTURE: Compost, peat and loam and an abundance of sand. Position, large pots or tubs, well drained, in shady stove, greenhouse or conservatory. Repot Feb. or March. Temp. stove, Sept. to March 50° to 65°, March to Sept. 65° to 75°. Greenhouse, Sept. to March 45° to 55°, March to Sept. 55° to 65°. Shade in summer essential. Water moderately Oct. to March, freely afterwards.

PROPAGATION: By spores sown at any time on surface of finely-sifted loam and peat in shallow, well-drained pans; cover with sheet of glass and keep moist in shady position in temp. 75° to 85°.

STOVE SPECIES CULTIVATED: *C. Dregei*, 10 to 12 ft., Trop. Africa; *insignis*, to 8 ft., Jamaica.

GREENHOUSE SPECIES CULTIVATED: *C. dealbata*, 10 ft. and more, New Zealand, etc.; *medullaris*, ' Sago Fern ', 15 to 20 ft., New Zealand.

Cyathodes—*Epacridaceae*. Hardy, evergreen, dwarf flowering shrubs.

CULTURE: Soil, peaty, lime-free. Position, semi-shade or north aspect, cool.

PROPAGATION: Seeds taken when ripe; cuttings in July and Aug.

SPECIES CULTIVATED: *C. Colensoi*, white, berries red, 6 to 9 in., May to June, New Zealand; *divaricata*, pink or red berries, 3 to 4 ft., Tasmania; *empetrifolia*, white, fragrant, prostrate, May to June, New Zealand; *ericoides* (syn. *C. Leucopogon*), white, fragrant, May to June, New Zealand; *Fraseri*, white, fragrant, 6 in., May, New Zealand; *glauca*, white or pink berries, 2 to 3 ft., Tasmania; *parviflora*, deep red berries, 4 to 5 ft., Tasmania; *pumila*, red berries, dwarf, New Zealand; *robusta*, flowers inconspicuous, berries pink, dwarf shrubby habit, Chatham Islands, for sheltered gardens.

Cybistetes—*Amaryllidaceae*. Tender bulbous plant.

CULTURE: As Brunsvigia.

PROPAGATION: As Brunsvigia.

SPECIES CULTIVATED: *C. longifolia* (syn. *Ammocharis falcata*, *Brunsvigia falcata*), pale or dark pink, March, 9 in., S. Africa.

Cycas (Sago Palm)—*Cycadaceae.* Stove plants with ornamental, feather-shaped, dark green leaves.

CULTURE: Compost, two parts turfy loam, one part silver sand. Position, well-drained pots in moist plant stove. Repot, Feb. and March. Water moderately Oct. to March, freely afterwards. Temp., March to Sept. 75° to 80°, Sept. to March 55° to 65°. *C. revoluta* may stand outdoors in sheltered position from June to Sept.

PROPAGATION: By seeds sown 1 in. deep in light soil in temp. 85° to 90° in March or April; suckers obtained from base of plant inserted in small pots in temp. 80° to 85° at any time.

SPECIES CULTIVATED: *C. circinalis,* 8 ft., E. Indies; *revoluta,* 6 to 8 ft., China.

Cyclamen (Sowbread)—*Primulaceae.* Hardy and greenhouse, tuberous-rooted perennial flowering plants. First introduced late sixteenth century.

CULTURE OF GREENHOUSE SPECIES: Compost, two parts loam, one part leaf-mould and sand. Position, pots in greenhouse Sept. to May; cold frame other times. Repot, July or Aug.; corm to be above surface of soil. Water moderately until new growth begins, then increase supply, decreasing it when plants have ceased to flower, keeping roots nearly dry and cool May or July. Apply liquid manure when in flower. Temp., Sept. to April 50° to 55°. Corms should not be grown for more than two years. Best results obtained from seedling plants one year old. Shade from sun essential.

CULTURE OF HARDY SPECIES: Soil, rich, friable loam containing plenty of leaf-mould. Position, sheltered, partially shady nooks of rockery or in turf under trees. Plant, Aug. or Sept., 2 or 3 in. apart and 1½ in. deep. Top-dress with cow manure and rich soil annually after leaves die down, first removing old soil as far as corms. May also be grown in pots or pans in cold greenhouse or frame.

PROPAGATION: Greenhouse kinds by seed sown ½ in. deep and 1 in. apart in well-drained pans of light soil in temp. of 55° Aug. to Nov., or Jan. to March; species by seeds sown similarly in cold frame in Oct. or Nov., transplanting seedlings following spring. Cover surface of soil in seed pans with layer of moss to keep soil uniformly moist. Seeds take several weeks to germinate.

GREENHOUSE SPECIES CULTIVATED: *C. persicum,* ' Florist's Cyclamen ', white, purple and rose, leaves usually variegated with white, 6 to 12 in., Greece to Syria. There are many large-flowered hybrid strains in cultivation.

HARDY SPECIES CULTIVATED: *C. africanum,* red and white, autumn, 6 in., N. Africa; *Atkinsii,* purple and white, hybrid; *coum,* red, Feb. to Mar., 4 in., S. Europe to Persia; *graecum,* rose-red, autumn, 3 in., S.E. Europe; *hederifolium,* red or white, summer or autumn, Europe (Br.); *ibericum,* red, Feb. to Mar., 3 in., Caucasus; *repandum,* rosy-red, March to May, 4 in., Medit. Region.

Cycnoches (Swan Orchid)—*Orchidaceae.* An epiphytic genus with stoutly cylindrical pseudo-bulbs. The spikes are often pendent with numerous flowers. As in Catasetum, the sexes are in separate flowers, the female are more uniform than the males. There are two sections , one in which the lip is entire, the other in which it is divided into slender finger-like lobes in the male flowers. In both the column is slender and curved.

CULTURE: Compost, etc., as for Catasetums.

PROPAGATION: By division of plants when potting in spring.

SPECIES CULTIVATED: With entire lips—*C. chlorochilon,* large, yellow or yellowish-green, lip creamy-white with a black-green blotch, summer, Brazil, Demarara; *Loddigesii* (syn. *C. cucullatum*), large, greenish, suffused purple-brown, lip whitish, red spotted, summer, Brazil.

With divided lips, smaller flowers but more numerous: *Cooperi,* greenish and mahogany-red, lip marked with white, various, Peru; *Egertonianum,* greenish suffused dull purple, summer, autumn, Mexico, Guatemala; *Forgetii,* green, pale brown, summer, Peru; *maculatum,* yellowish or greenish-buff, spotted red-purple, lip white, summer, Mexico; *pentadactylon,* fragrant, yellowish-green, whitish, barred and blotched brown, variable seasons, summer, Brazil; *peruviana*, pale green, spotted purplish-brown, lip white, summer, Peru.

Cydonia (Common Quince)—*Rosaceae*. A small, deciduous, much-branching tree from Persia and Turkistan, grown for its edible fruit, and as rootstock for pears. For flowering quince, see Chaenomeles.

CULTURE: Soil, ordinary. Position, sunny shrubberies or walls. Plant, Nov.

PROPAGATION: By seed, layers, cuttings or suckers.

SPECIES CULTIVATED: *C. oblonga* (syns. *C. vulgaris, Pyrus Cydonia*), to 20 ft., flowers white or pale pink, pear or apple-shaped fruits, fragrant.

Cymbalaria—*Scrophulariaceae*. Creeping herbaceous perennials, often included in the genus Linaria.

CULTURE: Soil, ordinary. Position, moist and partly shady; sunny or shady walls for *C. muralis* and *C. pallida*. Plant, autumn or spring.

POT CULTURE OF C. MURALIS: Compost, two parts loam, one part of equal proportions of dried cow manure, old mortar and sand. Sow seeds $\frac{1}{16}$ in. deep in 3 or 5 in. pots in March or April. Place pots in shady window or greenhouse until seedlings appear, then remove to light and suspend in a basket. Water moderately at first, freely afterwards; keep nearly dry during winter.

PROPAGATION: By division; seeds.

SPECIES CULTIVATED: *C. aequitriloba*, pale violet, summer, trailing, S. Europe; *hepaticifolia*, lilac, summer, trailing, France, Corsica; *muralis* (syn. *Linaria Cymbalaria*) 'Kenilworth Ivy', 'Ivy-leaved Toadflax', 'Mother o' Millions', lilac, summer, Europe (Br.); *pallida*, blue, summer, 3 ins., Italy; *pilosa*, lavender and yellow, summer, 2 to 3 ins., Italy.

Cymbidium—*Orchidaceae*. A genus of epiphytic, semi-epiphytic and terrestrial orchids; with exceptions the pseudo-bulbs are short, stout, clustered, sheathed and surmounted by long persistent leaves. The spikes are produced from the base of the pseudo-bulbs and in many carry large long-lasting flowers. On the whole the genus is of great horticultural value, and of late years an immense number of hybrids have been produced and, to an extent, superseded the species as a much greater variety of colour is present and the flowers appear in late autumn to April and May. These hybrids are so numerous and vary so greatly that if special colours are desired it is necessary either to see the flowers or secure authenticated varieties, or divisions. All, however, are as easily cultivated as the species.

CULTURE: Compost, largely of rough but fibrous loam, with a little sphagnum moss and finely broken potsherds. Peat may be added. Pots are suitable, tubs for large plants, drainage about 2 in. Repot, if necessary, in early spring, as growth appears, earlier if extra heat can be maintained. Usually growths or flower spikes are present through the winter and water must be given. Winter temp. should be 50° or a little higher, but falls to 45° or even lower do no harm if the atmosphere is kept fairly dry, and within reason the compost is dry. Admit night air whenever conditions are favourable. Syringe freely in summer, the temp. can then rise by sun heat to 70° to 80°. From April to September weak liquid manure may be sprinkled on the floor spaces in the evening.

PROPAGATION: By division of plants or healthy back bulbs may be removed and placed on compost, or potsherds, in a damp position. Pot when growth is seen.

SPECIES CULTIVATED: A selection—*C. Ballianum*, flowers 3 to 7, white, winter, spring, Burma, Annam; *Dayanum*, segments narrow, whitish with a purplish stripe, Assam, Annam; *Devonianum*, flowers small, many, greenish to purple, spring, Assam, Sikkim; *eburneum*, flowers 1 to 3, large, white, very fragrant, winter, early spring, N. India, Burma, var. *Dayanum*, marginal purple spots on lip; *ensifolium*, yellowish-brown, very fragrant, autumn, N. India; *erythrostylum*, glistening white, red column, and reddish stripes on lip, autumn, Annam; *Finlaysonianum*, tawny red, long pendent spikes, summer, Malaya, Borneo; *giganteum*, yellowish-green, striped red-brown, autumn, N. India, Annam; *grandi-*

florum (syns. *C. Griffithianum* and *C. Hookerianum*), large, green lip spotted red, winter, spring, Himalaya; *I'ansonii* (syn. *C. mandaianum*), tawny yellow, veined and suffused purplish-brown, winter, spring, Burma, Annam; *insigne* (syn. *C. Sanderi*), variable, white, suffused with rose-lilac, dotted in places with crimson, spikes erect, early spring, Annam; *Lowianum*, flowers 15 to 36, yellowish-green suffused with reddish-brown, lip widely bordered with crimson-red, spring, early summer, Burma, var. *concolor*, yellow, tinted green; *Parishii*, white, purple spotted chiefly on lip margins, summer, Burma, var. *Sanderae*, flowers 3 to 6, purple spots, bolder, Annam; *sinense*, very fragrant, like *ensifolium*, autumn, China; *tigrinum*, dwarf, 2 to 5 flowered racemes, yellowish, marked crimson, lip yellowish, striped crimson, summer, Burma; *Tracyanum*, large, very fragrant, yellowish with red-brown lines, lip cream colour spotted red, softly haired, autumn, Burma.

Cymbopogon—*Gramineae.* Stove ornamental flowering grass. First introduced late eighteenth century.

CULTURE: Compost, two parts loam, one part leaf-mould and sand. Position, pots in stove. Pot, March. Water freely March to Oct., moderately afterwards. Temp., March to Oct. 75° to 85°, Oct. to March 55° to 65.

PROPAGATION: By division in March.

SPECIES CULTIVATED: *C. Martinii*, to 2 ft., foliage lemon scented, India.

Cynara—*Compositae.* Coarse, hardy, herbaceous perennials. Immature flower heads of artichoke and blanched stalks and midribs of leaves of cardoon used as vegetables.

CULTURE OF CARDOON: Soil, light, deep, rich and moist. Position, open and sunny. Prepare trenches 2 ft. deep, 18 in. wide as for celery, in March. Fork 6 in. of rotted manure into the soil in bottom of trench and cover with 3 in. soil. Sow seed 20 in. apart in early May 1½ in. deep. Place a stake to each plant when a foot high, and secure the leaves loosely to this. Soak roots once a week with diluted liquid manure and water copiously. Blanch in Aug., winding brown paper round stems for 6 in. when leaves are tied together at top. Increase blanched area in 6 in. steps each week, covering paper with a hayband and mulch of soil. Plants are sufficiently blanched for cooking eight weeks after earthing up. Seeds may be sown two in a 3 in. pot filled with ordinary soil, placed in temp. 55° to 65° in March, hardened off in April, and planted out in May.

CULTURE OF GLOBE ARTICHOKE: Soil, deep, rich loam, liberally manured and trenched three spits deep. Position, open and sunny. Plant suckers, *i.e.* offshoots, 4 in. deep in triangular groups 9 in. from plant to plant, 2 ft. apart in rows 4 ft. asunder, early in April. Keep well watered first season. In Nov. surround each plant with dry litter and in severe weather cover with similar material, uncovering in mild weather. Fork surface over in March, and mulch with decayed manure. Apply liquid manure freely to established plants during summer. Gather flower heads for use when fully developed. Seaweed an excellent manure. Apply in spring. Replant bed every four years.

PROPAGATION: By suckers removed in Nov. and stored in boxes with a little soil in a cold frame and planted out in April. Seedlings are variable.

SPECIES CULTIVATED: *C. Cardunculus*, ' Cardoon ', purple, Aug., 4 to 6 ft., S. Europe; *Scolymus*, ' Globe Artichoke ', Sept., 3 to 6 ft., Europe.

Cynoglossum—*Boraginaceae.* Hardy perennials and alpines.

CULTURE: Soil, well-drained loam with sand and leaf-mould. Position, sunny beds and rock gardens.

PROPAGATION: *C. Wallichii* by division. *C. amabile* is best treated as a biennial, raising a fresh stock each year from seed sown in a cold frame in March or April.

SPECIES CULTIVATED: *C. amabile*, blue, June, 2 ft., S.W. China; *Wallichii*, sky blue, summer, 8 in., Himalaya. See also Omphalodes.

Cynorchis—*Orchidaceae.* A genus of terrestrial orchids with fleshy or tuberous roots. Leaves deciduous in several species. The flowers have their labellums shaped much as those of Calanthe.

CULTURE: Compost, half fibrous loam, half osmunda fibre and sphagnum moss for the warm-growing kinds. Three parts loam, one part sphagnum moss, finely crushed potsherds added for the cool growing kinds which require a rather decided rest. Pans.

PROPAGATION: By division, if possible, in spring.

SPECIES CULTIVATED: *C. compacta*, small, clustered, white, cool, early spring, S. Africa; *grandiflora*, variable, greenish, lip rose-purple, spur slender, winter, Madagascar; *Lowiana*, greenish, lip purple, winter, Madagascar; *purpurascens*, flowers up to 25, greenish, lip purplish and whitish, basket, spring, Madagascar; *villosa*, lilac-purple, lip whitish, hairy, late summer, Madagascar.

Cypella—*Iridaceae*. Half-hardy bulbs. Suitable for cool greenhouse and outdoor culture. First introduced early nineteenth century.

OUTDOOR CULTURE: Soil, light, rich sandy. Position, sunny well-drained border. Plant, Sept. to Jan., placing bulbs 4 in. deep and 2 in. apart. Lift and replant bulbs annually. Mulch surface of bed in March with cow manure.

POT CULTURE: Compost, two parts sandy loam, one part leaf-mould or decayed cow manure. Pots, 4½ in. in diameter, well drained. Place five bulbs, 3 in. deep, in each pot in Nov., and cover with moss or leaves, in cold frames or under cool greenhouse stage until growth begins. Water moderately from time bulbs begin to grow until flowers fade, then gradually cease, keeping bulbs dry till Jan. Temp., Sept. to March 40° to 50°, other times 50° to 60°.

PROPAGATION: By offsets treated as advised for bulbs or by seeds sown as soon as ripe in a cool house.

SPECIES CULTIVATED: *C. Herbertii* (syn. *Tigridia Herbertii*), yellow, summer, 1 ft., S. America; *peruviana*, yellow and brown, summer, 1 ft., Peru; *plumbea*, greyish-blue and yellow, autumn, 3 ft., Brazil.

Cyperus (Galingale)—*Cyperaceae*. Greenhouse and hardy grass-like perennials.

CULTURE OF GREENHOUSE SPECIES: Compost, two parts loam, one part leaf-mould and sand. Position, pots in shady greenhouse. Water moderately in winter, freely other times. Repot, Feb. to March. Temp., March to Sept. 55° to 65°, Sept. to March 45° to 55°.

CULTURE OF HARDY SPECIES: Soil, heavy loam. Position, margins of lakes, ponds, etc. Plant, Oct. to March.

PROPAGATION: By seeds sown in shallow boxes or pans of light soil in temp. 55° to 65° in March or April; division of roots in March or April.

GREENHOUSE SPECIES CULTIVATED: *C. alternifolius*, ' Umbrella Plant ', 2½ ft., leaves green, Africa, vars. *variegatus*, leaves striped with white, *gracilis*, a dwarfer, more elegant form; *Haspan*, 1 to 3 ft., Trop. America, etc., var. *adenophorus*, 18 in.; *Papyrus* (syn. *Papyrus antiquorum*), ' Papyrus ', 8 to 10 ft., leaves green, Trop, Africa.

HARDY SPECIES CULTIVATED: *C. esculentus*, ' Chufa ', producing underground edible tubers, 2 to 3 ft., N. America, Europe and Asia; *longus*, 4 ft., Europe; *vegetus* (syn. *C. Eragrostis*), crowded heads of mahogany-coloured flowers, autumn and winter, Chile.

Cyphomandra—*Solanaceae*. Greenhouse evergreen shrub. Fruit, large, egg-shaped, red and edible, ripe in Aug. and Sept. First introduced early nineteenth century.

CULTURE: Compost, two parts loam, one part leaf-mould and sand. Position, pots in light, sunny greenhouse. Pot, March or April. Water moderately Oct. to March, freely afterwards. Temp., Oct. to March 45° to 55°, March to Sept. 55° to 65°. Prune plants into shape March or April.

PROPAGATION: By seeds sown ⅛ in. deep in light soil in temp. 75° to 85° in March or April; cuttings of side shoots 3 in. long inserted in sandy soil under bell-glass in temp. 75° to 80° in spring or early summer.

SPECIES CULTIVATED: *C. betacea*, ' Tree Tomato ', purple and green, spring, 6 to 10 ft., S. America.

Cypress, see Cupressus; **Bald-,** see *Taxodium distichum*; **Montezuma-,** see *Taxodium mucronatum*; **-Spurge,** see *Euphorbia Cyparissias*; **-Vine,** see *Quamoclit pennata.*

Cypripedium (Lady's Slipper Orchid; Moccasin Flower)—*Orchidaceae.* A generic name which has unfortunately been misused. Led away by the pouch-like formation of their labellums four different genera have become familiarised under this name. The so-called Selenipediums of orchid collections are often included in this genus. The name Cypripedium was first applied to a hardy species (correctly it should have been Cypripedilum) characterised by plicate deciduous leaves, which, more or less, ascend the flowering stems. The species are distributed in both hemispheres. The greenhouse and stove plants known as Cypripediums should correctly be termed Paphiopedilums. All are Eastern, from India to Hong Kong, their leaves are of greater consistency than those of Cypripediums and persistent, conduplicate, often mottled. The so-called Selenipediums (correctly Phragmipedium of gardens) differ again, their leaves are more numerous, not tessellated, narrower and tapered. The stems bear several flowers more or less in succession. Some Paphiopedilums bear 3 to 5 flowers on their scapes but in Phragmipedium the dorsal sepal, though it may be attenuated, is on the whole smaller than that in Paphiopedilums and the flowers are never warted or spotted. Of true Selenipediums there are only three or four species and they have never appeared in cultivation. Botanical differences in floral structure also serve to differentiate the four genera. The greater number of Cypripediums should be hardy but in their home the seasons are more consistent than ours and growths are delayed till frost is past. Snow often affords complete protection to the roots in their native habitat. Here an early start is often fatal.

CULTURE: Compost, two parts peat, one part leaf-mould, one or two parts fibrous loam and an addition of sharp sand and chopped sphagnum moss. A north-west aspect is often preferable to one which might appear more favourable. A mulching of leaves may be given in winter. Species may also be grown in pans in a frost-proof frame or house during winter and placed out of doors in the summer, not too sunny.

PROPAGATION: By division of the plants (the rhizomes often branch).

SPECIES CULTIVATED: A selection—*C. arietinum*, yellowish-green, shaded brown and whitish, the lateral sepals are free, they form one organ in others, spring to summer, Canada; *Calceolus*, dark brown, lip yellow, spring, summer, England, Europe, N. Asia, var. *pubescens*, large, greenish-yellow or yellowish, lip sometimes marked with red-brown, early summer; *candidum*, solitary, greenish-brown, lip white or rose-veined, early summer, N. America; *japonicum*, solitary, large, greenish-white, red dotted, lip white and crimson, summer, Japan; *macranthum*, variable, large, 1 to 2 red-purple, lip pink and purple-red, summer, N. Asia; *Reginae* (syn. *C. spectabile*), large, white or rose-flushed, lip rose to purplish-rose, succeeds in damp places or bog gardens, summer, N. America, Canada; *tibeticum*, large solitary, greenish-yellow and dark purple, lip blackish-purple in front, summer, Tibet, China.

Cyrilla—*Cyrillaceae.* Hardy evergreen flowering shrub. Flowers borne in tufts on the ends of old wood. Seldom planted. First introduced mid-eighteenth century.

CULTURE: Soil, loam and peat. Position, warm, sheltered nooks. Plant, Sept. or April.

PROPAGATION: By cuttings in silver sand under bell-glass in temp. 55° to 65°.

SPECIES CULTIVATED: *C. racemiflora*, ' Leatherwood ', white, summer, 6 ft., Southern U.S.A.

Cyrtanthus—*Amaryllidaceae.* Greenhouse bulbous plants with fragrant flowers. First introduced mid-eighteenth century.

CULTURE: Compost, two parts loam, one part sand and peat. Position, well-drained pots on shelf in light greenhouse. Pot bulbs in Oct. to Nov., 2 in. deep.

Water freely March to Oct., very little other times. Temp., Nov. to April 50° to 55°, April to Nov. 60° to 65°.

PROPAGATION: By offsets in Nov. or seeds sown as soon as ripe in a temp. of 55° to 60°.

SPECIES CULTIVATED: *C. angustifolius*, orange, summer, 1 ft., S. Africa; *carneus*, red, summer, 1 ft., S. Africa; *collinus*, red, Aug., 1 ft., S. Africa; *epiphyticus*, red, 1½ ft., Natal; *Flanaganii*, yellow, 9 in., S. Africa; *Mackenii*, white, Dec. to March, 1 ft., Natal, var. *Cooperi* (syn. *C. lutescens*), yellow; *obliquus*, yellow and red, 9 to 24 in., S. Africa; *O'Brienii*, pale scarlet, 1 ft., S. Africa; *parviflorus*, bright red, 1 ft., S. Africa; *rhododactylus*, rose, 6 in., S. Africa; *sanguineus*, red, summer, 1 ft., S. Africa.

Cyrtomium—*Polypodiaceae.* Greenhouse ferns.

CULTURE: Compost, equal parts loam, leaf-mould, peat and sand. Pot, March. Water freely in summer, moderately in winter. Shade from strong sun. Temp., Sept. to March 45° to 55°, March to Sept. 55° to 65°. These ferns also make good room plants provided the atmosphere is not too dry.

PROPAGATION: By division of roots in March, also by spores sown on fine sandy peat in temp. 60° at any time.

SPECIES CULTIVATED: *C. caryotideum*, 1 to 2 ft., fronds drooping, Japan, India; *falcatum* (Holly fern), 2 to 3 ft., fronds spreading or erect, Asia.

Cyrtopodium—*Orchidaceae.* About thirty terrestrial and epiphytic species. First introduced early nineteenth century. Pseudo-bulbs are fusiform, short or tall; scapes bracteate produced from their base with the young growth, often tall and panicled. Leaves deciduous in some. *C. Andersonii* and *punctatum* are the finest species in cultivation.

CULTURE: Compost, as for Cymbidiums but with more peat or osmunda fibre, a little sphagnum and crushed potsherds. Pots or pans, well drained. Pot March or April. Water freely April to Aug., moderately Aug. to Nov., afterwards keep nearly or quite dry. Expose to full light in autumn; winter temp. 60°, summer 70° to 80°. Resting period when bulbs are matured in a light position.

PROPAGATION: By division of plants large enough in spring.

SPECIES CULTIVATED: *C. Andersonii*, tall, panicled, yellow and greenish-yellow, lip rich yellow, many, 1½ in. diameter, spring, early summer, Brazil, W. Indies, var. *cardiochilum* (syn. *C. cardiochilum*), flowers more closely set; *punctatum* (syn. *C. speciosum*), yellow, red spotted and marked, lip yellow and chestnut, crest and base spotted red, bracts greenish-yellow and often spotted bright red-brown, spring, S. America; *virescens*, greenish-yellow and red-chocolate, lip marked red-purple, spring, Brazil.

Cystopteris (Bladder Fern)—*Polypodiaceae.* Hardy deciduous ferns.

CULTURE: Soil, rich, deep, sandy loam, freely mixed with pieces of limestone or dried mortar. Position, well-drained, shady, sheltered rockery. Plant, March or April. Water moderately in dry weather.

POT CULTURE: Compost, two parts good loam, one part leaf-mould mixed with old mortar or sand. Position, well-drained, cold frame or cold greenhouse in shade. Repot, March or April. Water freely April to Sept., moderately Sept. to Nov., nearly dry afterwards.

PROPAGATION: By spores sown on surface of fine sandy soil in shallow boxes or pans, cover with sheet of glass and place in cold frame at any time; division of plants in March or April.

SPECIES CULTIVATED: *C. bulbifera*, 6 to 12 in., N. America; *fragilis*, 6 to 8 in., fronds deeply cut, widely distributed and variable, Europe, Newfoundland, Arizona, and var. *alpina*, small finely cut fronds, Asia Minor; *montana*, 6 to 8 in., Europe and N. America.

Cytisus (Broom)—*Leguminosae.* Greenhouse and hardy deciduous and evergreen flowering shrubs. ' Genista ' of florists is *C. canariensis*. The named varieties, in great numbers, provide wonderful colouring.

Culture of Greenhouse Species: Compost, two parts turfy loam, one part lumpy peat and sharp sand. Position, pots in greenhouse. Pot, May or June. Prune shoots to within 2 in. of base directly after flowering and place plants in temp. 50° to 55° to make new growth before repotting. Place plants in sunny place outdoors from end July to Oct. to ripen growth. Water freely March to May, moderately during May and June, freely June to Nov., moderately afterwards. Apply weak liquid or artificial manure to plants during the time they are in bloom. Temp., Nov. to Feb. 45° to 50°, Feb. to May 50° to 55°, May to June 55° to 60°.

Culture of Hardy Species: Soil, ordinary. Brooms will thrive in hungry light and stony soils and enjoy dry root conditions and full sun. Position, sunny rockery for *C. Ardoinii, C. kewensis,* etc.; shrubbery borders for *C. multiflorus, C. praecox, C. purpureus, scoparius,* var. *Andreanus,* and choice kinds; rough banks, woodlands, etc. for *C. scoparius.* Plant, Oct. to Dec. Prune directly after flowering, shortening old shoots to base of promising young ones but avoid cutting into old wood. Transplant best when young. *C. praecox, C. purpureus* and *C. scoparius* var. *Andreanus* make excellent pot plants for flowering early in cold greenhouse.

Propagation: Greenhouse species by cuttings of young shoots 3 in. long with small portions of branches attached in sandy soil in well-drained pots under bell-glass in temp. 75° to 80° in March, April or May; seeds sown ¼ in. deep in well-drained pots of light soil in temp. 65° to 70° in March; hardy species by seeds outdoors in March or April; August cuttings in sandy soil; grafting in March or April. Seeds of common broom may be scattered broadcast on banks or in woodlands.

Greenhouse Species Cultivated: *C. canariensis* (syn. *Genista canariensis*), yellow, fragrant, spring and summer to 6 ft., Canary Is., and var. *ramosissimus,* small leaved; *filipes,* white, March, 4 to 6 ft., Canary Is.; *fragrans* (syn. *Genista fragrans*), yellow, summer, 2 to 3 ft., Canary Is., var. *elegans,* yellow, 4 ft.

Hardy Species Cultivated: *C. albus,* ' White Spanish Broom ', white, May, 6 to 10 ft., Spain; *Ardoinii,* yellow, spring, 4 to 6 in., Maritime Alps; *Beanii,* deep yellow, May, 6 to 18 in., hybrid; *Battandieri,* 10 ft., newer species, hardy in south, golden, scented, June, foliage and shoots covered with silky hairs, Morocco; *Burkwoodii,* 4 to 5 ft., flowers red, hybrid; *decumbens,* yellow, May to June, 4 to 6 in., S. Europe; *hirsutus,* yellow, 1 to 2 ft., S. Europe; *kewensis,* creamy white, May, prostrate, hybrid; *monspessulanus,* yellow, May, 5 to 7 ft., S. Europe; *multiflorus* (syn. *C. albus*), ' White Spanish Broom ', white, May, to 10 ft., Spain, N. Africa; *nigricans,* yellow, June, 4 to 6 ft., Europe; *praecox,* creamy yellow, May, 4 to 6 ft., hybrid; *purgans,* deep yellow, April to May, 3 to 4 ft., France and Spain; *purpureus,* purple, May, 1 to 1¼ ft., E. Europe; *ratisbonensis,* yellow, May, 4 to 6 ft., Europe; *scoparius,* ' Common Broom ', yellow, April to July, 5 to 10 ft., Europe (Br.), var. *Andreanus,* yellow and red; *sessilifolius,* yellow, June, 5 to 6 ft., S. Europe and N. Africa; *versicolor,* yellowish-purple, May, 2 to 3 ft., hybrid.

Daboecia—*Ericaceae.* Evergreen flowering shrub of heath-like appearance.

Culture: Compost, sandy peat and loam free from lime. Best planted in clumps 15 in. apart each way. Position, sunny banks or rockeries. Plant, Sept., Oct., March or April.

Propagation: By cuttings inserted in sandy soil in summer under hand-light; layers of shoots in autumn.

Species Cultivated: *D. azorica,* 6 in., bright rose, June, Azores; *cantabrica* (syn. *D. polifolia, Menziesia polifolia*), ' Irish Heath ', ' St. Dabeoc's Heath ', 18 in., purple, July, Connemara and S.W. Europe. There are various forms: *alba,* white; *atropurpurea,* rich, reddish purple; and *bicolor,* some flowers white, others purple, and some mixed on the same plant.

Dacrydium—*Taxaceae* (or *Podocarpaceae*). Rather tender, ornamental, evergreen trees. First introduced early nineteenth century.

CULTURE: Soil, sandy peat. Position, as specimens in open places or upon lawns in mildest districts only. Plant, Sept. to Oct. and April to May.
PROPAGATION: By cuttings of ripened wood in cold frame in Aug. or Sept.; seeds sown in sandy peat in pans in cool greenhouse during Feb. or March.
SPECIES CULTIVATED: *D. cupressinum*, ' New Zealand Rimu ', 80 to 100 ft., New Zealand; *Franklinii*, ' Huon Pine ', 80 to 100 ft., Tasmania.

Dactylis (Cock's-foot Grass)—*Gramineae*. Hardy ornamental grass.
CULTURE: Soil, ordinary. Position, margins of flower beds or borders in sun or shade, or mixed with bedding plants. Plant, Oct. or April, 3 to 6 in. apart.
PROPAGATION: By division of plants in Oct. or April.
SPECIES CULTIVATED: *D. glomerata variegata*, silver and green variegation, 6 to 8 in., Britain.

Daemonorops—*Palmae*. Stove, ornamental-leaved, climbing palms. Useful for table decoration.
CULTURE: Compost, equal parts loam, peat, leaf-mould and sand. Position, pots in a young state; in beds or tubs with shoots trained up pillars when large. Pot or plant in March. Water freely in summer, moderately in winter. Syringe daily; moist atmosphere essential. Temp., March to Oct. 75° to 85°, Oct. to March 60° to 65°.
PROPAGATION: By seeds sown in sand or sandy soil in spring.
SPECIES CULTIVATED: *D. Lewisianus*, Penang; *melanochaetes*, Malaya; *palembanicus*, Sumatra; *periacanthus*, Sumatra; *plumosus*, India.

Daffodil, see *narcissus PseudoNarcissus*; **-Orchid,** see *Ipsea speciosa*.

Dahlia—*Compositae*. Half-hardy, herbaceous, tuberous-rooted perennials. First introduced late eighteenth century.
TYPES—Show : Flower, large, circular; florets, quilled; colour, all one tint. Fancy: Flower, large, circular; florets, quilled; colour, florets tipped, striped or flaked different tint to ground colour. Cactus: Flower, high in centre, circular; florets, long, narrow, pointed, not quilled or fluted, reflexed at edges. Pompon: Flower, small, circular; florets and colours like those of show and fancy types. Single: Flower, circular; florets, broad, flat, eight in number, overlapping each other, rounded, recurving at tips. Collarette: Flowers, single, with ' collar ' of very shortened florets; outer florets broad and flattened. Peony-flowered: Flower, semi-double; outer florets, broad; inner ones, short and narrow. Charm and Miniature Peony-flowered: Flower, semi-double; florets, broad and more or less flattened; plants bushy and branching; colours very varied. Decorative: Flower, semi-double; florets, flat. Anemone-flowered: Flowers, double; outer florets, broad and flattened; inner florets, short and densely packed. Star: Flowers, semi-double; florets, long, narrow, pointed, reflexed at edges and incurving towards centre. Orchid: Flowers, single; florets, broad, flattened and twisted. Dwarf Bedding: Flowers, single or semi-double; florets, broad and more or less flattened; habit, dwarf and branching, very free flowering. Forms of garden origin include Cactus, Semi-cactus, Decorative (tall), Pompon, Charm, Dwarf Cactus (medium), Bedding, double and single (dwarf).
OUTDOOR CULTURE: Soil, ordinary, well enriched with manure. Position, open sunny beds or borders. Plant tubers 3 in. deep in April, or start them in pots in temp. 55° in March, planting outdoors in May or June. Thin shoots to three on each plant in July; flower buds to one on each shoot in Aug. Apply liquid manure occasionally in July, Aug. and Sept. Lift and store tubers in frost-proof place in Oct., just covering them with soil or coconut-fibre refuse. Cut down stems to within 6 in. of tubers before lifting.
CULTURE IN POTS: Compost, two parts turfy loam, one part decayed manure. Place tubers in well-drained 6 in. pots in March, in temp. 55°. Water moderately and keep close to glass. Transfer to 8 in. pots in May. Stand plants outdoors in June. Apply liquid manure in July. Thin shoots to three on each plant, flower

buds to one on each shoot in Aug. Withhold water after flowering and store away in frost-proof place.

PROPAGATION: By seeds sown ⅛ in. deep in light soil in temp. 65° to 75° in March; cuttings of shoots 3 in. long issuing from tubers, inserted in 2 in. pots of sandy soil, in temp. 65° to 70° in Feb., March or April; division of tubers in spring.

SPECIES CULTIVATED: *D. coccinea*, scarlet, autumn, 4 ft., parent of Single Dahlia; *coronata*, scarlet, Mexico; *excelsa*, purplish-pink, summer, 15 to 20 ft.; *gracilis*, orange-scarlet, autumn, 5 ft.; *imperialis*, white, lilac and red, Oct., 10 to 12 ft.; *Juarezii*, parent of Cactus Dahlias, scarlet, autumn, 3 ft.; *Merckii*, lilac and yellow, Oct., 3 ft.; *pinnata* (syn. *D. variabilis*), parent of Show, Fancy and Pompon Dahlias, scarlet, autumn, 4 ft.

Daisy, see Bellis;   **-Bush,** see *Olearia Haastii*.

Dalechampia—*Euphorbiaceae*. Stove flowering evergreen shrubs. First introduced mid-eighteenth century.

CULTURE: Compost, equal parts loam, peat, leaf-mould and sand. Position, shady part of plant stove. Pot, March. Water moderately Sept. to April, freely afterwards. Temp., Sept. to March 55° to 65°, March to Sept. 70° to 80°.

PROPAGATION: By cuttings inserted in sandy peat under bell-glass in March, April or May, in temp. 85°.

SPECIES CULTIVATED: *D. Roezliana*, yellow, insignificant, bracts rose, 12 in., Mexico; *scandens*, 18 in., Trop. America; *spathulata*, 12 to 18 in., Mexico, and var. *rosea*.

Damask Rose, see *Rosa damascena*.

Damasonium (Starfruit)—*Alismaceae*. Shallow-water aquatics closely allied to Alisma.

CULTURE: Position, wet soil or shallow water.

PROPAGATION: Seed sown in March in shallow pans of loam just covered with water.

SPECIES CULTIVATED: *D. Alisma*, white or yellow flowers, star-like fruit, very rare British plant.

Dame's Rocket or **Dame's Violet,** see *Hesperis matronalis*.

Damson, see *Prunus domestica* var. *insititia*.

Danae—*Liliaceae*. Hardy evergreen berry-bearing shrub with bamboo-like growth. Introduced early eighteenth century.

CULTURE: Soil, ordinary, medium or light, moist. Position, under shade of trees; good carpeting shrub. Plant in autumn.

PROPAGATION: By seeds sown outdoors in autumn; by division in spring.

SPECIES CULTIVATED: *D. racemosa* (syn. *Ruscus racemosus*), ' Alexandrian Laurel ', greenish-white flowers, succeeded by red berries, 2 to 3 ft., sprays used for indoor winter decoration, S. Europe.

Dandelion, see Taraxacum.

Daphne—*Thymelaeaceae*. Greenhouse and hardy deciduous and evergreen shrubs with fragrant flowers.

CULTURE OF GREENHOUSE SPECIES: Compost, two parts loam, one part peat and sand. Position, airy greenhouse from Sept. to June, outdoors June to Sept. Pot, Feb., pinch out points of young shoots in June. Water moderately Sept. to April, freely afterwards. Temp., Sept. to March 40° to 50°, March to Sept. 55° to 65°.

CULTURE OF HARDY SPECIES: Soil, sandy peat. Position, drooping over front of rockeries for trailing species; summit of rockery or open border for erect species. Plant, Oct., Nov., March or April. *D. Mezereum* is very free flowering, easy of culture and can be raised from seed.

PROPAGATION—Greenhouse species : By cuttings of side shoots in well-drained pots or pans of sandy peat under bell-glass in temp. 50° to 55°; layers in March

or April; grafting on *D. Laureola* and *D. pontica* in spring. Hardy species: By layering shoots in autumn and seed sown as soon as ripe.

GREENHOUSE SPECIES CULTIVATED: *D. odora*, purple, Jan. to March, 2 to 3 ft., Japan, very strongly fragrant, bushes will succeed in the open in the extreme S.W.

HARDY SPECIES CULTIVATED: *D. Blagayana*, white, March to April, fragrant, 9 to 12 in., E. Europe; *Burkwoodii*, 3 ft., creamy white flushed pink, April, May, hybrid; *Cneorum*, ' Garland Flower ', pink, May, fragrant, 10 to 12 in., Cent. and S. Europe; *collina*, purplish rose, March to June, fragrant, 2 to 3 ft., Italy and Asia Minor; *hybrida*, reddish-purple, spring and autumn, fragrant, 2 to 4 ft., hybrid; *Laureola*, yellowish-green, Feb. to March, fragrant, S. and W. Europe (Br.); *oleoides*, purplish-rose to white, 2 to 3 ft., S. Europe; *petraea*, bright pink, June, fragrant, 3 to 5 in., S. Tyrol; *pontica*, yellowish-green, April, fragrant, 2 to 3 ft., Asia Minor; *retusa*, rose, purple and white, May, fragrant, 1 to 2 ft., W. China.

HARDY DECIDUOUS SPECIES CULTIVATED: *D. acutiloba*, 4 ft., white, July, W. China; *alpina*, white, May to June, fragrant, 6 to 18 in., Alps; *caucasica*, white, May to June, fragrant, 3 to 4 ft., Caucasus; *Mezereum*, ' Mezereon ', purplish-red or white, Feb. to March, fragrant, 3 to 5 ft., Europe and Siberia, and vars. *alba*, white, *grandiflora*, autumn flowering.

Daphniphyllum—*Euphorbiaceae.* Hardy evergreen shrubs. Flowers unisexual and sexes on separate plants, unattractive. First introduced late nineteenth century.

CULTURE: Soil, ordinary rich. Position, moist shady borders or shrubberies. Plant, Nov.

PROPAGATION: By cuttings of nearly ripe wood in close frame in July.

SPECIES CULTIVATED: *D. humile*, blue-black fruits, 1½ to 2 ft., Japan; *macropodum*, blue-black fruits, 8 to 12 ft., Japan.

Darling River Pea, see *Swainsona coronilliflora.*

Darlingtonia—*Sarraceniaceae.* Hardy, herbaceous, insectivorous plant. Pitchers borne on summit of leaves, hood-like, bright green, mottled with white and pink. First introduced mid-nineteenth century.

GREENHOUSE CULTURE: Compost, equal parts peat, chopped sphagnum, sharp sand and sifted loam. Position, shady greenhouse, plunge pots in live sphagnum. Pot, Feb. or March. Water freely during growing season. Syringe daily March to Sept.

OUTDOOR CULTURE: Compost, spongy fibrous peat and chopped sphagnum moss. Position, damp, by side of stream, or in bog exposed to sun, but sheltered from cold winds. Plant, March or April. Protect in winter with hand-light.

PROPAGATION: By seeds sown on surface of mixture of fibrous peat, charcoal, sphagnum and sand in a pan standing partly in water and covered with a bell-glass in cool greenhouse in April or May; division of side shoots inserted in small pots at any time of year.

SPECIES CULTIVATED: *D. californica*, ' Californian Pitcher Plant ', yellow and green, April, 12 in., California.

Darwinia—*Myrtaceae.* Greenhouse evergreen shrubs. First introduced early nineteenth century.

CULTURE: Compost, equal parts loam, peat and sand. Position, well-drained pots in airy greenhouse. Pot firmly in Feb. or March. Water moderately Sept. to March, freely March to Sept. Prune, Feb. or March. Temp., Sept. to March 40° to 50°, March to Sept. 50° to 60°.

PROPAGATION: By cuttings of young shoots 2 or 3 in. long inserted in sandy peat under bell-glass in temp. 40° to 50° in April or May.

SPECIES CULTIVATED: *D. diosmoides*, white, 3 ft., Australia; *fascicularis*, red, 3 to 5 ft., Australia; *fimbriata*, rose, June, 5 ft., Australia; *Hookeriana*, resembles *macrostegia* but usually smaller; *macrostegia* (syn. *Genetvllis tulipifera*), crimson, May, 3 ft., Australia.

Dasylirion—*Liliaceae.* Greenhouse evergreen plants. Leaves, glaucous green, with spiny margins. First introduced early nineteenth century.

CULTURE: Compost, two parts loam and peat, one sand. Position, pots or tubs in airy greenhouse, dwelling-rooms or outdoors in beds May to Sept. Pot firmly Feb. or March. Water very little Oct. to March, freely afterwards. Temp., Sept. to March 40° to 50°, March to Sept. 50° to 60°.

PROPAGATION: By seeds sown in sandy peat in well-drained pans or pots under bell-glass in temp. 50° to 60° in March, April or May.

SPECIES CULTIVATED: *D. acrotriche,* 6 to 8 ft., Mexico; *glaucophyllum.* 10 ft., Mexico; *Hookeri,* 3 ft., Mexico; *serratifolium,* Mexico.

Date Palm, see *Phoenix dactylifera;* **-Plum,** see *Diospyrus Lotus.*

Datisca—*Datiscaceae.* Hardy herbaceous perennial. Male and female flowers borne on separate plants. Leaves, pinnate, green. First introduced mid-eighteenth century.

CULTURE: Soil, deep rich, ordinary. Position, open and sunny border. Plant, Oct., Nov., March and April. Female plant most effective.

PROPAGATION: By seeds sown $\frac{1}{16}$ in. deep in fine soil outdoors in March, April or May, transplanting seedlings to permanent positions any time.

SPECIES CULTIVATED: *D. cannabina,* ' False Hemp ', greenish-white, summer, 3 to 6 ft., W. Asia.

Datura (Trumpet Flower)—*Solanaceae.* Half-hardy and greenhouse annuals, shrubs and trees.

CULTURE OF ANNUAL SPECIES: Soil, light sandy. Position, sunny borders outdoors. Plant, May.

CULTURE OF SHRUBBY SPECIES: Compost, equal parts loam, fibrous peat, well-rotted manure and silver sand. Position, pots, tubs, or borders well drained in sunny greenhouse. Pot or plant, March. Prune freely Sept. or Oct. Water very little Oct. to March, freely afterwards. Temp., Sept. to March 45° to 55°, March to Sept. 55° to 65°. Place plants outdoors in sunny position June to Sept. Apply liquid manure occasionally while plants are in flower.

PROPAGATION: Annuals by seed $\frac{1}{8}$ in. deep in light sandy soil in well-drained pots in temp. 55° to 65° in March or April, and transfer the seedlings to small pots until planting time; shrubby species by cuttings of shoots 6 in. long inserted in sandy soil under bell-glass in temp. 65° to 75° in spring or autumn.

ANNUAL SPECIES CULTIVATED: *D. ceratocaula,* white, July, 3 ft., Trop. America; *Metel* (syn. *D. fastuosa*), blue and white, summer, 2 ft., Tropics; *Stramonium,* ' Thorn Apple ', white, July, 2 ft., Britain, etc.

SHRUBBY SPECIES CULTIVATED: *D. arborea,* white, Aug., 7 to 10 ft., Peru; *chlorantha,* ' Yellow-flowered Thorn-apple ', native country unknown; *cornigera,* ' Horn of Plenty ', creamy white, summer, 10 ft., Organ Mountains; *meteloides* (syn. *D. Wrightii*), bluish-violet, summer, 2 ft., California; *sanguinea* (syn. *Brugmansia sanguinea*), orange-yellow, summer, 4 to 6 ft., Peru; *suaveolens,* white, fragrant, Aug., 8 to 10 ft., Mexico and var. *Knightii.*

Daucus—*Umbelliferae.* Hardy annual or biennial. A well-known edible rooted vegetable. Reputed to be first introduced into England by the Flemings in time of Queen Elizabeth. Types—Shorthorn: Roots short, conical. Stump-rooted: Roots medium, blunt at ends. Intermediate: Root spindle-shaped, midway in length between a shorthorn and long-rooted carrot. Long-rooted: Roots long, and tapering.

CULTURE: Soil, deep and well manured in previous year. Fresh manure causes forking. Make early sowings of shorthorn type in sheltered border in Feb. Sow intermediate and long-rooted types in March to July, sowing main crops for storing in late May. Thin plants 4 to 6 in. apart when 2 in high. Store in clumps or in frost-proof shed in boxes of sand or soil. Crop matures in 20 to 24 weeks. For exhibition, long-rooted types are sown in specially prepared stations, a good friable compost being used to fill holes made by a crowbar.

CULTURE IN FRAMES: The shorthorn or French forcing types may be sown in 6 in. of good compost over a hotbed in frames from Oct. or Jan. to Feb. Sufficient water will run down the lights in winter but beds must be kept moist in spring, soaking with warm water. Ventilate even in mid-winter, closing the lights in the afternoon; protect with straw nets when frosty.

SPECIES CULTIVATED: *D. Carota*, white, summer, Europe (Br.), var. *sativa*, ' Carrot '.

Davallia—*Polypodiaceae.* Stove and greenhouse evergreen ferns.

CULTURE OF STOVE SPECIES: Compost, two parts loam, one part leaf-mould, peat, pounded charcoal and sand. Pot, Feb., March or April. Position, pots or hanging baskets in light part of plant stove. Water moderately Oct. to Feb., freely afterwards. Temp., Sept. to March 55° to 60°, March to Sept. 65° to 75°.

CULTURE OF GREENHOUSE SPECIES: Compost, as above. Pot, March or April. Position, pots or baskets in partial shade. Water moderately Sept. to March, freely afterwards. Temp., Sept. to March 40° to 50°, March to Sept. 50° to 60°.

PROPAGATION: By spores sown on surface of sandy peat in pans under bell-glass in temp. 55° to 75° at any time; division of rhizomes in Feb. or March.

STOVE SPECIES CULTIVATED: *D. denticulata*, fronds to 2 ft. long; *hymenophylloides*, creeping, 9 to 12 in., Ceylon, Java, etc.; *solida*, to 2 ft., Malaya.

GREENHOUSE SPECIES CULTIVATED: *D. bullata*, ' Squirrel's-foot Fern ', dwarf, creeping, Japan; *canariensis*, ' Hare's-foot Fern ', 1½ ft. long, Canary Is. to Spain and N. Africa; *dissecta*, trailing Java; *pyxidata*, to 1 ft., Australia.

Davidia—*Nyssaceae.* Handsome, hardy, deciduous tree, unusual subject with the bearing of a lime tree. First introduced late nineteenth century.

CULTURE: Soil, ordinary. Position, as specimens on lawns or at back of shrub borders. Plant, Nov.

PROPAGATION: By seed sown in pans in cold frame in Feb., or cuttings of ripened wood in Oct.

SPECIES CULTIVATED: *D. involucrata*, large creamy-white bracts, May, 40 to 65 ft., Cent. and W. China, and var. *Vilmoriniana*, glabrous leaves.

David's Harp, see *Polygonatum multiflorum*; **-root,** see *Celastrus scandens*.

Daviesia—*Leguminosae.* Greenhouse evergreen flowering shrubs. First introduced early nineteenth century.

CULTURE: Compost, equal parts loam, peat and silver sand. Position, well-drained pots in airy greenhouse. Pot firmly March or April. Water very little Oct. to March, moderately other times. Temp., Sept. to March 40° to 50°, March to Sept. 50° to 60°.

PROPAGATION: By cuttings of firm young shoots inserted in sand under bell-glass in temp. 50° to 55° in spring; seeds sown 1/16 in. deep in sandy peat in temp. 55° in March.

SPECIES CULTIVATED: *D. alata*, ' Australian Hop ', yellow, summer, 3 ft., Australia; *cordata*, yellow, summer, 3 ft., Australia; *latifolia*, orange-yellow, summer, 2 to 5 ft., Australia; *ulicina*, yellow, summer, 2 ft., Australia.

Day Flower, see Commelina; **-Lily,** see Hemerocallis.

Dead Nettle, see Lamium.

Decaisnea—*Berberidaceae* (or *Lardizabalaceae*). Hardy deciduous ornamental shrub. First introduced late nineteenth century.

CULTURE: Soil, rich loamy. Position, sunny shrubberies sheltered from north and east winds. Plant, Nov.

PROPAGATION: By seeds sown in pans of sandy soil in Feb. or March.

SPECIES CULTIVATED: *D. Fargesii*, yellowish-green, large dull blue fruits, 3 ft. pinnate leaves, 7 to 10 ft., W. China.

Deciduous Cypress, see *Taxodium distichum*.

Decodon—*Lythraceae.* Handsome shrubby perennial for shallow water, with purple flowers and willow-like leaves.

CULTURE: Soil, ordinary. Position, pond margin. Plant, spring.

PROPAGATION: Divisions or soft cuttings in very moist soil.

SPECIES CULTIVATED: *D. verticillatus* (syn. *Nesaea verticillata*), ' Swamp Loose strife ', ' Water-Willow ', rose-purple, July to Sept., 8 ft., N. America.

Decumaria—*Saxifragaceae* (or *Hydrangeaceae*). Hardy, deciduous, fragrant, flowering twiner. First introduced late eighteenth century.

CULTURE: Soil, light rich. Position, against south or west walls, arbours or trellis work. Plant, Oct. to Dec. Prune away weak and dead shoots in Feb.

PROPAGATION: By cuttings of shoots inserted in ordinary soil under hand-light in shady position outdoors in summer.

SPECIES CULTIVATED: *D. barbara*, white, June, 10 to 20 ft., United States.

Deer Fern (*Blechnum spicant*); **-Grass** (*Rhexia virginica*).

Deinanthe—*Saxifragaceae* (or *Hydrangeaceae*). Herbaceous perennial plants related to Hydrangea.

CULTURE: Soil, sandy peat. Position, cool, north aspect or shade, not exposed to morning sun.

PROPAGATION: By seed; careful division of roots in spring when growth commences.

SPECIES CULTIVATED: *D. caerulea*, blue, 12 in., June, China.

Delonix—*Leguminosae* (or *Caesalpiniaceae*). Stove evergreen flowering tree with graceful, fern-like, green leaves. First introduced early nineteenth century.

CULTURE: Compost, two parts peat or loam, one part leaf-mould, half a part silver sand. Position, pots in light part of stove or outdoors during July and Aug. Pot, Feb. or March. Water freely March to Oct., moderately afterwards. Temp., March to Oct. 70° to 85°, Oct. to March 55° to 65°.

PROPAGATION: By seeds sown in light, sandy soil in temp. of 75° to 85° in spring; cuttings of short young shoots inserted singly in small pots filled with pure sand under bell-glass in temp. 75° to 85° in summer.

SPECIES CULTIVATED: *D. regia* (syn. *Poinciana regia*), ' Peacock Flower ', ' Flamboyant ', crimson, summer, 20 to 30 ft., Madagascar. See also Caesalpinia.

Delosperma—*Aizoaceae*. Greenhouse succulent plants formerly included in Mesembryanthemum.

CULTURE: As Mesembryanthemum.

PROPAGATION: As Mesembryanthemum.

SPECIES CULTIVATED: *D. echinatum* (syn. *Mesembryanthemum echinatum*), yellow, Aug., 1 ft., S. Africa; *robustum*, much branched shrub to 10 in., flowers reddish-gold above, red below, S. Africa.

Delphinium (Larkspur)—*Ranunculaceae*. Hardy annuals and herbaceous perennials. Showy plants for border culture.

CULTURE OF ANNUAL SPECIES: Soil, ordinary, rich. Position, open beds or borders. Sow seeds ⅛ in. deep where plants are to flower in April, or in light soil in shallow boxes in temp. 55° in March, pricking out seedlings when large enough to handle and transplanting, outdoors in May.

CULTURE OF PERENNIAL SPECIES: Soil, deep, rich. Position, sunny beds or borders. Plant 3 ft. apart in Sept., Oct., March or April. Cut down flower stems in Oct. Feed liberally with liquid manures in summer, and mulch with decayed manure in early spring. Lift and replant every three years in March.

PROPAGATION: By seeds sown ⅛ in. deep outdoors in April, or in pans or boxes of light soil in temp. 55° in March; cuttings of young shoots, 3 in. long, inserted in 2 in. pots of sandy soil in cold frame in spring; division of roots in Sept. or March.

ANNUAL SPECIES CULTIVATED: *D. Ajacis* (syn. *D. Gayanum*), blue, white or rose-blue, summer, 1 to 2 ft., Europe; *Consolida*, blue, summer, 2 ft., Europe; *orientale*, ' Rocket Larkspur ', violet, white or rose, 1 to 2 ft., E. Europe. Many beautiful strains of annual kinds to be found in trade lists.

PERENNIAL SPECIES CULTIVATED: *D. Brunonianum*, light purple, 12 to 18 in.,

Tibet; *cardinale*, scarlet, summer, 3 to 6 ft., California; *cashmerianum*, blue,
July, 18 in., Kashmir; *cheilanthum*, dark blue, summer, 2 to 3 ft., Dahuria, var.
formosum (syns. *D. Belladonna*, *D. Bellamosum*), rich blue; *elatum*, blue, June, 2 to
3 ft., Alps; *grandiflorum* (syn. *D. chinense*), blue or white, June to Sept., 1 to 3 ft.,
Siberia; *nudicaule*, red, Aug., 12 to 18 in., California; *Pylzowii*, violet blue,
summer, 6 to 10 in., China; *Ruysii*, reddish or pink, summer, 2 to 4 ft., hybrid;
tatsienense, azure blue, summer, 12 to 18 in., China; *trolliifolium*, bright blue, April
to May, 1½ to 3 ft., N.W. America; *Zalil*, yellow, summer, 6 ft., Afghanistan.
See trade lists for varieties. The popular garden delphiniums are hybrids between
several species such as *D. elatum*, *D. cheilanthum*, *D. formosum*, etc.

Dendrobium—*Orchidaceae*. Probably 1000 species are included in this widely-
spread Eastern genus and naturally considerable variation is present in both the
flower and plants. Some very small, tufted in habit with stems rather than pseudo-
bulbs, some resemble Bulbophyllums, others have stem-like pseudo-bulbs several
feet in height, usually with hard persistent leaves. A number have distinctly
noded stems, with membraneous leaves often nearly or quite deciduous. Flowers
may be produced from the nodes as in *D. nobile*, in twos or threes to a considerable
number, axillary and then often solitary, from or near the apices of the pseudo-
bulbs often in many flowered spikes. In many of the hard-bulbed, apical-flower-
ing kinds 3 or 5 spikes may be produced together, or some, or all of the eyes may
remain dormant until favourable conditions supervene. This character occurs in
many far-eastern species and also in the Burmese forms, with many flowers in
thyrse-like formation. It is, however, present in other species. Many beautiful
and free-flowering hybrids have been obtained, chiefly from *D. nobile*, and special
varieties of that species with *D. aureum*, *Wardianum*, *pendulum*, *Findlayanum* and
between the hybrids themselves. Great variation exists. Treatment should be
as for *D. nobile*, but the winter night temp. can be slightly higher.

CULTURE: General compost, three parts of osmunda fibre to one part of
sphagnum moss, rather more moss for any kinds of soft texture. Pots or pans,
well drained and as small as the plant size allows should be used. The shorter-
growing species may be suspended, the pendent-growing kinds suspended in
baskets. So varied is the genus, and so widely distributed that only general direc-
tions can be given. Much will be gained by studying the character of the individual
species. Shading is required in summer for the majority, not heavy, and very
light for the hard-bulbed, hard-leaved kinds. Expose to full light in autumn,
especially the deciduous kinds. Water freely in summer, when the temp. for the
majority can rise to 85° by sun-heat, with a humid atmosphere in the day. With
exceptions the far eastern species (Borneo, Java, etc.) require a winter night temp.
of 65° to 70° with moderate humidity, deciduous kinds, especially those from
Burma, a more decided rest in winter, a minimum of 50°. In none allow the
pseudo-bulbs to shrivel or the leaves approach flaccidity.

PROPAGATION: By division of plants. By young plants produced on the pseudo-
bulbs in some species, taken off when roots are seen. Some of the noded stems
may be cut in pieces with not less than two nodes, laid on sand or coconut fibre,
in shallow pans or boxes and placed in a propagating case with bottom heat.

SPECIES CULTIVATED: A selection—*D. aggregatum*, dwarf, bright yellow, decided
rest, spring, Burma, N. India, and var. *majus*; *albo-sanguineum*, creamy-white, lip
with crimson blotch, large, spring, Moulmein; *amethystoglossum*, small, numerous,
white, lip amethyst, autumn, winter, Philippines; *atroviolaceum*, creamy-white,
purple spotted, lip violet-purple, spring, various seasons, New Guinea; *aurantiacum* (syn. *D. chryseum*), orange-yellow, stems slender, spring, Assam, Burma;
aureum (syn. *D. heterocarpum*), from nodes, amber-yellow and velvet-brown,
fragrant, spring, Ceylon, Burma, India; *Bensoniae*, from upper nodes, white, lip
with two maroon blotches, spring, Burma; *bigibbum*, apical spikes, magenta-
purple, autumn, winter, N. Australia; *Bronckartii*, flushed rose, season various,
Annam; *Brymerianum*, 3 to 5 golden, lip with a large beard-like fringe, spring,
Burma; *chrysanthum*, from nodes, orange-yellow, lip with two maroon blotches,

basket, spring, autumn, N. India, Burma; *chrysotoxum*, yellow-orange, apical spikes, severe rest, spring, Burma, var. *suavissimum* (syn. *D. suavissimum*), fragrant, maroon blotch on lip; *clavatum*, golden, lip with maroon blotch, from upper parts of stem, summer, Assam; *Coelogyne*, solitary, large, greenish-yellow, lip dull purple, raft, autumn, various seasons, Burma; *crepidatum*, from nodes, rose-pink, winter, spring, Burma; *crumenatum*, 'Pigeon Orchid', one or two from bare elongations of the bulbs, white, pink-flushed, fugitive, fragrant, various seasons, Malaya; *crystallinum*, from nodes, white, tipped magenta, spring, summer, Moulmein; *cymbidioides*, 5 to 12, not large, yellowish, purplish marks on lip, spring, various seasons, Java, Sumatra; *Dearei*, 5 to 12, or more, clustered, white, lip with green, summer, autumn, Philippines; *densiflorum*, orange-yellow in thyrses, spring, Assam, Burma; *Devonianum*, stems pendulous, from nodes, creamy-white, magenta, orange and yellow, basket, spring, India, Burma; *Falconeri*, solitary, large, white, rose-flushed, amethyst and orange, never allow to get really dry, tilted basket, spring, summer, Assam, Burma; *falcorostrum*, very fragrant, white or purple dotted, Australia; *Farmeri*, yellow, flushed pink to rose, spring, early summer, India, Burma; *fimbriatum*, from upper parts of stem, 5 to 15, orange-yellow, spring, summer, Nepal, Burma, var. *oculatum*, lip with maroon blotch; *Findlayanum*, from nodes, whitish, tipped magenta, lip with orange centre, winter, spring, Burma; *formosum*, large, white, orange-yellow in lip, fragrant, autumn, Burma, Assam, Andaman Isles, var. *giganteum*, larger, Burma; *gratiotissimum*, from upper nodes, white and rose-purple, spring, Burma; *Griffithianum*, near *D. densiflorum*, racemes longer, spring, summer, Burma, var. *Guibertii* (syn. *D. Guibertii*), brighter; *Harveyanum*, golden-yellow, petals and lip fringed, spring, Burma; *infundibulum*, white, lip stained yellow, no decided rest, spring to summer, Burma; *Jamesianum*, near *infundibulum*, but stain is usually cinnabar red, Burma; *Johnsoniae*, pure white, purple marked on lip, in apical spikes, summer to autumn, New Guinea; *Kingianum*, small, purplish, spring, Australia, var. *album*, white; *lituiflorum*, from indistinct nodes, rose-purple, purple, spring, Assam, Burma; *Loddigesii*, creeping, from nodes, rose-lilac, purplish-orange, shallow pan or raft, spring, China, Yunnan; *luteolum*, pale yellow, from upper nodes, spring, Moulmein; *Lyonii*, 15 to 30, chestnut rose, give full light, decided rest, erroneously known as *D. acuminatum*, early summer, Philippines; *Macarthiae*, 2 to 5, whitish, rose-pink, purple, a moist warm atmosphere, careful shading, spring, summer, Ceylon, national flower of Ceylon; *moschatum*, large, from near apices, yellowish, flushed rose, lip with two blackish blotches, spring, summer, Burma, var. *Calceolaria*, lip more slipper shaped, apricot or copper colour, usually smaller; *nobile*, beautiful and variable, parent of many hybrids, from nodes, whitish, passing to rose or amethyst, lip purple on disk, winter to spring, N. India, China, Burma, vars. *album*, white, and *Cooksonianum*, petals very similar to lip, Many other named vars.; *ochreatum* (syn. *D. Cambridgeanum*), from nodes, orange-yellow, lip with maroon blotch, spring, N. India; *Parishii*, from nodes, purplish-rose, lip with two purplish blotches, decided rest, spring, Burma; *pendulum* (syn. *D. crassinode*), from nodes, white, tipped purple, lip orange-yellow, white and purple, spring, Burma; *phalaenopsis*, very variable 5 to 20 from apices, rose-red to magenta-purple, late summer, autumn, N. Australia, New Guinea, var. *Schneiderianum*, a type with larger flowers and longer spikes, very light shading; *Pierardii*, from nodes, blush white, rose to primrose yellow on lip, basket, winter to spring, N. India, Burma; *pulchellum* (syn. *D. Dalhousieanum*), 5 to 12, large, from upper parts of stout stems, yellowish, shaded rose, lip with two maroon-crimson blotches, spring, summer, Burma, N. India; *regium*, rose colour, near *D. nobile*, summer, Lower Hindustan; *Sanderae*, clustered, white, lip purple-lined, variable, autumn, Philippines; *sanguinolentum*, clustered, fawn, tipped purple, summer, autumn, Malacca; *senile*, yellow, 1 to 2, plant white-haired, spring, Moulmein; *speciosum*, whitish, spotted purple, many, in apical spikes, decided rest, various seasons, Australia; *spectabile*, yellow, gold and crimson-red, segments twisted, winter, New Guinea; *superbiens*, crimson, purple, near *D. phalaenopsis*, autumn, winter, N. Australia; *superbum*, from indistinct nodes, large, variable, magenta-rose-purple, basket, spring, Philippines, Malacca; *teretifolium*, white, 10 to 20, basket, summer, autumn, Australia; *thyrsiflorum*, white, lip yellow, in thyrses, spring, Burma; *tortile*, white, rose-flushed, lip yellowish, purple, from nodes, spring, summer, Burma, Siam; *Victoriae Reginae*, 3 to 5, whitish to purplish-blue, raft or fern stem, summer, Philippines; *Wardianum*, white, amethyst purple, lip yellow, white, with two crimson-red blotches, large, from nodes, basket, winter, spring, Assam, Burma, var. *giganteum*, larger, richly coloured; *Williamsonii* (syn. *D. cariniferum*), fawn-yellow, whitish, lip reddish, spring, Assam, Burma.

Dendrochilum—*Orchidaceae.* About 150 epiphytic species. Pseudo-bulbs small usually clustered, and single leaved. Flowers small, numerous, the rachis often pendulous from an erect, laterally inclined, slender peduncle. Sometimes included in the genus Platyclinus.

CULTURE: Compost, two to three parts of osmunda fibre cut fine to one part of sphagnum moss with pounded potsherds and a very little addition of half-decayed oak leaves. Pans which can be suspended, free drainage. Water freely when growing, fairly frequently in winter. The greater number require a winter night temp. of 65°, 70° to 85° in summer. Position near the glass.

PROPAGATION: By division of the plants in spring.

SPECIES CULTIVATED: A selection—*D. Cobbianum*, creamy-white, autumn, Philippines; *cucumerinum*, greenish-yellow, autumn, winter, Philippines; *filiforme*, ' Golden Chain Orchid ', yellow, fragrant, early summer, Philippines; *glumaceum*, cream or whitish, very fragrant, spring, Philippines; *latifolium*, creamy-white, tinted green, spring, Philippines; *uncatum*, green to brown, winter, Philippines.

Dendromecon (Tree Poppy)—*Papaveraceae.* Rather tender, semi-woody, deciduous shrub. First introduced mid-nineteenth century.

CULTURE: Soil, light and unenriched, with sand and mortar rubble. Position, borders at the foot of south walls. Plant, Nov.

PROPAGATION: By cuttings of well-ripened growth placed singly in sandy soil in small pots during July and Aug. They should be placed in a propagator with a little bottom heat till rooted.

SPECIES CULTIVATED: *D. rigida*, yellow, summer, fragrant, 2 to 10 ft., California.

Dentaria (Toothwort)—*Cruciferae.* Hardy perennials and alpines.

CULTURE: Soil, peaty loam with leaf-mould and sand. Position, moist shady banks and margins of woodland. Plant, Oct. or March.

PROPAGATION: By division in spring.

SPECIES CULTIVATED: *D. bulbifera* (syn. *Cardamine bulbifera*), pale purple, April, 1 to 2 ft., Britain; *digitata*, purple-rose, April to May, 9 to 18 in., Alps, Pyrenees; *enneaphylla*, creamy-white, April to May, 9 to 12 in., Alps.

Deodar, see *Cedrus Deodara.*

Desert Rod, see Eremostachys.

Desfontainea—*Loganiaceae.* Rather tender evergreen flowering shrub. Leaves oval, dark shiny green, with spiny margins resembling those of holly. First introduced mid-nineteenth century.

OUTDOOR CULTURE: Compost, equal parts peat and loam. Position, sheltered borders outdoors, or against south wall. Plant, Oct., Nov. or April.

GREENHOUSE CULTURE: Compost, equal parts peat, loam, charcoal and sand. Position, well-drained pots, tubs or borders. Pot or plant, March or April. Water moderately Oct. to March, freely afterwards.

PROPAGATION: By cuttings inserted in sandy peat and loam in well-drained pots under bell-glass or hand-light in temp. 55° to 65° in spring.

SPECIES CULTIVATED: *D. spinosa*, scarlet and yellow, waxy 2 in. flowers, 6 ft., spreading, Chile and Peru.

Desmodium—*Leguminosae.* Hardy and stove flowering perennials and semi-woody shrub dying to ground level each winter. Leaves of stove species (*D. motorium*) animated, especially in sunshine.

CULTURE OF STOVE SPECIES: Compost, equal parts peat, loam and silver sand. Position, pots in plant stove. Pot, Feb. or March. Water moderately Oct. to Feb., freely afterwards. Temp., Sept. to March 55° to 65°, March to Sept. 65° to 75°.

CULTURE OF HARDY SPECIES: Soil, ordinary. Position, open sunny borders. Plant, March.

CULTURE OF SHRUBBY SPECIES: Soil, light or chalky, well drained. Position, sunny banks. Plant, Nov. to March.

PROPAGATION: Stove species by seeds sown in light sandy soil in temp. 75° to 80° in Feb. or March, or by cuttings inserted in sandy peat under bell-glass in temp. 75° to 80° in March or April; hardy perennial species by division in March; hardy shrubby species by division in spring.

STOVE SPECIES CULTIVATED: *D. motorium* (syn. *D. gyrans*), ' Telegraph Plant ', violet, July, 2 to 3 ft., India.

HARDY PERENNIAL SPECIES CULTIVATED: *D. canadense*, ' Tick Trefoil ', purple, July, 3 ft., N. America.

HARDY SHRUB SPECIES CULTIVATED: *D. tiliaefolium*, pale lilac to deep pink, Aug. to Oct., 2 to 4 ft., Himalaya. See also Lespedeza.

Deutzia—*Saxifragaceae* (or *Hydrangeaceae*). Hardy, deciduous, easily grown, flowering shrubs of great beauty.

CULTURE: Soil, ordinary. Position, sunny well-drained border. Plant, Oct. to Feb. Prune, June, shortening shoots that have flowered only.

POT CULTURE OF *D. gracilis*: Compost, two parts loam, one part decayed manure and sand. Pot, Oct. or Nov. Position, cold frame Nov. to Feb.; greenhouse, Feb. to May; outdoors afterwards. Water very little Oct. to Feb., moderately Feb. to April, freely April to Oct. Temp., Feb. to May 55° to 65°. Plants will flower in cold greenhouse without heat if desired. Plant out deutzias that have flowered in heat in open garden for a year, then lift and repot.

PROPAGATION: By cuttings of young shoots 3 in. long in sandy soil under bell-glass in cold frame in June or July, or firm young shoots 10 to 12 in. long in ordinary soil in Nov. to Jan.

SPECIES CULTIVATED: *D. gracilis*, ' Japanese Snowflower ', white, April, 4 ft., Japan, and var. *aurea*, leaves yellow; *kalmiaeflora*, 5 ft., charming graceful hybrid with saucer-shaped carmine flowers, June; *Lemoinei*, white, May, 7 ft., hybrid; *longifolia*, purplish-rose, June, 4 to 6 ft., W. China, var. *Veitchii*, probably the best-coloured deutzia; *magnifica*, a fine hybrid, double white, June, 8 ft.; *purpurascens*, white and purple, June, 6 to 7 ft., W. China; *rosea*, pinkish, 4 ft., a beautiful hybrid, vars. *carminea*, *campanulata*, *venusta*; *scabra* (syn. *D. crenata*), white, June, 7 ft., Japan, and vars. *Fortunei*, *mirabilis*, *Watereri*; *setchuenensis*, white. May to June, 6 ft., China; *Sieboldiana*, white, June, 3 to 4 ft., Japan; *Vilmoriniae*, white, 8 ft., W. China; *Wilsonii*, white, May to June, 4 to 6 ft., hybrid.

Devil-in-a-Bush, see *Nigella damascena.*

Devil's Apple, see *Mandragora officinarum*; **-Walking Stick,** see *Aralia spinosa.*

Dewberry, see *Rubus caesius.*

Diacrium—*Orchidaceae.* A small epiphytic genus, allied to Epidendrum. Pseudo-bulbs hollow, ribbed, peduncles terminal.

CULTURE: Compost and general conditions as for Cattleyas but give more exposure especially in autumn, and a decided rest in winter. Baskets or pans, which can be suspended near the glass, are preferable.

PROPAGATION: By division if plants are large enough.

SPECIES CULTIVATED: *D. bicornutum* (syn. *Epidendrum bicornutum*), 5 to 20, white, with a few purple spots on lip, summer, autumn, W. Indies, Brazil, var. *indivisum*, white, smaller.

Dianella (Flax Lily; Paroo Lily)—*Liliaceae.* Slightly tender fibrous-rooted perennials. First introduced early eighteenth century.

OUTDOOR CULTURE: Soil, equal parts loam and peat. Position, sheltered borders in S. of England only. Plant, Oct., March or April.

INDOOR CULTURE: Compost, equal parts peat, loam and leaf-mould, and sand. Position, well-drained pots in unheated greenhouse. Pot, Feb., March or April. Water moderately Sept. to March, freely afterwards.

PROPAGATION: By division in Oct. or March; seeds in heat in spring.

SPECIES CULTIVATED: *D. caerulea,* blue, May, 2 ft., Australia, Tasmania; *ensifolia* (syn. *D. nemorosa*), blue or white, spring, 2 to 6 ft., S.E. Asia; *laevis,* blue, spring, 2 ft., Australia, Tasmania.

Dianthera (Water Willow)—*Acanthaceae.* Greenhouse flowering plant.

CULTURE: Compost, equal parts fibrous loam, peat, leaf-mould and sand. Position, well-drained pots in light airy greenhouse June to Sept.; warm greenhouse Sept. to June. Pot, March to April. Water moderately Sept. to March, freely other times. Temp., Sept. to March 55° to 65°, March to June 65° to 75°. Stop young plants once or twice during early stages of growth to promote bushy habit. Apply liquid or artificial manure twice a week to plants when established or in flower.

PROPAGATION: By cuttings of young shoots inserted in pots of sandy soil under bell-glass or in propagating frame, temp. 70° March to June.

SPECIES CULTIVATED: *D. nodosa,* pink, winter, 18 in., India.

Dianthus—*Caryophyllaceae.* Annual, biennial and perennial plants, many of which are fragrant.

TYPES: Border Carnations subdivided into—Cloves; Selfs; Fancies; White-ground Fancies; Yellow-ground Fancies; Flakes and Bizarres; Yellow-ground Picotees; White-ground Picotees. Margaret or Marguerite Carnations, a race of hybrids with fragrant fringed flowers of all shades. Jacks, coarse-growing, mostly singles. Tree, Perpetual or American Carnations, habit tall, flowers self-coloured, striped or flaked appearing all the year round. Malmaison Carnations, habit sturdy, flowers large, self-coloured. Pinks sub-divided into—Garden, Show and Laced. Sweet Williams, Show-type—smooth-edged petals with dark centres; Auricula-eyed, smooth-edged petals with white eye, surrounded crimson or other tints.

CULTURE OF CARNATIONS AND PICOTEES: Soil, three parts decayed turfy loam, one part equal parts well-decayed cow manure and sand for exhibition kinds, good, well-drained, ordinary, rich soil for border kinds. Position, sunny beds or borders. Plant 12 in. apart in Oct. or March. Top-dress with manure or compost in April. Thin flower buds to one on each shoot in June, and in July place rubber band round calyx of flower to prevent bursting. Stake flower stems in May. Apply liquid manure once a week when buds form. Shade exhibition blooms from hot sun. Pot culture, compost as advised for exhibition culture. Position, cold frame Oct. to Feb., cold greenhouse afterwards. Plant singly in 3 in. pots in Oct., then two in 8 in. pot in Feb. Water moderately Oct. to March, freely afterwards. Apply liquid manure once a week April to July. Thin buds to three on each shoot in May. Give plenty of air.

CULTURE OF TREE OR PERPETUAL CARNATIONS: Insert cuttings of side shoots 3 in. long from midway up the flowering stems with a few of the lower leaves removed in well-drained pots of pure sand, Nov. to March. Place in box or propagator, keep moist and shaded from sun till rooted. Temp. 50° and slight bottom heat. When rooted, transfer to small pots in compost of two parts sandy loam and one part leaf-mould and sand. Stand in temp. 45° to 55° till pots are filled with roots, then transfer to larger pots in compost of four parts fibrous loam, one part mortar rubble, sand and leaf-mould. Add carnation fertiliser at rate suggested by makers. Bonemeal, 4 oz. to a bushel of soil, is sometimes used instead of the fertiliser. Stop or pinch shoots at third or fourth joint after first potting; again at intervals when shoots are a few inches long till early July. Feed with liquid manure when well rooted. Place outdoors May to Sept. Winter temp. 45° to 55°. Ventilate freely in fine weather. Syringe daily during spring and summer. May also be grown outdoors like border carnations.

CULTURE OF MALMAISON CARNATIONS: Layer shoots in July. Plant rooted layers in small pots in Aug. or Sept., place in cold frame or greenhouse and transfer to 5 or 6 in. pots in Oct. Water moderately during winter. Temp. 40° to 45°. Feed with liquid manure when buds form. Shade in spring from sun. Admit air freely on fine days.

CULTURE OF PINKS: Soil, ordinary, rich. Position, sunny borders. Plant 9 in. apart in autumn or spring. Thin shoots to four on each plant to ensure fine blooms. Feed with liquid manure in May and June.

CULTURE OF ANNUAL AND BIENNIAL SPECIES: Sow seeds in gentle heat in spring, harden off seedlings in cold frame and plant out in beds and borders in May to flower same season; or sow in open border in April and plant out in July to flower following year. Sweet Williams, although perennial, are usually grown as biennials.

CULTURE OF PERENNIAL SPECIES: Soil, sandy loam. Position, sunny rockeries or borders. Plant, Oct. or March.

PROPAGATION: Carnations, pinks and picotees by seeds in sandy soil in heat or in cold frame in spring; pinks by cuttings or pipings in cold frame in summer; perpetual carnations by cuttings as already explained; border carnations and picotees by layering in July or Aug. Annuals and biennials by seed; perennials by seed in cold frame in spring or cuttings in July.

SPECIES CULTIVATED: *D. alpestris*, pink, summer, 6 in., Alps; *alpinus*, rose to crimson, summer, 3 to 4 in., Alps; *anatolicus*, pale pink and yellow, summer, 1 to 3 ft., Asia Minor; *arenarius*, white, summer, 6 in., N. Europe; *barbatus*, ' Sweet William ', various, 1 to 2 ft., S. Europe; *callizonus*, pale pink and maroon, 2 to 4 in., Alps; *carthusianorum*, crimson, 1 to 2 ft., Europe; *Caryophyllus*, ' Clove Pink ', ' Carnation ', various, 1½ to 2 ft., Britain, Europe; *chinensis*, ' Chinese or Indian Pink ', various, 6 to 12 in., biennial, Portugal to China and Japan, var. *Heddewigii*, hardy annual pink of gardens; *cruentus*, scarlet, summer, 18 in., E. Europe; *deltoides*, ' Maiden Pink ', rose and white, summer, 6 to 9 in., Britain to Japan; *fimbriatus*, rose, summer, 12 to 16 in., Europe and Asia; *fragrans*, white, summer, 6 in., Caucasus; *glacialis*, ' Glacier Pink ', purple, summer, 4 in., S. Europe; *graniticus*, pink, June to Sept., trailing, Europe; *gratianopolitanus* (syn. *D. caesius*), ' Cheddar Pink ', rose, fragrant, July, 3 to 6 in, Britain to Germany and S. France; *Knappii*, yellow, May to July, 6 in., Europe; *microlepis*, pink or white, summer, cushion, Bulgaria; *monspessulanus*, pink, June to July, 9 to 12 in. S. Europe; *neglectus*, rose, summer, 2 in., Pyrenees; *Noeanus* (syn. *Acanthophyllum spinosum*), white, fragrant, June to July, 6 to 9 in., densely tufted, S. Europe to S.W. Asia; *petraeus*, rose, summer, 6 in., E. Europe; *plumarius*, ' Cottage Pink ', various, 12 in., Britain, E. Europe; *squarrosus*, white or pink, summer, 9 to 12 in., Russia, Siberia; *Sternbergii*, rose, summer, 6 in., S. Europe; *superbus*, ' Fringed Pink ', rose, summer, 9 to 18 in., Europe; *sylvestris*, ' Wood Pink ', rose, May to July, 9 to 12 in., Alps. There are many hybrid forms of Dianthus in cultivation.

Diapensia—*Diapensiaceae*. Hardy, dwarf, evergreen, tufted plants. First introduced, early nineteenth century.

CULTURE: Soil, deep sandy peat mixed with stones. Position, sunny rock garden. Plant, March to April. Water freely June to Aug.

PROPAGATION: By division of plants in March and April.

SPECIES CULTIVATED: *D. lapponica*, white, July, 3 in., Northern Regions.

Diascia—*Scrophulariaceae*. Half-hardy annual. First introduced mid-nineteenth century.

INDOOR CULTURE: Compost, two parts sandy loam and one part leaf-mould and sand. Sow seeds in a temp. of 60° in March or April. Transplant seedlings when the third leaf forms, four or five in a 4½ in. pot. Grow on shelf near the glass.

Water freely when flower buds form. Give weak liquid manure occasionally. Shoots may require to be supported by twiggy sticks.

OUTDOOR CULTURE: Sow seeds in temp. of 60° in March or April. Transplant in pots or boxes when large enough to handle. Gradually harden off in cold frame, and plant out in good ordinary soil in sunny position at the end of May.

SPECIES CULTIVATED: *D. Barberae*, rosy pink, summer, 1 ft., S. Africa.

Dicentra—*Fumariaceae*. Hardy, herbaceous, tuberous and fibrous-rooted perennials. Formerly known as Dielytra. First introduced early eighteenth century.

CULTURE: Soil, deep, light, rich, sandy. Position, warm sheltered borders; dwarf species on rockeries. Plant, Oct., Nov., March or April. Protect during winter by covering with layers of ashes or manure. Top-dress with decayed manure in March.

POT CULTURE OF D. SPECTABILIS: Compost, equal parts loam, leaf-mould and sand. Pot, Oct. or Nov. Position, cold frame Oct. to Feb.; greenhouse Feb. to May, afterwards planting out in borders. Water moderately when new growth begins, freely when in full growth. Apply liquid manure once or twice weekly when flower buds appear.

FORCING: Pot, Oct. Place in cold frame till Jan. Transfer to temp. 55° to 65° in Jan. After forcing, plant out in open border. Plants should only be forced in pots one year.

PROPAGATION: By dividing the crowns in Feb. to April; cuttings of fleshy roots 2 in. long inserted in sandy soil in temp. 55° in March or April.

SPECIES CULTIVATED: *D. canadensis*, white, May, 6 in., N. America; *chrysantha*, ' Golden Eardrops ', deep yellow, May to June, 2 to 3 ft., California; *Cucullaria*, ' Dutchman's Breeches ', white and yellow, spring, 6 in. United States; *eximia*, reddish purple, April to Sept., 12 in., N. Carolina; *eximia × formosa*, reddish purple, April to Sept., 9 to 12in., garden hybrid; *formosa*, red, May, 6 in., N. America; *peregrina*, white, May to June, 3 in., Japan; *spectabilis* (syn. *Dielytra spectabilis*), ' Chinaman's Breeches ' or ' Bleeding Heart ', ' Lyre Flower ', rosy crimson, spring and summer, 2 ft., Siberia and Japan, var. *alba*, white form.

Dichaea—*Orchidaceae*. Small tufted epiphytal orchids. Stems slender, erect or pendulous, clothed with small leaves. Flowers small, axillary, solitary. The lip corner often prolonged into a short tendril.

CULTURE: Compost, two parts of osmunda fibre and one part of sphagnum moss, small pans, which can be suspended and tilted for the pendulous kinds. Pots or pans for the erect growing. Position not too sunny, shade carefully in summer. Water freely in summer, moderately in winter. No decided rest. Winter temp. for the species given 60° to 65° in a moist atmosphere, summer up to 80°.

PROPAGATION: By division of plants in spring.

SPECIES CULTIVATED: *D. picta*, green and purple, winter, Trinidad; *Bradeorum*, green, red-flecked, whitish, summer, Costa Rica; *glauca*, whitish, autumn, W. Indies; *vaginata*, white, small, summer, Mexico.

Dichelostemma, see Brodiaea.

Dichorisandra—*Commelinaceae*. Stove ornamental-leaved and flowering perennials.

CULTURE: Compost, one-third each of peat, loam and leaf-mould, and a little silver sand. Position, pots in shady part of stove. Pot in March. Water freely March to Oct., moderately afterwards. Syringe daily in spring and summer. Temp., March to Oct. 75° to 85°, Oct. to March 55° to 65°.

PROPAGATION: By seeds in spring; division in March.

SPECIES CULTIVATED: *D. mosaica*, leaves green marked with white, 2 ft., Peru; *pubescens taeniensis*, leaves striped with white, 2 ft., Brazil; *thyrsiflora*, blue, autumn, 5 to 10 ft., Brazil; *vittata*, leaves purplish-green, striped white, Brazil.

Dicksonia—*Dicksoniaceae*. Greenhouse tree ferns. First introduced late eighteenth century.

CULTURE: Compost, peat and loam and an abundance of sand. Position, large pots or tubs well drained in shady greenhouse or conservatory. Repot, Feb. to March. Water moderately Oct. to March, freely afterwards. Syringe trunks daily March to Sept. Temp., Sept. to March 45° to 55°, March to Sept. 55° to 65°, or more from sun heat with shade and ventilation. Shade in summer essential.

PROPAGATION: By spores sown at any time on surface of finely sifted loam and peat in well-drained pots covered with a sheet of glass and kept moist.

SPECIES CULTIVATED: *D. antarctica*, 'Australian Tree Fern', 18 to 20 ft., Tasmania; *squarrosa*, 'New Zealand Tree Fern', 15 to 20 ft., length of frond nearly equalling height of plant, New Zealand.

Dicranostigma—*Papaveraceae*. Hardy perennial herbs.

CULTURE: Any good loamy soil, well drained, and a sunny, warm position in border or rock garden.

PROPAGATION: By seeds sown in spring.

SPECIES CULTIVATED: *D. Franchetianum*, yellow, 12 to 18 in., summer, China; *lactucoides*, yellow, 12 in., June to July, Himalaya.

Dictamnus—*Rutaceae*. Hardy herbaceous perennial with fragrant foliage. First introduced late sixteenth century.

CULTURE: Soil, ordinary, dryish. Position, sunny or partially shady borders. Plant, Oct., Nov., March or April.

PROPAGATION: By seeds sown ⅛ in. deep in light soil outdoors in Aug. or Sept.; cuttings of fleshy roots inserted 2 in. deep in frame in March or April; divisions of roots in Oct., Nov. or March.

SPECIES CULTIVATED: *D. albus* (syn. *D. Fraxinella*), 'Burning Bush', 'Dittany', 'Fraxinella', 'Gas Plant', white, May, 3 ft., Europe, and vars. *caucasicus*, giant form, *albus purpureus*, purplish, May, 3 ft., *purpureus*, dark flowers, and *rubra*, rosy-red.

Dictyosperma—*Palmae*. Stove feather-leaved palms. First introduced early nineteenth century.

CULTURE: Compost, equal parts loam, leaf-mould and sand. Position, pots in shady moist plant stove. Pot, Feb. or March. Water freely at all times. Temp., March to Sept. 70° to 85°, Sept. to March 60° to 65°.

PROPAGATION: By seeds sown 1 in. deep in pots of sandy peat in temp. 85° in Feb., March or April.

SPECIES CULTIVATED: *D. album*, 15 to 20 ft., Mauritius, and vars. *aureum*, *furfuraceum* and *rubrum*.

Didymocarpus—*Gesneriaceae*. Stove perennial herbs. First introduced mid-nineteenth century.

CULTURE: Compost, equal parts peat and loam, one-fourth part cow dung and sand. Position, well-drained pots in moist plant stove. Pot, Feb., March or April. Water moderately Oct. to Feb., freely afterwards. Temp., Sept. to March 55° to 65°, March to Sept. 65° to 75°.

PROPAGATION: By cuttings of young side shoots inserted in sandy soil under bell-glass in temp. 80° to 85° in March or April.

SPECIES CULTIVATED: *D. Humboldtiana*, lilac, autumn, 3 to 4 in., Ceylon; *malayana*, yellow, summer, 4 to 6 in., Malaya.

Didymochlaena—*Polypodiaceae*. Greenhouse fern. First introduced mid-nineteenth century.

CULTURE: Compost, two parts loam, one part peat, pounded charcoal and sand. Pot, Feb. or March. Position, well-drained pots in shady part of greenhouse. Water moderately Oct. to Feb., freely afterwards. Temp., Sept. to March 45° to 50°, March to Sept. higher with sun heat, shade and ventilation.

PROPAGATION: By spores sown on surface of sandy peat under bell-glass in temp. 70° to 80° at any time.

SPECIES CULTIVATED: *D. truncatula* (syn. *D. lunulata*), tree-like habit, Tropics.

Dieffenbachia (Dumb Cane)—*Araceae*. Stove evergreen perennials with oblong variegated leaves. First introduced mid-nineteenth century.

CULTURE: Compost, equal parts peat and loam, one-fourth part decayed manure and silver sand. Position, well-drained pots in moist plant stove. Pot, Feb. or March. Water moderately Sept. to Feb., freely afterwards. Syringe daily June, July and Aug. Shade in summer essential. Temp., Sept. to Feb. 55° to 65°, Feb. to Sept. 65° to 85°.

PROPAGATION: By cuttings of stems 1 to 2 in. long inserted in sandy soil under bell-glass in temp. 75° to 85° in spring.

SPECIES CULTIVATED: *D. Bausei*, leaves yellowish-green, blotched dark green and spotted white, hybrid; *Bowmannii*, leaves blotched dark and light green, Japan; *Carderi*, leaves variegated, Colombia; *Chelsonii*, leaves green and yellow, Colombia; *picta*, leaves dull green and white or yellow, S. America, vars. *Jenmannii*, leaves veined and spotted with white, *magnifica*, leaves spotted along veins; *picta*, leaves green, white and yellow, 4 ft., S. America; *Regina*, leaves white and green, S. America; *Seguine*, leaves green and white, Brazil, and vars. *irrorata*, *liturata* and *nobilis*.

Dielytra, see Dicentra.

Dierama (Wandflower)—*Iridaceae*. Hardy bulbous-rooted plant with sword-shaped leaves and long graceful flower stems.

CULTURE: Soil, light or sandy. Position, well-drained border at base of a south wall. Plant bulbs 3 in. deep and 3 in. apart in Nov. Lift and replant every third year.

PROPAGATION: By offsets from old bulbs.

SPECIES CULTIVATED: *D. pendulum*, lilac, Sept., 4 ft., S. Africa; *pulcherrimum* (syn. *Sparaxis pulcherrima*), blood-red, Sept., 3 to 4 ft., var. *album*, white flowers.

Diervilla (Bush Honeysuckle)—*Caprifoliaceae*. Deciduous low-growing stoloniferous shrubs suitable for holding banks, colonising or as tall ground cover. For other species sometimes listed under this name, see Weigela. First introduced early eighteenth century.

CULTURE: Soil, ordinary, moist. Position, sun or partial shade. In native surroundings grows on banks, rocks and hillsides.

PROPAGATION: By removal of suckers.

SPECIES CULTIVATED: *D. Lonicera*, yellow, to 4 ft., N. America; *rivularis*, lemon-yellow, to 6 ft., N. America; *sessilifolia*, sulphur-yellow, July to Aug., 2 to 3 ft., N. America; *splendens*, similar to *D. sessilifolia*, hybrid.

Digitalis (Foxglove)—*Scrophulariaceae*. Hardy biennial and perennial herbs.

CULTURE OF PERENNIAL SPECIES: Soil, rich, ordinary. Position, open shady border, or naturalised in woodlands and wild gardens. Plant, Oct. or April.

CULTURE OF BIENNIAL SPECIES: Sow seeds ¹⁄₁₆ in. deep in shady border outdoors in April. Transplant seedlings 3 in. apart in shady bed in June. Transfer seedlings to flowering position in Oct. or Nov.

PROPAGATION: Perennials by seeds sown as directed for biennials; division of plants in March.

PERENNIAL SPECIES CULTIVATED: *D. dubia*, rose, June, 1½ ft., Balearic Isles; *grandiflora* (syns. *D. ambigua*, *D. ochroleuca*), yellow, July and Aug., 3 ft., Europe; *Thapsii*, rosy-purple, June to Aug., 2 to 4 ft., W. Europe.

BIENNIAL SPECIES CULTIVATED: *D. lanata*, grey and white or purple, summer, 2 to 3 ft., S.E. Europe; *purpurea*, ' Common Foxglove ', purple, July to Sept., 3 to 5 ft., Europe (Br.); *purpurea gloxiniaeflora*, has longer racemes and more open flowers. There are numerous varieties and hybrid strains to be found in trade lists.

Dill, see *Anethum graveolens*.

Dillwynia—*Leguminosae*. Greenhouse, evergreen, flowering, heath-like shrubs. First introduced late eighteenth century.

CULTURE: Compost, equal parts fibrous peat and loam, one-fourth part sand.

Position, pots in sunny greenhouse. Pot, March or June; firm potting essential.
Prune straggling shoots a little after flowering. Water freely March to Sept.,
moderately afterwards. Temp., March to Sept. 60° to 65°, Sept. to March 45° to
50°. Place plants outdoors July to Sept. to mature growth.

PROPAGATION: By seeds sown $\frac{1}{16}$ in. deep in light sandy compost in temp. 65°
to 70° in March; cuttings inserted in pots of sandy peat under bell-glass in temp.
65° in summer.

SPECIES CULTIVATED: *D. ericifolia*, yellow and red, spring, 2 ft., Australia;
floribunda, yellow and red, spring, 18 in., Australia; *hispida*, orange and red,
spring, 1 ft., Australia.

Dimorphotheca (Cape Marigold)—*Compositae*. Half-hardy annuals and perennials from S. Africa. Usually grown as annuals. First introduced mid-eighteenth
century.

INDOOR CULTURE: Compost, three parts sandy loam, one part leaf-mould and a
liberal addition of silver sand. Pot, March or April. Grow in cool sunny greenhouse. Water freely during spring and summer, moderately in autumn and
winter. Temp., Oct. to March 40° to 50°.

OUTDOOR CULTURE: Soil, ordinary, sandy. Position, sunny, warm border.
Plant, May and June.

PROPAGATION: By seeds sown in a temp. of 55° in sandy soil in early spring.

SPECIES CULTIVATED: These are now placed in four genera as follows:

CASTALIS: *C. nudicaulis* (syn. *Dimorphotheca nudicaulis*), white with purple exterior,
summer, 6 to 12 in., S. Africa; *spectabilis*, mauve, 6 to 12 in., Transvaal; *Tragus*
(syn. *Dimorphotheca flaccida, D. aurantiaca* D.C. non hort.), orange yellow, 6 to 12 in.,
S. Africa.

CHRYSANTHEMOIDES: *C monilifera* (syn. *Osteospermum moniliferum*), yellow, 3 to
6 ft., S. Africa, but introduced into New Zealand and Tasmania, a shrub with
small edible fruits.

DIMORPHOTHECA: *D. chrysanthemifolia* (syn. *Calendula chrysanthemifolia*), yellow,
summer, 2 to 3 ft., S. Africa; *D. cuneata* (syn. *Calendula viscosa*), white with bluish
or copper exterior, summer, 2 to 3 ft., S. Africa; *pluvialis* (syn. *D. annua*), white
and violet, summer, 1 ft., S. Africa, the opening and closing of the flowers (really
dependent on temperature) was once thought to indicate rain; *sinuata* (syn. *D.
aurantiaca* hort. non D.C., *D. pseudaurantiaca*), orange, summer, 1 ft., S. Africa, the
most popular species; *turicensis* (syn. *D. aurantiaca hybrida, D. calendulacea dubia*),
light yellow, violet-tinged, 1 ft., summer, hybrid.

OSTEOSPERMUM: *O. amplectens* (syn. *Tripteris amplectens*), yellow, summer, 1 to
3 ft., S. Africa; *Barberiae* (syn. *Dimorphotheca Barberiae, D. lilacina*), purple,
summer, 1 to 2 ft., S. Africa; *Ecklonis* (syn. *Dimorphotheca Ecklonis*), white, with
violet-blue exterior, purple disk, summer, 1 to 3 ft., S. Africa; *hyoseroides* (syn.
Tripteris hyoseroides), orange with dark purple disk, summer, 2 ft., S. Africa;
Vaillantii (syn. *Tripteris Vaillantii*), yellow, summer, 1 to 2 ft., S. Africa.

Dionaea—*Droseraceae*. Greenhouse, herbaceous, insectivorous, perennial plants.
Are fringed with sensitive hairs closing together when touched.

CULTURE: Compost, equal parts peat and living sphagnum. Position, pots or
pans well drained and partly immersed in pans of water, and placed under glass in
cool greenhouse. Pot, March or April. Water freely always. Temp., Oct. to
March 40° to 45°, March to Sept. 45° to 55°.

PROPAGATION: By seeds sown in mixture of sphagnum moss and peat, kept
moist under bell-glass in March or April; division of plants in March.

SPECIES CULTIVATED: *D. muscipula*, ' Venus's Fly-Trap ', white, July and Aug.,
6 in., Carolina.

Dionysia—*Primulaceae*. Evergreen alpine cushion plants. Similar to Androsace.

CULTURE: Soil composed of loam, leaf-mould, grit and sharp sand in equal
proportions. Best grown in the alpine house or cold frame. Keep very dry in
winter.

PROPAGATION: By seeds sown in compost as above; cuttings of tiny shoots carefully taken in spring.

SPECIES CULTIVATED: *D. bryoides*, pink, sessile, spring, Persia; *curviflora*, red, sessile, spring, Persia; *ianthina*, yellow, sessile, spring, Persia; *oreodoxa*, yellow, sessile, spring, Persia.

Dioscorea (Yam)—*Dioscoreaceae.* Hardy tuberous-rooted climbing perennials. Tubers, large, milky, edible, cooked like potatoes.

CULTURE: Soil, ordinary. Position, sunny, open. Plant small tubers 3 in. deep and 12 in. apart in March. Fix stakes or branches for shoots to climb on. Lift and store tubers in frost-proof place in Oct.

PROPAGATION: By cuttings of stems 1 in. long with leaf attached, inserted ¼ in. deep in sandy soil under bell-glass in temp. 55° in summer.

SPECIES CULTIVATED: *D. Batatas*, ' Chinese Yam ', white, summer, 12 ft., Philippines; *sativa*, ' Cultivated Yam ', Tropics.

Diosma—*Rutaceae.* Greenhouse evergreen flowering shrub with fragrant leaves.

CULTURE: Compost, two parts fibrous peat, one part loam and silver sand. Pot, May, June. Pinch off points of vigorous shoots in July and Aug. Water very little Oct. to March, moderately afterwards. Temp., Sept. to March 40° to 45°, March to Sept. 50° to 55°.

PROPAGATION: By cuttings inserted in sandy peat under bell-glass in temp. 55° to 65° in March, April or May.

SPECIES CULTIVATED: *D. ericoides*, white, spring, 2 to 3 ft., S. Africa. For *D. uniflora* see Adenandra.

Diospyros—*Ebenaceae.* Deciduous or evergreen trees and shrubs with juicy edible fruits. Date plum introduced late sixteenth century, persimmons early twentieth century.

CULTURE: Soil, ordinary. Position, shrubberies for *D. armata*, *D. Lotus* and *D. virginiana*; south wall for *D. Kaki*, except in extreme S. of England. Plant, Oct. to Feb. Prune similarly to apple trees.

PROPAGATION: By seeds sown 1 in. deep outdoors in Sept. or Oct.

SPECIES CULTIVATED: *D. armata*, yellow fruits, 20 ft., half-evergreen, Cent. China; *Kaki*, ' Chinese Persimmon ', yellowish-white, spring, yellow fruits, to 40 ft., China; *Lotus*, ' Date Plum ', reddish white, July, purple or yellow fruits, to 45 ft., W. Asia. China and Japan; *virginiana*, ' Persimmon ', yellow, July, pale yellow and red fruits, to 50 ft. or more, N. America.

Dipelta—*Caprifoliaceae.* Hardy deciduous shrubs with flowers resembling those of Diervilla. First introduced early twentieth century.

CULTURE: Soil, moist loam. Position, sunny sheltered shrubberies. Plant, autumn. Prune away dead wood only.

PROPAGATION: By cuttings inserted in cold frame in autumn.

SPECIES CULTIVATED: *D. floribunda*, pink and yellow, fragrant, May and June, 10 to 15 ft., W. China; *ventricosa*, deep rose and orange, May, 6 to 15 ft., W. China; *yunnanensis*, cream with orange markings, 10 ft., China.

Diphylleia—*Berberidaceae.* Hardy herbaceous perennial. First introduced early nineteenth century.

CULTURE: Soil, peaty. Position, moist shady borders. Plant, Oct. to March.

PROPAGATION: By division of plants in March or April.

SPECIES CULTIVATED: *D. cymosa*, ' Umbrella Leaf ', white, May, 1 ft., N. America.

Diplacus, see Mimulus.

Dipladenia—*Apocynaceae.* Stove flowering evergreen climbers. First introduced mid-nineteenth century.

CULTURE: Compost, rough fibrous peat and one-fourth silver sand. Position, well-drained pots, with shoots trained to roof of stove or to wire trellis. Pot, Feb. or March. Prune, Oct., cutting away shoots that have flowered only. Water very little Oct. to Feb., moderately Feb. to April, freely afterwards. Temp., Oct. to Feb. 55° to 60°, Feb. to Oct. 65° to 75°.

PROPAGATION: By cuttings of young side shoots 3 in. long inserted in pots of sandy peat under bell-glass in temp. 80° in Feb., March or April.

SPECIES CULTIVATED: *D. atropurpurea*, purple, summer, 10 ft., Brazil; *boliviensis*, white and yellow, summer, 8 to 10 ft., Bolivia; *Sanderi* (syn. *Mandevilla Sanderi*), rose, summer, 10 ft., Brazil; *splendens*, white, rose and purple, summer, 8 to 12 ft., Brazil, and vars. *amabilis*, rosy crimson, *Brearleyana*, crimson, *hybrida*, crimson-red, and *profusa*, carmine. See also Odontodenia.

Diplarrhena—*Iridaceae*. Rather tender perennial plants.
CULTURE: Deep sandy loam and full sun in the border.
PROPAGATION: By seeds; division of old plants.
SPECIES CULTIVATED: *D. Moraea*, white, purple and gold, 2 ft., summer, Australia.

Disa—*Orchidaceae*. A genus of terrestrial, tuberous-rooted orchids, chiefly African. The upper sepal is often the largest segment, often hood-like and developed into a short spur at its base. The S. African species are the most commonly cultivated. The leaves are often in rosette formation.

CULTURE: Compost, three parts of finely shredded osmunda fibre or peat, two parts sphagnum moss and a few half-decayed leaves with potsherds pounded to dust, or sand. A very little loam fibre may be added. A cool moist atmosphere is necessary and the compost must never approach dryness. They may grow in a cold frame in summer with shading but require a winter temp. of 45° to 50°. The Odontoglossum house often suits. Air must be given but draughts avoided. Spikes leafy from centre of growth. Species from warmer parts of Africa need much more warmth and a winter rest.

PROPAGATION: The stronger crowns form offsets which may be carefully removed in early spring and potted. Success is occasionally obtained from seeds sown on compost.

SPECIES CULTIVATED: *D. racemosa*, rose-purple or whitish to rose, summer, S. Africa; *tripetaloides*, whitish, suffused and dotted rose-pink, summer, S. Africa; *uniflora* (syn. *D. grandiflora*), flowers 3 to 7, large, crimson, shaded yellow, spring, summer, S. Africa. From these three species a number of beautiful hybrids have been derived.

Dishcloth Gourd, see Luffa.

Disporum—*Liliaceae*. Hardy herbaceous perennials.
CULTURE: Soil, cool, preferably lime-free. Position, half-shade or cool spot.
PROPAGATION: By seed; division of roots in spring.
SPECIES CULTIVATED: *D. Hookeri*, greenish-yellow, early summer, 4 to 6 in., California; *lanuginosum*, pale yellow, summer, 6 in., N. America.

Ditch Moss, see *Anacharis canadensis*.

Dittany, see *Dictamnus albus*.

Diuris—*Orchidaceae*. A terrestrial tuberous genus of Australasia, 30 or more species. The flowering stem rises from the centre of the leaves. The lateral sepals are often longer than the other segments.

CULTURE: Compost, three parts sandy loam to one part of decayed leaves. Water may be required occasionally in the winter. Temp. then 50° to 55°. Considerably higher in summer by sun-heat, with shading.

PROPAGATION: Uncertain, as with nearly all tuberous orchids, offsets may occur.

SPECIES CULTIVATED: *D. alba*, 1 to 8, white, or marked with lilac to purple, autumn, Queensland; *longifolia*, yellow or purplish, spring, Australia; *maculata*, 2 to 10, yellow, spotted or flushed purplish-brown, spring, Queensland.

Divi-Divi, see *Caesalpinia coriaria*.

Dizygotheca (False Aralia)—*Araliaceae*. Tender greenhouse shrubs. Formerly included in Aralia. First introduced mid-seventeenth century.

CULTURE: Compost, equal parts loam, peat, leaf-mould, charcoal and sand. Pot, Feb. to March. Water freely March to Oct., moderately afterwards. Temp., March to Sept. 70° to 80°, Sept. to March 60° to 70°.

PROPAGATION: By grafting; cuttings in heat; portions of roots in April.

SPECIES CULTIVATED: *D. elegantissima*, thread-like drooping leaflets, Pacific Isles; *Kerchoveana*, prominently notched leaflets, Pacific Isles; *Veitchii*, leaves toothed or wavy-margined, reddish beneath, Pacific Isles.

Dock, see Rumex.

Dodecatheon (American Cowslip)—*Primulaceae*. Hardy herbaceous perennials. First introduced early eighteenth century.

OUTDOOR CULTURE: Soil, light loam enriched with plenty of leaf-mould. Position, sheltered beds on rockeries, or in borders under shade of trees. Plant, Jan. or Feb. Top-dress in Feb. with well-decayed manure.

POT CULTURE: Compost, equal parts loam, leaf-mould and sand. Position, 6 in. pots, well drained, in cold frame Nov. to March, then in unheated greenhouse till after flowering, when place outdoors. Pot, Nov. Water moderately when new growth appears, freely when in full growth.

PROPAGATION: By seeds sown in pots of light sandy soil in cold frame in Sept. or March; division of crowns in Oct. or March.

SPECIES CULTIVATED: *D. Clevelandii*, violet blue, May, 1 ft., California; *Hendersonii*, crimson and yellow, March, 6 in., Oregon; *Jeffreyi*, purple-rose, spring, 6 in., California; *Meadia*, rosy purple, white and lilac, April, 1 ft., N. America, var. *album*, white, *lilacinum*, lilac, *radicatum*, rose, 6 in., April, Kansas to N. Mexico.

Dog Rose, see *Rosa canina*; **-Violet,** see *Viola canina*; **-wood,** see Cornus.

Dog's-Tooth Violet, see *Erythronium Dens-canis*.

Dolichos—*Leguminosae*. Greenhouse evergreen twiner. First introduced mid-eighteenth century.

CULTURE: Compost, equal parts loam and peat, little sand. Position, well-drained pots, shoots twining round trellis, posts or pillars. Pot, Feb. Water moderately in winter, freely in summer. Temp., Sept. to March 50° to 55°, March to Sept. 55° to 65°.

PROPAGATION: By seeds sown in light soil in temp. 65° in March; cuttings inserted in sandy soil under bell-glass in temp. 65° in April.

SPECIES CULTIVATED: *D. Lablab*, ' Bonavist ' ' Hyacinth Bean ', rosy purple, July, 1 to 2 ft., Tropics.

Dombeya—*Sterculiaceae*. Stove ornamental evergreen trees. First introduced early nineteenth century.

CULTURE: Compost, equal parts sandy loam and fibrous peat. Position, large pots or borders in warm greenhouse. Temp., March to Oct. 75° to 90°, Oct. to March 65° to 75°. Water freely during growing season.

PROPAGATION: By cuttings of nearly ripe wood in sandy soil under hand-light in April. Temp. 80°.

SPECIES CULTIVATED: *D. Burgessiae*, white and rose, 10 ft., S. Africa; *Cayeuxii*, bright pink, 10 ft., Madeira; *Mastersii*, white, fragrant, Trop. Africa; *natalensis*, white, fragrant, Natal; *spectabilis*, white, 20 to 30 ft., East Trop. Africa; *Wallichii*, scarlet, 20 to 30 ft., Madagascar.

Doodia—*Polypodiaceae*. Greenhouse evergreen ferns. First introduced early nineteenth century.

CULTURE: Compost, two parts loam, one part leaf-mould, charcoal and sand. Pot, Feb., March or April. Position, pots in shady part of greenhouse. Water moderately Sept. to March, freely afterwards. Temp., Sept. to March 40° to 50°, March to Sept. 50° to 60°.

PROPAGATION: By spores sown on surface of sandy peat in pans under bell-glass in temp. 65° to 75° at any time.

SPECIES CULTIVATED: *D. aspera*, 6 to 8 in., Australia; *caudata*, 6 to 12 in., Australia; *lunulata* (syn. *D. media*), 12 to 18 in., Australia; *maxima* (syn. *D. Blechnoides*), 12 to 18 in., N.S.W.

Doritis—*Orchidaceae*. An epiphytic genus; though allied to Phalaenopsis there are discrepancies with that genus.

CULTURE: Compost and conditions as for Phalaenopsis, but the species, though variable, is of harder nature and so more exposure to light and fewer waterings in winter are required.

PROPAGATION: Side shoots seldom or never develop, though the stems are taller than those of Phalaenopsis.

SPECIES CULTIVATED: *D. pulcherrima* (syn. *Phalaenopsis Esmeralda*), flowers many, 1 in. or more across, lilac or light or dark amethyst, lip purple or amethyst, very variable, late summer, leaves 5 to 8 in. long, rounded, scapes erect, slender up to 30 in. high, simple or branched, Cochin-China, Moulmein, Siam.

Doronicum (Leopards-bane)—*Compositae*. Hardy herbaceous perennials.

CULTURE: Soil, ordinary, rich. Position, open borders, banks, or under shade of trees. Plant, Oct., Nov., March or April. This genus also does well in pots for early flowering in cold greenhouse.

PROPAGATION: By division of roots in Oct. or March.

SPECIES CULTIVATED: *D. austriacum*, yellow, March, 18 in., Europe; *caucasicum*, yellow, April, 1 ft., Europe; *cordatum*, deep yellow, April to May, 9 in., Europe and Asia Minor; *Pardalianches*, yellow, May, 2 ft., Europe (Br.); *plantagineum*, yellow, March, 3 ft., Europe (Br.), var. *giganteum*, more robust with larger flower heads.

Doryanthes—*Amaryllidaceae*. Greenhouse flowering plants. First introduced early nineteenth century.

CULTURE: Equal parts loam and leaf-mould, little sand. Position, well-drained pots in light airy greenhouse. Pot, Feb., March or April. Water very little Sept. to April, moderately afterwards. Temp., Sept. to March 50° to 55°, March to Sept. 65° to 70°.

PROPAGATION: By suckers removed from old plants and placed in small pots in temp. 55° to 65° at any time.

SPECIES CULTIVATED: *D. excelsa*, ' Australian Giant Lily ', scarlet, summer, 8 to 12 ft., N.S. Wales; *Guilfoylei*, crimson, summer, 12 to 15 ft., Queensland; *Palmeri*, ' Spear Lily ', red, summer, 12 ft., Queensland.

Dorycnium—*Leguminosae*. Hardy and half-hardy shrubby plants.

CULTURE: Good loam and sunny position.

PROPAGATION: By seeds; cuttings of well-ripened shoots after flowering.

SPECIES CULTIVATED: *D. hirsutum*, pink, 18 in., summer, S. Europe.

Double Bladder Pod, see *Physaria didymocarpa*.

Douglasia—*Primulaceae*. Hardy tufted evergreen plants. First introduced early nineteenth century.

CULTURE: Compost, equal parts peat and loam. Position, sunny rockery. Plant, Oct., Nov., March or April.

PROPAGATION: By seeds sown $\frac{1}{16}$ in. deep in sandy peat in cold frame, or under hand-light in March or April; division of plants in autumn.

SPECIES CULTIVATED: *D. laevigata*, rosy pink, March to Sept., 1 in., Oregon Mountains; *montana*, pink, 2 in., spring, U.S.A., var. *praetutiana*, yellow, spring; *nivalis*, pink, April, 1 in., Rocky Mountains; *Vitaliana* (syn. *Androsace Vitaliana*), yellow, May to July, 2 in., Alps.

Dovedale Moss, see *Saxifraga hypnoides*.

Dove Flower, see *Peristeria elata*.

Downingia—*Lobeliaceae.* Hardy annuals. First introduced early nineteenth century.
CULTURE: Soil, ordinary, rich. Position, sunny beds or borders. Sow seeds in April where plants are to flower. Thin seedlings to 6 in. apart in May or June.
POT CULTURE: Compost, equal parts loam, leaf-mould and sand. Sow seeds $\frac{1}{16}$ in. deep in 5 or 6 in. pots placed in temp. 55°, or in cold frame in April or May. Water moderately. Apply weak liquid manure until plants are in flower. Place plants when in flower in cool greenhouse or window.
SPECIES CULTIVATED: *D. elegans* (syn. *Clintonia elegans*), blue and white, summer, 6 in., N.W. America; *pulchella* (syn. *Clintonia pulchella*), blue, white and yellow, summer, 6 in., W. America.

Down Thistle, see *Onopordum Acanthium.*

Draba (Whitlow Grass)—*Cruciferae.* Hardy perennial plants.
CULTURE: Soil, ordinary. Position, crevices in sunny rockeries, or on old walls. Plant, March or April.
PROPAGATION: By seeds sown where plants are to grow or in pans of sandy soil in April; division of roots in March.
SPECIES CULTIVATED: *D. aizoides*, yellow, March, 3 in., Europe (Br); *Aizoon*, yellow, April, 3 in. W. Europe; *alpina*, yellow, April, 3 in., N. Europe and Asia; *bruniifolia*, yellow, June, 3 in., Caucasus; *bryoides*, yellow, 2 in., April to May, Caucasus, var. *imbricata*; *Dedeana*, white, May, 2 to 3 in., Spain; *Mawii*, white, early spring, 3 in., Spain; *mollissima*, soft yellow, 2 in., early spring, Caucasus; *olympica*, golden, 3 in., spring, Asia Minor; *polytricha*, yellow, 2 in., spring, Turkish Armenia; *rigida* (syn. *D. diacranioides*), yellow, 3 in., spring, Asia Minor; *stylaris*, yellow, 3 to 4 in., April to May, Europe; *vesicaria*, yellow, 2 in., May, Lebanon.

Dracaena—*Liliaceae.* Stove evergreen plants grown in greenhouse for the handsome, often variegated, foliage. Some species were formerly known as Pleomele. First introduced early seventeenth century.
CULTURE: Compost, two parts loam, one part peat and one part leaf-mould and sand. Position, well-drained pots in light part of stove. Pot, Feb. to March. Water moderately Oct. to March, freely afterwards. Temp., March to Sept. 75° to 85°, Sept. to March 55° to 65°.
PROPAGATION: By seeds in sandy soil in temp. 85° in March; cuttings of main stem cut into lengths of 1 to 2 in. and partially buried horizontally in sandy peat in March or April; cuttings or ' toes ' of fleshy roots in sandy peat in spring; tops of stems in sand in March or April.
SPECIES CULTIVATED: *D. concinna*, leaves green, margined with red, 4 to 6 ft., Madagascar; *deremensis*, leaves long and pointed, 10 to 15 ft., Trop. Africa; *Draco*, ' Dragon Tree ', leaves glaucous, hardy in Cornwall and Scilly Isles, 40 to 50 ft., Canary Islands; *fragrans*, leaves green, 15 to 20 ft., Trop. Africa, and vars. *Lindenii, Massangeana, Victoriae,* garden form; *Godseffiana*, leaves white and green, 3 ft., W. Trop. Africa; *Goldieana*, leaves green and white, 4 to 6 ft., W. Trop. Africa; *Sanderiana*, leaves white and green, 5 ft., W. Trop. Africa.

Dracocephalum (Dragonhead)—*Labiatae.* Hardy annual and perennial herbs. First introduced late sixteenth century.
CULTURE: Soil, light, ordinary. Position, cool, partially shady borders. Plant, Oct., Nov., March or April.
PROPAGATION: Annual and perennial species by seeds sown $\frac{1}{8}$ in. deep in light sandy soil outdoors in April; cuttings of young shoots inserted in light sandy soil under hand-light or in cold frame in April or May; division of roots in Oct., Nov. or March.
ANNUAL SPECIES CULTIVATED: *D. Moldavica*, ' Moldavian Balm ', blue, July and Aug., 12 to 18 in., E. Siberia; *Isabellae*, 2 ft., purple-blue, China; *Purdomii*, purple-blue, May, 9 in., Asia.

PERENNIAL SPECIES CULTIVATED: *D. austriacum*, blue, summer, 12 to 18 in., Europe; *bullatum*, 9 in., bright blue, July, China; *grandiflorum*, blue, summer, 6 to 9 in., Siberia; *Hemsleyanum*, light blue, summer, 1½ to 2 ft., Tibet; *palustre*, rose, 12 to 15 in., for waterside; *Ruyschiana*, purplish-blue, June, 12 to 18 in., Alps; *sibiricum* (syns. *Nepeta macrantha*, *N.* ' Souvenir d'André Chaudron '), blue, July, 4¼ ft., Siberia; *speciosum*, lilac, June, 18 in., Himalaya; *Stewartianum* violet, summer, 1½ ft., China. See also Physostegia.

Dracunculus (Dragon Arum)—*Araceae*. Hardy tuberous-rooted perennial. Unisexual flowers on spadices surrounded by spathes, very offensive odour when in bloom. First introduced early sixteenth century.

CULTURE: Soil, sandy. Position, well-drained sunny border. Plant tubers 3 in. deep in Oct. or Nov.

PROPAGATION: By division of tubers in Oct. or March.

SPECIES CULTIVATED: *D. vulgaris* (syn. *Arum Dracunculus*), chocolate-brown, July, 3 ft., S. Europe.

Dragon Arum, see, Dracunculus;   **-Tree,** see *Dracaena Draco.*

Dragonhead, see Dracocephalum;   **False-,** see Physostegia.

Drimys—*Magnoliaceae*. Tender ornamental deciduous tree. First introduced early nineteenth century.

CULTURE: Soil, good loamy. Position, warm, sheltered borders in favoured localities only. Plant, Oct.

PROPAGATION: By cuttings of ripened wood inserted in a cold frame in autumn, or by layering in spring.

SPECIES CULTIVATED: *D. Winteri*, ivory white, aromatic, April to May, 12 to 40 ft., S. America.

Drooping Urn Flower, see *Urceolina pendula.*

Dropwort, see *Filipendula vulgaris.*

Drosera—*Droseraceae*. Greenhouse and hardy perennial insectivorous plants.

CULTURE: Compost, equal parts living sphagnum moss, peat, charcoal, sand and potsherds. Position, well-drained pots in moist position in sunny greenhouse. Water freely except in winter.

PROPAGATION: By seeds sown on surface of living sphagnum moss and peat in well-drained pots under bell-glass in temp. 55° to 65° at any time; division of the crowns in March or April; cuttings of roots ⅛ to 1 in. long embedded in pan of moss and peat under bell-glass in temp. 65° to 75°.

SPECIES CULTIVATED: *D. binata*, white, June to Sept., 3 to 4 in., Australia; *capensis*, purple, June to July, 3 to 4 in., Cape of Good Hope; *longifolia*, white, July, 3 in., Europe (Br.); *rotundifolia*, ' Sundew ', white, July, 4 in., Europe (Br.).

Drosanthemum—*Aizoaceae*. Greenhouse succulent plants, formerly included in Mesembryanthemum.

CULTURE: As Mesembryanthemum.

PROPAGATION: As Mesembryanthemum.

SPECIES CULTIVATED: *D. floribundum* (syn. *Mesembryanthemum floribundum*), pink July, 6 in., S. Africa.

Drosophyllum—*Droseraceae*. Greenhouse sub-shrubby insectivorous plants. First introduced mid-nineteenth century.

CULTURE: Soil, light sandy loam and fibrous peat. Position, well-drained pots close to glass in light airy greenhouse. Water moderately summer, little winter. Temp., Sept. to March 40° to 50°, March to Sept. 50° to 60°.

PROPAGATION: By seeds sown on the surface of sandy loam in well-drained pots in spring.

SPECIES CULTIVATED: *D. lusitanicum*, ' Portuguese Sundew ', yellow, May, 1 ft., Portugal.

Dryas—*Rosaceae*. Hardy evergreen creeping or trailing plants.

CULTURE: Soil, moist peat. Position, sunny rockery or borders. Plant, Oct., Nov. or March.

PROPAGATION: By seeds sown $\frac{1}{16}$ in. deep in sandy peat in shallow pans or boxes in cold frame April or May; cuttings of shoots 2 in. long inserted in sandy soil in cold frame in autumn; division of plants in Oct., Nov. or March.

SPECIES CULTIVATED: *D. Drummondii*, yellow, June, 3 in., N. America; *octopetala*, ' Mountain Avens ', white, June, 3 in., trailing, Europe, vars. *minor*, Europe (Br.), *vestita*, white, leaves felted grey, Alps; *Suendermannii*, white, June, 3 to 4 in., hybrid.

Dryopteris—*Polypodiaceae*. Stove, greenhouse and hardy ferns. Many ferns previously known as Aspidium, Lastrea, Nephrodium and Thelypteris are now included in this genus.

CULTURE OF STOVE SPECIES: Compost, equal parts loam, leaf-mould, peat and sand. Position, well-drained pots in shady part of stove. Pot, March. Water moderately Oct. to March, freely afterwards. Temp., Sept. to March 55° to 60°, March to Sept. 65° to 75°.

CULTURE OF GREENHOUSE SPECIES: Compost, equal parts loam, leaf-mould, peat and sand. Position, well-drained pots, borders or rockeries in shade. Pot or plant, Feb., March or April. Water moderately Oct. to Feb., freely afterwards. Temp., Oct. to March 40° to 50°, March to Oct. 55° to 65°.

CULTURE OF HARDY SPECIES: Soil, ordinary, light, rich. Position, shady borders or rockeries. Plant, April. Water freely in dry weather May to Sept. Top-dress annually with leaf-mould or well-decayed manure. Protect in severe weather with bracken or litter. Do not remove dead fronds until April.

PROPAGATION: Stove and greenhouse species by spores sown on surface of fine sandy peat under bell-glass in temp. 75° to 85° any time; division of plants at potting or planting time. Hardy species by spores sown on surface of sandy soil in shady cold frame; division in April.

STOVE SPECIES CULTIVATED: *D. dissecta* (syn. *Nephrodium dissectum*), Tropics; *orientalis* (syn. *Nephrodium albo-punctatum*), Mascarene Is.

GREENHOUSE SPECIES CULTIVATED: *D. concolor*, India, Brazil; *decomposita* (syn. *N. decompositum*), Australia, etc.; *effusum*, Jamaica; *erythrosora*, Japan; *khasiana* (syn. *N. cuspidatum*), Ceylon; *lepida*, Polynesia; *otaria*, Japan; *parasitica* (syn. *N. molle*), Tropics and Subtropics; *patens*, Tropics and Subtropics; *pubescens*, Jamaica; *refracta*, Brazil; *Richardsii*, New Caledonia; *Sieboldii*, Japan.

HARDY SPECIES CULTIVATED: *D. aemula*, ' Hay-scented Fern ', Britain; *cristata*, Britain and N. America; *Filix-mas*, ' Male Fern ', Britain and Temp. Zone, and numerous vars.; *fragrans*, N. America; *Goldiana* (syn. *Aspidium Goldianum*), N. America; *Linnaeana* (syn. *Polypodium Dryopteris*), Europe, Britain etc.; *marginalis*, (syn. *Aspidium marginale*), Canada; *Phegopteris*, ' Beech Fern ', Britain; *rigida*, Europe; *spinulosa*, N. Temp. Zone (Br.); *Thelypteris* (syns. *Aspidium Thelypteris*, *Thelypteris palustris*), N. America, Europe, Asia.

Drypis—*Caryophyllaceae*. Hardy herbaceous perennial. First introduced mid-eighteenth century.

CULTURE: Soil, ordinary. Position, sunny rockeries or borders. Plant, Oct., Nov., March, April.

PROPAGATION: By seeds sown in light soil in cold frame or under hand-light in March or April; cuttings inserted in sandy soil under hand-light or in cold frame in Sept. or Oct.

SPECIES CULTIVATED: *D. spinosa*, blue, summer, 9 in., Medit. Region.

Duck Potato, see *Sagittaria latifolia*.

Ducksfoot, see *Podophyllum peltatum*.

Duke of Argyll's Tea-plant, see *Lycium chinense*.

Dusty Miller, see *Primula auricula* and *Senecio Cineraria*.

Dutch Agrimony, see *Eupatorium cannabinum;* **-Myrtle,** see *Myrica Gale;* **-Woodbine,** see *Lonicera Periclymenum* var. *belgica.*

Dutchman's Breeches, see *Dicentra Cucullaria;* **-Pipe,** see *Aristolochia durior.*

Dwarf Sunflower, see *Actinea grandiflora.*

Dyckia—*Bromeliaceae.* Greenhouse, succulent, ornamental, foliage plants. First introduced mid-nineteenth century.

CULTURE: Compost, two parts loam, one part leaf-mould and little sand. Position, pots in light airy greenhouse; outside June to Sept. Water moderately April to Aug., little afterwards. Repot every five or six years; good drainage essential. Temp., Sept. to March 50° to 55°, March to Sept. 55° to 65°.

PROPAGATION: By offsets or suckers inserted in small pots in greenhouse at any time.

SPECIES CULTIVATED: *D. altissima,* yellow, autumn, 2 ft., Brazil; *brevifolia,* yellow, Aug., 1 ft., Brazil; *frigida,* orange-yellow, spring, 1 to 2 ft., Brazil; *rariflora,* orange, summer, 2 ft., Brazil.

Dyer's Greenweed, see *Genista tinctoria.*

Earthnut, see *Arachis hypogaea.*

Ebenus—*Leguminosae.* Slightly tender evergreen sub-shrubs.

CULTURE: Soil, poorish, well drained. Position, warm, sheltered ledges in the rock garden.

PROPAGATION: Seeds; cuttings.

SPECIES CULTIVATED: *E. cretica,* pink, 2 ft., summer, Crete; *Sibthorpii,* pink, 1 to 2 ft., summer, Greece.

Eccremocarpus—*Bignoniaceae.* Half-hardy climbing plant. Stems herbaceous in the open. First introduced early nineteenth century.

CULTURE: Soil, light, rich. Position, against south or south-west walls. Plant, June. Protect roots in Oct. by layer of cinder-ashes on surface of soil; base of plant in severe weather by mats.

PROPAGATION: By seeds sown $\frac{1}{16}$ in. deep in well-drained pots of light sandy soil in temp. 55° to 65° in March or April.

SPECIES CULTIVATED: *E. scaber,* ' Chilean Glory Flower ', scarlet and yellow, summer, 15 to 20 ft., Chile.

Echeveria—*Crassulaceae.* Greenhouse and half-hardy succulent plants, by some authors included in the genus Cotyledon.

CULTURE OF GREENHOUSE SPECIES: Compost, two parts loam, one part sand and fine brick rubble. Position, in well-drained pots close to glass in window or greenhouse. Repot, March or April. Water freely March to Sept., very little afterwards. Temp., Sept. to March 50° to 55°, March to Sept. 60° to 70°. Can be grown outdoors June to Sept.

CULTURE OF HALF-HARDY SPECIES: Soil, ordinary. Position, sunny rockeries or as edgings to beds. Plant in May, place in boxes in cold frame in Oct.

PROPAGATION: By seeds in temp. 55° to 65° in March; cuttings of leaves with base inserted in well-drained pots of sandy soil in Aug. to Oct. in temp. 55° to 60°. Do not water leaves or cuttings until they begin to shrivel.

SPECIES CULTIVATED: *E. agavoides,* orange, Sept., 1 ft., Mexico; *caespitosa* (syn. *Cotyledon californica*), yellow, summer, 1 ft., California; *coccinea,* red, Oct., 2 ft., Mexico; *farinosa,* orange-red, summer, leaves silvery-white, California; *gibbiflora,* red, autumn, 2 ft., Mexico; *glauca,* red and yellow, autumn, 1 ft., Mexico; *retusa,* bright red, autumn, 1 ft., Mexico.

HALF-HARDY SPECIES CULTIVATED: *E. secunda,* reddish, summer, 1 ft., Mexico.

Echinacea (Purple Cone Flower)—*Compositae.* Hardy herbaceous perennials. First introduced late eighteenth century.

CULTURE: Soil, deep, rich, light loam. Position, well-drained sunny borders. Plant, Oct. or March.

PROPAGATION: By seeds sown ½ in. deep in boxes of light soil in temp. 50° to 55° in March, or outdoors in sunny position in April; division in Oct., March or April; root cuttings in Feb.

SPECIES CULTIVATED: *E. angustifolia*, purplish-red, summer, 1 to 2 ft., N. America; *purpurea* (syn. *Rudbeckia purpurea*), purplish-red, Aug., 3 ft., N. America.

Echinocactus—*Cactaceae*. Greenhouse succulent plants. Many species formerly included in this genus have been transferred to other genera including Gymnocalycium, Notocactus, Pediocactus, Pyrrhocactus, Stenocactus, etc. First introduced late eighteenth century.

CULTURE: Compost, two parts fibrous sandy loam, one part brick rubble, old mortar and sand. Position, well-drained pots in sunny greenhouse or window. Repot every three or four years in spring. Water occasionally Sept. to April, once a week afterwards. Temp., Sept. to March 50° to 65°, March to Sept. 65° to 75°.

PROPAGATION: By seeds sown ⅛ in. deep in well-drained pans of sandy soil in temp. 75° in March, keeping soil moderately moist; cuttings of stems inserted in small pots of sandy soil kept barely moist, in summer; grafting on common kinds in April.

SPECIES CULTIVATED: *E. Grusonii*, red and yellow, summer; *Visnaga*, yellow, summer, 5 ft., Mexico.

Echinocereus—*Cactaceae*. Greenhouse plants with fleshy, spiny stems, without leaves. Formerly included in the genus Cereus. First introduced late seventeenth century.

CULTURE: Compost, two parts fibrous loam, one part coarse sand and broken brick. Position, well-drained pots in sunny greenhouses or windows. Pot every two or three years as required, water sparingly. Temp., Sept. to March 50° to 55°, March to Sept. 55° to 65°.

PROPAGATION: By seeds sown in well-drained pots or pans; cuttings of stems inserted in pots of sand and kept just moist; grafting on other kinds in spring.

SPECIES CULTIVATED: *E. Blanckii*, purple, Texas, Mexico; *coccineus* (syn. *Cereus aggregatus*), scarlet, Sept., U.S.A.; *conglomeratus*, Mexico; *enneacanthus*, purple, Mexico, Texas; *Fendleri*, purple, Mexico; *pentalophus*, rose, Mexico, Texas; *Richenbachii* (syn. *Cereus caespitosus*), rose, summer, U.S.A.

Echinocystis—*Cucurbitaceae*. Half-hardy annual climber, bearing small prickly cucumber-like fruits.

CULTURE: Sow seeds in heat in spring, and plant out in moist rich soil in May against a sunny trellis, fence or arch.

SPECIES CULTIVATED: *E. lobata*, ' Wild Balsam Apple ', greenish-white, summer, 8 to 10 ft., United States.

Echinodorus—*Alismaceae*. Waterside plants akin to Alisma.

CULTURE: Soil, any wet mud. Plant, in spring.

PROPAGATION: Seeds or division in spring.

SPECIES CULTIVATED: *E. ranunculoides*, rosy-white, tapering leaves, Europe (Br.), N. Africa.

Echinops (Globe Thistle)—*Compositae*. Hardy biennials and perennials. First introduced mid-sixteenth century.

CULTURE: Soil, ordinary. Position, well-drained sunny borders. Plant, Oct., Nov. or March.

PROPAGATION: By seeds sown ½ in. deep in sunny position outdoors in April; division of roots in Oct. or March; root cuttings.

PERENNIAL SPECIES CULTIVATED: *E. bannaticus*, violet blue, summer, 2 to 3 ft., Hungary; *Ritro*, blue, summer, 3 ft., S. Europe; *sphaerocephalus*, pale blue, summer, 3 to 4 ft., Europe.

Echinopsis—*Cactaceae.* Greenhouse succulent plants. First introduced early nineteenth century.

CULTURE: Compost, two parts fibrous sandy loam, one part brick rubble, old mortar and sand. Position, well-drained pots in sunny greenhouse or window. Repot every three or four years in spring. Water occasionally Sept. to April, once a week afterwards. Temp., Sept. to March 50° to 55°, March to Sept. 65° to 75°.

PROPAGATION: By seeds sown ⅛ in. deep in well-drained pans of sandy soil in temp. 75° in March, keeping soil moderately moist; cuttings of stems inserted in small pots of sandy soil, kept barely moist in summer; grafting on common kinds in April.

SPECIES CULTIVATED: *E. cristata*, creamy-white, summer, 1 ft., Bolivia; *Eyriesii*, white, fragrant, July, 4 to 6 in., Mexico; *leucantha* (syn. *E. campylacantha*), rose, summer, 1 ft., Chile; *multiplex*, rose, July, Brazil; *oxygona*, rose, summer, 6 ins., Brazil; *tubiflora*, white, summer, 4 in., Mexico.

Echites—*Apocynaceae.* Stove evergreen flowering and climbing shrub. First introduced mid-nineteenth century.

CULTURE: Compost, rough fibrous peat and one-fourth silver sand. Position, well-drained pots, with shoots trained to roof of stove or to wire trellis. Pot, Feb. or March. Prune, Oct., cutting away shoots that have flowered only. Water very little Oct. to Feb., moderately Feb. to April, freely afterwards. Temp., Oct. to Feb. 55° to 60°, Feb. to Oct. 65° to 75°.

PROPAGATION: By cuttings of young side shoots 3 in. long inserted in pots of sandy peat under bell-glass in temp. 80° in Feb., March or April.

SPECIES CULTIVATED: *E. rubro-venosa*, emerald green leaves, speckled red or yellow, Brazil.

Echium (Viper's Bugloss)—*Boraginaceae.* Hardy annuals, biennials and perennials.

CULTURE: Soil, ordinary. Position, sunny well-drained borders or wild garden. Plant, Aug. or April.

PROPAGATION: By seeds sown ⅛ in. deep in sunny position outdoors in April or Aug.

ANNUAL OR BIENNIAL SPECIES CULTIVATED: *E. creticum*, violet, July, 12 to 18 in., S. Europe; *plantagineum*, bluish-purple, summer, 2 to 3 ft., S. Europe (Br.); *vulgare*, purple or blue, summer, 3 to 4 ft., Britain; *Wilderetii*, rose, summer, 3 ft., Canary Isles.

PERENNIAL SPECIES CULTIVATED: *E. albicans*, rose or violet, summer, 1 ft., Spain.

Edelweiss, see *Leontopodium alpinum.*

Edgeworthia—*Thymelaeaceae.* Slightly tender, deciduous, early-flowering shrub bearing dense heads of fragrant little yellow flowers in Feb. or March. Allied to Daphne, and can be grown outdoors in milder counties and maritime districts. The bast is a source of soft tough paper.

CULTURE: Compost, two parts sandy loam and one part turfy peat. Good drainage and a liberal supply of water in summer are essential.

PROPAGATION: By cuttings in sandy soil under bell-glass in spring.

SPECIES CULTIVATED: *E. papyrifera* (syns. *E. chrysantha*, *E. Gardneri*), 'Paper Bush', 'Mitsumata', yellow, Feb. to March, 4 to 6 ft., China, Japan.

Edraianthus—*Campanulaceae.* Hardy low tufted perennial plants.

CULTURE: Soil, any open, gritty medium. Position, warm and sunny.

PROPAGATION: By seeds; cuttings made from soft tips.

SPECIES CULTIVATED: *E. dalmaticus*, purple-blue, cluster-headed, 6 in., summer, Dalmatia; *graminifolius*, blue, cluster-headed, 9 in., summer, Europe; *pumilio*, blue, 2 to 3 in., June, Dalmatia; *serpyllifolius*, deep purple-blue, prostrate, May to June, Dalmatia; *tenuifolius*, blue, fine-leaved, May, 3 to 4 in., Europe.

Eel Grass, see Vallisneria.

Egeria, see Anacharis.

Eggplant or **Aubergine,** see *Solanum Melongena* var. *esculentum.*

Eglantine, see *Rosa Eglanteria.*

Egyptian Lotus, see *Nymphaea Lotus.*

Eichhornia—*Pontederiaceae.* Tender floating aquatic perennials. First introduced mid-nineteenth century.

CULTURE: Float on water during summer months. In Sept. pot number closely together in bowls of sifted loam and charcoal and fill with water. Reduce water gradually till plants are in wet soil only during winter months. Store away from frost and restart in temp. 60° about March. Multiplies rapidly in temp. 60° to 70°.

PROPAGATION: By division in early summer, or by severing the stolons from natural runners.

SPECIES CULTIVATED: *E. azurea,* runs lengthwise, 5 to 6 ft., lavender-blue and yellow, S. America; *crassipes* (syn. *E. speciosa*), ' Water Hyacinth ', rounded habit, swollen petioles make it buoyant, pale violet, peacock eye, Africa, Australia, Trop. America.

Elaeagnus—*Elaeagnaceae.* Hardy deciduous and evergreen shrubs with insignificant but mostly fragrant silver-coloured flowers resembling small fuchsias. First introduced mid-seventeenth century.

CULTURE: Soil, ordinary. Position, open sheltered dryish borders or against south or west walls. Plant deciduous species in Oct. to Dec., evergreen species in April or Sept.

PROPAGATION: By seeds in boxes of light soil in temp. 55° in March; cuttings in sandy soil in cold frame in Sept.; layering in spring.

EVERGREEN SPECIES CULTIVATED: *E. glabra,* white, Aug., 4 to 6 ft., China, Japan; *macrophylla,* yellow, Nov., very fragrant, 6 ft., Japan; *pungens,* yellow, autumn, 6 ft., China, Japan, vars. *aurea, maculata,* golden-leaved, *variegata,* leaves bordered yellow.

DECIDUOUS SPECIES CULTIVATED: *E. angustifolia,* ' Oleaster ', silvery white and yellow, June, 15 to 20 ft., Europe, W. Asia; *commutata,* yellow, July, 8 ft., N. America; *multiflora,* creamy, April to May, 6 to 10 ft., Japan; *umbellata,* strong growing and spreading, May, fruits silver then red, 15 ft., Himalaya, Japan.

Elaphoglossum—*Polypodiaceae.* Stove and greenhouse evergreen ferns, formerly included in the genus Acrostichum.

CULTURE: As Acrostichum.

PROPAGATION: As Acrostichum.

STOVE SPECIES CULTIVATED: *E. Aubertii,* 1 ft., Nata, Guatemala, etc.; *conforme,* 6 in., Tropics; *crinitum,* ' Elephant-ear Fern ', 4 to 18 in., W. Indies; *decoratum,* 1 ft., W. Indies; *Herminieri,* 1 to 2 ft., W. Indies; *magnum,* 1 to 2 ft., Brit. Guiana; *muscosum,* 6 to 12 in., Trop. America; *scolopendrifolium,* 1 ft., Brazil; *squamosum,* 8 to 12 in., Sumatra, Sandwich Is., Azores, etc.; *viscosum,* 6 to 12 in., Cuba, Trop. America.

GREENHOUSE SPECIES CULTIVATED: *E. Bluemeanum,* 4 to 6 in., Assam.

Elder, see Sambucus.

Elderberry, see *Sambucus nigra.*

Elecampane, see *Inula Helenium.*

Eleocharis (Spike Rush)—*Cyperaceae.* Marsh grasses.

CULTURE: Soil, aquarium compost. Plant, any time.

PROPAGATION: Division, any time during growing season.

SPECIES CULTIVATED: *E. acicularis,* the elegant appearance makes it suitable for growing submerged in an aquarium, Europe (Br.), Australia.

Elephant-ear Fern, see *Elaphoglossum crinitum.*

Elephant's Foot, see *Testudinaria elephantipes*.

Elisena—*Amaryllidaceae*. Warm greenhouse bulbous plant. First introduced early nineteenth century.

CULTURE: Compost, two parts light sandy loam, one part leaf-mould and one part of coarse sand. Position, well-drained pots in warm, sunny greenhouse. Pot, autumn. Water freely during growing period. Keep nearly dry when at rest. Temp., Sept. to March 55° to 65°, March to Sept. 65° to 75°.

PROPAGATION: By offsets removed and treated as parent bulbs at potting time.

SPECIES CULTIVATED: *E. longipetala*, white, spring, 3 ft., Peru.

Elisma, see Luronium.

Elm, see Ulmus.

Elodea—*Hydrocharitaceae*. Useful oxygenating plants for the aquarium or pond.

CULTURE: Soil, aquarium compost or loam. Plant any time during spring or summer, weight clumps with lead or stone and sink in position.

PROPAGATION: Slips taken any time during growing season.

SPECIES CULTIVATED: *E. callitrichoides*, Argentine, Australia; *densa* (syn. *Anacharis canadensis* var. *gigantea*), small white flowers enclosed by broad loose spathe, S. America. For *E. crispa* see Lagarosiphon.

Elsholtzia—*Labiatae*. A semi-woody shrub, with growths usually dying back in winter but throwing up flowering stems each summer. First introduced early twentieth century.

CULTURE: Ordinary, rich garden soil, full sun. Prune back dead shoots in April.

PROPAGATION: Aug. cuttings in frames.

SPECIES CULTIVATED: *E. Stauntonii*, rose-lilac flowers in panicles, autumn, 5 ft., China.

Embothrium—*Proteaceae*. Rather tender evergreen shrub. First introduced mid-nineteenth century.

OUTDOOR CULTURE: Soil, sandy peat, dislikes lime. Position, against south walls outdoors S. of England, pots in cold greenhouse N. of England. Protect with mats in severe weather. Plant, March or April.

GREENHOUSE CULTURE: Compost, two parts peat, one part loam, and one part sand. Pot, March. Prune, March. Water moderately Oct. to April, freely in summer. Place plants in sunny position outdoors May to Oct.

PROPAGATION: By cuttings inserted in sandy peat under bell-glass in temp. 55° in spring; also by cuttings of roots inserted in sandy peat in temp. 75° in spring; by grafting young shoots on portions of its own roots in spring; also by sowing imported or home-saved seeds in sandy peat, in temp. 75°, in spring.

SPECIES CULTIVATED: *E. coccineum*, 'Firebush', bright scarlet, honeysuckle-shaped, of great beauty, May to June, 10 to 30 ft., Chile, var. *longifolium*, probably more hardy.

Emilia—*Compositae*. Half-hardy annual.

CULTURE: Soil, rich loam. Position, sunny beds and borders. Sow seed in boxes or pans in warm greenhouse in Feb. or March, pricking out seedlings into boxes as soon as large enough to handle, and hardening off for planting out in May.

SPECIES CULTIVATED: *E. sagittata* (syn. *E. flammea*, *Cacalia coccinea*), scarlet, summer, 1 to 2 ft., Trop. America.

Empetrum—*Empetraceae*. Hardy evergreen fruiting shrub with black edible berries ripe in Sept.

CULTURE: Soil, boggy. Position, damp, moist, shady. Plant, March or April.

PROPAGATION: By cuttings inserted in June, July or Aug. in sandy peat under bell-glass in shady position.

SPECIES CULTIVATED: *E. nigrum*, 'Crowberry', pink, May, 8 to 10 in., N. Hemisphere, var. *purpureum*, red or purple fruits.

Encephalartos (Caffer Bread)—*Cycadaceae.* Greenhouse evergreen plants. First introduced early nineteenth century. Leaves, feather-shaped, bluish-green.

CULTURE: Compost, two parts good loam, one part sand. Position, well-drained pots in light part of greenhouse. Repot, March. Water liberally April to Aug., very little afterwards. Growth may appear to cease for a few years. Temp., Sept. to April 55° to 60°, April to Sept. 65° to 75°.

PROPAGATION: By seeds sown ¼ in. deep in light soil in temp. 85° to 95° in March or April.

SPECIES CULTIVATED: *E. Altensteinii*, 8 ft., S. Africa; *caffra*, ' Caffer Bread ', 8 to 10 ft., S. Africa; *horridus*, 8 to 10 ft., S. Africa.

Endive, see *Cichorium Endivia.*

Enkianthus—*Ericaceae.* Hardy deciduous shrubs with small bell-shaped flowers in spring and autumn-tinted foliage.

CULTURE: Soil, ordinary, moist, with a little peat and leaf-mould. Position, warm, sheltered shrubberies or beds. Plant, Sept. or April. No pruning required.

PROPAGATION: By cuttings of firm shoots in sandy soil in heat in spring, or seed sown in peaty soil in spring.

SPECIES CULTIVATED: *E. campanulatus*, cream, May, 20 ft., Japan, var. *Palibinii*, flowers red; *cernuus*, cream, May, 12 ft., Japan, var. *rubens*, flowers deep red; *chinensis* (syn. *E. sinohimalaicus*), a strong-growing species, salmon-orange, May, W. China; *perulatus* (syn. *E. japonicus*), 4 ft., white, Japan.

Eomecon—*Papaveraceae.* Hardy, rhizomatous, herbaceous, poppy-like perennial. First introduced late nineteenth century.

CULTURE: Soil, sandy peat and leaf-mould. Position, sunny, well-drained border. Plant, Oct. to March. Water freely in very dry weather.

PROPAGATION: By division of the roots in March or early April.

SPECIES CULTIVATED: *E. chionantha*, ' Snow Poppy ', white, summer, 1 to 2 ft., China.

Epacris (Australian Heath)—*Epacridaceae.* Greenhouse evergreen flowering shrubs. First introduced early nineteenth century.

CULTURE: Compost, three-fourths fibrous peat, one-fourth silver sand. Position, light airy greenhouse Sept. to July, sunny place outdoors July to Sept. Repot, April, May or June; good drainage essential. Prune shoots of erect kinds to within 1 in. of base directly after flowering; pendulous kinds about half-way. Water moderately at all times. Syringe plants daily March to July. Temp., Sept. to March 45° to 50°, March to July 55° to 60°. Stimulants not essential.

PROPAGATION: By seeds sown immediately they ripen on surface of sandy peat under bell-glass in temp. 55°; cuttings of ends of shoots inserted in pots of sandy peat covered with bell-glass placed in cool greenhouse in Aug. or April.

SPECIES CULTIVATED: *E. impressa*, white and red, March, loosely branched, Australia; *longiflora*, crimson and white, May and June, 2 to 4 ft., Australia, var. *splendens*, red, tipped white; *purpurascens*, white and red, winter, 2 to 3 ft., Australia. Numerous vars. and hybrids will be found in trade lists.

Ephedra (Shrubby Horsetail)—*Ephedraceae.* Hardy evergreen shrubs resembling the wild horse-tail, of little ornamental value.

CULTURE: Soil, a well-drained loam. Position, sunny banks where the branches can sprawl about. Plant in autumn.

PROPAGATION: By layering the branches in summer.

SPECIES CULTIVATED: *E. distachya*, branchlets rigid, 3 to 4 ft., S. Europe; *Gerardiana*, branchlets slender and spreading, 2 ft., Himalaya, etc.; *minuta*, prostrate, 3 to 6 in., China; *major* (syn. *E. nebrodensis*), branchlets prostrate, 3 ft. N. Africa; *procera*, to 6 ft., Greece to Caucasus.

× **Epicattleya**—*Orchidaceae.* Bigenic hybrid between Epidendrum and Cattleya. The habit is intermediate between the two genera. Flowers borne in terminal spikes.

CULTURE: Similar to Cattleyas with consideration regarding temp. if a cross between a cool-growing species and one requiring more warmth.

Epidendrum—*Orchidaceae.* Epiphytic orchids, native in Trop. America. Allied to Cattleya. Probably over 1000 species, very variable, including some of dwarf habit. Decided pseudo-bulbs in many, in others stemlike, slender or stout, short or tall, fleshy stems and fleshy leaves or otherwise. The inflorescence terminal with a few exceptions, flowers solitary, racemose or in panicles. A number of hybrids have been raised.

CULTURE: The hard-bulbed, hard-leaved species must have a decided rest in winter, most of them about 50°. In summer, rising to 80° or more with sun heat. The stemmed section mostly needs a winter temp. of 60° and a more humid atmosphere throughout the year, rising in summer to 80° or more with shading. Variation is so great that slight differences are necessary in treatment. The Nanodes section needs a moist atmosphere throughout the year, though high temps. may not be needed. Compost as for Cattleyas. The Cattleya house provides suitable conditions for a large number but the Barkeria section is suited in the cool house, suspended near the glass and though with slender pseudo-bulbs needs only occasional waterings, if any, in winter.

PROPAGATION: By division of plants. Stemmed kinds which emit stem roots by cuttings taken off below roots.

SPECIES CULTIVATED: A selection only—*E. advena* (syns. *E. Caprartianum*, *E. osmanthum*), summer, Brazil; *aromaticum*, very fragrant, in panicles, yellowish, lip whitish with red striations, summer, Mexico, Guatemala; *atropurpureum* (syn. *E. macrochilum*), dark brownish, lip white, crimson-purple, very variable, var. *album*, has a pure white lip; *Brassavolae*, yellow, lip whitish and purple, spring, summer, Guatemala; *ciliare*, white, lip fringed, various seasons, Trop. America; *cyclotellum* (syn. *Barkeria cyclotellum*), spring, Mexico, Guatemala; *dichromum*, whitish, rose-flushed, crimson-purple, summer, Brazil, var. *amabile* (syn. *E. amabile*), rosy, crimson-purple, white; *Endresii*, whitish, rose, violet spots on lip, purplish streaked, various seasons, Costa Rica; *fragrans*, dwarf, white, lip purple streaked, various seasons, Cent. America; *Frederici Gulielmii*, crimson-purple, summer, Peru; *ibaguense*, orange-yellow to red, various seasons, Colombia, Ecuador; *Lindleyanum* (syn. *Barkeria Lindleyana*), rose-purple, variable, autumn, Mexico; *Mathewsii* (syn. *Nanodes Mathewsii*), dwarf, purplish, Peru, Cent. America; *Medusae* (syn. *Nanodes Medusae*), yellowish-green, lip purple-brown, fringed, Costa Rica; *melanocaulon* (syn. *Barkeria melanocaulon*), rose-red, late summer, Mexico; *nemorale*, rose-mauve, lip whitish and purple, decided rest, summer, Mexico, var. *majus*, larger, lip whitish, rose-bordered; *oncidioides* (syn. *E. Mooreanum*), yellowish, red-brown, lip white and purplish, spring, summer, Brazil; *pentotis* (syn. *E. fragrans megalanthum*), in twos, creamy-white, lip purple-striped, very fragrant, autumn, Brazil; *prismatocarpum*, yellowish-white, purplish-spotted, summer, Cent. America; *radicans* (syn. *E. rhizophorum*), orange-scarlet, various seasons, Mexico, Guatemala; *Skinneri* (syn. *Barkeria Skinneri*), deep rose, autumn, Guatemala; *Stamfordianum*, variable, flowers on abortive basal growths, yellow, red-spotted, lip lobed, fringed, fragrant, spring, summer, Cent. America; *Wallisii*, golden-yellow, maroon-spotted, lip feathered with purple, various seasons, Colombia; *xanthinum*, yellow or orange-yellow, various seasons, Brazil.

Epigaea—*Ericaceae.* Hardy evergreen perennial with woody creeping stems. First introduced mid-eighteenth century.

CULTURE: Soil, sandy peat. Position, shady borders or rockeries. Plant, Sept., Oct. or April.

PROPAGATION: By division of plant in Oct. or April; seeds sown as soon as ripe.

SPECIES CULTIVATED: *E. asiatica*, pink, May, Japan; *intertexta*, pink, May, hybrid; *repens*, 'American Ground Laurel', 'New England Mayflower', 'Trailing Arbutus', white, fragrant, May, trailing, N. America.

× **Epilaelia**—*Orchidaceae.* Bigeneric hybrid between Epidendrum and Laelia.

The habit is intermediate between the genera. Flowers are borne on erect scapes. About 30 hybrids have been raised.

CULTURE: As Cattleyas, but when derived from a warm growing and cool house species the individual plant must be studied as one species may slightly predominate.

Epilobium (Willow Herb)—*Onagraceae.* Hardy perennial herbs. Showy plants for wild gardens.

CULTURE: Soil, ordinary. Position, shady or sunny borders, or sides of water-courses. Dwarf species in sunny rock gardens. Plant, Oct. or March

PROPAGATION: By seeds sown ⅛ in. deep in shady position outdoors in March, April or Aug.; division of roots in Oct. or March.

SPECIES CULTIVATED: *E. angustifolium,* ' Rose Bay ' or ' French Willow ', crimson, July, 4 to 8 ft., Europe (Br.), var. *album,* white; *Dodonaei* (syn. *Chamaenerion palustre*), rosy purple, Aug., 9 to 12 in., Europe; *Hectori,* pale pink, summer, 4 to 6 in., New Zealand; *hirsutum,* ' Codlins and Cream ', pink or white, July, 4 ft., Britain; *luteum,* yellow, summer, 6 in., N. America; *macropus,* creamy-white, summer, creeping, New Zealand; *obcordatum,* rosy purple, summer, 6 in., California.

Epimedium (Barrenwort)—*Berberidaceae.* Hardy herbaceous perennials. First introduced late sixteenth century.

CULTURE: Soil, sandy loam, preferably enriched with leaf-mould or peat. Position, cool shady border or rock garden; will do well under trees. Plant, autumn or spring.

PROPAGATION: By division of rhizomes in autumn.

SPECIES CULTIVATED: *E. alpinum,* ' Bishop's Hat ', garnet-red and yellow, April, 9 in., S. Europe; *diphyllum* (syn. *Aceranthus diphyllus*), white, April, 6 in., Japan; *grandiflorum* (syn. *E. macranthum*), pale violet and white, April, 9 in., Japan, and vars. *flavescens,* pale yellow, *violaceum,* violet; *Perralderianum,* bright yellow, April, 9 in., Algeria; *pinnatum colchicum,* bright yellow, April, 9 in., Caucasus; *pubigerum,* white, pink and yellow, April, 15 in., Bulgaria, Turkey, Caucasus; *rubrum* (syn. *E. alpinum rubrum*), crimson and yellow, April, 9 in., hybrid; *versicolor,* old rose and yellow, April, 12 in., hybrid, and vars. *neo-sulphureum* and *sulphureum* (syn. *E. sulphureum*), sulphur-yellow; *warleyense,* coppery-red and yellow, April, 12 in., hybrid; *Youngianum* (syn. *Bonstedtia Youngiana*), greenish-white, 9 in., April, Japan, and vars. *niveum* (syn. *E. niveum*), white, 6 in., *roseum* (syn. *E. concinnum*), rose, 6 in.

Epipactis—*Orchidaceae.* Hardy terrestrial orchids.

CULTURE: For the British species: Position, moist, shady borders or near ponds or rivulets. Plant in early autumn. Collect wild specimens directly after flowering.

PROPAGATION: By division of plant in March or April.

SPECIES CULTIVATED: *E. gigantea,* green and rose, striped red, June to Aug., 3 ft., W.N. America and Mexico; *helleborine* (syn. *E. latifolia*), ' Helleborine ', purple, July, 1 ft., gravelly loam, Europe (Br.); *palustris,* purple, July, 1 ft., moist, marshy ground on limestone or chalk, Europe (Br.).

× **Epiphronitis**—*Orchidaceae.* Bigeneric hybrid between Sophronitis and Epidendrum.

CULTURE: As for stemmed Epidendrums. So far only two crosses have been recorded, temp., etc., may depend on the Epidendrum species used; if one with decided pseudo-bulbs, temp. and winter treatment must be modified. *E. Veitchi* is a cross between *Sophronitis coccinea* (syn. *E. grandiflora*) and *Epidendrum radicans*; it succeeds best in a temp. of 60° in winter and near that in summer, but the individual plants vary slightly.

SPECIES CULTIVATED: *E. Veitchii,* short, leafy, often branched stems terminating in scarlet flowers.

Epiphyllum—*Cactaceae.* Succulent greenhouse plants. Some species formerly included in this genus have now been transferred to Nopalxochia, Schlumbergera, Zygocactus, etc. First introduced early nineteenth century.

CULTURE: Compost, equal parts turfy loam, peat and leaf-mould, one-fourth part silver sand. Position, light warm greenhouse Sept. to June, sunny place outdoors or cold frame June to Sept. Water moderately Sept. to April, little more freely other times. Temp., Nov. to March 50° to 60°, March to June 55° to 65°, Sept. to Nov. 40° to 45°.

PROPAGATION: By cuttings of stems in sand; seeds sown in well-drained pans.

SPECIES CULTIVATED: *E. anguliger*, yellow, fragrant, autumn, 1 to 2 ft., Mexico; *crenatum*, white, fragrant, summer, Honduras; *Hookeri*, white, fragrant, summer, 2 to 3 ft., Brazil.

Episcia—*Gesneriaceae.* Stove herbaceous perennials. First introduced mid-nineteenth century.

CULTURE: Compost, equal parts fibrous loam, peat and leaf-mould with sharp sand added. Position, large pans or hanging baskets in shady part of stove or warm greenhouse. Pot or plant, March or April. Water moderately at all times. Feed with liquid manure when plants established. Temp., March to Sept. 65° to 85°, Sept. to March 55° to 65°.

PROPAGATION: By cuttings inserted in sandy peat in temp. 75° to 85° in March or April.

SPECIES CULTIVATED: *E. chontalensis*, lilac, white and yellow, autumn, winter, trailing, Nicaragua; *fulgida*, scarlet, July, trailing, Colombia.

Equisetum (Horsetail; Fox-tailed Asparagus)—*Equisetaceae.* Hardy deciduous herbaceous perennials. Leaves, green, narrow, rush-like.

CULTURE: Soil, ordinary. Position, bogs, margins of ponds, moist shady corners, or in pots in a cool shady greenhouse. Plant or pot, April. Water plants in pots freely while growing, moderately at other times.

PROPAGATION: By division of rootstocks in March or April.

SPECIES CULTIVATED: *E. maximum* (syn. *E. Telmateia*), 2 to 6 ft., Britain; *praealtum* (syn. *E. robustum*), to 11 ft., N. America, Asia.

Eragrostis—*Gramineae.* Hardy annual flowering grasses. Native to Temperate Regions. Inflorescence, light, feathery and graceful.

CULTURE: Soil, ordinary. Position, open sunny beds or borders.

PROPAGATION: By seeds sown ⅛ in. deep where plants are to grow in April. Gather inflorescence in July and dry for winter use.

SPECIES CULTIVATED: *E. abyssinica*, 2 to 3 ft., N. Africa; *maxima*, 2 to 3 ft., Madagascar; *pilosa*, 1 to 1½ ft., Europe; *suaveolens*, 2 to 3 ft., W. Asia; *tenella* (syn. *E. elegans*), 2 to 3 ft., Japan.

Eranthemum—*Acanthaceae.* Stove flowering plants with ornamental foliage. First introduced late eighteenth century.

CULTURE: Compost, equal parts peat, leaf-mould, loam and sand. Position, well-drained pots in light stove Sept. to June, sunny frame June to Sept. Pot, March or April. Water moderately in winter, freely other times. Temp., Sept. to March 55° to 65°, March to June 65° to 75°. Prune shoots to within 1 in. of base after flowering. Apply liquid or artificial manure occasionally to plants when well rooted in final pots.

PROPAGATION: By cuttings of young shoots inserted in sandy peat under bell-glass in temp. 75° March to July.

SPECIES CULTIVATED: *E. Andersonii*, white and purple, autumn, 1 ft., Malaya; *cinnabarinum*, scarlet, winter, 3 ft., Burma; *Cooperi*, white and purple, June, 2 ft., New Caledonia; *Moorei*, canary yellow, distinct, Polynesia; *nervosum*, blue, April, to 4 ft., India; *purpurescens*, pale blue, 18 in., Trop. Africa; *tricolor*, green, purple and pink, Polynesia; *variabile*, white, crimson and pink, Australia; *Wattii*, purple, 12 in., Trop. Africa.

Eranthis (Winter Aconite)—*Ranunculaceae.* Hardy tuberous-rooted perennial. First introduced late sixteenth century.

CULTURE: Soil, ordinary. Position, shady borders, beds, lawns, under trees or on rockeries. Plant 2 in. deep and 2 in. apart in Oct. to Dec. Tubers should not be lifted, but left permanently in the soil.

POT CULTURE: Compost, equal parts leaf-mould, loam and sand. Position, 3 in. pots or large pans in cool greenhouse or window. Plant tubers ½ in. deep and close together in pots or pans in Oct. or Nov. Water moderately. After flowering, plant tubers out in borders.

PROPAGATION: By division of tubers in Oct. or Nov.

SPECIES CULTIVATED: *E. hyemalis*, yellow, Jan. to March, 3 to 4 in., Europe (Br.), var. *cilicica*, broader sepals; *sibirica*, yellow, Jan. to March, 2 to 3 in., Siberia; *Tubergenii*, large, shiny, golden-yellow, hybrid.

Ercilla—*Phytolaccaceae*. Hardy evergreen creeping or climbing shrub. First introduced early nineteenth century.

CULTURE: Soil, sandy loam. Position, south walls or old tree trunks; sunny. Plant, Sept. or April. Prune after flowering, cutting away weak and shortening strong shoots one-fourth. Shoots cling to the wall like those of ivy.

PROPAGATION: By cuttings or layers in autumn.

SPECIES CULTIVATED: *E. spicata* (syn. *Bridgesia spicata*), purple, spring, berries, 10 to 15 ft., Chile.

Eremostachys (Desert Rod)—*Labiatae*. Hardy perennial. First introduced early eighteenth century.

CULTURE: Soil, light, rich. Position, sunny well-drained borders. Plant, Oct. or April. Cut off spikes after flowering.

PROPAGATION: By seeds sown ⅟₁₆ in. deep in light soil in sunny position outdoors in April; division of roots in Oct. or April.

SPECIES CULTIVATED: *E. laciniata*, yellow, summer, 2¼ ft., Asia Minor.

Eremurus—*Liliaceae*. Hardy herbaceous perennials with thick fibrous or cord-like roots. First introduced early nineteenth century.

CULTURE: Soil, light, deep, rich, sandy, well-manured loam. Position, sunny well-drained beds or borders. Plant, Sept. or Oct. Transplanting must not be done oftener than is really necessary. Mulch freely with well-decayed manure in autumn. Water copiously in hot weather. Protect in winter by a covering of bracken or dry litter.

PROPAGATION: By division of roots in Oct. or March; seeds sown in heat in spring, growing seedlings on in cold frame for first three years. Seeds sometimes take a long time to germinate.

SPECIES CULTIVATED: *E. Bungei*, yellow, June and July, 1 to 3 ft., Persia; *himalaicus*, white, May and June, 8 ft., Himalaya; *Kaufmannii*, yellow, June, 4 ft., Turkistan; *Olgae*, lilac-purple, fragrant, 2 to 4 ft., Turkistan; *robustus*, ' Fox-tail Lily ' pink, May and June, 6 to 10 ft., Turkistan; *Shelfordii*, orange, July, 3 to 4 ft., hybrid; *spectabilis*, yellow and orange, June, 2 to 4 ft., Siberia. A number of hybrids are offered in trade lists.

Erepsia—*Aizoaceae*. Greenhouse, shrubby, succulent plants, formerly included in Mesembryanthemum.

CULTURE: As Mesembryanthemum.

PROPAGATION: As Mesembryanthemum.

SPECIES CULTIVATED: *E. Haworthii* (syn. *Mesembryanthemum Haworthii*), purple, summer, 1¼ ft., S. Africa; *inclaudens* (syn. *M. inclaudens*), purplish-pink, June, 1¼ ft., S. Africa.

Eria—*Orchidaceae*. A large epiphytal genus allied to Dendrobium, but of less importance. In many the flowers, though freely produced, are small and have little attraction. Considerable variation is present in the genus. Pseudo-bulbs and stems are present. Inflorescence terminal, near the apices of the pseudo-bulbs, with the young growths lateral or axillary.

CULTURE: Compost, etc., as for Dendrobium, the nature of the species must have consideration as regards resting. The intermediate house with winter night temp. around 60° is suitable for the majority, but species from the Far East should be kept at 70°. The floral bracts in some are showy.

PROPAGATION: By division of plants in spring.

SPECIES CULTIVATED: A selection—*E. bicolor*, white, bracts yellowish, spring, Ceylon; *bractescens*, white, red, bracts yellowish, summer, Burma, Java; *convallarioides*, creamy-white, small, many, summer, India, Burma; *globifera*, single, inverted, creamy-white, reddish, winter, Annam; *ornata*, fuscous-brown, reddish, bracts large, orange-cinnabar, summer, Malaya, Java; *pannea*, curious, white, lip orange, red, pendent habit, woolly, small raft, various seasons, Burma; *rhyncostyloides*, white, rose-flushed, up to 300, summer, autumn, Java; *vestitia*, whitish, yellowish, pendent habit, brown-haired, summer, Malaya, Philippines.

Erianthus (Woolly Beard Grass)—*Gramineae*. Hardy ornamental perennial grass. Inflorescence similar to pampas plumes.

CULTURE: Soil, deep loam. Position, sunny well-drained lawns or borders. Plant, March or April.

PROPAGATION: By division of roots in March or April.

SPECIES CULTIVATED: *E. Ravennae*, ' Ravenna Grass ', 6 to 12 ft., S. Europe to India.

Erica (Heath)—*Ericaceae*. Hardy and greenhouse flowering shrubs. The hardy kinds are of great garden value, suitable selections providing colour the whole year round. The majority of these are dwarf-growing but a few species reach small-tree dimensions.

CULTURE OF HARDY SPECIES: A peaty soil, preferably light and well-drained, but at any rate lime-free. *Erica carnea* and its vars. and *E. darleyensis* will grow in chalky soils. Choose open situation and plant in clumps or drifts on rockeries or margins of borders or massed on banks or in the wild garden. If compact growth is desired, remove spent stems after flowering.

CULTURE OF GREENHOUSE SPECIES: Compost, two-thirds fibrous peat, one-third silver sand. Position, well-drained pots in light airy greenhouse Oct. to July, sunny place outdoors July to Oct. Repot autumn- and winter-flowering kinds in March, summer-flowering kinds in Sept. Press the compost firmly in pots. Water carefully always, giving sufficient to keep soil uniformly moist; rain, not spring water, essential. Prune shoots to within 1 or 2 in. of base immediately after flowering. Temp., Oct. to March 40° to 45°, March to July 45° to 55°. Soot-water best stimulant.

PROPAGATION: Greenhouse species by cuttings of shoots 1 in. long inserted in well-drained pot of sandy peat under bell-glass in temp. 60° to 70° in spring; hardy species by cuttings inserted in sandy peat under bell-glass or hand-light in gentle bottom heat during July and August; division of plants in Oct.; layering shoots in spring.

HARDY SPECIES CULTIVATED: *E. arborea*, ' Tree Heath ', white, fragrant, May, handsome grey foliage, 10 to 20 ft., hardy only in south, Medit., var. *alpina*, similar, but hardy, 8 ft., Spain; *australis*, ' Spanish Heath ', rather tender, rosy red, April, May, 3 to 4 ft., Spain; *carnea*, dwarf to 18 in., winter flowering, Cent. Europe, in many vars.; *ciliaris*, ' Dorset Heath ', 1 ft., summer, rosy-red, S.W. Europe and S.W. England, with var. *Maweana*, rosy crimson; *cinerea*, ' Bell Heather ', 1 ft., June till Sept., purple, W. Europe, including British moorland, with vars. *alba*, *atropurpurea*, *atrorubens* and *fulgida*; *darleyensis* (syn. *E. mediterranea hybrida*), very easily grown, rose-lilac, Nov. till May, 18 in., hybrid; *lusitanica* (syn. *E. codonodes*), rather tender, pretty foliage, pale rose, Feb. to April, S.W. Europe; *mediterranea*, hardiest of tree heaths, 6 to 10 ft., rosy-lilac, honey-scented, March to May, W. Europe, vars. *alba*, *superba*; *stricta* (syn. *E. corsica*), ' Corsican Heath ', hardy tree heath, 8 ft. to 10 ft., erect, pale rose, June to Sept., Spain, Italy, Corsica; *Tetralix*, ' Cross-leaved Heath ', to 18 in., rose-pink, June to Oct., Europe, including Britain, with vars. *mollis*, silver foliage, white flowers, and *rubra*, dark red; *umbellata*, trailing, cerise, May, not fully hardy, Spain; *vagans*, ' Cornish Heath ', 2 ft., spreading to 5 ft. wide, rosy-lilac, July to Oct., with numerous vars.; *Veitchii*, a hybrid between *lusitanica* and *arborea*, a vigorous counterpart of the former.

GREENHOUSE SPECIES CULTIVATED: *E. Bergiana* (syn. *E. cupressina*) red, May to June, 1 to 3 ft., S. Africa; *caffra*, white, May, 18 in., S. Africa; *canaliculata* (often cult. as *E. melanthera*), rose, winter, 2 to 5 ft., S. Africa; *Cavendishiana*, yellow, May, 4 ft., hybrid; *coccinea*, scarlet, June, 1 ft., S. Africa; *glauca* (syn. *E. elegans*), rose and green, Aug., 6 in., S. Africa; *gracilis*, reddish-purple, 1 ft., S. Africa; *hyemalis*, pink, Dec. to March, hybrid; *mammosa*, reddish-purple, July to Oct., 2 ft., S. Africa; *melanthera*, rose, winter, 2 to 3 ft., S. Africa; *Pageana*, yellow, 1 to 2 ft., Sept. to Oct., Cape; *regerminans*, pale red, May to Aug., to 2 ft., S. Africa; *subdivaricata* (syn. *E. persoluta*), purple, April, 16 in., S. Africa; *ventricosa*, pink, June, 1 ft., S. Africa, and numerous vars.

Erigeron (Fleabane)—*Compositae*. Hardy herbaceous perennials. First introduced early seventeenth century.

CULTURE: Soil, ordinary. Position, sunny moist rockeries or borders. Plant, Oct. or March. Cut down stems after flowering.

PROPAGATION: By seeds sown ⅛ in. deep in light soil in shady position outdoors in April, May or June; division of roots in Oct. or March.

SPECIES CULTIVATED: *E. alpinus* (syn. *E. Roylei*), purple and yellow, Aug., 12 in., Northern Regions; *aurantiacus*, ' Orange Daisy ', orange, summer, 12 in., Turkistan; *aureus*, bright gold, spring onwards, 4 in., N. America; *compositus*, purple, summer, 3 in., N. America; *Karvinskianus* (syn. *E. mucronatus*), white, pink, and yellow, summer, 12 in., more or less trailing, Mexico; *leromerus*, lavender, summer, 3 to 4 in., N.W. America; *macranthus*, violet-blue, June to Sept., 1 ft., N.W. America; *philadelphicus*, lilac-pink, summer, 1 to 2 ft., N. America; *speciosus* (syn. *Stenactis speciosa*), violet blue, summer, 1½ to 2 ft., N. America; *trifidus*, deep lavender, May to June, 2 to 3 in., N. America; *ursinus*, rich purple, gold centre, May to July, 6 in., N. America.

Erinacea—*Leguminosae*. Dwarf deciduous spring-flowering shrub. Introduced mid-eighteenth century.

CULTURE: Soil, loam and peat. Position, sunny rockeries, or borders at base of a south wall. Plant, May or Sept.

PROPAGATION: By cuttings in sandy loam and peat in a cold frame in autumn; seed.

SPECIES CULTIVATED: *E. Anthyllis* (syn. *E. pungens*), ' Hedgehog Broom ', pale blue, spring, 1 ft., Spain.

Erinus—*Scrophulariaceae*. Hardy tufted perennial. First introduced early eighteenth century.

CULTURE: Soil, decayed vegetable mould and old mortar. Position, crevices of old sunny walls or dryish rockeries. Plant, March or April.

PROPAGATION: By seeds sown where plants are to grow in April; division of plants in April.

SPECIES CULTIVATED: *E. alpinus*, violet-purple, spring, 6 in., Pyrenees, and vars.

Eriobotrya—*Rosaceae*. Rather tender evergreen flowering shrub. The edible fruit of loquat is about the size of a green walnut, pale orange-red, downy, borne in bunches.

OUTDOOR CULTURE: Soil, light, deep loam. Position, against south walls S. and S.W. of England and Ireland only. Plant, Sept. to Nov., April or May. Prune, April. Protect in severe weather with mats or straw hurdles.

INDOOR CULTURE: Soil, two parts sandy loam, one part leaf-mould. Position, beds against back wall of cold or slightly heated sunny greenhouse. Plant, Oct. or April. Water moderately Sept. to April, freely afterwards. Syringe daily May to Sept. Prune straggling shoots in April.

PROPAGATION: By seeds sown ½ in. deep in pots of light soil in cold greenhouse or frame, spring or autumn; cuttings of firm shoots inserted in sandy soil in cold frame or greenhouse, Aug.

SPECIES CULTIVATED: *E. japonica* (syn. *Photinia japonica*), ' Loquat ', white, summer, 10 to 30 ft., China and Japan.

Eriodendron, see Ceiba.

Eriogonum—*Polygonaceae.* Hardy herbaceous perennial.
CULTURE: Soil, ordinary. Position, open borders. Plant, Oct. or March.
PROPAGATION: By seeds sown ⅛ in. deep in light soil outdoors in April; division of roots in March.
SPECIES CULTIVATED: *E. Allenii,* bronze, late summer, 9 to 12 in., N. America; *depressum,* white, summer, 3 to 4 in., N. America; *Jamesonii,* cream, June to July, 9 in., N. America; *ovalifolium,* yellow turning purplish, 3 in., summer, W.N. America; *subalpinum,* white flushed rose, late summer, 9 in., N. America; *umbellatum,* golden yellow, summer, 12 in., N.W. Africa.

Eriophorum (Cotton Grass)—*Cyperaceae.* Hardy aquatic perennials. Inflorescence borne in spikelets, with cottony tufts on their extremities.
CULTURE: Soil, ordinary. Position, margins of ponds. Plant, March.
PROPAGATION: By seeds sown where plants are to grow; division of plants in March.
SPECIES CULTIVATED: *E. alpinum,* 1 ft., N. Hemisphere; *angustifolium,* 15 in., Britain; *latifolium,* 12 to 18 in., N. Temp. and Frigid Regions; *vaginatum,* 1 ft., Britain.

Eriophyllum—*Compositae.* Hardy perennial herb with white tomentose leaves.
CULTURE: Soil, ordinary. Position, sunny border. Plant, Oct. to April.
PROPAGATION: By seeds sown ⅛ in. deep outdoors in April or division in March.
SPECIES CULTIVATED: *E. caespitosum* (syn. *Bahia lanata*), yellow, May to Aug., 12 to 18 in., California.

Eriopsis—*Orchidaceae.* An epiphytic evergreen genus with stout pseudo-bulbs from the base of which long flower spikes are produced, many flowers one inch or more across.
CULTURE: Compost, three parts osmunda fibre, one part sphagnum moss. Baskets or well-drained pans. Rest in winter with occasional waterings, 60°. Summer temp. 65° to 80°. Water freely, moderate shading, expose to light in autumn.
PROPAGATION: By division of plants in spring.
SPECIES CULTIVATED: *E. biloba* (syn. *E. Schomburgkii*), dark yellow to brown, lip purple-spotted, summer, Peru, Guiana, Brazil; *Heleniae,* yellow, orange-yellow, red, purplish-red, pots, summer, Peru; *rutidobulbon,* orange, purplish, lip purple-dotted, summer, Colombia.

Eriostemon—*Rutaceae.* Greenhouse evergreen shrubs. First introduced early nineteenth century.
CULTURE: Compost, equal parts sandy loam and peat. Position, well-drained pots in light airy greenhouse. Repot, March, pressing soil down firmly. Water moderately Sept. to April, freely afterwards. Prune straggly growths in Feb. Temp., Sept. to April 45° to 50°, April to Sept. 50° to 60°. Ventilate greenhouse freely in summer.
PROPAGATION: By cuttings 2 in. long inserted in sandy peat under bell-glass in temp. 60° in March; grafting on *Correa alba* in March.
SPECIES CULTIVATED: *E. buxifolius,* pink, May or June, 3 to 4 ft., Australia; *intermedius,* white and pink, April, 3 ft., garden origin; *myoporoides,* rose, March, 1 to 2 ft., Australia; *pulchellus,* pink, May, 2 to 3 ft., hybrid; *salicifolius,* red, spring, 2 ft., Australia.

Eritrichium—*Boraginaceae.* Hardy perennial alpine plant. First introduced mid-nineteenth century.
CULTURE: Compost, equal parts broken limestone, sandstone, fibrous loam, peat and sand. Position, sheltered crannies of open rockeries, where foliage can

be protected from excessive moisture in winter. Plant, April. Protect by panes of glass in rainy weather.

PROPAGATION: By division of plants in April; seeds sown in gentle heat in spring.

SPECIES CULTIVATED: *E. nanum*, ' Fairy Borage ', ' Fairy Forget-me-not ', sky-blue and yellow, summer, 2 to 3 in., N. Temp. Regions; *strictum*, blue, 6 in., all summer, Asia.

Erodium (Heron's Bill)—*Geraniaceae*. Hardy perennial herbs. First introduced early seventeenth century.

CULTURE: Soil, sandy. Position, dry sunny borders or rockeries. Plant, March or April. Transplant very seldom.

PROPAGATION: By seeds sown ⅛ in. deep in pots of sandy soil in temp. 55° in March or April, transplanting seedlings outdoors in June or July; division of roots in April.

SPECIES CULTIVATED: *E. absinthioides* (syn. *E. olympicum*), rosy lilac, summer, 6 in., Asia Minor; *chamaedryoides*, white and pink, April to Sept., 2 to 3 in., Balearic Islands; *chrysanthum*, pale yellow, summer, 6 in., Greece; *corsicum*, pink, summer, trailing, Corsica and Sardinia; *guttatum*, pink, summer, 6 in., Medit. Region; *macradenum* violet, flesh and purple, summer, 6 in., Pyrenees; *Manescavii*, purplish-red, summer, 1 to 2 ft., Pyrenees; *Mouretii*, 6 to 12 in., white, red veining, Morocco; *trichomanefolium*, violet-veined rose, summer, 4 to 6 in., Syria.

Eryngium—*Umbelliferae*. Hardy perennial herbs with spiny-toothed leaves; flower heads surrounded by spiny, coloured bracts.

CULTURE: Soil, light sandy. Position, sunny borders. Plant, Oct., Nov., March or April.

PROPAGATION: By seeds sown ¹⁄₁₆ in. deep in boxes of sandy soil in cold frame in April or May; division of plants in Oct. or April; root cuttings.

SPECIES CULTIVATED: *E. alpinum*, blue and white, summer, 1 to 2 ft., Europe; *amethystinum*, purple, July and Aug., 12 to 18 in., Europe; *Bourgatii*, blue, June to Aug., 1 to 2 ft., Spain; *giganteum*, blue, summer, 3 to 4 ft., Armenia, usually treated as a biennial; *maritimum*, ' Sea Holly ', bluish-white, July to Oct., 1 to 2 ft., Britain; *Oliverianum*, blue, summer, 2 to 4 ft., Orient; *pandanifolium*, purplish, summer, 10 to 15 ft., Uruguay; *planum*, blue, summer, 1 to 2 ft., Europe; *Spinalba*, white, summer, 1 ft., Europe; *Zabelii*, amethyst blue, summer, 1½ ft., hybrid.

Eryngo, see Eryngium.

Erysimum (Alpine Wallflower)—*Cruciferae*. Hardy annuals, biennials and perennials. First introduced early nineteenth century.

CULTURE: Soil, ordinary. Position, dryish sunny beds or rockeries. Plant, March or April.

PROPAGATION: Annual species, by seeds sown where plants are required to grow in April; biennials, by seeds sown in sunny place outdoors in June, transplanting seedlings to flowering positions in Aug.; perennials, by seeds sown as advised for biennials, also by cuttings inserted in sandy soil under hand-light or cold frame in Aug.; division of plants in March or April.

ANNUAL SPECIES CULTIVATED: *E. Perofskianum*, reddish-orange, spring to autumn, 1 ft., Afghanistan.

BIENNIAL SPECIES CULTIVATED: *E. Allionii* (syns. *E. Marshallii*, *Cheiranthus Allionii*), ' Siberian Wallflower ', orange, spring and summer, 1 to 2 ft., origin unknown, possibly hybrid; *asperum*, orange or yellow, spring and early summer, 1 to 2 ft., N. America; *linifolium* (syn. *Cheiranthus linifolius*), rosy lilac, summer, 1 to 1½ ft., Spain; *ochroleucum*, sulphur-yellow, fragrant, April to July, 1 ft., Europe; *pumilum*, sulphur-yellow, spring and early summer, 6 in., Europe; *purpureum*, purple, spring and summer, 6 in., Asia Minor; *rupestre*, sulphur-yellow, fragrant, spring, 1 ft., Greece; *suffrutescens*, pale yellow, spring and early summer, 1¼ to 2 ft., California.

Erythraea, see Centaurium.

Erythrina—*Leguminosae.* Half-hardy herbaceous perennials and greenhouse deciduous shrubs, usually thorny. First introduced late seventeenth century.

CULTURE OF SHRUBBY SPECIES: Compost, equal parts loam, peat, well-decayed manure and sand. Position, pot in warm greenhouse, or at base of south wall S. of England. Pot or plant, March. Prune shoots close to old wood in Oct. Water freely April to Sept., keep almost dry thereafter. Temp., Sept. to March 45° to 50°, March to Sept. 55° to 65°. Store plants in pots on their sides in greenhouse during winter. Place in light part of structure March to June, then in sunny position outdoors. Protect outdoor plants with covering of ashes.

CULTURE OF HERBACEOUS SPECIES: Compost, same as above. Position, pot in warm sunny greenhouse. Pot, March. Cut down flowering stems in autumn. Water freely April to Sept., keep nearly dry afterwards. Temp., Sept. to March 45° to 55°, March to Sept. 60° to 70°.

PROPAGATION: Shrubby species by cuttings of young shoots removed in spring with portion of old wood attached and inserted singly in well-drained pots of sandy peat in temp. 75°; herbaceous species by division in spring.

SHRUBBY SPECIES CULTIVATED: *E. Crista-galli*, 'Coral Tree', scarlet, June to Aug., 6 to 8 ft., Brazil.

HERBACEOUS SPECIES: *E. herbacea*, scarlet, June to Sept., 3 to 4 ft., W. Indies.

Erythronium—*Liliaceae.* Hardy bulbous perennials. First introduced late sixteenth century.

CULTURE: Compost, equal parts loam, peat and leaf-mould. Position, sheltered rockeries, beds, borders, or under shade of trees. Plant bulbs 3 in. deep and 2 in. apart in Aug. Transplant very seldom. Top-dress annually with decayed manure.

POT CULTURE: Compost, same as above. Plant bulbs 1 in. deep and ½ in. apart in well-drained pots in Aug. Store pots in cold frame during winter. Water very little until Feb., then give a moderate supply. Place plants in greenhouse or window in March to flower.

PROPAGATION: By offsets in Aug.; seeds.

SPECIES CULTIVATED: *E. albidum*, white and yellow, April, 6 in., N. America; *americanum*, 'Yellow Adder's-tongue', golden yellow and purple, May, 6 in., N. America; *californicum*, creamy-white, spring, 9 to 12 in., California; *citrinum*, yellow, orange, and pink, spring, 6 in., Oregon; *Dens-canis*, 'Dog's-tooth Violet', rose, spring, 6 in., Europe, and vars.; *grandiflorum*, yellow, spring, N.W. America, *Helenae*, white, yellow base, Aug., 9 in., California; *Hendersonii*, purple-rose, March, 6 in., Oregon; *Howellii*, yellow and orange, spring, 6 in., Oregon; *multiscapoideum* (syn. *E. Hartwegii*), white to pale yellow, 6 in., California; *oregonum* (syn. *E. giganteum* hort.), white, yellow base, 6 to 18 in., Oregon to Br. Columbia; *purpurascens*, yellow, purple, and orange, spring, California; *revolutum*, rose-pink, spring, 8 to 12 in., California, and vars. *albiflorum* (syn. *E. Watsonii*), white and maroon, and *Johnsonii*, rosy pink; *tuolumnense*, deep, golden yellow, April, 9 to 12 in., California.

Escallonia—*Saxifragaceae* (or *Escalloniaceae*). Slightly tender evergreen or deciduous shrubs. First introduced early nineteenth century.

CULTURE: Soil, ordinary, rich, well drained. Position, against south walls in Midlands and in open garden S. of England. May also be planted against back walls of cold greenhouses. Suitable for hedges in mild districts and are excellent maritime shrubs. Plant, Oct. or April. Prune straggly shoots only in April. The named hybrids available are generally more reliable than the species.

PROPAGATION: By seeds; cuttings inserted in sandy soil under bell-glass Aug. or Sept.; layering shoots in Oct.; suckers removed and replanted in April.

EVERGREEN SPECIES CULTIVATED: *E. exoniensis*, white or rose-tinted, June to Oct., 15 to 20 ft., hybrid; *floribunda*, white, late summer and autumn, 10 ft., S. America; *illinita*, white, Aug., 10 to 12 ft., Chile; *langleyensis*, rosy carmine, one of the most popular, does well on a north wall, June, 8 ft., hybrid; *macrantha*, crimson-red, June, 6 to 10 ft., Chile; *montevidensis* (syn. *E. floribunda*), white,

July, 10 ft., Montevideo; *organensis*, rosy red, Sept., 4 to 6 ft., Brazil; *ptero-cladon*, white, June to Aug., 4 to 8 ft., Patagonia; *pulverulenta*, white, July to Sept., 10 to 12 ft., Chile; *punctata*, red, July, 6 to 10 ft., Chile; *revoluta*, white, June to Aug., 15 to 20 ft., Chile; *rubra*, red, July to Sept., 6 ft., Chile; *viscosa*, white, June to Aug., 10 ft., Chile.

DECIDUOUS SPECIES CULTIVATED: *E. virgata* var. *Philippiana*, 6 to 8 ft., white, June to July, hardy, Chile.

Eschscholtzia (Californian Poppy)—*Papaveraceae*. Hardy annuals. Sometimes spelled Eschscholzia. First introduced late eighteenth century.

CULTURE: Soil, ordinary. Position, sunny well-drained beds or borders.

PROPAGATION: By seeds sown $\frac{1}{16}$ in. deep in April where plants are to flower. Thin seedlings out to 2 in. apart when 1 in. high.

SPECIES CULTIVATED: *E. californica*, orange-yellow, summer, 1 to 2 ft., California. Numerous vars. will be found in trade lists.

Esparto Grass, see *Stipa tenacissima*.

Euanthe, see *Vanda Sanderiana*.

Eucalyptus (Gum)—*Myrtaceae*. Greenhouse and slightly tender evergreen trees. Fragrant leaves, mostly ovate-lanceolate. First introduced early nineteenth century.

CULTURE: Compost, two parts fibrous loam, one part leaf-mould, charcoal and sand. Position, pots in greenhouse heated to temp. 45° to 50° in winter, 55° to 60° other times; dwelling rooms, sunny beds outdoors during summer, sheltered positions outdoors all the year S. England. Pot, March or April. Plant, outdoors June, lift October. Water plants in pots moderately Oct. to April, freely afterwards. Pruning not required.

PROPAGATION: By seeds sown $\frac{1}{8}$ in. deep in pots of sandy soil in temp. 65° in Feb., March or April; for pot culture young plants should be raised annually.

SPECIES CULTIVATED: *E. amygdalina*, 'Almond-leaved' or 'Peppermint Gum', Australia, and vars. *angustifolia*, *numerosa*, *regnans*, 'Giant Gum'; *coccifera*, Tasmania; *cordata*, Tasmania; *coriacea*, Australia; *globulus*, 'Blue Gum', 15 to 20 ft., Australia; *Gunnii*, 15 to 20 ft., Australia; *maculata*, var. *citriodora*, 'Citron-scented Gum', 15 to 20 ft., Australia; *resinifera*, 30 to 60 ft., Australia; *viminalis*, 'Manna Gum', Australia.

Eucharidium, see Clarkia.

Eucharis—*Amaryllidaceae*. Stove, bulbous, flowering, evergreen plants. Firs introduced mid-nineteenth century.

CULTURE: Compost, two parts fibrous loam, one part peat, decomposed sheep manure and sand. Position, well-drained pots on a bed or stage heated beneath to temp. 85° in plant stove. Pot in June or July, placing six bulbs in a 10 in. pot. Press down compost firmly. Repotting not needed more often than once every three or four years. Water moderately Oct. to April, freely afterwards. Syringe freely in summer. Apply liquid manure twice a week after flower stems appear. Top-dress established plants annually in March with rich compost. Temp., March to Sept. 70° to 80°, Sept. to Dec. 55° to 65°, Dec. to March 65° to 75°.

PROPAGATION: By seeds sown $\frac{1}{2}$ in. deep in sandy soil in temp. 85° in Feb. or March; offsets removed from old bulbs and placed singly in 3 in. pots in June or July.

SPECIES CULTIVATED: *E. candida*, white, autumn, 1 ft., Colombia; *grandiflora* (syn. *E. amazonica*), 'Amazon Lily', white, March to Dec., 1 to 2 ft., Colombia; *Lowii*, white, spring, 1 to 2 ft., hybrid; *Mastersii*, white, spring, 12 to 18 in., Colombia; *Sanderiana*, white and yellow, spring, 12 to 18 in., Colombia; *Stevensii*, white and yellow, spring, 1 ft., hybrid; *subedentata*, Colombia.

Eucomis—*Liliaceae*. Half-hardy bulbous flowering plants. First introduced mid-eighteenth century.

POT CULTURE: Compost, two parts sandy loam, one part well-decayed manure and sand. Position, well-drained pots in light, warm greenhouse. Pot, Oct. or March, placing one bulb in a 5 in. pot. Water very little Sept. to March, moderately March to May, freely afterwards. Temp., Sept. to March 45° to 50°, March to Sept. 55° to 65°. Apply liquid manure occasionally when flower spike shows.

OUTDOOR CULTURE: Soil, ordinary, light, rich. Position, sunny well-drained border. Plant, Sept., Oct. or March, placing bulbs 6 in. below surface and 6 in. apart. Protect in winter by covering of ashes, coconut-fibre refuse or manure.

PROPAGATION: By offsets removed and transplanted in Sept. or Oct.

SPECIES CULTIVATED: *E. bicolor*, greenish-yellow, Aug., 1 to 2 ft., Natal; *comosa* (syn. *E. punctata*), 'Pineapple Flower', green and brown, Aug., 18 in. to 2 ft.; *pallidiflora*, greenish-white, 2 ft., S. Africa; *regia*, ' King's Flower ', green and purple, 2 ft., S. Africa.

Eucryphia—*Eucryphiaceae.* Hardy and slightly tender evergreen and deciduous flowering trees of great beauty.

CULTURE: Soil, ordinary, light, with plenty of peat or leaf-mould. Position, warm open shrubberies with preferably some shade for roots. *E. cordifolia* will grow on chalky soils.

PROPAGATION: Layers in autumn, or seed sown in peaty soil in spring.

SPECIES CULTIVATED: *E. cordifolia*, evergreen, 10 to 15 ft., Sept. to Oct., white flowers, requires warm locality, Chile; *glutinosa* (syn. *E. pinnatifolia*), partially deciduous, 12 to 18 ft., July to Aug., white, hardy, Chile; *nymansensis*, a vigorous hybrid between the two species, evergreen, July to Sept., white, hardy.

Eugenia (Fruiting Myrtle)—*Myrtaceae.* Stove and greenhouse flowering evergreen shrubs. The dried flower buds of *E. aromatica* provide the cloves of commerce. First introduced mid-eighteenth century.

CULTURE: Compost, two parts sandy loam, one part leaf-mould and sand. Pot, Feb. or March. Position, pots in stove or greenhouse. Water moderately Oct. to April, freely afterwards. Syringe April to Aug. Prune straggling shoots in March. Temp. for stove species, 55° to 65° Sept. to March, 65° to 75° March to Sept.; for greenhouse species, 40° to 50° Oct. to March, 55° to 65° March to Oct.

PROPAGATION: By cuttings of firm shoots inserted in sandy soil under bell-glass in temp. 55° to 75° in summer.

STOVE SPECIES CULTIVATED: *E. aromatica*, ' Clove Tree ', 20 ft., Moluccas; *Jambos*, ' Rose Apple ', white, summer, 20 ft., Trop. Asia; *malaccensis*, ' Malay Apple ', scarlet, summer, 15 to 20 ft., Malaya. See also Myrtus.

GREENHOUSE SPECIES CULTIVATED: *E. apiculata* (syn. *Myrtus Luma*), white, freely borne, summer, cinnamon-coloured branches, 20 ft., Chile; *myriophylla*, leaves narrow and elegant, 6 ft., Brazil.

Eulalia, see Miscanthus.

Eulophia—*Orchidaceae.* A large genus of epiphytal or semi-epiphytal and terrestrial orchids; widely distributed. Few are of sufficient interest to warrant their cultivation.

CULTURE: Usually pseudo-bulbs are present and the spikes produced from their bases; a decided rest should be given to hard-bulbed and hard-leaved species. A winter temp. of 60° is sufficient for such species. Around 70° for species from tropical Africa and Madagascar. All revel in a tropical atmosphere in summer. Compost, two parts osmunda fibre, two parts fibrous loam, one part sphagnum. Well-drained pots are suitable.

PROPAGATION: By division of plants in spring.

SPECIES CULTIVATED: *E. epidendroides* (syn. *E. virens*), whitish, violet-crested, spring, Ceylon, India; *guineensis*, purplish, green, lip whitish, flushed crimson, summer, autumn, W. Africa; var. *purpurata*, rose; *lurida*, small, yellowish-brown, autumn, W. Africa; *nuda*, greenish, lilac, yellow, rose, spring, India, China; *Saundersiana*, yellowish, green, marked black-purple, spring, Africa. Many other species but few in orchid collections.

Eulophiella—*Orchidaceae.* Only three species are known in this epiphytic genus. Spikes from base of pseudo-bulbs. Flowers fleshy, beautiful.

CULTURE: Compost, two parts of osmunda fibre, one part of crushed potsherds and sphagnum moss. A warm moist atmosphere is required throughout the year. Compost must not get dry, nor waterlogged in winter; temp. 70°, higher in summer, with shading.

PROPAGATION: By division of plants. The rhizome may be cut, behind at least four pseudo-bulbs, and growths may develop.

SPECIES CULTIVATED: *E. Elizabethiae*, many, white, rose-flushed, purplish, lip with golden disk, spring, summer, basket, Madagascar; *Pectersiana* (syn. *E. Roemplerianum*), violet, purplish-rose, lip paler, centrally, disk orange-yellow, spring, summer, raft, Madagascar; *Rolfei*, a beautiful hybrid between the above species.

Euonymus (Spindle-tree)—*Celastraceae.* Hardy and slightly tender deciduous and evergreen shrubs. Leaves mostly oval-shaped, green, or variegated with white and yellow, in the evergreen kinds; the deciduous ones being grown for the great beauty of their autumn fruits.

CULTURE: Soil, ordinary. Position, deciduous species in shrubberies; evergreen species against south or west walls, edgings to beds, window boxes, hedges and front of shrubberies. Plant deciduous species in Sept., Oct. or Nov.; evergreen in Sept., Oct., March or April. Prune, Oct. or April. Good seaside shrubs.

POT CULTURE OF EVERGREEN SPECIES: Compost, two parts loam, one part leaf-mould and sand. Position, well-drained pots in cool greenhouse, corridors, balconies, windows. Pot, Sept., Oct. or March. Water moderately in winter, freely other times. Syringe foliage frequently in summer.

PROPAGATION: By cuttings of shoots of current year's growth, well ripened, inserted in sandy soil in cool greenhouse, window or frame, in Sept. or Oct.; *E. radicans* by division at planting time. Deciduous kinds from seed sown in spring.

DECIDUOUS SPECIES CULTIVATED: *E. alatus*, 6 to 8 ft., China and Japan; *europaeus*, 10 to 15 ft., Europe (Br.) and Siberia, 'Common Spindle-tree', well known for its brilliant red and orange autumn fruits, with vars. *atropurpureus*, coloured foliage, *fructu-albo* and *fructu-coccineo*, white and scarlet fruits respectively; *latifolius*, 10 ft., a fine European species with large fruits; *sachalinensis* (syn. *E. planipes*), 10 ft., very similar to *E. latifolius*, Japan; *yedoensis*, 15 ft., fruit pink, Japan.

EVERGREEN SPECIES CULTIVATED: *E. japonicus*, leaves green, 4 to 6 ft., China and Japan, and vars. *albo-marginatus*, leaves margined with white, *aureus*, leaves yellow, *albo-variegatus*, leaves broad and variegated with white; *radicans*, 1 ft., Japan, and its silver- and golden-leaved forms.

Eupatorium—*Compositae.* Hardy and slightly tender herbaceous and greenhouse shrubby plants.

CULTURE OF GREENHOUSE SPECIES: Compost, equal parts loam and dried cow manure with a little sand. Position, pots in light greenhouse Sept. to June, cold frame June to Sept. Pot, March to April. Prune immediately after flowering. Water moderately Sept. to March, freely afterwards. Temp., Sept. to March 45° to 50°, March to June 55° to 60°. Apply liquid manure frequently to plants in flower. May be planted out in the open garden in June, the shoots should be frequently pinched. Lift and repot for flowering in greenhouse.

CULTURE OF HARDY SPECIES: Soil, ordinary. Position, in open borders or shrubberies. Plant, Oct., Nov., March or April.

PROPAGATION: By cuttings of young shoots in sandy soil in temp. 55° to 65° in March or April. Hardy species by division in Oct. or March.

GREENHOUSE SPECIES CULTIVATED: *E. atrorubens*, red, Jan. to March, 12 to 18 in., Mexico; *ligustrinum* (syn. *E. micranthum*, *E. Weinmannianum*), white, autumn, 8 ft., Mexico; *riparium*, white, spring, 2 to 3 ft., Mexico; *sordidum* (syn. *E. ianthinum*), purple, winter, 2 ft., Mexico.

HARDY SPECIES CULTIVATED: *E. cannabinum*, 'Hemp Agrimony', reddish-purple, July, 2 to 4 ft., Britain; *purpureum*, 'Joe-Pye Weed', purplish, autumn,

3 to 6 ft., N. America; *rugosum* (syn. *E. ageratoides*), white, summer, 2 to 4 ft., N. America.

Euphorbia (Spurge)—*Euphorbiaceae*. Stove and hardy flowering shrubs or herbs.

CULTURE OF WARM HOUSE SPECIES: Compost, equal parts fibrous loam and peat with liberal amount of sand. Position, sunny dry part of stove, with shoots trained up roof, wall, or on trellis. Pot, March or June. Water moderately Sept. to Jan.; keep almost dry Jan. to May, freely afterwards. Temp., Jan. to May 50° to 55°, May to Sept. 65° to 75°, Sept. to Jan. 55° to 65°. Prune *E. fulgens* in June, cutting shoots back to within 1 in. of base.

CULTURE OF POINSETTIA: Flowers, insignificant. Bracts, scarlet, white; winter. Foliage, green or variegated with creamy-white. Compost, four parts fibrous loam, one part decayed cow manure, and half a part silver sand. Position, pots or beds with shoots trained to back wall of stove. YOUNG PLANTS: Place old plants in temp. 65° to 75° in May. Remove young shoots when 2 to 3 in. long, insert singly in 2 in. pots filled with sandy loam and peat, and plunge to the rims in bottom heat of 85°, under a bell-glass or in propagator. When rooted, place singly in 4 in. pots, plunge again in bottom heat for a few days, then remove to shelf near glass. As soon as well rooted, transfer to 6 or 8 in. pots, keep near glass for week or so, then gradually harden. Place in cold sunny frame until Sept., when remove to temp. 55°. Shade from midday sun when in cold frame. Water freely. Syringe twice daily. Ventilate freely on fine days. Transfer plants into temp. 60° to 65° end of Sept. Water moderately. Apply stimulants twice a week. After flowering remove to a temp. of 40° to 45°, keep roots quite dry and store pots on their side under staging. OLD PLANTS: Prune shoots, unless required for producing cuttings, to second latent bud or eye from their base, end of April. When new shoots are 1 in. long, turn plants out of their pots, remove old soil from roots, cut off the straggling ends of latter, and repot in pots just large enough to take roots and little compost. Place in temp. 65° to 75° from pruning time. Repot into larger size when small pots are filled with roots. Place in cold sunny frame or pit during July and Aug. Water and syringe freely. Remove to temp. 55° to 60°, Sept., 60° to 70°, Oct. onwards. Apply stimulants twice a week Oct., until bracts are fully developed, then cease. After flowering treat as advised for young plants. Beds: Compost, as above. Plant, July. Train the shoots thinly to wall. Water freely while growing; after flowering keep quite dry. Prune shoots to within one latent bud of their base, end of Sept. Temp., April to Sept. 65° to 75°, Sept. to April 55° to 60°. Average height of a well-grown young plant 12 to 18 in. Average diameter of a well-grown head of bracts 10 to 15 in.

CULTURE OF HARDY SPECIES: Soil, ordinary. Position, dry borders, banks, sunny rockeries. Plant, March or April.

PROPAGATION: Stove species by cuttings of young shoots 3 in. long inserted in well-drained pots of sandy compost in temp. 70° in May, June or July; hardy species by cuttings inserted in sandy soil in cold frame in summer, seeds sown in dryish positions outdoors in April, division of plants in Oct. or April.

STOVE SPECIES CULTIVATED: *E. fulgens* (syn. *E. jacquinaeflora*), scarlet, autumn and winter, 2 to 3 ft., Mexico; *Milii* (syn. *E. splendens*), red, summer, 4 ft., Madagascar; *pulcherrima* (syn. *Poinsettia pulcherrima*), 'Poinsettia', scarlet, autumn, 3 to 6 ft., Mexico.

HARDY SPECIES CULTIVATED: *E. amygdaloides*, yellow, late summer, Europe and Orient; *Cyparissias*, 'Cypress Spurge', yellow, June, 2 ft., Europe; *epithymoides*, soft yellow, early spring, 9 in., Europe; *Lathyrus*, 'Caper Spurge', yellow, June and July, 3 to 4 ft., biennial, Europe; *Myrsinites*, yellow, summer, trailing, S. Europe; *pilosa major*, yellow, spring, 1 to 1½ ft., Europe, N. Asia; *polychroma*, yellow, spring, 12 in., Europe; *sikkimensis*, yellow, 2 ft., E. Himalaya; *Wulfenii* yellow, summer, 3 ft., Europe.

Eupritchardia—*Palmae*. Warm greenhouse fan palms. First introduced late nineteenth century.

CULTURE: Compost, two parts peat and one part of loam and sand. Position, well-drained pots in light part of stove. Pot, Feb. to April. Water moderately Oct. to March, freely afterwards. Syringe twice daily March to Sept., once daily Sept. to March. Temp., March to Sept. 65° to 75°, Sept. to March 55° to 65°.

PROPAGATION: By seeds sown ¼ in. deep in light, rich soil in temp. 80° to 90° Feb., March or April.

SPECIES CULTIVATED: *E. Martii*, 4 to 10 ft., Sandwich Islands; *pacifica*, 20 to 30 ft., Fiji; *Thurstonii*, 4 to 10 ft., Fiji.

European Palm, see *Chamaerops humilis.*

Eurya—*Theaceae* (or *Ternstroemiaceae*). Slightly tender evergreen shrubs.

CULTURE: Compost, two parts loam, one part peat and sand. Position, pots in cool greenhouse, dwelling-rooms or windows. Pot, March or April. Water moderately in winter, freely other times. *E. japonica* may be grown outdoors in S. of England and Ireland. Requires protection when young.

PROPAGATION: By cuttings of young shoots inserted in sandy soil in temp. 60° to 65° in spring.

SPECIES CULTIVATED: *E. japonica*, 5 ft., India, China and Japan, var. *variegata*, leaves green and creamy-white. For *E. ochracea*, see Cleyera.

Eurycles—*Amaryllidaceae*. Stove bulbous plants. First introduced mid-eighteenth century.

CULTURE: Compost, three parts sandy loam, one part leaf-mould and sand. Position, well-drained pots in light part of stove. Pot, Feb. Water freely March to Sept., keep nearly dry remainder of time. Temp. for stove species, Sept. to March 50° to 55°, March to Sept. 65° to 75°.

PROPAGATION: By offsets removed and placed singly in small pots in Feb.

SPECIES CULTIVATED: *E. Cunninghamii*, 'Brisbane Lily', white, July, 1 ft., Australia; *sylvestris*, white, spring, 1 to 1½ ft., Malaya and Australia.

Euterpe—*Palmae*. Stove ornamental-leaved palms. First introduced mid-seventeenth century.

CULTURE: Compost, equal parts loam, peat, leaf-mould and sand. Pot, Feb. to March. Position, pots in shady part of stove. Water freely always. Shade from sun. Temp., March to Sept. 70° to 85°, Sept. to March 60° to 65°.

PROPAGATION: By seeds sown 1 in. deep in above compost, in temp. 85° in spring.

SPECIES CULTIVATED: *E. edulis*, 10 to 20 ft., Trop. America; *oleracea*, 10 to 20 ft., Brazil.

Evening Primrose, see *Oenothera biennis.*

Evergreen Candytuft, see Iberis sempervirens; **-Oak, see** *Quercus Ilex.*

Everlasting Flowers, see Ammobium, Anaphalis, Antennaria, Helipterum, Helichrysum, Limonium and Xeranthemum; **-Pea, see** *Lathyrus latifolius.*

Exacum—*Gentianaceae*. Stove annuals and perennials. First introduced midnineteenth century.

CULTURE: Compost, equal parts peat, loam and sand. Position, pots in light part of plant stove. Water freely. Temp., 65° to 75°.

PROPAGATION: By seeds sown on surface of fine compost in temp. 75° to 80° in April, transplanting seedlings when large enough to handle into small pots and thence into a larger size later on; perennial species also by cuttings.

PERENNIAL SPECIES CULTIVATED: *E. affine*, bluish-lilac, fragrant, June to Oct., 6 in., Socotra.

BIENNIAL SPECIES CULTIVATED: *E. macranthum*, purplish-blue, 2 ft., Ceylon; *zeylanicum*, violet-purple, autumn, 2 ft., Ceylon.

Exochorda (Pearl Bush)—*Rosaceae*. Hardy deciduous flowering shrubs of great beauty, somewhat neglected in gardens. First introduced mid-nineteenth century.

CULTURE: Soil, ordinary. Position, shrubberies, full sun, but not too dry. Plant, Oct. to Feb. Prune after flowering.

PROPAGATION: By seeds sown in sandy soil in cold frame in spring or autumn; cuttings of young shoots inserted in sandy soil under bell-glass in summer.

SPECIES CULTIVATED: *E. Giraldii*, white, May, 10 ft., N. and W. China, and var. *Wilsonii* with very large flowers; *Korolkowii* (syn. *E. Albertii*), white, May, 12 ft., probably the best species, grows well in chalk, Turkistan; *macrantha*, hybrid between *E. racemosa* and *E. Korolkowii*, 15 ft., vigorous upright habit, white, April, May; *racemosa* (syn. *E. grandiflora*), white, May, 10 ft., very free flowering, N. China.

Fabiana (False Heath)—*Solanaceae.* Rather tender flowering evergreen shrubs with heath-like foliage and flowers. First introduced early nineteenth century.

CULTURE: Soil, ordinary. Position, protected by south or west walls; cool greenhouses N. of England. Plant, Oct. or April. Water plants in pots moderately in winter, freely in summer. Repot, March or April.

PROPAGATION: By cuttings of firm young shoots inserted in sandy soil under bell-glass in cold greenhouse, or in cold frame in March or April.

SPECIES CULTIVATED: *F. imbricata*, white, May, only hardy in the south, or sheltered positions elsewhere, to 8 ft., Chile, vars. *prostrata*, a fairly hardy form for the rockery, and *violacea*, newer form, more hardy than the type.

Fagopyrum—*Polygonaceae.* Hardy annual. Grown for seed for pheasant and poultry feeding; also for ploughing or digging in as a green manure. Good bee plant.

CULTURE: Soil, light, sandy or well drained; clay unsuitable. Sow in May in shallow drills 6 in. to 8 in. apart. Harvest when greatest amount of seed has matured, as seeds do not ripen all at once. Cut early in morning when moist with dew. Dig in as green manure when flowering begins.

SPECIES CULTIVATED: *F. esculentum*, ' Buckwheat ', pink and white, summer, 3 ft., Cent. Asia.

Fagus (Beech)—*Fagaceae.* Hardy deciduous trees.

CULTURE: Soil, sandy or chalky, and gravelly loam. Position, open dryish shrubberies, lawns, copses; also good seaside tree. Plant, Oct. to Feb. Common species (*F. sylvatica*) is a good hedge shrub; plant 9 in. apart and keep sides closely trimmed. Timber used for making joiners' tools, gun stocks, saddle trees and wheel felloes.

PROPAGATION: By seeds sown 1 in. deep in rows 15 in. apart in March or April, transplanting seedlings when two years old; variegated kinds by grafting in March on common species.

SPECIES CULTIVATED: *F. sylvatica*, ' Common Beech ', 70 to 80 ft., deciduous, Europe (Br.), and vars. *atropunicea*, ' Copper Beech ', *laciniata*, ' Cutleaf Beech ', *pendula*, ' Weeping Beech ', *purpurea*, ' Purple Beech '.

Fair Maids of February, see *Galanthus nivalis*; **-of France, -of Kent,** see *Ranunculus aconitifolius.*

Fairy Moss, see Azolla.

False Aralia, see Dizygotheca; **-Acacia,** see Robinia; **-Dragonshead,** see Physostegia; **-Hellebore,** see Veratrum; **-Indigo,** see Baptisia; **-Mitrewort,** see *Tiarella cordifolia*; **-Plantain,** see *Heliconia Bihai*; **-Solomon's Seal,** see Smilacina; **-Spiraea,** see Sorbaria; **-Tamarisk,** see Myricaria.

Farewell-to-Spring, see *Godetia amoena.*

Fatsia—*Araliaceae.* Hardy or slightly tender evergreen shrub. A popular room or greenhouse plant. First introduced early nineteenth century.

GREENHOUSE CULTURE: Compost, two parts sandy loam, one part leaf-mould, decayed manure and sand. Position, well-drained pots in cool greenhouse or dwelling room. Pot or plant, Feb. to April. Water moderately Sept. to April freely afterwards. Temp., Sept. to April 40° to 50°, April to Sept. 55° to 65°.

OUTDOOR CULTURE: Soil, ordinary, well drained. Position, sheltered, partially-shaded shrubberies, requires protection in severe weather. Plant, May.

PROPAGATION: By cuttings of roots in light soil in temp. 80° in March or April; variegated kinds by grafting on common species in temp. 75° in March or April, tall plants by stem-rooting in spring.

SPECIES CULTIVATED: *F. japonica* (syn. *Aralia Sieboldii, A. japonica*), 'Japanese Aralia' or 'Figleaf Palm', leaves green, palmate, 6 to 15 ft., Japan, and variegated vars.

Faucaria—*Aizoaceae.* Greenhouse succulent plants.

CULTURE: Compost, six parts sharp sand, three parts rich loam, two parts leaf-mould, one part each mortar rubble and crushed brick. Position, well-drained pots in sunny greenhouse or window, or bed on greenhouse staging. Plant or pot, May. Water freely in autumn and winter, less freely spring and summer. Temp., Oct. to Mar. 45° to 55°, April to Sept. 55° and over.

PROPAGATION: By seeds sown in close atmosphere, temp. 55° to 60°, April or Sept.; stem cuttings, which should first be dried, May or June, temp. 60°.

SPECIES CULTIVATED: *F. albidens*, yellow, Aug. to Nov., S. Africa; *Britteniae*, yellow, Aug. to Nov., S. Africa; *felina* (syn. *Mesembryanthemum felinum*), yellow, Aug. to Nov., S. Africa; *lupina* (syn. *M. lupinum*), yellow, Aug. to Nov., S. Africa; *tigrina* (syn. *M. tigrinum*), yellow, Aug. to Nov., S. Africa; *tuberculosa* (syn. *M. tuberculosum*), yellow, Aug. to Nov., S. Africa.

Fauria—*Gentianaceae* (or *Menyanthaceae*). Hardy aquatic perennial, allied to Menyanthes.

CULTURE: Soil, ordinary mud or bog. Position, shallow stream pools, ponds, marshes, bogs.

PROPAGATION: By inserting pieces of creeping stem in the mud, March to Oct.

SPECIES CULTIVATED: *F. Crista-galli* (syn. *Menyanthes Crista-galli, Nephropyllidium Crista-galli*), white, 1 to 2 ft., N. America to Alaska.

Feather Grass, see Stipa; **-Hyacinth,** see *Muscari comosum* var. *monstrosum.*

Feathery Bamboo, see *Bambusa vulgaris.*

Fedia—*Valerianaceae.* Hardy annual. First introduced late eighteenth century.

CULTURE: Soil, ordinary. Position, open beds, rockeries or borders.

PROPAGATION: By seeds sown in boxes or pots of light soil in temp. 55° in March, transplanting into borders in May; or outdoors in April where plants are to grow.

SPECIES CULTIVATED: *F. Cornucopiae*, 'Horn of Plenty', red, lilac, rose, and carmine, July, 6 to 12 in., S. Europe.

Feijoa—*Myrtaceae.* Half-hardy evergreen flowering tree. First introduced late nineteenth century.

CULTURE: Compost, equal parts sandy loam and leaf-mould with a liberal addition of well-decayed manure. Position, well-drained pots in cool greenhouse, outdoors on south wall, or sheltered shrubberies in mild districts. Water freely during growing season.

PROPAGATION: By seeds sown in sandy soil during Feb. or March in temp. 55° to 60°; cuttings of young growth during June or July under bell-glass in gentle bottom heat.

SPECIES CULTIVATED: *F. Sellowiana*, white and purplish, autumn, to 18 ft., S. America.

Felicia—*Compositae.* Half-hardy annuals or biennials and sub-shrubs.

CULTURE: Soil, ordinary. Position, sunny beds or borders, or sunny greenhouse. Sow seeds thinly in well-drained pans during Feb. or March in temp. 55° to 60°. Prick out when large enough to handle and harden off for planting out in May. Shrubby species by cuttings of young shoots March or Aug. in sandy soil, temp. 55° to 65°.

SPECIES CULTIVATED: *F. amelloides* (syn. *Agathaea coelestis*), 'Blue Marguerite', blue, June to Aug., 12 to 18 in., sub-shrub, S. Africa; *Bergeriana*, blue, dwarf, summer, annual, S. Africa; *petiolata*, rose to blue, summer, prostrate sub-shrub, S. Africa; *tenella* (syn. *F. fragilis*), pale blue, summer, 12 to 14 in., annual, S. Africa.

Fendlera—*Saxifragaceae* (or *Hydrangeaceae*). Slightly tender deciduous flowering shrub; does not suceed well in this climate. First introduced late nineteenth century.

CULTURE: Soil, sandy loam. Position, sunny rockeries or against S. or S.W. walls. Plant, Nov. to Feb.

PROPAGATION: By cuttings of young growth during June or July under bell-glass in gentle bottom heat.

SPECIES CULTIVATED: *F. rupicola*, white or rose-tinted, May to June, 3 to 6 ft., S.W. United States.

Fennel, see *Foeniculum vulgare*; **-Flower**, see Nigella.

Fenugreek, see *Trigonella Foenum-Graecum*.

Ferocactus (Hedgehog Cactus)—*Cactaceae*. Greenhouse succulent plants, formerly included in the genus Echinocactus.

CULTURE: Compost, two parts fibrous sandy loam, one part brick rubble, old mortar rubble and sharp sand. Position, well-drained pots or pans in sunny greenhouse or window. Repot every two or three years in spring. Water only occasionally Sept. to April, once a week afterwards. Temp., Sept. to March 50° to 55°, March to Sept. 65° to 75°.

PROPAGATION: By seeds sown ⅛ in. deep in well-drained pots or pans of sandy soil in temp. 75° in spring, keeping soil moderately moist; cuttings of stems inserted in small pots of sandy soil kept barely moist in summer; grafting on common kinds in April.

SPECIES CULTIVATED: *F. acanthodes* (syn. *F. Lecontei*), lemon-yellow, summer, Mexico; *cylindraceus*, yellow, summer, Colorado; *latispinus* (syn. *F. cornigera*), purple, summer, Mexico.

Ferraria (Black Iris)—*Iridaceae*. Half-hardy deciduous bulbous plant. First introduced mid-eighteenth century.

CULTURE: Compost, two parts sandy loam, one part peat. Position, cool greenhouse. Pot, Nov. Place bulbs with point just below surface and 1 to 2 in. apart. Water occasionally Nov. to Feb; moderately Feb. to June; keep quite dry July to Nov. Temp., Nov. to Feb. 40° to 45°, Feb. to June, 50° to 60°.

SPECIES CULTIVATED: *F. antherosa*, green and brown, June, 6 in., S. Africa; *undulata*, brown and purple, March and April, 6 to 8 in., S. Africa.

Ferula—*Umbelliferae*. Hardy herbaceous plants with elegant, fern-like, deep green foliage. First introduced late sixteenth century.

CULTURE: Soil, ordinary. Position, open, margins of shrubberies, borders, ponds, isolated on lawns and summits of rockeries or banks. Plant, Nov. to March.

PROPAGATION: By seeds sown in Sept. or Nov. in light soil outdoors, transplanting seedlings following summer; division of roots in Oct. or Nov.

SPECIES CULTIVATED: *F. communis*, ' Giant Fennel ', yellow, June, 8 to 12 ft., Medit. Region, var. *glauca*, yellow; *tingitana*, yellow, June, 6 to 8 ft., N. Africa.

Fescue, see Festuca.

Festuca—*Gramineae*. Hardy perennial grass.

OUTDOOR CULTURE: Soil, ordinary. Position, edgings of flower beds or borders. Plant, Sept., Oct., March or April.

POT CULTURE: Compost, two parts good soil, one part leaf-mould and sand. Position, cold or warm greenhouses and windows. Pot, March or April. Water moderately in winter, freely other times.

PROPAGATION: By seeds sown outdoors in April; division in March or April.

SPECIES CULTIVATED: *F. ovina glauca*, ' Fescue Grass ', leaves bristly, glaucous green, 6 in., Britain.

Feverfew, see *Chrysanthemum Parthenium*.

Ficus (Fig)—*Moraceae*. Stove, greenhouse and hardy deciduous and evergreen trees and shrubs. Flowers unisexual, borne inside the fruit. *F. Carica* bears the edible fruit of commerce.

CULTURE OF TENDER SPECIES: Compost, three parts loam, one part peat and sand. Position, erect species (*F. elastica*, etc.) in pots in stove, greenhouse or dwelling rooms; creeping species (*F. pumila*) in beds with shoots clinging to walls, rockeries, etc. Pot or plant, Feb., March or April. Water moderately Oct. to March, freely afterwards. Syringe stove species daily Feb. to Aug. Temp. for stove species, 55° to 65° Oct. to Feb., 75° to 85° Feb. to Oct.; for greenhouse species, 50° to 55° Sept. to March, 60° to 70° March to Sept.

CULTURE OF INDIARUBBER PLANT IN ROOMS: Compost, see above. Position, light, near window, away from draughts. Pot, March or April. Water once a week Nov. to March, twice and three times weekly other times. Temp., Sept. to April 40° to 50°, April to Sept. 55° to 60°. Sponge leaves weekly.

OUTDOOR CULTURE IN SUMMER: Plunge pots to rim in sunny beds middle of June. Lift and place in greenhouse again in Sept. Water freely daily.

OUTDOOR CULTURE OF FIG: Compost, two parts fibrous loam, one part brick rubbish and old mortar. Position, against south or south-west walls. Plant, April, in border 2 ft. deep and 3 ft. wide, enclosed with brick or concrete wall. Mode of bearing: Entire length of previous year's shoots; only one crop borne outdoors in England. Prune, April or July, simply removing deformed, dead, or very weak branches. Pinch points off vigorous young shoots in July. Apply liquid manure once in Aug. to trees bearing heavily. Figlets size of filberts remove in Sept. or Oct. Protect branches in Dec. with straw or mats, removing both in April.

CULTURE OF FIG UNDER GLASS: Compost, position, border, time of planting as above. Branches trained up roof or against wall. Mode of bearing: On shoots of previous year's growth for first crop; those of current year for second crop. Prune and pinch as above. Disbud young shoots when too many are forming. Water and syringe freely in summer. Apply liquid manure occasionally in summer. Temp. for forcing, 50° to 65°.

POT CULTURE OF FIG: Compost, turfy loam, little bonemeal. Position, ordinary greenhouse, vinery or forcing house. Pot, Nov. to April. Size of pots, 10 or 12 in. Water freely when growing, very little when not. Apply liquid manure twice weekly to trees bearing fruit. Syringe daily when in growth. Pinch points off young shoots when latter are 9 in. long. Protect pots with covering of straw Nov. to Jan. and partially expose branches to the air.

PROPAGATION: Tender species by cuttings of shoots inserted in sandy peat in a temp. of 75° in spring or summer; cuttings of stem 1 in. long, and with one leaf attached, slightly burying stem portion in soil and supporting leaf with a stake, and placing in above temp.; stem rooting in case of tall india-rubber plants in spring. Expose cuttings to air for a short time to allow base to dry before inserting in soil. Fig by seeds sown in light soil in a temp. of 65° to 70° in Jan., afterwards growing seedlings on in pots until they bear fruit and it can be seen if they are worth growing; cuttings of previous year's shoots 6 in. long and having a heel of older wood attached at base, inserted in a warm border outdoors or in pots in gentle heat between Oct. and March; cuttings of young shoots, 3 or 4 in. long, removed with a heel of older wood, and inserted in pots of light sandy soil in a propagating frame (temp. 70°) in June; layering shoots in summer; grafting by approach just after tree comes into leaf; budding in July; suckers in autumn.

TENDER SPECIES CULTIVATED: *F. benghalensis*, ' Banyan Tree ', fruits round, red, 30 to 40 ft., India; *Cannonii*, leaves bronzy-red, Society Islands; *Chauvieri*, leaves green and yellow, origin unknown; *diversifolia*, leaves bright green, Malaya; *elastica*, ' India-rubber Plant ', leaves green, India, var. *variegata*, leaves variegated; *lyrata* (syn. *F. pandurata*) leaves fiddle-shaped, green, Tropical Africa; *macrophylla*, ' Morton Bay Fig ', leaves green, Australia; *Parcellii*, leaves green and white, Polynesia; *pumila* (syn. *F. repens*), leaves green, shoots creeping, a good plant for covering walls, Japan, var. *minima*, smaller; *radicans variegata*, leaves variegated with silver; *rubiginosa* (syn. *F. australis*), leaves with a rusty appearance underneath, Australia, and var. *variegata*.

HARDY SPECIES CULTIVATED: *F. carica*, ' Fig ', Medit. Region; introduced mid-sixteenth century.

Field Balm see *Glecoma hederacea.*

Fig Marigold, see (Mesembryanthemum); **-Tree, see** Ficus.

Filbert, see *Corylus maxima.*

Filipendula (Meadowsweet)—*Rosaceae.* Hardy herbaceous perennials, formerly included in Spiraea.

CULTURE: Soil, ordinary, well manured for *F. Ulmaria.* Position, open sunny borders and wild gardens. Plant, Oct. to Nov., or March to April.

PROPAGATION: By division in spring.

SPECIES CULTIVATED: *F. camtschatica* (syns. *Spiraea camtschatica, F. kamtschatica*), white, June, 6 to 8 ft., Manchuria, Kamtchatka; *hexapetala* (syns. *Spiraea* and *Ulmaria Filipendula*), ' Dropwort ', white, June, 2 to 3 ft., Europe; *palmata* (syn. *Spiraea digitata*), white, 2 to 3 ft., July and Aug., N.E. Asia; *purpurea* (often cultivated as *Spiraea palmata*), pink or purple, 2 to 4 ft., July and Aug., Japan, var. *elegans*, white; *rubra* (syns. *Ulmaria rubra, Spiraea lobata*), ' Queen of the Prairie ', pink, 4 to 8 ft., N. America, var. *venusta* (syn. *Spiraea venusta*), deep pink, *Ulmaria* (syn. *Spiraea Ulmaria*), ' Common Meadowsweet ', white, June, to 6 ft., Europe (incl. Britain), W. Asia, var. *plenum*, double; *vulgaris* (syns. *F. hexapetala, Spiraea Filipendula*), ' Dropwort ', white, June, 1 to 3 ft., Europe (incl. Britain), var. *plenum*, double.

Finocchio, see *Foeniculum vulgare* var. *dulce.*

Fir, see Abies; **-Club Moss,** see *Lycopodium Selago.*

Fire Bush, see *Embothrium coccineum*; **-Pink,** see *Silene virginica*; **·thorn,** see Pyracantha; **-weed** see *Epilobium angustifolium.*

Fire-cracker Flower, (*Oichelostemma Ioa-Maia*), see Brodiaea.

Fishbone Thistle, see *Cirsium Diacantha.*

Fittonia—*Acanthaceae.* Warm greenhouse, ornamental, perennial, trailing plants with white or coloured veins on the leaves. First introduced mid-nineteenth century.

CULTURE: Compost, equal parts peat, loam and sand. Position, shallow pans, pots, or surface of beds in shady part of plant stove. Water moderately Nov. to Feb., freely afterwards. Temp., Oct. to March 55° to 60°, March to Oct. 65° to 75°.

PROPAGATION: By cuttings of firm shoots inserted in sandy soil in temp. 75° to 85° under bell-glass in Feb., March or April; division of plants in Feb. or March.

SPECIES CULTIVATED: *F. gigantea*, leaves green, veined with red, 12 to 15 in., Peru; *Verschaffeltii*, leaves green, veined with red, 8 in., Peru, vars. *argyroneura*, leaves veined white, and *Pearcei*, leaves glaucous below with carmine veins.

Flag, see *Iris germanica.*

Flamboyant, see *Delonix regia.*

Flame Flower, see *Tropaeolum speciosum.*

Flamingo Plant, see Anthurium.

Flannel Flower, see *Actinotus Helianthi*; **-Plant,** see *Verbascum Thapsus.*

Flax, see Linum.

Fleabane, see Erigeron.

Floating Fern, see Ceratopteris; **-Heart,** see Nymphoides; **-Water Plantain,** see Luronium.

Flower-of-an-hour, see *Hibiscus Trionum*; **-of-the-West-Wind,** see Zephyr. anthes.

Flowering Ash, see *Fraxinus Ornus*; **-Currant,** see *Ribes sanguineum*; **-Dogwood,** see *Cornus florida*; **-Moss,** see *Pyxidanthera barbulata*; **-Nutmeg,** see *Leycesteria formosa*; **-Rush,** see *Butomus umbellatus*; **-Seakale,** see *Crambe cordifolia*.

Fly Honeysuckle, see *Lonicera Xylosteum*; **-Orchis,** see *Ophrys muscifera*.

Foam Flower, see *Tiarella cordifolia*.

Foeniculum—*Umbelliferae.* Hardy perennial and annual herbs. Leaves used for sauces and garnishing.

CULTURE: Soil, ordinary. Position, sunny border. Plant *F. vulgare*, March or April, 12 in. apart in rows 15 in. asunder. Sow seeds of *F. dulce* in drills 18 in. apart where plants are required, thinning out seedlings to 6 in. asunder. Remove flower stems as soon as seen, unless seed is wanted.

PROPAGATION: *F. vulgare* by seeds sown ¼ in. deep in drills 6 in. apart in March; division of roots in March.

SPECIES CULTIVATED: *F. vulgare*, ' Fennel ', yellow, autumn, 2 ft., Europe (Br.), var. *dulce*, 2½ ft., annual, Italy.

Fontanesia—*Oleaceae.* Hardy deciduous shrubs. First introduced late eighteenth century.

CULTURE: Soil, ordinary. Position, sunny shrubberies, or as hedge plants. Plant, Nov. to Feb.

PROPAGATION: By cuttings inserted in sandy soil in cold frame during late summer.

SPECIES CULTIVATED: *F. Fortunei*, greenish-white, summer, 10 to 15 ft., China; *phillyreoides*, greenish-white, June, 6 to 10 ft., Orient.

Fontinalis (Willow Moss; Water Moss)—*Fontinalaceae.* Hardy aquatic perennials. *F. gracilis* is sometimes considered a variety of *F. antipyretica*.

CULTURE: Usually grows on wood or stone in running water. A piece of this should be detached with the plant and dropped in the pond or aquarium; each portion must be attached separately to a similar material. Plant, spring.

PROPAGATION: By division.

SPECIES CULTIVATED: *F. antipyretica*, Britain; *gracilis*, Europe.

Forget-me-not, see Myosotis.

Forsythia (Golden Bells)—*Oleaceae.* Hardy deciduous flowering shrubs. Popular for their early blossoms of yellow and gold. First introduced mid-nineteenth century.

OUTDOOR CULTURE: Soil, ordinary. Position, against south or west walls, or in sheltered parts of shrubbery. Plant, Oct. to Feb. Prune after flowering.

POT CULTURE: Compost, two parts loam, one part leaf-mould and sand. Position, well-drained pots in cool or warm greenhouse Dec. to May, outdoors remainder of year. Pot, Oct. to Dec. Water very little till March, then apply freely.

PROPAGATION: By cuttings inserted in sandy soil under bell-glass, July and Aug.; or in cold frame, Oct. or Nov.; layering in Oct. or Nov.

SPECIES CULTIVATED: *F. intermedia*, 10 ft., of upright growth, rich yellow, March to April, a good hybrid but inferior to its var. *spectabilis*, the best of all forsythias, with larger, more numerous, and more richly-coloured flowers, also vars. *densiflora*, free flowering, and *Vitellina*, canary yellow; *ovata suspensa*, 10 ft., as a bush, rather sprawling, and higher when trained to a wall, April, bright yellow, China, var. *atrocaulis*, an excellent form with lemon flowers on purplish stems; *viridissima*, yellow, April, 6 ft., China.

Fortunella (Kumquat)—*Rutaceae.* Small evergreen fruiting shrubs often grown as decorative pot plants. Small orange-like fruits used for preserves and eaten raw. May be hybridised with Citrus species.

CULTURE: As Citrus. *F. japonica* makes a good ornamental pot plant, the fruit of which is eaten skin and all.

PROPAGATION: As Citrus.

SPECIES CULTIVATED: *F. japonica* (syn. *Citrus japonica*), ' Round or Marumi Kumquat ', sweetly scented, fruit orange 1¼ in. round, sweet, foliage glossy, to 10 ft., China; *margarita*, ' Oval or Nagami Kumquat ', fruit oblong or oval, to 1 in. diameter, China.

Fothergilla (American Wych-Hazel)—*Hamamelidaceae*. Hardy deciduous flowering shrubs. First introduced mid-eighteenth century.

CULTURE: Compost, well-drained soil, sandy peat. Position, borders. Plant, Oct. to March. Prune after flowering.

PROPAGATION: By seeds sown ¹⁄₁₆ in. deep in pans of moist sandy peat in temp. of 45° to 55° in March or April; layering shoots in Oct. or Nov.

SPECIES CULTIVATED: *F. Gardenii* (syn. *F. alnifolia*), white, fragrant, May, 3 ft., United States; *major*, pinkish-white and yellow, May, 6 to 8 ft., Virginia and S. Carolina; *monticola*, white and yellow, May, 6 ft., N. America. These species have no petals, colour being provided by the stamens alone; the foliage sometimes colours well in autumn.

Foxglove, see Digitalis.

Fragaria (Strawberry)—*Rosaceae*. Low perennial herbs with rooting runners and edible fruits. Virginian strawberry first introduced early in the seventeenth century. The first large-fruited strawberry introduced in England was a seedling of *F. chiloensis* raised by Keens in 1806. Large-fruited varieties now in cultivation are all hybrids. Plants certified as virus-free should always be bought.

CULTURE OF STRAWBERRY: Soil, rich in organic matter and slightly acid, trenched 2 ft. deep. Position, open plots or borders; alpine kinds under shade of trees or on banks. Plant, Aug., Sept. or March, 18 in. apart in rows 2½ ft. asunder; alpines 6 in. apart. Mulch annually with manure or compost in late Feb. and give a light dressing of nitrate of soda after picking. Straw down under the leaves as the fruit begins to swell. Remove runners when they appear. No digging between rows necessary. Renew beds every three or four years.

FORCING: Royal Sovereign is the variety usually used for forcing, and runners are best rooted in early summer into 3 in. pots; when full of roots the pots are lifted and plunged in ashes until ready for potting on in July to 48 size pots towards the side, so that trusses rest on rim. May be potted again to 6 or 7 in. pots in Sept. Compost, equal parts loam and compost or peat, with a little bonemeal plus some dry cow manure for finals. Frames, Oct. to Jan., greenhouse or vineries after Jan. Water moderately till Oct., very little till Jan., freely afterwards. Fertilise blossoms by means of camel-hair brush. Thin fruit when set to a few on each plant. Feed with liquid manure after fruit has set until it begins to ripen. Plant out in garden after fruiting. Temp. for forcing, Jan. to March 45° to 55°, March to ripening period 65° to 75.

PROPAGATION: By runners on plants from which blossom trusses were removed. Peg runners in 3 in. pots in June or July, or into open ground around plants. Some alpine varieties that do not produce runners, by division or by seeds sown ¹⁄₁₆ in. deep in light soil outdoors, or in boxes in greenhouse in March or April.

SPECIES CULTIVATED: *F. chiloensis*, parent of large-fruited garden vars, white, May, 8 in., fruit crimson, ¾ in., Chile, var. *ananassa*, ' Pine Strawberry '; *moschata* (syn. *F. elatior*), ' Hautbois Strawberry ', white, summer, 6 in., fruit red, aroma musky, edible, Europe; *vesca* (syn. *F. alpina*), ' Alpine Strawberry ', white, May to Aug., 6 to 12 in., fruit small, scarlet, edible, Europe and N. America; *virginiana*, ' Scarlet Strawberry ', white, May, fruit light scarlet, edible, United States—another parent of the many forms of garden strawberries.

Franciscea, see Brunfelsia.

Francoa (Maiden's Wreath; Bridal Wreath)—*Saxifragaceae*. Hardy and half-hardy perennial plants. First introduced early nineteenth century.

OUTDOOR CULTURE: Soil, light rich loam. Position, sunny sheltered borders, banks, or rockeries. Plant, March or April.

POT CULTURE: Compost, two parts loam, one part leaf-mould and sand. Position, well-drained pots in cool greenhouse, frame or window. Pot, March or April. Water moderately Oct. to April, freely afterwards. Apply little liquid manure to plants in flower. Temp., Oct. to April 40° to 50°, April to Sept. 55° to 65°.

PROPAGATION: By seeds sown on the surface of a well-drained pan of sandy peat under bell-glass in temp. of 50° to 55° in Feb., March or April; division of plants at potting time.

SPECIES CULTIVATED: *F. appendiculata*, red, July, 1 to 2 ft., Chile; *ramosa*, white, July and Aug., 2 ft., Chile; *sonchifolia*, pink, summer, 2 ft., Chile.

Frangipani-plant, see Plumeria.

Frankenia—*Frankeniaceae*. Hardy evergreen flowering creeping plant.

CULTURE: Soil, light sandy. Position, sunny dry rockeries or borders. Plant, Oct. to April.

PROPAGATION: By division of plants in Oct. or April; seeds in cold frame in April.

SPECIES CULTIVATED: *F. laevis*, rose, July and Aug., Europe (Br.); *pulverulenta*, ' Sea Heath ', pink, 2 in., June, Medit.; *thymifolia*, pink, 1 to 2 in., July, Spain, Algiers.

Franklinia—*Theaceae* (or *Ternstroemiaceae*). Rare and beautiful, rather tender, deciduous flowering shrub. Sometimes included in the genus Gordonia. First introduced mid-eighteenth century.

CULTURE: Soil, peat and leaf-mould. Position, warm sheltered borders or against a south wall, in mildest southern districts only. Plant in November.

PROPAGATION: By layering shoots in spring.

SPECIES CULTIVATED: *F. alatamaha* (syn. *Gordonia pubescens*), large white camellia-like flowers, fragrant, late summer, 4 to 6 ft., N. America.

Fraxinella, see *Dictamnus albus*.

Fraxinus (Ash)—*Oleaceae*. Hardy deciduous trees. Ornamental foliage and flowering. Flowers, white, green, yellow; March to May.

CULTURE: Soil, ordinary. Position, dryish, sheltered. Suitable for seaside gardens, towns, chalky or gravelly situations. Plant, Oct. to Feb. Prune, Oct. to March. Timber used for tool handles, wooden rakes, ploughs, hoops, dairy utensils, and agricultural implements; also by cabinet makers for furniture making. Average life, 300 years. Timber reaches maturity at 70 years.

PROPAGATION: By seeds stratified and sown the following year; transplant seedlings when a year old; grafting on common species in March.

SPECIES CULTIVATED: *F. americana*, ' White Ash ', to 120 ft., Canada; *angustifolia*, 60 to 70 ft., S. Europe and N. Africa; *excelsior*, ' Common Ash ', 100 to 140 ft., Europe (Br.), and vars. *crispa*, ' Curl-leaved Ash ', *aurea*, ' Golden Ash ', *pendula*, ' Weeping Ash '; *floribunda*, white, to 120 ft., Himalaya, slightly tender; *Ornus*, ' Flowering or Manna Ash ', 50 to 65 ft., S. Europe; *pennsylvanica*, 40 to 60 ft., Eastern N. America; *Spaethiana*, one of the most striking ashes on account of its yellow-tinged foliage, 30 to 50 ft., Japan; *velutina*, of neat growth yet leafy and suitable for street planting, 30 to 40 ft., S.W. United States; *xanthoxyloides*, ' Afghan Ash ', unusual small tree, with winged leaf stalks, Afghanistan.

Freesia—*Iridaceae*. Greenhouse bulbous plants with very fragrant flowers.

INDOOR CULTURE: Compost, equal parts decayed manure, loam, leaf-mould and sand. Position, pots in cool greenhouse, frame or window. Pot, Aug. to flower in Jan., Oct. for Feb., Nov. for March, Dec. for April. Plant bulbs 1 in. deep and 2 in. apart. Suitable sized pot, 4½ in. diameter. Stand pots in cool position and give very little water until growth commences. Water freely when growth well advanced and until plants have flowered, then gradually decrease supply, keeping soil quite dry till July. Temp., not lower than 40°. Apply weak liquid or artificial manure to plants showing flower. Repot annually.

OUTDOOR CULTURE: Soil, light, rich, sandy. Position, sunny well-drained borders S. of England only. Plant bulbs 2 in. deep and 2 in. apart in Aug. or Sept. Protect in winter.

PROPAGATION: By seeds sown ¼ in. deep in pots or pans of light sandy soil in cool greenhouse or frame as soon as ripe, or in March or April; by offsets at potting time. Do not transplant seedlings first year.

SPECIES CULTIVATED: *F. alba* (syn. *F. refracta* var. *alba*), white, to 1½ ft., S. Africa; *Armstrongii*, rosy pink with yellow tube, 10 to 15 in., S. Africa; *corymbosa* (syn. *F. odorata*), yellow and orange, 5 to 18 in., S. Africa; *refracta*, white and orange, May to Aug., 1 ft., S. Africa; *xanthospila*, white with yellow blotch, 6 to 10 in., S. Africa, var. *Leichtlinii*, yellow and orange. There are many hybrids.

Fremontia—*Sterculiaceae*. Slightly tender deciduous flowering shrub. First introduced mid-nineteenth century.

CULTURE: Soil, sandy loam. Position, against west or north walls or fences, or in shrubberies S. of England. Plant, Oct. to March.

PROPAGATION: By seeds sown ⅛ in. deep in well-drained pots of sandy soil under bell-glass or frame in March or April.

SPECIES CULTIVATED: *F. californica*, golden mallow-like flowers, May to Aug., very handsome, to 10 ft. on a wall, or more in warm localities, California.

French Honeysuckle, see *Hedysarum coronarium*; **-Marigold,** see *Tagetes patula;* **-Mulberry,** see *Callicarpa americana*; **-Rose,** see *Rosa gallica*.

Fringe Tree, see *Chionanthus virginica*.

Fritillaria (Fritillary)—*Liliaceae*. Hardy bulbous plants.

OUTDOOR CULTURE: Soil, ordinary, deep rich. Position, shady borders for Crown Imperial; Snake's-head Fritillary, borders, or naturalised in turf; well-drained open borders for other species. Plant, 4 to 6 in. deep and 6 to 8 in. apart, Sept. to Nov. Top-dress annually with decayed manure. Do not transplant bulbs oftener than once in four years.

POT CULTURE: Compost, equal parts loam, peat, leaf-mould, decayed manure and sand. Position, well-drained pots in cold frame or cold greenhouse. Pot, Sept. or Oct., placing one bulb in centre of 5, 6 or 8 in. pot. Water very little till growth begins, then give moderate supply. Apply liquid manure when plants show flower. After flowering gradually withhold water, keeping soil quite dry after foliage has died.

PROPAGATION: By seeds sown ⅛ in. deep in pots or pans of sandy soil in cold frame or greenhouse as soon as ripe, or in spring; offsets at planting time. Do not transplant seedlings first year. Seedlings do not flower until four to six years old.

SPECIES CULTIVATED: *F. aurea*, yellow and brown, 6 in., May, Asia Minor; *citrina*, green and yellow, 8 in., May, Asia Minor; *Elwesii*, green and brown, May, 1 ft.; *imperialis*, ' Crown Imperial ', yellow, May, 2 to 3 ft., Orient, and vars.; *meleagris*, ' Snake's-head ', ' Chequered Daffodil ', purple, yellow, and white, May, 12 to 18 in., Europe (Br.), var. *alba*, white; *pallidiflora*, yellow, rose and purple, May, 9 in., Siberia; *persica*, ' Persian Lily ', violet blue, May, 2 ft., Asia Minor; *pudica*, golden yellow, April, 6 in., N.W. America; *pyrenaica*, plum, olive, and maroon, summer, 1¾ ft., Pyrenees; *recurva*, orange-scarlet, May, 2 ft., California; *ruthenica*, black, May, 1 ft., Caucasus.

Fritillary, see *Fritillaria meleagris*.

Frogbit, see *Hydrocharis Morsus-ranae*.

Fruiting Myrtle, see Eugenia.

Fuchsia—*Onagraceae*. Greenhouse and slightly tender flowering shrubs. First introduced late eighteenth century.

CULTURE OF GREENHOUSE SPECIES: Compost, two parts good fibrous loam, one part well-decayed manure and leaf-mould, with liberal quantity of silver or river sand. Position, shady part of greenhouse or window March to July; sunny place outdoors July to Oct.; cool dry part of greenhouse or room remainder of year. Pot old plants in Feb. or March, young ones when needed. Prune old plants in Feb. Water moderately March to May, freely May to Oct., very little at other times. Temp., Oct. to Feb. 40° to 45°, Feb. to Oct. 55° to 65°. Apply liquid or artificial manure to healthy plants showing flower. Pinch out points of shoots frequently in spring and early summer to induce bushy growth. When repotting old plants, remove soil from roots and place in small pots till growth begins, then shift into large size. Syringe foliage Feb. to May. Can be planted outdoors in June and potted and returned to greenhouse in Sept.

CULTURE OF SLIGHTLY TENDER SPECIES: Soil, ordinary, deep rich. Position, well-drained borders, base of south or west walls, or in sheltered position in the open S. of England. Plant, Oct. or April. Prune shoots off close to base in Feb. Protect in winter with layer of dry litter or leaves.

PROPAGATION: By seeds sown $\frac{1}{16}$ in. deep in well-drained pots of light sandy soil in temp. 55° in March or April; cuttings of young shoots inserted singly in small pots of sandy soil in temp. 70° to 80° in Jan., Feb. or March, or in cool greenhouse or window in April, May or June.

GREENHOUSE SPECIES CULTIVATED: *F. alpestris*, crimson, summer, 12 to 18 ft., Brazil; *arborescens*, pink, summer, 10 to 15 ft., Mexico; *bacillaris*, rose, summer, 5 ft., Chile; *boliviana*, rose, summer, 5 ft., Bolivia; *cordifolia*, orange, summer, 5 ft., Mexico; *corymbiflora*, deep red, summer, 6 ft., Peru; *dominiana*, scarlet, summer, 5 ft., garden hybrid; *exoniensis*, scarlet, summer, garden hybrid, *fulgens*, scarlet, July, 3 to 4 ft., Mexico; *parviflora*, red, summer, Mexico; *procumbens*, yellow and blue, summer, magenta-crimson berries, habit trailing, New Zealand; *serratifolia*, scarlet and green, summer, Peru; *simblicicaulis* crimson, summer, Peru; *splendens*, scarlet, summer, 6 ft., Mexico; *superba*, scarlet; summer, garden hybrid; *triphylla*, cinnabar red, summer, 1 to 1½ ft., Mexico.

SLIGHTLY TENDER SPECIES CULTIVATED: *F. magellanica* (syn. *F. macrostemma*), scarlet and purple, July, 10 to 20 ft., S. America, and vars. *conica*, scarlet, *discolor*, purple and red, *globosa*, purplish-red, *gracilis*, scarlet and purple, *Riccartonii*, scarlet.

Fuchsia-flowered Gooseberry, see *Ribes speciosum.*

Fumaria (Fumitory)—*Fumariaceae.* Hardy annual climber.

CULTURE: Soil, ordinary. Position, against south-east or west walls, in open borders with shoots running up sticks, or against arbours and trellis-work.

PROPAGATION: By seeds sown $\frac{1}{16}$ in. deep in April where plants are to flower.

SPECIES CULTIVATED: *F. officinalis*, purple, tipped crimson, summer, 3 to 4 ft., Europe (Br.).

Fumitory, see Fumaria.

Funkia, see Hosta.

Furcraea—*Amaryllidaceae.* Greenhouse succulent plants with leaves in basal rosettes and whitish or greenish flowers in terminal panicles on tall scapes. First introduced late seventeenth century. Leaves, long, fleshy, spined.

CULTURE: Compost, two parts loam, one part old mortar and river sand. Position, pots or tubs in greenhouses; may stand outside June to Sept. Water moderately April to Aug., little afterwards. Pot every five or six years; good drainage essential. Temp., winter 50° to 55°, summer 55° to 65°.

PROPAGATION: By offsets inserted in small pots at any time.

SPECIES CULTIVATED: *F. Bedinghausii*, green, May to Nov., to 15 ft., Mexico; *cubensis*, greenish, Oct. to Nov., 20 ft., Trop. America; *gigantea*, greenish, to 25 ft., Trop. America; *inermis*, 10 ft., Trop. America; *longaeva*, greenish, 30 to 40 ft., Mexico; *macrophylla*, greenish, 30 ft., origin uncertain; *Selloa*, greenish, 15 to 20 ft., Mexico, Colombia, and var. *marginata.*

Furze, see Ulex.

Gagea—*Liliaceae.* Small hardy bulbous plants.

CULTURE: Soil, sandy. Position, sunny borders, or in turf. Plant 3 in. deep and 3 in. apart, Aug. to Nov. Lift only when bulbs unhealthy.

PROPAGATION: By offsets, treated as advised for bulbs.

SPECIES CULTIVATED: *G. Liottardii*, yellow, 4 in., April to May, Europe; *lutea* (syn. *G. silvatica*), ' Yellow Star of Bethlehem ', yellow, March to May, 6 in., Europe (Br.).

Gaillardia—*Compositae.* Hardy annual and perennial herbaceous plants. First introduced late eighteenth century.

CULTURE: Soil, moderately light, rich. Position, sunny well-drained beds or borders. Plant, March or April. Apply weak liquid manure to plants in flower. Mulch beds with decayed manure in summer.

PROPAGATION: Annual and perennial species by seeds sown $\frac{1}{16}$ in. deep in shallow boxes of light soil in temp. 55° to 65° in April, transplanting seedlings outdoors in June; perennials by cuttings of shoots issuing from roots, inserted in sandy soil under hand-light or in cold frame Aug. to Oct., division of plants Oct. or March, cuttings of roots laid in shallow boxes of sandy soil, Feb. or March.

ANNUAL SPECIES CULTIVATED: *G. amblyodon*, red, autumn, 2 to 3 ft., Texas; *pulchella*, crimson and yellow, 2 to 3 ft., summer, N. America, var. *picta*, orange, red, and yellow, double 1 ft.

PERENNIAL SPECIES CULTIVATED: *G. aristata*, ' Blanket Flower ', yellow, autumn, 18 in., N. America, and vars. *grandiflora* and *maxima*. There are many named vars. to be found in trade lists.

Galanthus (Snowdrop; Fair Maids of February)—*Amaryllidaceae.* Hardy bulbous flowering plants.

OUTDOOR CULTURE: Soil, ordinary rich. Position, margins of beds; groups in open or shady borders; banks, rockeries, or in turf. Plant bulbs 2 in. deep and 1 in. apart, Sept. to Dec. Bulbs must only be lifted when they show signs of deterioration.

POT CULTURE: Compost, two parts ordinary soil, one part leaf-mould and sand. Position, cold or warm greenhouse, frame or window. Pot, Sept. to Nov., placing bulbs 1 in. deep and 1 in. apart in 4 or 5 in. pots or shallow pans. Place pots, etc., in cold frame or outdoors and cover with cinder ashes until growth begins. Water moderately till after flowering, then gradually cease. Plant bulbs outdoors following autumn.

PROPAGATION: By seeds sown as soon as ripe ¼ in. deep and 2 in. apart in shallow boxes filled with light sandy soil and placed at base of north wall outdoors; offsets treated as bulbs. Seedlings flower when three years old.

SPECIES CULTIVATED: *G. Allenii*, white, Feb. and March, 6 to 9 in., Asia Minor; *byzantinus*, green and white, Feb., 9 to 12 in., S.E. Europe; *caucasicus*, white and green, March, 6 in., Caucasus; *Elwesii*, white, Feb., 9 to 12 in., Asia Minor, and vars.; *Fosteri*, white, Feb., 6 in., Asia Minor; *Ikariae*, white, Feb., 8 in., Nikaria; *nivalis*, ' Common Snowdrop ', white, Jan. to March, 6 in., Europe, and vars.; *platyphyllus* (syn. *G. latifolius*), white and green, Feb. and March, 6 in., Caucasus; *plicatus*, ' Crimean Snowdrop ', white, Jan. to Feb., 10 to 12 in., Caucasus.

Galax—*Diapensiaceae.* Hardy evergreen perennial. First introduced mid-eighteenth century.

CULTURE: Compost, equal parts peat, leaf-mould and silver sand. Position, ledges of moist rockery or margin of rhododendron beds. Plant, Oct. to March.

PROPAGATION: By division of plants Oct. to March; seeds sown in peaty soil in cold frame in spring.

SPECIES CULTIVATED: *G. aphylla*, ' Wand Plant ', ' Carpenter's Leaf ', white, July, 3 to 6 in., N. America.

Galaxia—*Iridaceae.* Greenhouse bulbous plants. First introduced late eighteenth century.

CULTURE: Compost, two parts sandy peat, one part light loam. Position, well-drained pots in cold frame or greenhouse. Pot, Aug. to Nov., placing bulbs with apex just below surface, one in a 5 in. or three in a 6 in. pot. Cover pots with ashes till growth begins. Water moderately when growth commences, freely afterwards, cease after flowering. Repot, annually.

PROPAGATION: By seeds sown ⅛ in. deep in well-drained pans or shallow boxes of sandy peat in cool greenhouse or frame Aug. or Sept.; by offsets treated as bulbs Aug. to Nov.

SPECIES CULTIVATED: *G. graminea*, yellow, July, 6 in., S. Africa; *ovata*, yellow, autumn, 6 in., S. Africa.

Gale, see *Myrica Gale.*

Galeandra—*Orchidaceae.* An epiphytic and terrestrial genus. Pseudo-bulbs generally leafy, stem-like. Racemes terminal. Flowers moderately large and attractive.

CULTURE: Compost, three parts of osmunda fibre or peat, with crushed potsherds, one part sphagnum moss, one part loam fibre. Expose in autumn to light, then rest in 60° with occasional waterings. Summer temp. near tropical.

PROPAGATION: By division of plants in spring.

SPECIES CULTIVATED: A selection—*G. Batemanii* (syn. *G. Baueri* (Bateman)), yellowish, whitish, rose-purple, spur yellow, summer, Guatemala, Mexico; *Baueri* (Lindl.), yellowish, flushed purple-brown, spur horizontal, summer, autumn, Brazil; *Devoniana*, brownish-purple, purple, whitish, summer, autumn, Brazil; *flaveola*, yellowish, summer, Brazil, Venezuela; *lacustris* (syn. *G. d'Escagnolleana*), brownish, white and sulphur-yellow, purple rose, summer, Brazil; *lagoensis*, purple and yellow, terrestrial, summer, Brazil; *nivalis*, olive-green, white, summer, Brazil.

Galega—*Leguminosae.* Hardy perennial herbs. First introduced mid-sixteenth century.

CULTURE: Soil, ordinary. Position, open borders or shrubberies. Plant, Oct. to March. Cut down flower stems in Oct. Replant every two or three years.

PROPAGATION: By seeds sown ¼ in. deep in April in ordinary soil in sunny position; division of roots Oct. to March.

SPECIES CULTIVATED: *G. officinalis*, 'Goat's Rue', blue, summer, 3 to 5 ft., S. Europe, and vars. *alba*, white, *Hartlandii*, blue; *orientalis*, blue, summer, 2 to 3 ft., Caucasus.

Galingale, see Cyperus.

Galium (Bedstraw)—*Rubiaceae.* Hardy herbaceous perennials.

CULTURE: Soil, ordinary. Position, sunny borders or rock gardens. Plant, Oct. or March.

PROPAGATION: By division when planting or by seeds sown outdoors in April.

SPECIES CULTIVATED: *G. Mollugo*, white, summer, 3 ft., Europe; *olympicum*, white, summer, 2 to 3 ft., Medit. Region; *purpureum*, brownish-red, summer, 9 to 12 in., S. Europe; *pyrenaicum*, white, 1 to 2 ft., summer, Pyrenees; *rubrum*, brown-red, 1½ ft., midsummer, S. Europe.

Galtonia (Spire Lily)—*Liliaceae.* Hardy bulbous flowering plant.

OUTDOOR CULTURE: Soil, ordinary rich, well drained. Position, open sunny borders. Plant, Oct. to March, placing bulbs 6 in. deep and 6 in. apart. Lift and replant only when the bulbs show signs of deterioration.

POT CULTURE: Compost, two parts loam, one part decayed manure and silver sand. Position, cold or warm greenhouse. Pot, Oct. to Dec. to flower in spring; Feb. to April to flower in autumn. Place one bulb with apex just showing through surface of soil in a well-drained 6 in. pot. Cover with ashes in cold frame until growth begins. Water moderately when leaves appear, freely when in full growth; keep nearly dry after flowering. Apply weak liquid manure occasionally to plants in flower. Bulbs not capable of flowering second time in pots.

PROPAGATION: By seeds sown ⅛ in. deep in shallow boxes of sandy soil in cold frame Oct. or March; offsets treated as bulbs in autumn. Seedlings flower when four or five years old.

SPECIES CULTIVATED: *G. candicans* (syn. *Hyacinthus candicans*), white, fragrant, summer, 2 to 3 ft., S. Africa.

Garcinia—*Guttiferae*. Stove evergreen trees. The fruit of one species is edible and juice of others yields the gamboge of commerce. First introduced late eighteenth century.

CULTURE: Compost, two parts peat, one part loam and sand. Position, pots or boxes in light part of plant stove. Pot and prune, Feb. to March. Temp., March to Oct. 65° to 85°, Oct. to March 55° to 65°. Water moderately Sept. to April, freely other times.

PROPAGATION: By cuttings of firm shoots 2 to 3 in. long inserted in silver sand under bell-glass in temp. 75° to 85° in spring or summer.

SPECIES CULTIVATED: *G. Cambogia*, 'Gamboge-tree', yellow, Nov., 40 ft., E. Indies; *Mangostana*, 'Mangosteen-tree', red, June, 6 to 10 ft., Molucca Islands; *Morella*, 'Ceylon Gamboge', yellowish, 30 ft., India, Malaya.

Gardenia—*Rubiaceae*. Stove evergreen flowering shrubs or small trees. First introduced mid-eighteenth century.

CULTURE: Compost, one part loam, one part peat, one part well-decayed manure and charcoal. Position, well-drained pots, or beds in plant stove. Pot or plant, Feb. or March. Prune into shape, Feb. or March. Temp., March to Sept. 65° to 85°, Sept. to March 55° to 65°. Water moderately Oct. to Feb., freely afterwards. Syringe daily (except when in bloom), March to Sept. Apply liquid manure occasionally to healthy plants in flower. Plants one to two years old produce the best blooms.

PROPAGATION: By cuttings of firm young side shoots 2 to 3 in. long, inserted in well-drained pots of sandy peat under bell-glass in temp. 75° to 85°, Jan. to April.

SPECIES CULTIVATED: *G. grandiflora*, white, fragrant, 20 ft. or more, Cochin-China; *intermedia*, white, fragrant, origin unknown; *jasminoides* (syn. *G. florida*), 'Cape Jasmine', white, fragrant, summer, China and Japan, and vars. *florepleno*, double white, *radicans*, white, fragrant; *Thunbergia*, white, fragrant, Jan. to March, to 10 ft., S. Africa. See also Mitriostigma. For named hybrids see trade lists.

Garland Flower, see *Hedychium coronarium*.

Garlic, see *Allium sativum*.

Garrya—*Garryaceae*. Slightly tender evergreen shrubs. Flowers (pendulous catkins), male and female borne on separate trees. First introduced early nineteenth century.

CULTURE: Soil, ordinary, well drained. Position, against south or west walls outdoors; sheltered shrubberies S. of England. Plant, Oct. to Nov., or March to May. Male plant only cultivated; female plant very rare in gardens.

PROPAGATION: By cuttings of firm shoots 3 to 4 in. long inserted in sandy soil under hand-light or cold frame Aug. to Sept.; layering shoots in Sept.

SPECIES CULTIVATED: *G. elliptica*, silvery catkins up to 12 in. long, Nov. to Feb., 6 to 12 ft., California; *Thuretii*, a vigorous hybrid with insignificant catkins, but useful as a very fast growing windbreak in maritime and warm localities, 15 ft.

Gas Plant, see *Dictamnus albus*.

Gasteria—*Liliaceae*. Greenhouse succulent plants, stemless, or nearly so, with long thick leaves in rosettes, and flowers in loose racemes. First introduced early eighteenth century.

CULTURE: Compost, two parts loam, one part peat, old mortar and river sand. Position, well-drained pots in sunny greenhouse or window. Pot, March or April. Water moderately April to Sept. Temp., March to Sept. 55° to 65°, Sept. to March 50° to 55°.

PROPAGATION: By seeds sown $\frac{1}{16}$ in. deep in well-drained pots or pans of sandy soil, temp. 65°, March to Aug.

SPECIES CULTIVATED: *G. acinacifolia*, orange, summer, S. Africa; *brevifolia*, red, July, S. Africa; *carinata*, red, summer, S. Africa; *Croucheri*, rose, Aug., S. Africa; *lingua* (syn. *G. disticha*), scarlet, July, S. Africa; *pulchra*, scarlet, summer, S. Africa; *verrucosa*, red, July, 3 to 4 in., S. Africa.

× **Gaulnettya**—*Ericaceae.* Hardy evergreen shrub. Bigeneric hybrid between Pernettya and Gaultheria.

CULTURE: Soil, peaty, cool. Position, semi-shaded or north-facing.

PROPAGATION: By cuttings taken in Aug.; layers.

SPECIES CULTIVATED: *G. wisleyensis*, white, 1 to 2 ft., May to June, hybrid.

Gaultheria—*Ericaceae.* Hardy or half-hardy evergreen shrubs with red, purple or blue berries. First introduced mid-eighteenth century.

CULTURE: Soil, peaty. Position, moist rockeries or margins of open or shady shrubberies and beds. Plant, Sept. to Nov., or March to May.

PROPAGATION: By seeds sown $\frac{1}{4}$ in. deep in bed of peaty soil outdoors in autumn, or removal of rooted offsets in spring.

SPECIES CULTIVATED: *G. adenothrix*, white, June, berries red, 1 ft., Japan; *codonantha*, greenish white, summer, 7 ft., Assam, cool greenhouse; *cuneata*, white, June, 9 in., W. China; *Forrestii*, white, June, berries blue, 3 ft., W. China; *Miqueliana*, white or pinkish, June, berries white, 1 ft., Japan; *nummularioides*, white and pink, summer, trailing, Himalaya; *procumbens*, 'Canada Tea' 'Partridge Berry', 'Creeping Wintergreen', white, July, creeping, N. America; *Shallon*, 'Shallon', white and red, May, 4 ft., N.W. America; *tetramera*, white, June, berries varying shades of blue, W. China; *trichophylla*, pink, May, 3 to 6 in., Himalaya; *Veitchiana*, white, early summer, 1 to 3 ft., W. China.

Gaura—*Onagraceae.* Hardy perennial, but usually grown as an annual.

CULTURE: Position, sunny well-drained beds or borders. Plant, March or April.

PROPAGATION: By seeds sown $\frac{1}{16}$ in. deep in light soil outdoors April.

SPECIES CULTIVATED: *G. Lindheimeri*, white and rose, July to Oct., 3 to 4 ft., Texas.

Gaya, see Hoheria.

Gaylussacia (Huckleberry)—*Ericaceae.* Evergreen or deciduous berry-bearing shrubs. First introduced mid-eighteenth century.

CULTURE AND PROPAGATION: As for Vaccinium.

SPECIES CULTIVATED: *G. baccata* (syn. *G. resinosa*), reddish, fruits black, 1 to 3 ft., Eastern N. America; *brachycera*, white or pink, berries blue, 6 to 12 in., Eastern U.S.A.; *dumosa*, white to red, berries black, 1 to 2 ft., Eastern N. America; *frondosa*, greenish-purple, berries blue, 3 to 6 ft., Eastern U.S.A.

Gazania (Treasure-flower)—*Compositae.* Half-hardy perennials. First introduced mid-eighteenth century.

CULTURE: Compost, two parts loam, one part peat and sand. Position, well-drained pots in sunny part of greenhouse, or planted outdoors in summer in sunny place on rockery, edging to beds, etc. Pot, March or April. Plant outdoors June. Water very little Oct. to March, moderately other times. Prune into shape, March. Temp., March to Sept. 55° to 75°, Sept. to March 45° to 55°.

PROPAGATION: By cuttings of side shoots removed from base of plant and inserted in boxes of sandy soil or in a bed in cold frame July to Sept.; cuttings may remain in cold frame if protected from frost; seeds sown in sandy soil during early spring in temp. 65°.

SPECIES CULTIVATED: *G. montana*, yellow and black, summer, 6 to 8 in.; *Pavonia*, yellow, brown, and white, summer, 12 in., S. Africa; *rigens*, yellow and black, June, 1 ft., S. Africa; *splendens*, orange, black, and white, summer, 1 ft., hybrid, var. *variegata*, foliage creamy-white, flowers orange, black, and white. Also many hybrid vars. of varying colours.

Genista (Broom)—*Leguminosae*. Hardy deciduous flowering shrubs of high orna" mental value, and easily grown; excellent for dry banks and stony ground.

CULTURE: Soil, ordinary. Position, shrubbery for tall species, rockery for dwarf. Plant, Oct. to March. Prune after flowering.

PROPAGATION: By seeds sown ¼ in. deep outdoors in March or April; grafting on laburnum in March; budding on similar stocks in July.

SPECIES CULTIVATED: *G. aethnensis*, yellow, June to Aug., 6 to 12 ft., Sicily; *anglica*, ' Needle Furze ', yellow, May and June, 1 to 2 ft., Britain; *hispanica*, ' Spanish Broom ', yellow, May to July, fragrant, 1 to 2 ft., rounded, N.W. Europe; *pilosa*, yellow, May to June, 1 to 1½ ft., Europe (Br.); *radiata*, yellow, summer, 2 to 4 ft., S. Europe; *silvestris*, spiny, yellow, June and July, S.E. Europe, var. *pungens* (syn. *G. dalmatica*), more spiny; *tinctoria*, ' Dyer's Greenweed ', yellow, July to Sept., 1 to 2 ft., Britain, var. *virgata*, more vigorous than type.

Gentiana (Gentian)—*Gentianaceae*. Hardy perennials.

CULTURE: Compost, two parts good loam, one part peat, one part grit or broken limestone and coarse sand. Position, sunny rock garden for dwarf kinds, borders for tall species. All should be kept fairly dry in winter, moist in summer. Plant, Sept., Oct., March or April, top-dress with rotted leaf-mould in March. *G. amoena, Andrewsii, Cachemirica, calycosa, depressa, Farreri, hexa-Farreri, hexaphylla, Kurroo, Lawrencei, Loderi, ornata, Pneumonanthe, prolata, sikkimensis, sino-ornata, strangulata and Waltonii* dislike lime.

PROPAGATION: By seeds sown ⅟₁₆ in. deep in well-drained pots or pans of sandy soil in cold frame in March; division of plants in March. Seeds sometimes take one or two years to germinate and soil must be kept moderately moist.

SPECIES CULTIVATED: *G. acaulis*, ' Gentianella ', blue, spring, 3 in., Europe, and numerous vars.; *amoena*, white and blue, late summer, 3 in., Himalaya; *Andrewsii*, blue, 12 in., June to July, prefers a north aspect, N. America; *asclepiadea*, ' Willow Gentian ', blue, 2 ft., July to Aug., Europe, and var. *alba*; *bavarica*, blue, 1 to 2 in., spring, Europe; *bellidifolia*, white, 6 in., late summer, New Zealand; *brachyphylla*, blue, 2 in., spring, Europe; *cachemirica*, blue, 4 to 6 in., late summer, Kashmir; *calycosa*, blue, 12 in., July, N. America; *depressa*, blue, 3 in., Aug., Himalaya; *Farreri*, Cambridge blue, 4 in., Aug. to Sept., Asia; *Froelichii*, light blue, 2 to 3 in., June to July, Austria; *glauca*, deep blue, 2 to 3 in., July, N. America; *gracilipes*, blue, procumbent, July to Aug., China; *hascombensis*, blue, 12 in., late summer, hybrid; *hexa-Farreri*, blue, 3 to 4 in., autumn, hybrid; *hexaphylla*, blue, 3 in., late summer, Asia; *Kurroo*, blue, 6 to 9 in., late summer, Kashmir; *Lawrencei*, blue, procumbent, late summer, Asia; *Loderi*, blue, 4 to 6 in., late summer, Kashmir; *lutea*, yellow, 3 ft., summer, Europe; *Olivieri* (syn. *G. dahurica*), pale blue, 9 in., late summer, Asia Minor; *ornata* (syn. *G. Veitchiorum*), blue, 2 in., autumn, Nepal; *Pneumonanthe*, blue, 9 in., late summer, Europe (Br.); *prolata*, blue, 1 to 2 in., late summer, Sikkim; *pumila*, blue, 2 in., May, Europe; *punctata*, yellow, spotted purple, 18 in., July to Aug., Europe; *pyrenaica*, blue, 3 in., spring and summer, Pyrenees; *saxosa*, white, 3 in., summer, New Zealand; *septemfida*, blue, 9 to 12 in., late summer, Asia, and var. *Lagodechiana*, blue, single flowers on prostrate stems; *sikkimensis*, blue, prostrate, late summer, Sikkim; *sino-ornata*, blue, 3 in., autumn, China; *strangulata*, blue, prostrate, autumn, Tibet; *verna*, blue, 2 to 3 in., spring, Europe (Br.), and var. *alata*, larger, finer form; *Waltonii*, blue, 9 to 12 in., late summer, Tibet. There are numerous hybrids between the Asiatic species, all of which are lime haters and autumn flowering. The name *G. acaulis*, no longer used by botanists, covers two wild species (*G. Clusii* and *G. Kochiana*) and *G. excisa* (syn. *G. hortorum*); the plant commonly cultivated as ' *G. acaulis* ' is probably a hybrid.

Geodorum—*Orchidaceae*. A terrestrial genus with tuberous rootstocks. Leaves deciduous or nearly so. Scapes usually basal with the new growth.

CULTURE: Much as for Phaius. Compost, three parts fibrous loam, one part chopped sphagnum, one part peat fibre, with sand. A rest must be given in winter, temp. 55° to 60°. Summer temp. 65° to 80° with shading. Well-drained pots; water freely.

PROPAGATION: By offsets if they occur.

SPECIES CULTIVATED: *G. candidum*, white, lip marked red and yellow, summer, Moulmein; *citrinum*, greenish-white, lip yellowish, summer, autumn, Burma, etc.; *dilatatum*, whitish, flesh colour, summer, India, Burma; *pictum*, variable, pink to rose, red-veined on lip, summer, New Guinea, Australia.

Geonoma—*Palmae*. Stove palm with feather-shaped pale green leaves. First introduced early nineteenth century.

CULTURE: Compost, two parts peat, one part loam, sand and charcoal. Position, pots in moist shady part of plant stove. Pot, Feb. or March. Water freely Oct. to Feb., abundantly other times. Syringe daily. Temp., Sept. to March 55° to 65°, March to Sept. 65° to 70°.

PROPAGATION: By seeds sown 1 in. deep in above compost in pots in temp. 85°, March; offshoots from base of plants in small pots in temp. 80° to 85°, any time.

SPECIES CULTIVATED: *G. gracilis*, 6 ft., Costa Rica; *pumila*, dwarf species, Colombia.

Geranium (Cranesbill)—*Geraniaceae*. Hardy herbaceous perennials. For greenhouse ' Geraniums ' see Pelargonium.

CULTURE: Soil, ordinary rich. Position, tall kinds in sunny well-drained borders, dwarf kinds on sunny rockeries. Plant, Oct., Nov., March or April. Apply weak liquid manure occasionally to established plants in flower.

PROPAGATION: By seeds sown ½ in. deep in ordinary soil in sunny position outdoors, March or April, or in shallow boxes of sandy soil in cold frame or greenhouse, March; division of roots, Oct., Nov., March or April.

SPECIES CULTIVATED: *G. argenteum*, rose, summer, 1 ft., Alps, var. *purpureum*, intense crimson-red; *cinereum*, red, summer, 6 in., Pyrenees, var. *album*, white; *dalmaticum* (syns. *G. macrorrhizum dalmaticum*, *G. microrrhizum*), light rose, June, 4 in., Dalmatia; *Endressii*, rose, summer, 1 ft., Pyrenees; *Farreri*, pink, May, 3 in., Asia; *grandiflorum*, bluish-mauve, June to Sept., 6 in., Himalayas; *ibericum*, blue, summer, 1 ft., Caucasus; *phaeum*, purplish-brown, May to July, 1 ft., Europe; *pratense*, blue, summer, 2 to 3 ft., Britain, and its double blue and double white vars.; *psilostemon* (syn. *G. armenum*), purple, June and July, 2 ft., Orient; *Pylzowianum*, pale pink, summer, 6 to 9 in., Tibet; *Robertianum*, ' Herb Robert ,' annual or biennial, red-purple, 1½ ft., N. America; *sanguineum*, crimson, summer, 2 ft., Britain, and vars. *album*, white, *prostratum*, dwarf form; *sylvaticum*, blue, summer, 2 to 3 ft., Britain; *tuberosum*, purple, June, 9 in., S. Europe.

Gerbera (Transvaal Daisy)—*Compositae*. Greenhouse perennial herbs. First introduced late nineteenth century.

CULTURE: Grow in a compost of sandy loam and peat in a temp. of 45° to 50° from Nov. to May, without artificial heat afterwards. Water sparingly from Nov. to April; freely afterwards. Repot annually in spring. No shade required. *G. Jamesonii* may be grown outdoors in warm nooks in mild districts.

PROPAGATION: By seeds sown in sandy peat in March in temp. of 55°; cuttings of side shoots in spring.

SPECIES CULTIVATED: *G. asplenifolia*, purple, summer, 1 ft., S. Africa; *Jamesonii*, ' Barberton Daisy ', orange-scarlet, June to Oct., 18 in., S. Africa. Also various coloured hybrids.

German Catchfly, see *Lychnis Viscaria*; **-Iris,** see *I. germanica*; **-Ivy,** see *Senecio mikanioides*.

Germander, see Teucrium.

Gesneria—*Gesneriaceae*. Stove tuberous-rooted herbaceous perennials. Flowering and ornamental foliage. Some authorities have transferred these plants to Corytholoma or Smithiantha. First introduced mid-eighteenth century.

CULTURE: Compost, two parts fibrous peat, one part loam, one part leaf-mould, with a little decayed manure and silver sand. Position, well-drained pots or pans in shady part of plant stove. Pot, March to flower in summer; May to flower in autumn; June to flower in winter. Place tubers 1 in. deep singly in 5 in. pots, or 1 to 2 in. apart in larger sizes. Water moderately from time growth begins until plants are 3 or 4 in. high, then freely. After flowering gradually withhold water till foliage dies down, then keep dry till potting time. Apply weak liquid manure once or twice a week when flower buds show. Syringing not required. Temp., March to Sept. 65° to 85°, Sept. to March 55° to 65°. Store when foliage has died down on their sides under stage till potting time in temp. of 50° to 55°.

PROPAGATION: By seeds sown on surface of well-drained pots of sandy peat, in temp. 75°, March or April; cuttings of young shoots inserted in pots of sandy peat in temp. 75° to 85° in spring; fully matured leaves pegged on surface of pots in sandy peat in temp. 75° to 85°; stalk ends of leaves inserted vertically in pans of sandy peat in temp. 75° to 85°.

SPECIES CULTIVATED: *G. cardinalis*, scarlet and white, autumn, 12 to 18 in.; *Cooperi*, scarlet, drooping habit, May, Brazil; *Donklarii*, red and yellow, 2 ft., summer, Colombia; *Douglasii*, red and yellow, autumn, 18 in., Brazil; *exoniensis*, orange, scarlet and yellow, winter, 1 ft., hybrid; *Leopoldii*, scarlet, summer, 1 ft., Brazil; *Lindleyi*, yellow and scarlet, July, 1 ft., Brazil; *naegelioides*, rosy pink, autumn, 18 in.; *refulgens*, violet and white, summer, 18 in.; hybrid; *tuberosa*, scarlet, 1 ft., Brazil. See also Isoloma and Naegelia.

Gethyllis—*Amaryllidaceae*. Greenhouse bulbous plants. First introduced mid-eighteenth century.

CULTURE: Compost, equal parts peat, loam and sand. Position, well-drained pots in cold greenhouse or frame. Pot, Aug. to Nov., placing bulbs singly in 5 in. pots, with points just below surface. Cover with ashes in cold frame or greenhouse till growth begins. Water moderately from time growth begins till flowers fade; keep quite dry after foliage has died down until potting time. Repot, annually.

PROPAGATION: By seeds sown ¼ in. deep in well-drained pots of sandy soil in cold frame or greenhouse, March or April; offsets treated as bulbs at potting time.

SPECIES CULTIVATED: *G. afra*, red and white, summer, 6 in., S. Africa; *ciliaris*, white, summer, 6 in., S. Africa; *lanceolata*, white, June, 9 in., S. Africa; *spiralis*, ' Cape Crocus ', white, autumn, 9 in., S. Africa; *villosa*, white, June and July, 9 in. S. Africa.

Geum (Avens)—*Rosaceae*. Hardy perennial flowering herbs.

CULTURE: Soil, ordinary rich. Position, tall species in sunny borders, dwarf species on sunny rockeries. Plant, Oct. to April. Cut down flower stems in Sept.

PROPAGATION: By seeds sown 1/16 in. deep in shallow boxes or well-drained pots of light soil in cold frame, March or April, or in sunny positions (similar depth and soil) outdoors, April or July; division of plants, Oct. to April.

SPECIES CULTIVATED: *G. Borisii* (of gardens), orange, summer and autumn, 9 to 12 in.; *chiloense* (syn. *G. coccineum*), scarlet, summer, 2 ft., Chile, and var. *plenum*, and numerous garden forms; *Heldreichii*, orange-red, July, 1 ft.; *montanum*, yellow, May, 2 ft., Europe; *reptans*, yellow, summer, trailing, Europe; *rivale*, old rose, summer, 9 to 12 in., Britain.

Gevuina (Chilean Nut, Chile Hazel)—*Proteaceae*. Half-hardy, evergreen shrub or small tree. Native of Chile. Often wrongly spelt Guevina.

CULTURE: Soil, good loamy. Position, sheltered, semi-shady. May be grown outdoors in Cornwall and similar mild climates but elsewhere needs the protection of a greenhouse in winter. No pruning required.

SPECIES CULTIVATED: *G. Avellana*, white, summer, 10 to 20 ft., occasionally more.

Giant Bellflower, see Ostrowskia; **-Fennel,** see *Ferula communis*; **-Fern Palm, see** *Macrozamia Peroffskyana*; **-Groundsel,** see *Ligularia Wilsoniana*; **-Lily, see**

Cardiocrinum giganteum; **-Sequoia,** see *Sequoiadendron giganteum*; **-Reed,** see *Arundo Donax*; **-Water Thyme,** see Lagarosiphon.

Gilia—*Polemoniaceae.* Annuals, biennials and sub-shrubs, some hardy, including species formerly known as Hugelia and Linanthus. First introduced early nineteenth century.

CULTURE OF HARDY ANNUALS: Soil, ordinary. Position, sunny beds or borders. Sow seeds $\frac{1}{16}$ in. deep in April where plants are to flower, thinning seedlings in May to 3 in. apart.

CULTURE OF BIENNIALS: Soil, ordinary. Position, sunny beds or borders. Sow in pans or boxes in January in temp. 55° to 60°, pricking out seedlings as soon as large enough to handle and hardening off for planting out in May.

CULTURE OF SUB-SHRUBS: Compost, equal parts fibrous loam, leaf-mould and sand. Sow in pans or boxes in late summer or early autumn in temp. 60° to 65°. Prick out seedlings when large enough and grow on in same temp., either hardening off plants in spring for planting outdoors or else potting them singly for flowering in the greenhouse.

ANNUAL SPECIES CULTIVATED: *G. achilleaefolia*, purplish-blue, Aug., 1 ft., California; *androsacea*, lilac, pink, and white, Aug., 1 ft., California; *densiflora* (syn. *Hugelia densiflora*), lilac, June, 6 in., var. *alba*, white; *dianthoides* (syn. *Fenzlia dianthiflora*), lilac and yellow, July, 4 in., California; *liniflora*, white, summer, 1 ft., California; *micrantha* (syn. *Leptosiphon roseus*), rose, summer, 9 in., California; *tricolor*, orange and purple, June, 1 ft., California.

BIENNIAL SPECIES CULTIVATED: *G. rubra* (syn. *G. coronopifolia*), scarlet, summer, 9 to 18 in., California.

SUB-SHRUBBY SPECIES CULTIVATED: *G. californica*, ' Prickly Phlox ', pink, July, 3 ft., California; *montana* (syn. *Linanthus montanus*), white, to 10 in., California, Oregon.

Gillenia—*Rosaceae.* Hardy perennials. First introduced early eighteenth century.

CULTURE: Soil, peaty. Position, moist shady bed or border. Plant, Oct. to Dec. or March. Cut down flowering stems in Sept.

PROPAGATION: By division of roots in March or April.

SPECIES CULTIVATED: *G. stipulata*, white, June, 1 to 2 ft., N. America; *trifoliata*, ' Indian Physic ', red or white, July, 2 ft., N. America.

Gillyflower, see *Dianthus Caryophyllus* and *Cheiranthus Cheri.*

Ginkgo (Maidenhair Tree)—*Ginkgoaceae.* Hardy deciduous coniferous tree with ornamental foliage attractively tinted in autumn. First introduced mid-eighteenth century.

CULTURE: Soil, ordinary, well drained. Position, sheltered shrubberies or lawns in the south, against south or west walls elsewhere. Plant Oct. to Feb.

PROPAGATION: By seeds in light sandy soil in cold frame Oct. to March.

SPECIES CULTIVATED: *G. biloba* (syn. *Salisburia adiantifolia*), fruit small, globular, 60 to 80 ft., China, **var.** *pendula*, ' Weeping Maidenhair Tree '.

Ginseng, see Panax.

Gladiolus (Sword Lily)—*Iridaceae.* Half-hardy bulbous flowering plants. First introduced late sixteenth century.

TYPES: Large flowered—Habit vigorous; colours various; height, 2 to 4 ft.; individual flowers open, 4 to 8 in. in diameter. Primulinus: Habit less vigorous but free flowering; colours various; height, 1½ to 3 ft.; individual flowers hooded, 1 to 2 in. in diameter. There are now many hybrids intermediate between these two classes. Colvillei: Flowers small, widely open, early, usually grown under glass.

OUTDOOR CULTURE: Soil, deep rich, liberally manured. Position, sunny well-drained beds or borders. Plant in late March or April. Place corms 4 in. deep and 6 in. apart. Apply liquid manure when flower buds form. Fix sticks to spikes when 2 or 3 in. high. Lift corms in Nov., dry off in a frost-proof shed or greenhouse, remove old shrivelled corms, which are useless, from the base of the new corms and store latter in shallow trays in an airy place secure from frost.

POT CULTURE: Compost, two parts loam, one part well-decayed manure and river sand. Position, pots in cold frame, cool greenhouse or window. Pot Colvillei vars. Oct. or Nov., placing five corms 1 in. deep in a 6 in. pot; late kinds March or April, one 1 in. deep in a 6 in. pot or three 1 in. deep in an 8 in. pot. Place pots in cold frame till flower spikes show, then remove to greenhouse or window. Water moderately at first, freely afterwards. Apply liquid manure when flower spikes show. After flowering gradually withhold water till foliage dies, then clean of. corms and store in trays as with those grown outdoors. Forcing: Pot early kinds Oct. to Dec. Temp., 55° to 65°.

PROPAGATION: By seeds sown ½ in. deep in pans of light rich soil in Feb., in temp. 55° to 65°; by bulbils (spawn) growing at base of corms, planted 2 in. deep and 6 in. apart in sunny border outdoors, March. Seedlings flower when three years old; bulbils when two years old.

SPECIES CULTIVATED: *G. blandus*, white, red, and yellow, June, 18 in., S. Africa; *byzantinus*, red and purple, June, 2 ft., Asia Minor; *cardinalis*, scarlet, July and Aug., 3 to 4 ft., S. Africa; *Colvillei*, crimson and white, summer, 2 ft., hybrid; *communis*, ' Corn Flag ', rose, June to Aug., 1 to 2 ft., S. Europe; *cruentus*, scarlet and white, Sept., 2 to 3 ft., Natal; *primulinus*, ' Maid of the Mist ', golden yellow, fragrant, Aug., 3 to 4 ft., Trop. Africa; *psittacinus*, scarlet and yellow, summer, 3 ft., S. Africa; *purpureo-auratus*, yellow and purple, Aug., 3 to 4 ft., S. Africa; *Saundersii*, crimson, pink and white, autumn, 2 to 3 ft., S. Africa; *tristis*, red and yellow, July, 1 ft., Natal. There are many hybrids and vars. in trade catalogues. See also Watsonia and Acidanthera.

Gladwyn, see *Iris foetidissima.*

Glastonbury Thorn, see *Crataegus monogyna* var. *biflora.*

Glaucidium—*Ranunculaceae.* Herbaceous perennial plants.
CULTURE: Soil, deep, cool, peaty or leaf-mould, perfectly drained. Position, north aspect or partial shade.
PROPAGATION: By careful division of old plants when growth commences.
SPECIES CULTIVATED: *G. palmatum*, deep lilac, 12 in., April to May, Japan.

Glaucium (Horned Poppy; Sea Poppy)—*Papaveraceae.* Hardy biennials.
CULTURE: Soil, ordinary rich. Position, sunny well-drained beds or borders.
PROPAGATION: By seeds sown $\frac{1}{16}$ in. deep in beds of light soil outdoors in May, transplanting seedlings into flowering position in July or Aug.
SPECIES CULTIVATED: *G. corniculatum*, crimson and black, summer, 9 in., Medit. Region, and var. *rubrum* red; *flavum* (syn. *G. luteum*), yellow, summer, 1 to 2 ft., Europe (Br.), etc.

Glecoma—*Labiatae.* Creeping hardy perennial, useful for ground cover in both exposed and shady places.
CULTURE: Soil, ordinary. Position, sunny or shady. *G. hederacea* makes a good basket plant for a cool greenhouse or window or for draping staging in greenhouse.
PROPAGATION: By seeds; division.
SPECIES CULTIVATED: *G. hederacea* (syns. *Nepeta Glechoma, N. hederacea*), ' Ground Ivy, ' Field Balm ', light blue, leaves silvery, trailing, Europe (Br.), and var. *variegata*, leaves variegated.

Gleditsia—*Leguminosae* (or *Caesalpiniaceae*). Hardy ornamental deciduous trees with green, feather-shaped leaves and shoots armed with exceptional spines, up to 6 in. long on *G. caspica*. First introduced early eighteenth century.
CULTURE: Soil, ordinary. Position, sheltered borders or shrubberies. Plant, Oct. to Feb.
PROPAGATION: By seeds sown in light soil outdoors in March, transplant seedlings when two years old.
SPECIES CULTIVATED: *G. aquatica* (syn. *G. monosperma*), ' Water Locust ', green,

July, 20 to 30 ft., United States; *caspica*, green, 20 to 30 ft., N. Persia; *triacanthos*, ' Honey Locust ', ' Three-thorned Acacia ', green, summer, 30 to 60 ft., attractive frond-like leaves, United States.

Gleichenia (Umbrella Fern; Net Fern)—*Gleicheniaceae.* Ornamental stove and greenhouse ferns with feather-shaped fronds and creeping stems. First introduced early nineteenth century.

CULTURE: Compost, two parts fibrous peat, one part fibrous loam, charcoal and sand. Position, well-drained pans in shady stove or greenhouse. Pot, Feb. or March. Water moderately in winter, freely at other times. Syringing unnecessary. Temp. stove species, Sept. to March 55° to 65°, March to Sept. 65° to 75°; greenhouse species, Sept. to March 45° to 50°, March to Sept. 55° to 65°.

PROPAGATION: By spores sown on surface of sandy peat in well-drained pots under bell-glass at any time of year; division of creeping stems, Feb. or March.

STOVE SPECIES CULTIVATED: *G. cincinnata* (syn. *G. microphylla*), 6 ft., Australia, New Zealand, Malay; *dicarpa*, 6 ft., Australia, New Zealand; *linearis* (syn. *G. dichotoma*), 6 ft., Tropics; *rupestris*, 6 ft., Tropics.

Globularia (Globe Daisy)—*Globulariaceae.* Hardy sub-shrubs and perennial herbs. First introduced early seventeenth century.

CULTURE: Soil, ordinary moist. Position, sunny rockeries or margins of borders. Plant, Oct., Nov., March or April. *G. Alypum* may be grown in a greenhouse.

PROPAGATION: By seeds sown on surface in boxes of light sandy soil in cold frame in March or April; division of plants, Oct. or April.

SPECIES CULTIVATED: *G. Alypum*, blue, Aug., 2 ft., shrubby, S. Europe; *cordifolia*, blue, June, 6 in., shrubby, S. Europe; *incanescens*, blue, 6 in., summer, S. Europe; *nudicaulis*, blue, summer, 6 in., herbaceous, Europe; *repens* (syn. *G. nana*), blue, 1 in., summer, Europe; *stygia*, blue, 4 in., summer, Greece; *trichosantha*, blue, summer, 6 to 8 in., herbaceous, Asia Minor; *vulgaris*, blue, summer, 6 to 12 in., herbaceous, S. Europe.

Globe Amaranth, see *Gomphrena globosa*; **-Artichoke,** see *Cynara Scolymus*; **-Flower,** see *Trollius europaeus*; **-Mallow,** see Sphaeralcea; **-Thistle,** see Echinops.

Gloriosa—*Liliaceae.* Stove flowering, deciduous, tuberous-rooted climbers. First introduced late seventeenth century.

CULTURE: Compost, equal parts loam, peat, leaf-mould, decayed manure and silver sand. Position, well-drained pots, with shoots trained to roof or trellis. Pot, Feb., placing tubers 2 in. deep, one in a 6 in. pot or several in an 8 or 12 in. pot. Water moderately till growth is well advanced, then freely. After flowering gradually withhold water and keep soil quite dry till potting time. Temp., Feb. to Sept. 70° to 85°, Sept. to Feb. 55° to 65°.

PROPAGATION: By seeds inserted singly ¼ in. deep in 3 in. pots filled with light soil in temp. 75° in Feb. or March; offsets removed from large tubers at potting time.

SPECIES CULTIVATED: *G. Carsonii*, yellow and brown, 6 to 8 ft., Trop. Africa; *Rothschildiana*, ruby red and yellow, summer, Uganda; *superba*, ' Glory Flower ', orange and red, summer, 6 to 10 ft., Tropics; *virescens*, ' Mozambique Lily ', yellow and red, summer, 5 ft., Trop. Africa, and vars. *Plantii* and *grandiflora.*

Glory Bower, see Clerodendron; **-Flower,** see Eccremocarpus; **-Lily,** see Gloriosa; **-of-the-Marsh,** see *Primula helodoxa*; **-of-the-Snow,** see Chionodoxa; **-of-the-Sun,** see *Leucocoryne ixioides*; **-Pea,** see *Clianthus Dampieri.*

Glottiphyllum—*Aizoaceae.* Greenhouse succulent plants.

CULTURE: Compost, six parts sharp sand, three parts rich loam, two parts leaf-mould, one part each mortar rubble and crushed brick. Position, well-drained pots in sunny greenhouse or window, or bed on greenhouse staging. Between June and Sept. may be put outside in sunny, very sandy position, not watered, and protected from excess rain. Plant or pot, June. Water sparingly, June to

Jan.; keep dry rest of year. Temp., Oct. to Jan. 40° to 55°, Feb. to Mar. 35° to 45°, April to Sept. 45° and over.

PROPAGATION: By seeds sown in close atmosphere, temp. 55° to 60°, April or Sept.; stem cuttings, which should first be well dried, June, temp. 60°.

SPECIES CULTIVATED: (A selection). *G. depressum*, yellow, Sept. to Jan., S. Africa; *linguiforme* (syn. *Mesembryanthemum linguiforme*), yellow, Sept. to Jan., S. Africa; *longum* (syn. *M. longum, M. pustulatum*), yellow, Sept. to Jan., S. Africa.

Gloxinia, see Sinningia.

Glycine—*Leguminosae.* Erect or twining plants grown for human food, forage and oil. Much grown in the East.

CULTURE: As for French Bean, but a sunny and sheltered position should be chosen.

PROPAGATION: By seed.

SPECIES CULTIVATED: *G. Max* (syns. *G. Soja, G. hispida, Soja Max*), ' Soybean ', ' Soya ', white or purple, inconspicuous, pods to 3 in. long, brown and hairy, erect to 1 to 6 ft., annual, China, Japan.

Glycyrrhiza—*Leguminosae.* Hardy herbaceous perennials. Liquorice is obtained from the roots of *G. glabra.* First introduced mid-sixteenth century.

CULTURE: Soil, deep, rich sandy. Position, open sunny. Plant, Feb. or March, 18 in. apart and 3 in. deep in rows 3 ft. asunder. Cut down foliage and remove creeping stems close to root in Nov. Roots ready for use the third year.

PROPAGATION: By division of creeping stems in Feb. or March.

SPECIES CULTIVATED: *G. glabra*, ' Liquorice ', blue, May to Sept., 3 ft., Medit. Region; *lepidota*, ' Wild Liquorice ', yellow, to 5 ft., N. America.

Gnidia—*Thymelaeaceae.* Greenhouse evergreen flowering shrubs. First introduced mid-eighteenth century.

CULTURE: Compost, two parts fibrous peat, one part loam and silver sand. Position, well-drained pots near glass in airy greenhouse during autumn, winter and spring, cold frame June to Sept. Pot, March. Press compost firmly in pots. Prune straggling shoots into shape directly after flowering. Water carefully, giving sufficient to keep soil uniformly moist, rain, not spring, water essential. Temp., Oct. to March 40° to 45°, March to July 45° to 55°.

PROPAGATION: By cuttings of young shoots 2 in. long in sandy peat in well-drained pots under bell-glass in temp. 45° to 55° in March, April or May.

SPECIES CULTIVATED: *G. denudata*, yellow, summer, 18 in., S. Africa; *pinifolia*, white, fragrant, spring, 2 ft., S. Africa.

Goat Root, see *Ononis Natrix*; **-Willow,** see *Salix caprea.*

Goat's Beard, see *Aruncus sylvester*; **-Rue,** see *Galega officinalis*; **-Thorn,** see *Astragalus Tragacantha.*

Godetia—*Onagraceae.* Hardy annuals, related to Oenothera and formerly included in that genus.

CULTURE: Soil, ordinary. Position, sunny or partly shady.

POT CULTURE: Compost, two parts good soil, one part leaf-mould, one part well-decayed manure and sand. Position, well-drained 6 in. pots in cold frame, greenhouse or window. Water moderately at first, freely when in full growth. Apply liquid manure twice weekly when flower buds appear.

PROPAGATION: Sow seeds in March or April where they are to bloom, thin outdoor seedlings to 6 in. apart in June.

SPECIES CULTIVATED: *G. amoena*, ' Farewell to Spring ', rose and crimson, summer, 1 to 2 ft., California; *grandiflora* (syn. *Oenothera Whitneyi*), red, crimson or white, summer, 6 to 12 in., California; *viminea*, purple and crimson with dark centre, short branched, to 2 ft., California. See trade lists for numerous vars.

Goethea—*Malvaceae.* Stove evergreen shrubs. First introduced mid-nineteenth century.

CULTURE: Compost, two parts loam, one part peat and sand. Pot, March Shady position desirable. Water freely from March to Sept., moderately in winter. Syringe freely during summer months. Temp., March to Sept. 65° to 75°, Sept. to March 55° to 65°.

PROPAGATION: By cuttings in sandy soil under bell-glass in steady bottom heat.

SPECIES CULTIVATED: *G. intermedia*, white, 2 ft., hybrid; *kermesina*, white, 1 ft., hybrid; *makoyana*, crimson, 2 ft., Brazil; *strictiflora*, yellowish, tinged red, Aug., 1½ ft., Brazil. See also Pavonia.

Gold Dust, see *Alyssum saxatile*; **-thread**, see Coptis; **-Fern**, see *Pityrogramma calomelanos* var. *aureo-flava*.

Golden Aster, see Chrysopsis; **-Bells**, see Forsythia; **-Chain**, see *Laburnum anagyroides*); **-Club**, see *Orontium aquaticum*; **-Feather**, see *Chrysanthemum Parthenium* var. *aureum*); **-Hair**, see *Chrysocoma coma-aurea*; **-Larch**, see Pseudolarix; **-Lily**, see *Lycoris aurea*; **-Marguerite**, see *Anthemis tinctoria*; **-Rain**, see *Laburnum anagyroides*; **-rod**, see Solidago; **-Saxifrage**, see Chrysosplenium; **-Thistle**, see *Scolymus hispanicus*; **-Star**, see *Chrysogonum virginianum*; **-Wattle**, see *Acacia pycnantha*.

Goldilocks, see *Linosyris vulgaris*.

Gomeza—*Orchidaceae*. An epiphytic genus of about 10 species, allied to Odontoglossum. Scapes often arched from base of pseudo-bulbs. Flowers many, not large, often fragrant.

CULTURE: Compost, etc., as for Odontoglossums. Winter temp. should be 55°, no decided rest, but in winter must not be watered too frequently.

PROPAGATION: By division of plants in spring.

SPECIES CULTIVATED: *G. Barkeri*, greenish-yellow, spring, Brazil; *crispa*, greenish-yellow, primrose scented, winter, spring, Brazil; *planifolia*, greenish-yellow, fragrant, spring, summer, Brazil.

Gomphia—*Ochnaceae*. Stove evergreen flowering shrub.

CULTURE: Compost, two parts fibrous loam, one part peat, little silver sand. Position, pots in light part of plant stove. Pot, Feb. or March. Press compost down firmly in pot. Prune into shape Feb. or March. Water moderately Oct. to March, freely afterwards. Syringe daily in summer. Temp., March to Oct. 65° to 75°, Oct. to March 50° to 60°.

PROPAGATION: By cuttings of firm young shoots, 2 to 3 in. long, inserted in pots of silver sand under bell-glass in temp. 75° in spring.

SPECIES CULTIVATED: *G. decorans*, yellow, spring, 10 to 15 ft., Brazil; *theophrasta*, golden-yellow, May, 10 to 12 ft., Brazil.

Gompholobium—*Leguminosae*. Greenhouse, evergreen, trailing and erect, flowering shrubs. First introduced early nineteenth century.

CULTURE: Compost, two parts rough peat, one part rough loam, charcoal and sand. Position, well-drained pots in light part of greenhouse. Pot, Feb. or March. Prune into shape after flowering. Water carefully at all times. Temp., Sept. to April 45° to 50°, April to Sept. 50° to 60°. Ventilate greenhouse freely in summer.

PROPAGATION: By cuttings of young shoots 2 in. long inserted in well-drained pots of sandy peat under bell-glass in temp. 45° to 55° in March or April.

SPECIES CULTIVATED: *G. grandiflorum*, yellow, June, 2 ft., Australia; *polymorphum*, yellow, scarlet and purple, spring, 2 ft., Australia; *venustum*, purple, spring, 3 ft., Australia.

Gomphrena—*Amaranthaceae*. Greenhouse flowering annual. First introduced early eighteenth century.

CULTURE: Compost, two parts fibrous loam, one part leaf-mould, well-decayed cow manure and sand. Position, warm greenhouse, exposed to light. Sow seeds ⅟₁₆ in. deep in well-drained pots of light soil in temp. 75° in March. Transplant seedlings 1 in. apart when 1 in. high in light soil in well-drained pots and keep in temp. of 60° to 75°. When seedlings have formed four leaves place singly in 4 in. pots. Transfer them in June to 5 in. pots and keep near the glass. Water moderately. Syringe foliage twice daily. Apply liquid manure when flowers appear. Summer temp., 55° to 65°. Cut flowers immediately they are fully developed for drying for winter decoration.

SPECIES CULTIVATED: *G. globosa*, ' Globe Amaranth ', white, red or purple, summer, 12 to 18 in., India, and vars. *aurea superba*, yellow, *carnea*, flesh, *purpurea*, purple, and *nana*, dwarf.

Gongora—*Orchidaceae*. An epiphytic genus with stout ribbed pseudo-bulbs. Spikes usually arched from their base. Flowers often many, grotesque in shape, gaining the title ' Punch and Judy Orchids '.

CULTURE: Compost, temps., etc., as for Stanhopeas, and baskets are preferable.
PROPAGATION: By division of plants in spring.
SPECIES CULTIVATED: A selection—*G. armeniaca* (syn. *Acropera armeniaca*), yellow, summer, Nicaragua; *atropurpurea*, purplish-brown, variable, various seasons, Brazil, British Guiana; *bufonia*, yellowish-white, spotted dull purple, various seasons, Brazil; *galeata* (syn. *Acropera Loddigesii*), tawny yellow, brownish-red, variable, summer, Mexico; *gratulabunda*, yellow, dotted dull red, various seasons, Colombia; *grossa*, whitish or yellowish, spotted purple, summer, Ecuador; *portentosa*, buff yellow, purple spotted, deep yellow, spring, Columbia; *quinquenervis*, yellowish, marked brown-purple, summer, Guatemala, Peru, Brazil; *Sanderiana*, yellowish, brown, rose, lip bright yellow, summer, Peru; *scaphephorus*, yellowish-white, blotched purple-brown and purple, summer, Peru.

Goniophlebium, see Polypodium.

Good King Henry, see *Chenopodium Bonus-Henricus*.

Goodyera—*Orchidaceae*. Terrestrial orchids of the Anoectochilus group in which many species with ornate foliage are included. The habit is that of Anoectochilus. The flowers are small.

CULTURE: Compost for the tropical species as for Anoectochilus, and similar conditions should be given. The hardy species given a compost of leaf-mould, peat and sand. Position, rather shady in drained pockets in rockery. The cool house species: Similar compost and position in well-drained pans. A cool fernery is often suitable.
PROPAGATION: As for Anoectochilus.
SPECIES CULTIVATED: A selection with leaf coloration—*G. colorata*, greenish brown, nerved red-brown, Java; *hispida*, green with rose-red veins, Himalaya; *japonica*, velvet-green, shaded brown, mid-rib white or pink-flushed; *macrantha*, dark green, pale green, bordered yellow, Japan; *pubescens*, green with grey or yellowish stripe and reticulations, N. America; *repens*, dark green with or without green marbling, spiralled, Britain, N. Hemisphere.

Gooseberry, see *Ribes Grossularia*.

Gordonia—*Theaceae* (or *Ternstroemiaceae*). Slightly tender evergreen shrubs with snowy white flowers. First introduced mid-eighteenth century.

CULTURE: Soil, peat and leaf-mould. Position, warm sheltered borders or against south walls. Plant, April.
PROPAGATION: By seeds; layers in spring; greenwood cuttings under glass.
SPECIES CULTIVATED: *G. axillaris* (syn. *G. anomala*), white, summer, 15 ft., S. China; *Lasianthus*, ' Loblolly Bay ', white, to 60 ft., N. America. See also Franklinia.

Gorse, see Ulex.

Gossypium (Cotton-plant)—*Malvaceae*. Stove perennial herbs. Fruit (capsule) furnishes cotton of commerce. First introduced late sixteenth century.

CULTURE: Compost, equal parts loam, leaf-mould and little sand. Position, well-drained pots in sunny part of stove. Pot, March or April. Water moderately Sept. to April, freely afterwards. Temp., March to Oct. 65° to 75°, Oct. to March 55° to 65°.

PROPAGATION: By seeds sown $\frac{1}{16}$ in. deep in light soil in temp. 65° to 75°, March or April. Transplant seedlings when 1 in. high singly into 2 in. pots.

SPECIES CULTIVATED: *G. barbadense*, yellow and purple, Sept., 5 ft., Tropics; *herbaceum*, yellow and purple, summer, 3 to 4 ft., E. Indies.

Grammanthes—*Crassulaceae*. Half-hardy annual. First introduced mid-eighteenth century.

CULTURE: Soil, light sandy. Position, sunny rockeries.

PROPAGATION: By seeds sown on surface of sandy soil in well-drained pans in temp. 60° to 65° in March. Transplant seedlings outdoors in May.

SPECIES CULTIVATED: *G. chloraeflora*, orange-yellow and red, summer, 3 to 4 in., S. Africa.

Grammatocarpus—*Loasaceae*. Half-hardy annual climber.

CULTURE: Sow seeds in gentle heat in March, harden seedlings off later on, and plant in June. Ordinary soil Suitable for low sunny trellises, vases, etc.

SPECIES CULTIVATED: *G. volubilis*, yellow and red, summer, 3 ft., Chile.

Grammatophyllum—*Orchidaceae*. An epiphytic genus in two contrasting sections, one with tall, stout, stem-like pseudo-bulbs forming huge plants, the other with much shorter, stouter pseudo-bulbs; the long spikes are produced from the base. Under cultivation neither of the species given here completes growth in one season.

CULTURE: Compost, three parts of osmunda fibre, one part loam fibre, one part sphagnum moss with potsherds broken according to size of plant. A warm moist atmosphere for all throughout the year, tropical in summer, 65° in winter for the pseudo-bulbed kinds, and a moderate rest. Tall-stemmed species 70° in winter with waterings. Pots well drained, or tubs for the large growing. Shading is required in summer.

PROPAGATION: By division of the plants in spring.

SPECIES CULTIVATED: The following are very similar, so much so that several are considered forms of G. *scriptum*. *G. Fenzlianum*, greenish-yellow, chocolate, summer, Amboina; *Guilielmitii*, greenish, blotched reddish-brown, summer, New Guinea; *Measuresianum*, bright green, purplish, chocolate, Philippines; *multiflorum*, greenish-yellow suffused and marked purple-brown, summer, Philippines; *Rumphianum* (syn. *G. Seegeranum*), pale yellowish-green, blotched brown, lip lined purple, summer, Moluccas, Borneo; *scriptum*, greenish-yellow, spotted dark brown, summer, Moluccas. Species with pseudo-bulbs up to 10 ft. high, scapes 6 or 7 ft. : *papuanum*, large, green, spotted brown-red, the basal flowers are abortive, spring, New Guinea; *speciosum*, large, yellow, blotched and marked wine-purple, Malaya, Moluccas.

Granadilla, see *Passiflora quadrangularis* and *P. edulis*.

Grape, see Vitis; **-Fern,** see *Botrychium Lunaria*; **-Fruit,** see *Citrus paradisi*; **-Hyacinth,** see Muscari.

Grass of Parnassus, see *Parnassia palustris*.

Greek Valerian, see *Polemonium caeruleum*.

Greenbriar, see Smilax.

Green Man Orchis, see Aceras.

Greenovia—*Crassulaceae*. Tufted perennial herbs, natives of Canary Islands, formerly included in Sempervivum.

CULTURE: As Aeonium.

PROPAGATION: As Aeonium.

SPECIES CULTIVATED: *G. diplocycla*, to 8 in., rosette 10 in.; *dodrentalis*, to 10 in., many long-stemmed offsets.

Grevillea—*Proteaceae*. Greenhouse and hardy, evergreen, flowering shrubs. First introduced late eighteenth century.

CULTURE OF GREENHOUSE SPECIES: Compost, equal parts fibrous peat, turfy loam and silver sand. Position, well-drained pots in airy greenhouse, window or dwelling-room. *G. rosmarinifolia* may be grown outdoors in the south. Pot, March or April. Water moderately Sept. to April, freely afterwards. Prune off points of shoots occasionally to induce bushy growth. Temp., March to Oct. 55° to 65°, Oct. to March 45° to 55°.

CULTURE OF HARDY SPECIES: Soil, peaty. Position, sheltered shrubberies S. of England; against south walls other parts. Plant, Oct. or April. Prune, April. Protect in severe weather.

PROPAGATION: Greenhouse species by seeds sown ¼ in. deep in well-drained pots of light soil in temp. 65° to 70° in March; cuttings of young shoots 3 in. long, with small heels of old wood attached, inserted in sandy soil in well-drained pots under bell-glass in temp. 75° to 80° in March, April or May; hardy species by seeds sown ¼ in. deep outdoors in March or April; layers in Oct. or Nov.; grafting in March.

GREENHOUSE SPECIES CULTIVATED: *G. acanthifolia*, reddish, June, 4 ft., Australia; *asplenifolia*, pink, July, 12 to 15 ft., Australia; *Banksii*, red, Aug., 15 ft., Australia; *punicea*, deep red, July, 6 ft., Australia; *robusta*, 'Silk Bark Oak', orange, summer, 10 to 20 ft., Australia; *rosmarinifolia*, red, summer, 6 ft., Australia.

HARDY SPECIES CULTIVATED: *G. juniperina* (syn. *G. sulphurea*), yellow, summer, 10 ft., Australia.

Griffinia—*Amaryllidaceae*. Stove evergreen bulbous flowering plants. First introduced early nineteenth century.

CULTURE: Compost, two parts fibrous loam, one part peat, decomposed sheep manure and sand. Position, well-drained pots on a bed or stage heated beneath to temp. 85° in plant stove. Pot, June or July. Press compost down firmly. Repotting not needed more often than once every three or four years. Water moderately Oct. to April, freely afterwards. Syringe freely in summer. Top-dress established plants annually in March with rich compost. Temp., March to Sept. 70° to 80°, Sept. to Dec. 55° to 65°, December to March 65° to 75°.

PROPAGATION: By seeds sown ⅛ in. deep in sandy soil in temp. 85° in Feb. or March; offsets removed from old bulbs and placed singly in 3 in. pots at potting time.

SPECIES CULTIVATED: *G. Blumenayia*, white with pale rose, summer, 1 ft., Brazil; *hyacinthina*, 'Blue Amaryllis', blue, summer, 18 in., Brazil; *ornata*, bluish-lilac, summer, 18 in., Brazil.

Grindelia—*Compositae*. Coarse hardy perennial plants.

CULTURE: Soil, ordinary. Position, sunny beds or borders. Plant 6 ft. apart in March or April.

PROPAGATION: By seeds sown in warm greenhouse in Feb. or March; division at planting time.

SPECIES CULTIVATED: *G. chiloensis* (syn. *G. speciosa*), shrubby, 18 in., orange-yellow, Argentine; *integrifolia*, yellow, summer, to 3 ft., N. America; *robusta*, 'Californian Gum Plant', yellow, summer, to 2 ft., California.

Griselinia—*Cornaceae*. Slightly tender evergreen shrubs. Male and female flowers produced on separate plants, berries seldom seen. First introduced mid-nineteenth century. Excellent near the sea and useful hedge shrubs.

CULTURE: Soil, ordinary, poor, including chalk. Maritime shrubs. Plant, Oct., Nov., March and April. Prune into shape in April.

PROPAGATION: By cuttings in sandy soil in sheltered border or cold frame Sept. to Nov.

SPECIES CULTIVATED: *G. littoralis*, green, spring, 20 to 30 ft., New Zealand, and var. *variegata*, with white variegation; *lucida*, green, spring, 10 to 12 ft., New Zealand.

Grobya—*Orchidaceae*. An epiphytic genus, three species. Pseudo-bulbs clustered, small, scapes from their base. Flowers rather small.

CULTURE: Compost, three parts osmunda fibre, one part sphagnum moss. Peat and sand can be added. Pans or small baskets. Can be grown in the cool house, but winter temp. should be 55°. Water should then be very infrequently given.

PROPAGATION: By division of the plants in spring.

SPECIES CULTIVATED: *G. Amherstiae*, yellowish-brown, spotted purplish-brown, lip purplish, autumn, Brazil; *fascifera*, ochre yellow, purple spots, spring, Brazil; *galeata*, greenish-yellow, shaded purple, early autumn, Brazil.

Gromwell, see *Lithospermum prostratum.*

Grossularia, see Ribes.

Ground Ivy, see *Glecoma hederacea*; **-nut,** see *Arachis hypogaea.*

Groundsel, see Senecio.

Guava, see *Psidium Guajava.*

Guelder Rose, see *Viburnum Opulus* var. *roseum.*

Guernsey Lily, see *Nerine sarniensis.*

Gum Arabic, see *Acacia Senegal*; **-Cistus,** see *Cistus cyprius*; **-Plant,** see Grindelia; **-Tree,** see Eucalyptus.

Gumbo, see *Hibiscus esculentus.*

Gunnera (Prickly Rhubarb)—*Haloragidaceae.* Hardy herbaceous perennials. First introduced mid-nineteenth century.

CULTURE: Soil, ordinary rich. Position, damp, sunny sheltered margins of ponds or bogs. Plant, March or April. Protect with leaves in winter. Water abundantly in dry weather.

PROPAGATION: By seeds sown $\frac{1}{16}$ in. deep in pans of light soil in temp. 55° to 65° in March, transplanting seedlings outdoors in June; division of plants in spring.

SPECIES CULTIVATED: *G. chilensis* (syn. *G. scabra*), 'Chile Rhubarb', leaves 4 to 6 ft. in diameter, 6 to 10 ft., Chile; *manicata*, leaves 5 to 10 ft. in diameter, 4 to 10 ft., Brazil; *magellanica*, very dwarf, 3 in., S. Chile.

Guzmania—*Bromeliaceae.* Stove, terrestrial or epiphytic herbs with stiff leaves in basal rosettes, and yellow or white flowers in spikes, often showily bracted. First introduced early nineteenth century.

CULTURE: Compost, equal parts fibrous loam, rough peat and leaf-mould. Pot, March. Water freely always. Good drainage essential. Temp., Sept. to March 60° to 70°, March to Sept. 70° to 80°.

PROPAGATION: By offshoots inserted in small pots at any time.

SPECIES CULTIVATED: *G. Bevansayana*, white with scarlet bracts, 1 ft., Ecuador; *lingulata*, yellowish-white, summer, 1 ft., bracts purplish-red, epiphytic, Trop. America; *musaica* (syn. *Tillandsia musaica*), yellowish, stemless, bracts yellow and rose, terrestrial, Colombia. See also Tillandsia.

Gymnadenia—*Orchidaceae.* A tuberous terrestrial genus resembling Orchis, but very near to Habenaria to which many species have been referred.

CULTURE: *G. conopsea*, prefers a rather moist position in a well-drained, rather sandy loam; *albida*, a peaty loam.

PROPAGATION: Seldom effected.

SPECIES CULTIVATED: *G. albida*, small, creamy-white, spur shorter than ovary, early summer, Britain, Europe, Asia; *conopsea*, small, variable, usually mauve, early summer, Britain, Europe, Japan.

Gymnocalycium—*Cactaceae.* Greenhouse succulent plants, sometimes included in Echinocactus.

CULTURE: As Echinocactus.

PROPAGATION: As Echinocactus.

SPECIES CULTIVATED: *G. gibbosum*, white, June, 4 in., Mexico; *multiflorum*, white, summer, 5 in., Mexico; *Weissianum*, pink, campanulate, Argentine.

Gymnocladus—*Leguminosae.* Slightly tender deciduous trees with feather-shaped, bluish-green leaves. First introduced mid-eighteenth century.

CULTURE: Soil, ordinary, well drained. Position, shady shrubberies or lawns. Plant, Oct. to Feb. Prune young trees, Jan.

PROPAGATION: By imported seeds sown in light soil in shady, cool greenhouse in Oct., Nov., March or April; root cuttings in March.

SPECIES CULTIVATED: *G. dioica* (syn. *G. canadensis*), ' Coffee Tree ', white, May to July, 60 ft., N. America, var. *folia-variegata*, variegated foliage.

Gymnogramma, see Pityrogramma and Coniogramme.

Gymnothrix, see Pennisetum.

Gynura—*Compositae.* Stove perennials with ornamental foliage and purple-tinted leaves.

CULTURE: Compost, equal parts peat, loam, leaf-mould and sand. Position, pots in partial shade. Pot in March. Water freely March to Oct., moderately afterwards. Temp., March to Oct. 70° to 80°, Oct. to March 55° to 65°.

PROPAGATION: By cuttings in spring.

SPECIES CULTIVATED: *G. aurantiaca,* 2 ft., Java; *bicolor,* 3 ft., Moluccas.

Gypsophila—*Caryophyllaceae.* Hardy perennial and annual herbs. Flowers valuable for cutting. First introduced mid-eighteenth century.

CULTURE: Soil, ordinary, freely mixed with old mortar or brick rubbish. Position, dryish well-drained borders for erect species; sunny rockeries and margins of borders for dwarf species. Plant, Oct., Nov., March or April. Cut down flower stems in Oct.

PROPAGATION: Annual species by seeds sown in April on surface of soil where plants are to flower, thinning seedlings out to 3 to 6 in. apart when 1 in. high; perennial species by seeds sown in sunny position outdoors in April, transplanting seedlings to permanent position in June, July or Aug.; *G. paniculata* by cuttings of secondary laterals, 2 in. long, in silver sand under bell-glass in gentle bottom heat during June and July; trailing species by division in spring and cuttings.

ANNUAL SPECIES CULTIVATED: *G. elegans,* white, June to Oct., 12 to 18 in., Caucasus; *viscosa* (syn. *G. rosea*), rose, fragrant, summer, 12 to 18 in., Asia Minor.

PERENNIAL SPECIES CULTIVATED: *G. acutifolia,* white or rosy, autumn, 4 ft., Caucasus; *aretioides,* white, spring, 1 in., Caucasus; *cerastioides,* white, veined red, May to Sept., 2 in., Himalaya, var. *flore-pleno,* double flowers, and numerous improved garden forms; *Oldhamiana,* 2½ ft., pinkish, Japan; *paniculata,* ' Chalk Plant', white, summer, 2 to 3 ft., Europe; *repens,* white, summer, 6 in., Alps, and vars. *rosea* and *monstrosa*; *Rokejeka,* 2 ft., pink or violet, Egypt, Asia Minor; *Stevenii,* white, summer, 2 ft., Caucasus; *tenuifolia,* soft pink, summer, 6 in., Caucasus.

Habenaria—*Orchidaceae.* A very large terrestrial deciduous genus, in both hemispheres. Roots usually tuberous. The differences between Habenaria, Platanthera and Bonatea are so slight that for horticultural purposes they may be regarded as one, and are so treated here. The flowers in some are remarkable for the development of the rostellum lobes and the lobe-like division of the petals.

CULTURE: The British species are amenable in outdoor gardens, and not particular as to soil, preferring a sandy loam. The North American species given might be hardy but early growths are liable to receive damage by frost. Compost for exotic species, three parts loam, one part leaf-mould, with sand. The kinds generally cultivated need a decided rest; when dormant the pots should be placed on a shelf near the glass. Temp. around 60°. Repot early in spring. Summer temp. up to 80° with shade. Water frequently as the growths gain strength.

PROPAGATION: Seldom effected. Occasionally by separation of the tubers when repotting.

HARDY SPECIES CULTIVATED: A selection—*H. bifolia,* fragrant, white, green-tinged, spur twice as long as ovary, summer, Britain, Europe, N. Asia, var. *chlorantha,* greener, summer; *blephariglottis,* white, summer, N. America; *ciliaris,* yellowish, lip fringed, summer, N. America; *cristata*, golden yellow, summer, N. America; *dilatata*, white, summer, N. America, and var. *leucostachys*; *Elwesii*, greenish, yellow, lip in 3 lobes, summer, Nilgiri Hills; *fimbriata*, lilac-rose, summer; *pusilla* (syn. *H. militaris*), greenish, red, lip scarlet or cinnabar-red, autumn, Cochin-China; *viridis*, small, greenish or yellowish, early summer, Britain, Europe, N. Asia.

The following group is attractive and popular: *H. carnea*, rose-flesh, autumn, Penang; *pusilla* (syn. *H. militaris*), greenish, red, lip scarlet or cinnabar-red, autumn, Cochin-China.

Haberlea—*Gesneriaceae*. Hardy herbaceous tufted perennial. First introduced late nineteenth century.

CULTURE: Soil, fibrous sandy peat. Position, vertical fissures of rockery in shade. Plant, Oct., March or April. Water freely in dry weather.

PROPAGATION: By seeds sown $\frac{1}{16}$ in. deep in well-drained pots or pans of sandy peat in cold frame in March or April; by division of plants in March or April.

SPECIES CULTIVATED: *H. Ferdinandi-Coburgii*, white and lilac, 4 to 6 in., May, Bulgaria; *rhodopensis*, lavender and white, 6 in., May, Balkans, var. *virginalis*, white.

Hablitzia—*Chenopodiaceae*. Rather uninteresting hardy herbaceous climber. First introduced early nineteenth century.

CULTURE: Soil, ordinary. Position, base of naked trunks of trees, south or west trellises, arbours, walls or fences. Plant, Oct. or March. Cut down stems to the ground in Oct.

PROPAGATION: By seeds sown $\frac{1}{16}$ in. deep in sunny place outdoors in March or April, or similar depth in boxes of light soil in greenhouse or cold frame in March, transplanting seedlings outdoors in May or June; by division of roots Oct. or April.

SPECIES CULTIVATED: *H. tamnoides*, green, summer, 8 to 10 ft., Caucasus.

Habranthus—*Amaryllidaceae*. Slightly tender bulbous plants, sometimes included in the genus Zephyranthes.

CULTURE: Soil, light sandy loam. Position, well-drained sunny beds, borders or rockeries. Plant, Aug. to Nov., placing bulbs 3 to 4 in. deep and 4 in. apart. Protect in winter by a layer of cinder ashes. Lift and replant only when bulbs show signs of deterioration.

PROPAGATION: By offsets.

SPECIES CULTIVATED: *H. Andersonii* (syn. *Zephyranthes Andersonii*), golden yellow, summer, 6 in., S. America; *brachyandrus* (syn. *Hippeastrum brachyandrum*), orchid-pink above, shading to dark reddish-purple below, to 12 in., S. America; *robustus*, rose-red, to 9 in., Argentina.

Hackberry, see Celtis.

Hacquetia—*Umbelliferae*. Hardy herbaceous perennial.

CULTURE: Soil, ordinary. Position, sunny rockery or margin of border. Plant in March.

PROPAGATION: By division of the roots in March.

SPECIES CULTIVATED: *H. Epipactis* (syn. *Dondia Epipactis*), yellow, spring, 3 to 6 in., Europe.

Haemanthus (Blood Lily; Red Cape Tulip)—*Amaryllidaceae*. Stove and greenhouse bulbous plants. First introduced early eighteenth century.

CULTURE: Compost, two parts sandy loam, one part peat, well-decayed manure and sand. Position, well-drained pots exposed to full sun in stove or greenhouse whilst growing; sunny shelf or frame whilst at rest. Pot early-flowering species Aug. to Nov.; late-flowering species March or April. Place bulbs half their depth in compost. Water very little till growth begins, then moderately; gradually withhold it when flowers fade, and keep soil quite dry from time foliage turns yellow till repotting time. Apply weak liquid manure once or twice weekly to plants in flower. Temp., greenhouse species, Sept. to March 45° to 55°, March to Sept. 55° to 65°; stove species, Sept. to March 55° to 65°, March to Sept. 65° to 75°. Bulbs flower best when only repotted every three or four years.

PROPAGATION: By offsets removed at potting time and placed in small pots.

STOVE SPECIES CULTIVATED: *H. cinnabarinus*, red, April, 1 ft., S. Africa; *coccineus*, ' Blood Flower ', scarlet, autumn, 1 ft., S. Africa; *multiflorus* (syn. *H. Kalbreveri*), scarlet, April, 1 ft., S. Africa.

GREENHOUSE SPECIES CULTIVATED: *H. albiflos*, white, autumn, 1 ft., S. Africa, and var. *pubescens*; *Katharinae*, red, spring, 1 ft., S. Africa; *natalensis*, green, purple and yellow, Feb., 1 ft., S. Africa; *puniceus*, orange-scarlet, summer, 1 ft., S. Africa.

Hair Grass, see Aira.

Hakea—*Proteaceae.* Tender evergreen shrubs. First introduced late eighteenth century.

CULTURE: Compost, equal parts fibrous loam, leaf-mould and sharp sand. Position, well-drained large pots, tubs or borders in unheated glasshouse, or sheltered borders in the open in the mildest parts of the country.

PROPAGATION: By cuttings of half-ripened wood in July under hand-light in slight bottom heat, or by seeds sown in sandy peat in temp. 60° in spring.

SPECIES CULTIVATED: *H. dactyloides*, white, July, 7 ft., Australia; *ferruginea*, creamy-white, May to June, 3 to 4 ft., Australia; *saligna*, white, spring, 6 to 8 ft., Australia; *suaveolens*, white, fragrant, summer, 10 ft., W. Australia.

Halesia (Silver Bell)—*Styracaceae.* Hardy flowering deciduous trees. First introduced mid-eighteenth century.

CULTURE: Soil, deep sandy loam. Position, sheltered borders, shrubberies or lawns. Plant, Oct. to Feb. Prune into shape after flowering.

PROPAGATION: By cuttings of roots inserted in sandy soil outdoors in March or Oct.; by layering shoots in Oct. or Nov., or by seeds sown in spring.

SPECIES CULTIVATED: *H. carolina* (syn. *H. tetraptera*), ' Snowdrop Tree ', white, May, 15 to 20 ft., N. America; *diptera*, white, May, to 30 ft., N. America: *monticola*, similar to *H. carolina* but stronger growing and with larger flowers, N. America.

× **Halimiocistus**—*Cistaceae.* Hardy dwarf evergreen shrubs. Bigeneric hybrid between Halimium and Cistus.

CULTURE: Soil, dry, light. Position, full exposure to sun.

PROPAGATION: By cutting of half-ripened wood.

SPECIES CULTIVATED: *H. Ingwersenianus*, white, 18 in., all summer, Portugal; *Sahucii*, white, 12 in., May to autumn.

Halimium—*Cistaceae.* Hardy evergreen shrubs, similar to Helianthemum and formerly included in that genus.

CULTURE: Soil, dry. Position, sunny. Subject to damage in severe winters.

PROPAGATION: By seed sown in heat in April; cuttings in sandy soil in frames in August.

SPECIES CULTIVATED: *H. alyssoides*, yellow, May to July, 2 ft., Spain and Portugal; *lasianthum* (syn. *H. formosum*), yellow, June, 3 to 4 ft., Portugal; *halimifolium*, yellow, May to June, 2 to 3 ft., S. Europe; *ocymoides* (syn. *Helianthemum ocymoides*), flowers bright yellow with maroon blotch, erect growing to 3 ft., young shoots downy, summer, Spain and Portugal.

Halimodendron (Salt Tree)—*Leguminosae.* Hardy deciduous flowering shrub. First introduced mid-eighteenth century.

CULTURE: Soil, deep sandy. Position, shrubberies and open borders. Plant, Oct. to Feb. Prune into shape in Nov.

PROPAGATION: By seeds outdoors in March or April; grafting on to stocks of caragana, to which it is related, in spring.

SPECIES CULTIVATED: *H. halodendron* (syn. *H. argenteum*), grey-spined leaves and pink pea-shaped flowers, a good maritime shrub, June to July, 4 to 6 ft., Siberia.

Hamamelis (Wych-Hazel)—*Hamamelidaceae.* Hardy winter and early spring flowering deciduous shrubs. First introduced early eighteenth century.

CULTURE: Soil, deep, rich loam. Position, as lawn specimens or in shrubberies where they can have plenty of space, being open habited.

PROPAGATION: By layering in Oct. or Nov.; grafting rare species on stocks of *H. virginiana*, which is raised from seed, in April.

SPECIES CULTIVATED: *H. japonica*, lemon yellow, Dec. to Feb., 12 ft., Japan, and vars. *arborea* and *Zuccariniana*; *mollis*, yellow, Jan. and Feb., the best species with spicily fragrant flowers and autumn-tinted foliage, 10 ft., China; *virginiana*, yellow, Dec. to Feb., N. America.

Hard Fern, see *Blechnum spicant.*

Hardenbergia (Australian Sarsaparilla-tree)—*Leguminosae.* Greenhouse flowering evergreen twining plants. First introduced late eighteenth century.

CULTURE: Compost, equal parts loam and peat, little silver sand. Position, pots, with shoots trained to trellis, or planted out in beds, and shoots trained up rafters. Pot or plant, Feb. or May. Water freely March to Sept., moderately at other times. Prune straggling plants into shape in Feb. Apply weak stimulants occasionally to healthy plants in flower. Temp., March to Sept. 55° to 65°, Sept. to March 40° to 50°.

PROPAGATION: By seeds sown ⅛ in. deep in well-drained pots of light sandy soil in temp. of 55° to 65° in March or April; cuttings of firm young shoots, 2 to 3 in. long, inserted in well-drained pots of sandy peat under bell-glass in temp. 55° to 65°, March to July.

SPECIES CULTIVATED: *H. Comptoniana*, purple, March, 10 ft., S. Australia; *violacea* (syns. *H. monophylla*, *H. bimaculata*), ' Australian Lilac ', purple, April, 8 to 10 ft., S. Australia, and var. *rosea*.

Harebell, see *Campanula rotundifolia.*

Hare's-foot Fern, see *Davallia canariensis.*

Hare's-tail Grass, see *Lagurus ovatus.*

Haricot Bean, see *Phaseolus vulgaris.*

Hart's-tongue Fern, see *Phillitis Scolopendrium.*

Hartwegia—*Orchidaceae.* About five small epiphytic species. Pseudo-bulbs stem-like, terminating in a spike of small bright flowers. Leaf single, persistent.

CULTURE: Compost, temps. as for Cattleyas. Requires a rest but not severe. Position, pans hung near the glass.

PROPAGATION: By division of plants in spring.

SPECIES CULTIVATED: *H. gemma*, amethyst-purple, summer, autumn, Cent. America; *purpurea*, rose-purple, summer, autumn, Guatemala, Mexico.

Hatchet Cactus, see *Pelecyphora aseliiformis.*

Hautbois Strawberry, see *Fragaria moschata.*

Hawkweed, see Hieracium.

Hawk's Beard, see *Crepis aurea.*

Haworthia—*Liliaceae.* Low succulent greenhouse plants with or without a short stem. Leaves in rosettes or overlapping, arranged in several rows, short, blunt, pointed or even truncate, fleshy, often covered with pearly tubercles or even more or less transparent. Flowers in long loose racemes, small and inconspicuous, whitish-green. Flowering almost any time. Attractive easily-grown little succulents suitable for room culture.

CULTURE: Soil, well drained, rich, sandy. Position, room or cool house, winter temp. not above 55°. Rather liable to sunburn. Water freely in summer, less in winter but should not be dried out for too long.

PROPAGATION: By offshoots. May easily be raised from seed but not recommended on account of hybridisation.

SPECIES CULTIVATED: *H. arachnoides* (syn. *Aloe arachnoidea*), stemless rosettes, oblong leaves with bristly tip, Cape; *cymbiformis*, rosettes stemless making offsets freely, leaves 1¼ to 2 in., S. Africa; *herbacea* (syn. *H. atrovirens*), stemless rosettes forming clumps, S. Africa; *marginata* (syn. *H. albicans*), leaves 3 to 4 in., S. Africa; *margaritifera*, stemless rosettes making many offsets, leaves 3 in. long with large roundish pearly tubercles, S. Africa; *Reinwardtii*, rosettes elongated, leaves to 1¼ in. long, upper side with a few tubercles, beautiful species, S. Africa; *tortuosa*, rosette elongated to 5 in., stems branching from the base leaves in three spiral overlapping rows, S. Africa; *viscosa*, rosette to 8 in. long, leaves in three rows, overlapping, erect, S. Africa.

Hawthorn, see *Crataegus Oxyacantha*; **Water-,** see *Aponogeton distachyus*.

Hazelnut, see *Corylus Avellina.*

Heartsease, see *Viola tricolor.*

Heath, see Erica.

Heather, see Calluna.

Heavenly Bamboo, see *Nandina domestica.*

Hebe—*Scrophulariaceae.* Slightly tender and hardy evergreen flowering shrubs from New Zealand. Formerly included in Veronica.

CULTURE: Soil, ordinary, or loam and peat. Position, sunny rockeries, borders or beds near the sea coast or in inland sheltered districts south of the Trent. Plant, Sept. or April, prune straggly plants into shape in April.

PROPAGATION: Cuttings of young growth inserted in sandy soil under a bell-glass in June or July; cuttings of nearly ripened growth under hand-light or in cold frame in summer.

SPECIES CULTIVATED: *H. amplexicaulis*, white, July to Aug., 1 to 3 ft.; *Andersonii variegata*, foliage margined with white, 2 to 3 ft., hybrid; *angustifolia*, white, July to Sept.; *anomala*, white or pale pink, July to Aug., 3 to 5 ft.; *Bidwillii*, white veined pink, summer, 6 in.; *Buchananii*, white, July to Aug., 1 ft.; *buxifolia*, white, 9 to 12 in., summer; *carnosula*, white, July to Aug., 1 to 3 ft.; *catarractae*, white and pink, summer, 6 to 9 in.; *chathamica*, purple, summer, 1 to 1¼ ft.; *Colensoi*, white, July to Aug., 1 to 1½ ft.; *cupressoides*, pale blue, summer, 1 to 6 ft.; *Darwiniana*, white, July to Aug., 2 to 3 ft.; *decumbens*, white, July to Aug., to 3 ft.; *diosmaefolia*, white or pale blue, July to Aug., to 5 ft.; *elliptica*, white, summer, to 20 ft.; *epacridea*, white, 4 to 6 in., summer; *Hectori*, white or pink, July to Aug., 6 to 12 in.; *Hookeriana*, white, summer, 8 to 12 in.; *Hulkeana*, lilac, 4 to 6 ft.; *Lewisii*, pale blue, summer, 4 to 6 ft.; *loganioides*, white, July to Aug., 4 to 12 in.; *lycopodioides*, white, July, 1 to 2 ft.; *macrantha*, large white flowers, 12 to 15 in., June to July; *pimeleoides*, purplish-blue, June to Aug., 1 to 1½ ft.; *pinguifolia*, white, July to Aug., 1 to 3 ft.; *salicifolia*, white, summer, 6 to 10 ft.; *speciosa*, reddish-purple, July to Sept., to 5 ft.; *Traversii*, white, summer, 4 to 6 ft.; *tetrasticha*, white, 9 in., summer; *vernicosa*, white, June to Aug., 1 to 2 ft.

Hebenstretia—*Scrophulariaceae.* Half-hardy perennial treated as an annual.

CULTURE: Soil, good ordinary. Position, sunny borders. Sow seeds in heat in March, harden seedlings off early in May, and plant out late in May, 12 to 18 in. apart in groups. Seeds may also be sown thinly where required to flower, about the middle of April.

SPECIES CULTIVATED: *H. comosa*, white with tinge of orange, summer, 2 to 3 ft., S. Africa.

Hedera (Ivy)—*Araliaceae.* Hardy evergreen climbing shrubs with insignificant green flowers followed by purplish-black, orange or yellow berries. Tree Ivies represent the adult stage of growth of many kinds; the climbing habit is lost and a large, rounded, free-flowering bush is formed. The types usually grown are *H. Helix arborescens*, ' Common Tree Ivy ', and *H. colchica arborescens*, the best large-leaved tree ivy.

CULTURE: Soil, ordinary. Position, against walls of all aspects, railings, tree stumps, arbours, etc., on banks and under shade of trees. Plant, Sept. to Nov., or Feb. to April. Peg shoots to surface of soil when first planted in any position. Prune, April, cutting off old leaves and straggling shoots. Apply stimulants if vigorous growth is desired.

POT CULTURE: Compost, two parts loam, one part leaf-mould or decayed manure and sand. Position, well-drained pots in unheated greenhouse, balcony or window. Pot, Oct. or March. Water moderately Oct. to March, freely afterwards. Prune into shape, April. Apply stimulants to established plants in summer.

PROPAGATION: By cuttings of firm shoots 6 to 8 in. long in ordinary soil at base of north wall or fence, Sept. to Nov.; in well-drained pots in cold frame in Oct., or in temp. 55° to 65° Sept. to Nov.; tree and variegated kinds by cleft grafting on common species in temp. 55° in Feb.

SPECIES CULTIVATED: *H. canariensis*, large leathery leaves to 8 in. across, Canary Is., N. Africa, and var. *variegata*; *colchica*, largest-leaved of all ivies up to 10 in. across, Caucasus, Persia, and var. *dentata variegata*, attractively mottled and streaked with gold; *Helix*, ' Common Ivy ', Europe, including Britain, usually represented in gardens by improved vars. *arborescens*, shrubby, *hibernica*, ' Irish Ivy ', coarse and vigorous, good for shade under trees.

Hedge Hyssop, see Hydrotrida.

Hedgehog Cactus, see Ferocactus; **-Holly,** see *Ilex Aquifolium ferox*.

Hedychium (Ginger Lily)—*Zingiberaceae.* Stove and greenhouse herbaceous perennials with fragrant flowers. First introduced late eighteenth century.

CULTURE: Compost, two parts peat, one part loam, one part sand. Position, well-drained pots, tubs or boxes, or planted in beds in stove or warm greenhouse. Pot plants may be stood outdoors July to Aug. Pot, March or April. Water freely April to Nov., occasionally other times. Apply liquid manure twice a week to plants in flower. Temp., stove species, March to Nov. 65° to 75°, Nov. to March 50° to 55°; greenhouse species, March to Nov. 55° to 65°, Nov. to March 45° to 50°. Cut down flower stems immediately after flowering. *H. Gardnerianum* suitable for outdoor culture in summer. Plant, May, in rich soil. Water freely in dry weather. Apply liquid manure when in flower. Lift roots in Oct. and store in frost-proof place till planting time.

PROPAGATION: By division of rhizomes in March or April.

STOVE SPECIES CULTIVATED: *H. coronarium*, ' Fragrant Garland Flower ', white, summer, 5 ft., India.

GREENHOUSE SPECIES CULTIVATED: *H. flavum*, yellow and orange, July, 5 ft., Himalaya; *Gardnerianum*, lemon-yellow, summer, 4 ft., Himalaya; *Greenei*, red, summer, 6 ft., Himalaya.

Hedysarum—*Leguminosae.* Hardy perennials or sub-shrubs with pea-shaped flowers. First introduced late sixteenth century.

CULTURE: Soil, ordinary. Position, sunny rockeries, banks, etc., for dwarf species; sunny well-drained borders for tall kinds. Plant, Oct., March or April.

PROPAGATION: By seeds sown outdoors in April, transplanting to final position in June; division in Oct. or April; sub-shrubby kinds by layering in spring or cuttings in August.

SPECIES CULTIVATED: *H. coronarium*, ' French Honeysuckle ', red, summer, 3 to 4 ft., S. Europe, var. *album*, white; *microcalyx*, crimson-violet, June to July, 2 to 3 ft., Himalaya; *multijugum*, magenta, all summer, 4 ft., shrubby, Mongolia, and var. *apiculatum*; *obscurum*, crimson, summer, 6 to 12 in., Europe.

Hedyscepe—*Palmae.* Stove palm with feather-like leaves. A good room plant.
CULTURE: Compost, equal parts loam and peat, little silver sand. Position, well-drained pots in shady plant stove. Pot, Feb., March or April. Water freely March to Oct., moderately afterwards. Syringe twice daily March to Sept. Temp., March to Sept. 70° to 85°, Sept. to March 60° to 65°.
PROPAGATION: By seeds sown 1 in. deep in light soil, in temp. 70° to 80°, in Feb. or March.
SPECIES CULTIVATED: *H. Canterburyana* (syn. *Kentia Canterburyana*), Lord Howe's Island.

Helenium (Sneezeweed)—*Compositae.* Hardy herbaceous perennials and annuals. First introduced early eighteenth century.
CULTURE OF PERENNIAL SPECIES: Soil, ordinary rich. Position, sunny well-drained borders. Plant, Oct., Nov., March or April. Cut down flower stems in Oct.
PROPAGATION: By seeds sown ⅛ in. deep outdoors in April, transplanting seedlings in June or July; division of roots in Oct. or March.
CULTURE OF ANNUAL SPECIES: Soil, ordinary. Position, sunny borders. Sow seeds in patches in borders in March or April.
PERENNIAL SPECIES CULTIVATED: *H. autumnale*, yellow, July to Oct., 3 to 5 ft., N. America, and vars. *pumilum*, 1 ft., *striatum*, yellow and brown, 4 ft.; *Bigelovii*, yellow and brown, Aug. to Oct., 4 ft., California; *Bolanderi*, yellow and brown, summer, 18 in., California; *Hoopesii*, yellow, summer, 2 ft., N. America. There are several named vars.
ANNUAL SPECIES CULTIVATED: *H. tenuifolium*, yellow, summer, 1½ to 2 ft., N. America.

Helianthemum (Sun Rose)—*Cistaceae.* Hardy flowering evergreen shrubs. A number of the species are now referrred to Halimium.
CULTURE: Soil, light sandy. Position, sunny banks or rockeries. Plant, Oct., March or April. Prune into shape in March.
PROPAGATION: By seeds sown 1/16 in. deep in light soil outdoors in April; cuttings of shoots 1 to 2 in. long inserted in well-drained pots of sandy soil in cold frame Aug. or Sept.; division of plants Oct. or April.
SPECIES CULTIVATED: *H. apenninum*, white, summer, to 15 in., Europe, Asia Minor; *guttatum*, yellow with red spot at base, 6 in., Medit.; *nummularium* (syn. *H. vulgare*), yellow, June, trailing, and numerous double and single vars.; *Tuberaria* (syn. *Tuberaria vulgaris*), yellow, summer, trailing, S. Europe.

Helianthus (Sunflower)—*Compositae.* Hardy annual or perennial herbs; tubers of Jerusalem Artichoke edible.
CULTURE OF ANNUAL SPECIES: Soil, ordinary. Position, sunny borders. Sow seeds ¼ in. deep in April where plants are to flower, or in pots in temp. 55° to 65° in April, transplanting seedlings outdoors in June. Apply stimulants occasionally when flower buds form.
CULTURE OF PERENNIAL SPECIES: Soil, ordinary rich. Position, sunny well-drained borders. Plant, Oct., Nov. or April. Cut down flower stems in Oct. Water in dry weather. Apply stimulants occasionally when plants show flower buds. Replant every third year.
CULTURE OF JERUSALEM ARTICHOKE: Soil, ordinary rich. Position, open or shady. Plant, Feb. or March, placing tubers 6 in. deep and 12 in. apart in rows 3 ft. asunder. Earth up when stems are 6 in. high. Lift tubers in Nov. and store in sand or dry soil in outhouse, or leave in ground and dig as required.
PROPAGATION: Annual and perennial species by seeds sown ¼ in. deep in sunny place outdoors in March or April; perennials by division of roots, Oct., March or April; Jerusalem Artichoke, by tubers treated as above.
ANNUAL SPECIES CULTIVATED: *H. annuus*, 'Common Sunflower', yellow, summer, 6 to 10 ft., N. America; *argophyllus*, yellow, 6 ft., N. America; *debilis* (syn. *H. cucumerifolius*), yellow, 3 to 4 ft.

PERENNIAL SPECIES CULTIVATED: *H. atrorubens*, yellow, disk purple, Aug. to Sept., 5 to 6 ft., N. America; *decapetalus*, sulphur yellow, summer, 4 to 6 ft., Canada, and vars. *grandiflorus*, double, *maximus*, large; *doronicoides*, yellow, summer, 7 ft., roots tuberous, N. America; *laetiflorus*, yellow, autumn, 5 to 7 ft., N. America; *rigidus* (syn. *Harpalium rigidum*), yellow, Aug., 5 ft., N. America; *salicifolius* (syn. *H. orgyalis*), yellow, Aug., 6 ft., N. America; *tuberosus*, ' Jerusalem Artichoke ', yellow, 6 ft., N. America. There are numerous sunflower vars. to be found in trade lists.

Helichrysum (Everlasting-flower; Immortelle-flower)—*Compositae*. Half-hardy annuals, hardy perennials and greenhouse shrubs.

CULTURE OF ANNUAL SPECIES: Soil, ordinary. Position sunny. Sow seeds in gentle heat in March and plant out in May; or sow outdoors in April. Gather flowers for winter decoration directly they are fully expanded.

CULTURE OF PERENNIAL SPECIES: Soil, rich loam. Position, sunny well-drained borders and rock gardens. Plant, March or April.

CULTURE OF HARDY SHRUBBY SPECIES: Soil, rich loam. Position, sunny well-drained borders or sheltered shrubberies. Plant, Sept. or Oct. Protect in very severe weather.

PROPAGATION: Hardy species by seeds sown outdoors in April or cuttings in cold frame in spring; greenhouse species by cuttings in fine sand under bell-glass in spring; shrubby species by cuttings of half-ripened wood in frame in Aug.

ANNUAL SPECIES CULTIVATED: *H. bracteatum*, colours various, summer, 3 to 4 ft., Australia.

PERENNIAL SPECIES CULTIVATED: *H. angustifolium*, white, summer, to 1 ft.. Medit. Region; *arenarium*, ' Yellow Everlasting ', yellow, summer, 6 to 12 in,, Europe; *bellidioides*, silvery white, summer, 3 to 4 in., New Zealand; *lanatum*, yellow, summer, to 15 in., S. Africa.

HARDY SHRUBBY SPECIES CULTIVATED: *H. diosmifolium* (syn. *Ozothamnus rosmarinifolium*), white, summer, 6 to 9 ft., Tasmania.

Helicodiceros (Dragon's Mouth)—*Araceae*. Hardy tuberous-rooted perennial. Flowers, arum-like, with an unpleasant odour.

CULTURE: Soil, ordinary, well drained. Position, sunny borders. Plant in autumn or early spring.

PROPAGATION: By offsets in autumn.

SPECIES CULTIVATED: *H. muscivorus* (syn. *Arum crinitum*), spathe purplish-brown, summer, 2 ft., S. Europe.

Heliconia (False Plantain)—*Musaceae*. Stove herbaceous perennials. Leaves, green and stem striped with black, green and yellow. First introduced late eighteenth century.

CULTURE: Compost, two parts fibrous loam, one part leaf-mould, peat and sand. Position, pots in shady part of plant stove. Pot, Feb. or March. Water freely March to Sept., moderately Sept. to Nov., none Nov. to March. Syringe daily March to Sept. Temp., Feb. to Sept. 65° to 75°, Sept. to Nov. 60° to 70°, Nov. to Feb. 55° to 65°.

PROPAGATION: By division of roots in Feb. or March.

SPECIES CULTIVATED: *H. angustifolia* (syn. *H. bicolor*), flowers white and green, spathes scarlet, 3 ft., Brazil; *aureo-striata*, green and yellow leaves, 3 ft., New Guinea; *illustris*, green and red leaves, 3 ft., South Sea Islands; *Sanderi*, variegated, 2 ft., New Guinea; *triumphans*, green and black striped leaves, 3 ft., Trop. America.

Heliophila—*Cruciferae*. Hardy annuals. First introduced late eighteenth century .

CULTURE: Soil, ordinary. Position, sunny well-drained borders. Water in dry weather.

PROPAGATION: By seeds sown $\frac{1}{16}$ in. deep in pans or boxes of light soil in temp.

55° in March, transplanting seedlings outdoors end of May, or similar depth in April where plants are to flower.

SPECIES CULTIVATED: *H. linearifolia*, blue, 18 to 24 in., S Africa.

Heliopsis—*Compositae.* Hardy, herbaceous, sunflower-like perennials. First introduced early eighteenth century.

CULTURE: Soil, ordinary rich. Position, sunny well-drained borders. Plant, Oct., Nov., March or April. Cut down flower stems in Oct. Water in dry weather. Apply stimulants occasionally when plants show flower buds.

PROPAGATION: By division of plants, Oct., March or April.

SPECIES CULTIVATED: *H. helianthoides* (syn. *H. laevis*), ' North American Ox-eye ', yellow, autumn, 5 ft., N. America, perennial, and var. *Pitcheriana*; *scabra*, yellow, July to Sept., 4 ft., U.S.A., and vars. *magnifica, major, incomparabilis, patula,* and *zinniaeflora.*

Heliosperma, see Silene.

Heliotropium (Heliotrope)—*Boraginaceae.* Greenhouse fragrant flowering shrub. First introduced mid-eighteenth century.

CULTURE: Compost, equal parts light loam, leaf-mould and sand. Position, pots or beds, with shoots growing loosely or trained to trellis, walls, pillars, or rafters in greenhouse; in sunny beds outdoors June to Sept., or in pots in windows. Pot, Feb. to May. Plant outdoors, June. Lift and repot, Sept. Water freely March to Oct., moderately afterwards. Apply liquid or artificial manure to healthy plants in flower. Prune old plants closely in Feb. Training: Nip off points of main, also lateral shoots when 3 in. long to form dwarf plants; points of main shoots when 12 in. long, and side shoots when 3 to 6 in. long, to form pyramids; points of main shoots when 2 ft. long, and of lateral shoots at apex when 3 to 6 in. long—all side shoots to within 4 in. of apex to be removed altogether —to form standards. Temp., Feb. to Oct. 60° to 70°, Oct. to Feb. 50° to 55°. Pot plants do best in cold frame or sunny position outdoors July and Aug.

PROPAGATION: By seeds sown $\frac{1}{16}$ in. deep in well-drained pots or pans of light soil in temp. 65° to 75° in March; by cuttings of shoots 2 to 3 in. long inserted in pots of sandy soil under bell-glass, or in propagator in temp. 65° to 75° in March, April, Aug. or Sept.

SPECIES CULTIVATED: *H. amplexicaulis* (syn. *H. anchusaefolium*), lavender, 1 ft., summer, Peru; *arborescens* (syn. *H. peruvianum*), ' Cherry Pie ', blue and white, spring to winter, 1 to 6 ft., Peru, and numerous vars.

Helipterum (Australian Everlasting: Immortelle-flower)—*Compositae.* Hardy annuals. First introduced mid-nineteenth century.

CULTURE OF H. HUMBOLDTIANUM: Soil, light rich. Position, sunny well-drained borders.

PROPAGATION: By seeds sown ½ in. deep in well-drained pots of light soil, in temp. 55° in March, transplanting seedlings outdoors end of May or early in June.

CULTURE OF H. MANGLESII AND H. ROSEUM: Soil, ordinary. Position, sunny beds or borders. Sow seeds ½ in. deep in light sandy soil in temp. 55° to 65° in March or April, harden off in May, and plant out in June. Gather blooms when fully grown and dry thoroughly in summer for winter decorations.

POT CULTURE: Compost, any good well-drained soil. Sow seeds thinly in pots in temp. 50° in Sept. for spring flowering, and in March for summer blooming. Water moderately at first, freely later on. Apply weak stimulants once a week when seedlings are 6 in. high. Support with neat stakes when 3 to 6 in. high. No shade required. Winter temp., 45° to 55°.

SPECIES CULTIVATED: *H. Humboldtianum* (syn. *H. Sandfordii*), yellow, summer, 1 ft., Australia; *Manglesii* (syn. *Rhodanthe Manglesii*), rosy pink and yellow, summer, 12 to 18 in., Australia; *roseum* (syn. *Acroclinium roseum*), rose, summer, 2 ft., Australia.

Hellebore, see Helleborus.

226

Helleborine see *Epipactis latifolia.*

Helleborus (Hellebore)—*Ranunculaceae.* Hardy evergreen and deciduous perennials with thick fibrous roots.

OUTDOOR CULTURE: Soil, rich loamy. Position, shady well-drained east border. Plant, Oct., Nov. and March, 12 in. apart. Mulch with well-decayed manure in April. Water freely in dry weather. Apply liquid manure occasionally May to Sept. Disturb roots as little as possible. Protect with hand-lights, cloches or frames, or cover surface of bed with moss when in bloom. Manure freely prior to planting.

POT CULTURE: Compost, two parts fibrous loam, one part decayed manure. Position, cold frame, or greenhouse heated to temp. 40° to 50°. Pot, Oct. Lift fresh plants annually for pot culture, replanting old ones outdoors in April or May. Water moderately. Size of pot for single plants, 6 to 8 in.

PROPAGATION: By seeds sown ⅛ in. deep in shallow boxes of sandy soil in cold frame Oct. or March, transplanting seedlings outdoors when a year old; by division of roots in March.

SPECIES CULTIVATED: *H. abchasicus*, purplish-green, Jan. to March, 1 ft., Caucasus; *antiquorum*, rose-pink, Feb. to April, 1½ ft., Caucasian Region; *caucasicus*, pale green, Feb. to April, 2 ft., Caucasus; *colchicus*, deep purple, Jan. to March, 1½ ft., Asia Minor; *cyclophyllus*, 1 ft., green, E. Medit. Region; *foetidus*, ' Stinking Hellebore ', green and purple, Feb., 2 to 3 ft., Britain; *guttatus*, white and crimson, Jan. to April, 1½ ft., Caucasus; *lividus*, green, March, 2 ft., Corsica; *multifidus*, 1 ft., much divided leaves, green, Balkans; *niger*, ' Christmas Rose ', white, winter, 6 to 15 in., Europe, and vars. *altifolius*, white and purple, *angustifolius*, white, and *major*, white; *odorus*, ' Fragrant Hellebore ', green, March, 1½ ft., Hungary; *olympicus*, purple, Feb. to April, 1 to 2 ft., Greece; *orientalis*, ' Lenten Rose ', rose, Feb. to May, 1 to 2 ft., Greece; *vesicarius*, 1 ft., greenish, inflated fruits, N. Syria; *viridis*, ' Green Hellebore ', green, March, 1½ ft., Europe. Many vars. will be found in trade lists.

Helmet or **Bucket Orchid,** see Coryanthes.

Helonias (Stud-flower)—*Liliaceae.* Hardy tuberous-rooted perennial. First introduced mid-eighteenth century.

CULTURE: Soil, sandy loam and peat. Position, moist, shady borders or margins of lakes or ponds. Plant, Oct., March or April.

PROPAGATION: By seeds sown 1/16 in. deep in a well-drained pan of sandy peat in cold shady frame in March or April; division of roots, Oct. or March.

SPECIES CULTIVATED: *H. bullata*, ' Swamp Pink ', purplish-rose, summer, 18 in. N. America. See also Zygadenus.

Helxine (Baby's Tears)—*Urticaceae.* Hardy perennial with creeping or trailing shoots.

CULTURE: Soil, ordinary, mixed with a little leaf-mould and sand. Position, in pots suspended in windows or as edgings to beds, or carpeting small beds on rockery in sun or shade. Pot in spring, or plant out in May. Water moderately those grown in pots.

PROPAGATION: By division in spring.

SPECIES CULTIVATED: *H. Solierolii*, 2 to 3 in., tiny neat green leaves, very invasive, Corsica.

Hemerocallis (Day Lily)—*Liliaceae.* Hardy herbaceous perennials. First introduced late sixteenth century.

CULTURE: Soil, ordinary deep rich. Position, moist borders, open or slightly shady. Plant, Oct., March or April, singly or in groups. Lift and replant only when they become unhealthy. Mulch established clumps with decayed manure in April or May.

PROPAGATION: By division of roots, Oct. or March.

SPECIES CULTIVATED: *H. aurantiaca major*, ' Japanese Day Lily ', apricot, summer, 3 ft., Japan; *Dumortieri,* orange-yellow, July, 2 ft., Japan; *flava,* orange-yellow, fragrant, July, 2 to 3 ft., S. Europe; *fulva,* yellow, June, 2 to 3 ft., Europe and Japan, and vars. *Kwanso,* double flowered, *longituba,* and *rosea*; *Middendorffii,* golden yellow, summer, 2 ft., Siberia and Japan; *minor* (syn. *H. graminea*), yellow, fragrant, 8 in., Siberia and Japan; *Thunbergii,* yellow, July, fragrant, 2 ft., Japan. There are also many fine hybrids.

Hemionitis—*Polypodiaceae.* Warm greenhouse evergreen ferns. Fronds heart- or hand-shaped. First introduced late eighteenth century.

CULTURE: Compost, two parts peat, one part sand. Position, small well-drained pots in shade. Pot, Feb. or March. Water moderately March to Sept., occasionally other times. Syringing not required. Temp., March to Sept. 60° to 70°, Sept. to March 55° to 60°.

PROPAGATION: By spores sown on surface of pans of sandy peat under bell-glass in temp. 65° to 75° at any time.

SPECIES CULTIVATED: *H. arifolia* (syn. *H. cordata*), 6 in., Ceylon, etc.; *palmata,* 8 in., W. Indies.

Hemiptelia—*Cyatheaceae.* Stove and greenhouse evergreen tree ferns with feather-shaped fronds. First introduced early nineteenth century.

CULTURE: Compost, equal parts peat, loam and sand. Position, well-drained pots or tubs in shade. Pot, March. Water freely March to Sept., moderately afterwards. Syringe trunks daily March to Sept. Temp., Sept. to March 55° to 65°, March to Sept. 65° to 75°, for stove species; Sept. to March 45° to 55°, March to Sept. 55° to 65°, for greenhouse species.

PROPAGATION: By spores sown at any time on surface of finely sifted loam and peat in shallow well-drained pans under bell-glass in moist, shady position in temp. 75° to 85°.

STOVE SPECIES CULTIVATED: *H. horrida,* 6 to 10 ft., W. Indies.

GREENHOUSE SPECIES CULTIVATED: *H. capensis,* 6 to 10 ft., S. Africa; *Smithii,* 'Smith's Tree Fern', 10 to 12 ft., New Zealand; *Walkerae,* 4 to 6 ft., Ceylon.

Hemlock, see Tsuga; **-Spruce,** see Tsuga.

Hemp, see *Cannabis sativa*; **-Agrimony,** see *Eupatorium cannabinum.*

Hepatica—*Ranunculaceae.* Hardy perennial herbs, sometimes included in the genus Anemone.

CULTURE: Soil, rich, well drained. Position, thin woodland, useful for colonising.

PROPAGATION: By seeds; division of roots.

SPECIES CULTIVATED: *H. americana* (syn. *Anemone Hepatica*), blue, Feb. to March, 6 in., Europe, N. America; *transsilvanica* (syn. *Anemone transsilvanica*), rose, spring, 3 to 5 in., Hungary, Romania, and various colour forms.

Heracleum (Cow Parsnip)—*Umbelliferae.* Coarse hardy perennial herbs with large, feather-shaped, green leaves.

CULTURE: Soil, ordinary. Position, open or sheltered shrubberies, borders, margins of ponds, lakes, etc. Plant, Oct. or Nov. Remove flower stems immediately they appear early in June if fine, healthy foliage is desired.

PROPAGATION: By seeds sown ¼ in. deep in ordinary soil outdoors, March or April; division of roots, Oct. or March.

SPECIES CULTIVATED: *H. Mantegazzianum,* white, summer, very large leaves, 7 to 9 ft., Caucasus; *villosum* (syn. *H. giganteum*), ' Cartwheel Flower ', white and yellow, summer, 10 to 12 ft., Caucasus.

Herb Christopher, see *Actaea spicata*; **-of-Grace,** see *Ruta graveolens*; **-Paris,** see *Paris quadrifolia*; **-Patience,** see *Rumex Patientia*; **-Robert,** see *Geranium Robertianum.*

Hercules' Club, see *Aralia spinosa* and *Zanthoxylum Clava-Herculis.*

Herminium (Musk Orchis)—*Orchidaceae*. Hardy terrestrial orchid with musk-scented flowers.
CULTURE: Soil, light turfy loam with plenty of chalk or old mortar and leaf-mould added. Position, sunny rockeries, or in pots in cold frame. Plant wild roots directly flowers have faded, pot-grown roots in early spring.
PROPAGATION: By division in spring.
SPECIES CULTIVATED: *H. monorchis*, green and yellow, July, 6 in., Britain.

Hermodactylus (Snakeshead Iris)—*Iridaceae*. One tuberous species closely allied to Iris.
CULTURE: As tuberous iris.
PROPAGATION: By seed; division.
SPECIES CULTIVATED: *H. tuberosus* (syn. *Iris tuberosa*), violet, black and green, March, 9 to 12 in., Medit.

Herniaria (Rupture-wort)—*Illecebraceae*. Hardy perennial trailing herbs.
CULTURE: Soil, ordinary. Position, sunny or shady rockeries, or as edgings to carpet-beds, or for carpeting surfaces of beds containing choice bulbs. Plant, Oct., Nov., March to June.
PROPAGATION: By seeds sown $\frac{1}{16}$ in. deep in light sandy soil outdoors, March or April; division of plants, Oct., Nov., March, April or May.
SPECIES CULTIVATED: *H. glabra*, leaves dark green, 1 in., Europe (Br.), var. *aurea*, leaves golden; *hirsuta*, leaves hairy, prostrate, Europe.

Heron's Bill, see Erodium.

Herpetospermum—*Cucurbitaceae*. Half-hardy annual climbing plants.
CULTURE : As for Cucurbita.
PROPAGATION: As for Cucurbita.
SPECIES CULTIVATED: *H. pedunculosum*, yellow, summer, N. India.

Hesperantha (Evening-flower)—*Iridaceae*. Greenhouse bulbous flowering plants with fragrant flowers opening in the evening. First introduced late eighteenth century.
CULTURE: Compost, two parts fibrous loam, one part leaf-mould or decayed cow manure, and little sand. Position, well-drained pots in cold frame, cool greenhouse or window till growth begins, then remove to temp. 45° to 55°. Pot, Nov., placing five bulbs 3 in. deep in a 5 in. pot. Cover pots with coconut-fibre refuse or cinder ashes till growth begins. Water moderately from time growth commences till flowers fade, then gradually withhold, keeping bulbs quite dry from Sept. to Jan.
PROPAGATION: By offsets treated as advised for bulbs.
SPECIES CULTIVATED: *H. cinnamomea*, white, April and May, 6 in.; *falcata*, brown and white, May, 10 in.; *pilosa*, white and red, April, 6 in.; *radiata*, white and red, May, 6 in.

Hesperis—*Cruciferae*. Hardy perennial and biennial herbs with fragrant flowers. First introduced late sixteenth century.
CULTURE OF PERENNIAL SPECIES: Soil, ordinary rich moist. Position, sunny beds or borders. Plant, Oct., Nov., March or April. Mulch with decayed manure in May. Apply liquid manure occasionally in summer to double varieties. Cut down flower stems in Oct. Lift and replant double kinds every second year.
PROPAGATION: Single kinds by seeds sown $\frac{1}{4}$ in. deep in sunny position outdoors in April, transplanting seedlings in June or July; double kinds by cuttings of young shoots 3 in. long inserted in sandy soil in shady position outdoors, July to Sept., or under hand-light or in cold frame, Sept. or Oct., transplanting in March; also by division of roots, Oct. or March.
CULTURE OF BIENNIAL SPECIES: Soil, ordinary. Position, well-drained borders or old walls. Sow seeds where plants are to flower, in July thinning seedlings to 6 to 12 in.
PERENNIAL SPECIES CULTIVATED: *H. matronalis*, ' Sweet Rocket ', ' Dame's

Violet ', ' Dame's Rocket ', white or lilac, May to July, 2 to 3 ft., S. Europe, and its double white and purple flowered vars.

BIENNIAL SPECIES CULTIVATED: *H. tristis,* white, cream or purplish, summer, 1 to 2 ft., S. Europe.

Hesperochiron—*Hydrophyllaceae.* Hardy herbaceous perennials.
CULTURE: Soil, sandy loam, deep and well drained. Position, sunny sheltered pocket in the rock garden.
PROPAGATION: By seeds sown in spring in soil as above.
SPECIES CULTIVATED: *H. californicus,* white, 6 to 9 in., summer, N. America; *pumilus,* white, pink or lavender, 4 to 6 in., summer, N. America.

Hesperoscordum, see Brodiaea.

Hessea—*Amaryllidaceae.* Greenhouse bulbous flowering plants. First introduced mid-eighteenth century.
CULTURE: Compost, two parts sandy soil, one part leaf-mould or decayed cow manure, and little sand. Position, well-drained pots in cold frame, cool greenhouse, or window till growth begins, then remove to temp. 45° to 55°. Pot, Nov., placing five bulbs 3 in. deep in a 5 in. pot. Cover pots with peat or cinder ashes till growth begins. Water moderately from time growth commences till flowers fade, then gradually withhold, keeping bulbs quite dry till potting time. Repot annually. May be grown outdoors in sunny borders in the mildest parts of the country.
PROPAGATION: By offsets treated as bulbs.
SPECIES CULTIVATED: *H. crispa,* pink, summer, 3 in., S. Africa; *gemmata,* yellow, Aug., 10 in., S. Africa.

Heteranthera (Mud Plantain)—*Pontederiaceae.* Tender aquatics for indoor tanks or aquariums.
CULTURE: Soil, rich loam. Position, full sun in very shallow water. Plant, March to June.
PROPAGATION: Cuttings in shallow water or division during growing season.
SPECIES CULTIVATED: *H. graminea,* yellow, bronze growth, used in aquariums, S. America; *limosa,* blue or white, Trop. America; *reniformis,* scrambling growth, pale blue, S. and Trop. America; *zosterifolia,* aquarium oxygenator, blue flowers, S. America.

Heteromeles—*Rosaceae.* Slightly tender evergreen shrub. First introduced late eighteenth century.
CULTURE: Soil, well-drained open loam. Position, sheltered shrubberies or walls in mild districts. Large well-drained pots in cool greenhouse elsewhere.
PROPAGATION: By seeds sown in sandy soil in pans during Feb. in temp. 60° to 65°; cuttings of partially ripened shoots during July under bell-glass in gentle bottom heat; layers.
SPECIES CULTIVATED: *H. arbutifolia* (syn. *Photinia arbutifolia*), ' Christmas Berry ', white, Aug., small red berries in clusters, seldom formed in this climate, 15 ft., California, var. *chrysocarpa,* yellow berries.

Heuchera (Alum-root)—*Saxifragaceae.* Hardy perennial herbs. *H. tiarelloides* is now *Heucherella tiarelloides.* First introduced mid-seventeenth century.
CULTURE: Soil, ordinary, light, rich or peaty; not suited for clay soils. Position, open sunny well-drained borders. Plant, Oct., Nov., March or April.
PROPAGATION: By division of roots or crowns, March to May; also by seeds sown in light soil in cold frames in spring, transplanting seedlings into small pots and planting out following spring.
SPECIES CULTIVATED: *H. americana,* red, summer, 18 in., N. America; *brizoides,* pink, summer, 1 ft., hybrid; *micrantha,* yellowish-white, summer, 2 ft., N. America; *pubescens,* pale red and yellow, summer, brown-mottled foliage, 2 to 3 ft., N. America; *sanguinea,* ' Coral Bells ', red, summer, 12 to 18 in., Mexico. There are several vars. to be found in trade lists.

× **Heucherella**—*Saxifragaceae.* A bigeneric hybrid between Heuchera and Tiarella. Sometimes included in Heuchera and similar to *H. sanguinea*, but with stamens varying from 5 to 10. Hardy herbaceous perennials.

CULTURE: Soil, ordinary. Position, sun or half-shade. Plant, Oct., to Nov., or March to April.

PROPAGATION: By division.

SPECIES CULTIVATED: *H. alba*, white, leaves longer than broad, May to June, to 2 ft.; *tiarelloides* (syn. *Heuchera tiarelloides*), pink or red, bell-shaped, summer, 8 to 12 in.

Hibbertia—*Dilleniaceae.* Greenhouse evergreen flowering climbers. First introduced early nineteenth century.

CULTURE: Compost, equal parts loam and peat, and little sand. Position, pots, tubs or beds; shoots trained up rafters. Pot or plant, Feb. or March. Prune straggling shoots, Feb. Water abundantly March to Sept., moderately afterwards. Temp., March to Oct. 55° to 75°, Oct. to March 45° to 55°.

PROPAGATION: By cuttings of moderately firm shoots to 3 in. long inserted in well-drained pots of sandy peat under bell-glass in temp. 55° to 65°, April to Aug.

SPECIES CULTIVATED: *H. dentata*, yellow, summer, trailing or twining, Australia; *perfoliata*, pale yellow, summer, trailing, Australia; *volubilis*, yellow, summer, strong climber, Australia.

Hibiscus (Rose Mallow)—*Malvaceae.* Stove evergreen and hardy deciduous flowering shrubs, hardy annuals and perennials. First introduced late sixteenth century.

CULTURE OF STOVE SPECIES: Compost, equal parts fibrous peat and loam, with charcoal and sand. Position, well-drained pots or beds with shoots trained to wall. Pot or plant, Feb. or March. Prune into shape, Feb. Water abundantly March to Oct., moderately afterwards. Temp., March to Oct. 65° to 75°, Oct. to March 55° to 65°. *H. Manihot* makes a useful pot plant treated as a tender annual and grown in the greenhouse for summer flowering.

CULTURE OF ANNUAL SPECIES: Soil, ordinary. Position, sunny beds or borders.

CULTURE OF SHRUBBY SPECIES: Soil, rich light loam. Position, sheltered, sunny, well-drained border. Plant, Oct. Prune after flowering, only thinning out weak and dead wood.

PROPAGATION: Stove species, by seeds in well-drained pots of sandy peat under bell-glass in temp. 75° in March; cuttings of firm shoots in sandy peat under bell-glass in temp. 75° in spring or summer; grafting in March. Perennial species, by seeds sown outdoors in April, or division of roots in March. Annual species, sow seeds of *H. Trionum* in April where plants are to flower, seeds of other annuals in well-drained pans during Feb. in temp. 60° to 65° and grow on in pots in greenhouse or planted outdoors in June. Shrubby species, by cuttings in sandy peat in cold frame in summer, or grafting in March.

STOVE SPECIES CULTIVATED: *H. Archeri*, hybrid between *H. schizopetalus* and *H. Rosa-sinensis*; *Cameronii*, rose, July, 4 to 5 ft., Madagascar; *coccineus*, scarlet, 10 ft., America; *Manihot*, with 6 in. yellow flowers with large blotch of maroon, 10 ft., Tropics; *Rosa-sinensis*, 'Blacking Plant', crimson, summer, to 25 ft., Asia; *schizopetalus*, orange-red, 10 ft., E. Trop. Africa.

ANNUAL SPECIES CULTIVATED: *H. diversifolius*, white with maroon centre, Africa, Australia, Pacific Isles; *esculentus*, 'Okra', 'Gumbo', yellow, to 6 ft., immature fruit used as a vegetable in America, Tropics; *Trionum* (syn. *H. africanus*), white with violet eye, 2 ft., Africa, N. America.

SHRUBBY SPECIES CULTIVATED: *H. syriacus* (syn. *Althaea frutex*), 'Shrubby Althaea', various colours, Aug. to Sept., to 10 ft., India and China, and many vars.

Hickory, see Carya.

Hidalgoa—*Compositae.* Half-hardy climbing perennial. First introduced late nineteenth century.

OUTDOOR CULTURE: Raise plants from seed or cuttings in heat in spring and plant out against a sunny trellis or arch late in May. Water freely, and feed with liquid manure when plants begin to bloom. Cut down shoots in Sept., lift roots, and place them in pots in a heated house to furnish cuttings in spring.

GREENHOUSE CULTURE: Grow in equal parts loam and leaf-mould, with plenty of sand. Water freely in spring and summer, little at other seasons. Train shoots up roof.

PROPAGATION: By cuttings of young shoots in spring.

SPECIES CULTIVATED: *H. Wercklei*, ' Climbing Dahlia ', scarlet and yellow, summer, 12 to 15 ft., Costa Rica.

Hieracium (Hawkweed)—*Compositae*. Hardy perennial herbs.

CULTURE: Soil, ordinary. Position, sunny banks or elevated borders. Plant, Oct. or March.

PROPAGATION: By seeds sown $\frac{1}{16}$ in. deep outdoors in March or April; division of roots any time in spring.

SPECIES CULTIVATED: *H. aurantiacum*, orange-red, summer, 12 to 18 in., Cent. Europe, naturalised in Britain; *bombycinum*, yellow, silver leaves, 9 in., June, Europe; *brunneocroceum* (syn. *H. aurantiacum* hort.), brownish-orange, 9 to 18 in., Cent. Europe, naturalised in Britain; *villosum*, yellow, May to July, 1 ft., Europe.

Hierochloe (Holy Grass)—*Gramineae*. Hardy perennial grasses. Inflorescence chestnut-coloured, fragrant, borne in panicles; May to July.

CULTURE: Soil, ordinary. Position, damp, shady borders or margins of ponds. Plant, March or April.

PROPAGATION: By seeds sown in damp positions outdoors in spring; division of plants in March.

SPECIES CULTIVATED: *H. odorata* (syn. *H. borealis*), 1 to 2 ft., Europe (Br.).

Himalayan Honeysuckle, see *Leycesteria formosa*; **-Poppy,** see *Meconopsis betonicifolia*.

Himantoglossum—*Orchidaceae*. Hardy terrestrial orchid.

CULTURE: As Ophrys.

PROPAGATION: As Ophrys.

SPECIES CULTIVATED: *H. hircinum*, ' Lizard Orchid ', green or greenish-white, lip with few red marks, goat-scented, summer, Europe, Britain, N. Africa.

Hindsia—*Rubiaceae*. Stove evergreen flowering shrubs. First introduced mid-nineteenth century.

CULTURE: Compost, equal parts rough fibrous peat, light loam, silver sand and charcoal. Position, well-drained pots in light stove. Pot, Feb. or March. Water freely April to Sept., moderately afterwards. Prune into shape, Feb. Temp., Feb. to Aug. 65° to 75°, Aug. to Nov. 60° to 70°, Nov. to Feb. 55° to 65°.

PROPAGATION: By cuttings of firm shoots inserted in well-drained pots of pure silver sand under bell-glass in temp. 65° to 75° from March to June.

SPECIES CULTIVATED: *H. longiflora*, blue, summer, 2 to 3 ft., Brazil, and var. *alba*, white; *violacea*, violet blue, May, 3 ft., Brazil.

Hippeastrum—*Amaryllidaceae*. Stove bulbous plants, popularly known as Amaryllis. First introduced mid-seventeenth century.

CULTURE: Compost, two parts turfy loam, one part river sand and a few crushed bones. Position, well-drained pots in light part of stove. Pot, Jan., burying bulb about two-thirds of its depth. Water freely from time growth begins (about Feb.) until July, when keep quite dry. Apply liquid manure when flower spike shows. Top-dress large bulbs annually and repot every three or four years only. Temp., Feb. to Sept. 65° to 75°, Sept. to Feb. 50° to 55°.

PROPAGATION: By seeds sown $\frac{1}{16}$ in. deep in well-drained pots of sandy loam in temp. 65° to 70° in March, placing seedlings singly in 2 in. pots and keeping them moderately moist all the year round for three years; by offsets treated as old bulbs. Seedlings are three years or so before they flower.

SPECIES CULTIVATED: *H. aulicum*, crimson and orange, winter, 2 ft., Brazil;

pardinum, green, yellow and scarlet, spring, 2 ft., Peru; *pratense*, scarlet, spring and early summer, Chile; *procerum*, bluish-mauve, 3 ft., spring, Brazil; *psittacinum*, orange and scarlet, summer, 2 ft., Brazil; *puniceum* (syn. *H. equestre*), 'Barbados Lily', red, summer, 18 in., Trop. America; *Reginae*, red and white, spring, 2 ft., S. America; *reticulatum*, rose or scarlet, spring, 1 ft., Brazil; *rutilum*, bright crimson and green, spring, 1 ft., S. Brazil; *vittatum*, crimson and white, spring, 2 ft., Peru. Numerous hybrids, more beautiful than the species, will be found in trade lists.

Hippocrepis—*Leguminosae.* Hardy evergreen trailing herb.
CULTURE: Soil, ordinary. Position, sunny rockeries or elevated borders. Plant, March or April.
PROPAGATION: By seeds sown $\frac{1}{16}$ in. deep in fine soil in sunny position outdoors in March or April; division of roots in March.
SPECIES CULTIVATED: *H. comosa*, 'Horseshoe Vetch', yellow, May to Aug., Europe, Africa.

Hippophae (Sea Buckthorn)—*Elaeagnaceae.* Hardy deciduous berry-bearing shrub. Male and female flowers borne on separate plants. Both must be grown to ensure a crop of berries.
CULTURE: Soil, ordinary. Position, open or shady shrubberies and inland or seaside gardens. Plant, Oct. to Feb.
PROPAGATION: By seeds sown $\frac{1}{2}$ in. deep outdoors in Nov. or Dec.; by cuttings of roots inserted in Feb. or March in ordinary soil outdoors; layering shoots in autumn.
SPECIES CULTIVATED: *H. rhamnoides*, silver foliaged and partly spined shrub or small tree, most useful for seaside planting, but also highly ornamental in inland gardens for its long-persisting orange berries, to 20 ft., sometimes more, Europe, including Britain.

Hippuris (Mare's Tail)—*Haloragidaceae.* Hardy aquatic perennial. Leaves, narrow, strap-shaped; in circles round the stem.
CULTURE: Soil, mud. Position, bogs, ponds or damp places. Plant, March to June.
PROPAGATION: By division of roots, March.
SPECIES CULTIVATED: *H. vulgaris*, 8 to 12 in., Europe (Br.).

Hoffmannia—*Rubiaceae.* Warm greenhouse herbaceous perennials and shrubs. First introduced mid-nineteenth century.
CULTURE: Compost, equal parts fibrous loam and leaf-mould, with liberal addition of sharp sand. Position, large well-drained pots in sunny greenhouse. Water freely during growing season, sparingly at other times. Temp., March to Sept. 60° to 70°, Sept. to March 55° to 60°.
PROPAGATION: By cuttings of young growth inserted in sandy soil in propagating frame with brisk bottom heat.
SPECIES CULTIVATED: *H. discolor*, red, foliage shining green above, purple beneath, 6 in., Mexico; *Ghiesbreghtii*, red and yellow, foliage velvety green above, purple beneath, 4 ft., Mexico, and var. *variegata*; *refulgens*, pale red, foliage green and red, reddish beneath, 1 to 2 ft., Mexico; *regalis*, yellow, foliage deep green above, purplish-red beneath, 1 ft., Mexico.

Hog Plum, see *Spondias Mombin.*

Hoheria—*Malvaceae.* Slightly tender flowering evergreen and deciduous shrubs.
CULTURE: Soil, rich, deep loam. Position, sheltered borders in favoured localities in the south and other districts.
PROPAGATION: By cuttings of half-ripened shoots in July in sandy soil with gentle bottom heat.
SPECIES CULTIVATED: *H. glabrata* (syns. *Gaya Lyallii* and *Plagianthus Lyallii*), tall shrub or small tree, 1 in., pure white fragrant flowers, deciduous, July, New Zealand; *populnea*, 30 ft., evergreen, fast growing, white, Sept. to Oct., New

Zealand; *sexstylosa* (syn. *H. populnea lanceolata*), similar to preceding, flowering freely in July to Aug., New Zealand.

Hoho, see *Pseudopanax chathamicum.*

Holboellia—*Berberidaceae* (or *Lardizabalaceae*).   Cool greenhouse flowering evergreen climber.   First introduced mid-nineteenth century.
CULTURE: Compost, two parts loam, one part of equal proportions of leaf-mould and silver sand. Position, large pots or tubs, shoots trained up roof. Prune away weak shoots in autumn.   Water freely during spring and summer, moderately in winter.   Syringe freely when not in flower.   Temp., Sept. to March 40° to 50°, March to Sept. 50° to 60°.
PROPAGATION: By cuttings inserted in sandy soil in gentle heat in spring.
SPECIES CULTIVATED: *H. latifolia* (syn. *Stauntonia latifolia*), white, fragrant, spring, 10 to 20 ft., Himalaya.

Holcus—*Gramineae.* Hardy ornamental perennial grass.
CULTURE: Soil, ordinary. Position, edgings to beds or borders, or in clumps in borders. Plant, Oct., March or April.
PROPAGATION: By division of plants in Oct., March or April.
SPECIES CULTIVATED: *H. lanatus*, 6 to 12 in., Britain.

Holly, see Ilex; **-Oak,** see *Quercus Ilex.*

Hollyhock, see *Althaea rosea.*

Holm Oak, see *Quercus Ilex.*

Holodiscus—*Rosaceae.* Hardy deciduous flowering shrubs, formerly included in Spiraea.
CULTURE: Soil, good ordinary well drained.   Position, sunny.
PROPAGATION: By seeds; layers.
SPECIES CULTIVATED: *H. discolor* (syn. *Spiraea discolor*), creamy-white, July, 8 to 14 ft., W. North America, var. *ariaefolius* (syn. *Spiraea ariaefolia*), leaves grey, pubescent beneath; *dumosus*, flowers in panicles, 8 ft., Southern N. America.

Holy Ghost, see Archangelica; **-flower,** see *Peristeria elata.*

Holy Thistle, see *Silybum Marianum.*

Homalocladium—*Polygonaceae.* Greenhouse shrub with flat, articulated, striate stems, usually leafless in the flowering stage.   Grown as a curiosity and sometimes included in the genus Muehlenbeckia.
CULTURE: As Muehlenbeckia.
PROPAGATION: As Muehlenbeckia.
SPECIES CULTIVATED: *H. platycladum* (syn. *Muehlenbeckia platyclados*), ' Centipede Plant ', to 10 ft., Solomon Islands.

Homeria—*Iridaceae.* Handsome greenhouse bulbous plants.   First introduced late eighteenth century.
POT CULTURE: Compost, loam, leaf-mould and sand in equal parts. Place bulbs 1 in. apart and 1 in. deep in 5 in. pots during Sept. and Oct. Stand in a cold frame and cover with a few inches of coconut-fibre refuse till growth begins, then remove to greenhouse. Plant in pots near the glass. Water freely during active growth. Keep nearly dry after flowers fade to ripen bulbs. Repot annually in autumn.
OUTDOOR CULTURE: Plant bulbs 3 to 4 in. deep in light, rich, well-drained soil in a south border between Oct. and Jan.   Protect with bracken litter in winter.
PROPAGATION: By offsets removed at planting time.
SPECIES CULTIVATED: *H. collina* (syn. *Moraea collina*), red and yellow, spring, 1 ft., S. Africa, var. *aurantiaca*, orange, red and yellow, spring, 1 ft., S. Africa; *elegans*, yellow, brown and orange, summer, 1 ft., S. Africa; *lineata*, red and yellow, spring, 1 ft., S. Africa; *miniata*, red, spring, 6 to 8 in., S. Africa.

Homogyne—*Compositae.* Dwarf evergreen perennial rock plants.

CULTURE: Almost any reasonably good soil. Position, sunny.
PROPAGATION: By seeds; division of plants in spring or autumn.
SPECIES CULTIVATED: *H. alpina*, pink, 3 in., summer, S.E. Europe; *discolor*, pink, leaves with silver reverse, 3 in., summer, Alps.

Honesty, see *Lunaria biennis*.

Honey Locust, see Gleditsia.

Honeysuckle, see Lonicera.

Honeywort, see Cerinthe.

Hoodia—*Asclepiadaceae*. Greenhouse succulent flowering plants. Stems, cylindrical, prickly, leafless. First introduced mid-nineteenth century.
CULTURE: Compost, equal parts sandy loam, old mortar, broken bricks and dry cow manure. Position, well-drained pots, fully exposed to sun in warm greenhouse. Repot every three or four years in Feb. or March. Water moderately March to Oct., keep quite dry Oct. to March. Temp., April to Sept. 65° to 75°, Sept. to April 45° to 55°.
PROPAGATION: By portions of fleshy stems 3 in. long cut clean at base and laid on sunny shelf to dry for several days; then insert in small well-drained pots of sandy soil in temp. of 55° to 65°, April to Aug.
SPECIES CULTIVATED: *H. Bainii*, yellow, Aug., 1 ft., S. Africa; *Gordonii*, yellow and purple, July, 18 in., S. Africa.

Hookera, see Brodiaea.

Hop, see Humulus; **-Hornbeam,** see Ostrya; **-tree,** see *Ptelea trifoliata*.

Hordeum—*Gramineae*. Hardy annual flowering grass. Inflorescence barley-like, borne in spikes, June to Sept., very useful for cutting. First introduced late eighteenth century.
CULTURE: Soil, ordinary. Position, open dryish borders.
PROPAGATION: By seeds sown ⅛ in. deep in March or April in borders where plants are required to flower.
SPECIES CULTIVATED: *H. jubatum*, ' Squirreltail Grass ', 2 ft., N. America.

Horehound, see Marrubium.

Horminum—*Labiatae*. Hardy herbaceous perennial. First introduced early nineteenth century.
CULTURE: Soil, ordinary. Position, open well-drained borders. Plant, Oct., March or April.
PROPAGATION: By seeds sown 1/16 in. deep outdoors in March or April; by division of roots, Oct. to March.
SPECIES CULTIVATED: *H. pyrenaicum*, 'Pyrenean Dead Nettle', blue, summer, 1 ft., Pyrenees.

Hornbeam, see *Carpinus Betulus*.

Horn of Plenty, see *Fedia Cornucopiae* and *Datura Metel*.

Hornwort, see Ceratophyllum

Horned Poppy, see Glaucium; **-Rampion,** see *Phyteuma orbiculare*; **-Violet,** see *Viola cornuta*.

Horse Chestnut, see *Aesculus Hippocastanum*; **-mint,** see Monarda; **-radish,** see *Armoracia rusticana*; **-shoe Vetch,** see *Hippocrepis comosa*; **-tail,** see Equisetum.

Hosta (Plantain Lily)—*Liliaceae*. Hardy herbaceous flowering plants with ornamental foliage, formerly known as Funkia. First introduced late eighteenth century.
CULTURE: Soil, ordinary, with decayed manure. Position, open sunny well-drained borders. Plant, Oct. or March. Top-dress annually with decayed manure.
POT CULTURE: Compost, two parts loam, one part well-decayed manure and sand. Position, pots in cold frame Oct. to March, greenhouse or window March

to Oct. Pot, March or April. Water moderately Oct. to March, freely other times. Apply liquid manure to healthy plants when in flower.

PROPAGATION: By division of crowns in Oct., March or April.

SPECIES CULTIVATED: *H. crispula* (syn. *H. Fortunei albo-marginata*), whitish, July, 2½ ft., Japan; *decorata*, dark lilac, July, 2 ft., Japan; *erromena*, whitish, July, 2½ ft., Japan; *Fortunei* (syn. *Funkia Fortunei*), whitish, July, 2 ft., Japan; *glauca* (syn. *Funkia glauca*), whitish, July, 1½ ft., Japan; *lancifolia* (syn. *Funkia lancifolia*), lilac, Aug., 2 ft., Japan; *plantaginea* (syn. *Funkia subcordata*), ' Corfu Lily ', white, fragrant, Sept., 2½ ft., China; *rectifolia*, dark lilac, Aug., 2 ft., Japan; *tardiflora*, lilac, 9 in., Oct., Japan; *undulata*, whitish, July, 2½ ft., Japan; *ventricosa* (syn. *H. caerulea, Funkia ovata*), dark violet, July, 3 ft., China.

Hottentot Fig, see *Carpobrotus edulis*; **-Bread,** see *Testudinaria elephantipes*.

Hottonia (Water Violet)—*Primulaceae.* Hardy aquatic perennial herb.

CULTURE: Soil, ordinary. Position, shallow water in aquarium, ponds and rivulets or in bogs. Plant, March to July.

PROPAGATION: Division, setting each plant separately in a pot and lowering in the water or weighting individually.

SPECIES CULTIVATED: *H. palustris*, pinnate foliage, in whorls round stem, lilac flowers in whorls 8 to 10 in. above water level, Europe (Br.).

Houlletia—*Orchidaceae.* Evergreen epiphytal orchids. Flowers fragrant, on usually erect spikes from base of pseudo-bulbs which carry generally but one leaf. Flowers rather large. Lip more or less spear-shaped, horned at base.

CULTURE: Compost and temps. as for Stanhopeas. Pots are preferable to baskets. Rest, after growth is matured, not too severe.

PROPAGATION: By division of plants when, or just before, growth commences.

SPECIES CULTIVATED: *H. Brocklehurstiana*, brown and yellow, summer, 2 ft., Brazil; *odoratissima*, red, white, summer, 2 ft., Colombia, var. *antioquensis*, larger, lip with more yellow; *picta*, cinnamon brown, yellow, summer, Colombia; *Sanderi*, creamy-white to yellow, malodorous, summer, Peru; *Wallisii* (syn. *H. chrysantha*), yellow, chocolate and crimson, summer, 2 ft., Colombia.

Houpara, see *Pseudopanax Lessionii.*

Houstonia—*Rubiaceae.* Hardy herbaceous perennials. First introduced late eighteenth century.

CULTURE: Soil, leaf-mould and sand. Position, partially shaded crevices, nooks and crannies of moist rockeries. Plant, March or April.

PROPAGATION: By seeds sown $\frac{1}{16}$ in. deep in pans of leaf-mould and sand in cold frame in spring or autumn; division of roots in Sept. or Oct.

SPECIES CULTIVATED: *H. caerulea*, ' Bluets ', blue, May to July, 4 to 6 in., Virginia, var. *alba*, white; *purpurea*, white to pink, summer, 6 to 12 in., N. America; *serpyllifolia*, white, summer, 3 in., N. America.

Houseleek, see Sempervivum.

Houttuynia—*Saururaceae.* Hardy aquatic perennial for the waterside. First introduced early nineteenth century.

CULTURE: Soil, heavy loam. Position, boggy or wet ground or in shallow water. Plant, spring.

PROPAGATION: By division in spring.

SPECIES CULTIVATED: *H. cordata*, white flowers, heart-shaped leaves, 18 to 24 in., China and Japan.

Hovea—*Leguminosae.* Greenhouse evergreen flowering shrubs. First introduced early nineteenth century.

CULTURE: Compost, three parts peat, one part loam and little silver sand. Position, well-drained pots in light airy greenhouse. Pot, Feb. or March. Nip off points of young shoots in spring to induce bushy growth. Water freely April to Sept., moderately Sept. to April. Temp., March to July 55° to 65°, Sept. **to**

March 45° to 50°. Place plants outdoors from July to Sept. to mature flowering shoots for following year.

PROPAGATION: By seeds sown $\frac{1}{16}$ in. deep in well-drained pots of sandy peat in temp. of 55° to 65° in March or April; cuttings inserted in sandy soil under bell-glass in temp. 55°, April to July.

SPECIES CULTIVATED: *H. Celsii*, blue, spring, 3 ft., Australia; *longifolia*, purple, spring, 5 ft., Australia; *pungens*, blue, spring, 1 to 2 ft., Australia.

Howea—*Palmae.* Greenhouse palms with feather-shaped, graceful leaves. Elegant plant for house decoration.

CULTURE: Compost, equal parts loam and peat, little silver sand. Position, well-drained pots in greenhouse, or in dwelling rooms during summer. Pot, Feb. or March. Temp., Sept. to March 45° to 55°, March to Sept. 55° to 65°. Water moderately Oct. to Feb., freely afterwards. Apply weak liquid manure to healthy plants once a week May to Sept. Syringe plants daily. Sponge leaves of those grown in dwelling rooms once weekly.

PROPAGATION: By seeds sown 1 in. deep in light soil in temp. 80°, Feb. or March.

SPECIES CULTIVATED: *H. Belmoreana* (syn. *Kentia Belmoreana*), 6 to 10 ft., Lord Howe's Island; *Forsteriana* (syn. *Kentia Forsteriana*), 6 to 15 ft., Lord Howe's Island.

Hoya—*Asclepiadaceae.* Stove and greenhouse climbing, flowering evergreen plants. First introduced early nineteenth century.

CULTURE: Compost, equal parts peat and loam, little charcoal and sand. Position, well-drained pots, beds or hanging baskets, with shoots trained round trellises, up rafters, or against walls, and fully exposed to the light. Pot or plant, Feb. or March. Water freely March to Sept., moderately Sept. to March. Temp., stove species, 65° to 75° March to Oct., 55° to 65° Oct. to March; greenhouse species, 55° to 65° March to Sept., 45° to 55° Sept. to March. Prune into shape, Feb. Foot stalks of flowers should not be removed after blooming, as these will produce a second crop of flowers.

PROPAGATION: By cuttings of shoots of preceding year's growth inserted in well-drained pots of sandy peat under bell-glass in temp. of 75° to 85° in March, April or May; layering shoots in pots of sandy peat in spring or summer.

STOVE SPECIES CULTIVATED: *H. bella*, white and crimson, summer, 3 ft., Burma.

GREENHOUSE SPECIES CULTIVATED: *H. australis* (syn. *H. Dalrympliana*), white, tinged pink, October, Australia; *carnosa*, 'Honey Plant', 'Wax Flower', pink and white, summer, 10 to 12 ft., China and Australia, and var. *variegata*.

Huckleberry, see Gaylussacia.

Hudsonia—*Cistaceae.* Slightly tender evergreen flowering shrubs. First introduced early nineteenth century.

CULTURE: Compost, two parts peat and one of sea sand. Position, well-drained rock gardens, full sun, sheltered from winds; or in pots for unheated greenhouse. A difficult plant to establish, but sometimes succeeds in a slightly saline soil.

PROPAGATION: By cuttings of firm shoots 1 to 2 in. long inserted in well-drained pots of silver sand under bell-glass in greenhouse, April to Aug.; layering in Sept. and Oct.

SPECIES CULTIVATED: *H. ericoides*, yellow, May to July, 6 to 8 in., U. States; *tomentosa*, yellow, June, 1 ft., N. America.

Hugelia, see Gilia.

Humata—*Polypodiaceae.* Stove and greenhouse ferns, formerly included in the genus Davallia.

CULTURE: As Davallia.

PROPAGATION: As Davallia.

STOVE SPECIES CULTIVATED: *H. heterophylla* (syn. *Davallia heterophylla*), dwarf, creeping, Malay; *repens* (syn. *Davallia pedata*), dwarf, India, Malaya, etc.

GREENHOUSE SPECIES CULTIVATED: *H. Tyermannii*, ' Bear's-foot Fern ', creeping, W. Africa, etc.

Humble-plant, see *Mimosa pudica*.

Humea—*Compositae*. Half-hardy biennial. First introduced early nineteenth century.

GREENHOUSE CULTURE: Compost, two parts sandy loam, half a part decayed manure, half a part charcoal and silver sand. Position, well-drained pots in cold frame during summer; airy greenhouse in winter and when in flower. Sow in June or July for blooming the following year. Water freely March to Oct., very little afterwards. Syringing unnecessary. Temp., Oct. to April 50°, April to Oct. 55° to 65°. Discard plants after flowering. Fine plants can be obtained in 8 in. pots.

OUTDOOR CULTURE: Soil, ordinary rich. Position, sunny well-drained beds or borders. Plant out in June. Water freely in dry weather.

PROPAGATION: By seeds sown on surface of fine soil in well-drained pots or pans, covering seeds slightly with fine soil, in June, in cold frame or greenhouse, potting seedlings singly in 2 in. pots when large enough to handle.

SPECIES CULTIVATED: *H. elegans*, ' Amaranth Feathers ', red, pink and crimson, in feathery panicles, June to Oct., 3 to 10 ft., Australia.

Humulus—*Moraceae*. Hardy annual and perennial twining climbers. Male blooms borne in axillary panicles, and female blooms in cones in clusters on separate plants; the latter form the hop of commerce and are the more ornamental.

CULTURE OF ANNUAL SPECIES: Soil, ordinary rich. Position, sunny or shady walls, fences, arbours, trellises or tree stumps. Plant, May or June. Water freely in dry weather. This species is an excellent plant for covering unsightly objects rapidly in summer.

CULTURE OF PERENNIAL SPECIES: Soil, deep, rich and well-manured loam. Position, sunny walls, fences, arbours, trellises, tree stumps, or in open ground with shoots trained round poles. Plant in groups of three, or 6 or 12 in. apart in rows 4 to 5 ft. asunder, Feb. or March. Top-dress annually with decayed manure in Feb. or March. Water freely in dry weather. Gather female flowers (hops) in Sept. for drying. Cut down plants in Oct.

PROPAGATION: Annual species by seeds sown ⅛ in. deep in pots of ordinary soil in cool or heated greenhouse in April, or where plants are required to grow in May; perennial species by seeds sown ⅛ in. deep in ordinary soil outdoors in March or April; division of roots in March.

ANNUAL SPECIES CULTIVATED: *H. japonicus variegatus*, ' Japanese Hop ', 8 to 10 ft., green and white variegated foliage, Japan.

PERENNIAL SPECIES CULTIVATED: *H. Lupulus*, ' Hop ', 10 to 15 ft., Europe; the golden-leaved form, *aureus*, is superior for garden cultivation.

Hunnemannia—*Papaveraceae*. Half-hardy herbaceous perennial. First introduced early nineteenth century.

CULTURE: Soil, ordinary rich. Position, sunny well-drained border at base of south wall. Plant, March. Protect with dry litter in winter.

PROPAGATION: By seeds sown as soon as ripe in a cold frame, planting out seedlings following June.

SPECIES CULTIVATED: *H. fumariifolia*, yellow, Aug., 2 ft., Mexico.

Huntleya—*Orchidaceae*. An epiphytic genus, separated from Zygopetalum, as pseudo-bulbs are absent. The scapes bear a single handsome flower with a raised transverse crest.

CULTURE: Compost, two parts of osmunda fibre, two parts of sphagnum moss. Pots or pans well drained. Water throughout the year and keep the atmosphere moist. Winter temp. 65°, summer to 75° by sun heat with shading.

PROPAGATION: By division of plants in spring.

SPECIES CULTIVATED: *H. albido-fulva*, whitish, brown, rose-crimson, summer, Brazil, Trinidad; *Burtii* (syn. *Batemannia Burtii*), whitish, yellow, red-brown, summer, Costa Rica; *meleagris* (syn. *Batemannia meleagris*), yellowish, yellow, red-brown and white, summer, Brazil; *Wallisii*, variable, green, brown, yellowish, scarlet streaks on petal bases, summer, Colombia, Costa Rica; *Wallisii major*, much larger and darker.

Huon Pine, see *Dacrydium Franklinii.*

Hutchinsia—*Cruciferae.* Hardy annual and perennial herbs.
CULTURE: Soil, sandy. Position, open sunny rockeries or margins of borders. Plant, March or April.
PROPAGATION: Annual species, by seeds sown and slightly covered with fine soil where plants are required to grow in March or April; perennial species, by seeds sown similarly, or by division of plants in March or April.
SPECIES CULTIVATED: *H. alpina* (syn. *H. Auerswaldii*), white, spring, 1 to 3 in., perennial, Alps; *H. petraea*, white, spring, 3 in., annual, Britain.

Hyacinth, see Hyacinthus; **-Bean,** see *Dolichos Lablab.*

Hyacinthus (Hyacinth)—*Liliaceae.* Hardy bulbous flowering plants. First introduced late sixteenth century.
CULTURE OF COMMON HYACINTHS IN POTS: Compost, fibrous loam, leaf-mould and sharp sand. Position, first plunge under cinder ashes in cold frame or outdoors, afterwards in window or greenhouse. Pot, Sept. to early Nov., placing one bulb half its depth in a 6 in. pot or three in an 8 in. pot. Water only when growth begins, and with increasing liberality afterwards. Apply liquid manure occasionally when flower spikes form. After flowering plant bulbs outdoors.
CULTURE IN GLASSES: Place bulbs in glasses so that base just touches water. Time, Sept. to Oct. Water, soft or rain, and little charcoal; add fresh as required. Put in dark position until roots form, then remove to light. No stimulant needed.
CULTURE IN BEDS: Soil, ordinary, enriched with manure previous autumn. Position, open, sunny. Plant bulbs 3 to 4 in. deep and 8 in. apart, Sept. to Oct. Protect surface of bed by covering with peat. Apply liquid manure once or twice when flower spikes appear. Lift and dry bulbs in June, storing in cool place till planting time.
CULTURE OF ROMAN HYACINTH: Compost, as advised above. Position, pots under ashes in cold frame or outdoors till rooted, then in heated greenhouse or window. Pot, Aug., Sept. and Oct., placing three in a 5 in. pot. Depth for planting, 1 in. Water only when removed from the ashes, and regularly afterwards. Temp. when in greenhouse or window, 55° to 65°.
CULTURE OF SPANISH HYACINTH: Soil, light rich. Position, well-drained sunny borders. Plant, Sept. or Oct. Top-dress annually with decayed cow manure in Feb. Lift and replant only when bulbs show signs of deterioration.
PROPAGATION: By seeds sown ½ in. deep in light sandy soil in boxes in cold frame or outdoors in Sept.; by offsets removed from old bulbs when lifted and planted 6 in. apart each way outdoors in Oct. Seedling bulbs flower when three years old, and attain full size when seven years old.
SPECIES CULTIVATED: *H. amethystinus,* ' Spanish Hyacinth ', blue, spring, 1 ft., Pyrenees, var. *albus*, white; *candicans*, see *Galtonia candicans*; *ciliatus* (syn. *H. azureus*), sky blue, 6 in., Asia Minor; *orientalis*, ' Common Hyacinth ', various colours, spring, Medit. Region, var. *albulus*, ' Roman Hyacinth ', white.

Hydrangea—*Saxifragaceae* (or *Hydrangeaceae*). Greenhouse and hardy deciduous flowering shrubs. First introduced early eighteenth century.
POT CULTURE: Compost, two parts rich loam, one part well-decayed manure and sharp sand. Position, cool greenhouse, frame or room Oct. to March; greenhouse, window or warm terrace March to Oct. Pot, Feb. or March. Water abundantly March to Oct., moderately afterwards. Prune, Aug. or Sept., cutting out all weak shoots and those that have flowered. Flowers are produced on shoots arising from vigorous growths of the previous year. Best blooms are obtained on plants propagated by cuttings annually in August. Apply liquid manure frequently to plants showing flower. Temp. for early flowering (Jan. to May) 55°

to 65°. Blue flowers may be obtained in many kinds by planting in acid soil or by use of one of the proprietary blueing powders. The kinds grown for decoration in pots are mainly vars. of the Hortensia section of the Japanese *H. macrophylla*; many are suitable for outdoor cultivation and once established are hardier than is generally supposed.

OUTDOOR CULTURE: Soil, ordinary, rich. Position, sunny or semi-shaded borders, preferably with protection and slight shade from the east. *H. paniculata* in any open situation and *H. petiolaris* against a west wall in well-drained border. Young growth of *H. Sargentiana* is liable to be injured by early spring frosts. Plant, Oct. to Nov. or March to April. Top-dress annually. Prune straggling or dead shoots in March. *H. arborescens* and *H. paniculata* should be pruned annually to within 1 in. of the base in March or April. Water freely in dry weather and apply liquid manure when flower buds appear.

PROPAGATION: By cuttings of young shoots inserted singly in 2 in. pots of light sandy soil under bell-glass in temp. 55° to 65° in March or April; cuttings of points of firm shoots 2 to 3 in. long in well-drained pots of sandy soil in cold frame in August; suckers separated from parent plant in Nov. or March; layering in spring for *H. quercifolia*.

SPECIES CULTIVATED: *H. arborescens grandiflora*, white, July to Sept., hardy, 4 ft., East U.S.A.; *Bretschneideri*, white, 8 to 10 ft., June, July, a good hardy species, China; *heteromalla*, white, 10 ft., June, July, downy leaves, Himalaya; *macrophylla*, blue, pink and white, to 12 ft., June, July, China, Japan, and vars. *Hortensia*, pink to blue all sterile, *Mariesii*, rose-pink slightly toothed, *Otaksa*, dwarfer form, etc.; *paniculata*, whitish in panicles, 30 ft., Aug. to Sept., China, Japan, vars. *grandiflora*, the common outdoor hydrangea with long panicles of whitish flowers, nearly all sterile, *praecox*, flowers about six weeks earlier than the type; *petiolaris*, self-clinging climbing species, white, June, July, to 50 ft., Japan; *quercifolia*, white, June, July, scalloped leaves, 6 ft., rather tender, S.E. United States; *Sargentiana*, pale violet, July, August, 6 ft., large velvety leaves, rather tender, China; *xanthoneura*, white in convex corymbs, July, to 15 ft., W. China, var. *Wilsonii*, oblong leaves lustrous above.

Hydrilla—*Hydrocharitaceae*. Tender, submerged, oxygenating perennials resembling Elodea, with bristly leaves in whorls up the stem.

CULTURE: Soil, loam or aquarium compost. Position, tropical tank. Plant, spring or early summer.

PROPAGATION: Cuttings in shallow tanks in growing season.

SPECIES CULTIVATED: *H. verticillata*, India and Ceylon.

Hydrocharis (Frog-bit)—*Hydrocharitaceae*. Hardy aquatic floating perennial.

CULTURE: Soil, muddy. Position, shallow ponds, lakes or rivulets. Plant, by dropping on water, March to June.

PROPAGATION: By autumn buds which appear naturally and drop to the bottom in autumn and rise again in spring.

SPECIES CULTIVATED: *H. Morsus-ranae*, green and white, summer, Europe (Brit.).

Hydrocleys (Water Poppy)—*Butomaceae*. Half-hardy aquatic perennial. First introduced early nineteenth century.

CULTURE: Soil, two parts loam and one part leaf-mould. Position, sunny, shallow ponds or tubs sunk in ground. Plant 6 in. below surface of water in March. In cold districts plants best wintered in frost-proof greenhouse.

PROPAGATION: By seeds in pots of rich soil sunk in water or division of roots in spring.

SPECIES CULTIVATED: *H. nymphoides* (syn. *Limnocharis Humboldtii*), yellow, rounded floating leaves, July to Sept., Brazil.

Hydrocotyle—*Umbelliferae* or *Hydrocotylaceae*. Creeping perennial plants.

CULTURE: Any reasonably good soil, excellent ground coverers in a cool position.

PROPAGATION: By seeds; cuttings; layers.

SPECIES CULTIVATED: *H. moschata*, flowers inconspicuous, neat evergreen carpets, slightly invasive, New Zealand.

Hydrolea—*Hydrophyllaceae*. Annual or perennial sub-shrubby stove plants. Introduced late eighteenth century.

CULTURE: Soil, rich. Position, margin of indoor pool or in pot standing in pan of water. Plant, spring.

PROPAGATION: By cuttings in very sandy soil under glass; seed.

SPECIES CULTIVATED: *H. spinosa*, 1 to 2 ft., pale blue, thorns in axils of leaves, Trop. America; *zeylanica*, blue and white, Trop. America.

Hydrotrida (Hedge Hyssop)—*Scrophulariaceae*. Low-growing tender aquatics used for marginal work or in tropical aquariums. Sometimes known as Herpestis. First introduced late eighteenth century.

CULTURE: Soil, soft mud at pond edge or submerged in fish tank. Plant, spring or summer.

PROPAGATION: Seeds sown in shallow pans submerged just below water level; cuttings in spring; or division.

SPECIES CULTIVATED: *H. Caroliana* (syn. *Herpestis amplexicaulis*), 6 to 18 in., soft blue flowers, N. America; *Monnieria*, prostrate, pale blue, cosmopolitan.

Hymenanthera—*Violaceae*. Hardy semi-evergreen berry-bearing shrub. First introduced mid-nineteenth century.

CULTURE: Soil, loam, peat and leaf-mould. Position, margin of a rhododendron or azalea bed, or on a sunny rockery. Plant, May or September. Prune to remove dead wood only.

PROPAGATION: By cuttings of ripened shoots in sandy peat in a cold frame in autumn.

SPECIES CULTIVATED: *H. crassifolia*, yellow, pansy-like flowers, succeeded by pearly-white berries in autumn, 3 to 4 ft., New Zealand.

Hymenocallis—*Amaryllidaceae*. Stove and greenhouse bulbous evergreen and deciduous plants. Flowers, fragrant. First introduced mid-eighteenth century.

CULTURE: Compost, two parts sandy loam, one part decayed manure and half a part silver sand. Position, well-drained pots in sunny part of stove and greenhouse. Margins of indoor pools for *H. crassifolia*. Pot, March. Repotting necessary every three or four years only. Water abundantly April to Sept., moderately Sept. to Dec., keep quite dry Dec. to March. Apply liquid manure once or twice a week May to Sept. Temp. for stove species, 70° to 80° March to Sept., 55° to 65° Sept. to March; greenhouse species, 55° to 65° April to Sept., 45° to 50° Sept. to April.

PROPAGATION: By offsets removed from old bulbs in March and treated as above.

STOVE SPECIES CULTIVATED: *H. crassifolia*, white, fragrant, strap-shaped leaves, Kentucky; *eucharidifolia*, white, spring, 2 ft., Trop. America; *macrostephana*, white, spring, 2 ft., hybrid; *ovata*, white, autumn, 1 ft., W. Indies; *speciosa*, white, spring, 1 ft., W. Indies.

GREENHOUSE SPECIES: *H. calathina*, white, spring, 1 ft., Peru.

Hymenophyllum—*Hymenophyllaceae*. Stove, greenhouse and half-hardy ferns with delicate, feathery, membraneous fronds.

CULTURE OF STOVE AND GREENHOUSE SPECIES: Compost, equal parts peat, loam, leaf-mould, charcoal, sandstone and silver sand. Position, moist, shady, in recesses of rockeries, under bell-glasses or in cases. Plant, March. Water freely March to Oct., moderately afterwards. Atmospheric moisture must be maintained always. Shade is most essential. Temp. stove species, March to Oct. 65° to 75°, Oct. to March 55° to 65°; greenhouse species, Sept. to March 45° to 55°, cool through summer.

CULTURE OF HALF-HARDY SPECIES: Compost, as above. Position, deep, moist, shady frames or tubs, etc., away from direct light and sunshine. Plant, March. Water freely in summer, moderately other times. Always maintain atmospheric moisture. Protect in severe weather.

CULTURE IN CASES IN ROOMS: Compost, as above. Position, shady window, not exposed to sun. Plant, March. Top-dress with fresh compost annually in March. Water freely April to Sept., moderately afterwards. Ventilate case a few minutes daily.

PROPAGATION: By spores sown on surface of sandy peat in shallow pan covered with bell-glass in temp. 65° to 75° at any time; by division of plant at potting time.

STOVE SPECIES CULTIVATED: *H. caudiculatum*, Chile; *dichotomum*, Chile; *polyanthos*, beautiful, slender fern, W. Indies; *sericeum*, soft, long, narrow, Jamaica.

GREENHOUSE SPECIES CULTIVATED: *H. demissum*, New Zealand, Malaya; *flabellatum*, Australia.

HALF-HARDY SPECIES CULTIVATED: *H. tunbridgense*, ' Tunbridge Fern ', withstands frost better than drought, Britain.

Hyophorbe—*Palmae*. Stove palm with feather-shaped, deep green leaves. First introduced mid-nineteenth century.

CULTURE: Compost, equal parts peat, loam, leaf-mould and sand. Position, shady, moist. Pot, Feb. or March. Water abundantly March to Sept., moderately afterwards. Temp., March to Sept. 70° to 85°, Sept. to March 60° to 65°.

PROPAGATION: By seeds sown 1 in. deep in pots of light soil in temp. 85° in March.

SPECIES CULTIVATED: *H. amaricaulis*, 6 to 10 ft., Mauritius; *indica*, 8 ft. Mascarene Islands; *Verschaffeltii*, 5 to 10 ft., Mascarene Islands.

Hypericum (St. John's Wort)—*Guttiferae* (or *Hypericaceae*). Evergreen and deciduous shrubs and sub-shrubs, and a few hardy perennials, some species slightly tender, the rest hardy.

CULTURE: Soil, ordinary, well drained. Position, sunny. *H. calycinum* on banks or in full shade under trees, the tender kinds require wall protection. *H. elodes* at edges of outdoor pools in S. England. Plant, Oct. to Nov. or Feb. to March. Prune *H. calycinum* and *H. Moserianum* almost to ground in March, other kinds should have frost-damaged wood removed in March.

PROPAGATION: By seed in most cases; Aug. cuttings in sandy soil in cold frame; division in spring for *H. calycinum*.

SPECIES CULTIVATED: *H. Androsaemum*, ' Tutsan ', 3 ft., half-woody, will grow in semi-shade, June to Aug., yellow, Europe, inc. Br.; *calycinum*, ' Rose of Sharon ', ' Aaron's Beard ', low-growing evergreen, flowering all summer, 18 in., S.E. Europe, Asia Minor; *Coris*, sub-shrub, yellow, summer, 6 to 9 in., S. Europe; *Dyeri* (syn. *H. lysimachioides*), half-evergreen, yellow, 3 ft., summer, Himalaya; *elatum*, yellow, summer, 5 ft., leaves aromatic, Canary Is.; *elodes*, ' Marsh Hypericum ', yellow, downy leaves, creeping, Europe (Br.); *empetrifolium*, rather tender, yellow, July to Sept., 1 ft., Greece; *fragile*, sub-shrub, pale gold, July to Aug., 6 in., Greece; *frondosum* (syn. *H. aureum*), deciduous, bright yellow, summer, 4 ft., Georgia; *hircinum*, evergreen, semi-woody, very hardy and attractive, yellow, Aug. to Oct., Medit. Region, and var. *pumilum*, a good dwarf form; *Hookerianum*, half-evergreen, yellow, Aug., to 6 ft., hardy except in bleak situations, Himalaya and Assam; *Moserianum*, best dwarf garden form, golden-yellow, July to Oct., 18 in., hybrid; *olympicum*, large-flowered, golden-yellow, June to Aug., 1 ft., Asia Minor; *patulum*, golden-yellow, July to Sept., 4 ft., deciduous, hardy, Yunnan, and vars. *Henryi*, more vigorous, *Forrestii*, larger flowers, probably the best of all shrubby hypericums, *uralum*, smaller flowers and leaves; *repens*, prostrate perennial with heath-like growth, bright yellow, June to Aug., 6 to 8 in., Asia Minor; *reptans*, prostrate, yellow flowers, reddish buds, Aug. to Oct., vigorous bright green close tufts of foliage, Sikkim.

Hypolepis—*Polypodiaceae*. Stove and greenhouse evergreen ferns. Fronds, feather-shaped. First introduced early nineteenth century.

CULTURE OF STOVE SPECIES: Compost, equal parts loam, leaf-mould and sand. Position, well-drained pots or hanging baskets in shady part of stove. Pot, March. Water freely March to Sept., moderately afterwards. Syringing undesirable. Temp., March to Sept. 65° to 75°, Sept. to March 55° to 65°.

CULTURE OF GREENHOUSE SPECIES: Compost, as above. Position, well-drained pans or beds in shade. Pot, March. Water freely March to Sept., moderately afterwards. Temp., March to Sept. 55° to 65°, Sept. to March 45° to 55°.

PROPAGATION: By spores sown on surface of well-drained pans of sandy peat and leaf-mould under bell-glass in temp. 65° to 75° at any time; division of creeping rhizomes in March.

STOVE SPECIES CULTIVATED: *H. repens,* creeping rhizomes, Trop. America, Jamaica.

GREENHOUSE SPECIES CULTIVATED: *H. Bergiana,* creeping rhizomes, S. Africa; *ternifolia,* New Zealand.

Hypoxis (Star Grass)—*Amaryllidaceae.* Greenhouse bulbous-rooted plants. First introduced mid-eighteenth century.

CULTURE: Compost, two parts peat, one of leaf-mould and sand. Position, well-drained pots, or beds in cold frame. Pot, Aug. to Nov., covering pots with cinder ashes in cold frame or greenhouse till growth begins. Water moderately from time bulbs begin to grow until flowers fade, then gradually withhold it, keeping bulbs dry until growth recommences. Temp., Sept. to Feb. 40° to 50°, 50° to 60° afterwards.

PROPAGATION: By offsets, removed at potting time and treated as old bulbs.

SPECIES CULTIVATED: *H. hirsuta,* yellow, 12 in. N. America; *hygrometrica* (syn. *Rhodohypoxis hygrometrica*), ' Golden Weatherglass ', yellow, to 6 in., Australia; *stellata,* white, striped green outside, spring, 6 to 12 in., S. Africa.

Hypsela—*Lobeliaceae.* Creeping perennial rock plants.

CULTURE: Soil, well drained. Position, cool.

PROPAGATION: By division of plants in spring.

SPECIES CULTIVATED: *H. longiflora,* white and pink, ½ in., spring and summer, Chile.

Hyssopus (Hyssop)—*Labiatae.* Hardy evergreen shrub. Leaves, narrow, aromatic. Shoots and flowers, infused in water, are largely used as an expectorant; also for distilling for yielding oils for perfumery and flavouring liquors. First introduced mid-sixteenth century.

CULTURE: Soil, ordinary, light. Position, dry, warm borders. Plant, March to May, 12 in. apart each way. Prune into shape, April. Gather shoots for medicinal purposes at any season; when flowers open for distilling.

PROPAGATION: By seeds sown $\frac{1}{16}$ in. deep outdoors in April—transplant June or July; cuttings of shoots inserted in shady position in April or May; division of roots in Feb., March, Sept. or Oct.

SPECIES CULTIVATED: *H. officinalis,* blue, June to Sept., 1 to 2 ft., S. Europe.

Iberis (Candytuft)—*Cruciferae.* Hardy annuals and evergreen perennials.

CULTURE OF ANNUAL SPECIES: Soil, ordinary. Position, sunny beds or borders. Sow seeds ⅛ in. deep in patches or lines in March to May for flowering in summer, Aug. or Sept. for spring flowering. Thin out seedlings to 2 in. apart in June.

POT CULTURE: Compost, two parts good soil, one part decayed manure, leaf-mould and sand. Size of pots, 5 in. in diameter. Sow seeds ⅛ in. deep in April or May. Place pots in cold frame till June, then stand outdoors. Thin seedlings to an inch apart in June. Water moderately. Apply weak liquid manure occasionally when flowers show.

CULTURE OF PERENNIAL SPECIES: Soil, light sandy loam. Position, fissures or ledges of sunny rockeries or margins of well-drained sunny borders. Plant, Oct., March or April.

PROPAGATION: Annual species by seeds sown as above; perennial species by seeds sown $\frac{1}{16}$ in. deep in shallow boxes of sandy soil in cold frame in April; cuttings of partially ripened shoots, from 1 to 2 in. long, inserted in well-drained pots in cold frame or in beds under handlight outdoors, July to Oct.; division of roots, Oct. or March.

ANNUAL SPECIES CULTIVATED: *I. amara*, ' Rocket Candytuft ', white, summer, 1 ft.; *umbellata*, ' Common Candytuft ', purple, summer, 1 ft., S. Europe, and several vars.

SHRUBBY SPECIES CULTIVATED: *I. gibraltarica*, lilac, 12 in. spring, Spain, Morocco; *Jordanii*, white, 4 in., May, Asia Minor; *saxatilis*, white, tinged purple, 4 to 6 in., May, S. Europe; *sempervirens*, white, 9 in., May, S. Europe, Asia Minor, and a number of garden vars.

Ibicella—*Martyniaceae*. Coarse, viscid-pubescent herbs. Flowers in dense, compact terminal racemes. The fruit may be used for pickles as in Proboscidea.

CULTURE: Soil, ordinary rich. Position, warm.

PROPAGATION: By seed in warm house in March.

SPECIES CULTIVATED: *I. lutea* (syns. *Martynia lutea, Proboscidea lutea*), greenish-yellow without and deeper yellow to orange within, sometimes red-blotched, Aug., to 1½ ft., annual, Brazil to Argentina.

Iboza—*Labiatae*. Greenhouse perennial flowering plant with nettle-like foliage, formerly known as Moschosma.

CULTURE: Compost, equal parts loam and decayed manure, little sand. Position, greenhouse, Sept. to June; cold frame, June to Sept. Pot, March. Water freely March to Oct., moderately afterwards. Apply stimulants occasionally a month after repotting until flowers expand, then cease. Temp., Sept. to March 45° to 55°, March to June 55° to 65°. Cut down shoots to within 3 in. of their base after flowering. Young plants: insert cuttings 3 in. long of young shoots in light, sandy soil in temp. 65° in Feb. or March. When rooted, place singly in 3½ in. pots. Nip off point of main shoots, also of succeeding shoots when 3 in. long. Shift into 5 or 6 in. pots when former pots are filled with roots. Water freely. Apply stimulants occasionally. Place in cold frame, June to Sept.

PROPAGATION: By cuttings inserted in sandy soil in temp. 65° in spring.

SPECIES CULTIVATED: *I. riparia* (syn. *Moschosma riparium*), white and purple, winter, 2 to 3 ft., S. Africa.

Ice Plant, see *Cryophytum crystallinum*.

Idesia—*Flacourtiaceae*. Hardy deciduous flowering tree with heart-shaped leaves. Flowers in panicles. Male flowers orange, female green, borne on separate trees. Berries, small, purplish-black.

CULTURE: Soil, ordinary, sandy. Position, well-drained shrubberies. Plant, Oct. to Feb. Prune into shape after flowering.

PROPAGATION: By seeds sown ⅛ in. deep in sandy soil in temp. 65° to 75° in March; cuttings of firm shoots, 3 to 4 in. long, inserted in well-drained pots of sandy soil under bell-glass in temp. 65° to 75° in March or Sept.

SPECIES CULTIVATED: *I. polycarpa*, 10 to 15 ft., Japan.

Ilex (Holly)—*Aquifoliaceae*. Hardy and tender evergreen and deciduous shrubs or trees. Greenish flowers sometimes bisexual and sometimes male and female borne on separate plants, which accounts for some specimens not berrying. Leaves, dark green, or variegated with white and yellow. Timber white, used for cabinet-making and turnery purposes. Bark used for making birdlime. Wood sometimes dyed black and used as substitute for ebony. Average weight of wood per cubic foot, 47½ lb. One bushel of seeds will yield about 17,000 plants.

CULTURE OF GREENHOUSE SPECIES: Soil, two parts loam, one part peat and sand. Position, well-drained pots exposed to full light. Pot, March. Prune, Feb. Water freely in summer, occasionally other times. Temp., March to Oct. 55° to 65°, Oct. to March 45° to 50°.

CULTURE OF HARDY SPECIES: Soil, ordinary. Position, well-drained shrubberies, banks, exposed slopes, etc., or near the sea. Plant, May or Sept. Hollies are not always easy to move and must be well watered and constantly damped overhead if dry weather follows transplanting. Prune or clip from May until July.

HEDGE CULTURE: Soil, ordinary, trenched 2 ft. deep and 3 ft. wide. Plant hollies (18 in. high) 18 in. apart in May or Sept.

PROPAGATION: By seed stratified and planted the following Oct. for common species; variegated kinds by budding on common species; grafting in March; cuttings of half-ripened side shoots with heel of older wood under bell-glass with slight bottom heat.

GREENHOUSE SPECIES CULTIVATED: *I. Cassine*, red berries, S. United States; *paraguariensis*, ' Paraguay Tea ', 10 to 15 ft., Brazil.

HARDY SPECIES CULTIVATED: *I. Aquifolium*, ' Common Holly ', 10 to 30 ft., red berries, Europe (Br.), and numerous horticultural forms including *bacciflava*, yellow fruit, *ferox*, ' Hedgehog Holly ', leaves with short teeth and spines on surface, *heterophylla*, leaves entire, *pendula*, pendulous branches, *pyramidalis*, probably the best berrying var., *variegata*, leaves variegated with silver and gold; *cornuta*, 20 to 30 ft., red berries, China; *crenata*, small leaves, black berries, 5 ft., Japan; *glabra*, ' Ink Berry ', unarmed leaves, black berries, 2 to 3 ft., U.S.A.; *latifolia*, large-leaved, 20 ft., tender in exposed places, Japan; *opaca*, 20 to 40 ft., U.S.A.; *Pernyi*, red berries, 15 to 30 ft., C. and W. China; *serrata*, deciduous, 10 ft., heavy crops of very small scarlet berries, Japan; *verticillata*, deciduous, red berries, 6 to 10 ft., Eastern N. America.

Illicium (Aniseed Tree)—*Magnoliaceae*. Slightly tender evergreen shrubs with fragrant flowers and leaves with an odour of aniseed. First introduced mid-eighteenth century.

CULTURE: Compost, equal parts sandy loam and peat. Position, sheltered shrubberies or against south walls in S. of England, in pots in cold greenhouses elsewhere. Plant outdoors April, Sept. or Oct. Pot, Oct. Water plants in pots freely in summer, moderately in winter. Prune into shape, April or May.

PROPAGATION: By layers of young shoots in well-drained pots of sandy soil under bell-glass in temp. 55° to 65°, May to Aug.

SPECIES CULTIVATED: *I. anisatum* (syn. *I. religiosum*), yellowish-white, March to May, 4 ft., China and Japan; *floridanum*, purple-red, summer, 8 ft., Florida; *verum*, ' Star Anise ', greenish-yellow, March to May, 4 ft., China.

Immortelles, see Helichrysum, Xeranthemum and Heliperum.

Impatiens—*Balsaminaceae*. Stove, greenhouse and hardy annuals and perennials.

CULTURE OF STOVE SPECIES: Compost, equal parts peat, loam, leaf-mould and sand. Position, well-drained pots in light part of stove Sept. to May; greenhouse, June to Sept. Pot., Feb. or March. Water moderately March to Sept., occasionally afterwards. Temp., Oct. to March 55° to 65°, March to June 65° to 75°. Prune into shape, Feb. May be grown in the flower garden during the summer.

CULTURE OF BALSAM (*I. Balsamina*): Sow seeds ⅛ in. deep in light soil in temp. 65° to 75° in March or April. Transplant seedlings singly into 2 in. pots when 1 in. high. Compost, equal parts loam, leaf-mould and sand. Position, near glass in greenhouse, not shaded. Transfer from 2 in. into 5 in., and then into 6 and 8 in. pots. Apply liquid manure daily to plants showing flower. Water freely. Temp., March to June 55° to 65°. May be grown in flower garden during the summer. Plant, June. Soil, ordinary. Position, sunny borders.

CULTURE OF HARDY SPECIES: Sow seeds ⅛ in. deep in April where plants are to grow. Soil, ordinary. Position, sunny borders. Thin seedlings to 6 in. apart when 1 in high.

PROPAGATION: Stove species by seeds sown 1/16 in. deep in light rich soil in temp. 65° in March; cuttings of side shoots inserted in small pots of light sandy soil in temp. 75° March to Aug.

STOVE SPECIES CULTIVATED: *I. auricoma*, yellow, summer, 2 ft., Comoro Isles; *grandiflora*, rosy-pink to purple, summer, 2 ft., Madagascar; *Hawkeri*, carmine, summer, 2 ft., Sunda Islands; *Holstii*, brick-red, summer, 3 ft., E. Trop. Africa; *Hookeriana*, white, summer, 2 ft., Ceylon; *kewensis*, orange-scarlet, summer, 2 ft., hybrid; *Marianiae*, purplish-red, summer, 2 ft., India; *mirabilis*, pink, succulent, spring, 3 to 4 ft., Trop. Africa; *Oliveri*, pale lavender, summer, 2 to 3 ft., Trop. Africa; *Petersiana*, rose, summer, 1½ ft., Trop. Africa; *platypetala*, rose, summer, 1½ ft., Java; *Sultanii*, scarlet, summer, 1 ft., Zanzibar. All perennials.

GREENHOUSE SPECIES CULTIVATED: *I. Balsamina*, 'Balsam', rose, scarlet, and white, summer, 2 ft., annual, Trop. Asia.

HARDY SPECIES CULTIVATED: *I. amphorata*, purple, Aug., 5 ft., Himalaya; *Noli-tangere* (syn. *I. Noli-me-tangere*), yellow, 1 to 1½ ft., annual, Europe; *Roylei* (syn. *I. glandulifera*), purple, summer, 6 ft., Himalaya.

Incarvillea—*Bignoniaceae*. Hardy herbaceous perennials. First introduced mid-nineteenth century.

OUTDOOR CULTURE: Soil, light, rich and well-drained. Position, sunny and sheltered borders. Plant in March or April. Protect crowns of the plant in winter by a covering of dry litter. Apply weak liquid manure occasionally in summer.

INDOOR CULTURE: Compost, two parts loam, one part of equal proportions of leaf-mould, decayed manure and silver sand. Position, fairly large pots, well drained, in cool or cold greenhouse. Pot in Oct. or March. Water freely in spring and summer; keep nearly dry in autumn and winter; give weak liquid manure occasionally in summer.

PROPAGATION: By seeds sown in a temp. of 55° in March, or in cold frame in April, and transplant seedlings outdoors in June. Sow also in Sept. in cold frame and plant out seedlings following April. Divide large plants in autumn.

SPECIES CULTIVATED: *I. Delavayi*, rose, summer, 2½ ft., China; *grandiflora*, rose, summer, 1½ to 2 ft., China, and var. *brevipes*, crimson; *Olgae*, purple, summer, 3 to 4 ft., Turkestan; *variabilis*, rose-purple, Aug., 18 in., W. China.

Incense Cedar, see Libocedrus; **-Juniper,** see *Juniperus thurifera*.

India Rubber Plant, see *Ficus elastica*.

Indian Azalea, see *Rhododendron Simsii*; **-Bean,** see *Catalpa bignonioides*; **-Corn,** see *Zea Mays*; **-Fern,** see Ceratopteris; **-Fig,** see *Opuntia Ficus*, var. *indica*; **-Hawthorn,** see *Raphiolepis indica*; **-Lilac,** see *Melia Azedarach*; **-Physic,** see *Gillenia trifoliata*; **-Paint-brush,** see *Castilleja californica*; **-Pink,** see *Dianthus chinensis*; **-Poke,** see *Phytolacca americana*; **-Shot,** see *Canna indica*.

Indigofera (Indigo)—*Leguminosae*. Stove, greenhouse and hardy evergreen and deciduous shrubs with pea-shaped flowers. First introduced early eighteenth century.

CULTURE OF STOVE AND GREENHOUSE SPECIES: Compost, equal parts turfy loam, leaf-mould and sand. Position, well-drained pots or beds. Pot or plant, Feb. or March. Prune into shape, Feb. or March. Water freely March to Oct., moderately other times. Temp. stove species, March to Oct. 65° to 75°, Oct. to March 55° to 65°; greenhouse, March to Oct. 55° to 65°, Oct. to March 45° to 55°; place plants outdoors June to Sept.

CULTURE OF HARDY SPECIES: Soil, ordinary rich, but not heavy. Position, well-drained bed or border in full sun, shoots may be trained against south wall. Plant, Oct. to Feb. Prune moderately after flowering, removing only those shoots that have flowered; those planted in open border will probably have to be cut to ground level annually in spring.

PROPAGATION: By seeds or cuttings in heat.

STOVE SPECIES CULTIVATED: *I. tinctoria*, red, summer, 4 to 6 ft., Tropics.

GREENHOUSE SPECIES CULTIVATED: *I. australis*, rose, spring, 4 ft., Australia.

HARDY SPECIES CULTIVATED: *I. Gerardiana*, racemes of rosy purple flowers, July to Sept., 4 to 8 ft., Himalaya; *hebepetala*, brownish crimson and rose, Aug. to Sept., 4 to 10 ft., N.W. Himalaya; *incarnata* (syn. *I. decora*), pretty dwarf species for rockery, white and pink, July to Aug., 18 in., China; *Kirilowii*, rose, July to Aug., 2 to 4 ft., N. China; *pendula*, wine-coloured, summer, 3 to 5 ft., W. China; *Potaninii*, very free flowering, pink, July to Sept., 4 to 5 ft., N.W. China.

Inkberry, see *Ilex glabra*.

Inula—*Compositae*. Hardy herbaceous perennials.

CULTURE: Soil, ordinary rich. Position, moist sunny beds or borders. Plant, Oct., Nov., March or April. Cut down flower stems in Oct. Top-dress with well-decayed manure in April.

PROPAGATION: By seeds sown $\frac{1}{16}$ in. deep in partially shady border outdoors in April; division of roots, Oct. or March.

SPECIES CULTIVATED: *I. acaulis*, yellow, spring and early summer, 2 in., Asia Minor; *ensifolia*, yellow, Aug., 10 in., S. Europe; *glandulosa*, yellow, Aug., 2 ft., Caucasus; *grandiflora*, yellow, July to Sept., 2 ft., Himalaya; *Helenium*, ' Ele- campane ', yellow, July to Sept., 6 to 8 ft., Europe; *Hookeri*, yellow, Aug. and Sept., 2 ft., Himalaya; *Oculus-Christi*, yellow, summer, 18 in., Europe; *Royleana*, deep golden-yellow, Aug. to Sept., 2 ft., Himalaya.

Ionopsidium—*Cruciferae*. Hardy annual. First introduced early nineteenth century.

OUTDOOR CULTURE: Soil, ordinary. Position, ledges of rockeries or as edgings to flower beds. Sow seeds where plants are to grow in April, just covering with fine soil.

POT CULTURE: Compost, any good mixture, not too light. Position, shady window, cold frame or greenhouse. Sow seeds $\frac{1}{16}$ in. deep in 5 in. pot well drained and filled with above compost, in April or Sept. Thin seedlings to 1 in. apart. Water moderately. Apply liquid manure occasionally when flower buds show.

SPECIES CULTIVATED: *I. acaule*, ' Carpet Plant ', lilac, white and violet, summer, 3 in., Portugal.

Ionopsis—*Orchidaceae*. Epiphytic orchids. Pseudo-bulbs absent or very small, racemes simple or branched. Flowers not large but attractive.

CULTURE: Compost, osmunda fibre and sphagnum moss in equal parts. Posi- tion, in shallow pans suspended from roof. Repot Feb. or March. Water freely March to Sept., moderately other times. Syringe freely in summer, expose to light in autumn. Temp., Oct. to Feb. 55° to 60°, Feb. to Oct. 60° to 75° or higher.

PROPAGATION: By division of plants in spring.

SPECIES CULTIVATED: *I. paniculata*, white, purple and yellow, winter, 6 in., Brazil; *teres* (syn. *I. pulchella*), white, shaded yellow, purplish on lip, summer, Brazil, W. Indies; *utricularioides*, white, rose-flushed, purple on lip, autumn, Trop. America.

Ipheion, see Brodiaea.

Ipomoea (Morning Glory)—*Convolvulaceae*. Stove, greenhouse and hardy peren- nial and half-hardy annual climbers. Some species formerly included here have been transferred to Calonyction and Quamoclit. First introduced late sixteenth century.

CULTURE OF STOVE SPECIES: Compost, equal parts fibrous loam, leaf-mould, decayed manure and silver sand. Position, pots, beds or borders in stove; shoots trained up roof, or on trellises. Pot or plant, Feb., March or April. Temp., March to Sept. 65° to 75°, Sept. to March 55° to 65°. Water freely April to Sept., moderately afterwards. Prune straggling growths of perennials into shape, Feb. Sow three seeds of the annual species $\frac{1}{8}$ in. deep in a $2\frac{1}{2}$ in. pot in temp. 65° in March. Transfer seedlings when 2 in. high into 5 in. pots. Train shoots to trellis or sticks.

CULTURE OF HALF-HARDY ANNUALS: Soil, light rich. Sow seeds $\frac{1}{8}$ in. deep in pots in temp. 65° in March. Transfer seedlings to cold frame in May. Plant, June. Position, sunny walls or borders; shoots trained to trellis or to sticks.

CULTURE OF HARDY PERENNIAL SPECIES: Soil, ordinary. Position, sunny walls, fences or arbours. Plant, Oct. or Nov.

CULTURE OF SWEET POTATO: Compost, two parts loam and one part decayed manure. Plant tubers singly in 6 in. pots in Feb., in temp. 65°, or 6 in. deep and 8 in. apart in prepared border in greenhouse. Water moderately Feb. to May, freely May to Sept., then give none, keeping tubers dry. Tubers are edible.

PROPAGATION: Annual species by seeds as above; perennials by cuttings of side shoots inserted in sandy peat under bell-glass in temp. 75° to 85°, March to Aug., or grafting in March; sweet potato by division of tubers in Feb.; *I. pandurata* by cuttings of young shoots in April.

STOVE SPECIES CULTIVATED: *I. Horsfalliae*, rose, winter, 10 to 15 ft., W. Indies; *Leari*, ' Blue Dawnflower ', blue, summer, 10 ft., Trop. America; *paniculata* (syn. *I. digitata)* rose, 20 ft., Tropics; *tricolor* (syn. *I. rubro-caerula*), red, Mexico.

GREENHOUSE SPECIES CULTIVATED: *I. Batatas*, ' Sweet Potato ', white, summer, 2 to 4 ft., tubers edible, Tropics.

HALF-HARDY SPECIES CULTIVATED: *I. hederacea*, blue or pale purple, summer, twining, Trop. America; *purpurea*, purple, summer, twining, Trop. America.

PERENNIAL SPECIES CULTIVATED: *I. pandurata*, ' Wild Sweet Potato Vine ', white and purple, summer, climber, N. America.

Ipsea—*Orchidaceae*. Terrestrial, tuberous, deciduous orchid. Flowers, fragrant. First introduced mid-nineteenth century.

CULTURE: Compost, one part leaf-mould, three parts fibrous loam, one part chopped sphagnum moss and small crocks. Position, light part of cool or intermediate house. Pot, Feb. or March in well-drained pots. Water freely March to Aug., moderately Aug. to Oct., none afterwards. Temp., March to Sept. 60° to 65°, Sept. to March 50° to 55°. In Sept. expose to light.

PROPAGATION: Can seldom be effected, offsets from tubers are rare.

SPECIES CULTIVATED: *I. speciosa*, ' Daffodil Orchid ', yellow, spring, 12 to 18 in., Ceylon.

Iresine—*Amarantaceae*. Stove and half-hardy plants with brilliantly coloured leaves. First introduced mid-nineteenth century.

POT CULTURE: Compost, equal parts peat, loam, leaf-mould and sand. Position, sunny part of stove. Pot, Feb. or March. Water freely March to Sept., moderately other times. Temp., March to Oct. 65° to 75°, Oct. to March 55° to 65°.

OUTDOOR CULTURE: Soil, ordinary. Position, edgings to sunny beds or borders. Plant, June. Lift, repot and remove to stove in Sept. Pinch off points of shoots frequently to induce bushy growth.

PROPAGATION: By cuttings of young shoots inserted in pots or pans of light sandy soil in temp. of 65° to 75°, Feb., March, April, Sept. or Oct.

SPECIES CULTIVATED: *I. brilliantissima*, leaves red and crimson, 1 ft., Brazil; *Herbstii*, leaves maroon and crimson, 1 ft., Brazil, var. *aureo-reticulata*, leaves green, gold and red; *Lindenii*, leaves blood-red, 1 ft., Ecuador.

Iris—*Iridaceae*. Hardy evergreen rhizomatous and bulbous-rooted perennials. Sections: Tall Bearded, Dwarf Bearded, Beardless, Cushion, Japanese and Bulbous-rooted.

CULTURE OF TALL BEARDED SECTION: Soil, ordinary, well drained, and with plenty of lime or old mortar rubble. Position, sunny borders. Plant in July, Oct. or March, keeping rhizomes near surface. Top-dress with superphosphate of lime in April at the rate of 1 to 2 oz. per sq. yd. Lift and replant every fourth year.

CULTURE OF DWARF BEARDED SECTION: Soil, as above. Position, sunny well-drained borders. Plant and treat as advised for foregoing section.

CULTURE OF BEARDLESS SECTION: Moist soil and margins of ponds or streams for *I. versicolor, sibirica, ochroleuca* and *Pseudacorus*. Plant, Oct. or March. Cool, deep soil well supplied with humus and a partially shady position for *I. gracilipes*. Plant, March or April. Ordinary rich soil and sunny borders or rockeries for other species. Plant in Oct. or March.

CULTURE OF JAPANESE SECTION: Rich loamy soil on the margins of ponds, or in a half cask filled with loam and sunk in garden in sunny spot. Plant in Oct. or March. Apply liquid manure in growing season.

CULTURE OF CUSHION SECTION: Soil, light, rich loam with a liberal addition of old mortar rubble. Position, raised bed against a south wall. Plant in Oct. Protect by a cold frame or hand-light in winter. Lift rhizomes in July and store in dry sand in sunny shed or greenhouse until Oct.

CULTURE OF BULBOUS-ROOTED SECTION: Plant choice kinds in a compost of equal parts fibrous loam, leaf-mould and sharp sand. Place bulbs 3 in. deep and

3 in. apart. Plant in Aug. or Sept. Spanish and English kinds to be planted in ordinary soil in sunny beds or borders in Sept. or Oct., placing bulbs 3 in. deep and 6 in. apart. Lift and replant every third year.

POT CULTURE OF BULBOUS SPECIES: Compost, equal parts loam, leaf-mould and silver sand. Place in cold frame till growth begins, when remove to cold greenhouse or leave in frame to flower. Pot in Oct., placing five bulbs of the Spanish or English kinds, and *I. tingitana* in a 5 in. pot. Three bulbs of *I. reticulata* may be placed in a 3 in. pot. Give water only when growth has begun. Withhold water after leaves begin to decay. Spanish and English iris must not be placed in artificial heat. *I. tingitana* can be gently forced to flower from January onwards.

PROPAGATION: All the species by seeds in sandy soil in cold frame as soon as ripe; division of rhizomes immediately after flowering; offsets in autumn.

TALL BEARDED IRISES CULTIVATED: *I. albicans*, white, 2 to 3 ft., Spain; *Billiottii*, purple, white, and yellow, May to June, 3 ft., Asia Minor; *Cengialtii*, violet and orange, May, 18 in., Tyrol; *germanica*, ' Flag Iris ', purple and lilac, fragrant, May, 2 to 2½ ft., S. Europe, and var. *florentina*, ' Orris Root '; *kashmiriana*, creamy white, lavender, or purple, May to June, 2 ft., Kashmir; *pallida*, lilac, purple, and white, May, fragrant, 3 ft., Southern Tyrol; *squalens*, lilac, purple and yellow, May, 3 ft., Europe, natural hybrid; *trojana*, purple and violet, 3 ft., Asia Minor; *variegata*, yellow and chestnut, May, 18 in., E. Europe. A large number of forms will be found described in trade lists.

DWARF BEARDED IRISES CULTIVATED: *I. aphylla*, purple, May, 9 to 15 in., E. Europe, a plant with many synonyms such as *biflora*, *bifurca*, *bohemica*, *breviscapa*, *extrafoliacea*, *falcata*, *Fieberi*, *furcata*, *hungarica*, *nudicaulis*, *reflexa*, *rigida*, *Schmidtii* and *subtriflora*; *Chamaeiris*, yellow or purple, April, 4 to 6 in., S. Europe; *pumila*, ' Crimean Iris ', lilac purple, April, 4 in., S. Europe, and its many vars., which range in colour from white to purple.

BEARDLESS IRISES CULTIVATED: *I. crocea* (syn. *I. aurea*) golden-yellow, June to July, 4 ft., Kashmir; *chrysographes*, violet purple, veined gold, 1½ to 2 ft., S.W. China; *confusa*, white tinged mauve and gold, 3 ft., China, often grown as *I. Wattii*; *cristata*, lilac, white, and orange, May, 6 to 12 in., S.E. United States; *ensata*, slate-blue or white, sometimes with a creamy ground, 18 in., Temp. Asia; *foetidissima*, ' Gladwin Iris ', purple, June, 18 to 24 in., Britain; *brevicaulis* (syn. *I. foliosa*), blue, lavender, and greenish-white, June, 1 ft., S.E. United States; *Forrestii*, clear yellow, June, 18 in., N.W. Yunnan; *fulva*, coppery maroon, June to July, 18 to 24 in., banks of Mississippi near New Orleans; *gracilipes*, lilac pink, May, 9 to 12 in., Japan; *graminea*, blue and purple, June, 4 to 10 in., S. Europe; *Grant-Duffii*, sulphur yellow, May, 6 in., Palestine; *innominata*, deep yellow, 30 in., Oregon; *japonica* (syn. *I. fimbriata*), amethyst blue and gold, April, 18 in., Japan and China; *longipetala*, violet and white, June, 2 ft., California; *Milesii*, reddish purple with darker mottlings, June to July, 24 to 36 in., Himalaya; *Monnieri*, lemon yellow, fragrant, June, 3 ft., Crete; *monspur*, lilac blue, June, 4 ft., hybrid; *ochroleuca*, white and yellow, June to July, 4 to 5 ft., Western Asia Minor; *orientalis*, blue-purple, May to June, 1½ to 2 ft.; Manchuria and Japan; *Pseudacorus*, ' Yellow Water Flag ', yellow, May and June, 3 ft., Britain; *setosa*, purplish blue, May, 8 to 24 in., N. Siberia, Japan, Alaska and Labrador; *sibirica*, blue and white, May and June, 3 ft., Cent. Europe and Russia; *spuria*, blue to reddish purple, June, 3 ft., Europe; *tectorum*, ' Japanese Roof Iris ', lilac or blue-purple, 1 ft., Cent. and S.W. China; *unguicularis* (syn. *I. stylosa*), ' Algerian Iris ', lavender blue, Jan. and Feb., 1 ft., Algeria; *verna*, lilac blue, fragrant, April to May, 3 in., N. America; *versicolor*, purple, May to June, 2 ft., E. Canada and Eastern U.S.A.; *Wattii*, pale lavender, 3 to 6 ft., China; *Wilsonii*, yellow, June, 2 ft., China. Here also numerous vars. exist which may be found in trade lists.

CUSHION IRISES CULTIVATED: *I. Barnumiae*, vinous red, May, 2 to 6 in., N.E. Asia Minor; *Bismarckiana*, purple, yellow, blue, and white, May, 12 to 15 in., Mt. Lebanon; *Gatesii*, grey, purple, and white, May, 12 to 18 in., Kurdistan; *Hoogiana*, grey-blue or blue-purple, May, 18 to 24 in., Turkistan; *iberica*, lilac, white, and purple, May, 6 in., Caucasus; *Korolkowii*, creamy white and olive green, May, 1 ft., Turkistan; *Lortetii*, crimson and cream, May, 1 ft., S. Lebanon; *paradoxa*, blue-purple, white, and purplish black, May, 4 to 6 in., Persia; *susiana*, 'Mourning Iris', brown, black, and lilac, May, 1 ft., habitat uncertain.

JAPANESE IRISES CULTIVATED: *I. Kaempferi*, reddish purple and yellow, June to July, 18 to 30 in., Manchuria, Korea and Japan; *laevigata*, blue-purple, June, 15 to 18 in., E. Siberia, Manchuria and Korea.

BULBOUS-ROOTED IRISES CULTIVATED: *I. alata*, lilac purple and yellow, Oct., 1 ft., S. Europe; *Aucheri* (syn. *I. sindjarensis*), azure blue and pale yellow, Feb. and March, 9 to 12 in., Mesopotamia; *Bakeriana*, white, violet, and blue, fragrant, Jan., 6 to 12 in., Almeria; *bracteata*, yellow and purple, May, 4 to 6 in., Oregon; *bucharica*, white and yellow, April, 12 to 18 in., Bokhara; *filifolia*, red-purple, blue, and orange, June, 10 to 15 in., S. Spain and N. Africa; *Graebbriana*, mauve and cobalt blue, March and April, 6 to 12 in., Turkistan; *Histrio*, bright blue and yellow, Dec. and Jan., 1 ft., Asia Minor; *histrioides*, blue-purple, white, and yellow, Jan., 1 ft., N. Asia Minor; *orchioides*, yellow, April, 9 in., Turkistan; *persica*, white, greenish blue, purple, and orange, Feb., 1 to 2 in., Persia; *reticulata*, violet, purple and yellow, violet scented, Feb., 6 in., Caucasus; *tingitana*, lilac blue, deep blue, and yellow, March, 2 ft., Tangier; *Vartanii*, slate grey or white, Dec. and Jan., 6 to 12 in., Nazareth; *xiphioides*, 'English Iris', various colours, 1 to 2 ft., Pyrenees; *Xiphium*, 'Spanish Iris', various colours, June, 1 to 2 ft., S. Europe and N. Africa. The plant known in gardens as *Iris pavonia* is actually *Moraea pavonia*, *q.v.*

Irish Heath, see *Daboecia cantabrica.*

Ironweed, see Vernonia.

Ironwood, see *Ostrya virginiana.*

Isoetes (Quillwort)—*Isoetaceae.* Rush-like plants sometimes used in the water garden.

CULTURE: Soil, sandy loam. Position, pond margin, or submerged forms in very deep water. Plant, spring.

PROPAGATION: By division.

SPECIES CULTIVATED: *I. lacustris*, tufts of quill-like leaves, for cold water aquariums, or may be used as an oxygenator in deep clear-water pools, N. Temp. Regions including Britain.

Isoloma—*Gesneriaceae.* Stove flowering tuberous-rooted plants. The plants formerly known as Tydaeas are now merged in this genus.

CULTURE: Compost, two parts fibrous peat, one part loam, one part leaf-mould, with a little decayed manure and silver sand. Position, well-drained pots or pans in shady part of plant stove. Pot, March to flower in summer, May to flower in autumn, June to flower in winter. Place tubers 1 in. deep singly in 5 in. pots, or 1 to 2 in. apart in larger sizes. Water moderately from time growth begins until plants are 3 or 4 in. high, then freely. After flowering, gradually withhold water till foliage dies down, then keep dry till potting time. Apply weak liquid manure once or twice a week when flower buds show. Syringing not required. Temp., March to Sept. 65° to 85°, Sept. to March 55° to 65°. When foliage has died down, store on their sides under stage till potting time in temp. of 50° to 55°.

PROPAGATION: By seeds sown on surface of well-drained pots of sandy peat, in temp. 75°, March or April; cuttings of young shoots inserted in pots of sandy peat in temp. 75° to 85° in spring; fully matured leaves pegged on surface of pots of sandy peat in temp. 75° to 85°.

SPECIES CULTIVATED: *I. amabile*, rose and purple, 1 to 2 ft., Colombia; *bogotense*, yellow and red, 1 to 2 ft., origin unknown; *digitaliflorum*, rose, purple, and white, winter, 1 ft.; *hirsutum*, crimson spotted white, rose and purple, 2 to 3 ft., W. Indies; *hondense*, yellow and red, winter, 1 ft., New Grenada; *Lindenii* (syn. *Tydaea Lindenii*), white and violet, winter, 1 ft., Ecuador.

Isopyrum—*Ranunculaceae*. Hardy herbaceous perennial with finely divided foliage, somewhat like maidenhair fern. First introduced mid-eighteenth century.

CULTURE: Soil, ordinary. Position, sunny or shady rockery, bed or border. Plant, Oct. or March.

PROPAGATION: By seeds outdoors in April or May; division of roots in Oct. or Nov.

SPECIES CULTIVATED: *I. thalictroides*, white, spring, 8 in., Europe. See also Paraquilegia.

Isotoma—*Lobeliaceae*. Greenhouse flowering perennial. Formerly included in the genus Lobelia. First introduced early nineteenth century.

CULTURE: Compost, equal parts loam, leaf-mould and sand. Position, pots or baskets in shady part of greenhouse. Pot, March to July. Water freely in summer, moderately other times. Feed with stimulants when plants are well rooted in final pots.

PROPAGATION: By seeds sown thinly on the surface of sandy soil in temp. 60° in Feb. or March. Cuttings of young shoots inserted in pots of sandy soil in gentle heat in spring or autumn.

SPECIES CULTIVATED: *I. axillaris*, blue, 1 ft., autumn, Australia, and var. *subpinnatifida*.

Itea—*Saxifragaceae* (or *Escalloniaceae*). Evergreen and deciduous flowering shrubs First introduced early eighteenth century.

CULTURE: Soil, peaty. Position, moist sheltered shrubberies. Plant, Oct. to Feb. Prune moderately after flowering.

PROPAGATION: By seeds sown ¼ in. deep in sandy soil outdoors in April; suckers removed in Oct. or Nov.; cuttings in August in sandy soil and given close treatment and gentle bottom heat.

SPECIES CULTIVATED: *I. ilicifolia*, 9 in. pendulous racemes of greenish-white flowers in August, evergreen, rather tender, 8 to 15 ft., W. China; *virginica*, 'Virginian Willow', erect racemes, creamy-white fragrant flowers, July, 5 ft., hardy, deciduous, Eastern U.S.A.

Italian Corn Salad, see *Valerianella eriocarpa*; **-Starwort,** see *Aster Amellus*.

Ivy, see Hedera.

Ixia (African Corn Lily)—*Iridaceae*. Half-hardy bulbous plants with fragrant flowers. First introduced early eighteenth century.

OUTDOOR CULTURE: Soil, light, rich, sandy. Position, sunny well-drained border. Plant, Sept. to Jan., placing bulbs 4 in. deep and 2 in. apart. Lift and replant bulbs annually. Mulch surface of bed in March with cow manure.

POT CULTURE: Compost, two parts sandy loam, one part leaf-mould or decayed cow manure. Pots, 4½ in. in diameter, well drained. Place five bulbs, 3 in. deep, in each pot in Nov., and cover with coconut-fibre refuse in cold frame or under cool greenhouse stage until growth begins. Water moderately from time bulbs begin to grow until flowers fade, then gradually cease, keeping bulbs dry till Jan. Temp., Sept. to March 40° to 50°, other times 50° to 60°.

PROPAGATION: By offsets, treated as advised for bulbs.

SPECIES CULTIVATED: *I. flexuosa*, pink, spring, 1 ft., S. Africa; *campanulata* (syn. *I. speciosa*), purple and crimson, summer, 1 ft., S. Africa; *maculata*, orange yellow, spring, 1 ft., S. Africa; *patens*, pink, spring, 1 ft., S. Africa; *viridiflora*, green, spring, 1 ft., S. Africa.

Ixiolirion—*Amaryllidaceae*. Half-hardy bulbous plant. First introduced early nineteenth century.

CULTURE: Soil, light sandy loam. Position, well-drained sunny border at foot of south wall. Plant bulbs 3 in. deep and 4 in. apart in March. Mulch surface of bed with cow manure in April. After flowering cover with bell-glass or hand-light to ensure thorough ripening of bulbs. Lift bulbs in Sept. and store in dry sand in cool, frost-proof place till planting time.

PROPAGATION: By offsets removed at any time, planted and treated as advised for normal bulbs. May also be grown in pots as advised for Ixias.

SPECIES CULTIVATED: *I. montanum*, blue, June, 1 ft., W. Asia.

Ixora—*Rubiaceae*. Stove flowering evergreen shrubs with fragrant flowers. First introduced late seventeenth century.

CULTURE: Compost, two parts good fibrous peat, one part fibrous loam and silver sand. Position, shady part of stove whilst growing, light situation when at rest. Pot, Feb. or March; good drainage indispensable. Prune into shape in Feb. Water freely March to Sept., moderately afterwards. Syringe twice daily March to Aug. Apply liquid manure once or twice a week to healthy plants in flower. Temp., March to Sept. 75° to 85°, Sept. to March 55° to 65°.

PROPAGATION: By cuttings of firm young shoots 2 to 3 in. long, inserted singly in small pots in sandy peat under bell-glass in temp. 75° to 85°, March to May.

SPECIES CULTIVATED: *I. acuminata*, white, summer, 3 to 5 ft., Himalaya; *coccinea*, orange-scarlet, summer, 3 to 4 ft., India; *congesta*, orange, summer, 4 ft., Burma, Malaya; *lutea*, yellow, summer, 3 to 4 ft., origin unknown; *macrothyrsa* (syn. *I. Duffii*), deep red, tinged crimson, summer, 10 to 12 ft., Sumatra; *splendens*, coppery-scarlet, 4 ft., origin unknown; *stricta*, light orange, summer, 2 to 3 ft., China. Numerous vars. and hybrids.

Jaborosa—*Solanaceae*. Half-hardy herbaceous perennial. First introduced early nineteenth century.

● CULTURE: Soil, rich loamy. Position, well-drained border at base of south wall. Plant, Oct. to March. Protect in winter with covering of ashes or litter.

PROPAGATION: By seeds sown $\frac{1}{16}$ in. deep in light sandy soil in well-drained pots in temp. 55° to 65° in March or April; cuttings of young shoots inserted in sandy soil under bell-glass, hand-light, or in cold frame, July to Sept.; division of creeping stems in March or April.

SPECIES CULTIVATED: *J. integrifolia*, white, summer, 9 in., Buenos Ayres.

Jacaranda—*Bignoniaceae*. Stove evergreen flowering tree with downy, fern-like leaves. First introduced early nineteenth century.

CULTURE: Compost, equal parts peat, fibrous loam and silver sand. Position, well-drained pots in light part of plant stove Sept. to April, sunny place outdoors July to Sept. Pot, Feb. to March. Prune into shape, Feb. Water freely March to Oct., moderately Oct. to March. Temp., Sept. to March 55° to 65°, March to July 70° to 80°. Plants form decorative specimens when 1 to 3 ft. high; flowering specimens when grown as standards, 10 to 15 ft. high.

PROPAGATION: By seeds sown $\frac{1}{8}$ in. deep in light sandy peat in well-drained pots under bell-glass in temp. of 75° to 85°, Feb. to June; cuttings of firm shoots inserted in sandy peat under bell-glass in temp. of 75°, June to Sept.

SPECIES CULTIVATED: *J. acutifolia* (syns. *J. mimosaefolia*, *J. ovalifolia*), blue, to 50 ft., Brazil.

Jack-go-to-bed-at-noon, see *Ornithogalum umbellatum*; **-in-prison,** see *Nigella damascena*; **-fruit,** see *Artocarpus integra*.

Jacobaea, see *Senecio elegans*.

Jacobean Lily, see *Sprekelia formosissima*.

Jacobinia—*Acanthaceae*. Stove flowering plants. First introduced mid-eighteenth century.

CULTURE: Compost, equal parts peat, loam, leaf-mould and sand. Position, well-drained pots in light stove Sept. to June, sunny frame June to Sept. Pot, March to April. Water moderately Sept. to March, freely other times. Temp., Sept. to March 55° to 65°, March to June 65° to 75°. Prune shoots to 1 in. of base after flowering. Nip off points of young shoots occasionally, May to Aug., to induce bushy growth. Apply liquid or artificial manure twice a week to plants in flower.

PROPAGATION: By cuttings of young shoots inserted singly in small pots or sandy soil under bell-glass in temp. 75°, March to July.

SPECIES CULTIVATED: *J. carnea*, flesh-coloured, Aug. and Sept., 3 to 4 ft., Brazil; *chrysostephana*, yellow, winter, 3 ft., Mexico; *Ghiesbreghtiana* (syn. *Justicia Ghiesbreghtiana*), scarlet, Dec., 2 ft., Mexico; *pauciflora* (syn. *Libonia pauciflora*), scarlet and yellow, winter, 2 ft., Brazil; *Pohliana*, pink, 4 ft., Sept., Brazil, and var. *velutina*; *suberecta*, orange, 1 ft., summer, Uruguay.

Jacob's Ladder, see *Polemonium caeruleum*; **-rod,** see Asphodeline.

Jalap, see *Mirabilis Jalapa*.

Jamesia—*Saxifragaceae* (or *Hydrangeaceae*). Hardy deciduous flowering shrub. First introduced early nineteenth century.

CULTURE: Soil, ordinary. Position, sunny rockeries or borders. Plant, Oct. to Feb. Prune directly after flowering.

PROPAGATION: By cuttings inserted under hand-light or in cold frame in autumn.

SPECIES CULTIVATED: *J. americana*, white, spring, mildly fragrant, 6 to 8 ft., Rocky Mountains.

Japanese Cedar, see *Cryptomeria japonica*; **-Laurel,** see *Aucuba japonica*; **-Maple,** see *Acer palmatum*; **-Pagoda Tree,** see *Sophora japonica*; **-Snowflower,** see *Deutzia gracilis*; **-Windflower,** see *Anemone hybrida*.

Jasione (Sheep's-bit Scabious)—*Campanulaceae*. Hardy biennials and herbaceous perennials.

CULTURE OF ANNUAL SPECIES: Soil, ordinary. Position, well-drained sunny beds or borders. Sow seeds $\frac{1}{16}$ in. deep in April or Sept. where plants are to grow.

CULTURE OF PERENNIAL SPECIES: Soil, good light loam. Position, sunny well-drained borders. Plant, March.

PROPAGATION: By seeds sown $\frac{1}{16}$ in. deep in light soil outdoors, April to Sept.; division of roots, March.

ANNUAL SPECIES CULTIVATED: *J. montana*, lilac blue, summer, 1 ft., Europe (Br.).

PERENNIAL SPECIES CULTIVATED: *J. humilis*, blue, July to Aug., 6 in., Pyrenees; *Jankae*, blue, July to Sept., 9 to 12 in., E. Europe; *perennis*, blue, June, 18 in., W. Europe.

Jasmine, see Jasminum; **-Nightshade,** see *Solanum jasminoides*.

Jasminum (Jasmine; Jessamine)—*Oleaceae*. Tender and hardy climbing and trailing, shrubby, flowering plants; mostly evergreen. First introduced midixteenth century.

CULTURE OF STOVE AND GREENHOUSE SPECIES: Compost, equal parts loam, peat and leaf-mould, with little sand. Position, well-drained pots, beds or borders with shoots trained to walls, rafters or trellis. Pot or plant, Feb. or March. Prune moderately in Feb. Water freely March to Oct., moderately afterwards. Temp. stove species, March to Sept. 65° to 75°, Sept. to March 55° to 65°, syringe daily Mar. to Aug.; greenhouse species, March to Sept. 45° to 55°, March to June 55° to 65°, sunny place outdoors June to Sept.

CULTURE OF HARDY AND SLIGHTLY TENDER SPECIES: Soil, ordinary, rich. Position, well-drained borders at base of south or south-west walls. Plant, Oct., Nov., Feb. or March. Prune moderately after flowering, only removing shoots that have flowered.

PROPAGATION: Stove and greenhouse species by cuttings of firm shoots in well-drained pots of sandy peat under bell-glass in temp. 65° to 75°, March to Sept. Hardy species by cuttings of shoots 3 to 6 in. long in pots of sandy soil in cold frame or in sheltered borders outdoors, Sept. to Dec.; layering in spring or summer.

STOVE SPECIES CULTIVATED: *J. gracillimum*, white, winter, 4 ft., Borneo; *Sambac*, ' Arabian Jasmine ', white, autumn, 6 ft., Trop. Asia.

GREENHOUSE SPECIES CULTIVATED: *J. officinale grandiflorum*, white, autumn, 10 ft., Malaya; *Mesnyi* (syn. *J. primulinum*), yellow, winter, 6 to 10 ft., China.

HARDY AND SLIGHTLY TENDER SPECIES CULTIVATED: *J. Beesianum*, strong-growing deciduous climber, fragrant rose-coloured flowers, June to July, shining black berries, W. China; *floridum*, half-evergreen loose-growing shrub better for wall protection, 4 to 8 ft., bright yellow, July to Sept., China; *Giraldii*, deciduous shrub, 5 ft., large downy leaves, yellow flowers, summer, Cent. China; *humile*, half-evergreen low shrub to 4 ft., yellow, July to Aug., W. China; *nudiflorum*, 'Winter Jasmine', deciduous, hardy, yellow, Nov. to March, best trained to wall, any aspect, China; *officinale*, ' Common Jasmine ', vigorous deciduous climber to 30 ft., better for wall protection in cold districts, white, very fragrant, June to Oct., Persia, Kashmir and China; *stephanense*, hybrid, pink, June to July, black fruits.

Jeffersonia—*Berberidaceae*. Hardy perennial herb. First introduced late eighteenth century.

CULTURE: Soil, peaty. Position, shady edges of rockery or borders. Plant, Oct., March or April.

PROPAGATION: By seeds sown $\frac{1}{16}$ in. deep in sandy soil in cold frame, July to Sept.; division of roots, Oct. or March.

SPECIES CULTIVATED: *J. diphylla*, ' Twin Leaf ' (syn. *J. binata*), white, spring, 6 in., N. America; *dubia* (syn. *Plagiorhegma dubium*), deep lilac, spring, 9 in., Asia Minor.

Jerusalem Artichoke, see *Helianthus tuberosus*; **-Cherry,** see *Solanum Pseudo-Capsicum*; **-Cross,** see *Lychnis chalcedonica*; **-Sage,** see *Phlomis fruticosa*.

Jessamine, see Jasminum.

Jewel Orchid, see Anoechtochilus.

Jew-bush, see *Pedilanthus tithymaloides*.

Jew's Mallow, see *Kerria japonica*.

Job's Tears, see *Coix Lacryma-Jobi*.

Jonquil, see *Narcissus Jonquilla*.

Judas Tree, see *Cercis Siliquastrum*.

Juglans (Walnut)—*Juglandaceae*. Hardy deciduous nut-bearing trees. First introduced late sixteenth century.

CULTURE OF WALNUT: Soil, sandy and calcareous, or stiff loams on gravelly subsoil. Position, S. or S.W., open, not shaded by trees or buildings. Plant, Oct. or Nov., placing roots 3 to 4 in. below surface of ground previously deeply trenched. Pruning unnecessary. Gather nuts for pickling before shell gets too hard. Place ripe nuts in thin layers in dry position till husks fall off, then pack in alternate layers with sand in barrels or casks, or sprinkled with salt in jars. Grafted or budded trees bear earlier than seedlings. Culture of other species, same as above. Walnuts planted for fruit production should be grafted specimens of named vars. of known cropping powers. Thus for pickling during July, kinds such as Leeds Castle, which bears in clusters, should be selected. For dessert, French types such as Mayette and Parisienne are best. *J. regia maxima* is the ' Double Walnut '.

USEFUL DATA: *Juglans regia* and *nigra* good for town gardens. Timber used for making gun stocks, furniture and veneering. One bushel of nuts will yield about 5,000 seedlings. Average life of a walnut tree, 300 years. Average weight of timber per cubic foot, 47 lb.

PROPAGATION: By seed (nuts) sown 2 in. deep in light soil outdoors in Nov., transplanting seedlings following Oct.; budding in Aug.; grafting in March for named vars. which do not come true from seed

SPECIES CULTIVATED: *J. cinerea*, ' Butter-nut ', 50 to 60 ft., N. America; *nigra*,

'Black Walnut', 80 to 100 ft., N. America;   *regia*, 'Walnut', 50 to 60 ft., Caucasus to Himalaya .

Juncus (Rush)—*Juncaceae*.   Hardy bog-plants.

CULTURE: Soil, ordinary.   Position, wet ground or pond margin.   Plant, spring or autumn.

PROPAGATION: By division.

SPECIES CULTIVATED: *J. effusus*, 18 in., stems twisted in corkscrew fashion, N. America, Europe, Asia, var. *spiralis*; *follicularis*, 2 ft, variegated stems, var. *variegatus*

Jujube, see *Zizyphus Jujuba*

June-berry, see *Amelanchier canadensis*

Juniperus (Juniper)—*Pinaceae* (or *Cupressaceae*).   Hardy evergreen coniferous trees.   Habit, pyramidal or bushy.   Leaves, needle-shaped, narrow, scale-like.

CULTURE: Soil, good ordinary.   Position, open, well-drained shrubberies or lawns for erect species, rockeries or banks for dwarf species.   Plant, Sept., Oct. or April.

PROPAGATION: By seeds sown ½ in. deep in beds of light soil in cold frame in April, transplanting seedlings singly into small pots when 2 in. high and planting outdoors a year afterwards; cuttings of young branches inserted in sandy soil in cold frame or under hand-light in Sept. or Oct.

SPECIES CULTIVATED: *J. chinensis*, to 60 ft., China and Japan, and vars. *aurea*, upright growth, young shoots gold, *Pfitzeriana*, wide horizontal spreading branches for covering banks or large rocks, *Sargentii*, a prostrate form with creeping stems for the rockery, *variegata*, compact growth, tipped creamy white, also numerous dwarf forms such as *globosa*, *japonica* and *plumosa*; *communis*, 'Common Juniper', 30 to 40 ft., Europe, and vars. *hibernica*, 'Irish Juniper', and *compressa*, very dwarf; *excelsa*, pyramidal habit, 30 to 40 ft., Asia Minor, and var. *stricta*, upright growing; *Sabina*, 'Savin', 5 to 10 ft., Europe and N. America, and var. *tamariscifolia*, spreading habit; *squamata*, 2 ft., Himalaya and China, and var. *Meyeri*, dense habit and metallic blue colouring; *thurifera*, 'Incense Juniper', 30 to 40 ft., S.W. Europe and N. Africa; *virginiana*, 'Red Cedar', 40 to 50 ft., N. America, and vars. *bedfordiana*, columnar, *aureo-variegata*, golden variegated, *glauca*, blue foliage, *pendula*, branches drooping, and *Schottii*, columnar habit, bright green foliage.

Jupiter's Beard, see *Anthyllis Barba-Jovis*.

Jussiaea (Primrose Willow)—*Onagraceae*.   Bog and water plants, mostly tender, with yellow Oenothera-like flowers.   First introduced early nineteenth century.

CULTURE: Soil, any good loam.   Position, sunny, in shallow water.   Plant, spring.

PROPAGATION: By seeds sown in shallow pans of loam and charcoal and submerged just below water level, or cuttings struck in a sandy compost, kept very damp.

SPECIES CULTIVATED: *J. grandiflora*, hardy in the south, 1 ft., Carolina; *peruviana* (syn. *J. Sprengeri*), evergreen, 5 to 6 ft., tender, woolly leaves, S. America; *repens*, hardy, creeping, large flowers, N. America; *suffruticosa*, 2 to 3 ft., reddish stems, tender, S. America.

Justicia, see *Jacobinia Ghiesbrechtiana*.

Kadsura—*Magnoliaceae*.   Slightly tender, evergreen, climbing, flowering shrub. First introduced mid-nineteenth century.

CULTURE: Soil, peaty.   Position, well-drained borders against south or west walls in warm districts only.   Plant, Sept., Oct. or April.   Prune straggling shoots moderately in April.

PROPAGATION: By cuttings of firm shoots 2 to 3 in. long, inserted in silver sand under bell-glass in cold greenhouse or frame, July to Oct.

SPECIES CULTIVATED: *K. japonica*, yellowish-white, June to Sept., followed by scarlet berries, climbing, Japan and Korea, and var. *variegata*, leaves variegated, creamy white.

Kaempferia—*Zingiberaceae*. Stove herbaceous perennial with fragrant flowers. First introduced early eighteenth century.

CULTURE: Compost, equal parts fibrous loam and peat with little silver sand and charcoal. Position, well-drained pots in light part of stove during growing period; on their sides under staging in dry part of house during resting period. Pot, Feb. or March. Water freely March to Sept., keep almost dry afterwards. Temp., March to Sept. 65° to 75°, Sept. to March 55° to 60°. Growing period, Feb. to Oct. Resting period, Oct. to Feb.

PROPAGATION: By division of rootstocks in Feb.

SPECIES CULTIVATED: *K. Gilbertii*, leaves variegated white and green, 1 ft., Burma; *Kirkii*, rosy purple, Aug., 6 in., Zanzibar; *ornata*, yellow and orange, July, Borneo; *Roscoeana*, white and reddish-violet, July to Aug., Burma; *rotunda*, white and violet, Aug., 1 ft., India.

Kaffir Lily, see Clivia and Schizostylis.

Kaki, see *Diospyros Kaki*.

Kalanchoe—*Crassulaceae*. Greenhouse succulent perennial plants with fragrant flowers. First introduced late eighteenth century.

CULTURE: Compost, equal parts sandy loam, brick rubble, dried cow manure and river sand. Position, well-drained pots in light greenhouse, close to glass. Pot, March. Water freely April to Aug., moderately Aug. to Nov., very little afterwards. Prune old plants after flowering, shortening shoots to 1 in., and repot when new shoots are 1 in. long. Temp., March to Sept. 55° to 65°, Sept. to March 45° to 50°.

PROPAGATION: By seeds sown in well-drained pots or pans of sandy soil, just covered with fine soil, in temp. 60° to 70° in March or April, seedlings to be kept close to glass and have little water; cuttings of shoots 2 to 3 in. long exposed to sun for few days, then inserted in June, July or Aug. in well-drained pots of sandy soil, placed on greenhouse shelf, and given very little water, leaves laid on surface of moist sand.

SPECIES CULTIVATED: *K. Bentii*, pink and white, June, 3 ft., Arabia; *Blossfeldiana*, scarlet, summer, 1 ft., Madagascar; *flammea*, orange-scarlet, summer, 2 ft., Somaliland; *marmorata*, white, summer, 2 ft., Abyssinia; *pinnata* (syns. *Bryophyllum calycinum*, *B. pinnatum*), green and purple, summer, 3 ft., Tropics; *Schimperiana*, white, May, 2 ft., Abyssinia; *thyrsiflora*, yellow, May to June, 2 ft., S. Africa; *verticillata* (syn. *Bryophyllum tubiflorum*), salmon, winter, 3 ft., S. Africa, notable for plantlets formed on the slender, mottled leaves.

Kale, Scotch, see *Brassica fimbriata*; **Field-,** see *B. oleracea* var. *acephala*.

Kalmia—*Ericaceae*. Hardy evergreen or deciduous flowering shrubs with clusters of waxy, rose or pink blossoms in late spring. First introduced early eighteenth century.

CULTURE: Soil, sandy peat and leaf-mould free from lime or chalk. Position, moist and cool, partially shaded. Plant, Sept., Oct., April or May. Pruning unnecessary. Foliage of *K. latifolia* poisonous to cattle.

POT CULTURE: Compost, two parts sandy peat, one part leaf-mould and sand. Position, well-drained pots in greenhouse (temp. 45° to 55°) from Nov. to May; sunny place outdoors afterwards. Water moderately in winter, freely other times.

PROPAGATION: By seed sown in April or Oct., $\frac{1}{16}$ in. deep, in well-drained shallow pans of sandy peat in cold frame; cuttings of young shoots inserted in pots of sandy peat under bell-glass in shady cold frame, April to Aug.; layers in spring.

SPECIES CULTIVATED: *K. angustifolia*, 'Sheep Laurel', crimson, June, 3 ft., evergreen, N. America, and vars. *nana*, dwarf, *rosea*, pink, and *rubra*, red; *cuneata*, white, June to July, 3 to 4 ft., deciduous or partially evergreen, South-eastern

U.S.A.; *glauca*, lilac purple, May, 2 ft., N. America; *latifolia*, 'Calico Bush', 'American Laurel', 'Mountain Laurel', the best species for general cultivation, beautiful clear rose-pink, June, 6 to 10 ft., N. America, and var. *myrtifolia*, a good dwarf form for a confined space.

Kalmiopsis—*Ericaceae*. Hardy evergreen dwarf shrub, beautiful and uncommon. First introduced early twentieth century.

CULTURE: Soil, as for Kalmia. Position, in the rockery or heath garden, full sun or very slight shade. No pruning.

PROPAGATION: By cuttings, July or August, in acid, sandy soil, kept in close conditions.

SPECIES CULTIVATED: *K. Leachiana*, to 15 in., small Kalmia-like blossoms of bright pink, June onwards, N.W. and N. America.

Karatas—*Bromeliaceae*. Stove flowering evergreen foliage plant. Bracts, green, red or crimson. Leaves, strap-shaped, green above, purplish or whitish beneath, spiny. First introduced early eighteenth century.

CULTURE: Compost, equal parts fibrous loam, rough peat, leaf-mould and silver sand. Position, well-drained pots in light, moist part of stove. Pot, Feb. or March. Water moderately in winter, freely at other times. Temp., March to Sept. 70° to 80°, Sept. to March 65° to 75°.

PROPAGATION: By large-sized offshoots inserted singly in small pots of sandy peat, in temp. of 85°, Feb. or April.

SPECIES CULTIVATED: *K. Plumieri*, purple, summer, 18 in., Trop. America. See also Aregelia, Canistrum and Nidularium, as many species formerly included in Karatas are now placed in these genera.

Kenilworth Ivy, see *Cymbalaria muralis*.

Kelseya—*Rosaceae*. Hardy evergreen perennial cushion plants.

CULTURE: Good, well-drained soil with ample sharp grit, full sun. Probably best grown in alpine house or cold frame.

PROPAGATION: By seeds, if obtainable, or by carefully made small cuttings of side growths in spring and early summer.

SPECIES CULTIVATED: *K. uniflora*, pink, ½ in., summer, N. America.

Kennedia—*Leguminosae*. Greenhouse flowering and twining evergreen plants. First introduced late eighteenth century.

CULTURE: Compost, equal parts peat and loam, little silver sand. Position, pots, with shoots trained to trellis, or planted out in beds, and shoots trained up rafters. Pot or plant, Feb. or May. Water freely March to Sept., moderately at other times. Prune straggling plants into shape in Feb. Apply weak stimulants occasionally to healthy plants in flower. Temp., March to Sept. 55° to 65°, Sept. to March 40° to 50°.

PROPAGATION: By seeds sown ⅛ in. deep in well-drained pots of light sandy soil in temp. of 55° to 65° in March or April; cuttings of firm young shoots, 2 to 3 in. long, inserted in well-drained pots of sandy peat under bell-glass in temp. 55° to 65°, March to July.

SPECIES CULTIVATED: *K. coccinea*, scarlet, summer, 10 to 15 ft., Australia; *nigricans*, purple-black and green, large climber, Australia; *prostrata*, 'Coral Creeper', scarlet, spring, prostrate, Australia; *rubicunda*, dark red, May, 10 to 15 ft., Australia. See also Hardenbergia.

Kentia, see Howea.

Kerria (Jew's Mallow)—*Rosaceae*. Hardy deciduous flowering shrub   First introduced early eighteenth century.

CULTURE: Soil, good ordinary. Position, against south, west or even north walls or fences, or in mixed shrubberies. Plant, Oct. to March. Prune in May or June, cutting off old or weak shoots only.

POT CULTURE: Compost, two parts loam, one part leaf-mould and sand. Pot, Oct. Place in cold greenhouse and water moderately. After flowering place plants in sunny position outdoors till Oct. Forcing: place plants in temp. 55° to 65° in Jan. Water moderately. Transfer plants to sunny position outdoors after flowering.

PROPAGATION: By cuttings of young shoots, 2 to 3 in. long, in sandy soil under bell-glass or in cold frame in summer; layering shoots in spring.

SPECIES CULTIVATED: *K. japonica* (syn. *Corchorus japonicus*), yellow, May, 6 to 10 ft., China, and var. *pleniflora*, double, golden yellow; there is a variegated form which is partially tender, requiring a protected position. See also Rhodotypos.

Kickxia—*Scrophulariaceae*. Annual creeping herbs, sometimes planted for ground-cover in rockeries, formerly included in Linaria.

CULTURE: Soil, ordinary. Position, rockeries. Plant, autumn or spring.

PROPAGATION: By division; seed.

SPECIES CULTIVATED: *K. Elatine* (syn. *Linaria Elatine*), yellowish, purple outside, summer, creeping, Europe (Br.); spuria (syn. *Linaria spuria*), yellowish, upper lip purple, summer, creeping, Europe (Br.).

Kidney Bean, see *Phaseolus vulgaris*; **-bean Tree,** see *Wisteria sinensis*; **-Vetch,** see *Anthyllis Vulneraria*.

Kingcup, see *Caltha palustris*.

King's Spear, see *Asphodeline lutea*.

Kirengeshoma—*Saxifragaceae*. One hardy, herbaceous perennial.

CULTURE: Soil, rich, leafy or peaty, moist. Position, cool, partially shaded beds or borders. Plant, March or April.

SPECIES CULTIVATED: *K. palmata*, yellow, Aug. to Oct., 3 to 4 ft., Japan.

Kitaibelia—*Malvaceae*. Hardy perennial herb with vine-like foliage. First introduced early nineteenth century.

CULTURE: Soil, ordinary. Position, open, large border or shrubbery. Plant, Oct. or April.

PROPAGATION: By division of roots in Oct. or April; seeds sown outdoors in April.

SPECIES CULTIVATED: *K. vitifolia*, white and rose, summer, 6 to 8 ft., E. Europe.

Kleinia—*Compositae*. Greenhouse perennials with fleshy cylindrical bluish-grey leaves. First introduced mid-eighteenth century.

CULTURE: Compost, equal parts loam, peat, leaf-mould, broken crocks, and silver sand. Pot in spring. Position, sunny part of greenhouse or near windows in rooms. *K. repens* is used for carpet bedding in summer. Temp., Oct. to March 45° to 50°, March to Oct. 55° to 60°. Water sparingly Oct. to March, freely in summer. For outdoor culture, plant out late in May and lift again in Oct.

PROPAGATION: By cuttings of shoots dried for a few hours before insertion and then inserted in gritty compost any time during summer.

SPECIES CULTIVATED: *K. articulata*, ' Candle Plant ', yellow, 18 in., summer, S. Africa; *ficoides*, white, summer, creeping, S. Africa; *fulgens*, orange and red, May, 2 ft., S. Africa; *Galpinii*, orange, autumn, 1 ft., S. Africa; *neriifolia*, yellow, winter, 4 ft., Canaries; *repens*, white, June, creeping, S. Africa.

Klugia—*Gesneriaceae*. Stove evergreen flowering plant. First introduced mid-nineteenth century.

CULTURE: Compost, equal parts sandy loam and peat. Position, well-drained pots in shaded part of warm greenhouse or stove. Water freely March to Oct., moderately at other times.

PROPAGATION: By cuttings of young shoots inserted in sandy peat under bell-glass in spring.

SPECIES CULTIVATED: *K. zeylanica* (syn. *K. Notoniana*), blue, summer, 1 ft., Ceylon.

Knautia—*Dipsaceae*. Hardy perennial herbs, sometimes included in Scabiosa.

CULTURE: Soil, ordinary. Position, sunny. Plant, Oct. to Nov., or Mar. to April.

PROPAGATION: By seed; division.

SPECIES CULTIVATED: *K. arvensis* (syn. *Scabiosa arvensis*), ' Field Scabious ', pale lilac-purple, summer, 1 to 3 ft., Europe, including Britain; *macedonica* (syn. *Scabiosa lyrophylla*), dark red, summer, 2 ft., Balkans.

Kniphofia (Torch Lily; Club Lily)—*Liliaceae.* Hardy herbaceous perennials. Formerly known under the generic name of Tritoma.

CULTURE: Soil, sandy, well enriched with manure. Position, sunny well-drained borders. Plant, April or May. Top-dress annually in April with well-decayed manure. Water freely in dry weather during spring and summer. Apply liquid manure once a week to established plants in summer. Protect in severe weather by covering of dry leaves or straw. Dwarf species suitable for the rock garden.

PROPAGATION: By seeds sown ⅛ in. deep in sandy soil in shallow boxes in cold frame in March or April; transplanting seedlings outdoors when large enough to handle; division of roots in April.

SPECIES CULTIVATED: *K. Burchellii*, scarlet, yellow and green, autumn, 3 ft., S. Africa; *caulescens*, reddish-salmon, July, 4 to 5 ft., S. Africa; *comosa*, apricot-yellow, Sept., 2 ft., Abyssinia; *corallina*, scarlet, autumn, 3 ft., hybrid; *Galpinii*, red, summer, 2½ ft., Abyssinia; *gracilis*, orange-red, 2½ ft., S. Africa; *Leitchlinii*, red and yellow, Aug., 4 ft., Abyssinia; *Macowanii*, orange-red, Aug., 2 ft., S. Africa; *Nelsonii*, orange-scarlet and yellow, Aug., 18 to 24 in., Orange River Colony; *Northiae*, yellow and red, July, 4 to 5 ft., S. Africa; *pauciflora*, canary yellow, Aug., 1½ to 3 ft., Natal; *pumila*, orange-red, Aug., 18 in., S. Africa; *Rooperi*, orange-red, summer, 2 ft., S. Africa; *rufa*, red and yellow, Aug., 2 ft., Orange River Colony; *Snowdonii*, 4 to 5 ft., coral scarlet, sheltered border, Uganda; *Tuckii*, yellow and red, June, 4 ft., Cape Colony; *Tysonii*, rosy scarlet and yellow, Aug., 3 to 4 ft., S. Africa; *Uvaria* (syn. *K. alooides*), ' Red-hot Poker Plant ', red and yellow, autumn, 4 ft., S. Africa, and vars. *erecta*, coral scarlet, lower flowers pointing upwards, and *maxima*, 6 to 7 ft.

Knotweed, see Polygonum.

Kochia—*Chenopodiaceae.* Hardy annual. Flowers, uninteresting. Leaves, narrow and green, changing to a brilliant crimson-purple tint in early autumn.

CULTURE: Soil, ordinary. Position, sunny borders. Sow seeds in light soil in a temp. of 55° in March; transplant seedlings into pots or boxes, harden off in a cold frame, and plant out 2 ft. apart each way in June.

SPECIES CULTIVATED: *K. scoparia trichophila*, ' Summer Cypress ', 2 to 3 ft., Europe.

Koelreuteria—*Sapindaceae.* Hardy deciduous flowering tree. A graceful subject for lawn or shrubbery. First introduced mid-eighteenth century.

CULTURE: Soil, ordinary. Position, open but sheltered. Plant, Oct. to March. Pruning unnecessary

PROPAGATION: By cuttings of young shoots inserted in sandy soil under hand-light or in cold frame in April or May; sowing of imported seeds in spring.

SPECIES CULTIVATED: *K. paniculata*, 1 ft. panicles of yellow flowers, July, followed by bladder-like fruits, good autumn-tinted foliage, 30 to 60 ft., China.

Kohleria—*Gesneriaceae.* Greenhouse herbaceous perennial with scaly, catkin-like, underground stolons or tubercles.

CULTURE: Compost, two parts fibrous loam and peat, one part leaf-mould and sand. Start tubercles into growth in Feb., placing them 2 in. apart, 2 in. deep, in pots, pans or boxes. Repot into 5 in. pots when 2 in. high, subsequently repotting into 6 in. or 7 in. pots as required. Water moderately at first, freely after growth is active. After flowering, gradually withhold water from roots and when foliage dies down place pots on a shelf and allow them to rest until Feb.

PROPAGATION: By seeds sown in sandy soil, temp. 70°, March; cuttings of young shoots in April; division of the tubercles in Feb.

SPECIES CULTIVATED: *K. spicata* (syn. *Campanea Oerstedii*), scarlet, summer, 3¾ ft., Costa Rica.

Kohlrabi, see *Brassica caulorapa.*

Kolkwitzia—*Caprifoliaceae.* Deciduous hardy shrub with flowers resembling those of Abelia. First introduced early twentieth century.
CULTURE: Soil, ordinary, well drained. Position, full sun.
PROPAGATION: By Aug. cuttings in sandy soil in cold frame.
SPECIES CULTIVATED: *K. amabilis,* ' Beauty Bush ', upright to 5 ft., pink with yellow throat, May and June, Cent. China.

Kowhoi, see *Sophora tetraptera.*

Kumquat, see Fortunella.

Labichea—*Leguminosae.* Greenhouse evergreen flowering shrub. First introduced early nineteenth century.
CULTURE: Compost, equal parts peat, loam and sand. Position, well-drained pots in light, sunny greenhouse. Pot, March. Prune into shape, Feb. Water moderately Oct. to April, freely afterwards. Temp., March to Sept. 55° to 65°, Sept. to March 45° to 55°. Requires plenty of air April to Oct.
PROPAGATION: By cuttings of firm shoots inserted in sand under bell-glass in cool greenhouse, June to Aug.
SPECIES CULTIVATED: *L. lanceolata,* yellow, spring, 4 to 6 ft., Australia.

Labrador Tea, see *Ledum groenlandicum.*

+**Laburnocytisus**—*Leguminosae.* Hardy deciduous flowering tree. A bigeneric graft-hybrid between the genera Laburnum and Cystisus, interesting but of little ornamental value.
CULTURE: As Laburnum.
PROPAGATION: As Laburnum.
SPECIES CULTIVATED: *L. Adamii,* yellow or purple, spring, 15 to 20 ft.

Laburnum—*Leguminosae.* Hardy deciduous flowering trees. First introduced late sixteenth century.
CULTURE: Soil, ordinary. Position, sunny shrubberies or may be trained over pergolas, arches, etc. Plant, Oct. to March. It is advisable to remove seed pods after flowering to ensure regular flowering and to maintain healthy vigour. The seeds are poisonous.
PROPAGATION: By seeds outdoors in March or April; layers, Oct. or Nov.; varieties by grafting in March or budding in July on seedlings of common species grown in pots. These stocks are also extensively used for grafting flowering brooms.
SPECIES CULTIVATED: *L. alpinum,* ' Scottish Laburnum ', yellow, June, 15 to 20 ft., Europe, and var. *fragrans,* more strongly scented, June; *anagyroides* (syn. *L. vulgare*), ' Golden Chain ', yellow, spring, 20 to 30 ft., Europe, and vars. *aureum,* golden-leaved, *quercifolium,* oak-leaved, *Carlieri,* long racemes, and *pendulum,* weeping; *Watereri* (syn. *L. Vossii*), longest racemes, semi-weeping, hybrid.

Lace-bark, see *Hoheria Lyallii;* -**Fern,** see *Cheilanthes gracillima.*

Lachenalia (Cape Cowslip)—*Liliaceae.* Greenhouse bulbous flowering plants. First introduced mid-eighteenth century.
CULTURE: Compost, two parts fibrous sandy loam, half part leaf-mould, half part decayed cow manure, and one part river or coarse silver sand. Position, well-drained pots, pans or baskets; light. Pot, Aug., placing six bulbs ½ in. deep in a 5 in. pot or 1 to 2 in. apart in pans or baskets. After potting water and place pots in cold frame until Nov., then remove to airy shelf in greenhouse. Temp., 45° to 55°. Water moderately when growth begins, freely when well advanced. Apply weak stimulants occasionally when flower spikes form, discontinue when in bloom. After flowering gradually withhold water, place pots in sunny position

outdoors, and keep quite dry to ripen bulbs. Growing period, Sept. to June; resting period, June to Sept. Forcing (*L. tricolor*): Pot and treat as above until Nov., then remove into temp. of 55° to 65°.

PROPAGATION: By offsets, removed and placed in separate pots at potting time.

SPECIES CULTIVATED: *L. glaucina*, white tinged with orange, May, 6 in., S. Africa; *orchioides*, pale yellow tinged red, April to May, 9 in., S. Africa; *pendula*, yellow, red, and purple, April to May, 8 to 12 in., S. Africa; *tricolor* (syn. *L. aurea*), ' Leopard Lily ', red and yellow, spring, 1 ft., S. Africa, and vars. *aurea*, bright orange-yellow, *buteola*, brown-yellow, *Nelsonii*, yellow, and *quadricolor*, yellow, green, and reddish-purple. Many named hybrids are to be found in trade lists.

Lactuca—*Compositae.* Hardy border annuals and perennials and salad vegetables. Edible lettuce introduced mid-sixteenth century.

CULTURE OF EDIBLE LETTUCE: Soil, light, rich, deeply dug, well manured. Position, south borders for spring and winter crops; open, sunny for summer crops. Make selection of garden vars. to suit season of sowing. Sow seeds ⅛ in. deep in light soil in temp. 65° in Jan., Feb. or March for planting outdoors in March, April and May; in bed of rich soil in sunny spot outdoors in March, April, May and June, for planting out in April, May, June and July; outdoors in Aug. and Sept., for planting out in Sept. and Oct.; in cold frames in Oct., for planting out in March. Plant 10 in. apart in rows 12 in. asunder. Blanch cos vars. by tying bast round outside a week before required for use. Water freely when first planted, if weather dry. Cabbage vars. best for poor dry soil, cos for heavy and rich soil. Crop reaches maturity in 10 or 12 weeks. There are some vars. suitable for forcing in greenhouses, and ordinary crops will mature more quickly given frame or cloche protection.

CULTURE OF FLOWERING LETTUCE: Soil, sandy loam. Position, open, sunny, dryish border. Plant, Oct. or March.

PROPAGATION: Flowering lettuce by seeds sown ⅛ in. deep outdoors in April; division of roots in March. Edible species by seed.

SPECIES CULTIVATED: *L. alpina* (syn. *Mulgedium alpinum*), blue, Aug., 3 ft., N. Europe; *Plumieri* (syn. *Mulgedium Plumieri*), purple, summer, 8 ft., Pyrenees; *sativa*, ' Lettuce ', yellow, summer, 3 to 4 ft., and vars. *asparagina*, ' Asparagus Lettuce ', *capitata*, ' Cabbage Lettuce ', *crispa*, ' Curled Lettuce ', *longifolia*, ' Cos Lettuce.

Lad's Love, see *Artemisia Abrotanum.*

Lady Bell, see Adenophora; **-Fern,** see *Athyrium Filix-femina.*

Lady's Mantle, see Alchemilla; **-Slipper,** see Cypripedium.

Lady-smock, see *Cardamine pratense.*

Laelia—*Orchidaceae.* An epiphytic genus closely allied to Cattleya, with which genus very many hybrids have been produced, also with Brassavola, Epidendrum, etc.

CULTURE: Compost, as for Cattleyas for all. Broadly there are two sections, one much like the *Cattleya labiata* group requiring the same conditions. The second with smaller, often ovoid, pseudo-bulbs and rather tall, slender scapes terminating in several flowers, usually smaller than those of the first section. This section succeeds in the cool house, but can be grown with the others suspended near the glass in pans, during the summer and given a rather severe rest in the cool house in winter, temp. 50°. In each section the spikes are terminal to the pseudo-bulb.

PROPAGATION: By division of plants in spring.

SPECIES CULTIVATED: A selection: clavate-bulbed species—*L. crispa* (syn. *Cattleya crispa*), white, purple flushed, lip purple, variable, summer, Brazil; *grandis*, yellow shaded buff, lip dusky rose-purple with deeper veins, summer, Brazil; *lobata* (syn. *L. Boothiana*), rose-purple, lip amethyst-purple, summer, Brazil; *Perrinii*, rose or rose-lilac, lip intense purple, crimson on mid lobe autumn, winter, Brazil, and var. *alba*, white; *purpurata*, variable, white, rose-flushed, lip rich crimson-purple, spring, summer, Brazil, very many vars.; *tenebrosa* (syn. *L. grandis tenebrosa*), bronze and copper shaded, lip dusky brown-purple, summer, Brazil; *xanthina*, yellow, lip whitish suffused purple, variable, spring, summer, Brazil.

Species requiring more decided rest, enjoying sun heat and a moist atmosphere in the summer—*L. albida*, very variable, white, rose-flushed, winter, Mexico, and several named vars.; *anceps*, very variable, pale to deep rose, lip crimson, purple-crimson, yellow keels, winter, Mexico, and many named vars.; *autumnalis*, rose-purple, whitish, variable, autumn, winter, Mexico, and var. *atrorubens*, a type with much darker flowers; *Gouldiana*, deep rose-purple, winter, Mexico; *rubescens*, lilac-rose, winter, Mexico; *speciosa* (syn. *L. majalis*), lilac, lip whitish, purple, blotched purple-lilac, spring, summer, Brazil.

Species suited to the Odontoglossum house, not rested.—*L. harpophylla*, orange-red, slender habit, winter, spring, Brazil; *Jongheana*, large, lilac-purple, lip rose-purple, yellow, winter, spring, Brazil, should be similarly treated; *pumila*, dwarf-growing, variable, rose-purple to deep purple, and many vars. occur under the name *Dayana*, a varietal type, slightly smaller, mauve, deep purple, also has many named vars, as has var. *major* (syn. var. *praestans*), a third type, mauve to red-purple, autumn, Brazil.

× **Laleiocattleya**—*Orchidaceae*. Bigeneric hybrids between the genera Cattleya and Laelia. Some 2,000 distinct hybrids have been recorded and further additions are being made. Nature had antedated the artificial hybrids and several Laeliocattleyas have been imported, including the variable *L. elegans* (syns. *Laelia elegans* and *Laeliocattleya Schilleriana*).

CULTURE: Compost, conditons, temperatures, as for Cattleyas.

Lagarosiphon (Giant Water Thyme)—*Hydrocharitaceae*. Submerged aquatics which are excellent oxygenators. First introduced early twentieth century.

CULTURE: Any soil. Position, outdoor pools, tropical and cold water aquariums. Plant, any time during growing season.

PROPAGATION: Slips pulled off and rooted in mud.

SPECIES CULTIVATED: *L. major* (syn. *Elodea crispa*), reflexed leaves in whorls up branching stems, S. Africa.

Lagenaria (Bottle Gourd; Trumpet Gourd)—*Cucurbitaceae*. Hardy orn. fruiting annual. Fruit not edible, oblong, bottle-like, 1 to 6 ft. long. First introduced late sixteenth century.

CULTURE: Soil, rich, ordinary. Position, beds at foot of low sunny walls, fences or arbours, or on the summits of sunny banks, shoots growing at will. Plant, June. Water freely and apply stimulants when fruit has formed. No pinching of shoots required. May also be grown in pots in sunny greenhouses, training shoots up roof.

PROPAGATION: By seeds sown ½ in. deep in light soil in temp. 55° to 65° in April.

SPECIES CULTIVATED: *L. siceraria* (syn. *L. vulgaris*), white, summer, 10 ft., Trop. Asia and Africa.

Lagerstroemia—*Lythraceae*. Stove and greenhouse evergreen flowering shrubs. First introduced late eighteenth century.

CULTURE: Compost, equal parts loam and peat, little sand. Position, well-drained pots in light part of greenhouse or stove. Pot, Feb. or March. Prune, slightly in Oct. or Nov. Water freely March to Oct., very little Oct. to March. Syringe twice daily March to Sept. Temp., stove species, 55° to 60° Oct. to March, 65° to 75° March to Oct.; greenhouse species, Oct. to March 45° to 55°, March to Oct. 60° to 70°.

PROPAGATION: By cuttings of firm shoots inserted in sandy peat under bell-glass in temp. of 70° to 80° in March, April, Aug. or Sept.

STOVE SPECIES CULTIVATED: *L. speciosa* (syn. *L. Flos-Reginae*), rose purple, summer. 50 to 60 ft., Trop. Asia.

GREENHOUSE SPECIES CULTIVATED: *L. indica,* ' Crape Myrtle ', pink, summer, 6 to 10 ft., Trop. Asia; *indica alba,* white.

Lagunaria—*Malvaceae.* Greenhouse evergreen flowering tree. First introduced late eighteenth century.
CULTURE: Compost, fibrous loam, peat and sand. Position, well-drained pots in light greenhouse, also planted out in a border of well-drained soil. Water freely March to Oct., moderately Nov. to Feb.
PROPAGATION: By cuttings of half-ripened shoots in sandy peat under bell-glass or in propagating frame, in gentle heat during May.
SPECIES CULTIVATED: *L. Patersonii,* reddish-white, summer, 20 ft., Australia.

Lagurus—*Gramineae.* Hardy ornamental annual grass. Inflorescence borne in egg-shaped heads, white, downy, June to Sept. Very useful in dried state for winter decorations.
CULTURE: Soil, ordinary. Position, open dryish borders. Gather inflorescence for drying in Aug.
PROPAGATION: By seeds sown ¼ in. deep outdoors in April where plants are required to grow.
SPECIES CULTIVATED: *L. ovatus,* ' Hare's Tail Grass ', 1 ft., S. Europe (Br.).

Lallemantia—*Labiatae.* Small annual or biennial herbs with opposite toothed leaves and small two-lipped flowers in whorls.
CULTURE: Soil, ordinary well drained. Position, sunny.
PROPAGATION: By seed.
SPECIES CULTIVATED: *L. canescens,* blue, summer, to 1½ ft., biennial, W. Asia.

Lamarckia—*Gramineae.* Hardy ornamental annual grass. Inflorescence plumelike, silky and golden, June to Sept. Useful in a dried state for winter decorations. First introduced mid-eighteenth century.
CULTURE: Soil, ordinary. Position, patches in open sunny borders. Gather inflorescence for winter use in Aug.
PROPAGATION: By seeds sown ¼ in. deep outdoors in April where plants are required to grow, or in well-drained pans of light soil in cold frame in Oct., planting outdoors in April.
SPECIES CULTIVATED: *L. aurea,* 8 in., S. Europe.

Lamb's Ear, see *Stachys lanata;* **-Lettuce,** see *Valerianella olitoria.*

Lamium (Dead-Nettle)—*Labiatae.* Hardy perennial flowering herb. Leaves, egg- or heart-shaped, with serrated margins.
CULTURE: Soil, ordinary. Position, dryish, sunny borders. Plant, Oct. or April.
PROPAGATION: By division of roots, Oct. or March.
SPECIES CULTIVATED: *L. maculatum aureum,* leaves variegated with golden yellow, 1 ft., Europe (Br.).

Lampranthus—*Aizoaceae.* Greenhouse succulent plants, formerly included in Mesembryanthemum.
CULTURE: Compost, equal parts old mortar, pounded crocks, sandy loam, well-decayed manure or leaf-mould, and sand. Position, well-drained pots in sunny greenhouse or window, may be planted in sunny borders outdoors from June to Sept. Pot, March to May. Water freely April to Sept., keep nearly dry during winter. Temp., March to Oct. 55° to 65°, Oct. to March 40° to 50°.
PROPAGATION: By seed; cuttings in temp. 55° to 65°, March to Sept.
SPECIES CULTIVATED: *L. aurantiacus* (syn. *Mesembryanthemum aurantiacum*), bright orange, summer, 1 to 2 ft., S. Africa; *aureus* (syn. *M. aureum*), yellow, June, 1 ft., S. Africa; *blandus* (syn. *M. blandum*), white, June, 18 in., S. Africa; *Brownii* (syn. *M. Brownii*), orange-red, summer, 1 ft., S. Africa; *coccineus* (syn. *M. coccineum*), scarlet, July, 18 in., S. Africa; *emarginatus* (syn. *M. violaceum*), purple, July, 1 ft., S. Africa; *roseus* (syn. *M. roseum*), pale rose, July, 1½ to 2 ft., S. Africa; *spectabilis* (syn. *M. spectabile*), red, May, 1 ft., S. Africa.

Land Cress, see *Barbarea verna.*

Lantana—*Verbenaceae.* Greenhouse and half-hardy evergreen flowering shrubs. First introduced late seventeenth century.

POT CULTURE: Compost, two parts loam, one part peat, leaf-mould or decayed manure, little sand, and charcoal. Position, well-drained pots in light greenhouse. Pot, firmly, March. Water freely April to Oct., moderately Oct. to April. Prune into shape, Feb. Temp., Oct. to March 45° to 55°, March to Oct. 55° to 65°. Apply weak stimulants once or twice weekly, May to Sept.

OUTDOOR CULTURE: Soil, rich sandy. Position, sunny, dryish beds or borders. Plant, June. Lift in Sept., repot and replace in greenhouse for winter.

PROPAGATION: By seeds sown $\frac{1}{16}$ in. deep in well-drained pots or pans of sandy peat and leaf-mould, in temp. of 70° to 80°, in Feb., March or April; by cuttings of firm shoots, 2 to 3 in. long, inserted in small pots of sandy peat under bell-glass in temp. of 55° to 65° in Aug. or Sept.; or by cuttings of young side shoots 2 in. long inserted as above in temp. 60° to 70°, March or April.

SPECIES CULTIVATED: *L. Camara,* violet, summer, 4 ft., Trop. America; *Chelsonii,* orange-red, summer, 2 ft., S. America; *montevidensis* (syn. *L. Selloviana*), rosy lilac, summer, 3 ft., S. America; *nivea,* white, summer, 2 to 3 ft., Trop. America. Numerous vars. superior to species in trade lists.

Lapageria—*Liliaceae.* Greenhouse and half-hardy evergreen flowering climber. First introduced early nineteenth century.

INDOOR CULTURE: Compost, three parts fibrous peat, one part loam, one part equal proportions of sand and charcoal. Position, shady in large, well-drained pots, tubs, beds, or borders, with shoots trained to trellises or up walls or rafters of greenhouse. Pot or plant, Feb. or March. Good drainage very essential. Water freely April to Sept., moderately afterwards. Syringe daily from March until flowers develop. Prune away dead or sickly shoots only in March. Ventilate freely April to Oct. Temp., Oct. to March 40° to 50°, March to Oct. 55° to 65°. Foliage must be kept free from insects.

OUTDOOR CULTURE: Soil, equal parts peat and loam. Position, west walls, sheltered, in S. of England only. Plant, Oct. or March, in well-drained bed. Protect in severe weather. Water freely in dry weather.

PROPAGATION: By seeds sown $\frac{1}{8}$ in. deep in well-drained pots or pans of sandy peat and leaf-mould in temp. of 55° to 65° in March or April; by layering strong shoots in sandy peat in spring or autumn.

SPECIES CULTIVATED: *L. rosea,* ' Chilean Bellflower ', rose, summer, 15 to 20 ft., Chile, and vars. *albiflora,* white, and *superba,* crimson.

Lapeirousia—*Iridaceae.* Hardy and half-hardy bulbous flowering plants. First introduced late eighteenth century.

OUTDOOR CULTURE: Soil, sandy loam and leaf-mould. Position, sunny well-drained borders or rockeries. Plant bulbs 4 in. deep and 3 in. apart, Sept. to Oct.

POT CULTURE: Compost, equal parts sandy loam, leaf-mould and sand. Position, cold frame Sept. to Feb., cool or cold greenhouse afterwards. Pot, Sept., placing six bulbs in a 6 in. pot, and cover with cinder ashes till growth begins. Water moderately when new growth commences; keep dry after flowering till potting time.

PROPAGATION: By offshoots removed at planting or potting time and treated as old bulbs.

SPECIES CULTIVATED: *L. cruenta* (syn. *Anomatheca cruenta*), crimson, summer, 1 ft., hardy, Cape of Good Hope; *grandiflora,* red and yellow, summer, 1 ft., tender, best grown in pots., Cape of Good Hope.

Laportea—*Urticaceae.* Stove perennial herb, with ornamental fruits. Plants possess stinging hairs and require to be handled with great care.

CULTURE: Compost, rich loam and fibrous peat or leaf-mould with sharp sand. Position, well-drained pots in warm greenhouse. Water carefully at all times.

PROPAGATION: By seeds sown in sandy soil in temp. 65° to 70° in spring. Cuttings placed in sand under bell-glass in heat.
SPECIES CULTIVATED: *L. crenulata*, India.

Larch, see Larix.

Lardizabala—*Lardizabalaceae.* Slightly tender evergreen flowering climber. First introduced mid-nineteenth century.
CULTURE: Soil, equal parts sandy loam and peat. Position, well-drained border at base of south or west walls in mild districts. Plant, Sept., Oct., March or April. Prune away dead or straggling shoots only in April. Suitable also for growing against walls in cold greenhouses or conservatories.
PROPAGATION: By cuttings of firm shoots, 1 to 2 in. long, inserted in sandy loam and peat in well-drained pots under bell-glass in temp. 45° to 55°, July or Aug.
SPECIES CULTIVATED: *L. biternata*, vigorous to 30 or 40 ft., large leathery leaves, flowers unisexual, dark purple, fruits 3 in. long, edible.

Larix (Larch)—*Pinaceae.* Hardy deciduous trees. Grown largely for timber purposes. First introduced early seventeenth century.
CULTURE: Soil, any except heavy clay. Position, hill slopes or banks, sheltered from north; low, damp situations not suitable. Plant in autumn. Distance for planting, 3 to 4 ft. each way. Also make fine specimen trees planted singly on lawns or in open places. Best age to plant, two years old. Land best trenched a good spit deep before planting. Number of trees required to plant an imperial acre at 3 ft., 4,840; at 4 ft., 2,722. Thinning should commence at five years old. Each imperial acre should contain about 1,200 trees at tenth year; 900 at fifteenth year; 600 at twentieth year; 450 at twenty-fifth year; and 300 in thirtieth year; latter number to be permanent crop. Trees attain maturity when 30 to 70 years old. Bear seeds when 30 to 40 years old. Number of seeds in a pound, 5,000. Weight of a bushel of seed, 14 lb. Weight of timber per cubic foot, 38 lb. Timber used for fencing, pit wood, scaffold poles, and boat building. Quantity of seeds to sow 100 ft. square of bed, 8 oz.
PROPAGATION: By seeds sown 1 in. deep in March. Transplant seedlings when two years old.
SPECIES CULTIVATED: *L. decidua* (syn. *L. europaea*), ' European Larch ', 60 to 120 ft., Europe, and var. *pendula*; *Griffithii*, 40 to 60 ft., Himalaya; *laricina* (syn. *L. americana*), to 60 ft., America; *leptolepis*, ' Japanese Larch ', 80 to 100 ft., Japan; *Gmelinii* (syn. *L. dahurica*), 50 to 80 ft., Siberia; *occidentalis*, 100 to 200 ft., N. America; *sibirica*, ' Siberian Larch ', to 100 ft., Siberia.

Larkspur, see Delphinium.

Lasiandra, see Tibouchina.

Lasthenia—*Compositae.* Hardy annuals. First introduced early nineteenth century.
CULTURE: Soil, ordinary. Position, warm, sheltered rockeries, beds or borders.
PROPAGATION: By seeds sown ⅛ in. deep in April where plants are required to grow for summer flowering; in Sept. to Oct. similarly for spring flowering.
SPECIES CULTIVATED: *L. glabrata*, yellow, summer, 1 ft., California.

Lastrea, see Dryopteris.

Latania—*Palmae.* Stove palms with fan-shaped, bright green leaves.
CULTURE: Compost, two parts loam, one part peat and a little charcoal and sand. Position, well-drained pots in shady part of stove. Pot, Feb. or March. Water freely March to Sept., moderately afterwards. Syringe once daily in winter, twice other times. Temp., March to Sept. 65° to 75°, Sept. to March 55° to 65°.
PROPAGATION: By seeds sown ½ in. deep in rich light soil in temp. of 80° to 90°, Feb., March or April.
SPECIES CULTIVATED: *L. Commersonii*, 7 ft., Mauritius and Bourbon; *Ver-*

schaffeltii (syn. *L. aurea*), 7 ft., Mauritius. See also *Livistona chinensis*, which is frequently erroneously named *Latania borbonica*.

Lathraea—*Orobanchaceae.* Herbaceous, perennial, leafless, parasitic plants.

CULTURE: Plant seeds on the roots of Willow, Poplar or Hazel.

SPECIES CULTIVATED: *L. clandestina*, purple, 3 in., spring, Europe; *Squamaria*, purplish, Britain.

Lathyrus—*Leguminosae.* Hardy annuals and herbaceous perennial climbers. Sweet Pea introduced early eighteenth century.

CULTURE OF SWEET PEA: Soil, rich ordinary, well manured. Position, groups in sunny borders, shoots supported by tree branches or bamboo canes; against sunny walls or fences; in sunny window boxes; in rows in open garden. Sow seeds, three or four, in a 3 in. pot in light soil in temp. 50 to 55° in Feb., transplanting seedlings outdoors in April; or 2 in. deep and 3 to 6 in. apart in Oct. or March where plants are to grow. Water liberally in dry weather. Apply liquid manure once or twice weekly to plants in flower. Remove seed pods as they form to ensure plenty of flowers.

POT CULTURE: Sow four seeds 1 in. deep in 3 in. pots in temp. 55° in Jan. or Feb. Compost, two parts loam, one part leaf-mould and sand. Transfer four seedlings, when 2 in. high, to a 5 in. pot. Support shoots with small twigs or bamboo canes. Water liberally. Apply liquid manure when buds show. Grow in cool greenhouse, conservatory or window when in flower.

EXHIBITION OR SPECIAL CULTURE: Grow in rows 8 ft. apart. Dig trenches 18 in. wide and 2 ft. deep. Fork into subsoil 2 in. of rotting manure, then fill up trench to within 2 in. of top with ordinary soil and good loam. Add a handful each of superphosphate and kainit to each linear yard of trench and fork in. Sow seeds 1 in. deep and 3 in. apart in Oct., or five seeds in a 3 in. pot of good soil in cold frames in Oct., and plant out seedlings 6 in. apart in April. Stake early, using bamboo canes at least seven feet high. Feed with half-ounce of sulphate of ammonia to gallon of water. Give 3 gallons to each group or linear yard of row once a week. Remove all side growths, keeping each plant to a single stem. Nip off points of shoots when top of sticks is reached, or, alternatively, untie each plant, loop the old growth round the bottom of its stake, and allow the growing point to climb to the top once more. Remove spent blooms daily.

CULTURE OF PERENNIAL SPECIES: Soil, ordinary deep rich. Position, against sunny walls, fences, arbours, or tree stumps or banks. Plant, Oct., Nov., March or April. Apply liquid manure occasionally in summer. Water freely in dry weather. Prune away stems close to ground in Oct. Top-dress with decayed manure in March.

PROPAGATION: Annuals by seed; perennials by seed or division of roots in March or April.

ANNUAL SPECIES CULTIVATED: *L. odoratus*, ' Sweet Pea ', various, 6 to 10 ft., Italy; *sativus azureus*, blue, summer, 2 ft., S. Europe; *tingitanus*, ' Tangier Pea ' purple and red, summer, 4 to 6 ft., Tangier.

PERENNIAL SPECIES CULTIVATED: *L. grandiflorus*, rosy crimson, summer, 5 ft., S. Europe; *latifolius*, ' Everlasting Pea ', red, crimson, and violet, 8 to 10 ft., Europe; *latifolius albus*, white; *magellanicus*, ' Lord Anson's Pea ', purple, June to Sept., 6 to 8 ft., Straits of Magellan; *pubescens*, pale blue, July to Sept., 3 to 5 ft., Chile; *rotundifolius*, rosy pink, summer, 6 ft., Asia Minor; *splendens*, carmine red, summer, California, rather tender; *undulatus*, rosy purple, May and June, 2 to 3 ft., Dardanelles; *vernus* (syn. *Orobus vernus*), purple and blue, spring, 1 ft., Europe.

Laurel, see Laurus; **Alexandrian-**, see *Danae racemosa*; **Californian-**, see *Umbellularia californica*; **Cherry-**, see *Prunus cerasifera*; **Mountain-**, see *Kalmia latifolia*; **Portugal-**, see *Prunus lusitanica*; **Sheep-**, see *Kalmia angustifolia*; **Spurge-**, see *Daphne Laureola*.

Laurus (Bay Tree)—*Lauraceae.* Hardy evergreen shrub or small tree. Insignificant yellow flowers, male and female borne on separate plants; berries, dark purple. The dark green aromatic leaves are used for flavouring. First introduced mid-sixteenth century.

CULTURE: Soil, ordinary. Position, open sunny lawns, sheltered shrubberies or borders. Plant, Sept., March or April. Good subject for clipping to formal shape, may be purchased as pyramids or standards. Trim between May and July.

CULTURE IN TUBS: Compost, two parts loam, one part leaf-mould and sand. Plant, Sept., Oct., March or April. Water sparingly Oct. to April, freely afterwards. May stand in sunny sheltered position for the winter or in a cold greenhouse. Although perfectly hardy, severe weather may cause a browning of the leaves.

PROPAGATION: By cuttings of shoots 3 to 4 in. long in sandy soil under handlight in shady place outdoors, Aug. to Oct.; layering shoots Sept. or Oct.

SPECIES CULTIVATED: *L. nobilis*, ' Sweet Bay ', ' Victor's Laurel ', ' Poet's Laurel ', 20 to 40 ft., S. Europe.

Lavandula (Lavender)—*Labiatae*. Hardy evergreen fragrant flowering shrubs. The flowers are highly esteemed for their fragrance in a dried state and for distilling for perfumery, being grown commercially for the latter purpose. First introduced mid-sixteenth century.

CULTURE: Soil, ordinary light. Position, warm, dry and sunny. Plant, March or Sept. Prune straggly plants into shape in March or April; this should be done regularly to lavender hedges to prevent them from getting bare at the base. Gather blossoms for drying just as they come into bloom and for distilling about a week later.

PROPAGATION: By cuttings in ordinary soil in shaded frame in August or out of doors in sheltered border Sept to Oct.

SPECIES CULTIVATED: *L. officinalis* (syn. *L. Spica*), lavender, grey foliage, July to Aug., 3 to 4 ft., Medit. Region, and vars. *alba*, white, *compacta*, low and compact.

Lavatera (Tree Mallow)—*Malvaceae*. Hardy flowering sub-shrubs and annuals.

CULTURE OF SHRUBBY SPECIES: Soil, ordinary. Position, warm, dryish borders. Plant, June. *L. arborea*, the Tree Mallow, is not fully hardy inland, but quickly naturalises itself in maritime districts.

CULTURE OF ANNUAL SPECIES: Soil, ordinary light rich. Position, sunny beds or borders. Sow seed ⅛ in. deep where plants are required to grow, in Sept. or April.

PROPAGATION : Shrubby species by seeds sown in pots or boxes of light soil in temp. of 55° to 60° in Feb. or March ; or in sunny position outdoors, April or May; variegated species by cuttings of young shoots inserted in sandy soil under bell-glass in gentle bottom heat during June or July.

SHRUBBY SPECIES : *L. assurgentiflora*, purple, summer, 6 to 10 ft., S. California ; *arborea* ' Tree Mallow ', purple, autumn, 8 to 10 ft., Europe (Britain), and its variety *variegata*, leaves mottled with white ; *Olbia*, rosy pink, summer and autumn, 6 ft., S. Europe.

ANNUAL SPECIES : *L. trimestris* (syn. *L. rosea*), rose, 4 to 6 ft., S. Europe, var. *alba*. white.

Laurustinus, see *Viburnum Tinus*.

Lavender, see Lavandula; **-Cotton**, see *Santolina Chamaecyparissus*.

Lawson's Cypress, see *Chamaecyparis Lawsoniana*.

Layia—*Compositae*. Hardy annuals. First introduced early nineteenth century.

CULTURE: Soil, ordinary. Position, sunny beds or borders.

PROPAGATION: By seeds sown 1/16 in. deep in light mould in temp. 45° to 55° in April, transplanting seedlings outdoors end of May; or outdoors in April where plants are required to grow.

SPECIES CULTIVATED: *L. calliglossa*, yellow, summer, 1 ft., California; *chrysanthemoides* (syn. *Oxyura chrysanthemoides*), yellow and white, summer, 1 ft., California; *elegans*, ' Tidy Tips ', yellow and white, summer, 1 ft., California:

glandulosa, white, summer, 6 to 18 in., N. America; *platyglossa* (syn. *Callichroa platyglossa*), yellow, summer, 1 ft., California.

Lead Plant, see *Amorpha canescens*; **-wort,** see Plumbago.

Leaf-flowering Cactus, see Schlumbergera and Zygocactus.

Leatherwood, see *Cyrilla racemiflora*.

Lebanon Candytuft, see *Aethionema coridifolium*.

Ledum—*Ericaceae.* Hardy evergreen flowering shrubs. First introduced mid-eighteenth century.

CULTURE: Soil, ordinary, but rich in humus and free from lime. Position, open, but not too dry, beds or borders in company with azaleas, kalmias, etc. Plant, Oct., Nov. or March, disturbing roots as little as possible.

PROPAGATION: By seeds sown $\frac{1}{16}$ in. deep in a well-drained pan of sandy peat in a cold frame in March; by layering in Sept.; division of roots in Sept. or Oct.

SPECIES CULTIVATED: *L. groenlandicum* (syn. *L. latifolium*), 'Labrador Tea', white, April, 3 ft., N. America, the prettiest species with scented leaves, woolly beneath; *palustre*, 'Marsh Rosemary', white, May, 2 ft., N. Europe. See also Leiophyllum.

Leea—*Vitaceae.* Stove shrub with pinnate leaves. Leaves, feather-shaped, bronze green, striped with white above and dark red below. First introduced late nineteenth century.

CULTURE: Compost, two parts loam, one part well-decayed manure or leaf-mould and one part sharp silver sand. Position, well-drained pots in shade. Pot, Feb. or March. Temp., March to Sept. 65° to 75°, Sept. to March 55° to 65°. Water freely March to Sept., moderately afterwards. Syringe daily April to Aug.

PROPAGATION: By cuttings of side shoots inserted in sandy soil under bell-glass in temp. 75° to 85° in spring.

SPECIES CULTIVATED: *L. amabilis*, 3 ft., Borneo, and var. *splendens*, superior form; *coccinea*, scarlet, summer, 1 ft., Burma.

Leek, see *Allium Porrum*.

Leiophyllum (Sand Myrtle)—*Ericaceae.* Hardy evergreen flowering shrubs. First introduced early eighteenth century.

CULTURE: Soil, light, lime-free, rich in humus. Position, rockeries, heath gardens or in front of azaleas. Plant, Oct., Nov., or March.

PROPAGATION: By seeds sown $\frac{1}{16}$ in. deep in well-drained pan of sandy peat in a cold frame in March; Aug. cuttings in gentle bottom heat.

SPECIES CULTIVATED: *L. buxifolium*, compact, rich pink buds opening rose, May and June, to 18 in., East N. America; *Lyonii* (syn. *L. buxifolium prostratum*), prostrate, densely branched, N. Carolina.

Lemon, see *Citrus Limonia*; **-scented Verbena,** see *Lippia citriodora*.

Lens—*Leguminosae.* Hardy annual. Leaves, feather-shaped. Pods, about $\frac{3}{4}$ in. long, $\frac{1}{4}$ in. broad, containing two seeds. Seeds, a cheap and nutritious source of food in some countries. Vines sometimes used as forage. Introduced mid-sixteenth century.

CULTURE: Soil, light ordinary. Position, sunny borders. Sow seeds 2 in. deep and 2 in. apart in drills 18 in. asunder early in April. Allow the plants to grow till quite yellow, then pull up, dry thoroughly in the sun, gather pods and store in a dry place till required for use. Thrash as required.

SPECIES CULTIVATED: *L. esculenta*, 'Lentil', white, June to Aug., 1 ft., S. Europe.

Lent Lily, see *Narcissus Pseudo-Narcissus*.

Lentil, see *Lens esculenta*.

Lenten Rose, see *Helleborus orientalis*.

Leonotis—*Labiatae.* Greenhouse and half-hardy evergreen flowering shrub. First introduced early eighteenth century.

INDOOR CULTURE: Compost, two parts rich loam, one part equal proportions of leaf-mould, charcoal and silver sand. Position, well-drained pots in light, airy part of greenhouse, Sept. to June; sunny place outdoors, June to Sept. Pot, March or April. Prune into shape after flowering. Water moderately April to Sept., very sparingly afterwards. Temp., Sept. to April 40° to 50°, April to June 55° to 65°.

OUTDOOR CULTURE: Soil, sandy loam. Position, warm, sheltered border in mild southern districts only. Plant, May. Protect in winter with bracken or straw.

PROPAGATION: By cuttings of shoots inserted in light sandy soil in temp. 55° to 65° in March or April. Young plants require tops of shoots to be removed occasionally.

SPECIES CULTIVATED: *L. Leonurus,* ' Lion's Ear ', orange-scarlet, summer, 3 to 5 ft., S. Africa.

Leontice—*Berberidaceae.* Hardy tuberous-rooted perennials. First introduced late sixteenth century.

CULTURE: Soil, equal parts sandy loam, leaf-mould and sand. Position, sheltered, sunny rockery. Plant tubers in Sept. or Oct.; base only of tuber to be buried in the soil, leaving the upper part exposed. Mulch with peat or decayed leaves in summer and protect tubers with covering of ashes in winter.

PROPAGATION: By offsets, removed and planted in Sept. or Oct.

SPECIES CULTIVATED: *L. Albertii,* ' Lion's Turnip ', brown and yellow, spring, 6 to 8 in., Turkistan; *Leontopetalum,* ' Lion's Leaf ', yellow, spring, 1 ft., Caucasus.

Leontopodium—*Compositae.* Hardy perennial herb. First introduced mid-eighteenth century.

CULTURE: Soil, well-drained, sandy. Position, exposed sunny rockeries. Plant, March or April. Protect from heavy rains in autumn and winter by placing a square of glass, supported by sticks at each corner, a few inches above the plants. Gather flowers in Aug. and dry for preserving. Best results are obtained by raising fresh plants from seed annually, or by dividing old plants in spring.

PROPAGATION: By seeds sown in March in a well-drained pan of fine loam, leaf-mould and granite chips, placed under a hand-light, or in a cold frame in a cool shady spot, transplanting seedlings outdoors in Aug. or Sept.; by division in April.

SPECIES CULTIVATED: *L. alpinum,* ' Edelweiss ', yellow, May to July, surrounded by star-shaped, white, cottony involucre, 6 in., Alps; *calocephalum,* white, May, 9 in., China; *crassense,* white, May, 4 in., Bulgaria; *haplophylloides* (syn. *L. aloysiodorum*), ' Lemon-scented Edelweiss ', grey-white, June, 6 in., China; *japonicum,* white, May, 9 in., China, Japan; *leontopodioides,* white, spring, 6 to 9 in., Siberia; *nivale,* white, May, 3 in., Balkans; *Palibinianum,* white, May, 9 in., Asia.

Leopard's-bane, see Doronicum.

Lepachys—*Compositae.* Hardy perennials. First introduced early nineteenth century.

CULTURE: Soil, ordinary. Position, sunny beds or borders. Plant, Oct., or March to April. Sometimes grown as an annual.

PROPAGATION: By seeds sown in well-drained boxes in cool greenhouse or frame during March or April.

SPECIES CULTIVATED: *L. columnifera* (syn. *L. columnaris*), yellow and brown, late summer, 2 to 2½ ft., N.W. America; *pinnata,* yellow and brown, late summer, 3 to 5 ft., N. America.

Lepidium (Cress)—*Cruciferae.* Hardy annual. Leaves, finely divided, agreeably flavoured and largely used in conjunction with mustard for salads. First introduced early sixteenth century.

OUTDOOR CULTURE: Soil, ordinary. Position, open borders. Sow seeds on surface of soil, water, and cover with mats or boards until they germinate; or in drills ½ in. deep and 6 in. apart. Make first sowing end of March, follow with successional sowings every 10 days until Sept., then cease. Gather for salading when 1 in. high. Two crops sufficient off one piece of ground.

INDOOR CULTURE: Sow seed on surface of light soil in shallow boxes, moisten with tepid water, cover with sheet of paper, slate, or board, and place in warm position in greenhouse or room. Sow for succession every 7 days. Two crops may be grown in same soil. Seeds may be sown on flannel kept moist in a warm room, at any time of year.

SPECIES CULTIVATED: *L. sativum*, ' Common Cress ', white, 3 to 6 in., Persia.

Leptarrhena—*Saxifragaceae.* Perennial evergreen herbs.
CULTURE: Soil, cool, slightly moist, and a not-too-hot position in the rock garden or woodland.
PROPAGATION: By division of old plants in spring or autumn.
SPECIES CULTIVATED: *L. pyrolifolia* (syn. *L. amplexifolia*), white, summer, 9 in., N. America.

Leptochilus—*Polypodiaceae.* Stove evergreen ferns, sometimes included in Acrostichum.
CULTURE: As Acrostichum.
PROPAGATION: As Acrostichum.
SPECIES CULTIVATED: *L. auritum*, 1 to 2 ft., Philippines; *flagelliferum*, 1 ft., Tropics; *nicotianaefolium*, 1 to 2 ft., Cuba; *virens*, 1 ft., Trop. Asia.

Leptopteris—*Osmundaceae.* Greenhouse evergreen ferns with finely or coarsely divided fronds, dark green, mostly semi-transparent, previously known as Todea. First introduced mid-nineteenth century.
CULTURE: Compost, equal parts peat, loam, leaf-mould, charcoal, sandstone and silver sand. Position, moist, shady, in damp recesses of rockeries, under bell-glasses or in cases. Plant, March. Water freely March to Oct., moderately Oct. to March. Moist atmosphere and shade most essential but syringing unsatisfactory. Temp., March to Sept. 55° to 65°, Sept. to March 45° to 55°. *L. superba* and *L. hymenophylloides* suitable for cold houses.
CULTURE IN CASES: Compost, as above. Position, shady window, not exposed to sun. Pot or plant, March. Top-dress with fresh compost annually in March. Water freely April to Sept., moderately afterwards. Ventilate case few minutes daily. Suitable species are *L. superba* and *L. hymenophylloides*.
PROPAGATION: By spores sown on surface of sandy peat in shallow pan covered with bell-glass in temp. 65° to 75° at any time; by division of plants at potting time.
SPECIES CULTIVATED: *L. barbata*, S. Africa, Australia and New Zealand; *hymenophylloides* (syn. *Todea hymenophylloides*), New Zealand; *superba*, ' Prince of Wales's Feather Fern ', New Zealand; *Wilkesiana*, Fiji and New Hebrides.

Leptospermum—*Myrtaceae.* Slightly tender evergreen flowering shrubs. First introduced mid-nineteenth century.
CULTURE: Soil, ordinary, but light and well drained. Position, sheltered gardens near the seaside or against a south wall in the southern counties, but not suitable for cold districts. Plant in April or May. Prune slightly in April when required.
PROPAGATION: By cuttings in sandy peat, in pots, in a cold frame in autumn.
SPECIES CULTIVATED: *L. scoparium*, ' South Sea Myrtle ', white, May and June, 6 ft., or more in warmest localities, Australia and New Zealand, and vars. *Chapmanii*, pink, *grandiflora*, larger flowers, *myrtifolium*, of comparative hardiness, *Nichollsii*, crimson, and *prostratum*, white flowered and the hardiest of all.

Leptosyne—*Compositae.* Hardy annuals and perennials.
CULTURE: Soil, ordinary. Position, sunny well-drained beds or borders. Plant, perennial species in Oct. or March; annual species, May or June.
PROPAGATION: All species by seeds sown ⅛ in. deep in light soil in temp. 55° **to**

60° in March; transplant seedlings when 1 in. high, 2 in. apart in boxes of light soil, and keep in cool greenhouse till May or June, then plant outdoors.

SPECIES CULTIVATED: *L. calliopsidea*, yellow, Sept., 18 in., California; *Douglasii*, yellow, autumn, 1 ft., California; *maritima*, perennial, yellow, autumn, 1 ft., California; *Stillmanii*, yellow, autumn, 1 ft., California.

Leptotes—*Orchidaceae*. Dwarf-growing epiphytal orchids, allied to Laelia. Flowers terminating the short fleshy stem, leaves solitary, fleshy, terete.

CULTURE: Compost, temp., etc., as for Cattleyas. Only occasional waterings are required in winter, the temp. then 55° to 60°. Expose to light in autumn. Pans which can be suspended are preferable.

PROPAGATION: By division of plants in March.

SPECIES CULTIVATED: *L. bicolor* (syn. *Tetramicra bicolor*), white and purple, winter, 3 to 7 in., Brazil, and vars. *brevis*, white, lip lined purple basally, *serrulata* (syn. *L. serrulata*), larger, white, lip with purple-lilac lines, its side lobes serrulate.

Leschenaultia—*Goodeniaceae*. Greenhouse flowering evergreen shrubs. First introduced early nineteenth century.

CULTURE: Compost, two parts fibrous peat and one part silver sand. Pot, March or April. Position, well-drained pots in light, sunny greenhouse. Temp., Sept. to March 40° to 50°, March to Sept. 55° to 65°. Water sparingly Oct. to April, moderately afterwards; use soft water only. Manures or stimulants not required. After flowering nip off the points of the shoots. Repotting only necessary every second year. Firm potting essential. Ventilate freely in fine weather.

PROPAGATION: By cuttings of young growth inserted in sandy peat under bell-glass in temp. 50° to 55° from April to July.

SPECIES CULTIVATED: *L. biloba*, blue, summer, 1 ft., Australia, and var, *major*, large-flowered; *formosa*, scarlet, summer, 1 ft., Australia; *linarioides*, yellow, Aug., Australia.

Lespedeza (Bush Clover)—*Leguminosae*. Uncommon hardy sub-shrubs of herbaceous habit, similar in appearance and growth to Desmodium and Indigofera.

CULTURE: Soil, sandy loam. Position, sheltered, sunny borders. Plant, Oct. or Nov., Feb. or March. Prune slightly after flowering.

PROPAGATION: By seeds sown ½ in. deep in light soil in a sheltered position outdoors in Feb. or March; cuttings inserted in heat in spring; layering in spring.

SPECIES CULTIVATED: *L. bicolor*, rosy purple, Sept., 3 ft., China and Japan, and var. *alba*, white; *cuneata*, white and blue, Sept., 2 to 3 ft., Himalaya, China and Siberia; *Thunbergii* (syn. *L. Sieboldii*), purple, autumn, 5 ft., China and Japan.

Lettuce, see Lactuca.

Leucadendron—*Proteaceae*. Greenhouse evergreen tree with silvery silky leaves. In Cape Colony the leaves are utilised for ornamental purposes, especially by painting local scenes thereon. First introduced late seventeenth century.

CULTURE: Compost, equal parts sandy loam and peat, with some charcoal and sand. Position, light, airy greenhouse, free from damp in winter. Pot in March. Water moderately in summer, very little in winter. Temp., March to Oct. 60° to 65°, Sept. to March 40° to 50°.

PROPAGATION: By seeds sown in sandy peat in a temp. of 55° to 65° directly they are imported; by cuttings of firm shoots in sand in a temp. of 55° in summer.

SPECIES CULTIVATED: *L. argenteum*, 'Cape Silver Tree', yellow, Aug., 15 ft., S. Africa.

Leucocrinum—*Liliaceae*. Hardy herbaceous perennials.

CULTURE: Sandy loam and a sunny pocket in the rock garden.

PROPAGATION: By seeds in sandy compost.

SPECIES CULTIVATED: *L. montanum*, 'Sand Lily', white, May, 6 in., N. America.

Leucocoryne—*Liliaceae* (or *Amaryllidaceae*). Half-hardy bulbous-rooted perennial. First introduced early nineteenth century.

OUTDOOR CULTURE: Soil, light rich sand. Position, sunny well-drained border. Plant, Sept. to Jan., placing bulbs 4 in. deep and 2 in. apart. Lift and replant annually.

POT CULTURE: Compost, two parts sandy loam and one part leaf-mould. Place five bulbs 3 in. deep in pot 4½ in. in diameter. Plunge pots in peat in cold frame or under staging in cool greenhouse in sunny part of greenhouse or frame. Water moderately from time bulbs commence to grow until flowers fade, then gradually cease, keeping bulbs dry till growth recommences. Temp., Sept. to March 40° to 50°, March to Sept. 50° to 60°. Pot, Sept. to Oct.

PROPAGATION: By seeds sown in Feb. or March in sandy soil in temp. 55° to 60°; by offsets detached when bulbs are lifted and grown on in same way.

SPECIES CULTIVATED: *L. ixioides* (syn. *L. odorata*), ' Glory of the Sun ', blue, May to June, 12 to 18 in., Chile.

Leucogenes—*Compositae.* Hardy evergreen, dwarf, semi-shrubby plants.

CULTURE: Deep, well-drained gritty loam and a slightly shaded position or a cool aspect.

PROPAGATION: By seeds sown in spring or by cuttings of inch-long side shoots in early summer.

SPECIES CULTIVATED: *L. grandiceps*, ' New Zealand Edelweiss ', white, early summer, 6 to 9 in., New Zealand.

Leucojum (Snowflake)—*Amaryllidaceae.* Hardy bulbous plants.

CULTURE: Soil, ordinary rich. Position, Summer Snowflake (*L. aestivum*) in sunny or shady borders or woodlands; Spring Snowflake (*L. vernum*) in shady borders or on rockeries. Both may also be naturalised in grass. Plant bulbs 4 in. deep and 3 in. apart, Aug. to Nov. Bulbs do not usually flower first year after planting, and only require to be lifted and replanted every five to eight years.

PROPAGATION: By offsets, removed and replanted in Sept. or Oct.

SPECIES CULTIVATED: *L. aestivum*, ' Summer Snowflake ', white and green, May, 1 ft., Europe (Br.); *autumnale*, white and pink, autumn, 4 in., Medit. Region; *hyemale*, white and green, April, 9 in., Italy and S. France; *pulchellum* (syn. *L. Hernandezii*), white and green, May, 1 ft., Balearic Isles; *roseum*, rosy red, Sept. to Oct., 4 in., Corsica; *vernum*, ' Spring Snowflake ', white and green, March, 1 ft., Europe, and var. *carpaticum*, white and yellow.

Leucopogon—*Epacridaceae.* Greenhouse flowering evergreen shrubs. First introduced early nineteenth century.

CULTURE: Compost, three parts fibrous peat, one-part silver sand. Position, light, airy greenhouse Sept. to July; sunny place outdoors July to Sept. Repot, April, May or June; good drainage essential. Water moderately at all times. Syringe plants daily March to July. Temp., Sept. to March 40° to 50°, March to July 55° to 60°. Stimulants not essential.

PROPAGATION: By seeds sown immediately they ripen on surface of sandy peat under bell-glass in temp. 55°; cuttings of ends of shoots inserted in pots of sandy peat covered with bell-glass placed in cool greenhouse in Aug. or April.

SPECIES CULTIVATED: *L. australis*, white, spring, 2 to 4 ft., Australia; *lanceolatus*, white, May, 8 to 10 ft.; *Reichei*, ' Australian Currant ', white, May, 4 to 6 ft.; *verticillatus*, white or pink, summer, 3 to 6 ft., Australia.

Leucothoe—*Ericaceae.* Hardy evergreen flowering shrubs. First introduced mid-eighteenth century.

CULTURE: Soil, peaty loam, lime-free. Position, open, sheltered borders. Plant, Sept., Oct., March or April. Pruning not necessary.

PROPAGATION: By seeds sown ¹⁄₁₆ in. deep in sandy peat in cold frame, Feb. or March; layering shoots in Sept.; division, Oct. or Nov.

SPECIES CULTIVATED: *L. Catesbaei* (syn. *Andromeda Catesbaei*), white, May, 3 to 6 ft., an attractive shrub with arching growths, Georgia; *Davisii*, erect, sturdy habit, white, July, 3 ft., California; *Keiskei*, newer species, prettily coloured, young foliage, flowers large, white, July, Japan; *racemosa* (syn. *Andromeda racemosa*), deciduous, free flowering, white, June, 6 ft., East U.S.A. See also Lyonia.

Lewisia (Bitter-wort)—*Portulacaceae.* Hardy herbaceous perennials. First introduced early nineteenth century.

CULTURE: Soil, equal parts sandy loam, peat and sand. Position, crevices of moist sunny rockeries. Plant, Sept., Oct., March or April. Water occasionally in dry weather. Leaves wither at the time of flowering, or may not be produced at all. Growing period above ground, about six weeks.

PROPAGATION: By seeds sown in well-drained pans of sandy loam and peat in a cool shady frame in March or April; division of the roots in March or April.

SPECIES CULTIVATED: *L. brachycalyx*, white or pink, May, 2 in., U.S.A.; *columbiana*, pale pink, May, 9 in., U.S.A., and vars. *alba* and *rosea*; *Cotyledon*, salmon-pink, May, 9 in., U.S.A.; *Finchii*, rose, May, 9 to 12 in., U.S.A.; *Heckneri*, salmon-pink, May, 9 in., U.S.A.; *Howellii*, apricot-pink, early summer, 3 in., Oregon; *Leana*, white or soft pink, May to June, 6 in., U.S.A.; *nevadensis*, pink, May, 3 in., U.S.A.; *oppositifolia*, white, May, June, 6 to 9 in., U.S.A.; *pygmaea*, pink or white, May, 2 in., U.S.A.; *rediviva*, ' Spatlum ', soft pink, May to June, 1 to 2 in., U.S.A.; *Tweedyi*, salmon-pink, May, 6 in., U.S.A.; *yosemitense*, white or rose, May, 4 to 6 in., U.S.A.

Leycesteria—*Caprifoliaceae.* Hardy deciduous flowering shrub. First introduced early nineteenth century.

CULTURE: Soil, ordinary. Position, sunny or shaded borders. Plant, Oct., Nov., Feb. or March. Prune hard back to old wood annually in April.

PROPAGATION: By seeds sown $\frac{1}{16}$ in. deep in light soil in temp. 45° to 55° in March or April; cuttings of firm shoots inserted in sandy soil under hand-light in Sept. or Oct.

SPECIES CULTIVATED: *L. formosa*, ' Himalayan Honeysuckle ', ' Flowering Nutmeg ', half-woody green stems, attractive in winter, wine-coloured bracts and white flowers, very ornamental and useful for covert planting, June to September, Himalaya.

Lhotzkya—*Myrtaceae.* Greenhouse evergreen heath-like shrubs, limited to Australia. First introduced early nineteenth century.

CULTURE: Compost, equal parts sandy peat and loam. Position, well-drained pots in cool sunny greenhouse. Water copiously March to September, moderately at other times. Feed established plants with liquid manure.

PROPAGATION: By cuttings made from the young shoots when the base is firm, and inserted in pots of sandy peat under bell-glass during spring or late summer.

SPECIES CULTIVATED: *L. acutifolia*, yellow, June, 1½ ft., Australia; *ericoides*, pale yellow, June to July, 2 to 3 ft., Australia; *violacea*, purplish, June, 1½ ft., Australia.

Liatris (Blazing Star)—*Composita.* Hardy perennial herbs of strikingly erect habit. First introduced early eighteenth century.

CULTURE: Soil, light, rich, ordinary. Position, open, sunny beds or borders. Plant, Sept., Oct., March or April. Cut off decayed stems in Oct. Mulch with decayed manure in April. Water freely in dry weather.

PROPAGATION: By seeds sown $\frac{1}{16}$ in. deep in light sandy soil outdoors in Aug. or Sept., transplanting seedlings the following May; division of plants in March or April.

SPECIES CULTIVATED: *L. elegans*, white, July to Sept., 3 to 4 ft., N. America; *graminifolia*, rosy mauve, July to Sept., 2 to 3 ft., N. America, and var. *dubia*, taller; *ligulistylis*, purple, summer, 1 to 1½ ft., Colorado; *pycnostachya*, ' Button Snake-root ', purple, Aug., 3 to 4 ft., N. America; *scariosa*, purple, Aug., 2 to 3 ft., N. America; *spicata*, purple, Aug., 4 to 5 ft., N. America.

Libertia—*Iridaceae.* Hardy evergreen perennials with sword-shaped or grass-like, graceful, dark green leaves. First introduced early nineteenth century.

CULTURE: Soil, equal parts sandy loam, peat and leaf-mould. Position, well-drained sunny borders or, preferably, rockeries. Plant, Sept., Oct., March or April. Protect, Nov. to April, by covering with dry fern, tree leaves or strawy manure.

PROPAGATION: By seeds sown ⅛ in. deep in sandy soil in cold frame or greenhouse, Aug. to Nov.; division of creeping rhizomes, March or April.

SPECIES CULTIVATED: *L. formosa*, white, June, 2 to 3 ft., Chile; *grandiflora*, white, June, 2 to 3 ft., New Zealand; *ixioides*, white, June, 2 ft., New Zealand.

Libocedrus—*Pinaceae* (or *Cupressaceae*). Hardy and slightly tender evergreen coniferous trees with scale-like leaves and small oblong cones. Pyramidal or columnar in habit. First introduced mid-nineteenth century.

CULTURE: Soil, rich loam with gravelly subsoil. Position, warm, sheltered. As specimens on lawns in mild districts in S. England only for *L. chilensis*, but *L. decurrens* is quite hardy. *L. plumosa* is only suitable for conservatory and winter-garden cultivation. Plant, Sept. to Nov.

PROPAGATION: By seeds in sandy soil in cold frame or greenhouse, Oct. to April; cuttings of firm shoots or branchlets in sandy soil in cold frame or under hand-light in Aug. or Sept.

SPECIES CULTIVATED: *L. chilensis*, 60 to 80 ft., Chile; *decurrens*, ' Incense Cedar ', 100 to 150 ft., California; *plumosa* (syn. *L. Doniana*), 70 to 100 ft., New Zealand.

Libonia, see *Jacobinia pauciflora*.

Licuala—*Palmae*. Stove palms with fan-shaped green leaves. First introduced early nineteenth century.

CULTURE: Compost, two parts peat and one of loam and sand. Position, well-drained pots in light part of stove. Pot, Feb. to April. Water moderately Oct. to March, freely afterwards. Syringe twice daily March to Sept., once daily Sept. to March. Temp., March to Sept. 65° to 75°, Sept. to March 55° to 65°.

PROPAGATION: By seeds sown ¼ in. deep in light rich soil in temp. 80° to 90°, Feb., March or April.

SPECIES CULTIVATED: *L. grandis* (syn. *Pritchardia grandis*), 10 ft., New Britain; *spinosa* (syn. *L. horrida*), 10 to 15 ft., Malaya, sometimes erroneously cultivated as *L. peltata*.

Ligularia—*Compositae*. Hardy herbaceous perennials, sometimes included in the genus Senecio.

CULTURE: Soil, loamy. Position, partly shady, moist border. *L. japonica* at edge of pond or lake or in damp soil nearby.

PROPAGATION: By seeds; cuttings; division.

SPECIES CULTIVATED: *L. clivorum*, orange-yellow, July to Sept., 4 to 5 ft., China and Japan; *Hessei*, orange, Aug. to Sept., 5 ft., hybrid; *japonica*, orange-yellow, July, 5 ft., Japan; *stenocephala*, orange-yellow, late summer, 4 ft., China and Japan; *tussilaginea* (syn. *L. Kaempferi*, *Senecio Kaempferi*), yellow, 1 to 2 ft., Japan, and vars. *aureo-maculata* and *argentea*; *Veitchiana*, yellow, summer, 3 ft., W. China; *Wilsoniana*, golden yellow, summer, 3 to 5 ft., China.

Ligustrum (Privet)—*Oleaceae*. Hardy deciduous and evergreen shrubs. Insignificant white flowers in panicles, odorous but not always pleasantly so, followed by black or yellow berries. Of no great ornamental value but useful for screening in shady places, in sunless town gardens and as pheasant cover.

CULTURE: Soil, ordinary. Position, common species in shrubberies, under shade of trees or as hedges; others in open shrubberies. Plant deciduous kinds Oct. to Feb., others Oct. to April. Prune deciduous species in autumn, evergreen in April.

HEDGE CULTURE: Soil, ordinary, trenched two spits deep and 3 ft. wide. Plant privet (1 to 3 ft. high), 1½ to 2 ft. apart, Oct. to April. Trim into shape in June and July. Privet and hawthorn planted alternately make a splendid hedge. The best evergreen species for screening is *L. lucidum*, and *L. ovalifolium* and its vars. for hedges.

PROPAGATION: By seeds in open ground in Nov., transplanting the largest seedlings the following Oct., the remainder the next year; cuttings of young shoots in shady position or under hand-light in summer; cuttings of firm shoots 8 to 12 in. long in shady position outdoors, Sept. to Nov.

SPECIES CULTIVATED: *L. lucidum*, broad, lustrous foliage, 10 to 18 ft., China, and vars. *tricolor*, variegated leaves, *compactum*, dense growth, etc.; *ovalifolium*, semi-evergreen, Japan, and vars. *aureo-marginatum*, ' Golden Privet ', *variegatum*, variegated; *Quihoui*, 6 to 10 ft., deciduous, China; *sinense*, 10 to 20 ft., deciduous, the best flowering species, white, July, China; *vulgare*, ' Common Privet ', deciduous, 6 to 10 ft., Britain, and var. *xanthocarpum*, yellow berried.

Lilac, see Syringa; **Californian-,** see *Ceanothus integerrimus*.

Lilium (Lily)—*Liliaceae*. Hardy and half-hardy bulbous flowering plants, Some species formerly included in Lilium are now referred to other genera; see Cardiocrinum for *L. giganteum*, Nomocharis for *L. apertum*, Notholirion for *L. Thomsonianum*. First introduced in Middle Ages (before 1400).

CULTURE: Soil, ordinary well drained, with decayed leaf-mould and sand added if soil is at all heavy, for *L. amabile, bulbiferum, bulbiferum croceum, candidum, chalcedonicum, concolor, dauricum, Davidii, formosanum, Hansonii, Henryi, hollandicum, longiflorum, maculatum, Martagon, pomponium, pumilum, pyrenaicum, regale, tigrinum* and *testaceum*. Lime-free loam, fibrous peat, leaf-mould and sand for *L. auratum, Brownii, Humboldtii, speciosum* and *sulphureum; L. monadelphum* and *Szovitsianum* do well in rather heavy loam if it is well drained. Peaty loam, leaf-mould and sand, well drained but with abundant moisture in summer and a half-shady position for *L. canadense, Grayi, japonicum, michiganense, pardalinum, Parryi, philadelphicum, rubellum, superbum* and *Washingtonianum*. Plant *L. candidum* in Aug. or Sept., others Oct. or Nov.; see that basal roots are damaged as little as possible. Plant stem-rooting lilies, such as *L. amabile, auratum, Brownii, bulbiferum croceum, Davidii, Hansonii, hollandicum, Henryi, Horfordii, leucanthum, maculatum, philippinense, primulinum, pumilum, regale, Sargentiae, speciosum, sulphureum* and *tigrinum*, 6 in. deep and 6 in. or more apart and draw soil round the stems as growth progresses. Only just cover the bulb of *L. candidum* with soil. Other lilies plant 4 in. deep. Place a handful of silver sand under each bulb and a little round it. Mulch with leaf-mould in April. Protect *L. leucanthum, philadelphicum*, etc., against excessive wet in winter by a pane of glass or other cover above the bulbs. Do not cut down flower stems before the leaves have turned yellow. Water freely in very dry weather. To prevent spread of virus diseases spray continually against aphides. Any plants showing signs of virus infection (e.g. mottling or streaking and twisting of leaves or deformity of flowers due to adhering of petal tips) should be burned as soon as possible. Do not handle a healthy plant after touching a virus-infected one. Many lilies become virus-infected in the propagating frame when diseased stock and healthy stock are propagated side by side. *L. tigrinum* often carries virus disease.

POT CULTURE: Compost, equal parts loam, leaf-mould, decayed manure and sand. Pot, Sept. to March, placing one bulb in a 5 or 6 in. pot or three in an 8 or 10 in. pot. For stem-rooting kinds put ¼ drainage, then half-fill with compost, place bulbs thereon and cover them with ½ in. of compost, top-dress with similar compost as growth progresses. Other kinds may be potted about 3 in. deep in the ordinary way. After potting, place pots in cold frame, greenhouse or shed and cover with 2 in. of cinder ashes or peat. Allow them to remain thus till growth begins, then remove to light airy part of greenhouse or to window or cool room till they flower, then stand outdoors. Water moderately when growth begins, freely when in full growth. Temp. for forcing *L. longiflorum, neilgherrense* and *philippinense*, 55° to 65°. Repot *L. longiflorum* annually in Sept., others in Oct. or Nov. and treat as advised for first potting. After flowering, place plants in sunny position outdoors, gradually withhold water and keep quite dry from Oct. to Feb. *L. longiflorum*, however, should never be kept quite dry—only moderately so for six weeks then watered as before. Species most suitable for indoor culture are *L. longiflorum, neilgherrense, primulinum, philippinense, speciosum* and *sulphureum.*

PROPAGATION: By seeds sown $\frac{1}{16}$ in. deep in well-drained pans or boxes of sandy soil in cold frame in autumn or spring, transplanting seedlings when large enough to handle into similar soil in boxes and, when two years old, into specially prepared bed outdoors; offsets or bulbils planted 1 in. deep and 2 or 3 in. apart in boxes of sandy soil, or in similar soil in sunny cold frame, in autumn; plump scales, broken from bulb just after flowering, planted in drills 2 in. deep outdoors or in boxes of sand and moist peat. Take care not to injure roots when transplanting.

TENDER SPECIES CULTIVATED: Those best grown under glass are—*L. Bakerianum,* white, June, 1 to 3 ft., Burma, and vars. *aureum,* yellow, *Delavayi,* greenish-yellow, *rubrum,* rose, *yunnanense,* white; *formosanum,* white, 2 to 6 ft., Formosa; *longiflorum,* ' Easter Lily ', white, 1 to 3 ft., Japan, and many vars. including *eximium* (syn. *L. Harrisii*), 'Bermuda Lily'; *neilgherrense,* white, 2 to 3 ft., Aug. to Sept., S. India; *nepalense,* greenish-yellow and purple-brown, May to July, 3 ft., N. India (Himalaya); *nobilissimum,* white, July, 1½ to 2 ft., Japan; *philippinense,* white, July to Sept., 1 to 3 ft., Philippine Islands (Luzon); *primulinum,* yellow, July to Sept., 2 to 8 ft., Burma, and vars. *burmanicum,* primrose yellow, *ochraceum,* heavily blotched with purple in the throat; *sulphureum,* deep yellow inside, often pink-flushed outside, tips white, 4 to 10 ft., Burma W., China; *Wallichianum,* white, Sept., 2 to 6 ft., N. India (Himalaya).

HARDY SPECIES CULTIVATED: *L. amabile,* red, July, 1½ to 3 ft., Korea, and var. *luteum,* yellow; *auratum,* ' Golden-rayed Lily ', white, yellow and crimson, Aug. to Sept., 3 to 8 ft., Japan, and many vars.; *aurelianense,* yellow-orange and white, July, 4 to 8 ft., hybrid; 'Backhouse Hybrids', orange, yellow, cream or pink, June to July, 5 to 6 ft., hybrid; ' Bellingham Hybrids ', red, orange or yellow, spotted brown or red, July, 4 to 7 ft., hybrid; *Bolanderi,* brick-red, July, 1 to 3 ft., Oregon, California; *Brownii,* white, rose-purple outside, July, 3 to 4 ft., China, and var. *viridulum* (syn. *L. Brownii colchesteri*) and *australe,* white, greenish or purplish outside; *bulbiferum,* red and orange, July, 3 to 4 ft., Cent. Europe, and var. *croceum* (syns. *L. croceum, L. aurantiacum*), orange; *Burbankii,* saffron-yellow, July, 2 to 7 ft., hybrid; *callosum,* dull red, Aug., 1 to 3 ft., China, Japan; *canadense,* yellow and red, July, 2 to 5 ft., Eastern N. America; *candidum,* ' Madonna Lily ', white, July, 4 to 6 ft., E. Medit. Region; *carniolicum,* red, July, 1 to 3 ft., Balkan Peninsula, and var. *Jankae,* yellow; *cernuum,* purplish pink, June to July, 1 to 3 ft., Korea, Manchuria; *chalcedonicum,* red, July, 3 to 4½ ft., Greece, and var. *maculatum,* red, black-spotted; *columbianum,* orange-yellow, July to Aug., 2 to 5 ft., Western N. America; *concolor,* scarlet, June to July, 1 to 3 ft., Cent. China, and many vars.; *Dalhansonii,* reddish maroon, June to July, 4 to 6 ft., hybrid; *dauricum,* red, June, 1 to 2½ ft., N.E. Asia; *Davidii,* orange, July to Aug., 3 to 4½ ft., W. China, and var. *unicolor* (syns. *L. sutchuenense* hort, *L. Willmottiae* var. *unicolor*) and *Willmottiae* (syn. *L. Willmottiae*); *Duchartrei* (syn. *L. Farreri*), white, purple-spotted, July, 2 to 4 ft., W. China; *formosanum* (syn. *L. philippinense* var. *formosanum*), white, often purplish outside, Aug. to Sept., 2 to 6 ft., Formosa, and var. *Pricei,* 1 to 2 ft.; *Grayi,* crimson and orange, July, 2½ to 4 ft., Eastern N. America (Alleghanies); *Hansonii,* orange, June to July, 4 to 5 ft., Korea; *Henryi,* orange, Aug., 4½ to 10 ft., Cent. China; *hollandicum* (syn. *L. umbellatum* hort.), yellow, orange, apricot or red, June to July, 1½ to 2½ ft., hybrid; *Horsfordii,* orange, July to Aug., 4 to 6 ft., hybrid; *Humboldtii,* orange, maroon-spotted, July, 4 to 6 ft., California, and var. *Bloomerianum,* 2 to 3 ft., and *ocellatum* (syn. var. *magnificum*), 4 to 6 ft.; *imperiale* (syn. *L. princeps*), white, yellow in throat, purplish outside, July, 4 to 6 ft., hybrid; *iridollae,* yellow, Aug., 3 to 5 ft., S.E. United States; *japonicum* (syns. *L. Krameri, L. Makinoi*), rose-pink, 1½ to 3 ft., Japan; *Kelloggii,* pinkish-mauve, July, 1½ to 4 ft., California, Oregon; *Kesselringianum,* straw-yellow, July, 2 ft., Caucasus; *lankongense,* rose, July to Aug., 2 to 4 ft., W. China; *Leichtlinii,* yellow, Aug., 2 to 4 ft., Japan, and var. *Maximowiczii* (syns. *L. pseudo-tigrinum, L. Maximowiczii*), cinnabar-red, 2 to 8 ft.; *leucanthum,* white, July to Aug., 3 to 4 ft., Cent. China, and var. *centifolium,* white, rose-purple outside, 4 to 9 ft.; *maculatum* (syns. *L. elegans*, *L. Thunbergianum*), yellow, orange, apricot or red, June to July, 9 to 24 in., Japan; *Manglesii*, orange, dark-spotted, July, 4 to 5 ft., hybrid; *maritimum*, dark reddish-orange, July, 1½ to 3 ft., California; *Martagon*, dull purple, July, 3 to 6 ft., Europe, N. Asia, and many vars. including *album*, white, *Cattaniae*, dark red unspotted, *sanguineo-purpureum*, dark purple, spotted, *plenum*, dull purple, double; *medeoloides*, red, July, 1 to 3 ft., Japan to Kamchatka; *Michauxii* (syn. *L. carolinianum*), orange-red, 1 to 3½ ft., Eastern U.S.A.; *michiganense*, orange-red, July, 2 to 5 ft., E. Canada and U.S.A.; *monadelphum*, yellow, June to July, 4 to 5 ft., Caucasus; *nevadense* (syn. *L. pardalinum nevadense*), orange-yellow, July, 2 to 5 ft., California; *occidentale*, orange-red, July, 2 to 6 ft., California, Oregon; *papilliferum*, dark red, July, 1 to 3 ft., W. China; *pardalinum*, ' Panther Lily ', ' Leopard Lily ', orange and crimson, July, 4 to 7 ft., California, and many vars. including *giganteum*, ' Sunset Lily ', 3 to 8 ft.; *Parkmannii*, white and crimson, Aug., 4 ft., hybrid; *Parryi*, yellow, July, 2 to 6 ft., California, Arizona; *parvum*, orange, yellow or dark red, July, 3 to 4 ft., California, Oregon; *philadelphicum*, orange-scarlet, boldly spotted, June to July, 1½ to 3 ft., N. America; *polyphyllum*, white, lilac-spotted, July, 1½ to 4 ft., Himalaya; *pomponium*, red, June to July, 1½ to 2½ ft., Maritime Alps; *ponticum*, dull yellow and purple, July, 3 to 4½ ft., Caucasus; *pumilum* (syn. *L. tenuifolium*), red, June, 1 to 2 ft., E. Asia; *pyrenaicum*, greenish-yellow, May to June, 1 to 4½ ft., Pyrenees, and var. *rubrum*, red; *regale*, white with yellow throat and rose-purple exterior, July, 3 to 6 ft., W. China; *rubellum*, rose-pink, May to June, 1½ to 2¾ ft., Japan; *rubescens*, pinkish-purple, June to July, 2 to 4 ft., California, Oregon; *Sargentiae*, white, yellow throat and purple-brown exterior, July, 4 to 5 ft., W. China; *Scottiae*, orange, June, 1½ to 2½ ft., hybrid; *speciosum* (syn. *L. lancifolium* hort.), white and crimson, Aug. to Sept., 3 to 6 ft., Japan, and many vars.; *sulphureum*, white with yellow throat, often flushed pink outside, Aug. to Sept., 4 to 8 ft., China; *superbum*, orange with crimson tips, July, 5 to 9 ft., Eastern U.S.A.; *Szovitsianum*, yellow, June, 2½ to 5 ft., Caucasus; *taliense*, white, purple-spotted, June, 2 to 4 ft., W. China; *testaceum*, ' Nankeen Lily ', pale apricot, June to July, 4 to 6 ft., hybrid; *tigrinum*, ' Tiger Lily ', orange, July to Sept., 4 to 6 ft., China, Japan, and many vars. including *Fortunei* and *splendens*; *tsingtauense*, orange, June, 1½ to 3 ft., China, Korea; *Wardii*, rose-pink, July to Aug., 3 to 5 ft., S.E. Tibet; *Washingtonianum*, white to lilac-purple, June to July, 4 ft., California, Oregon.

Lily, see Lilium; **-of the Valley,** see Convallaria; **Flax-,** see Dianella;

Paroo-, see Dianella; **-Thorn,** see *Catesbaea spinosa*.

Lime Fruit, see *Citrus aurantifolia*; **-Tree,** see Tilia.

Limnanthemum, see Nymphoides.

Limnanthes—*Limnanthaceae*. Hardy annual. First introduced early nineteenth century.

CULTURE: Soil, ordinary. Position, in masses, edges of sunny beds, or on rockeries. Sow for spring flowering in Sept., for summer flowering in April.

PROPAGATION: By seeds sown where plants are required to flower, Sept. or April.

SPECIES CULTIVATED: *L. Douglasii*, yellow and white, April to Sept., 1 ft., fragrant, N.W. America.

Limnobium—*Hydrocharitaceae*. Tender floating aquatics used in tropical aquariums.

CULTURE: Soil, loam and charcoal covered with several inches of water. Position, in small pans, prepared as above, in light place on window-sill, greenhouse bench or dropped on surface of warm water aquariums. Temp., March to Oct. 70° to 85°, Oct. to March 60° to 70°. Plant, any time.

PROPAGATION: By division.

SPECIES CULTIVATED: *L. Boscii* (syn. *L. spongia*), resembles the native Frogbit,

Trop. America; *stoloniferum* (syn. *Trianea bogotensis*), fleshy, dark green, Trop. America.

Limnocharis—*Butomaceae.* Stove aquatic perennial. First introduced early nineteenth century.

CULTURE: Compost, sandy loam. Position, in shallow tubs, cisterns or aquariums in sunny place. Plant 3 to 6 in. below surface of water, in March or April. Temp., March to Sept. 60° to 70°, Sept. to March 50° to 60°.

PROPAGATION: By seeds sown in soil below water in March or April; division of plants in April.

SPECIES CULTIVATED: *L. flava* (syns. *L. emarginata* and *L. Plumieri*), yellow, July, S. America. See also Hydrocleys.

Limonium (Sea Lavender)—*Plumbaginaceae.* Greenhouse evergreens and half-hardy and hardy herbaceous perennials. Formerly known as Statice.

CULTURE OF GREENHOUSE SPECIES: Compost, two parts sandy fibrous loam, one part fibrous peat and one part sand. Pot, March or April. Position, light airy sunny greenhouse, Sept. to May; cold frame, May to Sept. Water freely April to Sept., moderately afterwards. Apply weak stimulants occasionally in summer to healthy established plants. Temp., Sept. to April 40° to 50°, April to May 55° to 65°. Good drainage in pots indispensable.

CULTURE OF PERENNIAL SPECIES: Soil, sandy loam. Position, sunny rockeries or borders. Plant, March or April.

CULTURE OF ANNUAL SPECIES: Soil, ordinary sandy. Position, sunny borders or rockeries. Sow seeds in well-drained pots filled with sandy loam, cover slightly with fine soil, place in temp. 55° to 65°, Feb. or March. Transplant when large enough to handle; harden off and plant outdoors in May.

PROPAGATION: By seeds sown in pans of sandy soil in temp. 55° to 60° in Feb. or March; cuttings of roots inserted in similar soil and cold frame in Feb. or March.

GREENHOUSE SPECIES CULTIVATED: *L. fruticans*, blue, summer, Canaries; *imbricatum*, blue, summer, 1½ ft., Teneriffe; *macrophyllum* (syn. *L. Halfordii*), blue, June, 1 to 2 ft., Canaries; *profusum*, blue, summer, 2 to 3 ft., hybrid.

PERENNIAL SPECIES CULTIVATED: *L. bellidifolium* (syn. *Statice caspia*), lavender, summer, 6 in., Europe; *eximium*, rosy lilac, summer, 1 ft., Cent. Asia; *Gmelinii*, blue and rose, summer, 1 to 2 ft., Caucasus; *latifolium*, blue, 2 to 3 ft., Bulgaria, and var. *grandiflorum*; *Mouretii* (syn. *S. Mouretii*), brown and white, summer, 1 to 2 ft., Morocco; *sinense*, yellow, summer, 1 ft., China; *tataricum*, red and white, summer, 1 ft., Caucasus; *vulgare* (syn. *Statice Limonium*), ' Common Sea Lavender ', purple, summer, 1 ft., Europe (Br.).

ANNUAL SPECIES CULTIVATED: *L. Bonduellii*, yellow, summer, 1 to 2 ft., Algeria; *sinuatum*, blue and cream, summer, 1 to 2 ft., Medit. Region, and several colour forms, really a perennial but always grown as an annual; *spicatum*, rose or white, summer, 6 in., W. Asia; *Suworowii*, lilac and pink, summer, 18 in., Cent. Asia.

Limnophila—*Scrophulariaceae.* Tender aquatic or semi-aquatic plants for the tropical tank or aquarium.

CULTURE: Soil, loam with charcoal or aquarium compost. Position, fair amount of light for the semi-aquatics, more subdued for the under-water forms. plant, spring or summer.

PROPAGATION: By division.

SPECIES CULTIVATED: *L. gratioloides*, blue, resinous smell, 6 in., India; *heterophylla* (also known as Ambulia), submerged for aquarium, feathery leaves, Trop. Asia; *sessiliflora*, fleshy stems and leaves, bluish-white, Trop. Asia.

Linanthus, see Gilia.

Linaria (Toadflax)—*Scrophulariaceae.* Hardy annual and perennial herbs. Some species formerly included in this genus have been transferred to Cymbalaria, Kickxia and Chaenorrhinum.

CULTURE OF PERENNIAL SPECIES: Soil, ordinary, mixed with grit or old mortar. Position, moist rockeries or margin of borders; open, sunny borders for *L. dalmatica, purpurea, vulgaris* and *triornithophora*. Plant, Oct., Nov., March or April.
CULTURE OF ANNUAL SPECIES: Soil, ordinary. Position, sunny beds or borders. Sow seeds $\frac{1}{16}$ in. deep in patches in April for flowering in summer; in Aug. for flowering in spring. *L. tristis*, a pretty dwarf annual for beds or rockeries.
PROPAGATION: By seeds sown where plants are required to flower, Sept. or April.
ANNUAL SPECIES CULTIVATED: *L. bipartita*, violet-purple with orange, summer, 1 ft., Portugal, N. Africa, and vars. *alba*, white, *splendida*, deep purple; *Broussonnetii* (syn. *L. multipunctata*), yellow and brown, summer, 6 in., Medit. Region; *delphinioides*, red-violet to pale lilac, summer, 1½ ft., Spain; *faucicola*, deep lavender, all summer, 4 in., Spain; *heterophylla* (syn. *L. aparinoides*), straw-coloured and yellow, summer, 1 to 3 ft., Morocco; *maroccana*, red-purple, June, 9 to 12 in., Morocco; *reticulata*, purple and yellow, summer, 2 to 4 ft., Portugal; *tristis*, yellow and brown, July, 12 in., Medit. Region.
PERENNIAL SPECIES CULTIVATED: *L. alpina*, blue, violet and yellow, summer, 6 in., Alps; *dalmatica*, yellow, summer, 3 to 5 ft., S.E. Europe; *purpurea*, purple, summer, 2 to 3 ft., S. Europe; *supina*, yellow, all summer, 6 in., Spain; *triornithophora*, purple and yellow, summer, 1 to 3 ft., Portugal, Spain; *ventricosa*, pale yellow with red-brown veining, summer, 3 ft., Morocco; *vulgaris*, ' Common Toadflax ', ' Butter and Eggs ', yellow, summer, 2 ft., Europe (Br.).

Lincolnshire Asparagus, see *Chenopodium Bonus-Henricus.*

Lindelofia—*Boraginaceae.* Hardy perennial herb. First introduced early nineteenth century.
CULTURE: Soil, ordinary. Position, sunny well-drained borders. Plant, Oct., March or April. Cut off flower stems, Sept. Apply weak liquid manure occasionally during flowering period, or dig decayed manure into surface of soil round base of plants in March or April.
PROPAGATION: By seeds sown $\frac{1}{16}$ in. deep in sandy soil in sunny position outdoors in April or May, transplanting seedlings following Aug. or Sept. for flowering the next year; division of roots in March.
SPECIES CULTIVATED: *L. longifolia* (syn. *L. spectabilis*), ' Himalayan Lung-wort ', purple, July, 18 in., Himalaya.

Linden, see Tilia.

Lindera—*Lauraceae.* Hardy and slightly tender deciduous and evergreen flowering trees; aromatic, but of little ornamental value. The genus was at one time known as Benzoin. First introduced late seventeenth century.
CULTURE: Soil, ordinary. Position, open, sunny shrubberies or borders. Plant, Oct. to Feb. Prune into shape when necessary after flowering.
PROPAGATION: By cuttings of shoots, 6 to 8 in. long, inserted in sandy soil in shady, sheltered position outdoors, Oct. to Nov.; layering in spring.
SPECIES CULTIVATED: *L. Benzoin*, ' Benjamin Bush ', ' Spice Bush ', deciduous, yellow, spring, 15 to 20 ft.; *megaphylla*, evergreen, black fruits, 15 to 20 ft., Cent. China; *obtusiloba*, deciduous, yellow, black fruits, March to April, 20 to 25 ft., Japan and Korea; *praecox*, yellow, March, 8 ft., Japan and Korea.

Lindsaya—*Polypodiaceae.* Greenhouse evergreen ferns. Fronds, feather-, kidney- or arrow-shaped. First introduced early nineteenth century.
CULTURE: Compost, two parts turfy loam, one part lumpy peat, and one part equal proportions of broken crocks, charcoal and sand. Position, moist, shady part of stove, in wardian case, or under bell-glasses. Pot very firmly in well-drained pots, Feb. or March. Water abundantly March to Oct., moderately afterwards. Temp., March to Sept. 55° to 65°, Sept. to March 50° to 55°.
PROPAGATION: By spores sown on fine sandy peat, in well-drained pans under bell-glass, in temp. 55° to 65° at any time.

SPECIES CULTIVATED: *L. cuneata* (syn. *L. trichomanoides*), 6 in., New Zealand; *linearis*, 6 in., New Zealand.

Ling, see *Calluna vulgaris.*

Linnaea—*Caprifoliaceae.* Dainty creeping hardy shrub, found wild in N.E. Britain.

CULTURE: Soil, light. Position, shady, moist, suitable for rockery or wild garden.

PROPAGATION: By seed sown in sandy soil in frame, April.

SPECIES CULTIVATED: *L. borealis*, 'Twin-flower', creeping, pink or white, fragrant, summer, circumpolar, and var. *americana*, slightly larger and more easy to grow.

Linseed Oil Plant, see *Linum usitatissimum.*

Lion's-ear, see *Leonotis Leonurus.*

Linum (Flax)—*Linaceae.* Hardy annuals, perennials and shrubs.

CULTURE OF ANNUAL SPECIES: Soil, ordinary. Position, sunny beds or borders. Sow seeds $\frac{1}{8}$ in. deep in April, in lines or masses where plants are required to flower.

CULTURE OF PERENNIAL SPECIES: Soil, good ordinary. Position, sunny rockeries, borders or banks. Plant, Oct. to Nov. or Feb. to April.

CULTURE OF HARDY SHRUBBY SPECIES: Soil, sandy loam, leaf-mould, peat and sand. Position, warm, sheltered rockeries or dry walls. Plant, Oct. or Nov. Prune straggling shoots into shape, March or April.

CULTURE OF L. GRANDIFLORUM IN POTS: Soil, any good compost. Sow seeds $\frac{1}{16}$ in. deep in April in 6 in. pots. Place pots in cold frame or shady window till seedlings appear, then remove to full light. Water moderately at first, freely afterwards. Support shoots by inserting small twiggy branches between them. Sow again in July, plunging pots to rim in garden soil, and keep well supplied with water to flower in autumn.

PROPAGATION: Perennial species by seeds sown $\frac{1}{2}$ in. deep outdoors in April, also by division in March or April; shrubby species by cuttings of young shoots inserted in sandy soil under bell-glass in brisk bottom heat during June or July.

ANNUAL SPECIES CULTIVATED: *L. grandiflorum*, rose, summer, 1 ft., Algeria, and vars. *coccineum*, scarlet, *splendens*, rose, and *rubrum*, red; *usitatissimum*, 'Linseed Oil Plant', blue, June, 18 in., Europe.

PERENNIAL SPECIES CULTIVATED: *L. alpinum*, blue, summer, 6 in., Europe; *campanulatum*, yellow, summer, 1 ft., Europe; *capitatum*, yellow, June to July, 6 to 9 in., Europe; *flavum*, yellow, summer, 18 in., Austria; *monogynum*, white, June to Oct., 1 to 2 ft., New Zealand; *narbonnense*, blue, May to July, 2 ft., S. Europe; *perenne*, blue or white, summer, 18 in., Britain; *salsoloides*, white, tinged pink, June to July, 9 in., S.W. Europe. See also Reinwardtia.

SHRUBBY SPECIES CULTIVATED: *L. arboreum*, yellow, June, 1 ft., Crete.

Liparis—*Orchidaceae.* A large terrestrial and epiphytic genus, very variable, widely distributed. Pseudo-bulbs may be evident, or the leaf base forms a short stem, more or less swollen. Flowers in terminal racemes, often numerous, usually very small.

CULTURE: Compost, three parts of osmunda or peat fibre, two parts of sphagnum moss with crushed potsherds. Terrestrial kinds should have an addition of loam. Species from tropical countries require a warm moist atmosphere and rather shady position. Winter temp. 60° to 65°, higher in summer. Rest requires consideration, with very few should it be drastic but must vary with the species. If the foliage remains fresh, none, for kinds in which the leaves are not persistent, or with pseudo-bulbs, dryer, cooler conditions. The English representative, though said to be inclined to be epiphytic, has succeeded in a mixture of leaf-mould and brick dust. It grows in spongy bogs.

PROPAGATION: By the division of suitable plants in spring.

SPECIES CULTIVATED: A selection—*L. atropurpurea*, purple, summer, Ceylon;

atrosanguinea (syn. *L. tabulare*), purple-maroon, summer, Perak; *elata*, variable, 1 ft. or more high, greenish, reddish-purple or yellowish-white, summer, America; *fulgens*, deep red, summer, Philippines; *lacerata*, yellowish, lip reddish, lacerated, summer, Borneo; *Loeselii*, small, yellowish, Europe (Br.), N. America; *reflexa*, yellowish-green to orange, autumn, Australia; *tricallosa*, yellowish changing to purple, summer, Malaya, Borneo; *Walkeriae*, dwarf, purplish, green shaded, summer, Ceylon.

Lip Fern, see Cheilanthes.

Lippia—*Verbenaceae.* Greenhouse deciduous shrub. First introduced late eighteenth century.

CULTURE: Compost, two parts loam, one part leaf-mould and sand. Position, pots in windows or greenhouse; beds outdoors against south walls in S. England and Ireland only. Pot or plant, March. Water freely March to Sept., little afterwards. Prune shoots Feb. to within an inch of base. Temp., 45° to 50° in winter, 50° to 55° other times.

PROPAGATION: By cuttings pulled off stem when 4 in. long and inserted in sandy soil under bell-glass in temp. 65° in March.

SPECIES CULTIVATED: *L. citriodora* (syn. *Aloysia citriodora*), ' Lemon Scented Verbena ', lilac, Aug., foliage fragrant, 10 to 15 ft., Argentine, Chile.

Liquidambar—*Hamamelidaceae.* Hardy deciduous flowering trees. Flowers greenish-yellow, inconspicuous; spring. Leaves, downy, very fragrant, palmate, First introduced late seventeenth century.

CULTURE: Soil, deep, moist loam. Position, sheltered in shrubberies or on lawns. Plant, Oct. to Dec. Prune into shape when necessary in Nov.

PROPAGATION: By seeds sown ⅛ in. deep in sandy soil outdoors, Oct., Nov., March or April, transplanting seedlings two to three years afterwards; layering shoots, in spring.

SPECIES CULTIVATED: *L. formosana* (syn. *L. acerifolia*), 60 to 80 ft., China; *orientalis*, 80 to 100 ft., Asia Minor; *Styraciflua*, ' Sweet Gum ', 100 to 150 ft., U. States. In this country these trees do not usually attain more than half the heights stated.

Liquorice-plant, see *Glycyrrhiza glabra.*

Liriodendron—*Magnoliaceae.* Hardy deciduous tree with tulip-shaped flowers and bright green leaves turning gold in autumn. First introduced mid-seventeenth century.

CULTURE: Soil, deep rich loam. Position, sunny, sheltered shrubberies, or as specimen on lawn. Plant, Oct. to Feb. Prune straggling shoots into shape Nov. or Dec.

PROPAGATION: By seeds in moist, sandy loam in sheltered position outdoors, Sept. to Nov.; layering in spring.

SPECIES CULTIVATED: *L. Tulipifera*, ' Tulip Tree ', yellow, 100 to 200 ft., N. America, numerous forms in cultivation including *aureo-maculatum*, bright gold-mottled leaves, and *fastigiatum*, columnar in habit.

Liriope—*Liliaceae.* Hardy evergreen perennials. Grass-like foliage in tufts First introduced early nineteenth century.

CULTURE: Soil, sandy loam. Position, as an edging to beds in the open or as a small pot plant in cool greenhouse or conservatory. Plant or pot, March to April.

PROPAGATION: By division at planting time.

SPECIES CULTIVATED: *L. Muscari*, lilac, autumn, 1 to 1½ ft., Japan and China; *spicata*, pale lilac to white, autumn, creeping, China and Japan.

Lissochilus—*Orchidaceae.* Terrestrial orchids. About 100 tuberous-rooted or with rhizomatous pseudo-bulbs, just below or on the soil surface. Spikes simple, from rhizome or base of pseudo-bulbs. Flowers showy, many.

CULTURE: Compost, three parts fibrous loam, one part leaf-mould, silver sand and chopped sphagnum. Position, shallow pans or well-drained pots in warm, moist part of stove during the growing period and cool part when at rest. Pot, Feb. or March. Water freely March to Sept., moderately Sept. to Nov., keeping quite dry Nov. to March. Temp., March to Oct. 65° to 80°, Oct. to March 60° to 65°. Growing period, March to Oct.; resting period, Oct. to March. Expose to full light in autumn, and in summer shade lightly.

PROPAGATION: By division of plants, March.

SPECIES CULTIVATED: A selection—*L. arenarius*, green, suffused brown-red, mauve-purple, yellow, variable, summer, Trop. Africa, Natal; *bellus*, greenish-yellow, reddish, spring, autumn, Nyasaland; *giganteus*, rose-lilac, lip bright purple, autumn, 10 to 16 ft., River Congo; *Horsfallii*, purple, rose, violet, summer, autumn, 4 to 6 ft., W. Africa; *Krebsii*, yellow, red-brown, lip with two purple blotches, spring, summer, 2 to 4 ft., Natal, and var. *purpuratus*, purplish-brown, yellow; *roseus*, brown, deep rose, summer, Sierra Leone; *speciosus*, variable, fragrant, yellow, purplish, lip whitish, purple feathered, 3 to 7 ft., summer, S. Africa.

Listera—*Orchidaceae*. A terrestrial genus, widely distributed. Stems from fibrous roots.

CULTURE: The two English species are not very exigent as to soil and situation, but *L. cordata* prefers rather boggy ground. Some of the exotic species might be hardy.

PROPAGATION: By offsets if they occur.

SPECIES CULTIVATED: *L. cordata*, small, brownish, greenish-brown, summer, Europe (Br.), N. America; *ovata*, 'Twayblade', many, small, green to yellowish-green, curiously scented, spring, summer, Europe (Br.), and var. *variegata*, leaves banded yellow.

Lithodora, see Lithospermum.

Lithops (Stone-face, Living Stones)—*Aizoaceae*. Greenhouse succulent plants.

CULTURE: Compost, six parts sharp sand, four parts rich loam, one part each mortar rubble and brick dust. Position, well-drained pots in sunny greenhouse or window, or bed on greenhouse staging; very light in winter. Plant or pot, April or May, burying ¼ of plant-body. Keep fairly moist May to Nov., completely dry Dec. to April. Temp., Dec. to April 60°, May to Nov. 60° or over.

PROPAGATION: By seeds sown in close atmosphere, temp. 55° to 60°, April or Sept.; the plant-bodies can be used as cuttings, leaving a short section of stem below the body and removing skin from same; dry well before insertion, May or June, temp. 65°.

SPECIES CULTIVATED: *L. bella* (syn. *Mesembryanthemum bellum*), white, Sept. to Nov., S.W. Africa; *Comptonii*, yellow, Sept., S.W. Africa; *Lesliei* (syn. *M. Lesliei, M. ferrugineum*), yellow, Sept., S.W. Africa; *olivacea*, yellow, S.W. Africa; *pseudotruncatella* (syn. *L. farinosa, M. pseudotruncatellum*), yellow, Sept. to Oct., S.W. Africa.

Lithospermum (Gromwell)—*Boraginaceae*. Hardy dwarf, trailing, evergreen flowering shrubs and perennials.

CULTURE: Soil, sandy or loamy. Position, margins of sunny borders or on ledges of sunny rock gardens. Plant, Oct., Nov., March or April. *L. diffusa* is an excellent plant for draping stones on rockeries.

PROPAGATION: By seeds in well-drained pots of sandy soil in cold frame in March or April, transplanting seedlings when an inch high singly into 2 in. pots and growing in frame till following spring; cuttings of ripened shoots, 2 to 3 in. long, in well-drained pots of sandy soil in cold frame in Aug. to Oct.; layering shoots in Sept.

SPECIES CULTIVATED. These have now been separated into three genera as follows: LITHOSPERMUM—*L. canescens*, yellow, July, 9 to 12 in., N. America; *Gastonii*, blue, summer, 1 ft., Pyrenees; *purpureo-caeruleum*, blue-purple, June to Aug., Europe. LITHODORA—*L. diffusa* (syn. *Lithospermum diffusum* and *prostratum*), blue, all summer, 6 in., Spain, Portugal; *oleifolia* (syn. *Lithospermum oleifolium*), sapphire-blue, May to June, 6 to 9 in., Pyrenees; *rosmarinifolia* (syn. *Litho-*

spermum rosmarinifolium), blue, winter, 12 in., slightly tender, Italy. Moltkia—*M. intermedia* (syn. *Lithospermum intermedium*), blue, summer, 9 to 12 in., hybrid; *petraea* (syn. *Lithospermum petraeum*), violet, June to July, 2 ft., half-evergreen bushy shrub, S.E. Europe; *suffruticosa* (syn. *Lithospermum graminifolium*), blue, June to Aug., 1 ft., Italy.

Littonia—*Liliaceae.* Greenhouse herbaceous perennial climber. First introduced mid-nineteenth century.

Culture: Compost, two parts loam, one part each of leaf-mould, peat and silver sand. Position, well-drained pots or bed in warm greenhouse. Pot or plant, March. Train shoots up roof or wall. Water freely during spring and summer, moderately autumn and winter. Syringe morning and evening during early period of growth. Plant likes plenty of sunshine. Temp., March to Sept. 65° to 75°, Sept. to March 50° to 60°.

Propagation: By division of the plant at potting time.

Species Cultivated: *L. modesta*, orange, April, 3 to 4 ft., S. Africa, and var. *Keitii.*

Liver Leaf, see Hepatica.

Living Stones, see Lithops, Pleiospilos.

Livistona—*Palmae.* Warm greenhouse palms. First introduced early nineteenth century.

Culture: Compost, two parts loam, one part peat, little sand. Position, well-drained pots in warm greenhouse, Sept. to June; outdoors or in cool greenhouse in summer. Pot, Feb. or March. Water freely March to Sept., moderately afterwards. Syringe twice daily March to Oct., once Oct. to March. Temp., March to Sept. 60° to 70°, Sept. to March 55° to 60°.

Propagation: By seeds sown ½ in. deep in rich light soil in temp. 80° to 90° in Feb. or March.

Species Cultivated: *L. australis*, 40 to 50 ft., Australia; *chinensis*, 30 to 50 ft., leaves large, fan-shaped, China, Japan; *humilis*, 6 to 15 ft., Australia; *rotundifolia*, to 80 ft., Java.

Lizard's-tail, see Saururus.

Lloydia (Mountain Spider-wort)—*Liliaceae.* Hardy bulbous flowering plant.

Culture: Soil, sandy loam. Position, sunny, dryish borders or rockeries. Plant, Sept. or Oct. Depth for bulbs, 3 to 4 in. Lift and replant when unhealthy only.

Propagation: By offsets, removed and planted in Sept. or Oct.

Species Cultivated: *L. serotina*, white and green, June, 6 in., Britain (Snowdon).

Loasa—*Loasaceae.* Greenhouse and half-hardy annual climbing and twining plants. First introduced early nineteenth century.

Outdoor Culture: Sow seeds ¹⁄₁₆ in. deep in light soil in temp. 65° in Feb. or March. Transplant seedlings singly in 3 in. pots when 1 in. high and grow in temp. 55° till June, then plant outdoors. Position, against sunny walls or fences. Soil, ordinary.

Indoor Culture: Sow seeds as above. Transplant seedlings singly into 3 in. pots, and when 6 in. high into 5 in. size, or place three in an 8 in. size. Compost, two parts sandy loam, one part leaf-mould and sand. Train shoots round wire trellis or stakes inserted in the soil. Water moderately at first, freely afterwards. Apply stimulants occasionally to plants in bloom. Temp., 55° to 65°. All the species are furnished with stinging hairs and hence should not be touched by naked hands.

Species Cultivated: *L. urens* (syn. *L. hispida*), yellow, to 1½ ft., Peru; *vulcanica*, white, yellow, and red, summer, 2 to 3 ft., Ecuador.

Lobelia—*Lobeliaceae.* Hardy and half-hardy herbaceous perennials. First introduced early seventeenth century.

Outdoor Culture of Hardy Species: Soil, ordinary rich. Position, sunny, moist borders. Cool rock garden for *L. linnaeoides*. Plant, March or April. *L. Dortmanna* is an aquatic for very still, deep water such as lakes. On cold, damp soils all the species (except *L. siphilitica* and *linnaeoides*) best lifted in Oct., placed in pots, stored in cold frame till March, then replanted.

POT CULTURE: Compost, two parts sandy loam, one part leaf-mould and sand. Pot, Oct. or March. Position, cold frame, Oct. to March; cool greenhouse, March, till past flowering, then outdoors. Water very little Oct. to March, freely afterwards. Apply stimulants, May to Aug.

CULTURE OF HALF-HARDY SPECIES: Soil, ordinary. Position, pots in greenhouse heated to temp. 55°, Oct. to June; as edgings to beds, etc., outdoors, June to Oct. Plant, June, 3 to 6 in. apart. Lift plants in Sept., place in small pots, and store in greenhouse to furnish cuttings in spring. Cut off flower stems a fortnight before lifting.

POT CULTURE: Compost, equal parts good soil, leaf-mould and sand. Position, dwarf kinds in 4 or 5 in. pots and trailing kinds in pots or baskets, in shady or sunny greenhouse or window. Pot, March to July. Water freely in summer, moderately other times. Apply stimulants to plants in flower.

PROPAGATION: Hardy perennial species by seeds sown $\frac{1}{16}$ in. deep in sandy loam and leaf-mould in cold frame in Sept. or Oct., or in temp. 55° in March; cuttings of shoots inserted in small pots in temp. 55° in spring; division in March. Half-hardy species by seeds sown in heat in Feb., transplanting seedlings 2 in. apart in boxes, hardening off in cold frame, and planting out in May; cuttings of young shoots inserted in sandy soil in temp. 65° to 75° in spring; division in March or April.

HARDY PERENNIAL SPECIES CULTIVATED: *L. cardinalis*, 'Cardinal Flower', scarlet, summer, 3 ft., N. America; *Dortmanna*, 'Water Lobelia', light blue, 9 to 12 in., Europe (Br.), N. America; *fulgens*, scarlet, May, 1 to 3 ft., Mexico; *Gerardii*, violet, July, 3 to 4 ft., hybrid; *laxiflora*, red and yellow, summer, 4 to 5 ft., Mexico; *splendens*, scarlet, 2 to 3 ft., N. America; *siphilitica*, blue, July, 2 to 3 ft., N. America; *Tupa*, red, Aug. to Sept., 4 to 6 ft., Chile. See also Pratia.

HALF-HARDY PERENNIAL SPECIES CULTIVATED: *L. Erinus*, blue and white, summer, 6 in., parent of bedding vars., S. Africa; *tenuior*, bright blue, Sept., 12 to 18 in., W. Australia. There are several named vars.

Loblolly Bay, see *Gordonia Lasianthus*.

Lobularia—*Cruciferae*. Perennial herbs and sub-shrubs differing from Alyssum in technical points and formerly included in that genus.

CULTURE: As Alyssum.

PROPAGATION: As Alyssum.

SPECIES CULTIVATED: *L. maritima* (syn. *Alyssum maritimum*), 'Sweet Alyssum', white, sometimes violet, fragrant flowers produced over a long season, to 12 in., perennial but grown as an annual, Medit. Region.

Lockhartia—*Orchidaceae*. An epiphytic genus. Stems tufted, clothed with small often glaucous, leaves. Flowers, solitary or few, small, from upper parts of stems, or terminals, often with large bracts.

CULTURE: Compost, two parts osmunda fibre, two parts sphagnum moss with crushed potsherds. Pans for the smaller growing, pots for the larger, well drained. A moist, warm atmosphere is needed, summer temp. 70° and upwards. Winter temp. around 60°, watering then not as frequent as in summer. Shading is required in summer.

PROPAGATION: By division of plants in spring.

SPECIES CULTIVATED: *L. acuta* (syn. *Fernandezia acuta*), bright yellow, red marked, several, summer, Trinidad; *lunifera*, yellow, lip dotted red, variable, up to 15 in., summer, Brazil; *robusta*, golden yellow, lip red-spotted and streaked, summer, Costa Rica, Guatemala; *verrucosa* (syn. *Fernandezia robusta*), bright yellow, lip marked red, warted, summer, autumn, Guatemala.

Locust Tree, see *Robinia Pseudoacacia*

Loganberry, see *Rubus ursinus* var. *loganobaccus.*

Loiseleuria (Alpine Azalea)—*Ericaceae.* Hardy trailing evergreen flowering shrub.

CULTURE: Soil, deep, sandy peat. Position, open, moist rockeries. Plant, Sept. to Nov.

PROPAGATION: By layering shoots, Sept. to Nov.

SPECIES CULTIVATED: *L. procumbens* (syn. *Azalea procumbens*), rose to white, May. Subarctic Regions.

Lomaria, see Blechnum.

Lomatia—*Proteaceae.* Greenhouse evergreen shrubs. Orn. foliage. Leaves, feather- or egg-shaped, green or glaucous. First introduced late eighteenth century.

CULTURE: Compost, equal parts peat, loam and sand. Position, well-drained pots in sunny, airy greenhouse, or sheltered borders in Cornwall and similar mild districts. Pot, Feb. to April. Prune into shape when necessary, Feb. Water moderately Sept. to April, freely afterwards. Ventilate freely April to Sept., moderately afterwards. Temp., March to Oct. 55° to 65°, Oct. to March 45° to 55°.

PROPAGATION: By cuttings of firm shoots, 2 to 3 in. long, inserted in sandy peat under bell-glass in temp. 60° to 70°, June to Sept.

SPECIES CULTIVATED: *L. ferruginea* (syn. *L. pinnatifolia*), rosy red and white, 10 to 12 ft., Chile; *longifolia*, 8 to 10 ft., N.S. Wales; *obliqua*, white, to 20 ft., Chile; *silaifolia*, white, May to June, 3 ft., Australia; *tinctoria*, 2 to 3 ft., Australia.

Lonas—*Compositae.* Hardy annual. Introduced late seventeenth century.

CULTURE: Soil, ordinary. Position, sunny borders.

PROPAGATION: By seeds sown outdoors in April where plants are required to grow.

SPECIES CULTIVATED: *L. inodora*, yellow, June to Aug., 1 ft., N.W. Africa.

London's Pride, see *Saxifraga umbrosa.*

Lonicera (Honeysuckle)—*Caprifoliaceae.* Hardy and slightly tender deciduous and evergreen shrubs, some twining, others of shrubby nature. Flowers most fragrant.

CULTURE OF TWINING SPECIES: Soil, rich ordinary. Position, as far as possible choose a shaded and cool position for the roots, but where the top growth can reach full sun. North-west or west walls are good, also the shaded side of pergolas or tree stumps. For the more tender evergreen kinds choose a partially shaded wall. Plant, Oct. or March. Mulch annually with compost or well-decayed manure. Any pruning necessary to restrict size should be done in early spring.

POT CULTURE: Compost, two parts sandy loam, one part leaf-mould or well-decayed manure and sand. Pot, Oct. to Dec. Position, cold frame or green-house, Nov. to Feb.; warm greenhouse, Feb. to June; sunny place outdoors, June to Nov. Water freely Feb. to Oct., moderately afterwards. Apply stimulants occasionally when in flower. Prune previous year's shoots to within 1 or 2 in. of base in June.

CULTURE OF L. SEMPERVIRENS IN GREENHOUSE: Compost, same as for pot culture. Plant, Oct. to March. Position, small well-drained bed or tub, with shoots trained up rafter or trellis. Prune slightly after flowering. Water freely March to Sept., moderately afterwards. Temp., March to Sept. 55° to 65°, Sept. to March 40° to 50°.

CULTURE OF SHRUBBY SPECIES: Soil, ordinary, well drained. Many are winter-and early spring-flowering, others subject to damage by spring frosts. Choose sheltered positions in shrubbery, sun or part shade. Plant, Oct., Nov. Pruning, thin out some of the older wood occasionally after flowering. *L. nitida,* bushy, evergreen, suitable for hedges to 5 ft. high. Plant young specimens only up to 18 in. high, 18 in. apart, Oct. or April. Trim, June to July.

PROPAGATION: All kinds strike readily from July, Aug. cuttings in sandy soil in shaded frame; layering shoots, Aug. to Nov.; seeds, where available, in well-drained pots in temp. 55° to 60°, Feb. or March.

TWINING SPECIES CULTIVATED: *L. Brownii*, hybrid, semi-evergreen, vigorous to 15 ft., orange-scarlet, June to July, scentless; *Caprifolium*, ' Goat-leaf Honeysuckle ', deciduous, creamy yellow tinged red, June, July, fragrant, Europe (Br.); *etrusca*, nearly evergreen, very vigorous, creamy yellow tinged red, July, very fragrant, tender in colder districts, Medit.; *Giraldii*, evergreen, vigorous, tender in colder districts, purplish-red, China; *Heckrotii*, hybrid, rather spreading habit, deep yellow and pink, June, July, hardy; *Henryi*, evergreen, vigorous, purplish-red, July, dark blue fruits, China; *Hildebrandtiana*, ' Giant Honeysuckle ', tender, and only for extreme south and south-west gardens, and then requiring wall protection, flowers up to 6 in. long, cream fading to deep yellow, fragrant, Burma; *implexa*, ' Minorca Honeysuckle ', 8 ft., semi-evergreen, rather tender, cream and white, June, July, S. Europe; *japonica*, vigorous and reliable small-leaved climber to 30 ft., very fragrant, June to Aug., Japan, more usually seen in one of its forms, *aureo-reticulata*, golden, variegated, and *Halliana*, flowers white and yellow, very fragrant all summer; *Periclymenum*, ' Wild Honeysuckle ', ' Woodbine ', and its improved garden forms, *belgica*, ' Early Dutch ', and *serotina*, ' Late Dutch '; *sempervirens*, ' Trumpet Honeysuckle ', vigorous, evergreen, only suited to mild parts of the country, orange and scarlet, summer, scentless, S.E. United States; *Tellmanniana*, hybrid, the most reliable of the trumpet-flowered types, deciduous, vigorous, pale orange tipped red, June, July, flowers large; *tragophylla*, hardy, deciduous, vigorous, large bright yellow flowers, June, July, China.

SHRUBBY SPECIES CULTIVATED: *L. alpigena*, yellow, tinged red, April to May, 6 ft., Europe; *angustifolia*, pinkish white, April to May, 8 to 10 ft., Himalaya; *chaetocarpa*, primrose yellow, June, 3 to 5 ft., Cent. China; *chrysantha*, yellowish-white, April, to 12 ft., N.E. Asia to Japan; *fragrantissima*, creamy white, Dec. to March, 6 to 8 ft., partially evergreen, China; *hispida*, yellow, May to June, 3 to 5 ft., Turkistan; *Ledebouri*, orange yellow and red, June, 8 to 9 ft., California; *Maackii*, white or yellow, May to June, to 10 ft., Manchuria and China; *Morrowii*, white to yellow, May to June, 6 to 8 ft., China and Japan; *nitida*, evergreen with neat foliage, 4 to 6 ft., W. China; *Purpusii*, vigorous hybrid, winter flowering, fragrant; *pyrenaica*, rose and white, May to June, 2 to 3 ft., Pyrenees; *Standishii*, creamy white, Nov. to March, 6 to 8 ft., partially evergreen, China; *syringantha*, lilac, May to June, to 8 ft., China and Tibet; *tatarica*, pink or white, May, 8 to 10 ft., Siberia, etc.; *quinquelocularis*, creamy white, June, 12 to 15 ft., Himalaya and China; *Xylosteum*, ' Fly Honeysuckle ', yellow, May, 4 to 6 ft., Europe. All these bush honeysuckles have fragrant flowers and, frequently, attractive crops of red berries.

Loofah Gourd, see Luffa.

Loosestrife, see Lysimachia; **Purple-,** see *Lythrum Salicaria.*

Lopezia—*Onagraceae.* Half-hardy annual and perennial. First introduced early nineteenth century.

CULTURE: Soil, ordinary. Position, sunny borders.

PROPAGATION: By seeds sown $\frac{1}{16}$ in. deep in light soil in temp. 55° to 65° in March, transplanting outdoors in May.

SPECIES CULTIVATED: *L. albiflora*, pinkish-white, late summer and autumn, 2 ft., Mexico, perennial, this may be grown in pots for flowering in the greenhouse; *coronata*, red, Aug., 1 ft., annual, Mexico.

Loquat, see *Eriobotrya japonica.*

Lord Anson's Pea, see *Lathyrus magellanicus.*

Lords and Ladies, see *Arum maculatum.*

Loropetalum—*Hamamelidaceae.* Slightly tender evergreen flowering shrubs, closely resembling the Wych-Hazel, but flowers white. First introduced late nineteenth century.

OUTDOOR CULTURE: Soil, ordinary, light rich. Position, warm, sheltered borders. Plant, Oct. to Feb. Prune to maintain good shape after flowering.

GREENHOUSE CULTURE: Compost, two parts sandy loam, one part leaf-mould and a liberal amount of sand. Position, pots in cold, sunny greenhouse; must not be forced. Water freely between March and Oct., moderately afterwards. Pot in Oct.; place outdoors in full sun from June to Oct. to ripen wood.

PROPAGATION: By cuttings in sandy soil in a cold frame in summer or autumn; by seeds in similar soil in a cold frame at any time.

SPECIES CULTIVATED: *L. chinense,* white, winter, 5 to 6 ft., China.

Lotus—*Leguminosae.* Greenhouse and hardy perennials.

CULTURE OF GREENHOUSE SPECIES: Compost, two parts sandy loam, one part leaf-mould, half part each pounded charcoal and sand. Pot, Feb. or March. Position, pots in light, airy part of sunny greenhouse. Water moderately March to Sept., very little afterwards. Apply weak stimulants to healthy plants in flower. Temp., March to Sept. 55° to 65°, Sept. to March 45° to 55°.

CULTURE OF HARDY SPECIES: Soil, ordinary rich. Position, sunny rockeries or elevated beds. Plant, March or April.

PROPAGATION: Greenhouse species by seeds sown $\frac{1}{16}$ in. deep in sandy soil in well-drained pot or pan in temp. 55° to 65° in March or April; cuttings of shoots inserted in well-drained pots of sandy soil under bell-glass in temp. 55° to 65° in summer. Hardy species by seeds sown $\frac{1}{16}$ in. deep in April where plants are required to grow; division of plants in March or April.

GREENHOUSE SPECIES CULTIVATED: *L. Berthelotii* (syn. *L. peliorhynchus*), scarlet, summer, 2 ft., Canaries.

HARDY SPECIES CULTIVATED: *L. aegaeus,* yellow, red-veined, summer, 1 to 2 ft., Balkan Peninsula; *corniculatus,* ' Bird's-foot Trefoil ', yellow, summer, creeping, Britain, var. *pleniflorus,* double, yellow.

Lotus, see Nymphaea and Nelumbo; **-Tree,** see *Diospyros Lotus.*

Love Apple, see *Lycopersicon esculentum*; **-in-a-Mist,** see *Nigella damascena*; **-lies-bleeding,** see *Amaranthus caudatus.*

Luculia—*Rubiaceae.* Greenhouse evergreen flowering shrubs. First introduced early nineteenth century.

CULTURE: Compost, equal parts fibrous loam, peat, charcoal and sand. Position, in large well-drained pots, or preferably in beds 2 to 3 ft. wide and 18 in. deep. Put 6 in. of drainage into latter. Pot or plant, Feb., March or April. Prune young shoots moderately after flowering to a length of 2 or 3 in. Water freely April to Nov., withhold entirely afterwards. Syringe foliage twice daily April to Sept. Temp., April to Sept. 60° to 70°, Sept. to Dec. 55° to 65°, Dec. to April 45° to 55°.

PROPAGATION: By seeds sown $\frac{1}{16}$ in. deep in well-drained pans of light, sandy soil in temp. of 60° to 70° in Feb., March or April; cuttings of young shoots inserted in sandy soil under bell-glass in temp. 70° to 80° in June or July. Seedlings flower when three to five years old.

SPECIES CULTIVATED: *L. gratissima,* rose, autumn, 8 to 10 ft., Himalaya; *Pinceana,* rose, autumn, 10 ft., Himalaya.

Ludwigia—*Onagraceae.* Creeping aquatic plants used at pond margin and extensively for aquarium work. Glossy, privet-like leaves, insignificant yellow, axillary flowers.

CULTURE: Soil, sandy or plain loam. Position, submerged in aquarium or at pond margin. Plant, spring outdoors, any time in aquarium.

PROPAGATION: By seeds sown in pans of loam just covered with water in March or April; division or cuttings.

SPECIES CULTIVATED: *L. Mulerttii*, most widely grown, foliage bronzed, not hardy, S. America; *palustris*, greener, Europe (Br.).

Luffa (Loofah; Dish-cloth Gourd)—*Cucurbitaceae*. Stove climbing annual, bearing curious gourd-like fruits.

CULTURE: Sow seeds in a compost of equal parts leaf-mould and loam in a temp. of 75° in Feb. Transfer seedlings when third leaf forms singly into 3 in. pots, and later on to 8 or 10 in. pots, using three parts of loam to one of leaf-mould. Train shoots up roof. Water freely. Syringe daily. Feed with weak liquid manure when fruit has formed.

SPECIES CULTIVATED: *L. acutangula*, yellow, summer, India, Malaya; *cylindrica* (syn. *L. aegyptiaca*), yellow, summer, fruits club-shaped, Tropics. There are numerous garden forms.

Luisia—*Orchidaceae*. An epiphytic genus, allied to but not comparable, in floral beauty, with Vanda. The tufted stems and leaves terete. Flowers few, almost sessile.

CULTURE: Compost and temp. as for Vanda. Winter waterings should be infrequent, when falls of temp. to 55° would do no harm.

PROPAGATION: By severance of the stem below roots or division of plants.

SPECIES CULTIVATED: *L. Amesiana*, yellow, brownish, lip spotted maroon, summer, Burma, India; *brachystachys*, greenish rose-purple and yellow, summer, autumn, Burma; *Psyche*, greenish-yellow, lip reticulated violet-purple, summer, 12 in., Burma; *teretifolia*, variable, dull purplish-brown, sometimes whitish, widely distributed in the East; *trichorhiza*, green, brown, lip purplish-brown, various, N. India.

Lunaria—*Cruciferae*. Annual and perennial flowering plants. Seed pods flat, oval, containing a satiny partition; very useful for drying for winter decorations. First introduced late sixteenth century.

CULTURE OF ANNUAL SPECIES: Soil, ordinary. Position, partially shaded borders or margins of shrubberies. Plant, Aug. to Oct., singly or in groups of three or six. Discard plants after flowering.

CULTURE OF PERENNIAL SPECIES: Soil, light, rich ordinary. Position, partially shaded borders. Plant, Oct., March or April.

PROPAGATION: Annual species by seeds sown in shallow drills or patches outdoors in sunny position in April, transplanting seedlings when third leaf is formed 6 in. apart each way; perennial species by seeds similarly, or by division of roots in March or April.

ANNUAL SPECIES CULTIVATED: *L. annua* (syn. *L. biennis*), ' Honesty ', ' Money Flower ', ' Satin Flower ', lilac, white, or purple, May and June, 2 to 3 ft., Europe.

PERENNIAL SPECIES CULTIVATED: *L. rediviva*, purple, fragrant, June, 2 to 3 ft., Europe.

Lungwort, see Pulmonaria.

Lupin, Lupine, see Lupinus.

Lupinus (Lupin)—*Leguminosae*. Hardy shrubby and herbaceous perennials and annuals. First introduced late sixteenth century.

CULTURE OF SHRUBBY PERENNIALS: Soil, sandy loam. Position, sunny shrubberies, or open, sheltered borders. Plant, Oct. or April. Prune into shape after flowering.

CULTURE OF HERBACEOUS PERENNIALS: Soil, ordinary rich. Position, open sunny or partially shaded borders. Plant, Oct., March or April. Mulch with decayed manure in April. Cut down flower stems in Oct. Dislikes lime.

CULTURE OF ANNUAL SPECIES: Sow seeds ½ in. deep and 1 in. apart in April in patches where required to flower. Thin seedlings in May to 6 to 12 in. apart. Remove seed pods directly they form to ensure continuous display of flowers. Apply stimulants when in flower. Water freely in dry weather.

PROPAGATION: Perennial species by seeds sown ¼ in. deep outdoors in April, transplanting seedlings into flowering positions June to Aug.; cuttings of young growth taken in March before they become hollow, and rooted in sandy soil in unheated frame.

SHRUBBY SPECIES CULTIVATED: *L. arboreus*, ' Tree Lupin ', yellow, fragrant, summer, 6 to 9 ft., and var. *albus*, white; *Paynei*, blue, pink, or white with yellow blotch, spring, to 8 ft., California.

HERBACEOUS SPECIES CULTIVATED: *L. nootkatensis*, blue, purple, and yellow, summer, 1 ft., N. America; *polyphyllus*, ' Perennial Lupin ', blue, summer, 3 to 6 ft., California, and vars. *albus*, white, *roseus*, pink. There are also many named vars. to be found in trade lists.

ANNUAL SPECIES CULTIVATED: *L. densiflorus* (syn. *L. Menziesii*), yellow, fragrant, Aug., 2 ft., California; *Hartwegii*, blue, white, and rose, Aug. to Sept., 2 to 3 ft., Mexico; *hirsutissimus*, reddish-purple, July, 9 in., California; *hirsutus*, blue and white, July to Aug., 1¼ to 2¾ ft., Medit. Region; *luteus*, yellow, June to Aug., 1 to 2 ft., S. Europe; *mutabilis*, white, blue, and yellow, fragrant, summer, 3 to 4 ft., Colombia, and var. *Cruckshanksii*, violet and purple; *nanus*, lilac and blue, summer, 1 ft., California; *pubescens*, violet blue and white, July to Sept., 1½ to 3 ft., Mexico and Guatemala, and vars. *albococcineus*, *atrococcineus*, *Dunnettii*, *elegans*, *speciosus*, *superbus*, *tricolor*, etc.; *subcarnosus*, blue and yellow, summer, 1 ft., Texas.

Luronium (Floating Water Plantain)—*Alismaceae*. Dainty aquatic for shallow water, pond edges or submerged in aquarium.

CULTURE: Soil, indifferent. Plant, spring.

PROPAGATION: Division.

SPECIES CULTIVATED: *L. natans* (syn. *Elisma natans*), 1 to 2 in., white flowers, tiny leaves, Europe.

Luzula—*Juncaceae*. Ornamental hardy grass-like plants.

CULTURE: Any reasonable soil. Position, in sun or semi-shade, on dryish banks or by stream-side.

PROPAGATION: By seeds; division of old plants in spring or autumn.

SPECIES CULTIVATED: *L. maxima*, ornamental grass-like tufts, 1 to 2 ft., Europe; *nivea*, flower heads creamy-white, summer, 2 in., Europe.

Lycaste—*Orchidaceae*. A terrestrial and epiphytic genus (often on rocks), not large but of great importance. The majority have beautiful flowers. All are of easy cultivation. Stout, ovoid pseudo-bulbs, scapes single-flowered, freely produced from their base. Leaves plicate, deciduous in some species, nearly so in others.

CULTURE: Compost, fibrous loam, with a little sphagnum moss and finely pounded potsherds. Peat may be added; if in quantity, use more potsherds. Pots with free drainage. Repot, if necessary, in spring. As with all plicate-leaved orchids, the syringe should not be used until the leaves are fully expanded. Light shading in summer. Whenever weather allows, admit air at night, in reason, by top vents. The plants should mature in autumn and then be exposed to full light. A decided rest should be given in winter, especially to deciduous. Winter night temp. 50°. If dry they will withstand lower, but at 50° a slight humidity can be maintained. Summer temp. 60°, or near, at night, with sun heat higher in the day. Avoid draughts but air freely without losing humidity. When growths first commence, water infrequently but thoroughly, freely in summer.

PROPAGATION: By division of plants when repotting, or by sound back bulbs, removed singly, placed in a small pot, filled with small potsherds and surfaced with sphagnum. Pot when roots are seen.

SPECIES CULTIVATED: A selection—*L. aromatica* (syn. *Maxillaria aromatica*), orange-yellow, rather small, very fragrant, winter, spring, Mexico, and var. *majus*, larger, often with reddish stain at lip base; *brevispatha*, very variable, pale green, whitish, spotted, flushed rose, lip white, spotted rose-purple, winter, spring, summer, Costa Rica, Guatemala, and var. *Lawrenceana* (syn. *L. Lawrenceana*), heavily spotted and flushed with rose, variable; *costata* (Lindl), large, ivory white, lip margins fimbriate, summer, Peru; *cruenta* (syn. *L. Maxillaria*), larger than *aromatica*, orange-yellow, with a sanguineous blotch at base of lip, sometimes fragrant, spring, summer, Guatemala; *Deppei* (syn. *L. Maxillaria*), green, red-spotted, white, lip yellow, winter, spring, Mexico; *Dyeriana*, plant and flowers pendent, green, lip fringed, summer, Peru; *fulvescens*, large, yellowish-brown, lip orange-brown, fringed, summer, various, Colombia; *gigantea*, large, olive green, lip chocolate, orange-yellow, margins denticulate, summer, various, Ecuador; *lanipes*, greenish-white, ivory white, lip margins shortly fimbriate, autumn, Brazil, Peru, Ecuador; *lasioglossa*, sepals red-brown, petals yellow,.mid-lobe of lip woolly haired, winter, spring, Guatemala; *leucantha*, greenish, creamy white, variable, various, Costa Rica; *locusta*, green, lip margin with short white hairs, spring, summer, Peru; *longiscapa*, green, scapes 2 ft. high, spring, various, rare; *Luscianii*, a natural hybrid, spring, Guatemala; *macrobulbon*, much larger than *L. cruenta*, yellow to orange-yellow, tinged green, spring, summer, Colombia; *macrophylla* (syn. *L. plana*), greenish, shaded red, petals white, rose spotted, lip white crimson-spotted, variable, spring, various, Brazil, Peru; *Skinneri* (syn. *Maxillaria Skinneri*), variable, very beautiful, large, sepals whitish, rose-flushed, petals rose, lip flushed rose to purple, the vars. are endless, colour from pure white to crimson, winter, spring, Guatemala.

Lychnis (Campion)—*Caryophyllaceae*. Hardy annuals and perennials. By some authors certain species are placed in separate genera: Melandrium, Viscaria and Agrostemma.

CULTURE OF PERENNIAL SPECIES: Soil, light rich loam for *L. alpina*; open, dryish beds, borders or banks for other species. Plant, Oct. and Feb. to May. Cut down flower stems of *L. chalcedonica* and *L. alba* in Oct. or Nov. Top-dress border species with well-decayed manure in March or April. Apply weak liquid manure occasionally to border species when in flower. Lift and replant border species every other year.

CULTURE OF ANNUAL SPECIES: Soil, ordinary. Position, sunny beds or edgings to or masses in borders. Sow in March or April for summer, Sept. for spring flowering.

PROPAGATION: By seeds sown ⅛ in. deep in light soil in sunny position outdoors in March or April, transplanting seedlings into flowering position Aug. to Nov.; division of perennials, Sept. to Dec. and Feb. to April.

PERENNIAL SPECIES CULTIVATED: *L. alba* (syns. *L. vespertina, Melandrium album*), ' White Campion', white, May to Aug., 3 ft., Britain; *alpina* (syn. *Viscaria alpina*), rosy pink, summer, 6 in., Europe (Br.); *Arkwrightii*, scarlet, summer, 1½ ft., hybrid; *chalcedonica*, ' Scarlet Lychnis ' or ' Jerusalem Cross ', scarlet, summer, 3 ft., Russia, and vars. *alba*, white, and *flore-pleno*, double; *Coronaria* (syn. *Agrostemma Coronaria*), ' Rose Campion ', crimson, July and Aug., 2 to 3 ft., S. Europe, and vars. *atrosanguinea*, crimson red, *alba*, white, and *flore-pleno*, red; *dioica* (syns. *Melandrium dioicum, rubrum* and *sylvestre*), ' Red Campion ', purple, rose, summer, 3 ft., Britain; *Flos-cuculi* (syn. *A. Flos-cuculi*), ' Ragged Robin ', rose, May and June, 1 to 2 ft., Britain, and double var. *flore-pleno*; *Flos-Jovis* (syn. *A. Flos-Jovis*), bright pink, summer, 1½ to 2 ft., Europe; *fulgens*, vermilion, May to Sept., 6 to 12 in., Siberia; *Haageana*, scarlet, summer, 9 to 12 in., hybrid; *Viscaria* (syn. *V. viscosa*), ' German Catchfly ', reddish-purple, summer, 1 ft., Europe (Br.), and vars. *splendens*, red, *alba*, white, *flore-pleno*, rose, double.

ANNUAL SPECIES CULTIVATED: *L. Coeli-rosa* (syn. *Agrostemma Coeli-rosa*), ' Rose of Heaven ', rose and purple, summer, 1 ft., Levant, and vars. *alba*, white, *kermesina*, red, and *oculata*, purple-eyed.

Lycium (Box-thorn)—*Solanaceae*. Hardy erect and climbing deciduous flowering shrubs with branches more or less spiny. First introduced late seventeenth century.

CULTURE Soil, ordinary. Position, not worthy of place of importance, but useful for dry poor soil, and especially seaside cliffs, quite attractive when berrying well. Plant, Oct. to Feb. Prune, Oct. to Feb., removing weak shoots entirely and shortening vigorous ones a little.

HEDGE CULTURE: Trench ground two spits deep and 3 ft. wide. Plant 12 in. apart in single rows, Oct. to Feb. Trim into shape, June and July.

PROPAGATION: By cuttings of firm shoots, 6 to 8 in. long, inserted in ordinary soil in shady position in Sept. or Oct.; layering shoots, spring; by removing suckers with roots attached, Oct. to Feb.

SPECIES CULTIVATED: *chinense*, 'Common Box-thorn', 'Duke of Argyll's Tea-tree', purple and yellow, summer, 10 to 12 ft., succeeded by scarlet berries, China; *L. halimifolium*, lilac-purple, May to July, 8 to 9 ft., S.E. Europe and W. Asia; *pallidum*, green and purple, June to July, 5 to 6 ft., South-eastern U.S.A.

Lycopersicon (Tomato)—*Solanaceae*. Tender perennials treated as half-hardy annuals.

CULTURE OUTDOORS: Set out plants, in early June, in the open. Plant 18 in. apart with separate stakes, remove all side shoots and stop when four trusses formed. Bush vars. may grow freely, planted 3 ft. apart. Water freely and feed weekly with tomato fertiliser after first fruits set. Gather remaining fruit in late Sept. and ripen indoors.

CULTURE IN FRAMES AND CLOCHES: Set out plants first week in May, choosing short-jointed vars. Either train them horizontally along stakes or remove protection when plants grow.

CULTURE IN HEATED HOUSES: May be grown in borders, troughs, boxes or pots. Compost, five parts good turfy loam, one part well-decayed stable manure to which is added 1 lb. each of lime, hoof and horn, sulphate of potash and bonemeal per bushel. Plant when 3½ in. pot well supplied with roots about 10 weeks after sowing. Stake or tie to strings. Water in and keep soil moist; when fruit is set, two heavy waterings daily may be needed. Temp. at planting should be 60° at night and 65° to 70° by day. Set fruit by damping overhead in the mid-morning from time first flowers open. Feed with tomato fertiliser weekly after fruits set. Ventilate during day when day temp. reaches 65° and at night when temp. reaches this level.

PROPAGATION: Any time when night temp. of 60° can be maintained, avoiding short dull days of November and December. Sow in sterilised compost, water and cover boxes with glass and paper. Germination, 8 days. Keep house moist and when 2 in. high pot into 3½ in. pots. Keep well watered and space out plants as they grow. 1 oz. of seed will yield about 2,000 plants.

SPECIES CULTIVATED: *L. esculentum*, 'Tomato', fruits red or yellow, Western S. America, and vars. *cerasiforme*, 'Cherry Tomato', *pyriforme*, 'Pear Tomato'; *pimpinellifolium*, 'Currant Tomato', trusses of very small fruits. Used in crosses with other species to produce heavy cropping, dwarf and leaf-mould resistant vars.

Lycopodium—*Lycopodiaceae*. Stove and hardy perennial mosses, creeping or erect, closely allied to ferns. Foliage, ornamental. Stems clothed with scale-like, dark green leaves.

CULTURE OF STOVE SPECIES: Compost, equal parts loam, peat, limestone and silver sand. Position, well-drained shallow pans under bell-glass or in beds in wardian cases and are especially suitable for teakwood baskets. Pot or plant, Feb. to April. Water freely March to Sept., moderately afterwards. Syringe once or twice daily April to Sept. Shade from direct sun. Temp., March to Sept. 65° to 75°, Sept. to March 55° to 65°.

CULTURE OF HARDY SPECIES: Soil, deep, moist, sandy peat. Position, low bed on moist rockery in shade. Plant, March or April. Water freely in dry weather. In wardian cases: compost, two parts peat, one part leaf-mould, one part charcoal and liberal quantity of limestone chips or tufa, bed to be well drained. Plant, Feb. to April. Water once or twice a week, April to Sept., fortnightly Sept. to Dec. and once a month Dec. to April. Syringe or dew over daily April to Oct. Shade from sun. Ventilate a little daily.

PROPAGATION: By division, Feb. to April.

STOVE SPECIES CULTIVATED: *L. squarrosum*, 2 ft. or more, India; *taxifolium* W. Indies; *verticillatum*, Tropics.

HARDY SPECIES CULTIVATED: *L. Billardieri*, free-growing creeper, New Zealand; *clavatum*, ' Club Moss ', ' Stag's-horn Moss ', creeping, Britain; *complanatum*, fan-like growth, N. America; *lucidulum*, grows erect to 6 to 8 in., glossy green, N. America; *Selago*, ' Fir Club Moss ', 3 in., Britain; *tristachyum*, creeping, Europe.

Lycoris—*Amaryllidaceae*. Greenhouse flowering bulbs. First introduced mid-eighteenth century.

CULTURE: Compost, two parts sandy loam, one part equal proportions of leaf-mould and cow manure. Pot dry bulbs Sept. to Dec., afterwards repotting annually immediately after flowering. Bury bulbs about two-thirds of their depth. Water moderately from time flowers show till leaves appear, then freely; keep quite dry after leaves·fade. Temp., Sept. to April 55° to 65°. Place pots from April to Sept. in light, sunny, cool position.

PROPAGATION: By offsets, treated as bulbs, Sept. to Dec.

SPECIES CULTIVATED: *L. aurea* (syn. *Amaryllis aurea*), ' Golden Lily ', yellow, Aug., 1 to 2 ft., China; *radiata* (syn. *Nerine japonica* and *Amaryllis radiata*), scarlet, June, 18 in., China and Japan, and vars. *alba*, white, and *variegata*, crimson and white; *sanguinea*, crimson, summer, 2 ft., Japan; *squamigera*, rosy lilac, fragrant, summer, 2 ft., Japan.

Lygodium (Climbing Fern)—*Schizaeaceae*. Stove and greenhouse climbing ferns, deciduous and evergreen. Fronds slender, twining, divisions lingulate or palmate. First introduced late eighteenth century.

CULTURE: Compost, equal parts peat, loam, sand and charcoal. Position, well-drained pots or beds in shade with fronds twined round sticks, pillars, string or trellis. Plant or pot, Feb. to April. Water freely Feb. to Oct., moderately afterwards. Temp. stove species, Sept. to March 55° to 65°, March to Sept. 65° to 75°; greenhouse, Sept. to March 45° to 50°, March to Sept. 55° to 65°.

PROPAGATION: By spores sown on surface of fine sandy peat under bell-glass in temp. 75° to 85° any time; division of plants at potting time.

STOVE SPECIES CULTIVATED: *L. circinatum* (syn. *L. dichotomum*), Trop. Asia; *reticulatum*, Polynesia.

GREENHOUSE SPECIES CULTIVATED: *L. japonicum*, E. Asia; *palmatum*, U. States; *scandens*, the most generally grown species, E. Asia.

Lyonia—*Ericaceae*. Hardy deciduous flowering shrub of no great garden merit. First introduced mid-eighteenth century.

CULTURE: Soil, peaty. Position, moist, shady borders. Plant, Sept. to Nov. and Feb. to April. Pruning unnecessary.

PROPAGATION: By seeds sown on surface of sandy peat under bell-glass in shade in cold frame or greenhouse in Oct. or April; layering shoots, Sept. or Oct.

SPECIES CULTIVATED: *L. ligustrina*, white, June, 4 to 8 ft., N. America. See also Leucothoe.

Lyre Flower, see *Dicentra spectabilis*.

Lysimachia (Loosestrife)—*Primulaceae*. Hardy herbaceous perennials.

CULTURE: Soil, ordinary rich. Position, moist shady borders or margins of ponds, etc. Plant, Oct. to April. Cut down flower stems of tall kinds in Nov.

CULTURE OF CREEPING JENNY IN POTS: Compost, two parts good soil or loam, one part leaf-mould, decayed manure or compost and one part sand. Position, well-drained pots or baskets suspended in shady window or cool greenhouse. Pot, March to May. Water freely April to Sept., moderately afterwards.

PROPAGATION: By division of plants in spring or autumn.

SPECIES CULTIVATED: *L. atropurpurea*, red, summer, to 2 ft., Greece; *clethroides*, white, July to Sept., 3 ft., China, Japan; *Ephemerum*, white, summer, 3 ft., Medit. Region; *Fortunei*, white, summer, 1½ ft., China, Japan; *Nummularia*, ' Creeping Jenny ', ' Moneywort ', yellow, summer, creeping, Britain; *phyllocephala*, yellow, summer, 1 ft., China; *punctata* (syn. *L. verticillata*), yellow, summer, 2 to 3 ft., Britain; *thyrsiflora*, yellow, June to July, 3 ft., Britain, Asia, N. America; *vulgaris*, ' Yellow Loosestrife ', yellow, July to Aug., 3 ft., Britain, Europe, Asia.

Lysionotus—*Gesneriaceae.* Dwarf evergreen shrub.
   CULTURE: Soil, deep, cool, lime-free, composed principally of peat or well-rotted leaf-mould. Position, cool, semi-shaded aspect or alpine house.
   PROPAGATION: By cuttings made of half-ripened growths in late summer.
   SPECIES CULTIVATED: *L. pauciflorus*, white and lavender, late summer, 6 to 9 in., Japan.

Lythrum (Loosestrife)—*Lythraceae.* Hardy herbaceous and shrubby perennials.
   CULTURE: Soil, ordinary. Position, moist shady borders or margins of ponds or streams. Plant, Oct. or Feb. to April. Cut down flower stems in Nov. Water freely in dry weather. Top-dress with well-decayed manure, March or April. Lift, divide, and replant every third year.
   PROPAGATION: By division of plants, Oct. or April.
   SPECIES CULTIVATED: *L. alatum*, purple, July to Oct., 2 to 4 ft., N. America; *Salicaria*, ' Purple Loosestrife ', reddish-purple, July, 3 to 4 ft., Britain, and vars. *roseum, superbum* and *tomentosum*; *virgatum*, purple, summer, 3 ft., Europe.

Maackia—*Leguminosae.* Hardy deciduous flowering tree of little garden merit. First introduced mid-nineteenth century.
   CULTURE: Soil, loamy. Position, sunny shrubberies. Plant, Nov. to Feb.
   PROPAGATION: By seeds sown in well-drained pans in temp. 55° to 60° during Feb. or March; cuttings of roots placed in pans in similar temp. and at same season.
   SPECIES CULTIVATED: *M. amurensis* (syn. *Cladrastis amurensis*), white, July to Aug., 15 to 40 ft., Manchuria and Japan.

Mace, see Myristica; **Reed-,** see *Typha latifolia.*

Mackaya—*Acanthaceae.* Greenhouse deciduous flowering shrub. First introduced mid-nineteenth century.
   CULTURE: Compost, two parts fibrous loam, one part dried cow manure, half-part sharp silver sand. Position, light airy greenhouse. Pot, March. Prune after flowering, shortening shoots to 2 or 3 in. Water freely March to Sept., moderately Sept. to Nov., keep quite dry Nov. to March. Temp., April to Oct. 55° to 65°, Oct. to April 45° to 55°.
   PROPAGATION: By cuttings inserted singly in 2 in. pots filled with sandy soil, June to Aug. Transfer to 5 in. pots when rooted. Prune closely in April and shift into 8 and 10 in. pots. Plants flower when two to three years old.
   SPECIES CULTIVATED: *M. bella* (syn. *Asystasia bella*), lilac, veined purple, April to June, 4 to 6 ft., Natal.

Macleania—*Ericaceae.* Greenhouse trailing evergreen flowering shrubs. First introduced mid-nineteenth century.
   CULTURE: Compost, equal parts turfy loam, peat and sand. Position, well-drained pots with shoots drooping over front of staging, or in suspended baskets. Pot, March or April. Water freely March to Sept., moderately afterwards. Prune straggling shoots into shape, March. Temp., March to Sept. 55° to 65°, Sept. to March 45° to 55°.
   PROPAGATION: By cuttings inserted in fine sand in temp. 55° to 65° in summer.
   SPECIES CULTIVATED: *M. pulchra*, yellow and scarlet, spring, 8 to 10 ft., Colombia; *punctata*, rosy red, white, and yellow, November, Ecuador; *speciosissima*, yellow and scarlet, spring, trailing, Colombia.

Macleaya—*Papaveraceae.* Hardy herbaceous perennials. Sometimes included in the genus Bocconia. First introduced late eighteenth century.
   CULTURE: Soil, rich loamy, well manured. Position, open, sunny, sheltered from cold winds. Plant, April. Cut down flower stems after blooming. Good plant for pot culture in cool greenhouse or window. Compost, two parts loam, one part leaf-mould and sand. Pot, March. Water freely spring and summer, moderately other times.
   PROPAGATION: By cuttings of young shoots growing out of axils of leaves, inserted

in small pots of sandy soil, temp. 55° under bell-glass, June to Aug.; by suckers removed from root, placed in pots in cold frame in July; by root cuttings in winter.

SPECIES CULTIVATED: *M. cordata* (syn. *Bocconia cordata*), ' Plume Poppy ', ' Tree Celandine ', buff or whitish, July, 6 to 8 ft., China; *microcarpa* (syn. *Bocconia microcarpa*), yellowish buff, June, 6 to 7 ft., N. China.

Maclura—*Moraceae.* Hardy deciduous spiny tree. Flowers, yellowish green, inconspicuous. Sexes borne on separate trees. Fruit, round, golden yellow, 3 to 5 in. in diameter; rarely borne in this country. Leaves, egg-shaped, bright green. Wood used for longbows. First introduced early nineteenth century.

CULTURE: Soil, ordinary. Position, in open, sheltered shrubberies or hedges. Plant, Oct. to Feb. Prune into shape when necessary, Nov. to Feb.

HEDGE CULTURE: Plant 12 in. apart in single row. Soil to be trenched two spits deep and 3 ft. wide. Trim into shape, July and Nov.

PROPAGATION: By cuttings, 6 to 8 in. long, inserted in ordinary soil in shady position, Oct. to March.

SPECIES CULTIVATED: *M. pomifera* (syn. *M. aurantiaca*), ' Osage Orange ', 20 to 40 ft., N. America.

Macradenia—*Orchidaceae.* An epiphytic genus of dwarf habit, pseudo-bulbs small, the usually pendulous inflorescence from their bases.

CULTURE: Compost and general conditions as for Oncidiums, pans or small baskets are suitable. Position near the glass but careful shading is necessary. The winter rest must not be severe, but watering should be far less frequent than in summer. The Cattleya house gives the requisite temp.

PROPAGATION: By division of the plants in spring.

SPECIES CULTIVATED: *M. lutescens*, yellowish-green, marked with red-brown on inner surfaces, summer, autumn, Florida, W. Indies; *modesta* (syn. *Serastylis modesta*), red-brown, margined yellow, lip whitish, purple streaked, spring, summer, Brazil; *triandra*, greenish, purplish-red, lip yellowish, purple streaked, spring, summer, Surinam, Guiana.

Macrozamia—*Cycadaceae.* Greenhouse evergreen perennials with feather-shaped, green leaves. First introduced early nineteenth century.

CULTURE: Compost, equal parts peat, loam and sand. Position, well-drained pots, in light greenhouse, shaded from sun. Pot, Feb. or March. Water freely April to Oct., moderately afterwards. Syringe daily April to Sept. Temp., March to Sept. 60° to 70°, Sept. to March 55° to 60°.

PROPAGATION: By seeds sown in sandy peat in temp. 75° in March; division of plants in March; offsets in Feb. or March.

SPECIES CULTIVATED: *M. Fraseri*, ' Swan River Fern Palm ', W. Australia; *Hopei*, Australia; *Peroffskyana*, ' Giant Fern Palm ', Australia; *tenuifolia*, Australia.

Madagascar Jasmine, see *Stephanotis floribunda*; **-Lace Plant**, see *Aponogeton fenestralis*; **-Periwinkle**, see *Vinca rosea*.

Madeira Vine, see *Boussingaultia baselloides*.

Madia—*Compositae.* Hardy annuals. First introduced late eighteenth century.

CULTURE: Soil, ordinary. Position, shady borders.

PROPAGATION: By seeds sown ⅛ in. deep in April in patches where required to flower, thinning out seedlings when 2 in. high, to 3 in. apart.

SPECIES CULTIVATED: *M. elegans*, yellow, Aug., 1 ft., N.W. America; *sativa*, yellow, Aug., 1 ft., Chile.

Madwort, see Alyssum.

Magnolia—*Magnoliaceae.* Hardy deciduous and evergreen flowering trees and shrubs. Contrary to popular belief there are many kinds of easy culture suitable for small gardens, which flower when quite small. First introduced seventeenth century.

GREENHOUSE CULTURE: Compost, two parts sandy loam, one part peat or leaf-mould and sand. Position, well-drained pots or tubs, or against walls in sunny greenhouse. Pot or plant, March. Water freely in summer, moderately other times. Syringe daily March to Sept. Temp. for forcing, 55° to 65°. Prune straggling shoots into shape, March or April. *M. Campbellii, Soulangeana* and *stellata* are suitable for greenhouse culture.

CULTURE: Soil, rich, deep, sandy loam, mulch annually with peaty compost until established. Position, sheltered parts of lawn or pleasure garden, or against south or south-west walls, evergreen kinds against south or west walls. Plant, March or April. When necessary prune evergreen species in spring, deciduous species after flowering. Protect evergreen species in very severe weather.

PROPAGATION: By seeds in well-drained sandy soil in cold frame or greenhouse in spring or autumn; layering in summer or autumn; grafting in heat in July or Aug.

SPECIES CULTIVATED: *M. acuminata*, 'Cucumber Tree', greenish-yellow, red fruits, quick growing, 60 to 90 ft., Eastern N. America; *Campbellii*, clear rose-pink 8 in. flowers in March, vigorous but slow to flower, to over 100 ft., Himalala ; *denudata* (syn. *M. conspicua*), 'Yulan', white, March to May, fragrant, 30 ft., China; *Kobus*, white, April, quick growing, 30 to 60 ft., Japan; *mollicomata*, pink, spring, flowers when young, large tree, Himalaya; *obovata* (syn. *M. hypoleuca*), 8 in. creamy white, fragrant, June, to 50 ft., Japan; *salicifolia*, white, April, distinct narrow foliage, 15 to 20 ft., Japan; *Sieboldii* (syn. *M. parviflora*), waxy-white with crimson centre, fragrant, May to August, flowering when young, easily grown, Japan and Korea; *sinensis*, white, crimson centre, fragrant, summer, to 20 ft., W. China; *Soulangeana*, white, purple stained without, flowering when young, easily grown, spreading, hybrid, to 20 ft., and vars. *alba*, white, *Lennei*, rosy purple, *nigra*, white stained deep wine, slow growing, easy for small gardens; *stellata*, white fading pink, March, April, very free flowering when young, slow growing to 15 ft., Japan; *tripetala*, 'Umbrella Tree', creamy white, May to June, large leaves, 30 ft., Eastern N. America; *Watsonii*, large, white, crimson centre, very fragrant, May to July, Japanese hybrid; *Wilsonii*, white, crimson centre, June to July, 20 ft., W. China; *virginiana* (syn. *M. glauca*), 'Swamp Bay', 'Beaver Tree', white, July to Aug., shrub to 15 ft., Eastern U.S.A.

EVERGREEN SPECIES CULTIVATED: *M. Delavayi*, creamy white, June, requires wall protection, 20 to 30 ft., S.W. China; *grandiflora*, white, fragrant, July to Aug., freely planted evergreen, slow in flowering, 15 to 20 ft., South U.S.A.

× **Mahoberberis**—*Berberidaceae*. A bigeneric hybrid between *Mahonia Aquifolium* and *Berberis vulgaris*. Sub-evergreen shrub of little ornamental value, not known to bloom.

CULTURE: As Berberis.

PROPAGATION: Vegetative.

SPECIES CULTIVATED: *M. Neubertii* (syn. *Berberis Neubertii*), nearly evergreen, to 6 ft., and var. *latifolia*, broader leaves.

Mahogany, see Swietenia.

Mahonia—*Berberidaceae*. Hardy evergreen shrubs. Formerly included in the genus Berberis.

CULTURE: Soil, good garden. Position, excellent as ground cover, has attractive and durable foliage.

PROPAGATION: By seeds, suckers, layers and cuttings of half-ripe wood under glass.

SPECIES CULTIVATED: *M. Aquifolium* (syn. *Berberis Aquifolium*), yellow, spring, winter coloured leaves useful for cutting, useful for banks, to 3 ft., West N. America; *Bealei* (syn. *Berberis Bealei, Mahonia japonica*), yellow, blue berries, to 12 ft., China; *lomariifolia*, yellow, 1 to 2 ft., China; *napaulensis*, to 10 ft., Himalaya; *pinnata* (syn. *M. fascicularis*), like a taller *M. Aquifolium*, sea-green foliage, to 12 ft., Western N. America.

Maianthemum—*Liliaceae.* Hardy herbaceous perennial. Leaves and habit similar to the Lily of the Valley.
    CULTURE: Soil, ordinary rich. Position, shady borders in the open or under shrubs. Plant, Sept. and Oct. Water freely in dry weather.
    PROPAGATION: By division of creeping rootstocks in Sept. or April.
    SPECIES CULTIVATED: *M. bifolium* (syn. *M. Convallaria, Smilacina bifolia*), white, May, 6 in., N. Europe.

Maiden's Wreath, see Francoa.

Maid-of-the-Mist, see *Gladiolus primulinus.*

Maidenhair Fern, see Adiantum;   **-Spleenwort,** see *Asplenium Trichomanes;* **-Tree,** see *Gingko biloba.*

Maize, see *Zea Mays.*

Majorana (Marjoram)—*Labiatae.* Perennial herbs and sub-shrubs with aromatic foliage.
    CULTURE OF SWEET MARJORAM: Soil, ordinary, rich. Position, sunny border. Gather shoots when coming into flower, dry in shade and store for winter use.
    CULTURE OF POT OR COMMON MARJORAM: Soil, ordinary. Position, sunny.
    PROPAGATION: Sweet Marjoram: Sow seeds ¹⁄₁₆ in. deep in light soil in shallow boxes in temp. 55° to 65° in March, transplanting seedlings when 2 in. high to 6 in. apart in rows 9 in. apart in April outdoors. Common or Pot Marjoram: By seed in sunny position outdoors in March or April; division of roots March or April.
    SPECIES CULTIVATED: *M. hortensis* (syn. *Origanum Majorana*), ' Sweet Marjoram ', purple or white, summer, to 2 ft., Europe; *Onites,* ' Common ' or ' Pot Marjoram ', white, summer, 1 ft., S.E. Europe.

Malay Apple, see *Eugenia malaccensis.*

Malcomia—*Cruciferae.* Hardy annual. First introduced early eighteenth century.
    CULTURE: Soil, ordinary. Position, edging to sunny beds, masses on sunny borders, or on banks or rockeries. Sow seeds for summer flowering ¹⁄₁₆ in. deep in March, April, May or June where plants are required to grow, and similar depth in Sept. for flowering in spring.
    POT CULTURE: Compost, any good soil. Position, in 5 in. pots, well drained, in cold, sunny greenhouse or window. Sow seeds ¹⁄₁₆ in. deep in above pots in March, April or May. Water moderately when first sown, freely when in full growth. Thin seedlings to ½ in. apart when 1 in. high.
    SPECIES CULTIVATED: *M. maritima,* ' Virginia Stock ', various colours, summer, 6 in., S. Europe.

Male Fern, see *Dryopteris Filix-mas.*

Mallow, see Malva;   **Rose-,** see Hibiscus;   **Tree-,** see Lavatera.

Malope—*Malvaceae.* Hardy annuals. First introduced early eighteenth century.
    CULTURE: Soil, rich ordinary. Position, sunny beds, or in masses in borders. Water freely in dry weather. Apply stimulants occasionally when plants show flower.
    PROPAGATION: By seeds sown ⅛ in. deep in pots or boxes of light soil in temp. 50° in March, transplanting into flowering positions in May or June; or by seeds sown ¼ in. deep and 4 to 6 in. apart where required to grow, in April or May.
    SPECIES CULTIVATED: *M. trifida,* purple, summer, 2 to 3 ft., Spain, and vars. *alba,* white, *grandiflora,* crimson.

Malpighia—*Malpighiaceae.* Stove evergreen flowering shrubs or small trees. Some species cultivated for their cherry-like fruits. First introduced early eighteenth century.
    CULTURE: Compost, equal parts sandy loam and fibrous peat. Position, well-

drained pots in stove or planted out in border of well-drained soil in warm green-house. Pot-grown specimens should be watered freely March to Oct., moderately afterwards.

PROPAGATION: By half-ripened cuttings inserted in sandy soil in propagating frame with bottom heat during summer, or under bell-glass with bottom heat. Repot, autumn or spring. Temp., March to Oct. 65° to 75°, Oct. to March 55° to 65°.

SPECIES CULTIVATED: *M. coccigera*, pale pink, June to Aug., 2 ft., W. Indies; *glabra*, ' Barbados Cherry ', purplish-rose, March to Sept., 8 to 12 ft., Trop. America; *nitida*, pink, March to July, 10 ft., Venezuela; *urens*, pink, June to Oct., 3 to 5 ft., W. Indies.

Malus (Apple)—*Rosaceae*. Hardy deciduous, spring-flowering, fruit-bearing trees and shrubs. Formerly included in Pyrus.

CULTURE OF APPLE: Soil, deep loam. Position, open or sheltered gardens, trained on walls, fences, etc. Plant, Nov. to March. Distance for planting: Cordons, 24 in.; dwarf pyramids, pillars, 5 ft.; bush-trained trees, 12 ft.; pyramids, 12 ft.; fan-trained trees, 15 ft.; espaliers, 18 ft.; standards, 21 to 24 ft. Distance from paths: pyramids, 5 ft.; bush-trained, 2½ ft. Mode of bearing: On spurs formed on older branches and base of shoots of previous year's growth. Fruit buds may be distinguished from growth buds by their plumpness and round-ness. Summer pruning for trained trees; shorten side shoots 4 to 6 in. during July and Aug.; leave the leader unpruned. Secure to the wall suitably placed young shoots of fan-trained trees to form future branches, and summer-prune remaining ones. Standards and bush trees require no summer pruning. Winter pruning: Spur back summer-pruned shoots to within 1 to 2 in. of their base in dormant season. Leave extension shoots on espalier tiers unpruned. Bend cordons to a sharper angle to accommodate extension growth which is not shortened. Central leader of dwarf pyramid is shortened by half growth to opposite bud each year to keep it straight. About 5 in. of growth is allowed on each side branch cutting back to an under-bud. Prune laterals on bush trees according to vigour. Weak growths can be spurred back hard, those of medium vigour shortened by one-third of their growth and vigorous wood either removed or left unpruned. These long laterals will spur up at the base and can be shortened back to a fruit bud in later years. Simply thin out branches of standards, keeping the centre open, removing dead, diseased and crossing wood. Mulch newly-planted trees with thick layer of manure. Root-prune vigorous, unfruitful trees in Oct. or Nov. Gather fruit when, on lifting it by the hand from a vertical to a horizontal position, it readily parts from the tree. Store in dark, cool, frost-proof room. Manuring: Apply rotted farmyard manure as a mulch to extent of branch spread in spring and dig it in during following autumn. Use chemical fertilisers with regard to condition of the trees. Nitrogen to encourage growth, potash if leaves appear dried out, with ash-grey or brown margins. A good balanced mixture would be ¾ lb. sulphate of ammonia, ½ lb. superphosphate and 10 oz. sulphate of potash per in. of trunk diameter, hoed in lightly to beyond spread of branches in spring.

CULTURE OF ORNAMENTAL SPECIES: Soil, ordinary. Position, sunny borders or shrubberies or as specimens in open places. Plant, Nov. to Feb.

PROPAGATION: By seed sown outdoors in March for new sorts; grafting estab-lished vars. in March; budding in July and Aug. Ornamental species by seeds sown 3 in. deep in sandy soil in sunny position outdoors in Oct.; cuttings of shoots 8 to 12 in. long in ordinary soil outdoors in autumn; layering in autumn. Root stocks: budded in July or Aug. or grafted when sap is rising in April. Selected stocks of known vigour numbered by East Malling Research Station are: M IX Jaune de Metz, very dwarfing, used for cordons and other restricted forms; M VII, semi-dwarfing, used for cordons of tip-bearing vars. and for pyramid trees; M II Doucin, fairly vigorous and reliable for bush trees; M I English Broadleaf, less reliable than M II, especially on dry soils; M XVI Ketziner Ideal, vigorous stock suitable for standard trees; Malling Crab C, another suitable vigorous stock for standard trees.

APPLE SPECIES CULTIVATED: *M. pumila* (syns. *M. sylvestris*, *M. communis*, *Pyrus Malus*), white or pink, fruits cultivated in many orchard vars., to 40 ft. or more, Europe, W. Asia.

ORNAMENTAL SPECIES CULTIVATED: *M. adstringens*, many forms of crab apple, some of them hybrids with *M. pumila*; *atrosanguinea*, rose-purple, 18 ft., hybrid; *baccata*, ' Siberian Crab Apple ', white or pinkish, fruit yellow and red, to 40 ft., Siberia; *coronaria*, ' Garland Crab Apple ', rose to white, sweet-scented, fruit yellow, hard, acid, to 30 ft., United States; *floribunda*, rose-red changing to white, fruit red, to 25 ft., Japan or China, and var. *Scheideckeri*, pale pink, semi-double, fruit yellow, 20 to 25 ft. ' Hall Crab Apple ', deep rose, fruit purple, to 18 ft., China, and var. *Parkmanii*, double; *ioensis*, white or pink, fruit greenish, 30 ft., N. America; *prunifolia*, white, fruit yellow or red, 15 to 20 ft., N.E. Asia, and var. *Rinkii*, pink, fruit red; *pumila* and vars. *Niedzwetzkyana*, deep red, fruit skin and flesh-purple-red, bark and leaves reddish, *paradisiaca*, ' Paradise Apple ', shrubby form; *purpurea*, leaves purple when young, fruit small, purple, 15 to 20 ft., hybrid, and vars. *aldenhamensis*, partly double, light red, fruit purple-red, *Lemoinei*, dark crimson, small red fruits, brown-red leaves; *Sargentii*, white, fruit dark red, 6 ft., Japan; *Sieboldii*, pink, small red or yellowish fruits, 15 ft., Japan, and var. *arborescens*, white, to 30 ft.; *spectabilis*, showy, pink, fruit yellow, to 25 ft., China; *toringoides*, creamy white, fruit yellow and reddish, 25 ft., China; *yunnanensis*, white, fruit red, leaves orange and red in autumn, to 25 ft., W. China, and var. *Veitchii*, white, fruit red spotted white.

Malva (Mallow)—*Malvaceae*. Hardy annual and perennial flowering plants.

CULTURE OF PERENNIAL SPECIES: Soil, ordinary. Position, sunny or partially shaded beds or borders. Plant, Oct. or March. Mulch with manure in autumn.

CULTURE OF ANNUAL SPECIES: Soil, ordinary. Position, sunny. Plant, May or June.

PROPAGATION: Annual species by seeds sown ⅛ in. deep in light, sandy soil in temp. 55° in March or April; perennial species by seeds sown similarly, or by cuttings inserted in cold frame in July or Aug.

ANNUAL SPECIES CULTIVATED: *M. crispa*, white and purple, summer, 3 to 6 ft., Europe; *sylvestris*, purple-rose, summer, 2 to 3 ft., Europe, biennial usually grown as annual, var. *mauritiana*, purple, summer, 3 to 4 ft.

PERENNIAL SPECIES CULTIVATED: *M. Alcea*, rosy purple, summer, 4 ft., Europe, best grown as an annual; *moschata*, ' Musk Mallow ', rose, summer, 3 ft., Britain, and var. *alba*, white. See also Malvastrum.

Malvastrum (False Mallow)—*Malvaceae*. Hardy perennials. First introduced early nineteenth century.

CULTURE: Soil, ordinary. Position, sunny rockeries for dwarf species; sunny well-drained borders for tall species. Plant, Oct. or March. Protect in severe winters with a layer of cinder ashes or leaf-mould.

PROPAGATION: By seeds sown ⅛ in. deep in light, sandy soil in temp. 55° in March or April; cuttings inserted in cold frame in July or Aug.

SPECIES CULTIVATED: *M. coccineum*, scarlet, July to Sept., 6 in., U. States; *Gilliesii*, red, summer, 6 in., S. America; *lateritium* (syn. *Malva lateritia*), salmon-pink, summer, 1 ft., Uruguay.

Malvaviscus—*Malvaceae*. Greenhouse evergreen shrubs. First introduced early eighteenth century.

CULTURE: Compost, two parts fibrous loam, one part fibrous peat and leaf-mould with a liberal admixture of broken charcoal and silver sand. Positon, well-drained pots or border in warm greenhouse. Pot or plant during spring. Prune into shape after flowering. Water moderately Oct. to March, freely at other times. Temp., March to Sept. 65° to 75°, Sept. to March 55° to 65°.

PROPAGATION: By cuttings of side shoots inserted in sandy soil under bell-glass or in propagating case in heat, spring or summer.

SPECIES CULTIVATED: *M. arboreus*, scarlet, summer, 12 ft., S. America; *Conzattii*, scarlet, winter, 10 to 15 ft., Mexico.

Mammillaria—*Cactaceae*. Greenhouse succulent perennials. Flowers generally expanding about 11 a.m. and closing at 1 p.m.; somewhat fugitive. Stems leafless, cylindrical or globular, bearing small tubercles or teats crowned with rosettes or stars of spines evenly spaced over their surface. First introduced late seventeenth century.

CULTURE: Compost, equal parts sandy loam, rough old mortar and pounded bricks. Position, sunny, airy greenhouse or window. Pot, March or April, in well-drained pots just large enough to accommodate roots. Repot every third or fourth year only. Water moderately March to Sept., once a fortnight, Sept. to Dec., none afterwards. Syringe on evenings of warm days June to Sept. Apply soot-water to healthy plants June to Sept. Ventilate freely in summer. Temp., March to Sept. 60° to 70°, Sept. to March 50° to 55°.

PROPAGATION: By seeds sown ⅛ in. deep in well-drained pans or pots of sandy soil in temp. 75° in March, keeping soil moderately moist; by cuttings of the tops of the plants inserted in small pots of sandy, gritty compost in spring; by grafting on *Cereus speciossimus* at any time.

SPECIES CULTIVATED: *M. compressa* (syn. *M. augularis*), rosy purple, summer, 4 to 8 in., Mexico; *echinaria*, rose, summer, 6 in., Mexico; *elongata* (syn. *M. Stella-aurata*), yellow, summer, 3 in., Mexico; *floribunda*, rose, summer, 5 in., Chile; *geminispina* (syn. *M. bicolor*), purple, June, 6 to 12 in., Mexico; *Haageana*, carmine rose, June, 4 in., Mexico; *multiceps*, yellow and red, summer, 1 ft., Mexico; *Neumanniana*, rose, summer, 6 in., Mexico; *pulchra*, rose, June, 4 in., Mexico; *pycnacantha*, yellow, July, 6 in., Mexico; *Schelhasei*, white and rose, summer, 4 in., Mexico; *Schiedeana*, white, summer, 3 in., Mexico; *sempervivi*, 3 in., Mexico; *spinosissima* (syn. *A. sanguinea*), crimson, June, 6 in., Mexico; *tetracantha*, rose, July, 9 in., Mexico; *turbinata*, yellow, June, Mexico; *uncinata*, purple, May and June, 4 in., Mexico; *vetula*, yellow, May and June, 3 in., Mexico; *villifera*, rose and purple, May, 3 in., Mexico; *viridis*, yellow, May and June, 4 in., Mexico; *Wildii*, rose, summer, 3 to 4 in., Mexico; *Wrightii*, purple, May, Mexico; *Zuccariniana*, purple, May and June, 3 in., Mexico.

Mammoth Tree of California, see *Sequoiadendron giganteum*.

Mandevilla—*Apocynaceae*. Greenhouse flowering deciduous climber. First introduced early nineteenth century.

CULTURE: Compost, equal parts peat and loam, half-part each of sand and pounded charcoal. Position, well-drained beds or borders; shoots trained up trellis, pillars, or roof of sunny greenhouse. Plant, Feb. Water freely Feb. to Sept., moderately Sept. to Dec., none afterwards. Syringe twice daily Feb. to July. Temp., Feb. to Sept. 55° to 65°, Sept. to Dec. 45° to 55°, Dec. to Feb. 40° to 50°. Prune shoots to within two buds of their base immediately after flowering.

PROPAGATION: By seeds sown in pans or bed of sandy peat slightly covered with fine soil in a temp. of 65° to 75°, Feb. to April; cuttings of firm side shoots, 2 to 3 in. long, inserted in sand under bell-glass in temp. of 70° to 85° in summer.

SPECIES CULTIVATED: *M. laxa* (syn. *M. suaveolens*), 'Chilean Jasmine', white, fragrant, summer, 15 to 30 ft., Buenos Ayres.

Mandragora (Mandrake)—*Solanaceae*. Hardy perennial herbs. First introduced early sixteenth century.

CULTURE: Soil, deep rich. Position, well-drained sunny borders. Plant, Oct. or March.

PROPAGATION: By seeds sown in pans or boxes in cool greenhouse in March; careful division in March.

SPECIES CULTIVATED: *M. autumnalis*, violet, Sept., 6 to 12 in., S. Europe; *officinarum*, 'Devil's Apple', greenish yellow, May, 1 ft., S. Europe.

Manettia—*Rubiaceae*. Greenhouse evergreen climber. First introduced early nineteenth century.

CULTURE: Compost, equal parts loam and peat, with a liberal admixture of pounded charcoal and silver sand. Position, well-drained pots or beds; shoots trained to trellises, round pillars, or up rafters. Plant, Feb. to March. Prune slightly after flowering. Water freely March to Sept., moderately afterwards. Syringe daily March to Sept. Temp., Feb. to Oct. 55° to 65°, Oct. to Feb. 45° to 55°.

PROPAGATION: By seeds sown in shallow pans of sandy soil, slightly covered with fine soil, and placed in temp. 55° to 65°, Feb. or March; cuttings of young shoots, 2 to 3 in. long, inserted in small pots of sandy soil in temp. 65° to 75° in summer.

SPECIES CULTIVATED: *M. bicolor*, scarlet and orange, Brazil; *glabra*, scarlet, Aug. to Oct., S. America; *inflata*, scarlet and orange, March to Dec., 10 to 15 ft.. Paraguay and Uraguay.

Mangel, Mangold, see *Beta vulgaris.*

Mangosteen Tree, see *Garcinia Mangostana.*

Manihot—*Euphorbiaceae.* Stove and greenhouse herbs or evergreen shrubs with ornamental foliage. Some species of great economic value. First introduced early eighteenth century.

CULTURE: Compost, equal parts fibrous loam, peat and leaf-mould, with sharp sand and crushed charcoal added. Position, well-drained pots or tubs in warm greenhouse or stove, or planted out in border of well-drained soil. Pot or plant, March or April. Water freely March to Sept., moderately afterwards. Keep deciduous type dry at roots during winter. Temp., March to Oct. 65° to 75°, Oct. to March 50° to 60°.

PROPAGATION: By cuttings of firm young shoots inserted in sand or sandy peat under bell-glass or in a warm propagating case with bottom heat in spring.

SPECIES CULTIVATED: *M. dulcis*, shrub to 9 ft. with edible roots, S. America, and var. *Aipi*, ' Sweet Cassava '; *esculenta* (syn. *M. utilissima*), ' Tapioca ', ' Cassava ', yellowish with attractive foliage, summer, 3 ft., Brazil, and var. *variegata*, a most handsome ornamental plant; *Glaziovii*, ' Ceara Rubber ', tree to 30 ft., Brazil.

Manila Hemp, see *Musa textilis.*

Maple, see Acer; **Flowering-,** see Abutilon.

Maranta—*Marantaceae.* Stove herbaceous perennials with ornamental foliage. First introduced early eighteenth century.

CULTURE: Compost, two parts fibrous peat, one part rich loam, one part sand. Position, well-drained pots in shady part of stove. Pot, Feb. or March. Water abundantly March to Sept., moderately Sept. to Dec., keep nearly dry afterwards. Syringe daily March to Sept. Apply weak stimulants occasionally during summer. Temp., Feb. to Oct. 65° to 75°, Oct. to Feb. 55° to 65°. Repot annually.

PROPAGATION: By division of tubers or rhizomes in Feb. or March.

SPECIES CULTIVATED: *M. arundinacea*, ' Arrowroot ', white, to 6 ft., Trop. America, and var. *variegata*, leaves green and white; *bicolor*, leaves olive green, 1 ft., Brazil; *leuconeura*, leaves light green, white, and purple, 1 ft., Brazil, and vars. *Kerchoveana*, leaves spotted with red, and *Massangeana*, leaves purple beneath. See also Calathea.

Marattia—*Marattiaceae.* Greenhouse evergreen ferns with long, feather-shaped fronds; leaflets twice or three times divided. First introduced late eighteenth century.

CULTURE: Compost, two parts peat, one each of loam, leaf-mould and sand. Position, large well-drained pots or moist beds. Pot or plant, Feb. or March. Shade from sun essential. Water freely March to Oct., moderately afterwards. Syringing not required. Temp., Feb. to Oct. 60° to 70°, Oct. to Feb. 50° to 60°.

PROPAGATION: By spores sown on surface of sandy peat in shallow, well-drained pans placed under bell-glass in temp. 65° to 75° any time.

SPECIES CULTIVATED: *M. alata*, Cent. America; *attenuata* (syn. *M. Cooperi*), fronds to 4 ft., New Caledonia; *fraxinea*, 'Ash Leaf Fern', fronds to 12 ft., S. Africa, Malaya, New Zealand; *laxa*, large, fleshy fronds, Mexico.

Mare's Tail, see Hippuris.

Marguerite, see *Chrysanthemum frutescens*; **Blue-,** see *Felicia amelloides*; **Golden-,** see *Anthemis tinctoria.*

Marigold, see Tagetes; **Pot-** or **Scotch-,** see Calendula.

Marica, see Neomarica.

Margyricarpus—*Rosaceae.* Hardy evergreen trailing shrub. First introduced early nineteenth century.
CULTURE: Soil, equal parts leaf-mould, loam and sand. Position, sunny rockery, with shoots trailing over stones. Plant, Feb. to May.
PROPAGATION: By seeds sown $\frac{1}{16}$ in. deep in shallow boxes of light, sandy soil in cold frame in autumn or spring; cuttings of young shoots, 1 to 2 in. long, inserted in sandy peat under bell-glass in cold frame in summer; layering branches in Sept. or Oct.
SPECIES CULTIVATED: *M. setosus*, 'Pearl Fruit', green, summer, berries white, prostrate, Chile.

Marjoram, see Majorana.

Marmalade Plum, see *Achras Zapota.*

Marrubium (Horehound)—*Labiatae.* Hardy perennial medicinal herb. Leaves and young shoots used as a popular remedy for coughs.
CULTURE: Soil, ordinary. Position, sunny, dry borders. Plant, March or April.
PROPAGATION: By seeds sown $\frac{1}{8}$ in. deep in shady position outdoors, March to May; cuttings inserted in shady border in April; division of roots in March.
SPECIES CULTIVATED: *M. vulgare*, white, June to Sept., 1 ft., Britain.

Marsh Calla, see *Calla palustris*; **-Fern,** see *Dryopteris Thelypteris*; **-Hypericum,** see *Hydrocleys elodes*; **-Mallow,** see *Althaea officinalis*; **-Marigold,** see *Caltha palustris*; **-Rosemary,** see *Ledum palustre* and *Andromeda polifolia*; **-Trefoil,** see *Menyanthes trifoliata.*

Markhamia—*Bignoniaceae.* Tropical trees and shrubs with large, persistent, pinnately compound leaves and tubular-funnel shaped flowers in panicles.
CULTURE: Compost, ordinary. Position, warm or cool greenhouse.
PROPAGATION: By seed.
SPECIES CULTIVATED: *M. platycalyx*, yellow, Aug. to Sept. tree to 35 ft. or more, Cent. Africa.

Martynia—*Martyniaceae.* Half-hardy annual. See also Ibicella and Proboscidea.
CULTURE: Sow seed in warm house in March, prick off and grow on in genial warmth until danger of frost is past, when they can be planted out in warm position.
SPECIES CULTIVATED: *M. annua*, reddish-purple, summer, Cent. America, W. Indies.

Marvel of Peru, see *Mirabilis Jalapa.*

Maryland Dittany, see *Cunila origanoides*; **-Pink Root,** see *Spigelia marilandica.*

Masdevallia—*Orchidaceae.* A large epiphytic genus, pseudo-bulbs absent, stems short, clustered, peduncles sheathed from their base, leaves single. Several sections are made. Flowers brightly coloured in many. Some made more distinctive by the sepals, the larger of the segments having their extremities developed into tails. The Chimaera section has the sepals spreading, the lip in evidence. In many of the others, their bases assume a more or less tubular form, concealing, or nearly so, the smaller petals and lip. In the coccinea group, the two lower sepals are spread and are brightly coloured, the tails on the lower sepals very short. Variations and gradations occur throughout.

CULTURE: Compost and general treatment and temp. should be as for Odontoglossums of the *O. crispum* type. As all are pseudo-bulbless, rest is prohibited. At no time should the compost be allowed to become really dry. Pans or well-drained pots suit the majority. A moist atmosphere should be maintained. Shading is necessary. The Chimaera section should not fall below 50° in the winter, 55° is better, but during the spring, summer and early autumn the Odontoglossum house suits. Their flowers are often produced in succession on thin wiry peduncles, often laterally inclined, hence small baskets for them are better than pots. If pans are used, slightly mound the compost centrally. Suspend them near the glass, night air should be admitted whenever weather allows. Draughts must be avoided. A black smudge sometimes seen, principally on the backs of the leaves, is often due to lack of sweet air. A change of position often benefits. Stale compost may also be the cause. Several hybrids have been raised and a few occur naturally.

PROPAGATION: By division of plants in early spring.

SPECIES CULTIVATED: A selection—*M. amabilis*, orange-red to orange-yellow, with crimson veins, tails dull red, spring, summer, Colombia; *angulata*, large, dull crimson-red, tails short, autumn, Ecuador; *Barlaeana*, tube bent, coral-red above, tails red, lower sepals carmine, lined crimson, summer, Peru; *bella*, solitary, large, yellowish, thickly spotted chocolate-red, upper tail 3 or 4 in. long, lip shell-shape, ribbed, autumn, various vars. Colombia; *caloptera*, small, 2-3 whitish, violet purple, tails short, yellow, various, Peru; *calura*, chocolate-red, tails orange-yellow, the lower shorter, spring, summer, Costa Rica; *Carderi*, bell-shaped, whitish, blotched purple-brown, tails yellow, pendent, summer, autumn, Colombia; *caudata*, dwarf, tube open, large, yellow, spotted and marked red, lower sepals mauve-purple mottled white, tails divergent, yellow, and var. *xanthocorys*, smaller, yellow, rose spotted and flushed; *Chestertonii*, comparatively small, in succession, greenish-yellow, marked black-purple, lip yellowish, ribs red, tails short, blackish, summer, autumn, Colombia; *Chimaera*, variable, large, in succession, yellowish, hispid, with dark red spots, lip slipper-shape, ribbed, tails reddish, 3 to 4 in. long, various seasons, Colombia, and many vars.; *coccinea* (syn. *M. Harryana*), beautiful, very variable, magenta-purple, tube short, upper sepal smaller than lower, tails erect, spring, Colombia, among the many named vars. are *alba*, creamy white, *armeniaca*, apricot, *atrosanguinea*, blood-red, *Gravesiae*, white, tinged buff, *Lindenii*, lilac-magenta, *Sanderae*, white, yellow tinged, *coriacea*, tube rather large, tails short, broad, whitish, yellow shaded, purple spotted, *corniculata*, brownish-red, tails yellow, large bract behind, summer, Colombia; *Davisii*, yellow with orange marking, tail erect, spring, summer, Peru; *deorsa*, pendent habit, buff yellow and purplish-brown, upper tail 2½ in. long, yellow, lower, shorter, summer, Colombia; *elephanticeps* (syn. *M. Gargantua*), large, scape short, tube large, yellowish, purplish-red, tails yellow upper 2 to 3 in. long, variable, malodorous, various seasons, Colombia; *ephippium* (syn. *M. trochilus*), scape 3-sided, yellowish-brown to chestnut-brown, lower sepals forming a ribbed cup, tails yellow, 3 to 4 in. long, flowers in succession, autumn, Colombia; *ignea*, cinnabar red, crimson veined, dorsal tail always inclined downwards, spring, Colombia, and var. *militaris* (syn. *M. militaris*), brilliant red and scarlet; *muscosa*, scape erect with short stiff hairs, flowers, 1 or 2, brownish, tails short, yellowish, lip projecting, on being touched by an insect it snaps up enclosing the insect for a short time, spring, autumn, Colombia; *polysticta*, scapes erect, flowers rather small, tube short, white, purple spotted, tails stiff, yellow, spring, Peru; *Schroderiana*, whitish to purple, tails yellow, tube campanulate, spring, Colombia; *tovarensis*, pure white, winter, Venezuela; *trinema* (syn. *M. Lowii*), whitish, thickly spotted red-purple, lip small, various, Colombia; *Veitchiana*, very fine, large, brilliant orange, with crimson-purple papillae on outer halves of lower sepals, upper tail 1 to 2 in. long, spring, Peru, and var. *grandiflora*, larger, more brilliant.

Maskflower, see Alonsoa.

Mastic, see *Pistacia Lentiscus*.

Masterwort, see Astrantia.

Mathiola (Stock)—*Cruciferae.*· Annual, biennial or perennial herbs. Sometimes spelt Matthiola. First introduced early eighteenth century.

CULTURE OF TEN-WEEK STOCK OUTDOORS: Soil, deep, rich, well manured. Position, open, sunny beds or borders. Sow seeds 1/16 in. deep in light soil in temp. 50° to 55° in March, transplanting seedlings outdoors end of May; or in cold frame or outdoors in April, transplanting seedlings in June. Plant, dwarf kinds 9 in. and tall kinds 12 to 15 in. apart each way. Mulch surface of soil after planting, with decayed manure. Remove seed pods as they form.

POT CULTURE OF TEN-WEEK STOCK: Sow seeds as above advised. Transplant three seedlings 1 in. high into a 3 in. pot, and when 3 to 4 in. high into a 5 in. pot. Compost, two parts good soil, one part decayed manure and sand. Position, cold frame during May; afterwards outdoors. Water freely.

CULTURE OF WALLFLOWER-LEAVED STOCK: As for Brompton.

CULTURE OF NIGHT-SCENTED STOCK: Soil, ordinary. Position, sunny beds or borders. Sow seeds 1/8 in. deep in April where required to flower.

CULTURE OF INTERMEDIATE STOCK: Sow seeds 1/8 in. deep in light soil in well-drained pots or boxes in cold frame in June or July. Transplant seedlings when 1 in. high singly in a 2 in. pot or four in a 4 in. pot, or in sheltered border out of doors. Compost, equal parts loam, leaf-mould and old mortar. Plunge pots to rim in cinder ashes in sunny, cold frame. Water sparingly. Ventilate freely in fine weather. Plant out in rich soil in March, or transfer single plants to a 5 in. or three plants to a 6 in. pot. Water moderately. For autumn flowering, sow seeds in March or April and plant out in June.

CULTURE OF BROMPTON AND QUEEN STOCKS: Sow seeds 1/8 in. deep in light soil in cold frame in June or July. Transplant seedlings when 1 in. high 8 to 12 in. apart where required to flower following year; or place singly in 2 in. pots, keep in cold frame, and plant out in March. Seed saving: Largest percentage of double flowers obtained from plants grown in poor soil and of the dwarfest habit.

SPECIES CULTIVATED: *M. bicornis*, 'Night-scented Stock', lilac, summer, fragrant at night, 1 ft., annual, Greece; *incana*, 'Brompton Stock', purple varying to yellow, white, blush, fragrant, often double, spring to summer, 1 to 2 ft., biennial or perennial, S. Europe, and var. *annua* (syn. *M. annua*), 'Ten-Week Stock', 'Intermediate Stock', annual.

Matricaria—*Compositae*. Hardy perennial herb.

CULTURE: Soil, ordinary. Position, open, sunny beds or borders. Plant, Oct., March or April.

PROPAGATION: By cuttings inserted in ordinary soil in shady position outdoors in spring; division of roots in March.

SPECIES CULTIVATED: *M. inodora plenissima*, 'Double Mayweed', white, double, summer, 1 ft., Britain.

Matteuccia, see Pteretis.

Matrimony Vine, see Lycium.

Maurandia—*Scrophulariaceae*. Half-hardy climbing perennials. First introduced late eighteenth century.

INDOOR CULTURE: Compost, equal parts loam and leaf-mould and little sand. Pot, March to May. Position, well-drained pots with shoots draping over front of stage, or trained up trellises, walls, or rafters, or suspended in baskets in sunny greenhouse. Water freely March to Sept., moderately Sept. to Nov., keep nearly dry afterwards. Apply stimulants to healthy plants in flower only. Temp., March to Sept. 55° to 65°, Sept. to March 45° to 55°.

OUTDOOR CULTURE: Soil, ordinary rich. Position, against south walls or in sunny vases or window boxes. Plant, June. Lift, repot and place in greenhouse in Sept. Water freely in dry weather.

PROPAGATION: By seeds sown $\frac{1}{16}$ in. deep in ordinary light soil in temp. of 60° to 70° in March, transplanting seedlings when 1 in. high singly into 2 or 3 in. pots; cuttings of young shoots inserted in sandy soil under bell-glass in temp. 55° to 65°, March to Aug.

SPECIES CULTIVATED: *M. Barclaiana*, violet-purple, summer, Mexico; *erubescens* (commonly grown as *M. scandens*), rose and white, summer, Mexico; *Purpusii*, violet, summer, to 2 ft., Mexico; *scandens*, purple and violet, summer, Mexico.

Maxillaria—*Orchidaceae*. An epiphytic genus, over 200 species, varying greatly, many of minor interest and attraction, others of considerable size and beauty. Pseudo-bulbs general, absent in a few. Scapes, single flowered, from base. A few are scandent or ascendent in habit, others bear a single, rather large, leaf, keeled behind, at the apex of the pseudo-bulbs, the greater number have more or less ovoid pseudo-bulbs with one or two strap-shaped, persistent leaves.

CULTURE: The variation demands slight differences in treatment. Compost for all can consist of three parts osmunda fibre, one part sphagnum moss. Peat may be used but should have finely crushed potsherds incorporated. Pots, well drained, are suitable, but the very small-growing kinds should have pans and, more moss. The winter rest must be governed by the nature of the plant. For hard-bulbed, hard-leaved species it should be decided, occasional waterings may be required. For the species with strongly keeled leaves, e.g. *M. venusta*, *M. Sanderiana*, water can seldom be withheld for more than a week or two, and their winter temp. should not fall below 55° nor should the syringe be used too freely on them or brown spots appear on their foliage. On other forms it may be freely used as soon as the leaves are free. Like Lycaste, they are well suited to the cool house, with a winter night temp. of 50°, no pipe heat in the summer, light shading is required, air at night when favourable. Summer temp. with humidity and by sun heat with shading can rise to 75° or 80°.

PROPAGATION: By division of the plants in spring.

SPECIES CULTIVATED: A selection—*M. acutipetala*, orange-yellow, blotched red, lip whitish, spring, Cent. America; *crocea*, yellow segments, tapered, autumn, spring, Brazil; *dichroma*, fleshy, white, flushed fawn and red in parts, autumn, winter, Ecuador; *elegantula*, white, chrome-yellow, chocolate-red and red spots, lip margined red, usually summer, Ecuador; *Fletcheriana*, large, cream-white, purplish-red lined, lip large, yellow, purple marked, spring, Peru; *fractiflexa*, sepals and petals 6 in. long, twisted, white, flushed purple, various, Ecuador; *fucata*, white, terra cotta, yellow, red spotted, lip red-brown, yellow, spring, summer, Ecuador; *grandiflora*, white, lip yellowish with flushes and streaks of crimson, spring, Ecuador, Brazil, Peru; *iridifolia*, pendent, small, yellowish, spring, summer, Brazil, W. Indies; *lepidota*, sepals long, tapered, yellow to purple-brown, petals yellow, autumn, Colombia; *Lindeniae*, large, white, lip margined red, winter, Ecuador; *luteo alba*, large, white and tawny yellow, spring, various, Venezuela; *macrura* (syn. *M. longisepala*), dark red, sepals and petals narrow, long, drooping, summer, various, Venezuela; *nigrescens*, brownish wine-purple, winter, spring, Colombia; *oceophylla*, large, old gold, copper-brown, mid-lobe of lip white, various, habitat unknown; *ochroleuca*, fragrant, segments narrow, whitish, yellowish, scapes fasciated, spring, summer, Brazil; *praestans*, yellowish, red dotted, spring, Guatemala; *Sanderiana*, very large, whitish, blotched blood-red, variable, basket, spring, Ecuador; *scurrilis*, segments narrow, long, white, blotched blackish brown, summer, Colombia; *striata*, large, yellow, striped and streaked chocolate-red, autumn, Ecuador, and var. *grandiflora*, larger, more richly coloured; *tenuifolia*, ascendant habit, dark red, broken with yellow, needs a support, summer, autumn, Mexico; *venusta*, very fragrant, large, white, segments tapered, autumn, Colombia, Venezuela.

May, see *Crataegus Oxyacantha*; **-Apple,** see Podophyllum; **-flower,** see *Epigaea repens*; **-Lily,** see Convallaria.

Mazus—*Scrophulariaceae.* Hardy dwarf perennial herbs, suitable for rockery culture. First introduced late eighteenth century.

CULTURE: Soil, moist, sandy loam. Position, sunny rockery. Plant in spring.

PROPAGATION: By seeds sown in sandy soil in April in a cold frame, the seedlings being grown on until the following spring before planting out; by division of the tufts in spring.

SPECIES CULTIVATED: *M. Pumilio,* purplish blue, May to Oct., 2 in., New Zealand; *reptans,* rosy lavender, white and brown, May to Oct., 1 in., Himalaya; *japonicus* (syn. *M. rugosus*), lilac-blue, summer, Asia.

Meadow Beauty, see Rhexia; **-Rue,** see Thalictrum; **-sweet,** see Filipendula.

Meconopsis—*Papaveraceae.* Hardy monocarpic and perennial herbs.

CULTURE OF MONOCARPIC SPECIES: Sow seeds $\frac{1}{16}$ in. deep in light, sandy soil in temp. 60° to 70° in March or April. Transplant seedlings when large enough to handle into a cold frame and plant out in permanent positions as soon as they have formed tufts of seven or eight leaves each. Soil, deep loam with sand, leaf-mould and peat. Position, well-drained sunny rockery. Water freely in summer; keep dry as possible in winter. Monocarpic species flower when two to four years old and afterwards die.

CULTURE OF PERENNIAL SPECIES: Soil, deep rich loam mixed freely with decayed manure and leaf-mould. Position, sunny, sheltered borders or rockeries. Plant, March or April. Water, as above advised.

PROPAGATION: Perennial species by seeds sown $\frac{1}{16}$ in. deep in light, sandy soil in temp. 55° to 60° as soon as ripe or in Feb. or March, transplanting as advised above for monocarpic species.

MONOCARPIC SPECIES CULTIVATED: *M. aculeata,* pale blue and violet, 12 to 16 in., N.W. Himalaya; *Delavayi,* violet, 6 to 8 in., W. China; *horridula,* blue, to 5 ft., Cent. and E. Asia; *integrifolia,* primrose yellow, May to Aug., 18 in., W. China; *lancifolia,* violet, 3 to 6 in., Cent. Asia; *paniculata,* yellow, July to Aug., 5 to 6 ft., W. China; *punicea,* crimson, late autumn, 1 to 1½ ft., Tibet; *pseudo-integrifolia,* sulphur yellow, 6 to 8 in., W. China; *racemosa,* lavender blue or violet, 18 in., W. China and Tibet; *rigidiuscula,* blue, 2 to 2½ ft., E. Asia; *simplicifolia,* sky blue, summer, 2 ft., Himalaya; *sinuata,* pale blue, May to June, 1 to 1½ ft., E. Himalaya.

PERENNIAL SPECIES CULTIVATED: *M. betonicifolia,* 'Himalayan Poppy', 'Tibetan Poppy', 'Blue Poppy', azure blue, June and July, 3 to 4 ft., Himalaya, and var. *Baileyi* (syn. *M. Baileyi*), the form usually cultivated; *cambrica,* 'Welsh Poppy', yellow, summer, 1 ft., Europe (Br.), and var. *plena,* double-flowered; *grandis,* violet blue or slaty blue, June, 3 ft., Sikkim; *napaulensis* (syn. *M. Wallichii*), 'Satin Poppy', blue, summer, 4 to 6 ft., Himalaya; *quintuplinervia,* lavender blue, May, 12 to 18 in., Tibet; *regia,* yellow flowers, ornamental foliage, summer, 2 ft., Nepal.

Medicago—*Leguminosae.* Hardy annual. Flowers succeeded by curiously twisted legumes. First introduced early nineteenth century.

CULTURE: Sow seeds $\frac{1}{8}$ in. deep in ordinary soil in sunny position outdoors, April or May. Thin seedlings when 1 in. high to 6 in. apart. Water freely in dry weather.

POT CULTURE: Compost, any good soil. Sow seeds thinly in 5 in. pots filled with above compost. When seedlings are 1 in. high, thin to 3 in each pot. Water moderately. Position, sunny window or greenhouse.

SPECIES CULTIVATED: *M. Echinus,* 'Calvary Clover', yellow, summer, 6 in., S. Europe.

Medinilla—*Melastomaceae.* Stove evergreen flowering shrubs. First introduced early nineteenth century.

CULTURE: Compost, two parts fibrous peat, one part loam, half part sand, half part well-decayed manure. Position, sunny, moist part of stove Feb. to Sept.; light and moderately dry part afterwards. Pot, Feb. Temp., Feb. to Sept. 75° to 85°, Sept. to Nov. 70° to 80°, Nov. to Feb. 65° to 75°. Water freely March to Sept., moderately afterwards. Syringe twice daily March to Sept. Moist atmosphere very essential. Apply stimulants when plants commence flowering. Prune straggling shoots into shape, Jan. or Feb.

PROPAGATION: By cuttings of firm young side shoots, 3 to 4 in. long, inserted in sandy peat and leaf-mould under bell-glass in temp. 85° in spring or summer.

SPECIES CULTIVATED: *M. Curtisii*, white, Sumatra; *javanensis*, pale pink, winter, 4 ft., Java; *magnifica*, rosy pink, May, 4 ft., Philippines, and var. *superba*; *Teysmannii* (syn. *M. amabilis*), rosy pink, spring, 4 ft., Java.

Medlar, see *Mespilus germanica*.

Megaclinium—*Orchidaceae*. An epiphytic genus, allied to Bulbophyllum. Flowers similar in structure to those of Bulbophyllum, small, placed generally on both sides of a curiously enlarged, flattened rachis, on the central rib. In many the rachis, 3 to 6 in. long, is bent at right-angles to the peduncle. The majority in cultivation are small-growing, with hard bulbs and leaves.

CULTURE: Compost, as for Bulbophyllum. Coming from Africa they enjoy a warm moist atmosphere. Pans are preferable to pots as they can be suspended near the glass. A rather decided rest should be given. Winter temp. 60° to 70°.

PROPAGATION: By division of the plants in spring.

SPECIES CULTIVATED: A selection—*M. Clarkei*, greenish, purplish, brown, spring, West Coast of Africa; *eburneum*, ivory white, yellow, spring, Gold Coast; *falcatum*, reddish-brown, Sierra Leone; *leucorachis*, yellow, summer, Upper Guinea; *maximum*, yellowish, variable, often spotted red-brown, summer, Sierra Leone; *purpureo-rachis*, yellowish shaded brown, spotted purple-red, broad, spiralled, 2 ft. high, spring, various, West Coast of Africa.

Megasea, see Bergenia.

Melaleuca—*Myrtaceae*. Greenhouse flowering shrubs. First introduced late eighteenth century.

CULTURE: Compost, equal parts peat, loam and silver sand. Position, pots in greenhouse or well-drained borders in the open at base of south wall in the mildest counties. Pot or plant, March or April. Prune shoots a little after flowering. Water freely April to Sept., moderately afterwards. Temp., March to Sept. 55° to 65°, Sept. to March 40° to 50°.

PROPAGATION: By cuttings of nearly ripened shoots inserted in sandy peat under hand-light in temp. 55° to 65° during July or Aug.

SPECIES CULTIVATED: *M. armillaris*, white, June, 10 to 30 ft., Australia; *decussata*, lilac, Aug., 15 to 20 ft., Australia; *ericifolia*, yellowish white, July to Sept., 15 to 20 ft., Australia; *hypericifolia*, rich red, July to Aug., 10 to 20 ft., Australia; *Leucadendra*, 'Cajuput-tree', creamy white, 20 ft., or more, Australia; *linariifolia*, white, 15 to 20 ft., Australia; *striata*, pink, June, 4 ft., Australia; *thymifolia*, purple, June to Sept., 2 ft., Australia.

Melandrium, see Lychnis.

Melia (Bead-tree)—*Meliaceae*. Slightly tender deciduous flowering tree with graceful, feather-shaped, green leaves. First introduced mid-seventeenth century.

CULTURE: Soil, sandy loam. Position, large well-drained pots in cool greenhouse or conservatory, or sheltered shrubberies outdoors south of England. Pot or plant, Oct. to Feb. Water freely (in pots) March to Oct., little afterwards.

PROPAGATION: By cuttings inserted in sand under bell-glass in temp. 55° to 65°, summer or autumn.

SPECIES CULTIVATED: *M. Azadirachta*, bluish, summer, to 20 ft., India; *Azedarach*, 'Indian Lilac', lilac, summer, leaves fragrant, to 40 ft., India and China, and var. *umbraculiformis*, 'Texas Umbrella Tree'.

Melianthus—*Melianthaceae*.   Slightly tender evergreen shrubs with graceful, feather-shaped, green leaves.   First introduced late seventeenth century.

Pot Culture: Compost, two parts loam, one part leaf-mould and sand. Position, well-drained pots in sunny greenhouse.   Pot, Feb. or April.   Water freely March to Oct., moderately afterwards.   Temp., March to Sept. 55° to 65°, Sept. to March 40° to 50°.

Outdoor Culture: Soil, ordinary rich.   Position, sunny beds or borders. Plant, May or June.   Cover roots and base of plant with dry litter in late Sept. as protection from frost or else lift, pot and winter in cool greenhouse or conservatory. May be grown entirely outdoors in warm, sheltered parts of England.

Propagation: By seeds sown $\frac{1}{16}$ in. deep in light, sandy soil in temp. 65° to 75° in Jan., Feb. or March, or in similar soil in temp. 55° to 65° in Aug. or Sept.; by cuttings inserted in light, sandy soil under bell-glass in temp. 55° to 65° in spring or summer.

Species Cultivated: *M. comosus*, orange-red and green, autumn, 3 to 5 ft., S. Africa; *major*, ' Cape Honey Flower ', brown, summer, 4 to 6 ft., S. Africa; *minor*, dark brown, Aug., 5 ft., S. Africa; *pectinatus*, scarlet, winter, 6 to 10 ft., S. Africa.

Meliosma—*Sabiaceae*.   Deciduous trees and shrubs.   Hardy, or nearly so, with panicles of spiraea-like flowers.   First introduced late nineteenth century.

Culture: Soil, good loamy.   Position, sheltered shrubberies, or as specimen plants on lawns.   *M. myriantha* requires protection when young in all but the mildest parts of the country.

Propagation: By cuttings of half-ripened shoots inserted in sandy soil and slight bottom heat during July.

Species Cultivated: *M. cuneifolia*, yellowish white, fragrant, summer, to 20 ft., W. China; *myriantha*, yellowish white, fragrant, June to July, 20 ft., Japan, etc.; *Veitchiorum*, white, purplish-black berries, 30 to 40 ft., W. China.

Melissa (Balm)—*Labiatae*.   Hardy herbaceous perennials with lemon-scented leaves; used in seasoning and liqueurs, and also as medicine.

Culture: Soil, ordinary light.   Position, warm, sunny beds or borders.   Plant, Oct. or March in groups or 12 in. apart in rows.   Gather stems when flowers open for drying for winter use.   Cut stems off close to ground after flowering.

Propagation: By seeds sown $\frac{1}{8}$ in. deep outdoors in March; division of roots in Oct. or March.

Species Cultivated: *M. officinalis*, ' Balm ', white or yellow, summer, 3 ft., Europe (Br.), and var. *variegata*, leaves golden.

Melittis—*Labiatae*.   Hardy perennial.

Culture: Soil, ordinary rich.   Position, partially shaded beds or borders. Plant, Oct., March, or April.

Propagation: By division of roots directly after flowering.

Species Cultivated: *M. Melissophyllum*, ' Bastard Balm ', creamy white and pink, May, 18 in., Europe (Br.).

Melocactus (Cactus)—*Cactaceae*.   Greenhouse succulent perennial with globular, ribbed, spiny stems surmounted by a cylindrical cap.   First introduced late eighteenth century.

Culture: Compost, two parts fibrous sandy loam, one part brick rubble, old mortar and sand.   Position, well-drained pots in sunny greenhouse or window. Repot every three or four years in March.   Water once a month Sept. or April; once a week afterwards.   Temp., Sept. to March 50° to 55°, March to Sept. 65° to 75°.

Propagation: By seeds sown $\frac{1}{8}$ in. deep in well-drained pans of sandy soil in temp. 75° in March, keeping soil moderately moist; cuttings of stems inserted in small pots of sandy soil kept barely moist in summer; grafting on common kinds in April.

SPECIES CULTIVATED: *M. Broadwayi*, ' Turk's Cap Cactus ' or ' Melon Cactus ', rosy red, summer, 12 to 18 in., W. Indies.

Melon, see *Cucumis Melo*;   **Water-,** see *Citrullus vulgaris.*

Menispermum (Moon Seed)—*Menispermaceae.* Hardy deciduous flowering climber. First introduced late seventeenth century.

CULTURE: Soil, ordinary rich. Position, moist, shady borders with shoots twined up walls, arbours, pergolas, or trellises. Plant, Oct. or March. Prune away weak or unhealthy shoots, Nov. to Feb.

PROPAGATION: By cuttings of young shoots inserted in sandy soil in shady position outdoors, or under hand-light in spring; division of roots, Oct. to March.

SPECIES CULTIVATED: *M. canadense*, yellow, summer, 10 to 15 ft., N. America.

Mentha (Mint)—*Labiatae.* Hardy aromatic herbs grown for oil and as garden herbs and as ornamental creeping plants.

CULTURE OF CULINARY MINTS: Soil, moist, rich. Renew beds every three years. Cut to ground level in late June and a second crop will develop. Spread thinly on trays and dry in a heat of 90° F. Force one-year-old uncropped runners by planting under glass in Oct. There are many fragrant mints grown as herbs for flavouring.

CULTURE OF MEDICINAL MINTS: Peppermint is usually grown for its valuable oil. In gardens, culture as for culinary mints, but on a commercial scale it is usual to plant on raised beds. Cut when in flower and partially dried before distilling.

CULTURE OF OTHER SPECIES: Soil, light rich. Position, partly-shaded borders. Plant, March or April. *M. Requienii* is an excellent creeping plant for covering surface of soil or paving in moist places. *M. Pulegium* var. *gibraltarica* should be wintered in a cold frame and planted out in April or May.

PROPAGATION: By summer cuttings in moist soil under a hand-light; division in Feb. or March; runners with some species.

SPECIES CULTIVATED: *M. aquatica*, ' Water Mint ', mauve, summer, 2½ ft., Europe (Br.); *piperita*, ' Peppermint ', purple, autumn, to 3 ft., Europe (Br.), var. *vulgaris*, ' Black Mint ', has purple stems and dark foliage; *Pulegium*, ' Pennyroyal ', var. *gibraltarica*, deep green, sometimes variegated leaves, 2 in., carpet bedding, W. Asia; *Requienii*, pale mauve, small creeping herb, Europe (Br.); *rotundifolia*, ' Apple Mint ', ' Round-leaved Mint ', robust and not very susceptible to rust, to 2 ft., Europe (Br.); *spicata* (*M. viridis* of trade lists), ' Green Pea Mint ' ' Lamb Mint ', ' Spearmint ', purple, Aug., 2 ft., Europe (Br.).

Mentzelia—*Loasaceae.* Hardy annuals. First introduced early nineteenth century.

CULTURE: Sow seeds ⅛ in. deep in light, sandy soil in temp. 55° to 65° till May; place in cold frame and plant outdoors in June; or sow outdoors in sunny borders in April or May. Soil, ordinary. Position, sunny well-drained borders.

SPECIES CULTIVATED: *M. bartonioides*, yellow, summer, 1 ft., U. S.; *decapetala*, white, fragrant, Aug., 1 ft., N. America; *Lindleyi* (syn. *Bartonia aurea*), golden yellow, summer, 1 ft., California.

Menyanthes—*Gentianaceae* (or *Menyanthaceae*). Hardy perennial aquatics.

CULTURE: Soil, ordinary mud or bog. Position, shallow streams, pools, or ponds, marshes and bogs. Plant, Sept. to Nov. and March or April.

PROPAGATION: By inserting pieces of creeping stems in the mud, March to Oct.

SPECIES CULTIVATED: *M. trifoliata*, ' Buck Bean ', ' Bog Bean ', ' Marsh Trefoil ', pinkish, fringed, fragrant, March to June, Europe (Br.).

Menziesia—*Ericaceae.* Hardy deciduous flowering shrub. First introduced early nineteenth century.

CULTURE: Soil, peaty loam. Position, sunny or partially shady shrubberies, borders or rock gardens. Plant, Nov. to Feb.

PROPAGATION: By seed sown in sandy peat in well-drained pans during Feb. in temp. 55° to 60°; cuttings of current year's growth during July in sandy soil and gentle bottom heat.

Species Cultivated: *M. ciliicalyx*, yellowish green, purple-tipped, May to June, 3 to 6 ft., Japan; *pilosa* (syn. *M. globularis*), yellowish white, May to June, 3 to 6 ft., Eastern N. America; *purpurea*, bright rosy purple, May to June, to 3 ft., Japan. See also Daboecia and Phyllodoce.

Mercury, see *Chenopodium Bonus-Henricus.*

Merendera (Pyrenean Meadow Saffron)—*Liliaceae.* Hardy bulbous perennials with fragrant flowers. First introduced early nineteenth century.

Culture: Soil, light, sandy loam enriched with decayed manure or leaf-mould Position, moist beds or rockeries, shrubbery borders, or lawns near shade of trees Plant bulbs 3 in. deep and 3 in. apart in July or Aug. Foliage dies down in June and July and does not reappear until after plant has flowered.

Propagation: By seeds sown ½ in. deep in bed of fine soil outdoors in Aug. or Sept., or in pans or boxes of similar soil in cold frame at same time, transplanting seedlings 3 in. apart when two years old; division of bulbs in Aug. Seedling bulbs do not flower until four or five years old.

Species Cultivated: *M. montana* (syn. *M. Bulbocodium*), rosy lilac, autumn, 3 in., Spain; *caucasica*, white, spring, 3 in., Caucasus; *persica*, lilac, Nov., 3 in., Persia; *sobolifera*, white, flushed pink, spring, 3 to 4 in., Asia Minor.

Mertensia—*Boraginaceae.* Hardy perennial herbs.

Culture: Soil, sandy peat and loam. Position, partially shady rockeries or borders. Plant, Oct. and Nov., March and April. Lift and replant in fresh soil every four or five years. *M. sibirica* will thrive in ordinary soil in partial shade.

Propagation: By seeds sown 1/16 in. deep in sandy peat in cold frame in autumn; division of roots in Oct. or March.

Species Cultivated: *M. brevistyla*, blue, spring, 9 in., Utah; *echioides*, blue, May to June, 6 in., Himalaya; *lanceolata* (syn. *M. coriacea*), turquoise-blue, May, 4 to 6 in., Colorado; *maritima*, blue, spring, 6 in., Europe (Br.); *moltkioides*, blue, May, 6 in., Himalaya; *primuloides*, blue, April to May, 9 in., Himalaya; *sibirica*, blue, May, 6 in., N. America; *stomatechoides*, blue, 9 in., May, California; *tibetica*, blue, spring, 6 to 9 in., Himalaya; *virginica* (syn. *M. pulmonarioides*), ‘ Virginian Cowslip ’, blue, May to June, 12 in., N. America.

Mesembryanthemum (Fig Marigold)—*Aizoaceae.* Greenhouse succulent plants. Many species formerly included here have been transferred to other genera including Aptenia, Carpobrotus, Conophytum, Cryophytum, Delosperma, Drosanthemum, Erepsia, Faucaria, Glottiphyllum, Lampranthus, Lithops, Pleiospilos, Ruschia and Trichodiadema.

Culture: Compost, equal parts old mortar, pounded crocks, sandy loam, well-decayed manure or leaf-mould and sand. Position, well-drained pots in sunny greenhouse or window; may be planted in sunny borders outdoors from June to Sept. Pot, March to May. Water freely April to Sept, keep nearly dry during winter. Temp., March to Oct. 55° to 65°, Oct. to March 40° to 50°.

Propagation: By seed; stem-cuttings in temp. 55° to 65°, March, Sept.

Species Cultivated: *M. alboroseum*, white, shrubby to 5 in., S. Africa; *album*, white, to 8 in., S. Africa; *bifoliatum*, rose-purple, stems branching underground, S. Africa; *paardebergense*, rose in dense cymes, decumbent or ascending to 8 in., S. Africa; *pachyphyllum*, rose-purple, branches crowned, S. Africa; *Putterillii*, rose-purple, solitary, shrubby, ascending or decumbent branches to 9 in., S. Africa; *Stanleyi*, yellow, solitary, fragrant, shrubby to 4 in., S. Africa; *verruculatum*, yellow, branches twisted or crooked to 1 ft. or more, S. Africa.

Mespilus—*Rosaceae.* Hardy, ornamental deciduous tree. Flowers, white or tinted pink, solitary; cultivated for its fruits.

Culture: Soil, ordinary. Position, sunny shrubberies, or as specimens on lawns. Plant, Nov. to Feb. Prune out weak and overcrowding wood in winter. Pick fruit before advent of frosts and store until over-ripe or bletted.

Propagation: By seeds sown in the open during March or April; germination slow, grafting in April on seedling stock or on pear, quince or hawthorn; budding on same stocks in July.

SPECIES CULTIVATED: *M. germanica* (syn. *Pyrus germanica*), ' Medlar ', white, May and June, fruits brown, to 20 ft., Europe and Asia Minor.

Metrosideros—*Myrtaceae.* Greenhouse evergreen flowering trees. First introduced early nineteenth century.

CULTURE: Compost, peaty loam and sand. Position, large well-drained pots or borders in cool greenhouse. Plant or pot, Oct. or April. Water freely during summer months. Temp., March to Sept. 55° to 65°, Sept. to March 40° to 50°.

PROPAGATION: By cuttings of young growth during May, inserted in sandy soil under hand-light in gentle bottom heat.

SPECIES CULTIVATED: *M. lucida*, bright red, to 60 ft., New Zealand; *robusta*, dark red, May, to 100 ft., New Zealand; *scandens*, white, Aug., to 40 ft., New Zealand; *tomentosa*, dark red, July, to 70 ft., New Zealand.

Meum—*Umbelliferae.* Hardy perennial aromatic herb.

CULTURE: Soil, ordinary. Position, sunny beds, borders, banks, or rockeries. Plant, Oct., March or April. Cut down flower stems, Sept. Water freely in dry weather.

PROPAGATION: By division of the roots, Oct., Nov., March or April.

SPECIES CULTIVATED: *M. athamanticum*, ' Baldmoney ', ' Spignel ', white, May, 1 ft., Europe (Br.).

Mexican Cigar-flower, see *Cuphea platycentra*; **-Clover,** see *Richardia scabra*; **-Orange-flower,** see *Choisya ternata*; **-Poppy,** see *Argemone mexicana*; **-Sunflower,** see *Tithonia rotundifolia*.

Mezeron, see *Daphne mezereum.*

Michaelmas Daisy, see Aster.

Michauxia—*Campanulaceae.* Hardy perennials. First introduced late eighteenth century.

CULTURE: Soil, moist, sandy loam. Position, warm, sheltered, sunny borders. Plant in Oct. or March. Best grown as biennials.

PROPAGATION: By seeds sown ⅛ in. deep in sunny position outdoors in April, transplanting seedlings into flowering position following July or Aug.; or by sowing seeds in April where plants are required to grow.

SPECIES CULTIVATED: *M. campanuloides*, white, July, 4 to 6 ft., Asia Minor; *Tchihatchewii* (syn. *M. Tchihatcheffii*), white, July to Sept., 5 to 7 ft., Asia Minor.

Michelia—*Magnoliaceae.* Rare evergreen flowering trees and shrubs, closely allied to Magnolia. First introduced late nineteenth century.

CULTURE: Soil, rich, deep, sandy loam. Position, border against south or west wall. Plant, March or April.

PROPAGATION: By seeds sown singly in small pots during Feb., in temp. 55° to 60°.

SPECIES CULTIVATED: *M. compressa*, pale yellow, fragrant, to 40 ft., Japan; *Doltsopa*, creamy white, April, 40 ft., Japan; *fuscata*, yellowish green and purple, very fragrant, June, 15 ft., Japan.

Miconia—*Melastomaceae.* Stove evergreen plants with broad leaves, upper surface velvety green, under side reddish purple. First introduced mid-nineteenth century.

CULTURE: Compost, equal parts fibrous peat and leaf-mould, fourth part silver sand. Position, pots in moist, shady plant stove. Pot, Feb. or March. Water moderately in winter, freely other times. Syringe foliage March to Sept. Temp., March to Sept. 75° to 85°, Sept. to March 60° to 70°.

PROPAGATION: By seeds sown in fine light compost in temp. 85° in March or April; cuttings of shoots of stems inserted in light soil in temp. 80° to 90° in spring.

SPECIES CULTIVATED: *M. flammea*, leaves green, 1 to 2 ft., Brazil; *Hookeriana*, leaves green and white, 1 to 2 ft.; *magnifica*, leaves bronzy green, 2 to 3 ft., Mexico.

Microcachrys—*Taxaceae*. Dwarf evergreen coniferous plants.
CULTURE: Deep, well-drained loam. Cool position in sheltered rock garden or in the alpine house.
PROPAGATION: By cuttings made from well-ripened, short side growths in late summer.
SPECIES CULTIVATED: *M. tetragona*, small crimson cones, 18 to 24 in., Antipodes.

Microglossa—*Compositae*. Hardy shrubby perennial. First introduced late nineteenth century.
CULTURE: Soil, ordinary. Position, sunny borders. Plant, Oct., March or April.
PROPAGATION: By seeds sown ⅛ in. deep in sunny position outdoors, March or April, or in sandy soil in cold frame, April; division of roots in March.
SPECIES CULTIVATED: *M. albescens*, ' Shrubby Starwort ', lilac blue or bluish white, autumn, 2 to 3 ft., Himalaya.

Microlepia—*Polypodiaceae*. Stove ferns, similar to Davallia, and formerly included in that genus.
CULTURE: As Davallia.
PROPAGATION: As Davallia.
SPECIES CULTIVATED: *M. hirta cristata*, spreading, South Sea Is.; *platyphylla* (syn. *Davallia lonchitidea*), erect to 4 ft., India, Ceylon, Japan.

Micromeria—*Labiatae*. Half-hardy shrubby perennials.
CULTURE: Soil, ordinary. Position, sunny rockeries. Plant, Oct., Nov., March or April. Protect in winter with hand-lights.
PROPAGATION: By cuttings inserted in ordinary sandy soil under hand-light in cold frame, Sept. to Nov.
SPECIES CULTIVATED: *M. Chaminonis* (syn. *M. Douglasii*), flowers inconspicuous, fragrant leaves, trailing, N. America; *croatica*, pale rose, spring, 6 in., Croatia; *Piperella*, purple, summer, 4 to 6 in., S. Europe.

Microstylis—*Orchidaceae*. A large genus, distributed in both hemispheres. A few species are said to be epiphytic but it is usually classed as a terrestrial genus. Allied to Malaxis and Liparis, the inflorescence is terminal to a leafy stem, which may be thickened into pseudo-bulbs, then often deciduous.
CULTURE: The species given all require a warm, moist atmosphere and liberal waterings in the summer, winter temp. 65°. The deciduous species, given a decided rest, 60°. Compost, three parts of osmunda fibre to one part of sphagnum moss. A few decayed oak leaves may be added and a little loam fibre to the stronger growing. Repotting should be effected every spring. Shading is needed.
PROPAGATION: With the bulbed species, bulbs may be separated when two have been formed. The stemmed species by offsets when formed, or such species as *M. commelynaefolia*, by separating rooted pieces from the main plant.
SPECIES CULTIVATED: A selection—*M. calophylla*, greenish, leaves variously marked in green and rich brown, summer, E. Indies; *commelynaefolia*, forms a creeping mass, purplish, leaves green, small, various, Java, Sumatra; *discolor*, yellow, red marked, leaves metallic brown, green bordered, summer, Ceylon; *Josephiana*, yellow, red flecked, comparatively large, leaves olive-copper and green, spring, summer, Sikkim; *Lowii*, purple, leaves copper-brown, with a whitish central band, Borneo; *macrochila*, yellowish, lip, red purple, leaves mottled in cream, light brown and yellowish, summer, Malaya; *metallica*, yellow, rose, leaves glossy, purplish-red, summer, Borneo; *purpurea*, yellowish, purple, leaves metallic red, Ceylon, Java; *Scottii*, greenish or purplish, leaves polished, reddish, centrally passing to grey and green, flecked with red-brown and silver, near to *M. calophylla*, summer, Burma.

Mignonette. see *Reseda odorata*.

Mikania—*Compositae*. Half-hardy perennial twining climber. First introduced early nineteenth century.

OUTDOOR CULTURE: Soil, good ordinary. Position, against south or west walls, sunny arbours, or trellises. Plant, May. Lift in Oct. and store in pots in frost-proof greenhouse or frame.

INDOOR CULTURE: Compost, two parts loam, one part leaf-mould or well-decayed manure and little sand. Position, well-drained pots with shoots trained round trellises, or up rafters or in suspended baskets with shoots hanging down, in sunny greenhouse or window. Pot, Feb. or March. Water freely March to Oct., moderately afterwards. Apply stimulants occasionally May to Sept. Temp., March to Oct. 55° to 65°, Oct. to March 40° to 50°.

PROPAGATION: By cuttings of shoots inserted in sandy soil in temp. 55° to 65° in spring.

SPECIES CULTIVATED: *M. scandens*, ' German Ivy ', ' Parlour Ivy ', yellow and white, summer, 6 to 8 ft., Trop. America.

Milfoil, see *Achillea Millefolium*.

Milk Thistle, see *Silybum Marianum*; **-Vetch,** see Astragalus; **-wort,** see Polygala.

Milla, see Brodiaea.

Miltonia—*Orchidaceae*. An epiphytic genus, not large but every species with attractive flowers. Allied to Odontoglossum. Many beautiful hybrids have been raised with them, Cochlioda and Oncidium and with the hybrids resulting between *M. vexillaria* and its close allies *M. Phalaenopsis*, *M. Roezlii* and *M. Endresii*; a large number of garden crosses have been made, the spreading labellums of *M. Roezlii* and *vexillaria* and the variation of the latter species, with the purple colouring in the lip of *M. phalaenopsis* have produced hybrids, some with flowers of a rich crimson, all beautiful. The habit is not unlike that of Odontoglossum.

CULTURE: Compost, as for Odontoglossums. Treatment is very similar to that for Odontoglossums but slightly more heat should be given to obtain the best results, particularly for those hybrids derived, even remotely, from *M. Roezlii* and *M. Phalaenopsis*. A winter night temp. of 55° to 58° or 60° suits them and the species; though some may be grown with Odontoglossums they do not object to the increased heat. Summer temps. should be as given Cattleyas. Use as little pipe heat as possible, but with shading, take advantage of all sun heat. *M. vexillaria* may be potted in early spring or early in September, the other species in early spring, the hybrids in spring or into summer. Avoid winter potting. Pots or pans, well drained, may be used. A few of the species with rather hard pseudo-bulbs are the better for rather infrequent waterings in winter, but growths are often present. Use syringe freely in summer.

PROPAGATION: By division of the plants when they are repotted.

SPECIES CULTIVATED: *M. candida*, chestnut-brown, and yellow, lip partly con-volute, white, autumn, Brazil; *Clowesii*, chestnut-brown, barred yellow, lip pandurate, violet-purple, white, various, Brazil; *cuneata*, chestnut-brown, tipped yellow, lip , white, spring, Brazil; *Endresii* (syn. *Odontoglossum Warscewiczii*), white, rose-purple in blotches, spring, summer, Costa Rica; *flavescens* (syn. *Cyrtochilum flavescens*), yellowish white, starry, summer, Brazil; *Karwinskii* (syn. *Odontoglossum Karwinskii*), yellow, brown, lip violet-lilac, white, 3 ft. high, autumn, Mexico; *laevis* (syn. *Odontoglossum laeve*), greenish yellow, barred brown, lip rose, purplish, or white, 3 ft. high, spring, Mexico, Guatemala; *Phalaenopsis* (syn. *Odontoglossum Phalaenopsis*), white, lip white, with two radiating crimson-purple blotches, variable, summer, Colombia; *Regnelii* (syn. *M. cereola purpurea*), white, rose-flushed, lip white, rosy, rose-purple, summer, autumn, suffused rose-purple, Brazil; *Reichenheimii*, near *M. Karwinskii*, lip purple; *Roezlii*, large, sepals white, petals purple basally, lip white, autumn, Colombia; *Schroderiana*, chestnut-brown and yellow, lip rose-purple, white, summer, Costa Rica; *spectabilis*, usually soli-tary, large, cream-white, rose-flushed basally, lip rose-purple to whitish, variable, spring, summer, Brazil; *vexillaria*, beautiful, variable, large, light rose to deep rose, lip often darker, spring, summer, Colombia; *Warscewiczii*, brownish-red, whitish, narrow, lip rose-purple round a brown-purple glossy disk, scape often branched, variable, spring, Colombia.

× **Miltonioda**—bigeneric hybrid between Miltonia and Cochlioda.

Mimosa—*Leguminosae* (or *Mimosaceae*). Stove perennials with feather-shaped, green, sensitive leaves. The spring flower sold as Mimosa is *Acacia decurrens* var. *dealbata*. First introduced early seventeenth century.

CULTURE: Compost, equal parts peat, loam and sand. Position—For sensitive plants (*M. pudica* and *M. sensitiva*), well-drained pots in light part of stove; *M. marginata*, similar, but with shoots trained up roof. Pot, Feb. or March. Water freely March to Sept., moderately afterwards. Temp., March to Oct. 65° to 75°.

PROPAGATION: By seeds sown 1/16 in. deep in light soil in temp. 65° to 75°, Feb. or March; cuttings of young shoots inserted in sandy soil in temp. 65° to 75° at any time. *M. pudica* and *M. sensitiva*, though strictly perennials, are generally treated as annuals.

SPECIES CULTIVATED: *M. marginata*, pink, summer, 5 to 10 ft., Mexico; *pudica*, ' Sensitive Plant ' or ' Humble Plant ', rose, summer, 12 to 18 in., Brazil; *sensitiva*, purple, summer, 3 to 6 ft., Brazil.

Mimulus (Monkey-flower; Musk)—*Scrophulariaceae*. Hardy annual and perennial herbs. First introduced early nineteenth century.

CULTURE OF ANNUAL SPECIES: Sow seeds on surface of light soil and slightly cover with fine soil, place in temp. of 55° to 65°, Feb., March or April. Transplant seedlings when three leaves have formed, 1 in. apart, in shallow boxes of light soil. Place in temp. 55° until May, then transfer to cold frame. Plant outdoors, 4 in. apart, June. Position, shady bed or border. Soil, light, moist, well enriched with decayed manure. Mulch with compost or decayed manure. Apply stimulants occasionally, July to Sept.

CULTURE OF PERENNIAL SPECIES: (*M. cardinalis*, etc.). Soil, ordinary rich. Position, moist shady border. Plant, March to June. Apply stimulants occasionally, June to Oct. May be grown in pots.

PROPAGATION: By seeds sown, Feb. to May, on surface of light soil and covered with a little sand or fine soil, in temp. 55° to 60°; cuttings of young shoots inserted in light sandy soil in temp. 55° to 65° at any time; division of roots, Feb. to May, by cuttings of shoots, 2 in. long, inserted in sandy soil under bell-glass in temp; 55° to 65° in March, or in cool greenhouse or window during summer.

ANNUAL SPECIES CULTIVATED: *M. brevipes*, yellow, summer, 1½ to 2 ft., California; *Fremontii*, crimson, summer, 6 to 8 in., California.

PERENNIAL SPECIES CULTIVATED: *M. cardinalis*, ' Cardinal Monkey Flower ', scarlet, summer, 1 to 2 ft., N. America; *guttatus* (syn. *M. Langsdorfii*), often known as *luteus*, yellow, spotted red, summer, 1 to 1½ ft., N. America, *luteus*, smooth leaves and botanical differences from *guttatus*, Chile; *Lewisii*, rose, July to Oct., 1 ft., N.W. America; *ringens*, violet, summer, 2 to 4 ft., N. America. See also Mazus.

Mint, see Mentha; **Apple-,** see *M. rotundifolia*; **Pepper-,** see *M. piperita*; **Spear-,** see *M. spicata*; **Water-,** see *M. aquatica*.

Mirabilis—*Nyctaginaceae*. Half-hardy tuberous-rooted perennials. First introduced late sixteenth century.

CULTURE: Soil, good ordinary. Position, sunny beds or borders. Plant tuberous roots in April, seedlings in June. Apply stimulants occasionally when plants are flowering. Lift tubers in Oct. and store in sand, peat, or cinder ashes in frost-proof place until April.

PROPAGATION: By seeds sown ½ in. deep in light soil in temp. 65° to 75°, Feb. or March, transferring seedlings to cold frame in May and planting out in June; division of tubers at planting time. Marvel of Peru may be treated as an annual.

SPECIES CULTIVATED: *M. hybrida*, various colours. summer. 2 ft., hybrid;

Jalapa, ' Marvel of Peru ', various colours, summer, fragrant, 2 to 3 ft., Trop. America; *longiflora*, various colours, summer, fragrant, 3 ft., Mexico; *multiflora*, purple, summer, 2 to 3 ft., N.W. America.

Miscanthus—*Gramineae*. Tall hardy perennial grasses.
CULTURE: Soil, ordinary. Position, pots in cold or heated greenhouse; in groups on lawns, or sunny borders. Pot or plant, March or April. Water plants in pots moderately in winter, freely in summer. Variegated kinds best adapted for pot culture.
PROPAGATION: By division of plants in March or April.
SPECIES CULTIVATED: *M. saccharifer* (syn. *Eulalia saccharifer*), leaves with prominent white mid-rib, 6 ft., Japan; *sinensis* (syn. *Eulalia japonica*), ' Eulalia ', green with white mid-rib, 6 to 10 ft., China and Japan, and vars. *gracillimus*, dwarf and narrow-leaved, *variegatus*, leaves striped yellow or white, and *zebrinus*, ' Zebra-striped Rush ', leaves cross-banded yellow.

Misopates, see Antirrhinum.

Mistletoe, see *Viscum album*; **-Cactus,** see *Rhipsalis ceriscula*.

Mitchella—*Rubiaceae*. Hardy evergreen trailing herb. Flowers succeeded by small scarlet berries. First introduced mid-eighteenth century.
CULTURE: Soil, equal parts peat and leaf-mould. Position, shady borders or rockeries. Plant, Oct., Nov., March or April.
PROPAGATION: By division of roots in Oct. or March.
SPECIES CULTIVATED: *M. repens*, ' Chequer Berry ', ' Deer Berry ', ' Partridge Berry ', white and purple, fragrant, summer, 3 in., N. America.

Mitella (Bishop's Cap)—*Saxifragaceae*. Hardy perennial herb. First introduced early eighteenth century.
CULTURE: Soil, sandy peat. Position, partially shaded rockeries. Plant, March.
PROPAGATION: By division of the roots, March or April.
SPECIES CULTIVATED: *M. diphylla*, ' Mitre-wort ', white, spring, 6 in., N. America.

Mitraria—*Gesneriaceae*. Half-hardy evergreen flowering shrub. First introduced mid-nineteenth century.
CULTURE: Soil, two parts fibrous peat, one part sand. Position, moist, sheltered, shady borders or walls. Plant, Sept. or April.
POT CULTURE: Compost, two parts sandy peat, one part leaf-mould and sand. Pot, Sept. or Oct. Position, well-drained pots in shady, cold greenhouse or fernery. Water freely March to Oct., moderately afterwards.
PROPAGATION: By cuttings of shoots inserted in light soil under bell-glass in cold, shady frame or greenhouse, April to Sept.; division of roots in April.
SPECIES CULTIVATED: *M. coccinea*, ' Mitre Flower ', scarlet, May to Aug., scandent, Chiloe Island.

Mitre Flower, see *Mitraria coccinea*; **-wort,** see Mitella.

Mitsumata, see *Edgeworthia papyrifera*.

Mocassin Flower, see Cypripedium.

Mock Orange, see Philadelphus; **-Plane,** see *Acer Pseudo-Platanus*.

Mocker Nut, see *Carya tomentosa*.

Mohria—*Schizaeaceae*. Greenhouse evergreen fern. Fronds, feather-shaped, green, fragrant. First introduced early nineteenth century.
CULTURE: Compost, two parts peat, one part small lumps of sandstone, one part silver sand. Position, well-drained pots in shady part of greenhouse, or in beds in wardian cases in dwelling room. Pot or plant, Feb. or March. Water moderately Oct. to Feb., freely afterwards. Temp., March to Sept. 55° to 65°, Sept. to March 45° to 55°.

PROPAGATION: By spores sown on surface of fine sandy peat in pans and placed in temp. 75° to 85° any time.

SPECIES CULTIVATED: *M. caffrorum* (syn. *M. thunifraga*), S. Africa.

Moldavian Balm, see *Dracocephalum Moldavica.*

Molinia—*Gramineae.* Hardy perennial grass. Leaves, smooth, rigid, variegated with white.

CULTURE: Soil, ordinary. Position, open or shady, as edgings to beds or borders. Plant, Oct. or March to June.

PROPAGATION: By division of roots, autumn or spring.

SPECIES CULTIVATED: *M. caerulea*, ' Indian Grass, ' Lavender Grass ', 2 to 3 ft., Britain.

Molopospermum—*Umbelliferae.* Hardy perennial with fern-like graceful leaves. First introduced late sixteenth century.

CULTURE: Soil, deep rich. Position, sunny, fully exposed borders, or naturalising in wild garden. Plant in March.

PROPAGATION: By seeds sown outdoors when ripe, or in cold frame in March; also by division of roots in April.

SPECIES CULTIVATED: *M. cicutarium*, yellow and white, May, 3 to 4 ft., Central Europe.

Moltkia, see Lithospermum.

Molucella—*Labiatae.* Half-hardy annuals or biennials. First introduced mid-sixteenth century.

CULTURE: Soil, sandy loam. Position, sunny beds or borders. Sow seeds in pans or boxes during Feb. or March in temp. 50° to 55°. Prick out when large enough to handle and gradually harden off for planting outdoors in May.

SPECIES CULTIVATED: *M. laevis*, ' Shell-flower ', white, Aug., 2 to 3 ft., W. Asia; *spinosa*, white, summer, 6 to 8 ft., S. Europe and Syria.

Momordica—*Cucurbitaceae.* Half-hardy climbing annuals. Fruit, round, oblong, or cylindrical, reddish orange; Sept. First introduced mid-sixteenth century.

INDOOR CULTURE: Compost, two parts decayed turfy soil, one part horse droppings or decomposed manure. Position, pots or beds with shoots trained up roof of sunny greenhouse. Pot or plant, April or May. Size of pots, 8 or 10 in. Water freely. Syringe twice daily. Moist atmosphere essential. Apply stimulants occasionally when fruit forms. Nip off point of shoot at first joint beyond fruit. Shade from hot sun. Temp., 65°.

OUTDOOR CULTURE: Soil, ordinary rich. Position, against sunny walls, trellises, arbours, or trailing over banks. Plant, June. Water freely in dry weather. Apply stimulants occasionally when fruit forms. Pruning of shoots not required.

PROPAGATION: By seeds sown singly in 2 in. pots filled with light soil in temp. 65° to 75° in Feb. or March.

SPECIES CULTIVATED: *M. Balsamina*, ' Balsam Apple ', yellow, June, 4 ft., Tropics; *Charantia*, ' Balsam Pear ', yellow, June, 4 to 6 ft., Tropics.

Monarda (Horsemint)—*Labiatae.* Hardy aromatic herbaceous perennials. First introduced mid-seventeenth century.

CULTURE: Soil, ordinary. Position, singly, or in masses in open or partially shaded borders. Plant, Oct., March or April. Top-dress with decayed manure in autumn or spring.

PROPAGATION: By seeds sown $\frac{1}{16}$ in. deep in light soil in partially shaded position outdoors, March or April, or in boxes of light soil in cold frame or greenhouse in March; division of roots in Feb. or March.

SPECIES CULTIVATED: *M. didyma*, ' Bee Balm ', ' Oswego Tea ', ' Sweet Bergamot ', scarlet, summer, 1 to 2 ft., N. America; *fistulosa*, ' Wild Bergamot ', purple, summer, 3 to 4 ft., N. America.

Monardella—*Labiatae.* Hardy annual and perennial fragrant-leaved herbs. First introduced mid-nineteenth century.

CULTURE: Soil, ordinary. Position, open or partially shaded borders. Plant, Oct., March or April. Sow annual species outdoors where required to grow, in March or April. Top-dress with decayed manure in autumn or spring.

PROPAGATION: By seed sown $\frac{1}{16}$ in. deep in light soil in partially shaded position outdoors, March or April, or in boxes of light soil in cold frame or greenhouse in March; division of roots, Oct. or March.

ANNUAL SPECIES CULTIVATED: *M. candicans*, white, summer, 1 ft., N. America.

PERENNIAL SPECIES CULTIVATED: *M. macrantha*, scarlet, autumn, fragrant, 6 in., N. America.

Money Flower, see Lunaria; **-wort,** see *Lysimachia Nummularia*.

Monkey Flower, see Mimulus; **-Nut,** see *Arachis hypogaea*; **-Puzzle,** see *Araucaria araucana*.

Monkshood, see *Aconitum Napellus*.

Monochaetum—*Melastomaceae*. Greenhouse evergreen flowering shrubs.

CULTURE: Compost, two parts fibrous peat, one part light loam, one part leaf-mould, and little sand. Position, well-drained pots in light greenhouse, Sept. to June; cold, sunny frames, June to Sept. Pot March. Prune shoots moderately close immediately after flowering. Water moderately Oct. to March, freely afterwards. Syringe twice daily March to June. Apply stimulants occasionally June to Oct. Temp., Sept. to March 45° to 55°, March to June 55° to 65°.

PROPAGATION: By cuttings of shoots, 2 to 3 in. long, inserted in well-drained pots of sandy peat under bell-glass in temp. 65° to 75°, March or April. Nip off points of shoots of young plants occasionally, April to Aug., to induce bushy growth.

SPECIES CULTIVATED: *M. alpestre*, red, winter, 2 ft., Mexico; *Hartwegianum*, rose, winter, 2 ft., Peru; *Humboldtianum*, red and purple, winter, 2 ft., Caracas; *Lemoineanum*, rose and violet, winter, 2 ft.; *sericeum multiflorum*, mauve, spring, 2 ft., New Grenada.

Monsonia—*Gerâniaceae*. Greenhouse ornamental herbs. First introduced mid-eighteenth century.

CULTURE: Compost, sandy loam and leaf-mould. Position, well-drained pots or pans in sunny greenhouse. Water carefully at all times. Repot March or April.

PROPAGATION: By seeds sown in light sandy soil in spring in gentle heat; cuttings inserted in sandy soil under bell-glass in spring or late summer.

SPECIES CULTIVATED: *M. lobata*, purple, red and white, spring, 1 ft., S. Africa; *speciosa*, rose and purple, spring, 9 in., S. Africa.

Monstera (Shingle Plant)—*Araceae*. Stove evergreen ornamental climbers. Leaves, large, handsome, perforated, dark green. Stems, creeping, furnished with aerial roots. Fruit, cylindrical, fragrant, pineapple-flavoured; ripe in autumn.

CULTURE: Compost, equal parts peat, leaf-mould and loam, little sand. Position, well-drained border against damp wall of stove or warm fernery. Plant, Feb. to April. Water freely March to Oct., moderately afterwards. Syringe twice daily March to Sept., once daily afterwards. Temp., March to Sept. 65° to 75°, Sept. to March 55° to 65°.

PROPAGATION: By cuttings of the stems inserted in light soil in temp. 70° to 80° any time.

SPECIES CULTIVATED: *M. acuminata* (syn. *M. tenuis* and *Gravia paradoxa*), yellow, summer, Trop. America; *deliciosa*, yellow, summer, Mexico; *pertusa* (syn. *M. Adamsonii*), yellow and white, May, Trop. America.

Montbretia—*Iridaceae*. Half-hardy cormous plants. The common Montbretia of gardens is *Crocosmia crocosmiiflora*.

CULTURE: Soil, sandy loam. Position, well-drained borders. Plant 3 in. deep and 2 in. apart in groups during March or April. Lift plants in Oct. and place in shallow boxes filled with dry soil in unheated frame or greenhouse until planting time. In sheltered gardens corms may be left in the ground with covering of dry litter during winter. Lift, divide and replant every three years.

PROPAGATION: By offsets.

SPECIES CULTIVATED: *M. laxiflora*, cream to flesh-pink, Sept. to Nov., **6 to 18** in., Cape.

Montia—*Portulacaceae.* Soft annual herbs with rather fleshy leaves and small flowers.

CULTURE: Soil, ordinary. Position, rockery or moist, shady border. Sow seed in April.

PROPAGATION: By seed.

SPECIES CULTIVATED: *M. parviflora* (syn. *Claytonia* and *Limnia parviflora*), pink or white, summer, 2 to 3 in., N. America; *perfoliata* (syn. *Claytonia* and *Limnia perfoliata*), ' Winter Purslane ', white, June, 6 in., N. America.

Moon Creeper, see Calonyction; **-Daisy,** see *Chrysanthemum Leucanthemum*; **-Fern,** see *Botrychium Lunaria*; **-flower,** see Calonyction; **-Seed,** see Menispermum; **-wort,** see Botrychium and Lunaria.

Moraea (Butterfly Iris)—*Iridaceae.* Half-hardy bulbous plants. First introduced late sixteenth century.

CULTURE: Soil, light, rich, sandy. Position, sunny well-drained border. Plant Sept. to Jan., placing bulbs 4 in. deep and 2 in. apart. Lift and replant bulbs annually. Mulch surface of bed in March with cow manure.

POT CULTURE: Compost, two parts sandy loam, one part leaf-mould or decayed cow manure. Pots, 4¼ in. in diameter, well drained. Place five bulbs 3 in. deep in each pot in Nov. and cover with peat in cold frame or under cool greenhouse stage until growth begins. Water moderately from time bulbs begin to grow until flowers fade, then gradually cease, keeping bulbs dry till Jan. Temp., Sept. to March 40° to 50°, other times 50° to 60°.

PROPAGATION: By offsets, treated as advised for bulbs.

SPECIES CULTIVATED: *M. bicolor*, yellow and brown, summer, 2 ft., S. Africa; *glaucopis*, white and blue-black, 1 to 2 ft., S. Africa; *iridioides*, white and yellow, 1 to 2 ft., S. Africa; *pavonia* (syn. *Iris pavonia*), ' Peacock Iris ', red and blue-black, 1 to 2 ft., S. Africa; *Robinsoniana* (syn. *Iris Robinsoniana*), ' Wedding Flower ', white, summer, 4 to 6 ft., Lord Howe's Island; *spathacea*, yellow and purple, 1 to 2 ft., S. Africa.

Moricanda, see Orychophragmus.

Morina (Whorl Flower)—*Dipsaceae.* Hardy perennial herbs. First introduced early nineteenth century.

CULTURE: Soil, deep, moist, sandy loam. Position, partially shaded, sheltered borders. Plant, Sept., Oct., March or April. Protect, Nov. to March, by covering of litter.

PROPAGATION: By seeds sown ¹⁄₁₆ in. deep in sandy peat and leaf-mould in cold frame in Sept. or Oct., March or April; division of roots, Sept.

SPECIES CULTIVATED: *M. Coulteriana*, yellow, June, 18 in., Himalaya; *longifolia*, white to crimson, July, 2 to 3 ft., Himalaya; *persica*, red and white, 1 to 2 ft., Himalaya.

Morisia—*Cruciferae.* Hardy dwarf alpine perennial. Introduced late nineteenth century.

CULTURE: Soil, sandy, gritty loam. Position, in the moraine or in a moist bed of stone chippings and sand. Requires full exposure to the sun. Plant in spring.

PROPAGATION: By seeds sown in sandy soil in a cold frame or by root cuttings laid in sand in spring.

SPECIES CULTIVATED: *M. monanthos* (syn. *M. hypogaea*), golden yellow, early spring, prostrate, Corsica and Sardinia.

Mormodes—*Orchidaceae.* An epiphytic genus allied to Catasetum. Both sexes are present in the same flower and the pseudo-bulbs are usually more slender. Scapes produced from old and new pseudo-bulbs, flowers several, attractive, in some almost contorted, the segments spreading their margins often revolute, the lip tip often touching the column apex, which is sensitive, releasing the pollinia when touched.

CULTURE: Compost, temp., rest, etc., as for Catasetums.

PROPAGATION: By division of the plants as growth commences.

SPECIES CULTIVATED: A selection—*M. aromatica*, yellow, spotted red-brown, fragrant, summer, autumn, Mexico; *atropurpurea*, purple-brown or reddish-purple, autumn, Panama; *badia*, red to purplish-crimson, lip brownish, winter, Peru, var. *lutea*, yellow; *buccinator*, very variable, often yellowish suffused red-brown, lip trumpet-shaped, autumn, winter, Mexico, Colombia, Venezuela, var. *aurea*, orange-yellow; *Cartonii*, yellow, lined and spotted red, summer, autumn, Colombia; *colossus*, large, rose, yellow, lip red-dotted, spring, summer, Cent. America; *ignea*, orange or fiery red, variable, winter, Cent. America; *Lawrenceana*, large, orange-yellow, greenish, lip yellow, purple-brown, Colombia; *luxata*, yellowish, sometimes purple-spotted, summer, Mexico, var. *eburnea*, ivory white, var. *purpurata*, mauve-purple; *pardina*, yellow, spotted brown-red, summer, autumn, Mexico; *vernixia*, blackish purple, lip spotted, winter, Roraima.

Morning Glory, see Ipomoea.

Morus (Mulberry)—*Moraceae*. Grown for edible fruits and for foliage to feed silkworms. Flowers, greenish white, May to July. Fruit, oblong, white, red or black berries; ripe Sept. and Oct. First introduced mid-sixteenth century.

CULTURE OF MULBERRY: Specimen trees of *M. nigra* sometimes grown for edible fruits. Soil, warm, deep and well drained, moist loam. Position, sunny, sheltered from north winds, against south walls in north. Plant, Nov. to March, roots 6 in. below surface; avoid exposure and drying out and do not cut back fleshy roots as bleeding results. Pruning: thin overcrowded branches in Feb. and shorten straggling ones. With wall trees shorten to 6 in. in July young shoots growing at right angles to wall. Top-dress area of soil equal to spread of branches with well-decayed manure in Oct. or Nov. Gathering: allow to drop on to a layer of straw or lawn mowings.

CULTURE OF OTHER SPECIES: Soil, ordinary. Position, sunny sheltered shrubberies or singly on lawns. Plant, Nov. to March. Prune, as advised for mulberry.

PROPAGATION: Named vars. by cuttings 12 in. or more long, inserted half their depth in light soil in sheltered position outdoors, Sept., Oct. or March; layering shoots in Oct.; grafting in March.

SPECIES CULTIVATED: *M. alba*, ' White Mulberry ', to 40 ft., China, Europe, N. America, and vars. *globosa*, compact, *pendula*, ' Weeping Mulberry ', leaves used for silkworms; *nigra*, 'Black Common Mulberry ', to 30 ft., W. Asia; *rubra*, ' Red ' or ' American Mulberry ', to 60 ft., less hardy in England than previous species, Cent. U.S.

Moschosma, see Iboza.

Moss Campion, see *Silene acaulis*; **-Pink,** see *Phlox subulata* and *Silene acaulis*.

Mountain Ash, see *Sorbus aucuparia*; **-Fringe,** see *Adlumia cirrhosa*; **-Holly,** see *Olearia ilicifolia*; **-Laurel,** see *Kalmia latifolia*; **-Snow,** see *Arabis albida*; **-Tobacco,** see *Arnica montana*.

Mousetail Plant, see Arisarum.

Mouth Root, see Coptis.

Mud Plantain, see Heteranthera.

Muehlenbeckia—*Polygonaceae*. Slightly tender deciduous shrub with wiry, tangled stems and climbing or clambering habit, flowers insignificant. First introduced early nineteenth century.

CULTURE: Soil, ordinary. Position, sunny, may be trained to walls, or allowed to stray over large rocks or tree stumps. Both species liable to curtailment by severe frost.

PROPAGATION: By Aug. cuttings in cold frame; division of rootstock in spring.

SPECIES CULTIVATED: *M. axillaris*, creeping and dwarf habit, suitable for rockery or rock walls, spreading, to 3 in., Antipodes; *complexa*, 'Wire Vine', 15 ft., New Zealand. For *M. platyclados*, see Homalocladium.

Mugwort, see *Artemisia vulgaris.*

Mulberry, see Morus.

Mulgedium, see Lactuca.

Mullein, see *Verbascum Thapsus.*

Musa (Banana)—*Musaceae.* Stove herbaceous perennials. Some species grown for fruit, *M. Ensete* for garden decoration in summer and *M. textilis* for fibre. First introduced late seventeenth century.

CULTURE: Compost, two parts good loam, one part well-decayed manure and one part sand. Position, pots, tubs or beds in lofty, sunny stove. Pot or plant, Jan. to April. Water copiously Feb. to Oct., about once a fortnight afterwards. Syringe twice daily Feb. to Sept., once daily Sept. to Feb. Moist atmosphere essential. Apply stimulants twice or three times weekly March to Oct. Temp., March to Oct. 70° to 85°, Oct. to March 60° to 70°.

OUTDOOR CULTURE OF M. ENSETE: Position, sunny, sheltered borders or nooks. Place in position first or second week in June, plunging pot or tub to its rim in the ground. Water copiously. Apply stimulants once a week. Lift and replace in stove in Sept. May also be planted in ordinary rich soil in June, freely watered, lifted in Sept., and roots stored close together in temp. 45° to 55° until following June.

PROPAGATION: By suckers removed from parent plant and placed in pots in temp. 75° to 85° any time of year.

SPECIES CULTIVATED: *M. Ensete*, 20 to 40 ft., Abyssinia; *nana*, 'Dwarf Banana', grown commercially in Bermuda, Canary Islands, etc., S. China; *paradisiaca*, 'Plantain', to 30 ft., Trop. Asia, var. *sapientum*, 'Banana'; *superba*, handsome species, to 14 ft., India; *textilis*, 'Manila Hemp', to 20 ft., Philippine Islands.

Muscari (Grape Hyacinth)—*Liliaceae.* Hardy bulbous flowering plants.

OUTDOOR CULTURE: Soil, deep, sandy loam. Position, sunny beds, borders, or rockeries. Plant, Aug. to Nov., in lines or masses. Depth for planting: small bulbs 2 in. deep and 1 in. apart; large bulbs 4 in. deep and 3 to 4 in. apart. Mulch with decayed manure, Nov. Lift, divide and replant every third year.

POT CULTURE: Compost, two parts sandy loam, one part leaf-mould or well-decayed cow manure, and one part river sand. Pot, Aug. to Nov., placing 18 to 20 small bulbs, 1 in. apart, in a 5 in. pot; or 3 to 5 large-sized bulbs 1 in. deep in similar pots. Position, under layer of cinder ashes from time of potting till growth commences, then in cold frame, cool greenhouse, or window till past flowering, afterwards in sunny spot outdoors. Water moderately from time growth commences till foliage fades, then keep dry. Repot annually. Apply weak stimulants once or twice during flowering period.

PROPAGATION: By seeds sown $\frac{1}{16}$ in. deep in light, sandy soil in boxes or cold frames, or outdoors in Sept.; offsets from old bulbs removed when lifting and planted as advised for full-sized bulbs. Seedlings flower when three to four years old.

SPECIES CULTIVATED: *M. botryoides*, blue, spring, 6 in., Europe, var. *album*, white; *comosum* (syn. *Leopoldia comosa*), 'Tassel Hyacinth', blue, April, 8 in., Europe, var. *monstrosum*, 'Feather Hyacinth', blue, April, 8 in.; *conicum*, April, 8 in., S. Europe; *Heldreichii*, blue, May, 8 in., Greece; *macrocarpum* (syn. *M. moschatum flavum*), yellow, April, 8 in., Aegean Islands; *Muscerinii* (syn. *M.*

moschatum), ' Musk Hyacinth ', dull violet, April, 8 in., Asia Minor; *racemosum*, ' Starch Hyacinth ', blue, April, 6 in., Europe; *Tubergenianum*, light blue, spring, 8 in., Persia.

Mushroom, see *Agaricus hortensis*.

Musk, see Mimulus.

Mussaenda—*Rubiaceae*. Stove evergreen flowering shrubs. First introduced early nineteenth century.

CULTURE: Compost, equal parts peat, loam, leaf-mould and silver sand. Position, well-drained pots in light, moist stove. Pot, Feb. to April. Prune moderately after flowering. Temp., Feb. to Oct. 65° to 85°, Oct. to Feb. 55° to 65°. Water freely April to Sept., moderately Sept. to Nov. and Feb. to April, keep somewhat dry Nov. to Feb. Syringe daily Feb. to Oct.

PROPAGATION: By cuttings of young shoots in sandy soil under bell-glass in temp. 70° to 80°, May to July.

SPECIES CULTIVATED: *M. erythrophylla*, yellow, bracts crimson, winter, 1 ft., Trop. Africa; *frondosa*, yellow, Aug., 2 to 3 ft., India; *luteola*, bright yellow, autumn and winter, 5 to 6 ft., Trop. Africa; *macrophylla*, orange, May, 4 to 6 ft., Nepal.

Mustard, White, see *Brassica hirta*; **Black-,** see *B. nigra*; **Leaf-,** see *B. juncea*; **Purple-,** see *B. purpuraria*.

Mutisia—*Compositae*. Greenhouse or hardy climbing flowering shrubs. First introduced early nineteenth century.

CULTURE OF GREENHOUSE SPECIES: Compost, two parts loam, one part leaf-mould, half-part sand. Position, pots or beds; shoots trained up rafters or round trellises. Pot or plant, Feb. or March. Prune slightly after flowering. Water freely March to Sept., moderately afterwards. Apply stimulants occasionally May to Sept. Temp., March to Sept. 55° to 65°, Sept. to March 40° to 50°.

CULTURE OF HARDY SPECIES: Soil, ordinary rich. Position, well-drained border against sheltered, partially shaded wall. Plant, Oct., March or April. Water freely in dry weather. Protect from slugs by placing layer of fine coke or cinders round base of stems.

PROPAGATION: Greenhouse species by cuttings of half-ripened shoots inserted in sand under bell-glass in temp. 55° to 65°, May or June; hardy species by cuttings of similar shoots inserted in sand in shady, cold frame or greenhouse, April or May.

GREENHOUSE SPECIES CULTIVATED: *M. Clematis*, scarlet, summer, 20 to 30 ft., Peru; *ilicifolia*, white or rose, summer, 8 to 12 ft., Chile; *speciosa*, red, July, 10 ft., Ecuador; *subulata*, reddish-brown, summer, to 10 ft., Chile.

HARDY SPECIES CULTIVATED: *M. decurrens*, orange, summer, 6 to 10 ft., Chile.

Myosotidium—*Boraginaceae*. Hardy herbaceous perennial. First introduced mid-nineteenth century.

CULTURE: Soil, ordinary. Position, cool, damp, sheltered border. Plant, Oct. or March. Water freely in dry weather.

PROPAGATION: By seeds sown $\frac{1}{16}$ in. deep in April where plants are required to grow. This plant should be disturbed as little as possible.

SPECIES CULTIVATED: *M. Hortensia* (syn. *M. nobile*), ' Chatham Island Forget-me-not ', blue and white, spring, 12 to 18 in., Chatham Islands.

Myosotis (Forget-me-not)—*Boraginaceae*. Hardy perennials.

CULTURE OF M. ALPESTRIS: Soil, moist, gritty loam. Position, partially shady rockery, surrounded by small pieces of sandstone. Plant, March or April.

CULTURE OF OTHER SPECIES: Soil, ordinary. Position, as edgings to or in masses in partially shady beds or borders. Plant, Oct., Feb. or March, 4 to 6 in. apart. These are best treated as biennials—namely, raised from seed sown outdoors in April, May or June and transplanted into the beds or borders in Oct. to flower following year.

PROPAGATION: By seeds sown $\frac{1}{16}$ in. deep outdoors in spring or summer;

cuttings inserted in sandy soil under hand-light in June or July; division of roots in March or Oct.

SPECIES CULTIVATED: *M. alpestris* (syn. *M. rupicola*), blue and white, fragrant, June and July, 6 to 8 in., Europe, and its many selected forms; *azorica*, blue, summer, 6 to 10 in., Azores; *cespitosa*, blue and yellow, June to July, 3 to 6 in., Europe; *dissitiflora*, sky blue, March to July, 8 to 10 in., Alps, var. *alba*, white; *scorpioides* (syn. *M. palustris*), sky blue, May to July, 6 to 12 in., Britain, var. *semperflorens*, long flowering; *sylvatica*, blue and yellow, summer, 1 to 2 ft., Britain.

Myrica—*Myricaceae.* Hardy deciduous and evergreen shrubs with small catkin flowers of no beauty. Leaves, lance-shaped, green, highly fragrant.

CULTURE: Soil, moist, sandy peat. Position, open, sheltered borders. Plant, Oct. to March. Prune deciduous species, Nov. to Feb.; evergreen species, April.

PROPAGATION: By seeds sown ⅛ in. deep in ordinary soil in sheltered position outdoors in autumn; cuttings inserted in sandy soil in sheltered position outdoors, Sept. or Oct.; layering shoots in Sept. or Oct.; division of plants, Oct. to March.

SPECIES CULTIVATED: *M. californica*, evergreen to 15 ft., rather tender, waxy white berries, California; *cerifera*, ' Candle-berry ' or ' Wax Myrtle ', brown, May, 20 to 40 ft., America; *Gale*, ' Sweet Gale ', brown, May, 4 ft., N. Europe (Br.). See also Comptonia.

Myricaria (False Tamarisk)—*Tamaricaceae.* Hardy deciduous flowering shrub. First introduced mid-sixteenth century.

CULTURE: Soil, ordinary sandy. Position, open, sunny borders or banks. Plant, Oct. to March. Prune into shape, Nov. to Feb.

PROPAGATION: By cuttings of firm young shoots inserted in sandy soil outdoors, Oct., Nov.

SPECIES CULTIVATED: *M. germanica* (syn. *Tamarix germanica*), pink, July, 6 to 8 ft., Europe.

Myriophyllum (Water Milfoil)—*Haloragidaceae.* Pretty feathery submerged and shallow-water aquatics much used in ponds and aquariums.

CULTURE: Soil, pond or aquarium compost. Plant, spring and summer in pans, dropping these gently into the water or planting individual specimens in the aquarium. Waterside kinds, plant at the pond edges.

PROPAGATION: By slips broken from parent plant inserted in pans containing a little loam and several inches of water.

SPECIES CULTIVATED: *M. gracile*, Australia; *heterophyllum*, bronze-green, N. America; *hippuroides*, hair-like, S. and N. America; *proserpinacoides*, ' Parrot's Feather ', grow at pond margin, feathery stems trail over sides of pool or fountain, hardy, S. Africa; *pinnatum*, Trop. America; *verticillatum*, Britain.

Myrrhis (Myrrh)—*Umbelliferae.* Hardy perennial aromatic herb. Leaves finely divided, fern-like, fragrant.

CULTURE: Soil, ordinary. Position, open, sunny borders. Plant, Oct. or March.

PROPAGATION: By seeds sown ⅛ in. deep in ordinary soil outdoors, Sept. or April; division of roots, Oct. or March.

SPECIES CULTIVATED: *M. odorata*, ' Sweet Cicely ', white, May, 3 ft., Europe (Br.).

Myristica (Nutmeg)—*Myristicaceae.* Stove or warm greenhouse evergreen tree. The seed furnishes the nutmeg of commerce and commercial mace is obtained from the aril surrounding the seed. First introduced late eighteenth century.

CULTURE: Compost, fibrous loam, leaf-mould, peat and sand. Position, large pots or planted out in prepared border in warm greenhouse. Temp., March to Oct. 65° to 75°, October to March 55° to 65°.

PROPAGATION: By cuttings of ripened shoots inserted in sand under bell-glass or in propagating case over bottom heat.

SPECIES CULTIVATED: *M. fragrans*, pale yellow, June, to 30 ft., Moluccas.

Myrtus (Myrtle)—*Myrtaceae.* Greenhouse and slightly tender evergreen shrubs.

Hardy in open extreme south-west, requiring wall protection in the south, leaves fragrant when crushed, flowers also fragrant.

CULTIVATION: Soil, ordinary, well drained. Position, very sheltered borders, or against south walls in southern counties. May be grown in pots or tubs in conservatories and are sometimes formally trained as pyramids or standards.

PROPAGATION: cuttings in sandy soil with gentle bottom heat, Aug. May be clipped to formal shapes, May to July. Prune to shape after flowering.

SPECIES CULTIVATED: *M. bullata* (syn. *M. communis*), ' Common Myrtle ', to 10 ft., white, fragrant, summer, W. Asia, with vars. *microphylla*, smaller leaved, *tarentina*, a smaller-growing dainty form, and *variegata*; *Ralphii*, 8 to 10 ft., New Zealand; *Ugni* (syn. *Eugenia Ugni*), to 10 ft., white, fragrant, summer, berries which are pleasant to eat, freely borne, Chile.

Naegelia, see Smithiantha.

Nailwort, see Paronychia.

Nancy-Pretty, None-so-Pretty, see *Saxifraga umbrosa.*

Nandina—*Berberidaceae.* Half-hardy evergreen flowering shrub. First introduced early nineteenth century.

CULTURE: Soil, peat and loam. Position, sheltered, moderately moist beds or borders in mild districts only. Plant in May or Sept.

PROPAGATION: By cuttings inserted in sandy peat in gentle bottom heat in summer. Rooting is slow.

SPECIES CULTIVATED: *N. domestica,* ' Heavenly Bamboo ', white, summer, 6 to 8 ft., leaves assume reddish tint in autumn, red berries sometimes borne, China.

Narcissus—*Amaryllidaceae.* Hardy spring flowering bulbs.

R.H.S. CLASSIFICATION: Division 1—Trumpet. Distinguishing characters, one flower to a stem; trumpet or corona as long as or longer than the perianth segments: (*a*) perianth coloured; corona coloured, not paler than the perianth: (*b*) perianth white; corona coloured: (*c*) perianth white; corona white, not paler than the perianth: (*d*) any colour combination not falling into (*a*), (*b*) or (*c*).

Division II—Large-cupped. Distinguishing characters, one flower to a stem, cup or corona more than one-third, but less than equal to the length of the perianth segments: (*a*) perianth coloured; corona coloured but not paler than the perianth: (*b*) perianth white; corona coloured: (*c*) perianth white; corona white, not paler than the perianth: (*d*) any colour combination not falling into (*a*), (*b*) or (*c*).

Division III—Small-cupped. Distinguishing characters, one flower to a stem; cup or corona not more than one-third the length of the perianth segments: (*a*) perianth coloured; corona coloured, not paler than the perianth: (*b*) perianth white; corona coloured: (*c*) perianth white; corona white, not paler than the perianth: (*d*) any colour combination not falling into (*a*), (*b*) or (*c*).

Division IV—Double. Distinguishing character, double flowers.

Division V—Triandrus. Distinguishing characters, characteristics of *Narcissus triandrus* clearly evident: (*a*) cup or corona not less than two-thirds the length of the perianth segments: (*b*) cup or corona less than two-thirds the length of the perianth segments.

Division VI—Cyclamineus. Distinguishing characters, characteristics of *Narcissus cyclamineus* clearly evident; (*a*) cup or corona not less than two-thirds the length of the perianth segments; (*b*) cup or corona less than two-thirds the length of the perianth segments.

Division VII—Jonquilla. Distinguishing characters, characteristics of any of the *Narcissus Jonquilla* group clearly evident; (*a*) cup or corona not less than two-thirds the length of the perianth segments; (*b*) cup or corona less than two-thirds the length of the perianth segments.

Division VIII—Tazetta. Distinguishing characters, characteristics of any of the *Narcissus Tazetta* group clearly evident.

Division IX—Poeticus. Distinguishing characters, characteristics of the *Narcissus poeticus* group without admixture of any other.

Division X—Species, etc. All species and wild, or reputedly wild, forms and hybrids.

Division XI—Miscellaneous. All narcissi not falling into any of the foregoing divisions.

OUTDOOR CULTURE: Soil, ordinary for common kinds; sandy loam for *N. bulbocodium* and vars.; peaty soil for *N. cyclamineus*. No animal manure must be applied. Position, partially or quite shady beds or borders facing north or north-east for robust kinds; rockeries sheltered from north or north-east winds for choice or dwarf kinds. Plant, Aug. to Nov. Depth for planting robust kinds, 3 to 4 in. on heavy soils; 6 in. on light soils. Distance apart, 4 to 6 in. Rock garden narcissus, 2 to 3 in. deep and the same apart. Lift *N. Bulbocodium* in July and re-plant in Oct.; other kinds every three or four years in July. Do not remove foliage until quite dead. Manures: 4 oz. of basic slag or 4 oz. of bonemeal for heavy soils; ¼ oz. of sulphate of potash for sandy soils. Apply above quantities per square yard before planting.

CULTURE IN TURF: Make holes 2 to 3 in. wide, 3 in. deep. Place one bulb in each and cover with soil and turf. Plant, Aug. to Oct. Grass must not be cut until leaves turn yellow.

INDOOR CULTURE: Compost, two parts fibrous loam, one part well-decayed manure or leaf-mould, one part sand. Pot, Aug. to Nov., placing 3 large, 6 medium-sized, or 12 small bulbs in a 5 in. pot. Depth for planting: Allow apex to just appear above surface of soil. Position, under cinder ashes outdoors or in frame until growth begins, then remove to greenhouse or window. Water only when growth commences, moderately afterwards. Apply weak stimulants when flowers appear. Temp. for forcing, 55° to 65°. After flowering, plant bulbs, except those of *N. Bulbocodium* and *N. cyclamineus*, outdoors. Keep soil of the latter dry after flowering.

PROPAGATION: By seeds sown ⅛ in. deep in pans of sandy loam in cold frame in autumn, transplanting seedlings following year 1 in. apart in bed of sandy soil in shady position outdoors; by offsets, removed from old bulbs in July or Aug. and replanted at once as advised for parent bulbs. Seedling bulbs flower when three to eight years old.

SPECIES CULTIVATED: *N. biflorus*, white and yellow, May, 1 ft., Europe; *Bulbocodium* (syn. *N. cantabricus*), 'Hoop-petticoat Daffodil', yellow, April, 6 in., S. Europe, and vars. *citrinus*, lemon-yellow, *Graellsii*, whitish, *monophyllus*, white; *cyclamineus*, lemon and yellow, spring, 1 ft., Portugal; *gracilis*, yellow, April, 1 ft., S. France; *incomparabilis*, 'Chalice Cup Narcissus', yellow, April, 1 ft., Europe; *Jonquilla*, 'Jonquil', yellow, April, 9 in., S. Europe and Algeria; *juncifolius*, yellow, spring, 6 to 8 in., S. Europe; *maximus*, yellow, April, 1 ft., Europe; *minimus*, 'Pygmy Daffodil', sulphur yellow, spring, 4 in., Europe; *moschatus*, 'Musk Daffodil', white, April, 1 ft., Pyrenees; *odorus*, 'Campernelle', yellow, May, 1 ft., France and Spain; *poetaz*, 'Poetaz Narcissus', like *N. Tazetta* but larger and more fragrant, hybrid; *poeticus*, 'Poet's Narcissus', 'Pheasant Eye Narcissus', white, May, 1 ft., France to Greece, var. *ornatus*, early flowering form; *Pseudo-Narcissus*, 'Daffodil', 'Trumpet Narcissus', 'Lent Lily', yellow, March, 1 ft., Europe (Br.), var. *bicolor*, yellow and white; *serotinus*, white and yellow, Sept. to Oct., 1 ft., S. Europe; *Tazetta*, 'Polyanthus Narcissus', white and yellow, March, 1 ft., Canary Isles to Japan, var. *orientalis*, 'Chinese Sacred Lily'; *triandrus*, 'Angel's Tears', white, April, 6 to 9 in., Spain, var. *calathinus*, pale yellow.

Nard, see *Valeriana celtica.*

Narthecium (Bog Asphodel)—*Liliaceae.* Hardy herbaceous perennial.

'CULTURE: Soil, ordinary. Position, moist beds, borders, or margins of ponds. Soil, ordinary, or boggy peat. Plant, Oct. or March.

PROPAGATION: By seeds sown in March or April where plants are required to grow; division of roots in Oct. or March.

SPECIES CULTIVATED: *N. ossifragum*, yellow, July, 6 in., Europe (Br.).

Nasturtium (Watercress)—*Cruciferae.* Hardy perennial aquatic herb. Leaves, green or brown; largely used for salads. The annual known in gardens as Nasturtium is *Tropaeolum majus.*

CULTURE IN BEDS IN WATER: Soil, ordinary. Position, open. Dimensions of beds, 3 to 4 ft. wide; 3 to 6 in. deep; no limit as to length. Depth of soil, 1½ to 3 in. Depth of water, 1¾ in. when first planted; 3 in. when growing freely; 6 in. in winter. Water must flow through beds, not be stagnant. Plant, May and June for gathering in Aug. to Feb.; Sept. to Nov. for gathering in Feb. to May. Replant beds twice annually. Distance for planting, 6 in. apart in rows, 2 ft. between rows. Soil must be removed each planting. Gather the tops once a week; cut, not break, them off.

CULTURE IN PANS: Soil, ordinary. Position, tubs or tanks of water in open air or under glass. Sow seeds ¹⁄₁₆ in. deep in March or Sept. and partly immerse pan in water; wholly when seedlings appear. Insert cuttings 2 to 3 in. apart in spring or autumn; partly immerse at first, wholly after.

CULTURE IN TRENCHES: Soil, ordinary. Position, sunny. Dig trench 2 ft. wide, 1 ft. deep. Put 6 in. decayed manure in, and 3 in. of soil on this. Sow seeds thinly ⅛ in. deep in April and Aug. Keep well watered. Cress sown in April gather June to Sept.; in Aug., Nov. to May.

PROPAGATION: For beds by seeds sown in a shady border in April, and kept moist; division of the plants in May or Aug.

SPECIES CULTIVATED: *N. officinale* (syn. *Rorippa Nasturtium-aquaticum*), white, June, Britain.

Navelwort, see Omphalodes and Umbilicus.

Nectarine, see *Prunus Persica* var. *nectarina.*

Needle Furze, see *Genista anglica.*

Nectaroscordum, see Allium.

Neillia (Nine Bark)—*Rosaceae.* Hardy deciduous flowering shrubs. First introduced mid-nineteenth century.

CULTURE: Soil, ordinary. Position, open, sunny shrubberies or banks. Plant, Oct. to March. Prune moderately after blooming.

PROPAGATION: By seeds sown ⅛ in. deep in sandy soil in sheltered position outdoors, autumn or spring; cuttings of half-ripened shoots, 2 to 3 in. long, inserted in sand under bell-glass during July and Aug. which strike readily; rooted offsets.

SPECIES CULTIVATED: *N. longiracemosa*, rose pink, July, 6 to 8 ft., W. China; *sinensis*, white, June, 6 ft., Cent. China; *thibetica*, pink, July, 6 ft., W. China; *thyrsiflora*, white, July, 3 ft., Sikkim.

Nelumbium, see Nelumbo.

Nelumbo (Lotus)—*Nymphaeaceae.* Greenhouse aquatic rhizomatous-rooted perennials with fragrant flowers and bluish-green, shield-shaped leaves 1 to 2 ft. in diameter. *N. nucifera* is one of the two plants known as the ' Lotus of the Nile ', the other being *Nymphaea caerulea.* First introduced late eighteenth century.

CULTURE: Compost, two parts loam, one part well-decayed manure. Position, tanks or tubs of water heated to a temp. of 60° to 65°. Plant rhizomes 1 to 2 in. below surface of water in Feb. or March. Temp., March to Oct. 55° to 60°, Oct. to March 45° to 55°. Draw off water from tank in Oct. and keep rhizomes dry till Feb.

PROPAGATION: By seeds sown in sandy soil, 2 to 3 in. below surface of water heated to temp. 60° to 70° any time of year, file seeds to facilitate germination; division of rhizomes in Feb.

SPECIES CULTIVATED: *N. nucifera* (syns. *Nelumbium speciosum, N. Nelumbo*), white and rose, Trop. Asia, and many vars. including double white, white edged red or green, rose, double rose and pygmy forms; *pentapetala* (syn. *N. lutea*), ' Sacred Bean ', sulphur-yellow, slow to establish itself (5 to 6 years), S. United States.

Nemastylis—*Iridaceae.* Half-hardy flowering bulbs. First introduced mid-nineteenth century.

OUTDOOR CULTURE: Soil, light, rich, sandy. Position, sunny well-drained border. Plant, Jan., placing bulbs 4 in. deep and 2 in. apart. Lift and replant bulbs annually. Mulch surface of bed in March with cow manure.

POT CULTURE: Compost, two parts sandy loam, one part leaf-mould or decayed cow manure. Pots, 4½ in. in diameter, well drained. Place five bulbs, 3 in. deep, in each pot in Nov. and cover with peat in cold frame or under cool greenhouse stage until growth commences. Water moderately from time bulbs begin to grow until flowers fade, then gradually cease, keeping bulbs dry till Jan. Temp., Sept. to Mar. 40° to 50°, other times 50° to 60°.

PROPAGATION: By offsets, treated as advised for bulbs.

SPECIES CULTIVATED: *N. geminiflora*, purplish blue, May to June, 2 ft., California.

Nemesia—*Scrophulariaceae.* Half-hardy annuals. First introduced mid-eighteenth century.

CULTURE: Soil, ordinary. Position, sunny beds or well-drained borders.

PROPAGATION: By seeds sown in April $\frac{1}{16}$ in. deep in well-drained pots or pans filled with light fibrous loam and little wood ashes. Place in temp. 55°, transplanting seedlings when they have formed three leaves 1 in. apart in well-drained pots, placing in temp. of 55°, and planting into flowering position outdoors in June, or repot into 6 in. pots for flowering in the greenhouse; also seeds sown in May $\frac{1}{16}$ in. deep in patches outdoors where plants are required to flower, afterwards thinning seedlings to at least 4 in. apart.

SPECIES CULTIVATED: *N. strumosa*, various colours, summer, 1 ft., S. Africa, and many dwarf vars. are now available; *versicolor*, many colours, summer, 8 to 12 in., S. Africa. There are several hybrid races to be found in trade lists.

Nemophila—*Hydrophyllaceae.* Hardy spreading annuals. First introduced early nineteenth century.

OUTDOOR CULTURE: Soil, ordinary. Position, in masses or in lines as edgings to sunny beds or borders. Sow seeds $\frac{1}{16}$ in. deep in March or April for flowering in summer; in Aug. or Sept. for flowering in spring. Thin seedlings to 3 in. apart when ½ in. high.

POT CULTURE: Compost, any well-drained soil. Sow seeds thinly, slightly covering with fine soil, and place pots in cool, shady frame or window. Water moderately at first, freely when seedlings appear. Apply weak stimulants once or twice weekly when plants begin to flower. Position when in flower, cold, sunny greenhouse, window or frame.

SPECIES CULTIVATED: *N. maculata*, white and purple, summer, 6 in., California; *Menziesii* (syn. *N. insignis*), ' Baby Blue-eyes ', white or blue, summer, spreading, California.

Neobenthamia—*Orchidaceae.* A terrestrial orchid. The one species has slender stems, often 6 ft. high and branched, clothed with leaves, flowers in terminal heads.

CULTURE: Compost, two parts osmunda fibre, one part loam fibre, one part sphagnum moss, well-drained pots. A warm moist atmosphere and waterings throughout the year. Winter temp. 65°, higher in summer. Shading required.

PROPAGATION: By division of plants or rooted branches.

SPECIES CULTIVATED: *N. gracilis*, white, lip rose-spotted, spring to summer, Zanzibar, E. Africa.

Neomarica—*Iridaceae.* Stove herbaceous perennials, formerly known as Marica. First introduced late eighteenth century.

CULTURE: Compost, equal parts peat, leaf-mould and sand. Position, well-drained pots in light part of stove. Pot, Feb. or March. Water freely March to

Oct., keep dry Nov. to Feb. Apply weak stimulants occasionally when in flower. Temp., 65° to 75° March to Sept., Sept. to March 55° to 65°.

PROPAGATION: By division of rhizomatous roots, Feb. or March.

SPECIES CULTIVATED: *N. gracilis*, bluish-white, spotted with reddish-brown, summer, 2 ft., Trop. America; *Northiana*, white, yellow, and red, summer, 3 to 4 ft., Trop. America.

Neomoorea—*Orchidaceae.* Only one species is known in this genus, a large-growing epiphyte. The stout pseudo-bulbs carry large leaves up to 3 ft. long. Scapes with the young growth, flowers many. Originally known as Moorea.

CULTURE: Compost, three parts osmunda fibre, one part sphagnum moss, with loam fibre, one part, for strong plants. Pots well drained. Position, shade from bright sunlight. Winter temp. 60° to 65°, water then given infrequently. Summer 70° to 80°, water freely. A moist atmosphere throughout the year.

PROPAGATION: By division of plants in spring, or by separating sound back bulbs and treating as for Cymbidiums but in heat.

SPECIES CULTIVATED: *N. irrorata* (syns. *Moorea irrorata, Neomoorea Wallisii*), many, cup-shaped, orange-brown, yellowish, white, lip 3-lobed, barred purple-brown, mid-lobe spotted red, spring, Colombia.

Nepenthes (Pitcher-plant)—*Nepenthaceae.* Stove evergreen sub-shrubby perennials. Flowers, greenish, dioecious, insignificant. Leaves, oblong or lance-shaped, variously mottled with red, brown and crimson, terminating in a pitcher-like appendage. First introduced late eighteenth century.

CULTURE: Compost, two parts good brown fibrous peat, one part sphagnum moss. Position, in baskets suspended from roof in shady part of stove. Plant, Feb. or March. Temp., March to Sept. 70° to 85°, Sept. to March 65° to 75°. Water copiously March to Sept., moderately afterwards. Syringe twice daily all the year round. Moist atmosphere very essential. Shade from sun.

PROPAGATION: By seeds sown on surface of mixture of fibrous peat and sphagnum moss in well-drained pan covered with bell-glass and placed in a moist frame heated to temp. of 80° to 85°; cuttings of one-year-old shoots inserted singly in small pots plunged in bottom heat of 85° any time.

SPECIES CULTIVATED: *N. albomarginata*, green and white, Singapore; *atro-sanguinea*, pale green and reddish-purple, hybrid; *Dicksoniana*, green marked with purple, hybrid; *Dominii*, mottled green and purple, hybrid; *Henryana*, red, mottled, hybrid; *Hookeriana*, pale green and red, Borneo; *intermedia*, green spotted with purple, hybrid; *Mastersiana*, crimson with purple spots, hybrid; *maxima* (syn. *N. Curtisii*), green, crimson, and purple, Borneo; *mirabilis* (syn. *N. Rafflesiana*(, green, red, and brown, India; *sanguinea*, blood-red, Malaya; *Sedenii*, pitchers contracted in middle, hybrid; *Veitchii*, green, Borneo; *ventricosa*, green, brown, and crimson, Philippines.

Nepeta—*Labiatae.* Hardy herbaceous perennials with toothed, more or less heart-shaped leaves, mostly aromatic. The plant most commonly cultivated in gardens as *N. Mussinii* is in reality a hybrid, *N. Faassenii*, the flowers are on longer spikes than in the true species.

CULTURE: Soil, ordinary. Position, sunny beds, borders or rockeries. Plant, Oct. to March.

PROPAGATION: By seeds sown where plants are to grow, March to May; division of roots, Oct. to March.

SPECIES CULTIVATED: *N. Cataria*, ' Catmint ', whitish to pale purple, summer, to 3 ft., Europe (Br.); *Faassenii* (syn. *N. pseudomussinii*), lavender-blue, summer, to 2 ft., hybrid; *Mussinii*, lavender-blue, summer, 18 in., Caucasus, Persia; *nervosa*, pale blue, summer, to 2 ft., Himalaya. See also Glechoma.

Nephrodium, see Dryopteris.

Nephrolepis—*Polypodiaceae.* Stove evergreen ferns. Fronds linear, narrow, once divided, plain or crested. First introduced late eighteenth century.

CULTURE: Compost, equal parts loam, leaf-mould and sand, two parts lumpy peat. Position, in baskets suspended from roof, or in well-drained pots or beds in shady part of stove. Pot or plant, Feb. or March. Water moderately Oct. to March, freely afterwards. Temp., Sept. to March 55° to 60°, March to Sept. 65° to 75°. *N. cordifolia* will thrive in warm greenhouse.

PROPAGATION: By spores sown on surface of pans of sandy peat under bell-glass and placed in temp. 75° to 85° any time; division of plants, Feb. to April; or by pegging down creeping stems bearing young plants and removing when rooted.

SPECIES CULTIVATED: *N. acuminata* (syn. *N. davallioides*), 2 to 3 ft., Java; *biserrata* (syn. *N. acuta*), 2 to 4 ft., Tropics; *cordifolia* (syn. *N. tuberosa*), 1 to 2 ft., Tropics and Subtropics; *Duffii*, 1 ft., Australia; *exaltata*, ' Ladder Fern ', 2 to 3 ft., Tropics, and many fine crested and plumose vars.; *hirsutula* (syn. *N. refescens*), 2 to 3 ft., Tropics.

Nephrophyllidium, see Fauria.

Nerine—*Amaryllidaceae*. Greenhouse bulbous plants, natives of S. Africa, which flower from June well on into the autumn. First introduced late seventeenth century.

CULTURE: Compost, two parts sandy loam, one part well-decayed cow manure or leaf-mould, one part coarse sand. Pot, Aug. to Nov., placing one bulb half its depth in a 4½ in. pot or three in a 6 in. pot; good drainage essential. Position, light, cool greenhouse, Sept. to May; cold frame or sunny spot outdoors, May to Sept. Water moderately Sept. to May, or as soon as flower spikes show; keep quite dry May to Sept. Apply stimulants occasionally during growth. Top-dress annually with equal parts sandy loam, decayed cow manure, and sand, in Aug. Repotting only necessary every three or four years. Season of growth, Sept. to May; season of rest, May to Sept.

CULTURE OUTDOORS: Soil, light sandy, enriched with decayed cow manure. Position, sunny well-drained borders at base of south wall. Plant, Aug. to Nov., 2 to 3 in. deep. Protect, Nov. to April, with covering of dry litter. Top-dress annually in Aug. with leaf-mould or decayed cow manure. Lift and replant every four or five years.

PROPAGATION: By offsets, removed when repotting and treated as old bulbs.

SPECIES CULTIVATED: *N. Bowdenii*, pink, 1½ ft.; *curvifolia*, scarlet, 1 ft., var. *Fothergillii*, deep scarlet; *filifolia*, red, 1 ft.; *flexuosa*, pink, 2 ft.; *humilis*, purplish rose, 18 in.; *sarniensis*, ' Guernsey Lily ', salmon, 2 ft., and vars. *corusca*, orange-scarlet, 1 ft., *Plantii*, crimson, *rosea*, rose, and numerous hybrids. See also Lycoris.

Nerium—*Apocynaceae*. Greenhouse evergreen flowering shrubs. First introduced late sixteenth century.

CULTURE: Compost, two parts sandy loam, one part well-decomposed manure, one part leaf-mould, and one part sand. Position, pots, tubs, or well-drained beds in light, sunny greenhouse or window, place pot or tub plants outdoors, June to Sept. Pot or plant, Feb. or March. Prune immediately after flowering, or in Oct. shortening shoots of previous year's growth to within 3 or 4 in. of their base. Temp., Sept. to March 45° to 55°, March to June 55° to 65°. Water copiously March to Sept., moderately Sept. to Nov., keep nearly dry Nov. to March. Apply stimulants once or twice weekly May to Sept. Remove young shoots that issue from base of flower trusses as soon as they appear. No shade required. Syringe twice daily March to June.

PROPAGATION: By cuttings of firm young shoots, 3 to 6 in. long, inserted singly in 2 in. pots in a compost of equal parts peat, loam, leaf-mould, and sand, placed under bell-glass in temp. 60° to 70°, spring or summer.

SPECIES CULTIVATED: *N. Oleander*, ' Oleander ' or ' Rose Bay ', white, red, or purple, summer, to 20 ft., Orient, and numerous vars.; *indicum* (syn. *N. odorum*), rose-pink or white, sweet-scented, June to Aug., 6 to 8 ft., Persia and Japan.

Nertera—*Rubiaceae*. Greenhouse and half-hardy creeping perennial herb with orange berries. First introduced mid-nineteenth century.

INDOOR CULTURE: Compost, two parts sandy loam, one part leaf-mould and sand. Position, small well-drained pots or pans in shady part of greenhouse. Pot, Feb. or March. Water freely March to Sept., moderately afterwards. Temp., March to Oct. 50° to 60°, Oct. to March 40° to 50°.

OUTDOOR CULTURE: Soil, ordinary, light rich. Position, moist, sheltered ledges of shady rockery. Plant, March or April. Water in dry weather. Protect in severe weather with bell- or hand-glass.

PROPAGATION: By seeds sown $\frac{1}{16}$ in. deep in light, sandy soil in temp. 55° to 65°, March or April; division of plants in March or April.

SPECIES CULTIVATED: *N. granadensis* (syn. *N. depressa*), ' Bead Plant·', ' Fruiting Duckweed ', 1 in., flowers green, S. America, Australasia.

Neviusia—*Rosaceae.* Hardy deciduous flowering shrub. First introduced late nineteenth century.

CULTURE: Soil, good ordinary. Position, sunny, sheltered shrubbery. Plant in autumn.

PROPAGATION: By cuttings of half-ripened shoots inserted in sandy soil in cold frame in summer; also by layering in autumn.

SPECIES CULTIVATED: *N. alabamensis*, ' Alabama Snow Wreath ', white, May, 6 ft., Alabama.

New Jersey Tea-Plant, see *Ceanothus americanus.*

New Zealand Broom, see Notospartium;   **-Bur,** see *Acaena microphylla;* **-Daisy Bush,** see Olearia;   **-Flax,** see *Phormium Tenax;*   **-Glory· Pea,** see *Clianthus Dampieri;*   **-Holly,** see *Olearia ilicifolia;*   **-Kowhoi,** see *Sophora tetraptera;* **-Mountain Buttercup,** see *Ranunculus Lyallii;*   **-Palm,** see *Rhopalostylis sapida;* **-Penwiper Plant,** see *Notothlaspi rosulatum;*   **-Spinach,** see *Tetragonia expansa;* **-Tree Fern,** see *Dicksonia squarrosa.*

Nicandra—*Solanaceae.* Hardy annual. First introduced mid-eighteenth century.

CULTURE: Soil, ordinary. Position, sunny, open borders.

PROPAGATION: By seeds sown $\frac{1}{8}$ in. deep in pots or boxes of light soil in temp. 55° in March, transplanting seedlings 3 ft. apart outdoors in May; or by sowing seed in sunny position outdoors in April, transplanting seedlings in June.

SPECIES CULTIVATED: *N. Physalodes*, ' Apple of Peru ', blue and white, summer, 18 in. to 2 ft., Peru.

Nicotiana (Tobacco Plant)—*Solanaceae.* Half-hardy annuals. *N. Tabacum* is the tobacco of commerce. First introduced mid-sixteenth century.

POT CULTURE: Compost, two parts loam, one part leaf-mould or decayed manure, and one part sand. Position, sunny or shady greenhouse or window. Water freely when in full growth, moderately at other times. Temp., March to Sept. 55° to 60°, Sept. to March 40° to 50°.

OUTDOOR CULTURE: Soil, ordinary. Position, sunny beds or borders. Plant in June in groups of three or six. Protect *N. alba* in winter with covering of cinder ashes, tan, or decayed manure. Will only survive winter in well-drained soils.

CULTURE OF TOBACCO PLANT: Soil, ordinary. Position, sunny beds or borders. Plant, June. Gather leaves of *N. Tabacum* in Sept. for drying. Water freely in dry weather.

PROPAGATION: By seeds sown on the surface of fine light soil in a shallow box or pan in shade, in a temp. of 55° to 60°, in March or April.

SPECIES CULTIVATED: *N. alata*, var. *grandiflora* (syn. *N. affinis*), ' Sweet-scented Tobacco ', white, fragrant, summer, 3 to 5 ft., strictly a perennial, Brazil; *Sanderae*, red, pink, carmine, etc., summer, 2 to 3 ft., hybrid; *suaveolens*, white, summer, 2 ft., S. America; *sylvestris*, white, summer, 3 to 4 ft., Argentina; *Tabacum*, ' Tobacco Plant ', rose, summer, 4 ft., S. ·America, var. *macrophylla* (syn. *N. macrophylla*), red, rose, or purple, summer; *tomentosa* (syn. *N. colossea*), pale green and yellow, tinged red, 10 to 20 ft., S. America.

Nidularium—*Bromeiaceae.* Stove plants with green, red or crimson bracts, **and** leaves in dense basal rosetter. First introduced early nineteenth century.

CULTURE: Compost, equal parts fibrous loam, rough peat, leaf-mould and silver sand. Position, well-drained pots in light, moist part of stove. Pot, Feb. or March. Water moderately in winter, freely at other times. Temp., March to Sept. 70° to 80°, Sept. to March 65° to 75°.

PROPAGATION: By largish offshoots inserted singly in small pots of sandy peat in temp. of 85°, Feb. or April.

SPECIES CULTIVATED: *N. fulgens*, white and violet, leaves spotted dark green, 9 to 12 in., Brazil; *Innocentii*, white, leaves tinted brown or red, Brazil; *purpureum*, red, leaves flushed purple-brown, Brazil; *striatum*, white, to 1 ft., Brazil. See also Canistrum and Aregelia.

Nierembergia (Cup-flower)—*Solanaceae*. Hardy and half-hardy creeping perennial herbs. First introduced early nineteenth century.

CULTURE OF HARDY SPECIES: Soil, equal parts sandy loam and leaf-mould. Position, sunny or moist border or ledges of rockery. Plant, Oct., March or April. Water freely in dry weather. Top-dress annually in March with decayed cow manure. Protect in very severe weather with covering of litter.

CULTURE OF HALF-HARDY SPECIES: Compost, two parts sandy loam, one part well-decomposed cow manure, and one part sand. Position, well-drained pots or pans in shady part of greenhouse or cold frame all the year round, or outdoors in shady spot, May to Oct. Pot, Feb. or March. Water freely March to Sept., moderately afterwards.

PROPAGATION: By seeds sown in light, sandy soil in temp. 55° to 65° Nov. to April; cuttings inserted in sandy soil under bell-glass in shady part of cool greenhouse in Aug., transferring when well rooted singly into 2 in. pots and placing in light, airy position in greenhouse or window.

HARDY SPECIES CULTIVATED: *N. patagonica*, pink, summer, 1 in., Patagonia; *repens* (syn. *N. rivularis*), white, summer, 1 in., S. America.

HALF-HARDY SPECIES CULTIVATED: *N. frutescens*, white and yellow, tinged blue, summer, 1 to 3 ft., Chile, and var. *atroviolacea*, dark violet;   *gracilis* (syn. *N. filicaulis*), white and yellow, tinged purple, summer, 6 to 9 in., S. America; *hippomanica*, white, tinged rose, 3 to 12 in., var. *violacea* (syn. *N. caerulea*), violet-blue, summer, Argentine.

Nigella (Fennel-flower)—*Ranunculaceae*. Hardy annuals. Flowers surrounded by a green mossy involucre. Foliage, green, graceful, feathery. First introduced mid-sixteenth century.

CULTURE: Soil, ordinary. Position, sunny, open beds or borders.

PROPAGATION: By seeds sown ⅛ in. deep in lines, bands or masses in March or April; thin seedlings out 6 in. apart each way, May or June.

SPECIES CULTIVATED: *N. damascena*, ' Love-in-a-Mist ', ' Devil-in-a-Bush ', blue, summer, 1 to 2 ft., S. Europe, vars. *flore-pleno*, double, blue, *alba*, white; *hispanica*, blue, summer, 1 to 2 ft., Spain; *sativa*, pale blue, summer, 1½ ft., Medit. Region (cultivated for seeds, which are used in seasoning and known as black cummin).

Night-scented Stock, see *Mathiola bicornis*.

Nine Bark, see Physocarpus.

Nippon Bells, see *Shortia uniflora*.

Nolana (Chilean Bell-flower)—*Nolanaceae*. Hardy annuals. First introduced mid-sixteenth century.

CULTURE: Soil, ordinary. Position, open, sunny beds, borders, or rockeries.

PROPAGATION: By seeds sown 1/16 in. deep in patches in March or April where plants are required to grow, thinning seedlings to 2 or 3 in. apart in May or June.

SPECIES CULTIVATED: *N. atriplicifolia* (syn. *N. grandiflora*), blue and white, summer, trailing, Peru; *lanceolata*, blue, white, and green, summer, 6 in., Peru.

Nolina, see Beaucarnea.

Nomocharis—*Liliaceae*. Hardy bulbous flowering plants, sometimes included in Lilium. First introduced early twentieth century.

CULTURE: Soil, well drained, with leaf-mould or peat added. Position, sun or half-shade.

PROPAGATION: By seeds sown $\frac{1}{16}$ in. deep in Jan. or Feb. under glass, transplanted soon after germination or grown in deep seed pan and planted outdoors the next spring or the spring following.

SPECIES CULTIVATED: *N. aperta* (syn. *Lilium apertum*), rose, boldly blotched with crimson, June to July, 1 to 3 ft., W. China; *Farreri*, white with crimson spots, June to July, 2 to 3 ft., N. Burma; *Mairei*, white, usually spotted with red-purple, June to July, 2 to 2½ ft., W. China; *pardanthina*, pink with purple-brown spots, 1½ to 3 ft., W. China; *saluenensis*, white, pale yellow or pale rose, purplish-spotted, 2 to 3 ft., W. China.

Nopalxochia—*Cactaceae*. Greenhouse succulent plants, sometimes included in Epiphyllum.

CULTURE: As Epiphyllum.

PROPAGATION: As Epiphyllum.

SPECIES CULTIVATED: *N. Ackermannii*, crimson, summer, 3 to 4 ft., Mexico; *phyllanthoides*, rose or red, Mexico.

Norfolk Island Palm, see *Rhopalostylis sapida*; **-Pine**, see *Araucaria excelsa*.

Nothofagus (Southern Beech)—*Fagaceae*. Slightly tender evergreen or deciduous trees. First introduced early nineteenth century.

CULTURE: Soil, moist loam. Position, specimens on lawns or in open spaces in milder counties such as Devon and Cornwall. Plant deciduous species Nov. to Feb., evergreen species Sept. or April.

PROPAGATION: By layering in spring.

DECIDUOUS SPECIES CULTIVATED: *N. antarctica*, 40 to 60 ft., S. America; *obliqua*, 50 to 100 ft., Chile.

EVERGREEN SPECIES CULTIVATED: *N. betuloides*, 40 to 60 ft., S. America; *cliffortioides*, 30 to 50 ft., New Zealand; *Cunninghamii*, 40 to 60 ft., Tasmania; *fusca*, 50 to 100 ft., New Zealand; *Menziesii*, 40 to 60 ft., New Zealand; *Moorei*, tinted young foliage, to 150 ft., Australia.

Notholaena—*Polypodiaceae*. Stove and greenhouse ferns. Fronds divided, upper surface green, under covered with white powder or scales. Height from 3 to 18 in. First introduced mid-eighteenth century.

CULTURE: Compost, equal parts loam, leaf-mould, peat and sand, with little charcoal and finely broken sandstone. Position, pots in shady part of house. Pot, Feb. or March. Water moderately Oct. to Feb., freely afterwards. Syringing not required. Temp. stove species, Sept. to March 55° to 65°, March to Sept. 65° to 75°. Greenhouse, Sept. to March 45° to 50°, March to Sept. 55° to 65°. *N. bonariensis* is impatient of water on fronds.

PROPAGATION: By spores sown on surface of fine sandy peat in pans under bell-glass in temp. 75° to 85° any time; division at potting time.

STOVE SPECIES CULTIVATED: *N. bonariensis* (syn. *N. tomentosa*), species of great charm, fronds 1 ft., almost yellow, Mexico; *scariosa* (syn. *N. squamosa*), fronds 6 in., Mexico; *sinuata*, Trop. America; *trichomanoides*, Jamaica and Cuba.

GREENHOUSE SPECIES CULTIVATED: *N. Hookeri*, N. America; *Marantae*, S. Europe, N. Africa, etc.; *Newberryi*, California; *vellea* (syn. *N. languinosa*), S. Europe and Australia.

Notholirion—*Liliaceae*. Hardy bulbous plants, sometimes included in Lilium.

CULTURE: Soil, well drained, enriched with leaf-mould. Position, sheltered, cool, in half-shade, except *N. Thomsonianum*.

PROPAGATION: By seed; bulblets formed round base of flower stems, these should be separated and planted apart after flowering.

SPECIES CULTIVATED: *N. campanulatum*, crimson, June, 2½ to 4 ft., N. Burma, Tibet, W. China; *bulbitinum* (syn. *N. hyacinthinum*), lavender, June, 2½ to 3½ ft.,

N. India (Himalaya), Tibet, W. China; *macrophyllum*, pale mauve or lavender, May, 7 to 12 in., N. India; *Thomsonianum* (syns. *Lilium Thomsonianum, L. roseum*), pale mauve, May, 2 to 3 ft., N. India, Afghanistan.

Nothopanax—*Araliaceae.* Tender, fast-growing evergreen shrubs with large palmate leaves.
CULTURE: Soil, light well drained. Position, sheltered borders in mildest districts only.
PROPAGATION: By seeds sown in sandy soil in a frame in spring.
SPECIES CULTIVATED: *N. arboreum*, 15 ft., New Zealand; *laetum*, 20 ft., New Zealand.

Notocactus—*Cactaceae.* Greenhouse succulent plants, sometimes included in Echinocactus.
CULTURE: As Echinocactus.
PROPAGATION: As Echinocactus.
SPECIES CULTIVATED: *N. apricus*, yellow, Uruguay; *concinnus*, yellow, summer, 4 in., Mexico; *Scopa*, yellow, spring, 12 to 18 in., Brazil, var. *ruberrimus*, crimson-red central spines.

Notospartium—*Leguminosae.* Slightly tender evergreen flowering shrub. First introduced late nineteenth century.
CULTURE: Soil, light well-drained loam. Position, sunny sheltered border. Plant, April or May. Prune in April, thinning out weak wood only.
PROPAGATION: By seeds sown in sandy soil in a cold frame in spring; cuttings in a cold frame in autumn.
SPECIES CULTIVATED: *N. Carmichaeliae*, ' New Zealand Broom ', pink, Aug., 4 to 10 ft., New Zealand.

Notothlaspi—*Cruciferae.* Monocarpic alpine plants.
CULTURE: Difficult to grow. Demands perfectly drained scree soil, very stony, and warm, sunny position. Bitterly resents root disturbance and should be sown one or two seeds in a small, deep pot and left undisturbed. Best in alpine house or cold frame.
PROPAGATION: By seeds.
SPECIES CULTIVATED: *N. rosulatum*, ' New Zealand Penwiper Plant ', white, fragrant, summer, 9 in., New Zealand.

Nuphar (Yellow Water Lily)—*Nymphaeaceae.* Hardy aquatic perennials.
CULTURE: Soil, six parts strong rich loam, one part well-decayed manure. Position, sunny, shallow streams, ponds or lakes. Depth of water, 6 to 12 in.; plants will live in 4 to 6 ft. of water, but rarely bloom in such depths. Plant, March or Oct. Methods of planting: (1) Strap the root between two turves turned grass-side inwards and lower gently into the water. (2) Plant firmly in a wicker basket in loam, rather on the wet side, and drop into position.
PROPAGATION: By division of the plants in March.
SPECIES CULTIVATED: *N. advenum*, ' Common Spatterdock ', yellow, May till Sept., N. America, var. *variegatum*, variegated leaves; *japonicum*, yellow, arrow-shaped leaves above and crimped ones below water, still water, Japan, var. *rubrotinctum*, orange-scarlet, reddish stamens; *lutea*, ' Brandy Bottle ', yellow, June to Sept., Europe (Br.); *minimum* (syn. *N. pumilum*), yellow, for rock garden pools, July, Europe.

Nutmeg, see Myristica; **Californian-,** see *Torreya californica.*

Nuttallia, see Osmaronia.

Nymphaea (Water-lily)—*Nymphaeaceae.* Stove and hardy aquatic tuberous-rooted perennials.
CULTURE OF STOVE SPECIES: Six parts rich turfy loam and one part well-decayed manure. Position, large pots or tubs immersed 8 to 12 in. below surface of water in tanks fully exposed to light. Plant, Feb. to April. Temp. of atmo-

sphere 65° to 75° March to Sept., 50° to 60° Sept. to March. Temp. of water 65° to 75° March to Sept., 55° to 65° Sept. to March. Repot annually in Feb. or March. Reduce water as soon as foliage dies off and leave tubers in mud all winter. Alternatively, lift tubers end of Oct., dry off and store in moist sand until spring; beware of rats during this period.

CULTURE OF HARDY SPECIES: Compost, six parts strong, rich loam, one part well-decayed manure or bonemeal at rate of one 5 in. potful per bushel of loam. Depth of water 18 in. to 2 ft. for strong growing kinds, 12 to 18 in. for medium kinds and 9 to 12 in. for the pygmies. Position, open sunny ponds or lakes. Plant, March to June. Methods of planting: (1) Place plant in small wicker basket containing above compost and lower to the bottom of pond or lake. (2) Pack layer of compost 4 in. deep over floor of emptied pool with 1 in. plain loam above it and plant direct into this. Run water in very gradually and at intervals —taking six to eight weeks to fill the pool if growth is slow. (3) Enclose root between turves turned grass-side inwards and strap round or cover with matting and lower carefully into position. (Only use this method if there is a natural mud bottom to the pond).

PROPAGATION: Stove species by seeds sown ⅛ in. deep in pots of soil immersed in water heated to a temp. of 65° to 75°, March or April. Hardy species by division of tubers or rhizomes, March or April.

HARDY SPECIES CULTIVATED: *N. alba*, ' Common Water-lily ', white, summer, Europe (Br.), and vars. *candidissima*, white, and *rosea*, rose; *Barkleyi rosea*, deep rose, hybrid; *candida*, white, Bohemia; *fennica*, white, Finland; *Gladstoniana*, white, hybrid; *Laydekeri*, rose, purplish, suitable for pot culture, hybrid, many named forms, series of hybrids of different parentage raised in France; *Moorei*, yellow, hybrid; *odorata*, white, summer, N. America, and vars. *rosea*, pink, *sulphurea*, yellow; *tetragona* (syn. *N. pygmaea*), white, June; *tuberosa*, white, July, N. America, and var. *Richardsonii*, double.

STOVE SPECIES CULTIVATED: *N. ampla*, white, July, W. India; *Bissettii*, rose, night-flowering, hybrid; *Burtii*, yellow, Tanganyika; *caerulea*, ' Blue Lotus of the Nile ', blue, N. and Cent. Africa; *capensis*, ' Cape Blue Waterlily ', sky-blue, summer, S. and E. Africa, Madagascar, and vars. *zanzibariensis*, dark blue, *azurea*, blue, and *rosea*, deep rose; *Daubeniana*, viviparous hybrid, will grow in small bowl, blue; *Deaniana*, pink, hybrid; *flavovirens* (syn. *N. gracilis*), white, summer, Mexico; *gigantea*, sky-blue, summer, Australia; *Lotus*, ' White Lotus of the Nile ', white, night-blooming, scented, Egypt and Africa; *micrantha*, viviparous, bluish-white, small, W. Africa; *polychroma*, bright blue, summer, Tanganyika; *rubra*, foliage bronze, flowers bright red, nocturnal, India, and var. *devoniensis*; *scutifolia*, blue, summer, Africa; *stellata*, light blue, summer, S.E. Asia, Philippines; *Stuhlmannii*, yellow, Aug., Sept., scented, Africa.

Nymphoides (Floating Heart; Bean Lily)—*Gentianaceae* (or *Menyanthaceae*). Hardy and greenhouse floating perennial aquatics. Formerly known as Limnanthemum.

CULTURE OF GREENHOUSE SPECIES: Soil, loam and leaf-mould. Position, tub or tank of water in greenhouse. Temp., Oct. to March 45° to 55°, March to Oct. 55° to 65°. Plant in spring.

CULTURE OF HARDY SPECIES: Soil, ordinary. Position, ponds or shallow lakes. Plant in March.

PROPAGATION: Tender species by seeds sown in pots of light soil immersed in water in temp. 65° in spring, or division of the plants in March; hardy species by seeds sown in mud in spring, or division of roots in March.

SPECIES CULTIVATED: *N. indica*, ' Water Snowflake ', fringed white flowers just above water, floating, round leaves 1 to 2 in. dia., tender, very beautiful, Florida; *peltata* (syns. *Limnanthemum nymphaeoides*, *Villaisia nymphaeoides*), ' Water Fringe ', hardy, 6 to 18 in. water, flowers golden, summer, leaves mottled, floating, Europe, N. America; *trachysperma*, white, floating, tubers hanging in water, tender, Mexico.

Nyssa (Tupelo)—*Nyssaceae*. Hardy deciduous trees. Grown for the beauty of their rich scarlet-tinted foliage in August. Flowers and fruits insignificant.
CULTURE: Soil, ordinary. Position, margins of streams, lakes, etc. Plant in autumn.
PROPAGATION: By layering in autumn.
SPECIES CULTIVATED: *N. aquatica*, white, May, 40 to 50 ft., U. States; *sinensis*, white, May, 30 ft., Cent. China; *sylvatica*, white, June, 30 to 100 ft., N. America.

Oak, see Quercus.

Oat, see Avena.

Ocimum—*Labiatae*. Half-hardy annual aromatic herbs. Leaves, egg-shaped, aromatic; used for flavouring stews, soups and salads. First introduced early sixteenth century.
CULTURE: Soil, ordinary light rich. Position, sunny well-drained border. Plant, 6 in. apart in rows 9 to 12 in. asunder in May. Shade from sun first few days after planting. Water freely in dry weather. Gather leaves and tops when coming into flower, dry and reduce to powder for winter use.
PROPAGATION: By seeds sown $\frac{1}{16}$ in. deep in light soil in shallow box in temp. 55° to 60° in March, transplanting seedlings when three leaves are formed 1 in. apart in similar soil and gradually hardening off in cold frame.
SPECIES CULTIVATED: *O. Basilicum*, ' Sweet Basil ', white, summer, 1 ft., Trop. Asia; *minimum*, ' Bush Basil ', white, summer, 6 in., Trop. Asia.

Octomeria—*Orchidaceae*. A rather large epiphytic genus allied to Pleurothallis, dwarf, tufted habit, stems slender, monophyllous. Flowers, small, terminal to stems.
CULTURE: Compost, as for *Odontoglossum crispum*. Temps. similar. Species with hard-textured leaves need fewer waterings in winter, and a few require a higher temp.
PROPAGATION: By division of plants in spring.
SPECIES CULTIVATED: A selection—*O. Baueri*, yellow, clustered, whitish-yellow, autumn, winter, W. Indies; *crassifolia* (syn. *O. graminifolia*), whitish-yellow, lip with purplish blotch, autumn, Brazil; *diaphana*, white, almost trans-lucent, spring, summer, Brazil; *grandiflora*, few, pale to deep yellow, summer, autumn, Brazil; *Saundersiana*, pale yellow, lip marked purple, in pairs, winter, Brazil.

Odontadenia—*Apocynaceae*. Stove flowering climber. First introduced mid-nineteenth century.
CULTURE: Compost, rough turfy loam, peat, sharp sand and a little broken charcoal. Position, well-drained pots, with shoots trained to roof of stove or to wire trellis. Pot, Feb. or March. Prune, Oct., cutting away shoots that have flowered only. Water very little Oct. to Feb., moderately Feb. to April, freely afterwards. Temp., Oct. to Feb. 55° to 60°, Feb. to Oct. 65° to 75°.
PROPAGATION: By cuttings of young side shoots, 3 in. long, inserted in pots of sandy peat under bell-glass in temp. 80° in Feb., March or April.
SPECIES CULTIVATED: *O. speciosa* (syn. *O. grandiflora*), yellow and orange, fragrant, summer, climbing, Trinidad.

× **Odontioda**—*Orchidaceae*. Bigeneric hybrid between Cochlioda and Odonto-glossum. A great number have been raised. The Cochliodas, particularly *C. densiflora* (syn. *C. Noezliana*), have imparted brilliant coloration to the flowers, and secondary and subsequent crosses, with the primary hybrids and Odonto-glossum hybrids, have given size and varied floral colour. Culture, as for the Odontoglossums of the *O. crispum* type.

Odontoglossum—*Orchidaceae*. A large epiphytic genus, so popular that often a house is devoted to them. Of late years, many hybrids, now outnumbering the species, have been produced. Crosses with Cochliodas, in particular *C.*

densiflora (*Noezliana*), have imparted brilliant colours to many hybrids, and secondary and subsequent crosses have added large and varied coloration. The genus is variable—many have pseudo-bulbs of fairly soft texture, others hard. Spikes from the base of the leading pseudo-bulbs may be few- or many-flowered, usually simple, sometimes branched. All have beautiful flowers The leaves are persistent, from thin textures to the coriaceous. A number of natural hybrids occur.

CULTURE: Compost, two parts osmunda fibre, two parts sphagnum moss, rather more fibre for large plants, a few half-decayed oak or beech leaves rubbed to pieces, and sand should be added. Polypodium or other fibres may be added but these should be cut into short lengths. For *O. crispum* and similar-textured plants, and most of the hybrids, a sweet moist atmosphere, as far as possible equable, should be maintained. 60° is a guide, necessarily lower in winter and higher in summer. Summer temps. can often be kept reasonably low by manipulation of blinds and ventilation—never allow humidity to escape by opening vents too widely. Admit air at night whenever weather permits. Syringing and damping can be freely practised in warm weather. Pipe heat can usually be dispensed with from May to Sept., earlier or later. These conditions can only be approximated in winter. Pipe heat is resented but is then necessary. A night temp. of 50° to 55° should be aimed at and allows moderate humidity in the atmosphere. Below 50° plants and atmosphere must be dryer. Whenever possible admit a little air to freshen atmosphere, and increase the day temp. Avoid draughts at all times. Watering is required throughout the year with consideration in cold weather. Differentiation must be made with the harder-bulbed kinds. They may be grown in the same house but should be hung near the glass and the extremes, e.g. *O. grande*, *O. citrosum*, placed on a shelf, as, if they are matured by late autumn, water may be needed but once or twice, if at all, from the end of Oct. to Feb. For *O. Rossii*, *Cervantesii* and similar, a decided rest but not as severe.

Repotting may be effected with the majority of species in spring as growth is seen. Hybrids may be at slight variance with this season, but never pot in the cold months. Both flowers and plants are susceptible to attacks from thrips. Occasional sprayings with weak insecticides deter, but when their presence is evident, dipping should be performed—immerse the plants one by one up to, but not touching, the compost, swirl lightly and then lay the plant on the stage in such a position that the liquid drains from it before returning the plant to its proper place. Choose a rather dull day for the operation. Fumigations also deter, the best time to fumigate is in the evening—beforehand withhold the use of the syringe that the foliage may be fairly dry.

PROPAGATION: By division of plants when potting. Each division should have four bulbs and a growth evident or incipient. Sound back bulbs may be removed singly or in twos, laid on a rather shady part of a shingle-covered stage, or placed in pans or shallow boxes, filled with small potsherds kept damp till growth is seen, then pot using a very small pot.

SPECIES CULTIVATED: A selection—*O. Adrianiae*, a natural hybrid, yellow or white broken with red-brown, spring to summer, Colombia, and many named vars.; *apterum* (syn. *O. nebulosum*), few, white with red-brown spots, brightest on lip, spring to summer, Mexico, var. *candidulum*, without spots; *aspidorhinum*, yellow, blotched red-brown, lip white blotched purple, small, pretty, summer to autumn, Colombia; *bictoniense*, yellowish-green blotched chestnut-brown, lip rose, 2 to 3 ft., autumn, Guatemala, Mexico, var. *sulphureum*, yellow, white; *blandum*, white marked red-purple, pretty, spring, variable, Colombia; *cariniferum* (syn. *O. fuscatum*), brown-yellow, scape branched, Costa Rica, Panama; *Cervantesii*, white or rosy, basal halves with concentric chocolate-red bars, spring, Mexico, Guatemala, vaı. *decorum*. larger, bars purplish-red; *cirrhosum*, white spotted purplish-crimson, segments tapered, scapes often branched, spring to summer, Ecuador, var. *Hrubyana*, white faintly spotted; *citrosum*, white or rose flushed, lip usually rose, scapes long, pendulous, spring to summer, very variable, Mexico, vars. *album*, white, *punctatum*, rose flushed dotted purple; *constrictum*, yellow blotched red-brown, lip white rose blotched, segments tapered, scapes branched, winter to spring, Venezuela, var. *Sanderianum*, larger and brighter; *Coradinei*, yellow, chestnut blotched, segments narrow, variable, spring, hybrid, var. *mirabile*, larger, finer; *cordatum*, pseudo-bulbs monophyllous, chestnut-brown, broken yellow, lip white brown spotted, scapes sometimes branched, spring, various, Mexico; *coronarium*, chestnut-red bordered yellow, lip bright yellow, requires raft, Colombia, vars. *brevifolium*, leaves and scapes shorter, various, *chiriquense*, larger, scapes taller; *crispum*, white or rose tinged or blotched red, long season, Colombia; *excellens*, yellow blotched chestnut-brown, beautiful, variable, scapes often branched, spring, hybrid, many vars. have been named; *gloriosum*, yellow blotched chestnut-brown, fragrant, segments narrow acuminate, scape often branched, spring to summer, Colombia; *grande*, large yellow chestnut-brown, lip whitish or yellowish with reddish blotches and spots, autumn, Guatemala, var. *aureum*, light and dark yellow; *Hallii*, large brown-red and yellow, lip fringed, segments acute, scapes 2 to 4 ft., spring, Ecuador, Peru, Colombia; *Harryanum*, large, chestnut-brown, yellow, white, spring to summer, Colombia; *harvengtense*, variable, beautiful, yellow spotted cinnamon, hybrid; *hastilabium*, greenish-yellow, purplish-brown, lip white and purplish, segments tapered, spring to summer, Colombia; *Horsmannii*, variable hybrid, white or yellowish, blotched brown, lip base spotted purplish-red, spring, Colombia; *Kegeljanii* (syn. *O. polyxanthum*), yellow blotched cinnamon, lip dark brown, spring, Ecuador; *Krameri*, dwarf, white, light violet, lip purplish-violet, winter to summer, Costa Rica, var. *album*, white; *Lindleyanum*, yellow-brown, segments narrow, spring, Colombia; *luteo-purpureum*, large, yellow, chestnut-brown, lip yellowish, often fringed, spring, very variable, Colombia; *maculatum*, segments acute, spring, Mexico; *maxillare* (syn. *O. madrense*), white, purple-brown blotch at base, lip orange, white, spring to summer, Mexico; *mulus*, yellow, blotched brown, very variable, spring, Colombia; *naevium*, resembles a small *O. cirrhosum*, spring to summer, Colombia; *nobile* (syn. *O. Pescatorei*), white or rose flushed, often purple spotted, scape often branched, spring, Colombia, many named vars.; *odoratum*, golden-yellow, fragrant, spring, Venezuela; *Oerstedii*, dwarf, white, winter to spring, Venezuela; *pulchellum*, small, white, lip uppermost, spring, fragrant, Guatemala, Costa Rica, var. *majus*, larger, strongly scented; *ramosissimum*, white, dotted mauve, scapes tall, branched, spring, Colombia, var. *liliflorum*, rose-purple, white; *Rossii*, dwarf, pretty, white or rose flushed, lip rose flushed, very variable, spring, Mexico; *Schlieperianum*, yellow, barred brown, lip wedge-shaped, late summer to autumn, Costa Rica; *tripudians*, yellow, chestnut-brown, lip white, blotched rose or purple, crest bristled, autumn, spring, Colombia, Peru; *triumphans*, golden-yellow, chestnut-brown, lip white, handsome, variable, spring, Colombia; *Uroskinneri*, greenish, chestnut-brown, lip rose marbled white, scape 2 to 3 ft., spring to summer, Guatemala, vars. *album*, lip white, *splendens*, lip purplish-rose; *Wilckeanum*, large, yellow blotched red-brown, very variable, many vars., all beautiful, spring, Colombia; *Williamsianum*, greenish-yellow barred cinnamon-brown, lip creamy-white, summer, Costa Rica. Many other species and natural hybrids.

Odontonema—*Acanthaceae*. Greenhouse evergreen flowering plants. First introduced mid-nineteenth century.

CULTURE: Compost, equal parts fibrous loam, peat, leaf-mould and sand. Position, well-drained pots in greenhouse Sept. to June, sunny frame or pit June to Sept. Pot, March or April. Water moderately at all times. Temp., Sept. to March 55° to 65°, March to June 65° to 70°. Shorten growths after flowering. Plants may be grown on for second year to form large specimens. Feed with liquid manure or an approved plant food when plants are established in final pots.

PROPAGATION: By cuttings of young shoots inserted in small pots of sandy soil under bell-glass or in propagating frame in temp. 75° March to June.

SPECIES CULTIVATED: *O. Schomburgkianum* (syn. *Thyrsacanthus rutilans*), scarlet-crimson, winter, 3 to 5 ft., Colombia.

× **Odontonia**—*Orchidaceae.* Bigeneric hybrid between Odontoglossum and Miltonia. Culture, as for Odontoglossums, minimum temp. 55°.

Odontosoria—*Polypodiaceae.* Tropical ferns, formerly included in Davallia.
CULTURE: As Davallia.
PROPAGATION: As Davallia.
SPECIES CULTIVATED: *O. aculeata*, climbing, 6 ft., W. Indies; *chinensis* (syn. *Davallia tenuifolia*), drooping habit, Malaya.

Oenothera—*Onagraceae.* Hardy annuals, biennials and herbaceous and shrubby perennials. First introduced early seventeenth century.
CULTURE OF ANNUAL SPECIES: Soil, ordinary. Position, sunny where plants are to flower, or in boxes of light soil in temp. 55° to 65° in April, transplanting seedlings outdoors in May. Thin seedlings sown outdoors to 6 in. apart in June.
POT CULTURE: Compost, two parts good soil, one part leaf-mould, well-decayed manure and sand. Position, well-drained 6 in. pots in cold frame, greenhouse or window. Thin seedlings when 1 in. high to six or eight in each pot. Water moderately at first, freely when in full growth. Apply liquid manure twice a week when plants show flower.
CULTURE OF BIENNIAL SPECIES: Soil, ordinary. Position, sunny beds or borders. Sow seeds $\frac{1}{16}$ in. deep in shady position outdoors in April, transplanting seedlings when 1 in. high, 3 in. apart each way, in sunny border, again transplanting into flowering position following Sept. or March.
CULTURE OF PERENNIAL SPECIES: Soil, light, sandy loam. Position, sunny well-drained borders, beds or rockeries. Plant, Oct., March or April. Water freely in dry weather. Mulch annually with decayed cow manure. Lift and replant every three or four years. Prune away straggling shoots of shrubby species after flowering.
PROPAGATION: Perennial species by seeds sown in light soil in shallow box or well-drained pans in cold frame or under hand-light in March or April, transplanting outdoors end of May or June; cuttings of young shoots inserted in sandy soil under hand-light in shade in spring or summer; suckers removed with roots attached, spring or autumn; division of roots, March or April.
ANNUAL SPECIES CULTIVATED: *O. bistorta*, yellow and red, summer, 1 ft., California; *Drummondii*, yellow, June to Oct., 1 to 2 ft., Texas; *odorata*, yellow, summer, nocturnal, 2 to 3 ft., Chile, and var. *grandiflora*; *tetraptera*, white, summer, 1 ft., Mexico, and var. *rosea*, pink, sometimes erroneously named *O. mexicana rosea*.
BIENNIAL SPECIES CULTIVATED: *O. biennis*, ' Evening Primrose ', yellow, fragrant, June to Oct., 4 to 5 ft., N. America, and vars. *grandiflora*, *Lamarckiana*, similar to *O. biennis* but flowers larger; *Clutei*, soft yellow, summer, 3 to 4 ft., Arizona.
PERENNIAL SPECIES CULTIVATED: *O. acaulis* (syn. *O. taraxacifolia*), white or blush, summer, prostrate, Chile, sometimes a biennial; *caespitosa*, white, fragrant, July, 4 to 9 in., California; *fruticosa*, ' Sun-drops ', golden yellow, summer, 1 to 2 ft., U.S.A. and vars. *major* and *Youngii*; *glauca*, yellow, summer, 2 to 3 ft., Southern U. States, and var. *Fraseri*; *linearis*, yellow, summer, 12 to 18 in., U.S.A. *missouriensis* (syn. *O. macrocarpa*), yellow, summer, trailing, N. America; *Nuttallii*, white or pink, summer, 6 to 9 in., California; *ovata*, golden yellow, May, 6 in., U.S.A.; *perennis*, yellow, summer, 9 to 18 in., N. America; *rosea*, rose, summer, 1 to 2 ft., Texas and New Mexico; *speciosa*, white or pink, summer, 1 to 2 ft., U.S.A.

Oftia—*Myoporaceae.* Greenhouse evergreen shrub. First introduced early eighteenth century.
CULTURE: Compost, sandy loam, leaf-mould and peat. Position, large pots or planted out in prepared border in conservatory or cool greenhouse. Water moderately in winter, freely at other times. Temp., March to Oct. 55° to 60°, Oct. to March 50° to 55°.
PROPAGATION: By cuttings of the young side growths inserted in sandy soil in heated propagating case during spring.

SPECIES CULTIVATED: *O. africana*, white, Feb. to Aug., 3 to 6 ft., S. Africa.

Okra, see *Hibiscus esculentus.*

Old Man, see *Artemisia Abrotanum.*

Old Man's Beard, see *Clematis Vitalba.*

Olea—*Oleaceae.* Slightly tender evergreen flowering shrub. Fruiting in most favoured localities only. First introduced mid-sixteenth century.

CULTURE: Soil, sandy loam. Position, sheltered, sunny borders, or against south or west walls S. of England only. Plant, Sept., Oct. or April. Prune when necessary, April. Protect in very severe weather with litter or mats.

POT CULTURE: Compost, two parts sandy loam, one part leaf-mould and sand. Position, cool greenhouse, Sept. to May; outdoors, June to Sept. Temp., Sept. to May 40° to 50°. Water moderately in winter, freely in summer. Syringe daily April to Sept.

PROPAGATION: By seeds sown $\frac{1}{16}$ in. deep in sandy peat in greenhouse in spring or autumn; cuttings inserted in sandy soil under bell-glass in shade in greenhouse in summer.

SPECIES CULTIVATED: *O. europaea*, ' Olive ', white, fragrant, summer, 20 to 40 ft., Asia Minor and Syria.

Oleander, see *Nerium Oleander.*

Olearia (New Zealand Daisy Bush)—*Compositae.* Hardy and slightly tender evergreen flowering shrubs from Australia and New Zealand. First introduced late eighteenth century.

CULTURE: Soil, sandy or chalky loam. Position, sunny borders or walls. Not suitable for outdoor culture in N. England, etc. Plant, Sept. to Nov. or April. Protect those grown against walls during severe weather by covering with straw or mats. Pruning not required except to remove dead or unhealthy shoots in April. Useful maritime shrubs.

PROPAGATION: By cuttings of firm young shoots, 2 to 3 in. long, inserted in well-drained pots of sandy soil under bell-glass in cold, shady frame in summer.

SPECIES CULTIVATED: *O. albida*, fairly hardy, white, summer, 15 ft.; *Haastii*, ' Victoria Snow Bush ', the hardiest species, white, July, 5 to 8 ft., compact; *ilicifolia*, ' Mountain Holly ', ' New Zealand Holly ', hardy, white, summer, 6 to 10 ft.; *lineata*, white, fragrant, summer, slender to 10 ft.; *macrodonta*, white, summer, good maritime screen, 15 ft.; *myrsinoides*, white, May to June, 5 ft., for low walls; *nummularifolia*, curious round yellowish leaves, 5 ft.; *odorata*, fragrant, summer, slender, to 10 ft.; *paniculata* (syn. *O. Forsteri*), white, summer, wavy apple-green foliage, 20 ft.; *semi-dentata*, mauve, July, 5 to 8 ft.; *stellulata* (syn. *O. Gunniana*), white, May to June, 6 ft., Tasmania, var. *splendens*, mauve to rose pink; *virgata*, fragrant, July, slender, 8 ft.

Oleaster, see *Elaeagnus angustifolia.*

Olive, see *Olea europaea.*

Omphalodes (Navel-wort)—*Boraginaceae.* Hardy annual and perennial herbs. First introduced early seventeenth century.

CULTURE OF ANNUAL SPECIES: Soil, ordinary. Position, partially shaded borders. Sow seeds in masses where required to grow—in April to flower in June, June to flower in Sept., and Sept. to flower in spring.

CULTURE OF PERENNIAL SPECIES: Soil, ordinary rich, moist. Position, partially shaded, well-drained borders or rockeries, or in rhododendron beds. Plant, Oct., Nov., March or April. Water copiously in dry weather. Mulch with decayed cow manure annually in spring.

PROPAGATION: By seeds sown $\frac{1}{8}$ in. deep in light, rich soil in semi-shaded position in April, transplanting seedlings when 1 in. high; division of roots, March or April.

ANNUAL SPECIES CULTIVATED: *O. linifolia,* ' Venus Navel-wort ', white, June, 6 to 9 in., S. Europe.

PERENNIAL SPECIES CULTIVATED: *O. cappadocica* (syn. *O. cornifolia*), blue, early summer and autumn, 6 to 9 in., S. Europe; *Lojkae,* blue, spring, 6 in., Caucasus; *Luciliae,* ' Rock Forget-me-not ', blue, summer, 6 in., Asia Minor; *nitida,* blue, May, 6 to 9 in., Portugal; *verna,* ' Creeping Forget-me-not ', ' Blue-eyed Mary ', blue, spring, 6 in., Europe, and var. *alba,* white.

Omphalogramma—*Primulaceae.* Small Asiatic genus allied to Primula.
CULTURE: Moist, deep, rich soil and a north or half-shaded position.
PROPAGATION: By seeds sown as soon as ripe in compost as above.
SPECIES CULTIVATED: *O. Coxii,* purplish-rose, summer, 6 in., Burma and China; *vinciflorum,* violet-purple, summer, 9 to 12 in., China.

× **Oncidioda**—bigeneric hybrid between Oncidium and Cochlioda.

Oncidium—*Orchidaceae.* A large polymorphic genus, over 500 species, epiphytal, with minor exceptions. Many handsome species are included, pseudo-bulbs are present in the greater number and the scapes, simple, panicled or with one or few flowers, are produced from the base of the new pseudo-bulb or in the practically pseudo-bulbless, monophyllous species, from their rhizome bases. The distinguishing feature of the flowers is a swelling at or near the base of the column and a toothed or warted crest on the lip base. Great variation is present.
CULTURE: With such a varied group the individual kinds must be studied. Compost for all may be as for Odontoglossum, the dwarf-growing kinds placed in pans, the larger in pots. Drainage must be ample from one-eighth to one-quarter of the pot in depth. Species with hard coriaceous leaves and/or pseudo-bulbs must have a decided rest, *O. splendidum* at least two months; the cool house species may require a few soakings during the winter. Kinds suited to the Odontoglossum house treated as for Odontoglossums but with fewer winter waterings. All when in vigorous growth need frequent waterings and particularly with the cool house species, as soon as matured, the plants should be exposed to full light in autumn, the smaller should be hung near the glass throughout the year. Though a rest is advocated for the pseudo-bulbed and coriaceous-leaved kinds, neither leaves nor bulbs must be allowed to shrivel for want of water.
PROPAGATION: By division of plants in spring. Pseudo-bulbs can be separated as suggested for Odontoglossums, Cymbidiums, etc., but do not respond as readily. A few species produce young plants on the flower spikes.
SPECIES CULTIVATED: A selection, suited to the Odontoglossum house. The following have long flexuous scapes, extending to 12 ft. or more, in some. In several the petal tips, owing to their serrated margins, interlock apically. The lips are small, fleshy and usually contrast in colour with the sepals and petals. *O. annulare,* rich chestnut-brown and yellow, various, Colombia; *Baldeviamae,* polished ochre-brown, yellow blotched, summer, Colombia; *Claesii,* sepals brown, petals flushed purple, summer, Colombia; *corynephorum,* rose, violet-rose, whitish, lip crimson-purple (*O. volubila* may be the correct name), various, Peru; *falcipetalum,* dark brown, yellow, autumn, Venezuela; *grandiflorum,* rich brown; *lamelligerum,* light brown, light yellow, variable, summer, Ecuador; *Leopoldianum,* white, rose-purple, various, Peru; *loxense,* chocolate-brown, barred yellow, lip broad, orange-yellow, spring, summer, Ecuador; *macranthum,* a fine variable species, sepals yellow shaded olive-brown, petals yellow, spring, summer, Ecuador, Peru; *metallicum,* metallic chestnut-brown, borders marked yellow, spring, Colombia; *Rolfeanum,* brown, yellow, summer, Colombia; *Sanderianum,* chocolate-brown, yellow and golden, summer, Peru; *superbiens,* sepals red-brown, petals whitish, with brown bars, spring, various, Colombia, Venezuela; *undulatum,* bronze-brown, petals white blotched purplish, summer, Colombia.
Other species suited to the Odontoglossum house but smaller. Should be hung near the glass and consideration given to the frequency or infrequency of winter waterings. *O. acrobotryum,* brown and yellow, lip wedge-shaped, small, many, spring, summer, Brazil; *cheirophorum,* bright yellow, fragrant, small,

densely set, autumn, winter, Colombia; *macrochilum*, crimson, purple, W. Indies; *nubigenum*, brownish, lip white, yellowish, violet; *olivaceum* (syn. *O. cucullatum*), scapes 1 to 2 ft. high, olive green or chestnut brown, lip light rose-purple and purple crimson, very variable, pretty, spring, Colombia into Ecuador; *ornithorynchum*, rose-lilac, small, fragrant, many, branched drooped scapes, early winter, Mexico, Guatemala; *phalaenopsis*, creamy white, deep purple, violet-crimson; *Waluewa*, whitish, banded pale purple, lip yellowish, spotted rose, spring, Brazil.

COOL HOUSE SPECIES: Winter night temp. 50°, summer temp. 60° to 80°, light shading. Infrequent, if any waterings in winter. *O. aureum*, yellow, brown, spring, Colombia; *Batemannianum*, bright yellow, crest purplish, scape up to 4 ft., various, Brazil; bicolor, yellow, dotted chestnut, autumn, Brazil; *bifolium*, dwarf, yellow, marked red-brown, early summer, Brazil; *bracteatum*, yellowish, spotted black-purple, lip yellow, 3 to 4 ft., spring, summer, Costa Rica, Colombia; *caloglossum* yellow, dark brown, various, Brazil; *candidum*, white, lip hiding the lower sepals from view, summer, Guatemala; *concolor*, canary yellow, scape drooping, spring, summer, Brazil; *crispum*, large, greenish-brown, chestnut-brown, broken with yellow, autumn, winter, Brazil; *curtum*, 2 to 3 ft., chestnut-brown, broken and edged with yellow, lip yellow with margin of chestnut spots, spring, Brazil; *dastyle*, yellow, red-brown, crest curious, the 'parson-in-the-pulpit' orchid, spring, Brazil; *dichromum*, bronze-red, shaded yellow, lip clear yellow, spring, Peru; *elegantissimum*, yellow spotted chestnut-brown, hybrid; *excavatum*, variable, yellow, barred brown, autumn, Peru, Brazil; *Forbesii*, rich chestnut broken with yellow, autumn, Brazil; *Gardneri*, (*dastyle* × *Forbesii*), chestnut-brown, yellow, various, Brazil; *Harrisonianum*, dwarf, yellow, red-spotted, mid-lobe of lip spreading, autumn, Brazil; *hastatum*, variable, yellowish-green, brown, claret-red, summer, autumn, Mexico; *incurvum*, purplish, white, many, fragrant, autumn, Mexico; *Mantinii*, chestnut-brown, yellow, winter, Brazil; *Marshallianum*, variable, handsome, yellow, red-brown, spring, Brazil; *leucochilum*, yellowish, greenish, dark brown, lip white, various, Mexico; *Martianum*, yellow, chestnut-brown, spring, summer, Brazil; *praetextum*, light chestnut-brown, yellow, spring, summer, Brazil; *spiloptrume*, yellow, brown, disk of lip magenta-purple, tubercled, spring, Brazil; *suave*, yellow, red-brown, fragrant, summer, autumn, Mexico; *tigrinum*, yellow, chestnut-brown, lip yellow, fragrant, autumn, winter, Mexico; *varicosum*, yellow, barred red-brown, lip large, yellow, autumn, winter, Brazil; *Wentworthianum*, yellow, blotched red-brown, summer, Guatemala; *Wheatleyanum*, chestnut-brown, crimson, yellow, various, Brazil.

The following selection should have the same conditions as Cattleyas. Rest given according to the nature of the leaf or pseudo-bulbs. *O. altissimum*, tall, yellow, brown, summer, W. Indies; *Baueri*, near *altissimum*, spikes branched from near their base, summer, W. Indies, Brazil; *bicallosum*, greenish, yellow lip bright yellow, winter, Guatemala; *carthaginense*, cream-white, spotted purplish-rose, variable, summer, Trop. America; *Cavendishianum*, yellow, bright yellow, winter, spring, Trop. America; *Cebolleta*, yellow, spotted red-brown, lip yellow, leaves terete, spring, summer, Brazil, Trop. America; *divaricatum*, chestnut, yellow, many, summer, autumn, Brazil; *fimbriatum*, yellow, red, small, many, spring, Brazil; *flexuosum*, red-brown, yellow, lip yellow, rhizome ascendant, support required, various Brazil; *Jonesianum*, white, yellow, chestnut-brown and red spotted, variable, beautiful, leaves terete, autumn, Paraguay; *Lowii*, yellow, spotted red-brown, spring, Mexico; *microhilum*, brown, broken with yellow, white and purple, small, many, summer, autumn, Guatemala; *oblongatum*, yellow, reddish-brown, variable, winter, Guatemala, Mexico; *obryzatum*, yellow, red-brown, winter, Peru; *phymatochilum*, 'The Gnat Orchid', creamy-white, marked red, many, summer, Mexico; *pubes*, red-brown, yellow, small, many, summer, Brazil; *pulvinatum*, red-brown, yellow, many, scape needs support, summer, Brazil; *pyramidale*, bright yellow, red spotted, summer, Colombia; *sarcodes*, chestnut-brown, broken with yellow, spring, summer, Brazil; *sphacelatum*, dark chestnut-brown, yellow, summer, Mexico, Guatemala.

A selection for the stove house, winter temp. not less than 65°. *O. ampliatum*, yellow, blotched red-brown, lip canary yellow, spring, Panama, Costa Rica, etc.; *citrinum*, yellowish, lip citron yellow, autumn, Trinidad; *haematochilum*, rare, yellowish and chestnut brown, lip blood-red, autumn, Trinidad; *Kramerianum*, scapes noded, flowers in succession, upper sepal and petals narrow, erect, reddish-brown, lower sepals larger, orange-red and yellow, lip yellow, margin spotted red-brown, frilled, small pans, various, Colombia, Ecuador; *Lanceanum*, yellow, greenish, red spotted, lip rose-purple, handsome, summer, Trinidad; *Linninghii*, ochre, brown, yellow and red marked flowers, in succession, raft or tree fern stem, summer, Venezuela, Brazil; *luridum*, many yellow, greenish, blotched red, variable, spring, W. Indies; *Papilio*, ' Butterfly Orchid ', near *O. Kramerianum*, scape flattened on upper portion, flowers larger, upper sepals and petals red, barred dull yellow, lower sepals chestnut-red, barred yellow, lip yellow bordered red, various, Trinidad, Venezuela; *pulchellum*, white, flushed rose, variable, pseudo-bulbs absent, summer, W. Indies, Brazil; *pusillum* (syn. *O. iridifolium*), yellowish, sometimes purple zoned, lip purplish, pseudo-bulbs absent, summer, autumn, Trop. America; *quadripetalum*, chestnut-brown, barred yellow, lip whitish, red, pseudo-bulbs absent, spring, summer; *Sanderae*, allied to *O. Papilio*, clear yellow, red-brown, column wings in filaments, various, Peru; *splendidum*, yellowish, blotched rich brown, lip canary yellow, large, midwinter, Guatemala, Brazil; *triquetrum*, habit of *O. pulchellum*, purplish, green, whitish, purple spotted, autumn, Jamaica; *urophyllum*, near *pulchellum*, small, many, yellow, blotched chestnut, lip yellow, summer, autumn, W. Indies.

Onion, see *Allium Cepa*; **Everlasting-**, see *A. Cepa* var. *perutile*; **Potato-**, see *A. Cepa* var. *aggregatum*; **Tree** or **Top-**, see *A. Cepa* var. *viviparum*; **Welsh-**, see *A. fistulosum*.

Onoclea—*Polypodiaceae*. Hardy deciduous ferns. Fronds, barren ones, broad, once-divided, green; fertile ones, narrow, contracted, once-divided, brown. First introduced late eighteenth century.

OUTDOOR CULTURE: Soil, two parts good loam, one part leaf-mould. Position, semi-shaded, cool, moist border or margins of ponds. Plant, April.

POT CULTURE: Compost, two parts fibrous loam, one part leaf-mould, one part sand. Position, well-drained pots in shady cold frame or greenhouse. Pot, March or April. Water copiously April to Sept., moderately Sept. to Nov., keep nearly dry Nov. to March. Repot annually.

PROPAGATION: By spores sown on surface of well-drained pan of sandy peat and leaf-mould covered with square of glass, and kept moderately moist in shady position in cold frame or greenhouse; division of plants, March or April.

SPECIES CULTIVATED: *O. sensibilis*, ' Sensitive Fern ', 2 to 3 ft., N. America and N. Asia.

Ononis (Rest-harrow)—*Leguminosae*. Hardy herbaceous perennials and deciduous shrubs. First introduced mid-sixteenth century.

CULTURE OF PERENNIAL SPECIES: Soil, ordinary. Position, sunny borders, banks or rockeries. Plant, Oct., Nov., March or April. Cut down flower stems, Oct. Mulch with manure, March. Lift and replant in fresh soil every four or five years.

CULTURE OF SHRUBBY SPECIES: Soil, ordinary. Position, sunny borders or banks. Plant, Oct. to Feb. Prune into shape, Jan. to Feb.

PROPAGATION: By seeds sown $\frac{1}{16}$ in. deep in ordinary soil in semi-shady position outdoors, March or April; or in shallow boxes or pans in cold frame or greenhouse in March; perennials by division of roots, Oct. to March.

PERENNIAL SPECIES CULTIVATED: *O. cenisia*, pink, summer, 6 in., Europe; *Natrix*, ' Goat Root ', yellow and red, summer, 1 to 2 ft., S. Europe; *spinosa* (syn. *O. arvensis*), rose and white, summer, 6 in., Europe (Br.).

SHRUBBY SPECIES CULTIVATED: *O. fruticosa*, purple, summer, 2 ft., Europe; *rotundifolia*, rose-pink, May to Aug., 1½ ft., Europe.

Onopordum—*Compositae.* Hardy biennial and perennial thistle-like herbs.

CULTURE OF BIENNIAL SPECIES: Sow seeds ⅛ in. deep in ordinary soil in sunny position outdoors, March or April. Transplant seedlings following Sept. to where required to flower.

CULTURE OF PERENNIAL SPECIES: Soil, ordinary rich. Position, well-drained sunny borders. Plant, Oct. or March.

PROPAGATION: By seeds sown ⅛ in. deep in ordinary soil in sunny position outdoors, March or April, transplanting seedlings to flowering position Sept. or Oct.

BIENNIAL SPECIES CULTIVATED: *O. arabicum*, 8 to 10 ft., S. Europe; *illyricum*, 6 ft., S. Europe.

PERENNIAL SPECIES CULTIVATED: *O. Acanthium*, ' Cotton Thistle ', ' Scotch Thistle', 5 ft., Europe (Br.).

Onosma (Golden Drop)—*Boraginaceae.* Hardy perennial herbs. First introduced late seventeenth century.

CULTURE: Soil, two parts sandy loam, one part grit or small stones. Position, sunny rockery where roots can descend close to cool, moist stones and shoots trail over edge. Plant, March or April. Place a few small stones on surface of soil round plant. Water occasionally in dry weather. Mulch annually with decayed cow manure in March or April.

PROPAGATION: By seeds sown 1/16 in. deep in sandy loam and grit in shallow pans in shady, cold frame of cool greenhouse in March, planting outdoors in May; cuttings of shoots inserted in sandy soil in close, shady frame or under hand-light in July or Aug.

SPECIES CULTIVATED: *O. albo-roseum*, white and rose, summer, 6 in., Asia Minor; *Bourgaei*, white, summer, 6 in., Armenia; *cassium*, yellow, summer, 18 in., N. Syria; *Sieheana*, pink, summer, 9 in., E. Europe; *stellulatum*, yellow and white, May, 6 in., Europe, var. *tauricum*, yellow, May, 1 ft., Europe; *Waddellii*, blue, summer, 9 in., Himalaya.

Onychium—*Polypodiaceae.* Stove and greenhouse evergreen ferns. Fronds green, light and graceful, four times divided.

CULTURE: Compost, two parts peat and loam, leaf-mould and sand in equal parts. Position, well-drained pots, beds or rockeries in shade. Pot or plant, Feb. or March. Water copiously March to Sept., moderately afterwards. Moist atmosphere essential. Temp. stove species, March to Sept. 65° to 75°, Sept. to March 55° to 65°; greenhouse species, March to Sept. 55° to 65°, Sept. to March 40° to 50°.

PROPAGATION: By spores sown on surface of fine sandy peat in well-drained pans in shade and temp. 70° to 80° any time; division of plants at potting time.

STOVE SPECIES CULTIVATED: *O. siliculosum* (syn. *O. auratum*), 1 ft., Malaya.

GREENHOUSE SPECIES CULTIVATED: *O. japonicum*, 1 ft., Japan, Himalaya.

Ophioglossum—*Ophioglossaceae.* Hardy deciduous fern. Barren fronds, egg-shaped, pale green; fertile ones contracted, spike-like.

OUTDOOR CULTURE: Soil, moist, loamy. Position, in tufts of grass on partially shaded rockery. Plant, April to Aug. Lift plants growing wild with large sod attached and plant fern and sod together. Water freely in dry weather.

POT CULTURE: Compost, sandy loam and leaf-mould in equal parts. Position, shallow pans, well drained, in cold, shady frame. Plant, April to Aug. Water freely March to Sept., keep just moist afterwards.

PROPAGATION: By spores gathered when ripe in July and sown on surface of pans of above soil, covered with a sheet of glass, and placed in a cool, moist frame or greenhouse; division of plants in April.

SPECIES CULTIVATED: *O. vulgatum*, ' Adder's Tongue Fern ', 4 to 6 in., in moist meadows, Britain, several forms or vars., some of which have led to other questionable specific names.

Ophiopogon (Snake's-beard)—*Liliaceae.* Hardy evergreen perennial herbs. First introduced late eighteenth century.

OUTDOOR CULTURE: Soil, sandy loam. Position, edgings to or groups in sunny borders. Plant, Oct. or March. Lift, divide and replant every four or five years.

POT CULTURE: Compost, two parts sandy loam, one part leaf-mould or decayed manure, and one part sand. Position, well-drained pots or in small beds in cold or heated greenhouses, conservatories, ferneries or windows. Adapted for sun or shade. Pot or plant, Feb. or March. Water copiously March to Oct., moderately afterwards. Apply stimulants once or twice weekly April to Sept.

PROPAGATION: By division of plants in Feb. or March.

SPECIES CULTIVATED: *O. Jaburan*, white, July, 1 ft., Japan; *japonicus*, white, hidden among the 6 to 15 in. long, dense, grassy leaves, summer, Japan.

Ophrys—*Orchidaceae*. A terrestrial genus distributed in south and mid-Europe and Mediterranean border. A few in England. Though all are deciduous, the continental species are not altogether suited to English gardens, and an alpine house has advantages in that the early growths are protected. Several natural hybrids are known.

TREATMENT: The greater number prefer a well-drained loam in limestone or chalk foundation, hence nodules of old mortar rubble should be mixed in the compost which should consist chiefly of loam and sand. A fairly sunny position should be given, particularly for the Italian species. While growing, water may be given liberally, but the tubers enjoy a rather dry rest. Both outdoor and indoor treatments are similar. The tubers are impatient of disturbance under glass; they should be repotted every second year, just before growth is expected.

PROPAGATION: Can seldom be effected, but secondary tubers are sometimes developed.

BRITISH SPECIES CULTIVATED: A selection—*O. apifera*, ' Bee Orchid ', stem 12 in., greenish, rosy, lip velvet-brown, early summer, variable, var. *alba*, white or yellowish white; *fuciflora* (syn. *O. arachnites*), stem 8 to 15 in., rosy with greenish lines, early summer; *insectifera* (syn. *O. muscifera*), ' Fly Orchid ', stems 4 to 20 in. high, greenish, reddish, lip purplish-brown, velvety with a glossy area, spring, summer; *sphegodes* (syn. *O. aranifera*), ' Spider Orchid ', stem 6 to 15 in., yellowish green, rose tinged, lip brown or purplish brown, velvety with yellowish spots or lines, spring.

EXOTIC SPECIES CULTIVATED: *O. Bertolonii*, stem 4 to 12 in., rose or whitish red, nerved, lip velvety purple, with a bluish area, S. Europe, Italy; *bombylifera,* ' Humble-Bee Orchid ', stem 4 to 8 in., green, purplish flushed, lip velvety-brown, spring, Mentone, etc.; *cornuta*, stem 8 to 15 in., rose-red, petals haired, lip brown, white marked, spring, summer, Caucasus; *fusca*, stem 4 to 12 in., yellowish-green, lip yellowish-brown, velvety with two glossy areas, spring, S. Europe; *lutea*, stem 4 to 12 in., yellowish-green, lip yellow, or brownish-yellow, velvety, two glossy areas, spring, S. Europe; *Philippei*, greenish, lip margined brown, France; *Scolopax*, ' Woodcock Ophrys ', stem 4 to 15 in., rosy, lip purplish, velvety, with yellow-bordered glossy areas, spring, S. Europe.

Oplismenus—*Gramineae*. Greenhouse perennial, trailing grass. Flowers insignificant. Stems, small, wiry, trailing. Leaves, green, variegated with white and pink. First introduced mid-nineteenth century.

CULTURE: Compost, equal parts peat, loam, leaf-mould and sand. Position, small pots with shoots draping front of staging, or in baskets suspended from roof; sun or shade. Pot, March. Water freely March to Oct., moderately afterwards. Apply stimulants occasionally in summer. Temp., March to Sept. 60° to 75°, Sept. to March 55° to 65°.

PROPAGATION: By cuttings of young shoots inserted in light, sandy soil in small pots under bell-glass or hand-light in temp. 65° to 75° at any time.

SPECIES CULTIVATED: *O. compositus* (syn. *O. Burmannii*, *O. hirtellus*), ' Basket Grass ', trailing, Tropics.

Oplopanax—*Araliaceae*. Prickly deciduous shrub formerly included in Fatsia.

CULTURE: As Fatsia.

PROPAGATION: As Fatsia.

SPECIES CULTIVATED: *O. horridus* (syn. *Fatsia horrida*), 'Devil's Club', spiny stems and leaves, 6 ft., spreading, deciduous, N.W. America and Japan.

Opuntia (Prickly Pear)—*Cactaceae*. Greenhouse and hardy succulent plants. Stems, fleshy, flat, bristly. Leaves, small, unimportant, fugacious. First introduced late sixteenth century.

CULTURE OF GREENHOUSE SPECIES: Compost, two parts sandy loam, one part powdered brick rubbish and old mortar. Position, sunny, airy greenhouse or window. Pot, March or April in pots filled ⅛ of depth with potsherds and just large enough to accommodate roots. Repot every three or four years only. Water moderately March to Sept., once a fortnight Sept. to Nov., none afterwards. Apply stimulants to healthy plants June to Sept. Ventilate freely in summer. Temp., March to Sept. 60° to 70°, Sept. to March 50° to 55°.

CULTURE OF HARDY SPECIES: Soil, sandy loam freely interspersed with powdered brick or old mortar. Position, sunny well-drained rockeries. Plant, March or April. Cover surface of soil between plants with small pieces of stone. Sprinkle soot freely between plants occasionally to keep away slugs. Apply weak liquid manure occasionally during summer to healthy plants only.

PROPAGATION: By seeds sown ⅛ in. deep in well-drained pots or pans of sandy soil in temp. 75° in March. Keep soil moderately moist; cuttings of portions of stems exposed for a few days, then inserted in small, well-drained pots of lime and brick dust in temp. 65° to 75°, summer; delicate species by grafting on robust kinds in April.

GREENHOUSE SPECIES CULTIVATED: *O. Bigelovii*, flowers not known, 10 ft., California; *brasiliensis*, yellow, June, 10 to 30 ft., Brazil; *cylindrica*, scarlet, summer, 4 to 6 ft., Peru, and var. *cristata*, crested; *echinocarpa*, green, summer, 18 in., U. States; *Ficus-indica*, 'Indian Fig', yellow, May, 2 ft,, Trop. America, *glaucophylla*, yellow, 2 ft., Mexico; *imbricata*, purple, June, 5 to 30 ft., South United States and Mexico; *leucotricha*, yellow, June, Mexico; *maxima* (syn. *O. decumana*), orange, summer, 10 to 15 ft., S. America; *Pottsii* (syn. *O. filipendula*), purple, May and June, 2 ft., Texas; *Stanlyi* (syn. *O. Emoryi*), yellow and purple, Aug. to Sept., 18 in., Mexico; *Tuna*, reddish-orange, July, 10 to 20 ft., S. America; *Whipplei*, red, June, U.S.A.

HARDY SPECIES CULTIVATED: *O. compressa* (syn. *O. Rafinesquei*), yellow and red, June, 1 ft., N. America; *Engelmannii*, yellow, May to June, 6 in., South U.S.A.; *polycantha* (syn. *O. missouriensis*), yellow, May and June, 6 in., N. America; *rhodantha*, carmine, June, Colorado; *vulgaris*, 'Barbary Fig', yellow, 2 ft., U.S.A.

Orach, see *Atriplex hortensis*.

Orange, see *Citrus sinensis*; **-ball Tree,** see *Buddleia globosa*; **-Daisy,** see *Erigeron aurantiacus*; **Mandarin** or **Tangerine-,** see *Citrus nobilis* var. *deliciosa*; **Osage-,** see *Maclura pomifera*; **Seville-,,** see *Citrus Aurantium*.

Orchis—*Orchidaceae*. A rather large, deciduous, terrestrial genus allied to Ophrys and Habenaria. Several natural hybrids occur. Habit as in Ophrys, a stem rising from a tuber which supports and forms another, lip spurred. The genus is widely distributed in England, Africa and N. America.

CULTURE: The English species are more amenable in our gardens than Ophrys and several are suitable for rockeries. A well-drained loam with sand suits the majority but it is well to make a compost similar to that in which the species grow. Exotic species may be treated as exotic Ophrys, but if possible ascertain the nature of the soil in which particular species grow.

PROPAGATION: As for Ophrys.

SPECIES CULTIVATED: *O. ericetorum* (syn. *O. elodes*), flowers densely set, stem 8 to 10 in., summer, Britain, Europe; *Fuchsii* (syn. *O. maculata*), lilac or whitish, rose or purple streaked, spotted darker colour, very variable, summer, Britain, Europe, *latifolia* (syn. *O. incarnata*), flesh colour or rose, lip darker, spring, stem 10 to 20 in., Britain, Europe; *maderensis* (syn. *O. foliosa*), purple, summer, 1 to 2 ft., Madeira:

mascula, purplish-crimson, variable, disk or lip downy, damp loam, spring, stem 8 to 24 in., Britain, Europe, Siberia, Africa; *militaris,* reddish, striped purple, lip purplish-white or rosy, spring, summer, stem 1 to 2 ft., S. England, Europe; *Morio,* purplish, petals green veined, lip broad, spring to summer, Britain, Europe; *pallens,* many pale and deep yellow, spring, stem 12 to 15 in., Europe; *pardalina,* purple-red to white, variable, spring to summer, stem 8 to 24 in., Britain, Europe, Asia; *purpurella,* dark purple, summer, 4 to 6 in., England, Holland; *pyramidalis,* (correctly *Anacamptis pyramidalis*) rose or purplish-red, summer, 1 ft., Britain; *sambucina,* yellow or purple, spring to summer, 6 to 9in., Europe; *simia,* 'Monkey Orchis', greenish-white, lip often crimson, variable, summer, England, Europe; *spectabilis,* pinkish-purple, spring to summer, 4 to 7 in., N. America; *tridentata,* purplish-rose, lip flesh colour red spotted, spring to summer, S. Europe; *ustulata,* 'Scorched Orchis', brownish-purple, lip whitish, chalky loam, spring, summer, 4 to 8 in., Britain, Europe, W. Siberia.

Oreopanax—*Araliaceae.* Stove evergreen ornamental-foliaged plants or shrubs. First introduced mid-seventeenth century.

CULTURE: Compost, equal parts loam, peat and leaf-mould, with charcoal and sand added. Pot, Feb. to April. Water freely March to Oct., moderately afterwards. Temp., March to Sept. 70° to 80°, Sept. to March 60° to 70°.

PROPAGATION: By grafting in heat during spring on to stocks of *O. reticulatum.* Cuttings inserted in sand in propagating case and by portions of the roots in April.

SPECIES CULTIVATED: *O. capitatum* (syn. *Aralia catalpifolia*), S. America; *guatemalense,* Guatemala; *nymphacifolium,* locality unknown; *platanifolium* (syn. *Aralia platanifolium*), Andes; *reticulatum* (syn. *Aralia reticulata*), S. America; *Sanderianum,* Guatemala; *Xalapense* (syn. *O. Thibautii*), Mexico.

Origanum—*Labiatae.* Perennial herbs cultivated for the aromatic foliage and attractive small purple-pinkish flowers borne in spikes. Sometimes listed as Amaracus. See also Majorana.

CULTURE: Compost, two parts sandy loam, one part leaf-mould and sand. Position, well-drained warm borders or greenhouse. Pot, Feb. or March, plant out late May.

PROPAGATION: Division of roots in March or April.

SPECIES CULTIVATED: *O. Dictamnus,* 'Cretan Dittany', pink, summer, 1 ft., Crete; *hybridus,* pink, late summer, 12 in., hybrid; *pulchellum,* purple, summer, 6 to 9 in., Greece.

Ornithidium—*Orchidaceae.* A genus of about twenty epiphytic species. In some the pseudo-bulbs are carried on ascendant or pendulous rhizomes. The flowers fascicled, small, produced in the axils of the leaves. In others a cushion-like habit is assumed, the flowers being solitary. Erect stems are also present, from the midst of smaller growths, carrying the flowers in axillary fascicles.

CULTURE: Compost, as for Maxillarias. Species with pendulous habit should be placed in baskets. In summer the temp. then can reach the sub-tropical, with shading and a moist atmosphere. Water is required throughout the year, not too frequently in winter. Winter temp. 50° to 55° to 60°.

PROPAGATION: By division of plants in spring.

SPECIES CULTIVATED: *O. coccineum* (syn. *Cymbidium coccineum*), coral-red to scarlet-red on leafy growths, winter, spring, W. Indies; *densum* (syn. *Maxillaria densa*), greyish-white, tinged purple, reddish, in fascicles on growths, 2 ft. high, Guatemala, Mexico; *sophronitis,* bright scarlet, cushion-like habit, shallow pans, spring, cool house, Venezuela.

Ornithocephalus—*Orchidaceae.* An epiphytic genus, many of the species are of botanical interest only. Pseudo-bulbs small or absent. Flowers small, usually with a large rostellum.

TREATMENT: Compost of finely cut osmunda fiibre and equal bulk of chopped sphagnum. Small pans, suspended near glass. Shade carefully. A moist atmosphere and water are required throughout the year.

PROPAGATION: By division of plants, if large enough, in spring.

SPECIES CULTIVATED: *O. grandiflorus*, white and green, usually twenty, attractive, pseudo-bulbs small, early summer, Brazil; *multiflorus*, allied to preceding, smaller, white, summer, Brazil; *Tonduzii*, pseudo-bulbs absent, small, crystalline white, lip green, leaves pretty, summer, Costa Rica.

Ornithochilus—*Orchidaceae.* A small epiphytic genus allied to Phalaenopsis. Only one species is met with in orchid collections, resembling Phalaenopsis in habit, racemes lateral often branched.

TREATMENT: Compost, etc., as for Phalaenopsis.

PROPAGATION: Can seldom, if ever, be effected.

SPECIES CULTIVATED: *O. fuscus* (syns. *Aerides difforme, A. hystrix*), yellow, greenish-yellow, streaked or suffused red, lip usually reddish and generally fimbriated, spur yellowish, spring, summer, Himalaya, Burma, Hong Kong.

Ornithogalum—*Liliaceae.* Hardy and greenhouse bulbous plants.

OUTDOOR · CULTURE: Soil, rich ordinary, sandy. Position, sunny borders, rockeries or turf. Plant, Aug. to Nov., placing small bulbs 3 in. and large bulbs 4 to 6 in. below surface and 2 to 3 in. apart. Mulch annually in March with decayed manure. Apply weak stimulants occasionally in summer.

INDOOR CULTURE: Compost, two parts sandy loam, one part equal proportions leaf-mould, peat and sand. Position, pots in sunny greenhouse or window. Pot, Sept. to Feb., placing several small or one large bulb in a 5 or 6 in. pot. Good drainage essential. Water moderately when growth begins, freely when in full growth, gradually withholding when foliage turns yellow and keeping dry till new growth begins. Apply stimulants occasionally while in full growth. Repot annually. Temp., March to Sept. 55° to 65°, Sept. to March 40° to 50°.

PROPAGATION: By offsets, removed from old bulbs and repotted, Sept. to Feb.

GREENHOUSE SPECIES CULTIVATED: *O. arabicum*, white, fragrant, summer, 2 ft., S. Europe, hardy in sheltered borders with slight winter protection; *biflorum*, white, April, 1 ft., Chile and Peru; *lacteum*, ' Chincherinchee ', white, summer, 1½ ft., S. Africa; *longibracteatum*, white, May, 1 to 2 ft., S. Africa, and var. *variegatum*.

HARDY SPECIES CULTIVATED: *O. nutans*, silvery grey and pale green, spring, 1 ft., Europe (Br.), var. *Boucheanum*, a superior form; *narbonense*, white, early summer, 2 ft., Medit. Region, and var. *pyramidale*; *pyrenaicum*, yellowish-green, June, 2 ft., S. Europe; *umbellatum*, ' Star of Bethlehem ', white, May, 1 ft., Europe.

Orobus, see Lathyrus and Vicia.

Orontium—*Araceae.* Hardy aquatic perennial. First introduced mid-eighteenth century.

CULTURE: Soil, boggy. Position, margins of shallow ponds or rivulets or in water 12 in. deep. Plant, March to June, placing roots 6 to 12 in. below surface of water.

PROPAGATION: By division of rootstock in Oct. or March; seed sown in spring in shallow pans.

SPECIES CULTIVATED: *O. aquaticum*, ' Golden Club ', yellow and white, glaucous leaves, May, 1 to 1½ ft., N. America.

Orphanidesia—*Ericaceae.* Evergreen shrub with large hirsute leaves, related to Epigaea.

CULTURE: Soil, well drained, lime-free. Position, considerable shade.

PROPAGATION: By seed.

SPECIES CULTIVATED: *O. gaultherioides*, pale pink with darker veins, low shrub with prostrate branches, Asia Minor.

Orphium—*Gentianaceae.* A monotypic genus, the species being an erect greenhouse shrub.

CULTURE: Compost, fibrous loam and peat with plenty of sharp sand and crock chippings. Position, well-drained pots in sunny greenhouse. Water

carefully at all times, especially in winter. Pot, March or April; the plants should never be over-potted, thriving best when grown in comparatively small receptacles. Temp., March to Oct. 50° to 55°, Oct. to March 45° to 50°.
PROPAGATION: By cuttings of the young side growths inserted in sandy peat under bell-glass or propagator in gentle heat during spring.
SPECIES CULTIVATED: *O. frutescens*, red, showy, summer, 1 to 2 ft., S. Africa.

Orris Root, see *Iris germanica* var. *florentina*.

Osage Orange, see *Maclura pomifera*.

Osier, see *Salix viminalis*.

Orychophragmus—*Cruciferae.* Hardy annual or biennial, sometimes placed in the genus Moricandia.
CULTURE: Soil, ordinary. Position, sunny.
PROPAGATION: By seed.
SPECIES CULTIVATED: *O. violaceus* (syns. *Moricandia sonchifolia, O. sonchifolius*), pale violet-blue, spring, 1 to 2 ft., China.

Osbeckia—*Melastomaceae.* Greenhouse herbs or sub-shrubs. First introduced early nineteenth century.
CULTURE: Compost, equal parts loam and peat, sand and crushed charcoal. Position, well-drained pots or pans in warm greenhouse or stove. Water moderately in summer, carefully at other times. Temp., March to Oct. 60° to 70°, Oct. to March 55° to 60°.
PROPAGATION: By cuttings inserted during spring in pots of sandy soil, in warm propagating case, or under bell-glass.
SPECIES CULTIVATED: *O. chinensis*, purple, July, 2 ft., India; *glauca*, red or purple, July, 2 ft., India; *rostrata*, rosy pink, summer, 2 to 3 ft., Bengal; *stellata*, rosy purple, July and Aug., 2 ft., Himalaya.

Osmanthus (Fragrant Olive)—*Oleaceae.* Hardy and half-hardy evergreen flowering shrubs. *O. Delavayi* is now *Siphonosmanthus Delavayi*, which see. First introduced mid-eighteenth century.
CULTURE: Soil, loamy. Position, sheltered, sunny borders or against south or west walls. *O. fragrans* in sunny, unheated greenhouse. Plant, Sept., Oct. or April. Prune, when necessary, April, May. *O. ilicifolius* may be planted as a hedge or clipped formally.
POT CULTURE: Compost, two parts sandy loam, one part leaf-mould and sand. Position, unheated, sunny greenhouse Sept. to June, outdoors June to Sept. Pot, Sept. or Oct. Water freely April to Oct., moderately other times. Temp., Sept. to May 40° to 50°.
PROPAGATION: By seeds sown $\frac{1}{16}$ in. deep in sandy peat in cold frame in spring or autumn; cuttings of firm young shoots in sandy soil under hand-light outdoors or in frame, in summer.
SPECIES CULTIVATED: *O. armatus*, creamy white, autumn, 8 to 15 ft., W. China; *Fortunei*, white, fragrant, autumn, 6 ft., hybrid; *Forrestii*, large leaves, white, summer, 15 ft., W. China; *fragrans* (syn. *Olea fragrans*), tender, powerfully fragrant, 6 to 10 ft., China and Japan; *ilicifolius* (syn. *O. Aquifolium*), white, Sept. to Oct., 10 to 20 ft., Japan, and numerous vars. See also Osmarea.

× **Osmarea**—*Oleaceae.* Bigeneric hybrid between Siphonosmanthus and Phillyrea. Hardy evergreen shrub.
CULTURE: Soil, ordinary. Position, open or partially shaded borders, excellent for hot dry soils. Makes good screen or useful clipped hedge. Plant, Sept., Oct. or April. Clip when required in May.
PROPAGATION: By cuttings of firm young shoots in well-drained sandy soil in shaded frame in Aug., Sept.
SPECIES CULTIVATED: *O. Burkwoodii*, white, April, very fragrant, hardy, 6 to 10 ft., English origin.

Osmaronia—*Rosaceae.* Hardy deciduous flowering shrub. Fragrant flowers succeeded by purplish plum-like fruits. Previously known as Nuttallia. First introduced mid-nineteenth century.

CULTURE: Soil, ordinary. Position, shady or sunny shrubberies. Plant, Oct. to Feb. Prune, when necessary, immediately after flowering.

PROPAGATION: By seeds sown ⅛ in. deep in ordinary soil in shady position outdoors in spring or autumn; suckers removed from parent plant in Oct. or Nov.; cuttings of ripened shoots in cold frame in autumn; layering in autumn.

SPECIES CULTIVATED: *O. cerasiformis*, ' Osoberry ', white, strongly almond-scented, March, 6 to 10 ft., California.

Osmunda—*Osmundaceae.* Greenhouse and hardy evergreen and deciduous ferns. Fronds, feather-shaped, plain or crested; fertile portions contracted.

CULTURE OF GREENHOUSE SPECIES: Compost, equal parts turfy loam and peat, little sand. Position, pots or beds in moist, shady part of greenhouse or fernery. Pot or plant, March or April. Water copiously April to Oct., moderately afterwards. Temp., 55° to 65° April to Sept., 45° to 55° Sept. to April.

CULTURE OF HARDY SPECIES: Soil, one part each loam, leaf-mould and sand, two parts peat. Position, bases of sheltered, moist rockeries or margins of ponds in shade or partial shade. Plant, April. Top-dress annually in April with compost of peat, leaf-mould and loam. Remove dead fronds in March. Water plants growing elsewhere than on the margins of ponds copiously in dry weather.

PROPAGATION: By spores sown on surface of sandy peat and leaf-mould in well-drained pans covered with sheet of glass or hand-light in shady part of cool greenhouse at any time; offsets from established plants in April.

GREENHOUSE SPECIES CULTIVATED: *O. javanica*, 2 to 4 ft., Java; *Mildei* (syn. *O. bipinnata*), 2 ft., Hong Kong.

HARDY SPECIES CULTIVATED: *O. cinnamomea*, 2 to 4 ft., N. America, E. Indies, etc.; *Claytoniana*, 2 to 3 ft., N. America and Himalaya; *gracilis*, a smaller, more slender plant than *O. regalis*, N. America; *regalis*, ' Royal Fern ', 3 to 6 ft., Britain, etc., and numerous vars.

Osoberry, see *Osmaronia cerasiformis*.

Osteomeles—*Rosaceae.* Slightly tender evergreen shrubs. First introduced late nineteenth century.

CULTURE: Soil, loamy. Position, well-drained borders against sheltered wall with sunny aspect. In warmest counties in open border. Prune lightly after flowering.

PROPAGATION: By cuttings of half-ripened shoots during June and July, inserted in sandy soil under bell-glass in gentle bottom heat.

SPECIES CULTIVATED: *O. Schwerinae* (syn. *O. anthyllidifolia*), white, June, 8 to 10 ft., W. China, var. *microphylla*, a dainty dwarf form, probably hardier; *subrotunda*, white, June, 4 ft., China.

Ostrich Fern, see Pteretis.

Ostrowskia (Giant Bell-flower)—*Campanulaceae.* Hardy perennial flowering herb. First introduced late nineteenth century.

CULTURE: Soil, deep, sandy loam. Position, warm, sheltered border. Cover with hand-light after foliage has died down. Carrot-like roots penetrate the soil to a depth of 2 ft. Plant in March.

PROPAGATION: By seeds sown in light soil in a cold frame in spring. Seedlings take several years to flower.

SPECIES CULTIVATED: *O. magnifica*, mauve-lilac or white, summer, 4 to 5 ft., Cent. Asia.

Ostrya (Hop Hornbeam)—*Betulaceae.* Hardy deciduous trees closely resembling hornbeam. First introduced early seventeenth century.

CULTURE: Soil, ordinary moist. Position, by the side of streams, lakes, or in shrubberies in damp situations. Plant, Oct. to Feb.

PROPAGATION: By seeds stratified and sown outdoors in spring in sandy soil;

by cuttings inserted outdoors in autumn; by layering in summer; by grafting on the Hornbeam (*Carpinus Betulus*) in March.

SPECIES CULTIVATED: *O. carpinifolia*, greenish-white, May, 50 to 60 ft., S. Europe; *virginiana*, 'Iron-wood', greenish-white, May, 30 to 50 ft., N. America.

Oswego Tea-plant, see *Monarda didyma*.

Otaheite Apple, see *Spondias cytherea*; **-Gooseberry,** see *Phyllanthus acidus*.

Othonna (African Ragwort)—*Compositae*. Greenhouse trailing herb. First introduced mid-nineteenth century.

CULTURE: Compost, two parts sandy loam, one part leaf-mould and one part sand. Position, small well-drained pots or baskets suspended from roof. Pot, March or April. Water freely April to Oct., moderately afterwards. Apply stimulants to healthy plants occasionally during summer. Full exposure to light and sun essential.

PROPAGATION: By cuttings of shoots inserted in sandy soil in cool greenhouse or frame in summer; division of plants in April.

SPECIES CULTIVATED: *O. crassifolia*, yellow, summer, trailing, S. Africa.

Othonnopsis—*Compositae*. Half-hardy rock plant. First introduced mid-eighteenth century.

CULTURE: Soil, sandy loam. Position, warm, sunny rock gardens. Protect in severe weather.

PROPAGATION: By division in March or April or cuttings of young growth when three or four inches in length in sandy soil under bell-glass.

SPECIES CULTIVATED: *O. cheirifolia*, yellow, spring and summer, 1 ft., N. Africa.

Ourisia—*Scrophulariaceae*. Hardy perennial creeping herb. First introduced mid-nineteenth century.

CULTURE: Soil, moist, loamy. Position, partially shaded rockery, with its roots placed close to a lump of soft, porous stone. Plant, March or April. Water freely in dry weather. Must not be exposed to sunshine.

PROPAGATION: By division of roots in March or April.

SPECIES CULTIVATED: *O. caespitosa*, lilac, 1 to 2 in., summer, New Zealand; *coccinea*, scarlet, early summer, 9 in., Chile; *elegans*, commonly cult. as *O. coccinea*, much more robust grower than the true *O. coccinea*; *macrophylla*, white and lilac, summer, 6 to 9 in., New Zealand.

Our Lady's Thistle, see *Silybum Marianum*.

Oxalis (Wood Sorrel)—*Oxalidaceae*. Greenhouse and hardy annuals, herbaceous perennials and bulbous-rooted plants. *O. corniculata* can be a troublesome weed.

CULTURE OF GREENHOUSE SPECIES: Compost, sandy loam. Position, well-drained pots in sunny greenhouse or window. Pot autumn-flowering kinds in Aug.; winter-flowering kinds in Sept. or Oct.; spring-flowering kinds, Jan. or Feb., and summer-flowering kinds, March or April. Pot bulbs ½ in. deep and ¼ in. apart in 5 in. pots. After potting place in warm part of greenhouse or window. Water moderately till leaves appear, then freely. Apply stimulants occasionally when flowers form. Gradually withhold water when flowers fade, and keep quite dry and cool till growth begins. Repot annually.

CULTURE OF HARDY SPECIES: Soil, sandy loam. Position, edgings to sunny borders or on rockeries. Cool, deep soil for *O. enneaphylla*. Plant *O. adenophylla* and *O. enneaphylla* Aug. to Nov., other species in March or April. Lift *O. floribunda* and *Deppei* in Sept. or Oct. Store in sand in cool, frost-proof place till March, then plant out.

PROPAGATION: By seeds sown 1/16 in. deep in light, sandy soil in temp. 55° to 65° in spring; division of roots or offsets at potting or planting time.

GREENHOUSE SPECIES CULTIVATED: *O. carnosa*, yellow, autumn, 6 in., Chile; *cernua*, 'Bermuda Buttercup', yellow, spring, 6 in., S. Africa, Europe; *hirta*; red, summer, 3 in., S. Africa; *rosea*, rose, spring, 6 to 8 in., Chile; *tetraphylla*, red, summer, 6 in., Mexico; *variabilis*, red, white, or crimson, autumn, 3 in.,

S. Africa. The following are bulbous-rooted: *O. cernua, floribunda, Deppei* and *tetraphylla.*

HARDY SPECIES CULTIVATED: *O. Acetosella,* ' Wood Sorrel ', white, spring, 1 to 2 in., Britain, and var. *rosea,* pink; *adenophylla,* rose-pink, May to June, 3 in., Chile; *Bowieana,* rose-purple, autumn, 3 in., S. Africa; *corniculata,* yellow, creeping, all summer, Europe; *Deppei,* red, March, 6 in., S. America; *enneaphylla,* blush-white, May to June, 2 to 3 in., Falkland Isles, and var. *rosea; floribunda,* rose, March, 9 in., Brazil, and var. *alba; lobata,* yellow, autumn, 3 in., Chile; *magellanica,* white, summer, 1 in., S. America; *montevidensis* (syn. *O. chrysantha*), yellow, all summer, 6 in., S. America; *oregana,* deep rose-red, May to June, 4 in., N. America; *valdiviensis,* yellow, summer, 4 to 6 in., Chile, often grown as an annual; *vespertilionis,* pink, summer, 6 in., Mexico.

Oxeye, see Bupthalmum; **-Chamomile,** see *Anthemis tinctoria;* **-Daisy,** see *Chrysanthemum Leucanthemum.*

Oxlip, see *Primula elatior.*

Oxycoccus, see Vaccinium.

Oxydendrum—*Ericaceae.* Hardy deciduous tree. First introduced mid-eighteenth century.
   CULTURE: Soil, lime-free loam, peat and sand. Position, as specimens on lawns or in open places. Plant, Nov. to Feb.
   PROPAGATION: By seeds sown during Feb. or March in well-drained pans in compost of sandy peat. Cover very lightly and place in greenhouse or frame.
   SPECIES CULTIVATED: *O. arboreum* (syn. *Andromeda arborea*), ' Sorrel Tree ', white, June to July, autumn tints, 10 to 30 ft., Eastern N. America.

Oxypetalum—*Asclepiadeae.* Stove and warm greenhouse evergreen climbers. First introduced early nineteenth century.
   CULTURE: Compost, equal parts fibrous peat, loam and sand. Position, well-drained pots; shoots trained up roof. Pot, March or April. Water freely in summer, moderately autumn and winter. Syringe morning and evening in springtime. Prune into shape, Feb. Repot, March. Temp., March to Sept. 65° to 75°, Sept. to March 55° to 65°.
   PROPAGATION: By seeds sown in sandy peat in a temp. of 75° in spring, or by cuttings placed in sand under a bell-glass over bottom heat in spring.
   SPECIES CULTIVATED: *O. caeruleum* (syns. *Tweedia caerulea* and *T. versicolor*), blue, summer, fragrant, 3 ft., Argentina; *solanoides,* blue, rose, orange, and purple, fragrant, summer, 6 ft., Brazil.

Oxytropis (Oxytrope)—*Leguminosae.* Hardy low perennial herbs or sub-shrubs.
   CULTURE: Soil, dry, gravelly or sandy loam. Position, open, sunny rockeries. Plant, March or April. Lift and replant only when unhealthy.
   PROPAGATION: By seeds sown ⅛ in. deep in April or May where required to grow; division of roots in March.
   SPECIES CULTIVATED: *O. campestris,* pale yellow and purple, July, 3 to 6 in., Northern and Arctic Regions (Scotland); *cyanea,* purple and blue, summer, 6 in., Caucasus; *Lambertii,* white, blue and purple, summer, 1 ft., N. America; *montana,* reddish-purple, July, 6 in., Alps; *pyrenaica,* purple and lilac, summer, 6 in., Pyrenees; *uralensis* (syn. *O. Halleri*), purple, summer, 4 in., Europe (Scotland).

Oyster Plant, see *Tragopogon porrifolius.*

Ozothamnus, see Helichrysum.

Pachyphragma—*Cruciferae.* Hardy herbaceous perennials suitable for carpeting shrubbery or rock garden.
   CULTURE: Soil, ordinary. Position, sun or shade.
   PROPAGATION: By division; seed.

Species Cultivated: *P. macrophyllum* (syns. *Thlaspi macrophyllum* and *T. latifolium*), white, May, leaves heart-shaped, 6 in., Caucasus.

Pachyphytum—*Crassulaceae.* Greenhouse succulent plants, sometimes included in the genus Cotyledon.
Culture: As Echeveria.
Propagation: As Echeveria.
Species Cultivated: *P. compactum*, reddish, 16 in., Mexico.

Pachysandra—*Buxaceae.* Hardy evergreen or deciduous procumbent sub-shrubs. First introduced early nineteenth century.
Culture: Soil, moist loam. Position, shady borders or rock gardens. Plant, Nov. to Feb.
Propagation: By cuttings of nearly ripened growths in sandy soil under bell-glass in July or Aug.
Species Cultivated: *P. procumbens*, greenish-white, March, 6 in., nearly deciduous, S.E. United States; *terminalis*, white, May, to 12 in., Japan, and var. *variegata*, leaves bordered and variegated with white, used for ground-cover.

Pachystachys—*Acanthaceae.* Warm greenhouse flowering and ornamental-leaved perennial.
Culture: Compost, equal parts loam, leaf-mould, peat and sand. Position, well-drained pots in light greenhouse; temp., Sept. to March 55° to 65°, March to Sept. 65 to 75 . Prune shoots to 1 in. of base after flowering. Nip off points of young shoots occasionally May to Aug. to induce bushy growth. Apply liquid manure once a week to plants in flower.
Species Cultivated: *P. coccinea* (syns. *Jacobinia coccinea, Justicia coccinea*), scarlet, summer, 3 to 6 ft., Trinidad and South America.

× **Pachyveria**—*Crassulaceae.* Bigeneric hybrids between Echeveria and Pachyphytum.

Paederota—*Scrophulariaceae.* Hardy rock garden plants.
Culture: Soil, well-drained gritty loam. Position, full sun.
Propagation: By seeds; cuttings; division in spring.
Species Cultivated: *P. Bonarota*, blue, summer, 4 to 6 in., Europe; *lutea* (syn. *P. Ageria*), yellow, summer, 4 to 6 in., Europe.

Paeonia (Peony; Paeony)—*Ranunculaceae* (or *Paeoniaceae*). Hardy herbaceous and shrubby perennials.
Culture: Soil, moist loam, well enriched with cow manure and trenched 3 ft. deep. Position, sunny or shady borders. Plant, Sept., Oct. or March, 4 ft. apart each way with 2 in. of soil over crown. Top-dress annually with decayed manure lightly forked in, Oct. or Nov. Mulch in April on dry soils. Apply liquid artificial manures occasionally April to Aug. Water copiously in dry weather. Shade blooms required for exhibition.
Culture of Tree Peonies: Soil, two parts loam, one part rotted cow manure. Position, sheltered nooks and sunny shrubberies or borders. Plant, Sept., Oct. or March. Bury point of union between stock and scion 3 in. below surface. Mulch in spring with thick layer of cow manure. Protect in severe weather with covering of litter. Plants flower three years after planting.
Propagation: Herbaceous species by seeds in cold frame in Sept.; also by division of roots in Sept. or March. Tree species by grafting in Aug.; layering in Sept. or Oct.; offsets, March or April.
Species Cultivated: *P. anomala*, crimson, May, 1 to 1¼ ft., Europe, Russia, Cent. Asia, var. *intermedia* (syn. *P. intermedia*), similar; *arietina*, dark purplish-red, May, 1½ to 2 ft., S.E. Europe, Asia Minor; *Bakeri*, purplish-red, April to May, 2 ft., origin unknown; *Broteri*, purplish-red, May, 1 to 1½ ft., Spain, Portugal; *cambessedesii*, deep rose, April to May, 1 to 1½ ft., Balearic Isles; *Clusii* (syn. *P. cretica*), white, May, 9 to 12 in., Crete; *coriacea*, rose, April, 1½ ft., Spain, Morocco; *daurica* (syn. *P. triteranta*), purplish-rose, 1 to 2 ft., Crimea;

Delavayi, dark red, May, 5 ft., shrubby, **W. China**; *emodi*, white, May, 1 to 2 ft., W. Himalaya; *festiva* (syn. *P. officinalis*), double red, hybrid; *humilis*, purplish-rose, May, 1 ft., S.W. Europe; *lactiflora* (syns. *P. albiflora* and *P. edulis*), various, to 3 ft., Siberia, Manchuria, N. China, Mongolia; *Lemoinei*, shrubby, hybrid; *lutea* (syn. *P. Delavayi* var. *lutea*), yellow, June, 3 ft., shrubby, **W. China**, S.E. Tibet; *mascula* (syn. *P. corallina*), crimson, May, 3 ft., S. Europe, W. Asia; *Mlokosewitschii* (syn. *P. Mlokosiewiczii*), yellow, April, 3 ft., Caucasus; *officinalis* (syn. *P. feminea*), crimson, May, 2 to 3 ft., S. Europe; *obovata*, white to rose-purple, May, 1½ to 2 ft., S.E. Asia, var. *Willmottiae* (syn. *P. Willmottiae*), white; *peregrina* (syns. *P. decora, lobata* and *romanica*), deep red, to 2 ft., S.E. Europe, Asia Minor; *Potaninii* (syn. *P. Delavayi* var. *angustiloba*), deep maroon, **W. China**, and vars· *alba*, white, *trollioides*, yellow; *suffruticosa* (syns. *P. arborea* and *P. Moutan*), ' Tree Peony ', rose, May, 3 to 6 ft., shrubby, China; *tenuifolia*, crimson, May, 1 to 1½ ft., Europe; *Veitchii*, purplish-red, to 2½ ft., China, var. *plena*, purplish-rose, *Woodwardii*, rose; *Wittmanniana*, yellow, May, 2 ft., Caucasus, and var. *tomentosa*.

Pak-Choi, see *Brassica chinensis*.

Paliurus—*Rhamnaceae*. Hardy deciduous flowering shrub with spiny branches and ornamental fruit. First introduced late sixteenth century.

CULTURE: Soil, ordinary. Position, shrubberies or walls. Plant, Oct. to Nov.

PROPAGATION: By seeds sown ¼ in. deep in ordinary soil outdoors, Oct. to Nov.; cuttings of roots inserted 3 in. deep and 6 in. apart, Oct. to Feb.; layering shoots Sept. to Nov.; removing suckers with roots attached Sept. to Dec.

SPECIES CULTIVATED: *P. Spina-Christi* (syn. *P. aculeatus*), greenish-yellow, July, Aug., 15 to 20 ft., S. Europe to N. China.

Palma Christi, see *Ricinus communis*.

Palmetto, see Sabal.

Pampas Grass, see Cortaderia.

Panax (Ginseng)—*Araliaceae*. Low perennial greenhouse herbs with greenish flowers and berry-like fruits, grown for the roots which are employed in medicine.

CULTURE: Compost, equal parts loam, peat or leaf-mould, charcoal and sand. Pot, Feb. to March. Water freely March to Oct., moderately afterwards. Temp., March to Sept. 70° to 80°, Sept. to March 60° to 70°.

PROPAGATION: By grafting in heat in spring; roots-cuttings in light soil in temp. 80° in April.

SPECIES CULTIVATED: *P. quinquefolium* (syn. *Aralia quinquefolia*), ' American Ginseng ', to 1½ ft., N. America; *Schinseng* (syn. *P. Ginseng*), ' Asiatic Ginseng ', white bristles on veins of leaves, Manchuria, Korea; *trifolium* (syn. *Aralia trifolia*), ' Dwarf Ginseng ', ' Groundnut ', to 8 in., N. America.

Pancratium—*Amaryllidaceae*. Stove and hardy evergreen bulbous plants. First introduced late sixteenth century.

CULTURE OF STOVE SPECIES: Compost, two parts sandy loam, one part decayed manure and half a part silver sand. Position, well-drained pots in sunny part of stove. Pot, March. Repotting necessary every three or four years only. Water abundantly April to Sept., moderately Sept. to Dec., keep quite dry Dec. to March. Apply liquid manure once a week May to Sept. Temp., 70° to 80° March to Sept., 55° to 65° Sept. to March.

CULTURE OF HARDY SPECIES: Soil, three parts sandy loam, one part leaf-mould. Position, warm, exposed, well-drained borders. Plant bulbs 3 to 4 in. deep, Oct., Nov. or March. Protect in winter by layer of decayed manure, peat or cinder ashes. Mulch after growth commences with decayed cow manure. Apply weak stimulants occasionally during summer. Lift, divide and transplant every three years.

PROPAGATION: Greenhouse and stove species by offsets removed from old bulbs in March; hardy kinds similarly when replanting.

STOVE SPECIES CULTIVATED: *P. canariense*, white, Oct. and Nov., 18 in., fragrant, Canary Isles; *zeylanicum*, white, June, 1 ft., Trop. Asia.

HARDY SPECIES CULTIVATED: *P. illyricum*, white, summer, 1 to 2 ft., S. Europe; *maritimum*, ' Mediterranean Lily ' or ' Sea Daffodil ', white, June, 2 to 2½ ft., Medit. Region.

Pandanus (Screw Pine)—*Pandanaceae*. Stove evergreen shrubs with narrow, strap-like, serrated leaves. First introduced mid-eighteenth century.

CULTURE: Compost, two parts sandy loam, one part equal proportions leaf-mould, charcoal and sand. Pot, Jan. to April. Position, sunny, moist part of stove. Water moderately Oct. to Feb., freely afterwards. Syringe twice daily March to Sept. Temp., March to Sept. 65° to 85°, Sept. to March 55° to 65°.

PROPAGATION: By suckers, Feb. to April.

SPECIES CULTIVATED: *P. Baptistii*, leaves yellow and green, 4 to 6 ft., New Britain, and var. *variegata*; *Candelabrum*, leaves green, 15 to 30 ft., Trop. Africa; *furcatus*, leaves bright green, 10 to 15 ft., India, Malaya; *Sanderi*, leaves green and yellow, 3 ft., Timor; *utilis*, leaves glaucous green with reddish spines, 30 to 60 ft., Madagascar; *variegatus*, leaves green and white, 2 to 3 ft., Polynesia; *Veitchii*, leaves green and white, 3 ft., Polynesia.

Pandorea—*Bignoniaceae*. Greenhouse evergreen shrubs, climbing or clambering by tendrils and petioles. Funnel-shaped, white or pink flowers, and fruit an oblong pod, leaves pinnate.

CULTURE: Compost, two parts loam, one part peat and silver sand. Position, large well-drained pots or beds 3 ft. square 18 in. deep for one plant, in sunny greenhouse, shoots trained up roof. Pot or plant, Feb. or March. Good drainage essential. Prune in Feb. Water copiously April to Oct., keep nearly dry Oct. to April. Apply weak stimulants occasionally during summer to established plants. No shade required at any time. Admit air freely during summer and early autumn to thoroughly ripen wood. Temp., April to Oct. 55° to 65°, Oct. to April 40° to 50°.

PROPAGATION: By cuttings of young wood under glass; seed.

SPECIES CULTIVATED: *P. jasminoides* (syns. *Bignonia* and *Tecoma jasminoides*), ' Bower Plant ', white with pink throat, Aug., 10 to 20 ft., Australia, var. *alba*, white, and *rosea*, pink; *pandorana* (syns. *P. australis*, *Bignonia* and *Tecoma australis*), ' Wonga-wonga Vine ', yellowish-white spotted purple, summer, 10 to 20 ft., Australia, var. *rosea*, pale rose.

Panicum—*Gramineae*. Hardy and half-hardy annual and perennial grasses.

CULTURE OF HARDY ANNUALS: Soil, ordinary. Position, sunny borders. Sow seeds ⅛ in. deep in patches where required to flower, in March or April. Thin seedlings when 1 in. high to 2 in. apart. Gather inflorescence in July or Aug. and dry for winter use.

CULTURE OF HARDY PERENNIALS: Soil, good ordinary. Position, sunny borders. Plant, Oct. or April. Lift, divide and replant every two or three years.

PROPAGATION: Stove species by division; hardy kinds by seeds sown outdoors in April or May; division of roots in Oct. or March.

ANNUAL SPECIES CULTIVATED: *P. capillare*, 2 ft., W. Hemisphere.

PERENNIAL SPECIES CULTIVATED: *P. bulbosum*, 5 ft., Mexico; *virgatum*, ' Switch Grass ', 3 to 4 ft., N. America. See also Oplismenus.

Pansy, see Viola.

Papaver (Poppy)—*Papaveraceae*. Hardy annual and perennial herbs.

CULTURE OF ANNUAL SPECIES: Soil, good ordinary. Position, sunny beds or borders. Sow seeds 1/16 in. deep in patches where required to grow—in April for flowering in summer, Sept. for flowering in spring. Thin seedlings to 1 or 2 in. apart when ½ in. high.

CULTURE OF PERENNIAL SPECIES: Soil, deep, sandy loam. Position, sunny borders for tall species, rockeries for *P. alpinum*. Plant, Oct., March or April.

Top-dress with decayed manure in March or April. *P. alpinum* and *nudicaule* are best grown as annuals or biennials.

PROPAGATION: Annual species by seeds as above; perennial species by seeds sown in sunny place outdoors in March or April; division of roots in March or April or root cuttings in winter.

ANNUAL SPECIES CULTIVATED: *P. glaucum*, ' Tulip Poppy ', crimson, summer, 18 in., Syria; *laevigatum*, scarlet, black, and white, summer, 2 ft., Greece; *pavoninum*, ' Peacock Poppy ', scarlet and black, 18 in., Afghanistan; *Rhoeas*, ' Corn ' or ' Shirley Poppy ', various colours, 18 in., Britain, and var. *umbrosum*, red and black; *somniferum*, ' Opium Poppy ', various colours, summer, 3 ft., Europe and Asia.

PERENNIAL SPECIES CULTIVATED: *P. alpinum*, ' Alpine Poppy ', yellow, orange, salmon, and white, summer, 6 in., Europe; *californicum*, orange, June, 1 ft., California; *nudicaule*, ' Iceland Poppy ', yellow, orange, and white, summer, 1 ft., Arctic Regions; *orientale*, ' Oriental Poppy ', orange-scarlet, June, 3 ft., Asia Minor; *pilosum*, orange, summer, 2 ft., Greece; *rupifragum*, ' Spanish Poppy ', terra-cotta, summer, 2 ft., Spain.

Papaw, see *Asimina triloba.*

Papaya, see *Carica Papaya.*

Paper Mulberry, see Broussonetia; **-Bush,** see *Edgeworthia papyrifera.*

Paphinia—*Orchidaceae.* Small-growing epiphytic orchids at one time placed in Lycaste. Flowers large, beautiful, on short pendulous scapes from the base of the small, clustered pseudo-bulbs. Leaves two to three.

CULTURE: Compost, three parts of osmunda fibre or substitute, two parts sphagnum moss with finely broken crocks and nodules of charcoal. Small pans are preferable, suspended near the glass, the compost should be slightly mounded centrally. A moist atmosphere should be maintained. Water liberally when growth is vigorous, infrequently in winter. Careful shading is necessary and the syringe should not be used. Winter night temp. 60° to 65°, summer 70° and higher.

PROPAGATION: By division of plants when they are large enough, which is very seldom. When potting, in spring, a healthy back bulb may be removed and may emit a growth.

SPECIES CULTIVATED: *P. cristata*, yellowish, barred with chocolate, mid-lobe of lip purplish or chestnut with a tuft of white hairs, summer, autumn, Trinidad, Guiana, Brazil, var. *Randii*, reddish-brown, Brazil; *grandiflora* (syn. *P. grandis*), creamy white, purplish spotted and flushed, mid-lobe of lip with creamy white shaggy hairs, autumn, Brazil; *Lindeniana*, purplish, marked with creamy white, mid-lobe of lip white, with hair and teat-like processes; *rugosa*, yellow, dotted red, mid-lobe of lip red-purple with a tuft of white bristle-like hairs, autumn, Colombia.

Paphiopedilum—*Orchidaceae.* Terrestrial or epiphytic orchids without pseudo-bulbs. Some 3,000 hybrids have been raised from the species and between the hybrids themselves. Many are suited to a moderately cool temp. and many are winter flowering.

CULTURE: Compost for both species and hybrids; for the green-leaved kinds, e.g. *P. insigne*, three parts fibrous loam, one part peat or osmunda fibre, one part sphagnum moss. For the tropical green-leaved species and hybrids and those with mottled foliage, more moss and much less loam, crushed potsherds added to all. *P. niveum, concolor, bellatulum, Godefroyae*, should have fibrous loam, a little fibre and sphagnum and nodules of old mortar rubble. This section requires less frequent waterings in winter. About 2 in. of drainage is required by all. Temps., all enjoy a moist atmosphere and though *P. insigne, villosum, Spicerianum* and similar can grow in a winter night temp. of 50° to 55°, 60° is better as it allows rather more humidity. The more tender tropical species need a winter night temp. of 65° to 70°, 60° to 65° for species from Burma, Annam, etc. Temps. for hybrids are governed by their parentage, 55° to 60° is sufficient for many, 60° is safer. These temps. will be exceeded in summer with shading and by sun heat, night air should be admitted whenever conditions are favourable.

PROPAGATION: By division of plants with not less than four growths, six are preferable.

SPECIES CULTIVATED: *P. Appletonianum* (syn. *P. sublaeve*, hort.), greenish-white, lilac-mauve, spring, summer, Siam; *Argus*, greenish, purple, veined brownish-purple, summer, Philippines; *barbatum*, greenish, white, striped and flushed brown-purple, summer, Malacca, many vars.; *bellatulum*, cream, spotted purple-maroon, spring, Burma, var. *album*, white; *callosum*, large, variable, white, purple striped, brown-purple, winter, summer, Siam, Cochin-China, var. *Sanderae*, white; *Chamberlainianum*, greenish, petals spiralled, rose or greenish-rose, lip rose-purple, New Guinea; *Charlesworthii*, dorsal sepal suffused rose, summer, Burma; *ciliolare*, whitish, green veined, purplish-brown, spring, summer, Philippines, Malaya; *concolor*, small, 1 to 2, 5 in some vars., yellow, dotted red, summer, autumn, Siam, Burma; *Curtisii*, large, greenish-purplish, petals spotted, Sumatra, var. *Sanderae*, whitish, green striped; *Dayanum*, greenish-white, dull rose, brownish-purple, summer, Borneo; *Druryi*, yellowish with black median lines, spring, early summer, Travancore; *exul*, yellowish, dorsal white-margined, Siam; *Fairieanum*, small, very pretty, whitish, purple striped and flushed, summer, winter, Assam; *glaucophyllum*, up to 20 in succession, greenish, dull purple, Java; *Godefroyae*, whitish or yellowish, irregularly marked, brown-purple, lip with small spots, variable, summer, Cochin-China, Tonkin, var. *leucochilum*, lip without spots; *Gratrixianum*, near to *exul*, larger, dorsal black spotted, hybrid; *Haynaldianum*, 3 to 6 segments, narrow, rose, yellowish-green, brown-purple, spotted, spring, summer, Philippines; *hirsutissimum*, large, greenish shaded brown-purple, petals partially purplish, autumn, Annam, N. India; *Hookerae*, yellowish-green to purplish, summer, Borneo, var. *Bullenianum* (syn. *P. Bulleni-anum*); *insigne*, variable, large, greenish, spotted on the white-margined dorsal with brown-purple, shading to brown, winter, N. India, Assam, Burma, of great use to hybridists, many named vars.; *javanicum*, greenish to brownish-green, summer, autumn, Java; *Lawrenceanum*, large, variable, white, striped purple-red, petals horizontal, greenish lip shaded brown-purple, summer, Borneo; *Lowii*, epiphytic, near to *Haynaldianum*, petals violet-purple apically, summer, Borneo; *Mastersianum*, greenish-yellow shading to copper, spring, summer, Amboina; *papuanum*, veined and shaded with dull crimson, summer, New Guinea; *Parishii*, 3 to 7 greenish-yellow, petals twisted, drooped, shading to brown, lip slender, summer, Moulmein; *philippinense* (syn. *P. Robelinii*), 3 to 5, dorsal, yellowish, striped brown-purple, petals twisted, tapered, black-warted, lip tawny to brown-green, summer, autumn, Philippines; *purpuratum*, white, shaded green, shading to purplish-red, dorsal striped, summer, Hong Kong; *Rothschildi-anum* (syns. *P. neoguinense*, *Nicholsonianum*), 2 to 7, large, dorsal yellowish, shaded white with blackish stripes, petals outstretched, tapered, lip reddish-brown, very fine, spring, summer, Sumatra, Borneo; *Sanderianum*, 3 to 5, yellowish, shaded green and brown-purple, petals ribbon-like, 18 to 27 in. long, summer, autumn, Malaya; *Spicerianum*, dorsal white with purplish median stripe, lip brownish-purple, winter, Assam; *Stonei*, 3 to 5 dorsal pink-flushed, striped black-crimson, petals twisted, tawny yellow, lip dull rose, autumn, Borneo; *superbiens* (syn. *P. Veitchianum*); *tonsum*, greenish-white, veined green, flushed brownish, summer, Sumatra; *venustum*, whitish, green veined, petals purple-flushed apically, lip yellowish, winter, N. India; *Victoriae Mariae*, many in succession, green shaded red, lip purplish-rose, summer, Sumatra; *villosum*, large, dorsal, white-margined, petals and lip yellow-brown, variable, winter, spring, Burma, Moulmein; *Wardii*, dorsal whitish, veined green, petals thickly spotted red-brown, autumn, winter, Upper Burma.

Paprika, see *Capsicum frutescens* var. *longum.*

Papyrus, see *Cyperus Papyrus.*

Paradisea—*Liliaceae.* Hardy herbaceous perennials. First introduced early seventeenth century.

CULTURE: Soil, ordinary, well enriched with leaf-mould and decayed manure. Position, partially shady borders. Plant, Oct. or March.

PROPAGATION: By division of roots in Oct. or March; seeds sown in cold frame or greenhouse in spring.

SPECIES CULTIVATED: *P. Liliastrum* (syn. *Anthericum Liliastrum*), ' St. Bruno Lily ', white, fragrant, May and June, 1 to 2 ft., Alps, var. *major*, 4 to 5 ft., larger flowers than the parent.

Para Nut, see Bertholletia.

Paraquilegia—*Ranunculaceae.* Hardy herbaceous perennials.

CULTURE: Cool crevices or narrow ledges in the rock garden or in rich scree soil in a cool corner of the scree.

PROPAGATION: By seeds or careful division of old plants in spring.

SPECIES CULTIVATED: *P. anemonoides* (syns. *P. grandiflora, Isopyrum grandiflorum*), rich lavender-blue, summer, 6 to 9 in., Cent. Asia, China.

Paris—*Liliaceae.* Hardy perennial rhizomatous herb.

CULTURE: Soil, sandy loam. Position, shady borders, woods or shrubberies. Plant, Oct. to March.

PROPAGATION: By seeds sown in moist position outdoors in autumn; division of roots, Oct. or March.

SPECIES CULTIVATED: *P. quadrifolia*, ' Herb Paris ', green, summer, 6 in., Britain.

Parlour Palm, see *Aspidistra lurida.*

Parnassia—*Saxifragaceae.* Hardy perennial herbs.

CULTURE: Soil, peaty or boggy. Position, moist, shady borders, bogs, or margins of streams or ponds. Plant, March or April.

PROPAGATION: By seeds sown in moist, boggy peat in shady position outdoors in autumn or spring; division of roots in March or April.

SPECIES CULTIVATED: *P. caroliniana*, white, summer, 6 in., N. America; *grandifolia*, white, summer, N. America; *palustris*, ' Grass of Parnassus', white and green, summer, 6 in., Britain.

Parochetus (Shamrock Pea)—*Leguminosae.* Hardy trailing herbaceous perennial. First introduced early nineteenth century.

CULTURE: Soil, ordinary. Position, moist, partially shady banks or rock gardens. Plant, Oct., March or April.

PROPAGATION: By seeds sown $\frac{1}{16}$ in. deep in light, sandy soil in cold frame in March; division of plants in March.

SPECIES CULTIVATED: *P. communis*, blue, March to June, trailing, Himalaya.

Paronychia (Nail-wort; Whitlow-wort)—*Caryophyllaceae.* Dwarf creeping perennial herbs. Flowers, white, surrounded by silvery bracts, produced in June. First introduced late nineteenth century.

CULTURE: Soil, ordinary. Position, dry, sunny banks or rockeries, or for carpeting surfaces of beds. Plant, March to June.

PROPAGATION: By seeds sown in sunny spot outdoors in March or April; division of plants, Oct. or March.

SPECIES CULTIVATED: *P. argentea*, trailing, S. Europe; *dichotoma*, trailing, Portugal; *nivea*, prostrate, S. Europe; *pyrenaica*, mat-forming, Pyrenees; *serpyllifolia*, trailing, S. Europe.

Parrotia—*Hamamelidaceae.* Hardy deciduous tree, leaves brilliantly coloured in autumn.

CULTURE: Soil, good ordinary. Position, open shrubberies or as lawn specimen. Plant, Oct. to Feb.

PROPAGATION: By seeds sown $\frac{1}{8}$ in. deep in well-drained pots of sandy soil in cold frame in autumn or spring; layering shoots in autumn; cuttings.

Species Cultivated: *P. persica*, to 15 ft., flowers, insignificant, before leaves, Persia.

Parrotiopsis—*Hamamelidaceae.* Hardy deciduous tree.
Culture: Soil, good ordinary. Position, open shrubberies, etc. Plant, Oct. to Feb.
Propagation: By seeds, layers and cuttings of green wood under glass.
Species Cultivated: *P. Jacquemontiana* (syn. *Parrotia Jacquemontiana*), leaves to 3 in. long, turning pale yellow in autumn, flowers in dense heads surrounded by large white bracts, to 20 ft., Himalaya.

Parrot's Bill, see *Clianthus puniceus*; **-Feather,** see *Myriophyllum proserpinacoides.*

Parsley, see *Petroselinum crispum*; **-Fern,** see *Cryptogramma crispa* var. *acrostichoides.*

Parsnip, see *Pastinaca sativa.*

Parson-in-the-Pulpit Orchid, see *Oncidium dastyle.*

Parthenocissus—*Vitaceae.* Shrubs, mainly deciduous, climbing by tendrils used to cover walls, fences and trees. Formerly included in genera Ampelopsis and Vitis.
Culture: Soil, ordinary. Position, against walls, etc. Plant, Oct. to March.
Propagation: Hardwood cuttings Sept. under glass; spring, outdoors; softwood cuttings in moderate heat in summer.
Species Cultivated: *P. Henryana* (syn. *Ampelopsis Henryana*), tall, leaflets bright green with silver and pink variegation colouring to red, China; *quinquefolia* (syn. *Ampelopsis quinquefolia*), 'Virginia Creeper', mid-America, var. *Englemannii*, better clinger on bare walls; *tricuspidata* (syn. *Ampelopsis tricuspidata*), 'Japanese' or 'Boston Ivy', furnished with short-branched tendrils that can hold fast to any surface, var. *Veitchii* (syn. *Ampelopsis Veitchii*), 'Small-leaved Virginia Creeper', leaves purple when young, Japan.

Partridge Berry, see Mitchella.

Pasque Flower, see *Anemone Pulsatilla.*

Passerina—*Thymeliaceae.* Woody, prostrate or dwarf sub-shrubs for the rock garden.
Culture: Well-drained, gritty loam or scree soil, full sun.
Propagation: By cuttings of ripened wood in Aug.
Species Cultivated: *P. nivea*, yellow, fragrant, all summer, 1 to 2 in., Europe.

Passiflora (Passion Flower)—*Passifloraceae.* Stove, greenhouse and slightly tender climbing plants. *P. edulis* and *P. quadrangularis* produce edible fruit. First introduced early seventeenth century.
Culture of Stove Species: Compost, equal parts loam and peat, one-fourth part silver sand. Pot, Feb. or March. Prune, Feb., thinning out weak shoots and shortening strong ones one-third. Position, well-drained tubs or pots, or beds 18 in. deep and 2 ft. wide; shoots trained up rafters or walls; sunny. Water copiously March to Sept., moderately afterwards. Syringe daily April to Sept. Apply stimulants occasionally to healthy plants when in flower. Temp., March to Oct. 65° to 75°, Oct. to March 55° to 65°.
Culture of Greenhouse Species: Compost, as above. Position, grown in pots, tubs or beds, and shoots trained up rafters. Prune, pot and water as advised for stove species. Temp., March to Oct. 55° to 65°, Oct. to March 45° to 50°.
Culture of Slightly Tender Species: Soil, good ordinary, mixed with a little decayed manure. Position, south or south-west walls. Plant, Oct. or March. Prune in Feb., shortening small shoots. Water freely in dry weather. Apply liquid manure to healthy plants once a month in summer. Protect base of plant with straw or dry bracken during severe weather.
Propagation: Stove and greenhouse species by seeds sown ¼ in. deep in pots of sandy soil in temp. 65° to 75° at any time; by cuttings of young shoots 4 to 6 in. long in sandy soil under bell-glass in temp. 65°, April to Sept. Half-hardy

species by similar cuttings in cold frame in summer; layering young shoots in summer.

STOVE SPECIES CULTIVATED: *P. alata*, crimson, white and purple, summer, 15 to 20 ft., Peru; *edulis*, ' Purple Granadilla ', white and purple, summer, 20 ft., Brazil; *exoniensis*, red and pink, summer, 20 to 30 ft., hybrid; *quadrangularis* ' Giant Granadilla ', red, violet and white, fragrant, summer, 20 ft., Trop. America; *racemosa* (syn. *P. princeps*), red, white and purple, summer, 20 ft., Brazil.

GREENHOUSE SPECIES CULTIVATED: *P. antioquiensis* (syn. *Tacsonia Van-Volxemii*), crimson, autumn, 30 ft., Colombia; *mixta* (syn. *Tacsonia mixta*), pink, summer, 20 ft., Trop. America; *mollissima* (syn. *Tacsonia mollissima*), rose, summer, 20 to 30 ft., Andes; *pinnatistipula* (syn. *Tacsonia pinnatistipula*), pale rose, Sept. 30 ft., Chile.

SLIGHTLY TENDER SPECIES CULTIVATED: *P. caerulea*, pale pink, white and purple, summer, 20 to 25 ft., Brazil, and vars.

Passion Flower, see Passiflora.

Pastinaca—*Umbelliferae*. Hardy biennial esculent-rooted vegetable.

CULTURE: Soil, rich ordinary, deeply dug and manured for the previous crop. Position, open and sunny. Sow when ground can be worked in March in drills 1 in. deep, 15 in. apart. Place seeds in groups of five at 9 in. intervals. Thin to leave sturdiest seedling at each station. Leave in ground until required for use, but lift when growth recommences and store in heaps of sand. In shallow soils prepare individual stations, making a hole with a crowbar and filling with good rich soil. Seed retains its vegetative powers for one year only. Quantity required for a row 50 ft. long, ½ oz. Crop reaches maturity in 24 to 27 weeks, but flavour improves if left in the ground. Seed takes 15 to 20 days to germinate.

SPECIES CULTIVATED: *P. sativa* (syn. *Pencedanum sativum*), ' Parsnip ', yellow, July and Aug., 4 ft., Europe.

Patrinia—*Valerianaceae*. Hardy perennials with graceful foliage and attractive flowers. First introduced mid-eighteenth century.

CULTURE: Soil, light, rich, ordinary. Position, sunny borders. Plant in Oct., March or April. Grow in groups of three or six.

PROPAGATION: By seeds sown outdoors in April; division of the plants in autumn or spring.

SPECIES CULTIVATED: *P. intermedia*, yellow, fragrant, May, 1 ft., Siberia; *scabiosifolia*, ' Eastern Valerian ', yellow, June and July, 2 ft., Siberia; *triloba*, June and July, 9 in., Japan.

Paullinia—*Sapindaceae*. Stove evergreen twining plant with finely divided, green, downy leaves. First cultivated early nineteenth century.

CULTURE: Compost, two parts loam, one part each leaf-mould and sand. Position, well-drained pots, with shoots trained round wire trellis or up rafters of roof. Pot, March. Prune slightly in Jan. and Feb. Water moderately Oct. to Feb., freely afterwards. Syringe twice daily March to Sept.

PROPAGATION: By cuttings of firm shoots, 2 to 3 in. long, inserted in small pots of sandy soil under bell-glass in temp. 75° to 85° any time.

SPECIES CULTIVATED: *P. thalictrifolia*, pink, Sept., 10 to 15 ft., Brazil.

Paulownia—*Scrophulariaceae*. Hardy deciduous tree with ornamental foliage and foxglove-shaped flowers of striking beauty. First introduced mid-nineteenth century.

CULTURE: Soil, rich well-drained loam. Position, sunny, sheltered shrubberies or lawns. Plant, Oct. to Feb. Prune shoots annually in Feb. to within 2 or 3 in. of base if only foliage is desired; leave unpruned for flowering.

PROPAGATION: By seeds sown ⅛ in. deep in sandy loam in cold frame in spring or autumn; cuttings of roots inserted in sandy soil in frame in Feb.

SPECIES CULTIVATED: *P. lilacina*, pale violet striped pale yellow, June, 30 to 50 ft., W. China; *tomentosa* (syn. *P. imperialis*), violet, June, 30 to 50 ft., China.

Pavetta—*Rubiaceae.* Stove and greenhouse evergreen shrubs. First introduced late eighteenth century.

CULTURE: Compost, two parts good fibrous peat, one part fibrous loam and silver sand. Position, shady part of warm greenhouse whilst growing, light situation when at rest. Pot, Feb. or March; good drainage indispensable. Prune into shape in Feb. Water freely from March to Sept., moderately afterwards. Syringe twice daily March to Aug. Apply liquid manure once or twice a week to healthy plants in flower. For *P. caffra*, March to Sept. 60° to 70°, Sept. to March 50° to 55°.

PROPAGATION: By cuttings of firm young shoots, 2 to 3 in. long, inserted singly in small pots in sandy peat under bell-glass in temp. 75° to 85°, March to May.

SPECIES CULTIVATED: *P. caffra*, white, June to Aug., 3 to 4 ft., Cape of Good Hope; *indica*, white, Aug. to Oct., 3 to 4 ft., Trop. Asia, Trop. Australia; *obovata*, white, summer, 3 ft., Natal.

Pavia, see *Aesculus Pavia.*

Pavonia—*Malvaceae.* Stove evergreen plants. First introduced mid-eighteenth century.

CULTURE: Compost, two parts loam, one part peat and sand. Pot, March. Position, pots in shade. Water freely March to Sept., moderately afterwards. Syringe daily in summer. Temp., March to Sept. 65° to 75°, Sept. to March 55° to 65°.

PROPAGATION: By cuttings in fine sand under bell-glass in temp. 75° at any time.

SPECIES CULTIVATED: *P. intermedia*, white, origin unknown, var. *kermesina*; *multiflora* (syn. *P. Wioti*), purple, autumn, 1 to 2 ft., Brazil; *rosea*, rosy red, 1 to 2 ft., Trop. America; *spinifex*, yellow, 10 to 20 ft., Trop. America.

Pawpaw, see *Carica Papaya.*

Pea, see *Pisum sativum*; **-Tree,** see Caragana.

Peanut, see *Arachis hypogaea.*

Peach, see *Prunus Persica.*

Peacock Flower, see *Delonix regia.*

Pear, see Pyrus.

Pearl Berry, see *Margyricarpus setosus*; **-Bush,** see Exochorda; **-Grass,** see *Briza maxima*; **-wort,** see Sagina.

Pecan, see *Carya Pecan.*

Pearly Everlasting, see *Anaphalis margaritacea.*

Pedilanthus—*Euphorbiaceae.* Stove succulent shrub. First introduced mid-nineteenth century.

CULTURE: Compost, two parts sandy loam, one part brick rubbish, half a part decayed cow manure and silver sand. Pot, March or April. Position, dry, sunny part of stove. Temp., Sept. to March 60° to 70°, March to Sept. 60° to 80°. Water once in three weeks from Sept. to March, once a week afterwards. No syringing or stimulants required.

PROPAGATION: By cuttings of shoots, 2 to 3 in. long, exposed to sun for one or two days, then inserted singly in sand in 2 in. pots, and placed on a shelf near the glass, any time during summer.

SPECIES CULTIVATED: *P. macrocarpus*, bright red, 5 ft., California; *tithymaloides*, ' Jew Bush ', ' Slipper Spurge ', bright red or purple, 6 ft., Trop. America, also var. *variegatus.*

Pediocactus—*Cactaceae.* Greenhouse succulent plant, sometimes included in Echinocactus.

CULTURE: As Echinocactus.

PROPAGATION: As Echinocactus.

SPECIES CULTIVATED: *P. Simpsonii*, ' Snowball Cactus ', pinkish, radial spines white and needle-like, hardy species, can be grown out of doors in S. England, Mexico.

Pelargonium—*Geraniaceae*. . Greenhouse and hardy herbaceous, evergreen, shrubby and tuberous-rooted perennials. Flowering and ornamental foliage. Popularly known as ' Geraniums '. First introduced eighteenth century.

CLASSIFICATION OF TYPES: (1) Zonal: Leaves roundish, cordate, lobed, pubescent, green, with or without zone or horse-shoe mark near margin of upper surface. Subclasses: Bicolor—Leaves green edged with white or white edged with green. Tricolor—Leaves green, white, yellow and crimson. Bronze—Yellow, with bronze zone. (2) Show: Leaves palmately lobed, toothed margins, wrinkled, green; flowers large, with smooth or wrinkled edges. Subclass: Regal —Flowers semi-double. (3) Fancy: Leaves similar to show kinds; flowers smaller, spotted, or blotched. (4) Ivy-leaved: Leaves ivy-shaped, fleshy, five-angled, green or variegated; stems trailing or climbing. (5) Scented-leaved: Leaves variously shaped, scented. (6) Succulent: Stems fleshy, often contorted, leaves variously shaped, often with glandular teeth.

CULTURE OF HARDY HERBACEOUS SPECIES: Soil, sandy loam. Position, sunny well-drained rockery or border. Plant, March or April. Protect in winter with covering of coconut-fibre refuse.

CULTURE OF ZONAL PELARGONIUMS: For summer flowering: Insert cuttings in Aug. or Sept. singly in 2 in. pots. Place in temp. 45° till March, then transfer to 4 in. size. Nip off points of main shoot in Feb. or March, also of side shoots when 2 in. long. Transfer to 6 in. pots when roots reach side of 5 in. sizes. Pot firmly. Compost for first potting, two parts yellow fibrous loam, half a part well-decayed manure, half a part leaf-mould, one part coarse sand, and tablespoonful of super-phosphate or a quarter of a pint of bonemeal to each bushel; for final potting, same proportion of loam, manure and leaf-mould, quarter part each of coarse sand and charcoal, tablespoonful of superphosphate or pint of bonemeal to each bushel. Remove flower buds until fortnight after final potting. Water moderately first ten days after potting, freely afterwards. Apply stimulants month after final potting. Shade from sun when in bloom. Temp., Aug. to March 40° to 50°, March to May 55° to 60°; ordinary cool greenhouse or window afterwards. After flowering shorten shoots and keep soil just moist, repotting following spring to make large plants. For winter flowering: Insert cuttings singly in 2 in. pots in Feb. or March in temp. 55° to 65°. Transfer when well rooted into 4 in. and again into 6 in. in June. Nip off points of main shoot in April and of side shoots in May or June. Pinch off flower buds appearing before Sept. Stand in sunny, cold frame or plunge to rim of pots in cinder ashes in open position, June to Sept. Remove into greenhouse in Sept. Water freely outdoors, moderately indoors. Apply stimulants twice a week June to Sept., once a week afterwards. Compost, as above. Temp., Sept. to March 50° to 55°. Dry atmosphere essential to prevent damping of blooms. After flowering shorten shoots, keep moderately moist, and repot. Zonals, Bicolors and Tricolors for bedding: Insert cuttings in Aug. or Sept., several in 5 in. pots, or 2 in. apart in shallow boxes. Keep thus until Feb., then transfer singly to 3 in. pots, place in temp. 55° until April, then remove to cold frame, and plant outdoors in June. Lift plants in Sept., placing bicolors, tricolors and bronzes singly in 3 in. pots; zonals singly in similar pots, three in a 4 or 5 in. pot, or a few inches apart in shallow boxes, and storing in temp. 40° to 45°, in greenhouse, room or cellar. Specimen Zonals: Insert cuttings in Aug. or Sept., grow in 2 in. pots until March, then transfer to 4 in. sizes. Compost, as above. Nip off point of main shoot in March, also of side shoots when 3 in. long. Tie these firmly to wire fixed to rim of pot and allow young shoots to form in centre. Remove all blooms first year. Transfer to 6 in. pot in May or June. Grow in greenhouse near glass. Water freely during summer, moderately in winter. Apply stimulants June to Sept. Shorten shoots two-thirds in Jan. When new shoots form repot. Nip off points of shoots where necessary to ensure good shape. Compost, as above. Stimulants for Zonals: Liquid horse, cow, sheep or deer dung diluted with two-thirds water and applied twice a week in summer, once a week in winter; nitrate of soda, ¼ oz. to a gallon of water, applied once a week, when soil is moist only, for three or four weeks, then cease; sulphate of ammonia, same as nitrate of soda; soot-water (one peck each of sheep and cow dung and ½ peck of soot to 36 gall. of water), diluted with half water, applied twice a week.

CULTURE OF SHOW AND FANCY PELARGONIUMS: Insert cuttings of firm shoots, 2 to 3 in. long, in July or Aug., singly in 2 in. pots in cold frame or greenhouse. Sandy soil. When rooted transfer to 4 in. pots, and place on a shelf close to glass in temp. 45° to 50°. Nip off point of main shoot just before potting. When new shoots are 3 in. long nip off points. Transfer to 5 in. pots in Jan. Keep near glass. When flowers show apply liquid manure twice a week. Water moderately until March, then freely until June, when give less. Temp., Sept. to March 45° to 50°, March to May 50° to 55°. After flowering stand in sunny place outdoors. Prune shoots to within 1 in. of base in July. When new shoots form turn plants out of pots, remove loose soil, and repot in 4 or 5 in. pots. Replace in greenhouse in Sept. Transfer to 6 or 8 in. pots in Dec. or Jan. Compost, three parts good fibrous loam, one part decayed horse or cow dung, half a part coarse sand, and a tablespoonful of superphosphate to each bushel. Good drainage and firm potting essential. Stimulants as above.

CULTURE OF IVY-LEAVED PELARGONIUMS: Insert cuttings singly in 2 in. pots, or three or four in a 4 in. pot, in Aug. or Sept. Grow in greenhouse near glass until Feb. or March, then transfer to 4 in. pots. Nip off points of main shoots in Feb. or March. Repot in 5 in. pots in April or May. Train shoots to stakes or place plants in suspended baskets, and let them droop over sides. Water moderately Sept. to April, freely April to Sept. Apply stimulants May to Sept. Temp., Sept. to March 40° to 50°, March to Sept. 50° to 60°. Plant outdoors June. Prune old plants Feb. or March. Compost and stimulants as for zonals.

CULTURE OF FRAGRANT-LEAVED PELARGONIUMS: Compost, two parts loam, half a part each of decayed manure and leaf-mould, quarter part sand. Pot and treat as advised for zonals.

CULTURE OF SUCCULENT PELARGONIUMS: Compost, two parts sandy loam, half part crushed brick with plenty of sharp sand. Position, greenhouse with full exposure to sun. Water sparingly, little in winter.

PROPAGATION: By seeds sown 1/16 in. deep in a well-drained pot or pan filled with light, sandy soil in temp. 55° to 65°, Feb. to April; cuttings inserted as above directed in each section; grafting on common kinds in close frame or under bell-glass in temp. 55° to 65° in spring; tuberous-rooted kinds by division in spring.

HARDY HERBACEOUS SPECIES CULTIVATED: *P. Endlicherianum*, rose, July to Oct. 2 ft., Orient.

FRAGRANT-LEAVED SPECIES CULTIVATED: *P. capitatum*, ' Rose-scented ', rose and purple, summer, 2 to 3 ft., S. Africa; *citriodorum*, ' Citron-scented ', white, summer, 2 to 3 ft., hybrid; *crispum*, ' Lemon-scented ', rose, Sept., 2 to 3 ft., S. Africa; *denticulatum*, purple, summer, 1 ft., S. Africa, and var. *filicifolium*, ' Fern-leaved '; *fragrans*, ' Nutmeg-scented ', white and pink, summer, 2 to 3 ft., S. Africa; *graveolens*, rose and purple, 2 to 3 ft., S. Africa; *odoratissimum*, white, 1½ ft., S. Africa; *quercifolium*, ' Oak-leaved ', pink and purple, May, 3 ft., S. Africa; *Radula*, ' Balsam-scented ', rose and purple, summer, 2 to 3 ft., S. Africa; *tomentosum*, ' Peppermint-scented ', white, summer, 3 ft., S. Africa.

SUCCULENT SPECIES CULTIVATED: *P. ardens*, scarlet shaded crimson, stem thick, suffruticose, 1 ft., S. Africa; *Bowkeri*, yellow and purple, stem short, 18 in., S. Africa; *dasycaule*, creamy white, 18 in., S. Africa; *echinatum*, white spotted red, stem fleshy, armed with spine-like stipules, S. Africa; *Gibbosum*, greenish-yellow, stem gouty and swollen at the distant nodes, 18 in., S. Africa; *Stapletonii*, pinkish-white, 18 in., a hybrid with *echinatum*; *tetragonum*, pale pink, stems square and fleshy, 2 ft., S. Africa; *triste*, brownish-yellow with dark spots, stem short, S. Africa, and vars. *daucifolium* (syn. *P. millefoliatum*) and *filipendulifolium*.

OTHER SPECIES CULTIVATED: *P. grandiflorum*, white and red, summer, 2 ft., S. Africa; *inquinans*, scarlet, rose, or white, summer, 2 ft., S. Africa; *kewensis*, scarlet, 1 ft., origin unknown; *peltatum* (syn. *hederaefolium*), parent of the Ivy-leaved Geraniums, white and red, summer, S. Africa; *salmonium*, salmon pink, 1½ ft., S. Africa; *zonale*, ' Horseshoe ' or ' Zonal Geranium ', parent of the zonal, bicolor and tricolor geraniums, various colours, summer, 2 ft., S. Africa. The bedding and zonal pelargoniums of gardens are hybrids between *P. inquinans* and *P. zonale*.

Pelecyphora—*Cactaceae*.   Greenhouse succulent perennial.   First introduced early nineteenth century.

CULTURE: Compost, equal parts sandy loam, rough old mortar and pounded bricks. Position, sunny, airy greenhouse or windows. Pot, March or April in well-drained pots just large enough to accommodate roots. Repot every third or fourth year only. Water moderately March to Sept., once a fortnight Sept. to Dec., none afterwards. Syringe on evenings of warm days June to Sept. Apply soot-water to healthy plants June to Sept. Ventilate freely in summer. Temp., March to Sept. 60° to 70°, Sept. to March 50° to 55°.

PROPAGATION: By seeds sown ⅛ in. deep in well-drained pans or pots of sandy soil in temp. 75° in March, keeping soil moderately moist; by cuttings of the tops of the plants inserted in small pots of sandy, gritty compost in spring.

SPECIES CULTIVATED: *P. aselliformis*, ' Hatchet Cactus ', white and rose, June, 4 in., Mexico.

Pelican Flower, see *Aristolochia grandiflora*.

Pellaea (Cliff Brake Fern)—*Polypodiaceae*.   Greenhouse evergreen and deciduous ferns, embracing species formerly named Platyloma.   First introduced mid-eighteenth century.

CULTURE: Compost, equal parts loam, leaf-mould, peat and sand, with a little charcoal and sandstone. Pot or plant, March. Position, well-drained pots in shady part of greenhouse or in beds or rockeries in shade. Water moderately Oct. to Feb., freely afterwards. Temp., Sept. to March 45° to 55°, March to Sept. 60° to 65°. *P. atropurpurea* is sufficiently hardy to grow outside in sheltered rockeries if protected with litter or hand-light in winter.

PROPAGATION: By spores sown on surface of sandy peat in shallow pan in temp. 70° or 80° any time; division of plants in Feb. or April.

SPECIES CULTIVATED: *P. atropurpurea*, 1 ft., N. America; *Breweri*, 10 in., N. America; *dealbata*, N. America; *flexuosa*, fronds much branched, Colombia; *falcata*, to 1½ ft., India to New Zealand; *hastata* (syn. *P. calomelanos*), 2 ft., S. Africa; *rotundifolia*, good basket fern, to 1 ft., New Zealand; *tenera*, fronds blue-green, Chile; *ternifolia*, Trop. America; *viridis* (syn. *P. adiantoides*), 2 ft., Africa.

Pellionia—*Urticaceae*.   Stove creeping herbs.   Cultivated in greenhouses for their attractive coloured stems.   First introduced late nineteenth century.

CULTURE: Compost, two parts sandy loam, one part leaf-mould and sand. Pot or plant, March or April. Position, shallow pans, or on surface of beds or rockeries or under staging. Water moderately Oct. to Feb., freely afterwards. Temp., Sept. to April 55° to 65°, April to Sept. 65° to 75°.

PROPAGATION: By cuttings of creeping shoots inserted in sandy soil in small pots under bell-glass in temp. 75° to 85° in spring; division of plants in March or April.

SPECIES CULTIVATED: *P. Daveauana*, Cochin-China; *Heyneana*, India; *pulchra*, Cochin-China.

Peltandra (Arrow Arum)—*Araceae*.   Hardy perennial herbs with spearhead-shaped, broad, deep green leaves.   First introduced mid-eighteenth century.

CULTURE: Soil, rich, boggy or muddy. Position, moist bog or shallow pond. Plant, March or April, enclosing roots and small quantity of soil in piece of canvas or sacking and dropping the whole into the water.

PROPAGATION: By division of roots in spring.

Species Cultivated: *P. alba*, white, red berries, June, 18 in., E. America; *virginica*, green, green berries, June to July, 12 to 24 in., N. America.

Peltaria—*Cruciferae.* Hardy herbaceous perennial herb. Plant garlic-scented. First introduced early seventeenth century.

Culture: Soil, ordinary. Position, sunny borders, beds or rockeries. Plant, Oct., March or April.

Propagation: By seeds sown ⅛ in. deep outdoors, March or April, where plants are required to grow; division of plants in March or April.

Species Cultivated: *P. alliacea*, white, summer, 1 ft., E. Europe.

Pendulous Bellflower, see Symphyandra.

Pennisetum—*Gramineae.* Hardy perennial grasses. Sometimes known as Gymnothrix. Inflorescence very graceful and useful for cutting and drying for winter decoration.

Culture of P. latifolium: Soil, sandy loam. Position, sheltered, well-drained borders in warm parts of the country only. Plant, April. Protect in severe weather with covering of mats, or lift in Nov., place in large pots or tubs, and remove to greenhouse, replanting outdoors in April or May.

Culture of P. villosum: Soil, ordinary. Position, sunny borders. Sow seeds ¹⁄₁₆ in. deep in patches a foot or more in diameter, in March or April, where plants are to flower. Gather inflorescence for winter use, end of July. This species is best treated as an annual.

Propagation: *P. latifolium* by seed sown ¹⁄₁₆ in. deep in sandy soil in shallow boxes or pans in temp. 60° to 65°, March or April, transplanting seedlings outdoors in May or June; division of root in April.

Species Cultivated: *P. latifolium* (syn. *Gymnothrix latifolia*), 5 to 8 ft., Argentina; *villosum* (syn. *P. longistylum*), 12 to 18 in., Abyssinia.

Pennyroyal, see *Mentha Pulegium.*

Penstemon (Beard Tongue)—*Scrophulariaceae.* Hardy perennials, formerly spelled Pentstemon. First introduced late eighteenth century.

Culture: Soil, two parts rich loam, one part decayed manure or leaf-mould. Plant, March or April. Position, sunny beds or borders, well drained. Apply stimulants once or twice a week in summer. The kinds grown so largely in gardens were originally derived from hybrids between *P. Cobaea* and *P. Hartwegii.*

Propagation: By seeds sown ¹⁄₁₆ in. deep in a well-drained pot or pan of light soil in temp. 55° to 65° in Feb. or March, transplanting seedlings outdoors in May; cuttings of young shoots, 3 in. long, inserted in sandy soil in boxes or a bed under hand-light, or in cold frame in Aug., allowing them to remain there until April; division in April.

Species Cultivated: *P. angustifolia*, mauve or soft blue, July, 8 to 12 in., Western U.S.A.; *antirrhinoides*, lemon-yellow, July, 1 to 3 ft., S. California; *azureus*, blue, Aug., 1 ft., N. America; *barbatus* (syn. *Chelone barbata*), scarlet, summer, 3 ft., U.S.A.; *Bridgesii*, scarlet, July to Sept., 1 to 2 ft., N. America; *campanulatus*, rosy purple, violet, or white, June, 1 to 2 ft., Mexico and Guatemala; *centranthifolius*, scarlet, summer, 1 to 3 ft., California and W. Arizona; *Cobaea*, purple or white, Aug., 1 to 2 ft., U.S.A.; *confertus*, yellow, 1 ft., summer, Rocky Mountains; *cordifolius*, scarlet, summer, partially climbing, S. California; *diffusus*, blue or purple, summer, 1 to 2 ft., Western N. America; *Digitalis*, white or pink, 2 to 3 ft., U.S.A.; *Edithae*, rose-purple, May, 6 to 9 in., hybrid; *glaber* (syn. *P. Gordonii*), purple, summer, 1 to 2 ft., U.S.A., and vars. *alpinus* and *cyananthus*; *Hartwegii*, scarlet, summer, 2 ft., Mexico; *heterophyllus*, pinkish to sky blue, July, 1 to 3 ft., California; *hirsutus* (syn. *P. pubescens*), purple or violet, July, 1 to 3 ft., U.S.A.; *laevigatus*, 2 to 3 ft., U.S.A.; *Menziesii*, purple, June, 6 in., N.W. America; *ovatus*, blue to purple, Aug. to Oct., 2 to 3 ft., U.S.A.; *Richardsonii*, violet, summer, 1½ to 2 ft., U.S.A.; *rupicola*, ruby red, May, 2 to 3 in., N.W. America; *Scouleri*, lilac, May to June, 1 to 2 ft., U.S.A.; *spectabilis*, rose-purple or lilac, summer, 2 to 4 ft., Mexico and S. California.

Pentaglottis—*Boraginaceae.* Hardy perennial herb, formerly included in Anchusa but with botanical differences, sometimes known as Caryolopha.
CULTURE: As Anchusa.
PROPAGATION: As Anchusa.
SPECIES CULTIVATED: *P. sempervirens* (syn. *Anchusa sempervirens*), rich blue, spring and summer, to 2 ft., Europe.

Pentas—*Rubiaceae.* Stove evergreen flowering shrubs. First introduced early nineteenth century.
CULTURE: Compost, equal parts fibrous peat and leaf-mould, half part each light loam and sand. Pot, Feb. to April. Position, well-drained pots in light part of stove. Water moderately Sept. to April, freely at other times. Syringe daily April to Sept. Prune plants into shape immediately after flowering. Nip off points of young shoots occasionally during May, June and July to induce bushy habit of growth. Temp., Sept. to April 50° to 60°, April to Sept. 60° to 75°.
PROPAGATION: By cuttings of young shoots, 2 to 3 in. long, inserted singly in 2 in. pots filled with sandy compost and placed under bell-glass in temp. of 75°, spring or summer.
SPECIES CULTIVATED: *P. coccinea*, scarlet, spring, 18 in., Trop. Africa; *lanceolata* (syn. *P. carnea*), pink, winter, 18 in., Trop. Africa, var. *alba*, white; *parviflora*, orange-red, spring, 2 ft., Trop. Africa.

Peony, see Paeonia.

Peperomia—*Piperaceae.* Stove herbaceous creeping or erect perennials. First introduced early nineteenth century.
CULTURE: Compost, equal parts fibrous loam and peat with half a part sand. Pot, March or April. Position, small well-drained pots for erect species, shallow pans or beds for creeping species. Shade from sun. Water moderately in winter, freely in summer. Syringe daily April to Sept. Temp., April to Sept. 60° to 75°, Sept. to April 55° to 65°.
PROPAGATION: By cuttings of shoots or single joints with leaf attached inserted in sandy peat and plunged in bottom heat in temp. 65° to 75° in spring.
SPECIES CULTIVATED: *P. argyroneura*, leaves green and silver striped, Brazil; *brevipes*, leaves brown and light green, Trop. America; *maculosa*, leaves bright green, W. Indies; *metallica*, leaves green, Peru; *obtusifolia*, flowers red, leaves green with dark red margins, Trop. America; *rotundifolia* (syn. *P. nummulariaefolia*, rour'd, green leaves, Trop. America.

Pepper, see Piper and Capsicum; **-mint,** see *Mentha piperita*; **-Tree,** see Schinus.

Pereskia—*Cactaceae.* Stove succulent perennials. First introduced late seventeenth century.
CULTURE: Compost, equal parts loam, peat and leaf-mould, one-fourth sand. Pot, March. Position, small well-drained pots in light, dry part of stove, or in beds with shoots trained to dry wall. Water moderately Sept. to April, freely afterwards. Temp., Sept. to March 50° to 60°, March to Sept. 65° to 75°. *P. aculeata* and *P. Bleo* grown chiefly for stocks for grafting epiphyllums, zygocactus, etc.
PROPAGATION: By cuttings of stem inserted in 2 in. pots filled with sandy soil and placed·on a light, dry shelf in temp. 65° to 75° in spring. Allow one shoot only to grow for forming a stock, and train this to a stake fixed in soil until high enough, then graft.
SPECIES CULTIVATED: *P. aculeata*, ' Barbados Gooseberry ', 10 to 30 ft., W. Indies; *Bleo*, 10 to 15 ft., Mexico; *grandifolia*, 6 ft., usually cultivated under the name *P. Bleo*, Brazil.

Perilla—*Labiatae.* Half-hardy annual, cultivated for its attractive coloured foliage, something like Coleus. First introduced mid-eighteenth century.
CULTURE: Sow seeds $\frac{1}{16}$ in. deep in shallow boxes or pans filled with ordinary

light soil placed in temp. 65° to 75° in Feb. or March. Transplant seedlings, when three leaves have formed, singly into 2 in. pots, or 2 in. apart in shallow boxes. Keep in temp. 55° to 65° till May, then transfer to cold frame; gradually harden off and plant outdoors in June. Suitable for masses in borders or for lines in, or edgings to, beds.

SPECIES CULTIVATED: *P. frutescens crispa* (syn. *P. nankinensis*), leaves bronzy purple, 1 to 3 ft., China, Japan and Himalaya.

Periploca—*Asclepiadaceae.* Hardy deciduous twiner of little beauty. Quaint 5 in. narrow fruits in pairs with silky tassels. First introduced late sixteenth century.

CULTURE: Soil, ordinary. Position, walls, arbours, summer-houses, or trellises in any aspect. Plant, Oct., Nov., Feb. or March. Prune away very weak or old distorted shoots only in March.

PROPAGATION: By cuttings inserted under bell-glass or hand-light outdoors, July to Oct.; layering shoots, Sept. or Oct.

SPECIES CULTIVATED: *P. graeca*, ' Silk Vine ', green and brown, fragrant, July to Aug., 20 to 30 ft., S.E. Europe.

Peristeria (Dove Orchid)—*Orchidaceae.* The common name is from the dove-like shape assumed by the beaked column and basal lobes of the lip. An epiphytic genus. Pseudo-bulbs rather large and rounded. Spikes erect, arched or descending, from base of bulbs. Flowers moderately large, fleshy, not widely spreading, often fragrant. Leaves, three to four large, ribbed or veined.

CULTURE: Compost, osmunda or peat fibre, loam fibre and sphagnum moss. Rather deep pans or baskets should be used. *P. elata* should be placed in a pot as the many-flowered spike is erect. Water infrequently when growth first commences, liberally as the growths gain strength. In winter, if atmospheric moisture is correct, few, if any, waterings are required. Avoid syringing until the leaves are free. Drainage must be ample. Shading should be dispensed with in early autumn and exposure then to full light benefits. Winter temp. 60°. Increase the heat as growth appears. In summer, with sun heat, it may reach 80°. All the species are worth growing and usually flower early summer to summer. The plants should be given a position in full light during winter.

PROPAGATION: By division of large plants. When repotting, back bulbs may be taken off, leaving four in front, placed on crocks in a pan and potted if, and when, growth is seen.

SPECIES CULTIVATED: *P. aspersa*, fragrant, yellowish, spotted purplish-red, lip maroon or purplish, Brazil, Venezuela; *cerina*, fragrant, citron-yellow, Cent. America; *elata*, scapes 3 to 6 ft. high, flowers twenty or many more, fragrant, waxy white, lip dotted purple, Panama; *pendula*, fragrant, yellowish, flushed and spotted with purplish-red, usually autumn, Guiana, Brazil. Other species are known but seldom appear in cultivation.

Peristrophe—*Acanthaceae.* Greenhouse flowering plant. First introduced early nineteenth century.

CULTURE: Compost, equal parts peat, loam, leaf-mould and sand. Position, well-drained pots in sunny greenhouse, June to Oct., ordinary greenhouse conditions at other times. Water moderately Sept. to March, freely at other times. Temp., Sept. to March 50° to 60°, March to Sept. 60° to 65°. Nip off points of young shoots several times during growing season to induce bushy habit. Apply liquid manure when plants are established in final pots.

PROPAGATION: By cuttings inserted in pots of sandy soil placed in warm propagating case in spring.

SPECIES CULTIVATED: *P. speciosa*, rich carmine-purple, winter, 2 ft., Himalaya.

Periwinkle, see Vinca.

Pernettya (Prickly Heath)—*Ericaceae.* Hardy evergreen shrubs with brightly coloured berries persisting until spring. First introduced early nineteenth century.

OUTDOOR CULTURE: Soil, peaty. Position, moist rockeries or margins of open or shady shrubberies and beds. Plant, Sept. to Nov. or March to May.

POT CULTURE: Compost, two parts peat, one part leaf-mould and sand. Position, cold or cool greenhouse or dwelling room. Pot, Oct. or Nov. Water moderately. When berries shrivel or fall off plant outdoors.

WINDOW BOX CULTURE: Soil, ordinary. Position, sunny or shady. Plant, Sept. to Jan. Remove when berries shrivel.

PROPAGATION: By seeds sown ¼ in. deep in bed of peaty soil outdoors in autumn; layering shoots in March or April.

SPECIES CULTIVATED: *P. mucronata*, white, spring, 2 to 5 ft., Magellan Islands, and vars. *atrococcinea*, *alba* and *lilacina*; pumila, pink or white berries, small, prostrate, Falkland Is.

Perovskia—*Labiatae*. Hardy, deciduous, semi-woody shrub with striking, greyish-white shoots and leaves.

CULTURE: Soil, good, well-drained loam. Position, sunny borders or shrubberies, excellent for chalky soils and maritime localities. Plant, Nov. to Feb. in groups of three or four. Cut away dead growth in early spring.

PROPAGATION: By cuttings of nearly ripened growth in July, inserted in sandy soil under bell-glass.

SPECIES CULTIVATED: *P. atriplicifolia*, violet-blue, Aug. to Sept., 3 to 5 ft., Himalaya and Afghanistan.

Persea—*Lauraceae*. Stove evergreen shrub with edible pear-shaped fruit, purplish when ripe. First introduced early eighteenth century.

CULTURE: Compost, equal parts loam and peat and a little sand. Position, moist stove in pots. Pot in March. Water freely in summer, little in winter. Syringe daily in spring and summer. Temp., March to Sept. 75° to 85°, Sept. to March 55° to 65°.

PROPAGATION: By seeds sown in above compost in a temp. of 85°; by cuttings in sand under bell-glass in a similar temp. in spring.

SPECIES CULTIVATED: *P. americana* (syn. *P. gratissima*), ' Avocado Pear ', ' Alligator Pear ', green, summer, to 60 ft., W. Indies.

Persimmon, see *Diospyros virginiana*.

Peruvian Bark Tree, see Cinchona;   **-Lily,** see Alstroemeria;   **-Mastic Tree,** see *Schinus Molle*.

Pescatorea—*Orchidaceae*. An epiphytic genus, sometimes included in Zygopetalum. Pseudo-bulbs are absent, habit tufted. Large attractive flowers borne singly, scapes usually shorter than leaves. The lips bear a transverse ribbed crest.

CULTURE: Compost of half osmunda fibre or substitute, and half sphagnum moss with crushed crocks and nodules of charcoal. The pots should have drainage to a quarter of their depth. A moist atmosphere and water must be given throughout the year. Winter temp. 60°, not less; summer, 70° to 75°. In repotting see that all dead roots are cut cleanly away. The majority of species flower in summer.

PROPAGATION: By division of plants when repotting in spring.

SPECIES CULTIVATED: A selection—*P. cerina*, citron-yellow, crest tinted red, Trop. America; *Dayana*, creamy white tipped green, lip white and crimson, crest deep crimson, Colombia; *Klabochorum*, white, passing to brownish-purple, lip whitish with purplish-tipped hairs, crest white and crimson-purple, Colombia, Ecuador.

Petamenes—*Iridaceae*. Cormous plants, formerly included in Antholyza.

CULTURE: Soil, light sandy. Position, sunny well-drained borders or pots in cool greenhouse. Plant in Oct. Lift in Aug., dry and store in a cool place till planting time.

PROPAGATION: By offsets; seeds in slight heat in spring.

SPECIES CULTIVATED: *P. abbreviatus*, yellow and red, April, 2 to 3 ft., Cape Colony.

Petasites—*Compositae.* Hardy perennial herb. First introduced early nineteenth century.

CULTURE: Soil, ordinary. Position, shrubberies or woodland, partially shaded borders. Plant, Oct.

PROPAGATION: By division, Oct. or Nov.

SPECIES CULTIVATED: *P. fragrans*, ' Winter Heliotrope ', pale lilac, fragrant, Feb., 6 in., Medit. region; *japonicus*, violet, Feb., 6 ft., Sachalin, and var. *giganteus.*

Petrea—*Verbenaceae.* Stove-flowering deciduous shrubs and climbers. First introduced early eighteenth century.

CULTURE: Compost, equal parts loam, leaf-mould, peat and sand, little char-coal. Position, well-drained pot, bed or border, with shoots of climbing species trained up rafters or trellises in shady part of stove. Pot or plant, Feb. or March. Prune slightly, Feb. Water freely March to Sept., moderately afterwards. Syringe daily March to Sept. Temp., March to Sept. 65° to 75°, Sept. to March 55° to 60°.

PROPAGATION: By cuttings of firm young shoots inserted in sandy soil in well-drained pot under bell-glass in temp. 65° to 75°, spring and summer.

SPECIES CULTIVATED: *P. arborea*, violet-blue, summer, 12 ft., shrub, Colombia; *racemosa*, dark violet, summer, climber to 15 ft., Trop. America; *volubilis*, ' Purple Wreath ', purple, summer, climber, to 15 ft., Trop. America, and var. *albiflora.*

Petrophytum—*Rosaceae.* Prostrate evergreen shrubs suitable for rock gardens, sometimes included in Spiraea.

CULTURE: As Spiraea.

PROPAGATION: As Spiraea.

SPECIES CULTIVATED: *P. caespitosum* (syn. *Spiraea caespitosa*), white, summer, 3 in., N.W. America; *Hendersonii* (syn. *Spiraea Hendersonii*), white, mat-forming to 1 in., N.W. America.

Petroselinum—*Umbelliferae.* Biennial herbs with divided or curled leaves and sometimes edible roots.

CULTURE OF PARSLEY: Semi-shaded, ordinary, well-manured soil. Often grown as edgings to borders or in beds. Sow in the open in April and Aug. Seeds may take eight weeks to germinate. Thin seedlings to 9 in. Remove flower stems. Give protection to autumn sowing for winter supply. Summer and autumn pullings keep colour best when dried.

SPECIES CULTIVATED: *P. crispum*, ' Parsley ', yellow, summer, 1 to 2 ft., Europe, W. Asia, var. *radicosum*, ' Parsnip-rooted ' or ' Hamburg Parsley ', edible roots.

Pe-Tsai, see *Brassica pekinensis.*

Petunia—*Solanaceae.* Half-hardy herbaceous perennials. First introduced early nineteenth century.

INDOOR CULTURE: Compost, two parts decayed turfy loam, one part well-rotted manure, quarter part silver sand. Position, sunny greenhouse or window. Shade only from bright sun. Pot, Feb. to June, moderately firmly. Size of pots, 3, 5 and 6 in. Pinch out point of young shoots occasionally in spring to induce bushy growth. Prune shoots of old plants moderately closely in Feb. or March. Water moderately Sept. to April, freely afterwards. No syringing required. Apply stimulants to established plants when flower buds form. Train shoots to stakes. Suitable liquid manures: ¼ oz. nitrate of soda or sulphate of ammonia to 1 gallon of water, applied three or four successive times only; ½ oz. guano to a gallon of water, applied twice a week; weak, liquid, natural manure, applied as advised for guano. Temp., March to Oct. 55° to 65°, Oct. to March 40° to 50°.

OUTDOOR CULTURE: Soil, ordinary rich. Position, sunny beds, borders, vases or trellises. Plant, June. Lift, Sept., and store in pots in greenhouse to furnish cuttings in spring. Water freely in dry weather. Place in cold frame in May to harden before planting out. Apply stimulants as above.

PROPAGATION: By seeds sown on surface of a compost of equal parts good soil, leaf-mould and sand in a well-drained pot or pan, in temp. 65° to 75°, in Feb., March or April; by cuttings of young shoots inserted in light, sandy soil in pots, pans or boxes in temp. 55° to 65° any time in spring.

SPECIES CULTIVATED: *P. axillaris* (syn. *P. nyctaginiflora*), white, Aug., 2 ft., Argentine; *integrifolia*, purple, 18 in., Argentine; *violacea*, purple, summer, 6 to 10 in., Argentine. The garden vars. are hybrids between these species.

Peucedanum, see Anethum and Pastinaca.

Phacelia—*Hydrophyllaceae.* Hardy annuals. Good bee flowers. First introduced early nineteenth century.

CULTURE: Soil, ordinary rich. Position, sunny or partially shaded beds or borders. Sow seeds in patches or lines where required to grow in April. Thin seedlings to 6 or 8 in. apart in June.

SPECIES CULTIVATED: *P. campanularia*, blue, summer, 8 in., California; *congesta*, blue or lavender, June, 2 to 3 ft., Texas and New Mexico; *Parryi*, violet, summer, 1 ft., California; *tanacetifolia*, blue or lilac, July, 2 to 3 ft., California; *viscida* (syn. *Eutoca viscida*), blue and white, summer, 1½ to 2 ft., S. California; *Whitlavia* (syn. *Whitlavia grandiflora*), ' Californian Bluebell ', blue, Sept., 1 ft., California.

Phaedranassa (Queen Lily)—*Amaryllidaceae.* Greenhouse flowering bulbous plants. First introduced early nineteenth century.

CULTURE: Compost, two parts sandy loam, one part leaf-mould, and half a part sand. Position, well-drained pots near the glass, March to Oct.; in dry place under stage, Oct. to March. Pot, Feb. or March. Water moderately March to May, freely May to Oct., keep nearly dry Oct. to March. Apply stimulants May to Aug. only. Temp., March to Sept. 55° to 65°, Sept. to March 40° to 50°. Repot annually, removing old soil away from bulbs. Place in small pots first; shift into larger sizes later on. No shade required.

PROPAGATION: By seeds sown ⅛ in. deep in well-drained pots or pans of sandy soil in temp. of 60° to 65° in spring; offsets removed and treated as old bulbs at potting time.

SPECIES CULTIVATED: *P. Carmiolii*, red and green, summer, 2 ft., Costa Rica; *chloracea*, scarlet and green, summer, 18 in., Ecuador; *Lehmannii*, scarlet, summer, 2 ft., Colombia; *schizantha*, green and red, 18 in., Peru.

Phaenocoma—*Compositae.* Greenhouse evergreen flowering shrub. First introduced late eighteenth century.

CULTURE: Compost, two parts good brown fibrous peat, one part silver sand, and little charcoal. Position, well-drained pots in light part of greenhouse; no shade. Pot, March or April. Firm potting most essential. Prune straggling shoots only moderately in Feb. or March. Water moderately Sept. to April, freely afterwards. No syringing required. Admit air freely in summer. Shoots can be trained round stakes or trellis.

PROPAGATION: By cuttings of firm young shoots inserted in well-drained pots of sandy peat under bell-glass in temp. of 55° to 65°, summer.

SPECIES CULTIVATED: *P. prolifera*, crimson, rose, and purple, May to Sept., 3 to 4 ft., S. Africa, var. *Barnesii*, superior form.

× **Phaio-Calanthe**—*Orchidaceae.* Bigeneric hybrids between Phaius and Calanthe; none occurs naturally.

CULTURE:' Compost, as for Phaius. The hybrids between the deciduous Calanthes and Phaius usually assume a shabby appearance in winter as they are partially deciduous. A rest must then be given but water may occasionally be required. Winter temp. at night about 60°. Hybrids between the evergreen species should not be so strictly rested. Winter temp. 65° at night; both enjoy a higher temp, 70° to 80°, during summer and exposure to light in autumn. Shading should be very light for the first section, heavier for the second, which should have a moist atmosphere throughout the year. The syringe should not be used.

Phaius—*Orchidaceae*. A genus of terrestrial orchids (one species epiphytic). Pseudo-bulbs usually short, stout, clustered. Spikes from their base, often tall. Leaves large, veined. Flowers, generally large, and fairly showy.

CULTURE: Compost for the *P. grandifolius* section, principally fibrous loam, with a little osmunda fibre or peat, and sphagnum moss mixed with finely crushed crocks; 2 to 3 in. of drainage should be placed in the pots. Other than newly potted plants may have occasional applications of weak manure-water when growing, that made from cow manure and soot is preferable. Species from N. India and Burma should have a winter night temp. of 55° to 60°. Water will be required in the winter but not too frequently. Species from tropical countries, Malaya, etc., should have a winter temp. of 65° or slightly higher. Species from Madagascar, 70° and only a small proportion of loam fibre in their compost. Summer temps. for all, with shading, may reach 80°. The syringe should not be used until the foliage, infolded when young, is free, but a moist atmosphere is enjoyed. Several beautiful hybrids have been raised, particularly with *P. tuberculosus*.

PROPAGATION: By division of plants. Healthy back bulbs may be removed from some, and, placed in a propagating case, will often emit growths.

SPECIES CULTIVATED: A selection—*P. assamicus*, yellowish, lip white-bordered, spring, summer, Assam; *bicolor*, reddish-brown, lip white, rose, yellow, early summer, Ceylon; *Blumei*, buff yellow or brownish, lip whitish, yellowish and crimson-red, spring, Java; *callosus*, reddish-brown, whitish at tips, lip trumpet-shaped, yellowish-white, shaded pink, purple beneath, spur two-lobed, summer, Malaya, Java; *Cooperi*, near *P. callosus*, red-brown, lip whitish, blotched red-brown in throat, winter, Malaya; *flavus*, soft yellow, lip marked red-brown, much crisped, spring, N. India, Burma, Java; *grandifolius*, yellow-brown or reddish-brown, silvery behind, lip yellow-brown, rose-purple bordered white, variable, spring, India, China, Australia; *Humboltii*, rose-purple, shaded white, mid-lobe of lip spreading, rose-purple and whitish, summer, Madagascar; *mishmiensis*, stems elongated, spikes lateral, soft rose, lip with a central ridge of white hairs, winter, Mishmi Hills, Assam, Burma; *Roeblingii*, large, lemon-yellow to red-brown, lip yellow, red-streaked at base, then whitish, veined rose, summer, Khasia; *Sanderianus*, near *P. Blumei*, of which it is often termed a var., spikes 7 to 8 ft. high, flowers large, red-bronze, lip yellow, then dusky rose, white-margined, spring, Assam; *simulans*, epiphytic, whitish, lip with rose blotches, keels yellow, near base, circular tuft of yellow hairs, winter, Madagascar; *tuberculosus*, white, mid-lobe of lip with three yellow keels, behind them four rows of white hairs, winter, Madagascar; *Wallichii*, near *P. grandifolius*, but stronger, tawny-brown, yellow margined, mid-lobe of lip whitish with a yellow red-lined disk, winter, spring, N. India, var. *Mannii*, larger, more deeply coloured.

Phalaenopsis (Moth Orchids)—*Orchidaceae*. A beautiful epiphytic genus containing some of the most handsome of the *Orchidaceae*. Pseudo-bulbs are absent, stems short, leaves usually rather large and persistent, flatly inclined. A few species have erect, cylindrical leaves. In many the scapes are long and branched, in others simple. The flowers of some species have the front lobe of the lip narrowed and terminating in two long curved ' tendrils '. Variation exists.

CULTURE: Compost, two parts osmunda fibre or substitute, two parts sphagnum moss, a few decayed oak or beech leaves may be added. The roots are extensive and clinging. Pans or baskets are preferable and should be suspended about 18 in. from glass, so tilted that they preferably face the south-west. Drainage must be ample. The roots resent disturbance and the plants should not be disturbed until absolutely necessary. In the spring the old compost may be carefully picked out and new inserted. Later in the summer the operation may again be needed to a lesser degree. In winter the plants are practically dormant but require a moist and consistent atmosphere of 70° or near that. In summer, with shading, the temp. can rise to the tropical and the syringe be freely used, but not too late in the day. Water freely in summer and at no period should the compost be allowed to become really dry. Air must be carefully admitted, frequently by the bottom vents only, as draughts and loss of atmospheric moisture are detrimental. Shading is required and should be carefully given when young leaves are present. In autumn light should be freely given. Natural hybrids exist and several crosses have been artificially raised.

PROPAGATION: Young plants are sometimes produced on the flower spikes and occasionally on the roots. These, when rooted, can be potted.

SPECIES CULTIVATED: A selection—*P. amabilis*, ' Blume ', branched, large, pure white, lip yellow and red spotted at base of side lobes, mid-lobe with two tendrils, autumn, winter, variable, Malaya; *Aphrodite*, branched, pure white, lip with yellow stain and marked purple, tendrils long, spring, various, Philippines; *Boxallii*, scape short, yellow, traversed with red-brown, mid-lobe of lip anchor-shape, spring, Philippines; *Cornu-cervii*, scapes short, flowers in succession, yellow barred with red-brown, lip whitish, mid-lobe crescent-shaped, summer, Malaya; *intermedia* (syn. *P. Lobbii*), scapes branched, white or rose flushed, lip light amethyst-purple, winter, Philippines; *leucorrhoda*, white, flushed with rose-purple, lip white, with some red-purple spots and a yellow stain, summer, winter, natural variable hybrid, Philippines; *Lowii*, often deciduous, few, white, flushed purple, mid-lobe of lip deep purple, dwarf growing, summer, Burma; *Lueddemanniana*, whitish, barred with amethyst and cinnamon-brown, mid-lobe of lip amethyst, with a white-haired ridge, variable, various, Philippines; *Mannii*, dwarf, small, yellow, marked with chestnut-brown, lip yellow, mid-lobe anchor-shaped, spring, Assam; *Parishii*, dwarf, small, white, lip rose-purple, sometimes deciduous, summer, Burma; *rosea*, scapes branched, small, many, white, flushed rose-purple, lip rose-purple, variable, various, Philippines; *Sanderiana*, rose-pink to rose-purple, sometimes white-mottled, mid-lobe with two short tendrils, autumn, winter, Philippines; *Schilleriana*, many, light rose-purple, lower sepals dotted purple, mid-lobe of lip with two ' flukes ', very variable, winter, various, Philippines; *speciosa*, starry, amethyst-purple, blotched purple, mid-lobe of lip white, and purplish or purple, scapes branching, proliferous, variable, summer, Andamans; *Stuartiana*, many, white, sometimes dotted at bases with purple, lower sepals with their inner halves yellow, thickly spotted rose-purple, lip white, yellowish, purple spotted, mid-lobes, terminating in two white ' flukes ', winter, Philippines; *sumatrana*, yellowish, barred red-brown, mid-lobe of lip narrow, whitish, streaked purple, with a tuft of hair near apex of the keel, summer, variable, Sumatra; *tetraspis*, variable, ivory-white, mid-lobe of lip with a dense tuft of bristle-like hairs, summer, Andamans, Malaya; *Veitchiana*, white, flushed purple, lip chiefly crimson-purple, winter, Philippines; *violacea*, few, white, greenish, flushed violet-purple, in places mid-lobe of lip violet-purple, pointed, summer, variable, Sumatra, Malaya.

Phalaris—*Gramineae*. Hardy annual and perennial flowering ornamental grasses. Flowers, white, green, purple, borne in panicles, July. Leaves, green or variegated with white.

CULTURE OF ANNUAL SPECIES: Sow seeds $\frac{1}{8}$ in. deep in April where required to grow. Soil, ordinary. Position, sunny.

CULTURE OF PERENNIAL SPECIES: Soil, ordinary. Position, sunny or shady borders. Plant, Oct. to April. Lift, divide, and replant every two or three years.

PROPAGATION: Perennials by seeds sown outdoors in April, transplanting seedlings following Oct.; division of plants, Oct. to April.

ANNUAL SPECIES CULTIVATED: *P. canariensis*, ' Canary Grass ', 18 in., S. Europe.

PERENNIAL SPECIES CULTIVATED: *P. arundinacea variegata*, ' Gardener's Garters ', ' Lady's Garters ', ' Ribbon Grass ', ' Silver Grass ', leaves striped with silvery white, 3 to 6 ft., N. Regions.

Phaseolus (Bean)—*Leguminosae*. Stove and hardy perennials and annuals, extensively grown for edible seeds and pods. Kidney or French Bean introduced early sixteenth century, Runner Bean mid-seventeenth century.

CULTURE OF SNAIL FLOWER: Compost, equal parts loam and peat, little sand.

Position, well-drained pots, shoots twining round trellises, posts or pillars. Pot, Feb. Water moderately in winter, freely in summer. Temp., Sept. to March 50° to 55°, March to Sept. 55° to 65°.

PROPAGATION: By seeds sown in light soil in temp. 65° in March; cuttings inserted in sandy soil under bell-glass in temp. 65° in April.

CULTURE OF KIDNEY OR FRENCH BEAN: Soil, light, rich, well manured. Position, open, sunny. Draw drills 3 in. deep and 18 in. apart. Sow seeds 6 in. apart end of April, middle of May, beginning of June, and end of July. Protect early sowings with sticks or straw. Thin seedlings when three leaves appear to 12 in. apart, replanting thinnings to form another row or rows. Water the drills thoroughly, if soil be dry, before sowing the seeds. Mulch with manure when seedlings appear. Water freely in dry weather. Apply stimulants when pods form. Plants bear earlier if sown along centre of early celery ridges than if sown in open garden. Pick when young and tender. For haricot vars. pick whole plant when pods turn brown and hang in open shed to dry and ripen thoroughly before thrashing.

FORCING: Sow monthly from end of Sept. to April. Compost, two parts good soil, one part decayed manure. Size of pots, 8 in. Put 1 in. of crocks in bottom, next a layer of half-decayed tree leaves or fresh horse droppings, then enough compost to half-fill the pot. Dibble seeds ½ in. deep, five per pot. Moisten with tepid water. Water moderately when seeds sprout, freely when 1 in. high. Top-dress with equal parts soil and manure when plants reach rim of pot when pinch out growing points. Apply stimulants after top-dressing has been done a fortnight. Temp., 55° to 65°. Support shoots with small twigs. No shade required. Keep close to glass.

CULTURE OF RUNNER BEANS: Soil, light, deep, well manured. Position, sunny or partially shady garden, arbour, trellis, or fences; former best. Sow seeds first week in May, 4 in. apart and 3 in. deep in drills 6 ft. asunder; in double rows 9 in. apart and 8 ft. asunder; in trenches 9 in. wide, 12 in. deep containing 3 in. manure and 6 in. soil, seeds being dibbled 2 in. deep, 4 in. apart in two rows 6 in. asunder. Support plants with long stakes or trellises or strands of twine when 6 in. high, or nip off point of main shoot when 2 ft. high and subsequent shoots when 6 in. long to ensure dwarf habit. Mound up those sown in drills. Mulch with manure. Water freely in dry weather, otherwise flowers will fall off. Apply stimulants freely when pods form. Quantity of seed required for a row 50 ft. long: ½ pint of French beans, 1 pint of runner beans. Seeds retain their vegetative powers for three years and germinate in ten to twelve days. French beans reach maturity fourteen weeks after sowing and runner beans sixteen weeks afterwards.

ORNAMENTAL SPECIES CULTIVATED: *P. Caracalla*, ' Snail Flower ', lilac, summer, climbing perennial, Tropics.

CULINARY SPECIES CULTIVATED: *P. coccineus* (syn. *P. multiflorus*), ' Scarlet Runner Bean ', var. *albus*, ' Dutch Bean ', flowers white, Trop. America; *lunatus*, ' Lima Bean ', Guatemala; *vulgaris*, ' Kidney Bean ', ' Haricot Bean ', ' French Bean ', white or violet, var. *humilis*, non-climbing form.

Pheasant's-eye, see Adonis.

Phellodendron—*Rutaceae*. Hardy deciduous trees with aromatic, ash-like foliage and small black fruits. First introduced about mid-nineteenth century.

CULTURE: Soil, deep, rich loam. Position, as specimens on lawns and in other open places. Plant, Nov. to Feb.

PROPAGATION: By seed sown in pans in greenhouse or frame during Feb. or March or by cuttings of nearly ripe wood inserted under bell-glass in sandy soil during July.

SPECIES CULTIVATED: *P. amurense*, 20 to 40 ft., China, Japan; *japonicum*, 20 to 35 ft., China and Japan; *sachalinense*, fast growing, 30 to 50 ft., Japan, Korea and China.

Phenomenal Berry, see *Rubus loganobaccus*.

Philadelphus (Mock Orange)—*Saxifragaceae* (or *Hydrangeaceae*). Hardy deciduous flowering shrubs often incorrectly known as Syringa. First introduced late sixteenth century.

CULTURE: Soil, ordinary, well drained. Position, equally at home in full sun or partial shade in the border. Stronger kinds make good lawn specimens. Plant, Oct. to Feb. Prune immediately after flowering, thinning out shoots that have bloomed only. Small kinds suitable for pot culture.

POT CULTURE: Compost, two parts sandy loam, one part leaf-mould and sand. Repot annually after flowering. Position, cold greenhouse Dec. to May or warm greenhouse Dec. to April, outdoors in sunny spot afterwards, pots plunged to the rim in coal ashes or soil. Water moderately indoors, freely outside.

PROPAGATION: By cuttings of young shoots inserted in sandy soil in close, cold frame outdoors, Aug. or Sept.; hardwood cuttings of stronger growing kinds outdoors in Nov.; removal of rooted suckers.

SPECIES CULTIVATED: *P. californicus*, white, June, 10 ft., fragrant, California; *coronarius*, ' Common Mock Orange ', cream, early June, to 10 ft., very fragrant, S.E. Europe; *Coulteri*, ' Rose Syringa ', rather tender, purple-blotched petals, June, 6 ft., Mexico; *Delavayi*, violet calyx, very fragrant, 6 to 10 ft., W. China; *grandiflorus*, white, scentless, end June, 10 to 15 ft., S.E. United States; *hirsutus*, white, scentless, early June, 6 to 8 ft., S.E. United States; *Lemoinei*, hybrid, white, June, 5 to 7 ft., parent of many well-known vars.; *mexicanus*, white, tender, very fragrant, slow growing, 3 to 4 ft., June, Colorado and Arizona; *pekinensis*, slightly fragrant, cream, 6 to 8 ft., N. China to Korea, and vars. *brachybotrys*, stronger growing to 10 ft., *kansuensis*, fragrant, 10 ft., June; *pubescens*, scentless, white, 10 ft., June, U.S.A.; *purpurascens*, very fragrant, purple calyx, 8 to 10 ft., June, W. China; *tomentosus*, creamy white, early June, 6 to 8 ft., Himalaya. Named hybrids and vars. are probably more popular than the species and can be found in trade catalogues.

Philesia—*Liliaceae*. Half-hardy evergreen flowering shrub. First introduced mid-nineteenth century.

CULTURE: Compost, equal parts peat, loam and coarse silver sand. Position, against walls or in pots in cold or cool greenhouse; against walls or in sheltered nooks outdoors, S.W. of England or Ireland. Pot or plant, Feb. to April. Water freely March to Oct., moderately afterwards. Syringe foliage daily in greenhouse March to Oct. Prune directly after blooming.

PROPAGATION: By cuttings inserted in sandy peat under bell-glass in greenhouse in summer; suckers in spring.

SPECIES CULTIVATED: *P. magellanica* (syn. *P. buxifolia*), rosy crimson, June, 6 in. to 2 ft., S. Chile.

Phillyrea—*Oleaceae*. Hardy evergreen flowering shrubs. Leaves lance- or egg-shaped, dark green. First introduced late sixteenth century.

CULTURE: Soil, ordinary. Easily cultivated in any situation. Plant, Sept. to April. Prune straggly shoots only in April. With the exception of *P. decora* all kinds may be clipped to formal shapes or to form hedges.

PROPAGATION: By cuttings of firm shoots in sandy soil in frame in Sept.

SPECIES CULTIVATED: *P. angustifolia* 'Jasmine Box,' white, May, 8 to 10 ft., Mediterranean; var. *rosmarinifolia*, rosemary-leaved; *decora* (syn. *P. Vilmoriniana*), white, May, 8 to 10 ft., W. Asia; *latifolia*, white, May, 20 ft., Mediterranean, and varieties. See also Osmarea.

Philodendron—*Araceae*. Stove evergreen dwarf or climbing plants, grown in greenhouses as foliage plants. First introduced mid-eighteenth century.

CULTURE: Compost, equal parts peat, leaf-mould, loam and silver sand. Pot or plant, Jan. to April. Position, dwarf kinds in pots; tall ones in beds or borders, with shoots trained up walls or pillars. Water freely all the year round. Syringe daily. Temp., March to Sept. 70° to 80°, Sept. to March 65° to 70°.

PROPAGATION: By cuttings of stems inserted in light soil in temp. **75° at any** time.

SPECIES CULTIVATED: *P. Andreanum,* climber, spathe black, purple, and creamy white, Colombia;   *calophyllum,* spathe creamy white and crimson, Brazil, Guiana; *gloriosum,* leaves green, white, and pink, climbing, Colombia;   *giganteum,* broadly heart-shaped leaves, climbing, W. Indies;   *verrucosum* (syn. *P. Lindenii*), dwarf, Colombia.   Many other species of little interest.

Phlomis—*Labiatae.*   Hardy perennials and evergreen shrubs.   First introduced late sixteenth century.

CULTURE OF PERENNIAL SPECIES: Soil, ordinary.   Position, sunny beds, borders, rockeries or banks.   Plant, Oct. to April.   Lift, divide and replant every three years.

CULTURE OF SHRUBBY · SPECIES: Soil, well-drained, light or chalky loam. Position, sunny borders or rockeries.   Good maritime plant, not hardy in cold districts.   Plant, Oct. to April.

PROPAGATION: By seeds sown in light soil in warm greenhouse in March or sunny spot outdoors in April;   herbaceous kinds also by division, Oct. or March; shrubs by cuttings inserted in cold frame in Aug.

PERENNIAL SPECIES CULTIVATED: *P. cashmeriana,* lilac, July, 2 ft., Himalaya; *Herba-venti,* purple and violet, summer, 12 to 18 in., S. Europe;   *samia,* yellow and orange, May to Aug., 2 to 3 ft., N. Africa;   *tuberosa,* rose-purple, June, 3 to 5 ft., S. Europe and Asia Minor;   *viscosa* (syn. *P. Russelliana*), golden yellow, June, 2 to 3 ft., Syria.

SHRUBBY SPECIES CULTIVATED: *P. fruticosa,* ' Jerusalem Sage ', yellow, June, 3 to 4 ft., S. Europe.

Phlox—*Polemoniaceae.*   Hardy perennial and half-hardy annual plants.   First introduced early eighteenth century.

CULTURE OF ALPINE SPECIES: Soil, deep, rich, sandy loam containing a little leaf-mould or peat.   Position, edgings to sunny borders or on ledges of rockeries. Plant, March to May.   Lift and divide only when grown too large for their position, in March.

POT CULTURE: Compost, two parts sandy loam, one part leaf-mould and half a part sand.   Pot, March.   Position, cold frame or greenhouse.   Water moderately Oct. to April, freely other times.   Admit air freely always.

CULTURE OF HERBACEOUS PERENNIALS: Soil, deep, rich, moderately heavy loam, light soils not suitable.   Position, sunny or partly shaded borders.   Plant, Oct., Feb. or March.   Mulch liberally with decayed manure or compost in March or April.   Apply liquid manure frequently May to Sept.   Water freely in dry weather.   Cut down stems in Oct.   Lift, divide and replant in fresh rich soil triennially.

CULTURE OF ANNUAL SPECIES: Sow seeds in light soil in temp. 55° to 65° in March.   Transplant seedlings 2 in. apart in boxes or pots, gradually harden off and plant outdoors 6 in. apart in rich soil in sunny position, in June.   Nip off point of main shoot after planting to induce bushy growth.   Water freely in dry weather.   Mulch with manure or peat.

POT CULTURE: Compost, two parts loam, one part decayed manure or leaf-mould and little sand.   Plant four seedlings in 5 in. pot in April.   Keep in temp. 55° until June then place in cold frame or on outside window-sill.   Water freely. Apply stimulants when 3 in. high.   Nip off points of shoots when 3 in. high. No repotting required.

PROPAGATION: Annuals, by seed.   Herbaceous perennials, seeds sown in sandy soil in temp. 55° in autumn or spring;   cuttings of shoots from base of old plant in sandy soil in temp. 55° in March;   division of.plants in Oct. or March; cuttings of roots early in the year as precaution against eelworm disease.   Alpine species, by cuttings of shoots in sandy soil in cold frame in July;   division in March or April.

ALPINE SPECIES CULTIVATED: *P. adsurgens,* salmon-pink, May to June, 6 in., California, Oregon;   *alyssifolia,* pink, spring, 2 to 3 in., N. America;   *amoena,* pink, spring, 3 in., N. America;   *andicola,* white, spring, 3 to 4 in., N. America;

bryoides, white, spring, 1 in., N. America; *condensata*, white, spring, 1 in., N. America; *divaricata* (syn. *P. canadensis*), blue, May to June, 12 in., N. America; *Douglasii*, lavender to pink, spring, 2 to 3 in., N. America, numerous vars. and hybrids; *Hoodii*, white, May, ½ in., N. America; *nana*, rich soft rose, June, 9 in., one of the loveliest of alpine phlox, N. America; *ovata* (*P. carolina* of gardens), pink or red, summer, 12 to 15 in., N.W. America; *procumbens*, pink, spring, 6 in., hybrid; *stolonifera*, pink or purple, spring, 6 in., N. America; *subulata*, ' Moss Pink ', various, early summer, N. America, many vars. and hybrids.

PERENNIAL SPECIES CULTIVATED: *P. Arendsii*, lavender, summer, to 2 ft., hybrid; *glaberrima*, red, May to June, 1 to 2 ft., N. America; *carolina*, purple, rose and white, late summer, to 4 ft., N. America, early blooming vars. are widely cultivated as *P. suffruticosa*; *maculata*, ' Wild Sweet William ', purple, July, fragrant, 2 ft., N. America; *paniculata*, purple and white, Aug., fragrant, 3 to 4 ft., U.S.A., horticultural forms often known as *P. decussata*.

ANNUAL SPECIES CULTIVATED: *P. Drummondii*, various, summer, 1 ft., Texas, and many vars.

Phoenix—*Palmae.* Stove feather palms. Dates are the fruits of *P. dactylifera* First introduced late sixteenth century.

CULTURE: Compost, three parts good fibrous loam, one part old cow manure and a little coarse sand. Position, well-drained pots or tubs in sunny part of stove. Pot, Feb. or March. Water moderately Oct. to March, copiously March to Oct. Syringe foliage morning and evening daily April to Sept., morning only Sept. to April. Apply weak stimulants occasionally May to Sept. Place a lump of sulphate of iron on surface of soil occasionally to keep foliage of a rich, healthy green hue. Temp., March to Sept. 65° to 75°, Sept. to March 55° to 65°.

PROPAGATION: By seeds sown 1 in. deep in light, sandy soil under bell-glass or in propagator in temp. 75°, March or April.

SPECIES CULTIVATED: *P. acaulis*, 8 to 12 ft., India; *canariensis*, 30 to 40 ft., Canary Isles; *dactylifera*, ' Date Palm ', 80 to 100 ft., N. Africa; *humilis*, 3 to 6 ft., India; *reclinata*, 25 to 35 ft., S. Africa; *Roebelenii*, 4 to 6 ft., S.E. Asia; *rupicola*, 15 to 20 ft., Himalaya; *sylvestris*, 30 to 40 ft., India.

Pholidota—*Orchidaceae.* Epiphytes, allied to Coelogyne. The flowers small, many, usually arranged in two rows, each flower based by comparatively large bract often partially concealing the flower. Two sections are represented, in one the rhizome is creeping, usually carrying rounded pseudo-bulbs, often clustered. In the second the jointed stems are erect, with somewhat oblong pseudo-bulbs, the newer proceeding from near the top of the older. Support should be given.

CULTURE: Compost, as for Coelogynes. Winter night temp. about 60°, summer, with shading, 70° or more. Water liberally in summer; in winter the stemmed section requires more frequent watering than the dwarfer-growing hard-bulbed kinds, judgement must be used. A moist atmosphere is beneficial.

PROPAGATION: By dividing plants of the creeping species. By severing the topmost joint or two of the stemmed kinds, and potting in early spring, or by cuttings of two joints placed in a propagating case.

SPECIES CULTIVATED: Stemmed section—*P. articulata* (syn. *P. Khasyana*), yellowish-white, summer, autumn, Burma, India; *Lugardii*, whitish-tinged flesh, summer, Burma; *recurva*, creamy white, inflorescence one-sided, late summer, India, Burma. Creeping Section—*P. chinensis*, whitish to reddish-pink, summer, S. China; *conchoidea*, small, whitish, tinged pink, lip marked with ochre-yellow, summer, Philippines; *imbricata*, ' Rattlesnake Orchid ', greenish-yellow, bracts brownish, overlapping, summer, India, Burma, Australia; *pallida*, perhaps a var. of *imbricata*, whitish, smaller; *ventricosa*, strong-growing, inflorescence erect, yellowish-white, summer, Java. Other species are known.

Phormium—*Liliaceae.* Half-hardy perennial herbs. First introduced late eighteenth century.

INDOOR CULTURE: Compost, two parts turfy loam, one part each of leaf-mould and sand. Position, pots, tubs or beds in cold or warm greenhouse, conservatory, balcony or dwelling-room. Pot, Feb. to April. Water copiously April to Oct., moderately afterwards. May stand outdoors in sunny position June to Sept.

OUTDOOR CULTURE: Soil, light, deep loam. Position, margins of ponds or streams, isolated specimens on lawns, or in beds or borders S. and S.W. of England and Ireland only. In other districts plants must be put out in May, lifted in Oct. and stored in greenhouse until following May. Plant permanently in April or May. Water freely in dry weather. Protect those left outdoors all winter with straw or dried fern.

PROPAGATION: By seeds sown ⅛ in. deep in pots of sandy soil in greenhouse or frame in March; division of roots in April.

SPECIES CULTIVATED: *P. Colensoi* (syn. *P. Cookianum*), yellow and green, summer, 4 to 6 ft., New Zealand; *Hookeri*, green, summer, 5 ft., New Zealand; *tenax*, ' New Zealand Flax ', yellow, summer, 5 to 12 ft., New Zealand, and vars. *atropurpureum*, leaves purple, *variegatum*, leaves yellow, green, and white, and *Veitchii*, leaves creamy white.

Photinia—*Rosaceae*. Hardy and slightly tender deciduous and evergreen shrubs or small trees. Handsome foliage and hawthorn-like flowers and fruits. First introduced early nineteenth century.

CULTURE: Soil, light, rich, well drained. Situation, warm and sheltered.

PROPAGATION: By seed sown in March to April in well-drained pots in cold frame.

SPECIES CULTIVATED: *P. Davidsoniae*, evergreen, handsome young foliage, tinted bronze, 20 to 40 ft., fairly hardy, Cent. China; *parvifolia*, deciduous, scarlet berries, 6 to 8 ft., Cent. China; *serrulata*, ' Chinese Hawthorn ', evergreen, white April to May, scarlet fruits, copper young foliage, not hardy coldest areas, 30 ft., China; *villosa*, deciduous, handsome, autumn foliage and fruits, 12 to 15 ft., Japan and China.

Phragmipedium—*Orchidaceae*. *Selenipedium* of gardens. Terrestrial or epiphytic orchids without pseudo-bulbs. Scapes, several flowered. There are numerous hybrids.

CULTURE: As for Paphiopedilums, winter night temp. need never exceed 60°. Compost, half peat or osmunda fibre, one part fibrous loam, one part sphagnum.

PROPAGATION: As for Paphiopedilum.

SPECIES CULTIVATED: *P. caricinum*, 3 to 6, small, greenish-white, petals twisted, summer, Bolivia, Peru; *caudatum*, 1 to 4, whitish, creamy white, veined green, lip variable, petals ribbon-like up to 30 in. long, spring, summer, Peru, Ecuador, Cent. America; *Lindenii* (syn. *Uropedium Lindenii*), lip in a ribbon-like form; *Lindleyanum*, 3 to 7, greenish, veined and shaded with red-brown, petals twisted, winter, British Guiana, Demerara; *longifolium*, 6 to 10, green and rose, various seasons, Costa Rica; *Sargentianum*, near *P. Lindleyanum*, greenish-lilac, olive green, red marked, autumn, Pernambuco; *Schlimii*, 3 to 8, small, pretty, white, rose and carmine rose, various seasons, Colombia; *vittatum*, 2 to 7, greenish-white, shaded and spotted with brown-purple, leaves edged yellowish, various seasons, Brazil.

Phygelius—*Scrophulariaceae*. Slightly tender evergreen shrub with handsome penstemon-like flowers. First introduced mid-nineteenth century.

CULTURE: Soil, light, with some humus, well drained. Position, warm, sheltered corners or beneath walls, full sun, open borders extreme south-west. Prune in April, shortening back any growth damaged by frost.

PROPAGATION: By cuttings of half-ripened shoots with bottom heat, July, or seed sown in well-drained pots in cold frame, early spring, germination slow; division of rootstock in early spring.

SPECIES CULTIVATED: *P. capensis*, ' Cape Fuchsia ', scarlet, Sept., 2 to 6 ft., S. Africa, var. *coccineus*, brighter, cooler.

Phyllachne—*Stylidiaceae*. Perennial, cushion-forming, alpine plants.

CULTURE: For the skilled cultivator and best grown in the alpine house or cold frame. Very gritty scree soil containing some finely sifted leaf-mould and loam. Wedge between small stones in sun. Do not over-water in winter.

PROPAGATION: By seeds, if obtainable; small rosettes rooted as cuttings in early summer.

SPECIES CULTIVATED: *P. Colensoi*, white, summer, ½ in., New Zealand; *clavigera*, white, summer, ¼ in., New Zealand.

Phyllagathis—*Melastomaceae*. Stove flowering sub-shrub.

CULTURE: Compost, equal parts peat and sand with a little leaf-mould. Position, well-drained pots in heated greenhouse. Water abundantly during growing season, moderately at other times. Moist atmosphere essential during summer months. Temp., March to Sept. 75° to 85°, Sept. to March 65° to 70°.

PROPAGATION: By leaf cuttings inserted in sandy compost in temp. 85° and brisk bottom heat.

SPECIES CULTIVATED: *P. rotundifolia*, pink flowers surrounded by deep purple bracts, July, leaves large, glossy green tinged metallic blue and purple, red beneath, 1 to 2 ft., Sumatra.

Phyllanthus—*Euphorbiaceae*. Stove ornamental-foliaged plants. First introduced late seventeenth century.

CULTURE: Compost, equal parts sandy loam and fibrous peat, one part equal proportions of charcoal, dried cow manure, powdered brick and coarse silver sand. Position, well-drained pots in shady part of stove. Pot, Feb. or March. Water moderately Oct. to March, freely afterwards. Syringe morning and evening, April to Sept. Prune into shape, Jan. Temp., Sept. to March 60° to 65°, March to Sept. 70° to 80°.

PROPAGATION: By cuttings of firm shoots, 2 to 3 in. long, inserted singly in small pots of sandy soil under propagator or bell-glass in temp. 75°, spring or summer.

SPECIES CULTIVATED: *P. acidus* (syn. *P. distichus*), 'Otaheite Gooseberry', yellow, 15 to 20 ft., Trop. Asia; *Emblica* (syn. *P. mimosaefolius*), yellow, mimosa-like foliage, 20 to 30 ft., Trop. Asia; *pulcher* (syn. *Reidia glaucescens*), yellow, summer, leaves green, 3 to 4 ft., Malaya, a pretty table plant; *reticulatus*, red, Aug., 3 to 4 ft., Tropics; *speciosus*, white, Sept., 15 to 20 ft., Jamaica.

Phyllitis—*Polypodiaceae*. Hardy evergreen ferns. Fronds, strap-shaped, crested or contorted.

OUTDOOR CULTURE: Soil, one part each fibrous peat and loam, and one part of sand, broken oyster shells and limestone or mortar rubbish. Position, shady borders, rockeries, chinks of old stone or brick walls, or banks. Plant, April. Water copiously in dry weather.

INDOOR CULTURE: Compost, as above. Position, pots in cold frame, greenhouse or dwelling-room. Shade from sun essential. Pot, Feb. or March. Water freely March to Oct., moderately afterwards.

PROPAGATION: By spores sown on surface of fine peat in well-drained pans placed in temp. 75° any time; division of plants, March or April.

SPECIES CULTIVATED: *P. Scolopendrium* (syn. *Scolopendrium vulgare*), 'Hart's-tongue Fern', 6 to 18 in., Europe (Br.), etc., and numerous crisped, cristate and divided forms.

Phyllodoce—*Ericaceae*. Dwarf hardy evergreen shrubs.

CULTURE: Soil, sandy peat. Position, cool, well-watered spots in the rock garden. Plant, Sept. to Oct. and April to May.

PROPAGATION: By seeds, cuttings of nearly ripened shoots in July and Aug., or by layers in spring.

SPECIES CULTIVATED: *P. Breweri*, purplish-rose, May, 6 to 12 in., California; *caerulea*, bluish-purple, June to July, 6 to 9 in., Europe, Asia and N. America; *empetriformis*, reddish-purple, April, 6 to 9 in., Western N. America; *nipponica*, white and pink, May, 4 to 8 in., Japan, and var. *tsugaefolia*, white flushed pink, 6 in.

Phyllostachys—*Gramineae*. Half-hardy grasses with ornamental foliage, Natives of China and Japan. Inflorescence borne in panicles in summer. Leaves, narrow, lance-shaped, green. Sometimes included in Bambusa.

CULTURE: Soil, rich, deep, sandy loam. Position, moist, sheltered borders in south and west only. Protect in winter with dry fern fronds. Plant, March or April.

PROPAGATION: By division of plants in March or April.

SPECIES CULTIVATED: *P. aureus* (syn. *Bambusa aureus*), stems yellow, leaves green, 10 to 15 ft., Japan; *bambusoides* (syn. *P. Quilioi*), leaves bright green, 10 to 18 ft., China; *flexuosa*, leaves dark green, 6 to 8 ft., China; *niger* (syn. *P. puberula*), leaves dark green, stems yellowish-green, 12 to 14 ft., China, var. *Henonis*; (syn. *P. puberula*), leaves dark green, stems yellowish green, 12 to 14 ft.; *sulphurea*, leaves green, 12 to 20 ft., China, Japan; *viridi-glaucescens*, leaves green, stems yellowish, 14 to 18 ft., China.

× **Phyllothamnus**—*Ericaceae*. Small evergreen shrub. Bigeneric hybrid between Phyllodoce and Rhodothamnus.

CULTURE: Lime-free, peaty or leaf-mould soil. North aspect or cool position.

PROPAGATION: By cuttings of half-ripened wood in late summer.

SPECIES CULTIVATED: *P. erectus*, deep rose, 12 to 15 in., spring.

Physalis—*Solanaceae*. Greenhouse and hardy perennial herbs. Fruit of Cape Gooseberry edible—a berry enclosed in an inflated calyx.

CULTURE OF HARDY SPECIES: Soil, rich. Position, sunny well-drained border. Plant, March or April. Lift, divide and replant in fresh soil every third year. Gather stems bearing fruits in Sept. and dry for winter decorations.

CULTURE OF GREENHOUSE SPECIES: Soil, two parts loam, one part well-decayed manure or leaf-mould, and little sand. Position, singly in 5 or 6 in. pots, with shoots trained to sticks and placed close to front of sunny greenhouse, or planted in small beds and shoots trained up back wall. Pot or plant, Feb. or March. Water freely April to Sept., moderately afterwards. Apply weak stimulants once or twice a week May to Sept. Gather fruit when ripe and fully coloured.

PROPAGATION: Hardy species by seeds sown in sunny spot outdoors in April; division of roots in March or April. Greenhouse species by seeds sown $\frac{1}{16}$ in. deep in shallow pots or pans of light soil and placed in temp. 65° to 75°, Feb. or March; cuttings inserted singly in pots of light, sandy soil placed in propagator or under bell-glass in temp. 65° to 75°, Jan. to April.

HARDY SPECIES CULTIVATED: *P. Alkekengi* (syns. *P. Bunyardii*, *P. Franchettii*), ‘ Bladder Herb ’ or ‘ Winter Cherry ’, white, summer, fruit scarlet, 1 to 2 ft., S.E. Europe to Japan.

GREENHOUSE SPECIES CULTIVATED: *P. peruviana* (syn. *P. edulis*), ‘ Cape Gooseberry ’, white, summer, fruit edible, 3 ft., Tropics.

Physaria—*Cruciferae*. Tufted herbaceous plants.

CULTURE: Gritty scree soil and a sunny pocket in the rock garden.

PROPAGATION: By seeds sown in early spring in gritty, sandy compost.

SPECIES CULTIVATED: *P. didymocarpa*, ‘ Double Bladder Pod ’, ornamental, bladder-like seed pods, summer, 2 to 3 in., N. America.

Physosiphon—*Orchidaceae*. An epiphytic genus allied to Pleurothallis, habit similar. Flowers small, numerous, the sepals form a tube with tips free, petals and lip concealed in the tube.

CULTURE: Compost, temp., etc., as for Masdevallia but water is not required as frequently in winter, the leaves usually being harder in texture.

PROPAGATION: By division of plants in spring.

SPECIES CULTIVATED: *P. guatemalensis*, yellow and purple-red, spring to summer, Guatemala; *Lindleyi*, green and reddish, spring, Mexico; *Loddigesii*, height about 6 in., scapes longer, greenish and orange-brown, spring to summer, Mexico, Guatemala.

Physostegia (False Dragonhead)—*Labiatae*. Hardy herbaceous perennials. First introduced late seventeenth century.

CULTURE: Soil, light ordinary. Position, cool, partially shaded borders. Plant, Oct., March or April.

PROPAGATION: By seeds sown ⅛ in. deep in light, sandy soil outdoors in April; cuttings of young shoots inserted in light, sandy soil under hand-light or in cold frame, April or May; division of roots, Oct. or March; root cuttings in winter.

SPECIES CULTIVATED: *P. virginiana* (syn. *Dracocephalum virginianum*), rosy pink, June to Sept., 1 to 4 ft., N. America, and numerous vars.

Phyteuma (Horned Rampion)—*Campanulaceae*. Hardy perennial herbs.

CULTURE: Soil, deep, rich loam mixed with limestone grit and old mortar and leaf-mould or peat. Position, sunny rockeries for dwarf species, sunny borders for tall. Plant, March or April. Lift, divide and replant only when overgrown. Top-dress dwarf species with a mixture of peat, leaf-mould, lime, and a little old mortar annually in Feb. or March. Water freely in dry weather.

PROPAGATION: By seeds sown in light, sandy soil in shallow boxes in cold frame, Sept. or Oct., transplanting seedlings in permanent positions, April or May; division of plants in March or April.

SPECIES CULTIVATED: *P. comosum*, amethyst blue, July, 3 to 4 in., S. Europe; *Halleri*, violet, May to July, 6 to 12 in., Europe; *hemisphaericum*, blue, June to July, 3 to 4 in., Alps; *nigrum*, blue, summer, 18 in., Europe (Br.); *orbiculare*, blue, July, 6 to 12 in., Cent. Europe; *pinnatum* (syn. *Petromarula pinnata*), ' Rock Lettuce ', blue, 12 to 15 in., summer, Crete; *Scheuchzeri*, blue, summer, 1 ft., Europe; *serratum*, blue, summer, 2 to 3 in., Corsica; *Sieberi*, blue, summer, 6 to 8 in., Europe; *spicatum*, cream, summer, 3 to 4 ft., Europe; *tenerum*, blue, July, 6 to 12 in., W. Europe (Br.).

Phytolacca (Pokeberry)—*Phytolaccaceae*. Hardy herbaceous perennials. Flowers succeeded by deep purple berries in autumn. Broad, ovate, dark green leaves, changing to rich purple in autumn. First introduced mid-eighteenth century.

CULTURE: Soil, good ordinary. Position, sunny or shady borders in woodlands, banks or ferneries. Plant, Oct., March or April.

PROPAGATION: By seed sown ⅛ in. deep in sandy soil outdoors in spring or autumn; division of plants in Oct. or March.

SPECIES CULTIVATED: *P. acinosa*, ' Indian Poke ', white, summer, 5 ft., Himalaya; *americana* (syn. *P. decandra*), ' Virginian Poke ', ' Red-ink Plant ', ' Pigeon Berry ', white, summer, 5 ft., N. America.

Picea (Spruce)—*Pinaceae*. Hardy evergreen coniferous trees. Leaves needle-shaped, spirally arranged. Branches always produced in tiers to form pyramidal shape. Cones almost always pendulous. *Picea Abies*, the Common or Norway Spruce is the Christmas tree and also produces timber known as white deal. First introduced, probably sixteenth century.

CULTURE: Deep, rich, moist soil, preferring areas of heavy rainfall. Mostly timber trees but some species make handsome specimens up to 100 ft. or more and others are dwarf, suitable for rock gardens. Norway spruce is used as a shelter nurse to larch and other forest trees. Plant, Oct. to April.

PROPAGATION: By seeds sown ⅛ in. deep in sandy loam in cold frame in March, or in prepared beds outdoors in April, ¼ lb. seed sufficient to sow 100 sq. ft.; special forms grafted in March.

SPECIES CULTIVATED: *P. Abies* (syn. *P. excelsa*), ' Common Spruce ', 100 to 120 ft., N. Europe, and vars. *argentea*, leaves variegated white, *Clanbrasiliana*, dense, slow growing, *columnaris*, fastigiate habit, *Ellwangeriana*, broadly pyramidal, dwarf form, *Gregoryana*, very dwarf, conical to 2 ft., *pendula*, weeping, *virgata*, ' Snake Fir ', and numerous others; *asperata*, vigorous, grey-leaved, 50 to 70 ft., China; *bicolor* (syn. *P. Alcockiana*), 80 ft., Japan; *Breweriana*, eventual weeping habit, 80 to 100 ft., California; *Engelmannii*, fine hardy tree, blue-green, 100 to 150 ft., Western N. America; *glauca* (syn. *P. alba*), ' White Spruce ', 60 to 100 ft., N.E. America, and vars. *albertiana*, pyramidal to 150 ft., *aurea*, leaves tinged yellow, *caerulea*, glaucous form, and many dwarf forms including *conica*, *nana* and *compacta*; *jezoensis*, ' Yeddo Spruce ', not so hardy as var. *hondoensis*, 80 to 100 ft., Japan; *Koyamai*, narrowly pyramidal, 50 ft., Japan, Korea; *likiangensis*, 60 to 80 ft., W. China, with var. *Balfouriana*, violet-coloured cones; *mariana* (syn. *P. nigra*), ' Black Spruce ', 25 to 50 ft., young cones purple, N. America; *obovata*, ' Siberian Spruce ', 80 to 100 ft., Siberia, N.E. Russia; *Omorika*, ' Serbian Spruce ', easily grown, narrowly conical , leaves white beneath, to 100 ft., Serbia and Bosnia, var. *pendula*, attractive weeping form; *orientalis*, ' Oriental Spruce ', one of the best species, good habit, short dark green leaves, 100 ft., Caucasus, with vars. *aurea*, bronze coloured, and *aureo-spicata*, young growth bright yellow; *polita*, ' Tigertail Spruce ', stout prickly leaves, to 100 ft., Japan; *pungens*, ' Colorado Spruce ', not so common as its beautiful forms *Kosteriana* (syn. var. *glauca pendula*), ' Weeping Blue Spruce ', *glauca*, bluish, *Speckii*, bluish, etc., 50 to 100 ft., Colorado to N. Mexico; *rubens* (syn. *P. rubra*), ' Red Spruce ', 70 to 80 ft., N. America; *Schrenkiana*, to 100 ft., Cent. Asia; *sitchensis*, ' Sitka Spruce ', useful timber tree for moist places, to 150 ft., Alaska to California; *Smithiana* (syn. *P. Morinda*), ' West Himalayan Spruce ', 100 to 200 ft., Himalaya; *spinulosa*, ' East Himalayan Spruce ', pendulous branches, over 200 ft., Himalaya; *Wilsonii* (syn. *R. Watsoniana*), dense habit, to 70 ft., Cent. China.

Pickerel-weed, see *Pontederia cordata.*

Picotee, see *Dianthus Caryophyllus* var.

Pieris—*Ericaceae.* Hardy evergreen shrubs of great beauty with lily-of-the-valley-like flowers. Some of the species were previously included in Andromeda. First introduced early eighteenth century.

OUTDOOR CULTURE: Soil, lime-free loam such as suits rhododendrons but preferably light and moist. Position, partial shade with some shelter from the east. Plant, Sept. to Nov., or March. Prune straggling shoots only moderately after flowering. Water freely in dry positions during summer.

POT CULTURE: Soil, equal parts peat, leaf-mould and fine silver sand. Position, well-drained pots in cold greenhouse, Nov. to June; in shady position outdoors, June to Nov. Pot, Oct. to Nov. Water moderately Nov. to March, freely afterwards.

PROPAGATION: By seeds sown $\frac{1}{16}$ in. deep in sandy peat in cold frame Nov. or March; layering shoots in Sept.

SPECIES CULTIVATED: *P. floribunda*, white, spring, 4 to 6 ft., Virginia; *formosa*, white, spring, 8 to 12 ft., Himalaya; *Forrestii*, young growths red, flowers white, April, 6 ft., China; *japonica*, white, spring, 9 to 10 ft., Japan, and var. *variegata*; *nana* (syn. *Arcterica nana*), white, summer, 3 in., Japan; *taiwanensis*, excellent newer species, attractive young red shoots, flowers when small, white, March to April, 4 to 6 ft., Formosa.

Pigeon Berry, see *Phylolacca americana*; **-Orchid,** see *Dendrobium crumentalum.*

Pignut, see *Carya glabra.*

Pilea—*Urticaceae.* Stove perennial herbs. Flowers, insignificant; unexpanded buds burst when in contact with moisture and discharge pollen. First introduced late eighteenth century.

CULTURE: Compost, equal parts loam, leaf-mould and silver sand. Position, small pots in partially shaded part of stove. Pot, Feb. to April. Water freely April to Sept., moderately afterwards. Temp., Sept. to March 55° to 65°, March to Sept. 70° to 80°.

PROPAGATION: By seeds sown on surface of light, sandy soil slightly covered with fine soil and placed in temp. 65° to 75° in spring; cuttings inserted singly in small well-drained pots of sandy soil in temp. 65° to 75°, Jan. to May; division of plants, Feb. or March.

SPECIES CULTIVATED: *P. microphylla*, ' Artillery Plant ', 3 to 15 in. Trop. America; *nummulariifolia*, prostrate, W. Indies; *Spruceana*, 3 to 12 in., Peru.

Pimelea (Rice-flower)—*Thymelaeaceae.* Greenhouse evergreen flowering shrubs. First introduced late eighteenth century.

CULTURE: Compost, three parts fibrous peat, one part turfy loam, half a part silver sand. Position, well-drained pots in light, airy greenhouse. Prune moderately closely immediately after flowering. Pot soon as new growth commences. Firm potting essential. Nip off points of shoots of young plants occasionally to induce bushy growth. Water freely April to Oct., moderately afterwards. Grow in a moist atmosphere for a few weeks after potting, then gradually harden off and place in an airy greenhouse. Temp., Sept. to March 40° to 50°, March to Sept. 55° to 65°.

PROPAGATION: By seeds sown $\frac{1}{16}$ in. deep in light, sandy soil under bell-glass in temp. 55° to 65°, Feb. to May; cuttings of young shoots, 2 in. long, inserted in compost of one part peat, two parts silver sand, under bell-glass, in temp. 55° to 65°, March or April.

SPECIES CULTIVATED: *P. ferruginea* (syn. *P. decussata*), rose, May, 2 ft., Australia; *gnidia*, red, May, 1 to 5 ft., New Zealand; *ligustrina* (syn. *P. hypericina*), white, May, 5 to 6 ft., Australia; *rosea*, pink, June, 1 to 2 ft., Australia; *spectabilis*, white and pink, May, 4 ft., Australia.

Pimenta—*Myrtaceae.* Aromatic stove evergreen flowering trees. *P. officinalis* furnishes the allspice of commerce. The oil of *P. acris* is used in the preparation of bay rum. First introduced mid-eighteenth century.

CULTURE: Compost, two parts sandy loam, one part leaf-mould and one part sand. Position, well-drained pots or beds with branches trained to wall. Pot, Feb. or March. Water moderately Oct. to April, freely afterwards. Syringe April to Aug. Prune straggling shoots moderately in March. Temp., Sept. to March 60° to 65°, March to Sept. 65° to 75°.

PROPAGATION: By cuttings of firm shoots inserted in sandy soil under bell-glass in temp. 65° to 75° in summer.

SPECIES CULTIVATED: *P. acris*, ' Pimento ', white and pink, May, 20 to 30 ft., W. Indies; *officinalis*, ' Allspice ', white, summer, 20 to 40 ft., W. Indies.

Pimento, see *Pimenta officinalis.*

Pimpernel, see Anagallis.

Pimpinella—*Umbelliferae.* Hardy annual herb. Seeds used as a condiment.

CULTURE: Soil, well drained, ordinary. Position, warm beds or borders. Sow seeds thinly in April where plants are to remain.

SPECIES CULTIVATED: *P. Anisum*, ' Anise ', to 2 ft., Greece to Egypt.

Pinanga—*Palmae.* Stove, bamboo-like feather palms. First introduced mid-nineteenth century.

CULTURE: Compost, one part loam, two parts peat, half a part silver sand. Position, well-drained pots in shady, lofty stove. Pot, Feb. or March. Water copiously March to Oct., moderately afterwards. Syringe twice daily March to Sept., once daily afterwards. Place few crystals of sulphate of iron on surface of soil occasionally to ensure deep green foliage. Temp., March to Oct. 75° to 85°, Oct. to March 55° to 65°.

PROPAGATION: By seeds sown $\frac{1}{2}$ in. deep singly in 2 in. pots of sandy loam and peat under bell-glass in temp. 75° to 85° in spring.

SPECIES CULTIVATED: *P. disticha*, 6 ft., Malaya; *malayana*, 8 to 12 ft., Malaya.

Pincushion Flower, see Scabiosa.

Pine, see Pinus; **-Barren Beauty,** see *Pyxidanthera barbulata*; **-weed,** see *Hypericum gentianoides.*

Pineapple, see *Ananas comosus*; **-Flower,** see *Eucomis comosa.*

Pinella—*Araceae.* Hardy herbaceous perennial.

CULTURE: Soil, light, well drained. Position, sunny.

PROPAGATION: By tubers on lower part of leaf-stalk.

SPECIES CULTIVATED: *P. ternata* (syn. *P. tuberifera*), spathe and spadix green, summer, 1 ft., China, Japan.

Pinguicula (Butterwort)—*Lentibulariaceae.* Greenhouse and hardy perennial insectivorous herbs.

CULTURE OF GREENHOUSE SPECIES: Compost, equal parts fibrous peat, sphagnum moss, and clean crocks. Position, well-drained pots or shallow pans placed on inverted pots in saucer of water under bell-glass or hand-light in shade. Pot, March or April. Water freely April to Sept., moderately afterwards. Admit air for a few minutes daily every morning by tilting bell-glass or hand-light. Temp., March to Oct. 55° to 65°, Oct. to March 45° to 55°.

CULTURE OF HARDY SPECIES: Soil, rich loam for *P. grandiflora*; peat and rough gravel for *P. alpina*; moist peat or peaty loam for *P. vulgaris*. Plant, March or April. Water freely in dry positions in summer. Mulch with thick layer of leaf-mould in May.

PROPAGATION: By seeds sown on surface of shallow pans filled with equal parts of sphagnum moss, peat and sand, placed under bell-glass, and kept moist in temp. of 55° to 65°, Feb., March or April; division of plants at potting or planting time.

GREENHOUSE SPECIES CULTIVATED: *P. caudata*, carmine, autumn, 6 in., Mexico.

HARDY SPECIES CULTIVATED: *P. alpina*, white and yellow, May, 4 in., Europe (Br.); *grandiflora*, blue and violet, summer, 4 in., Europe (Br.); *vulgaris*, ' Bog Violet ', ' Butterwort ', violet, summer, 4 to 6 in., Britain.

Pink, see Dianthus; **-root,** see *Spigelia marilandica.*

Pinus (Pine)—*Pinaceae.* Hardy evergreen coniferous trees. Leaves needle-like, two to five in a whorl. Cones conical and erect.

CULTURE: Soil, preferably open and well drained. Position, *P. nigra*, *P. Mugo* and *P. Pinaster* suitable for seaside gardens and ordinary soil, *P. nigra* is a good town tree. *P. nigra*, *P. Cembra*, *P. Griffithii*, *P. Pinaster*, *P. Strobus* and *P. sylvestris* suitable for gravelly or sandy soils. *P. nigra* is a good shelter tree and *P. sylvestris*, will grow in the poorest soil and on rocky slopes. *P. sylvestris*, the Scots Pine, often erroneously called Scotch Fir, is famous for production of timber known as deal; it is the most widely distributed of pines. For a quick screen plant Austrian Pine and Lombardy Poplar alternately at 8 ft. apart and grub out the poplars when pines are reasonably established. Pines should be planted in their permanent quarters as early in life as possible. Plant, Sept. to Nov.

PROPAGATION: By seeds sown ⅛ in. deep in pots filled with sandy loam, placed in cold greenhouse or frame in April and seedlings transplanted outdoors the following spring; or ¼ in. deep outdoors in April in bed of moist, sandy soil, transplanting seedlings the next year; special vars. grafted on common species in April.

USEFUL FACTS: Average age, 150 years. Timber reaches maturity at 80 years. Weight per cubic ft., 30 lbs. Timber, close-grained and resinous, used in young state for pit-props, staves, etc.; when matured for deal flooring, etc. Seeds ripe in Nov.; 1 lb. seed will yield about 8,000 plants.

SPECIES CULTIVATED: *P. Armandii*, blue-green, 50 to 60 ft., W. China; *Ayacahuite*, 60 to 100 ft., Mexico; *Balfouriana*, 20 to 50 ft., California; *Banksiana*, ' Canadian Jack Pine ', 25 to 50 ft., Eastern N. America; *Bungeana*, ' Lace Bark Pine ', 70 ft., N. China; *Cembra*, ' Stone Pine ', 60 to 100 ft., Cent. Europe; *cembroides*, ' Nut Pine ', slow-growing, round tree with edible seeds, 20 ft., Mexico, and var. *edulis*, taller-growing; *contorta*, ' Beach Pine ' or ' Shore Pine ', twisted leaves and branches, 30 ft., West N. America; *Coulteri*, 50 to 70 ft., California; *densiflora*, 100 to 120 ft., Japan; *flexilis*, ' Limber Pine ', 40 to 80 ft., N.W. America, *Griffithii* (syns. *P. nepalensis*, *P. excelsa*), 100 to 150 ft., Himalaya; *halepensis*, 50 ft., Medit. Region; *koraiensis*, ' Korean Pine ', glaucous blue, slow growing, 50 to 100 ft., Korea, Japan; *Lambertiana*, ' Sugar Pine ', 70 to 200 ft., N.W; America; *monticola*, ' Mountain White Pine ', 100 to 125 ft., West. N. America.

Mugo (syn. *P. montana*), ' Mountain Pine ', varying in height from 5 to 60 ft., with var. *Mughus*, almost prostrate, Cent. Europe; *muricata*, ' Bishop's Pine ', 50 to 90 ft., California; *nigra* (syn. *P. Laricio*), ' Austrian Pine ', 70 to 100 ft., W. Asia; *parviflora*, 30 to 40 ft., Japan, and var. *pentaphylla*, the wild form; *Peuce*, ' Macedonian Pine ', Macedonia; *Pinaster*, ' Cluster Pine ', 100 to 120 ft., Medit. Region; *Pinea*, ' Italian Stone Pine ', edible seeds, 40 to 100 ft., Medit. Region; *ponderosa*, ' Western Yellow Pine ', 100 to 150 ft., N.W. America; *radiata* (syn. *P. insignis*), ' Monterey Pine ', 100 to 120 ft., California; *resinosa*, ' Red Pine ', 50 to 100 ft., East N. America; *rigida*, ' Northern Pitch Pine ', 50 to 80 ft., Eastern. N. America; *Sabiniana*, ' Digger Pine ', 40 to 80 ft., California; *Strobus*, ' White Pine ', 60 to 100 ft., N.E. America; *sylvestris*, ' Scots Pine ', to 100 ft., Europe, including Britain, and vars. *argentea*, ' Silver Scots Pine ', *pendula*, weeping, and *Watereri*, *pumila*, *globosa*, dwarf forms for rockeries; *Thungerii*, ' Japanese Black Pine ', 80 to 100 ft., Japan; *virginiana*, ' Scrub Pine ', for poor dry soil, 30 to 50 ft., Eastern N. America.

Pinxter Flower, see *Rhododendron nudiflorum*.

Piper (Pepper Plant)—*Piperaceae*. Stove and greenhouse evergreen shrubs with marbled or blotched leaves. The pepper of commerce is obtained from the dried berries of *P. nigrum*. First introduced mid-eighteenth century.

CULTURE OF STOVE SPECIES: Compost, two parts loam, one part leaf-mould, half a part sand. Position, well-drained pots in shade. Pot, Feb. to April. Prune slightly into shape, Feb. Water freely April to Oct., moderately afterwards. Syringe twice daily April to Sept., once daily afterwards. Temp., March to Oct. 75° to 85°, Oct. to March 55° to 65°.

CULTURE OF GREENHOUSE SPECIES: Compost, as for stove species. Position, well-drained pots in partial shade. Pot, March or April. Water moderately Oct. to April, freely afterwards. Temp., March to Oct. 55° to 65°, Oct. to March 50° to 55°.

PROPAGATION: By cuttings of half-ripened shoots inserted in small pots of sandy soil under bell-glass in temp. of 65° to 75°, March to July.

STOVE SPECIES CULTIVATED: *P. Betle*, green, climber, India; *nigrum*, ' Pepper ', green, 4 to 6 ft., India.

GREENHOUSE SPECIES CULTIVATED: *P. excelsum aureo-pictum*, leaves green and creamy white, 4 to 6 ft., Australia; *Futokadsura*, ' Japanese Pepper ', greenish, 4 to 6 ft., Japan.

Pipe Vine, see *Aristolochia durior*.

Piptanthus—*Leguminosae*. Slightly tender evergreen flowering shrub, loses its leaves during winter in colder districts. First introduced early nineteenth century.

CULTURE: Soil, rich, sandy loam. Position, warm, sheltered shrubberies S. and S.W. of England; against south walls N. of London. Plant, Sept., Oct., April or May. Prune straggling shoots moderately after flowering.

PROPAGATION: By seeds sown in sandy soil in cool greenhouse or cold frame in spring; cuttings of ripened shoots inserted in small pots of sandy soil under bell-glass or hand-light outdoors, Aug. or Sept.; layering shoots, Sept. or Oct.

SPECIES CULTIVATED: *P. laburnifolius* (syn. *P. nepalensis*), ' Nepal Laburnum ', yellow, May, 8 to 12 ft., Himalaya.

Piqueria—*Compositae*. Greenhouse flowering perennial. First introduced late eighteenth century.

CULTURE: Compost, loam, leaf-mould and sand. Position, pots in greenhouse or bedded out during the summer months. Pot, March or April. Plant in open May or June. Lift and repot in early Oct.

PROPAGATION: By cuttings in spring in gentle bottom heat; by division at potting time; by seeds sown in temp. 60° in Feb.

SPECIES CULTIVATED: *P. trinervia*, white, various seasons, 1 to 1½ ft., Mexico, etc., and var. *variegata*, leaves marked with white. This plant is frequently listed in catalogues as *Stevia serrata*.

Pistachio Nut, see *Pistacia vera.*

Pistacia (Pistachio-nut)—*Anacardiaceae.* Hardy evergreen and deciduous trees. No beauty of flowers which are without petals, but handsome foliage with brilliant autumn tints. First introduced mid-seventeenth century.

CULTURE: Soil, deep, well drained, ordinary. Position, sheltered shrubberies S. and S.W. England; against south walls N. of London. Plant evergreen species, Sept., Oct., April or May; deciduous species, Nov. to Feb.

PROPAGATION: By cuttings inserted in sandy soil in cold frame or under handlight, Sept. or Oct.; layering in Sept. or sowing of imported seeds in cold frame in March.

SPECIES CULTIVATED: *P. atlantica,* ' Mt. Atlas Mastic ', slightly tender, deciduous, 40 ft., N. Africa; *chinensis,* ' Chinese Pistachio ', deciduous, handsome pinnate leaves, best species, hardy, to 75 ft., China; *Lentiscus,* ' Mastic ', tender, evergreen, 15 to 20 ft., Medit.; *Terebinthus,* ' Chian Turpentine ', deciduous, 15 to 30 ft., Asia Minor and Medit.; *vera,* ' Pistachio ', tender, requiring warm wall, but not producing nuts in this country, 20 ft., Levant.

Pistia (Tropical Duck Weed)—*Araceae.* Stove floating aquatic perennial. Flowers, borne on spadix at base of wedge-shaped, notched, pale green, hairy leaves. First introduced early nineteenth century.

CULTURE: Plant in shallow tub or tank in stove. Place 2 in. layer of soil on bottom of tub or tank and plant on surface of water. Replenish with tepid water occasionally. Add fresh soil annually. Temp., March to Oct. 70° to 85°, Oct. to March 60° to 70°. A humid atmosphere is necessary.

PROPAGATION: By offsets.

SPECIES CULTIVATED: *P. stratiotes,* ' Water Lettuce ', yellowish-green ', 1 to 12 in., Jamaica.

Pisum (Pea)—*Leguminosae.* Hardy annual vegetables with edible seeds or pods.

CULTURE OF GARDEN PEAS: Soil, deeply cultivated and well manured. Position, open, sunny. Sow in sheltered site towards end of Feb. and follow at intervals of three weeks until June. There are dwarf and tall as well as early and late varieties. Draw out flat drills 6 to 8 in. wide, 2¼ in. deep and height of var. apart. Draw earth up to plants when 6 in. high and provide twiggy stakes. Mulch to width of 15 in. on each side of row with manure or apply balanced fertiliser when in full flower. Water copiously in dry weather. For very early pods sow under glass in 4½ in. pots in Jan., harden off in cold frame and plant outside in late Feb. or protect Jan. or Sept. sown rows with cloches. Round seeded peas are hardier than the sweeter marrowfat varieties. Quantity of seed required for a row 50 ft. long, 1 pint. Seeds retain their vegetative powers for 3 to 4 years and seeds germinate in 10 to 20 days. Crop reaches maturity in 18 to 24 weeks. Protect seeds from mice and birds by damping them with paraffin and then rolling in red lead.

CULTURE OF SUGAR PEAS: Soil, as for garden peas. Sow in March or April, 2½ in. deep in drills 6 in. wide and 6 ft. apart, and earth up and stake in the usual way. Gather pods when fully developed and cook like French beans.

SPECIES CULTIVATED: *P. sativum,* ' Garden Pea ', white, summer, Europe, Asia, vars. *arvense,* ' Field Pea ', pinkish, summer, climber, *humile,* ' Early Dwarf Pea ', low form with small pods, *macrocarpon,* ' Edible Podded Pea ', soft pods to 6 in.

Pitcairnia—*Bromeliaceae.* Stove perennial herbs. Leaves, narrow or sword-shaped; margins prickly. First introduced mid-eighteenth century.

CULTURE: Compost, equal parts fibrous loam, rough peat and leaf-mould. Pot, March. Water freely always. Good drainage essential. Temp., Sept. to March 60° to 70°, March to Sept. 70° to 80°.

PROPAGATION: By offshoots, inserted in small pots at any time.

SPECIES CULTIVATED: *P. albiflos,* white, Sept 1½ to 2 ft., Brazil; *alta,* red, Aug., 2 to 3 ft., W. Indies; *Andreana,* yellow and red, summer, 1 ft., Venezuela and Colombia; *angustifolia,* red, Sept., 2 to 3 ft., W. Indies; *aphelandrae-*

flora, red, summer, 1 ft., Brazil; *beycalema* (syn. *P. muscosa*), red, winter, 1 ft., Brazil; *staminea*, red, Jan., 1 to 2 ft., Brazil; *violacea*, violet, summer, 1 ft., Brazil. There are forty or more other species of botanical interest.

Pitcher–plant, see Sarracenia and Nepenthes.

Pittosporum (Parchment-bark)—*Pittosporiaceae*. Slightly tender flowering shrubs. Some species very fragrant but all flowers inconspicuous. Attractive foliage grown commercially for florists. First introduced late eighteenth century.

CULTURE IN GREENHOUSE: Compost, two parts fibrous loam, one part fibrous peat, half a part silver sand. Position, pots or tubs in light, airy, sunny greenhouse. Pot, March or April. Prune straggling shoots moderately immediately after flowering. Water moderately Sept. to April, freely afterwards. Syringe occasionally, except when in flower, during summer. Temp., Oct. to April 40° to 50°, April to Oct. 60° to 70°.

CULTURE OUTDOORS: Soil, ordinary, well drained, including chalk. Position, in the open in warmest maritime localities of the south; inland, requiring shelter of wall. Plant, April.

PROPAGATION: By cuttings of moderately firm shoots, 2 to 3 in. long, inserted singly in small pots of sandy soil under bell-glass in shade in temp. 55° to 65° in summer.

HALF-HARDY SPECIES CULTIVATED: *P. crassifolium*, 'Parchment-bark', purple, spring, 15 to 20 ft., New Zealand; *eugenioides*, greenish-yellow, 20 to 30 ft., New Zealand; *Ralphii*, dark purple, spring, 15 ft., New Zealand; *tenuifolium*, the hardiest species, bright green leaves, wavy margins, black stems, chocolate-purple, May, fragrant, 20 to 30 ft., New Zealand; *Tobira*, white, fragrant, summer, 10 to 20 ft., Japan and China; *undulatum*, 'Victorian Box', creamy white, May to July, 30 to 40 ft., Australia; *viridiflorum*, greenish-yellow, June, to 25 ft., S. Africa.

Pityrogramma (Gold and Silver Ferns)—*Polypodiaceae*. Stove ferns, sometimes known as Ceropteris and Gymnogramma. Bipinnate, tufted fronds, interesting for the white or bright yellow powder on the under surface. First introduced late eighteenth century.

CULTURE: Compost, one part fibrous peat, one part leaf-mould and loam, one part silver sand, charcoal and coarsely ground bones. Position, erect species in well-drained pots, drooping species in baskets. Pot, Feb. or March. Water moderately Oct. to Feb., freely afterwards. Syringing or shading not necessary. Temp., Sept. to March 55° to 65°, March to Sept. 65° to 75°.

PROPAGATION: By spores sown on surface of fine sandy peat under bell-glass in temp. 75° to 85° any time; division of plants at potting time; fronds with plantlets pegged on to surface of sandy peat under bell-glass in temp. 70° to 80° at any time.

SPECIES CULTIVATED: *P. calomelanos* (syn. *Gymnogramma calomelanos*), 'Silver Fern', fronds to 3 ft. long and 10 in. wide, powdery white beneath, Trop. America and Africa, var. *aureo-flava* (syns. *Gymnogramma chrysophyllum*, *P. chrysophylla*), 'Gold Fern', gold-coloured powder; *sulphurea* (syn. *Gymnogramma sulphurea*), 'Jamaica Gold Fern', fronds to 1 ft. and 5 in. wide, sulphur-yellow powder, W. Indies; *tartarea* (syn. *Gymnogramma tartarea*), fronds to 2½ ft. and 1 ft. wide, white powdery beneath, Trop. America; *triangularis* (syn. *Gymnogramma triangularis*), 'Californian Gold Fern', fronds to 7 in. long and 6 in. wide, golden-yellow powder beneath, or sometimes white, California to Alaska.

Placea—*Amaryllidaceae*. Greenhouse bulbs. First introduced early nineteenth century.

CULTURE: Compost, two parts sandy loam, one part well-decayed cow manure or leaf-mould, and one part coarse sand. Plant in borders in greenhouse during Aug. or Sept., placing point of bulb just below surface of soil. These plants do not thrive well when confined to pots. Repot annually in Aug. Season of growth,

Jan. to Aug.; season of rest, Aug. to Jan. Temp., Dec. to April 50° to 55°, April to Aug. 60° to 70°, Aug. to Dec. 35° to 40°.

PROPAGATION: By offsets in Aug.

SPECIES CULTIVATED: *P. Arzae*, yellow and purple, summer, 1 ft., Chile; *grandiflora*, white and crimson, summer, 1 ft., Chile; *ornata*, white and red, 1 ft., Chile.

Plagianthus—*Malvaceae*. Slightly tender deciduous flowering trees and shrubs. Some species formerly classified as Plagianthus have now been transferred to Hoheria. First introduced mid-nineteenth century.

CULTURE: Soil, sandy loam and leaf-mould. Position, sheltered border or against a south wall in southern counties only. Plant, Nov. to Feb.

PROPAGATION: By cuttings in sandy soil in a cold frame in autumn; layers in spring.

SPECIES CULTIVATED: *P. betulinus*, yellowish-white, dioecious, summer, 30 to 40 ft., deciduous, New Zealand; *divaricatus*, yellowish-white, May, 8 ft., New Zealand. For the plant often known as *P. Lyallii*, see Hoheria glabrata

Plagiorrhegma, see Jeffersonia.

Plane Tree, see Platanus; **London-**, see *Platanus acerifolia*; **Scotch-**, see *Acer Pseudoplatanus*.

Plantain, see *Musa paradisiaca*; **-Lily**, see Hosta.

Platanus (Plane-tree)—*Platanaceae*. Hardy deciduous trees with ornamental foliage and ball-like clusters of fruits hanging throughout winter, and characteristic peeling bark of trunks and branches. First introduced mid-sixteenth century.

CULTURE: Soil, deep, rich, moist loam. Position, parks, avenues, etc., for Oriental Plane; streets, squares in towns, or in open gardens or shrubberies in country for London Plane. Plant, Oct. to March. Prune into shape when desirable, Oct. to Feb. Plenty of moisture at roots essential; dry soil not suitable.

PROPAGATION: By seeds simply pressed into surface of soil in moist position outdoors in autumn; cuttings of shoots, 6 to 8 in. long, inserted in moist soil in sheltered position in Nov.

SPECIES CULTIVATED: *P. acerfolia*, ' London Plane ', 70 to 100 ft., habitat uncertain, probably a hybrid between following two species, with vars. *pyramidalis*, pyramidal habit, and *Suttneri*, leaves blotched creamy white; *occidentalis*, ' Buttonwood ' or ' American Plane ', seldom grown in England, to 150 ft., South U.S.A.; *orientalis*, ' Oriental Plane ', 80 ft. to 100 ft., S.E. Europe, Asia Minor.

Platycerium—*Polypodiaceae*. Stove and greenhouse evergreen ferns. Fronds, more or less broad, divided, resembling a stag's horn. First introduced early nineteenth century.

CULTURE: Compost, equal parts fibrous peat and sphagnum moss. Position, blocks of wood suspended from roof or sides of greenhouse or stove. Place plant on block of wood, cover roots with layer of moss and peat and secure in position by means of copper wire. Top-dress annually with fresh peat and moss in Feb. or March. Water copiously April to Sept., moderately afterwards. Shade from sun. Temp. for stove species, Oct. to March 55° to 65°, March to Oct. 70° to 80°; greenhouse species, Oct. to March 45° to 55°, March to Oct. 60° to 70°.

PROPAGATION: By offsets in Feb. or March ; also by spores sown in sandy peat in temp. 75° to 85°.

STOVE SPECIES CULTIVATED: *P. grande*, nearly glabrous, fronds stag-like to 6 ft., Australia; *Hillii*, deep green, fertile fronds erect to 1½ ft., Queensland; *Stemaria* (syn. *P. aethiopicum*), fertile fronds, white tomentose beneath, W. Trop. Africa; *Wallichii*, similar to *P. grande* but yellowish tomentose, Malaya; *Willinckii*, Java.

GREENHOUSE SPECIES CULTIVATED: *P. bifurcatum* (syn. *P. alcicorne*), ' Stag's horn Fern ', Australia, and var. *majus*, larger, greener, more leathery.

Platycodon (Balloon Flower)—*Campanulaceae*. Hardy herbaceous perennial. First introduced late eighteenth century.

CULTURE: Soil, ordinary rich. Position, sunny, well-drained borders or rockeries. Plant, Oct., Feb. or March.

PROPAGATION: By seeds sown $\frac{1}{16}$ in. deep in sandy soil in temp. 55°, March or Aug.; cuttings, 3 in. long, of young shoots inserted singly in small pots of light, sandy soil in temp. 55° in March or April; division of plants in April.

SPECIES CULTIVATED: *P. grandiflorum*, ' Chinese Bell-flower ', blue, July to Sept., 1 ft., China and Japan, and vars. *album*, white, *Mariesii*, dwarf white.

Platylobium (Flat Pea)—*Leguminosae*. Greenhouse flowering evergreen shrub. First introduced early nineteenth century.

CULTURE: Compost, three parts peat, one part loam, and little silver sand. Position, well-drained pots in light, airy greenhouse. Pot, Feb. or March. Nip off points of young shoots in spring to induce bushy growth. Water freely April to Sept., moderately Sept. to April. Temp., March to Sept. 55° to 65°, Sept. to March 45° to 50°. Stand plants outdoors from July to Sept. to mature flowering shoots for following year.

PROPAGATION: By seeds sown $\frac{1}{16}$ in. deep in well-drained pots of sandy peat in temp. of 55° to 65° in March or April; cuttings inserted in sandy soil under bell-glass in temp. 55°, April to July.

SPECIES CULTIVATED: *P. obtusangulum*, yellow and red, May, 1 ft., Australia; *triangulare*, yellow, May, 1 ft., Australia.

Platystemon—*Papaveraceae*. Hardy annual. First introduced early nineteenth century.

CULTURE: Soil, good ordinary. Position, sunny beds, borders or rockeries. Sow seed $\frac{1}{8}$ in. deep in patches where required to grow, in April. Thin seedlings 1 to 2 in. apart where $\frac{1}{2}$ in. high. Water freely in dry weather. Mulch with decayed manure or coconut-fibre refuse in June.

SPECIES CULTIVATED: *P. californicus*, ' Cream Cups ', yellow, July, 1 ft., California.

Plectranthus—*Labiatae*. Greenhouse perennial herbs and sub-shrubs allied to Coleus. First introduced early nineteenth century.

CULTURE: Compost, two parts fibrous loam, one part leaf-mould and sand. Position, pots in sunny greenhouse or frame. Pot, March to June. Water freely in summer, moderately at other times. Feed with liquid manure or an approved fertiliser when plants are established in final pots. Temp., March to Oct. 55° to 65°, October to March 45° to 55°.

PROPAGATION: By cuttings of side shoots inserted in sandy soil in propagating frame in temp. 55° to 60° during March or April.

SPECIES CULTIVATED: *P. chiradzulensis*, blue, to 3 ft., winter, Trop. Africa; *fruticosus*, blue, summer, 3 to 4 ft., S. Africa; *Mahonii*, purple, winter, 2 ft., Trop. Africa; *Oertendahlii*, whitish-lavender, Oct. to Nov., 6 in., creeping herb popular in Scandinavia as a window plant, prob. Trop. Africa; *purpuratus*, blue, winter, 18 in., Natal.

Pleioblastus—*Gramineae*. Shrubs with tufted or creeping rootstocks, formerly included in Bambusa and Arundinaria.

CULTURE: Soil, good, not too heavy and of reasonable depth. Position, must be sheltered from cold winds, and dry root conditions are disliked.

PROPAGATION: By division in April and May.

SPECIES CULTIVATED: *P. gramineus* (syn. *Arundinaria Hindsii*), hardy, quick-spreading, 8 ft., Japan; *humilis*, 2 to 5 ft., Japan; *pumilus*, 2 ft., Japan; *Simonii*, quick-growing, 15 ft., Japan.

Pleiocarpa—*Apocynaceae*. Stove flowering shrubs. Flowers fragrant, borne on old wood.

CULTURE: Compost, two parts fibrous loam, one part fibrous peat, one part leaf-mould and silver sand. Position, shady part of stove in summer, light position in winter. Pot, March or April; good drainage essential. Water freely March to Sept., moderately at other times. Syringe twice daily April to Sept. Temp., March to Sept. 75° to 85°, Sept. to March 55° to 65°.

PROPAGATION: By no means easy, but cuttings of firm young side shoots 3 in. long, root slowly in pots of sandy peat under bell-glass in temp. 75° to 85° during spring or late summer.

SPECIES CULTIVATED: *P. mutica*, white, winter, 5 ft., Trop. Africa.

Pleione (Indian Crocus)—*Orchidaceae*. A genus, epiphytic or partially so, and terrestrial. Allied to and at one time included in Coelogyne. Pseudo-bulbs small, rounded, often warted, some flask-shaped, enduring into the second year, but then dwindling as the growths, generally two from each bulb, gain vigour. Leaves deciduous. Flowers large, brightly coloured, in many produced before the leaves gain size, on very short stems.

CULTURE: Compost, two parts osmunda or peat fibre, two parts fibrous loam, two parts sphagnum moss with a little leaf-mould, sand and small charcoal. Repotting is necessary every year, before flowering, or shortly afterwards. Well-drained pans should be used. Several bulbs may be placed at intervals. Bases of the bulbs must not be buried. They may have to be supported in position for a time. Winter night temp. about 50°. Water may not be required throughout the winter. After repotting water infrequently till growths advance, then more often; less frequently as leaves mature. The syringe should not be used. Suspend pans near the glass, shade lightly, summer temp. may reach 75° to 80° by sun heat. Air may be admitted by night as well as day, avoid draughts.

PROPAGATION: Vigorous pseudo-bulbs emit two growths which after forming pseudo-bulbs again throw two growths.

SPECIES CULTIVATED: A selection—*P. Hookeriana*, whitish or rose-flushed, lip blotched brown-purple and yellow, crested, early summer, Sikkim; *humilis*, pale lilac, lip purple lined, veins fringed, margin white haired, small bulbils often produced on apex of parent bulbs, winter, N. India; *lagenaria*, lilac, lip purple-striped, the front blotched crimson-purple, disk yellow with five fringed ridges, variable, winter, early spring, Burma, Assam; *maculata*, white, lip streaked and blotched crimson-purple with five fringed thin keels, late autumn, N. India, Assam, var. *Arthuriana*, petals lined purple; *praecox*, rose-purple, lip paler, with five-toothed keels, margin fringed, winter, N. India, Burma, var. *alba*, white, lip with sulphur-yellow; *Pricei*, rose or lilac, lip whitish, winter, Formosa; *Reichenbachiana*, rose-lilac, lip whitish, with some purple spots, margin haired, disk with fringed keels, winter, Burma.

Pleiospilos (Living Stones)—*Aizoaceae*. Greenhouse succulent plants.

CULTURE: Compost, six parts sharp sand, 2 parts loam. Position, well-drained pots in sunny greenhouse or window, or bed on greenhouse staging. Plant or pot, August. Water freely, Aug. to Dec.; keep quite dry, Jan. to July. Temp., 60° or over at all times.

PROPAGATION: By seeds or cuttings; as Lithops.

SPECIES CULTIVATED: *P. Bolusii* (syn. *Mesembryanthemum Bolusii*), yellow, Sept. to Oct., S.W. Africa; *Hilmari*, yellow, Sept. to Oct., S.W. Africa; *magnipunctata* (syn. *M. magnipunctatum*), yellow, Sept. to Oct., S.W. Africa; *Purpusii*, yellow, Sept. to Oct., S.W. Africa; *simulans* (syn. *M. simulans*), yellow or orange, Sept. to Oct., S.W. Africa.

Pleomele, see Dracaena.

Pleurisy-root, see *Asclepias tuberosa.*

Pleurothallis—*Orchidaceae*. A large epiphytic genus about 500 species (a few terrestrial), widely distributed, Brazil to the W. Indies. Pseudo-bulbs are absent. Leaves solitary, persistent, carried on short or fairly long, slender stems. Flowers from junction of stem and leaf, one, few, clustered or many in a simple raceme, usually small. Habit tufted or creeping. The majority of value only for their freedom of flowering. Considerable variation exists.

CULTURE: Compost and temps. as for Masdevallias. A few may require a higher winter temp. but 50° at night is sufficient for most. Winter waterings are required but consideration must be given to the leaf texture; throughout the summer months water liberally. Light shading is necessary, with that and moisture. Summer temp. may, or may not, be higher than that advised for Odontoglossums and Masdevallias. Small pans or pots are usually suitable but some of the creeping species succeed well on small rafts obliquely inclined, covered with compost, their base fixed in a pot.

PROPAGATION: By division of plants when repotting in early spring. Young plants are in some produced from the base of the old inflorescence, and they may be potted if wanted.

SPECIES CULTIVATED: A selection—*P. astriophora*, very small, blackish-brown, whitish, crimson-purple, pretty, summer; *Birchenallii*, segments attenuated, reddish, greenish, mid-lobe of lip red-haired, spring, Colombia; *cardium*, leaves heart-shaped on slender stems, flowers, one or two, apparently resting on their surface, reddish-copper, lip red, summer, Venezuela; *crinita*, small, greenish, reddish-purple, lip whitish, purple spotted, leaves spotted purple-brown, small, rounded, creeping, raft, winter, Brazil; *grandis*, flowers up to fifty, greenish with a brownish-red suffusion, various, Costa Rica; *immersa*, base of flower spike concealed in two folds of the leaf, greenish-brown with darker stripes, lip dark red, spring, Colombia; *ornata*, small, red to purple-brown, sepal edged with white air-moved filaments, spring, Colombia; *Roezlii*, 15 in. high, scapes as long, flowers comparatively large, deep blackish-purple, lip whitely tomentose, showy, spring, Colombia; *scapha*, segments attenuated, yellowish-white, purple, lined brownish-purple, winter, Venezuela; *stenopetala*, spikes erect, yellowish or greenish-white, attractive, segments tapered, autumn, Brazil.

Plum, see Prunus.

Plumbago (Leadwort)—*Plumbaginaceae*. Stove and greenhouse evergreen flowering shrubs. For hardy species, see Ceratostigma. First introduced mid-eighteenth century.

CULTURE OF STOVE SPECIES: Compost, equal parts fibrous peat and leaf-mould, half a part each loam and sand. Position, pots, shoots trained to stakes or balloon trellis; or in borders, shoots trained to wall in light part of stove. Pot, Feb. to April. Prune shoots moderately in Jan. Water freely April to Oct., moderately afterwards. Syringe daily March to Sept. Shade from sun. Temp., March to Oct. 75° to 85°, Oct. to March 55° to 65°.

CULTURE OF GREENHOUSE SPECIES: Compost, two parts fibrous loam, half a part of silver sand. Position, pots, shoots trained to stakes or trellis; borders, with shoots trained up rafters, pillars, or walls in light part of house. Pot or plant, Feb. or March. Prune shoots to within 1 in. of base immediately after flowering; flowers borne on points of shoots of current year's growth. Water copiously March to Sept. moderately Sept. to Nov., very little afterwards. Syringe daily until flowering begins. Apply weak stimulants twice a week during flowering period. Shade only from very bright sun. Temp., March to Oct. 55° to 65°, Oct. to March 45° to 55°.

PROPAGATION: By seeds sown on surface of sandy peat and slightly covered with fine sandy soil in temp. 65° to 75° in Feb. or March; cuttings of side shoots, 2 to 3 in. long, inserted singly in 2 in. pots of sandy peat in temp. 60° to 70°, Feb. to Aug.

STOVE SPECIES CULTIVATED: *P. indica* (syn. *P. rosea*), purplish-red, winter, 2 ft., India, and var. *coccinea*, larger scarlet flowers; *zeylanica*, white, June, 1½ ft., Tropics.

GREENHOUSE SPECIES CULTIVATED: *P. capensis*, ' Cape Leadwort ', blue, summer, 10 to 15 ft., S. Africa, var. *alba*, white.

Plume Poppy, see *Macleaya cordata*;   **-Thistle,** see Circium.

Plumeria (Frangipani Plant)—*Apocynaceae*. Stove deciduous flowering shrubs. First introduced late seventeenth century.

CULTURE: Compost, two parts sandy loam, one part fibrous peat, half a part silver sand. Position, well-drained pots in light stove. Pot ,Feb. to April. Prune straggling shoots moderately close immediately after flowering. Water freely March to Oct., moderately afterwards. Syringe daily March and until flowers appear. Temp., March to Sept. 70° to 80°, Sept. to March 65° to 75°.

PROPAGATION: By cuttings of ripe shoots, 2 to 3 in. long, inserted in small pots filled with sand under bell-glass in temp. 65° to 75° in Feb.

SPECIES CULTIVATED: *P. bicolor*, white and yellow, July, 10 to 15 ft., S. America; *rubra*, 'Frangipani Plant', red, July, 10 to 15 ft., Trop. America, var. *acutifolia*, white and yellow, fragrant.

Podocarpus—*Taxaceae* (or *Podocarpaceae*). Hardy and slightly tender evergreen trees related to Yew. First introduced mid-nineteenth century.

CULTURE: Soil, good deep loam, well drained. Position, sunny, sheltered lawns or shrubberies. Tender species only suitable for southern gardens or sheltered districts. Plant, Oct. to Nov. or March to April.

PROPAGATION: By cuttings of firm young shoots in small pots of sandy loam under bell-glass in temp. 60° to 70° in summer.

SPECIES CULTIVATED: *P. alpinus*, hardy, 3 to 4 ft., Tasmania; *andinus* (syn. *Prumnopitys elegans*), 'Plum Fir', 'Chilean Yew', 40 to 50 ft., Chile; *dacrydioides*, 'Kahika', to 40 ft., New Zealand; *macrophyllus*, hardy, yellowish leaves, 15 to 25 ft., China, Japan; *nivalis*, 'Alpine Totara', hardy, 3 ft., New Zealand; *nubigena*, 20 to 30 ft., Chile; *salignus* (syn. *P. chilinus*), hardy, 15 to 30 ft., Chile; *spicata*, bronze foliage, 60 to 75 ft., New Zealand.

Podolepis—*Compositae*. Hardy annuals. First introduced early nineteenth century.

OUTDOOR CULTURE OF ANNUAL SPECIES: Soil, ordinary. Position, sunny, well-drained beds or borders or rock gardens. Sow seeds $\frac{1}{16}$ in. deep in well-drained pots of light soil in temp. of 50° in March, transplanting seedlings outdoors in flowering position, end of May; or sow outdoors in sunny position end of April where required to grow and flower, thinning seedlings to 6 to 8 in. apart when $\frac{1}{2}$ in. high.

SPECIES CULTIVATED: *P. acuminata*, yellow, summer, 1 ft., Australia; *aristata*, yellow and pink, summer, 1 ft., Australia.

Podophyllum—*Berberidaceae*. Hardy herbaceous perennials with large, shield-shaped, divided, ornamental foliage. First introduced mid-seventeenth century.

CULTURE: Soil, moist peat. Position, partially shaded borders, woods, marshes or bog gardens. Plant, March or April.

PROPAGATION: By division of roots in March or April.

SPECIES CULTIVATED: *P. emodi*, 'Himalayan May Apple', white, May, 1 ft., coral-red fruits, Himalaya; *peltatum*, 'Duck's Foot', 'May Apple', white, May, 12 to 15 in., yellow fruits, N. America.

Poellnitzia—*Liliaceae*. Greenhouse succulent-leaved plant, native of S. Africa.

CULTURE: As Haworthia.

PROPAGATION: As Haworthia.

SPECIES CULTIVATED: *P. rubriflora* (syn. *Apicra rubrifolia*), flowers red or orange.

Poet's Laurel, see *Laurus nobilis*; **-Narcissus,** see *Narcissus poeticus*.

Pogonia—*Orchidaceae*. A terrestrial genus. Species are seldom seen in cultivation.

CULTURE: Compost, three parts fibrous loam, two parts peat or osmunda fibre, one part sphagnum moss and a little sand. Drainage should be ample. Pots should be used; a rather decided rest is required in winter in a temp. of 55° for the species given here. Summer temp. 70° or more with shading.

PROPAGATION: Can seldom be effected, possibly only by division.

SPECIES CULTIVATED: *P. speciosa* (syn. *Cleistes speciosa*), 4 ft. high, large, few, purple-rose, lip purple-crimson at apex, keels yellow, summer, Brazil.

Poinciana—*Leguminosae* (or *Caesalpiniaceae*). Tender trees or shrubs with bi-pinnate leaves and showy flowers in racemes or panicles, native to warm regions.

CULTURE: As Caesalpinia.

PROPAGATION: As Caesalpinia.

SPECIES CULTIVATED: *P. pulcherrima* (syn. *Caesalpinia pulcherrima*), ' Barbados Pride ', ' Barbados Flower Fence ', orange or yellow with red stamens, pods 4 in. long, more or less prickly glabrous shrub to 10 ft., Tropics, var. *flava*, yellow. See also Delonix.

Poinsettia, see *Euphorbia pulcherrima.*

Poison Ivy, see *Rhus radicans*; **-Sumach,** see *Rhus vernix.*

Pokeberry, see Phytolacca.

Polemonium—*Polemoniaceae.* Hardy herbaceous perennials.

CULTURE: Soil, good ordinary or deep, rich, well-drained loam. Position, open, sunny borders for *P. caeruleum* and vars.; sunny, well-drained rockeries for other species. Plant, Oct., March or April. Cut off flower stems immediately after flowering. Top-dress annually in spring with well-decayed manure or leaf-mould.

PROPAGATION: *P. caeruleum* by division of plants in Oct.; other species by division in March or April.

SPECIES CULTIVATED: *P. caeruleum*, ' Jacob's Ladder ' or ' Greek Valerian ', blue, June, 2 ft., Europe (Br.), var. *album*, white; *carneum*, cream to rose, summer, 12 to 18 in., N.W. America; *confertum*, blue, summer, 6 to 8 in., N.W. America; *flavum*, yellow, summer, 3 ft., New Mexico; *Jacobae* (syn. *P. Richardsonii* hort.), lilac, white or violet-blue, May to Aug., 1 to 1½ ft., hybrid; *reptans*, blue, spring, 6 in., N. America.

Polianthes—*Amaryllidaceae.* Half-hardy, tuberous-rooted plant with fragrant flowers. First introduced early seventeenth century.

CULTURE: Compost, two parts fibrous loam, one part of equal proportions of leaf-mould, decayed manure and coarse silver sand. Pot, African kinds, Oct. to Dec., to flower following autumn; American or Pearl vars. Jan. to April, to flower following winter and spring. Plant bulbs about two-thirds of their depth singly in a 5 in. pot, or three in a 6 in. size. Pot firmly. After treatment: (*a*) Plunge pots to their rims in bottom heat, 75° to 85°, and give one application of water only until growth begins, then remove to a shelf near the glass in temp. 55° to 65°, and remove to temp. 50° to 55° when in bloom. (*b*) Place pots on bed of coal ashes in cold frame, cover with 4 in. peat and give no water until growth begins. After this remove the covering, water moderately, and transfer most forward plants to the greenhouse. (*c*) Pot bulbs in April, plunge pots just above rim in a sunny spot in garden, keep moderately moist, lift pots in Sept. or Oct., and place in greenhouse to flower. Water freely when in full growth. Syringe foliage frequently. Apply stimulants (¼ oz. guano or Clay's fertiliser) once a week when growing freely.

OUTDOOR CULTURE: Soil, ordinary rich. Position, warm, sunny border. Plant tubers 3 in. deep and 6 in. apart, March to April, to flower in Aug. and Sept. Plant fresh stock annually.

PROPAGATION: By offsets.

SPECIES CULTIVATED: *P. tuberosa*, ' Tuberose ', white, fragrant, autumn and winter, 3 ft., Mexico, and var. *flore-pleno*, double.

Polyanthus, see *Primula Polyantha.*

Polybotrya—*Polypodiaceae.* Stove and greenhouse evergreen ferns, formerly included in Acrostichum.

CULTURE: As Acrostichum.

PROPAGATION: As Acrostichum.

STOVE SPECIES CULTIVATED: *P. apiifolium*, 2 to 6 in., Philippines; *appendiculatum*, 6 to 18 in., India; *cervinum*, 2 to 4 ft., Trop. America; *osmundaceum*, 2 to 3 ft., Ecuador.

GREENHOUSE SPECIES CULTIVATED: *P. canaliculatum*, climbing, Venezuela; *Caenopteris*, climbing, Mexico.

Polygala (Milkwort)—*Polygalaceae*. Hardy herbaceous perennials, greenhouse and hardy evergreen flowering shrubs. First introduced mid-seventeenth century.

CULTURE OF HARDY SPECIES: Soil, sandy peat. Position, sunny border or rockery. Plant, Oct., Nov. or April. No pruning required.

CULTURE OF GREENHOUSE SPECIES: Compost, two parts fibrous peat, one part silver sand. Position, well-drained pots in cool, airy greenhouse. Pot, Feb. or March. Prune straggly shoots only into shape, Feb. Water freely April to Sept., moderately afterwards. No stimulants required. Shade unnecessary. Temp., March to Sept. 55° to 65°, Sept. to March 40° to 50°.

PROPAGATION: Hardy species by cuttings inserted in sandy peat under handlight or in cold frame in autumn, or by suckers removed in Sept.; greenhouse species by cuttings of young shoots inserted in small pots of sandy peat under bell-glass in temp. 55° to 65° in spring.

GREENHOUSE SPECIES CULTIVATED: *P. Dalmaisiana*, purplish-red, flowers continuously, 4 to 6 ft., hybrid, will grow in the open against a south wall; *myrtifolia grandiflora*, purple, spring, 4 to 6 ft., S. Africa.

HARDY SPECIES CULTIVATED: *P. calcarea*, blue, May, 2 in., Europe; *Chamaebuxus*, ' Bastard Box ', yellow, summer, 6 to 9 in., Alps, and var. *grandiflora*, crimson and yellow; *microphylla*, blue, summer, 4 to 6 in., S. Europe; *paucifolia*, pink, summer, 4 in., N. America; *Vayrediae*, pink, summer, 4 to 6 in., Spain.

Polygonatum (Solomon's Seal)—*Liliaceae*. Hardy herbaceous perennials.

CULTURE: Soil, ordinary light. Position, partially shaded beds, borders or woodlands. Plant, Oct., Feb. or March. Top-dress annually with decayed manure in March. Apply stimulants occasionally in summer.

POT CULTURE OF P. MULTIFLORUM: Pot roots in ordinary light soil in 6 or 8 in. pots in Nov. Cover with peat outdoors or in frame until growth begins, then remove to heated or cold greenhouse to flower. Water freely.

PROPAGATION: By division of roots in Oct. or March.

SPECIES CULTIVATED: *P. biflorum*, green and white, May, 1 to 3 ft., N. America; *Hookeri*, pink, Himalaya; *latifolium*, white, July, 2 to 3 ft., Europe; *multiflorum*, ' David's Harp ', white, June, 3 ft., Europe; *odoratum* (syn. *P. officinale*), ' Common Solomon's Seal ', white, May, 1 ft., Europe (Br.).

Polygonum (Knotweed)—*Polygonaceae*. Hardy annuals, herbaceous perennials and shrubby climbers.

CULTURE OF ANNUAL SPECIES: Soil, ordinary. Position, sunny, well-drained borders.

CULTURE OF PERENNIAL SPECIES: Soil, ordinary. The strong growing *P. cuspidatum* spreads quickly and is difficult to eradicate but is useful for wild gardens. *P. affine* and *P. vaccinifolium* are useful for rockery. Other species for borders. Plant, Oct. to Nov. or March to April.

CULTURE OF SHRUBBY SPECIES: Soil, ordinary. Position, sunny. Useful, for its quick and vigorous twining growth, to cover trellises, arbours or dead tree stumps.

PROPAGATION: Annuals by seed; perennials by seed or division; shrubby species by Aug. cuttings in sandy soil in shaded frame.

ANNUAL SPECIES CULTIVATED: *P. orientale*, rosy purple, Aug. 4 to 6 ft., Tropics, var. *variegata*, variegated form.

PERENNIAL SPECIES CULTIVATED: *P. affine* (syn. *P. Brunonis*), pink, Aug. to Oct., rich colouring of foliage in autumn and winter, 1 ft., Himalaya; *amplexicaule*, rose-red, autumn, 3 ft., Himalaya; *Bistorta*, pink, May to Aug., 2 ft., Europe; *cuspidatum*, white, summer, 5 to 8 ft., very spreading, Japan; *sachalinense*, white, summer, 10 ft., Island of Sakhalin; *sphaerostachyum*, crimson, July to Aug., 1 ft., Himalaya; *vaccinifolium*, rose-red, summer, trailing, half-shrubby species for moist position, Himalaya; *viviparum*, white or rose pink, May to June, 6 in., Arctic Regions.

SHRUBBY SPECIES CULTIVATED: *P. Aubertii*, white sometimes pink, Aug. to Oct., to 40 ft., not much grown, China; *baldschuanicum*, white tinged pink, to 20 ft. annually, July to Oct., popular vigorous climber, Bokhara.

Polypodium (Polypody)—*Polypodiaceae*. Stove greenhouse and hardy evergreen and deciduous ferns.

CULTURE OF STOVE AND GREENHOUSE SPECIES: Compost, equal parts loam, peat, leaf-mould and silver sand. Pot, Feb. to April. Position, pots, baskets or rock beds. Shade from sun essential. Moist atmosphere Feb. to Sept., moderately so afterwards. No syringing required. Water freely March to Sept., moderately Sept. to March. No stimulants. Temp. stove species, March to Oct. 65° to 75°, Oct. to March 55° to 65°; greenhouse, March to Oct. 55° to 65°, Oct. to March 40° to 50°.

CULTURE OF HARDY SPECIES: Soil, equal parts fibrous peat, decayed turf loam, leaf-mould and coarse silver sand for *P. vulgare* and vars. Position, *P. vulgare*, shady fernery, bank or rockery, other species anywhere in shade in ordinary soil. Plant, April. Water in dry weather. Top-dress annually in April with above compost.

POT CULTURE OF HARDY SPECIES: Compost, as above. Pot, March. Position, shady, airy, cold greenhouse, pit or frame. Water evergreen kinds freely in summer, moderately at other times; deciduous kinds freely whilst growing occasionally after foliage dies down. Repot annually.

PROPAGATION: By spores sown on surface of shallow pan or box filled with fine sandy peat covered with pane of glass and placed in temp. 65° to 75°; division of roots in March or April.

STOVE SPECIES CULTIVATED: *P. comans* (syn. *P. conjugatum*), Trop. Asia; *heracleum*, Java; *Meyenianum*, ' Bear's Paw Fern ', Philippines; *musifolium*, Malaya; *pectinatum*, W. Indies; *persicifolium*, Malaya; *Phymatodes*, E. India; *plumula*, W. Indies; *punctatum*, Old World Tropics; *verrucosum*, Philippines.

GREENHOUSE SPECIES CULTIVATED: *P. argutum*, fronds slender, dark green, to 3 ft., Nepal; *aureum*, W. Indies; *brasiliense* (syn. *Goniophlebium albo-punctatum*), fronds broad to 2 ft., Brazil; *Billardieri*, Australia; *Catharinae*, nearly erect to 1½ ft., Brazil; *fraxinifolium* (syn. *Goniophlebium deflexum*), 1½ ft., Brazil; *lepidopteris* (syn. *Goniophlebium sepultum*), narrow fronds to 1½ ft., S. America; *piloselloides*, creeping, W. Indies; *pustulatum*, ' Scented Polypody ', Australia and New Zealand; *subauriculatum* (syn. *Goniophlebium subauriculatum*), drooping fronds to 6 ft., good for large stout baskets, Java.

HARDY SPECIES CULTIVATED: *P. vulgare*, ' Adder's Fern ', ' Common Polypody ', Britain, etc., and many vars.

Polypody, see Polypodium.

Polyscias—*Araliaceae*. Stove evergreen and ornamental foliage plants and shrubs. First introduced mid-seventeenth century.

CULTURE: Compost, equal parts loam, peat, leaf-mould, charcoal and sand. Pot, Feb. to April. Water freely March to Oct., moderately afterwards. Temp., March to Sept. 70° to 80°, Sept. to March 60° to 70°.

PROPAGATION: By cuttings and portions of the roots in sandy soil in warm propagating frame in April.

SPECIES CULTIVATED: *P. Balfouriana* (syn. *Aralia Balfourii*), leaves green and creamy white, New Caledonia; *dissecta*, leaves finely segmented, origin unknown; *filicifolia*, fern-leaved, Pacific Islands; *fruticosa*, handsome pinnate leaves, Trop. Asia; *Guilfoylei*, ' Wild Coffee ', ' Coffee Tree ', Polynesia, and vars. *laciniata*, *monstrosa*, and *Victoriae*. See also Nothopanax and Pseudopanax.

Polystachya—*Orchidaceae*. An epiphytic genus, chiefly African and Eastern but represented in America. Very varied. Pseudo-bulbs pronounced in some, as thickened, often leafy, stems in others. Many are small-growing. The spikes are terminal. Flowers small, usually inverted, one to many. A few species are noteworthy from the bright colour and number of their blooms.

CULTURE: Compost, half osmunda or similar fibre, half sphagnum moss with sand and a few decayed leaves. Small pots or pans should be used. Species from the tropics should have a winter temp. of 65° to 70°. From cooler districts especially, if decided pseudo-bulbs are present, 55° to 60° is sufficient on winter nights. Temps. in summer, higher for all, with shading and moisture. Water freely in summer but decide winter waterings by the nature of the stems or bulbs.

PROPAGATION: By division of plants in spring. *P. paniculata* has been raised from seed.

SPECIES CULTIVATED: A selection—*P. affinis* (syn. *P. bracteosa*), many, yellow, brown marked and suffused, summer, W. Africa; *cucullala* (syn. *P. grandiflora*), 1 to 3, comparatively large, greenish-yellow, marked dull purple, summer, autumn, Sierra Leone; *leonensis*, light green, suffused purplish, lip whitish, autumn, Sierra Leone; *luteola*, often branched, yellowish-green, fragrant, various, Trop. America; *paniculata*, scape branched, small, many, red-orange and yellowish, various, Uganda; *Pobeguinii* (syn. *Epiphora pubescens*), scape long, many, rose-crimson, lip darker, shallow pan or raft, summer, Guinea.

Polystichum—*Polypodiaceae.* Stove greenhouse and hardy ferns. This genus includes many previously classed as Aspidium and Lastrea. Heights vary from 1 to 3 ft.

CULTURE OF STOVE AND GREENHOUSE SPECIES: Compost, two parts peat, one part loam, silver sand and charcoal. Pot, March. Water freely in summer, moderately in winter. Shade from sun. Temp. for stove species, Sept.' to March 60° to 70°, March to Sept. 55° to 65°.

CULTURE OF HARDY SPECIES: Compost, equal parts loam, peat, leaf-mould and coarse silver sand. Position, shady or partially shady spots. Plant in Oct. or April. Water freely in dry weather.

PROPAGATION: Stove and greenhouse species by spores sown in sandy peat any time; division in March. Hardy species by division of crowns in April, also by spores sown on sterilised loam and kept close under glass cover.

STOVE SPECIES CULTIVATED: *P. amabile*, India and Japan; *echinatum*, Jamaica; *macrophyllum*, Brazil and W. Indies; *viviparum*, W. Indies.

GREENHOUSE SPECIES CULTIVATED: *P. adiantiforme*, Tropics; *hispidum* (syn. *Nephrodium hispidum*), New Zealand; *lepidocaulon*, Japan; *pungens*, Cape Colony; *triangulum*, N. India; *vestitum*, New Zealand, Chile, etc.

HARDY SPECIES CULTIVATED: *P. acrostichoides*, N. America; *aculeatum*, Europe (Br.), and numerous vars.; *Lonchitis*, Europe (Br.); *munitum*, N. America.

Pomaderris—*Rhamnaceae.* Greenhouse flowering shrubs. First introduced early nineteenth century.

CULTURE: Equal parts sandy loam, peat and leaf-mould with sharp sand to ensure porosity. Position, well-drained pots or beds in greenhouse or conservatory. Pot or plant, March or April. Prune in Feb. or March. Temp., March to Sept. 65° to 75°, Sept. to March 55° to 65°. Water moderately Oct. to Feb., freely at other times. Syringe freely except when in flower. Feed liberally with liquid or artificial manure when established.

PROPAGATION: By cuttings of half-ripened shoots inserted in sandy soil under bell-glass in temp. 65° to 70°.

SPECIES CULTIVATED: *P. apetala*, greenish, June, 3 to 6 ft., Australia, New Zealand; *elliptica*, pale yellow, May and June, 6 ft., Australia, New Zealand; *phylicaefolia*, pale yellow, April, 2 ft., New Zealand.

Pomegranate, see *Punica Granatum.*

Poncirus (Hardy Orange)—*Rutaceae.* Hardy deciduous spiny shrub, allied to the orange. Formerly included in Aegle. Used as a rootstock for citrus fruits to improve their hardiness.

CULTURE: Deep, loamy soil. Position, sunny shrubberies or as a hedge plant.

PROPAGATION: By seeds sown ¼ in. deep in a frame or greenhouse in March; cuttings of half-ripened wood in a close frame in June or July.

Species Cultivated: *P. trifoliata* (syns. *Aegle sepiaria, Citrus trifoliata*), white, small bitter fruits similar in appearance to oranges, sharply spined, May, 8 ft., China, Japan.

Pond Weed, see Potamogeton.

Pontederia—*Pontederiaceae.* Hardy aquatic perennials. First introduced late sixteenth century.

Culture: Soil, rich loam. Position, shallow ponds or tanks containing water 6 to 12 in. in depth. Plant, March to June.

Propagation: By division of roots any time in spring.

Species Cultivated: *P. cordata,* ' Pickerel Weed ', blue, white, and green, summer, 2 ft., N. America, and var. *lancifolia* (syns. *P. angustifolia* or *P. lanceolata*). bright blue, not as hardy as the type, 4 to 5 ft.

Poor Man's Weather Glass, see *Anagallis arvensis.*

Popinac, see *Acacia Farnesiana.*

Poplar, see Populus.

Poppy, see Papaver and Meconopsis; **Californian-,** see *Eschscholtzia californica*; **Californian Tree-,** see *Romneya Coulteri*; **Horned-,** see Glaucium; **-Mallow,** see Callirhoe; **Matilija-,** see *Romneya Coulteri*; **Plume-,** see *Macleya cordata*; **Prickly-,** see *Argemone mexicana*; **Sea-,** see Glaucium; **Tree-,** see Dendromecon.

Populus (Poplar)—*Salicaceae.* Hardy deciduous trees. Flowers, catkin-shaped, March and April. Wood, soft, yellow or white; used for toy-making, spade handles, etc. Weight of timber per cubic foot, 30 lb.

Culture: Soil, ordinary, moist. Position, margins of ponds, lakes, rivers, moist shrubberies or woods. *P. deltoides and P. nigra italica*, good trees for forming screens in town or suburban gardens. Plant, Oct. to Feb. For screens, plant 4 to 6 ft. apart. Prune, Nov. to Feb. Dry soils not suitable.

Propagation: By cuttings of firm shoots, 8 in. long, inserted in ordinary soil outdoors in Oct. or Nov.; layering shoots in Oct.; suckers, Oct. to Feb.; weeping kinds by grafting on common poplars in March.

Species Cultivated: *P. alba,* ' White Poplar ', ' Abele ', leaves green above, white beneath, 50 to 90 ft., Europe (Br.), N. Asia, etc., and vars. *Richardii,* leaves dull yellow above, white beneath, and *Bolleana,* ' White Pyramidal Poplar '; *angulata,* heart-shaped leaves, 60 to 80 ft., probably hybrid; *berolinensis,* ' Berlin Poplar ', vigorous, columnar shape, to 70 ft., hybrid; *canadensis,* ' Carolina Poplar ', hybrid, and vars. *aurea,* leaves yellow, *marilandica,* vigorous quick growth, and *serotina,* to 100 ft., wide-spreading, ascending branches; *candicans,* ' Balm of Gilead ', very fragrant young foliage, 60 to 90 ft., origin unknown; *canescens,* ' Grey Poplar ', grey leaves, branches and trunk to 100 ft., W. Europe, including Britain; *deltoides* (syns. *P. balsamifera, P. monilefera*), ' Balsam Poplar ', ' Cotton-wood ', young foliage pleasantly balsam-scented, 70 to 100 ft., N. America; *Fremontii,* ' Fremont's Cottonwood ', 50 to 90 ft., California; *generosa,* very vigorous hybrid; *lasiocarpa,* immense leaves, red stalks, 40 to 60 ft., Cent. China; *laurifolia,* good for heavy soils, 40 to 50 ft., Siberia; *Maximowiczii,* large leathery leaves, white beneath, 70 to 90 ft., N.E. Asia and Japan; *nigra,* ' Black Poplar ', not so common as vars. *betulifolia,* ' Downy Black Poplar ', to 100 ft., *italica,* ' Lombardy Poplar ', well-known columnar tree, to 125 ft., and *thevestina,* similar to Lombardy but with a white trunk; *suaveolens,* balsam odour, 50 ft., Siberia; *tremula,* ' Aspen ', perpetually quivering leaves, 40 to 50 ft., Europe, including Britain, with vars. *pendula,* ' Weeping Aspen ' and *purpurea,* purple-tinged foliage; *tremuloides,* ' American Aspen ', not frequent in Britain, 50 to 100 ft., N. America; *trichocarpa,* ' Western Balsam ', ' Black Cottonwood ', the best of the Balsam Poplars, very quick growing, 75 to 150 ft., Western N. America.

Porcupine Rush, see *Scirpus Tabernaemontani* var. *zebrinus.*

Portlandia—*Rubiaceae.* Stove evergreen flowering shrubs. First introduced mid-eighteenth century.

CULTURE: Compost, equal parts fibrous loam and leaf-mould and half a part silver sand. Pot, Feb. or March. Position, well-drained pots in partially shaded part of stove. Prune into shape immediately after flowering. Water copiously April to Sept., moderately afterwards. Syringe twice daily March to Oct., once afterwards. Temp., March to Sept. 70° to 85°, Sept. to March 60° to 70°.

PROPAGATION: By cuttings of firm shoots, 2 to 3 in. long, inserted in sand under bell-glass in temp. 75° to 85° in summer.

SPECIES CULTIVATED: *P. coccinea*, scarlet, June, 2 to 3 ft., Jamaica; *grandiflora*, white, June, fragrant, 8 to 10 ft., W. Indies; *platantha*, white, summer, 1½ to 3 ft., habitat uncertain.

Portugal Laurel, see *Prunus lusitanica.*

Portulaca—*Portulacaceae.* Hardy and half-hardy annual flowering and edible-leaved plants. Leaves of purslane form an excellent summer salading. First introduced late sixteenth century.

CULTURE OF HALF-HARDY ANNUAL SPECIES: Soil, good ordinary. Position, sunny rockeries, raised beds or borders. Sow seeds thinly on surface of light, sandy soil in well-drained pot, box or pan, lightly cover with fine soil, and place in temp. 55° in March. Transplant seedlings when three leaves have formed into 2 in. pots, gradually harden off, and plant outdoors end of May. Water in dry weather. Plant 6 in. apart each way.

POT CULTURE: Compost, equal parts loam, leaf-mould, with a little silver sand. Raise plants from seeds as advised above. Transplant four seedlings into 5 in. pots, well-drained and filled with above compost. Grow near glass in temp. 55° to 65°. Water freely. Apply weak stimulants when in flower.

CULTURE OF PURSLANE: Soil, light, rich ordinary. Position, sunny, well-drained borders. Sow seeds thinly broadcast, middle of April, lightly rake in and keep well watered. To ensure a succession, sow at intervals of a month up to Aug. Gather shoots when 2 to 3 in. long, cutting them off close to the ground.

SPECIES CULTIVATED: *P. grandiflora*, ' Sun Plant ', red, yellow, rose, or white, 6 in., Brazil, and vars. *compacta*, various colours, *Thellusonii*, orange-scarlet, *Thornburnii*, yellow, and many others; *oleracea*, ' Purslane ', June, 6 in., Tropics.

Posoqueria—*Rubiaceae.* Stove evergreen flowering shrubs. First introduced early nineteenth century.

CULTURE: Compost, one part loam, one part peat, one part well-decayed manure and charcoal. Position, well-drained pots, or beds in plant stove. Pot or plant, Feb. or March. Prune into shape, Feb. or March. Temp., March to Sept. 65° to 85°, Sept. to March 55° to 65°. Water moderately Oct. to Feb., freely afterwards. Syringe daily (except when in bloom) March to Sept. Apply liquid manure occasionally to healthy plants in flower. Plants one to two years old produce the best blooms.

PROPAGATION: By cuttings of firm young side shoots, 2 to 3 in. long, inserted in well-drained pots of sandy peat under bell-glass in temp. 75° to 85°, Jan. to April.

SPECIES CULTIVATED: *P. formosa*, white, fragrant, summer, 15 to 20 ft., Venezuela; *fragrantissima*, white, fragrant, summer, 8 to 10 ft., Brazil; *latifolia*, white, Oct., 6 ft., Trop. America.

Potamogeton (Pondweed)—*Potamogetonaceae.* Large genus of hardy, under-water aquatics, used in pools and rivers for oxygenating water and as cover for fish.

CULTURE: Soil, mud at base of pond. Plant, spring to autumn, in boxes, or weight clumps of plant and sink in water.

PROPAGATION: By division.

SPECIES CULTIVATED: *P. crispus*, Britain; *pectinatus*, thread-like foliage, Europe; *perfoliatus*, bronze, Britain.

Potato, see *Solanum tuberosum*;   **Sweet-,** see *Ipomoea Batatas.*

Potentilla (Cinquefoil)—*Rosaceae*. Hardy herbaceous perennials or sub-shrubs. The hybrid garden potentillas are the result of crosses between *P. argyrophylla* and *P. nepalensis*.

CULTURE OF HERBACEOUS SPECIES: Soil, ordinary deep, rich, sandy. Position, sunny rockeries for dwarf species; sunny borders for tall. Plant, Oct., Nov., March or April. Mulch tall kinds with decayed manure annually in March. Water copiously in dry weather. Apply stimulants occasionally during flowering period. Lift, divide and replant border kinds in fresh soil every three or four years.

CULTURE OF SHRUBBY SPECIES: Soil, deep loam. Position, sunny shrubberies or borders. Plant, Nov. to Feb. Plants require abundant moisture. Mulch with strawy manure in May.

PROPAGATION: Herbaceous species by seeds sown $\frac{1}{16}$ in. deep in shallow pans or boxes of light, sandy soil in temp. 55° to 65°, March, transplanting seedlings outdoors in May or June, or similar depth in partially shaded border outdoors in April; division of roots, Oct., Nov., March or April; shrubby species by seeds treated as herbaceous kinds, or by cuttings of well-ripened wood during Aug. or Sept. in sandy soil in unheated frame.

ALPINE AND HERBACEOUS SPECIES CULTIVATED: *P. alba*, white, spring, 6 to 9 in., Europe (Br.); *alchemilloides*, white, summer, 9 to 12 in., Pyrenees; *alpestris* (syn. *P. Crantzii*), yellow, May to June, 6 in., Europe, Asia Minor, Caucasus, Arctic America; *argyrophylla*, yellow, summer, 2 to 3 ft., Himalaya; *atrosanguinea*, crimson, 2 to 3 ft., summer, Himalaya; *aurea*, yellow, summer, 4 to 6 in., Europe, and var. *plena*, double; *Clusiana*, white, June, 6 in., Europe; *coriandrifolia*, yellow, 4 to 6 in., summer, Himalaya, Yunnan; *cuneata* (syn. *P. ambigua*), yellow, summer, 4 to 6 in., Himalaya; *Detommasii*, yellow, 4 in., Europe, Asia Minor; *eriocarpa*, yellow, June to July, 2 in., Himalaya; *fragiformis*, yellow, summer, 9 in., Asia, Alaska; *fulgens*, crimson, summer, 9 to 12 in., Himalaya; *grandiflora*, yellow, summer, 12 in. Pyrenees; *Griffithii*, yellow, June, 12 in., Himalaya; *Hippiana*, yellow, summer, 12 in., N. America; *Hopwoodiana*, yellow and rose, summer, 18 in., hybrid; *multifoliata*, flowers inconspicuous, foliage fern-like, 6 to 9 in., Arizona; *nepalensis*, rose-red, summer, 18 in., Himalaya, and vars. *Roxana*, salmon-red, and *Willmottiae*, vivid rose; *nevadensis*, yellow, summer, 4 in., Spain; *nitida*, rose, June to July, 2 in., Europe, and var. *alba*; *recta-macrantha* (syn. *P. Warrenii*), yellow, June to July, 12 to 15 in., Europe, and var. *pygmaea*; *Tonguei*, terra-cotta, summer, 3 in., hybrid; *verna*, yellow, summer, 4 to 6 in., Europe, and var. *nana*, dwarf.

SHRUBBY SPECIES CULTIVATED: *P. fruticosa*, widely distributed throughout Europe, Asia and America, to 4 ft., yellow, summer, many vars., for which see trade lists.

Poterium—*Rosaceae*. Deciduous low shrub with branched spines. For other plants listed as Poterium, see Sanguisorba.

CULTURE: Soil, ordinary. Position, sunny or shady borders.

PROPAGATION: By cuttings.

SPECIES CULTIVATED: *P. spinosum*, red, to 1 ft., branched, S. Europe.

Pratia—*Lobeliaceae*. Hardy herbaceous perennial trailing plants. First introduced early nineteenth century.

OUTDOOR CULTURE: Soil, two parts peat, one part leaf-mould, and little sand. Position, sunny well-drained rockeries. Plant, March or April. Water freely in dry weather.

POT CULTURE: Compost, two parts sandy loam, half a part each leaf-mould and silver sand. Pot, March. Position, cool or cold greenhouse, frame or window. Water freely April to Sept., moderately afterwards. Apply weak stimulants occasionally when flowering. Shade from midday sun.

PROPAGATION: By seeds sown $\frac{1}{16}$ in. deep in equal parts loam, leaf-mould and sand in temp. 85°, March; cuttings of young shoots inserted in well-drained pots,

July to Sept., and stored in cold frame or greenhouse until March, then planted outdoors.

SPECIES CULTIVATED: *P. angulata* (syn. *Lobelia littoralis*), white, summer, 1 in., New Zealand; *nummularia* (syns. *P. begonifolia, Lobelia begonifolia*); *begonifolia* (syn. *Lobelia begonifolia*), blue, summer, Himalaya; *Treadwellii*, white, purple berries, creeping, New Zealand.

Prickly Ash, see *Zanthoxylum americanum*; **-Heath,** see Pernettya; **-Pear,** see Opuntia; **-Phlox,** see *Gilia californica*; **-Poppy,** see *Argemone mexicana*; **-Thrift,** see Acantholimon.

Primula (Primrose)—*Primulaceae.*   Greenhouse and hardy perennial plants. First introduced late sixteenth century.

CULTURE OF GREENHOUSE SPECIES: Sow seeds of *P. sinensis* and *P. obconica* from April to June, *P. malacoides* June to July, on surface of compost of two parts leaf-mould, one part loam and half a part sand pressed moderately firmly in a shallow pan, or 6 in. pot half filled with drainage material, cover seeds thinly with similar soil. Place pane of glass over pot and put in temp. 55° to 60°. Shade from sun and keep just moist. Transplant seedlings when large enough to handle 1 in. apart in well-drained pots or pans filled with same compost. When leaves of seedlings meet each other, place singly in 3 in. pots, keep in same temp. for a week then transfer to cold frame. Shade from sun, admit air freely and sprinkle foliage in evening. Transfer when well rooted to 5 in. pots filled with compost of one part fibrous loam, half a part each leaf-mould and decayed cow manure and half a part silver sand. Replace in frame, shade from sun, water moderately and sprinkle foliage as before. Apply liquid soot and cow or sheep manure twice a week when well rooted. Water freely and remove to temp. 50° to 55° in Sept. Admit air freely on fine days. When potting allow base of leaves just to touch the compost, pot moderately firmly. Apply artificial manure twice weekly to plants established in flowering pots. Temp. for flowering *P. sinensis*, 50° to 55°; *P. obconica* and *P. malacoides*, 45° to 55°. Single-flowered kinds are best raised from seed annually, rejecting old plants after flowering. Sow in June for spring flowering.

CULTURE OF HARDY SPECIES: Soil, open sandy loam containing peat and leaf-mould. Position, shaded rock gardens, beds or borders. Cool, shady banks and glades in rock garden for *P. farinosa, P. frondosa, P. glutinosa, P. Juliae* and *P. scotica.* Light, well-drained, peaty loam with plenty of sand and stone chippings in open position on sunny banks or crevices of rock garden for *P. carniolica, P. Clusiana, P. cottia, P. deorum, P. glaucescens, P. hirsuta, P. integrifolia, P. marginata, P. minima, P. Palinuri, P. pedemontana, P. spectabilis, P. viscosa* and *P. Wulfeniana.* All require abundant moisture. *P. Allionii, P. carniolica, P. Forrestii, P. frondosa, P. hirsuta, P. marginata, P. Menziesiana, P. nutans, P. pedemontana, P. Reidii, P. Reinii* and *P. Waltonii* are suitable for alpine house. The following species are suitable for waterside planting: *P. alpicola, P. aurantiaca, P. Beesiana, P. Bulleyana, P. burmanica, P. denticulata, P. Florindae, P. helodoxa, P. japonica, P. mollis, P. pulverulenta, P. rosea, P. sikkimensis, P. Veitchii, P. Waltonii.* Plant, Sept. to Oct. or March to April. Mulch beds containing choice kinds with decayed manure or compost in Feb. Lift those used for bedding directly after flowering, divide and replant 6 in. apart each way in shady border until Sept., then replant in beds.

POT CULTURE: Compost, two parts turfy loam, one part cow manure and leaf-mould, half a part silver sand. Position, airy frame or cool greenhouse in 3 in. pots. Pot, Feb. or March. Water moderately in winter, freely other times, apply weak liquid manure to plants in flower.

CULTURE OF AURICULA: Alpine type have blooms one colour, white or yellow eye, stems smooth and free from powder. Florists' type, stems and blooms covered with mealy powder, blooms with more than one colour, and white-, grey- or green-edged petals. Properties of Florists' Auriculas, stem erect, elastic, carrying truss well above foliage; stalk proportionately long to size of petals; pips (blooms), seven to each truss, round; anthers, bold; eye, white, smooth and round; colours, well defined, rich; edges, distinct. Compost, two parts turfy loam, one part cow manure and leaf-mould, half a part silver sand. Position, choice kinds in 3 in. pots in airy frame or cool greenhouse; others in rich soil in shady borders. Pot and plant, Feb. or March. Water those in pots moderately in winter, freely other times. Top-dress with rich soil in March plants that were not repotted. Apply liquid manure in weak solution to plants in flower.

CULTURE OF PRIMROSE AND POLYANTHUS: Soil, ordinary rich, moist. Position, partly or wholly shaded beds and borders. Plant, Oct. to Nov., Feb. to March. Mulch surface of beds containing choice kinds with rotted manure or compost in Feb. Lift those used for bedding directly after flowering, divide and replant 6 in. apart each way in shady border until Oct. then replant in beds. Polyanthus Classification: Gold-laced, centre and edges of bloom golden; fancy, blooms of various hues; hose-in-hose, semi-double, one bloom growing out of another; Jack-in-the-Green, bloom surrounded by a collar-like calyx; pantaloon, small, curiously coloured blooms.

PROPAGATION: By seed or division.

GREENHOUSE SPECIES CULTIVATED: *P. floribunda*, yellow, winter and spring, 9 in., Himalaya; *Forbesii*, rose or lilac, winter and spring, 12 in., China; *kewensis*, yellow, winter and spring, 9 to 12 in., hybrid; *malacoides*, lilac and rose, winter and spring, 12 to 18 in., China, and many vars.; *obconica*, lilac, winter and spring, 6 to 9 in., China, and vars. with white, pink, red and magenta flowers; *sinensis*, ' Chinese Primrose ', various, winter and spring, 9 in., China; *verticillata*, yellow, spring, 12 to 15 in., Arabia.

HARDY SPECIES CULTIVATED: *P. Allionii*, pink, spring, 2 in., Maritime Alps; *alpicola*, yellow, fragrant, 18 to 24 in., summer, Tibet; *anisodora*, deep purple, summer, 12 to 15 in., Yunnan; *amoena*, white to rich purple, spring, 9 to 12 in., Caucasus; *aurantiaca*, reddish-orange, summer, 9 to 12 in., China; *Auricula*, various, spring, 6 to 8 in., Alps; *auriculata*, red-purple, summer, 9 to 12 in., Asia Minor to Caucasus; *Beesiana*, rose-carmine, summer, 18 in., China; *Bulleyana*, orange, summer, 18 in., Yunnan; *burmanica*, reddish-purple, summer, 18 in., Burma; *capitata*, deep purple, fragrant, early summer, 9 to 12 in., Himalaya, Tibet; *carniolica*, rose, fragrant, spring, 4 to 6 in., Alps; *chionantha*, white, fragrant, summer, 12 to 15 in., Yunnan; *chungensis*, pale orange, summer, 12 in., Yunnan; *Clusiana*, rich rose, spring, 6 in., E. Alps; *Cockburniana*, rich orange, summer, 12 to 18 in., China; *cottia*, rose-pink, spring, 4 in., Cottian Alps; *denticulata*, white, spring, 12 to 15 in., China, and various coloured vars.; *deorum*, purple, spring, 6 in., Bulgaria; *elatior*, ' Oxlip ', yellow, spring, 9 in., Britain; *farinosa*, ' Bird's-eye Primrose ', rose, spring, 4 to 6 in., Europe (Br.); *Florindae*, yellow, summer, 24 in., Tibet; *Forrestii*, yellow, summer, 12 in., Yunnan; *frondosa*, pink, spring, 6 in., Bulgaria; *geraniifolia*, red to deep pink, summer, 9 in., Himalaya; *glaucescens*, blue, spring, 4 to 6 in., Alps; *glutinosa*, purple, fragrant, spring, 4 in., Alps; *helodoxa*, ' Glory of the Marsh ', yellow, summer, 2 to 3 ft., Yunnan; *heucherifolia*, red-purple, summer, 6 in., Himalaya; *hirsuta*, pink, lilac or white, 4 in., Alps; *integrifolia*, reddish-lilac, spring, 3 in., Alps; *involucrata*, white, fragrant, summer, 9 to 12 in., Himalaya; *japonica*, red, summer, 18 in., Japan, and many forms and vars.; *Juliae*, pink, spring, 2 to 3 in., Caucasus; *Juliana*, various, spring, 6 in., hybrid; *luteola*, sulphur-yellow, summer, 12 in., Caucasus; *marginata*, lavender, spring, 3 to 6 in., Alps; *Menziesiana*, purple, spring, 4 in., Bhutan; *minima*, pink, spring, 1 in., Alps; *mollis*, rose, 12 to 16 in., Himalaya; *Mooreana*, deep purple, summer, 9 in., Himalaya; *nutans*, deep lavender, fragrant, summer, China; *Palinuri*, yellow, spring, 9 in., S. Italy; *pedemontana*, pink, 2 to 3 in., spring, Alps; *Poissonii*, purple-crimson, summer, 12 to 18 in., China; *polyantha*, ' Polyanthus ', various, spring, 9 to 12 in., hybrid; *Pruhoniciana* (syns. *P. Julianae, P. Helenae*), lilac and magenta to white, Mar. to April, 1½ to 3 in., hybrid, many vars.; *pulverulenta*, red, summer, 12 to 18 in., China; *Reidii*, ivory-white, early summer, 4 to 6 in. Himalaya; *Reinii*, pink, 6 to 9 in., summer, Japan; *rosea*, crimson, spring, 6 to 9 in., Himalaya; *scotica*, bluish-purple, spring, 1 to 2 in., Scotland; *secundiflora*, deep rose-red, early summer, 12 in., Yunnan; *sibirica*, lilac, summer, 12 in., Asia to N. Europe; *Sieboldii*, various, summer, 12 in., Japan; *sikkimensis*, yellow, summer, 12 in., Sikkim; *sinopurpurea*, summer, 12 to 15 in., Yunnan; *Smithiana*, yellow, summer, 18 in., Himalaya; *spectabilis*, rose pink, spring, 4 in., Alps; *sphaerocephala*, deep purple, summer, 9 to 12 in., China; *Veitchii*, rose-purple, early summer, 9 to 12 in., China; *veris* (syn. *P. officinalis*), ' Cowslip ', yellow, spring, 6 to 9 in., Britain; *viscosa*, pink, fragrant, spring, 6 in., Alps; *vulgaris* (syn. *P. acaulis*), ' Primrose ', yellow, spring, 4 to 6 in., Britain; *Waltonii*, violet, spring, Tibet; *Wilsonii*, purple, summer, 12 to 15 in., Yunnan; *Winteri*, lavender, winter, 3 to 6 in., Himalaya; *Wulfeniana*, purple, spring, 4 in., E. Alps; *yargongensis*, white to deep mauve, summer, 9 to 12 in., China. There are many beautiful hybrids.

Prince of Wales's Feather Fern, see *Leptopteris superba*.

Prince's Feather, see *Amaranthus hybridus* var. *hypochondriacus*.

Prinsepia—*Rosaceae*. Hardy deciduous flowering shrubs armed with spines. First introduced early twentieth century.

CULTURE: Soil, ordinary loamy. Position, open shrubberies or borders. Plant, Nov. to Feb.

PROPAGATION: By seeds stratified and sown the following March or April in drills in the open; cuttings of young wood in gentle bottom heat; layering in spring.

SPECIES CULTIVATED: *P. sinensis* (syn. *Phagiospermum sinense*), yellow, Feb. to March, 3 to 6 ft., Manchuria; *uniflora*, white, March, 3 to 4 ft., N.W. China.

Prionium (Palmiet)—*Juncaceae*. Stove aquatic with ornamental leaves resembling those of a pineapple, grassy inflorescence.

CULTURE: Soil, rich loam with a little bonemeal or rotted manure. Position, indoor tank or in pot standing in vessel of water. Temp., 60° or more.

PROPAGATION: Division of the runners spring or summer.

SPECIES CULTIVATED: *P. Palmita* (syn. *P. serratum*), white and green, 3 to 4 ft., Aug., S. Africa, Australia.

Pritchardia, see Eupritchardia.

Privet, see Ligustrum.

Proboscidea—*Martyniaceae*. Half-hardy annuals. Fruit edible and used for making pickles. First introduced early eighteenth century.

POT CULTURE: Compost, equal parts loam, leaf-mould, decayed manure and sand. Sow seeds 1 in. deep singly in 2 in. pots and place in temp. of 60°, Feb. or March. Transfer to 5 in. pots in April or May; to 6 or 7 in. pots in June. Pot firmly. Position, light, sunny greenhouse or window. Water moderately at first, freely when in full growth. Apply weak stimulants occasionally to healthy plants in flower. Temp., Feb. to May 60°, afterwards 55°.

OUTDOOR CULTURE: Soil, ordinary rich. Position, sunny, well drained, sheltered beds or borders. Sow seeds 1 in. deep singly in 3 in. pots, or 3 in. apart in shallow boxes of light soil in temp. of 60° in Feb. or March, transplanting seedlings 8 to 12 in. apart early in June. Mulch with refuse or decayed manure after planting. Water in dry weather.

SPECIES CULTIVATED: *P. fragrans*, ' Unicorn Plant ', crimson-purple, summer, 2 ft., Mexico.

Promenaea—*Orchidaceae*. A small genus of pretty dwarf-growing epiphytes. At one time included in Zygopetalum. Habit similar in all, pseudo-bulbs small, clustered. Flowers comparatively large, usually one, sometimes two, freely produced on short, usually lateral, scapes, from pseudo-bulb bases.

CULTURE: Compost, as for Odontoglossums, in summer they enjoy the same temp. and atmosphere as Odontoglossums, but in winter should be infrequently watered and the temp. should not fall below 50° at night. Pans are preferable to pots and a position near the glass given, shading is required in summer.

PROPAGATION: By division of plants in late spring.

Species Cultivated: *P. guttata*, yellow, dotted purple, purplish on base of lip, Brazil; *lentiginosa*, greenish-white, spotted purple lip with three teeth on crest, autumn, Brazil; *Rollisonii* (syn. *Maxillaria Rollisonii*), yellow, lip paler, thickly red-spotted, summer, Brazil; *stapelioides*, greenish-white, thickly spotted purple-brown, mid-lobe of lip purplish, summer, autumn, Brazil; *xanthina* (syns. *P. citrina*, *Zygopetalum xanthinum*), golden yellow or lighter, summer, Brazil.

Prophet Flower, see *Arnebia echioides*.

Proserpinaca (Mermaid Weed)—*Haloragidaceae*. Hardy oxygenating aquatics for pool or cold water aquariums. Ornamental foliage—floating leaves differ from submerged. First introduced early nineteenth century.

Culture: Plant in pots and lower into water or weight each piece separately with small pieces of lead. Soil, sandy loam. Plant, spring.

Propagation: Soft cuttings in shallow bowls of loam covered with 2 in. of water, or by division.

Species Cultivated: *P. palustris*, green and white, July, N. America.

Prostanthera—*Labiatae*. Greenhouse flowering evergreen shrubs. First introduced early nineteenth century.

Culture: Compost, peaty loam and sand. Position, large well-drained pots in unheated greenhouse. Water freely during summer, moderately in spring and autumn, little in winter. Pot, Sept. to Oct. or April to May. *P. lasianthos* and *P. rotundifolia* may be grown in favoured districts out of doors when given the protection of a south wall.

Propagation: By cuttings of young growth in sandy soil under bell-glass with gentle bottom heat.

Species Cultivated: *P. lasianthos*, white, tinged red, June, 3 to 6 ft., Australia; *nivea*, white, May, 3 to 6 ft., Australia; *rotundifolia*, purple, May to June, 3 ft., Australia; *Sieberi*, lavender, March or April, 5 to 8 ft., Australia, Tasmania.

Protea—*Proteaceae*. Greenhouse evergreen shrubs; flowers enclosed in coloured bracts. First introduced mid-eighteenth century.

Culture: Compost, two parts light, well-decayed, turfy loam, one part equal proportions silver sand, charcoal, broken pots, freestone and peat. Position, light, airy greenhouse fully exposed to sunshine. Pot, March. Drain pots one-third of depth with broken potsherds. Pot firmly. Water moderately March to Sept., occasionally afterwards, keeping soil just moist. No syringing or stimulants required. Keep plants in sunny position outdoors during June, July and Aug. Temp., Sept. to March 40 to 50°, March to June 55° to 65°.

Propagation: By cuttings of firm shoots cut off close to a joint, pared quite smooth, inserted thinly in small pots half filled with drainage, and remainder with pure sand, placed under bell-glass in cool part of greenhouse in summer.

Species Cultivated: *P. cordata*, purple, spring, 18 in., S. Africa; *cynaroides*, white, Aug., 1 ft., S. Africa; *grandiceps*, bracts red to purplish, beard white, purple, orange-black, to 5 ft., S. Africa; *longiflora*, pink, early spring, 6 ft., S. Africa.

Prunella (Selfheal)—*Labiatae*. Hardy herbaceous perennials.

Culture: Soil, ordinary light, rich. Position, border or rockery. Plant, Oct. Nov., March or April. Lift, divide and replant every two or three years. Water in dry weather. Mulch with decayed manure in March.

Propagation: By division of roots, Oct., Nov. or March.

Species Cultivated: *P. grandiflora*, purple, July and Aug., 6 in., Europe, and vars. *alba* and *rubra*; *vulgaris laciniata*, purple, July, leaves finely cut, 1 ft., Britain; *Webbiana*, purple, summer, 6 in., botanical position uncertain.

Prunus—*Rosaceae*. A large genus of hardy shrubs and trees, mostly deciduous; the majority produce edible fruits with single stone.

Culture of Peach and Nectarine: (*a*) On walls outdoors. Soil, deep but not over-rich sandy loam, well-drained, and free from manure, to which has been added a generous supply of lime, preferably mortar rubble. Position, south or south-west walls fully exposed to sun. Height of wall, 12 to 14 ft. Plant, Oct. to Feb. Distances for planting, 15 ft. Depth of soil above roots, 4 to 6 in. Prune, Jan. or Feb. Spray with Bordeaux mixture or colloidal copper after pruning as a preventive of peach leaf curl. Fruit borne on shoots of previous year's growth. Do not shorten the latter unless very strong. Always cut back if possible to a triple bud. Train previous year's shoots 2 to 3 in. apart all over tree. Remove shoots annually that have borne fruit to make room for new ones. Fruit buds, conical, downy. Wood buds, pointed, narrow. Disbud, i.e. rub off young shoots, April, May and June, removing those growing out of front and back of branches, leaving one as replacement at base, one central and one extension shoot. Train young shoots to the wall when 3 to 6 in. long. Protect blossoms from frost by covering of tiffany or hessian in Feb. and March. Ensure pollination of flowers when open by dusting with a rabbit's tail each day for ten days. Thin fruit, when size of a hazel-nut, to 3 or 4 in. apart; again, when size of a walnut, to 10 to 12 in. apart. Average number of fruit for a full-grown tree to carry, about 240. Mulch established fruiting trees with decayed manure in March or April. Apply stimulants occasionally April to Aug. Vars. recommended—Peach: Hales Early, Peregrine, Bellegarde. Nectarine: Early Rivers, Lord Napier, Pineapple.

(*b*) In the open outdoors. May be grown successfully as bush or standard in the open in warmer gardens which do not lie in frost pockets. Plant 20 ft. apart and after shape of tree is formed, little pruning required, but always cut out dead wood. Heavy crops easily grown in this manner.

(*c*) Under Glass. The border should be about 10 ft. wide and soil dug out about 2 ft. 9 in. deep. Unless natural gravel subsoil, bottom must be concreted and drained. When planting young trees, first restrict border to about 5 ft., building a temporary turf wall to retain soil. Compost, fairly heavy loam best, chopped with a spade, with one barrow-load mortar rubble to each ton of soil, and a light dusting of ¼ in. bones. Enlarge to 8 ft. wide in third season. Once trees are established never allow border to become dry. Water well about once weekly and syringe the foliage twice daily. When carrying heavy crops manure water may be applied. Thin fruit as recommended for outdoor crops in two operations, leaving finally one fruit per sq. ft. of glass. The following temps. should be followed as closely as possible. Starting, 45° to 50°; flowering, 50° to 55°; first swelling, 55° to 60°; stoning, 60° to 65°; second swelling, 65° to 70°; ripening, 70° to 75°. These figures are for day, and may be dropped by 5° for night. Fire heat rarely needed before flowering. Do not syringe during flowering period, pollinate the flowers daily with rabbit's tail, or tap branches of free setters. After fruit is gathered, syringe freely to retain foliage as long as possible. When leaves have dropped, pruning should be done; this is simplified if disbudding has been properly done. Both operations as for outdoor trees. Discontinue fire heat after leaf-fall and if growth was unsatisfactory, top-dress the border. Following vars. recommended—Peaches: early, Alexander and Hales Early; mid-season, Noblesse and Bellegarde; late, Barrington and Sea Eagle. Nectarines: early, Early Rivers and Lord Napier; mid-season, Humboldt and Pineapple; late, Milton and Victoria. Note: It is strongly recommended that all peaches and nectarines indoors and outdoors should be sprayed every year whilst dormant (Dec. to Jan.) with tar oil wash (1 pint to 2½ gall. water) against leaf-curl, greenfly and scale insects.

PROPAGATION: By budding. The St. Julien plum is often recommended as a suitable rootstock for heavy soils and the almond for light. Peach seedlings may also be used.

CULTURE OF MYROBALAN PLUM: Used chiefly for hedges; occasionally as a stock for plums. Soil, ordinary. Position, sunny. Plant, Oct. to Feb. Distance apart to plant, 6 in. Plant out when two years old. Trim into shape, June or July. Makes an impenetrable hedge.

CULTURE OF PORTUGAL AND CHERRY LAURELS: Soil, good ordinary. Position, mixed shrubberies or hedges for cherry laurel; lawns or shrubberies for Portugal laurel. Plant, Sept. to Oct. or in May. Prune in April, merely shortening straggly growths.

HEDGE CULTURE OF CHERRY LAUREL: Trench site 3 ft. wide and 2 ft. deep, mixing plenty of rotted manure with soil. Plant, 12 to 24 in. apart. Prune in April.

CULTURE OF FLOWERING SPECIES: Soil, ordinary. The majority of prunus will grow more satisfactorily if provided with lime. Position, well-drained, sunny borders or shrubberies; almonds good town trees. Plant, Oct. to Feb. Prune only to cut away dead wood, or to shorten straggly growths after flowering.

POT CULTURE OF P. TRILOBA: Compost, two parts sandy loam, one part leaf-mould, half a part silver sand. Position, cold greenhouse, Jan. to June; outdoors, pots plunged to rim in garden soil, June to Nov.; sheltered corner or pit, Nov. to Jan. Pot, Nov. Repot annually. Water freely March to Oct., moderately afterwards. Apply stimulants occasionally April to Sept. Temp. for forcing, 55° to 65°. Prune severely after flowering.

PROPAGATION: Cherry by budding in July or Aug. on the Mahaleb cherry for dwarfs, or seedling cherry for standards; plums by budding in July or Aug. on the Brussel, Pershore, Common Plum, Myrobalan, St. Julien, Brompton and Common Mussel; damsons by seed; almonds by budding on seedling plums; other species by budding on the Myrobalan plum; laurels and Myrobalan plum by cuttings inserted in sheltered border or cold frame in autumn; flowering species by cuttings of half-ripened wood taken with a heel in July and Aug. and struck in sandy soil under bell-glass in gentle bottom heat. All kinds by seeds to produce new vars.

ORNAMENTAL SPECIES AND VARS. CULTIVATED: For the sake of simplicity these are dealt with in their separate sections.

SPECIES OF ALMONDS AND PEACHES: *P. Amygdalus*, ' Almond ', pale pink, March, April, 20 to 30 ft., S. Europe and Algeria, with vars. *Pollardii* large flowered, fine form, edible fruits, *amara*, ' Bitter Almond ', *dulcis*, ' Sweet Almond ', and *pendula*, weeping; *Davidiana*, white, Jan. to March, 20 to 30 ft., China; *Persica*, ' Peach ', pale pink, April, 20 to 30 ft., China, not as freely grown as double-flowered vars., e.g. *sanguinea plena*, carmine, *flore albo*, and *plena*, double white; *Pollardii*, fine hybrid between almond and peach, large, bright pink flowers, March, April, 25 ft.; *tenella* (syn. *P. nana*), ' Dwarf Russian Almond ', rosy red, April, 3 to 5 ft., S. Russia and S.E. Europe, with vars. *alba*, white, and *Gessleriana*, larger flowered; *triloba* (generally as double form, *P. triloba multiplex*), fine shrub, pink, March, April, prune hard after flowering, useful as small standard, 12 ft., China.

SPECIES OF CHERRIES: *P. avium*, ' Gean ' or ' Mazzard ', white, April, 30 to 60 ft., Europe, including Britain, with vars. *plena*, double, and *pendula*, weeping; *Cerasus*, ' Double Wild Dwarf Cherry ', May, white, 10 to 20 ft.,Europe, var. *Rhexii*; *Conradinae*, pale pink, Feb., March, 25 to 30 ft., Cent. China, with var. *incisa*, white, March, April, 6 to 15 ft., 20 to 25 ft., double flowers, a better form; *incisa*, white, March, April, 6 to 15 ft., spreading, stands pruning, Japan; *japonica*, white to pale pink, April, 4 ft., Cent. China, with var. *flore pleno*, double, much forced by florists, and a good garden plant; *Mahaleb*, ' St. Lucie Cherry ', white, in clusters, very fragrant, April, May, 30 to 40 ft., Cent. and S. Europe, with vars. *monstrosa*, dwarf, and *pendula*, beautiful semi-weeping form; *Sargentii*, rose pink, April, 20 to 40 ft., coloured spring and autumn foliage, Japan; *serrulata*, ' Japanese Cherry ', in numerous vars., generally grown as standards, making trees 15 to 30 ft., flowering April to May, as ' Amanagawa ' (*erecta*), semi-double, pink, very erect habit; ' Fugenzo ' (' J. H. Veitch '), double, deep pink, spreading habit; ' Hokusai ' (*roseo pleno*), semi-double, pale pink; ' Kiku Shidare ' (*rosea* or ' Cheal's Weeping '), double pink, early; ' Kwanzan ' (' Hisakura '), most popular, deep rose pink, young foliage copper, strong upright habit; ' Miyako ' (*longipes* or ' Shimidsu sakura '), double white, fragrant, late flowering, spreading habit; ' Sirotae ', semi-double, white, early; ' Tai-haku ', very fine var., large white, single, quick-growing, upright habit; ' Ukon ' (*grandiflora*), semi-double, pale sulphur, sparse habit, and ' Yoshino ', pink in bud to white, very free, March, April, with var. *pendula*, beautiful weeping form; *subhirtella*, ' Spring Cherry ' or ' Higan Sakura ', very free and beautiful, pale pink, April, 20 to 30 ft., Japan, with vars. *ascendens*, upright habit, *autumnalis*, Nov. to Dec. flowering, *pendula*, ' Weeping Rose-bud Cherry ', and *pendula rubra*, similar, red flowered; *tomentosa*, ' Downy Cherry ', pale pink, March, April, 4 to 6 ft., prune after flowering, N. and W. China.

SPECIES OF PLUMS: *P. cerasifera*, ' Cherry Plum ', ' Myrobalan ', white, Feb. to March, 15 to 25 ft., W. Asia, Caucasus, with var. *atropurpurea* (syn. var. *Pissardii*), popular tree, pink, March, brownish-claret foliage; *Bleiriana*, similar but less strong and double flowered; *nigra*, best form, deeper-coloured flowers and foliage; *insititia*, ' Bullace ', to 20 ft., Europe, including Britain; *spinosa*, ' Sloe ', ' Blackthorn ', March, white, 8 to 15 ft., Europe, including Britain.

SPECIES OF APRICOTS: *P. Armeniaca*, ' Apricot ', white or pale pink, March, to 20 ft., N. China, with ornamental var. *Ansu*, double, deeper pink; *dasycarpa*, ' Black Apricot ', probably hybrid between plum and apricot, white to pale pink, March, April, 20 to 25 ft., Japan, with vars. *alba*, white, *alba plena*, double white, and *pendula*, weeping.

SPECIES OF BIRD CHERRIES: *P. cornuta*, ' Himalayan Bird Cherry ', white, May, 40 to 50 ft., Himalaya; *Virginiana*, ' Western Choke Cherry ', white, May, purple fruits, 20 to 30 ft., Western N. America; *Padus*, ' Bird Cherry ', good woodland tree, white, fragrant, May, 30 to 50 ft., N. Europe, including Britain, N. Asia to Japan, with vars. which are superior garden forms, as *commutata*, early flowering, *plena*, good semi-double form, and *Watereri*, probably best form, single; *serotina*, ' Black Cherry ' or ' Rum Cherry ', white, May, black fruits, bright leaves, 30 to 60 ft., N. America.

SPECIES OF CHERRY LAURELS (these are all evergreen): *P. Laurocerasus*, ' Cherry Laurel ', quick-growing tree for screening or shelter in shady places, making handsome hedge or single specimen, dull white flowers, fruit black, to 20 ft. high, more in width, E. Europe and Asia Minor, with numerous vars., *caucasica*, fine large-leaved form, *magnoliaefolia*, leaves up to 12 in. long, *Mischiana* (dwarf form), *rotundifolia*, good for hedging, *schipkaensis*, pyramidal habit, very hardy, and *Zabeliana*, dwarf spreading, hardy; *lusitanica*, ' Portugal Laurel ', hardy, useful for hedging, white, June, 10 to 25 ft., Spain and Portugal, with vars. *azorica*, large-leaved, *myrtifolia*, dense form, and *variegata*, leaves margined silver.

Pseudocytisus—*Cruciferae*. Rather tender flowering shrubs. First introduced mid-eighteenth century.

CULTURE: Soil, ordinary light. Position, sheltered and rather dry border for *P. integrifolius*, sunny position in rock garden for *P. spinosus*. Plant, Oct. to Nov.

PROPAGATION: By cuttings of half-ripened wood in sandy soil under bell-glass in gentle bottom heat from June to Aug.

SPECIES CULTIVATED: *P. integrifolius* (syn. *Vella Pseudocytisus*), ' Cress Rocket ', rather tender, yellow and purple, May to July, 1 to 2 ft., evergreen, Cent. Spain; *spinosus* (syn. *Vella spinosa*), yellow and brown, June, 1 ft., deciduous, spiny, Spain.

Pseudolarix (Golden Larch)—*Pinaceae*. Hardy deciduous coniferous tree. First introduced mid-nineteenth century.

CULTURE: Soil, gravel or stony. Position, as specimens in open places or on lawns. Plant in autumn.

PROPAGATION: By seeds sown 1 in. deep in beds in the open during March, transplanting seedlings when two years old.

SPECIES CULTIVATED: *P. amabilis* (syn. *P. Fortunei* and *Larix Kaempferi*), 100 to 130 ft., foliage turns rich yellow in autumn, China.

Pseudopanax—*Araliaceae*. Greenhouse evergreen shrubs or small trees. First introduced mid-nineteenth century.

CULTURE: Compost, equal parts loam, peat or leaf-mould, charcoal and sand.

Pot, Feb. to March. Water freely March to Oct., moderately afterwards. Temp., March to Sept. 55° to 60°, Sept. to March 45° to 55°.

PROPAGATION: By cuttings of young shoots; inserting portions of roots in light soil in temp. 80° in April.

SPECIES CULTIVATED: *P. chathamicum*, ' Hoho ', 20 ft., New Zealand; *crassifolium*, 5 to 10 ft., New Zealand, and vars. *Abelii*, *Baueri*, *Knightiifolium*, *trifolium*; *discolor*, 15 ft., New Zealand; *ferox*, green, 5 to 10 ft., New Zealand; *Lessonii* (syn. *Panax Lessonii*), ' Houmapara ' or ' Houpara ', to 15 ft., New Zealand.

Pseudosasa—*Gramineae*. Shrubs with creeping rootstocks. Formerly included in Arundinaria and Sasa.

CULTURE: Soil, good, not too heavy and of reasonable depth. Position, must be sheltered from cold winds and dry root conditions are disliked.

PROPAGATION: By division in April and May.

SPECIES CULTIVATED: *P. japonica* (syn. *Bambusa Metake*), 10 ft., hardy, finely toothed leaves, shining above, glaucous beneath, Japan.

Pseudotsuga (Douglas Fir)—*Pinaceae*. Hardy evergreen coniferous tree. First introduced early nineteenth century.

CULTURE: Good deep loam. Position, as specimens in open places or on lawns. Thrives in districts where there is an abundant rainfall.

PROPAGATION: By seeds sown 1 in. deep in beds in the open during March, transplanting seedlings when two years old.

SPECIES CULTIVATED: *P. taxifolia* (syn. *P. Douglasii*), 200 to 250 ft., Western N. America, and vars. *glauca*, ' Colorado Douglas Fir ', leaves glaucous ', *pendula*, branches pendulous, and *Fretsii*, leaves short and broad.

Psidium—*Myrtaceae*. Stove evergreen flowering shrubs. Fruit (berries), yellow or claret-coloured, round or pear-shaped, aromatic, edible. First introduced late seventeenth century.

CULTURE: Compost, two parts fibrous sandy loam, one part equal proportions dry cow manure and silver sand. Position, well-drained pots, tubs or beds with shoots trained to back walls of stove, warm greenhouse or vinery. Pot or plant, Feb. or March. Prune into shape annually, Feb. Water freely April to Oct., moderately afterwards. Syringe freely, March, until fruit begins to ripen, then keep foliage dry. Apply weak stimulants occasionally after berries form until fruit ripens. Temp., March to Oct. 65° to 75°, Oct. to March 55° to 60°.

PROPAGATION: By cuttings of firm young shoots, 2 to 3 in. long, inserted in sand under bell-glass in temp. 75° to 80°, spring or summer.

SPECIES CULTIVATED: *P. Cattleianum*, ' Strawberry Guava ', white, June, 15 to 25 ft., fruits purplish-red, obovate to globose, Brazil; *Guajava*, ' Common Guava ', white, summer, 20 to 30 ft., fruits, yellow, globose, pyriform or ovoid, Trop. America.

Psoralea (Scurvy Pea)—*Leguminosae*. Greenhouse evergreen flowering scented shrubs. First introduced late seventeenth century.

CULTURE: Compost, equal parts fibrous loam, peat and silver sand. Position, pots in sunny, airy greenhouse. Pot, Feb. or March. Prune into shape, Feb. Water freely April to Sept., moderately afterwards. Good drainage essential. No stimulants or shade required. Temp., March to Sept. 55° to 65°, Sept. to March 40° to 50°.

PROPAGATION: By cuttings of firm shoots, 2 to 3 in. long, inserted in pots half filled with drainage, remainder layer of moss and pure sand, placed under bell-glass in shady part of greenhouse, May or June.

SPECIES CULTIVATED: *P. aculeata*, blue and white, summer, 3 ft., S. Africa; *aphylla*, blue and white, summer, 4 to 7 ft., S. Africa; *glandulosa*, white and blue, May to Sept., 4 ft., Chile; *pinnata*, blue, summer, 3 to 6 ft., S. Africa.

Psychotria (Wild Coffee)—*Rubiaceae*. Stove evergreen flowering shrub. Of similar habit to the Ixora. First introduced mid-nineteenth century.

CULTURE: Compost, two parts fibrous peat, one part fibrous loam, one part silver sand. Position, shady part of stove whilst growing; light one when at rest. Pot, Feb. or March. Prune into shape, Feb. Water freely March to Sept., moderately afterwards. Syringe morning and evening in spring and summer. Apply weak liquid manure once a week to healthy plants in flower. Temp., March to Sept. 75° to 85°, Sept. to March 55° to 65°.

PROPAGATION: By cuttings in sandy peat under bell-glass in temp. of 75° to 85° in spring.

SPECIES CULTIVATED: *P. capensis*, yellow, spring, 3 to 4 ft., S. Africa; *jasmini-flora* (syn. *Gloneria jasminiflora*), snow-white, summer, 3 ft., Brazil.

Ptelea—*Rutaceae*. Hardy deciduous flowering tree with elm-like fruits. First introduced early eighteenth century.

CULTURE: Soil, ordinary, well drained. Position, open shrubberies, plantations or woods. Plant, Nov. to Feb.

PROPAGATION: By seeds sown ¼ in. deep in sunny position outdoors in March or April; layering shoots in spring.

SPECIES CULTIVATED: *P. trifoliata*, ' Hop Tree ', ' Wafer Ash ', green, June to July, 15 to 20 ft., N. America, var. *aurea*, young leaves golden.

Pteretis (Ostrich Fern)—*Polypodiaceae*. Large hardy deciduous fern.

OUTDOOR CULTURE: Soil, two parts good loam, one part leaf-mould. Position, semi-shaded, cool, moist border or margin of pond. Plant, April.

POT CULTURE: Compost, two parts fibrous loam, one part leaf-mould, one part sand. Position, well-drained pots in shady, cold frame or greenhouse. Pot, March or April. Water copiously April to Sept., moderately Sept. to Nov., keep nearly dry Nov. to March. Repot annually.

PROPAGATION: By spores gathered just before the cases burst and sown on surface of well-drained pan of sandy peat and leaf-mould, cover with glass and keep moderately moist in a shady position in cold frame or greenhouse; division of plants March or April.

SPECIES CULTIVATED: *P. Struthiopteris* (syn. *Matteuccia Struthiopteris*), 3 to 5 ft., Europe.

Pteridium (Bracken)—*Polypodiaceae*. Hardy ferns useful as background in rock gardens, etc.

CULTURE: Soil, ordinary. Position, shady borders or woods. Plant, April.

PROPAGATION: By division; spores.

SPECIES CULTIVATED: *P. aquilinum* (syn. *Pteris aquilina*), fronds to 4 ft. long and 3 ft. wide, cosmopolitan, and vars. *languinosum* and *latiusculum*.

Pteris (Brake)—*Polypodiaceae*. Large genus of mostly tropical ferns. The hardy species formerly included here will be found under Pteridium.

CULTURE: Compost, equal parts loam, leaf-mould, peat and sand. Position, pots, beds or rockery in shady part of house. Pot, March or April. Water freely March to Oct., moderately other times. Temp., March to Sept. 55° to 65°, Sept. to March 50° to 55°.

PROPAGATION: By spores sown on fine sandy peat in well-drained pans in temp. 80° any time; dwarf species by division of plants, Oct. or April.

SPECIES CULTIVATED: *P. cretica*, fronds to 1 ft. long, Tropics and Subtropics, and numerous vars.; *ensiformis*, slender fertile fronds to 20 in., sterile fronds shorter, E. Asia, Malaya, Australia, var. *Victoriae*, segments banded with white; *serrulata* (syn. *P. multifida*), slender fronds to 1¼ ft. long, China, Japan, there are many crested and other vars.; *tremula*, ' Australian Brake ', fronds bright green to 3 ft. long, New Zealand, Australia.

Pteridophyllum—*Papaveraceae*. Hardy herbaceous rock garden plants.

CULTURE: Cool, well-drained loam. Position, north aspect or half-shade.

PROPAGATION: By division of old clumps when growth starts in spring.

SPECIES CULTIVATED: *P. racemosum*, white, July, 6 to 9 in., Japan.

Pterocarya (Wing Nut)—*Juglandaceae*. Hardy deciduous fast-growing trees resembling walnuts. Handsome, pinnate foliage. First introduced early nineteenth century.

CULTURE: Soil, deep loam. Position, as specimens in open places or on lawns. Require abundant moisture. Plant, Nov. to Feb. Young plants liable to damage by late spring frosts.

PROPAGATION: By seeds in open light soil during March; suckers in autumn.

SPECIES CULTIVATED: *P. fraxinifolia* (syn. *P. caucasica*), 50 to 100 ft., Caucasus; *hupeiensis*, 60 to 80 ft., W. China; *Rehderiana*, 40 ft., hybrid; *rhoifolia*, 'Japanese Wing Nut', 50 to 100 ft., Japan.

Pterocephalus—*Dipsaceae*. Annual and perennial herbs. Sometimes included in Scabiosa.

CULTURE: As Scabiosa.

PROPAGATION: As Scabiosa.

SPECIES CULTIVATED: *P. parnassi* (syn. *Scabiosa pterocephala*), purplish-pink, July, in composite heads, spreading, deep-rooted.

Ptychosperma—*Palmae*. Stove palm with feather-shaped, green, very graceful leaves. First introduced mid-nineteenth century.

CULTURE: Compost, equal parts loam and leaf-mould, half a part silver sand. Position, shady part of stove, warm greenhouse or conservatory; pots or tubs. Pot, Feb. or March. Water copiously March to Sept., moderately afterwards. Syringe freely daily March to Oct. Shade from sun. Top-dress large plants occasionally with layer of cow manure. Apply stimulants occasionally April to Sept. Temp., March to Oct. 60° to 75°, Oct. to March 55° to 60°.

PROPAGATION: By seeds sown ½ in. deep in light, rich soil in temp. 80° to 90°, Feb., March or April.

SPECIES CULTIVATED: *P. elegans*, 'Australian Feather Palm', 10 to 20 ft., Australia.

Pudding Pipe Tree, see *Cassia Fistula*.

Pulmonaria (Lung-wort)—*Boraginaceae*. Hardy herbaceous herbs. Ornamental foliage. Leaves, lance-shaped, green, sometimes spotted with white.

CULTURE: Soil, ordinary. Position, partially shaded rockeries or borders. Plant, Oct., Nov., March or April. Lift and replant in fresh soil every four or five years.

PROPAGATION: By seeds sown 1/16 in. deep in ordinary soil in shady position outdoors, March or April; division of roots, Oct. or March.

SPECIES CULTIVATED: *P. affinis*, red and purple, spring, 1 ft., Europe; *angustifolia*, 'Blue Cowslip', blue and pink, spring, 1 ft., Europe, and vars. *arvernensis*, purple-blue, and *azurea*, blue; *montana* (syn. *P. rubra*), brick red, spring, 9 to 12 in., Transylvania; *officinalis*, red and violet, spring, 1 ft., Europe (Br.); *saccharata*, 'Bethlehem Sage', pink, April to July, 1 ft., Europe.

Pulsatilla, see Anemone.

Pultenaea—*Leguminosae*. Greenhouse evergreen flowering shrubs. First introduced late eighteenth century.

CULTURE: Compost, two parts fibrous peat, one part equal proportions silver sand and pounded charcoal. Position, light, airy greenhouse. Pot, Feb. or March. Well-drained pots and firm potting essential. Water freely April to Sept., moderately other times. Use soft water only. No stimulants required. Shade unnecessary. Stand plants in sunny position outdoors during July and Aug. Temp., Sept. to March 40° to 50°, March to July 55° to 65°.

PROPAGATION: By seeds sown on surface of shallow, well-drained pans filled with sandy peat, slightly covered with fine peat, placed under bell-glass in temp. 55° to 65°, March or April; cuttings of firm shoots, 2 to 3 in. long, inserted in sandy peat under bell-glass in shade in temp. 55° to 65° in summer.

SPECIES CULTIVATED: *P. daphnoides*, orange-red, June and July, 2 to 3 ft., Australia; *obcordata*, yellow, April, 3 ft., Australia; *retusa*, yellow and purple,

April, 1 ft., Australia; *rosea*, pink, spring, 1 ft., Australia; *stricta*, yellow, spring, 3 ft., Australia; *villosa*, yellow, spring, 3 ft., Australia.

Pummelo, see *Citrus maxima.*

Pumpkin, see *Cucurbita moschata.*

Punch-and-Judy Orchid, see Gongora.

Punica—*Punicaceae.* Slightly tender deciduous small tree, ornamental flowers, seldom producing fruit. First introduced mid-sixteenth century.
CULTURE: Soil, ordinary, well drained. Position, full sun, warmest areas, sheltered position in open, elsewhere wall protection essential.
PROPAGATION: By seeds sown ¼ in. deep in well-drained pots in gentle heat, March; cuttings half-ripened wood, end July.
SPECIES CULTIVATED: *P. Granatum*, ' Pomegranate ', reddish-scarlet, June to Sept., 15 to 25 ft., Persia and Afghanistan, and vars. *albescens*, white, *Legrellii*, double, striped red and yellow, and *nana*, dwarf, 3 to 4 ft., grown in greenhouses.

Purple Rock Cress, see Aubrieta; **-Wreath,** see *Petrea volubilis.*

Purslane, see Portulaca; **Rock-,** see *Calandrinia umbellata.*

Puschkinia (Striped Squill)—*Liliaceae.* Hardy bulbous flowering plants. First introduced early nineteenth century.
CULTURE: Soil, ordinary light, sandy. Position, sunny, well-drained border or rockery. Plant bulbs 4 in. deep, 1 in. apart, Oct. or Nov. Protect immediately after planting with covering 1 in. deep of coconut-fibre refuse or decayed manure. After flowering remove protective material, fully exposing surface to sun to ripen bulbs. Lift and replant every two or three years.
PROPAGATION: By seeds sown ⅛ in. deep in shallow, well-drained pans filled with light, sandy soil in Aug. or Sept., placed in cold frame; offsets, removed and planted as advised for old bulbs, Oct. or Nov.
SPECIES CULTIVATED: *P. scilloides*, white, striped with blue, spring, 4 in., Asia Minor, vars. *compacta*, dwarf, and *alba*, all white.

Pussy Paws, see *Spraguea multiceps.*

Putoria—*Rubiaceae.* Slightly tender dwarf shrubby plants.
CULTURE: Warm, deep, sandy loam and a sheltered, sunny position. A good plant for a warm wall.
PROPAGATION: By seeds; cuttings of ripened growths in late summer.
SPECIES CULTIVATED: *P. calabrica*, red, summer, 9 in., Medit. Regions.

Pycnostachys—*Labiatae.* Greenhouse perennial.
CULTURE: Soil, loam, leaf-mould and sand. Position, well-drained pots in sunny greenhouse. Water freely during the growing season, sparingly other times. Temp., Sept. to March 45° to 55°, March to Sept. 60° to 65°.
PROPAGATION: By cuttings in sandy peat in warm propagating frame; seeds in a temp. of 65° in spring.
SPECIES CULTIVATED: *P. Dawei*, blue, winter, 4 to 6 ft., Uganda; *urticifolia*, blue, winter, 3 ft., Trop. Africa.

Pygmy Sunflower, see *Actinea grandiflora.*

Pyracantha (Firethorn)—*Rosaceae.* Hardy and slightly tender evergreen flowering and berried shrubs. First introduced early seventeenth century.
CULTURE: Soil, ordinary, well drained. Position, full sun or partial shade. May be trained as wall climbers or as hedges, or will make spreading border specimens. Excellent for screening. Resent transplanting. Plant, Sept. to Oct. and April to May. Prune or trim where necessary in March.
PROPAGATION: By seeds in boxes of sandy soil in cool greenhouse or frame during Feb. or March; cuttings of nearly ripened young growth in sandy soil in frame during Aug. or Sept.
SPECIES CULTIVATED: *P. angustifolia*, white, May to June, 10 to 12 ft., orange-

yellow berries, requires some protection, W. China; *atalantioides* (syn. *P. dis‾ color*), white, May to June, 10 to 20 ft., vigorous, hardy, scarlet berries, persisting' China; *coccinea* (syn. *Crataegus Pyracantha*), white, June, 10 to 15 ft., coral berries, S. Europe and Asia Minor, and its better known var. *Lalandii*, more vigorous, orange-red berries; *crenato-serrata*, white, May to June, berries coral-red, persisting, 10 to 15 ft., Cent. and W. China; *crenulata*, ' Nepalese White Thorn ', white, May, 10 to 15 ft., requires wall protection, orange-yellow berries, Himalaya, and var. *Rogersiana*, superior to the type, hardy, glossy foliage, creamy white, May, fruits reddish-orange to yellow.

Pyrenean Meadow Saffron, see Merendera.

Pyrethrum, see *Chrysanthemum coccineum.*

Pyrola—*Ericaceae.* Hardy perennial herbs.
CULTURE: Soil, equal parts peat, leaf-mould and sandy loam. Position, moist, partially shady borders or rockeries. Plant, March or April. Water freely in dry weather. Lift, divide and replant only when overgrown.
PROPAGATION: By seeds sown thinly and slightly covered with very fine sandy peat in position where intended to grow, March or April; division of roots, April.
SPECIES CULTIVATED: *P. elliptica*, white, summer, 6 in., N. America; *media*, white, summer, 6 in., Siberia; *rotundifolia*, white, June, 6 to 9 in., Europe, and var. *incarnata*, pink, N. America.

Pyrostegia—*Bignoniaceae.* Greenhouse climbing plants. First introduced early nineteenth century.
CULTURE: Compost, two parts fibrous loam, one part peat and silver sand. Pot, Feb. to April. Position, sunny greenhouse in well-drained border or bed, also large tubs. Prune away weak shoots and shorten by two-thirds strong shoots in February. Water freely March to Nov., slightly at other times. Temp., Oct. to Mar. 55° to 60°, March to Oct. 60° to 70°.
PROPAGATION: By cuttings of young shoots, 3 in. long, inserted in well-drained pots of sandy soil in temp. 65° to 70° in April.
SPECIES CULTIVATED: *P. ignea* (syn. *P. venusta*), orange-red, autumn, 20 ft. or more, Brazil.

Pyrrhocactus—*Cactaceae.* Greenhouse succulent plants, sometimes listed as Echinocactus.
CULTURE: As Echinocactus.
PROPAGATION: As Echinocactus
SPECIES CULTIVATED: *P. centeterius*, yellowish-red, nearly globose, summer, Chile.

Pyrus (Pear)—*Rosacae.* Hardy, deciduous, fruit-bearing and flowering trees, leaves usually turn red in autumn.
CULTURE OF PEARS: Soil, well drained and well supplied with humus to improve moisture-holding capacity. Position for cordon and horizontally-trained trees, south, west or east walls or fences. North walls for quick-ripening vars.; open sheltered garden for pyramids and bushes. Plant, autumn or spring. Cultural details, as advised for the apple (Malus). Potash is not so necessary for pears.
ROOTSTOCKS: Common pear for standards; quince for pyramids, bushes and cordons. Malling Quince A, good for dwarf trees and bushes, some incompatible vars. must be double-worked. Malling Quince B is similar to A. With Malling Quince C the mature tree is more dwarf than with other stocks.
CULTURE OF ORNAMENTAL SPECIES: Soil, ordinary. Position, sunny borders or shrubberies, or as specimens in open places. Plant, Nov. to Feb.
PROPAGATION: For new vars. by seeds stratified over winter and sown 3 in. deep outdoors in March; established vars. by grafting in March or budding in July and Aug.; layering in autumn.
FRUIT-BEARING SPECIES CULTIVATED: *P. communis*, ' Pear ', white, April to May, to 40 ft., Europe and W. Asia, var. *sativa*, collective name for cultivated

ғars., some of which are hybrids with *P. pyrifolia,* 'Sand Pear', 50 ft., hard, apple-shaped fruits, China and Japan.

ORNAMENTAL SPECIES CULTIVATED: *P. amygdaliformis,* 'Almond Pear', to 20 ft., flowers white, fruits yellowish, France to Asia Minor; *salicifolia,* 'Willow-leaved Pear', to 30 ft., flowers white, fruits yellowish, spring, 1 in., S.E. Europe, W. Asia.

Pyxidanthera—*Diapensiaceae.* Hardy evergreen creeping shrub. First introduced mid-nineteenth century.

CULTURE: Soil, equal parts sandy peat and leaf-mould. Position, sunny rockeries. Plant, Sept., Oct., March or April.

PROPAGATION: By seeds sown where required to grow, lightly covering with fine sandy peat, Sept., Oct. or March; division of plants, Oct. or March.

SPECIES CULTIVATED: *P. barbulata,* 'Flowering Moss', 'Pine Barren Beauty', white, rose, summer, 2 in., N. America.

Quaking Grass, see *Briza media.*

Quamash, see *Camassia Quamash.*

Quamoclit—*Convolvulaceae.* Stove greenhouse annual climber. Sometimes included in Ipomaea.

CULTURE: Compost, equal parts fibrous loam, leaf-mould, decayed manure and silver sand. Position, pots in warm greenhouse, with growths supported on twiggy stakes or trained to wires or trellis. Plant or pot, March or April. Temp., March to Sept. 65° to 70°. Water freely when established in final pots.

PROPAGATION: By seeds, $\frac{1}{8}$ in. deep, in pots in temp. 65° to 70° in March. Repot seedlings as required until they occupy 5 in. or 6 in. pots.

SPECIES CULTIVATED: *Q. lobata* (syn. *Mina lobata*), rosy crimson and yellow, summer, 6 to 8 ft., Mexico; *pennata* (syn. *Ipomaea Quamoclit*), 'Cypress Vine', red, summer, 6 ft., annual, Tropics.

Queen Lily, see Phaedranassa; **-of-the-Meadows,** see *Filipendula Ulmaria;* **-of-the-Prairie,** see *Filipendula lobata;* **-Palm,** see *Arecastrum Romanzoffianum;* **-Victoria Water Lily,** see Victoria.

Quercus (Oak)—*Fagaceae.* Hardy deciduous and evergreen trees and shrubs.

CULTURE: Soil, good deep loam, preferably rather moist. Position, shrubberies, fields and woods. *Q. Ilex* and *Q. Cerris* are suitable for planting near the sea. Plant evergreen kinds, Sept. to Nov. or April; deciduous ones, Sept., Oct., or April to end of May. Distance apart for deciduous oaks, 20 to 25 ft., evergreen species, used for shelter, 6 to 10 ft., for hedges, 4 to 6 ft. Prune deciduous oaks in Dec., evergreen kinds in April.

PROPAGATION: By acorns gathered in autumn, stored in sand until March and then sown 2 in. deep. Oaks transplant badly and are all the better for being sown where they are to grow. Choice kinds are grafted on common oak in March.

USEFUL DATA: Average extreme age of oak tree, 1,000 to 1,500 years, average spread of branches of largest trees, 180 ft. Flowers, greenish, male and female borne on same plant. Timber used for building, cabinet work, cartwheel spokes, fencing, etc., very durable. Weight of oak per cubic foot, 53 lb. One bushel of acorns will yield about 7,000 trees.

EVERGREEN SPECIES CULTIVATED: *Q. acuta,* 15 to 40 ft., Japan; *coccifera,* 10 to 12 ft., Medit. Region; *Ilex,* 'Holm Oak', 'Holly Oak', 60 ft., Medit. Region; *Suber,* 'Cork Oak', 50 to 60 ft., S. Europe, the source of the cork of commerce, only hardy in warmer districts.

DECIDUOUS SPECIES CULTIVATED: *Q. bicolor,* 'Swamp White Oak', 60 to 70 ft., Eastern N. America; *canariensis* (syn. *Q. Mirbeckii*), to 90 ft., one of the best oaks, handsome foliage retained till January, N. Africa and Portugal; *Cerris,* 'Turkey Oak', fast-growing, handsome ree, to 120 ft., S. Europe and Asia Minor; *coccinea,* 'Scarlet Oak', in true species leaves die off red and persist into winter, 60 to 80 ft., Eastern N. America, var. *splendens,* most handsome form;

Frainetto (syn. *Q. conferta*), good for chalk, large leaves warm-tinted in autumn, to 100 ft., S.E. Europe; *ilicifolia*, leaves white-felted beneath, 20 to 30 ft., Eastern U.S.; *imbricaria*, ' Shingle Oak ', long narrow leaves, autumn tints, 50 to 60 ft., Cent. U.S.; *lyrata*, ' Overcup Oak ', leaves to 12 in. long, 60 to 80 ft., N. America; *macranthera*, 60 ft., Caucasus and Persia; *macrocarpa*, enormous leaves, 40 to 50 ft., Eastern N. America; *marilandica*, ' Black Jack Oak ', slow growing, autumn tints, 30 to 40 ft., Eastern U.S.; *Muhlenbergii* (syn. *Q. castanea*), ' Chestnut Oak ', handsome, uncommon, 60 to 100 ft., Caucasus and Persia; *palustris*, ' Pin Oak ', quick growing, reliable, autumn tints, 75 to 100 ft., Eastern U.S.; *petraea* (syn. *Q. sessiliflora*), ' Durmast Oak ', British native species, generally found in elevated districts, 60 to 120 ft., Europe; *pontica*, large-ribbed leaves, to 20 ft., Armenia and Caucasus; *Robur* (syn. *Q. pedunculata*), ' Common Oak ', to 100 ft., sometimes more, Britain, Europe and Asia Minor, many vars. including *Concordia*, ' Golden Oak ', *fastigiata*, columnar habit, *heterophylla*, leaves variously shaped, *pendula*, weeping, *purpurascens*, leaves and young shoots tinged purple, *variegata*, leaves marked with white or yellow; *velutina*, ' Black Oak ', bark permeated yellow, used for tanning, 70 to 100 ft., Eastern and Cent. U.S.

Quick, see *Crataegus monogyna.*

Quillwort, see Isoetes.

Quince, see Cydonia and Chaenomeles.

Quinine, see Chinchona.

Quinoa, see *Chenopodium Quinoa.*

Quisqualis—*Combretaceae.* Stove climbing flowering deciduous shrubs. First introduced early nineteenth century.
CULTURE: Compost, two parts loam, one part peat and a little sand. Position, well-drained pot or tub, or in a bed with shoots trained up rafters. Pot, Feb. Prune shoots moderately closely after flowering. Water freely April to Oct., keep nearly dry remainder of year. Syringe daily April to Sept. Shade from midday sun only.
PROPAGATION: By cuttings of young shoots taken off with a small portion of old stem attached and inserted in sandy soil in small pots under a bell-glass in a temp. of 75° to 85° in spring.
SPECIES CULTIVATED: *Q. indica*, ' Rangoon Creeper ', white, changing to red, fragrant, summer, 10 to 15 ft., India.

Radish, see *Raphanus sativus.*

Raffenaldia—*Cruciferae.* Dwarf alpine perennial, sometimes known as Cossonia.
CULTURE: Very sandy soil in full sun.
PROPAGATION: By seeds sown in soil as above.
SPECIES CULTIVATED: *R. primuloides* (syn. *Cossonia africana*), yellow, summer, N. Africa.

Ragged Robin, see *Lychnis Flos-cuculi.*

Ragwort, see Senecio.

Ramonda—*Gesneriaceae.* Hardy perennial plants, sometimes spelled Ramondia. First introduced early eighteenth century.
CULTURE: Soil, light sandy peat, ample humus. Position, north or semi-shaded aspect in vertical or horizontal crevices, not on the flat. Water in very dry weather. For pot culture use similar soil and grow in cool position or in shaded cold greenhouse or frame.
PROPAGATION: By seeds sown in similar compost (germination and subsequent growth is hastened by slight heat where possible); by division of plants or by leaf cuttings made in summer.
SPECIES CULTIVATED: *R. Heldreichii* (syn. *Jankaea Heldreichii*), lavender, early summer, 3 in., Greece, and var. *alba*; *Myconi* ' Rosette Mullein ', deep lavender,

early summer, 4 in., Pyrenees, and vars. *alba*, white, *rosea*, pink; *Nathaliae*, rich lavender, June, 4 to 6 in., Macedonia, *serbica*, lavender, June, 4 in., Balkans, and var. *alba*.

Rampion, see *Campanula Rapunculus*.

Ramsons, see *Allium ursinum*.

Randia—*Rubiaceae*. Stove evergreen flowering climbing shrubs. First introduced early eighteenth century.

Culture: Compost, one part loam, one part peat, one part well-decayed manure and charcoal. Position, well-drained pots or beds in plant stove. Pot or plant, Feb. or March. Prune into shape, Feb. or March. Temp., March to Sept. 65° to 85°, Sept. to March 55° to 65°. Water moderately Oct. to Feb., freely afterwards. Syringe daily (except when in bloom) March to Sept. Apply liquid manure occasionally to healthy plants in flower. Plants one to two years old produce the best blooms.

Propagation: By cuttings of firm young side shoots, 2 to 3 in. long, inserted in well-drained pots of sandy peat under bell-glass in temp. 75° to 85°, Jan. to April.

Species Cultivated: *R. dumetorum*, yellowish-white, July, 5 ft., Trop. Asia; *macrantha*, yellow, summer, 20 to 30 ft., Trop. Africa; *maculata*, white, April, 10 to 15 ft., Trop. Africa; *malleifera*, white, July, 4 to 6 ft., Trop. Africa.

Rangoon Creeper, see *Quisqualis indica*.

Ranunculus (Buttercup; Crowfoot)—*Ranunculaceae*. Hardy and half-hardy, herbaceous, tuberous-rooted and aquatic perennials.

Culture of Tuberous-rooted Species (Turban, Persian, Dutch and Scotch Ranunculus): Soil, two parts good sandy loam and one part decayed cow manure for fine blooms; good ordinary soil enriched with rotted manure and leaf-mould for general culture. Position, open, sunny beds or borders. Plant Turban, Scotch and Dutch vars. in Oct. or Nov., in warm, sheltered districts, end of Feb. otherwise; Persian kinds, end of Feb. Place tubers claw-side downwards 2 in. deep and 3 in. apart if to be grown in beds; 2 in. deep and 4 in. apart in rows 5 in. asunder if to be grown in lines in border. Press tubers firmly in soil and cover with fine soil. Protect autumn-planted tubers with mulch of manure or leaves. Mulch in April with rotted manure or peat. Water copiously in dry weather. Sprinkle Peruvian guano on the bed at the rate of 1 oz. per square yard when leaves appear. Apply liquid manures—¼ oz. each of nitrate of soda, superphosphate, and sulphate of iron to 2 gall. of water—once a week from time leaves appear until flower buds open. Lift tubers when flowers fade and leaves turn yellow—generally early in July—dry them in the sun, and store away in sand in cool place till planting time.

Culture of Hardy Species: Soil, ordinary. Position, shady or partially shady border. Plant, Oct., Nov., March or April. Lift, divide and replant in fresh soil triennially. Mulch annually in March with decayed manure.

Propagation: By seeds sown as soon as ripe in autumn 1/16 in. deep in boxes or pans filled with equal parts loam, leaf-mould and sand and placed in a cold frame or cool greenhouse; herbaceous kinds by division in Oct. or March.

Tuberous-rooted Species Cultivated: *R. asiaticus*, 'Turban', 'Persian', 'French', 'Dutch' and 'Scotch Ranunculus', various colours, summer, 6 to 12 in., Orient.

Hardy Species Cultivated: *R. aconitifolius*, 'Fair Maids of Kent', white, May, 1½ to 2 ft., Europe, var. *flore-pleno*, 'Fair Maids of France', 'Bachelor's Buttons'; *acris*, yellow, spring, 1 to 2 ft., Europe (Br.), var. *flore-pleno*, double; *alpestris*, white, summer, 4 in., Europe; *amplexicaulis*, white, May, 6 to 12 in. S. Europe; *bulbosus*, yellow, spring, 1 ft., Europe (Br.), var. *flore-pleno*, double; *bullatus*, orange-yellow, May, 1 ft., rather tender, Medit. Region; *Callianthemum*, white, 3 in., Europe and Siberia; *crenatus*, white, April to July, Transylvania; *genariifolius*, yellow, May to June, 3 to 4 in., Europe; *glacialis*, white and rose, summer, 6 in., Arctic Regions; *gramineus*, yellow, spring, 6 to 8 in., Europe;

Lingua, ' Spearwort ', yellow, summer, 3 to 4 ft., Europe (Br.); *Lyallii,* ' New Zealand Mountain Buttercup ', white, spring, 2 to 3 ft., New Zealand; *monspeliacus,* yellow, spring, 1 ft., Medit. Region; *parnassifolius,* white, June, 6 in., Europe; *pyrenaeus,* white, summer, 6 in., S. Europe; *Seguieri,* white or rose-tinted, May to July, 4 in., Europe; *Thora* (syn. *R. carpaticus*), yellow, May to July, 6 in., S. Europe.

Ranzania—*Berberidaceae.* Hardy herbaceous perennials.
CULTURE: Woodland soil and half-shady aspect or north exposure.
PROPAGATION: By seeds sown in spring or by division of old plants in spring.
SPECIES CULTIVATED: *R. japonica,* lilac, April to May, 12 in., Japan.

Raoulia—*Compositae.* Small tufted or creeping perennial herbs.
CULTURE: Soil, sandy or gritty loam. Position, ledges of sunny rockeries or surface of moraine, suitable for carpeting the soil on rockeries; *R. eximia* and *R. grandiflora* in the Alpine House. Plant in spring.
PROPAGATION: By division in March; seeds.
SPECIES CULTIVATED: *R. australis,* silvery foliage, New Zealand; *eximia,* silver rosettes, New Zealand; *glabra,* emerald green foliage, New Zealand; *grandiflora,* silver foliage, New Zealand; *subsericea,* silvery foliage, very minute, New Zealand.

Rape, see *Brassica Napus.*

Raphanus—*Cruciferae.* Annual, biennial and perennial herbs, including the radish. First introduced mid-sixteenth century.
OUTDOOR CULTURE OF COMMON RADISH: Soil, any well-cultivated ground in good heart. Position, warm south border for first and last sowing; cool, partially shady ones for intermediate crops. Sow for first crop in Feb., either broadcast or in drills 6 in. apart; successional crops in similar manner at intervals of a fortnight until end of May. Make summer sowings in cool moist site or the plants will run to seed, but in suitable position sow each fortnight up to Oct. Long-rooted kinds best for spring sowing, round and oval ones for summer. *Forcing:* Make a hotbed of manure, cover with 4 in. of fine mould and place a frame over it. Sow seeds thinly, lightly cover with mould, moisten with tepid water and keep close until seedlings appear, then admit air daily. Thin early to ensure good roots. First sowing should be made in Dec., second in Jan., third in Feb. and fourth in March. Long-rooted vars. best for forcing. Seeds germinate in three to five days. Crop reaches maturity in five to six weeks.
CULTURE OF CHINESE RADISH: Sow seeds in drills 1 in. deep and 6 in. apart in July or Aug. Thin seedlings when 1 in. high to 6 in. apart. Water freely in dry weather. Lift roots in Nov. and store in sand in a cool shed to use as required.
CULTURE OF RAT-TAILED RADISH: Sow seeds in drills 1 in. deep and 6 in. apart in April, May or June. Thin to 6 in. apart when 1 in. high. Gather long seed pods when grown for pickling, mixing with salads, or cooking and eating, like asparagus.
SPECIES CULTIVATED: *R. sativus,* ' Common Radish ', white, purple, May, roots long, round or oval, crimson and white, Europe and Asia, var. *caudatus,* ' Rat-tail Radish ', roots not tuberous, pods 8 to 12 in. long, thick, used in pickles, *longipinnatus,* ' Chinese Radish ', roots long and durable, much grown in the Orient.

Raphiolepis—*Rosaceae.* Slightly tender and hardy evergreen flowering shrubs. First introduced early nineteenth century.
CULTURE: Soil, ordinary, well drained. Position, south and south-west walls or well-drained borders for tender species; sunny rockeries or sheltered borders for hardy species. Plant, Sept., Oct. or April. Prune straggling shoots into shape, April. Protect tender species in severe weather with mats or straw hurdles.
POT CULTURE OF TENDER SPECIES: Compost, equal parts peat, loam and coarse sand. Position, well-drained pots in cold greenhouse or pit, Sept. to May; sunny place outdoors, May to Sept. Pot, Feb. or March. Water copiously April to Oct., moderately afterwards.

PROPAGATION: By cuttings of firm shoots, 2 to 3 in. long, in compost of equal parts sand, peat and loam under bell-glass or hand-light in cold frame, Aug.

SPECIES CULTIVATED: *R. Delacouri*, tender, pink, May, 5 ft., hybrid; *indica*, 'Indian Hawthorn', tender, white, tinged pink, summer, 4 to 8 ft., China; *umbellata* (syn. *R. japonica*), hardy, withstands wind, white, fragrant, June, 10 ft., Japan.

Raspberry, see *Rubus idaeus*;   **Strawberry-,** see *Rubus illecebrosus*.

Rattan Palm, see Calamus.

Rattlesnake Fern, see *Botrychium virginianum*;   **-Plantain,** see Goodyera.

Ravenala—*Musaceae.* Stove evergreen perennials with palm-like trunks and very large leaves.

CULTURE: Compost, two parts good loam, one part well-decayed manure and one part sand. Position, pots, tubs or beds in lofty sunny stove. Pot or plant, Jan. to April. Water copiously Feb. to Oct., about once fortnightly afterwards. Syringe twice daily Feb. to Sept., once daily Sept. to Feb. Moist atmosphere essential. Apply stimulants twice or three times weekly March to Oct. Temp., March to Oct. 70° to 85°, Oct. to March 60° to 70°.

PROPAGATION: By suckers removed from parent plant and placed in pots in temp. 75° to 85° any time of year.

SPECIES CULTIVATED: *R. guianensis*, white, 15 ft., S. America; *madagascariensis*, 'Traveller's Tree', 15 to 30 ft., Madagascar.

Ravenea—*Palmae.* Stove palm with feather-shaped, green leaves. First introduced late nineteenth century.

CULTURE: Compost, equal parts peat, loam, leaf-mould and sand. Position, shady, moist. Pot, Feb. or March. Water abundantly March to Oct., moderately afterwards. Temp., March to Sept. 70° to 85°, Sept. to March 60° to 65°.

PROPAGATION: By seeds sown 1 in. deep in pots of light soil in temp. 85° in March.

SPECIES CULTIVATED: *R. Hildebrandtii*, 5 to 10 ft., Comoro Islands.

Ravenna Grass, see *Erianthus Ravenna*.

Redbird Cactus, see *Pedilanthes tithymaloides*.

Red-bud, see Cercis;   **-Chamomile,** see *Adonis annua*;   **-Chokeberry,** see *Aronia arbutifolia*;   **-Fir,** see *Abies magnifica*;   **-hot Cat-tail,** see *Acalypha hispida*; **-hot-poker,** see Kniphofia;   **-ink Plant,** see *Phytolacca americana*;   **-Sandal-wood Tree,** see *Adenanthera pavonina*;   **-Valerian,** see *Centranthus ruber*; **-wood,** see *Sequoia sempervirens*.

Reed Mace, see *Typha latifolia*.

Rehmannia—*Scrophulariaceae.* Half-hardy perennial herb. First introduced early nineteenth century.

OUTDOOR CULTURE: Soil, moist, sandy loam and peat. Position, partially shady borders, or at base of walls running east and west. Plant, March or April. Water freely in dry weather. Mulch liberally with leaf-mould or decayed manure in April. In cold districts it is best to lift plants in Oct., place in pots and store in cold frame or pit until following March, then plant out.

POT CULTURE: Compost, two parts sandy loam, one part peat, one part leaf-mould. Position, well-drained pots in cold frame, pit or greenhouse. Pot, Feb. or March. Water liberally April to Oct., moderately afterwards. Apply weak stimulants once a week during flowering period. Shade from bright sun essential.

PROPAGATION: By seeds sown in well-drained pans in warm greenhouse during Feb., or division in autumn.

SPECIES CULTIVATED: *R. angulata*, red and orange, 1 to 3 ft., China, var. *alba*, white, 1 to 3 ft.; *glutinosa* (syn. *R. chinensis*), purple, April, 1 to 2 ft., China and Japan.

Reineckia—*Liliaceae*. Hardy herbaceous perennial with creeping underground stems. First introduced late eighteenth century.

CULTURE: Soil, ordinary good. Position, sunny rockeries or borders; variegated var. as edgings to borders. Plant, March or April. Lift, divide and replant every three or four years. Water copiously in dry weather.

PROPAGATION: By division of creeping rhizomes in March or April.

SPECIES CULTIVATED: *R. carnea*, pink, fragrant, April, 6 in., China and Japan, var. *variegata*, variegated.

Reinwardtia—*Linaceae*. Greenhouse evergreen flowering shrubs. First introduced late eighteenth century.

CULTURE: Compost, equal parts loam and peat, little sand. Pot, March or April. Prune previous year's shoots to within 1 in. of their base in Feb. or March. Position, warm greenhouse Sept. to June; cold, sunny frame June to Sept. Water moderately Oct. to March, freely other times. Syringe twice daily Feb. to Sept. Apply weak stimulants occasionally when in flower. Temp., Sept. to Feb. 55° to 65°, Feb. to June 65° to 70°. Nip off points of young shoots in June to induce bushy growth.

PROPAGATION: By cuttings of shoots, 2 to 3 in. long, inserted in sandy soil under bell-glass in temp. 65° to 75° in April or May.

SPECIES CULTIVATED: *R. indica* (syn. *Linum trigynum*), ' Winter Flax ', yellow, autumn, 2 to 4 ft.; *tetragyna*, yellow, winter, 3 ft. Both natives of India.

Renanthera—*Orchidaceae*. An epiphytic genus. Few species, all with numerous showy flowers. Scapes usually branched. Flowers with narrow upper sepal and petals, and much broader lower sepals, lip small. Habit near to that of Vanda.

CULTURE: Compost, temps., etc., as for the warm-growing Vandas. The syringe may bef reely used in summer. Winter watering should be slightly more infrequent than with Vandas as the leaves are of harder texture.

PROPAGATION: As for Vandas, the stem severance being always made below stem roots.

SPECIES CULTIVATED: *R. annamensis*, small, orange-yellow and crimson, early summer, Annam; *coccinea*, vermilion-red with a little yellow, stem will reach a great length, summer, various, Burma, Cochin-China; *elongata*, small, many, yellow with suffusions of purple-red, autumn, Java, Sumatra; *Imschootiana*, many, upper segments yellow and vermilion, lower, vermilion, lip deeper in colour, spring, summer, 1 to 3 ft., Burma, Assam; *matutina*, orange-yellow, spotted scarlet-crimson, mid-lobe or lip hooked, autumn, winter, Java, Philippines; *pulchella*, yellow and crimson, summer, Burma; *Storiei*, stem up to 12 ft., many, large, upper segments orange-yellow to red, lower, dark crimson with lighter tints, lip crimson, yellow, whitish, summer, autumn, Philippines.

Reseda—*Resedaceae*. A perennial, but usually grown as an annual. First introduced mid-eighteenth century.

OUTDOOR CULTURE: Soil, ordinary, containing old mortar or slaked lime. Position, sunny beds, borders or rockeries. Sow seeds ⅛ in. deep in masses or rows in March or April. Thin seedlings when 1 in. high to 3 in. apart. Water freely in summer. Apply stimulants occasionally when in flower. In warm, dry positions plants will survive the winter outdoors for several years.

INDOOR CULTURE: Compost, any good potting soil containing lime. Sow March or April for summer flowering, July or Aug. for winter and spring. Fill 3 in. pots to within ¼ in. of rim, sow five or six seeds in each, cover with ¹⁄₁₆ in. of soil, and place in temp. 55°. When seedlings are 1 to 2 in. high transfer bodily to flowering pots (5 in.). Pot firmly and disturb roots as little as possible. Water moderately at first, freely afterwards. Pinch off points of main shoots when 3 in. high if abundance of bloom is required. Apply dilute farmyard manure water or fertiliser once a week in the growing season.

SPECIES CULTIVATED: *R. odorata*, ' Mignonette ', yellow and white, summer, 1 to 2 ft., N. Africa and Egypt.

Rest Harrow, see Ononis.

Restrepia—*Orchidaceae.* An epiphytic genus. One section (not in cultivation) has a branching creeping rhizome. A second section is of tufted habit much as in Pleurothallis, the stems bearing a solitary, usually heart-shaped, leaf. Flowers solitary, the upper sepal and petals narrow, often with a ' knob ' at their apices. The lower sepals are much larger, joined, except at their tips, the smaller lip lying on them. The flowers of some are brightly marked, in all freely produced.

CULTURE: Compost and general conditions as for Pleurothallis.

PROPAGATION: By division of the plants in spring.

SPECIES CULTIVATED: A selection—*R. antennifera*, yellowish-red marked, lower sepals each with seven purplish-red stripes, spring, summer, Colombia; *elegans*, small, whitish, purple streaked, lower sepals yellowish, purple spotted, spring, summer, Venezuela; *maculata*, comparatively large, yellow, red dotted, lower sepals yellow spotted with brown-purple, summer, Colombia; *pandurata*, whitish, spotted crimson-purple, various, Colombia; *striata*, maroon, lower sepals yellow, each with seven maroon stripes, various, Colombia; *trichoglotta*, whitish and purple, lower sepals cream, spotted crimson-purple, lip haired, summer, Colombia.

Resurrection Plant, see *Anastatica hierochuntica* and *Selaginella lepidophylla.*

Retinospora—Juvenile stages of Chamaecyparis and Thuja, not recognised as a genus.

Rhabdothamnus—*Gesneriaceae.* Dwarf slender greenhouse shrub. A monotypic genus from New Zealand.

CULTURE: Compost, equal parts sandy loam, peat and leaf-mould. Position, well-drained pots in shady part of greenhouse or frame. Water carefully Sept. to March, moderately at other times. Temp., March to Oct. 55° to 65°, Oct. to March 45° to 55°.

PROPAGATION: By seeds sown in sandy peat in temp. of 65° during spring; cuttings of young side shoots inserted in sandy peat under bell-glass or in propagating frame, temp. 60° to 65°.

SPECIES CULTIVATED: *R. Solandri*, orange, striped brownish-red, winter, 1 to 3 ft.

Rhamnus (Buckthorn)—*Rhamnaceae.* Hardy evergreen and deciduous trees and shrubs.

CULTURE: Soil, ordinary. Position, sunny or shady shrubberies; good seaside shrubs. Plant, Oct. to March. Prune, Feb.

PROPAGATION: By seeds sown outdoors in autumn; cuttings inserted outdoors in ordinary soil in Sept.; by layering in Sept. or March.

SPECIES CULTIVATED: *R. Alaternus*, 10 to 20 ft., evergreen, S.W. Europe, and vars. *angustifolia* and *argenteo-variegata*, leaves margined with creamy white, useful and attractive maritime shrub; *californica*, 10 to 15 ft., evergreen, Western N. America; *cathartica*, ' Buckthorn ', 5 to 10 ft., deciduous, Europe (Br.); *Frangula*, 15 to 20 ft., deciduous, Europe (Br.); *imeretina* (sometimes wrongly called *R. libanotica*), 10 ft., deciduous, fine autumn colour, Western Caucasus; *pumila*, 6 in., deciduous, Alps; *Purshiana*, ' Cascara Buckthorn ', drug obtained from bark, 40 to 50 ft., Western N. America.

Rhapis—*Palmae.* Greenhouse, fan-shaped palms. First introduced mid-eighteenth century.

CULTURE: Compost, two parts rich loam, one part decayed leaf-mould and sand. Position, well-drained pots in greenhouse or dwelling-room during summer. Pot, Feb. or March. Water copiously April to Oct., moderately afterwards. Apply weak stimulants occasionally during summer. Place small lumps of sulphate of iron on surface of soil to ensure deep healthy green foliage. Shade from sun essential. Syringe twice daily in summer, once other times. Temp., March to Sept. 55° to 65°, Sept. to March 45° to 55°.

PROPAGATION: By seeds sown 1 in. deep in light soil in temp. of 80° in Feb. or March; suckers removed in April or Aug.

SPECIES CULTIVATED: *R. excelsa* (syn. *R. flabelliformis*), 3 to 4 ft., China and Japan; *humilis*, 3 ft., China.

Rhazya—*Apocynaceae*. Hardy sub-shrub. First introduced late nineteenth century.

CULTURE: Soil, sandy loam. Position, sunny well-drained slopes or rock gardens. Plant, March to April.

PROPAGATION: By seeds sown in pans in greenhouse during Feb. or March.

SPECIES CULTIVATED: *R. orientalis*, blue, late summer, 9 to 12 in., Levant.

Rheum (Rhubarb)—*Polygonaceae*. Hardy herbaceous perennials. Ornamental foliage plants, one species cultivated for edible stalks. First introduced mid-sixteenth century.

CULTURE OF EDIBLE RHUBARB: Soil, light, deep, rich. Position, sunny, open. Plant single roots firmly with crowns at surface level, 3 ft. apart in rows 3 ft. asunder, in Nov., Feb. or March. Top-dress with manure in Nov. or Feb., forking it into surface of soil. Lift, divide and replant every four years. No stalks should be gathered the first year. Discontinue pulling after July. Remove flower stems directly they appear. *Forcing Roots*: Two- to five-year-old plants best for forcing. Cover crowns with pots, boxes or tubs, and place fresh manure and tree leaves over these in Jan. or Feb., or lift strong roots exposed to frost and then place close together in deep boxes underneath staging in warm greenhouse, in corners of dark cellars, or in mushroom houses, with a little soil between. Keep moist and dark. Temp., 55° to 75°. Water moderately at first, but freely as growth commences. Forcing season, Nov. to Feb. Reject roots after forcing.

PROPAGATION: By seeds sown ⅛ in. deep in ordinary soil outdoors in March or April; by division of roots with crowns or buds attached, Nov. to Feb.

CULTURE OF ORNAMENTAL-LEAVED SPECIES: Soil, deep, rich, ordinary. Position, isolated specimens on lawns, wild gardens, islands; sunny. Plant, Nov. to Feb. Water copiously in dry seasons. Apply stimulants occasionally in summer.

SPECIES CULTIVATED: *R. acuminatum*, 3 ft., Himalaya; *Collinianum*, 6 ft., China; *emodi*, 6 to 10 ft., Himalaya; *officinalis*, ' Medicinal Rhubarb ', 8 to 10 ft., Tibet; *palmatum*, 5 to 6 ft., N.E. Asia, and var. *tanguticum*; *Rhaponticum*, ' Edible Rhubarb ', to 6 ft., Siberia; *Ribes*, showy, blood-red fruits, 5 ft., Asia Minor to Persia.

Rhexia—*Melastomaceae*. Hardy perennial herb. First introduced mid-eighteenth century.

CULTURE: Soil, sandy peat or bog. Position, open, sunny bog, swamp, or moist border. Plant, Oct., Nov., March or April. The plants should not be disturbed too frequently and are often only hardy in sheltered positions.

PROPAGATION: By division of roots in March or April; seed sown in sandy soil in pans.

SPECIES CULTIVATED: *R. virginica*, ' Deer Grass ', ' Meadow Beauty ', purple, summer, 6 to 12 in., N. America.

Rhipsalis—*Cactaceae*. Greenhouse succulent shrubs. First introduced mid-eighteenth century.

CULTURE: Compost, equal parts sandy loam, leaf-mould, brick rubbish and coarse silver sand. Position, well-drained pots in light greenhouse. Pot, April or May; pots to be drained one-sixth depth for large plants, one-third for small plants. Press compost in firmly. Water moderately April to Aug., keep almost dry Aug. to April. Shade from bright sunshine. Temp., March to Sept. 55° to 65°, Sept. to March 50° to 55°.

PROPAGATION: By seeds sown ⅛ in. deep in well-drained sandy soil and placed in temp. 75°, March; keep soil moderately moist. By cuttings of stems inserted in small pots of sandy soil in summer; grafting on *Cereus speciosissimus*.

SPECIES CULTIVATED: *R. cassutha*, yellow, Sept., 1 ft., W. Indies; *cereuscula* (syn. *R. Saglionis*), ' Mistletoe Cactus ', yellow, March, 1 ft., Buenos Ayres; *crispata*, white, Dec., 1 ft., Brazil; *grandiflora* (syn. *R. funalis*), white, Feb., 3 ft., S. America; *Houlletiana*, yellow, winter, Brazil; *mesembryanthoides*, white, spring, 6 in., S. America; *pachyptera*, white, Feb., Trop. America; *prismatica* (syn. *Pseudorhipalis alata*), white, June, W. Indies; *sarmentacea*, white, spring, Argentina.

Rhodanthe, see *Helipterum Manglesii.*

Rhodochiton—*Scrophulariaceae.* Greenhouse climbing herb. First introduced early nineteenth century.

CULTURE: Compost, equal parts loam and leaf-mould and half a part silver sand. Position, well-drained pots, boxes, beds or borders, with shoots trained up trellis, walls or rafters of sunny greenhouse. Pot, March to May. Water freely March to Sept., moderately Sept. to March. Apply stimulants during flowering period. Shade from bright sun. Thin out and shorten shoots moderately in Feb. Temp., March to Sept. 55° to 65°, Sept. to March 45° to 55°.

PROPAGATION: By seeds sown $\frac{1}{16}$ in. deep in ordinary light soil in temp. 50° to 60°, March, transplanting seedlings when 1 in. high singly in 2 or 3 in. pots; cuttings of shoots inserted in sandy soil under bell-glass in temp. 45°, March to Aug.

SPECIES CULTIVATED: *R. atrosanguineum* (syn. *R. volubile*), ' Purple Bellerine ', reddish-purple, summer, 10 to 15 ft., Mexico.

Rhododendron—*Ericaceae.* Greenhouse and hardy evergreen and deciduous shrubs, including **Azalea.** *R. ponticum*, parent of hardy kinds, first introduced mid-eighteenth century; *R. Simsii* (Indian Azalea), early nineteenth century.

HARDY HYBRID RHODODENDRONS: In the main the hybrid garden races of evergreen rhododendrons have sprung from such species as *RR. catawbiense, ponticum, caucasicum, arboreum* and *Griersonianum.* A lesser part has been played by *R. maximum, Griffithianum, Fortunei, Thomsonii, Williamsianum, dicroanthum, haematodes, eriogynum, repens, neriiflorum, Elliottii, cinnabarinum, discolor* and *campylocarpum.* The deciduous hybrid azaleas have been obtained from *R. flavum, calendulaceum, nudiflorum, viscosum, occidentale, molle* and others. The Ghent azaleas are, in the main, derived from *R. flavum, viscosum, nudiflorum, calendulaceum* and *luteum.* The dwarf Japanese azaleas, such as Hinodgeri, are closely allied to *R. obtusum*, those known as ' Kurume Azaleas ' being forms raised over a period of many years by Japanese horticulturists round the city of Kurume, in the southern island of Kyushu, Japan. The greenhouse azaleas are, in the main, hybrids of *R. Simsii.*

CULTURE OF GREENHOUSE SPECIES: Compost, two parts turfy peat, one part silver sand. Position, well-drained pots or tubs, indoors all the year for stove species, greenhouse species may be stood outdoors on bed of cinders in sunny position from June to Sept. Pot, April or May, directly after flowering. Water freely April to Oct., moderately afterwards, preferably rain-water; water containing lime is injurious. A little artificial fertiliser may be applied to surface of soil when flower buds show. Repotting only necessary every three or four years. Temp. stove species, 55° to 65° Sept. to March, 70° to 80° March to Sept.; greenhouse species, 45° to 55° Sept. to March, 55° to 65° March to Sept.

CULTURE OF HARDY SPECIES: It is impossible to cover fully, in a confined space, the immense variety of species and hybrids and their individual requirements. The species vary from low-creeping shrubs to large trees, and natural conditions in which they are found vary from shaded and sheltered woodland to elevated dry and exposed moorland. For full details refer to *Rhododendron Year Books* and *Rhododendron Handbook* published by the Royal Horticultural Society. Only one species, *R. hirsutum*, will grow in soil containing free lime. General Cultivation: Lime-free soil essential; the majority like cool, moist and humus-rich soil, and both heavy and light soils should receive heavy dressings well dug in prior to planting. Hungry light soils should have some well-decayed manure mixed in also. All rhododendrons benefit from annual top-dressing; useful material consists of compost, half-decayed leaves or bracken. Best garden value for ordinary conditions found amongst the numerous named garden hybrids, which are easily grown. Position, in clumps or drifts in open border or semi-woodland glades.

Some species equally easy but others require specialised positions. Always remove developing seed pods at fading of flowers.

CULTURE OF INDIAN AZALEA: Compost, three parts peat, one part loam and one part equal proportions of leaf-mould and silver sand. Position, well-drained pots in sunny greenhouse from Oct. to June, in partial shade outdoors, June to Sept. Repot directly after flowering, firm potting essential. Prune only to shorten straggly growth. Syringe daily after flowering till plants are taken outdoors. Water moderately Oct. to March, freely afterwards, never allowing roots to get dry. Apply weak liquid manure when flower buds form. Temp., Oct. to March 45° to 55°, March to June 65°. Remove seed pods directly they form.

PROPAGATION: By seeds sown on surface of sandy peat from mid-Jan. to mid-Feb., slightly covered with fine sand and placed under bell-glass in temp. 55° to 60°, kept moderately moist; cuttings of firm shoots, 3 in. long, with a heel, taken from the end of June to Nov., inserted in three parts sand, one part granulated peat under bell-glass in temp. 45° to 55° at first, then 10° higher, steady bottom heat aids rooting of large-leaved kinds; small-leaved kinds can be rooted without heat; take cuttings of large-leaved kinds first and continue to smallest-leaved vars. last; layering in spring or summer; grafting on common species in a close frame or propagator in March. The hardiness of the different species is indicated by a letter following the specific name, as follows:

A.   Hardy anywhere in the British Isles and may be planted in full exposure if desired.
B.   Hardy anywhere in the British Isles but requires some shade to obtain the best results.
C.   Hardy along the seaboard and in warm gardens inland.
D.   Hardy in south and west but requires shelter even in warm gardens inland.
E.   Requires shelter in most favoured gardens.
F.   Usually a greenhouse shrub.
P.   Early flowering.

From B to E inclusive, planting in open spaces in woodland usually gives the best results.

SPECIES CULTIVATED: *R. ambiguum*, A, yellow, April to May, to 5 ft., W. China; *arboreum*, D, red, Jan. to April, 30 to 40 ft., Himalaya; *argyrophyllum*, A, white, May, to 20 ft., S.W. China; *Augustinii*, C, blue, early May, 10 ft., China; *auriculatum*, B, white, fragrant, July to Aug., 15 ft., China; *barbatum*, B, scarlet, March, 30 to 60 ft., Himalaya; *bullatum*, D, white, fragrant, April to May, 8 ft., Yunnan; *calophytum*, B, white or pink, deep blotch, March to April, 30 to 40 ft., China; *campanulatum*, B, rosy purple, April, 12 to 18 ft., Himalaya; *campylocarpum*, B, yellow, April to May, 4 to 8 ft., Himalaya; *campylogynum*, A, rose-purple to black-purple, May, 6 ft., W. Yunnan; *camtschaticum*, A, reddish-purple, dwarf, deciduous, May, N.E. Asia; *catawbiense*, A, magenta, June, 10 ft., N. Carolina; *caucasicum*, A, yellowish, May, 3 to 4 ft., Caucasus; *ciliatum*, C, white, March to April, 6 ft., spreading, Himalaya; *cinnabarinum*, B, bright red, May to June, to 6 ft., Himalaya; *concatenans*, C, apricot, April to May, Himalaya; *Dalhousiae*, F, white, flushed pink, 6 to 10 ft., Himalaya; *dauricum*, B, rose-purple, Feb., 8 ft., deciduous, N.E. Asia, var. *sempervirens*, evergreen; *Davidsonianum*, B, pink, spotted red, April to May, to 10 ft., China; *decorum*, B, white, sometimes shell pink, Mar. to May, 12 to 20 ft., China; *dichroanthum*, B, deep orange, May to June, 6 ft., Yunnan; *discolor*, B, pink or white, July, China; *Edgeworthii*, F, white, April to May, 8 to 10 ft., Himalaya; *Elliottii*, D, deep rosy purple, May to June, small straggling shrub, Manipur; *eriogynum*, D, clear bright red, June, 10 ft., Tibet; *euchaites*, C, crimson-scarlet, April to May, 15 to 20 ft., Yunnan and Burma; *Falconeri*, C, creamy white, April to May, 40 to 50 ft., Himalaya; *Fargesii*, B, bluish-pink, April, 20 ft., China; *fastigiatum*, A, light purple, May, erect shrublet, China; *ferrugineum*, A, rosy crimson, June, 3 to 5 ft., Switzerland; *fictolacteum*, B, white with dark crimson blotch, April, 15 to 45 ft., China; *flavidum*, A, pale yellow, March, small shrub, W. China; *formosum*, D, white, fragrant, May to June, to 8 ft., Himalaya;

Forrestii, B, dark crimson, April, creeping, China; *Fortunei*, B, pinky lilac, May, 15 to 20 ft., China; *fulgens*, B, bright scarlet, March, 6 to 12 ft., Himalaya; *fulvum*, B, white, flushed rose, crimson blotch, March to April, 20 ft., China; *glaucum*, B, pale old rose, May, aromatic foliage, 4 ft., Himalaya; *grande*, E, creamy white, purple blotch, Feb. to April, 30 ft., large leaves, Himalaya; *Griersonianum*, D, scarlet, June, 7 ft., China; *Griffithianum* (syn. *R. Aucklandii*), E, white, May, 14 to 20 ft., Himalaya; *haematodes*, B, scarlet-crimson, May, 3 to 4 ft., China; *Hanceanum*, C, pale yellow, April, 3 ft., China; *hippophaeoides*, A, lilac to rose, April, 2 to 3 ft., China; *hirsutum*, A, small rose pink, June, Mts. Europe; *Hookeri*, E, blood-red, March to April, 12 to 14 ft., Himalaya; *impeditum*, A, mauve or purplish-blue, April to May, to 1½ ft., Yunnan; *intricatum*, A, mauve, small shrublet, April to May, China; *javanicum*, F, red, bell-shaped, to 4 ft., Malaya; *Johnstoneanum*, C, pale yellow, fragrant, May, large bush, Manipur; *Keysii*, C, red, tipped yellow, June, 12 ft., Bhutan; *lacteum*, C, yellow, April to May, to 30 ft., Himalaya; *lapponicum*, A, purple, Jan. to Feb., to 1½ ft., Lapland; *ledoides*, C, clear rose, May, to 2 ft., Yunnan; *lepidotum*, A to C, pale yellow, pink or purple, June, 3 to 4 ft., Himalaya; *leucaspis*, C, white, Feb. to March, 1 to 2 ft., Tibet; *Loderi*, white to rose, fragrant, hybrid; *Ludlowii*, A, yellow, 1 to 2 ft., Bhutan; *lutescens*, C, pale yellow, Feb. to April, 5 ft., Caucasus; *Macabeanum*, C, pale yellow, purple spots, March, 45 ft., Assam; *Maddenii*, E, white-scented, June, 6 to 9 ft., Himalaya; *maximum*, A, light rose-purple or white, spotted yellow-green, July, 12 ft., N. America; *Metternichii*, B, rose, April, 3 to 8 ft., Japan; *micranthum*, A, small milky white, July, to 6 ft., China; *minus*, A, rose, June, to 10 ft., N. America; *moupinense*, B, white, sometimes pink, Feb., to 4 ft., W. China; *mucronulatum*, B, rosy purple, Jan., 7 to 8 ft., Korea and Japan; *myrtilloides*, A, small plum-coloured, May, 3 to 4 in., Burma; *neriiflorum*, C, scarlet, April, 3 to 9 ft., May to June; *niveum*, B, purple, April to May, 15 ft., Himalaya; *Nobleanum*, rose, hybrid; *Nuttallii*, F, light yellow, fragrant, April to May, 30 ft., Himalaya; *orbiculare*, B, rose-pink, April, 10 ft., W. China; *oreodoxa*, B, pink, March to April, shrub, W. China; *oreotrephes*, B, mauve, 7 ft., May, China; *pachytrichum*, C, white to pale rose, April, 6 to 18 ft., W. Szechuan; *parvifolium*, A, pale rosy magenta, to 1½ ft., Siberia, Korea; *pemakoense*, A, pinkish mauve, April, aromatic undershrub spreading by underground stolons, E. Tibet; *ponticum*, A, purple, June, to 10 ft., N. Asia Minor; *praecox*, rose-purple, March to April, hybrid; *racemosum*, A, pink, March to May, 3 to 4 ft., China; *radicans*, B, purple, May, 2 to 4 in., prostrate, Tibet; *repens*, A, scarlet, April to May, 6 to 12 in., creeping, W. China; *rubiginosum*, A, small rosy lilac, April to May, to 30 ft., Yunnan; *russatum*, A, blue-purple, April to May, to 4 ft., Yunnan; *sanguineum*, B, crimson, May, 3 ft., W. Yunnan; *scintillans*, A, lavender-blue, early April, 2 to 3 ft., Yunnan; *sinogrande*, D, creamy white, April, 20 to 30 ft., China; *Souliei*, B, white to soft rose, late May, 6 to 12 in., China; *spinuliferum*, C, crimson to brick-red, April, 6 to 8 ft., China; *strigillosum*, D, crimson-scarlet, March, 12 to 20 ft., China; *sutchuenense*, B, rosy lilac, sometimes lilac-white, Feb. to March, 10 to 20 ft., China; *Taggianum*, E, pure white, fragrant, April to May, 6 to 8 ft., China; *tephropeplum*, C, magenta-rose, April to May, 2 to 7 ft., S.E. Tibet; *Thomsonii*, B, blood-red, April, 6 to 14 ft., Himalaya; *triflorum*, D, light yellow, spotted green, Himalaya; *Veitchianum*, F, white, tinged green, 3 ft., Himalaya; *venator*, C, scarlet, end May, 8 to 12 ft., Tibet; *Wightii*, B, pale yellow, crimson blotch, April, 10 to 15 ft., Himalaya; *Williamsianum*, C, shell pink, April, 3 to 5 ft., W. China; *yunnanense*, B, pinkish or nearly white, end May, to 6 ft., China.

AZALEA SECTION: *R. arborescens* (syn. *A. arborescens*), A, white or pinkish, June to July, 8 to 17 ft., N. America; *calendulaceum* (syn. *A. calendulacea*), A, ' Flame Azalea ', yellow or orange to scarlet, May to June, 4 to 10 ft., N. America; *indicum* (syn. *A. indica*, but not the *A. indica* of the trade, which is *R. Simsii*), red to scarlet, June, 6 ft., evergreen, Japan, var. *balsaminaeflorum* (syn. *A. rosaeflora* of trade), double salmon-red; *linearifolium* (syn. *A. linearifolia*), B, rose-pink, April to May, to 4 ft., evergreen, Japan; *luteum* (syns. *A. pontica*, *R. flavum*), A, yellow, fragrant, May, 12 ft., Caucasus and E. Europe; *molle* (syns. *A. mollis, R. sinense*), C, yellow, May, 4 ft., China; *mucronatum* (syn. *A. ledifolia*), C, white, May, 6 to 10 ft., evergreen, Japan; *nudiflorum* (syn. *A. nudiflora*), A, pink or whitish, May, 2 to 8 ft., N. America; *obtusum* (syn. *A. obtusa*), A, purple through reds and pink to white, May, 3 ft., evergreen, Japan, vars. *japonicum*, ' Kurume Azalea ', *amoenum*, ' Amoenum Azalea '; *occidentale* (syn. *A. occidentalis*), A, white or pink with yellow blotch, June, 8 ft., N. America; *reticulatum* (syns. *A. reticulata, R. dilatatum, R. rhombicum*), A, bright purple, April to May, to 25 ft., Japan; *Schlippenbachii* (syn. *A. Schlippenbachii*), C, pale to rose-pink, April to May, 3 to 15 ft., Korea, Manchuria, Japan; *Simsii* (*A. indica* of trade), F, ' Indian Azalea ', rose-red, May, 5 ft., China; *Vaseyi* (syn. *A. Vaseyi*), B, pale pink to pink, May, N. Carolina; *viscosum* (syn. *A. viscosa*), A, white or suffused pink, July, 8 to 12 ft., N. America; *yedoense* (syn. *A. yodogava*), B, pale rosy purple, double, May, 2 to 6 ft., Japan.

Rhodohypoxis—*Amaryllidaceae.* Dwarf, hardy, bulbous plants.

CULTURE: Well-drained, sandy, moist loam and sunny position in rock garden.

PROPAGATION: By seeds sown in compost as above; offsets.

SPECIES CULTIVATED: *R. Baueri*, rose-red, early summer, 2 in., Natal; *platypetala*, white or soft pink, early summer, 2 in., Natal. There are also many variously coloured garden hybrids.

Rhodothamnus (Ground Cistus)—*Ericaceae.* Hardy evergreen flowering shrub. First introduced late eighteenth century.

CULTURE: Soil, equal parts peat, loam and sand. Position, fissures between pieces of limestone on rockeries. Plant, March or April. Water freely in dry weather.

PROPAGATION: By means of division at planting time, pulling off pieces with a few roots attached, as advised for rhododendron, and by seeds.

SPECIES CULTIVATED: *R. Chamaecistus* (syn. *Rhododendron Chamaecistus*), pink, spring, 6 to 12 in., Austrian Alps.

Rhodotypos—*Rosaceae.* Hardy deciduous flowering shrub with showy black berries in winter. First introduced mid-nineteenth century.

CULTURE: Soil, good ordinary. Position, against south or west walls or fences or in open border. Plant, Oct. to March. Prune in May or June, cutting off old or weak shoots only.

PROPAGATION: By cuttings of half-ripened shoots in sandy soil under bell-glass in brisk bottom heat.

SPECIES CULTIVATED: *R. scandens* (syn. *R. kerrioides*), white, May to July, 4 to 6 ft., China and Japan. This shrub is frequently erroneously called *Kerria japonica alba.*

Rhoeo—*Commelinaceae.* Greenhouse herbaceous perennial. First introduced mid-nineteenth century.

CULTURE: Compost, equal parts loam, leaf-mould and sand. Position, pots or baskets suspended from roof. Pot, Jan. to April. Water freely March to Oct., moderately afterwards. Shade from strong sunshine. Temp., Oct. to April 40° to 50°, April to Oct. 55° to 65°.

PROPAGATION: By cuttings of young shoots inserted in light soil under a bell-glass in above temp., March to Oct.

SPECIES CULTIVATED: *R. discolor* (syn. *Tradescantia discolor*), white, summer, creeping, Mexico, and var. *vittata* (syn. *Tradescantia variegata*), leaves striped with pale yellow.

Rhopalostylis—*Palmae.* Stove feather palms. First introduced early nineteenth century.

CULTURE: Compost, equal parts loam, peat, leaf-mould and sand. Position, pots or tubs in moist, shady greenhouse or conservatory. Pot, Feb. or March. Water copiously April to Oct., moderately afterwards. Apply stimulants occasionally May to Sept. Keep piece of sulphate of iron on surface of soil to ensure deep green foliage. Syringe twice daily April to Sept., once daily afterwards. Temp., March to Sept. 70° to 85°, Sept. to March 55° to 65°.

SPECIES CULTIVATED: *R. Baueri* (syn. *Areca Baueri*), 20 ft. or more, Norfolk Island; *sapida* (syns. *Areca* or *Kentia sapida*), 10 to 20 ft., New Zealand.

Rhubarb, see *Rheum Rhaponticum.*

Rhus (Sumach)—*Anacardiaceae.* Hardy deciduous flowering trees, shrubs and climbers with brilliantly coloured foliage in autumn. Two species hardy in this country, *R. radicans* and *R. vernix,* produce acrid and poisonous juices and should not be generally planted. A few species previously included in this genus have been transferred to Cotinus. First introduced early seventeenth century.

CULTURE: Soil, ordinary. Position, sunny borders or shrubberies; walls or old tree trunks for *R. radicans.* Plant, Oct. to Feb. Prune flowering species moderately after blooming, others in Nov. or Dec.

PROPAGATION: By cuttings of firm shoots, 6 to 8 in. long, in ordinary soil in cold frame or under hand-light, Oct. to Nov.; cuttings of roots, 2 or 3 in. long, planted 3 in. deep in sandy soil, Oct. or Nov.; layering shoots in autumn.

SPECIES CULTIVATED: *R. aromatica* (syn.*R. canadensis*), yellow, April, 3 to 5 ft., N. America; *copallina,* ' Shining Sumach ', yellowish, July to Aug., 3 to 5 ft., red fruits, Eastern N. America; *glabra,* ' Smooth Sumach ', 4 to 10 ft., close erect panicles of small fruits densely covered with crimson hairs, U.S.A., and var. *laciniata,* leaves finely cut; *radicans* (syn. *R. Toxicodendron*), ' Poison Ivy ', red-tinted foliage in autumn, 8 to 9 ft., Eastern U.S.A.; *typhina,* ' Stag's Horn Sumach ', 15 to 25 ft., crimson panicle of small fruits, var. *laciniata,* feathery foliage; *vernix,* ' Poison Sumach ', to 20 ft., leaves orange and scarlet in autumn but highly poisonous to the touch, U.S.A.

Rhynchostylis—*Orchidaceae.* An epiphytic genus, closely allied to Saccolabium and sometimes included in that genus. Leaves leathery. Flowers many, thickly set in axillary racemes, showy stems, stout, rather short.

CULTURE: Compost, temps., etc., as for Saccolabium but the leaf texture must have consideration in winter waterings. Baskets are preferable to pots, root disturbance can be avoided by picking out the old and stale compost and replacing with new as required.

PROPAGATION: Occasionally basal growths are produced but the plants resent disturbance. Sometimes imported plants may be carefully divided.

SPECIES CULTIVATED: *R. coelestis,* white, tipped deep blue, spike ascendant, summer, Siam; *retusa,* variable, fragrant, white, spotted amethyst-purple, lip purple in front, spike pendulous, summer, India, Burma, Java, etc., var. *guttata,* flowers smaller, more numerous, densely spotted.

Rhyncospermum, see Trachelospermum.

Ribbon Fern, see *Pteris serrulata;* **-Grass,** see *Phalaris arundinacea* var. *picta.*

Ribes—*Saxifragaceae.* Hardy deciduous fruit-bearing and flowering shrubs including Grossularia, which some botanists recognise as a separate genus. Berries oblong or globose, seeds plentiful.

CULTURE OF BLACKCURRANT: Soil, good ordinary. Position, sunny. Plant 5 ft. apart each way, Nov. to Feb. Fruit borne on shoots of previous year's growth. Pruning, thin out old shoots, Nov. to Feb. Tipping young shoots encourages large, even fruits.

CULTURE OF RED AND WHITE CURRANT: Soil, good ordinary. Position, sunny for early crops, against north walls or fences for late ones. Plant, Nov. to Feb., 5 to 6 ft. apart each way. Pruning, allow current year's branch extension shoots to remain and shorten others to within four leaves of their base in June or July. Cut back the extension shoots by half in young bushes or to leave only 1 in. of new growth in large old bushes, between Nov. and Feb.; at same time cut back summer-pruned laterals to ½ in. and cut out old or distorted branches. Fruit borne on spurs on older wood.

CULTURE OF GOOSEBERRY: Soil, good ordinary. Position, sunny for early crops, against north or east walls for late crops. Plant, Nov. to Feb., 5 to 6 ft. apart each way. Pruning, either spur all side shoots to 1 in. for large dessert fruit or allow long spurs for greater quantity of fruit. In each case keep centre of bush open to facilitate picking. Spur side shoots of cordon trees.

MANURES FOR CURRANTS AND GOOSEBERRIES: Blackcurrants are gross feeders and require plenty of nitrogen. Give an autumn mulch of compost mixed with chicken manure or of well-rotted stable manure or dress with a complete fertiliser 4 oz. per square yard and apply 1 oz. per square yard sulphate of ammonia in spring. Extra potash should be applied to red and white currants, and gooseberries, apply 2 oz. per square yard sulphate of potash in spring. Muriate of potash causes leaf scorch.

CULTURE OF FLOWERING CURRANTS: Soil, ordinary. Position, sunny. Plant, Oct. to Feb. Pruning, remove some of older wood after flowering. Top-dress occasionally with decayed manure in autumn.

PROPAGATION: By cuttings, 6 to 8 in. long, inserted in ordinary soil outdoors, Oct. to Feb.

FRUITING SPECIES CULTIVATED: *R. Grossularia*, ' English Gooseberry ', to 3 ft., Europe, N. Africa, S.W. Asia; *nigrum*, ' European blackcurrant ', to 6 ft., Europe, Asia; *rubrum*, ' Northern Redcurrant ', to 6 ft., Europe, Asia; *sativum* (syn. *R. vulgare*), ' Common Garden Currant ', fruit red or white, to 5 ft., W. Europe.

FLOWERING SPECIES CULTIVATED: *R. alpinum*, 'Alpine Currant', greenish-yellow, fruit scarlet, April and May, 8 ft., Europe; *americanum*, ' American Blackcurrant ', black fruits, crimson and yellow foliage in autumn, 3 to 4 ft., N. America; *aureum*, ' Buffalo Currant ', yellow, April, 6 to 8 ft., N. America; *Gordonianum*, yellow and red, April and May, 6 to 8 ft., hybrid; *sanguineum*, ' Flowering Currant ', rose, May, 6 to 8 ft., California, vars. *album*, white, *splendens*, fine deep red; *speciosum*, ' Fuchsia-flowered Gooseberry ', rich red flowers, April and May, 6 to 9 ft., California.

Riccia (Crystalwort)—*Ricciaceae*. Tender floating aquatics, much used by aquarists. Masses of tiny leaves tangled together in packs 1 to 2 in. deep at times.

CULTURE: No planting, simply drop on surface of water; temp. should not fall below 60°.

PROPAGATION: By division, any time.

SPECIES CULTIVATED: *R. fluitans*, Trop. America; *natans*, green, Trop. America.

Rice Flower, see Pimelea; **-paper Tree,** see *Tetrapanax papyriferum*.

Richardia, see Zantedeschia.

Ricinus—*Euphorbiaceae*. Half-hardy annual herb; in the Tropics a tree to 40 ft. high. Flowers insignificant. Large, greenish-purple, palmate leaves. First introduced early sixteenth century.

INDOOR CULTURE: Sow seeds, previously steeped for a few hours in tepid water, ½ in. deep in pots of light, sandy soil in temp. of 60° to 65° in March, transplanting seedlings when three leaves form, singly into 2 in. pots, and keep in similar temp. until well rooted, then transfer to 5 or 6 in. pots, after which remove to cool greenhouse or dwelling-room. Water moderately. Shade from sun.

OUTDOOR CULTURE: Sow seeds and transplant into small pots as above. Transfer to cold frame or pit in May to harden. Plant out, June. Position, sunny beds or borders.

SPECIES CULTIVATED: *R. communis*, ' Castor Oil Plant ', 3 to 6 ft., Trop. Africa, and several vars. *borboniensis arboreus*, *cambodgensis*, *Gibsonii*, *sanguineus*, *zanzibarensis*, etc.

Rivina—*Phytolaccaceae*. Greenhouse evergreen berry-bearing plant. Flowers succeeded by scarlet berries. Pretty for table decoration. First introduced late seventeenth century.

CULTURE: Compost, equal parts leaf-mould and sandy loam, half a part silver sand. Position, small, well-drained pots in light part of warm greenhouse (temp. 50° to 60°), Sept. to June; cold, sunny frames, June to Sept. Pot, Feb. or March. Water freely April to Oct., moderately afterwards. Apply weak stimulants occasionally Oct. to Feb. Shade from sun. Best results obtained by raising plants from seed or cuttings annually.

PROPAGATION: By seeds sown $\frac{1}{16}$ in. deep in well-drained pots or shallow pans of good light soil placed in temp. 55° to 65°, spring; cuttings of young shoots inserted in Feb., March or April in small pots of light, sandy soil in temp. of 65° to 75°, spring.

SPECIES CULTIVATED: *R. humilis* (syn. *R. aurantiaca*), ' Rouge Berry ', ' Blood Berry ', white, June, 1 to 3 ft., red fruits, Trop. America.

Robinia (False Acacia)—*Leguminosae.* Hardy deciduous flowering trees and shrubs. First introduced early seventeenth century.

CULTURE: Soil, ordinary. Position, sunny well-drained borders and shrubberies. Plant, Oct. to Feb. Prune, Nov. to Feb. Rose Acacia (*R. hispida*) may be grown against south or west walls, side shoots being pruned annually to 1 in. of base, Nov. or Dec. Not suitable for exposed places as shoots and branches are brittle.

PROPAGATION: Choice vars. by grafting on common species (*R. Pseudoacacia*) in March; other kinds by seeds sown $\frac{1}{2}$ in. deep in ordinary soil outdoors Nov. or March : suckers removed from parent tree and planted Oct. or Nov.

SPECIES CULTIVATED: *R. ambigua* var. *bella-rosea*, large rich pink flowers, June, 25 to 35 ft., hybrid origin; *Boyntonii*, rose pink, 6 to 8 ft., U.S.A.; *Elliottii*, purple and white, May to June, 5 ft., U.S.A.; *hispida*, ' Rose Acacia ', rose, May, 6 to 8 ft., Southern U.S.A., var. *macrophylla*, without prickles; *Kelseyi*, rose, June, 8 to 12 ft., Eastern U.S.A.; *Pseudoacacia*, ' Locust Tree ', white, June, 70 to 80 ft., Eastern U.S.A., and vars. *aurea*, golden-leaved, *Bessoniana*, larger but fewer leaflets, *Decaisneana*, pink-flowered, *inermis*, mop-headed, and *semperflorens*, flowering throughout the summer; *Slavinii*, lilac-pink, June, attractive habit, 15 to 20 ft., hybrid; *viscosa*, pale rose and yellow, June, 30 to 40 ft., Carolina.

Rocambole, see *Allium Scorodoprasum.*

Rochea—*Crassulaceae.* Greenhouse succulent plants. First introduced early eighteenth century.

CULTURE: Compost, equal parts sandy loam, brick rubble, dried cow manure and river sand. Position, well-drained pots in light greenhouse, close to glass. Pot, March. Water freely April to Aug., moderately Aug. to Nov., very little afterwards. Prune old plants after flowering, shortening shoots to 1 in., and repot when new shoots are 1 in. long. Temp., March to Sept. 55° to 65°, Sept. to March 45° to 50°.

PROPAGATION: By seeds sown in well-drained pots or pans of sandy soil, just covering seeds with fine soil, in temp. 60° to 70° in March or April; seedlings to be kept close to glass and have little water; cuttings of shoots, 2 to 3 in. long, exposed to sun for few days, then inserted in June, July or Aug. in well-drained pots of sandy soil, placed on greenhouse shelf, and given very little water.

SPECIES CULTIVATED: *R. coccinea*, scarlet, July, 1 ft., S. Africa; *jasminea*, white, spring, 6 to 9 in., S. Africa; *versicolor*, white and pink, spring, 2 ft., S. Africa. See also Crassula.

Rock Cress, see Arabis; **-foil,** see Saxifraga; **-Forget-me-not,** see *Omphalodes Luciliae*; **-Jasmine,** see Androsace; **-Lettuce,** see *Phyteuma pinnatum.*

Rocket, see Hesperis.

Rodgersia—*Saxifragaceae.* Hardy herbaceous perennials. Leaves very large, bronze-green. *R. tabularis* is sometimes placed in a separate genus, Astilboides. First introduced late nineteenth century.

CULTURE: Compost, two parts peat, one part loam. Position, partially shaded border. Plant, March or April. Water freely in dry weather. Protect in severe weather with covering of fern fronds or litter.

Propagation: By division, March or April.

Species Cultivated: *R. aesculifolia*, rosy white, summer, 2 to 3 ft., bronze foliage, China; *pinnata*, rosy crimson, summer, 2 to 3 ft., China; *podophylla*, 'Rodgers's Bronze Leaf', creamy white, summer, 3 ft., Japan; *tabularis*, creamy white, summer, 3 ft., bright green foliage, N. China.

Rodriguezia—*Orchidaceae*. An epiphytic genus. Pseudo-bulbs small, leaves rather leathery, a few inches long. Habit, tufted on the pseudo-bulbs at intervals, scapes from their base, often arched or pendulous. Flowers usually showy, the lower sepals generally joined and concealed, or partially so, by the lip. Some species were formerly known as Burlingtonia.

Culture: Compost, osmunda fibre or substitute and sphagnum moss in equal quantities. Baskets or pots, which can be suspended, preferably in pots. Species with extending rhizomes, a narrow trough-like raft. Water liberally in summer, and maintain a warm (70° or more) moist atmosphere with shading, drainage ample for all. Winter night temp. around 65°. Winter waterings are required but avoid a sodden or arid compost. The syringe may be used freely in summer days and in winter if pipe heat is excessive. Position, should be near the glass and watch must be kept against attacks of red spider and mealy bug.

Propagation: By division of plants, not too small, in spring.

Species Cultivated: A selection—*R. Batemannii*, fragrant, white, flushed or streaked rose, various, Brazil, Peru; *candida*, fragrant, white, lip large, with yellowish keels, spring, Brazil; *decora*, white, rose-flushed, red spotted, lip generally white, pseudo-bulbs at intervals, summer, Brazil; *maculata*, fragrant, yellow, cinnamon spotted, keels on lip unequally toothed, spring, summer, Brazil; *pubescens*, fragrant, white, lip emarginate, with yellow keels, column downy, summer, Brazil; *secunda*, many, comparatively small, rose-purple, summer, Brazil, Trinidad; *venusta*, fragrant, white, lip with yellowish centre, variable, summer, various, Brazil.

Roella—*Campanulaceae*. Greenhouse evergreen shrub. First introduced mid-eighteenth century.

Culture: Compost, equal parts of peat and loam and a fair quantity of sand. Position, pots in light and dry part of greenhouse. Pot, March. Water very carefully during spring and summer and give very little in autumn and winter. Syringing or wetting the foliage must be avoided at all seasons. Ventilate freely in summer and moderately at other times. Dry atmosphere essential in autumn and winter. Remove flowers directly they fade; also all blooms that form in autumn and winter. Temp., Sept. to April 40° to 45°, April to Sept. 50° to 60°.

Propagation: By cuttings of strong shoots, 2 in. long, inserted in moist sand in temp. 58° in spring. Shade from sun.

Species Cultivated: *R. ciliata*, 'South African Harebell', white and purple, summer, 1 ft., S. Africa.

Romanzoffia—*Hydrophyllaceae*. Hardy perennial herb. First introduced mid-nineteenth century.

Culture: Soil, ordinary. Position, sunny ledges of rockery. Plant, March or April.

Propagation: By division, March or April.

Species Cultivated: *R. sitchensis*, 'Sitcha Water-leaf', white, spring, 3 to 4 in., N.W. America; *Suksdorffii*, white, spring, 2 in., N. America; *unalaschkensis*, white, 3 in., Aleutian Islands.

Romneya—*Papaveraceae*. Slightly tender perennials. First introduced mid-nineteenth century.

Outdoor Culture: Soil, sandy loam with peat and leaf-mould. Position, well-drained border at base of south wall or sheltered sunny rockery. Plant, April or May. Protect in severe weather with covering of fern or litter.

Propagation: By seeds sown in sandy soil in well-drained pans during Feb. or

March in temp. 55°; root-cuttings in sandy compost during Feb. in temp. 55°, placing cuttings singly in small pots; suckers.

SPECIES CULTIVATED: *R. Coulteri*, ' Californian Tree Poppy ', white, fragrant, late summer and autumn, 4 to 6 ft., California, var. *trichocalyx*, white, fragrant, Aug. to Oct., 5 ft.; *hybrida* (syn. *R. Vandedenii*), white, July, Aug., 3 ft., California.

Romulea—*Iridaceae*. Hardy and half-hardy bulbous plants. First introduced early eighteenth century.

CULTURE: Soil, light, rich, sandy. Position, sunny well-drained border. Plant, Sept. to Jan., placing tubers 4 in. deep and 2 in. apart. Lift and replant tubers annually. Mulch surface of bed in March with cow manure.

PROPAGATION: By offsets.

SPECIES CULTIVATED: *R. Bulbocodium*, yellow and violet, March to April, 4 to 6 in., Europe; *Clusiana*, lavender and orange, spring, 9 in., Spain and Portugal; *parviflora*, lilac, May, 6 in., Europe; *ramiflora*, yellow and lilac, May, 6 to 8 in., Medit. Region; *Requienii*, violet, spring, 4 in., Corsica; *rosea*, carmine, March to May, 6 in., S. Africa.

Rondeletia—*Rubiaceae*. Stove evergreen flowering shrubs. First introduced mid-eighteenth century.

CULTURE: Compost, equal parts rough fibrous peat and loam, one part equal proportions charcoal lumps and coarse silver sand. Position, well-drained pots in light part of stove with shoots trained to sticks or trellis. Pot, Feb. or March. Prune moderately after flowering. Water freely April to Oct., moderately afterwards. Syringe daily March to Sept. Shade from bright sunshine. Temp., March to Sept. 70° to 80°, Sept. to March 55° to 60°.

PROPAGATION: By cuttings of firm shoots inserted in pure sand under bell-glass in temp. 75° to 85°, spring or summer.

SPECIES CULTIVATED: *R. amoena*, pink, summer, 3 to 4 ft., Mexico; *cordata*, pink or dull red, summer, 3 to 7 ft., Guatemala; *odorata* (syns. *R. splendens* and *speciosa*), orange-red and yellow, fragrant, summer, 4 to 6 ft., Cuba and Mexico.

Roripa, see Nasturtium and Armoracia.

Rosa (Rose)—*Rosaceae*. Hardy and slightly tender deciduous and evergreen flowering shrubs, mostly prickly.

CLASSIFICATION: Summer-blooming, Provence, Moss, Damask, Hybrid China, Hybrid Bourbon, Hybrid Noisette, Alba, Rugosa, Austrian Brier, Scotch, Sweetbrier, Ayrshire, Boursault, Banksian, Evergreen, Polyantha, Multiflora and Wichuraiana. Summer- and autumn-blooming, Hybrid Perpetual, Hybrid Tea, Tea, Noisette, China, Lawranciana, Bourbon Perpetual, Hybrid Musk, Hybrid Bracteata, Pernetiana, Hybrid Polyantha, Polyantha Pompon and Hybrid Rugosa.

CULTURE OF DWARF ROSES: Soil, deep, rich loam well enriched with decayed manure. Add clay and cow dung to light soils, road grit, leaf-mould, burnt refuse, horse dung and lime to heavy soils. Do not mix lime with manure but apply to surface after manure has been well dug in. Position, sunny beds or borders. Plant, Nov. or Feb. to March, average distance apart 18 in. to 2 ft. Depth of soil over roots should be 4 to 6 in. on heavy and 7 to 8 in. on light soils. Prune, end of March or early in April. Hybrid Perpetuals should have damaged and weak shoots removed and others shortened to dormant bud 9 to 18 in. from base, according to strength. After first flowering is finished in early July remove dead flowers by shortening young shoots by one-third to a strong bud facing outwards. Hybrid Teas, Teas and Pernetianas, remove damaged and weak shoots and shorten others to dormant bud 3 to 9 in. from base according to strength. Noisettes, thin out all weak and worn-out wood and shorten others a little according to strength, leaving the best of the previous year's growth full length. Bourbons, remove old and weakly growth but leave the best lateral bearing wood unpruned. Provence, Damask, Moss, Chinas and Pompons, thin out the oldest and weakest wood so as to make room for healthy new growth, which should be retained full length. Austrian and Scotch Briers, thin out weak or dead growths only. Hybrid Sweetbriers, thin out older shoots after flowering. Generally speaking, it is wise to prune more severely in the first spring after planting for all types, always cut to a bud facing outwards. Protect Tea, China and tender roses in winter by drawing soil to height of 6 in. round the base of each plant and place bracken or dry litter among the shoots.

CULTURE OF STANDARD ROSES: Soil, position and planting as for dwarfs. Distance apart, minimum 4 ft., or among bush roses from 4 to 6 ft. Pruning: Hybrid Perpetuals, Hybrid Teas, Teas, thin out weak shoots in centre of tree and shorten remaining shoots to 3 to 9 in. according to vigour.

CULTURE OF CLIMBING ROSES: Soil, as advised for dwarfs. Position, against walls, fences, arbours, pergolas, arches, tree trunks, trellises, pillars, etc. Distance apart to plant, 5 to 6 ft. Plant in Oct. or Nov. or in March. Pruning: Rambler type, cut away old flowering shoots after blooming and thin out dead or weakly growths in April, no further pruning required. Banksian type, thin out the strong young shoots not required to add to size of plant directly after flowering. Do not remove older or small shoots. Teas, Noisettes, Hybrid Teas, Singles, etc., grown as climbers, thin old flowering shoots after blooming and cut out dead or weak growths in April and, at the same time, cut off the unripened tips of shoots. Ayrshire, Boursault and Evergreen types only need to have weak growths thinned out in March.

CULTURE OF WEEPING ROSES: Soil and planting, as advised for dwarfs. Distance to plant, 10 ft. Pruning, thin out weak and old growths immediately after flowering and train in the young wood for next year's flowering, and, in March, remove soft unripened tips of shoots.

CULTURE OF ROSES IN POTS: Classes suitable for pot culture, Hybrid Perpetual, Hybrid Tea, Tea-scented and Polyantha. Compost, two parts turfy loam, two parts rotted cow or hotbed manure, one part sand. Pot, Oct. Repot annually in Aug. or Sept. Prune newly lifted and potted plants in Nov., shortening shoots to three, two or one ' eyes ' of the base according to size; established plants of Hybrid Perpetuals and Hybrid Teas to six, three and two ' eyes '; Tea-scented, Chinese, Fairy and Polyantha kinds to eight, six and four ' eyes ' in Nov. for early flowering, Dec. or Jan. for late flowering. Position, sheltered corner outdoors with pots protected from frost by straw, or in cold frame Oct. to Jan., greenhouse Jan. to May, sunny place outdoors afterwards. Water moderately Jan. to April, freely April to Dec., keep nearly dry Oct. to Jan. Apply stimulants once or twice during flowering period. Syringe freely in greenhouse. Temp. for forcing, 40° by night and 45° by day; Feb., 45° by night, 55° by day; March and onwards, 55° by night and 60° to 65° by day. Plants for forcing require to be established in pots one year.

CULTURE OF CLIMBERS IN GREENHOUSE: Compost, same as for pots. Beds or tubs for each plant 18 in. deep and 2 ft., wide, each to be provided with 3 in. of drainage. Plant, Sept. to Nov. or March. Prune each shoot first year to within 8 in. of its base at time of planting; second and future years thin out old wood and shorten young growth by a third or a half according to strength, immediately after flowering. Water freely March to Nov., keep nearly dry afterwards. Apply stimulants weekly, April to Sept., to established plants. Syringe daily in spring. Admit air freely in summer and autumn to ripen shoots.

MANURE FOR ROSES: Cow or pig dung for light soils, horse manure for heavy ones. Top-dress with above directly after pruning and lightly fork in. Suitable artificial manure—superphosphate of lime, 48 lb.; sulphate of potash, 20 lb.; sulphate of ammonia, 25 lb.; sulphate of iron, 4 lb. Mix thoroughly together and apply at the rate of 3 oz. per square yard directly after pruning; one dose a year is sufficient. Liquid soot-water, cow and sheep dung also good for roses outdoors or in pots, especially applied generously after the first summer blooming is over.

STOCKS FOR ROSES: For standards, the wild dog rose of the hedgerows, and

Rugosa; dwarfs and climbers, seedling and cutting wild dog rose, Manetti, de la Grifferae, Rugosa, Laxa and Multiflora (often known as Polyantha Simplex).

PROPAGATION: By seeds, preferably stratified, sown ⅛ in. deep in light sandy soil in cold frame in March or April, or ½ in. deep in ordinary soil outdoors in April, transplanting seedlings when a year old; cuttings, 6 to 8 in. long, in sheltered position outdoors, Sept. to Nov.; small side shoots of tea-scented and other kinds removed with a little old stem attached and inserted in small pots of light sandy soil in summer under a bell-glass or in a propagator; budding in July; grafting in Feb. or March in temp. 55° to 65°. Practically all nursery stock is budded. Seed provides new types, also stocks for budding. Cuttings will be found to provide useful new stock and are easily raised but scarcely as long-lived as budded plants.

SPECIES CULTIVATED: *R. acicularis*, large rose pink, May, 6 ft., for wild garden, Europe to Japan; *alba*, large single, white or blush, June, 6 ft., hybrid; *arvensis*, white, branches trailing, Europe, var. *Aireshirea*, ' Ayrshire Rose '; *Banksiae*, ' Banksian Rose ', double and single white and yellow, climbing to 20 ft., no pruning, for warm sunny districts, China; *Beggeriana*, silvery leaves, white, June, 6 ft., Afghanistan, N. Persia; *blanda*, rose, June, 4 to 6 ft., N. America; *borboniana*, ' Bourbon Rose ', purple, summer, 6 ft., hybrid; *bracteata*, large white, summer, to 20 ft., evergreen, for warm sunny walls, China; *canina*, ' Wild Rose ', ' Dog Rose ', pink, summer, Europe and W. Asia, used as stock for budding; *carolina*, crimson, June to Aug., 4 to 6 ft. for wild garden, Eastern N. America; *centifolia*, ' Cabbage Rose ', red, fragrant, summer, 6 ft., one of the oldest known roses, Caucasus, and vars. *muscosa*, ' Moss Rose ', and *parvifolia*, ' Burgundie Rose '; *chinensis*, ' China Rose ', white, blush to red, June to Sept., 3 to 4 ft., China, and vars. *minima* (syn. *R. Lawranceana*), a race of dwarf forms (*Roulettii*, with pink flowers, belongs here), and *viridiflora*, ' Green Rose '; *cinnamomea*, ' Cinnamon Rose ', red, May, 6 to 9 ft., spicily fragrant, Europe, N. China, Siberia, and var. *plena*, double; *damascena*, ' Damask Rose ', pink to red, June, 4 to 6 ft., Asia Minor. and vars. *trigintapetala*, cultivated in S. Europe for manufacture of attar, and *versicolor*, ' York and Lancaster Rose ', white, striped pink; *Davidii*, rose pink, June, bottle-shaped fruits, vigorous to 12 ft., W. China; *Dupontii*, large single, pale pink, July, 4 to 6 ft., attractive and graceful hybrid; *Ecae*, buttercup yellow, June, 3 to 4 ft., Afghanistan; *Eglanteria* (syn. *R. rubiginosa*), ' Sweetbrier ' or ' Eglantine ', pale pink, summer, fragrant leaves, 6 to 9 ft., Europe, including Britain, parent of Penzance Briers; *foetida* (syn. *R. lutea*), ' Austrian Brier ', yellow, June to July, 4 to 8 ft., beautiful climber, Asia Minor to Afghanistan, vars. *bicolor*, ' Austrian Copper ', copper red, *persiana*, ' Persian Yellow ', double yellow; *gallica*, ' French Rose ', the oldest rose of European cultivation, pink or crimson, to 4 ft., Europe, W. Asia, var. *officinalis*, ' Provence Rose '; *Helenae*, white, fragrant, large clusters, 12 to 15 ft., vigorous, Cent. China; *highdownensis*, hybrid of *R. Moyesii*, similar but vigorous and free-fruiting; *Hugonis*, single yellow, May, 8 ft., vigorous, W. China; *laevigata*, ' Cherokee Rose ', rather tender, 5 in. white flowers, May to June, climbing to 15 ft., China; *Lheritierana*, ' Boursault Rose ', red, 20 ft., hybrid; *macrophylla*, blush red, June, 8 to 10 ft., red pear-shaped fruits, Himalaya; *moschata*, ' Musk Rose ', large clusters cream flowers, June, 10 to 15 ft., S. Europe, India, China; *Moyesii*, beautiful dark velvety red, June, 6 to 10 ft., red bottle-shaped fruits, China; *multibracteata*, pink, June, 6 to 10 ft., fern-like foliage, orange-red fruits, W. China; *multiflora*, large clusters, white, June, 10 to 15 ft., vigorous, N. China and Japan, and var. *platyphylla*, ' Seven Sisters' Rose ', pink, also parent with *R. chinensis* of polyantha roses; *nitida*, rosy red, June, to 2 ft., autumn tints, Eastern N. America; *Noisettiana*, ' Noisette Rose ', white, large clusters, July to Aug., hybrid; *nutkana*, bright red, July, 6 to 10 ft., Western N. America; *odorata*, ' Tea Rose ', white, pale pink or yellow, almost evergreen, China; *omeiensis*, ' Mount Omi Rose ', white, May to June, ferny foliage, 10 to 12 ft., China, with vars. *chrysocarpa*, yellow fruits, *pteracantha*, striking red thorns; *pendulina* (syn. *R. alpina*), pink, June, thornless, Europe; *Primula*, primrose yellow, April to May, red twigs, 4 to 6 ft., Turkistan to N. China; *Richardii* (syn. *R. sancta*), pale pink, June to July, 4 ft., spreading, Abyssinia; *rubrifolia*, pink, June to July, 4 to 8 ft., striking glaucous purplish-tinted foliage, Cent. Europe; *rugosa*, ' Ramanas Rose ', red or white, fragrant, June to July, 4 to 7 ft., bright red fruits and autumn-tinted foliage, China and Japan, and many attractive vars. for shrub borders; *sericea*, white, May to June, 10 to 12 ft., spreading, India; *setigera*, ' Prairie Rose ', deep rose, July to Aug., rambling to 12 ft., Ontario to Florida; *setipoda*, purplish-rose, June to July, 6 to 10 ft., Cent. China; *Soulieana*, cream, July, 10 to 12 ft., vigorous and spreading, greyish foliage, W. China; *spinosissima*, ' Scotch or Burnet Rose ', white or pale pink, May to June, 3 to 4 ft., spreading, Europe, N. Asia, numerous vars. including *altaica*, creamy yellow, 6 ft., *lutea*, buttercup yellow, *myriacantha*, pale pink, very spiny; *Sweginzowii*, purplish-rose, June to July, 6 to 10 ft., oblong fruits, N.W. China; *virginiana*, pink, June to July, 3 to 6 ft., Eastern N. America; *Watsoniana*, finely cut foliage, trailing, for rockery, Japan; *Webbiana*, bright pink, June, glaucous stems, graceful habit, 4 to 6 ft., Himalaya; *Wichuraiana*, white, June to July, 8 to 12 ft., glossy foliage, Japan, parent of types such as Dorothy Perkins, Hiawatha and New Dawn; *Willmottiae*, rose, May to June, 6 to 10 ft., very spiny, W. China; *xanthina*, pale yellow, May, ferny leaves, 5 to 8 ft., N. China, Korea, var. *spontanea*, single flowered.

Rosary Pea, see *Abrus precatorius.*

Roscoea—*Zingiberaceae.* Dwarf hardy perennials of great charm and beauty. First introduced early nineteenth century.

CULTURE: Soil, sandy loam and leaf-mould. Position, woodland gardens or half-shady, sheltered borders. Plant the fleshy tuberous roots 6 in. deep in March.

PROPAGATION: By division of the roots in spring, or seed sown in warm greenhouse in Feb. or March.

SPECIES CULTIVATED: *R. alpina*, pink, summer, 6 in., Himalaya; *cautleoides*, yellow, summer, 12 in., China; *Humeana*, rose-purple, summer, 12 in., W. China; *purpurea*, purple, late summer, 12 in., Himalaya, and var. *pallida*, pale lavender.

Rose, see Rosa; **-Acacia,** see *Robinia hispida*; **-Apple,** see *Eugenia Jambos*; **-Bay Willow Herb,** see *Epilobium angustifolium*; **-Box,** see *Cotoneaster microphylla*; **-Campion,** see *Lychnis coronaria*; **-Mallow,** see Hibiscus; **-of China,** see *Hibiscus Rosa-sinensis*; **-of-Heaven,** see *Lychnis Coeli-rosa*; **-of Jericho,** see *Anastatica hierochuntica*; **-of Sharon,** see *Hypericum calycinum*; **-Root,** see *Sedum rosea.*

Rosemary, see Rosmarinus.

Rosinweed, see Silphium.

Rosmarinus (Rosemary)—*Labiatae.* Hardy evergreen fragrant shrub. First introduced mid-sixteenth century.

CULTURE: Soil, ordinary well drained. Position, dryish sunny border or shrubbery. Plant, April.

PROPAGATION: By cuttings of half-ripened young shoots in a cold frame in Aug. or Sept.

SPECIES CULTIVATED: *R. officinalis*, violet-blue, May, 4 to 7 ft., S. Europe, with vars. *prostratus*, trailing, rather tender, and *pyramidalis*, upright growth, useful for hedges.

Rosularia—*Crassulaceae.* Evergreen succulent plants, sometimes included in Cotyledon.

CULTURE: As Sempervivum, but requires protection from snow.

PROPAGATION: As Sempervivum.

SPECIES CULTIVATED: *R. pallida* (syns. *Cotyledon chrysantha*, *Sedum chrysanthum*, *Umbilicus chrysanthus*), whitish-yellow, Asia Minor to Himalaya.

Rouge Berry, see *Rivina humilis.*

Roupala—*Proteaceae.* Greenhouse evergreen flowering shrubs. Leaves, simple or feather-shaped, covered with brownish wool. First introduced early nineteenth century.

CULTURE: Compost, equal parts fibrous loam, leaf-mould, peat and little sand. Position, large pots or tubs in lofty sunny greenhouse or conservatory. Pot, Feb. or March. Water freely April to Sept., moderately afterwards. No syringing required. Temp., Sept. to March 45° to 50°, March to Sept. 55° to 65°. May stand outdoors in sunny position, June to Sept.

PROPAGATION: By cuttings of firm shoots inserted in pure silver sand in well-drained pots under bell-glass in temp. 55° to 65°, summer.

SPECIES CULTIVATED: *R. elegans*, 6 to 10 ft., Trop. America; *Pohlii*, 6 to 15 ft., Brazil.

Rowan Tree, see *Sorbus Aucuparia.*

Royal Fern, see *Osmunda regalis*; **-Water-lily,** see *Victoria regia.*

Rubus (Blackberry)—*Rosaceae.* Hardy fruit-bearing and flowering shrubs, perennial plants.

CULTURE OF RASPBERRIES: Soil, deep, rich, moist loam. Rows north to south if possible. Plant, Oct. to March. Distances for planting: Singly, 18 in. apart in the row and 5 ft. between the rows for training to wire trellis; in groups of two canes, 30 in. apart in row and 5 ft. between rows. Pruning: Cut canes off to within 10 in. of ground first year; succeeding years cut off old canes close to ground immediately after fruiting in order to allow young canes to ripen. Reduce the number of young canes at each root or stool to three or four of the strongest. Remove sappy tips of latter in early spring. Apply decayed manure annually in Nov., forking it in 3 in. deep only; on dry soil mulch with strawy manure in April. Water copiously with liquid manure during bearing period. Remove suckers appearing away from base of stools. Avoid deep digging near established plants. Sulphate of potash is an esssential manure for this crop and should be applied in autumn at ¾ oz. per square yard. Organic nitrogenous manures, such as meat or fish meal, can be applied at 2 oz. per square yard in March.

PROPAGATION: By seeds sown outdoors in a shady border as soon as ripe; division of roots in autumn. Propagate only virus-free strains.

CULTURE OF BLACKBERRIES: Soil, well-drained, deep, rich loam. Position, trained to sunny fences, or in rows in open garden, with shoots trained to a rough trellis. Plant in autumn, strong growers 12 ft. apart. Pruning, cut away shoots that have borne fruit directly after fruiting and remove tips of remaining shoots in March. Top-dress annually in winter.

PROPAGATION: By layering tips in summer, transplanting suckers in autumn; leaf-bud cuttings.

CULTURE OF WINEBERRY, LOGANBERRY AND OTHER HYBRID BERRIES: Soil, as for raspberries. Plant 10 ft. apart in autumn. Shorten shoots well back first season to encourage cane production. Train on fence or wire trellis or place four stakes round each plant at a distance of 3 ft. from the base, and train growths spirally round these. Prune after fruiting, cutting away shoots that have borne fruit and removing soft tips of remaining shoots in March. Top-dress with decayed manure in winter.

PROPAGATION: By layering shoots in summer; dividing the roots in autumn.

CULTURE OF HERBACEOUS SPECIES: Soil, sandy peat. Position, shady rockery. Plant, autumn or spring. Water freely in dry weather.

PROPAGATION: By division in spring.

CULTURE OF SHRUBBY SPECIES: Soil, good ordinary. Position, sunny or shady borders. Plant in Oct. Prune after flowering, cutting away old shoots.

PROPAGATION: By cuttings.

FRUIT-BEARING SPECIES CULTIVATED: *R. flagellaris*, ' American Dewberry ', fruit black, Canada, U.S.A.; *idaeus*, ' Raspberry ', white, May, berries red or yellow, 3 to 6 ft., Europe; *illecebrosus*, ' Strawberry Raspberry ', white, fragrant, fruits scarlet, sour, 5 to 8 ft., E. Asia; *innominatus*, pink, fruit orange-red, to 10 ft., China; *laciniatus*, ' Cut-leaved Blackberry ', white or pink, summer, berries black, 8 to 12 ft.; *loganobaccus*, ' Loganberry ', hybrid, origin uncertain, probably a cross between *R. ursinus* and a raspberry, berries deep red, 8 to 12 ft., introduced about 1897 from U.S.A.; *phoenicolasius*, ' Wineberry ', pink, summer, berries bright orange-red, 6 ft., China, Japan; *procerus*, ' Himalayan Blackberry ', introduced from Germany about 1899, white, berries black, 20 to 40 ft., Europe; *ulmifolius*, ' Evergreen Thornless Blackberry ', pink, fruit black, California, var. *inermis*.

HERBACEOUS SPECIES CULTIVATED : *R. arcticus* (syn. *R. stellatus*) mat-forming plant, rose, June, N. America; *Chamæmorus* ' Cloudberry ', white, 3 to 10 in.

SHRUBBY SPECIES CULTIVATED: *R. acuminatus*, white, Himalaya; *australis*, ' Lawyer Vine ', white, pink, or yellow, evergreen, 10 to 20 ft., New Zealand; *biflorus*, flowers inconspicuous, stems waxy white, 8 to 10 ft., spreading, Himalaya, var. *quinqueflorus*, more vigorous; *Cockburnianus* (syn. *R. Giraldianus*), purple, 8 to 10 ft., white stems, China; *deliciosus*, ' Rocky Mountain Flowering Raspberry ', white, May, 6 to 10 ft., Rocky Mountains; *Henryi*, climbing evergreen, pink, 3 to 6 ft., China, var. *bambusarum*, short-stalked leaflets; *lasiostylus*, purple-rose, July, 6 to 8 ft., Cent. China; *leucodermis*, white, June, 4 to 8 ft., yellowish canes, Western N. America; *odoratus* (syn. *Rubacer odoratum*), ' Flowering Raspberry ', unarmed, rose-purple, summer, 6 ft., N. America; *spectabilis*. ' Salmonberry ', rosy red, May, 6 ft., California.

Ruby Grass, see *Tricholaena rosea.*

Rudbeckia (Coneflower)—*Compositae.* Hardy annuals and herbaceous perennials. First introduced late seventeenth century.

CULTURE OF ANNUAL SPECIES: Soil, ordinary. Sow in boxes in cold frame in March, pricking seedlings out when large enough to handle into deeper boxes for hardening off and planting out in May; or sow in open ground where desired to flower in April, thinning the seedlings to 9 in. apart.

CULTURE OF PERENNIAL SPECIES: Soil, ordinary. Position, sunny well-drained borders. Plant, Oct., March or April. Mulch with decayed manure annually, Feb. or March. Lift, divide and replant in fresh position triennially.

PROPAGATION: By seeds sown ⅛ in. deep outdoors in ordinary soil and sunny position, March or April, transplanting seedlings into flowering positions following autumn; by division of roots, Oct., Feb., March or April.

ANNUAL SPECIES CULTIVATED: *R. amplexicaulis*, yellow and maroon, summer, 1 to 2 ft., N. America; *bicolor*, yellow and maroon, July to Sept., 1 to 2 ft., N. America; *hirta*, ' Black-eyed Susan ', yellow and dull brown, summer, 1 to 3 ft., N. America, biennial or annual; *triloba*, deep yellow and brown, summer, 2 to 5 ft., N. America, biennial or annual.

PERENNIAL SPECIES CULTIVATED: *R. californica*, yellow and brown, July to Sept., 4 to 6 ft., California; *fulgida*, yellow and dark purple, July to Sept., 1 to 2 ft., N. America; *laciniata*, yellow, summer, 3 to 6 ft., N. America, var. *portensis*, ' Golden Glow ', double; *maxima*, yellow and blackish-brown, late summer, 7 to 9 ft., N. America; *nitida*, yellow, late summer, 4 ft., N. America, var. *Herbstsonne*, 6 ft., golden-yellow, reflexed petals; *speciosa* (syn. *R. Newmannii*), orange-yellow, summer, 1½ to 3 ft., N. America; *subtomentosa*, yellow and purple, late summer, 3 to 5 ft., N. America. See also Echinacea and Lepachys.

Rue, see *Ruta graveolens.*

Ruellia—*Acanthaceae.* Stove perennial herbs or shrubs. First introduced late nineteenth century.

CULTURE: Compost, equal parts fibrous loam, leaf-mould, peat and silver sand. Pot, Feb. or March. Position, pot in shady part of stove or greenhouse. Water freely March to Oct., moderately afterwards. Syringe twice daily March to Sept., once daily other times. Apply weak stimulants during flowering period to perennial species. Temp., Sept. to March 55° to 65°, March to Sept. 65° to 75°.

PROPAGATION: By cuttings inserted in above compost in well-drained pots under bell-glass or in propagator in temp. 75° to 85°, spring or summer; perennial species by seeds sown in sandy soil in temp. 70° to 75°, Feb. or March.

SPECIES CULTIVATED: *R. Baikiei*, scarlet, winter, 2 to 3 ft., Brazil; *Devosiana*, white, winter, Brazil; *formosa*, scarlet, 2 ft., summer, Brazil; *Herbstii*, purplish-red, September, 3 ft., Brazil; *macrantha*, ' Christmas Pride ', rosy purple, winter, to 6 ft., shrubby, Brazil; *Portellae*, rose pink, winter, 1 ft., annual or perennial, Brazil; *solitaria*, purplish-lilac, winter, 2 ft., Brazil; *speciosa*, scarlet, July, to 10 ft., Brazil. See also Strobilanthes.

Rumex (Dock; Sorrel)—*Polygonaceae.* Hardy perennial herbs, mostly weeds, but a few grown for greens.

CULTURE OF HERB PATIENCE: Soil, ordinary, moist. Remove flower stems directly they appear and gather leaves frequently.

PROPAGATION: By seeds sown in March, 1 in. deep in drills 18 in. apart, thinning seedlings to 1 ft. apart in row in April; division of roots in March.

CULTURE OF SORREL: Soil, ordinary rich moist. Position, open borders. Plant, 1 ft. apart in rows 15 in. asunder in March. Gather leaves frequently. Remove flower stems. Water freely in dry weather.

CULTURE OF AQUATIC SPECIES: Soil, ordinary. Position, margins of water. Plant in spring. Increased by division in spring.

PROPAGATION: By seeds ½ in. deep in drills 15 in. apart in March, thinning seedlings to 12 in. apart in April; division of roots in March.

SPECIES CULTIVATED: *R. abyssinicus*, ' Spinach-Rhubarb ', leaves used as substitute for spinach, stems as rhubarb, 6 ft., Abyssinia; *Acetosa*, ' Sorrel ', green, summer, 18 in., leaves edible, Europe (Br.); *Hydrolapathum*, ' Water Dock ', 4 to 6 ft., Europe (Br.); *Patientia*, ' Herb Patience ', 4 ft., leaves used as substitute for spinach, S. Europe; *scutatus*, ' French Sorrel ', 1 to 2 ft., leaves edible, Europe and Asia.

Rupturewort, see Herniaria.

Ruschia—*Aizoaceae.* Half-hardy succulent plants, formerly included in Mesembryanthemum.

CULTURE: Compost, equal parts old mortar, pounded crocks, sandy loam, well-decayed manure or leaf-mould and sand. Position, well-drained pots in sunny greenhouse or window, may be planted in sunny borders outdoors from June to Sept. Pot, March to May. Water freely April to Sept., keep nearly dry during winter. Temp., March to Oct. 55° to 65°, Oct. to March 40° to 50°.

PROPAGATION: By seed; cuttings in temp. 55° to 65°, March to Sept.

SPECIES CULTIVATED: *R. multiflora* (syn. *Mesembryanthemum multiflorum*), white, Aug., 3 ft., S. Africa; *uncinata* (syn. *M. uncinatum*), red, summer, prostrate, S. Africa.

Ruscus—*Liliaceae* (or *Ruscaceae*). Hardy evergreen shrubs,

CULTURE: Soil, ordinary. Position, shady or sunny shrubberies, borders or woods; useful for dense shade. Plant, Sept., Oct. or April.

PROPAGATION: By suckers; division of roots in spring.

SPECIES CULTIVATED: *R. aculeatus*, ' Butcher's Broom ', green, May, 3 ft., Britain; *Hypoglossum*, yellow, inconspicuous, May, to 18 in., S. Europe. The Alexandrian Laurel, frequently known as *Ruscus racemosus*, is correctly *Danae racemosa*, q.v.

Russellia—*Scrophulariaceae.* Stove evergreen flowering shrubs, suitable plants for hanging baskets. First introduced early nineteenth century.

CULTURE: Compost, equal parts sandy loam, leaf-mould and silver sand. Position, in light part of stove. Pot, Feb. or March. Water freely April to Sept., moderately afterwards. Prune, Feb. Apply weak stimulants when in flower only. Syringe twice daily April to Oct., except when in flower. Temp., Sept. to March 55° to 65°, March to Sept. 65° to 75°.

PROPAGATION: By cuttings inserted in silver sand in temp. 75° in spring; layering shoots at any time.

SPECIES CULTIVATED: *R. equisetiformis* (syn. *R. juncea*), red, July, 3 to 4 ft., Mexico; *sarmentosa*, red, July, 4 ft., Trop. America. *R. Lemoinei* and *R. elegantissima* are hybrids between the two species.

Russian Vine, see *Polygonum baldschuanicum.*

Ruta (Rue)—*Rutaceae.* Hardy aromatic evergreen shrub. First introduced midsixteenth century.

CULTURE: Soil, ordinary. Position, in the herb garden or sunny border. Plant, March, 8 in. apart in rows 18 in. asunder or grow naturally as attractive foliage shrub in border; good for chalk soils. Prune the plants closely in April.

PROPAGATION: By seeds sown ⅛ in. deep in drills outdoors in April; cuttings inserted in shady frame, Aug., Sept.

SPECIES CULTIVATED: *R. graveolens*, ' Herb of Grace ', yellowish-green, summer, 3 ft., S. Europe.

Rutabaga, see *Brassica Napobrassica.*

Sabal—*Palmae.* Greenhouse fan palms. First introduced early nineteenth century.

CULTURE: Compost, two parts rich loam, one part decayed leaf-mould and sand. Position, well-drained pots in greenhouse or sheltered well-drained beds outdoors in S. of England. Pot, March. Plant, April. Temp., Sept. to March 45° to 55°, March to Sept. 55° to 65°. Water moderately in winter, freely in summer.

PROPAGATION: By seeds sown 1 in. deep in light soil in temp. of 80° in Feb. or March; suckers removed from parent plant in April or Aug.

SPECIES CULTIVATED: *S. Blackburnia*, 20 ft., Bermuda; *minor* (syn. *S. Adansonii*), 3 ft., Southern U.S.A.; *Palmetto*, ' Cabbage Palm ', 20 to 40 ft., Southern U.S.A.

Sabatia—*Gentianaceae.* Hardy biennial flowering herb. First introduced midnineteenth century.

CULTURE: Soil, equal parts good fibrous loam and finely-sifted leaf-mould and little sand. Position, moist, partially shaded borders or bogs. Sow seeds thinly in April where required to grow, lightly cover with soil, thin to 3 or 4 in. apart when an inch high; to flower following summer; or sow seed ¹⁄₁₆ in. deep in well-drained pots or shallow pans filled with equal parts sandy peat and leaf-mould; place in a pan partially filled with water and placed in cold frame or greenhouse. Transplant seedlings when an inch high, three in a 2 in. pot, in similar compost, keep in cold frame till following March, then plant out.

SPECIES CULTIVATED: *S. campestris*, rose, summer, 6 to 12 in., N. America.

Saccharum—*Gramineae.* Stove and hardy perennial flowering grasses. Inflorescence, silky, borne in pyramidal panicles, July. Leaves, ribbon-like, green, covered with silky hairs. First introduced late sixteenth century.

CULTURE OF SUGAR CANE: Two parts rich loam, one part leaf-mould or rotted manure and little sand. Position, large pots or tubs in lofty stove. Pot, Feb. or March. Water freely April to Sept., moderately afterwards. Syringe twice daily during spring and summer. Shade from midday sun essential. Temp., March to Oct. 70° to 85°, Oct. to March 55° to 65°.

PROPAGATION: Sugar cane by cuttings of stems inserted in light soil in temp. of 70° to 80° in spring, or by suckers removed in Feb. or March and potted singly in above compost.

SPECIES CULTIVATED: *S. officinarum*, ' Sugar Cane ', white, summer, 10 to 15 ft., Tropics, var. *violaceum*, stems violet tinted.

Saccolabium—*Orchidaceae.* An epiphytic genus, so variable that later revisions have made separations under generic names—Ascocentrum, Calceolare, Schoenorchis, Anota, Robiquetia, Malleola. The species given are all well known as Saccolabiums. The genus is allied to Vanda. Inflorescence axillary, racemose, somewhat clustered, solitary or many flowered.

CULTURE: Compost, as for Aerides, temps., etc., similar. As the genus contains hard and softer-leaved species, small and fairly large growing, winter treatment must be slightly varied, then a night temp. of 65° should be given. Winter waterings are required more frequently by the soft-textured species than by the hard, but the compost should never become really dry. In summer a moist warm atmosphere, 70° and more with shading. Liberal watering, exposure to light in autumn, varied. Pans may be used for the dwarf-growing kinds, hung near the glass in winter. Pots or hanging baskets for the larger.

PROPAGATION: The species do not make the tall stems seen in so many Aerides and Vandas, so that the method of propagation advised for them is very seldom possible. Very occasionally basal growths occur with some and division may then be carefully made.

SPECIES CULTIVATED: A selection—*S. acutifolium* (syn. *S. denticulatum*), greenish-yellow, spotted red-brown, lip white, yellow, spotted crimson, white fringed, summer, Burma, N. India; *ampullaceum*, many small, rose-red, summer, N. India, Burma; *bellinum*, yellow, blotched black-purple, lip white, yellow with a few purple spots, margins white fimbriated, spring, various, Burma; *bigibbum*, yellow, lip whitish, yellow centrally, margin ciliated, Burma; *calcolare*, yellow, lip white, orange-yellow, white fringed, summer, N. India, Burma; *curvifolium*, many, small, cinnabar-red, spur slender, summer, Burma; *gemmatum*, many, small, white and purple, leaves terete, raft, summer, N. India; *giganteum*, fragrant, many, white, purple blotched, lip amethyst-purple, racemes drooping, winter, various, Burma; *Hendersonianum*, small, many, rose-red, spur large, spring, summer, Borneo; *juncifolium*, near *S. gemmatum*, many, small, bluish-violet, lip yellowish, summer, Java; *lanatum*, many, small, purple, yellow, lip pink-white, spikes often branched, downy, summer, autumn, Burma; *longicalcaratum*, many, small, soft rose, spur comparatively long, leaves leathery, summer, Burma; *miniatum*, small, many, orange-red, mid-lobe of lip yellowish, spike erect, spring, Borneo, Java; *Mooreanum*, many, small, rose, rose-purple, tips green, stems drooping, raceme drooped, often branched, autumn, New Guinea; *penangiana*, many, small, yellow, red-brown, whitish, lip white and purple, summer, Penang, Burma; *violaceum*, near *S. giganteum*, many, fragrant, white, spotted amethyst, lip amethyst-purple, scapes drooping, winter, spring, Philippines.

Sadleria—*Polypodiaceae*. Stove tree fern. Fronds, feather-shaped. First introduced late nineteenth century.

CULTURE: Compost, two-thirds peat and loam and abundance of sand. Position, large pots or tubs, well drained, in shady stove or warm conservatory. Repot, Feb. or March. Water moderately Oct. to March, freely afterwards. Syringe trunks daily March to Sept. Temp., Sept. to March 55° to 65°, March to Sept. 65° to 75°. Shade in summer essential.

PROPAGATION: By spores sown at any time on surface of finely sifted loam and peat in shallow, well-drained pans. Cover with sheet of glass and keep moist in shady position in temp. 75° to 85°.

SPECIES CULTIVATED: *S. cyatheoides*, 5 to 8 ft., Sandwich Islands.

Safflower, see *Carthamus tinctoria*.

Saffron Crocus, see *Crocus sativus*.

Sage, see Salvia.

Sagina (Pearlwort)—*Caryophyllaceae*. Hardy perennial evergreen tufted herbs with creeping stems. *S. glabra* is used as a substitute for grass for forming lawns on sandy soils; golden-leaved variety used for carpet bedding.

CULTURE OF S. GLABRA ON LAWNS: Soil, sandy. Position, sunny. Plant small tufts 3 in. apart each way in March or April. Keep free from weeds and roll frequently. Requires frequent renewal.

CULTURE OF GOLDEN-LEAVED VARIETY: Soil, ordinary. Position, sunny beds, borders or rockeries. Plant small tufts in March, 2 in. apart, in lines, designs or masses.

PROPAGATION: By seeds sown in sandy soil in sunny position outdoors in March; division in March or April.

SPECIES CULTIVATED: *S. Boydii*, glossy green tufts, flowers inconspicuous, rare and choice, 1 in., Britain; *glabra*, white, summer, 2 in., Europe; *subulata* (syns. *S. pilifera, Spergula pilifera*), densely tufted, flowers white, July to Sept., Corsica, var. *aurea*, leaves marked yellow.

Sagittaria (Arrowhead)—*Alismaceae.* Hardy perennial aquatic herbs.

CULTURE: Compost, two parts strong, rich loam, one part well-decayed manure. Position, borders of open, sunny ponds or lakes for hardy species. Tender species in pots in warm greenhouse, Sept. to May; sunk in borders of ponds outdoors, May to Sept. Depth of water, 6 to 12 in. Plant, March to Oct. Methods of planting: (1) Place plant in small wicker basket containing above compost and lower to the bottom of pond or lake. (2) Enclose roots with soil and large stone in piece of canvas or matting, tie securely, and immerse as above. (3) Place large hillock or mound of compost at bottom of pond when dry and plant roots in centre, afterwards filling with water.

PROPAGATION: By seeds sown ¼ in. deep in rich soil in shallow basket and immersed in ponds or lakes in spring; division of plants March or April.

SPECIES CULTIVATED: *S. lancifolia*, white, summer, tender, 2 to 5 ft., America; *latifolia* (syn. *S. variabilis*), ' Duck Potato ', white, summer, 2 to 3 ft., N. America; *montevidensis*, white and purple, summer, 4 to 6 ft., tender, S. America; *natans* (syn. *S. pusilla*), for aquariums, white, 5 in., N. America; *sagittifolia*, white and purple, summer, 2 ft., Europe (Br.), and var. *flore-pleno*, double; *subulata*, aquarium carpeter, 3 in., N. America.

Sago Fern, see *Cyathea medullaris*; **-Palm,** see Cycas.

St. Augustine's Grass, see *Stenotaphrum secundatum.*

St. Bernard's Lily, see *Anthericum Liliago.*

St. Bruno's Lily, see *Paradisea Liliastrum.*

St. Dabeoc's Heath, see *Daboecia polifolia.*

St. John's Wort, see Hypericum.

Saintpaulia—*Gesneriaceae.* Warm greenhouse perennial. First introduced late nineteenth century.

CULTURE: Compost, equal parts of loam, leaf-mould, peat and sand. Pot, Feb. to May. Pots, 3 in. for small and 4½ in. for large plants, well drained. Water freely from April to Sept., moderately afterwards. Apply weak liquid manure occasionally during flowering season. Temp., Oct. to April 55° to 60°, April to Oct. 65° to 75°.

PROPAGATION: By seeds; leaf cuttings.

SPECIES CULTIVATED: *S. diplotricha* (syn. *S. kewensis*), violet, summer, 3 to 4 in., Trop. Africa; *ionantha*, ' African Violet ', violet, June to Oct., 3 to 4 in., Cent. Africa, and vars. *albescens*, white, *purpurea*, purple, and *violescens*, deep violet; *pusilla*, bluish-violet, summer, 3 to 6 in., Trop. Africa; *tongwensis*, violet, summer, N.E. Tanganyika, E. Africa.

Salix (Willow)—*Salicaceae.* Hardy deciduous trees and shrubs, many natives of Britain. Shoots more or less drooping, dioecious flowers and yellow, purple, red, orange or whitish bark

CULTURE OF ORNAMENTAL SPECIES: Soil, ordinary heavy or moderately heavy; light soils are not suitable. Position, damp, near margins of ponds, etc., for all species. Plant, Oct. to March. Prune, Nov. to Feb.

TIMBER CULTURE: Goat Willow is suitable for damp coppices, its wood being valuable for hoops, poles, crates, etc. White or Huntingdon Willow also suitable for damp soils, coppices, etc.; branches used for making scythe and rake handles, timber for lining carts and barrows. Wood of the Bat Willow used for making cricket bats. Plant in autumn. February is the time to pollard willows. Weight of timber per cubic foot, 33 lb.

PROPAGATION: By cuttings of shoots or stems of any age or size in moist soil, Oct. to March; choice kinds by budding on *S. caprea* in July, bandaging the bud with damp moss; or by grafting on a similar stock in March.

SPECIES CULTIVATED: *S. alba*, ' White Willow ', ' Huntingdon Willow ', 50 to 60 ft., Britain, Asia, N. Africa, vars. *calva* (syn. *S. caerulea*), ' Bat Willow ', *sericea*, ' Silver Willow ', *vitellina*, ' Golden Willow ', *vitellina pendula*, ' Golden Weeping Willow '; *babylonica*, ' Weeping Willow ', 30 to 50 ft., China; *Bockii*, 3 to 4 ft., W. China; *Caprea*, ' Goat Willow ', ' Sallow ', 15 to 20 ft., Britain, var. *pendula*, ' Kilmarnock Willow '; *daphnoides*, ' Violet Willow ', 30 to 40 ft., shoots covered with plum-coloured bloom, Britain, Europe, Asia; *discolor*, ' Pussy Willow ', to 20 ft., N. America; *fragilis*, ' Crack Willow ', 60 to 70 ft., shoots yellow and brown, Britain, Europe, N. Asia; *herbacea*, ' Dwarf Willow ', to 1 ft., Britain, Temp. Zone; *irrorata*, attractive white stems, red catkins, 8 to 10 ft., Colorado to N. Mexico; *lanata*, 2 to 3 ft., N. Europe, Britain; *magnifica*, 6 to 20 ft., W. China; *Matsudana*, pyramidal tree to 40 ft., good for dry soils, N. China, vars. *pendula*, weeping, and *tortuosa*, ' Corkscrew Willow ', spirally twisted leaves and branches; *Medemii*, large and early catkins, 12 to 18 ft., Armenia, Persia; *Medwedewii*, slender leaves, glabrous, 8 to 12 ft., Asia Minor; *nigra*, ' Black Willow ', dark brown, rough scaly bark, to 35 ft., N. America; *pentandra*, 20 to 50 ft., Britain, Europe, N. Asia; *purpurea*, ' Purple Osier ', shoots reddish-purple, 10 to 18 ft., Britain; *repens*, ' Creeping Willow ', to 3 ft., Britain, Europe, Asia; *reticulata*, 6 to 12 in., Britain, Labrador; *retusa*, 4 to 8 in., Europe; *viminalis*, ' Osier Willow ', the species grown to yield osiers, 12 to 20 ft., Europe, N. Asia.

Sallow, see *Salix Caprea.*

Salmonberry, see *Rubus spectabilis.*

Salpiglossis—*Solanaceae.* Half-hardy annual. First introduced early nineteenth century.

OUTDOOR CULTURE: Soil, sandy loam or good ordinary rich. Position, sunny beds or borders. Sow seeds in well-drained pots, pans, or shallow boxes filled with compost of equal parts loam, leaf-mould and sand placed in temp. of 55° to 60° in April. Cover seeds with thin sprinkling of fine soil. Transplant seedlings when three leaves have formed $\frac{1}{8}$ in. apart in well-drained pots or shallow boxes of above compost. Keep in temp. of 55° till May, then place in cold frame to harden and plant out in early June. Water freely in dry weather. Apply weak stimulants occasionally.

INDOOR CULTURE: Compost, four parts sandy loam, half a part each of leaf-mould and decayed cow manure and silver sand. Sow seeds as advised above for summer flowering; in July and Aug. for spring flowering. Transplant seedlings when three leaves have formed, one in a 2$\frac{1}{2}$ in. pot, and place on shelf close to glass in temp. 55° to 65°. When well rooted in small pots shift into 5 or 6 in. size. Water moderately until plants are well established. Nip off points of main shoots when 6 in. high to induce bushy growth. Place in cool greenhouse or window whilst in bloom.

SPECIES CULTIVATED: *S. sinuata*, ' Scalloped Tube Tongue ', various colours, 2 ft., Chile, parent of the beautiful strains grown in gardens.

Salsify, see *Tragopogon porrifolius.*

Salt Bush, see Atriplex; **-Tree,** see Halimodendron.

Salvia (Sage)—*Labiatae.* Greenhouse, hardy and half-hardy annuals, herbaceous perennials and evergreen shrubs.

CULTURE OF ANNUAL SPECIES: Soil, ordinary rich. Position, sunny borders for hardy kinds.

CULTURE OF GREENHOUSE SPECIES: Compost, equal parts loam and decayed manure, little sand. Position, greenhouse, Sept. to June; cold frame or sheltered position outdoors, June to Sept. Pot, March. Water freely March to Oct., moderately afterwards. Apply stimulants occasionally a month after repotting until flowers expand, then cease. Temp., Sept. to March 45° to 55°, March to June 55° to 65°. Cut down shoots to within 3 in. of their base after flowering. Plant rooted cuttings singly in 3½ in. pots. Nip off points of main shoots, also of succeeding shoots when 3 in. long. Shift into 5 or 6 in. pots when former pots are filled with roots. Water freely. Apply stimulants occasionally.

OUTDOOR CULTURE: Soil, rich ordinary. Position, sunny sheltered beds or borders. Plant, June. Lift in Sept., place in pots to flower in greenhouse in autumn. Water freely in dry weather. Apply stimulants occasionally. Lift tuberous roots of *S. patens* in Oct. and store in sand in frost-proof place. Start in heat in March and plant out in May.

CULTURE OF HARDY SPECIES: Soil, ordinary rich. Position, sunny border. Plant, Oct., Nov., March or April. Mulch annually with decayed manure in March. Cut down stems close to ground in Oct. Lift, divide and replant every third year.

CULTURE OF CLARY: Hardy biennial. Leaves used for flavouring soups. Used as border plant also. Soil, ordinary. Position, sunny. Sow seeds 1 inch deep in drills 18 in. apart in April. Thin seedlings when 2 in. high to 12 in. apart in row. Gather leaves in summer and dry for use following year.

CULTURE OF SAGE: Soil, ordinary rich, light, dryish. Position, sunny. Plant, March or April, 12 in. apart in rows 18 in. asunder. Nip off points of shoots first year to induce bushy growth. Water freely in dry weather first year after planting. Renew plantation every four years, as shrubs are inclined to become leggy with age.

PROPAGATION: Greenhouse species by cuttings 2 to 3 in. long of young shoots inserted in sandy soil in temp. 65° in spring. The popular vars. of scarlet salvia (*S. splendens*), although perennial, may be flowered in the first season from seed sown in Jan., Feb. or March in gentle heat, or grown on in pots for planting out in June; the blue *S. patens* may be similarly treated. Sage by seeds sown in 55° to 65° in March, transplanting seedlings outdoors in May or June, or by cuttings in a shady border or cold frame in April; miscellaneous hardy species by division in March or April. Annuals by seed.

GREENHOUSE SPECIES CULTIVATED: *S. azurea*, blue, winter, 6 ft., N. America; *caerulea*, blue, winter, 2 to 3 ft., S. Africa; *coccinea*, scarlet, autumn, 2 to 3 ft., N. America; · *farinacea*, violet-blue, summer, 3 ft., Mexico; *fulgens*, scarlet,, summer, 2 to 3 ft., Mexico; *Grahamii*, scarlet, July to Oct., 4 ft., Mexico; *Greggii*, carmine, Aug. to Nov., 3 ft., Mexico; *Heeri*, scarlet, winter, 2 to 3 ft., Peru; *interrupta*, violet-blue, winter, 3 to 4 ft., Morocco; *involucrata*, crimson, autumn, 3 to 4 ft., Mexico; *leucantha*, white, winter, 2 ft., Mexico; *patens*, blue, summer, 2 to 3 ft., Mexico; *rutilans*, red, winter, 2 to 3 ft., origin uncertain; *Sessei*, scarlet, winter, 4 to 5 ft., Mexico; *splendens*, scarlet, autumn, 2 to 3 ft., Brazil.

HARDY SPECIES CULTIVATED: *S. argentea*, white, foliage silvery, summer, 3 ft., Medit. Region; *bicolor*, bluish-violet and white, summer, 3 ft., Spain and N. Africa; · *Bulleyana*, yellow, June, July, 2 ft., Himalaya; *dichroa*, blue and white, summer, 4 to 6 ft., N. Africa; *farinacea*, violet-blue, July, Aug., 3 ft., Texas; *fulva*, red, requiring sheltered position, July, 2½ ft., Mexico; *glutinosa*, pale yellow, July to Sept., 3 ft., Europe; *grandiflora* (syn. *S. Pitcheri*), sky blue, summer, 3 ft., Mexico; *nutans*, blue, July, 2 ft., S.E. Europe; *officinalis*, ' Sage ', blue, shrubby, summer, 3 ft., S. Europe; *pratensis*, ' Meadow Sage ', violet, May, 3 ft., Britain; *Sclarea*, ' Clary ', bluish-white, summer, 2 ft., Medit. Region; *uliginosa*, azure blue, Aug. to Sept., 3 to 5 ft., Brazil.

ANNUAL SPECIES CULTIVATED: *S. carduacea*, half-hardy, lilac-blue, summer, 1 ft., California; *coccinea*, half-hardy, scarlet, autumn, 2 to 3 ft., N. America; *Horminium*, lilac, to purple, summer, 1½ ft., S.E. Europe.

Salvinia—*Salviniaceae*. Tender, floating, flowerless, annual aquatics. Rounded leaves, arranged in pairs and covered with silky hairs.

CULTURE: Soil, not necessary. Position, tanks or water in warm greenhouse or in indoor aquariums. Temp., March to Sept. 65° to 75°, Sept. to March 55° to 60°. Place in tanks any time.

PROPAGATION: By division during growing period. It is advisable to keep stock pans containing 3 in. sifted loam and charcoal and 1 in. of water; spores will drop into mud and keep the stock going.

SPECIES CULTIVATED: *S. auriculata* (syn. *S. brasiliensis*), pea-green foliage, Trop. America; *natans* (trade name), small, bright green, warm temp. regions excluding America.

Sambucus (Elder)—*Caprifoliaceae*. Hardy deciduous shrubs or small trees and, rarely, herbaceous perennials. Green, golden or white pinnate leaves, and black or scarlet berries which are extensively used in country districts for medicinal beverages and wines.

CULTURE: Soil, ordinary. Position, open shrubbery or hedgerows for common species; moist, sunny borders for variegated kinds, dry banks or shrubberies for herbaceous species. Plant, Oct. to March. Prune into shape, Nov. to Jan. Nip off points of young shoots of golden and silver elders during summer, also cut shoots closely back in March to ensure dwarf growth and rich colouring in foliage.

PROPAGATION: By cuttings, herbaceous species by division.

SPECIES CULTIVATED: *S. canadensis*, white, July, to 12 ft., Eastern N. America, and var. *acutiloba*, leaves deeply dissected; *Ebulus*, ' Dwarf Elder ', herbaceous, white, tinged pink, summer, 3 ft., Europe; *nigra*, ' Common Elder ', white, June, 20 ft., Britain, and vars. *aurea*, ' Golden Elder ', *laciniata*, ' Cut-leaved Elder ', *rosea flore-pleno*, flowers double, rosy tinted; *racemosa*, white, April, scarlet berries in summer, 8 to 12 ft., Europe, and vars. *plumoso-aurea*, toothed foliage golden-yellow, *tenuifolia*, leaflets finely dissected.

Samolus (Tasmanian Water Pimpernel)—*Primulaceae*. Hardy herbaceous perennial. First introduced early nineteenth century.

CULTURE: Soil, sandy peat. Position, moist bog or rockery. Plant, March or April. Water freely in dry weather in summer.

PROPAGATION: By division of the roots in spring.

SPECIES CULTIVATED: *S. repens*, white, Aug., 6 in., Australia.

Samphire, see *Crithmum maritimum.*

Sanchezia—*Acanthaceae*. Stove flowering shrub. First introduced mid-nineteenth century.

CULTURE: Compost, two parts peat and loam, one part decayed manure and sand. Position, light part of stove in winter; shady part in spring and summer. Pot, March. Syringe twice daily April to Oct., once daily afterwards. Water freely March to Oct., moderately other times. Apply weak stimulants occasionally during summer. Temp., Sept. to March 55° to 65°, March to Sept. 75° to 85°.

PROPAGATION: By cuttings of young shoots inserted under bell-glass in fine soil, March to July.

SPECIES CULTIVATED: *S. nobilis*, yellow and red, March to Oct., 3 to 4 ft., Ecuador, and var. *variegata*, leaves striped white or yellow.

Sand Lily, see *Leucocrinum montanum*; **-Myrtle,** see Leiophyllum; **-Verbena,** see Abronia; **-wort,** see Arenaria.

Sandersonia—*Liliaceae*. Stove climbing tuberous-rooted herb. First introduced mid-nineteenth century.

CULTURE: Compost, sandy loam with a little leaf-mould and well-decayed manure. Position, well-drained pots, with shoots trained to roof or trellis. Pot, Feb., placing tubers 2 in. deep, one in a 6 in. pot or several in an 8 or 12 in. pot. Water moderately till growth is well advanced, then freely. After flowering gradually withhold water and keep soil quite dry till potting time. Temp., Feb. to Sept. 70° to 85°, Sept. to Feb. 55° to 65°.

PROPAGATION: By seeds inserted singly, ¼ in. deep, in 3 in. pots filled with light soil in temp. 75° in Feb. or March; offsets removed from large tubers at potting time.

SPECIES CULTIVATED: *S. aurantiaca*, orange-yellow, July and Aug., 3 to 6 ft., Natal.

Sanguinaria—*Papaveraceae*. Hardy perennial low-growing herb with red juice. First introduced late seventeenth century.

CULTURE: Soil, sandy loam or peat. Position, sunny borders or rockeries. Plant, Oct., Nov., March or April. Water freely in dry weather. Top-dress annually with decayed cow manure in Feb. or March. Should be interfered with as little as possible.

PROPAGATION: By seeds sown $\frac{1}{16}$ in. deep in equal parts leaf-mould, peat and sand in cold frame or cool greenhouse in early autumn or spring, transplanting seedlings outdoors when large enough to handle; division of roots in Oct. or March.

SPECIES CULTIVATED: *S. canadensis*, ' Bloodroot ', white, early spring, 6 in., N. America, and var. *multiplex*, double flowers.

Sanguisorba (Burnet)—*Rosaceae*. Hardy perennial herbs, sometimes known as Poterium.

CULTURE: Soil, ordinary. Position, sunny or shady borders or by waterside. Appreciate abundant moisture during growing season. Plant, Oct. to Nov. or March to April.

PROPAGATION: By seed sown in pans in sandy soil during Feb. or March; division of roots in March or April.

SPECIES CULTIVATED: *S. canadensis* (syn. *Poterium canadense*), white, July to Sept., 4 ft., N. America; *obtusa* (syn. *Poterium obtusum*), pink, July to Sept., 2 to 3 ft., Japan, var. *alba*, white.

Sansevieria (Bowstring Hemp; Angola Hemp)—*Liliaceae*. Stove herbaceous perennials. Flowers, white, green, yellowish; insignificant. Leaves, narrow, ridged, green, long, margined or spotted with white. First introduced late seventeenth century.

CULTURE: Compost, equal parts loam, leaf-mould and sand. Position, pots in shady part of stove. Pot, Feb. to April. Water copiously March to Oct., moderately afterwards. Syringe freely in summer. Temp., March to Sept. 65° to 75°, Sept. to March 55° to 65°.

PROPAGATION: By division of plants, Feb. to April.

SPECIES CULTIVATED: *S. cylindrica*, white, Aug., 2½ to 5 ft., leaves banded dark green, Trop. Africa; *thyrsiflora* (syn. *S. guineensis*), greenish-white, Sept., 1 to 1½ ft., leaves banded pale green, S. Africa; *trifasciata* var. *Laurentii*, greenish-white, 2 ft., leaves striped golden yellow, W. Trop. Africa; *zeylanica*, greenish-white, 2 to 2½ ft., leaves banded light green, Ceylon.

Santolina (Lavender Cotton)—*Compositae*. Greyish evergreen aromatic shrubby plants. First introduced mid-sixteenth century.

CULTURE: Soil, ordinary sandy. Position, sunny borders or rockeries. Plant, Sept., Oct., March or April. *S. Chamaecyparissus* is one of the most useful of grey-foliaged shrubs, but requires annual hard pruning in spring to prevent legginess.

PROPAGATION: By cuttings of shoots, 2 to 3 in. long, pulled off with portion of stem attached and inserted in pots of sandy soil in cold frame, Sept. or Oct., or in sheltered position outdoors same time.

SPECIES CULTIVATED: *S. Chamaecyparissus* (syn. *S. incana*), yellow, July, 1 to 2 ft., S. Europe, leaves covered with cottony-grey down; *virens*, ' Holy Flax ', yellow, summer, 2 ft., leaves green, S. Europe.

Sanvitalia—*Compositae*. Hardy annual. First introduced late eighteenth century.

CULTURE: Soil, ordinary. Position, margins of sunny borders or rockeries. Sow seeds $\frac{1}{16}$ in. deep in light soil in cool temp. in March. Harden off seedlings in cold frame in April and plant outdoors in May; or in lines or patches in open ground end of April, thinning seedlings when 1 in. high to 4 or 5 in. apart. Water freely in dry weather and apply weak stimulants occasionally.

SPECIES CULTIVATED: *S. procumbens*, yellow and purple, summer to late autumn, trailing, Mexico, var. *flore-pleno*, flowers double.

Sapodilla, see *Sapota Achras*.

Saponaria (Soap-wort)—*Caryophyllaceae*. Hardy annuals and perennials. First introduced late sixteenth century.

CULTURE OF ANNUAL SPECIES: Soil, ordinary. Position, margins of sunny borders or in beds. Sow seeds in lines or patches ½ in. deep in April for summer flowering; in Sept. for spring flowering. Thin seedlings when 1 in. high to 2 or 3 in. apart. Water freely in dry weather and apply stimulants occasionally.

CULTURE OF PERENNIAL SPECIES: Soil, deep, rich loam. Position, sunny rockeries or borders for *S. ocymoides*; large, sunny or shady shrubbery borders or wild garden for *S. officinalis*. Plant, Oct. to April. Top-dress annually in Feb. with decayed manure. Water freely in dry weather.

PROPAGATION: Perennial species by seeds sown in shallow boxes of sandy soil in temp. of 55° in March, hardening seedlings in a cold frame in April, and planting out in May or June; or outdoors in April, transplanting seedlings in June and July; by cuttings inserted in sandy soil in cold frame, Sept. to Oct.; division of roots, Oct. to March.

ANNUAL SPECIES CULTIVATED: *S. calabrica*, rose, July to Sept., 6 to 12 in., Italy; *Vaccaria*, pink, summer, 2 to 3 ft., Europe, and var. *alba*.

PERENNIAL SPECIES CULTIVATED: *S. bellidifolia*, pale yellow, June to Aug., 9 to 12 in., E. Europe; *caespitosa*, rose, June to Aug., 4 in., Pyrenees; *lutea*, yellow, June to Aug., 3 to 6 in., Europe; *ocymoides*, ' Rock Soap-wort ', rosy purple, summer, trailing, Europe; *officinalis flore-pleno*, ' Bouncing Bet ', ' Fuller's Herb ', pink, Aug., 2 to 3 ft., Europe (Br.).

Sapota—*Sapotaceae*. Tender evergreen tree cultivated in the tropics for its fruit. The milky latex is the chief source of Gum Chicle, which, flavoured, is ' chewing gum '.

CULTURE: Compost, fertile sandy loam. Position, border in warm greenhouse.

PROPAGATION: By seeds; shield budding on common seedling stocks; grafting and layering are methods also used in India.

SPECIES CULTIVATED: *S. Achras* (syn. *Achras Sapota*), ' Sapodilla ', white, fruit brown, with yellow-brown translucent flesh and black shining seeds, to 75 ft., Trop. America.

Sapote, see *Achras Zapota*.

Sarcanthus—*Orchidaceae*. A large variable epiphytic genus. On the whole, of little horticultural value. Stems leafy, erect or pendent, varying in size, flowers often many, small, fleshy, racemes simple or branched. Species are met with in cultivation and a few have prettily coloured flowers.

CULTURE: As suggested for Saccolabiums, requiring the same consideration in winter for watering. The longer-stemmed forms require support.

PROPAGATION: The remarks under Saccolabium apply.

SPECIES CULTIVATED: A selection—*S. chrysomelas*, small, many, yellowish, with dark purplish centres to the sepals and petals, summer, Burma; *erinaceus*, dwarf, many, small, white to pink, lip deep rose, pretty, summer, Burma; *filiformis*, small, purplish, lip yellowish and rose, stems pendulous, long, leaves terete, summer, autumn, Burma, Siam; *hongkongensis*, many, small, lilac, lip purple, leaves terete, Hong Kong; *ornithorhynchus*, dwarf, many, small, yellowish, rose-purple centrally, lip amethyst-purple, pretty; *pallidus*, many, small, in a panicle, purplish-brown, margined yellow, lip white, various, India, Burma; *paniculatus*, many, small, yellowish, with one or two brown-red central stripes, various, China, Burma; *Williamsonii*, many, small, pink-lilac, lip lilac and amethyst, raceme often branched, leaves terete, pretty, summer, Andamans, Burma.

Sarcochilus—*Orchidaceae.* A large genus of epiphytic orchids. Pseudo-bulbs are absent, stems long or short, flowers usually racemose and small. There is great variation and many species are of no horticultural importance.

CULTURE: Compost, similar to that given Saccolabium, cultivation much the same. The temp. for tropical species as for Saccolabium and Phalaenopsis. The cooler-growing species, chiefly from Australia, succeed during summer in the Odontoglossum House but generally need a temp. of 60° and moist atmosphere in winter. Species with hard-textured leaves need less frequent watering in winter. Leafless species are known and they require a more decided rest.

PROPAGATION: As for Vandas but can seldom be effected.

SPECIES CULTIVATED: A selection—*S. Berkeleyi,* creamy white, lip with purple stain, stems short, raceme pendulous, summer, Nicobar Islands; *Ceciliae,* fragrant, few small pink, lip with white hairs, summer to autumn, Australia; *falcatus,* 3 to 10 fragrant whitish, lip with red and orange, spring, Australia; *Fitzgeraldii,* up to 12 comparatively large, white spotted red, lip spotted rose-purple, spring, Australia; *Hartmannii,* white spotted dark red, lip streaked red-purple, mid-lobe often yellowish, spring, Australia; *luniferus,* stem absent, leaves absent or fugitive, roots long, flowers yellow, spotted red, lip yellow, barred white or brown, spring to summer, N. India, Burma; *unguiculatus,* fragrant, creamy white or yellowish, lip streaked red, mid-lobe dotted crimson, flowers fugacious but borne in succession, summer, Philippines.

Sarcococca (Sweet Box)—*Buxaceae.* Hardy evergreen shrubs, fragrant unisexual flowers without petals produced in winter and early spring. First introduced early nineteenth century.

CULTURE: Soil, ordinary. Position, moist and shady, thrives well under trees. Plant, Sept. to Oct. and April to May.

PROPAGATION: By cuttings of ripened wood in sandy soil in cold frame during Sept. to Oct.

SPECIES CULTIVATED: *S. confusa,* white, fruits black, winter, up to 6 ft., origin unknown, probably China; *Hookeriana,* white, fruits black, winter, 2 to 3 ft., Himalaya; *humilis,* white, fruits black, winter, 2 ft., Cent. China; *ruscifolia,* white, fruits red, winter, to 4 ft., China; *saligna,* greenish, scentless, 4 to 5 ft., N. India, Himalaya.

Sarmienta—*Gesneriaceae.* Greenhouse evergreen creeper. First introduced mid-nineteenth century.

CULTURE: Compost, soft peat, charcoal and chopped sphagnum moss. Position, teak baskets or pans suspended from roof, or in pots with shoots growing up stems of dead tree ferns. Pot or plant, March. Water copiously April to Oct., moderately afterwards. Syringe freely daily March to Oct. Shade from sun. Temp., March to Sept. 60° to 70°, Sept. to March 45° to 55°.

PROPAGATION: By division of plants in March.

SPECIES CULTIVATED: *S. repens,* ' Chilean Pitcher Flower ', scarlet, creeping, summer, Chile.

Sarracenia (Pitcher-plant)—*Sarraceniaceae.* Half-hardy herbaceous perennials with tubular, pitcher-shaped, reticulated leaves. First introduced mid-eighteenth century.

INDOOR CULTURE: Compost, equal parts fibrous peat and chopped sphagnum moss with a little sifted loam and silver sand. Position, cool, moist corner of greenhouse or fernery, cold frame, or wardian case in dwelling-room. *S. flava* and *S. purpurea* are hardy grown under sheltered conditions in S. England. Pot, March. Pots to be two-thirds full of drainage. Place pot containing plant inside another pot two sizes larger and fill space between with sphagnum moss. Water freely April to Oct., very little in winter. Syringe foliage gently daily in summer. Shade from bright sun.

OUTDOOR CULTURE OF S. FLAVA AND S. PURPUREA: Compost, equal parts peat and sphagnum moss. Position, fully exposed bog garden or moist rockery. Plant,

March **or** April. Keep surface of soil covered with layer **of** moss. Water freely in summer and cover with frame-light in winter.

PROPAGATION: All the species and hybrids by division in March or April.

SPECIES CULTIVATED: *S. Drummondii*, flowers purple, June, leaves white, green, and purple, 2 ft., N. America; *flava*, ' Huntsman's Horn ', yellow, June, 2 ft., N. America; *minor* (syn. *S. variolaris*), flowers yellow, leaves spotted with white, N. America; *psittacina*, flowers purple, leaves veined red or purple, N. America; *purpurea*, ' Huntsman's Cup ', ' Indian Cup ', ' Sidesaddle Flower ', leaves veined purple, N. America ; *rubra*, flowers reddish, leaves veined purple, N. America. There are many hybrids.

Sarsaparilla, see Smilax.

Sasa—*Gramineae*. Bamboo-like shrubs. Formerly included in Arundinaria and Bambusa.

CULTURE: Soil, loam, leaf-mould and sand. Position, sheltered shrubberies or massed on lawns.

PROPAGATION: By division in April and May.

SPECIES CULTIVATED: *S. chrysantha* (syns. *Arundinaria* and *Bambusa chrysantha*), to 6 ft., slightly variegated, Japan; *Veitchii* (syns. *S. albo-marginata*, *Arundinaria* and *Bambusa Veitchii*), 3 ft., quick growing, Japan.

Sassafras—*Lauraceae*. Hardy deciduous aromatic tree **grown** for the foliage.

CULTURE: Soil, deep loam, situation sheltered. Plant, Oct. or March.

PROPAGATION: By imported seeds sown in well-drained pots in cold frame, March.

SPECIES CULTIVATED: *S. albidum* (syn. *S. officinale*), greenish-yellow, round, dark blue fruits, May, 50 to 70 ft., Eastern U.S.A.

Satin flower, see Lunaria; **-leaf,** see *Chrysophyllum oliviforme*; **-Poppy,** see *Meconopsis Wallichii*.

Satureja (Savory)—*Labiatae*. Hardy annual and perennial aromatic herbs and sub-shrubs. Some authors place certain species in a separate genus, Calamintha.

CULTURE: Soil, ordinary. Position, sunny rockeries or borders. Plant, Oct. or April.

PROPAGATION: **Annuals** by seed; perennials, division **or** cuttings of young shoots; shrubby species by cuttings.

SPECIES CULTIVATED: *S. Acinos* (syn. *Calamintha Acinos*), purple-blue, July, 6 in., annual, Europe; *alpina* (syn. *C. alpina*), purple, June, 6 in., Europe; *Calamintha* (syns. *C. officinalis*, *Clinopodium Calamintha*), ' Calamint ', lilac, June, 1 to 2 ft., Europe; *grandiflora*, purple, June, 1 ft., Europe; *hortensis* (syn. *C. hortensis*), ' Summer Savory ', pink, 1½ ft., annual, Europe; *intricata*, white, summer, tufted perennial, Spain; *montana* (syns. *S. cuneifolia*, *illyrica* and *pygmaea*, *C. montana*), ' Winter Savory ', white, 15 in., Europe, Asia; *rupestris*, flowers in dense whorls, sub-shrub, S.E. Europe.

Sauromatum (Monarch of the East)—*Araceae*. Half-hardy perennial with tuberous roots and arum-like flower spathes. First introduced early nineteenth century.

CULTURE: Purchase tubers in autumn, place them **in** a dry saucer in a warm room, and in a few weeks the flower spathe will appear. No soil or water needed. After flowering plant the tuber in a moist place outdoors to make its leaf growth. Lift in Aug., keep in a cool place, and again place in a saucer indoors. Repeat the operation year by year.

SPECIES CULTIVATED: *S. guttatum*, purple, yellow, and green, winter or spring, 1½ to 2 ft., Cent. Asia.

Saururus (Lizard's Tail)—*Saururaceae*. Hardy aquatic perennials. First introduced mid-eighteenth century.

CULTURE: Soil, heavy loam **with** peat and leaf-mould. Position, margins **of** ponds. Plant, April to May.

PROPAGATION: By division at planting time.

SPECIES CULTIVATED: *S. cernuus*, 'American Swamp Lily', white, fragrant, summer, 1 to 2 ft., N. America; *chinensis* (syn. *S. Loureirii*), yellowish-white, summer, 1 to 2 ft., China, Japan.

Saussurea—*Compositae*. Hardy perennial herbs. First introduced early nineteenth century.

CULTURE: Soil, ordinary. Position, sunny rockeries. Plant, Oct., Nov., March or April.

PROPAGATION: By seeds sown ⅛ in. deep in ordinary soil in sunny position outdoors, April, transplanting seedlings when three or four leaves have formed.

SPECIES CULTIVATED: *S. alpina*, purple, Aug., 6 in., Northern and Arctic Regions (Br.); *pygmaea*, purple, July, 4 in., Europe.

Savin, see *Juniperus Sabina*.

Savory, see Satureja.

Savoy, see *Brassica oleracea* var. *capitata*.

Saxifraga (Saxifrage; Rockfoil)—*Saxifragaceae*. A genus of about 300 species and as many hybrids. Mostly hardy perennial, rarely annual. Natives, generally alpine, north and south temperate and arctic zones and Asia, and very rare in S. America, absent from Australia, S. Africa and Southern Pacific. Flowers white, yellow, purple, pink or red, paniculate or corymbose. A dozen species are indigenous to Britain.

CULTURE: With few exceptions Saxifrages are among the easiest of plants to grow. As cultivation differs according to various sections, it is dealt with in each section.

PROPAGATION: By offsets or division of tufts, but some, especially hybrids of Kabschia and Engleria sections, are best increased by means of tiny cuttings rooted in a cold frame in a mixture of five parts sand to three parts finely-sieved moss peat; the cuttings should be taken as soon as the growths are long enough to handle after flowering in spring or early summer; also by seeds.

The genus falls botanically into fifteen sections and one sub-section (Engleria of horticulture equals sub-section Media of Kabschia section). These sections are numbered 1 to 16 and the section number appears in parentheses after each name in the list of species, and reference to the particular section will supply simple cultural needs of plants belonging to it. In so widely diverse a genus it is not possible in a limited space to give more than a broad general indication of the conditions preferred by each section:

1. **Boraphila.** All leaves at base forming a few-leaved, softly leathery rosette. Flowers in spikes or loose showers, white or spotted. Generally prefer cool or damp places and peaty soil.

2. **Hirculus.** Undivided, deciduous, oval leaves, mat, not rosette forming. Flowers yellow or orange on leafy stems. Require bog or damp scree conditions.

3. **Robertsonia.** More or less spoon-shaped, leathery leaves, entire, but variously toothed at margins. Mostly in basal rosettes. Flowers in loose, open showers, small, white, pink or spotted. All very easily grown in shady or slightly moist positions.

4. **Miscopetalum.** Tufted plants with leathery, round to oval leaves, stalked, and with variously-toothed margins. Stems upright and more or less leafy ending in open panicles of small, mostly white, but sometimes spotted flowers frequently having uneven petals. Shade lovers.

5. **Cymbalaria.** Small, freely-branching annuals with roughly ivy-shaped leaves and golden, or rarely white, star-shaped flowers. Cool shady spots for preference.

6. **Tridactylites.** Mostly unimportant annual or biennial plants with basal

rosettes of flimsy, undivided to three-pointed, leaves. More or less leafy, branching stems carry the small white flowers. Poor sandy soil in sun or shade.

7. **Nephrophyllum.** Deciduous plants, often bearing bulbils at the base or in the leaf axils of the flowering stems. Leaves mostly kidney-shaped of lax texture and variously marginally toothed. Flowers generally white.

8. **Dactyloides.** All the so-called ' Mossy ' Saxifrages belong to this group. All form more or less dense carpets or mats of rosettes of variously-cleft hairy or glabrous leaves. The freely-produced flowers may be white, pink, rose or deep red, or any intervening shade. Happiest away from scorching sun.

9. **Trachyphyllum.** Mostly small, mat-forming species with narrow, undivided, bristle-edged and pointed leaves. Flowers borne on sparsely branching stems, usually about 4 in. high. They are dingy white, pale, or almost orange-yellow. In nature seem to prefer lime-free positions.

10. **Xanthizoon.** This section embraces the many forms of *S. aizoides*, which is found all over the Northern Hemisphere with the exception of Asia. Loose mats of tangled stems set sparsely with narrow leaves which are scarcely rosetted. Leaves undivided but may be slightly notched or bristly at the margins. Flowers produced singly or in loose cymes, varying from pale and rich yellow to orange or even purple and deep red. In nature prefer shingly water margins but are tolerant of far less moist conditions in cultivation.

11. **Euaizoonia.** Contains all the broader-leaved, silver-encrusted species from *S. aizoon* to *S. longifolia*. All form rosettes which generally surround themselves with offset rosettes, forming clumps or cushions. All have tall, more or less branching, flower stems which are loosely or densely wreathed with flowers in early summer. Flowers mostly white but may be more or less heavily spotted with pink, red or purple, and soft pink, rich pink and even yellow flowers occur. Rosettes die after flowering. Nearly all avid lime-lovers and sun worshippers.

12. **Kabschia.** Contains the elite of the genus. All small, cushion-forming densely-tufted plants. Individual rosettes may consist of more or less sharply-spiny leaves or the leaves may be broader and more spreading and bluntly or roundly pointed. Flowers may be produced singly or several on a short, more or less branched, stem. May be pure white, soft or rich yellow, lilac, pink or soft red in colour, never spotted. Thirty-six known species, only half of which are in cultivation, and over 100 garden-raised hybrids.

13. **Engleria.** (Really sub-section *Media* of the *Kabschia* group.) Most of the species in this sub-group display a rosette formation resembling that of the *Euaizoon* section and all those in cultivation have leafy flower-stems ending in spikes or branched racemes of tiny flowers enveloped in usually highly-coloured calyces. Even the stem leaves may be more or less highly coloured.

14. **Porphyrion.** Creeping and mat-forming plants generally with purple flowers but a few whites and bicolor forms are known. Leaves opposite and only at the crowded ends of the creeping shoots do they approach the typical rosette formation of the genus. Gritty, porous soil and happiest in cool and slightly moist but not sunless positions. Frequent gritty top-dressing of old clumps is advisable.

15. **Tetrameridium.** Only one species of this group has ever been in cultivation. Differs from all the others in having only four sepals and apparently no petals. Solitary flowers on short stems. Dense, tufted habit and short, branching stems densely set with overlapping, opposite, narrow and tiny leaves.

16. **Diptera.** Tufts of broad-bladed, stalked leaves of leathery texture from which arise in autumn branching stems bearing odd-shaped flowers usually having one or two petals much elongated and often notched along the margin. Cool positions in soil containing much humus. Flowers pure white or occasionally spotted.

SPECIES CULTIVATED: *S. aizoides* (10), yellow, 3 to 4 in., summer, Europe, and vars. *atrorubens*, blood-red, *aurantia*, orange, and *autumnalis*, orange, autumn; *Aizoon* (11), white, 6 in., summer, Europe, and innumerable vars.; *Andrewsii* (3-11), pink, 9 in., summer, hybrid; *apiculata* (12), yellow, 4 in., spring, hybrid; *aquatica* (8), white, 12 in., early summer, Pyrenees; *Arco-Valleyi* (12), rose, 1 in., spring, hybrid; *aretioides* (12), yellow, 2 in., early summer, Pyrenees; *aspera* (9), yellow, speckled orange, 3 in., summer, Europe, and var. *bryoides*, smaller flowers spotted red; *assimilis* (12), white, 2 in., spring, hybrid; *Biasolettii* (13), red, 4 in., spring, hybrid; *biflora* (14), purple, 2 in., spring, Alps, no lime; *Bileckii* (12), yellow, 2 in., spring, hybrid; *Borisii* (12), yellow, 3 in., spring, hybrid; *Boryi* (12), white, 2 to 3 in., spring, Greece; *Boydii* (12), citron-yellow, 3 in., spring, hybrid; *Brunoniana* (2), yellow, 3 in., summer, Himalaya; *Burseriana* (12), white, 3 in., early summer, E. Alps, and many fine vars.; *bursiculata* (12), white, 3 in., spring, hybrid; *caesia* (12), white, 2 in., summer, Pyrenees, E. Alps; *Camposii* (8), white, 9 in., summer, Spain; *canis-dalmatica* (11), white, spotted red, 6 in., summer, hybrid; *cartilaginea* (11), white, 6 in., summer, Caucasus; *cebenensis* (8), white, 3 in., May, Cent. France; *Clibranii* (8), deep red, 6 in., early summer, hybrid; *cochlearis* (11), white, 6 in., summer, Maritime Alps; *conifera* (8), white, 1 to 2 in., summer, Pyrenees; *cortusaefolia* (16), white, 12 in., Sept., Japan; *corymbosa* (13), yellow, 4 in., early summer, Asia Minor, Bulgaria; *Cotyledon* (11), white, 18 to 24 in., summer, Alps, and numerous vars.; *crustata* (11), white, 3 to 4 in., summer, E. Alps; *cuneifolia* (3), white, 3 in., summer, Alps; *cuscutaeformis* (16), white flushed pink, 3 in., summer, India; *Cymbalaria* (5), yellow, 2 in., summer, Caucasus, Asia Minor, annual; *diapensioides* (12), white, 1 in., spring, Alps; *Elizabethae* (12), soft yellow, 3 in., spring, hybrid; *Engleri* (11), white, 9 in., summer, Carinthia, natural hybrid; *erioblasta* (8), white, 2 in., summer, Spain; *exarata* (8), cream, 3 in., spring, Pyrenees to Balkans; *Ferdinandi-Coburgii* (12), yellow, 4 in., spring, Bulgaria; *Fortunei* (16), white, 12 to 15 in., autumn, Asia; *Geum* (3), white, 4 to 6 in., summer, Europe (Br.); *Gordoniana* (12), yellow, 4 in., spring, hybrid; *granulata* (7), 'Meadow Saxifrage', white, 12 in., summer, Europe (Br.), and var. *florepleno*, double; *Grisebachii* (13), crimson, 9 in., summer, Greece; *Haagii* (12), yellow, 3 in., spring, hybrid; *Hirculus* (2), yellow, 6 in., summer, Europe (Br.); *Hostii*, cream, 12 in., summer, Europe; *hypnoides* (8), white, summer, 4 in., Europe (Br.), and many garden hybrids; *irrigua* (7), white, 12 to 18 in., summer, Crimea, biennial; *Irvingii* (12), pink, 2 in., spring, hybrid; *juniperifolia* (12), yellow, 3 in., spring, Caucasus; *Kellereri* (12-13), soft pink, 4 in., Feb., hybrid; *Kotschyi* (12), yellow, 3 in., spring, Asia Minor; *latepetiolata* (7), milk-white, 12 to 15 in., Spain, biennial; *lilacina* (12), lilac, ½ in., spring, Himalaya; *lingulata* (11), white, 9 to 12 in., summer, Maritime Alps, and numerous vars.; *longifolia* (11), white, 2 ft., summer, Pyrenees; *Macnabiana* (11), white, spotted red, 12 in., summer, hybrid; *marginata* (12), white, 4 in., early summer, Italy to the Balkans; *media* (13), pink, 6 in., spring, Pyrenees; *moschata* (8), white, pink, or pale yellow, 3 in., summer, Europe (parent of many garden hybrids); *muscoides* (8), white, 3 in., summer, Europe; *mutata* (11), yellow, 9 to 12 in., summer, E. Alps; *Obristii* (12), white, 4 in., spring, hybrid; *oppositifolia* (14), pink, 2 in., spring, Europe (Br.); *Paulinae* (8), yellow, 4 in., spring, hybrid; *pedemontana* (8), white, 4 in., summer, Europe; *pennsylvanica* (1), yellow-white, 2 to 3 ft., summer, N. America; *Petraschii* (12), white, 3 to 4 in., spring, hybrid; *porophylla* (13), pink, 6 in., summer, Italy; *retusa* (14), red, 1 in., summer, Alps; *rotundifolia* (4), white, speckled pink, 12 in., summer, Europe; *Salomonii* (12), white, 3 to 4 in., spring, hybrid; *sancta* (12), yellow, 4 in., summer, Asia Minor; *sarmentosa* (16), 'Mother of Thousands', white, pink spotted, 9 to 12 in., summer, Asia;

scardica (12), white, 4 in., summer, Macedonia; *Sibthorpii* (5), yellow, 2 in., summer, Greece, annual; *Spruneri* (12), white, 2 to 3 in., spring, Greece; *squarrosa* (12), white, 1 to 2 in., summer, Mts. Europe; *Stribrnyi* (13), pink, 4 in., summer, Bulgaria; *taygetea* (4), white, spotted pink, 2 to 3 in., summer, Greece; *tenella* (8), white, 2 to 3 in., summer, E. Alps; *tombeanensis* (12), white, 2 in., summer, Europe; *umbrosa* (3), 'London's Pride', pink, 9 in., summer, Europe (Br.), and many vars.; *valdensis* (11), white, 2 to 3 in., summer, Europe; *Vandellii* (12), white, 3 to 4 in., summer, Italy; *Veitchiana* (16), white, 9 in., late summer, China.

Scabiosa (Scabious; Pincushion Flower)—*Dipsaceae.* Hardy annual and perennial herbs. Flowers useful for cutting.

CULTURE OF ANNUAL SPECIES: Soil, good rich ordinary. Position, sunny beds or borders. Sow seeds $\frac{1}{16}$ in. deep in light, sandy soil in temp. of 60° to 70° in Feb. or March and plant out in May to ensure plants flowering same year, or outdoors in June or July, transplanting following March to flowering position. In cold districts lift the seedlings in Aug. and place in small pots; winter in cold frame and plant out in April.

CULTURE OF PERENNIAL SPECIES: Soil, ordinary deep rich. Position, sunny well-drained borders heavily dressed with lime for *S. caucasica*; sunny rockeries for *S. graminifolia*; ordinary borders for *S. Columbaria*, etc. Plant, March or April. Top-dress annually in Feb. or March with decayed manure. Lift, divide and replant every three or four years.

PROPAGATION: By division of roots, March, or cuttings of 2 in. growth.

ANNUAL SPECIES CULTIVATED: *S. atropurpurea*, 'Sweet Scabious' or 'Mournful Widow', various colours, single and double, July, 1 to 3 ft., S. Europe.

PERENNIAL SPECIES CULTIVATED: *S. caucasica*, 'Caucasian Scabious', light blue, summer, to 2 ft., Caucasus, and vars. *alba*, white, *goldingensis*, large lavender, *perfecta*, large and fringed; *Columbaria*, blue, 2 ft., Europe, Africa, Asia, and var. *rosea*, pink; *ochroleuca*, yellow, July, 1½ ft., Europe. See also Cephalaria, Knautea and Succisella.

Scarborough Lily, see *Vallota speciosa.*

Schaueria—*Acanthaceae.* Stove flowering and ornamental foliage plant. Formerly included in Justicia. First introduced early nineteenth century.

CULTURE: Compost, equal parts loam, peat, leaf-mould and sand. Position, well-drained pots in light stove or warm greenhouse Sept. to June, sunny frame or house June to Sept. Pot, March or April. Water moderately Sept. to March, freely other times. Temp., Sept. to March 55° to 65°, March to June 65° to 75°. Prune into shape after flowering. Stop growth several times during summer to induce bushy habit. Feed with diluted liquid manure or approved fertiliser when plants are established in final pots.

PROPAGATION: By cuttings of young shoots inserted in sandy soil in propagating case with bottom heat, March to July.

SPECIES CULTIVATED: *S. flavicoma* (syn. *S. calycotricha*), yellow, winter, 2 ft., Brazil. See also Jacobinia.

Schisandra—*Magnoliaceae.* Hardy deciduous aromatic climbing shrubs with large leaves and scarlet berries. Sometimes spelled Schizandra. First introduced mid-nineteenth century.

CULTURE: Soil, loam and peat. Position, sunny walls or arbours. Plant, Sept. and Oct. or April. Prune straggly shoots, April.

PROPAGATION: By cuttings of firm shoots inserted in sandy peat under bell-glass in cold frame, July to Oct.

SPECIES CULTIVATED: *S. chinensis*, pale rose, fragrant, April to May, 20 to 30 ft., E. Asia, Japan; *glaucescens*, orange-red, April to May, 10 to 20 ft., Cent. China; *grandiflora*, glabrous, W. China, var. *rubrifolia*, red, April; *Henryi*, white, April to May, climbing, W. China; *sphenanthera*, yellow, April to May, climbing, W. China.

Schismatoglottis—*Araceae.* Dwarf stove perennial herbs. Leaves, oblong or heart-shaped, green or striped with silver grey, purple or yellow. First introduced mid-nineteenth century.

CULTURE: Compost, equal parts sandy loam, fibrous peat, leaf-mould and silver sand. Position, well-drained pots in shady part of stove. Pot, Feb. or March. Water copiously April to Sept., moderately afterwards. Syringe daily April to Sept. Apply stimulants occasionally during summer. Temp., Sept. to March 60° to 65°, March to Sept. 75° to 85°.

PROPAGATION: By division, Feb. or March.

SPECIES CULTIVATED: *S. asperata*, leaves deep green dotted white above and black beneath, Borneo, and var. *albo-maculata* (syn. *S. crispata*), leaves silvery above; *concinna* (syn. *S. Lavellei*), leaves mottled with grey, Borneo; *neoguineensis*, leaves blotched with yellow, New Guinea; *pulchra*, leaves spotted with silvery white, Borneo. *S. siamensis* is a name frequently applied in catalogues to an unidentified plant, having leaves spotted with white and requiring the same treatment as Schismatoglottis.

Schizanthus (Butterfly or Fringe Flower)—*Solanaceae.* Half-hardy annual herbs. Natives of Chile. First introduced early nineteenth century.

OUTDOOR CULTURE: Soil, good ordinary rich. Position, sunny beds or borders. Sow seeds thinly in pots, pans, or boxes filled with light soil and place in temp. 65° to 75° in Feb. or March. Cover slightly with fine soil. Transplant seedlings when 1 in. high (four in a 3 in. pot), harden off in frame, and plant out in May. Sow also similarly in Aug., transplant three in a 3 in. pot, and place on shelf in light, airy greenhouse until following May, then plant out. Sow likewise outdoors end of April where required to grow.

POT CULTURE: Compost, one part loam, half a part each of decayed manure and leaf-mould, little sand. Sow seeds thinly in above compost in cool greenhouse or frame in Aug. Transplant seedlings singly in 3 in. pots and grow on shelf in greenhouse (temp. 45° to 55°) until Jan., then transfer to 6 in. pots and grow in light position. Water moderately in winter, freely other times. Apply weak stimulants occasionally whilst flowering. Support plants with stakes. For summer flowering sow seeds in temp. 55° to 65° in Feb. or March, transplanting when 1 in. high to 3 in. pots, then into 5 in. pots.

SPECIES CULTIVATED: *S. Grahamii*, lilac and orange, summer, 12 to 18 in., and many selected colour forms; *pinnatus*, rose, purple, and yellow, summer, 12 to 18 in., and many selected colour forms; *retusus*, rose, crimson, and orange, summer, 18 in., and several selected colour forms; *wisetonensis*, pink, white, and brown, summer, 1 ft., hybrid. The strains known as *S. hybridus grandiflorus* contain many colour forms.

Schizocentron—*Melastomaceae.* Greenhouse flowering plants of trailing habit. First introduced early nineteenth century.

CULTURE: Compost, equal parts sandy loam, peat and leaf-mould. Position, pots, pans or hanging baskets in shady greenhouse or conservatory. Water freely March to Oct., moderately at other times. Feed with diluted liquid manure when established.

PROPAGATION: By cuttings of young shoots inserted in pots of sandy soil under bell-glass or in propagating frame with gentle heat.

SPECIES CULTIVATED: *S. elegans* (syn. *Heeria elegans*), rose, trailing, spring, Mexico.

Schizocodon, see Shortia.

Schizopetalon—*Cruciferae.* Half-hardy annual. First introduced early nineteenth century.

CULTURE: Sow seeds in light, warm, rich soil in open border, April or May. Cover seeds lightly with fine soil. Thin seedlings when 1 to 2 in. high to 3 or 4 in. apart. Support plants when 6 in. high with small bushy twigs. Water freely in dry weather or sow thinly in well-drained pans filled with compost of loam, peat and sand placed in temp. of 50° to 55° in early April, transplanting seedlings three or four in 3 in. pots filled with above compost; harden off in cold frame and plant out in late May.

SPECIES CULTIVATED: *S. Walkeri*, white, almond scented, summer, 6 to 9 in., Chile.

Schizophragma—*Saxifragaceae* (or *Hydrangeaceae*). Hardy, deciduous, self-clinging, climbing, flowering shrubs of very great vigour, closely related to Hydrangea.

CULTURE: Soil, ordinary. Position, requiring space, high walls, tree trunks or pergolas. Easily cultivated. Plant, Oct. or April. Prune straggly shoots into shape, April.

PROPAGATION: By cuttings inserted in sand under a bell-glass in temp. 55° in spring.

SPECIES CULTIVATED: *S. hydrangeoides*, yellowish-white, July, 20 to 30 ft., Japan; *integrifolium*, white, July, to 40 ft., China.

Schizostylis (Kaffir Lily; Crimson Flag)—*Iridaceae*. Hardy bulbous or rhizomatous-rooted perennial. First introduced mid-nineteenth century.

OUTDOOR CULTURE: Soil, moist, loamy. Position, warm, sunny border. Plant, Oct. to March. Protect in severe weather by covering of dry litter. Water freely in dry weather in summer and apply stimulants occasionally.

POT CULTURE: Compost, two parts loam, one part decayed manure, little sand. Pot, Nov. to March. Position, cold frame, Dec. to April; plunged to the rim of pots in sunny border, April to Sept.; cold greenhouse, Sept. to Dec. Water copiously in summer, moderately other times. Apply stimulants occasionally in summer. Repot annually.

PROPAGATION: By division of rhizomes or roots in March or April.

SPECIES CULTIVATED: *S. coccinea*, crimson, Oct. and Nov., 1 to 3 ft., S. Africa, and vars.

Schlumbergera (Leaf-flowering Cactus)—*Cactaceae*. Greenhouse succulent plants. First introduced early in the nineteenth century under the name of Epiphyllum.

CULTURE: Compost, equal parts turfy loam, peat and leaf-mould, one-fourth part silver sand. Position, light warm greenhouse, Sept. to June, sunny place outdoors, or in cold frame June to Sept. Water moderately Sept. to April, a little more freely other times. Temp., Nov. to March 50° to 60°, March to June 55° to 65°, Sept. to Nov. 40° to 45°.

PROPAGATION: By cuttings inserted singly in 3 in. pots filled with sandy soil and brick dust in March or April; grafting on to stock of *Pereskia aculeata* or *P. Bleo* in temp. 65° to 75° in spring.

SPECIES CULTIVATED: *S. Gaertneri*, scarlet and violet, Brazil; *Russelliana*, rose, Brazil.

Schomburgkia—*Orchidaceae*. An epiphytic genus, strong growing, pseudobulbs solid, large. Leaves usually two, rather long, scapes long. Flowers with long whitish or red-tinted pedicels; often with long narrow bracts.

CULTURE: Compost, etc., as for Cattleyas. A rather decided rest should be given. The pots must be well drained, the leading growths may be allowed to extend beyond the pot rim for a season.

PROPAGATION: As for Cattleyas.

SPECIES CULTIVATED: *S. crispa*, many, brownish-yellow, lip whitish, or rosy, margins yellowish, variable, autumn, winter, British Guiana; *Lueddemanniana*, 12 to 20, rather thickly set, brown, lip rose-red, keels yellow, summer, Venezuela; *Lyonsii* (syn. *S. carinata*), many, white, purple spotted, lip rather small, tipped yellow, bracts long, summer, Jamaica; *marginata*, dull brick red, margined yellow, lip whitish, tinged pink, summer, autumn, Surinam; *splendida*, dark brownish-purple, lip rose-purple, autumn, winter, Colombia; *superbiens* (syn. *Laelia superbiens*), large, fragrant, rose or deep rose, mid-lobe of lip crimson, disk yellow, scape sometimes 9 ft. long, winter, Guatemala; *undulata* (syn. *S. violacea*), deep purplish-red, shaded brown, lip purplish, summer, Bogota.

Schubertia—*Asclepiadaceae*. Stove and greenhouse flowering evergreen climbers. First introduced early nineteenth century.

CULTURE: Compost, equal parts peat, loam, leaf-mould and sand. Position, pots or beds in greenhouse or conservatory. Shoots trained up roof or over trellis. Pot, Feb. or March. Water freely March to Sept., moderately afterwards. Syringe twice daily during spring and summer. Prune shoots during Jan. or Feb. Apply liquid manure occasionally during growing season. Temp., March to Oct. 65° to 75°, Oct. to March 55° to 65°.

PROPAGATION: By cuttings of firm side shoots in summer.

SPECIES CULTIVATED: *S. grandiflora* (syn. *Aranjia grandiflora*), white, fragrant, Oct., Brazil; *graveolens*, white, Sept., Brazil.

Sciadopitys (Umbrella Pine)—*Pinaceae* (or *Taxodiaceae*). Hardy evergreen conifer. False leaves, long, tapering, borne in tufts at the end of shoots, parasol-like; green, with yellow groove on their lower surface. First introduced mid-nineteenth century.

CULTURE: Soil, rich, moist, lime-free loam. Position, sheltered from piercing winds. Plant, Sept., Oct., March or April.

PROPAGATION: By imported seeds sown ⅛ in. deep in pots filled with moist, sandy loam and placed in cold frame or greenhouse, transplanting seedlings outdoors following spring; or ¼ in. deep outdoors in April in moist bed of sandy loam, transplanting seedlings next year.

SPECIES CULTIVATED: *S. verticillata*, ' Parasol Fir Tree ', slow growing, pyramidal shape, 80 to 120 ft., Japan.

Scilla (Squill)—*Liliaceae*. Greenhouse and hardy bulbous plants.

OUTDOOR CULTURE: Soil, deep, sandy loam. Position, sunny beds, borders, in grass on lawns, or rockeries. Plant, Aug. to Nov., in lines or masses. Depth for planting: Small bulbs 2 in. deep and 2 in. apart; large bulbs 4 in. deep and 3 to 4 in. apart. *S. peruviana* 4 to 6 in. deep in sheltered spot. Mulch with decayed manure, Nov. Lift, divide and replant every third year.

POT CULTURE: Compost, two parts sandy loam, one part leaf-mould or well-decayed cow manure, one part river sand. Pot, Aug. to Nov., placing small bulbs, 1 in. apart, in a 5 in. pot; or three to five large-sized bulbs, 1 in. deep, in similar pots. Position, under layer of cinder ashes from time of potting till growth commences, then in cold frame, cool greenhouse, or window till past flowering, afterwards in sunny spot outdoors. Water moderately from time growth commences till foliage fades, then keep dry. Repot annually. Apply weak stimulants once or twice during flowering period.

PROPAGATION: By seeds sown 1/16 in. deep in light, sandy soil in boxes or cold frame or outdoors in Sept.; offsets from old bulbs removed when lifting and planted as advised for full-sized bulbs. Seedlings flower when three to four years old.

SPECIES CULTIVATED: *S. amoena*, ' Star Hyacinth ', indigo blue, March to May, 6 to 9 in., Europe; *autumnalis*, rosy lilac, Aug. to Sept., 6 in., Europe (Br.); *bifolia*, blue, March, 6 in., Europe, and vars. *alba*, white, *rosea*, rose; *chinensis*, rose, Aug. to Sept., 6 in., China; *hispanica* (syns. *S. campanulata* and *S. patula*), ' Spanish Squill ', blue, May, 1 to 1½ ft., Europe, and vars. *alba*, and *rubra*; *nonscripta* (syns. *S. festalis* and *S. nutans*), ' Bluebell ', blue, April, 8 to 15 in., W. Europe (Br.); *peruviana*, lilac, May, 6 to 12 in., Algeria, and var. *alba*, white; *pratensis*, lavender, April to May, 6 in., E. Europe; *siberica*, ' Siberian Squill ', blue, Feb., 3 to 6 in., Asia Minor, and var. *alba*; *Tubergeniana*, light blue, spring, 6 in., Persia; *verna*, lilac blue, May, 3 in., W. Europe.

Scindapsus—*Araceae*. Stove evergreen climbers.

CULTURE: Compost, equal parts rough peat, sphagnum moss, and coarse sand with a little broken charcoal. Position, pots, with shoots trained to trunks of tree ferns or walls. Pot, Feb. or March. Water copiously March to Oct., moderately at other times. Syringe freely at all seasons. Temp., Sept. to March 60° to 65°, March to Sept. 80° to 85°. Shade from sun.

PROPAGATION: By division of roots at potting time.

SPECIES CULTIVATED: *S. aureus* (syn. *Pothos aureus*), leaves blotched with pale yellow, 20 ft., Solomon Islands; *pictus*, leaves glaucous, spotted dark green, 20 ft., E. Indies, and var. *argyraeus*, silver-spotted leaves.

Scirpus (Club Rush; Bulrush)—*Cyperaceae*. Greenhouse and hardy perennial marsh or water plants. *S. cernuus* really hardy but almost invariably cultivated as a greenhouse pot plant.

CULTURE OF HARDY SPECIES: Soil, ordinary. Position, margins of lakes, streams and ponds. Plant, Oct. to April.

PROPAGATION: By division, Oct. to April.

CULTURE OF GREENHOUSE SPECIES: Compost, equal parts loam, leaf-mould, and little sand. Position, small pots arranged along front of staging or in hanging baskets. Pot, Feb. or March. Water abundantly March to Oct., moderately other times. Temp., March to Oct. 55° to 65°, Oct. to March 45° to 55°.

PROPAGATION: By division of plants in March.

HARDY SPECIES CULTIVATED: *S. lacustris*, fat green rushes, 3 to 8 ft., chocolate inflorescence, Britain; *maritimus*, ' Sea Club Rush ', 3 to 5 ft., inflorescence golden brown, cosmopolitan; *Tabernaemontani*, glaucous stems, Europe, and var. *zebrinus* (syn. *Juncus zebrinus*), ' Porcupine Quill Rush ', ' Zebra Rush ', stems banded in green and white, 4 to 5 ft.; *triqueter*, triangular stems, 2 to 3 ft., Britain.

GREENHOUSE SPECIES CULTIVATED: *S. cernuus* (syn. *Isolepis gracilis*), ' Club Rush ', 6 to 12 in., stems slender and drooping, cosmopolitan.

Scleranthus—*Illecebraceae*. Hardy cushion-forming plants for the rock garden.

CULTURE: Gritty loam or scree soil. Position, full sun.

PROPAGATION: By division of old plants in spring or autumn.

SPECIES CULTIVATED: *S. biflorus*, flowers inconspicuous, green-gold hummocks, 1 in., Tasmania.

Scolopendrium, see Phyllitis.

Scolymus (Spanish Oyster Plant; Golden Thistle)—*Compositae*. Hardy biennial and perennial herbs. First introduced mid-seventeenth century.

CULTURE: Soil, ordinary. Position, sunny borders. Plant perennial species Oct. to April. Sow seeds of biennial species ⅛ in. deep where required to grow, in March or April. Thin seedlings to 8 or 12 in. apart when 2 in. high.

PROPAGATION: Perennial species by seeds sown as above; division of roots in April.

BIENNIAL SPECIES CULTIVATED: *S. hispanicus*, ' Spanish Oyster' or ' Golden Thistle ', yellow, Aug., 2 to 3 ft., roots edible, Europe.

PERENNIAL SPECIES CULTIVATED: *S. grandiflorus*, yellow, May, 3 ft., N. Africa.

Scorpion Senna, see *Coronilla Emerus*.

Scorzonera—*Compositae*. Hardy herbaceous perennial with edible roots. Roots, carrot-shaped, white with dark skin, sweet-flavoured. First introduced mid-sixteenth century.

CULTURE: Soil, ordinary, rich, deeply trenched, free from stones. Position, sunny, open. Sow seeds in groups of three or four, 12 in. apart, in drills ½ in. deep and 18 in. apart in April. Thin seedlings when 3 in. high to one in each group. Remove flower heads as soon as seen. Lift the roots in Oct., twist off their leaves, and store in layers with sand or soil between in cellar or outhouse until required for cooking. Artificial manures: 2¼ lb. kainit, 1 lb. sulphate of ammonia, 2½ lb. of guano, mixed, per square rod (30¼ square yards) applied before sowing in spring. Requires to be raised from seed annually for producing roots for culinary purposes. Seeds germinate in seven to twelve days and retain their vegetative powers for two to three years. Crop reaches maturity in eighteen weeks.

Species Cultivated: *S. hispanica*, ' Black Salsify ', yellow, June to Sept., 2 to 3 ft., S. Europe.

Scotch Heather, see *Calluna vulgaris*; **-Pine,** see *Pinus silvestris*; **-Thistle,** see *Onopordum Acanthium.*

Screw Pine, see Pandanus.

Scurvy Pea, see Psoralea.

Scutellaria (Helmet Flower; Skull Cap)—*Labiatae.* Stove and herbaceous perennials.

Culture of Stove Species: Compost, two parts loam, one part of equal proportions of leaf-mould, decayed manure and sand. Position, light part of stove Sept. to June; sunny cold frame remainder of year. Pot, Feb. or March. Prune shoots directly after flowering (Feb.) to within 3 in. of base. Good drainage essential. Nip off points of main shoots when 3 in. long, also of lateral shoots when of similar length, to induce bushy growth. Water freely Sept. to April, moderately afterwards. Syringe daily April to Sept. Apply stimulants once a week May to Dec. Temp., Sept. to March 55° to 65°, March to June 70° to 80°.

Culture of Hardy Species: Soil, ordinary. Position, open, sunny borders or rockeries. Plant, March or April. .Lift, divide and replant only when overgrown.

Propagation: Stove species by cuttings of firm shoots, 2 to 3 in. long, inserted in light, sandy soil under bell-glass in temp. 75° to 85° in spring; hardy species by seeds sown outdoors in April; division of roots in March or April.

Stove Species Cultivated: *S. coccinea*, scarlet, summer, 1 to 3 ft., Colombia; *javanensis*, violet-blue, summer, 1½ ft., China; *Mociniana*, scarlet and yellow summer, 2 to 3 ft., Mexico; *violacea*, violet-blue, summer, 2 ft., India and Ceylon.

Hardy Species Cultivated: *S. alpina*, purple, Aug., 6 to 8 in., S.E. Europe; *baicalensis*, blue, July to Sept., 6 to 12 in., E. Asia, and var. *coelestina*, bright blue; *indica japonica*, lavender, summer, 1 ft., Japan; *orientalis*, yellow, July to Aug. 6 to 12 in., Greece, Asia Minor.

Scuticaria—*Orchidaceae.* An epiphytic genus. Only two species are met with in cultivation. Two other named kinds are doubtful species, probably vars. Pseudo-bulbs short, small, each developed in a more or less terete leaf, scapes short from base of pseudo-bulbs. Flowers 1 to 3, comparatively large.

Culture: Compost, osmunda fibre or substitute and sphagnum moss in equal quantities. Water liberally in summer and maintain a moist atmosphere. Temp., 70° or more with shading. In winter less humidity, fewer waterings, night temp. 60°; *S. Hadwenii* can be accommodated in a pan suspended near the glass. *S. Steelii* should have a raft covered with compost, suspended if possible against a wall. The syringe may be freely used on both species in summer.

Propagation: The rhizome often branches and pieces with leaves and roots may be taken from it and potted as growth commences.

Species Cultivated: *S. Hadwenii* (syn. *Bifrenaria Hadwenii*), yellow, tinted green, blotched chocolate, lip with lighter spots and rosy spots on margin. Leaves erect, or nearly so, 9 to 18 in., variable, summer, Brazil; *Steelii*, larger, yellowish, spotted red-brown, lip with brown-crimson streaks, leaves 2 to 4 ft. long, summer, various, British Guiana.

Sea Buckthorn, see Hippophae; **-Holly,** see *Eryngium maritimum*; **-Lavender,** see Limonium; **-Onion,** see *Urginea maritima*; **-Pink,** see *Armeria maritima*; **-Poppy,** see Glaucium.

Seakale, see *Crambe maritima*; **-Beet,** see *Beta vulgaris* var. *Cicla.*

Sedge, see Carex.

Sedum (Stonecrop)—*Crassulaceae.* Succulent greenhouse and hardy evergreen and herbaceous perennials, biennials and annuals. *S. album* can become a troublesome weed.

Culture of Greenhouse Species: Compost, two parts sandy loam, one part brick rubbish, one part of equal proportions of dried cow dung and sand. Position, pots or pans in sunny greenhouse. Pot, Feb. to April. Water freely April to Oct., very little afterwards. Temp., Oct. to March 40° to 50°, March to Oct. 45° to 55°.

CULTURE OF HARDY PERENNIAL SPECIES: Soil, ordinary or sandy loam. Position, sunny, dry rockeries and borders. Plant, Nov. to April.

CULTURE OF ANNUAL SPECIES: Soil, ordinary. Position, sunny, dryish banks, rockeries or borders. Sow seeds thinly in April where required to grow and lightly cover with fine soil. Thin 3 to 6 in. apart when 2 in. high.

PROPAGATION: Greenhouse species by seeds sown in well-drained pots or pans filled with fine compost of equal parts brick rubble, sandy loam and sand and placed in temp. of 55°, Feb. to May; also by cuttings of shoots inserted in brick rubble, loam and sand in temp. 45° to 55° in summer; division of roots at potting time. Hardy species by seeds sown outdoors in April or division of the roots in March or April, or cuttings.

SPECIES CULTIVATED: *S. acre*, yellow, 2 in., May to June, Europe (Br.), and vars. *majus* and *aureum*; *Aizoon*, yellow, 12 in., summer, Asia; *alamosanum*, tender, pink, 2 in., summer, Mexico; *alboroseum*, white and rose, 18 in., late summer, Japan and China; *album*, white, 4 in., summer, Europe, Africa and Asia, and vars. *micranthum*, a miniature desirable form, *chloraticum*, greenish-white, 1 to 2 in., *murale*, deep purple leaves; *amecamecanum*, buff and orange, 6 in., summer, tender, Mexico; *Anacampseros*, greenish-purple, handsome stems and leaves, trailing, Alps; *anglicum*, white, tinged pink, 2 in., summer, Europe (Br.); *anopetalum*, rich cream, 6 in., summer, Europe; *bellum*, white and purple, 3 in., summer, Mexico, tender; *brevifolium*, blue-grey leaves, white flowers, ½ in., summer, Europe and N. Africa, and var. *quinquefarium*, twice as large; *cauticolum*, rose-crimson, 4 to 6 in., autumn, Japan; *Cepaea*, annual, white, 4 in., summer, Europe; *Chanetii*, white, 6 in., autumn, China; *caeruleum*, annual, blue, 2 to 3 in., late summer, S. Europe; *crassipes* (syn. *S. asiaticum*), white and purple, 9 in., summer, Himalaya; *cupressoides*, golden, 3 in., late summer, tender, Mexico; *dasyphyllum*, blush pink, 2 in., summer, S. Europe, and vars. *glanduliferum*, very hairy form, *macrophyllum*, twice as large as the type; *divergens*, golden, 2 to 3 in., summer, N. America; *Douglasii*, yellow, 12 in., July, N. America; *Ellacombianum*, yellow, 6 in., late summer, Japan; *Ewersii*, pink, 9 in., late summer, Himalaya, and var. *homophyllum*, condensed form; *floriferum*, yellow, 4 to 6 in., July to Aug., China; *gracile*, white, 2 in., summer, Caucasus; *gypsicolum*, white, 3 in., summer, Spain; *hirsutum*, white or pink, 3 in., summer, Europe; *hispanicum*, white, 2 in., summer, Europe and Persia; *Hobsonii* (syn. *S. Praegerianum*), deciduous, pink, summer, 1 in., Tibet; *humifusum*, yellow, 2 in., spring, tender, Mexico; *hybridum*, yellow, 4 in., spring and autumn, Siberia and Mongolia; *kamtschaticum*, orange-yellow, 6 in., late summer, Asia, and var. *variegatum*, variegated foliage; *lydium*, white, 2 in., June, Asia Minor; *magellense*, white, 4 in., spring, Italy; *maximum*, white, 2 ft., summer, annual, Europe, and var. *atropurpureum*, mahogany leaves and reddish flowers; *Middendorffianum*, yellow, late summer, 4 to 6 in., Siberia; *moranense*, white, 4 in., July, Mexico, and var. *arboreum*, like a miniature tree, 6 in.; *multiceps*, yellow, 4 in., summer, Algeria; *Nevii*, white, 3 in., summer, Eastern U.S.A.; *oaxacanum*, yellow, 2 in., summer, tender, Mexico; *oreganum*, golden, 3 in., late summer, N. America; *Palmeri*, yellow, 9 in., May to July, slightly tender, Mexico; *pilosum*, rose-red, 3 in., May to June, biennial, Asia Minor; *populifolium*, white, 9 in., late summer, Siberia; *primuloides*, white, 2 to 3 in., summer, China; *pulchellum*, pink, prostrate, summer, U.S.A.; *reflexum*, yellow, 6 to 9 in., summer, Europe, and var. *cristatum*, fasciated growths; *retusum*, white and pink, 6 in., summer, Mexico; *Rosea* (syns. *Rhodiola rosea*, *S. roseum*, *S. Rhodiola*), 'Roseroot', greenish-yellow, 12 to 15 in., summer, Europe, Asia, America; *rupestre*, yellow, 6 in., July, Europe (Br.); *sediforme* (syn. *S. altissimum*), pale yellow, summer, 12 to 18 in., Europe, etc.; *sempervivoides*, crimson, 4 to 6 in., June, biennial, Caucasus, Asia Minor; *sexangulare*, yellow, 2 in., summer, Europe; *Sieboldii*, rose-red, 9 in., June, Japan, and var. *variegatum*, variegated leaves;

spathulifolium, yellow, 3 to 4 in., May to June, N. America, and var. *purpureum*, leaves stained deep purple; *spectabile*, pink, 12 to 15 in., autumn, Japan, and var. *atropurpureum*, rich red flowers; *spurium*, pink, 2 in., summer, Caucasus, and var. *album*, white; *Stahlii*, yellow, 4 in., autumn, tender, Mexico; *stoloniferum*, rose, 6 in., June, Asia Minor; *Tatarinowii*, pink, 2 to 3 in., July to Aug., China; *Telephium*, pink, 12 in., summer, Europe (Br.); *tenuifolium* (syn. *S. amplexicaule*), yellow, summer, 4 to 6 in., S. Europe; *ternatum*, white, 4 in., spring, N. America; *trifidum*, purple-red, 9 in., late summer, China, and var. *album*, white; *Winkleri*, white, 3 in., summer, Spain.

Selaginella—*Selaginellaceae*. Stove and greenhouse evergreen moss-like plants, allied to ferns. Fronds creeping or erect, branched, green or variegated. First introduced mid-nineteenth century.

CULTURE: Compost, equal parts fibrous peat and chopped sphagnum moss. Position, pots, pans or rockeries in shade. Pot or plant, Feb. or March. Water copiously April to Sept., moderately afterwards. Syringe daily April to Sept. Shade from sun. Temp., stove species, Sept. to March 55° to 65°, March to Sept. 70° to 80°; greenhouse, Sept. to March 40° to 50°, March to Sept., 55° to 65°.

PROPAGATION: By cuttings of foliage stems inserted in above compost in well-drained pots and plunged in fibre refuse in a temp. of 80° at any season, or the smaller growers may be spread upon the surface of pans of compost and covered with glass until rooted.

STOVE SPECIES CULTIVATED: *S. cuspidata*, W. Indies; *Emmeliana*, erect branching, to 1 ft., Trop. America, and var. *variegata*; *erythropus*, 10 to 12 in., W. Indies; *flabellata*, 4 to 8 in., Tropics and Subtropics; *haematodes*, 1 to 2 ft., W. Indies; *lepidophylla*, 'Resurrection Plant', frequently sold as a curiosity, Texas; *Vogelii*, 1 to 2 ft., Africa; *Wallichii*, tall, erect, dense, Penang; *Wildenovii*, climbing, Trop. Asia.

GREENHOUSE SPECIES CULTIVATED: *S. apoda*, annual, Mexico to Texas; *Braunii*, 12 to 18 in., China; *caulescens* (syn. *S. amoena*), 1 to 2 ft., Malay, etc.; *Douglasii*, creeping, pale green, British Columbia to California; *Kraussiana*, creeping or trailing, S. Africa; *Martensii*, 6 to 12 in., Mexico; *rupestris*, dwarf, tufted, with white tips, E. America; *uncinata* (syn. *S. caesia*), trailing, China.

Selenicereus—*Cactaceae*. Greenhouse succulent plants with angled stems bearing bristles. Formerly included in Cereus. First introduced early eighteenth century.

CULTURE: Compost, two parts turfy loam, one part coarse sand and broken brick. Position, well-drained pots or pans in sunny greenhouse or window. Pot as required, Water sparingly. Temp., Sept. to March 50° to 55°, March to Sept. 55° to 60°.

PROPAGATION: By seeds sown in well-drained pots or pans; cuttings of stems in sand.

SPECIES CULTIVATED: *S. grandiflorus*, white, July, Jamaica, Cuba; *Macdonaldiae*, white and red, July, Honduras, Uruguay, Argentine; *pteranthus* (syn. *S. nycticallus*), white, autumn, Mexico. The species mentioned are all night flowering.

Selenipedium, see Phragmipedium. Most of the plants cultivated in greenhouses under this name are referred to Phragmipedium, probably no true Selenipediums are generally known to horticulture.

Selfheal, see Prunella.

Semiarundinaria—*Gramineae*. Erect bamboo-like shrubs, formerly included in Arundinaria.

CULTURE: Soil, good, not too heavy and of reasonable depth. Position, must be sheltered from cold winds and dry root conditions are disliked.

PROPAGATION: By division in April and May.

SPECIES CULTIVATED: *S. fastuosa* (syns. *Bambusa*, *Arundinaria* and *Phyllostachys fastuosa*), 20 ft., Japan.

Sempervivella—*Crassulaceae.* Hardy succulent-leaved perennials.
CULTURE: As for Sempervivum but rather less hot and dry.
PROPAGATION: By seeds; division; cuttings.
SPECIES CULTIVATED: *S. alba*, white, 2 in., spring and summer, Kashmir.

Sempervivum (Houseleek)—*Crassulaceae.* Hardy succulent-leaved perennials.
Tender species native to Canary Islands and Madeira have been transferred to
Aeonium, Aichryson and Greenovia.
CULTURE: Soil, ordinary, light sandy, containing a little old mortar. Position,
open and sunny, chinks, crevices or ledges of rockeries or as edgings to borders.
Plant, March to June, close together for edgings in single or double rows. Top-
dress annually in March. *S. tectorum*, suitable for growing on sunny roofs or
crevices of old walls, plant in mixture of cow dung and clay in March or April.
PROPAGATION: By seeds in spring in compost of equal parts sandy loam, leaf-
mould and old mortar in well-drained, shallow pans, lightly covered with fine
soil in temp. 55° to 65°; cuttings of shoots or leaves dried for a day or so after
removal from plant and inserted in above compost in summer; division of offsets
in March.
There are too many species with, in many instances, differences too slight for
brief descriptions to justify a detailed list here. The figures given in following list
refer to approx. diameter of rosettes.
SPECIES CULTIVATED: *S. Allionii*, 1 in., greenish-white, Alps; *arachnoideum*,
' Cobweb Houseleek ', red, ¾ in., Mts. S. Europe; *arenarium*, pale yellow, rosettes
globular, Tyrol; *atlanticum*, pale red in panicles, 3 in., Morocco; *ciliosum*,
greenish-yellow, 2 in., Bulgaria; *dolomiticum*, rose-red, 2½ in., tufted, Alps;
erythraeum, red-purple with white lines, 2 in. tufted, Bulgaria; *globiferum*, pale
yellow, 3 in., Russia; *grandiflorum*, yellow, 1¼ in., Alps; *Heuffelii*, pale straw,
2 in., Greece; *hirtum*, pale yellow, 1¼ in., S. Europe; *leucanthum*, pale or greenish
yellow, 3 in., leaves hairy and purple tipped, Bulgaria; *Kindingeri*, waxy-white,
reddish at base, 2½ in., Macedonia; *montanum*, purplish in hairy panicle, 1¾ in.,
Alps, Pyrenees; ·*Pittonii*, yellowish-white in hairy head, 1½ in., Syria; *pumilum*,
purple, 1 in., Caucasus; *ruthenicum*, pale yellow, filaments purple, 1½ in., E.
Europe; *soboliferum*, pale yellow in dense panicles, 1½ in., Austria; *tectorum*,
' Common Houseleek', pinkfsh on hairy branches, 3 to 4 in., Europe, Asia, and
numerous vars.; *Wulfenii*, pale yellow in dense hairy panicle 2 to 3 in. across,
2 in., Cent. Europe.

Senecio (Groundsel; Ragwort)—*Compositae.* Greenhouse and hardy annuals,
evergreen herbs or climbers, herbaceous perennials and evergreen shrubs. *S.
Smithii* is grown in the water garden. Florists' Cinerarias are hybrids or vars.
of *S. cruentus*. First introduced early eighteenth century. See also Ligularia.
CULTURE OF ANNUAL SPECIES: Soil, ordinary rich. Position, sunny beds or
borders. Sow seeds in April ⅛ in. deep in patches or lines where required to grow.
Thin seedlings 3 to 6 in. apart when 1 in. high.
POT CULTURE: Compost, two parts sandy loam, one part leaf-mould or well-
decayed manure and one part sand. Place in 6 in. pots, well drained, press
firmly, and sow seeds thinly in April, covering with fine mould. Stand pots in
cold greenhouse, window or frame. Thin seedlings when 1 in. high to 2 in.
apart. Water moderately and apply stimulants when flowers show.
CULTURE OF CLIMBING SPECIES: Compost, two parts sandy loam, one part well-
decayed manure or leaf-mould and one part sand. Position, well-drained pots in
sunny greenhouse or window; dwarf kinds on staging or inside window sills; tall
kinds trained up roof of greenhouse or round window frames. Pot, March or
April. Water freely April to Oct., very little afterwards. Apply stimulants
occasionally in summer. Temp., March to Oct. 55° to 65°, Oct. to March 40°
to 50°.
CULTURE OF HYBRID CINERARIAS (*S. cruentus*): Compost, two parts yellow loam,
one part leaf-mould and coarse silver sand. Sow seeds during May and June
1⁄16 in. deep in well-drained pans or pots of above finely-sifted compost. Cover

top of pot with square of glass, keep soil moist and shade from sun. Transplant seedlings when three leaves are formed singly in small pots; keep in cold frame and shaded. Shift into 4½ in. pots in July, 6 in. size in Aug. Remove to greenhouse in Oct., near glass. Apply weak liquid manure twice weekly from Sept. onwards. Liquid cow manure best for cinerarias. Fumigate frequently to destroy aphis. Temp., Oct. to time plants have ceased flowering, 45° to 50°. Sow in May for winter flowering, June for spring flowering. Double-flowered or choice single kinds may be increased by cuttings.

CULTURE OF S. CINERARIA: Compost, same as above. Pot, March. *S. Smithii* in water garden. Plant outdoors in June. Lift in Sept. Water moderately if grown in pots. Sometimes used for carpet bedding.

CULTURE OF HARDY SPECIES: Soil, deep, rich loam. Position, partially shady, moist border. *S. uniflorus* on sunny banks in the rock garden. Plant, March or April. Mulch with decayed manure annually in March. Water freely in dry weather.

CULTURE OF SHRUBBY SPECIES: Soil, ordinary. Position, warm, sunny borders sheltered from cold winds. Plant, Sept. to Oct. or April to May.

PROPAGATION: Greenhouse species by seeds sown in March or April, $\frac{1}{16}$ in. deep, in a compost of equal parts loam, leaf-mould and sand in well-drained pots or pans in temp. 65° to 75°; by cuttings inserted in similar soil and temp. in spring or early summer. Hardy species by seeds sown ⅛ in. deep outdoors in April; division of the roots in March or April. Shrubby species by cuttings of nearly ripe wood in sandy soil under bell-glass in July or Aug.

ANNUAL SPECIES CULTIVATED: *S. elegans* (syn. *Jacobaea elegans*), various colours, single and double, summer, 1 to 2 ft., S. Africa.

GREENHOUSE SPECIES CULTIVATED: *S. Cineraria* (syn. *Cineraria maritima*), ' Dusty Miller ', yellow, summer, leaves silvery, 1 to 2 ft., Medit. Region; *cruentus* (syn. *Cineraria cruenta*), parent of the well-known cinerarias, purple, summer, 1 to 2 ft., perennial but grown as an annual, Canaries; *grandiflora*, yellow, spring, to 5 ft., Mexico; *Heritieri*, white and purple, spring, scandent, Teneriffe; *leucostachys*, yellow, silver foliage, summer, 2 to 3 ft., Patagonia; *mikanioides*, ' German Ivy ', yellow, winter, climber, S. Africa; *multibracteatus*, purple, summer, 4 to 5 ft., S. Africa; *Petasites*, ' Velvet Groundsel ', yellow, spring, to 5 ft., Mexico.

HARDY SPECIES CULTIVATED: *S. adonidifolius*, orange, July to Aug., 8 to 12 in., Europe; *aurantiacus*, orange-yellow, summer, 1 to 1½ ft., Europe; *Doronicum*, yellow, summer, 1 ft., Europe; *incanus*, silver-grey cushions of foliage, Europe; *macrophyllus* (syn. *Jacobaea macrophylla*), golden yellow, summer, 4 to 5 ft., Caucasus; *pulcher*, red-purple, late summer, 2 to 4 ft., Uruguay and Argentine; *Smithii*, white, June, 3 ft., Cape Horn; *tanguticus*, golden yellow, July to Sept., 6 to 7 ft., W. China; *uniflorus*, yellow, July, 3 in., S. Europe.

SHRUBBY SPECIES CULTIVATED: *S. Greyi*, yellow, summer, 3 ft., New Zealand; *laxifolius*, yellow, June to Aug., 2 to 4 ft., New Zealand; *Monroi*, yellow, June to Aug., 2 ft., New Zealand.

Senna, see Cassia.

Sensitive Fern, see *Onoclea sensibilis*; **-Plant,** see *Mimosa pudica*.

Sequoia (Californian Redwood)—*Pinaceae* (or *Taxodiaceae*). Hardy evergreen coniferous trees. First introduced mid-nineteenth century.

CULTURE: Soil, deep loam. Position, sunny sheltered. Plant, Sept. to Oct. or April to May.

PROPAGATION: By seeds in sandy soil in cold frame in spring, transplanting seedlings when large enough to handle, 6 in. apart in rows 6 in. asunder; variegated kinds by grafting on common species.

SPECIES CULTIVATED: *S. sempervirens*, 200 to 300 ft., California.

Sequoiadendron (Wellingtonia)—*Pinaceae* (or *Taxodiaceae*). Tall evergreen coniferous tree with deeply furrowed spongy bark. First introduced mid-nineteenth century.

Culture: Soil, deep loam. Position, sunny sheltered.

Propagation: By seed; cuttings; grafting.

Species Cultivated: *S. giganteum* (syn. *Wellingtonia gigantea, Sequoia Wellingtonia*), 'Giant Sequoia', to 100 ft. or more, trunk many feet in diameter and bark to 20 in. thick, narrowly pyramidal when young, California.

Serjania—*Sapindaceae.* Tropical woody twining vines. Sometimes spelled Seriania.

Culture: Tropical conditions.

Propagation: By seed.

Species Cultivated: *S. reticulata*, white, reddish branches, S. America.

Serpent Gourd, see *Trichosanthes Anguina.*

Service Berry, see *Amelanchier canadensis*; **-Tree,** see *Sorbus Aria.*

Shadbush, see *Amelanchier canadensis.*

Shaddock, see *Citrus maxima.*

Shallon, see *Gaultheria Shallon.*

Shallot, see *Allium Cepa* var. *ascalonicum.*

Shamrock Pea, see *Parochetus communis.*

Shasta Daisy, see *Chrysanthemum maximum.*

Sheep Laurel, see *Kalmia angustifolia.*

Sheep's-bit Scabious, see Jasione.

Shepherdia—*Elaeagnaceae.* Hardy deciduous ornamental shrubs, producing male and female flowers on different plants. First introduced mid-eighteenth century.

Culture: Soil, ordinary. Position, open or shady shrubberies in inland or seaside gardens. Plant, Oct. to Feb.

Propagation: By seeds sown ½ in. deep outdoors in Nov. or Dec.; by cuttings of roots inserted in Feb. or March in ordinary soil outdoors; layering shoots in autumn.

Species Cultivated: *S. argentea*, 'Rabbit Berry', 'Buffalo Berry', greenish, spring, scarlet fruits, 8 to 10 ft., N. America; *canadensis*, greenish, spring, yellowish-red fruits, 3 to 6 ft., N. America.

Shibataea—*Gramineae.* Bamboo-like shrubs with flattened zigzag nearly solid stems. Sometimes included in Phyllostachys and Bambusa.

Culture: Soil, rich, deep, sandy loam. Position, moist sheltered borders in south and west only. Protect in winter with dry fern fronds. Plant, March or April.

Propagation: By division of plants in March or April.

Species Cultivated: *S. kumasaca* (syns. *Phyllostachys kumasaca, ruscifolia* and *viminalis, Bambusa kumasaca* and *viminalis*), leaves dark green, 1 to 2 ft., Japan.

Shield Fern, see Dryopteris; **-wort,** see Peltaria.

Shooting Stars, see *Dodecatheon Meadia.*

Shortia—*Diapensiaceae.* Hardy evergreen stemless herbs. Some species were formerly known as Schizocodon. First introduced late nineteenth century.

Culture: Soil, equal parts sandy peat and leaf-mould. Position, partially shady border, rhododendron bed or cold frame. Plant, April. Water freely in dry weather.

Propagation: By division of roots in April.

Species Cultivated: *S. galacifolia*, white, spring, 3 to 6 in., N. Carolina, and var. *rosea*; *soldanelloides*, deep rose, spring, 4 in., Japan, and vars. *alpina, alba*, and *ilicifolia*; *uniflora*, 'Nippon Bells', pink, spring, 6 in., Japan.

Shrimp Plant, see *Beloperone guttata.*

Shrubby Althaea, see *Hibiscus syriacus*; **-Starwort,** see Microglossa.

Siberian Squill, see *Scilla siberica*; **-Wallflower,** see *Erysimum Allionii.*

Sibthorpia—*Scrophulariaceae.* Greenhouse and hardy creeping perennial **herb.**
Culture: Compost, equal parts loam, leaf-mould, and little sand. Position, moist, partially shady borders or rockeries outdoors, or in pots or pans in cold frame, or cool, shady indoor fernery or greenhouse under bell-glass. Pot or plant, March or April. Water copiously in dry weather outdoors; also indoors April to Sept.; moderately other times. Moist atmosphere essential for indoor culture.
Propagation: By cuttings inserted in pots of light soil placed under bell-glass in cold greenhouse or frame in summer; division of plants in April.
Species Cultivated: *S. europaea,* ' Cornish Moneywort ', trailing, small pinkish flowers, W. Europe, and var. *variegata,* golden-green foliage.

Sidalcea—*Malvaceae.* Hardy perennial herbs. First introduced early nineteenth century.
Culture: Soil, ordinary. Position, sunny borders. Plant, Oct. or March. Lift, divide and replant every three or four years.
Propagation: By seeds sown ½ in. deep in light soil in April, transplanting seedlings when 1 in. high; division of roots, Oct. or March.
Species Cultivated: *S. candida,* white, summer, 3 ft., Rocky Mts.; *malvaeflora,* lilac, summer, 3 ft., California, and vars. *atropurpurea,* purple, *Listeri,* pink; *spicata,* rosy purple, July to Sept., 3 ft., California. There are numerous vars. and hybrids.

Sideritis—*Labiatae.* Perennial dwarf sub-shrubby plants.
Culture: Any reasonably good loamy soil and a warm, sunny aspect.
Propagation: By seeds sown in spring; cuttings made from half-ripened growths in summer.
Species Cultivated: *S. syriaca,* yellow, 9 to 12 in., summer, Crete.

Sigmatostalix—*Orchidaceae.* Small growing, small flowered epiphytic orchids. Pseudo-bulbs usually two-leaved, scapes from their base, free-flowering.
Culture: Compost, as for Odontoglossums. Small pans suit many, but *S. radicans* and others with extending rhizomes should be placed on a raft or piece of tree fern stem. All may be suspended near the glass, with shading. Temp. around 60° and a moist atmosphere should be given throughout the year. A decided winter rest should not be given.
Propagation: By division of plants in spring.
Species Cultivated: A selection—*S. Eliae,* small, many, yellow, spotted brown, summer to autumn, Peru; *guatemalensis* (syn. *S. costaricaensis*), greenish red-brown, yellowish, lip bright yellow and rich red-brown, autumn, Guatemala, Costa Rica; *radicans,* 10 to 15, greenish-white, shaded yellow, lip white with yellow disk, various, Brazil.

Silene (Catchfly)—*Caryophyllaceae.* Hardy annuals, biennials and herbaceous perennials.
Culture of Annual and Biennial Species: Soil, ordinary light or sandy. Position, sunny beds or borders. Sow seeds in Aug. or Sept., ⅛ in. deep, in a bed of light, rich soil, transplanting seedlings when 1 in. high 2 to 3 in. apart; and plant 6 in. apart in flowering position in March for spring blooming. Sow also in similar depth and position in April, transplanting when 1 in. high to flowering positions for summer blooming. Or sow where required to grow and flower in April, thinning out seedlings in May or June to 6 in. apart.
Culture of Perennial Species: Soil, sandy loam enriched with decayed cow dung. One-third loam, one-third peat, one-third stones for *S. Elizabethae, acaulis* and *rupestris*; ordinary soil for other kinds. Position, sunny crevices or ledges of rockeries for *S. acaulis, alpestris, rupestris, virginica, pensylvanica* and *Elisabethae*; open borders for *S. maritima flore-pleno.* Plant, March or April. Lift and replant only when absolutely necessary.

PROPAGATION: Perennials by seeds sown in pans or boxes of sandy loam and leaf-mould, lightly covered with fine mould, and placed in cold frame in March or April; cuttings of young shoots inserted in sandy loam in cold frame in summer; division in March or April.

ANNUAL SPECIES CULTIVATED: *S. Armeria*, pink, summer, 1 to 2 ft., S. Europe; *Asterias*, pink, summer, 12 to 18 in., Macedonia and Romania; *pendula*, pink, spring, 6 in., Medit. Region, and many vars.

BIENNIAL SPECIES CULTIVATED: *S. compacta*, pink, summer, 18 in., Asia Minor; *rupestris*, white, May, 4 to 6 in., Alps.

PERENNIAL SPECIES CULTIVATED: *S. acaulis*, ' Cushion Pink ', ' Moss Campion ', pink, June, 2 in., N. Temp. Zone, and var. *alba*, white; *alpestris* (syn. *Heliosperma alpestre*), ' Alpine Catchfly ', white, May, 6 in., Alps; *californica*, deep scarlet, late summer, 9 to 12 in., California; *caroliniana* (syn. *S. pensylvanica*), ' Wild Pink', pink, spring, 6 to 8 in., U.S.A.; *Elisabethae*, crimson-magenta, summer, 6 to 9 in., Tyrol; *Fortunei*, pink, June to Sept., 1½ ft., China; *Hookeri*, pink and white, summer, 2 in., California; *laciniata*, scarlet, summer, 8 to 10 in., N.W. America; *maritima* var. *flore-pleno*, ' Witch's Thimble ', white, double, summer, trailing, Europe; *Pumilio*, rose pink, summer, 2 to 3 in., Tyrol; *pusilla*, white, summer, 2 to 3 in., habitat unknown; *quadridentata* (syns. *S. monachorum, Heliosperma quadrifidum*), white, summer, 2 to 6 in., Europe; *Saxifraga*, white and brown, summer, 6 in., S. Alps; *Schafta*, purple, summer, 4 to 6 in., Caucasus; *vallesia*, white and brownish-red, summer, 3 to 4 in., Europe; *virginica*, ' Fire Pink ', crimson, June, 12 to 18 in., N. America.

Silk Cotton Tree, see *Ceiba pentandra*; **-Oak,** see *Grevillea robusta*; **-Vine,** see Periploca; **-weed,** see Asclepias.

Silphium—*Compositae.* Hardy perennials.

CULTURE: Soil, ordinary. Position, sunny borders. Plant, Oct. to April. Lift, divide and replant every two or three years.

PROPAGATION: By division of roots, Oct. or March.

SPECIES CULTIVATED: *S. laciniatum*, ' Compass Plant ', yellow, Aug. to Sept., 6 to 8 ft., N. America; *perfoliatum*, ' Cup Plant ', yellow, Aug. to Sept., 6 to 8 ft., N. America.

Silver Bell Tree, see Halesia; **-berry,** see *Elaeagnus commutata*; **-Bush,** see *Anthyllis Barba-Jovis*; **-Ferns,** see Pityrogramma; **-Wattle,** see *Acacia decurrens* var. *dealbata.*

Silybum—*Compositae.* Hardy annual or biennial herb. Leaves, large, variegated with broad white veins.

CULTURE: Soil, ordinary. Position, open borders. Sow seeds ⅛ in. deep in March where plants are to grow, thinning or transplanting seedlings to 2 ft. apart when large enough to handle.

SPECIES CULTIVATED: *S. Marianum*, ' Holy ', ' Our Lady's ' or ' Milk Thistle ', rose-purple, summer, 1 to 4 ft., Medit. Region.

Sinarundinaria—*Gramineae.* Erect, clump-forming, bamboo-like shrubs. Sometimes included in Arundinaria.

CULTURE: Soil, good, not too heavy and of reasonable depth. Position, must be sheltered from cold winds, and dry root conditions are disliked.

PROPAGATION: By division in April and May.

SPECIES CULTIVATED: *S. Murielae*, yellow stems with waxy bloom when young, to 8 ft., China; *nitida*, purple stems, hardy, quick growing, 8 ft., China.

Sinningia—*Gesneriaceae.* Stove tuberous-rooted deciduous flowering plant. First introduced early nineteenth century.

CULTURE: Compost, equal parts fibrous peat, fibrous loam, leaf-mould, well-decayed manure, and a little silver sand. Position, well-drained pots close to glass in plant stove while growing; greenhouse or conservatory when in flower. Pot, Jan., Feb. or March. Place tubers singly, and just below surface, in 3 or

4 in. pots, shifting into 5 or 6 in. pots when they have started growth. Water moderately till growth is well advanced, then freely. Apply weak liquid manure when flowers show. After flowering gradually withhold water till foliage dies down, then keep quite dry till potting time. Temp., Jan. to Oct. 65° to 75°, Oct. to Jan. 50° to 55°.

PROPAGATION: By seeds sown on surface of fine sandy peat and leaf-mould in well-drained pots or pans in temp. 65° to 75° in March; cuttings of shoots, 1 to 2 in. long, inserted in small pots of sandy peat under bell-glass in temp. of 65° to 75°; young leaves with stalk inserted in small pots of sandy soil treated as cuttings; matured leaves with mid-ribs cut and laid on surface of sandy peat in temp. 55° to 75°.

SPECIES CULTIVATED: *S. Concinna*, purple and white, Feb., 3 ft., Burma; *Helleri*, white, spotted red, June to July, 6 to 12 in., Brazil; *speciosa* (syn. *Gloxinia speciosa*), ' Gloxinia ', violet, autumn, 6 to 12 in., Brazil. Parent of the lovely strains of Gloxinias grown in gardens.

Siphonosmanthus—*Oleaceae.* Evergreen shrubs, formerly included in the genus Osmanthus but having botanical differences.

CULTURE: As Osmanthus.

PROPAGATION: As Osmanthus.

SPECIES CULTIVATED: *S. Delavayi* (syn. *Osmanthus Delavayi*), white, fragrant, April, 5 to 10 ft., China; *suavis*, white, midwinter, 12 ft., N. India.

Sisal Hemp, see *Agave sisalana.*

Sisyrinchium (Satin-flower)—*Iridaceae.* Hardy and half-hardy perennials. First introduced late seventeenth century.

CULTURE: Soil, two parts sandy loam, one part peat. Position, sunny, sheltered rock gardens. *S. californicum* does best in moist soil. Plant, Oct. or May.

PROPAGATION: By offsets, removed and potted in March; seeds.

SPECIES CULTIVATED: *S. angustifolium* (syn. *S. anceps*), blue, summer, 6 to 8 in., N. America; *Bermudiana*, blue, summer, 12 to 15 in., Bermuda; *californicum*, yellow, June, 12 in., California, rather tender; *chilense*, white and mauve, June, 9 in., America; *Douglasii*, ' Spring Bell ', ' Rush Lily ', purple, spring, 1 ft., N.W. America, and var. *album*, white; *filifolium*, ' Pale Maidens ', white, May, 6 in., Falkland Islands; *striatum*, yellow, veined purple, June, 1 to 2 ft., Argentine.

Sitcha Waterleaf, see *Romanzoffia sitchensis.*

Sium (Skirret)—*Umbelliferae.* Hardy esculent-rooted perennial. Cylindrical, clustered, white, sweet-flavoured roots. First introduced mid-sixteenth century.

CULTURE: Soil, ordinary fine, rich, deeply trenched, free from stones. Position, sunny, open. Sow seeds in groups of three or four, 12 in. apart, in drills ½ in. deep and 18 in. apart in April. Thin seedlings when 3 in. high to one in each group. Remove flower heads as soon as seen. Lift the roots in Oct., twist off their leaves, and store in layers with sand or soil between in cellar or outhouse until required for cooking. Artificial manures: 2¼ lb. kainit, 1 lb. sulphate of ammonia, 2¼ lb. of guano, mixed, per square rod (30¼ square yards), applied before sowing in spring. Requires to be raised from seed annually for producing roots for culinary purposes.

SPECIES CULTIVATED: *S. Sisarum*, white, Aug., 1 ft., E. Asia.

Skimmia—*Rutaceae.* Hardy evergreen berry-bearing shrubs with ornamental foliage. Flowers, inconspicuous but fragrant. Some species, notably *S. japonica* and *S. Laureola*, produce male and female flowers on separate plants. First introduced mid-nineteenth century.

CULTURE: Soil, ordinary, but not shallow and dry. Position, part shade or full sun, good for exposed positions. Plant, Sept., Oct., March or April.

PROPAGATION: By seeds sown when ripe in sandy loam and peat in cold frame; cuttings of firm shoots inserted under bell-glass in temp. 55° to 65° in spring or summer; layering shoots in autumn.

SPECIES CULTIVATED: *S. Foremanii*, white, spring, 3 ft., hybrid with herma-phrodite flowers; *japonica* (syn. *S. oblata*), white, April, 3 to 4 ft., spreading, Japan, and var. *fragrans*, large panicles, fragrant male flowers; *Laureola*, yellow, spring, 2 to 3 ft., Himalaya; *Reevesiana* (syn. *S. Fortunei*), white, April, 2 ft.. crimson pear-shaped fruits, China, and var. *rubella*, flowers pink, fragrant, male.

Skirret, see *Sium Sisarum.*

Skull Cap, see Scutellaria.

Slipper Flower, see Calceolaria and *Pedilanthus tithymaloides.*

Slippery Elm, see *Ulmus fulva.*

Sloe, see *Prunus spinosa.*

Smilacina—*Liliaceae.* Hardy perennials. First introduced early seventeenth century.

CULTURE: Soil, ordinary light, deep rich. Position, partially shady, moist shrubberies, woodlands, banks or borders. Plant, Oct., March.

PROPAGATION: By division of roots, Oct., March.

SPECIES CULTIVATED: *S. racemosa*, 'False Spikenard', white, May, 3 ft., N. America; *stellata*, 'Star-flowered Lily of the Valley', white, May, 2 ft., N. America. See also Maianthemum and Clintonia.

Smilax (Sarsaparilla Plant; Greenbriar)—*Liliaceae.* Hardy, half-hardy and stove evergreen and deciduous climbers. Shrubby and herbaceous. The Smilax of florists is *Asparagus asparagoides.* The sarsaparilla of commerce is yielded by the tuberous roots of several Trop. American species. First introduced mid-seventeenth century.

CULTURE OF STOVE SPECIES: Compost, light loam, leaf-mould and sand. Position, well-drained pots or borders in warm greenhouse, with shoots trained up wall or rafters. Water freely during growing season, moderately other times. Temp., March to Sept. 70° to 80°, Sept. to March 60° to 65°. Pot, Feb. or March.

CULTURE OF SHRUBBY SPECIES: Soil, ordinary. Position, sunny walls, arbours, trellises or banks. Plant, Sept. or Oct., March or April.

CULTURE OF HERBACEOUS SPECIES: Soil, ordinary. Position, sunny borders, with shoots trained to fences or rustic poles. Cut back dead shoots in autumn. Plant, March or April.

PROPAGATION: By division of roots at planting or potting time.

STOVE SPECIES CULTIVATED: *S. argyraea*, bright green leaves with white spots, climber, Peru; *australis*, white, 5 ft., Australia; *officinalis*, shining green leathery leaves, climber, Colombia.

SHRUBBY SPECIES CULTIVATED: *S. aspera*, 'Prickly Ivy', pale green, fragrant, July, 10 to 15 ft., evergreen, Medit. Region, and var. *maculata*, leaves blotched white; *Bona-Nox*, 'Stretchberry', greenish-white, 5 to 10 ft., Southern U.S.A.; *Cantab*, 'Cambridge Smilax', greenish, 12 ft., climber, probably a native of N. America; *China*, 'China Root', greenish-yellow, red berries, deciduous, 20 to 30 ft., China and Japan; *excelsa*, greenish-white, climber, S.W. Europe and W. Asia; *glauca*, green, black berries, tall climber, semi-evergreen, Eastern U.S.A.; *pseudo-china*, 'China Briar', dark green, 10 ft., climber, requires shelter, Southern U.S.A.; *rotundifolia*, greenish-yellow, black berries, to 25 ft., nearly evergreen, Eastern N. America.

HERBACEOUS SPECIES CULTIVATED: *S. herbacea*, greenish, bluish-black fruits, twining or semi-erect, N. America.

Smithiantha—*Gesneriaceae.* Stove tuberous-rooted herbaceous flowering peren-nials. Heart-shaped, green or crimson, velvety leaves. Formerly known as Naegelia. First introduced early nineteenth century.

CULTURE: Compost, two parts fibrous peat, one part loam, one part leaf-mould, with a little decayed manure and silver sand. Position, well-drained pots or pans in shady part of plant stove. Pot, March to flower in summer; May to flower in autumn; June to flower in winter. Plant tubers, 1 in. deep, singly in 5 in. pots, or 1 to 2 in. apart in larger sizes. Water moderately from time growth begins until plants are 3 or 4 in. high, then freely. After flowering gradually withhold water till foliage dies down, then keep dry till potting time. Apply weak liquid manure once or twice a week when flower buds show. Syringing not required. Temp., March to Sept. 65° to 85°, Sept. to March 55° to 75°. Store, when foliage has decayed, on their sides under stage till potting time in temp. of 50° to 55°.

PROPAGATION: By seeds sown on surface of well-drained pots of sandy peat, in temp. 75°, March or April; cuttings of young shoots inserted in pots of sandy peat in temp. 75° to 85° in spring; division of rhizomes at potting time.

SPECIES CULTIVATED: *S. cinnabarina* (syn. *Gesneria cinnabarina*), scarlet, summer, 2 ft., Mexico; *multiflora* (syn. *Gesneria amabilis*), white, Aug., 1¼ ft., Mexico; *zebrina*, yellow and scarlet, Oct., 2 ft., Mexico.

Smoketree, see *Cotinus Coggygria.*

Snail Flower, see *Phaseolus Caracalla.*

Snake Gourd, see *Trichosanthes Anguina;* **-root,** see *Cimicifuga racemosa.*

Snapdragon, see Antirrhinum.

Sneeze -weed, see Helenium; **-wort,** see *Achillea Ptarmica.*

Snowball Cactus, see *Pediocactus Simpsonii;* **-Tree,** see *Viburnum Opulus* var. *roseum.*

Snowberry Tree, see *Symphoricarpus albus.*

Snowdrop, see Galanthus; **-Tree,** see Halesia; **-Windflower,** see *Anemone sylvestris.*

Snowflake, see Leucojum.

Snow-in-summer, see *Cerastium tomentosum.*

Snow-on-the-mountain, see *Arabis albida.*

Snowy Mespilus, see *Amelanchier canadensis.*

Soap Plant, see *Chlorogalum pomeridianum;* **-wort,** see Saponaria.

Sobralia—*Orchidaceae.* A rather large, chiefly terrestrial, genus, with stiff leafy stems, set closely, varying in height, roots not tuberous. Flowers terminal in most, often five or six in succession from a thickened terminal head. In others the inflorescence is racemose, in a few lateral. In a number, though the individual flowers last but a few days, they are large and very handsome, not unlike a large Cattleya flower in shape.

CULTURE: All may be treated as terrestrials. Compost, rough fibrous loam, with about one-quarter of sphagnum moss and osmunda fibre or peat mixed with crushed crocks. Drainage, ample. Pots, fairly large. Water liberally in summer, less frequently in winter, but the compost should never get really dry. The intermediate house is suitable; winter temp. about 60°, higher in summer; shade and syringe; give full light in autumn.

PROPAGATION: By division of plants in early spring.

SPECIES CULTIVATED: A selection—*S. Cattleya*, purplish-brown, lip purplish, keels yellow, lateral, 12 ft. or more high, autumn, Colombia; *Charlesworthii* (syn. *E. Ruckeri*), racemose, larger, rose-purple, lip yellow and intense purple, 3 to 4 ft. high, summer, Colombia; *leucoxantha*, successive, large, creamy white, lip shaded yellow and orange, 2 to 5 ft., high, summer, Guatemala, Costa Rica; *liliastrum* (syn. *S. Elizabethae*), racemose, white or rose flushed, lip with yellow disk, 6 to 10 ft. high, winter, spring, Brazil, British Guiana, var. *rosea*, rose, lip with white veins; *Lowii*, successive, purple-rose, 1 to 3 ft. high, summer, Colombia; *macrantha*, successive, large, crimson-purple, lip with whitish throat and yellowish disk, very variable, 3 to 8 ft., high, summer, Mexico, Guatemala; *Ruckeri*, racemose, rose-purple, lip purple-crimson, summer, autumn, Colombia; *Sanderae*, sulphur-white, near *leucoxantha*, Cent. America; *violacea*, successive, fragrant, violet or violet-rose, keels on lip, yellow, 3 ft. high, autumn, Colombia, Peru; *violacea alba*, white, lip orange on throat and disk; *xantholeuca*, successive, creamy yellow, lip deep yellow, throat of lip brownish, 3 to 8 ft. high, summer, Cent. America. Several hybrids have been raised and some natural hybrids are strongly suspected.

Soja, see Glycine.

Solandra—*Solanaceae*. Stove climbing flowering shrubs. First introduced late eighteenth century.

CULTURE: Compost, two parts sandy loam, one part equal proportions fibrous peat and dry cow manure, and little sand. Position, pots or beds, with shoots trained up rafters or round trellises. Pot or plant, Feb. or March. Water freely April to Oct. Keep almost dry remainder of time. Syringe daily April to Sept. Prune weak shoots moderately closely and remove tips of stronger ones in Feb. Temp., Oct. to March 50° to 55°, March to Oct. 65° to 85°.

PROPAGATION: By cuttings inserted in light soil in coconut-fibre refuse in temp. of 65° to 75° in spring.

SPECIES CULTIVATED: *S. grandiflora*, 'Peach Trumpet Flower', cream and purple, spring, 10 to 15 ft., Trop. America; *longiflora*, white and purple, autumn, 4 to 6 ft., W. Indies; *nitida* (syn. *S. Hartwegii*), yellow, winter, 15 ft., Mexico; *viridiflora*, green, summer, 2 to 3 ft., Brazil.

Solanum—*Solanaceae*. A large genus including greenhouse and half-hardy flowering, berry-bearing and ornamental-leaved plants or shrubs, and vegetable and medicinal plants. Potato and Egg Plant first introduced late sixteenth century.

CULTURE OF THE POTATO: Classification—Kidney, oblong, white or coloured; round, roundish, white or coloured; pebble-shaped, flattish oblong, white or coloured. First earlies, varieties maturing in June; second earlies, varieties maturing in July and Aug.; late or maincrop, varieties maturing in Sept. and Oct. Soil, deep rich loam, or any kind except very heavy clay or bogland. Light soils best for very early crops. Dress at planting time with a balanced fertiliser. Position, sloping borders facing south for earlies, and open garden for second early and main crops. Never plant sets direct on farmyard manure in drills. If applied in spring, cover slightly with soil. Seaweed an excellent manure if dug in in autumn. Sets for planting: Best average size, 1½ to 2 in. wide and 3 in. long; weight, 2 to 3 oz. Larger tubers to be divided into three or four parts, each furnished with one good eye. Treatment of sets: Place tubers close together, eyed end suppermost, in shallow boxes in a cool, light spot early in the year, and allow each tuber to develop two strong shoots only, rubbing off all others. Plant early kinds in Feb., protecting young growth with straw if necessary; second earlies in March; maincrop in April. Draw drills 6 in. deep on heavy, and 7 in. deep on light soils. Rows to run north and south if possible, and be 15 in. apart for first earlies; 2¼ ft. for second earlies; and 3½ ft. for late kinds. Distances apart for early kinds, 6 to 8 in.; 1 ft. for medium growers; 1½ ft. for robust kinds. Never plant with a dibber. Fork or stir up soil between rows when shoots are 6 in. high; earth up when 6 to 8 in. high. Lift crop when haulm assumes a yellowish tinge. Avoid exposing tubers for eating too long to the light. Store in clamps in the open air or in cool cellars or dark sheds. Tubers for seed store in boxes, as above advised, in light, frost-proof position. Quantities of seed required: from 8 to 14 lb. per 100 ft. row, according to variety.

FORCING IN POTS: Compost, two parts loam and one part leaf-mould. Place one large crock over drainage hole, then add 2 in. of turf and enough compost to half-fill a 10 in. pot. Place one tuber in centre and fill pot to rim with soil pressed down moderately firmly. Place pots in temp. of 55°. Water carefully till shoots appear, then keep soil uniformly moist. When shoots are 6 in. high fill up remaining space in pot with compost. Increase temp. to 65° and feed twice a week with liquid manure. Expose plants fully to light. Time to plant, Jan. Crop ready for use in April or May.

CULTURE IN FRAMES: Early crops may be grown in frames on hotbeds or without heat. Compost, two parts good loam, one part well-rotted manure or leaf-mould, with a little wood ashes and bonemeal added. Depth of compost, 1 ft. Surface of soil from glass, 1 ft. Plant sets 1 ft. apart in rows 15 in. asunder; tubers, 4 in. deep. Time to plant, Feb. Earth up when 6 in. high. Give air when sun is shining. Keep soil uniformly moist, using tepid water. Protect frames at night in cold weather by means of mats or litter. Crop ready for use in May.

CULTURE OF AUBERGINE (EGG PLANT): Sow seed in well-drained pots Feb. to March, in temp. around 55°. Pot singly in small pots when sufficiently large, keep well syringed. Pot on to 5 or 6 in. pots in April, May, and in June move to cool house or conservatory. Water generously. Pinch out growing tip of plant when 6 in. high. Give air freely during blossoming period and eventually thin fruits to three or four per plant. In a warm season they will fruit freely out of doors beneath a sunny, sheltered wall. The purple- and black- fruited kinds are the best for culinary purposes.

CULTURE OF BERRY-BEARING SPECIES: Compost, equal parts loam, leaf-mould and silver sand. Pot, Feb. or March. Syringe daily, water freely, and grow in temp. of 55° to 65°. Pinch off points of shoots when 3 in. long. Transfer to cold frame in June, syringe morning and evening, and keep well watered. When berries set, give liquid manure twice a week. Admit air freely after first week. Remove to greenhouse middle of Sept. and grow in a temp. of 55°. Prune shoots back to 2 in. in Feb., and when new growth begins repot and grow as before. May also be planted outdoors in rich soil early in June, points of shoots removed early in July, and plants carefully lifted, potted and placed stood in shady, cold frame for a fortnight, then removed to greenhouse.

CULTURE OF CLIMBING SPECIES: Soil, loam, leaf-mould and silver sand. Position, pots, beds or tubs, shoots trained up rafters of greenhouse. *S. crispum* requires wall protection except in south, where it may be grown as a rampant bush. *S. jasminoides* will also thrive in the open in the south-west. Plant or pot in March. Prune away weak growths and shorten soft points of other shoots in Feb. Water indoor plants freely in spring and summer, moderately in autumn and winter. Temp., *S. Seaforthianum* and *S. Wendlandii*, Sept. to March 55° to 60°, March to Sept. 65° to 75°. *S. crispum* and *S. jasminoides* only require protection from frost.

CULTURE OF ORNAMENTAL-LEAVED SPECIES: Soil, ordinary. Position, sunny beds or borders. Plant out in June. Sow seeds annually in light soil in temp. of 75° in spring, grow seedlings on in pots in heat till May, then harden for planting out in June.

PROPAGATION: Berry-bearing species by seeds sown in temp. 65° to 75° in Feb., transplanting seedlings into small pots, and removing points of shoots when 3 in. high and later transferring to 5 in. pots. When shoots are 3 in. long remove their points, then allow them to grow naturally. From June onwards treat as advised for plants; also increased by cuttings inserted in sandy soil in temp. of 65° in spring, afterwards treating rooted cuttings as advised for seedlings. Climbing species by cuttings of young shoots in sandy soil under bell-glass, during Aug. or Sept. Ornamental-leaved species by seeds as above.

TUBEROUS-ROOTED SPECIES CULTIVATED: *S. tuberosum*, ' Potato ', white, violet, etc., summer.

FRUIT-BEARING SPECIES CULTIVATED: *S. Melongena*, ' Aubergine ', ' Andes ' or ' Egg Plant ', flowers blue, summer, 2 to 3 ft., fruit egg-shaped, white, yellow or purple, Tropics, var. *esculentum*.

BERRY-BEARING SPECIES CULTIVATED: *S. Capsicastrum*, ' Star Capsicum ', ' Winter Cherry ', flowers white, summer, fruits scarlet, winter, 1 to 2 ft., Brazil; *Pseudo-Capsicum*, ' Jerusalem Cherry ', white, summer, fruits scarlet or yellow, 2 to 4 ft., habitat uncertain, greenhouse evergreen shrubs. Wetherill's hybrids are the result of crosses between the two species.

CLIMBING SPECIES CULTIVATED: *S. crispum*, bluish-purple, fragrant, June to Sept., bush or climber, rampant, stands hard pruning, 15 to 25 ft., China, var. *autumnalis*, less strong, deeper colour, from May to Sept.; *jasminoides*, ' Jasmine Nightshade ', blue, summer, 15 to 20 ft., Brazil, var. *album*, white flowered, both lovely rampant climbers, rather tender; *Seaforthianum*, blue or purple, summer, 10 to 15 ft., Trop. America; *Wendlandii*, lilac and blue, summer, 15 to 20 ft.

ORNAMENTAL-LEAVED SPECIES CULTIVATED: *S. atropurpureum*, stems purplish, mid-ribs white, leaves prickly, Brazil; *marginatum*, stems woolly and prickly, leaves prickly, white beneath, green above and margined with white, N. Africa and Costa Rica; *robustum*, stems woolly, leaves velvety above, woolly beneath, and spiny, Brazil; *Warscewiczii*, stems hairy, red, and prickly, leaves green, mid-ribs prickly, S. America, shrubs, but best grown as half-hardy annuals.

Soldanella (Blue Moon-wort)—*Primulaceae*. Hardy perennial herbs. First introduced mid-seventeenth century.

CULTURE: Compost, equal parts peat and loam, with sharp sand. Position, sheltered, open, moist rockery. Plant, March or April. Mulch surface of soil in dry weather with leaf-mould.

PROPAGATION: By seeds sown in well-drained pans filled with equal parts sandy loam, peat and sand, lightly covered with fine soil and placed in a cold, shady frame, March or April; division of plants in March or April.

SPECIES CULTIVATED: *S. alpina*, blue, April and May, 3 in., Alps; *Ganderi*, palest lilac, March, 2 in., hybrid; *minima*, lilac and purple, April, 2 in., Europe; *montana*, lavender, April, 6 to 9 in., E. Europe; *neglecta*, lilac, spring, 3 to 4 in., hybrid; *pindicola*, lavender, spring, 3 in., Balkans; *pusilla*, pale lilac, April, 2 to 4 in., Alps.

Solidago (Golden Rod)—*Compositae*. Hardy herbaceous perennials.

CULTURE: Soil, ordinary. Position, sunny or shady borders or banks or margins of water. Plant, Oct. or March. Lift, divide and replant every three or four years.

PROPAGATION: By division of roots, Oct. or March; seeds sown outdoors in April.

SPECIES CULTIVATED: *S. brachystachys*, yellow, autumn, 6 to 12 in.; *canadensis*, yellow, Aug., 4 to 6 ft., N. America; *graminifolia* (syn. *S. lanceolata*), yellow, Sept., 2 to 4 ft., N. America; *virgaurea*, ' Common Golden Rod ', yellow, Aug., 2 to 3 ft., Europe (Br.).

× **Solidaster**—*Compositae*. A bigeneric hybrid of horticultural origin between *Aster ptarmicoides* and an unknown species of Solidago.

CULTURE: As Solidago.

PROPAGATION: As Solidago.

SPECIES CULTIVATED: *S. luteus* (syns. *Aster hybridus luteus* and *Solidago missouriensis* hort.), yellow, Aug., 2½ ft., scabrous.

Sollya—*Pittosporaceae*. Greenhouse evergreen twining shrubs. First introduced early nineteenth century.

CULTURE: Compost, two parts peat, one part turfy loam, and half a part silver sand. Position, well-drained pots or beds, with shoots trained to wire trellis or up rafters or pillars. Pot, Feb. or March. Water freely April to Sept., moderately afterwards. Syringe daily April to Aug. Shade not necessary. Temp., March to Sept. 55° to 65°, Sept. to March 40° to 50°.

PROPAGATION: By cuttings of shoots inserted in sand under bell-glass in temp. 65° to 75° in spring or summer.

SPECIES CULTIVATED: *S. heterophylla*, ' Australian Bluebell Creeper ', blue, July, 4 to 6 ft., Australia; *parviflora* (syn. *S. Drummondii*), blue, July, 4 to 6 ft., Australia.

Solomon's Seal, see Polygonatum.

Sonerila—*Melastomaceae*. Stove flowering perennial. Leaves, ovate or lanceolate, green or spotted with silvery white. First introduced mid-nineteenth century.

CULTURE: Compost, equal parts fibrous peat, chopped sphagnum, charcoal and sand. Position, well-drained pots or pans fully exposed to light. Pot, Feb. or March. Water freely April to Sept., moderately afterwards. Shade from sun and moist atmosphere essential. Temp., March to Sept. 70° to 85°, Sept. to March 55° to 65°.

PROPAGATION: By seeds sown in above compost and lightly covered with fine soil, Jan. to April, in a temp. of 75° to 85°; cuttings inserted in small pots under bell-glass in temp. 75° to 85°, Jan. to May.

SPECIES CULTIVATED: *S. argentea*, lilac-rose, leaves silvery grey, origin unknown; *margaritacea*, rose, summer, leaves white and green above, purplish beneath, Burma. There are numerous vars.

Sophora—*Leguminosae.* Hardy and slightly tender evergreen and deciduous shrubs and trees. Attractive pinnate foliage and ornamental flowers. First introduced mid-eighteenth century.

CULTURE: Soil, ordinary well-drained loam. Position, warm, with full sun. Some species require wall protection in all but warmest districts.

PROPAGATION: By seed sown in well-drained pots or boxes in a cold frame in March or April, or in gentle heat in Feb. Shrubby kinds by cuttings of half-ripened young shoots in shaded frame or under bell-glass, Aug. to Sept., or by layers, Oct. to Nov.

SPECIES CULTIVATED: *S. affinis*, hardy, white, tinged pink, summer, 12 to 18 ft., Arkansas and Texas; *japonica*, ' Japanese Pagoda Tree ', creamy white, Sept., young trees not flowering, 50 to 75 ft., China, with vars. *variegata*, leaves margined creamy white, and *violacea*, flowers rosy violet, all hardy; *macrocarpa*, evergreen, rather tender, yellow, June, 20 to 30 ft., Chile; *microphylla*, evergreen, yellow, June, 8 to 12 ft., New Zealand and Chile, var. *prostrata*, dwarf habit, both rather tender; *tetraptera*, ' Kowhai ', golden yellow, May to June, 15 to 25 ft. for warmer districts, New Zealand and Chile, with var. *grandiflora*, the best form, both evergreen in sheltered places; *visiifolia*, blue and white, June, hardy, 6 to 8 ft., attractive shrub, China.

× **Sophrocattleya**—*Orchidaceae.* Bigeneric hybrids between the genera Sophronitis and Cattleya.

× **Sophrolaelia**—*Orchidaceae.* Bigeneric hybrids between the genera Sophronitis and Laelia.

× **Sophrolaeliocattleya**—*Orchidaceae.* Trigeneric hybrids between the genera Sophronitis and Laeliocattleya.

Sophronitis—*Orchidaceae.* About eight dwarf-growing, pretty epiphytes, allied to Cattleyas. Pseudo-bulbs usually small, one-leafed, stout, with one or few terminal flowers.

CULTURE: Compost, as for Cattleyas, but finely cut. Pans, well drained, which can be suspended, preferable to pots. The temp. and atmosphere for Odontoglossums suit during summer. Winter growths and flowers are often produced with *S. coccinea* which should have 55° at night in winter. Infrequent waterings are needed during winter but the compost should not become really dry. Water freely when roots are active. Repot as growth commences, the period varies. Shade, but give full light in autumn.

PROPAGATION: The rhizomes branch and division can usually be made readily.

SPECIES CULTIVATED: *S. cernua*, small, cinnabar-red, lip paler at base, winter, spring, Brazil; *coccinea* (syn. *S. grandiflora*), comparatively large, variable, beautiful, flower 1 or 2 up to 3 in. across, bright scarlet, lip yellowish, red streaked, winter, spring, Brazil; *Lowii*, often placed as a var. of *S. coccinea*, smaller, dark chrome yellow, winter, Brazil; *pterocarpa*, near *S. cernua* in size and colour, perhaps synonymous, winter, Brazil; *violacea*, purple-violet, winter, Brazil.

Sorbaria (False Spiraea)—*Rosaceae.* Hardy deciduous shrubs, formerly included in Spiraea.

CULTURE: Soil, moist rich. Position, open sunny borders. *S. Aitchisonii* and *S. tomentosa* should have young wood shortened back, but may retain framework of old wood in March.

PROPAGATION: By seed; suckers; cuttings of ripe wood; root cuttings.

SPECIES CULTIVATED: *S. Aitchisonii* (syn. *Spiraea Aitchisonii*), white, July to Aug., 8 to 10 ft., W. Asia; *arborea*, white, to 18 ft., China; *sorbifolia*, white, July to Aug., 3 to 6 ft., N. Asia, Japan; *tomentosa* (syns. *S. Lindleyana*, *Spiraea Lindleyana*), white, July to Sept., 12 to 20 ft., Himalaya.

Sorbus—*Rosaceae*. Hardy deciduous ornamental trees with autumn berries, formerly included in Pyrus.

CULTURE: Soil, ordinary well drained. Position, sunny borders or as isolated lawn specimens, thrive in chalky soil. Plant, Nov. to Feb.

PROPAGATION: By seeds sown when ripe, or stratified; layers; rare kinds by budding or grafting on stocks of *S. Aucuparia*.

SPECIES CULTIVATED: *S. Aria* (syn. *Pyrus Aria*), ' Whitebeam ', flowers dull white, May, red berries, 30 to 50 ft., Europe, including Britain, with vars. *lutescens*, creamy white leaves, *majestica*, best form, grey leaves, scarlet fruits; *Aucuparia*, ' Mountain Ash ', ' Rowan ', white, May, scarlet fruits quickly eaten by birds, 30 to 50 ft., Europe and Asia, including Britain, many vars. including *tructu-luteo*, yellow fruited, *pendula*, weeping, *edulis*, larger fruits used for preserves; *commixta*, white, May, berries and foliage orange-red, Sept., upright habit, 15 to 25 ft., Japan, Korea; *discolor* (syn. *S. pekinensis*), white, May, brilliant autumn tints, white berries, 25 to 30 ft., N. China; *domestica* (syn. *Pyrus Sorbus*), ' Service Tree ', white, May, fruit green tinged red, 30 to 60 ft., S. and E. Europe; *Folgneri*, white, June, scarlet fruits, graceful habit, 15 to 20 ft., Cent. China; *Hostii*, natural hybrid, pale pink, June, 8 to 12 ft., Cent. Europe; *hupehensis*, white, May, white berries pink starred, brilliant autumn tints, 15 to 25 ft., W. China; *hybrida* (syn. *Pyrus pinnatifida*), white, May, round red fruits, natural hybrid, with vars. *fastigiata*, erect growing, *Gibbsii*, large clusters, bright fruits, and *Meinichii*, greyish leaves; *intermedia*, dull white, May, bright red berries, 20 to 40 ft., N. Europe, including Britain; *meliosmifolia*, attractive young growths, brownish-red fruits, 20 to 30 ft., W. China; *Sargentiana*, sticky terminal flower-buds, large bunches brilliant berries and good autumn tints, recent introduction, W. China; *scalaris*, grey leaves, reddish-brown berries, 10 to 15 ft., W. China; *tianshanica*, white, May, bright red fruits, 10 to 12 ft., Turkistan; *torminalis*, ' Wild Service Tree ', white, June, oval brown fruits, 30 to 40 ft., Europe; *Vilmorinii*, grey fern-like leaves, pink and white berries, 10 to 15 ft., W. China.

Sorrel, see Rumex; **-Tree**, see *Oxydendrum arboreum*.

Sour Sop, see *Annona muricata*.

South African Harebell, see *Roella ciliata*.

Southern Beech, see Nothofagus; **-wood**, see *Artemisia Abrotanum*.

Sowbread, see Cyclamen.

Soybean or **Soyabean**, see *Glycine Max*.

Spanish Bayonet, see *Yucca aloifolia*; **-Broom**, see *Spartium junceum*; **-Chestnut**, see *Castanea sativa*; **-Iris**, see *Iris Xiphium*; **-Moss**, see *Tillandsia usneoides*; **-Oyster Plant**, see *Scolymus hispanicus*; **-Squill**, see *Scilla hispanica*.

Sparaxis (African Harlequin Flower)—*Iridaceae*. Half-hardy bulbous plants. First introduced mid-eighteenth century.

OUTDOOR CULTURE: Soil, light, rich sandy. Position, sunny well-drained border. Plant, Sept. to Jan., placing bulbs 4 in. deep and 2 in. apart. Mulch surface of bed in March with cow manure. Cover with litter during winter months if not planted in sheltered border.

POT CULTURE: Compost, two parts sandy loam, one part leaf-mould or decayed cow manure. Pots, 4½ in. in diameter, well drained. Place five bulbs, 3 in. deep, in each pot in Nov. and cover with leaf-mould in cold frame or under cool greenhouse stage until growth begins. Water moderately from time bulbs begin to grow until flowers fade, then gradually cease, keeping bulbs dry till Jan. Temp., Sept. to March 40° to 50°, other times 50° to 60°.

PROPAGATION: By offsets, treated as advised for bulbs.

SPECIES CULTIVATED: *S. grandiflora*, violet-purple, spring, 1 to 2 ft., S. Africa; *tricolor*, orange-yellow and black, May, 1 to 2 ft., S. Africa. For vars. see trade lists. See also the genus Dierama.

Sparmannia—*Tiliaceae*. Greenhouse evergreen shrub. First introduced late eighteenth century.

CULTURE: Compost, two parts loam, one part peat, and little sand. Position, pots in light, airy greenhouse Sept. to June; sunny spot outdoors remainder of time. Pot, Feb. or March. Prune moderately close Nov. to Dec. Water copiously April to Oct., moderately afterwards. Apply stimulants April to Sept. No shade or syringing required. Temp., March to Sept. 55° to 65°, Sept. to March 40° to 50°.

PROPAGATION: By cuttings inserted singly in small pots filled with sandy soil under bell-glass in temp. 55° to 65°, spring or summer.

SPECIES CULTIVATED: *S. africana*, ' African Hemp ', white, summer, 10 to 15 ft., S. Africa, var. *flore-pleno*, double flowered.

Spartium—*Leguminosae*. Hardy deciduous flowering shrub. First introduced mid-sixteenth century.

CULTURE: Soil, ordinary. Position, sunny open borders or dry banks, excellent maritime shrub. Plant, Oct. to March. May be pruned, or even clipped if desired, in spring.

PROPAGATION: By seeds sown ¼ in. deep in drills in fine soil in sunny position outdoors, autumn or spring. Young plants should be pot grown until planted out.

SPECIES CULTIVATED: *S. junceum*, ' Spanish Broom ', yellow, summer, 6 to 10 ft., S. Europe.

Spathiphyllum—*Araceae*. Stove evergreen perennials. First introduced mid-nineteenth century.

CULTURE: Compost, leaf-mould and peat with a little loam, sand and charcoal. Water freely during growing season, moderately at other times. Maintain a humid atmosphere throughout the year, using the syringe freely. Temp., March to Sept. 75° to 85°, Sept. to March 65° to 70°.

PROPAGATION: By seeds sown in temp. 85° during Feb.; or by division, Feb. or March.

SPECIES CULTIVATED: *S. cochlearispathum*, white, large leaves with waved margins, 2 to 3 ft., Cent. America; *floribundum*, white and yellowish, foliage rich green, 1 ft., Colombia; *Ortgiesii*, green and white, 1½ ft., Mexico; *Patinii*, white and greenish, pale green foliage, 1 ft., Colombia.

Spathoglottis—*Orchidaceae*. An eastern terrestrial genus, about forty species. Pseudo-bulbs corm-like on a creeping rhizome. Leaves 1 to 5, tall, often broadly grass-like, deciduous in some. Scapes from near base of bulbs, tall, slender, the flowering portion elongating, more or less. Flowers, often many, not very large, but bright in colour, front lobe of lip spreading.

CULTURE: Compost, fibrous loam, a small quantity of leaf-mould, sand and chopped sphagnum moss added. Pots, well drained. Deciduous species should have their rhizomes and pseudo-bulbs just covered with the compost, evergreen kinds placed on the top and firmly pressed in but not covered. All the kinds need a stove temp. and moist atmosphere with shading when growing, expose to light in autumn but retain the far eastern in the stove during winter. The deciduous or nearly deciduous require a more decided rest and a winter temp. of 60°, or a little less, as do the Burmese and Indian kinds.

PROPAGATION: By division of the plants in spring.

SPECIES CULTIVATED: A selection—*S. aurea*, bright yellow, often reddish behind, lip red-spotted at base, autumn, Malacca; *Fortunei*, deciduous, yellow, lip red-spotted and marked, autumn, Hong Kong; *gracilis*, near *S. aurea*, mid-lobe of lip haired at base, spring, Borneo; *ixioides*, near *S. Fortunei*, golden yellow, lip disk red-spotted, keels haired, summer, E. Himalaya; *Kimballiana*, near *S. aurea*, finer, larger, golden yellow, copper-red behind, red spots on bases of the lip lobes, summer, Borneo; *Lobbii*, deciduous, sulphur-yellow, bases of lower sepals and lip marked red-brown, autumn, Burma; *plicata* (syn. *S. rosea*), variable, many, crowded, purplish or rose-purple, lip often whitish, summer, Malaya; *Vieillardii*, strong-growing, whitish, rose-flushed, many, comparatively large, variable, autumn, various, New Caledonia.

Spear Flower, see Ardisia; **-Grass,** see Aciphylla; **-Lily,** see Doryanthes; **-mint,** see *Mentha spicata*.

Specularia—*Campanulaceae.* Hardy annuals.
CULTURE: Soil, ordinary. Position, sunny beds or borders. Sow seeds in April thinly $\frac{1}{16}$ in. deep in patches or lines where required to grow. Thin seedlings when 1 to 2 in. high to 3 to 6 in. apart. Support plants with small twigs when 3 to 6 in. high.
SPECIES CULTIVATED: *S. pentagonia* (syn. *Campanula pentagonia*), blue, summer, 1 ft., Asia Minor; *perfoliata*, blue, June, 12 to 18 in., N. America; *Speculum-Veneris* (syn. *Campanula Speculum*), ' Venus's Looking Glass ', purple, summer, 1 ft., Europe. This genus was formerly known as Legousia.

Speedwell, see Veronica.

Spenceria—*Rosaceae.* Hardy perennial plants.
CULTURE: Soil, well-drained loam or scree mixture. Position, sunny pocket in the rock garden.
PROPAGATION: By seeds sown when ripe.
SPECIES CULTIVATED: *S. ramalana*, golden yellow, 12 in., July, Asia.

Sphaeralcea (Globe Mallow)—*Malvaceae.* Half-hardy perennial and greenhouse shrub. First introduced late eighteenth century.
CULTURE OF PERENNIAL SPECIES: Soil, ordinary. Position, sunny, dryish, sheltered banks or sheltered rock gardens. Plant, autumn or spring.
CULTURE OF SHRUBBY SPECIES: Compost, loam, leaf-mould and sand. Position, well-drained pots or borders in unheated greenhouse. Water freely during growth.
PROPAGATION: Perennial species by division at planting time; shrubby species by cuttings of young shoots inserted in sandy soil under bell-glass in gentle bottom heat.
SPECIES CULTIVATED: *S. angustifolia*, pink, Aug. to Sept., 3 to 4 ft., shrubby, Mexico; *Munroana*, bright scarlet, May to Nov., 1 to 2 ft., perennial, N. America.

Spice Bush, see *Lindera Benzoin*.

Spider Flower, see *Cleome spinosa*; **-wort,** see Tradescantia.

Spigelia—*Loganiaceae.* Hardy herbaceous perennial. First introduced late seventeenth century.
CULTURE: Soil, equal parts loam, leaf-mould, peat and sand. Position, partially shady border containing 2 ft. in depth of above compost. Plant, March or April. Water copiously during summer.
PROPAGATION: By division of roots, March or April.
SPECIES CULTIVATED: *S. marilandica*, ' Carolina Pink ', ' Maryland Pink Root ', red and yellow, summer, 1 ft., N. America.

Spike Heath, see *Bruckenthalia spiculifolia*; **-Rush,** see Eleocharis.

Spinach, see Spinacia; **New Zealand-,** see *Tetragonia expansa*; **-Beet,** see *Beta vulgaris* var. *Cicla*.

Spinacia—*Chenopodiaceae.* Hardy annual. Esculent-leaved vegetable. First introduced mid-sixteenth century.
CULTURE: Soil, deep, rich, moist ordinary for summer spinach; rich, moderately dry for winter kind. Position, sunny. Sow seeds of summer spinach at intervals of a fortnight, Feb. to May, in drills 1 in. deep and 12 in. apart; winter spinach, Aug. and Sept., in drills 1 in. deep and 15 in. asunder. Thin to 3 in. when large enough to handle then remove and use alternate plants. Seeds germinate in ten

to fifteen days; retain their germinating powers for five years. Crop reaches maturity eleven weeks after sowing.

SPECIES CULTIVATED: *S. oleracea*, ' Prickly-seeded ' or ' Winter Spinach ', S.W. Asia, var. *inermis*, ' Round-seeded ' or ' Summer Spinach ', S.E. Europe.

Spindle Tree, see *Euonymus europaeus*.

Spiraea—*Rosaceae*. Hardy deciduous flowering shrubs. Some species formerly included in this genus are now classified in Astilbe, Aruncus, Filipendula, Holodiscus and Sorbaria.

CULTURE: Soil, good ordinary or loamy. Position, open sunny borders or shrubberies. Plant, Sept. to March. Prune those which flower on young wood, such as *S. japonica*, *Bumalda*, ' Anthony Waterer ', *Margaritae*, *Menziesii*, etc., to ground level in March. Those which flower early on one-year-old wood, such as *S. arguta*, *prunifolia* and *Thunbergii*, should be pruned hard immediately after flowering. The later-flowering species, *S. bracteata*, *canescens*, *Vanhouttei*, *trichocarpa* and *Veitchii* should have some of the older wood thinned out in winter.

PROPAGATION: By cuttings of young shoots in sandy soil under hand-light, or in frame, in shade during summer; offsets removed and planted in autumn.

SPECIES CULTIVATED: *S. arguta*, white, April to May, 5 to 7 ft., hybrid; *brachybotrys*, pale rose, June, 4 to 8 ft., hybrid; *bullata*, deep rose, July, 12 to 15 in., Japan; *Bumalda*, carmine, July to Aug., 18 in., hybrid; *canescens*, white, 6 to 10 ft., Himalaya; *cantoniensis* (syn. *S. Reevesiana*), white, June, 4 to 6 ft., China and Japan, and var. *lanceata*, double flowers; *Chamaedrifolia*, white, June to July, 4 to 6 ft., E. Europe to Japan, var. *ulmifolia*, better form with larger flowers; *decumbens*, white, May, 3 to 8 in., S. Europe; *Douglasii*, purplish-rose, June to July, 4 to 6 ft., Western N. America; *Henryi*, cream, June, 6 to 8 ft., spreading, Cent. and W. China; *japonica* (syn. *S. callosa*), rosy red, July to Aug., 3 to 5 ft., Japan, China; *latifolia*, pale pink, June to July, 3 to 4 ft., Newfoundland and Canada; *Margaritae*, bright pink, July to Aug., 4 ft., hybrid; *Menziesii*, purplish-rose, July to Aug., 3 to 5 ft., Western N. America; *mollifolia*, white, June, 4 to 6 ft., silvery leaves, W. China; *nipponica* (syn. *S. bracteata*), pure white, June, 5 to 8 ft., Japan, var. *rotundifolia*, larger foliage and flowers; *prunifolia*, white, April to May, 6 ft., China, var. *plena*, double, autumn colouring; *salicifolia*, pink, June to July, 3 to 6 ft., spreading by suckers, S.E. Europe to N.E. Asia; *sanssouciana*, bright rose, July, 4 to 5 ft., hybrid; *Thunbergii*, white, March to April, 3 to 5 ft., China; *trichocarpa*, white, June, 4 to 6 ft., semi-weeping habit, Korea; *Vanhouttei*, white, June, 4 to 6 ft., hybrid; *Veitchii*, white, June, 10 to 12 ft., Cent. China; *Watsoniana*, rose, hybrid; *Wilsonii*, pure white, June to July, 6 to 8 ft., arching growths, Cent. and W. China.

Spiranthes—*Orchidaceae*. A large terrestrial genus, represented in Britain. Roots fleshy or thickened into tubers, stems erect, leafy or bracteate or without leaves when flowering. Flowers generally small, one-sided in the spikes or spiralled. Segments nearly equal, the upper sepal and petals hooded. Few species have appeared in cultivation.

CULTURE: With exotic species information should be obtained as to nature of soil, position and temp. If unknown, a compost of rough loam, peat, leaf-mould and sand should be made and the crown or tuber placed just beneath the surface. When dormant give infrequent waterings and a winter temp. about 60° to all from tropical countries, a higher temp. in summer with shading. British species require a similar compost to above with sometimes old mortar rubble added, but, if collected, a good ball of soil should be taken with them and both that and the position imitated as far as possible.

PROPAGATION: By division of crowns if more than one is present.

BRITISH AND EUROPEAN SPECIES CULTIVATED: *S. aestivalis*, small, white, summer, damp situation, height up to 15 in.; *Romanzoffiana*, white, fragrant, forming a spike 4 to 10 in. high, Ireland, Britain, N. Amecria; *spiralis* (syn. *S. autumnalis*), small, white, one-sided, fragrant, summer, autumn, chalky soil.

EXOTIC SPECIES CULTIVATED: A selection—*S. acaulis*, greenish-white or white within, variable, height 12 to 30 in., leaves rather large, green, with darker green markings, or whitish spots, spring, summer, Trop. America; *australis*, small, pinkish, lip white, summer, Europe to Australia; *bicolor*, white, with purplish streaks, height 1 to 3 ft., winter, W. Indies, Brazil; *cernua*, white, fragrant, spike cylindrical, N. America; *elata*, white or green shaded, spiralled, variable, summer, Trop. America; *gracilis*, white, spiralled, 12 to 18 in. high, N. America; *metallica*, green, lip whitish, leaves olive-green with paler spots, winter, spring, Brazil; *sauroglossum*, green, lip white, spike cylindrical, 2 to 3 ft. high.

Spire Lily, see Galtonia.

Spleenwort, see Asplenium.

Spondias—*Anacardiaceae*. Warm greenhouse trees. Cultivated for the edible fruits. First introduced early eighteenth century.

CULTURE: Compost, fibrous loam and sand. Position, well-drained borders in heated greenhouse or conservatory. Water freely during growing season, moderately at other times. Temp., March to Sept. 65° to 75°, Sept. to March 50° to 55°.

PROPAGATION: By cuttings of half-ripened shoots inserted in sandy soil under bell-glass in temp. 75°.

SPECIES CULTIVATED: *S. cytherea* (syn. *S. dulcis*), ' Otaheite Apple ', fruits 3 in. long, golden yellow, to 60 ft., Society Islands; *Mombin* (syn. *S. lutea*), fruits 1 to 2 in. long, yellow, to 60 ft., Tropics.

Spotted Laurel, see Aucuba.

Spraguea—*Portulacaceae*. Hardy perennial herb. First introduced mid-nineteenth century.

CULTURE: Soil, ordinary. Position, edges of sunny well-drained borders or rockeries. Plant, April or May.

PROPAGATION: By seeds sown, Feb. or March, in well-drained pots or pans, transplanting seedlings an inch apart in 3 in. pots when large enough to handle and planting out in May; cuttings of shoots inserted in sandy peat under bell-glass in spring.

SPECIES CULTIVATED: *S. multiceps*, ' Pussy Paws ', pink, summer, 2 in., N. America; *umbellata*, white, summer, 2 in., California.

Sprekelia—*Amaryllidaceae*. Warm house bulbous plants. First introduced mid-seventeenth century.

CULTURE: Compost, two parts turfy loam, one part river sand and a few crushed bones. Position, well-drained pots in light part of stove. Pot, Feb., burying bulb about two-thirds of its depth. Water freely from time growth begins (about Feb.) until Sept., when keep quite dry. Apply liquid manure when flower spike shows. Top-dress large bulbs annually and repot every three or four years only. Temp., Feb. to Sept. 65° to 75°, Sept. to Feb. 50° to 55°.

PROPAGATION: By seeds sown $\frac{1}{16}$ in. deep in well-drained pots of sandy loam in temp. 65° to 70° in March, placing seedlings singly in 2 in. pots, and keeping them moderately moist all the year round for three years; by offsets, treated as old bulbs. Seedlings are six to seven years before they flower.

SPECIES CULTIVATED: *S. formosissima* (syn. *Amaryllis formosissima*), ' Jacobean Lily ', crimson, June, 2 ft., Mexico and Guatemala.

Spring Beauty, see Claytonia; **-Starflower,** see *Ipheion uniflora* under Brodiaea

Spruce, see Picea.

Spurge, see Euphorbia; **-Laurel,** see *Daphne Laureola*.

Squash, see *Cucurbita maxima*.

Squirrel-foot Fern, see *Davallia bullata*; **-tail Grass,** see *Hordeum jubatum*.

Stachys (Woundwort; Betony)—*Labiatae*. Hardy and half-hardy perennials and one tuberous-rooted vegetable. First introduced late eighteenth century.

CULTURE OF CHINESE ARTICHOKE: Soil, ordinary, deeply dug. Position, sunny.

Plant tubers 9 in. apart, 4 in. to 6 in. deep in rows 18 in. asunder in March or April. Stir surface of soil between rows frequently. No earthing up required. Lift tubers in autumn as required for use. Cover surface of ground in severe weather.

CULTURE OF HARDY PERENNIALS: Soil, ordinary. Position, warm, sheltered border for *S. coccinea*; edgings to borders or beds for *S. lanata*; well-drained sunny rock gardens for *S. corsica* and *S. lavandulaefolia*. Plant, autumn or spring.

PROPAGATION: By division in autumn or spring.

SPECIES CULTIVATED: *S. coccinea*, scarlet, summer, 2 ft., Mexico; *corsica*, cream and pink, summer, 1 in., Corsica and Sardinia; *grandiflora* (syn. *S. Betonica*), violet, May to July, 1 ft., Asia Minor, and var. *robusta*, rosy pink; *lanata*, ' Lamb's Ear ', leaves white and woolly, 1 ft., Caucasus; *lavandulaefolia*, purplish-rose, July to Aug., 6 in., Caucasus and Asia Minor; *officinalis* (syns. *S. Betonica*, *Betonica officinalis*), purple, to 3 ft., Europe, Asia Minor; *Sieboldii* (syn. *S. tuberifera*), ' Chinese Artichoke ', pink, summer, 1 ft., roots white, spiral in shape and edible, Japan.

Stachyurus—*Stachyuraceae*. Hardy deciduous flowering shrubs, attractive warm coloured stems and sulphur-yellow blooms in Feb. First introduced mid-nineteenth century.

CULTURE: Soil, peat, leaf-mould and loam. Position, sheltered shrubberies. Plant, Nov. to Feb.

PROPAGATION: By cuttings with a heel removed in July and inserted in sandy soil under bell-glass in gentle bottom heat.

SPECIES CULTIVATED: *S. chinensis*, pale yellow, Feb. to March, 6 to 12 ft., China; *praecox*, pale yellow, Feb., 5 to 10 ft., Japan.

Staghorn Fern, see *Platycerium bifurcatum*; **-Sumach,** see *Rhus typhina*.

Stanhopea—*Orchidaceae*. Epiphytes, with clustered pseudo-bulbs, rather small, carrying a single leaf. Scapes from the bulb base, usually pendent. Flowers large, attractive, though lasting but a few days, among the most remarkable in the orchid family. Sepals and petals thin, lip wax-like. Variation is present but in the more popular kinds the base of the lip is cup-like (the hypochil), from this proceeds a fleshy, grooved extension (the mesochil) bearing two large curved horns, and terminating in a usually heart-shaped lobe (the epichil). Species are known which are hornless and in some the lip is so contorted that it is difficult to trace the three divisions.

CULTURE: Compost, two to three parts osmunda fibre, one part, or more, sphagnum moss. Teakwood baskets which can be suspended are preferable, drainage so placed as to allow exit for the spikes. While growing a moist atmosphere is needed and liberal watering, with shading, and as far as possible a tropical temp. In winter 60° to 65° is sufficient and a fairly moist atmosphere, water then being very infrequently needed. Remove shading early in autumn.

PROPAGATION: Division of large plants is the better method but two or three healthy back bulbs may be removed in spring, placed on small crocks in a pot, surfaced with sphagnum and put into a propagating case; gentle bottom heat is an aid to growth. Pot when roots are seen but return to case for a week or two.

SPECIES CULTIVATED: A selection—*S. Bucephalus*, variable, large, fragrant, yellow to orange-yellow, spotted purplish-crimson, lip usually yellow, late summer, Ecuador, Peru, Mexico, var. *guttata*, apricot, petals and hypochil blotched brown; *costaricensis*, large, yellow, with large purplish spots, hypochil purple-brown at base, variable, autumn, Costa Rica; *Devoniensis*, fragrant, creamy or fawn-yellow, marked brown-crimson, lip white, spotted purple, with three small teeth, summer, Mexico; *eburnea*, large, fragrant, white, hypochil with two short horns, mesochil hornless, summer, Trinidad, Guiana; *ecornuta*, white, yellow, lip hornless, not showing divisions, summer, Guatemala; *graveolens*, pale yellow, hypochil apricot-yellow, mesochil and horns ivory-white; epichil sometimes purple spotted, summer, Brazil; *insignis*, large, fragrant, variable, yellow, purple spotted, hypochil whitish, purple spotted, epichil similarly coloured, summer, Brazil, Peru;

Lowii, large, fragrant, cream or cream buff, lip ivory-white, hypochil suffused with maroon, hornless, winter, Colombia; *Madouxiana*, large, fragrant, creamy white, spotted rose, summer, Colombia; *Martiana*, large, whitish, petals spotted crimson-purple, epichil dimly three-toothed, summer, autumn, Mexico; *oculata*, large, fragrant, variable, yellow, with ocellated red spots, summer, Brazil, Guatemala, Mexico; *platyceras*, yellow, spotted red-purple, horns broad, sickle shape, summer, Colombia; *tigrina*, largest, showiest, very fragrant, deep crimson-red and yellow, hypochil orange-yellow, blotched maroon-purple, mesochil whitish, horns white, purple spotted, epichil often purple spotted, three-toothed in front, variable, summer, Brazil, Mexico, Guiana, Venezuela (the correct name but not in use is *Stanhopea Hernandezii*); *Wardii*, large, fragrant, yellow, spotted red-purple, hypochil orange, blotched maroon, horns sickle shape, summer, Guatemala, Venezuela, vars. *aurea*, deep orange-yellow, hypochil with two blotches, *amoena*, lemon-yellow, purple dotted, hypochil with two maroon blotches.

Stanleya—*Cruciferae*. Hardy perennial herb. First introduced early nineteenth century.

CULTURE: Soil, ordinary. Position, sunny border. Plant, Oct. or April.

PROPAGATION: By seeds sown in gentle heat in spring, planting out in May or June; also by division of the roots in Oct. or March.

SPECIES CULTIVATED: *S. pinnata*, yellow, summer, 4 ft., California.

Stapelia (Carrion Flower)—*Asclepiadaceae*. Greenhouse evergreen succulent-stemmed plants. Flowers disagreeably scented. First introduced late eighteenth century.

CULTURE: Compost, two parts sandy loam, one part broken rubbish or old mortar, and one part sand. Position, well-drained pots close to glass in light, sunny greenhouse or planted in prepared border between rocks. No shade required. Pot, March or April. Water moderately April to Oct., keep nearly dry remainder of year. Temp., Oct. to March 40° to 50°, March to Oct. 55° to 75°. Repot or plant only when absolutely necessary.

PROPAGATION: By cuttings of stems exposed to air on shelf in greenhouse for two or three days, then inserted singly in 2 in. pots half-filled with drainage, remainder with sand and brick rubbish; spring.

SPECIES CULTIVATED: *S. Asterias*, 'Star-fish Flower', violet, yellow, and purple, summer, 6 in., S. Africa; *deflexa*, green and red, summer, 4 to 6 in., S. Africa; *geminiflora*, dark brown, spotted yellow, Oct., 6 in., S. Africa; *gigantea*, yellow, red, brown, and purple, summer, 6 in., S. Africa; *grandiflora*, purple, autumn, 1 ft., S. Africa; *maculosa*, yellowish and red, July to Sept., 1 ft., S. Africa; *mutabilis*, greenish-yellow, purple and red, June and July, 6 in., S. Africa; *rufa*, violet-purple with red, June to Oct., 6 in., S. Africa; *variegata*, greenish-yellow and purplish-brown, Aug., 4 to 6 in., S. Africa, and var. *clypeta* (syn. *S. Bufonis*), 'Toad Flower', spotted and lined purple-brown.

Staphylea—*Staphyleaceae*. Hardy deciduous shrubs with ornamental flowers and foliage and curious inflated fruits. First introduced early seventeenth century.

CULTURE: Soil, moist, loamy. Position, sunny borders or shrubberies. Plant, Oct. to Feb. Prune straggling shoots moderately closely immediately after flowering.

CULTURE OF S. COLCHICA FOR FORCING: Compost, two parts sandy loam, one part leaf-mould. Pot, Oct. to Jan. Place in sheltered position outdoors, or in cold frame until Jan., then remove into forcing house, or end of Jan. into cold greenhouse. Temp., 65° to 75°. Water moderately when first placed in heat, afterwards more freely. Syringe daily until leaves expand. Transfer to cold frame after flowering. Harden and stand outdoors, May to Oct.

PROPAGATION: By seeds sown in sandy soil in sheltered position outdoors in Sept. or Oct.; cuttings of firm shoots, 6 to 8 in. long, inserted in sandy soil in cold frame or in sheltered corner outdoors in Sept.; layering shoots, Sept. or Oct.; suckers removed and planted, Oct. to Feb.

SPECIES CULTIVATED: *S. Bumalda*, greenish-white, autumn-tinted foliage, May to June, 2 to 3 ft., Japan and Cent. China; *colchica*, white, pleasantly fragrant conspicuous bladder fruits, May, 6 to 10 ft., Caucasus; *holocarpa*, white, May, 20 to 30 ft., Cent. China, with its more attractive var. *rosea*, pale pink, slightly larger flowers; *pinnata*, ' Bladder Nut ', white, May, 10 to 15 ft., Europe and Asia Minor; *trifolia*, dull white, least attractive species, May, 8 to 12 ft., Eastern U.S.A.

Star Anise, see *Illicium verum*; **-Apple,** see *Chrysophyllum Cainito*; **-fish Flower,** see *Stapelia Asterias*; **-flower,** see *Trientalis europaea*; **-fruit,** see Damasonium; **-Grass,** see Hypoxis; **-Jasmine,** see *Trachelospermum jasminoides*; **-of-Bethlehem,** see *Ornithogalum umbellatum*; **-Tulip,** see Calochortus; **-wort,** see Aster.

State Flower of Colorado, see *Aquilegia caerulea.*

Statice, see Limonium.

Stauntonia—*Berberideae* (or *Lardizabalaceae*). Slightly tender evergreen climbing shrubs with unisexual flowers; purple fruits, resembling walnuts, eaten by Japanese. First introduced mid-nineteenth century.
   CULTURE: Soil, deep, sandy loam. Position, south wall or trellis in southern counties; trained up trellis in conservatories or unheated greenhouses. Plant, Sept., Oct., March or April. Prune trailing shoots not required to produce flowers following season to two-thirds of their length in autumn.
   PROPAGATION: By cuttings of firm young shoots inserted in sandy soil under bell-glass in shady position outdoors in summer.
   SPECIES CULTIVATED: *S. hexaphylla*, white, tinged violet, April, 10 to 20 ft., China and Japan. See also the genus Holboellia.

Stelis—*Orchidaceae.* A large epiphytic genus allied to Pleurothallis which it resembles in habit. Flowers small. In one section the flowers open and close at different times in the day.
   CULTURE: Compost and conditions as for Pleurothallis.
   PROPAGATION: By division of plants when repotting in spring.
   SPECIES CULTIVATED: A selection—*S. barbata*, greenish, red-purple, sepals haired, various, Costa Rica; *ciliaris* (syn. *S. atropurpurea*), deep purple, whitish, sepals fringed, spring, Mexico; *grandiflora*, comparatively large, chocolate-brown, summer, Brazil; *Miersii*, very many, very small, greenish-white, summer, Brazil; *muscifera*, dark purple, summer; *ophioglossoides*, many, small, greenish-purple, arranged one-sidedly, autumn, Brazil, W. Indies.

Stellaria—*Caryophyllaceae.* Hardy perennial with golden foliage; used for carpet bedding.
   CULTURE: Soil, ordinary. Position, as edgings to or bands in summer beds. Plant in May.
   PROPAGATION: By division in autumn.
   SPECIES CULTIVATED: *S. graminea aurea*, pale yellow, 3 in. U.S.A.

Stenandrium—*Acanthaceae.* Stove flowering perennial, grown as a foliage plant in the greenhouse. First introduced late nineteenth century.
   CULTURE: Compost, equal parts peat, leaf-mould, loam and sand. Position, well-drained pots in light stove Sept. to June, sunny frame June to Sept. Pot, March or April. Water moderately in winter, freely other times. Temp., Sept. to March 55° to 65°, March to June 65° to 75°. Prune shoots to within 1 in. of base after flowering. Apply liquid manure occasionally to plants in flower.
   PROPAGATION: By cuttings of young shoots inserted in sandy peat under bell-glass in temp. 75°, March to July.
   SPECIES CULTIVATED: *S. Lindenii*, yellow, leaves dark green above veined with white or yellow-purple beneath, 6 to 12 in., Peru. See also Eranthemum.

Stenanthium—*Liliaceae.* Hardy perennials. First introduced mid-nineteenth century.
   CULTURE: Soil, sandy loam and peat. Position, well-drained, partially shaded beds or borders. Plant, Oct. or March and April.

PROPAGATION: By seeds sown in pans in cool greenhouse or frame during March or April; offsets, detached at planting time.

SPECIES CULTIVATED: *S. gramineum* (syn. *S. angustifolium*), greenish-yellow, June to July, 2 to 3 ft., N. America; *occidentale*, purple, summer, N.W. America; *robustum*, white, summer, 4 to 5 ft., N. America.

Stenocactus—*Cactaceae*. Greenhouse succulent plants, sometimes included in Echinocactus.

CULTURE: As Echinocactus.

PROPAGATION: As Echinocactus.

SPECIES CULTIVATED: *S. coptonogonus*, white and purple, May, 4 in., Mexico; *crispatus*, purple, summer, 8 in., Mexico; *heteracanthus*, greenish-yellow, Mexico; *Lloydii*, pale rose-pink, small, Mexico; *Ochoterenaus*, white to pale rose, Mexico; *Vaupelianus*, pale yellow, Mexico.

Stenoglottis—*Orchidaceae*. A terrestrial genus allied to Orchis. Only three species are known. Roots fascicled, tuberous. Leaves in rosette formation, deciduous. Spike from centre. Flowers rather small, numerous, pleasing.

CULTURE: Compost, chiefly fibrous loam with sand and a little leaf-mould and sphagnum moss. Water freely when in full growth, only occasionally, if at all, when dormant. Winter temp. 50°, can then be placed on a shelf. Summer temp. 60° to 70° or more, with shading.

PROPAGATION: Several crowns are often formed and can be separated and potted in early spring, as soon as growth is seen.

SPECIES CULTIVATED: *S. fimbriata*, ten to thirty, rosy or purplish-red, lip darker spotted, leaves brown spotted, autumn, S. Africa; *longifolia*, twenty-five to a hundred, rosy-mauve, spotted rose-purple, leaves green or brown spotted, height up to 2 ft., autumn, Natal, and vars. *alba*, white, *splendens*, stronger, rose-purple.

Stenotaphrum—*Gramineae*. Greenhouse ornamental-leaved grass. Leaves, narrow, grass-like, striped with yellow. First introduced late nineteenth century.

CULTURE: Compost, equal parts peat, loam, leaf-mould and sand or jadoo fibre. Position, warm and moist part of greenhouse. Pot, March. Water copiously March to Sept., fairly freely Sept. to March. Temp., Sept. to March 50° to 55°, March to Sept. 55° to 65°.

PROPAGATION: By cuttings of shoots or by division of roots in spring.

SPECIES CULTIVATED: *S. secundatum*, ' St. Augustine's Grass ', 1 ft., Carolina, var. *variegatum*, ' Variegated Grass'.

Stephanandra—*Rosaceae*. Hardy deciduous ornamental-leaved shrubs, stems attractive, sepia-tinted in winter. First introduced late nineteenth century.

CULTURE: Soil, moist loam. Position, in groups on the lawn, in the wild garden, or in the shrubbery. Plant in autumn.

PROPAGATION: By suckers or divisions; also by cuttings in summer under bell-glass.

SPECIES CULTIVATED: *S. incisa* (syn. *S. flexuosa*), greenish-white, June, fern-like foliage, 4 to 8 ft., Japan and Korea; *Tanakae*, yellowish-white, June to July, foliage turns orange in autumn, 4 to 6 ft., Japan.

Stephanotis—*Asclepiadaceae*. Stove evergreen twining shrubs. First introduced mid-nineteenth century.

CULTURE: Compost, equal parts good, light, fibrous loam and peat and one part equal proportions leaf-mould, well-decayed manure and coarse silver sand. Position, pots, tubs or beds, well drained, with shoots trained to wire trellis or up rafters of stove. Pot or plant, Feb. or March. Shade from sun. Water copiously March to Oct., moderately afterwards. Syringe daily March to Oct., except when in bloom. Apply stimulants once a week to healthy established plants between May and Sept. Prune straggling shoots moderately closely and thin out weak shoots freely, Jan. or Feb. Temp., March to Oct. 70° to 85°, Oct to March 55° to 65°.

PROPAGATION: By cuttings of the shoots of the previous year's growth inserted singly in 2 in. pots, filled with equal parts sand, peat and loam, placed under bell-glass in temp. 65° **to** 75° in spring.

SPECIES CULTIVATED: *S. floribunda*, ' Clustered Wax-flower ', ' Madagascar Jasmine ', white, fragrant, spring and summer, 10 to 15 ft., Madagascar, and var. *Elvastonii*, a dwarfer and more free-flowering form.

Sternbergia—*Amaryllidaceae*. Hardy bulbous plants. Leaves produced usually late in autumn or early in spring after flowering. First introduced late sixteenth century.

CULTURE: Soil, deep, fairly dry, good ordinary. Position, sunny sheltered border. Plant bulbs, Oct. or Nov., 4 to 6 in. deep and 2 or 3 in. apart. Lift and replant when bulbs show signs of deterioration. May also be grown in pots in cold greenhouse as advised for *Amaryllis Belladonna*.

PROPAGATION: By offsets, removed and planted Oct. or Nov.

SPECIES CULTIVATED: *S. colchiciflora*, produces its leaves in spring and its pale yellow flowers in autumn, Hungary; *Fischeriana*, 6 in. crocus-like flowers in April, Medit. Region; *lutea*, ' Winter Daffodil ', ' Yellow Star Flower ', yellow, autumn, Asia Minor, and var. *major*, flowers much larger than type; *macrantha*, yellow, autumn, S. Europe.

Stevensonia—*Palmae*. Stove palm with once-divided, wedge-shaped, green leaves. First introduced mid-nineteenth century.

CULTURE: Compost, two parts fibrous peat, one part equal proportions charcoal, turfy loam and sand. Position, moist, shady part of stove. Pot, Feb. or March. Syringe freely twice daily Feb. to Oct., once daily afterwards. Water freely at all times. Shade and moist atmosphere essential. Temp., March to Oct. 70° to 85°, Oct. to March 65° to 75°

PROPAGATION: By seeds sown 1 in. deep in peat and loam in small pots in temp. 75° to 85°, spring.

SPECIES CULTIVATED: *S. Borsigiana* (syn. *S. grandiflora*), 20 to 40 ft., Seychelles.

Stevia—*Compositae*. Slightly tender herbaceous perennials. First introduced early nineteenth century.

CULTURE: Soil, sandy loam. Position, well-drained sheltered borders. Protect with litter during the winter. Plant, Oct. or March and April.

PROPAGATION: By division in spring.

SPECIES CULTIVATED: *S. ivaefolia*, deep rose, summer, 1½ to 2 ft., Mexico; *ovata*, white, Aug., 2 ft., Mexico. The plant commonly listed as *S. serrata* is *Piqueria trinervia*.

Stewartia—*Theaceae* (or *Ternstroemiaceae*). Hardy deciduous flowering shrubs, allied to Camellia, with great beauty of flower in July and Aug., and attractive autumn foliage. Neglected in gardens. First introduced late eighteenth century.

CULTURE: Soil, ordinary loam, well drained but moist, and containing a generous addition of peat and leaf-mould or compost. Dry situations not suitable. Position, open sunny borders sheltered on north and east by walls, trees or shrubs. Plant, Oct. to Feb.

PROPAGATION: By cuttings of firm shoots inserted in sandy soil under hand-light in sheltered position outdoors in autumn; layering shoots in Sept. or Oct.; seeds sown ½ in. deep in sandy peat in temp. 75° as soon as ripe.

SPECIES CULTIVATED: *S. koreana*, white, hardy, July and Aug., 15 to 25 ft., Korea; *Malacodendron*, white, purple stamens, July and Aug., 12 to 20 ft., S.E. United States; *monadelpha*, ivory white, purple centred, July, 15 to 30 ft., Japan; *ovata* (syn. *S. pentagyna*), white, orange anthers, July, 10 to 15 ft., S.E. United States, with var. *grandiflora*, flowers larger, up to 4 in. across; *Pseudo-Camellia*, white, cup-shaped, requiring some shelter, July, 20 to 30 ft., Japan; *serrata*, white, flushed red on outside, July and Aug., 20 to 30 ft., Japan; *sinensis*, white, fragrant, decorative peeling bark, July, 20 to 30 ft., Cent. China.

Stifftia—*Compositae*. Stove evergreen shrub. First introduced early nineteenth century.

CULTURE: Compost, two parts fibrous loam, one part leaf-mould and sand. Position, light airy situation in stove or warm greenhouse. Water freely March to Sept., moderately afterwards. Syringe twice daily March to Aug. Feed with liquid manure when established in final pots or when planted out in beds. Temp., March to Sept. 75° to 80°, Sept. to March 55° to 65°.

PROPAGATION: By cuttings of the young growth inserted in sandy soil under bell-glass or in propagating frame, with bottom heat.

SPECIES CULTIVATED: *S. chrysantha*, orange-yellow, Feb. to April, 6 ft., Brazil.

Stigmaphyllon—*Malpighiaceae*. Stove evergreen climbing shrubs. First introduced late eighteenth century.

CULTURE: Compost, equal parts loam, leaf-mould, peat and sand. Position, well-drained pots, with shoots trained up roofs or round trellis. Pot, Feb. or March. Prune away weak growths and shorten strong ones moderately, Jan. Water freely March to Sept., moderately afterwards. Syringe daily in summer. Temp., March to Sept. 70° to 85°, Sept. to March 55° to 65°.

PROPAGATION: By cuttings of firm shoots inserted singly in small pots of sandy soil under bell-glass in temp. 65° to 75°, spring or summer.

SPECIES CULTIVATED: *S. ciliatum*, ' Golden Vine ', yellow, June to Sept., 8 to 10 ft., Brazil; *littorale*, yellow, autumn, 15 to 20 ft., Brazil.

Stinking Cedar, see *Torreya taxifolia*; **-Gladwyn,** see *Iris foetidissima*; **-Hellebore,** see *Helleborus foetidus*.

Stipa (Feather Grass)—*Gramineae*. Hardy perennial flowering grasses. Inflorescence borne in feathery panicles. *S. tenacissima* is grown for fibre for paper making.

CULTURE: Soil, ordinary. Position, dryish sunny borders for *S. pennata* and *S. tenacissima*; pots in unheated greenhouse for *S. elegantissima*. Plant or pot, March or April. Gather inflorescence for drying for winter decoration in July.

PROPAGATION: By seeds sown ⅛ in. deep in shallow boxes or pots filled with light soil placed in temp. of 55° to 65°, Feb. or March, hardening off seedlings and planting outdoors, May or June; or by sowing similar depth in ordinary soil in sunny position outdoors in April; also by division of roots in March or April.

SPECIES CULTIVATED: *S. elegantissima*, 3 ft., Australia; *pennata*, 2 ft., Europe; *tenacissima*, ' Esparto Grass ', 3 ft., Spain and N. Africa.

Stock, see Mathiola; **-Gilliflower,** see *Mathiola incana*; **Virginia-,** see *Malcolmia maritima*.

Stokesia (Stokes's Aster)—*Compositae*. Hardy perennial herb. First introduced mid-eighteenth century.

CULTURE: Soil, ordinary. Position, sunny well-drained borders. Plant, April. Protect in winter by covering with hand-light in cold districts. Plants may be lifted in Sept., placed in pots, and removed to greenhouse for flowering during autumn and winter, afterwards planting outdoors following April.

PROPAGATION: By division of roots, March or April.

SPECIES CULTIVATED: *S. laevis* (syn. *S. cyanea*), blue, Aug., 18 in., N. America, and vars. *alba, caerulea, elegans, lutea* and *rosea*

Stonecrop, see Sedum; **-wort,** see Chara.

Stone-face, see Lithops.

Storax, see Styrax.

Stranvaesia—*Rosaceae*. Hardy evergreen trees and shrubs with handsome foliage, white flowers, and hawthorn-like berries. First introduced early nineteenth century.

CULTURE: Soil, sandy loam. Position, partial shade or full exposure, useful for chalk soils and exposed and maritime localities.

PROPAGATION: By cuttings of half-ripened shoots in sandy soil under bell-glass in gentle bottom heat.

SPECIES CULTIVATED: *S. Davidiana*, white, June, 20 to 30 ft., scarlet berries, W. China, with var. *undulata*, 8 to 12 ft., spreading, coral berries; *salicifolia*, white, June, red fruits, 20 to 30 ft., upright habit, useful evergreen, W. China.

Stratiotes (Water Soldier)—*Hydrocharitaceae.* Hardy aquatic perennial.

CULTURE: Soil, ordinary. Position, shallow lakes or ponds. Plant, March to July, by just dropping plants into the water. They lie beneath the surface, coming to the top to flower about July.

PROPAGATION: By division in spring.

SPECIES CULTIVATED: *S. aloides*, white, July, 1 to 2 ft., Britain.

Strawberry, see Fragaria; **-Tree,** see *Arbutus Unedo.*

Strawflower, see *Helichrysum bracteatum.*

Strelitzia—*Musaceae.* Greenhouse flowering perennials. First introduced mid-eighteenth century.

CULTURE: Compost, two parts loam, one part peat and half a part silver sand. Position, pots or bed in sunny part of warm greenhouse. Pot or plant, Feb. or March. Water copiously April to Sept., moderately Sept. to Nov., keep nearly dry afterwards. No shade required. Temp., March to Oct. 65° to 75°, Oct. to March 55° to 65°.

PROPAGATION: By seeds sown in compost of leaf-mould, peat and loam in temp. of 65° to 75°, spring; offsets or division of old plants, Feb. or March.

SPECIES CULTIVATED: *S. augusta*, white and purple, spring, to 18 ft., S. Africa; *Nicolai*, white and blue, May, to 25 ft., S. Africa; *Reginae*, 'Bird of Paradise Flower', orange and blue, spring, 3 to 4 ft., S. Africa, var. *citrina*, yellow and blue.

Streptocarpus (Cape Primrose)—*Gesneriaceae.* Greenhouse herbaceous perennials. First introduced early nineteenth century.

CULTURE: Compost, two parts loam, one part of equal propotions leaf-mould, decayed manure and silver sand. Position, pots in light greenhouse. Pot, March or April. Temp., 40° to 50° Oct. to April, 55° to 65° April to Oct. Shade from sun. Water freely April to Oct., keep nearly dry afterwards. Apply weak stimulants when plants are in flower. Admit air freely in summer. Shady cold frame good position for young plants during summer.

PROPAGATION: By seeds sown in well-drained pots, pans or boxes with equal parts of finely sifted loam, leaf-mould, peat and sand. Cover the seeds thinly with a sprinkle of fine silver sand. Moisten the soil by holding the pot, pan or box nearly to its rim or edge in tepid water. Place a pane of glass over top of pot, pan or box and put in a temp. 55° to 65°. Transplant seedlings as soon as large enough to handle 1 in. apart in above compost, in pans or pots, and when seedlings touch each other place them singly in 3 in. pots, and ultimately into 5 or 6 in. pots. Seeds sown in Feb. will produce plants for flowering following July; in March or April, following Aug. or Sept.

SPECIES CULTIVATED: *S. caulescens*, pale lilac, summer, 12 in., Trop. Africa; *Dunnii*, rose, summer, 12 to 18 in., S. Africa; *Galpinii*, rosy-violet, Oct., 9 in., Transvaal; *grandis*, blue and white, 1½ to 2 ft., summer, S. Africa; *Holstii*, purple, mauve and white, summer, 18 in., Trop. E. Africa; *kewensis*, rosy purple, summer, 9 in., hybrid; *orientalis*, purple, summer, 12 in., Siam; *polyantha*, lavender, winter, 12 in., S. Africa; *Rexii*, blue, summer, 6 to 12 in., S. Africa; *Sandersii*, pale blue, Sept., 1 to 1½ ft., S. Africa; *Wendlandii*, blue, spring, 1½ to 2½ ft., S. Africa. Practically all the vars. cultivated to-day are hybrids between these species.

Streptosolen—*Solanaceae.* Greenhouse evergreen flowering shrub. First introduced early nineteenth century.

CULTURE: Compost, two parts sandy loam, one part leaf-mould and half a part silver sand. Position, well-drained pots close to glass in light, sunny greenhouse. Pot, Feb. to April. Prune shoots moderately closely after flowering. Water freely April to Oct., moderately afterwards. Apply weak stimulants occasionally during

summer. Shade only from bright sunshine. Temp., March to Oct. 60° to 70°,
Oct. to March 50° to 60°.

PROPAGATION: By cuttings inserted in light, sandy soil under bell-glass in temp.
55° to 65°, spring or summer.

SPECIES CULTIVATED: *S. Jamesonii* (syn. *Browallia Jamesonii*), orange, summer,
4 to 6 ft., Colombia.

Striped Squill, see *Puschkinia scilloides.*

Strobilanthes (Cone-head)—*Acanthaceae.* Stove evergreen flowering shrubs.
First introduced early nineteenth century.

CULTURE: Compost, equal parts loam and leaf-mould with a little silver sand.
Pot, March or April. Position, well-drained pots in moist, light part of heated
greenhouse. Temp., March to Sept. 75° to 85°, Sept. to March 60° to 65°. Prune
shoots closely, Feb. Water moderately Sept. to April, freely other times. Use
syringe frequently during the growing season. Apply liquid manure twice a
week to plants in flower.

PROPAGATION: By cuttings of moderately firm shoots, 2 to 3 in. long, inserted in
light, sandy compost under bell-glass in temp. 80°, Feb. to April.

SPECIES CULTIVATED: *S. anisophyllus* (syn. *Goldfussia anisophylla*), lavender blue,
Oct. to March, 1 to 3 ft., Himalaya; *Dyerianus*, violet and blue , autumn, 3 ft.,
Burma; *glomeratus*, purple, autumn, 2 to 4 ft., Himalaya, Burma; *isophyllus* (syn.
Goldfussia isophylla), blue and white, winter, 2 to 3 ft., India. See also *Ruellia.*

Stropholirion, see Brodiaea.

Stuartia, see Stewartia.

Studflower, see Helonias.

Stylidium—*Stylidiaceae.* Evergreen perennial plants.

CULTURE: Loam, leaf-mould and sand in equal proportions and some sharp
grit. Inclined to be spring tender and best grown in alpine house or cold frame.

PROPAGATION: By seeds sown in spring in compost as above.

SPECIES CULTIVATED: *S. caespitosum,* pink and white, June, 12 in., Australasia;
graminifolium, pink, June to July, 12 in., Australasia.

Stylophorum—*Papaveraceae.* Hardy perennial herb. First introduced mid-nineteenth century.

CULTURE: Soil, ordinary moist. Position, partially shaded beds or borders.
Plant, March or April.

PROPAGATION: By seeds sown ⅛ in. deep in ordinary soil in sunny position outdoors, March or April; division of roots, March.

SPECIES CULTIVATED: *S. diphyllum,* 'Celandine Poppy', yellow, June, 12 to
18 in., N.W. America.

Styrax (Storax, Snowbell)—*Styracaceae.* Hardy and slightly tender deciduous
flowering shrubs, flowers generally pendent, resembling snowdrops. First introduced late sixteenth century.

CULTURE: Soil, light peaty. Position, sheltered sunny borders or shrubberies,
or against south walls. Plant, Oct. to Feb.

PROPAGATION: By seeds sown in peaty soil in gentle heat in March; cuttings
of half-ripened wood in gentle heat in July; layers in spring or autumn.

SPECIES CULTIVATED: *S. americana,* white, June to July, 3 to 8 ft., S.E. United
States; *dasyantha*, white, July, 15 to 25 ft., requiring protection, Cent. China;
Hemslyana, white, June, 15 to 25 ft., Cent. and W. China; *japonica*, white,
fragrant, hardy, 12 to 25 ft., Japan and Korea; *Obassia*, white, fragrant, in
clusters, June, requiring shelter and some shade, 20 to 30 ft., Japan; *officinalis*,
white, June, fragrant, in clusters, for warmer localities only, 10 to 12 ft., Greece
and Asia Minor; *Wilsonii*, white, June, dense growth, flowering when very small,
4 to 8 ft., W. China.

Succisella—*Dipsaceae.* Hardy herbaceous perennial, closely related to Scabiosa·
CULTURE: Soil, ordinary. Position, sunny.
PROPAGATION: By seed; division.
SPECIES CULTIVATED: *S. inflexa* (syns. *Scabiosa inflexa*, *S. australis*), pale lilac,
summer, 1 to 3 ft., Cent. Europe; *Petteri* (syn. *Scabiosa Petteri*), pale lilac, summer,
1 to 3 ft., Dalmatia.

Sugar Cane, see *Saccharum officinarum*; -**Maple,** see *Acer saccharum.*

Sumach, see Rhus.

Summer Cypress, see *Kochia scoparia*; -**Savory,** see *Calamintha hortensis*;
-**Snowflake,** see *Leucojum aestivum.*

Sundew, see Drosera.

Sun Drops, see *Oenothera fruticosa*; -**flower,** see Helianthus; -**plant,** see
Portulaca grandiflora; -**rose,** see Helianthemum.

Supple Jack, see *Berchemia scandens.*

Swainsona (Darling River Pea)—*Leguminosae.* Greenhouse evergreen flowering
shrubs. First introduced early nineteenth century.
CULTURE: Compost, two parts fibrous loam, one part peat and half a part silver
sand. Position, well-drained pots in light, sunny greenhouse. Pot, Feb. or
March. Water freely March to Oct., moderately afterwards. Apply weak
stimulants occasionally in summer. Remove to cold frame or pit, June; replace
in greenhouse, Sept. Temp., Sept. to March 35° to 45°, March to June 55° to 65°.
PROPAGATION: By seeds soaked for about an hour in tepid water, then sown
⅛ in. deep in light soil in temp. 55° to 65°, March or April; cuttings of young
shoots, 2 to 3 in. long, inserted in silver sand under bell-glass in cool, shady part
of greenhouse in summer.
SPECIES CULTIVATED: *S. galegifolia*, purplish-red, summer, 3 to 4 ft., Australia,
var. *coronillaefolia*, violet.

Swan River Daisy, see *Brachycome iberidifolia*; -**Orchid,** see Cynoches; -**River
Everlasting,** see *Helipterum Manglesii.*

Swamp Bay, see *Magnolia glauca*; -**Cypress,** see *Taxodium distichum*; -**Honeysuckle,** see *Rhododendron viscosum*; -**Pink,** see *Helonias bullata.*

Swede, see *Brassica Napobrassica.*

Sweet Alyssum, see *Lobularia maritima*; -**Bay,** see Laurus; -**brier,** see *Rosa
Eglanteria*; -**Corn,** see *Zea Mays* var. *rugosa*; -**Cicely,** see *Myrrhis odorata*;
-**Fern,** see *Comptonia peregrina*; -**Flag,** see *Acorus Calamus*; -**Gale,** see *Myrica
Gale*; -**Gum Tree,** see *Liquidambar Styraciflua*; -**Maudlin,** see *Achillea Ageratum*;
-**Pea,** see *Lathyrus odoratus*; -**Pepper Bush,** see *Clethra alnifolia*; -**Potato,** see
Ipomoea Batatas; -**Scabious,** see *Scabiosa atropurpurea*; -**sop,** see *Annona squamosa*;
-**Sultan,** see *Centaurea moschata*; -**Vernal Grass,** see *Anthroxanthum odoratum*;
-**William,** see *Dianthus barbatus.*

Swertia (Marsh Fel-wort)—*Gentianaceae.* Hardy perennial herb.
CULTURE: Soil, equal parts peat and leaf-mould. Position, moist rockeries or
damp places. Plant, March to April. Water copiously in dry weather.
PROPAGATION: By seeds sown in well-drained pans filled with moist peat, placed
in shady, cold frame, March or April, transplanting seedlings outdoors in June;
division of roots in March.
SPECIES CULTIVATED: *S. perennis*, blue, greyish-purple and black, 1 ft., N.
Europe.

Swietenia (Mahogany)—*Meliaceae.* Stove evergreen tree with dark red wood
which furnishes the mahogany of commerce; of economic interest only. First
introduced early eighteenth century.
CULTURE: Soil, sandy loam. Position, well-drained borders in heated green·

house. Temp., March to Sept. 70° to 80°, Sept. to March 55° to 60°. Water freely during growing season, moderately at other times. Plant, April.

PROPAGATION: By cuttings of ripened shoots under bell-glass in temp. 75°.

SPECIES CULTIVATED: *S. Mahagoni*, to 75 ft., W. Indies and S. Florida.

Switch Grass, see *Panicum virgatum.*

Sword Lily, see Gladiolus.

Sycamore, see *Acer Pseudo-Platanus.*

Sycopsis—*Hamamelidaceae.* Hardy evergreen small winter-flowering tree, related to Wych-Hazel. First introduced early twentieth century.

CULTURE: Soil, ordinary. Position, shrubberies, or as isolated specimens.

PROPAGATION: By cuttings of half-ripened wood placed in gentle bottom heat, July.

SPECIES CULTIVATED: *S. sinensis,* red bracts, yellow stamens, Feb., 15 to 25 ft. Cent. and W. China.

Sydney Golden Wattle, see *Acacia longifolia.*

Symphoricarpos—*Caprifoliaceae.* Hardy deciduous flowering and berry-bearing shrubs. Flowers much sought after by bees. Frequently seen not at its best, existing in competition with roots of overgrowing trees. First introduced early eighteenth century.

CULTURE: Soil, ordinary. Position, sunny or shady borders, copses or woodlands. Plant, Oct. to Feb. Prune, Oct. to Feb., simply thinning out old or decayed wood.

PROPAGATION: By cuttings, 6 to 8 in. long, of firm wood inserted in ordinary soil in shady position outdoors, Oct. to Feb.; suckers removed and planted, Oct. to Feb.

SPECIES CULTIVATED: *S. albus* (syn. *S. racemosus*), ' Snowberry ', pink or rose, July, berries white, 8 to 10 ft., N. America, with var. *laevigatus,* larger berries, freely borne, the best garden form; *occidentalis,* ' Wolfberry ', pink, July, berries white, 4 to 6 ft., N. America; *orbiculatus,* white, Aug. to Sept., berries purplish-red, 3 to 7 ft., Eastern U.S.A.

Symphyandra (Pendulous Bell-flower)—*Campanulaceae.* Hardy perennials resembling Campanulas. First introduced early nineteenth century.

CULTURE: Soil, ordinary rich. Position, sunny well-drained borders or rockeries. Plant, Oct., March or April.

PROPAGATION: By seeds sown $\frac{1}{16}$ in. deep in ordinary light, sandy soil outdoors, April to May; cuttings of young shoots inserted in sandy soil in cold frame, March or April; division of roots, March.

SPECIES CULTIVATED: *S. Hofmannii,* white, summer, 1 to 2 ft., Bosnia; *pendula,* straw yellow, summer, 9 to 12 in., Caucasus; *Wanneri,* blue, summer, 6 in., S.E. Europe.

Symphytum (Comfrey)—*Boraginaceae.* Hardy herbaceous perennials. The common comfrey, *S. officinale,* is not suitable for garden culture. First introduced late eighteenth century.

CULTURE: Soil, ordinary. Position, sunny or shady, moist borders or margins of streams. Plant, Oct. to Nov. or March to April. Lift, divide and replant every three or four years.

PROPAGATION: By division of roots in spring.

SPECIES CULTIVATED: *S. asperum* (syn. *S. asperrimum*), ' Prickly Comfrey ', rose changing to blue, 3 to 6 ft., Caucasus; *caucasicum,* blue, 1 to 2 ft., Caucasus; *grandiflorum,* yellowish-white, 9 to 18 in., Caucasus; *Leonhardtianum,* pale yellow, summer, 6 to 12 in., Cent. Europe; *officinale,* ' Common Comfrey ', white or dull purple, 2 to 4 ft., Europe, including Britain, vars. *coccineum* (syn. *S. bohemicum*), crimson, *luteo-marginatum,* leaves bordered with yellow; *orientale,* creamy white, 2 ft., Turkey; *peregrinum,* rose changing to blue, 3 to 6 ft., Caucasus; *tauricum,* yellowish-white, 1 to 1½ ft., Crimea, S. Europe, Russia; *tuberosum*, yellowish-white, summer, 8 to 20 in., S.W. Europe, naturalised in Britain.

Synthyris—*Scrophulariaceae*. Hardy herbaceous perennial. First introduced late nineteenth century.

CULTURE: Soil, loamy. Position, partially shady beds or rock gardens. Plant, Oct. to Nov. or March to April. Water freely during summer months.

PROPAGATION: By division in spring; seeds sown in sandy soil in pans in cold greenhouse or frame during March and April.

SPECIES CULTIVATED: *S. laciniata*, blue, early summer, 6 in., N. America; *pinnatifida*, purple, summer, 6 to 9 in., N. America; *reniformis*, blue, early summer, 6 in., Western N. America; *rotundifolia*, blue, summer, 6 in., N. America, and var. *alba*, white.

Syringa (Lilac)—*Oleaceae*. Hardy deciduous flowering shrubs. The name Syringa is frequently erroneously applied to the Mock Orange, correctly named Philadelphus. First introduced late sixteenth century.

CULTURE: Soil, ordinary good. Position, sunny borders or shrubberies. Plant, Oct. to Feb. Prune moderately after flowering (June), removing all shoots with spent flowers, and thinning out the weaker shoots. Allow no suckers to grow from roots. The special coloured named vars. of the Common Lilac require feeding. Give annual dressing of bonemeal, 2 oz. per square yard in spring, or on lighter soils a generous mulch of manure or compost.

POT CULTURE FOR FORCING: Compost, two parts good sandy loam, one part leaf-mould and little sand. Pot, Oct. or Nov. Place plants after potting in sheltered corner outdoors, protecting pots from frost with litter until required for forcing. Transfer to temp. of 55°, Nov. to Feb. Syringe daily. Water moderately. Directly buds burst place in temp. of 60° to 65°; when expanded replace in temp. of 55°. Prune shoots that have flowered to within 2 in. of base directly after blooming. Keep plants in heat until May, then gradually harden and plant outdoors. Plants must not be forced two years in succession. Lilacs may be grown in cold greenhouse for flowering in April and May. Place in greenhouse in Nov.

PROPAGATION: Named vars. by layering in spring or autumn; grafting, either on common lilac or on privet is sometimes practised, from such plants suckers will be either common lilac or privet. Suckers from layered plants will resemble the parent. Cuttings of all types, of half-ripened wood in cold frame, Aug. to Sept. Removal of rooted suckers of common lilac or of species.

SPECIES CULTIVATED: *S. amuriensis*, ' Amur Lilac ', yellowish-white, June to July, to 12 ft., Manchuria, China, var. *japonica*; *chinensis*, ' Rouen Lilac ', mauve, May, 10 to 15 ft., elegant habit, hybrid, with vars. *alba*, white, *duplex*, double, *rubra*, deep rose, and *metensis*, slate blue; *emodi*, ' Himalayan Lilac ', white or purple tinted, June, 10 to 15 ft., Himalaya; *Josikaea*, ' Hungarian Lilac ', deep lilac, June, 10 to 12 ft., Hungary; *Julianae*, violet, May to June, 4 to 6 ft., very fragrant, W. China; *Komarowii*, purplish pink, 10 to 15 ft., W. China; *microphylla*, pale lilac, June, 3 to 5 ft., N. China; *pekinensis*, creamy white, June, slender habit, 15 to 25 ft., N. China, with var. *pendula*, graceful weeping form; *persica*, ' Persian Lilac ', mauve, May, fragrant, good miniature shrub for small gardens, 4 to 6 ft., Afghanistan, with vars. *alba*, white, and *laciniata*, cut-leaved; *reflexa*, rose pink, pendulous flower spikes, June, 10 to 12 ft., Cent. China; *Sweginzowii*, reddish to pale lilac, May to June, 6 to 9 ft., N.W. China; *tomentella*, pink, yellow anthers, May to June, 6 to 8 ft., W. China; *velutina*, lavender, June, 6 to 8 ft., N. China, Korea; *villosa*, lilac pink, early June, vigorous and free-flowering, N. China, with var. *alba*, flesh pink buds changing to white; *vulgaris*, ' Common Lilac ', very fragrant, May, 10 to 20 ft., E. Europe; *Wolfii*, lilac pink, May to June, large spikes and foliage, 10 to 15 ft., Manchuria and Korea; *yunnanensis*, ' Yunnan Lilac ', purplish-pink fading to white, June, 10 to 12 ft., Yunnan, with var. *rosea*, clear rose-pink.

Tabernaemontana—*Apocynaceae*. Stove evergreen flowering shrubs. First introduced mid-eighteenth century.

CULTURE: Compost, two parts sandy loam, one part fibrous peat, half a part silver sand. Position, well-drained pots in light stove. Pot, Feb. to April. Prune straggling shoots moderately closely immediately after flowering. Water freely March to Oct., moderately afterwards. Syringe daily March and until flowers appear. Temp., March to Sept. 70° to 80°, Sept. to March 65° to 75°.

PROPAGATION: By cuttings of ripe shoots, 2 to 3 in. long, inserted in small pots filled with sand under bell-glass in temp. 65° to 75° in Feb.

SPECIES CULTIVATED: *T. Barteri*, white, summer, 6 ft., Trop. Africa; *citrifolia*, yellow, summer, to 15 ft., W. Indies, Mexico; *grandiflora*, yellow, summer, to 6 ft., Venezuela and Guiana; *recurva* (syn. *T. gratissima*), yellowish-white, June, 6 ft., Chittagong and Tenasserim.

Tacca—*Taccaceae.* Stove perennial herbs. First introduced late eighteenth century.

CULTURE: Compost, equal parts loam, peat and sand. Position, well-drained pots in warm greenhouse. Water freely during summer months, very little during winter. Temp., March to Sept. 75° to 85°, Sept. to March 60° to 65°. Pot, Feb. or March.

SPECIES CULTIVATED: *T. cristata* (syn. *Ataccia cristata*), brownish-purple, summer, purplish-green foliage, 2 ft., Malaya; *laevis*, greenish-violet, July, 1 ft., India; *pinnatifida*, green and purple, June, 3 to 4 ft., Trop. Asia, Africa and Australia.

Tagetes (Marigold)—*Compositae.* Half-hardy annuals. First introduced late sixteenth century.

CULTURE: Soil, ordinary, well enriched with decayed manure. Position, sunny borders for African Marigold; sunny beds or borders for French and Mexican Marigolds; edgings to beds or borders for *T. signata pumila*. Sow seeds $\frac{1}{16}$ in. deep in light soil in temp. 55° in March, or in unheated greenhouse in April. Transplant seedlings when three leaves form 3 in. apart in light soil in shallow boxes, or in bed of rich soil in cold frame, gradually harden off in May, and plant out in June. Plant African Marigolds in groups of three or six, or 16 in. apart in rows; French Marigolds singly, or in groups in borders, or 15 in. apart in rows; Dwarf Marigolds (*T. signata pumila*) 6 in. apart in rows. African Marigold for exhibition to carry four blooms only. Thin shoots to four on each plant, each carrying one bloom. Water freely in dry weather. Apply stimulants when growing.

SPECIES CULTIVATED: *T. erecta*, ' African Marigold ', yellow, summer, 2 to 3 ft., Mexico; *lucida*, ' Mexican Marigold ', yellow, summer, 1 ft., Mexico; *patula*, ' French Marigold ', orange, red, and brown, summer, 1 to 1½ ft., Mexico, and var. *nana*; *signata*, yellow, summer, 1 to 1½ ft., Mexico, and var. *pumila*.

Talinum—*Portulacaceae.* Perennial, more or less fleshy herbs, sometimes woody at base.

CULTURE: As for Lewisia, to which they are nearly related.

PROPAGATION: By seeds sown in early spring.

SPECIES CULTIVATED: *T. okanaganense*, off-white, early summer, ¼ in., N. America; *spinescens*, pink, summer, 9 in., N. America.

Tamarind, see *Tamarindus indica.*

Tamarindus—*Leguminosae* (or *Caesalpiniaceae*). Stove evergreen flowering tree. First introduced mid-seventeenth century.

CULTURE: Compost, two parts fibrous loam, one part sand. Position, large well-drained pots or tubs in lofty stove. Pot or plant, Feb. Water copiously April to Oct., moderately afterwards. Syringe daily April to Sept. Shade from sun. Temp., April to Oct. 70° to 85°, Oct. to April 60° to 70°.

PROPAGATION: By seeds steeped for a few hours in tepid water and then sown ¼ in. deep in light soil in temp. 75° to 85° in spring; cuttings of shoots inserted singly in small well-drained pots placed under bell-glass in temp. 65° to 75°, March to Aug.

SPECIES CULTIVATED: *T. indica*, ' Tamarind ', pale yellow, summer, 40 to 80 ft., Tropics.

Tamarix (Tamarisk)—*Tamaricaceae*. Hardy evergreen and deciduous flowering shrubs.

CULTURE: Soil, ordinary or sandy. Position, shrubberies or hedges in seaside gardens; sunny banks or shrubberies in inland gardens south of the Trent. Plant, Sept. to April. Tamarisk makes an excellent seaside hedge interplanted with *Atriplex Halimus*; make a double row, planting 1 ft. apart each way. Prune *T. parviflora, juniperina* and *tetrandra* immediately after flowering in June, removing older wood. Other kinds should be pruned hard in winter or early spring, either to the ground or to a framework of older wood.

PROPAGATION: By cuttings of shoots, 4 to 6 in. long, inserted in sandy soil out of doors, Oct. to Nov. Hedges may be formed by planting stems up to a yard in length which will root readily.

EVERGREEN SPECIES CULTIVATED: *T. anglica*, ' Common Tamarisk ', white and pink, Aug. to Oct., 3 to 10 ft., Europe (Br.); *gallica*, pink, late summer and autumn, 10 to 30 ft., S. Europe.

DECIDUOUS SPECIES CULTIVATED: *T. hispida*, pink, glaucous foliage, Aug. to Sept., 3 to 4 ft., Caspian rather tender; *juniperina* (syn. *T. chinensis*), bright pink, May, 10 to 15 ft., N. China and Japan; *pentandra* (syn. *T. hispida aestivalis*), rosy pink, July to Aug., 12 to 15 ft., S.E. Europe and Asia Minor; *tetrandra*, pink, May, 10 to 15 ft., Medit. Region. (*Note*: This shrub is listed sometimes under such names as *africana, algerensis* and *caspica*.) See also Myricaria.

Tanacetum (Tansy)—*Compositae*. Hardy herbaceous perennials.

CULTURE: Soil, ordinary. Position, sunny beds for *T. vulgare*; open rock gardens for *T. argenteum* and *Herderi*. Plant *T. vulgare* 12 in. apart in rows 18 in. asunder in March or Oct.; remove flower stems as they form; replant every three or four years; leaves aromatic, used for flavouring puddings, etc., and for garnishing.

PROPAGATION: By seeds sown outdoors in spring; division of the roots in Oct. or March.

SPECIES CULTIVATED: *T. argenteum*, yellow, summer, silvery foliage, 9 in., Asia Minor; *Herderi*, yellow, summer, silvery-white foliage, 9 in., Turkistan; *vulgare*, yellow, summer, 3 ft., Britain, var. *crispum*, finer, more crisped leaves.

Tanakaea (Japanese Foam Flower)—*Saxifragaceae*. Dwarf evergreen perennial with leathery, fringed, rich green leaves.

CULTURE: Soil, light, containing plenty of humus. Position, woodland or partially shaded cool border. Plant in colonies in spring.

PROPAGATION: By division of tufts in March.

SPECIES CULTIVATED: *T. radicans*, white, April to June, 6 to 9 in., Japan.

Tansy, see Tanacetum.

Tape Grass, see Vallisneria.

Tapioca, see *Manihot esculenta*.

Taraxacum (Dandelion)—*Compositae*. Hardy perennial herb; a weed in most parts of the world and cultivated solely for its blanched leaves for saladings.

CULTURE: Soil, ordinary deep, free from recent manure. Position, sunny. Sow seeds, 1 in. deep, in drills 12 in. apart in April. Thin seedlings to 6 in. apart in rows in May. Remove flower stems directly they form. Lift roots in Nov. and store in sand in cool place. Plant roots almost touching in boxes or large pots in ordinary soil. Cover pots, etc., to exclude light. Place in warm greenhouse between Nov. and April. Keep soil moist and cut leaves when 3 to 6 in. long for salads. Destroy roots afterwards. Make a fresh sowing annually.

SPECIES CULTIVATED: *T. officinale*, yellow, spring, Britain.

Taro, see *Colocasia esculenta*.

Tarragon, see *Artemisia Dracunculus*.

Taxodium (Deciduous Cypress, Swamp Cypress)—*Pinaceae* (or *Taxodiaceae*). Hardy deciduous coniferous trees. Leaves, feather-shaped, deciduous, bright green, changing to dull red in autumn. Habit, pyramidal when young; broad, cedar-like when full grown. First introduced early seventeenth century.

CULTURE: Soil, moist loam. Position, margins of ponds and rivers or in damp places; growth less satisfactory in dry places. Plant, Oct. to Feb.

PROPAGATION: By seeds sown ⅛ in. deep in pans of light soil in cold frame in April, transplanting seedlings singly into small pots following spring, and planting outdoors the year after; cuttings of ripened shoots in shady, cold frame and sandy soil in Sept. or Oct., and kept moist; layering branches in spring.

SPECIES CULTIVATED: *T. distichum*, 70 to 100 ft., S.W. States, and var. *pendens*, branches drooping.

Taxus (Yew)—*Taxaceae*. Hardy evergreen trees. Timber used for cabinet making, but too slow in growth to cultivate for that purpose. Leaves poisonous to cattle. Estimated average age, 1000 to 2000 years.

CULTURE: Soil, good ordinary loam is the most suitable, although the yew will grow in any soil, including chalk, but cultivation should be deep prior to planting. Position, sunny or shady shrubberies for common kinds; sunny shrubberies, lawns or borders for variegated and Irish yews. Plant, Sept. to Nov., April to May. Prune, April or May.

POT CULTURE: Most suitable kind is *T. baccata elegantissima*. Pot, Oct. or Nov. Compost, two parts good ordinary soil, one part leaf-mould. Water moderately Nov. to April, freely afterwards. Keep in cold greenhouse, balcony or corridor, Oct. to May; outdoors afterwards, pots plunged to rims in cinders or soil.

HEDGE CULTURE: Suitable kinds—Common, gold and silver striped, upright English and Irish yews. Position, sunny. Soil, good moist ordinary, previously trenched two spits deep and 3 ft. wide. Plant, Oct., Nov., March or April. Distance for planting: 18 in. for trees 2 ft. high, 2 ft. for trees 3 ft. high, and 3 ft. for trees 3 to 5 ft. high. Clipping is best done twice yearly, in May and July. Do not carry out this work before the former or after the latter month. The common yew, or its golden form, is the best-known subject for training and clipping for topiary work. Previous instructions for trimming apply for these specimens also.

PROPAGATION: By seeds sown 1 in. deep in light soil outdoors in March, or ¼ in. deep in pans or boxes of light soil in cold frame or greenhouse in March, transplanting seedlings in nursery bed when large enough to handle; cuttings of shoots inserted in sandy soil under hand-light or in cold frame in Sept.; grafting variegated kinds on common yew in March; layering in Sept.

SPECIES CULTIVATED: *T. baccata*, 'Common Yew', 50 ft., Europe, N. Asia, numerous vars. including *aurea*, yellow leaves, *elegantissima*, compact, *erecta*, upright, bushy, *lutea*, yellow fruit, *stricta*, 'Irish Yew', *procumbens*, prostrate; *canadensis*, 'Canadian Yew', to 6 ft., Canada; *cuspidata*, 'Japanese Yew', to 50 ft., Japan, var. *nana*, shrubby.

Tea, see *Thea sinensis*; **-berry,** see *Gaultheria procumbens*.

Teak, see *Tectona grandis*.

Tecoma, see Bignonia, Campsis, Pandorea and Tecomaria.

Tecomaria—*Bignoniaceae*. Greenhouse evergreen shrubs, partly climbing, with yellow to scarlet, curved funnel-shaped flowers in dense terminal racemes or panicles.

CULTURE: As Pandorea.

PROPAGATION: By seed; cuttings.

SPECIES CULTIVATED: *T. capensis* (syn. *Tecoma capensis*), 'Cape Honeysuckle', orange-red or scarlet, summer, 10 to 20 ft., S. Africa.

Tecophilaea—*Haemodoraceae*. Half-hardy bulbous plant. First introduced mid-nineteenth century.

CULTURE: Soil, two parts sandy loam, one part decayed cow manure. Position, well-drained bed in cold frame or at foot of south wall, or pots in cool greenhouse. Plant bulbs 3 in. deep and 6 in. apart, Aug. to Nov. Pot, singly in 3½ in. pots or three in a 5 in. pot and 2 in. deep. Cover pot with ashes or fibre refuse till growth begins. Water moderately; keep dry after foliage turns yellow until growth recommences. No artificial heat required. Admit air freely to plants in pots and frames after Feb.

PROPAGATION: By offsets, removed at potting time.

SPECIES CULTIVATED: *T. cyanocrocus*, ' Chilean Crocus ', blue and white, fragrant, spring, 6 in., Chile, and var. *Leichtlinii*, blue.

Tectona—*Verbenaceae*. Stove tree, of economic interest only, furnishing the teak of commerce. First introduced mid-eighteenth century.

CULTURE: Soil, loam, leaf-mould and sand. Position, large well-drained tubs or borders in heated greenhouse. Temp., March to Sept. 75° to 85°, Sept. to March 60° to 65°. Plant or pot, March or April.

PROPAGATION: By seeds sown in sandy soil in temp. 85° during Feb. or March.

SPECIES CULTIVATED: *T. grandis*, ' Teak ', to 150 ft., India and Malaya.

Telanthera, see Alternanthera.

Telegraph Plant, see *Desmodium motorium*.

Tellima—*Saxifragaceae*. Hardy herbaceous hairy perennial. First introduced early nineteenth century.

CULTURE: Soil, ordinary. Position, open or partially shady borders or wild gardens. Plant, autumn or spring.

PROPAGATION: By division in spring.

SPECIES CULTIVATED: *T. grandiflora*, greenish, April to June, 2 ft., N. America.

Telopea—*Proteaceae*. Greenhouse evergreen shrub. First introduced late eighteenth century.

CULTURE: Soil, sandy loam. Position, well-drained pots or tubs in greenhouse. Water very freely during summer, sparingly in winter. Dryish atmosphere essential at all seasons. Temp., March to Sept. 55° to 65°, Sept. to March 45° to 55°.

PROPAGATION: By cuttings of young shoots inserted in sandy soil under bell-glass in gentle bottom heat during May or June.

SPECIES CULTIVATED: *T. speciosissima*, ' Waratah ', red, June, 8 ft., Australia.

Ternstroemia—*Theaceae* (or *Ternstroemiaceae*). Slightly tender evergreen flowering shrub with leathery shiny leaves, bronze-tinted when young.

CULTURE: Soil, ordinary, well drained. Position, sheltered shrubberies in southern counties or borders in conservatories and unheated greenhouses. Plant, Sept. to Oct. or April to May.

PROPAGATION: By cuttings of young shoots inserted in sandy soil under bell-glass in gentle bottom heat during May, June or July.

SPECIES CULTIVATED: *T. japonica*, yellowish-white, fragrant, July to Aug., to 20 ft., Japan.

Testudinaria—*Dioscoreaceae*. Greenhouse deciduous climber. *T. elephantipes* has a remarkable tuberous root, frequently as much as 3 ft. in diameter; it is sometimes cooked and eaten by natives. First introduced mid-eighteenth century.

CULTURE: Compost, equal parts fibrous loam, turfy peat and sand. Position, well drained in sunny greenhouse. Pot, Feb. or March. Water moderately April to Sept., keep nearly dry afterwards. No shade required. Temp., March to Sept. 55° to 65°, Sept. to March 40° to 50°.

PROPAGATION: By cuttings of firm side shoots inserted in sandy loam under bell-glass in temp. 45° to 55° in spring, or cuttings of young shoots when 1 to 2 in. long inserted in sandy loam under bell-glass in similar temp., spring or summer.

SPECIES CULTIVATED: *T. elephantipes*, ' Hottentot Bread ', ' Elephant's Foot ', yellow, summer, 5 to 10 ft., S. Africa.

Tetracentron—*Magnoliaceae*. Rare hardy deciduous ornamental tree with no beauty of flower but has elegant foliage. First introduced early twentieth century.

CULTURE: Soil, well-drained loam. Position, as specimens on lawns or in similar open places. Requires shelter from early spring frosts. Plant, Nov. to Feb.

PROPAGATION: By seeds sown ¼ in. deep in Feb. or March in well-drained pans of sandy soil in a cold frame or greenhouse; layering in spring.

SPECIES CULTIVATED: *T. sinense*, 50 to 90 ft., young growths purple-tinted, W. China.

Tetragonia—*Aizoaceae.* Annual with leaves and young shoots succulent, used as a summer vegetable as a substitute for spinach. First introduced mid-eighteenth century.

CULTURE: Site, trenched, well manured, porous soil in sunny position. Sow in boxes in warm greenhouse for early crops or outside end April. Thin to 1 ft.

SPECIES CULTIVATED: *T. expansa*, ‘ New Zealand Spinach ’, leaves 5 in., Japan, Australia, New Zealand, S. America.

Tetramicra, see *Leptotes bicolor.*

Tetrapanax (Rice-paper Tree)—*Araliaceae.* Evergreen greenhouse or half-hardy shrub; in Orient used for making rice-paper. First introduced mid-nineteenth century.

CULTURE: Compost, fibrous loam, peat, leaf-mould and sand. Pot, Feb. to April. Water freely March to Oct., moderately at other times. Temp., March to Sept. 60° to 70°, Sept. to March 50° to 60°.

PROPAGATION: By cuttings or portions of the stem in sand in propagating case in April.

SPECIES CULTIVATED: *T. papyriferum* (syns. *Aralia papyrifera, Fatsia papyrifera*), greenish shrub or small tree, Formosa. A useful subject for sub-tropical garden during summer.

Tetratheca—*Tremandraceae.* Greenhouse evergreen flowering shrubs and half-hardy perennial plants. First introduced early nineteenth century.

CULTURE OF GREENHOUSE SPECIES: Compost, two parts fibrous peat, one part turfy loam, one part equal amounts charcoal, broken pots and silver sand. Position, well-drained pots in light airy greenhouse. Pot, Feb. or March. Water moderately at all seasons; rainwater only to be used. Shade from sun June to Sept. Temp., Oct. to April 40° to 50°, April to Oct. 50° to 65°.

CULTURE OF HALF-HARDY SPECIES: Soil, rich loam, well drained. Position, warm, sunny and sheltered.

PROPAGATION: By cuttings of side shoots inserted in sand under bell-glass in shade in temp. 55° to 65° summer, for greenhouse species; seeds sown in spring for others.

GREENHOUSE SPECIES CULTIVATED: *T. ericifolia*, rose, summer, 1 ft., Australia; *thymifolia*, purple, July to Aug., 1 ft., Australia.

HALF-HARDY SPECIES CULTIVATED: *T. ciliata*, pink, summer, Tasmania; *glandulosa*, purple, 12 to 18 in., summer, Tasmania.

Teucrium (Germander)—*Labiatae.* Hardy perennial plants and slightly tender evergreen shrub.

CULTURE OF PERENNIAL SPECIES: Soil, ordinary. Position, sunny borders, sunny, dryish rockeries or old walls for *T. Marum*, etc. Plant, March or April.

CULTURE OF SHRUBBY SPECIES: Soil, light, well drained. Position, at base of sunny wall in sheltered gardens. Plant, Sept. to Oct. or April to May.

PROPAGATION: Shrubby species by cuttings of half-ripened shoots inserted in sandy soil in shaded frame in Aug.; perennial species by division in March or April.

PERENNIAL SPECIES CULTIVATED: *T. aureum*, yellow, July, 4 to 6 in., Medit. Region; *Chamaedrys*, rosy purple, July to Sept., 1 ft., Europe; *Marum*, ‘ Cat Thyme ’, purple, summer, 1 ft., S. Europe; *pyrenaicum*, cream and lilac, June to July, 1 to 2 in., Pyrenees; *Scordonia*, yellow, summer, to 2 ft., Britain, var. *variegatum*, variegated foliage.

SHRUBBY SPECIES CULTIVATED: *T. fruticans*, blue, summer and autumn, 7 to 8 ft., stems and undersides of leaves white, S. Europe.

Thalia—*Marantaceae.* Half-hardy aquatic perennials. First introduced late eighteenth century.
CULTURE: Soil, peaty loam. Position, tub in shallow pond. Plant in March. Requres a warm, sheltered spot. Place tubs in ponds in open from May to Sept. Remove tubs to frost-proof greenhouse, Sept. to May.
PROPAGATION: By division in spring.
HARDY SPECIES CULTIVATED: *T. dealbata*, purple, ornamental foliage, July, 6 ft., S. California.

Thalictrum (Meadow Rue)—*Ranunculaceae.* Hardy herbaceous perennials with foliage similar to Maidenhair Fern.
CULTURE: Soil, ordinary. Position, sunny borders for tall species, sunny rockeries for dwarf species. Plant, Oct. to March. Top-dress annually in Feb. or March with decayed manure. Lift, divide and replant only when absolutely necessary.
PROPAGATION: By division of roots in March or April.
SPECIES CULTIVATED: *T. alpinum*, yellowish-green, summer, 4 to 6 in., Northern and Arctic Regions; *aquilegifolium*, lilac, summer, 3 ft., Europe; *Chelidonii*, rosy lilac, summer, 6 in., Himalaya, requires sheltered position; *Delavayi*, lilac, June to July, 1½ to 3 ft., E. China; *dipterocarpum*, rosy lilac, summer, 5 to 7 ft., W. China, and var. *album*, white; *Fendleri*, yellowish-white, July, 2 to 3 ft., N. America; *flavum*, yellow, summer, 3 to 4 ft., Europe; *glaucum*, yellow, summer, 3 to 4 ft., S. Europe; *kiusianum*, rose purple, May to June, 6 in., Japan; *majus*, greenish-yellow, summer, 3 to 4 ft., Europe and Asia; *minus*, yellow, summer, 1 ft., Europe; *petaloideum*, white, June to Aug., 1½ ft., N. Asia.

Thea—*Theaceae* (or *Ternstroemiaceae*). Tender evergreen shrubs and trees. The tea of commerce is made from the leaves of *T. sinensis*.
CULTURE: As Camellia.
PROPAGATION: As Camellia.
SPECIES CULTIVATED: *T. cuspidata*, white, May, 6 ft., China; *sinensis* (syn. *Camellia Thea*), ' Tea ', to 30 ft., flowers white, fragrant.

Thelesperma—*Compositae.* Hardy annual. Flowers suitable for cutting.
CULTURE: Soil, ordinary. Position, sunny borders. Sow seeds outdoors in April where plants are required to grow.
SPECIES CULTIVATED: *T. Burridgeanum* (syn. *Cosmidium Burridgeanum*), yellow and red-brown, summer, 18 in., Texas.

Thelypteris, see Dryopteris.

Theobroma (Cocoa Tree; Chocolate Tree)—*Sterculiaceae.* Stove evergreen tree. Fruit, oval, yellow or reddish, from the seeds of which cocoa is obtained. First introduced early eighteenth century.
CULTURE: Compost, equal parts fibrous loam and sand. Position, well-drained pots in moist, warm stove. Pot, Feb. Water freely March to Oct., moderately afterwards. Syringe daily April to Sept. Shade from sun. Prune into shape, Feb. Temp., Oct. to March 55° to 65°, March to Oct. 70° to 85°.
PROPAGATION: By cuttings of half-ripened shoots inserted in sand under bell-glass in temp. of 75° to 85°, April to Aug.; seed sown in Feb. to March in temp. 80°.
SPECIES CULTIVATED: *T. Cacao*, rose and yellow, summer, 15 to 20 ft., Trop. America.

Thermopsis—*Leguminosae.* Hardy herbaceous perennials. First introduced early nineteenth century.
CULTURE: Soil, ordinary. Position, open sunny borders. Plant, March or April.
PROPAGATION: By seeds sown ⅛ in. deep in light, rich soil in sunny position out

doors in April, transplanting seedlings when large enough to handle; division in spring.

SPECIES CULTIVATED: *T. caroliniana*, golden yellow, summer, 4 to 5 ft., N. America; *fabacea*, yellow, June to July, 2 to 3 ft., Siberia; *montana*, golden yellow, summer, 1 to 2 ft., N. America.

Thlaspi—*Cruciferae*. Hardy perennial herbs. *T. latifolium* is now *Pachyphragma macrophyllum*. First introduced mid-eighteenth century.

CULTURE: Soil, ordinary. Position, sunny rock gardens. Plant, spring or autumn.

PROPAGATION: By seed sown in pans of sandy soil in cold frame or greenhouse during March or April; division at planting time.

SPECIES CULTIVATED: *T. alpinum*, white, spring, 3 to 4 in., Europe; *bellidifolium*, rose-purple, summer, 2 to 3 in., Macedonia; *rotundifolium*, rosy lavender, summer, 2 to 3 in., Alps.

Thorn, see Crataegus; **-Apple**, see *Datura Stramonium*.

Thrift, see Armeria.

Thrinax—*Palmae*. Stove fan palms. First introduced late eighteenth century.

CULTURE: Compost, two parts loam, one part peat, and little sand. Position, well-drained pots in moist part of stove. Water copiously April to Oct., moderately afterwards. Syringe daily April to Sept. Moist atmosphere essential. Shade from sun. Temp., March to Oct. 70° to 85°, Oct. to March 55° to 65°.

PROPAGATION: By seeds soaked for a few hours in tepid water and then sown ½ in. deep in sandy loam in temp. of 75° to 85° any time.

SPECIES CULTIVATED: *T. excelsa*, 6 to 8 ft., Panama; *Morrisii*, 3 to 4 ft., W. Indies; *multiflora*, 6 to 10 ft., Dominica; *parviflora*, ' Royal Palmetto Palm ', 25 to 30 ft., W. Indies.

Thuja (Arbor-Vitae)—*Pinaceae*. Hardy evergreen coniferous trees and shrubs, pyramidal in habit, leaves small and scale-like. Often spelled Thuya. First introduced late sixteenth century.

CULTURE: Soil, deep, moist loam. Position, open sunny shrubberies, lawns, banks or margins of water, dwarf forms suitable for rock garden. Plant, Sept. to Nov. and Feb. to April. Prune, April or Sept.

CULTURE IN POTS: Compost, two parts loam, one part leaf-mould. Pot, Sept. or Oct. Position, cold frame, window or cold greenhouse, Nov. to May; plunged to rim of pot in ashes or fibre in sunny spot outdoors afterwards. Water freely April to Oct., moderately afterwards.

HEDGE CULTURE: Soil, ordinary moist, previously trenched two spits deep and 3 ft. wide. Plant, Sept., Oct., March or April. Distance apart for planting: 2 ft. for trees up to 3 ft. high, 2¼ ft. for trees to 4 ft., and 3 ft. for taller specimens. Nursery stock generally available up to 10 ft. or more high. Training or clipping best done twice yearly between May and July inclusive. Suitable species, *T. plicata, occidentalis* and *orientalis*.

PROPAGATION: By seeds in sandy soil in temp. 55° in spring, transplanting seedlings in open ground when large enough to handle; cuttings of shoots, 2 to 3 in. long, in sandy soil under bell-glass or in cold frame in Sept.; grafting in March.

SPECIES CULTIVATED: *T. koraiensis*, leaves white beneath, spreading habit, to 20 ft., Korea; *occidentalis*, ' American Arbor-Vitae ', 50 to 60 ft., N.E. America, and vars. *Ellwangeriana*, low broad pyramid, *ericoides*, dwarf, *lutea*, bright yellow pyramidal form, *pendula*, branches drooping, *Vervaeneana*, small and dense, etc.; *orientalis* (syn. *Biota orientalis*), 30 to 40 ft., China, and vars. *elegantissima*, compact, bright yellow in spring, *decussata*, dwarf bushy form, *meldensis*, narrow pyramidal form, *stricta*, dense pyramid, etc.; *plicata* (syn. *T. Lobbii*), over 100 ft., N.W. America, and vars. *atrovirens*, leaves dark green, *fastigiata*, columnar form, *pendula*, drooping branches; *Standishii* (syn. *T. japonica*), 20 to 30 ft., Japan.

Thujopsis—*Pinaceae.* Hardy evergreen coniferous trees of pyramidal habit. Allied to Thuja.
CULTURE: See Thuja.
PROPAGATION: See Thuja.
SPECIES CULTIVATED: *T. dolabrata* (syn. *Thuja dolabrata*), to 50 ft., leaves dark green above, white patches below, Cent. Japan, and vars. *Hondai*, flat branches, taller growth, *nana*, dwarf, lighter green, *variegata*, tips creamy white.

Thunbergia—*Acanthaceae.* Stove and greenhouse evergreen flowering shrubs and perennials, mostly of climbing habit. First introduced late eighteenth century.
CULTURE OF T. ALATA AND T. GIBSONII: Compost, two parts loam, one part leaf-mould or decayed manure and one part sand. Sow seeds thinly in light compost in a well-drained pot, pan or box in temp. 65° to 75° in Feb. or March. Transplant seedlings when three leaves form singly in 3½ in. pots, and later on into 5 in. size. Place pots afterwards alongside of staging and let shoots hang down; or in baskets suspended from roof. May also be planted outdoors in June against sunny walls, in window boxes, or in vases. Water freely.
CULTURE OF OTHER SPECIES: Compost, equal parts leaf-mould or well-decayed manure, peat, fibrous loam and silver sand. Position, well-drained pots in shady part of stove during growing period; light part during the resting period for *T. erecta*; well-drained beds, with shoots trained up roof, for *T. mysoriensis*, etc. Pot, Feb. or March. Prune moderately, Feb. Water freely March to Sept., moderately Sept. to Nov., keep nearly dry Nov. to March. Syringe daily March to Sept. Apply stimulants occasionally May to Sept. Temp., Feb. to Oct. 65° to 75°, Oct. to Feb. 55° to 65°.
PROPAGATION: By seeds sown ¹⁄₁₆ in. deep in sandy peat and leaf-mould in temp. 75° to 85°, Jan. to May; cuttings of firm young shoots, 2 to 3 in. long, inserted in leaf-mould, peat and sand under bell-glass in temp. 75° to 85°, Feb. to June.
SPECIES CULTIVATED: *T. alata*, cream and dark purple, summer, 4 to 6 ft., Trop. Africa, and several colour forms; *chrysops*, purple with yellow eye, June, 3 ft., Trop. Africa; *coccinea*, scarlet, summer, 8 to 10 ft., India; *erecta* (syn. *Meyenia evecta*), purple and pale yellow, summer, 6 ft., Trop. Africa, and var. *alba*, white; *fragrans*, white, fragrant, summer, 8 to 10 ft., Trop. Asia; *Gibsonii*, orange, summer, 10 to 15 ft., Trop. Africa; *grandiflora*, blue, July to Sept., 10 to 15 ft., India, and var. *alba*, white; *laurifolia* (syn. *T. Harrisii*), pale blue and white, summer, 10 to 15 ft., Malaya; *mysorensis*, yellow and purple, spring, 10 to 15 ft., S. India; *natalensis*, yellow and blue, July, 2 to 3 ft., S. Africa; *Vogeliana* (syn. *Meyenia Vogeliana*), bluish-violet and yellow, summer, Trop. Africa.

Thunia—*Orchidaceae.* An epiphytal (terrestrial under suitable conditions) genus.
CULTURE: Compost, two-thirds of rough fibrous loam, the other third of sphagnum moss and peat with finely broken potsherds or sand. Well-drained pots. In summer, atmosphere should be tropical, if shading is required it should be very light. Syringe may be used freely and manure water given as for Calanthes, but continued until the leaves yellow after flowering. When foliage has fallen, or nearly so, place in a temp. about 50° in a light position. Withhold water.
PROPAGATION: In early summer the old stems may be cut into lengths, two or more nodes, and laid on sand or fibre in a propagating case, the growths being potted as roots are seen. The piece of the old stem may be removed.
SPECIES CULTIVATED: *T. alba*, white, lip white with yellow or purple-marked fringed keels, summer, N. India, var. *nivalis*, pure white; *Bensoniae*, amethyst-purple, lip with many yellow-fringed keels, very handsome, summer, Burma, var. *superba*, deep rose-purple, keel bronze; *Brymeriana*, white or purple-flushed, lip crimson-purple, keels yellow, tinted red, summer, Burma, a supposed hybrid.

Thuya, see Thuja.

Thymus (Thyme)—*Labiatae.* Hardy aromatic evergreen or semi-evergreen shrubs and sub-shrubs.
CULTURE OF GARDEN THYME: Shoots used largely for culinary purposes. Soil, light, rich ordinary. Position, sunny, warm border. Plant 4 in. apart in rows

8 in. asunder, March or April. Replant every three or four years. Gather shoots when blossoms appear and dry for winter use.

CULTURE OF OTHER SPECIES: Soil, light and poor with sand or gravel, well drained. Position, sunny rockeries and dry walls in full sun. Plant, Oct. or March. Excellent plants for carpeting bare spots over spring bulbs.

PROPAGATION: By seeds sown ⅛ in. deep in lines 8 in. apart in April, thinning seedlings to 4 in. apart in May or June; division of plants in March or April, each portion being furnished with a few roots; gold and silver kinds by cuttings in cold frames in summer.

SPECIES CULTIVATED: *T. carnosus*, white, Aug. to Sept., 9 in., Spain; *glabra* (syn. *T. Chamaedrys*), light purple, summer, 3 in., Europe; *Herba-barona*, light purple, summer, foliage scented like carraway seed, 6 in., Corsica; *nitidus*, rosy lilac, June, 9 in., Sicily; *pectinatus* (syn. *T. odoratissimus*), pale purple, summer, 2 in., Russia; *Serpyllum*, 'Wild Thyme', rosy purple, June, prostrate, Europe (Br.), and vars. *albus*, white, *coccineus*, carmine, *lanuginosus*, woolly-leaved, and *vulgaris* (syn. *T. citriodorus*), lemon scented; *vulgaris*, 'Garden Thyme', purple, June, 6 in., S. Europe.

Thyrsacanthus, see Odontonema.

Tiarella—*Saxifragaceae*. Hardy perennial herb. First introduced early eighteenth century.

CULTURE: Soil, ordinary. Position, cool, shady beds or rock gardens. Plant, March or April.

PROPAGATION: By division of roots in March or April.

SPECIES CULTIVATED: *T. cordifolia*, 'Foam Flower', 'False Mitrewort', white, June, 1 ft., Eastern N. America; *polyphylla*, white, summer, 1¼ ft., Himalaya, China; *unifoliata*, creamy white, summer, 2 ft., Western N. America; *Wherryi*, white, May to June, 1 ft., Eastern N. America.

Tibouchina (Brazilian Spider-flower)—*Melastomacea*. Greenhouse flowering shrubs. Evegreen. First introduced mid nineteenth century.

CULTURE: Compost, two parts turfy loam, one part peat, and one part charcoal and sand. Position, well-drained pots, tubs, or beds. Pot or plant, Feb. or March. Prune into shape after flowering. Water freely April to Sept., moderately afterwards. Temp. March or Sept. 60° to 70°; Sept. to March 50° to 60°

PROPAGATIO: By cuttings of firm side shoots, 3 in. long, inserted singly in small pots of sandy soil under bell-glass or in propagator in temp. of 70° to 80°. Feb. to Sept.

SPECIES CTLTIVATED: *T. elegans*, purple, June, 6 ft. Brazil; *semidecandra* (*Syn. Lasiandra or Pleroma macranthum*), purple, summer, 10 ft., Brazil.

Tick Clover, see Desmodium; **-Trefoil,** see Desmodium.

Tidytips, see *Layia elegans*.

Tiger Flower, see *Tigridia Pavonia*; **–Nut,** see *Cyperus esculentus*

Tigridia (Tiger Flower; Tiger Iris)—*Iridaceae*. Half-hardy or greenhouse bulbs. Blooms last in perfection one day only. First introduced late eighteenth century.

OUTDOOR CULTURE: Soil, equal parts rich loam and leaf-mould with a liberal addition of sand, in partially shaded bed prepared by digging out soil to depth of 24 in.; place 6 in. of brickbats or clinkers in bottom and remainder compost; or for ordinary culture an open, sunny border and any good soil. Plant bulbs 3 in. deep, 5 to 6 in. apart, placing little sand under and round each in April. Mulch with decayed manure and peat when 3 in. high. Water freely in dry weather. Lift bulbs in Oct., tie in small bundles, and suspend in cool, airy, frost-proof place until following April.

POT CULTURE: Compost, two parts sandy loam, one part peat and one part sand. Pot the bulbs singly in 4¼ in. pots in March or April. Cover pots with cinder ashes or peat in cold frame or under stage in cold greenhouse until growth begins, then remove to light. Water moderately after growth begins; freely when well advanced. Apply weak stimulants occasionally when flower stems show. Position when in flower, light airy greenhouse or cold sunny frame. After flowering gradually withhold water until foliage turns yellow, then keep quite dry. Remove bulbs from soil, tie into bundles, and suspend in cool place until potting time the following April.

PROPAGATION: By seeds sown ⅛ in. deep in light compost in temp. 55° to 65°, spring; offsets, removed and treated as advised for old bulbs in April.

SPECIES CULTIVATED: *T. Pavonia*, red, yellow, and purple, summer, 1 to 2 ft., Mexico, and vars. *alba*, white, *aurea*, yellow, and *conchiflora*, rich yellow, etc. See also Cypella.

Tilia (Lime Tree; Linden; Basswood)—*Tiliaceae*. Hardy deciduous trees.

CULTURE: Soil, good ordinary or loamy, moist. Position, sunny, as specimen trees on lawns or as screens. Also suitable for training over arches to form a shady path in summer; will stand severe pruning and may be trained (pleached) as mop-headed or other shaped specimens. Plant, Oct. to March. Prune, Nov. to Feb. Not suitable for dry soils or exposed places. Timber, soft, pale yellow or white, used chiefly for toy making, carving, leather-cutting boards, musical instruments, etc. Weight of cubic foot of timber, 28 lb. Number of seeds to a pound, 5000. Age at which timber reaches maturity, 30 years. Average life, 800 to 1000 years.

PROPAGATION: By seed sown in well-drained light soil in cold frame in March; layering shoots in autumn; grafting on common species in March for choice kinds.

SPECIES CULTIVATED: *T. americana*, ' American Lime ', large leaves, 60 to 120 ft., E. and Cent. N. America; *cordata*, ' Small-leaved Lime ', neat habit, slow growing, 50 to 90 ft., Europe, including Britain; *euchlora*, one of the handsomest, good foliage and habit, 40 to 60 ft., hybrid; *europaea* (syn. *T. vulgaris*), ' Common Lime ', unsatisfactory early shedding of leaves, to 130 ft., hybrid; *heterophylla* (syn. *T. Michauxii*), large leaves, white beneath, 70 to 80 ft., Eastern N. America; *Maximowicziana*, round leaves, hardy, 70 to 90 ft., Japan; *Moltkei*, very vigorous, pyramidal, 40 to 60 ft., hybrid; *mongolica*, ' Mongolian Lime ', very hardy and graceful small tree, 20 to 30 ft., N. China and Mongolia; *petiolaris*, ' Pendent Silver Lime ', graceful and very sweet scented, often overpowering bees, 60 to 90 ft., origin doubtful, possibly S.E. Europe; *platyphyllos*, ' Large-leaved Lime ', superior to Common Lime, to 120 ft., Cent. and S. Europe, with numerous vars. *laciniata*, cut-leaved, *rubra*, red-twigged lime, *aurea*, golden-twigged, *pyramidalis*, fastigiate habit, and *vitifolia*, leaves lobed; *tomentosa* (syn. *T. argentea*), ' White Lime ', leaves silvery beneath, handsome, broadly pyramidal tree, 60 to 100 ft., S.E. Europe.

Tillaea—*Crassulaceae*. Dwarf, annual aquatics used submerged in ponds or aquariums or as carpeting plants at borders of ponds or streams. Small green leaves, inconspicuous flowers.

CULTURE: Soil, muddy or sandy loam. Plant, spring, in soil at margins, or weight portions with small pieces of lead and sink into water if wanted for oxygenating purposes.

PROPAGATION: By division in spring.

SPECIES CULTIVATED: *T. aquatica*, 3 in., Europe; *recurva*, 4 in., Australia.

Tillandsia—*Bromeliaceae*. Stove epiphytal perennials.

CULTURE: Compost, equal parts fibrous loam, rough peat, silver sand and leaf-mould. Pot, Feb. or March. Water copiously March to Oct., moderately afterwards. Shade from sun. Syringe daily April to Sept. Moist atmosphere essential in summer. Temp., Sept. to March 60° to 70°, March to Sept. 70° to 80°.

PROPAGATION: By offsets, inserted in small pots of sandy peat in temp. 75° to 85° in spring. *T. usneoides* may be grown suspended from roof by a wire or fastened to a piece of wood; no soil required.

SPECIES CULTIVATED: *T. circinata* (syn. *T. streptophylla*), lilac, 1 ft., W. Indies and Cent. America; *fasciculata*, blue, 2 ft., W. Indies and Cent. America;

Lindeniana, bluish-purple, summer, 1 ft., Peru; *usneoides*, ' Spanish Moss' greenish-red, July, stems slender and pendent, to 20 ft. See also Cryptanthus, Vriesia and Guzmannia.

Tithonia—*Compositae*. Tender shrub, usually grown as half-hardy annual. First introduced early nineteenth century.

CULTURE: Soil, ordinary. Position, sunny beds or borders. Sow in boxes of sandy soil in greenhouse in temp. 60° during March. Prick out seedlings as soon as large enough to handle and gradually harden off for planting out in May.

SPECIES CULTIVATED: *T. rotundifolia* (syn. *T. speciosa*), ' Mexican Sunflower ', orange-yellow, Aug. to Sept., 3 to 6 ft., Mexico and Cent. America.

Toadflax, see Linaria; **-flower,** see *Stapelia variegata* var. *clypeata*; **-Lily,** see Tricyrtis.

Tobacco Plant, see Nicotiana.

Todea, see Leptopteris.

Tolmiea—*Saxifragaceae*. Hardy perennial herb. First introduced early nineteenth century.

CULTURE: Soil, ordinary. Position, shady beds or rock gardens. Plant, March.

PROPAGATION: By division of roots, March or April.

SPECIES CULTIVATED: *T. Menziesii*, green, April, 1 to 2 ft., N. America.

Tolpis (Yellow Garden Hawkweed)—*Compositae*. Hardy annuals. First introduced early seventeenth century.

CULTURE: Soil, ordinary. Position, sunny beds or borders. Sow seeds $\frac{1}{16}$ in. deep in patches or lines where required to grow; thin seedlings when 2 to 3 in. high to 6 or 8 in. apart.

SPECIES CULTIVATED: *T. barbata* (syn. *Crepis barbata*), yellow, June, 1 to 2 ft., S. Europe.

Tomato, see *Lycopersicum esculentum*.

Toothache Tree, see *Zanthoxylum Clava-Herculis*.

Toothwort, see Dentaria.

Torenia—*Scrophulariaceae*. Greenhouse annuals. First introduced early nineteenth century.

CULTURE: Compost, loam, leaf-mould and sand. Position, small pots, with shoots trained to sticks, or in baskets suspended from roof. Sow seeds thinly in boxes filled with sandy soil in temp. 60° from Feb. to April. Prick out seedlings when large enough to handle into the pots or boxes in which they are to flower. Nip off point of main shoot when 3 in. long, also of side shoots when 2 in. long, to induce bushy growth. Water freely.

SPECIES CULTIVATED: *T. asiatica*, blue and yellow, summer, trailing, India; *atropurpurea*, purple, trailing, summer, Malay Peninsula; *flava* (syn. *T. Baillonii*), yellow and red-purple, summer, 1 ft., Trop. Asia; *Fournieri*, blue, purple, yellow, and black, summer, 1 ft., Cochin-China, and vars. *grandiflora* and *speciosa*; *travancoria*, blue-purple and yellow, trailing, summer, Madras.

Torreya—*Taxaceae*. Rather tender evergreen coniferous tree. First introduced mid-nineteenth century.

CULTURE: Soil, light, sandy loam. Position, sheltered, sunny, well-drained shrubberies. Plant, Sept., Oct., March or April.

PROPAGATION: As advised for Taxus.

SPECIES CULTIVATED: *T. californica*, ' Californian Nutmeg ', 40 to 70 ft., California; *grandis*, 50 to 75 ft., China; *nucifera*, 50 to 80 ft., Japan; *taxifolia*, ' Stinking Cedar ', 30 to 40 ft., W. Florida.

Totara Pine, see *Podocarpus Totara*.

Townsendia—*Compositae*. Hardy perennial American aster-like plants.

Culture: Any good loam, gritty and well drained. Position, full sun in the rock garden.

Propagation: By seeds sown in early spring.

Species Cultivated: *T. exscarpa* (syn. *T. Wilcoxiana*), purple, spring, 4 in., N. America.

Trachelium (Blue Throat-wort)—*Campanulaceae*. Half-hardy herbaceous perennial herbs. First introduced early seventeenth century.

Culture: Compost, two parts sandy loam, one part leaf-mould. Position, sunny rock gardens or dry walls or as cool greenhouse pot plant, and for summer bedding. Plant, March or April. Protect in severe weather by covering with dry fern fronds.

Propagation: By seeds sown in above compost lightly covered with fine light soil, placing in temp. of 55° to 65°, spring, transplanting seedlings when large enough to handle, hardening in cold frame and planting out, May or June; cuttings of young shoots inserted in sandy soil under bell-glass in April or Sept. When grown as greenhouse pot plant or for bedding it is best raised annually from seed.

Species Cultivated: *T. caeruleum*, blue, Aug., 2 ft., S. Europe, and var. *album*.

Trachelospermum—*Apocynaceae*. Rather tender evergreen climbing shrubs with fragrant flowers. First introduced mid-nineteenth century.

Culture: Soil, light loam, well drained, with some leaf-mould or peat. *T. jasminoides* as wall plant in cool greenhouse, or outside in S.W. districts. *T. asiaticum*, south or west walls in S. of England only.

Propagation: By cuttings of half-ripened shoots in gentle bottom heat, July to Aug.

Species Cultivated: *T. asiaticum* (syns. *T. crocostemon* and *T. divaricatum*), yellowish-white, July, glossy leaves, hardiest species, 12 to 15 ft., Japan and Korea; *jasminoides* (syn. *Rhynchospermum jasminoides*), ' Chinese Jasmine ', white, very fragrant, July to Aug., leathery polished leaves, 10 to 12 ft., China, with vars. *variegatum*, foliage green, silver, and pink, and *Wilsonii*, narrow veined leaves.

Trachycarpus—*Palmae*. Greenhouse palm, hardy in southern parts of the kingdom. Leaves, fan-shaped and green. First introduced early nineteenth century.

Culture: Compost, two parts rich loam, one part decayed leaf-mould and sand. Position, well-drained pots in sunny greenhouse; sheltered place outdoors in the south. Pot, March. Temp., Sept. to March 40° to 50°, March to Sept. 50° to 60°. Water freely in spring and summer, moderately other times. Repotting only necessary every four or five years.

Propagation: By seeds sown 1 in. deep in a temp. of 75° to 80°; also by suckers removed from base of parent.

Species Cultivated: *T. Fortunei* (syn. *Chamaerops excelsa*), ' Windmill Palm ', 25 to 30 ft., China.

Trachymene (Blue Lace Flower)—*Umbelliferae*. Half-hardy annual. First introduced early nineteenth century.

Culture: Soil, ordinary. Position, sunny. Sow in temp. of 55° in March, transplant seedlings 2 in. apart in pots or boxes, harden off in cold frame in April, and plant out in May.

Species Cultivated: *T. caerulea* (syn. *Didiscus caerulea*), blue, summer, 8 in., Australia; *pilosa*, blue, summer, 6 in., Australia.

Tradescantia (Spiderwort)—*Commelinaceae*. Hardy herbaceous and stove perennials. First introduced early seventeenth century.

Culture of Hardy Species: Soil, ordinary. Position, partially shady or sunny borders or beds. Plant, Oct., March or April. Lift, divide and replant every three or four years. Excellent plants for town gardens.

Culture of Stove Species: Compost, equal parts loam and leaf-mould with liberal addition of sand. Position, well-drained pots in warm greenhouse. Pot, March or April. Water freely March to Sept., moderately at other times. Temp.,

March to Sept. 65° to 75°, Sept. to March 55° to 60°. *T. fluminensis* common under benches in greenhouse.

PROPAGATION: Hardy species by division in spring; stove species by cuttings inserted in sandy soil under bell-glass in temp. 75°, April to Aug.

HARDY SPECIES CULTIVATED: *T. virginiana*, ' Flower of a Day ', violet-purple, May to Sept., 1 to 2 ft., N. America, and several colour forms.

STOVE SPECIES CULTIVATED: *T. fluminensis*, ' Wandering Jew ', prostrate, small leaves, S. America; *Reginae*, leaves purplish-crimson and silver above, purple beneath, 1 ft., Peru. See also Rhoeo and Zebrina.

Tragopogon—*Compositae*. Hardy biennial esculent-rooted vegetable with long, tapering, white roots.

CULTURE: Soil, rich, deeply trenched, free from stones. Position, sunny, open. Thin seedlings when 3 in. high to one in each group. Remove flower heads as soon as seen. Lift the roots in Nov., twist off their leaves, and store in layers with sand or soil between in cellar or outhouse until required for cooking. Roots left in the ground all winter will provide tender stems in the spring.

PROPAGATION: By seeds sown in groups of three or four, 12 in. apart, in drills ½ in. deep and 18 in. apart in early April.

SPECIES CULTIVATED: *T. porrifolius*, ' Salsify ', ' Vegetable Oyster ', purple, May and June, 3 to 4 ft., S. Europe, N. America.

Trailing Arbutus, see *Epigaea repens*.

Transvaal Daisy, see *Gerbera Jamesonii*.

Trapa (Water Chestnut)—*Onagraceae*. Tender, annual, aquatic floating herbs with spiny edible fruit. First introduced late eighteenth century.

CULTURE: Soil, rich loamy. Position, sunny; shallow pots or tubs in cool greenhouse. Plant, April or May.

PROPAGATION: By seeds sown in loamy soil in water in temp. of 65° to 75° in spring.

SPECIES CULTIVATED: *T. bispinosa*, two to four spines, India, Ceylon; *natans* (syn. *T. bicornis*), ' Water Calthrops ', ' Jesuit's Nut ', reddish-white, summer, fruits edible, 2 in. in diameter, Europe; *verbanensis*, two-horned fruits, Italy.

Traveller's Joy, see *Clematis Vitalba*; **-Tree,** see *Ravenala madagascariensis*.

Treasure Flower, see Gazania.

Tree Celandine, see *Macleaya cordata*; **-Groundsel,** see *Baccharis halimifolia*; **-Heath,** see *Erica arborea*; **-Lupin,** see *Lupinus arboreus*; **-Mallow,** see Lavatera; **-of-Heaven,** see *Ailanthus altissima*; **-Onion,** see *Allium cepa* var. *viviparum*; **-Peony,** see *Paeonia suffruticosa*; **-Poppy,** see *Romneya Coulteri*; **-Purslane,** see *Atriplex Halimus*; **-Tomato,** see *Cyphomandra betacea*.

Trefoil, see Trifolium.

Trembling Fern, see *Pteris tremula*.

Trevesia—*Araliaceae*. Stove flowering shrub. First introduced early nineteenth century.

CULTURE: Compost, equal parts loam, leaf-mould and sand. Position, large well-drained pots in warm greenhouse. Temp., March to Sept. 70° to 80°, Sept. to March 60° to 65°. Moist atmosphere essential during the summer months. Shade from strong sun. Water freely during growing season, moderately at other times. Pot, Feb. or March.

PROPAGATION: By cuttings of half-ripened shoots inserted in sandy soil under bell-glass in temp. 80°.

SPECIES CULTIVATED: *T. palmata* (syn. *Gastonia palmata*), yellowish-white, spring, to 20 ft., Himalaya; *sundaica* (syn. *Gastonia sundaica*), yellowish, spring, 15 ft., Java, Sumatra.

Trianea, see Limnobium stoloniferum.

Trias—*Orchidaceae.* An epiphytic genus closely allied to Bulbophyllum. Pseudo-bulbs small, clustered, one-leaved. Scapes from base short. Flowers attractive, solitary, freely produced in the species given.

CULTURE: As for Bulbophyllum, pans.

PROPAGATION: As for Bulbophyllum.

SPECIES CULTIVATED: A selection—*T. disciflora,* comparatively large, sepals yellow, thickly spotted red, petals small dark red, autumn, Siam; *picta,* yellowish, densely spotted red-purple, winter, spring, Burma.

Trichodiadema—*Aizoaceae.* Greenhouse succulent plants, formerly included in Mesembryanthemum.

CULTURE: As Mesembryanthemum.

PROPAGATION: As Mesembryanthemum.

SPECIES CULTIVATED: *T. barbatum* (syns. *Mesembryanthemum barbatum* and *stelligerum*), red, summer, Cape; *densum* (syns. *M. densum* and *M. barbatum* var. *densum*), carmine-violet, winter and early spring, S. Africa; *stellatum* (syn. *M. stellatum*), pale violet, winter and early spring, tufted 2 to 4 in., S. Africa.

Tricholaena—*Gramineae.* Half-hardy annual grass.

CULTURE: Soil, ordinary. Sow seeds ½ in. deep and 1 in. apart in light, rich soil in well-drained pots or boxes in temp. 50° to 55°, Feb. or March; transfer seedlings when 2 in. high into boxes, then singly into 4½ in. pots. Place in cold frame to harden in May and plant outdoors in June. May also be grown in pots in any loamy compost. Water freely.

SPECIES CULTIVATED: *T. rosea,* ' Ruby Grass ', 3 to 4 ft., S. Africa.

Trichomanes—*Hymenophyllaceae.* Greenhouse filmy ferns. Fronds more or less divided, semi-transparent.

CULTURE: Compost, equal parts peat, loam, leaf-mould, charcoal, sandstone and silver sand. Position, moist, shady recesses of rockeries, under bell-glasses or in cases. Plant, March. Water freely March to Oct., moderately afterwards; syringing unsuitable. Damp atmosphere and shade most essential. Temp., March to Sept. 55° to 65°, Sept. to March 45° to 55°. The Killarney fern is best grown in a cool house, frame in complete shade or wardian case. Provide plenty of sandstone for rhizomes to cling to. Constant moisture essential.

CULTURE IN CASES IN ROOMS: Compost, as above. Position, shady window. Plant, March. Top-dress with fresh compost annually in March. Water freely April to Sept., moderately afterwards. Ventilate case a few minutes daily. Species most suitable is *T. radicans.*

PROPAGATION: By spores sown on surface of sandy peat in shallow pan covered with bell-glass in temp. 65° to 75° at any time; by division at potting time.

SPECIES CULTIVATED: *T. alatum,* W. Indies; *auriculatum,* Trop. Asia; *capillaceum* (syn. *T. trichoideum*), W. Indies; *Colensoi,* New Zealand; *exsectum,* Chile; *parvulum,* Tropics; *radicans,* ' Killarney Fern ', ' Bristle Fern ', Trop. and Temp. Regions; *reniforme,* New Zealand. Many other species are recorded, mainly belonging to hot swamps in tropical countries and scarcely known to cultivation.

Trichopilia—*Orchidaceae.* An epiphytic genus including some very handsome species. The single-leaved pseudo-bulbs usually set closely together; scapes from their base, usually arched, erect in the section Pilumna. The lip is the larger of the floral segments, the sepals and petals narrow, twisted in some; flowers are one or few.

CULTURE: Compost, two parts osmunda fibre or substitute, one part sphagnum moss, a very little loam fibre, with or without a few decayed oak or beech leaves, in pans which can be suspended. Pots for the erect spiked kinds, well drained. The Pilumnas can be grown in a cool or Odontoglossum house. Their winter temp. should be 50° to 55°. Species with drooped spikes should have a winter night temp. of 55° to 60°, higher in the summer. All with shading and a moist atmosphere and all exposed to light in autumn. Water freely when growing, but infrequently in winter. Less atmospheric moisture is then needed—a position near the glass usually meets their requirements.

PROPAGATION: By division of the plants if and when large enough in spring.

SPECIES CULTIVATED: A selection—*T. Backhousiana*, near *T. fragrans*, but larger, leaves dimly green mottled, summer, Colombia; *brevis*, yellow, blotched chestnut, lip white with yellow and purple marks, summer, Peru; *coccinea*, brownish-green with a reddish stripe, lip crimson within, whitish externally, the front blotched rose-carmine, margin sometimes whitish, variable, early summer, Costa Rica, Guatemala; *crispa*, crimson with whitish margins, lip typical, early summer, Cent. America; *fragrans*, two to five white, disk yellow, autumn, winter, Colombia, var. *nobilis*, larger; *Galeottiana*, one to two pale yellow, lip with a red-spotted disk, summer, Mexico; *hymenantha*, four to twelve, rather small, whitish or yellowish, lip white, red-dotted, fringed, summer, Colombia; *laxa*, four to twelve, scapes arching, fragrant, dull rose, greenish, lip white, various, Colombia; *sanguinolenta*, one to three, olive-green, barred and spotted with chestnut, lip white, red-purple marked at base, various, Ecuador; *suavis*, two to five, fragrant, large, white or rose spotted, lip spotted and blotched rose-pink, disk orange spotted, variable, spring, summer, Cent. America, Costa Rica; *tortilis*, one to two, rose, margined yellow-green, lip white, spotted red-brown, various, Mexico.

Trichosanthes—*Cucurbitaceae*. Greenhouse annual climber. Fruit, very long, cucumber-like, twisted. First introduced early eighteenth century.

CULTURE: Compost, equal parts sandy loam, leaf-mould and fibrous peat. Position, well-drained pots, with shoots trained up roof of sunny greenhouse. Sow seeds singly, 1 in. deep, in 2 in. pots filled with above compost placed in temp. 65° to 75°, Feb. or March. Transplant seedlings when three leaves form into 4½ in. pots, and when well rooted into 8 in. size. Water freely; use tepid water only. Syringe daily May to Sept. Shade from mid-day sun. Apply weak stimulants twice a week May to Sept. Temp., 60° to 70°.

SPECIES CULTIVATED: *T. Anguina*, ' Serpent Gourd ', ' Snake Gourd ', white, summer, 10 to 15 ft., Trop. Asia.

Tricuspidaria, see Crinodendron.

Tricyrtis—*Liliaceae*. Half-hardy perennials. First introduced mid-nineteenth century.

GREENHOUSE CULTURE: Compost, equal parts of sandy loam, peat and silver sand. Position, well-drained pots in cool greenhouse or cold frame. Pot, Oct. to March. Plunge pots to rim in peat or cinder ashes in cool greenhouse or cold frame and give no water till growth commences, then apply moderately. When stems are 3 in. high place plants in light, airy position in greenhouse. No shade required. Apply weak stimulants once a week during flowering period. After flowering gradually withhold water till foliage turns yellow, then keep dry, and store pots away in cold frame or under staging in cool greenhouse until Feb. or March.

OUTDOOR CULTURE: Soil, peaty. Position, partially shady, sheltered, moist border. Plant rhizomes 2 in. below surface, Oct. to March. Protect in severe weather with covering of litter. Plants grown outdoors do not flower until autumn.

PROPAGATION: By offsets, removed at planting or potting time.

SPECIES CULTIVATED: *T. hirta*, ' Japanese Toad Lily ', white and purple, autumn, 2 to 3 ft., Japan; *macropoda*, pale purple spotted blackish-purple, autumn, 2 to 3 ft., China and Japan, and var. *striata*, leaves striped white.

Trientalis—*Primulaceae*. Hardy herbaceous perennials.

CULTURE: Soil, ordinary light, rich. Position, shady borders, margins of rhododendron beds, rockeries or woodlands. Plant, Nov. to April.

PROPAGATION: By seeds sown in light, rich soil lightly covered with fine soil under hand-light in shady position outdoors in April; division of roots, Nov. or March.

SPECIES CULTIVATED: *T. borealis* (syn. *T. americana*), ' Starflower ', white, May,

6 to 9 in., N. America; *europaea*, ' Chickweed Winter Green ', pink and white, April to June, 6 to 8 in., N. Hemisphere.

Trifolium (Clover; Trefoil)—*Leguminosae*. Hardy perennials.
CULTURE: Soil, ordinary. Position, sunny borders or rock gardens. Plant, Oct. to April.
PROPAGATION: By division of plants, Oct. or March.
SPECIES CULTIVATED: *T. alpinum*, pale pink, May to July, 4 in., Europe; *badium*, golden yellow, summer, 6 in., Alps; *repens*, white, Europe (Br.), and vars. *album*, white, *purpureum*, leaves bronze-purple; *uniflorum*, deep pink, summer, 2 in., S. Europe.

Trigonella—*Leguminosae*. Hardy annuals. Leaves, feather-shaped. First introduced mid-sixteenth century.
CULTURE: Soil, ordinary. Position, sunny borders. Sow seeds in April in patches lightly covered with fine soil. Thin seedlings when three leaves form to 6 in. apart
SPECIES CULTIVATED: *T. caerulea*, blue, summer, 2 ft., E. Europe; *Foenum-Graecum*, ' Fenugreek ', white, summer, 18 in., S. Europe.

Trillium—*Liliaceae*. Tuberous-rooted perennials. First introduced mid-eighteenth century.
CULTURE: Soil, sandy peat. Position, shady, moist, well-drained border. Plant, Aug. to Oct. Top-dress annually in March with layer of decayed leaves. Lift and replant only when absolutely necessary.
PROPAGATION: By seeds sown in shallow, well-drained boxes or pans filled with sandy peat, covering seeds lightly with fine soil, and placing in shady, cold frame; division of tuberous roots, Aug. to Nov.
SPECIES CULTIVATED: *T. cernuum*, white, April, 1 ft., N. America; *erectum*, purplish-maroon, April, 1 ft., N. America; *grandiflorum*, ' Wake Robin ', ' American Wood Lily ', white, May, 1 to 1½ ft., N. America; *nivale*, ' Snow Wood Lily ', white, spring, 6 in., N. America; *ovatum*, white to pink, April, 1½ ft., N.W. America; *recurvatum*, maroon, April, 1 to 1½ ft., N. America; *rivale*, white and purple, March, 6 to 8 in., N. America; *sessile*, purple, March, 9 to 12 in., N. America; *undulatum* (syn. *T. erythrocarpum*), white and purple, May, 1 to 2 ft., N. America.

Triptilion—*Compositae*. Annual and perennial herbaceous plants. First introduced early nineteenth century.
CULTURE: Well-drained loamy soil. Postion, cool situation in the rock garden.
PROPAGATION: By seeds sown in spring; careful division of old plants in spring or autumn.
SPECIES CULTIVATED: *T. spinosum*, blue, summer, 9 in., Chile.

Tristania—*Myrtaceae*. Greenhouse evergreen flowering shrubs. First introduced early nineteenth century.
CULTURE: Compost, equal parts loam, peat and sand. Position, well-drained pots or borders in heated greenhouse. Pot, March or April. Water freely during growing season, moderately at other times. Temp., March to Sept. 55° to 65°, Sept. to March 45° to 55°.
PROPAGATION: By cuttings of half-ripened shoots inserted in sandy soil under bell-glass in gentle bottom heat during July or Aug.
SPECIES CULTIVATED: *T. conferta*, ' Brisbane Box ', yellow, July to Sept., 20 to 30 ft., Australia; *neriifolia*, yellow, July to Sept., 15 to 20 ft., Australia; *suaveolens*, yellow, Aug., 10 to 15 ft., Australia.

Trithrinax—*Palmae*. Stove hermaphrodite fan palms. First introduced mid-nineteenth century.
CULTURE: Compost, two parts loam, one part peat, and little sand. Position, well-drained pots in moist part of stove. Water copiously April to Oct., moderately afterwards. Syringe daily April to Sept. Moist atmosphere highly essential. Shade from sun. Temp., March to Oct. 70° to 85°, Oct. to March 55° to 65°.

PROPAGATION: By seeds soaked for a few hours in tepid water and then sown ⅛ in. deep in sandy loam in temp. of 75° to 85° any time.

SPECIES CULTIVATED: *T. acanthocoma*, 10 to 15 ft., Brazil; *brasiliensis*, 10 to 15 ft., Brazil.

Tritelia, see Brodiaea.

Tritoma, see Kniphofia.

Tritonia—*Iridaceae.* Hardy or half-hardy cormous plants. The common Montbretia of gardens is *Crocosmia crocosmaeflora* although often known as Tritonia.

CULTURE: Soil, sandy loam. Position, sunny well-drained borders. Plant 3 in. deep and 2 in. apart in groups during March or April. Water occasionally in very dry weather. Stimulants can be applied during flowering period. Lift plants in Oct. and place in shallow boxes filled with dry soil and keep in unheated frame or greenhouse until planting time. Practically no water required until growth commences in Feb. In sheltered gardens corms may be left in ground with covering of dry litter during winter.

POT CULTURE: Compost, two parts sandy loam, one part leaf-mould or decayed cow manure. Place five bulbs 3 in. deep in 4½ in. pots in Nov. and cover with peat in cold frame or under stage in cool greenhouse until growth begins. Water moderately from time plants begin to grow until flowers fade, then occasionally till plant dies down and keep dry till Jan. Temp., Sept. to March 40° to 50°, March to Sept. 50° to 60°.

PROPAGATION: By offsets.

SPECIES CULTIVATED: *T. crocata*, tawny red, summer, 2 ft., S. Africa; *flavida*, yellow, summer, 2 ft., S. Africa; *rosea*, bright red spotted yellow at base, summer, 3 ft., S. Africa.

Trochodendron—*Trochodendraceae.* Hardy evergreen flowering tree with handsome foliage and green flowers.

CULTURE: Soil, moist, peaty loam. Position, large shrubberies, or as specimens on lawns. Plant, Sept. to Oct. or April to May.

PROPAGATION: By cuttings of half-ripened shoots inserted in sandy soil under bell-glass in slight bottom heat during July or Aug.

SPECIES CULTIVATED: *T. aralioides*, bright green, April to June, 15 to 30 ft., Japan and Korea.

Trollius (Globe Flower)—*Ranunculaceae.* Hardy herbaceous perennials.

CULTURE: Soil, deep, moist ordinary, or preferably loam. Position, partially shady borders or margins of ponds or streams. Plant, Oct. or April. Water freely in dry weather. Lift, divide and replant every three or four years.

PROPAGATION: By seeds sown in moist, loamy soil in shady position outdoors in Sept. or April; division of roots, Oct. or April.

SPECIES CULTIVATED: *T. asiaticus*, orange, May, 18 in., Siberia; *caucasicus*, yellow, May to June, 2 to 3 ft., W. Asia; *chinensis*, yellow, May to June, 2 to 3 ft., N. China; *europaeus*, lemon-yellow, May to June, 1½ to 2 ft., Europe; *japonicus*, yellow, May to June, 6 to 8 in., Japan, and var. *flore-pleno*, double; *Ledebouri*, yellow, May to June, 1½ to 2 ft., Siberia; *pumilus*, yellow, May to June, 8 to 12 in., Himalaya, and var. *yunnanensis*, taller.

Tropaeolum—*Tropaeolaceae.* Greenhouse or hardy perennial dwarf or climbing herbs. Several treated as hardy annuals.

CULTURE OF CANARY CREEPER: Soil, good ordinary soil or sandy loam. Position, against sunny or shady wall, fence, arbour or trellis; does well in a north aspect. Sow seeds ½ in. deep in light soil in temp. 50° in March, harden off seedlings in cold frame in April, and plant outdoors in May; or ¼ in. deep outdoors in April where required to grow. Water freely in dry weather.

CULTURE OF NASTURTIUM: Soil, ordinary. Position, sunny. Sow seed 1 in. deep in April where plants are required to grow. Remove seed pods as they form to ensure free flowering.

POT CULTURE: Sow seeds ¼ in. deep and 2 in. apart in 5 in. pots filled with a compost of two parts good soil and one part decayed manure in April. Place pots in window or cold frame. Water moderately at first, freely when in full growth. Apply stimulants occasionally when in flower. Double vars. propagated by cuttings in temp. 55° in spring. Plant outdoors in May or June. May be grown in pots in a compost of four parts loam, one part leaf-mould, and a little sand. Pot in March or April. Water freely in summer, moderately other times. Temp., Oct. to March 40° to 50°, March to June 55° to 65°.

CULTURE OF T. PELTOPHORUM: Sow seeds in light soil in temp. 50° in March, harden seedlings off in cold frame in April, and plant out in June in sunny position against walls, fences, arbours, or in borders, placing tree branches to support the shoots; or outdoors ¼ in. deep in April where required to grow.

INDOOR CULTURE: Compost, two parts sandy loam, one part leaf-mould or decayed manure, and half a part sand. Position, well-drained pots or beds, training shoots up rafters. Water moderately Sept. to April, freely afterwards. Temp., Sept. to March 50°, March to Sept. 60°.

CULTURE OF GREENHOUSE TUBEROUS-ROOTED SPECIES: Compost, four parts turfy loam, one part leaf-mould, peat and silver sand. Position, well-drained pots in light, airy greenhouse. Pot, Aug. to Nov. Place one tuber only in a pot and bury this about 1 in. Water very little till plants grow freely, then give an abundant supply. Withhold water entirely when foliage turns yellow and until growth recommences. Apply stimulants occasionally when plants are in flower. Train shoots to wire trellis fixed in pots or up rafters. Temp., Nov. to Feb. 40° to 50°, Feb. to June 55° to 65°. After growth ceases store pots in cool place till potting time.

CULTURE OF HARDY SPECIES: Soil, light, sandy loam for *T. pentaphyllum*; ordinary soil for *T. polyphyllum*; equal parts loam, peat, leaf-mould and sand for *T. speciosum*; poorish soil for *T. tuberosum*. Position, south. wall or fence for *T. pentaphyllum*; sunny bank for *T. polyphyllum*; shaded wall or hedge facing north for *T. speciosum*; sunny border for *T. tuberosum*. Plant *T. tuberosum* in March or April; *T. polyphyllum*, Aug. to Nov.; *T. speciosum* and *T. pentaphyllum*, Oct. or March. Water freely in dry weather. Mulch with decayed manure in Oct. Lift tubers of *T. tuberosum* in Oct. and store in sand in frost-proof place till March; leave others undisturbed.

PROPAGATION: *T. peltophorum* by cuttings of shoots, 2 to 3 in. long, inserted in sandy soil in temp. 50° in spring. Greenhouse tuberous-rooted species by seeds sown in light, sandy soil in temp. 50° in spring; cuttings of shoots inserted in sandy soil and similar temp. in spring or summer. Hardy species by seeds sown in loam, leaf-mould and sand in cold frame in April; *T. majus* outdoors in April; division of roots at planting time.

ANNUAL SPECIES CULTIVATED: *T. majus*, ' Tall Nasturtium ', orange and brown, summer, 5 to 10 ft., Peru, and var. *nanum*, ' Tom Thumb Nasturtium '; *peregrinum* (syn. *T. canariense*), ' Canary Creeper ', yellow, summer, 3 to 10 ft., Peru. All these are strictly perennials but are best grown as annuals.

GREENHOUSE SPECIES: *T. azureum*, blue, green, and white, Oct., 3 to 6 ft., tuberous-rooted, Chile; *minus*, yellow and red, summer, trailing, S. America; *peltophorum* (syn. *T. Lobbianum*), orange-scarlet, summer and winter, 6 to 10 ft., S. America; *pentaphyllum*, vermilion and purple, summer, climbing, tuberous-rooted, Argentine; *tricolor*, vermilion, purple and yellow, summer, climbing, Chile.

HARDY PERENNIAL SPECIES CULTIVATED: *T. polyphyllum*, yellow, June, trailing, Chile; *speciosum*, ' Flame Flower ', crimson, summer, 10 ft., Chile; *tuberosum*, yellow and red, Sept., climbing, tuberous-rooted, Peru.

Trumpet Creeper, see Campsis; **-flower,** see Datura, *Bignonia capreolata*, and Clytostoma.

Tsuga (Hemlock)—*Pinaceae*. Hardy evergreen coniferous trees with handsome and elegant habit of growth. First introduced early eighteenth century.

CULTURE: Soil, deep, rich loam. Position, elevated, well-drained sites in parks or pleasure grounds, succeeding best in areas of heavy rainfall. Plant in autumn.

PROPAGATION: By seeds sown in sandy soil outdoors in April or in pans in gentle warmth in March; cuttings of ripened shoots inserted in sandy soil in cold frames during Sept. or Oct.

SPECIES CULTIVATED: *T. canadensis* (syn. *Abies canadensis*), 'Canadian' or 'Common Hemlock', the most satisfactory species, grows on chalk, 70 to 90 ft., Eastern N. America, with vars. *albo-spica*, young shoots tipped white, and *pendula*, beautiful weeping form, wider than high; *caroliniana*, 'Carolina Hemlock', compact habit, 40 to 60 ft., S.E. United States; *chinensis*, slow growing, elegant, to 150 ft., W. China; *diversifolia*, 'Japanese Hemlock', slow growing, pyramidal, to 70 ft., Japan; *heterophylla* (syn. *T. Albertiana*), 100 to 200 ft., Western N. America; *Mertensiana*, 'Mountain Hemlock', bluish-green leaves, purple cones, 70 to 110 ft., S. Alaska to California; *Sieboldii*, slow growing graceful tree, to 100 ft., Japan. (*Note*: The heights here given refer to trees in their native land, but some species, notably *T. chinensis*, *diversifolia* and *Sieboldii*, are as yet slow growing yet are singularly graceful small trees in this country.)

Tuberose, see *Polianthes tuberosa*.

Tulipa (Tulip)—*Liliaceae*. Hardy bulbous-rooted plants. First introduced late sixteenth century.

R.H.S. CLASSIFICATION: Early-flowering—(1) Duc van Thol, very early, rarely exceeding 6 in. in height; (2) Single Early, March, April; (3) Double Early, March, April; (4) Mendel, mid-season, single tall tulips of medium build; (5) Triumph, mid-season, single tall tulips of stouter build than Mendel and not so tall as Darwin. May-flowering—(6) Cottage, all tulips, including lily-flowered, which do not fall within the other classes; (7) Dutch Breeders, flower oval or cupped, brown, purple or red, but sometimes bronze, base white or yellow, but generally stained blue or green to blue-black; (8) English Breeders, flowers forming one-third to a half of a hollow ball when full expanded, base always white or yellow without trace of other colour; (9) Darwin, lower portion of flower usually rectangular in outline, segments of good substance, stems tall and strong; (10) Broken Dutch Breeders, as (7), but flowers striped or flaked; (11) Broken English Breeders, as (8), but flowers striped or flaked; (12) Rembrandt, as (9), but flowers striped or flaked; (13) Broken Cottage, as (6), but flowers striped or flaked; (14) Parrot, vars. with laciniate segments; (15) Late Double; (16) Species and first crosses between species.

CULTURE: Soil, ordinary light, enriched with manure or compost. Position, sunny beds, borders, rockeries or naturalised in grass. Plant 4 in. deep, 6 in. apart, Sept. to Nov., and mulch surface of soil with compost or manure. Bulbs grown in beds can be lifted directly after flowering and replanted at once into reserve border to finish growth, or left till July and then lifted, dried and stored away till planting time. Bulbs may be left in ground if desired, lifted, divided and replanted every three years.

POT CULTURE: Compost, two parts loam, one part rotted manure and little sand. Pot, Sept. to Nov., placing three bulbs in a 5 in. or four in a 6 in. pot and burying bulbs just below surface. Pot firmly. Place pots in cold frame and cover with cinders or peat for at least eight weeks. Remove to window, frame or greenhouse when growth begins and water freely. Temp. for forcing, 55° to 65°.

CULTURE FOR EXHIBITION: Compost, four parts good turfy loam, one part leaf-mould, one part decayed manure and one part sand mixed together and allowed to remain in heap for a year. Position, well-drained sunny bed containing about 18 in. of above compost. Plant bulbs 3 to 4 in. deep and 6 in. apart, end of Oct. or beginning of Nov. Surround each bulb with sand. Protect blooms with canvas awning. Lift bulbs when leaves turn brown. Store in cool shed to dry, after which remove loose skins and place in drawers till planting time.

PROPAGATION: By seeds sown in Feb. in light sandy soil in cold frame, transplanting following year to bed of rich soil outdoors; offsets removed from parent bulb and planted 3 in. deep in light rich soil in sunny position outdoors in Nov. Seedling bulbs flower when four to six years old, offsets when three to four years old.

SPECIES CULTIVATED: *T. acuminata*, ' Turkish Tulip ', yellow and red, May, 1 to 1¼ ft., Turkey; *australis* (syn. *T. Celsiana*), yellow and red, April, 1¼ ft., France to Algeria; *Batalinii*, yellow, May, 5 to 6 in., Asia Minor; *biflora*, cream and purplish-rose, March, 3 to 4 in., Caucasus; *Billettiana*, yellow, May, 2 ft., Italy; *chrysantha*, yellow and cherry red, April, 6 to 8 in., Persia; *Clusiana*, white, red, and black, April, 12 to 18 in., Portugal to Persia; *Didieri*, crimson and purplish-black, 8 to 12 in., S. Europe; *Eichleri*, scarlet and blue-black, April, 9 to 12 in., S.W. Asia; *elegans*, red and yellow, May, 1 ft., hybrid; *Fosteriana*, scarlet, yellow, and black, April, 12 to 18 in., Turkistan; *Gesneriana*, ' Common Tulip ', scarlet and black, May, fragrant, 2 ft., Armenia, Persia, and vars. *ixioides*, canary-yellow with black centre, *lutea*, yellow, *rosea*, rose, and *spathulata*, larger, red with purple blotch; *Gregii*, scarlet, yellow, and black, April, 6 to 9 in., Turkistan; *Hageri*, copper-red and olive, April, 4 to 6 in., Greece; *ingens*, vermilion and purplish-black, April, 10 to 12 in., Bokhara; *Kaufmanniana*, white, red, and yellow, March, 6 in., Turkistan; *Kolpakowskiana*, yellow and rose, April, 5 to 6 in., Turkistan; *linifolia*, crimson and blue-purple, May, 6 to 8 in., Bokhara; *montana*, crimson and black, June to July, 6 to 8 in., Persia; *Oculus-solis*, red, yellow, and black, April, 18 in., S. Europe; *Orphanidea*, dark orange, April, 8 to 10 in., Greece; *patens* (syn. *T. persica*), yellow, tinged green and red, May, 6 to 9 in., Siberia; *polychroma*, white, yellow, and grey, April, 4 in., Persia; *praecox*, red and black, April, 1½ ft., S. Europe; *praestans*, light scarlet, April, 10 to 12 in., Bokhara; *primulina*, yellow and red, spring, 6 in., Algeria; *pulchella*, mauve-red and yellow, March, 4 to 6 in., S.W. Asia; *saxatilis*, lilac and yellow, May, 9 to 12 in., Crete; *Sprengeri*, orange-scarlet and buff, June, 10 to 12 in., Armenia; *suaveolens*, ' Duc van Thol Tulip ', scarlet and yellow, fragrant, May, 6 in., S. Europe; *tarda* (syn. *T. dasystemon* hort.), white with yellow at base, May, 3 to 6 in., Turkistan; *Tubergeniana*, vermilion and purplish-black, May, 8 to 10 in., Bokhara; *violacea*, mauve, spring, 6 in., N. Persia.

Tulip Tree, see *Liriodendron Tulipifera*.

Tunica—*Caryophyllaceae.* Herbaceous wiry-stemmed perennials.

CULTURE: Soil, ordinary light. Position, sunny well-drained rock gardens or dry walls. Plant, Oct. or March.

PROPAGATION: By seed sown in sandy soil in boxes in cold frame during March; division at the same time.

SPECIES CULTIVATED: *T. Saxifraga*, pink, June to Sept., 6 in., Europe, and vars, *alba*, white, and *flore-pleno*, double.

Tupelo, see Nyssa.

Turfing Daisy, see *Matricaria Tchihatchewii.*

Turkey Beard, see Xerophyllum.

Turkish Hazelnut, see *Corylus Colurna*.

Turk's Cap Cactus, see *Melocactus communis.*

Turmeric, see *Curcuma longa*.

Turnip, see *Brassica Rapa.*

Turtlehead, see Chelone.

Tutsan, see *Hypericum Androsaemum.*

Twin-flower, see *Linnaea borealis*; **-leaf,** see *Jeffersonia diphylla.*

Typha (Cat-tail; Reed Mace)—*Typhaceae.* Hardy aquatic perennials.

CULTURE: Soil, ordinary. Position, margins of shallow rivers or ponds. They may be grown in 1 to 6 in. of water. Plant, Oct. or March.

PROPAGATION: By division or seed.

SPECIES CULTIVATED: *T. angustifolia*, brown, July, 8 to 10 ft., Europe; *latifolia*, brown, July, 6 to 8 ft., N. Temp. Region (Br.); *Laxmannii* (syn. *T. stenophylla*), brown, July, 2 to 4 ft., S.E. Europe to China; *minima*, brown, July, 12 to 18 in., E. Europe.

Typhonodorum—*Araceae.* Stove plant with ornamental arrow-like leaves and bright yellow arum-like flowers; very striking.

CULTURE: Soil, rich loam enriched with rotted manure. Position, tropical tank in warm greenhouse. Temp., Oct. to March 65° to 70°, March to Oct. 70° to 85°.

PROPAGATION: By division; seed sown in shallow pans in warm house.

SPECIES CULTIVATED: *T. Lindleyanum*, yellow spathe 1¾ to 2 ft. long, Aug., 4 to 10 ft., Trop. Africa, Madagascar.

Ulex (Furze; Gorse; Whin)—*Leguminosae.* Very spiny hardy evergreen shrubs.

CULTURE: Soil, poor and dry. Position, full sun, hot banks or rockeries. Overgrown or leggy plants may be hard cut in spring.

PROPAGATION: By seeds sown ¼ in. deep in light soil outdoors in April for common gorse, preferably where the plants are to grow as all forms transplant badly; cuttings inserted in sandy soil in cold frame during Aug. and kept close for the double form, which does not set seed. Grow in pots until planted out.

SPECIES CULTIVATED: *U. europaeus* ' Common Gorse ', gold, all the year round, 3 to 6 ft., Europe, including British Isles, of little garden value, but var. *plenus*, double-flowered, slow growing, compact, most ornamental shrub for dry places, fragrant; *Gallii*, yellow, Aug. to Oct., 2 ft., W. Europe, including Britain; *nanus*, ' Dwarf Gorse ', yellow, September, W. Europe. (*Note*: All three species abundant in heath land and waste areas in Britain.)

Ulmus (Elm)—*Ulmaceae.* Hardy deciduous trees. Flowers insignificant, appearing before the leaves. Some species are indigenous.

CULTURE: Soil, ordinary for common species, deep rich loam with gravelly subsoil for Wych-Elm, moist loam for American Elm. Position, open and sunny woodlands, parks or shrubberies for all species and vars. Not very suitable as garden trees owing to their extensive root systems which impoverish the soil. Large specimens of Common Elm are liable to shed branches without warning. Plant, Oct. to Feb. Timber fine, hard grain and brown in colour, used for making coffins, carts and wagons, furniture, etc. Average weight of timber per cubic foot, 43 lb. Average life of tree, 400 to 500 years. Will thrive to an altitude of 1500 ft.

PROPAGATION: By suckers removed and planted Oct. to Nov.; layering shoots in Sept. or Oct.; budding choice kinds on common species and choice variegated kinds on *U. glabra* in July, or by grafting similarly in March; seeds gathered as soon as ripe and sown in light soil in shade outdoors.

SPECIES CULTIVATED: *U. americana*, ' American ' or ' White Elm ', graceful habit, 100 to 120 ft., Central N. America; *carpinifolia* (syn. *U. nitens*), ' Smooth-leaved Elm ', deeply fissured bark, to 90 ft., Europe, W. Asia, and vars. *pendula*, weeping, *suberosa*, cork-barked, *variegata*, white markings at margins of leaves, *Webbiana*, pyramidal habit; *crassifolia*, ' Cedar Elm ', small thick leaves, slow growing, to 80 ft., S. United States; *fulva*, ' Slippery Elm ', large leaves, 60 to 70 ft., Cent. and Eastern N. America; *glabra* (syn. *U. montana*), ' Wych-Elm ', does not sucker, large rough leaves, 100 to 125 ft., N. Europe, and vars. *Camperdownii*, weeping, *crispa*, narrow leaves, slow growing, *fastigiata*, ' Exeter Elm ', upright growth, *lutescens*, leaves yellow, *pendula*, low growing, weeping, good lawn specimen, *purpurea*, leaves purple; *hollandica major* (syn. *U. major*), ' Dutch Elm ', quick growing, to 120 ft., hybrid, var. *vegeta*, vigorous tree with ascending branches; *procera* (syn. *U. campestris*), ' English Elm ', common in S. England, rarely sets seed, 100 to 150 ft., England and W. Europe, and vars. *argenteo-variegata*, leaves spotted white, *aurea*, yellow leaves, *australis*, pyramidal habit, thick leaves, *Berardii*, small tree, leaves coarsely toothed, *Vanhouttei*, yellow leaved; *Plotii*, ' Pilot Elm ', immense straight trunk, to 90 ft., Europe; *pumila*, dwarf, 10 to 30 ft., E. Siberia, N. China.

Umbellularia—*Lauraceae.* Slightly tender evergreen flowering tree; purple pear-shaped fruits in favoured localities. First introduced early nineteenth century.

CULTURE: Soil, loamy, well drained. Position, against sheltered walls or in the open in mild districts. Plant, Sept. to Oct. or April to May.

PROPAGATION: By seeds sown in pans of sandy soil in cool greenhouse during Feb. or March; layering in spring.

SPECIES CULTIVATED: *U. californica* (syn. *Oreodaphne californica*), yellowish-green, April, 20 to 80 ft., California and Oregon.

Umbilicus—*Crassulaceae.* Succulent perennial plants, sometimes included in the genus Cotyledon.

CULTURE: Soil, ordinary. Position, sunny beds or rock gardens. Plant, Oct. or March.

SPECIES CULTIVATED: *U. pendulinus* (syn. *Cotyledon Umbilicus*), ' Navelwort ', ' Pennywort ', greenish-yellow, June to July, 8 to 12 in., Britain.

Umbrella Leaf, see *Diphylleia cymosa*; **-Pine,** see *Sciadopitys verticillata*; **-Plant,** see *Cyperus alternifolius*; **-Tree,** see *Magnolia tripetala*.

Unicorn Plant, see Proboscidea.

Uniola—*Gramineae.* Hardy perennial grass. Inflorescence borne in large loose panicles, July and Aug.

CULTURE: Soil, ordinary. Plant, March or April. Position, open sunny borders. Gather inflorescence in Aug. and dry for winter use.

PROPAGATION: By seeds sown in light rich soil outdoors in April; division of roots in March.

SPECIES CULTIVATED: *U. latifolia*, ' Sea Oat ', 5 ft., N. America.

Urceolina—*Amaryllidaceae.* Greenhouse deciduous bulbous plants. First introduced early nineteenth century.

CULTURE: Compost, two parts turfy loam, one part river sand and a few crushed bones. Position, well-drained pots in light part of house. Pot, Feb., burying bulb about two-thirds of its depth. Water freely from time growth begins (about Feb.) until Sept., when keep quite dry. Apply liquid manure when flower spike shows. Top-dress annually and repot every three or four years only. Temp., Feb. to Sept. 55° to 65°, Sept. to Feb. 40° to 50°.

PROPAGATION: By seeds sown $\frac{1}{16}$ in. deep in well-drained pots of sandy loam in temp. 65° to 70° in March, placing seedlings singly in 2 in. pots, and keeping them moderately moist all the year round for three years; by offsets, treated as old bulbs.

SPECIES CULTIVATED: *U. miniata*, scarlet, Sept., 1 ft., Peru; *pendula* (syn. *U. aurea*), ' Golden Urn Flower ', ' Drooping Urn Flower ', yellow, summer, 1 ft., Peru.

Urginea—*Liliaceae.* Half-hardy bulbous plant. Source of the ' squill ' of commerce. First introduced early nineteenth century.

CULTURE: Soil, light loam, leaf-mould and sand. Position, well-drained pots in unheated greenhouse. Pot, Oct. to Nov. Water freely during the growing season.

PROPAGATION: By offsets, removed at potting time.

SPECIES CULTIVATED: *U. maritima* (syn. *U. Scilla*), whitish, late summer, to 3 ft., S. Europe and S. Africa.

Ursinia—*Compositae.* Half-hardy annuals. First introduced mid-eighteenth century.

CULTURE: Soil, ordinary. Position, sunny beds or borders. Sow seeds, Feb. or March, in ordinary light soil in pots, pans or boxes in temp. 55° to 65° and transplant seedlings when 1 in. high to 3 in. apart in shallow boxes; place in cold frame in April; harden off and plant outdoors, May or June. Also sow seeds in open ground in April where required to grow and thin seedlings to 4 or 6 in. apart when 1 to 6 in. high.

SPECIES CULTIVATED: *U. anethoides*, orange-yellow, summer, 1 ft., S. Africa; *anthemoides*, yellow and purple, summer, 1 ft., S. Africa; *pulchra* (syn. *Sphenogyne speciosa*), yellow and brown, summer, 1 to 2 ft., S. Africa; *pygmaea*, orange-yellow, summer, 4 to 6 in., S. Africa.

Utricularia (Bladderwort)—*Lentibulariaceae*. Hardy aquatic carnivorous herb.
CULTURE: Soil unnecessary. Position, ponds or tubs in about 2 ft. of water.
Plant, April to May.
PROPAGATION: By division at planting time.
SPECIES CULTIVATED: *U. vulgaris*, yellow, floating, Aug., Europe (Br.).

Uvularia (Bellwort)—*Liliaceae*. Hardy perennial plants. First introduced early eighteenth century.
CULTURE: Soil, moist peat. Position, partially shaded border. Plant, Oct. and Nov.
PROPAGATION: By division of roots in Oct.
SPECIES CULTIVATED: *U. grandiflora*, yellow, May, 1 ft., N. America; *perfoliata*, yellow, May, 1 ft., N. America; *sessilifolia* (syn. *Oakesia sessilifolia*), greenish-yellow, May, 1 ft., N. America.

Vaccinium—*Ericaceae*. Hardy deciduous and evergreen flowering and berry-bearing shrubs. Edible red or bluish-black berries in Aug. to Oct.
CULTURE: Soil, boggy peat, lime-free. Position, moist rock garden or shrubbery. Plant, Oct. to March or April.
PROPAGATION: By seeds, in moist sandy peat in temp. 55° to 65° in spring, transplanting seedlings outdoors in summer; cuttings of semi-matured shoots in sandy, moist peat under hand-light in shade in summer; layering in autumn; division, Sept. to March.
DECIDUOUS SPECIES CULTIVATED: *V. angustifolium*, greenish-white, April to May, 1 ft., N. America, var. *laevifolium* (syn. *V. pensylvanicum*), grown for fruit; *canadense*, white, tinged red, May, 1 to 2 ft., Eastern N. America; *caespitosum*, ' Dwarf Bilberry ', white or pink, May, 1 ft., black berries, N. America; *corymbosum*, ' American Blueberry ', pinkish, May, 4 to 12 ft., Eastern N. America; *erythrocarpum*, red, May, 3 to 6 ft., South-east U.S.A.; *hirsutum*, white, tinged pink, May, 3 ft., N. Carolina, etc.; *Myrtillus*, ' Bilberry ' or ' Whortleberry ', pale pink, May, 6 to 18 in., Europe (Br.), N. Asia; *parvifolium*, pinkish-white, 2 to 10 ft., Western N. America.
EVERGREEN SPECIES CULTIVATED: *V. macrocarpum* (syn. *Oxycoccus macrocarpus*), ' Large American Cranberry ', pink, June to Aug., creeping, N. America; *ovatum*, white or pink, June to July, 10 to 12 ft., Western N. America; *Oxycoccus* (syn. *Oxycoccus palustris*), ' European Cranberry ', pink, May to July, red berries, N. Hemisphere (Br.); *Vitis-idaea*, ' Cowberry ', pink or white, May to June, 6 to 8 in., N. Hemisphere (Br.).

Valerian, see Centranthus.

Valeriana—*Valerianaceae*. Hardy perennial herbs.
CULTURE: Soil, ordinary. Position, sunny borders for *V. Phu*; sunny rock gardens or the front of borders for other species. Plant, Sept. to April. Cut down flowering stems of *V. Phu* in Oct. and pick off flower buds as they form.
PROPAGATION: By seeds sown $\frac{1}{16}$ in. deep in light soil in sunny position outdoors in April; division of roots in March or April.
SPECIES CULTIVATED: *V. arizonica*, pink, March, 2 to 3 in., Arizona; *asarifolia*, red, June, 6 to 9 in., Crete; *celtica*, ' Nard ' or ' Spike ', brownish-yellow, June, 4 to 5 in., Europe; *montana*, rose pink, summer, 6 in., Europe; *Phu*, ' Cretan Spikenard ', white, Aug., 2 ft., Caucasus, var. *aurea*, young shoots golden yellow; *supina*, rose pink, spring and early summer, 3 to 4 in., Europe.

Valerianella—*Valerianaceae*. Hardy annual salad vegetables. Leaves largely used in winter and spring for salads.
CULTURE: Soil, ordinary. Position, sunny, dryish border. Sow seeds in drills, 1 in. deep and 6 in. apart, fortnightly during Aug. and Sept. Thin seedlings when

three leaves form to 6 in. apart in the row. Gather leaves either separately or by cutting off the entire plant. Matures in six to eight weeks.

SPECIES CULTIVATED: *V. eriocarpa*, ' Italian Corn Salad ', light blue, April, leaves to 5 in. long, S. Europe; *Locusta* (syn. *V. olitoria*), ' Corn Salad ' or ' Lamb's Lettuce ', blue, April, leaves to 3 in., Europe (Br.).

Vallisneria—*Hydrocharitaceae*. Half-hardy aquatic herb. In great demand by aquarists. First introduced early nineteenth century.

CULTURE: Soil, rich loam. Position, deep tubs, cisterns or aquariums. Plant in small pot or in heap of compost in bottom of tank, etc., March or April. Temp., Sept. to March 45° to 50°, March to Sept. 60° to 75°.

PROPAGATION: By seeds sown in moist loam in water, spring; division, spring.

SPECIES CULTIVATED: *V. spiralis*, ' Eel Grass ', ' Tape Grass ', minute, white, July, long narrow leaves, S. Europe, N. America, and vars. *gigantea*, and *torta*, with twisted foliage.

Vallota—*Amaryllidaceae*. Greenhouse evergreen bulbous plants. First introduced mid-eighteenth century.

CULTURE: Compost, equal parts good fibrous loam, leaf-mould and sand. Position, well-drained pots in light, sunny greenhouse or window. Pot imported bulbs, Oct., Nov., March or April. Repot established plants in June or July. Place bulbs with points just below the surface; pot firmly. Water moderately Sept. to March, freely March to June, keep nearly dry June to Sept. Apply stimulants once or twice a week March to June. Established plants do best placed in sunny, cold frame, or on layer of cinder ashes or slate, tile or board in open-air, May till flowering period. Repotting necessary every three or four years only. Temp., Sept. to March 40° to 50°, March to June 55° to 65°.

OUTDOOR CULTURE: Soil, light, sandy loam. Position, warm, well-drained border at foot of south wall. Plant bulbs, Oct., Nov., March or April, 6 in. deep and surround with sand. Press soil firmly round bulbs. Protect in winter with a covering of dry litter or fern fronds.

PROPAGATION: By offsets, removed at potting or planting time.

SPECIES CULTIVATED: *V. speciosa* (syns. *V. purpurea* and *Amaryllis purpurea*), ' Scarborough Lily ', red, Aug., 2 to 3 ft., S. Africa, var. *alba*, white.

Vancouveria—*Berberidaceae*. Hardy perennial with creeping rootstocks. First introduced mid-nineteenth century.

CULTURE: Soil, rich loam with leaf-mould or peat. Position, cool, shady beds or borders. Plant, autumn or spring.

PROPAGATION: By division in autumn.

SPECIES CULTIVATED: *V. chrysantha*, yellow, June, 9 in., Oregon; *hexandra*, white, spring, 12 to 18 in., N. America; *planipetala* (syn. *V. parviflora*), white, June, 12 in., California, Oregon.

Vanda—*Orchidaceae*. A large, important, epiphytic genus, widely distributed in the East; numerous species with beautiful flowers; variation is present in habit and flowers; many have tall stems clothed with leaves in two opposite rows. Spikes often long, lateral. As in Aerides, stem roots are emitted from many. Usually the floral segments are spreading and a twist is often noticeable in the petal bases, bringing their reverse surfaces into view; lip usually of much greater substance, smaller, the mid-lobes often ridged. See Vandopsis.

CULTURE: Compost, half part osmunda fibre or substitute, half part sphagnum moss, with a liberal addition of broken crocks, the larger the plant the larger the pieces, placed vertically in the compost; pieces of charcoal may be added and the pots filled to at least one-third with drainage. The wide distribution demands difference in their treatment. *V. Watsonii* should be grown with Odontoglossums, *V. Amesiana*, *Kimballiana*, *caerulea*, a winter temp. of 50° to 55° and very infrequent waterings if any. *V. teres* should also have a very decided rest in winter, but enjoys a moist tropical atmosphere when growing, as do the great majority. The

Far Eastern species should have a winter temp. of 65° to 70°; for some from Borneo and the Philippines, 70° is preferable. All require liberal watering when growing and the syringe may be freely used. In winter discretion must be exercised. The pipe heat used may cause a dry atmosphere with a correct temp.; the syringe, even in winter, is beneficial. With the exception of *V. teres, Amesiana, caerulea* and *Kimballiana*, compost in winter must not get dry. All the harder-leaved kinds should be exposed to light in autumn. At all times draughts should be avoided. Shading is needed in summer, varied according to leaf texture.

PROPAGATION: The taller stemmed kinds, in time, lose their bottom leaves and the stems can be severed below some healthy stem roots in spring. The severed portion may be potted carefully, guiding the roots into the compost. The base may remain in the old pot and usually develops growths which may eventually form a specimen or may be removed when rooted and potted singly. Basal growths are sometimes produced without severance of the stem.

SPECIES CULTIVATED: A selection— *V. Amesiana*, stem short, scape tall, branched, very fragrant, white, rose-flushed, lip deep rose to purple, winter, spring, Burma, N. India; *amoena*, bluish-grey, with deeper spots, lip white, violet-blue, probably a natural hybrid, summer, Burma; *Bensonii*, yellowish, marked chestnut, lip whitish, rose-purple, spring, autumn, Burma; *bicolor*, near *Bensonii*, yellowish-brown, lip whitish, mid-lobe lilac, spring, N. India; *Charlesworthii*, hybrid; *caerulea*, beautiful, variable, large, varying from a soft bluish-grey to deep blue, with darker veins, autumn, various, N. India, Assam, Burma, many named vars. are known; *caerulescens*, rather small, mauve-blue, lip violet-blue, pretty, spring, summer, Burma; *concolor*, fragrant, yellowish-brown, lip white, red, streaked brown, spring, summer, China, Java, Sumatra; *cristata*, dwarf, few, yellowish, mid-lobe reddish with whitish lines, summer, N. India; *Dearei*, tall, three to five large, fragrant, cream-yellow, summer, Borneo, Sunda Isles; *Denisoniana*, ivory white, summer, Burma; *helvola*, red to pale purple, spring, Java; *Hookeriana*, slender, beautiful, white, rose or purple flushed, petals purple spotted, lip white, spotted purple, leaves cylindrical, heat and moisture required all the year, autumn and various, Borneo, Malaya; *insignis*, yellow, with chocolate spots, lip, mid-lobe, rose-purple, concave, summer; *Kimballiana*, white or purplish flushed, lip amethyst-purple, scapes often branched, leaves cylindrical, tapered, autumn, various, Burma; *lamellata*, yellow, blotched chestnut, autumn, Philippines; *limbata*, cinnamon-brown, margined yellow, lip rose-lilac, margined white, summer, Java; *luzonica*, white, dotted and splashed with crimson-purple, lip crimson and white, autumn, Philippines; *Moorei*, a natural hybrid, lilac-purple, variable; *parviflora*, small, many, yellowish, lip whitish, purple marked, summer, N. India, Burma; *Roeblingiana*, brownish, veined yellowish, lip white, purple streaked, mid-lobe two-lobed, fringed, summer, Malaya; *Sanderiana* (syn. *Euanthe Sanderiana*), seven to fifteen, large, rose, whitish, tawny, red spotted and flushed, lip small, tawny yellow, red streaked, chocolate, purple, very variable, various, Philippines; *Stangeana*, greenish-yellow, suffused and marked red-brown, lip white and mauve, summer, Assam; *teres*, two to five, large, variable, whitish, rose, rose-magenta, lip funnel-like, orange, mid-lobe expanded, magenta-rose, stems 2 to 7 ft. or more, leaves cylindrical, no shading, spring, summer, N. India, Burma, many vars.; *tesselata* (syn. *V. Roxburghii*), fragrant, greenish, tessellated brown, mid-lobe of lip violet-purple, variable, summer, autumn, N. India, Burma, Ceylon; *tricolor*, handsome, very variable, typically yellow, with brownish-red spots, lip whitish, mid-lobe purplish, autumn, various, Java, so variable is the species that very many varietal names have been given; *Watsonii*, many, pure white, lip margin fringed, leaves and flowers set closely, various, Annam.

Vandopsis—*Orchidaceae.* An epiphytic genus. The name is applied to Vanda-like plants in which a distinction from that genus is that the obscurely three-lobed lip has its centre formed into a more or less prominent ridge. Authorities are not all agreed as to the limits of the genus.

CULTURE: Compost, temps. as for the warmer-growing Vandas. Waterings are required in the winter but consideration must be given to the hard-leaf texture of some.

PROPAGATION: As for Vandas.

SPECIES CULTIVATED: *V. gigantea* (syn. *Vanda gigantea*), large, fleshy, six to fifteen, yellow with chestnut brown spots, spring, summer, Burma; *lissochiloides* (syn. *Vanda Batemannii*), large, twelve to twenty, yellow, densely spotted with red-purple, crimson behind lip, buff yellow to purplish, summer, Philippines, Moluccas; *Parishii* (syn. *Vanda Parishii*), fragrant, yellowish, spotted red-brown, lip magenta-purple, leaves broad, almost oblong, summer, Burma.

Vanilla—*Orchidaceae*. Sixty or seventy species of climbing orchids, stems often long and branching, some losing all connection with the ground, some leafless, some with fleshy or leathery leaves. Scapes axillary or lateral. Flowers few or several, comparatively large in some species. One species, *V. fragrans*, is largely cultivated abroad, as the essence ' Vanilla ' is obtained from its seed pods.

CULTURE: Compost, two parts osmunda fibre or peat, two parts sphagnum moss, small pots well drained. The leafed species can be used as roof climbers. The leafless should be placed against a wall, failing that a pole or bar covered with a thin layer of compost. A moist, warm atmosphere is required throughout the year. The syringe freely used in summer, required less in winter. Winter temp. 70°, summer temp., with shading, considerably higher with sun heat.

PROPAGATION: The leafed species by cuttings, side branches may be taken off or the main stem cut into lengths as desired provided roots are present. The leafless species often resent attempts to propagate. Side branches, if any, may be attempted.

SPECIES CULTIVATED: A selection—*V. fragrans* (syn. *V. planifolia*), eight to twenty, fragrant, whitish-green or yellowish, yellow, summer, Mexico; *Humboltii*, large, light yellow, lip with crimson hairs in throat, leafless, summer, Madagascar; *Phalaenopsis*, six to seven, white, rose flushed, lip orange, pale rose, leafless, summer, Madagascar; *Pompona* (syn. *V. lutescens*), near *V. fragrans*, six to eight, yellow, summer, autumn, Brazil; *Walkerae*, many, white, leafless, Ceylon, India.

Variegated Laurel, see Aucuba.

Vegetable Marrow, see *Cucurbita Pepo*; **-Oyster, see** *Tragopogon porrifolius*.

Veltheimia—*Liliaceae*. Greenhouse bulbous plants. First introduced mid-eighteenth century.

CULTURE: Compost, two parts sandy loam, one part well-decayed cow manure, and little sand. Position, light, sunny greenhouse or window Sept. to June; sunny, cold frame remainder of year. Pot bulbs of *V. viridifolia* Aug. to Nov.; those of *V. glauca* Oct. to March. Place bulbs with point just below surface of compost. Press compost firmly in pots. Water moderately when new growth commences, freely when in full growth, keep nearly dry when leaves die off. Apply stimulants occasionally when the plants are growing freely. Temp., Sept. to March 40° to 50°, March to June 55° to 65°.

PROPAGATION: By offsets, removed from parent bulbs, placed in small pots, and treated as advised for large bulbs; by leaves removed close to bulbs and inserted singly in pots of sandy soil in spring or summer; by seeds sown as soon as ripe in sandy soil in temp. 55° to 65°.

SPECIES CULTIVATED: *V. Deasii*, pinkish, tinged green, winter, 1 ft., S. Africa; *glauca*, yellow, tinged red, March, 1 to 1½ ft., S. Africa; *viridifolia*, ' Unicorn-root ', yellow, tinged red, winter, 1 to 1½ ft., S. Africa.

Velvet Flower, see *Amaranthus caudatus*; **-Grass,** see *Holcus lanatus*.

Venidium—*Compositae*. Half-hardy annuals and perennials. All treated as half-hardy annuals.

CULTURE: Soil, ordinary. Position, sunny borders. Sow seeds in light soil in temp. 50° to 55°, March or April, transplanting seedlings outdoors May or June.

SPECIES CULTIVATED: *V. decurrens* (syn. *V. calendulaceum*), yellow and purplish-brown, summer, 2 ft., S. Africa, perennial treated as annual; *fastuosum*, orange and purplish-black, summer, 1½ to 2½ ft., S. Africa.

Venus's Flytrap, see *Dionaea muscipula*; **-Looking-glass,** see *Specularia Speculum-Veneris*.

Veratrum (False Hellebore)—*Liliaceae.* Hardy herbaceous perennials with large, much ribbed, green leaves and poisonous roots. First introduced mid-sixteenth century.

CULTURE: Soil, light ordinary or peaty. Position, partially shady, moist borders. Plant, Oct., March or April.

PROPAGATION: By seeds sown in peaty soil in deep pans in cool greenhouse during Feb. or March; division of roots, Oct. or April. Seed frequently takes several months to germinate.

SPECIES CULTIVATED: *V. album*, white, July, 3 to 4 ft., Europe; *californicum*, greenish-white, summer, to 6 ft., California; *nigrum*, maroon, summer, 4 to 5 ft., Europe; *viride*, yellowish-green, July, 5 to 8 ft., N. America.

Verbascum (Mullein)—*Scrophulariaceae.* Hardy biennial and perennial herbs.

CULTURE OF BIENNIAL SPECIES: Soil, ordinary. Position, sunny borders. Sow seeds in light, rich soil in sunny position outdoors in April, transplanting seedlings when three or four leaves form, 6 in. apart in sunny position until following April, then plant where required to flower.

CULTURE OF PERENNIAL SPECIES: Soil, deep, light, rich ordinary. Position, sunny borders. Plant, Oct., March or April.

PROPAGATION: By seeds, as advised for biennial species; division of roots in March or April; root cuttings taken early in the year.

BIENNIAL SPECIES CULTIVATED: *V. olympicum*, ' Olympic Mullein ', yellow, summer, 6 ft., Greece; *Thapsus*, yellow, summer, to 6 ft., Europe (Br.) and Asia.

PERENNIAL SPECIES CULTIVATED: *V. Chaixii*, ' Nettle-leaved Mullein ', yellow, summer, 3 ft., S.W. Europe; *longifolium*, yellow, July to Aug., 4 to 6 ft., Europe, and var. *pannosum*; *nigrum*, ' Dark Mullein ', yellow, summer, 3 ft., Europe (Br.); *Pestalozzae*, yellow, June, 4 to 6 in., Europe; *phoeniceum*, ' Purple Mullein ', violet and red, summer, 3 ft., Europe; *thapsiforme* (syn. *V. densiflorum*), yellow, summer, to 5 ft., Europe; *Wiedemannianum*, blue and purple, summer, to 3 ft., Asia Minor. There are numerous hybrids.

Verbena (Vervain)—*Verbenaceae.* Greenhouse half-hardy perennials. Present race of bedding verbenas originally derived from *V. teucrioides* and other species. First introduced mid-eighteenth century.

CULTURE OF V. TEUCRIOIDES: Compost, two parts good turfy loam and one part of equal proportions of decayed manure, leaf-mould and sharp silver sand. Position, pots in light greenhouse, or cold frames in summer. Pot, Feb. to May. Water freely April to Oct., moderately afterwards. Apply stimulants two or three times weekly to plants in flower. Nip off points of shoots during spring to induce bushy growth, discontinue six weeks before plants are required to flower. Young plants struck from cuttings or raised from seed best suited to pot culture. Temp., Oct. to March 40° to 50°, March to June 55° to 65°. Shade from sun.

OUTDOOR CULTURE: Soil, good ordinary, liberally enriched with decayed manure. Position, sunny beds or borders. Plant 12 in. apart each way in June. Water freely in dry weather. Peg shoots to surface of bed as they grow, and when they meet each other nip off their points.

CULTURE OF V. CANADENSIS, V. LACINIATA AND V. TENERA: Soil, ordinary. Sow seeds in pans of sandy soil in temp. 60° during Feb. or March, transplanting seedlings to deep boxes when large enough to handle and hardening off for planting outdoors in sunny beds or borders during May. Really perennials but are best treated as half-hardy annuals.

CULTURE OF V. RIGIDA and V. BONARIENSIS: Soil, ordinary rich. Position, sunny beds or borders. Plant, May. Lift roots in Oct., store in ordinary soil in boxes in frost-proof place until March, then place in temp. 55°, and when new shoots form remove these with portions of old roots, place in small pots, harden off, and plant out 12 in. apart in May; or plant old roots, dividing them, if neccessary, direct into beds in April. Peg shoots of *V. rigida* down as they grow. May be grown outdoors altogether in well-drained soils in sheltered districts.

CULTURE OF V. PERUVIANA: Soil, ordinary. Position, sunny beds or rock gardens. Insert cuttings of current year's growth in Aug. and Sept. in boxes filled with sandy soil and place in frost-proof frame or greenhouse until May, then plant in the open. Plants may survive outdoors in a mild winter.

PROPAGATION: Garden verbenas by seeds sown $\frac{1}{16}$ in. deep in pots, pans or boxes filled with a compost of equal parts loam and leaf-mould and little sand, placed in a temp. 65° to 75° in Jan., Feb. or March, transplanting seedlings when third leaf forms in boxes or pans, placing these on shelf near glass in temp. 55°, transferring when fairly strong singly in 2½ in. pots, and later on to a larger size; by cuttings inserted in a bed of sandy soil in cold frame in Aug., lifting cuttings when rooted and planting 2 in. apart in boxes or pans and storing in shelf in green-house until March, then potting off singly in small pots; or young shoots taken off in Feb. or March and inserted in damp sand under bell-glass in temp. 65°.

SPECIES CULTIVATED: *V. bonariensis*, purplish-lilac, summer, 4 to 5 ft., S. America; *canadensis* (syns. *V. Aubletia* and *V. Drummondii*), purple or lilac, summer, 1 ft., N. America; *laciniata*, lilac, summer, trailing, Peru; *peruviana*, scarlet, summer and autumn, trailing, Brazil, Peru, etc.; *radicans*, lilac, trailing, summer, Brazil; *rigida*, claret-purple, summer, 2 ft., Argentine; *tenera*, blue or lilac, summer, trailing, Southern S. America; *teucrioides*, yellowish-white or pink, summer, 1 ft., Brazil, etc.

Veronia (Ironweed)—*Compositae*. Hardy herbaceous flowering plants. First introduced early eighteenth century.

CULTURE: Soil, rich, sandy loam. Position, sunny borders. Plant, March or April. Top-dress with decayed manure in spring.

PROPAGATION: By seeds sown in sandy soil in a cold frame in March or April, or outdoors in a sunny border in April; also by division of the roots in March or April.

SPECIES CULTIVATED: *V. altissima*, purple and violet, autumn, 4 to 10 ft., U.S.A.; *crinita* (syn. *V. arkansana*), purple, autumn, 4 to 12 ft., N. America; *noveboracensis*, purple, summer, 4 to 9 ft., U.S.A.

Veronica (Speedwell)—*Scrophulariaceae*. Hardy herbaceous perennials. Shrubby New Zealand species have been transferred to Hebe.

CULTURE: Soil, ordinary rich. Position, sunny borders or rockeries; water-garden for *V. Anagallis* and *V. Beccabunga*. Plant, Sept. to Nov. or Feb. to May. Lift, divide and replant about every third year. Water freely in dry weather.

PROPAGATION: By division of roots in autumn or spring; seeds sown in light soil in shade outdoors in April.

SPECIES CULTIVATED: *V. Allionii*, violet-blue, June to July, 2 in., S.W. Europe; *Anagallis*, ' Water Speedwell ', pale blue, 6 to 18 in., Europe; *Beccabunga*, ' Brook Lime ', blue, succulent, 9 to 12 in., Europe; *caespitosa*, pink, May to June, 1 to 2 in., Greece; *canescens*, pale blue, July, prostrate, New Zealand; *cinerea*, pink, July to Aug., 3 to 4 in., Asia Minor; *filiformis*, china blue, May to June, 3 in., Asia Minor; *fruticans* (syn. *V. saxatilis*), blue, July, shrubby, 6 in., Europe; *gentianoides*, blue, June, 8 to 12 in., S.E. Europe, and var. *variegata*, leaves varie-gated with white; *incana*, blue, summer, 18 in., S. Europe; *latifolia* (syn. *V. Teucrium*), blue, May to June, 1½ ft., Europe, and vars. *dubia*, *prostrata* and *rosea*; *linifolia*, white or pale pink, June, 6 to 8 in., New Zealand; *maritima* (syn. *V. longifolia*), lilac-blue, Aug., 1½ to 2 ft., Europe, and var. *subsessilis*, deep blue; *orientalis*, pink, summer, 6 to 8 in., Asia Minor; *pectinata*, pale blue, May to June, 6 in., Caucasus; *repens*, pale blue, summer, 2 to 3 in., creeping, Corsica; *saturej-oides*, deep blue, April, 3 in., Dalmatia; *spicata*, blue, July, 12 to 18 in., Europe, and vars. *alba*, white, *corymbosa*, pale blue, and *rosea*, pink.

Verschaffeltia—*Palmae*. Stove palm with bright green roundish leaves, divided at tips. First introduced mid-nineteenth century.

CULTURE: Compost, two parts fibrous peat, one part equal proportions charcoal, turfy loam and sand. Position, moist, shady part of stove. Pot, Feb. or March. Syringe freely twice daily Feb. to Oct., once daily afterwards. Water freely at all times. Shade and moist atmosphere essential. Temp., March to Oct. 70° to 85°, Oct. to March 65° to 75°.

PROPAGATION: By seeds sown 1 in. deep in peat and loam in small pots in temp. 75° to 85°, spring.

SPECIES CULTIVATED: *V. splendida*, 12 to 80 ft., Seychelles.

Vervain, see Verbena.

Vesicaria—*Cruciferae*. Hardy perennial with large inflated pods following flowers. First introduced early eighteenth century.

CULTURE: Soil, ordinary. Position, sunny borders or rock gardens. Plant, autumn or spring.

PROPAGATION: By division; seed sown in spring.

SPECIES CULTIVATED: *V. utriculata*, yellow, May to June, large, inflated seed pods, to 1½ ft., Europe.

Vetch, see Vicia; **Kidney-,** see *Anthyllis Vulneraria*.

Viburnum—*Caprifoliaceae*. Extensive group of hardy deciduous and evergreen flowering shrubs. Some have beauty of blossom, others of fruit and autumn-tinted foliage.

CULTURE: Soil, deep moist loam, preferably rich. Many species thrive in partial shade. In borders, or as single specimens, in moderately sheltered positions. Avoid dry positions. No routine pruning, but avoid overcrowding on older specimens, removing weak shoots in winter.

CULTURE OF LAURUSTINUS: Soil, deep sandy loam. Position, warm, sheltered shrubberies, etc.; useful for town gardens. Plant, Sept., Oct. or April. Laurustinus makes a good hedge to 6 or 8 ft. high, flowering in winter. Space at 2 to 2¼ ft. apart, and clip or prune in April or May; is also suitable for pot culture for flowering in cold greenhouses in winter. Pot, spring. Position, outdoors in semi-shady position, May till Oct.; in cold greenhouse, Oct. to May. Water freely while outdoors, moderately in winter.

PROPAGATION: By cuttings of half-ripened shoots inserted in sandy loam under bell-glass in gentle bottom heat during July and Aug.; layering shoots in Sept. or Oct.

DECIDUOUS SPECIES CULTIVATED: *V. alnifolium*, ' Hobble Bush ', white, June, dark purple fruits, 6 to 10 ft., Eastern N. America; *betulifolium*, berries like red currants, freely borne, 10 to 15 ft., China; *bitchiuense*, pink and white, fragrant, May, resembling *V. Carlesii* but more straggling, 6 to 10 ft., Japan; *bodnantense*, pink and white, winter, fragrant, hybrid; *Carlesii*, blush in bud, opening white, very fragrant, April to May, 3 to 4 ft., Korea; *Carlcephalum*, as preceding, larger flowers, stronger growth, very fragrant, hybrid; *corylifolium*, red berries, autumn tints, 6 to 8 ft., Cent. and W. China; *dasyanthum*, red fruits, 6 to 8 ft., Cent. China; *dentatum*, ' Arrow Wood ', white, June, 15 ft., N. America; *dilatatum*, white, June, oval bright red berries, 6 to 9 ft., Japan and China; *erubescens*, pale pink, June, fruit red, changing to black, to 20 ft., Himalaya, W. China; *fragrans*, pale pink, fragrant, winter, 6 to 9 ft., N. China; *furcatum*, resembling *V. alnifolium*, more upright, 6 to 9 ft., China; *grandiflorum*, pink and white, winter, to 8 ft., Himalaya; *hupehense*, red berries, 5 to 8 ft., Cent. China; *ichangense*, white, small, numerous, May, red fruits, 4 to 6 ft., Cent. and W. China; *Juddii*, compact growth, hybrid; *kansuense*, pink, June, red fruits, maple-like foliage, 4 to 8 ft., China; *Lantana*, ' Wayfaring Tree ', white, June, fruits red, changing to black, autumn-tinted foliage, 10 to 15 ft., Europe, including Britain; *Lentago*, ' Sheepberry ', white, May to June, dark blue fruits, 20 to 30 ft., Canada to Georgia; *lobophyllum*, bright red berries, 10 to 15 ft., Cent. and W. China; *macrocephalum*, ' Chinese Snowball ', white, May, 12 to 15 ft., with var. *sterile*, flowers larger than our native Guelder Rose; *Opulus*, white, June, autumn tints and scarlet berries, 10 to 15 ft., Europe, N. Africa, N. Asia, and vars. *roseum* (syn. var. *sterile*), ' Snowball ', ' Guelder Rose ', large flowered, non-fruiting form of gardens, and *xanthocarpum*, fruits yellowish-amber; *trilobum*, ' Cranberry Bush ', scarlet fruits, 8 to 10 ft., U.S.A.; *tomentosum*, white, May, horizontal branches, 6 to 10 ft., China and Japan, and vars. *Mariesii* and *sterile*, ' Japanese Snowball ', both very free-flowering.

EVERGREEN SPECIES CULTIVATED: *V. Burkwoodii*, white, April to May, fragrant, attractive easily grown shrub, 6 to 8 ft., hybrid; *cinnamomifolium*, to 8 ft., W. China; *Davidii*, dull white, June, attractive turquoise-blue berries, leathery leaves, 2 to 3 ft., W. China; *Harryanum*, black fruits, small leaves, 5 to 8 ft., W. China; *Henryi*, white, June to July, fruits red, changing to black, free, 10 ft., China; *propinquum*, blue fruits, lustrous narrow leaves, 2 to 3 ft., Cent. and W. China; *rhytidophyllum*, dull white, May to June, fruits red then black, large wrinkled leaves, vigorous, 8 to 12 ft., Cent. and W. China, with var. *roseum*, flowers bright pink on back; *Tinus*, ' Laurustinus ', white, Nov. to April, to 10 ft., S.E. Europe, with vars. *hirtum*, larger leaves and taller, rather tender, *lucidum*, larger leaves, rather tender, and *variegatum*, leaves yellow variegated; *utile*, white, May, dark blue fruits, leaves white beneath, 4 to 6 ft., Cent. China.

Vicia (Vetch)—*Leguminosae*. Mostly tendril-climbing vines. The seeds of one species (Broad Bean) are used as a vegetable and some species cultivated as forage plants.

CULTURE OF BROAD BEANS: Soil, rich, well-manured, moist loam for main crops; lighter, rich soil for early ones. Position, south borders for early crops; open garden for main or late ones. Sow early longpod vars. in Feb., maincrop sorts in March and April. Distances, drills 3 in. deep and 1½ ft. apart. Seeds to be 9 in. apart in drills. Nip out growing points of plants when first flowers open. Mulch late crops with decayed manure, especially on light soils. Crop ready for use eighteen weeks after sowing. Seeds take twelve to fourteen days to germinate. Seeds retain their germinating powers one year. Quantity of seeds to sow a row 50 ft. long, 1 pint.

CULTURE OF PERENNIAL SPECIES: Soil, ordinary. Position, sunny rock garden or front of border. Plant, Oct. to Nov. or March to April.

PROPAGATION: Perennial species by seed sown in cold frame in March.

ANNUAL SPECIES CULTIVATED: *V. Faba*, ' Broad Bean ', white, June and July, 3 ft., N. Africa, S.W. Asia.

PERENNIAL SPECIES CULTIVATED: *V. oroboides* (syn. *Orobus lathyroides*), white or yellow, summer, 2 ft., Europe.

Victoria (Queen Victoria Water-lily)—*Nymphaceae*. Stove aquatic plant. Leaves, roundish, flat, with turned-up edges; bronze-green; 4 to 6 ft. diameter; floating. First introduced early nineteenth century.

CULTURE: Compost, two parts good, rich turfy loam, one part decayed cow manure. Position, large tank 6 ft. deep and 20 to 25 ft. wide. Plant, May. Temp. of water, 80° to 85°. Temp. of atmosphere, March to Sept. 75° to 85°, Sept. to March 65° to 70°. No shade required.

PROPAGATION: By seeds sown in pot of sandy loam submerged in water heated to temp. of 85° and placed near glass in light position, Jan. When seedlings appear above surface, transplant singly in small pots and place in water again until May, then plant out as above advised. *V. regia* is strictly a perennial, but thrives best treated as an annual in this country.

SPECIES CULTIVATED: *V. Cruziana*, will succeed in cooler temp., rose, Bolivia; *regia*, ' Royal Water-lily ', white, rose, and purple, summer, Trop. America.

Victoria Water-lily, see *Victoria regia*.

Victorian Box, see *Pittosporum undulatum*.

Villarsia—*Gentianaceae.* Hardy marsh and aquatic herbs with pretty yellow flowers. First introduced late eighteenth century.

CULTURE: Position, at pond margin in wet soil or shallow water. Soil, immaterial. Plant, spring.

PROPAGATION: By division in spring or autumn; seeds sown in pans of sandy loam standing in saucers of water.

SPECIES CULTIVATED: *V. ovata,* citron, July to Sept., 6 to 12 in., Africa; *parnassifolia* 1 to 2 ft., yellow, Australia. See also Nymphoides.

Vinca (Periwinkle)—*Apocynaceae.* Hardy and tender evergreen and deciduous trailing sub-shrubs or herbs.

CULTURE OF STOVE SPECIES: Compost, two parts fibrous loam, one part decayed manure and a little silver sand. Position, well-drained pots in stove Sept. to June, sunny cold frame or greenhouse remainder of year. Pot, Feb. or March. Prune shoots of old plants to within 1 or 2 in. of their base in Jan. or Feb. Water freely April to Oct., moderately afterwards. Apply weak stimulants occasionally during summer and autumn. Nip off points of shoots in young or old plants once or twice during July and Aug. to ensure bushy habit. Temp., March to June 65° to 75°, Sept. to March 55° to 65°. Alternatively, *V. rosea* may be treated as a tender annual. Sow seeds in temp. 70° during Feb. or March and transplant seedlings to small pots as soon as large enough to handle.

CULTURE OF HARDY SPECIES: Soil, ordinary. Position, flowers best in sunny places beneath hedges or on banks, also useful as ground cover in shady places beneath trees. Cut back in early spring.

PROPAGATION: By cuttings of young shoots removed when 2 or 3 in. long and inserted in sandy soil under bell-glass in temp. 65° to 75° in spring, or seed in temp. 70° during Feb. for *V. rosea*; hardy species, division in March or April.

STOVE SPECIES CULTIVATED: *V. rosea,* ' Madagascar Periwinkle ', rose, summer, 1 to 2 ft., Tropics, and var. *alba,* white.

HARDY SPECIES CULTIVATED: *V. difformis* (syn. *V. media*), pale lilac-blue, Dec. to March, 1 ft., for warmest districts, S.W. Europe; *major,* ' Large Periwinkle ', bright blue, May to Oct., trailing, 1 to 2 ft., Europe (Br.), and var. *variegata* (syn. var. *elegantissima*), leaves blotched and margined yellow-white; *minor,* ' Lesser Periwinkle ', blue, summer, trailing, Europe (Br.), and numerous vars.

Vine, see Vitis.

Viola (Violet; Pansy)—*Violaceae.* Hardy herbaceous perennial herbs.

CLASSIFICATION: Pansies in general—Any free-growing or free-flowering strain, self-coloured or variegated. Show Pansy—Blooms circular, flat and smooth, without wavy or crinkled edges, diameter 1½ in. Fancy Pansy—Blooms circular, flat and smooth, with wavy or crinkled edges. Tufted Pansy—A name applied to a class of pansies commonly called ' violas ', hybrids of the ordinary pansy and the Horned Violet (*V. cornuta*); blooms smaller than those of ordinary pansies; colours varied; habit, dwarf, not spreading as in the pansy. Violetta—Strain of very dwarf pansies, the result of a cross between a pansy and *Viola cornuta*; flowers, small, rayless and fragrant.

CULTURE OF SHOW, FANCY AND TUFTED PANSIES AND VIOLETTAS: Soil—(*a*) deep, rich, moist loam enriched with well-decayed cow manure; (*b*) two parts loam, one part of equal proportions of leaf-mould and sand; (*c*) ordinary light soil enriched with cow manure; (*d*) clay or heavy soils with decayed horse or cow manure. Soil best manured and dug previous autumn. Position, open, light, sheltered, away from roots and branches of trees, and shaded from mid-day sun. Plant pansies in Sept., Oct. or April, 12 in. apart each way; tufted pansies, March or April, 10 in. apart each way. Mulch with leaf-mould in May or June. Stir the surface frequently. Water copiously in dry weather, applying it in the evening. Remove all flower buds until plants are established. If exhibition blooms are desired allow only one bloom to grow on each shoot. Feed once a week during the growing season with a weak solution of a compound fertiliser.

CULTURE OF VIOLET: Soil, ordinary, previously well enriched with well-decayed manure. Clay soils require plenty of grit, decayed vegetable refuse and manure incorporated with them. Light and gravelly soils need a liberal amount of cow manure and loam or clay mixed with them. Position, border or bed on north or north-east side of hedge or under the shade of fruit trees. Full exposure to hot summer sun undesirable. Plant crowns 9 in. apart in rows 12 in. asunder, April. ' Crowns ' are portions separated from parent plant, each furnished with roots. Water when first planted and shade from sun. Apply manures recommended for pansies at intervals of three weeks during summer. Remove runners, *i.e.* shoots that issue from the crowns, as they form during summer and keep plants free from weeds. Lift plants for winter blooming in Sept. and replant, 6 to 8 in. apart, in equal parts good soil and leaf-mould in a cold, sunny frame. Water freely in fine weather. Protect from frost. In case of deep frames, decayed manure may be used to fill up space to within 12 in. of light, putting 6 in. of above soil on this. Replant annually.

POT CULTURE: Compost, two parts loam, one part leaf-mould and one part sand. Pot, April, placing six crowns in a 6 in. pot. Place in a shady frame and water moderately. Plunge pots to their rims outdoors in shade in May and let them remain till Sept., when remove to greenhouse. Water freely outdoors, moderately in winter. Winter temp., 40° to 50°.

CULTURE OF OTHER SPECIES: Soil, ordinary rich. Position, moist, partially shaded rockeries, beds or borders. Plant, March or April, 3 to 6 in. apart.

PROPAGATION: By seeds sown in light, sandy soil in boxes or pans in cold, shady frame in July or Aug., transplanting seedlings into flowering positions in Sept. or Oct.; cuttings inserted in cold, shady frames in Aug. or Sept.; divisions in Sept. or Oct.; violets by runners in April.

SPECIES CULTIVATED: *V. alpina*, purple, May, 3 in., E. Europe; *altaica*, ' Altaian Violet ', lilac-purple or yellow, May, 6 in., Taurus and Asia Minor; *arborescens*, lavender blue, 6 to 8 in., S. France; *Beckwithii*, purple and pale lilac, 3 to 4 in., California; *biflora*, ' Twin-flowered Violet ', yellow, June, 3 in., Europe and N. Asia; *calcarata*, ' Spurred Violet ', violet or variable, May to June, 4 in., Europe (Br.); *canadensis*, white, yellow, and violet, 12 in., N. America; *canina*, ' Dog Violet ', blue or white, May, 3 to 4 in., Europe (Br.); *cenisia*, violet-purple, 3 to 4 in., Alps; *cornuta*, ' Horned Violet ', blue, summer, 6 in., Pyrenees, one of the parents of the Garden Viola or Tufted Pansy; *cucullata*, ' Hollow-leaved Violet ', violet, spring, 3 to 4 in., N. America; *elegantula* (syn. *V. bosniaca*), rosy mauve, May to June, 4 in., S.W. Europe; *gracilis*, ' Olympian Violet ', violet-purple, June, 4 to 6 in., Macedonia and Asia Minor; *hederacea* (syn. *Erpetion reniforme*), purple and white, summer, 2 to 3 in., Australia; *lutea*, ' Mountain Violet ', yellow, June, 3 in., Europe (Br.); *Munbyana*, ' Munby's Violet ', violet or yellow, spring, 6 to 12 in., Medit. Region; *nummularifolia*, blue and blackish violet, summer, 3 to 4 in., Maritime Alps; *odorata*, ' Sweet Violet ', blue, spring, 6 in., Europe (Br.), and numerous vars.; *palustris*, ' Marsh Violet ', pale lilac to white, May, 3 to 4 in., N. Europe (Br.); *pedata*, ' Bird's-foot Violet ', violet and lilac, May, 6 in., N. America, and var. *alba*, white; *pedunculata*, orange-yellow, summer, 6 to 8 in., California; *pinnata*, rosy lilac, May to June, 2 to 3 in., Europe; *sylvestris*, ' Wood Violet ', blue, spring, 6 in., Europe; *tricolor*, ' Heartsease ', yellow, purple, and white, summer, 6 in., Europe (Br.), one of the parents of the Pansy.

Violet, see Viola.

Viper's Bugloss, see Echium.

Virginian Cowslip, see *Mertensia virginica;* **-Creeper,** see *Parthenocissus quinquefolia;* **-Poke,** see *Phytolacca americana;* **-Snowflower,** see *Chionanthus virginica;* **-Stock,** see *Malcomia maritima;* **-Willow,** see *Itea virginica.*

Virgin's Bower, see Clematis.

Viscaria, see Lychnis.

Viscum (Mistletoe)—*Loranthaceae.* Hardy evergreen parasitical plant with white berries; male and female flowers are borne on separate plants.

CULTURE: Cut a notch in bark on underside of branch and press ripe berry gently into it in March. Young plants grow slowly for two or three years. Trees suitable for mistletoe culture: Apple, hawthorn, poplar, lime, maple, mountain ash, cedar, larch and oak; two first most suitable.

SPECIES CULTIVATED: *V. album*, green, March, Europe (Br.).

Vitex—*Verbenaceae.* Slightly tender, deciduous, aromatic, flowering shrubs. First introduced mid-sixteenth century.

CULTURE: Soil, ordinary. Position, sheltered, warm border or against south wall in southern districts. In open, mildest areas only. Plant, Oct. to Feb. Prune out older wood, Feb.

PROPAGATION: By cuttings of shoots inserted in ordinary light, sandy soil under bell-glass in cool greenhouse or cold frame, Sept. or Oct.

SPECIES CULTIVATED: *V. Agnus-castus*, 'Chaste Tree', 'Tree of Chastity', violet blue, Sept. to Oct., to 10 ft., S. Europe, with var. *alba*, flowers white; *Negundo*, 'Chinese Chaste Tree', lavender blue, autumn, 10 ft., China, var. *incisa*, deeply toothed leaves.

Vitis (Vine)—*Vitaceae.* Hardy and greenhouse climbing shrubs, some species grown for fruit and others for screen or wall cover. Some species formerly included in this genus have been reclassified and will be found under Ampelopsis, Parthenocissus and Cissus.

CULTURE OF GRAPE VINE UNDER GLASS: A border should be prepared, 3 ft. deep and the length of the house, and 10 to 12 ft. wide, sloping slightly to the front. Surround this with brick or concrete so that the roots do not penetrate to unprepared soil. Provide drainage with a 9 in. layer of rubble and cover this with a layer of turves grass side downwards. Fill the border with a well-mixed compost of eight parts chopped turf, one part old mortar rubble, half a part wood ashes, quarter part charcoal broken to the size of peas. Add ½ lb. bonemeal to each bushel of the mixture. Purchase vine in Nov. and stand pot in house; cut back so that top eye is level with bottom pane of glass. Plant as growth commences in Feb. to March, covering upper roots with 2 in. of soil. Water in freely. Single rods 5 to 6 ft. apart. If the prepared border is outside the house take rod through a hole in brickwork near soil level and fill space with straw or sacking.

PRUNING: Vines are thinned and stopped periodically during the spring and summer and the laterals pruned back to within two buds of the main rod in winter.

STARTING VINES: Lower rods from training wires. Start between Jan. to March according to date when fruit required. Close ventilators and raise temp. by fire heat to 50° at night. Water the border and mulch with 3 in. rotted manure. Syringe with tepid water to maintain a moist atmosphere. Retie rods when growth starts. Thin berries each fortnight from time they form, using stick and scissors.

VENTILATION AND WATERING: Ventilate as freely as is consistent with maintenance of necessary temp. Keep moist atmosphere by syringing until colouring commences then allow temp. to rise slightly. Water border thoroughly whenever it appears dry on surface. Feed with vine fertiliser in winter and spring.

POT CULTURE: Two-year-old plants established in 10 or 12 in. pots best adapted for fruit in pots. No potting on required. Place in temp. 60°, Nov. to Feb. Give little water till buds break, then apply freely. Increase temp. to 65° after buds break, and to 75° when in flower; lower to 68° afterwards until stoning is completed, when again raise to 70°. Allow above temp. to be increased 5° to 10° by sun heat. Syringe daily until vines flower. Thin berries. Apply liquid stimulant three times weekly after berries form and until they are ripe. Allow each vine to carry six to eight bunches—8 to 10 lb. altogether.

CULTURE OF HARDY ORNAMENTAL VINES: Soil, good ordinary, enriched with decayed manure. **Position, walls or fences, arbours, trellises, poles, pergolas,** etc. Plant in autumn.

OUTDOOR CULTURE: Position, against a sunny south wall. Plant, Nov. to March in prepared border and treat as indoor plants though allowing rather freer growth, which is left to start naturally in the spring. Choose hardy early vars. as Brant, Royal Muscadine, Black Hambourg.

PROPAGATION: Grape vine by ' eyes ' inserted in sandy compost in temp. 65° to 75° in Jan., Feb. or March; cuttings of shoots, 6 in. long, in shady position outdoors, Oct. or Nov. Ornamental vines by seeds in heat in spring; cuttings of shoots, 6 to 8 in. long, in pots of sandy soil in cold frame in Sept. or Oct.; layering shoots in spring or summer.

FRUITING SPECIES CULTIVATED: *V. Bourguinia*, 'Southern Summer Grape', parent of some vineyard vars.; *cinerea*, ' Sweet Winter Grape ', fruit black, N. America; *Doaniana*, fruit black, with bloom, N. America; *Labruscana*, ' Labruscan Grape '; *rotundifolia*, ' Muscadine ', dull purple, thick skinned large grapes, a number of vineyard vars., N. America; *vinifera*, ' Wine Grape ', the cultivated grape of Europe and of history, fruit variable in form, size and colour, Caucasian Region, var. *apiifolia*, cut-leaved form.

ORNAMENTAL SPECIES CULTIVATED: *V. amurensis*, large leaves colouring to scarlet, Manchuria; *Champinii*, robust climber with glossy green leaves, Texas; *Coignetiae* (syn. *V. Kaempferi*), enormous leathery leaves colouring to yellow, orange and crimson, Japan; *Davidii*, shoots spiny, leaves dark green colouring scarlet, China; *flexuosa*, slender climber, small leaves a metallic bronze-green, Japan, China; *Longii*, ' Bush Grape ', Texas; *Thunbergii*, slender climber, rich autumn colour, China.

Vriesia—*Bromeliaceae*. Stove epiphytal perennials with variously coloured flowers and conspicuous bracts.

CULTURE: Compost, equal parts fibrous loam, rough peat, silver sand and leafmould. Pot, Feb. or March. Water copiously March to Oct., moderately afterwards. Shade from sun. Syringe daily April to Sept. Moist atmosphere essential in summer. Temp., Sept. to March 60° to 70°, March to Sept. 70° to 80°.

PROPAGATION: By offsets inserted in small pots of sandy peat in temp. 75° to 85° in spring.

SPECIES CULTIVATED: *V. fenestralis*, yellow, leaves marked brown, to 1½ ft., Brazil; *hieroglyphica*, yellowish, leaves banded dark green and brown, Brazil; *speciosa* (syn. *V. zebrina*), yellowish-white, leaves banded dark brown, to 3 ft., Guiana, and var. *major*, robust form. See also Tillandsia.

Wachendorfia—*Haemodoraceae*. Half-hardy tuberous-rooted plants. First introduced early eighteenth century.

OUTDOOR CULTURE: Soil, light, rich sandy. Position, sunny well-drained border. Plant, Sept. to Jan., placing bulbs 4 in. deep and 2 in. apart. Lift and replant bulbs annually. Mulch surface of bed in March with cow manure.

POT CULTURE: Compost, two parts sandy loam, one part leaf-mould or decayed cow manure. Pot, 4½ in. diameter, well drained. Place five bulbs, 3 in. deep, in each pot in Nov. and cover with peat in cold frame or under cool greenhouse stage until growth begins. Water moderately from time bulbs begin to grow until flowers fade, then gradually cease, keeping bulbs dry till Jan. Temp., Sept. to March 40° to 50°, other times 50° to 60°.

PROPAGATION: By offsets, treated as advised for bulbs.

SPECIES CULTIVATED: *W. paniculata*, yellow, April, 3 ft., S. Africa; *thyrsiflora*, yellow, May, 2 ft., S. Africa.

Wahlenbergia (Bell-flower)—*Campanulaceae*. Hardy perennial herbs.

CULTURE OF HARDY SPECIES: Soil, gritty, well drained, containing plenty of well-rotted leaf-mould. Position, sunny rockeries well supplied with moisture during the summer months. Protect Australasian species with hand-light during the winter. Plant, Oct. to April.

PROPAGATION: By seeds sown in a temp. of 55° in March or April; cuttings in summer; division in spring.

HARDY SPECIES CULTIVATED: *W. albo-marginata*, white or blue, summer, 3 to 6 in., New Zealand, frequently wrongly named *W. saxicola*; *gracilis*, blue, summer, 9 in., Australia; *hederacea* (syn. *Campanula hederacea*), ' Creeping Hare-bell ', blue, summer, trailing, Britain; *Mathewsii*, blue, July, 12 to 15 in., New Zealand; *saxicola*, white or pale blue, summer, 9 in., Tasmania; *vincaeflora*, light blue, summer, 1 ft., New Zealand. See also Edraianthus.

Wake Robin, see *Trillium grandiflorum.*

Waldsteinia—*Rosaceae.* Hardy perennial herbs. First introduced early twentieth century.

CULTURE: Soil, ordinary rich. Position, on sunny rockeries. Plant, Oct. to April. Cut away flower stems in Sept.

PROPAGATION: By seeds sown $\frac{1}{16}$ in. deep in shallow boxes or well-drained pots of light soil in cold frame, April or July, or in sunny positions (similar depth and soil) outdoors, April or Aug.; division of plants, Oct. to April.

SPECIES CULTIVATED: *W. fragarioides*, ' Barren Strawberry ', yellow, June, 6 in., N. America; *siberica* (syn. *W. trifolia*), yellow, summer, 3 to 4 in., Europe.

Wall Cress, see Arabis.

Wallflower, see Cheiranthus; **Alpine-,** see Erysimum; **Siberian-,** see *Erysimum Allionii.*

Wallichia—*Palmae.* Stove feather palms. First introduced early nineteenth century.

CULTURE: Compost, two parts rich loam, one part leaf-mould, little sand. Position, well-drained pots in moist part of stove. Pot, Feb. Water copiously Feb. to Oct., moderately afterwards. Syringe daily in summer. Shade from sun. Temp., March to Oct. 75° to 85°, Oct. to March 55° to 65°.

PROPAGATION: By suckers removed with roots attached, Feb. or March; seeds sown in temp. 80° in Feb. or March.

SPECIES CULTIVATED: *W. caryotoides*, 6 to 9 ft., Himalaya; *densiflora*, 8 to 12 ft., Himalaya; *disticha*, 10 to 15 ft., Himalaya.

Walnut, see Juglans.

Wandering Jew, see *Saxifraga sarmentosa* and *Zebrina pendula.*

Waratah, see *Telopea speciossima.*

Warley Rose, see *Aethionema warleyense.*

Warscewiczella—*Orchidaceae.* An epiphytic genus at one time included in Zygopetalum. Habit tufted, pseudo-bulbs absent, scapes one-flowered, freely produced, flowers attractive.

CULTURE: Compost and all conditions as for Bolleas, Pescatoreas, etc. Any known to come from comparatively cool localities should have a winter night temp. of 60°. With all, use small pans or well-drained pots and repot annually in spring.

PROPAGATION: By division of plants when repotting.

SPECIES CULTIVATED: A selection—*W. amazonica*, white, lip large, white, with forked purple lines, crest fan-shaped, variable, winter, spring, Amazon Basin, Peru; *candida*, white, lip margined violet, and with a central violet irregular blotch, variable, various, Brazil; *discolor*, ivory white, petals tinted purple, lip violet-purple, erect, toothed, variable, summer, Costa Rica; *flabelliformis*, fragrant, white, lip spreading, white, shaded violet, veins purple-violet, summer, Brazil, W. Indies; *marginata*, creamy white, lip margined rose, or rose-purple, disk striated violet-purple, summer, autumn, Colombia; *Wendlandii*, whitish or yellowish, lip white, violet-blue in centre, summer, autumn, Costa Rica, **var.** *discolor*, fragrant, yellowish-green, violet blotch on lip, larger, brighter.

Washingtonia—*Palmae.* Warm greenhouse palms. Leaves, roundish and fringed with filaments.
CULTURE: Compost, equal parts peat, loam and silver sand. Position, pots in partial shade. Repot, Feb. Water moderately Oct. to April, freely afterwards. Temp., Sept. to March 55° to 65°, March to Sept. 65° to 75°.
PROPAGATION: By seeds sown in above compost in temp. 85° in spring.
SPECIES CULTIVATED: *W. filifera* (syn. *Brahea* or *Pritchardia filamentosa*), 20 to 80 ft., California.

Water Arum, see *Calla palustris*; **-Calthrops,** see *Trapa natans*; **-Carpet,** see Chrysosplenium; **-Chestnut,** see Trapa; **-Cowslip,** see *Caltha palustris*; **-cress,** see *Nasturtium officinale*; **-Hawthorn,** see *Aponogeton distachyum*; **-Hyacinth,** see *Eichhornia crassipes*; **-Lettuce,** see *Pistia Stratiotes*; **-Lily,** see Nymphaea and Victoria; **-Locust,** see *Gleditsia aquatica*; **-Melon,** see *Citrullus vulgaris*; **-Milfoil,** see Myriophyllum; **-Plantain,** see *Alisma Plantago*; **-Poppy,** see Hydrocleys; **-Shield,** see *Brasenia Schreberi*; **-Snowflake,** see *Nymphoides indicum*; **-Soldier,** see *Stratiotes aloides*; **-Thyme,** see Anacharis; **-Trumpet,** see Cryptocoryne; **-Violet,** see *Hottonia palustris*; **-weed,** see *Anacharis canadensis*; **-Willow,** see Dianthera.

Watsonia (Bugle Lily)—*Iridaceae.* Half-hardy summer-blooming bulbous plants. First introduced mid-eighteenth century.
OUTDOOR CULTURE: Soil, deep, rich, liberally manured. Position, sunny, sheltered, well-drained beds or borders. Plant, March to May. Place corms 4 in. deep and 6 in. apart in groups of three, six or twelve; put a little silver sand under each corm. Protect in winter with layer of manure. Apply liquid manure when flower buds form. Fix stakes to spikes when 2 or 3 in. high. Lift corms in Sept. and store in cool place till planting time.
POT CULTURE: Compost, two parts loam, one part well-decayed manure and river sand. Position, pots in cold frame, cool greenhouse or window. Pot, Oct. to March, placing five corms 1 in. deep in a 6 in. pot. Place pots in cold frame till flower spikes show, then remove to greenhouse or window. Water moderately at first, freely afterwards. Apply liquid manure when flower spikes show. After flowering gradually withhold water till foliage dies, then keep quite dry till repotted.
PROPAGATION: By seeds sown ⅛ in. deep in pans of light, rich soil in Feb. in temp. 55° to 65°; bulbils planted 2 in. deep and 6 in. apart in sunny border outdoors, April.
SPECIES CULTIVATED: *W. angusta*, scarlet, to 4 ft., S. Africa; *coccinea*, scarlet, 1 ft., S. Africa; *densiflora*, rosy red, June, 1 ft., S. Africa; *Meriana*, pink, to 4 ft., S. Africa; *rosea*, rose, 3 to 6 ft., S. Africa.

Wattle, see Acacia.

Wax Plant, see *Hoya carnosa*.

Wayfaring Tree, see *Viburnum Lantana*.

Weeping Myall, see *Acacia pendula*.

Weigela—*Caprifoliaceae.* Hardy deciduous flowering shrubs, formerly included in Diervilla. First introduced early eighteenth century.
CULTURE: Any good garden soil with humus added to conserve moist root conditions. Mulch occasionally. Position, full sun or slight shade. Prune directly after flowering by shortening shoots that have borne flowers; no winter pruning required. For general cultivation the best value will be found among the numerous named hybrids, all grow to about 5 ft. with graceful arching branches.
PROPAGATION: By cuttings of young shoots in sandy soil under bell-glass or in cool greenhouse in spring; cuttings of firm shoots in north border under hand-light in Oct. or Nov.
SPECIES CULTIVATED: *W. coraeensis* (syn. *Diervilla grandiflora*), pale rose to carmine, June, glabrous branches and leaves, to 15 ft., Japan; *floribunda*, dark crimson, funnel-shaped, crowded on short branchlets, June, 6 to 10 ft., Japan;

515

florida (syn. *W. rosea*), rose, broadly funnel-shaped May, 6 to 8 ft., China; *hortensis*, carmine, bell-shaped, summer, 6 to 8 ft., Japan, var. *nivea*, white; *japonica*, pale rose, summer, 4 ft., Japan; *Middendorffiana*, sulphur-yellow, summer, 4 ft., Japan; *praecox*, earliest flowering species, rose colour, to 6 ft., Korea.

Weinmannia—*Cunoniaceae.* Slightly tender evergreen shrubs or trees with attractive fern-like foliage. First introduced early nineteenth century.

CULTURE: Soil, light, rich. Position, sheltered walls in southern counties, in the open in mildest areas, or well-drained borders in unheated greenhouse or conservatory. Plant, Sept. to Oct. or April to May. Water indoor plants freely during growing season.

PROPAGATION: By cuttings of half-ripened shoots in sandy soil under bell-glass in gentle bottom heat during July and Aug.

SPECIES CULTIVATED: *W. racemosa*, white or pink, June, 20 to 80 ft., New Zealand; *trichosperma*, creamy white, May to June, columnar habit, the hardier species, Chile. (*Note*: Heights given are for native countries, considerably less in Britain.)

Weldenia—*Commelinaceae.* Slightly tender herbaceous perennials.

CULTURE: Deep, well-drained loam, rather rich. Best grown in deep pots or pans in the alpine house or cold frame. Withhold water and plunge pots in dry peat or sand during winter. Water freely when growth commences in April.

PROPAGATION: By seeds. (These will be found at the base of the long flower tube, usually below ground level.)

SPECIES CULTIVATED: *W. candida*, white, May to July, 4 to 6 in., Mexico, Guatemala.

Wellingtonia, see Sequoiadendron.

Welsh Poppy, see *Meconopsis cambrica.*

Welwitschia—*Gnetaceae.* A curious hothouse plant of mushroom-like habit of growth with leaves fringed with ribbon-like filaments. A difficult plant to grow. First introduced mid-nineteenth century.

CULTURE: Equal parts brick rubble, loam and coarse sand. Avoid root disturbance at all times. Position, a well-drained bed in a hot, dry corner. Scarcely any water required. Full exposure to sun essential. Temp., 55° in winter, 75° in summer.

PROPAGATION: By imported seeds which are exceedingly difficult to obtain.

SPECIES CULTIVATED: *W. mirabilis*, Trop. Africa.

Westringia (Australian Rosemary)—*Labiatae.* Slightly tender evergreen flowering shrub. First introduced late eighteenth century.

CULTURE: Soil, light, rich loam. Position, sheltered shrubberies in southern gardens or unheated greenhouses and conservatories. Plant, Sept. to Oct. or April to May. Water indoor plants freely during the summer months.

PROPAGATION: By cuttings of half-ripened wood in shaded frame, Aug. to Sept.

SPECIES CULTIVATED: *W. rosmariniformis*, white, spotted purple, July to Aug., 3 to 5 ft., Australia.

Whin, see Ulex.

White Alder, see Clethra; **-beam,** see *Sorbus Aria*; **-Cedar,** see *Chamaecyparis, thyoides*; **-Hellebore,** see *Veratrum album*; **-Lotus-of-the-Nile,** see *Nymphaea Lotus*; **-Mustard,** see *Brassica alba.*

Whitlow Grass, see *Draba verna.*

Whorl Flower, see *Morina longifolia.*

Whortleberry, see *Vaccinium myrtillus.*

Widdringtonia (African Cypress)—*Pinaceae* (or *Cupressaceae*). Tender evergreen coniferous trees, suitable only for greenhouse cultivation in this country. Habit, elegant and graceful. First introduced mid-eighteenth century.

CULTURE: Compost, two parts sandy loam and one part leaf-mould with a liberal amount of silver sand. **Position**, pots in light, sunny greenhouse. Pot in March. Water freely March to Oct., moderately afterwards. Temp., March to Oct. 55° to 65°, Oct. to March 45° to 55°.

PROPAGATION: By seeds sown in gentle heat in spring, transferring seedlings singly to small pots as soon as large enough to handle.

SPECIES CULTIVATED: *W. cupressoides*, to 12 ft., S. Africa; *juniperoides*, to 60 ft., S. Africa; *Whytei*, leaves glaucous and graceful, to 140 ft, Cent. Africa.

Wigandia—*Hydrophyllaceae*. Stove foliage plants with large, very wrinkled, more or less downy leaves. First introduced early nineteenth century.

CULTURE: Soil, ordinary. Position, sunny sheltered beds outdoors May to Oct., warm greenhouse remainder of year. Plant, May or June. Lift, Sept. or Oct.

PROPAGATION: By seeds sown in light soil in temp. 65° to 75° in Feb.; cuttings inserted in sandy soil under bell-glass in temp. 75° in spring. Usually treated as an annual; seldom preserved during the winter.

SPECIES CULTIVATED: *W. caracasana*, 8 to 10 ft., Mexico, and var. *imperialis* vigorous; *Vigieri*, 4 to 6 ft., silvery foliage, origin uncertain.

Wild Coffee, see Psychotria; **-Rice,** see Zizania.

Willow, see Salix; **-Herb,** see Epilobium.

Windflower, see Anemone.

Windmill Palm, see *Trachycarpus Fortunei*.

Wine-Berry, see *Rubus phoenicolasius*; **-Palm,** see *Caryota urens*.

Winter Aconite, see *Eranthis hyemalis*; **-Cherry,** see *Physalis Alkekengi* and *Solanum Capsicastrum*; **-Cress,** see *Barbarea verna*; **-Daffodil,** see *Sternbergia lutea*; **-Green,** see *Gaultheria procumbens*; **-Heliotrope,** see *Petasites fragrans*; **-Savory,** see Calamintha; **-Sweet,** see *Acokanthera spectabilis* and *Chimonanthus praecox*.

Wire Vine, see *Muehlenbeckia complexa*.

Wisteria—*Leguminosae*. Hardy and slightly tender deciduous climbing flowering shrubs. Often, but not originally, spelt Wistaria. First introduced early eighteenth century.

CULTURE: Easily grown in ordinary soil, deep loam is best. Position, full sun essential. Walls with southern exposure, pergolas, arbours, trellis or scrambling over a tree. Easily trained as bush or standard. Plant, March or April. Prune, Jan. to March, shortening all young shoots not required for extending branches to within 1 in. of base. Do not prune those growing naturally over trees.

PROPAGATION: By layering young shoots, spring or summer.

SPECIES CULTIVATED: *W. floribunda*, violet-blue, spikes to 12 in. long, May to June, vigorous to 30 ft., Japan, with vars. *alba*, white flowered, *rosea*, pale rose, *macrobotrys* (syn. *W. multifuga*), flowers to 4 ft. long, *Russelliana*, flowers dark blue, and *violaceo-plena*, double violet flowers; *japonica*, cream, small, July, slender growth to 15 ft., rather tender, Japan; *sinensis*, ' Chinese Wisteria ', deep lilac, spikes to 12 in., May to June, vigorous, 30 to 40 ft., very free-flowering and most popular form, China, with vars. *alba*, white-flowered, and *flore pleno*, double lilac flowers; *venusta*, white, May to June, rather tender, Japan.

Wych–Hazel, see Hamamelis.

Wolfberry, see *Symphoricarpos occidentalis*.

Wolfsbane, see *Aconitum lycoctonum*.

Wood Anemone, see *Anemone nemorosa*.

Woodbine, see *Lonicera Periclymenum*.

Woodruff, see Asperula.

Woodsia—*Polypodiaceae*. Greenhouse and hardy deciduous and evergreen ferns. Fronds, feather-shaped.

CULTURE OF GREENHOUSE SPECIES: Compost, equal parts peat and loam with little silver sand and charcoal. Position, well-drained pots or beds in shady greenhouse. Pot or plant, Feb. or March. Water freely March to Oct., moderately afterwards. Syringing not required. Shade from sun. Temp., Sept. to March 45° to 50°, March to Sept. 50° to 60°.

CULTURE OF HARDY SPECIES: Compost, equal parts peat and loam. Position, shady borders or banks. Plant, April. Water copiously in dry weather. All the hardy species are suitable for greenhouse culture.

PROPAGATION: By spores sown on surface of fine peat in well-drained pans placed in temp. of 75° at any time; division of plants, March or April.

GREENHOUSE SPECIES CULTIVATED: *W. obtusa*, 1 ft., N. America; *polystichioides*, 6 to 9 in., Japan.

HARDY SPECIES CULTIVATED: *W. alpina*, 6 in., N. Temp. Zone; *glabella*, 6 in., N. America; *ilvensis*, 4 in., Arctic and N. Temp. Zone (Br.); *scopulina*, 8 in., N. America.

Wood Sorrel, see Oxalis.

Woodwardia (Chain Fern)—*Polypodiaceae.* Greenhouse evergreen ferns. First introduced mid-eighteenth century.

CULTURE: Compost, equal parts loam and leaf-mould or peat. Position, in well-drained pots, or on rockeries in cool greenhouse or fernery. Water freely in summer, moderately other times. Syringe daily in summer. *W. radicans* and *W. radicans cristata* suitable for suspending in baskets. Greenhouse species will also grow outdoors in sheltered positions, and with the protection of litter in winter.

PROPAGATION: By spores sown on surface of fine peat in well-drained pans placed in temp. of 75° any time; division of plants, March or April; by bulbils removed from fronds and placed in small pots in temp. of 65° to 70° until roots form.

SPECIES CULTIVATED: *W. areolata*, 1 to 1½ ft., U.S.A.; *Harlandii*, 1½ ft., Hong Kong; *japonica*, 1¾ to 2 ft., China and Japan; *radicans*, 3 to 8 ft., N. Temp. Zone, var. *orientalis* (syn. *W. orientalis*).

Wonga-wonga Vine, see *Pandorea pandorana.*

Wormwood, see *Artemisia Absinthium.*

Woundwort, see Stachys and *Anthyllis Vulneraria.*

Wulfenia—*Scrophulariaceae.* Hardy low herbaceous perennial herbs. First introduced early nineteenth century.

CULTURE: Soil, light, rich, sandy loam. Position, partially shady rockeries. Plant, March or April.

PROPAGATION: By seeds sown in light, sandy soil in shallow boxes in cold frame in March or April, transplanting seedlings when large enough to handle on to rockery; division of plants in March or April.

SPECIES CULTIVATED: *W. Amherstiana*, light blue, June to July, 9 to 12 in., Himalaya; *Baldaccii*, blue, summer, 9 in., Balkans; *carinthiaca*, blue, July, 1 ft., Carinthia.

Xanthisma—*Compositae.* Hardy annual. First introduced mid-nineteenth century.

CULTURE: Sow seeds in gentle heat in spring, harden off seedlings in May, and plant out in June, a foot apart, in bold groups in sunny borders.

SPECIES CULTIVATED: *X. texanum* (syn. *Centauridium Drummondii*), yellow, summer, 2 to 4 ft., Texas.

Xanthoceras—*Sapindaceae.* Hardy deciduous flowering tree. First introduced mid-nineteenth century.

CULTURE: Soil, ordinary. Position, sheltered sunny borders or shrubberies in milder districts, against walls in southern counties. Plant, Oct. to Feb.

PROPAGATION: By seeds sown in light soil outdoors in autumn or spring, or by root cuttings inserted in pans of sandy soil in cool greenhouse in Feb. or March.

Species Cultivated: *X. sorbifolium*, white, stained carmine, attractive, May, 10 to 20 ft., N. China.

Xanthorhiza—*Ranunculaceae*. Hardy deciduous flowering shrub. First introduced mid-eighteenth century.

Culture: Soil, moist loam. Position, thin woodlands or partially shady shrubberies. Plant, Nov. to Feb.

Propagation: By division in Feb.

Species Cultivated: *X. simplicissima* (syn. *X. apiifolia*), ' Yellow Root ', purple, March to April, 1 to 2 ft., Eastern U.S.A.

Xanthosoma—*Araceae*. Stove perennial herbs with thick arrow-shaped leaves, grown in the tropics for the edible roots. First introduced early eighteenth century.

Culture: Compost, equal parts turfy loam, peat, leaf-mould and silver sand. Position, well-drained pots in shade. Pot moderately firmly in pots just large enough to take tubers in Feb. or March; transfer to larger pots in April or May. Water moderately Feb. to April and Sept. to Sept., freely April to Sept., keep quite dry Nov. to Feb. Temp., Feb. to Sept. 70° to 80°, Sept. to Nov. 65° to 75°, Nov. to Feb. 55° to 65°.

Propagation: By dividing the tubers in Feb. or March.

Species Cultivated: *X. atrovirens*, leaves dark green above, greyish beneath, Venezuela; *Lindenii* (syn. *Phyllotaenium Lindenii*), bright green leaves with white veins and midribs, Colombia; *violaceum*, leaves green with purplish veins, W. Indies.

Xeranthemum (Immortelle)—*Compositae*. Hardy annuals. Flowers, single and double; suitable for winter decoration. First introduced mid-sixteenth century.

Culture: Soil, ordinary. Position, sunny beds or borders. Sow seeds in light soil in March in temp. 50° to 55°, planting out in June, or in open ground end of April. Gather flowers for winter decoration directly they are fully expanded.

Species Cultivated: *X. annuum*, purple, etc., summer, 2 ft., S. Europe, and vars. *ligulosum* (syn. *X. imperiale*), double, and *perligulosum* (syn. *X. superbissimum*), very double.

Xerophyllum (Turkey's Beard)—*Liliaceae*. Hardy perennial subaquatic herb. First introduced mid-eighteenth century.

Culture: Soil, moist, sandy peat. Position, boggy places near the margins of ponds or lakes or damp spots in the wild garden. Plant, March or April.

Propagation: By seeds sown in moist, peaty soil in April where required to grow or by division of roots in March or April.

Species Cultivated: *X. asphodeloides*, white, May, 3 to 5 ft., N. America.

Xylobium—*Orchidaceae*. An epiphytic genus, scapes erect from base of the closely-set, rather small, pseudo-bulbs, which carry one or two hard-textured leaves, flowers often numerous but not large, and dull in colour.

Culture: Compost, as for Maxillarias, but include a little loam fibre. Pots well drained, water liberally in summer, intermittently in winter, judge by the texture of pseudo-bulbs and leaves, expose to light in autumn. Winter temp. 50° to 55°, in summer up to 75° to 80° by sun heat. Shading moderate.

Propagation: By division of plants in spring.

Species Cultivated: A selection—*X. bractescens*, fifteen to twenty-five, greenish-yellow, lip marked brown, floral bracts 1 to 2 in. long, summer, autumn, Peru; *concavum* (syn. *Maxillaria concava*), small, pale yellow, mid-lobe of lip veined rose, spring, Guatemala; *elatum*, comparatively large, many, yellowish, red-brown, height 3 ft., spring, Peru; *hyacinthinum*, fifteen to twenty, fragrant, yellow, lip veined red, summer, Venezuela; *leontoglossum* (syn. *Maxillaria leontoglossa*), yellow, spotted red or purplish-red, mid-lobe of lip warted, summer, Colombia; *palmifolia*, ten to fifteen, yellowish, whitish, spring, W. Indies; *squalens*, fifteen to twenty-five, yellowish-white, often suffused brown-red, petals and lip dull purple, mid-lobe warted, summer, Venezuela.

Yam, see Dioscorea.

Yarrow, see Achillea.

Yellow Asphodel, see *Asphodeline lutea*; **-Centaury,** see Blackstonia; **-Flax,** see *Reinwardtia indica*; **-Root,** see *Xanthorhiza simplicissima*; **-Star Flower,** see *Sternbergia lutea*; **-Star of Bethlehem,** see *Gagea silvatica*; **-Water Flag,** see *Iris Pseudacorus*; **-Water Lily,** see Nuphar; **-wood,** see *Cladrastis*; **-wort,** see Blackstonia.

Yerba Mansa, see *Anemopsis californica*.

Yew, see Taxus.

Youth-and-old-age, see *Zinnia elegans*.

Yucca—*Liliaceae* (or *Agavaceae*). Greenhouse and hardy evergreen shrubs or small trees with rosettes of sword-shaped leaves. First introduced late sixteenth century.

CULTURE OF HARDY SPECIES: Soil, ordinary light, well drained. Position, sunny banks, mounds, rockeries, raised borders, or as single specimens on lawns. Plant, Oct. or April. Protect in severe weather with mats in coldest districts.

CULTURE OF GREENHOUSE SPECIES: Compost, two parts sandy loam, one part leaf-mould, and little sand. Position, light greenhouse Sept. to June; sunny position outdoors, pots plunged to rims in soil, June to Sept; or may be grown entirely in greenhouse. Pot, March. Water freely April to Sept., very little afterwards. Repotting only necessary when root-bound. Temp., Sept. to March 40° to 50°, March to Sept. 55° to 65°.

PROPAGATION: By offsets or suckers in March or April; cuttings of roots inserted in sand in temp. 55° in spring.

GREENHOUSE SPECIES CULTIVATED: *Y. aloifolia*, 'Spanish Bayonet', creamy white, summer, 15 to 25 ft., Southern U.S.A. and W. Indies, and vars. *draconis*, leaves drooping, *quadricolor*, leaves reddish, *tricolor*, leaves variegated with white, green, and yellow, and *variegata*, leaves striped with white; *baccata*, creamy white, summer, to 3 ft., Colorado and Texas.

HARDY SPECIES CULTIVATED: *Y. filamentosa*, 'Adam's Needle', creamy, July to Aug., 3 to 6 ft., Southern U.S.A., and var. *variegata*, leaves variegated yellow or white; *flaccida*, creamy, July to Aug., 3 to 4 ft., South-eastern U.S.A., and vars. *integra*, smaller leaves, and *orchioides*, unbranched inflorescence; *glauca* (syn. *Y. angustifolia*), creamy, July, Southern U.S.A.; *gloriosa*, 'Spanish Dagger', creamy, July, 6 to 9 ft., not very free flowering, Southern U.S.A., and var. *nobilis*, with greyish leaves and flowers tinged red on outside; *recurvifolia*, leaves recurving, creamy, summer, to 6 ft., hardy and of easy culture, Southern U.S.A.

Yulan, see *Magnolia denudata*.

Zaluzianskya—*Scrophulariaceae*. Half-hardy annuals. First introduced mid-eighteenth century.

CULTURE: Soil, rich, sandy loam. Position, warm, sunny borders or rockeries.

PROPAGATION: By seeds sown on surface of fine light soil and lightly covered with silver sand and placed in temp. 55° in March, transplanting seedlings outdoors in June; or sow seeds 1/16 in. deep outdoors in May where plants are required to flower. Water freely in dry weather. Mulch with layer of peat in June.

SPECIES CULTIVATED: *Z. capensis* (syn. *Nycterinia capensis*), white and purple, spring and summer, fragrant, 1 ft., S. Africa; *selaginoides* (syn. *Nycterinia selaginoides*), white and lilac, summer, 8 to 12 in., S. Africa.

Zamia—*Cycadaceae*. Stove or greenhouse evergreen palm-like plants with pinnate leaves. First introduced late seventeenth century.

CULTURE: Compost, equal parts loam and peat, little silver sand. Position, well-drained pots in shady part of stove. Pot, Feb. or March. Water copiously March to Oct. Syringe daily April to Sept. Moist atmosphere essential. Shade from sun. Temp., March to Oct. 70° to 75°, Oct. to March 55° to 60°.

PROPAGATION: By seeds sown in light soil in temp. 75° to 85°, spring; by offsets removed and placed in small pots under bell-glass in propagator in spring; by division, Feb. or March.

SPECIES CULTIVATED: *Z. furfuracea*, ' Jamaica Sago Tree ', 3 ft., W. Indies; *integrifolia*, 3 ft., W. Indies; *Lindenii*, 8 ft., Ecuador; *Wallisii*, Colombia.

Zantedeschia (Arum or Calla Lily)—*Araceae*. Greenhouse rhizomatous perennials. First introduced early eighteenth century.

CULTURE OF Z. AETHIOPICA (ARUM LILY): Compost, equal parts loam, cow manure, and coarse silver sand. Position, greenhouse or dwelling-room Oct. to May; outdoors remainder of year. Repot annually in Aug. or Sept. Water moderately Sept. to March, freely March to May. Apply stimulants once a week during flowering period. Plant 15 in. apart in ordinary rich soil in sunny position outdoors in May, lift and repot in Aug. or Sept., singly in 5 or 6 in. pots. Supply freely with water in dry weather when outdoors. Suitable stimulants: ½ oz. of Peruvian guano; 1 teaspoonful of Clay's fertiliser; or ¼ oz. nitrate of soda or sulphate of ammonia to 1 gall. of water. Temp., Sept. to March 40° to 55°, March to May 50° to 60°.

CULTURE OF OTHER SPECIES: Compost, same as for *Z. aethiopica*. Position, greenhouse Oct. to June; cold frame remainder of year. Repot annually in Feb. Water moderately Feb. to April and Aug. to Oct., freely April to Aug., keep nearly dry Oct. to Feb. Apply stimulants during flowering period. Temp., Oct. to March 55° to 65°, March to Oct. 65° to 75°.

PROPAGATION: By seeds sown ⅛ in. deep in loam, leaf-mould and sand in temp. 65° to 75° in spring; division of plants when planting outdoors or repotting; suckers removed at potting time.

SPECIES CULTIVATED: *Z. aethiopica* (syn. *Richardia africana*), white, winter and spring, 3 to 4 ft., S. Africa; *albo-maculata*, yellow or milk-white, summer, 2 ft., leaves spotted white, S. Africa; *Elliottiana*, yellow, Aug., 3 ft., S. Africa; *melanoleuca*, yellow and purple, summer, 18 in., S. Africa; *Rehmannii*, rosy purple, summer, 2 ft., Natal.

Zanthorhiza, see Xanthorhiza.

Zanthoxylum—*Rutaceae*. Hardy deciduous prickly shrubs or trees with aromatic young branches, flowers insignificant. First introduced mid-eighteenth century.

CULTURE: Soil, deep, loamy. Position, open shrubberies, or as specimens on lawns. Plant, Nov. to Feb.

PROPAGATION: By seeds sown in cool greenhouse in Feb.; by cuttings of half-ripened shoots in July under bell-glass; by root cuttings in cool greenhouse in Feb.

SPECIES CULTIVATED: *Z. alatum*, yellowish, spring, to 12 ft., Himalaya; *americanum*, ' Prickly Ash ', yellowish-green, spring, 10 to 25 ft., Eastern U.S.A.; *Clava-Herculis*, ' Toothache Tree ', ' Hercules' Club ', to 30 ft. or more, trunk and branches prickly, seeds black and shining, Southern N. America; *piperitum*, green, 10 to 20 ft., China and Japan; *simulans* (syn. *Z. Bungei*), handsome lustrous foliage, 6 to 8 ft., N. and Cent. China; *stenophyllum*, climbing 6 to 8 ft., W. China.

Zauschneria—*Onagraceae*. Half-hardy shrubby perennial. First introduced early nineteenth century.

CULTURE: Soil, sandy loam. Position, well-drained rockery or old wall. Plant, March or April.

PROPAGATION: By seeds sown in light, sandy soil, lightly covered with fine soil, March, transplant seedlings outdoors end of May or beginning of June; cuttings of young side shoots inserted in pots of sandy soil under bell-glass or hand-light in shady position outdoors in Sept., protecting cuttings in greenhouse until following April, then planting out; division of old plants in April.

SPECIES CULTIVATED: *Z. californica*, ' Californian Fuchsia ', scarlet, autumn, 1 ft., California; *cana* (syn. *Z. microphylla*), scarlet, to 2½ ft., California.

Zea—*Gramineae*. Half-hardy annual. Leaves, narrow, grass-like; green or variegated with white. First introduced mid-sixteenth century.

CULTURE: Soil, ordinary. Sow seeds ½ in deep and 1 in. apart in light, rich soil in well-drained pots or boxes in temp. 55°, March and April; transfer seedlings when 2 in. high singly into 2 in. pots, then into 4½ in. pots. Place in cold frame to harden in May and plant outdoors in June. May also be grown in pots in compost of equal parts good loamy soil and leaf-mould and a little sand. Water freely.

SPECIES CULTIVATED: *Z. Mays*, ' Maize ', ' Indian Corn ', 3 to 12 ft., habitat uncertain, and vars. *everta*, ' Pop Corn ', *gracillima*, dwarf, narrow-leaved, *japonica*, striped yellow, white, or pink, *japonica quadricolor*, striped, *japonica variegata*, variegated, and *rugosa* (syn. var. *saccharata*), ' Sweet Corn '.

Zebra Grass, see *Miscanthus sinensis* var. *zebrinus*;　**-Plant,** see *Calathea zebrina*.

Zebrina—*Commelinaceae*. Greenhouse herbaceous trailing perennial with ornamental, oval-oblong leaves, dark green, striped white above, purplish beneath. Stems creeping. First introduced mid-nineteenth century.

CULTURE: Compost, equal parts loam, leaf-mould and sand. Position, in pots or baskets suspended from roof, or in beds under stage or on rockeries. Pot or plant, Jan. to April. Water freely March to Oct., moderately afterwards. Shade from strong sunshine. Temp., 40° to 50° Oct. to April, 55° to 65° April to Oct. May be grown in windows as a pot or basket plant. Protect from frost in winter.

PROPAGATION: By cuttings of young shoots inserted in light soil under bell-glass in above temp., March to Oct.

SPECIES CULTIVATED: *Z. pendula* (syn. *Tradescantia zebrina*), ' Wandering Jew ', foliage striped white above, purple beneath, Mexico, and var. *quadricolor*, foliage striped with red and white.

Zelkova—*Ulmaceae*. Hardy deciduous trees.

CULTURE: Soil, deep, moist loam. Position, side of water-courses and in similar damp places. Plant, Oct. to Feb.

PROPAGATION: By seeds sown outdoors in autumn or spring; grafting in March.

SPECIES CULTIVATED: *Z. carpinifolia* (syn. *Z. crenata*), to 80 ft., Caucasus; *Serrata* (syn. *Z. acuminata*), to 100 ft., Japan.

Zenobia—*Ericaceae*. Hardy deciduous or half-hardy evergreen flowering shrub with attractive Lily of the Valley-like flowers. First introduced early nineteenth century.

CULTURE: Soil, peat or sandy loam, lime-free. Position, moist sheltered borders. Plant, Sept., Oct., March or April. Prune to prevent seed formation by cutting away, in early Aug., portions of shoots which have flowered.

PROPAGATION: By cuttings of half-ripe shoots inserted in sandy soil under bell-glass in gentle bottom heat during July.

SPECIES CULTIVATED: *Z. pulverulenta* (syns. *Z. speciosa, Andromeda pulverulenta*), white, waxy, June to July, fragrant, greyish-white foliage, 4 to 6 ft., N. Carolina to Florida, and var. *nuda*, leaves green, flowers smaller.

Zephyranthes (Zephyr Lily; Flower of the West Wind)—*Amaryllidaceae*. Hardy and half-hardy bulbous flowering plants. First introduced early seventeenth century.

CULTURE OF HARDY SPECIES: Soil, light, sandy loam. Position, well-drained sunny beds, borders or rockeries. Plant, Aug. to Nov., placing bulbs 3 to 4 in. deep and 4 in. apart. Protect in winter by a layer of cinder ashes. Lift and replant only when bulbs show signs of deterioration.

CULTURE OF HALF-HARDY SPECIES: Compost, two parts loam, one part peat, leaf-mould and silver sand. Position, well-drained pots in cold frame or greenhouse. Pot, Aug. to Nov., placing one bulb 2 in. deep in a 5 or 6 in. pot. Water very little till growth begins, then freely. Withhold water when flowers fade and keep soil quite dry till potting time.

PROPAGATION: By offsets, planted and treated as advised for large bulbs, Aug. to Nov.

HALF-HARDY SPECIES CULTIVATED: *Z. Atamasco*, ' Atamasco Lily ', white, tinged purple, May, 1 ft., N. America; *grandiflora* (syn. *Z. carinata*), pink, summer, 6 to 12 in., Cent. America and W. Indies.

HARDY SPECIES CULTIVATED: *Z. candida*, white, Sept., 6 to 12 in., La Plata.

Zingiber (Ginger)—*Zingiberaceae.* Stove perennial. Roots furnish the ginger of commerce. First introduced early seventeenth century.

CULTURE: Compost, equal parts loam, peat and sand. Position, pots in shady, moist part of stove. Pot, Feb. Water copiously March to Oct., keep nearly dry Oct. to March. Temp., March to Oct. 75° to 85°, Oct. to March 55° to 65°. Stems die down in autumn.

PROPAGATION: By division of the rhizomes in Feb.

SPECIES CULTIVATED: *Z. officinale*, yellowish-green and purple, July, to 3 ft., Trop. Asia.

Zinnia (Youth-and-old-age)—*Compositae.* Half-hardy annuals. First introduced mid-eighteenth century.

CULTURE: Soil, deep, loamy, liberally enriched with decayed manure. Position, sunny beds or borders. Sow seeds $\frac{1}{16}$ in. deep in light soil in temp. 55° early in April. Transplant seedlings when third leaf forms 2 in. apart in shallow boxes filled with loamy soil. Place box near the glass in temp. 55° until seedlings are established, then remove to a cooler house, and if possible plant out 4 in. apart in good rich soil in cold frame early in May. Shade from sun, keep moist, and gradually expose to air, end of month. Plant out 8 to 12 in. apart, second week in June. Sow also outdoors, middle of May. Prepare bed of rich soil in sunny position, sow three or four seeds at intervals of 12 in., and thin seedlings to one at each place when third leaf forms. Mulch all zinnias with decayed manure after planting. Water liberally in dry weather. Apply stimulants when the plants commence to flower. On dry soils take out soil to depth of 12 in., put 3 in. of decayed manure in, then replace soil.

SPECIES CULTIVATED: *Z. elegans*, various colours, summer, 2 to 3 ft., Mexico; *Haageana*, orange-scarlet, summer, 1 ft., Trop. America; *linearis*, golden yellow, summer, 9 to 12 in., Mexico; *pauciflora*, yellow or purple, summer, 1 ft., Mexico; *tenuiflora* (syn. *Z. multiflora*), scarlet, summer, 2 ft., Mexico.

Zizania (Canadian Wild Rice)—*Gramineae.* Hardy aquatic grass. First introduced late nineteenth century.

CULTURE: Soil, ordinary. Position, margins of shallow ponds or lakes. Plant, April or May.

PROPAGATION: By seeds sown in heat in spring, growing seedlings on under glass until May, then hardening off in cold frame.

SPECIES CULTIVATED: *Z. aquatica*, ' Water Rice ', ' Water Oats ', green and brown, summer, 6 to 10 ft., N. America.

Zizyphus (Jujube)—*Rhamnaceae.* Slightly tender deciduous small tree. Cultivated in Medit. region for the production of jujube fruits. First introduced mid-seventeenth century.

CULTURE: Soil, good loamy. Position, sheltered and sunny. Plant, Nov. to Feb.

PROPAGATION: By seeds stratified and sown the following spring; cuttings of the roots in cool greenhouse in Feb.

SPECIES CULTIVATED: *Z. Jujuba* (syn. *Z. sativa*), yellowish, fruits dark red, to 30 ft., branches spiny, S.E. Europe to China.

Zigadenus—*Liliaceae.* Hardy herbaceous plants with or without bulbs. First introduced mid-eighteenth century.

CULTURE: Soil, peat, leaf-mould and sand. Position, partially shady, moist border or bed. Plant, autumn. Lift and replant triennially.

PROPAGATION: By division of offsets in autumn; seeds sown in sandy soil in a cold frame in spring.

SPECIES CULTIVATED: *Z. angustifolius*, white and purple, June, 18 in., N.

America; *elegans*, green and white, July, 2 to 3 ft., N. America; *glaberrimus*, white, July, 2 to 3 ft., N. America; *Nuttallii*, white, June, 18 in., N. America.

Zygocactus (Leaf-flowering Cactus)—*Cactaceae*. Succulent greenhouse plants. First introduced, under the generic name Epiphyllum, early nineteenth century.

CULTURE: Compost, equal parts turfy loam, peat and leaf-mould, with silver sand and broken brick added. Position, light, warm greenhouse Sept. to June; sunny place outdoors or cold frame June to Sept. Water moderately Sept. to April, little more freely other times. Temp., Nov. to March 50° to 60°, March to June 55° to 65°, Sept. to Nov. 40° to 45°.

PROPAGATION: By cuttings inserted singly in 3 in. pots filled with sandy soil and brick dust in March or April; grafting on *Pereskia aculeata* or *P. Bleo* in temp. 65° to 75° in spring.

SPECIES CULTIVATED: *Z. truncatus*, ‘Crab Cactus’, ‘Christmas Cactus’, rosy red, Brazil.

× **Zygocolax**—*Orchidaceae*. Bigeneric hybrid between Zygopetalum and Colax, intermediate between the two in habit and floral characters.

Zygopetalum—*Orchidaceae*. An epiphytic genus which has been much confused through the inclusion of allied genera. True Zygopetalums have decided pseudo-bulbs carrying two to three leaves. The scapes, often tall with several flowers, are produced from the base of the pseudo-bulb, often with the young growths. Flowers fairly large, attractive, lip has a transverse crest. Some species are terrestrial in suitable environments. In a few the habit is scandent and the pseudo-bulbs are carried at intervals.

CULTURE: Compost, two parts loam fibre, two parts peat or osmunda fibre, one part sphagnum moss with finely broken crocks and a few decayed leaves. Well-drained pots for the majority; species with creeping stems should be placed in shallow baskets on rafts or tree fern stem, very little, if any, loam included in the compost for them. The Odontoglossum House is suitable for many during summer but the winter temp. should be 55° to 60°, as a dry atmosphere is inimical. Water liberally in summer, infrequently in winter, but guided by the state of the plant and pipe heat.

PROPAGATION: By division of the plants in spring, if large enough.

SPECIES CULTIVATED: *Z. Burkei*, three to eight, green, lined dark brown, lip white, crest ribbed purple-violet, winter, British Guiana; *coeleste*, blue-violet, yellow on lip, summer, without pseudo-bulb, Colombia; *intermedium*, four to ten yellowish-green, flushed or blotched red-brown, lip spreading, whitish with radiating lines and spots of violet-purple, very fine, autumn, Brazil; *Mackayi*, five to seven, fragrant, yellowish-green, blotched chestnut or purplish-brown, lip whitish with radiating lines of purple-violet, crest two-lobed, autumn to winter, Brazil; *maxillare*, five to eight, green blotched and barred chocolate-brown, lip violet-blue, crest darker, creeping, summer, various, Brazil, var. *Gautieri*, larger lip often spotted blue, crest purple.

SUPPLEMENT

Abies nobilis, up to 250 ft., Washington to California. See p. 1.

Aechmea marmorata, leaves marked brown, violet-blue flowers, greenhouse or room plant, Brazil. For culture see p. 11.

Agapetes—*Ericaceae.* Warm greenhouse evergreen flowering shrubs.
CULTURE: Compost, equal parts acid loam, peat and sand. Position, warm moist greenhouse with light shade in summer. Temp., Sept. to March 55° to 60°, March to Sept. 60° to 70°.
PROPAGATION: By cuttings of firm shoots in sandy soil in a propagating case with temp. of 65° to 70°.
SPECIES CULTIVATED: *A. macrantha,* fl. white, yellow and red, December, Nepal; *serpens* (syn. *Pentapterygium serpens*), fls. red with deeper markings, W. China.

Aloe plicatilis, greyish leaves, red flowers, greenhouse or room plant, Cape Province. For culture see p. 20.

Alsine verna, see *Arenaria verna,* p. 39.

Anemopaegma—*Bignoniaceae.* Warm greenhouse climber.
CULTURE: Compost, fibrous loam, decayed manure and sand. Plant in borders or large tubs with stems trained up greenhouse roof. Thin out the growths in summer and each spring cut back side growths. Temp., March to Oct. 60° to 75°, Oct. to March 55° to 60°.
PROPAGATION: By seed sown in pots of sandy soil in temp. 60° to 75°; cuttings of young shoots taken in late spring in sandy soil in a heated propagating case.
SPECIES CULTIVATED: *A. chamberlaynii,* yellow, Sept., Brazil.

Apricot, see Prunus, pp. 399 to 402.

Arabis albida (syn. *A. caucasica*), white, Jan. to May, 6 to 9 in., S.E. Europe; *flore-pleno,* double white or tinged pink; *variegata,* leaves variegated yellow. For culture see p. 36.

Bertholletia—*Lecythidaceae.* Tropical trees producing Brazil and Para nuts but of no ornamental value.
SPECIES CULTIVATED: B. *excelsa,* B. *nobilis,* S. America.

Blue-Eyed Grass, see *Sisyrinchium angustifolium,* p. 457.

Chionodoxa gigantea, violet-blue flowers, Asia Minor; there are also white and pink forms. For culture see p. 107.

Cinnamon Vine, see *Dioscorea batatas,* p. 165.

Cissus sicyoides, *C. striata;* popular green-foliaged room or greenhouse plants. For culture see p. 114.

Crassula perfoliata; white or red flowers, Cape Province; popular greenhouse or room plant. For culture see p. 133.

Cryptanthus undulatus, small, ornamental leaves, Brazil; popular room or greenhouse plant. For culture see p. 136.

Cyclamen neapolitanum, hardy, rose, July to Nov., Medit. Region; var. *album,* white-fld.; *roseum,* rose-fld. For culture see p. 142.

Cyperus diffusus, 1 to 2 ft., Tropics: popular greenhouse or room plant. For culture see p. 145.

Daphne odora, evergreen, to 6 ft., reddish purple, fragrant fls., Jan. to March, China, Japan; not fully hardy. For culture see p. 150.

Doxantha capreolata, (syn. *Bignonia capreolata, Anisostichus capreolatus*); see p. 30.

Endymion nonscriptus, 'Bluebell'; E. *hispanicus,* latest botanical names for *Scilla nonscripta* and *S. hispanica*; see p. 447.

Fatshedera—*Araliaceae.* Evergreen, hardy shrub, popular as room plant. A bi-generic hybrid between fatsia and hedera.
    CULTURE: Out of doors, well drained soil, shady position. Indoors, pot in a mixture of equal parts loam peat or sand; water freely in summer, sparingly in winter.
    PROPAGATION: Cuttings root readily in sandy soil in spring and summer.
    SPECIES CULTIVATED: *F. lizei,* dark green leaves, France; there is a variegated form.

Ficus *benjamina, F. heterophylla,* popular green-foliaged room or greenhouse plants. For culture see p. 195.

Four o'clock Plant, also known as Marvel of Peru, see *Mirabilis jalapa,* p. 313.

Gentiana macaulayi, deep blue, 2½in., Sept. to Oct., garden origin (*G. arreri* x *G. sino-ornata*) see p. 206.

Gherkin, see Cucumis, p. 137.

Ghost Tree, see *Davidia involucrata,* p. 153.

Handkerchief Tree, see *Davidia involucrata,* p. 153.

Helianthus multiflorus, see *Helianthus decapetalus,* p. 224.

Helleborus corsicus, yellowish green, March to April, 1½ ft., Corsica, Sardinia. For culture see p. 227.

Himalayan Blackberry, see *Rubus procerus,* p. 429.

Ixora fulgens, orange red, 3 to 4 ft., Java. For culture see p. 252.

Leptosiphon, see Gilia, p. 209.

Litchi (Lychee, Leechee)—*Sapindaceae.* Tender, evergreen tree grown in warm regions for edible fruits.
    CULTURE: Small plants can be grown in rooms or a frost-proof greenhouse for ornament. Compost, equal parts loam, peat and sand.
    PROPAGATION: By seed sown in spring or summer in a warm greenhouse.
    SPECIES CULTIVATED: *L. chinensis,* 30 to 40 ft., China.

Lysichitum (Skunk Cabbage)—*Araceae.* Hardy perennial waterside plants.
    CULTURE: Wet, marshy soil. Position, edges of streams or pools. Plant in early spring.
    PROPAGATION: By division in spring. *L. americanum* by seed.
    SPECIES CULTIVATED: *L. americanum,* yellow spathes, April 1 to 2½ ft., N. America; *camtschatcense,* spathes white, May, Japan.

Madonna Lily, see *Lilium candidum,* pp. 275 to 276.

Mangifera (Mango)—*Anacardiaceae.* Stove evergreen trees. Grown in the tropics for edible fruits.
    CULTURE: Compost equal parts loam, peat and sand. Temp. Sept. to March 55° to 60°, March to Sept. 60° to 75°.

PROPAGATION: By seeds or cuttings in a heated propagating case.
SPECIES CULTIVATED: *M. indica*, 60 ft., E. Indies, Malaya.

Mango, see Mangifera, p. 526.

Metasequoia—*Pinaceae.* Hardy deciduous conifer.
CULTURE: Soil, ordinary. Plant Oct. to Feb.
PROPAGATION: By seed or cuttings taken in late summer in a propagating case
with a temp. of 65° to 70°.
SPECIES CULTIVATED: *M. glyptostroboides*, 115 ft., China.

Mimulus glutinosus (syn. *Diplacus glutinosus*), fls. orange, crimson, to 5 ft.,
California. For culture see p. 313.

Mind-Your-Own-Business, see *Helxine solierolli*, p. 227.

Monarch of the East, see Sauromatum, p. 440.

Myrobalan Plum, see *Prunus cerasifera*, p. 402.

Neanthe—*Palmaceae.* Greenhouse or room palm.
CULTURE: Compost, peat, sand and loam in equal parts. Pot March. Water
moderately Sept. to March, freely afterwards. Feed occasionally in summer.
Temp. Sept. to March 50° to 60°, March to Sept. 60° to 70°.
PROPAGATION: By seeds sown in spring or summer in a heated greenhouse.
SPECIES CULTIVATED: *N. elegans* (syn. *Chamaedorea elegans, C. pulchella, Collinia
elegans*) 4 ft., Mexico.

Nepeta hederacea, see *Glechoma hederacea*, p. 210.

Nidularium rutilans, vermilion-red fls., spotted leaves, Brazil. For culture see
p. 328.

Pentapterygium, see Agapetes, p. 525.

Peperomia caperata, leaves small, white flowers, Brazil; *glabella*, leaves green,
trailing, Cent. America; *hederaefolia*, leaves marked silver, Brazil; *magnoliaefolia*,
leaves pale green and cream, W. Indies; *micropyhlla*, leaves small, trailing, Mexico;
sandersii, rounded leaves with silver markings, Brazil; *scandens*, leaves marked
white, Peru. For culture see p. 363.

Philodendron bipinnatifidum, leaves green, indented, Brazil; *erubescens*, leaves
bronzy-green, red beneath, Colombia; *fenzlii*, leaves green, three-lobed, Mexico;
leichtlinii, leaves green, perforated; *oxycardium*, leaves green, heart-shaped, C.
America; *pinnatifidum*, leaves green, indented, S. America; *scandens*, leaves green,
heart-shaped, C. America; *selloum*, leaves green, indented, Brazil; *wendlandii*,
leaves green, glossy, C. America. For culture see p. 371.

Phuopsis stylosa, see *Crucianella stylosa*, p. 136.

Pilea cadierei, ornamental leaves, silver markings, Vietnam. For culture see
p. 378.

Primula edgeworthii (syn. *P. winteri*), pale mauve, April, W. Himalaya; *alba*,
white flowers. For culture see p. 396.

Prunus—*Rosaceae.*
CULTURE OF PLUMS: Can be grown as fan-trained trees on walls and as standards
or half-standards in the open. Rootstocks, common plum (partially dwarfing),
common mussel (partially dwarfing), Brompton (vigorous) Myrobalan B (vigorous). Plant fan-trained trees 15 to 18 ft. apart; standards and half-standards
15 to 20 ft. apart. Good, well-drained soil needed and trees are best grown in
cultivated ground. Feed each spring with ½ oz. sulphate of ammonia and ½ oz.
sulphate of potash per sq. yd. Apply superphosphate of lime at 2 oz. per sq. yd.
only every 2 to 3 years. Mulch around trees each spring with farmyard manure,
compost or moist peat. Trees in the open, once the framework of branches is
formed, should be pruned as little as possible. None should be done in the winter
owing to the risk of infection from the silver leaf fungus disease. Prune only in

spring or before the end of the summer when wounds heal quickly. Cut out dead and diseased wood and thin overcrowded growths. The pruning of established fan-trained trees is done in the summer. Young shoots growing towards or away from the wall should be rubbed out. New shoots can be allowed to extend the framework of the tree and to fill bare spaces but other new side growths should have their tips pinched out when they have made about 6 leaves. These should be shortened by about half their length after picking the fruit. Plums are prone to suckering and these should be torn from their point of origin and not cut off—this will encourage more suckers to appear.

CULTURE OF CHERRIES: Fan-trained trees can be grown on walls (the acid Morello cherry does well on a North facing wall) or as standard trees in the open. Rootstocks, the Malling selection F12/1 can be used for all cherries. Plant fan-trained trees 18–24 ft. apart. Standard trees need to be spaced 30 to 40 ft. apart and are not suitable for small gardens. Good deep soil that is well drained is required; trees will not succeed in heavy, wet ground. Feed sweet cherries with ½ oz. sulphate of potash each spring and give a mulch of rooted manure or compost. Nitrogenous manures, such as sulphate of ammonia, will stimulate growth too much, and should only be given if growth is weak. Superphosphate of lime can be applied every 2 or 3 years at 1½ oz. per sq. yd. Feed acid cherries similarly to plums. Prune standard sweet cherries as for standard plums. Sweet cherries, trained as fans, are spur pruned in a similar manner to fan-trained plums. Acid cherries, trained as fan trees, are pruned similarly to peaches (p. 400). Standard acid cherries can be pruned in the spring by thinning out some of the older growths to encourage plenty of young shoots. It should be borne in mind that acid cherries fruit on growths made in the previous season, whereas sweet cherries produce fruit on young and old wood. Over vigorous trees growing against walls can be root-pruned in winter.

Pteris biaurita argyraea, ' Silver Fern ' (syn. *P. quadriaurita argyraea*), white-lined fronds, 3 ft., Central India; *P.b. tricolor*, fronds red with silver lines. For culture see p. 404.

Pussy Willow, see *Salix discolor*, p. 434.

Puya—*Bromeliaceae*. Warm and cool greenhouse perennials.

CULTURE: Compost, equal parts fibrous loam, peat and coarse sand. Pot, March, good drainage essential. Most species require a minimum winter temperature of 55° but *P. alpestris* is almost hardy and will succeed in a frost-proof greenhouse.

PROPAGATION: by seed or suckers removed from established plants.

SPECIES CULTIVATED: *P. alpestris*, metallic blue fls. 2 to 3 ft., Chile; *P. chilensis*, greenish-yellow fls., July, 2 to 3 ft., Chile.

Redcurrant, see ribes, p. 420.

Rhoicissus—*Vitaceae*. Evergreen climber for warm greenhouse or room.

CULTURE: Compost, equal parts loam peat and sand. Pot in spring and feed occasionally in summer with liquid fertiliser. Train shoots to supports. Temp., Oct. to April 45° to 55°, April to Oct. 55° to 65°.

PROPAGATION: Cuttings in spring in a heated propagating case or by layering.

SPECIES CULTIVATED: *R. rhomboidea* (syn. *Cissus rhomboidea*), small glossy green leaves, Natal.

Rhus cotinus, see *Cotinus coggygria*, p. 131.

Rock Rose, see Cistus, p. 114.

Schefflera (Umbrella Tree)—*Araliaceae*. Evergreen tree or plant for warm greenhouse or room.

CULTURE: Compost equal parts loam, peat and coarse sand. Pot in spring, feed in summer with liquid fertiliser. Light shade needed from strong sunshine.

Temp. Oct. to April 55° to 65°, April to Oct. 60° to 70°.
  PROPAGATION: Stem cuttings in propagating case, temp. 65° to 70°.
  SPECIES CULTIVATED: *S. actinophylla*, large ornamental leaves, Australia.

Schinus (Christmas Berry Tree)—*Anacardiaceae*. Evergreen, greenhouse tree.
  CULTURE: Compost, equal parts loam, peat and coarse sand. Temp. Oct. to
April 45° to 55°, April to Oct. 60° to 70°.
  PROPAGATION: By seeds.
  SPECIES CULTIVATED: *S. terebinthifolius*, fls. white, berries red, 20 ft., S. America.

Setcreasea—*Commelinaceae*. Perennials with ornamental leaves for warm green-
house or room.
  CULTURE: Compost, equal parts fibrous loam, peat and sand. Pot in spring and
grow in warm, light position. Temp. Oct. to April 55° to 60°, April to Oct. 60° to
70°.
  PROPAGATION: By cuttings of shoots in a warm propagating case.
  SPECIES CULTIVATED: *S. striata*, olive-green leaves with white stripes; *purpurea*,
' Purple Heart ', rosy-purple leaves, Mexico.

Spathiphyllum wallisii, popular room plant with ornamental leaves and flowers.
For culture see p. 465.

Skunk Cabbage, see Lysichitum, p. 526.

Syngonium (Goosefoot) *Araceae*. Greenhouse or room evergreen climbers.
  CULTURE: Compost, equal parts loam, peat and sand. Moist atmosphere
needed in summer. Temp. Oct. to March 55° to 60°, March to Oct. 60° to 75°.
  PROPAGATION: By cuttings of shoots in heated propagating case.
  SPECIES CULTIVATED: *S. podophyllum*, C. America; *vellozianum*, Brazil.

Tacsonia, see Passiflora, p. 356.

Tiger Lily, see *Lilium tigrinum*, p. 277.

Tradescantia blossfeldiana, green and purple leaves, warm greenhouse or room
plant, Argentine. For culture see p. 491.

Tree Fern, see Dicksonia, p. 161.

Venidio-Arctotis. A name applied to some hybrids between *Arctotis grandis* and
A. speciosa in which chance crossing with *Venidium fastuosum* is also believed to have
played a part. The flowers resemble those of arctotis, are in many shades of wine,
crimson, rose and orange and, as they are almost completely sterile, must be
increased by cuttings. These are taken at any time in summer and rooted in a
frame or cool greenhouse in which the plants should also be overwintered. Plant
out in May in a sunny, open situation and well-drained soil.

NOTES

NOTES

NOTES

NOTES

NOTES